COVID-19 Outbreak and Beyond: Psychological and Behavioral Responses and Future Perspectives

COVID-19 Outbreak and Beyond: Psychological and Behavioral Responses and Future Perspectives

Editors

Paolo Roma
Merylin Monaro
Cristina Mazza

MDPI • Basel • Beijing • Wuhan • Barcelona • Belgrade • Manchester • Tokyo • Cluj • Tianjin

Editors
Paolo Roma
Department of Human Neuroscience
Sapienza University of Rome
Roma
Italy

Merylin Monaro
Department of General Psychology
University of Padova
Padova
Italy

Cristina Mazza
Department of Neuroscience, Imaging and Clinical Sciences
University G.d'Annunzio
Chieti-Pescara
Italy

Editorial Office
MDPI
St. Alban-Anlage 66
4052 Basel, Switzerland

This is a reprint of articles from the Special Issue published online in the open access journal *International Journal of Environmental Research and Public Health* (ISSN 1660-4601) (available at: https://www.mdpi.com/journal/ijerph/special_issues/COVID-19_outbreak).

For citation purposes, cite each article independently as indicated on the article page online and as indicated below:

LastName, A.A.; LastName, B.B.; LastName, C.C. Article Title. *Journal Name* **Year**, *Volume Number*, Page Range.

ISBN 978-3-0365-3015-4 (Hbk)
ISBN 978-3-0365-3014-7 (PDF)

Contents

Preface to "COVID-19 Outbreak and Beyond: Psychological and Behavioral Responses and Future Perspectives"

The COVID-19 pandemic drastically changed our lifestyle when, on 30 January 2020, the World Health Organization declared the coronavirus disease outbreak a public health emergency of international concern. Since then, many governments have introduced unprecedented containment measures, hoping to slow the spread of the virus. International research suggests that both the pandemic and the related protective measures, such as lockdown, curfews, and social distancing, are having a profound impact on the mental health of the population. Among the most commonly observed psychological effects, there are high levels of stress, anxiety, depression, and post-traumatic symptoms, along with boredom and frustration. At the same time, the behavioral response of the population is of paramount importance to successfully contain the outbreak, creating a vicious circle in which the psychological distress impacts the willingness to comply with the protective measures, which, in turn, if prolonged, could exacerbate the population's distress. This book includes: i) original studies on the worldwide psychological and behavioral impact of COVID-19 on targeted individuals (e.g., parents, social workers, patients affected by physical and mental disorders); ii) studies exploring the effect of COVID-19 using advanced statistical and methodological techniques (e.g., machine learning technologies); iii) research on practical applications that could help identify persons at risk, mitigate the negative effects of this situation, and offer insights to policymakers to manage the pandemic are also highly welcomed.

Paolo Roma, Merylin Monaro, Cristina Mazza
Editors

International Journal of
Environmental Research and Public Health

MDPI

Article

How Does Social Class Affect Need for Structure during the COVID-19 Pandemic? A Moderated Mediating Model Analysis

Ting-Ting Rao †, Shen-Long Yang † and Xiaowen Zhu *

School of Humanities and Social Science, Xi'an Jiaotong University, Xi'an 710049, China; raotingtingpsy@stu.xjtu.edu.cn (T.-T.R.); yangsl@mail.xjtu.edu.cn (S.-L.Y.)
* Correspondence: xwzhu@mail.xjtu.edu.cn
† These authors contributed equally to this work.

Abstract: The COVID-19 pandemic is profoundly affecting the minds and behaviors of people worldwide. This study investigated the differences in the need for structure among people from different social classes and the psychological mechanisms underlying this need, as well as the moderating effect of the threat posed by the pandemic. Using data collected from non-student adults in China, we found that the lower an individual's social class, the lower their need for structure, and this effect was based on the mediating role of perceived control. However, the mediating effect was moderated by pandemic threat, and the above relationship existed only when this threat was low. When the level of pandemic threat was higher, neither the effect of social class nor of perceived control on the need for structure were significant. Specifically, in higher-threat situations, the need for structure among individuals from higher social classes and who had a higher sense of control increased significantly, meaning the mediating effect was no longer significant. This finding showed that under the threat of a pandemic, individuals who have a lower need for structure will still pursue and prefer structure and order. The theoretical and practical implications of the research are also discussed.

Keywords: need for structure; compensatory control; social class; COVID-19

Citation: Rao, T.-T.; Yang, S.-L.; Zhu, X. How Does Social Class Affect Need for Structure during the COVID-19 Pandemic? A Moderated Mediating Model Analysis. *Int. J. Environ. Res. Public Health* **2022**, *19*, 932. https://doi.org/10.3390/ijerph19020932

Academic Editors: Paolo Roma, Merylin Monaro and Cristina Mazza

Received: 31 October 2021
Accepted: 9 January 2022
Published: 14 January 2022

1. Introduction

Since the outbreak of the COVID-19 pandemic, our social culture and way of life have undergone profound changes [1,2]. Consequently, people are unknowingly experiencing the effects of this pandemic in their psychology and behavior. Many researchers have focused on the impact of COVID-19 on individuals' subjective feelings and objective life [3]. However, underlying these different psychological performances, there may be some common psychological basis worth exploring.

The need for structure, a basic need for human beings [4], may be one such basic psychological variable that deserves our attention. It refers to the psychological need to perceive one's existence and surroundings as clear, orderly, and predictable and not ambiguous or random [5], and could be the common inner psychological basis of many people's external manifestations. For example, the need for structure is concretely embodied in our desire for clarity from the obscure events, hope to find rules for our daily work, or our need to experience order in the products we purchase [6]. Researchers have found that the need for structure can predict conspiracy beliefs about important social events [7], preference for work [8], and people's understanding of news [9]. Compensatory control theory demonstrates that affirming social or physical structure is a means to compensate for personal control in an uncertain situation [10]. People who lack personal control are motivated to seek structure, order, and certainty in various ways [11]. As such, this motivation could be the underlying process that explains much of the psychological and behavioral performance of individuals during the COVID-19 pandemic.

It is worth noting that there are individual differences in this tendency. Previous studies have found that higher class individuals have a strong sense of personal control; therefore, their need for structure is relatively lower [7]. However, against the background of an uncertain environment, individuals tend to experience difficulty in maintaining their perceptions of a structured world, as demonstrated through belief in conspiracy theories [12], appeal of a dominant leader [13], and collective action [14], which may reinforce the need for structure. Therefore, it is worth exploring whether the level of the need for structure among individuals from different social classes has changed amidst the pandemic, and what is the mediating mechanism underlying this change. This will not only help us better understand the series of stress-related responses observed during the pandemic but also provide suggestions for pandemic prevention practice and management. Therefore, this study focused on the differences in the need for structure among individuals from higher and lower classes against the background of the COVID-19 pandemic, as well as the psychological mechanisms underlying this need.

1.1. Social Class, Perceived Control, and the Need for Structure

Studies focusing on the differences in the impact of the pandemic on individuals of higher and lower social classes in the USA [15] or in China [16,17] indicated that it imposed a significant negative impact on lower-class individuals. Moreover, previous research also found that perceived control positively affected individuals [18,19], while the need for structure negatively influenced them during the pandemic [20]. However, the relationship between social class, perceived control, and the need for structure is yet to be clarified. Subsequently, we explored their correlations from the existing literature (before the COVID-19 pandemic).

First, perceived control, the degree to which an individual feels that he or she is in control of the external world and not restricted by the environment [21], can negatively predict the need for structure. Research has shown that the lower an individual's perceived control, the higher their need for structure [22]. Compensatory control theory provides an explanation for this effect: According to the theory [6,11], feeling a sense of control is a basic human need and provides an important guarantee for people to feel that the world and their objective environment is safe and orderly. However, people are often faced with situations that are beyond their control. To compensate for this lack of control, individuals' needs for structure and order increase. Therefore, when confronted with incidents or uncertainty, individuals may upgrade their need for structure, with the lack of control as the psychological mediating factor. Many studies have supported this conclusion [23–25].

Second, social class, which refers to an individual's material resources as well as their perceptions of rank comparing with others in society [26], can positively predict perceived control. Despite the objective indicators used to define social class in existing literature, in recent years researchers tended to depict individuals' social class by integrating their perception of their own status in the social hierarchy with the traditional objective measurement. Therefore, several psychological studies on social class examined both the effect of objective class (some indices representing objective social status and material position, such as annual income, education level, and occupational reputation) and subjective class (a person's subjective assessment of where they are on the social ladder) [27]. Previous research suggests that higher class individuals are more likely to have a higher sense of control, based on both objective and subjective social class indicators [21,28]. The cognitive theory of social class [26] attempts an explanation of this effect: The theory argues that people who belong to higher classes are more likely to enjoy more resources in their life, and their living environment can provide them with more protection; thus, it is easier for such individuals to pursue and achieve important life goals and follow their own desires freely. Conversely, due to the shortage of material resources in their life, individuals who belong to lower classes are often subjects of their environment and must consider more environmental factors and the influence of others in their social lives. In the long run, individuals belonging to higher classes develop a relatively higher sense of control, while those of lower classes tend to possess a low sense of control [26]. These findings have been consistently supported by different studies with East Asian [7] and American participants [29].

Based on these two aspects, we can infer a mediating relationship among social class, perceived control, and the need for structure. In particular, the higher the social class of the individual, the higher their perceived control, which further leads to a lower need for structure. Research has already found a mediation model of "social class → perceived control → need for structure" [7]; however, the study only took college students as its participants and only examined the effects of the subjective class, which rendered its results less compelling. In the present study, we retested this issue by using data obtained from adults in the context of the COVID-19 pandemic and examining the effects based both on objective and subjective social classes. We proposed the following hypothesis:

Hypothesis 1. *Participants from lower social classes have lower levels of the need for structure than those from higher social classes, with perceived control playing a mediating role.*

1.2. Moderating Effect of the Threat of the Pandemic

The above hypothesis describes the general relationship among social class, perceived control, and the need for structure. However, considering the threat posed by the pandemic, we speculated that the relationship between the three variables will differ. Compensatory control theory demonstrates a lower sense of control leads individuals to seek structure, while also proposing some potential moderating variables that could remove the negative correlation between perceived control and the need for structure [6]. For example, individuals with lower perceived control indicated an increased preference for products that provide structure, but for individuals with a strong belief in God this effect was not significant [30]. The existing research on compensatory control theory has tended to focus on the conditions under which the need for structure will not increase among people with lower levels of perceived control [30,31]. Conversely, the present study examined whether the need for structure increases among people with a higher sense of control under the threat of a pandemic. Therefore, in addition to compensatory control theory, we introduced further theoretical perspectives to analyze this assumption.

The cognitive motivation model of stress [32] can provide a new perspective to investigate this issue. This theory focuses on the relationship between the stress experienced by individuals and their cognitive structure. Based on this model, the desire for certainty is one of the preconditions for individuals to construct cognitive structures in stressful situations. More importantly, the model suggests that when people feel stress and threat, their need for certainty increases. According to this view, we can conclude that in the context of a pandemic, people may feel pressure and threat, thus increasing their need for structure.

Further, there may be individual differences in the effects of this increase. Studies have shown that motivational threats most typically cause a specific motivation among people who have relatively lower general levels of that particular motivation [33–35]. That is, threat or stress from the environment may make the motivation salient for everyone, although it will have a stronger effect for those with low chronic motivation, thus causing them to become close to those that have high levels of that motivation. Therefore, if Hypothesis 1 holds true, people from higher social classes and with a higher sense of control will generally have a relatively lower need for structure. Therefore, we can further speculate that in a pandemic-threat situation, those individuals (from higher classes and/or with higher perceived control) are more likely to find their need for structure increases significantly than those from lower social classes and/or who have lower perceived control.

Based on the above analysis, we proposed the following three hypotheses regarding this moderating effect.

Hypothesis 2a. *The threat of a pandemic can moderate the relationship between perceived control and the need for structure: When the level of pandemic threat is lower, perceived control negatively predicts the need for structure; when the threat level increases, the need for structure among individuals with higher perceived control will increase significantly, so that the predictive effect of perceived control on the need for structure will no longer be significant.*

Hypothesis 2b. *The threat of a pandemic can moderate the relationship between social class and the need for structure: When the level of pandemic threat is lower, social class will negatively predict the need for structure; when the threat level increases, the need for structure among individuals from higher social classes will increase significantly, so that the predictive effect of social class on the need for structure will no longer be significant.*

Hypothesis 2c. *The threat of a pandemic can moderate the mediating relationship of "social class → perceived control → need for structure" proposed in Hypothesis 1: When the level of pandemic threat is lower, the mediating effect will be significant; when the threat is higher, the mediating effect will not be established because the predictive effect of both social class and perceived control on the need for structure will no longer be significant (Figure 1).*

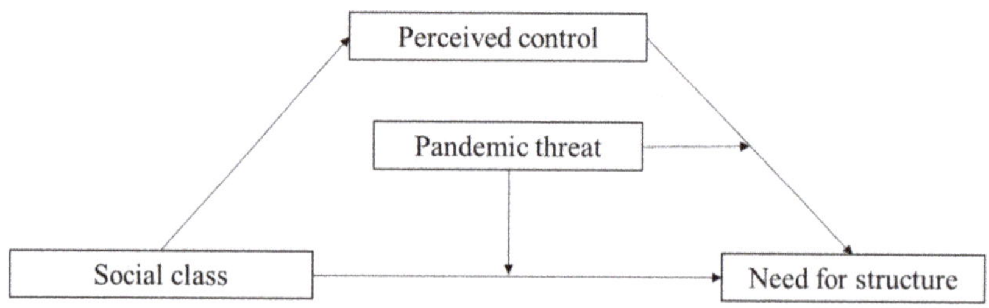

Figure 1. Hypothesized moderated mediating model.

1.3. Overview of the Present Study

The present study examined the effects of both subjective and objective classes to test the above hypotheses to obtain more robust results. Data were obtained from a survey of non-student adults in China, and the hypothesized variable relationships and models were examined using a cross-sectional study design. Until 20 July 2021, the daily number of confirmed new COVID-19 cases in China had remained extremely low for many months. However, from late July to August, there were small outbreaks of COVID-19 in several Chinese provinces. According to official standards, several areas in China were classified as high risk or medium risk during this period. Within this context, we distributed questionnaires through an online platform to adults (excluding students) in various Chinese provinces in August 2021 to collect their self-reported scores on the above variables. We considered the official pandemic risk level (including high-risk, medium-risk, and low-risk areas) as the index of objective pandemic threat. Since residents in different regions of China faced different risk levels during this period, this Chinese sample was especially suitable for testing the present study's hypotheses.

2. Materials and Methods

2.1. Participants

We recruited adult Chinese residents who were told this was a study on public social perceptions via Credamo (a Chinese questionnaire website, www.credamo.com (accessed on 10 January 2022). To thank them for their time, each participant who provided a valid response received ¥5. All participants were fully informed that their anonymity was assured, why the research was being conducted, and how their data would be used. As we aimed to test the effect of individuals' social class, only non-student participants' data were included. We included two questions to identify whether each participant's data were valid, namely, "Please choose 'strongly disagree' for this question," and "Please choose 'not sure' for this question," which confirmed whether the participants had read the questions carefully. Data from participants who failed to answer these questions correctly were deleted. Students (according to the participants' self-reported occupations) and participants who did not know the pandemic risk level in their area (according to the comparison between their self-reported risk level and the official risk level of the area where they lived) were also excluded (see also Section 2.2.5). In total, 92 participants with invalid data were excluded, leaving a final sample of 837 (43.8% male, $N = 367$, $M_{age} = 31.93$, $SD = 6.82$), which was higher than the recommended sample size ($N \approx 250$) for obtaining stable coefficients based on the average effect size ($r \approx 0.20$) in social and personality psychology [36,37].

2.2. Measures

2.2.1. Objective Social Class

Three indicators of the objective social class (i.e., educational attainment, occupation, and monthly income) were measured. First, participants reported their education level by choosing one of the following six options: 1 = "primary school or below", 2 = "junior high school", 3 = "High school diploma or equivalent", 4 = "junior college", 5 = "bachelor's degree", or 6 = "postgraduate degree or higher". Second, they reported their occupations in one of six categories, according to the classification criteria offered by previous Chinese research [38]: 1 = "student" (excluded); 2 = "temporary workers, unemployed people, unskilled workers, and agricultural workers, such as farmers"; 3 = "manual laborers, self-employed workers, skilled workers, and workers at the same level, such as industrial workers and service employees"; 4 = "general management personnel, general professional and technical personnel, and clerical staff, such as salespersons and drivers"; 5 = "middle management, middle-level professional and technical personnel, and assistant professional personnel, such as doctors, teachers, and engineers"; and 6 = "professional senior managers, senior professional and technical personnel, and professional supervisors, such as civil servants, company managers, and project managers." Third, monthly income was divided into seven categories: <1000 RMB, 1000–2000 RMB, 2000–4000 RMB, 4000–8000 RMB, 8000–16,000 RMB, 16,000–32,000 RMB, and 32,000 RMB or more, with an overall value ranging from 1 to 7. Following the methods of previous studies [39,40], the three scores were then standardized, and an exploratory factor analysis extracted one principal component for the three items. The factor loading for each item was multiplied by the respective item score, and these scores were summed. Eigenvalues were then used to divide this sum and create the final objective class score. Higher scores represented a higher objective class.

2.2.2. Subjective Social Class

The MacArthur Scale [41] was used to measure subjective social class. Participants were shown a 10-rung ladder and were asked to imagine that each level of the ladder represented different social classes in China (1 = the lowest class; 10 = the highest class). They were asked to consider their own social class and to choose a suitable number: a higher number indicated a participant's higher perceived social class.

2.2.3. Perceived Control

Perceived control was measured with a 12-item scale [21], which included items such as: "I can do just about anything I really set my mind to", "When I really want to do something, I usually find a way to succeed at it", "Whether or not I am able to get what I want is in my own hands", "What happens to me in the future mostly depends on me", "Other people determine most of what I can and cannot do", "There is little I can do to change many of the important things in my life", "I often feel helpless in dealing with the problems of life", "What happens in my life is often beyond my control", "There are many things that interfere with what I want to do", "I have little control over the things that happen to me", "There is really no way I can solve all the problems I have" and "I sometimes feel I am being pushed around in my life" (the last eight items were reverse scored). These items were rated on a 7-point Likert scale (1 = strongly disagree; 7 = strongly agree). The responses were then averaged across the 12 items, with higher scores indicating a higher level of perceived control. Cronbach's alpha in this study was 0.92.

2.2.4. Need for Structure

The need for structure was measured with an 11-item Personal Need for Structure scale [42], which included items such as: "It upsets me to go into a situation without knowing what I can expect from it", "I'm not bothered by things that interrupt my daily routine (reverse scored)", "I enjoy having a clear and structured way of life", "I like to have a place for everything and everything in its place", "I find that a well-ordered life with regular hours makes my life tedious (reverse scored)", "I don't like situations that are uncertain", "I hate to change my plans at the last minute", "I hate to be with people who are unpredictable", "I find that a consistent routine enables me to enjoy life more", "I enjoy the exhilaration of being in unpredictable situations (reverse scored)", and "I become uncomfortable when the rules in a situation are not clear". These items were rated on a 6-point Likert scale (1 = strongly disagree; 6 = strongly agree). The responses were averaged across the 11 items, with higher scores indicating a higher need for structure. Cronbach's alpha in this study was 0.89.

2.2.5. Pandemic Threat

We used a relatively objective standard to measure the threat of the COVID-19 pandemic. As the Chinese government released risk levels for each region daily to reflect the threat of the pandemic in each area of China, the participants were asked to choose one of four options to indicate the pandemic risk level in their area. The higher the number they chose, the higher the threat of the COVID-19 pandemic in their location. After they made their choices, we compared their self-reported risk ratings of where they lived with the official risk level. If these two levels were inconsistent, the participant's data were excluded (see also Section 2.1).

3. Results

3.1. Common Method Variance Test

This study not only used self-reported data, but also combined objective social class indicators and risk levels, which could help control for the effects of common methodological biases. Simultaneously, Harman's single-factor test was used to examine the common method variance [43]. The result showed that the first factor accounted for 26.34% of the total variance and did not explain most of the variance (<40%). Thus, there was no obvious common methodological bias in this study.

3.2. Preliminary Analyses

The means, standard deviations, and correlation coefficients for main research variables are displayed in Table 1. The results indicated that both objective and subjective social class were positively correlated with perceived control, and those three variables above were all negatively correlated with the need for structure.

Table 1. Descriptive statistics and correlations for all variables.

Variables	*M* (*SD*)	1	2	3	4
1.Objective social class	0.00 (1.00)	1			
2.Subjective social class	5.71 (1.41)	0.37 ***	1		
3.perceived control	4.98 (1.00)	0.24 ***	0.35 ***	1	
4.Pandemic threat	3.17 (0.70)	0.06	−0.04	−0.01	1
5.Need for Structure	4.32 (0.77)	−0.08 *	−0.13 ***	−0.17 ***	0.16 ***

Note: $N = 837$; * $p < 0.05$, *** $p < 0.001$; M = mean; SD = standard deviation.

3.3. Mediating Effect of Perceived Control (Objective Social Class as Independent Variable)

Mediating effect analysis in PROCESS [44] was used to test the mediation effect using 1000 bootstrapped samples. Figure 2 displays the paths in the proposed model. Objective social class positively predicted perceived control (b = 0.24, SE = 0.03, t = 7.03, p < 0.001) and negatively predicted need for structure (b = −0.06, SE = 0.03, t = −2.18, p = 0.03). When we added objective social class and perceived control to the model simultaneously, perceived control negatively predicted need for structure (b = −0.12, SE = 0.03, t = −4.57, p < 0.001) and objective social class could not predict need for structure significantly (b = −0.03, SE = 0.03, t = −1.06, p = 0.29). Furthermore, bootstrapping analyses showed that perceived control mediated the pathway from objective social class to need for structure (indirect effect = −0.03, SE = 0.01, 95% CI = [−0.05, −0.02]), and the ratio of the indirect effect to total effect is 50.55%.

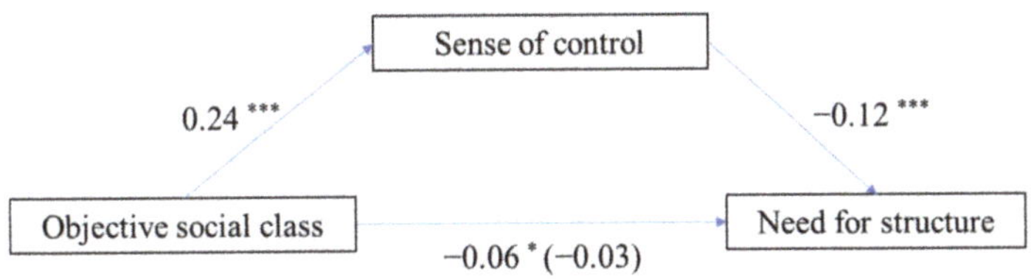

Figure 2. Model of the mediating role of perceived control in the association between objective social class and need for structure; * p < 0.05, *** p < 0.001.

3.4. Moderated Mediating Effect of Pandemic Threat (Objective Social Class as Independent Variable)

We next tested for the moderating role of pandemic threat. Moderated mediating effect analysis in PROCESS [44] was used to test the moderated mediation effect using 1000 bootstrapped samples. Results (see Table 2) showed that objective social class was significantly associated with perceived control. More importantly, pandemic threat significantly moderated the impact of objective social class on need for structure and the impact of perceived control on need for structure. This suggests that the mediating effect among objective social class, perceived control, and need for structure was moderated by the pandemic threat. We further tested the conditional indirect effects. For a lower pandemic threat, the indirect effect of objective social class on the need for structure was significant (indirect effect = −0.08, 95% CI [−0.16, −0.01]), and for a higher pandemic threat, the effect was not significant (indirect effect = 0.03, 95% CI [−0.03,0.09]).

Table 2. Multiple regression analyses of moderated mediation effect.

Predictors	Model 1 (Criterion = Need for Structure)		Model 2 (Criterion = Perceived Control)		Model 3 (Criterion = Need for Structure)	
	b	t	b	t	b	t
Objective social class	−0.07	−2.58 *	0.24	7.23 ***	−0.03	−1.23
Pandemic threat	0.17	4.81 ***			0.16	4.61 ***
Objective social class ×Pandemic threat	0.13	3.28 *			0.08	2.29 *
Perceived control					−0.12	−4.09 ***
Perceived control ×Pandemic threat					0.13	3.51 ***
R^2	0.04		0.06		0.08	
F	9.79 ***		52.25 ***		8.14 ***	

Note: * p < 0.05, *** p < 0.001.

We conducted simple slope tests to better understand the results regarding pandemic threat as a moderator. As depicted in Figure 3, when the pandemic threat was lower, the need for structure of the upper class individuals was significantly lower than that of lower class individuals ($b = -0.15$, $SE = 0.04$, $t = -3.69$, $p < 0.001$). However, when the pandemic threat was higher, this discrepancy disappeared ($b = 0.02$, $SE = 0.03$, $t = 0.77$, $p = 0.44$). Furthermore, for the lower objective class, pandemic threat could not predict the need for structure ($b = 0.14$, $SE = 0.05$, $t = 0.97$, $p = 0.33$), but for the higher objective class, the pandemic threat positively predicted the need for structure ($b = 0.30$, $SE = 0.06$, $t = 5.05$, $p < 0.001$).

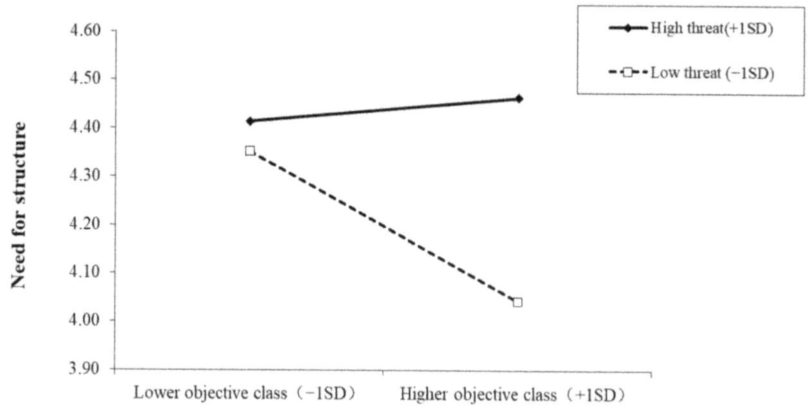

Figure 3. Interactive effect of pandemic threat and objective social class on need for structure. Note: Pandemic threat is graphed for two levels: high pandemic threat (1 *SD* above the mean) and low pandemic threat (1 *SD* below the mean).

Similarly, as depicted in Figure 4, when the pandemic threat was lower, people with higher perceived control reported a significantly lower need for structure than those with lower perceived control ($b = -0.21$, $SE = 0.04$, $t = -5.03$, $p < 0.001$). However, when the pandemic threat was higher, this discrepancy disappeared ($b = -0.02$, $SE = 0.04$, $t = -0.61$, $p = 0.54$). Furthermore, for individuals of lower perceived control, pandemic threat could not predict the need for structure ($b = 0.03$, $SE = 0.05$, $t = 0.57$, $p = 0.57$), but for those with higher perceived control, pandemic threat positively predicted the need for structure ($b = 0.29$, $SE = 0.06$, $t = 5.21$, $p < 0.001$).

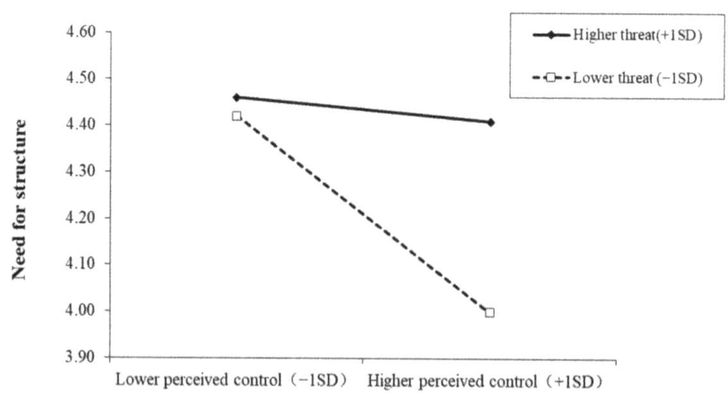

Figure 4. Interactive effect of pandemic threat and perceived control on need for structure. Note: Pandemic threat is graphed for two levels: higher pandemic threat (1 *SD* above the mean) and lower pandemic threat (1 *SD* below the mean).

3.5. Mediating Effect of Pandemic Threat (Subjective Class as Independent Variable)

Next, we used the subjective class as the independent variable, testing the same mediation model and moderated mediation model. Mediating effect analysis in PROCESS [44] was used to test the mediation effect using 1000 bootstrapped samples. Figure 5 displays the paths in the proposed model. Subjective social class positively predicted perceived control (b = 0.25, SE = 0.02, t = 10.82, p < 0.001) and negatively predicted need for structure (b = −0.07, SE = 0.02, t = −4.16, p < 0.001). When we added subjective social class and perceived control to the model simultaneously, perceived control negatively predicted need for structure (b = −0.11, SE = 0.03, t = −3.67, p < 0.001) and subjective social class significantly predicted need for structure (b = −0.04, SE = 0.02, t = −2.67, p = 0.008). Furthermore, bootstrapping analyses showed that perceived control mediated the pathway from subjective social class to need for structure (indirect effect = −0.03, SE = 0.01, 95% CI = [−0.04, −0.01]), and the ratio of the indirect effect to total effect was 37.07%.

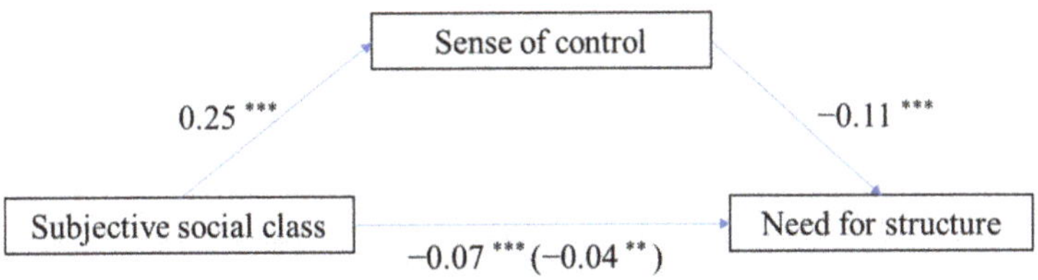

Figure 5. Model of the mediating role of perceived control in the association between subjective social class and need for structure; ** p < 0.01, *** p < 0.001.

3.6. Moderated Mediating Effect of Pandemic Threat (Subjective Social Class as Independent Variable)

We next tested for the moderating role of the pandemic threat. Moderated mediating effect analysis in PROCESS [44] was used to test the moderated mediation effect using 1000 bootstrapped samples. Results (see Table 3) showed that subjective social class was significantly associated with perceived control. More importantly, pandemic threat significantly moderated the impact of subjective social class on need for structure and the impact of perceived control on need for structure. This suggests that the mediating effect among subjective social class, perceived control, and need for structure was moderated by pandemic threat. We further tested the conditional indirect effects. For lower pandemic threat, the indirect effect of subjective social class on need for structure was significant (indirect effect = −0.05, 95% CI [−0.07, −0.03]), and for higher pandemic threat, the effect was not significant (indirect effect = 0.00, 95% CI [−0.02,0.01]).

Table 3. Multiple regression analyses of moderated mediation effect.

Predictors	Model 1 (Criterion = Need for Structure)		Model 2 (Criterion = Perceived Control)		Model 3 (Criterion = Need for Structure)	
	b	*t*	*b*	*t*	*b*	*t*
Subjective social class	−0.06	−3.82 **	0.25	10.82 ***	−0.03	−2.05 *
Pandemic threat	0.17	4.73 ***			0.16	−4.60 ***
Subjective social class ×Pandemic threat	0.09	3.52 **			0.06	2.64 **
Perceived control					−0.11	−3.63 ***
Perceived control ×Pandemic threat					0.13	3.40 ***
R^2	0.05		0.12		0.08	
F	12.45 ***		117.15 ***		8.96 ***	

Note: * p < 0.05, ** p < 0.01, *** p < 0.001.

We conducted simple slope tests to better understand the results regarding pandemic threat as a moderator. As depicted in Figure 6, when the pandemic threat was lower, the need for structure of the upper-class individuals was significantly lower than that of the lower-class individuals ($b = -0.13$, $SE = 0.03$, $t = -4.49$, $p < 0.001$). However, when the pandemic threat was higher, this discrepancy disappeared ($b = 0.00$, $SE = 0.02$, $t = -0.02$, $p = 0.98$). Furthermore, for lower subjective class, pandemic threat could not predict the need for structure ($b = 0.05$, $SE = 0.04$, $t = 1.12$, $p = 0.26$), but for those with higher subjective class, pandemic threat positively predicted the need for structure ($b = 0.30$, $SE = 0.06$, $t = 4.99$, $p < 0.001$).

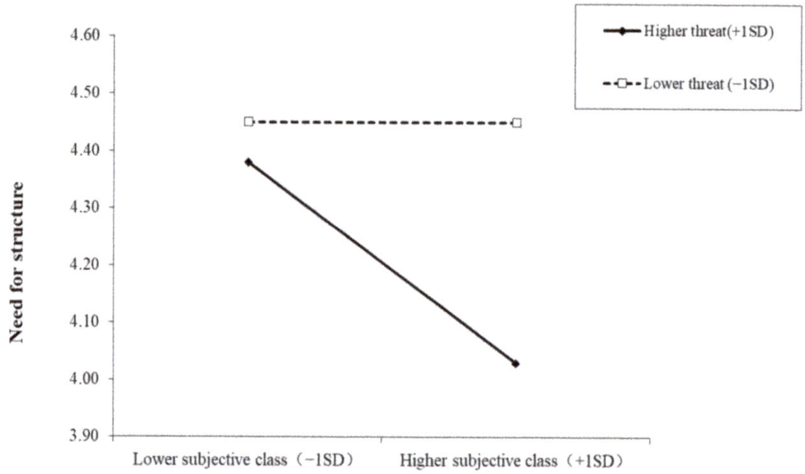

Figure 6. Interactive effect of pandemic threat and subjective social class on need for structure. Note: Pandemic threat is graphed for two levels: high pandemic threat (1 *SD* above the mean) and low pandemic threat (1 *SD* below the mean).

Similarly, as depicted in Figure 7, when the pandemic threat was lower, people with higher perceived control had significantly lower need for structure than those with lower perceived control ($b = -0.20$, $SE = 0.04$, $t = -4.61$, $p < 0.001$). However, when the pandemic threat was higher, this discrepancy disappeared ($b = -0.02$, $SE = 0.04$, $t = -0.45$, $p = 0.65$). Furthermore, for individuals of lower perceived control, pandemic threat could not predict the need for structure ($b = 0.03$, $SE = 0.05$, $t = 0.72$, $p = 0.47$), but for those with higher perceived control, pandemic threat positively predicted the need for structure ($b = 0.29$, $SE = 0.06$, $t = 5.13$, $p < 0.001$).

Therefore, based on both the results of objective and subjective social classes, all the above hypotheses were supported by these data. Perceived control played a mediating role between social class and the need for structure, and pandemic threat moderated the mediating model.

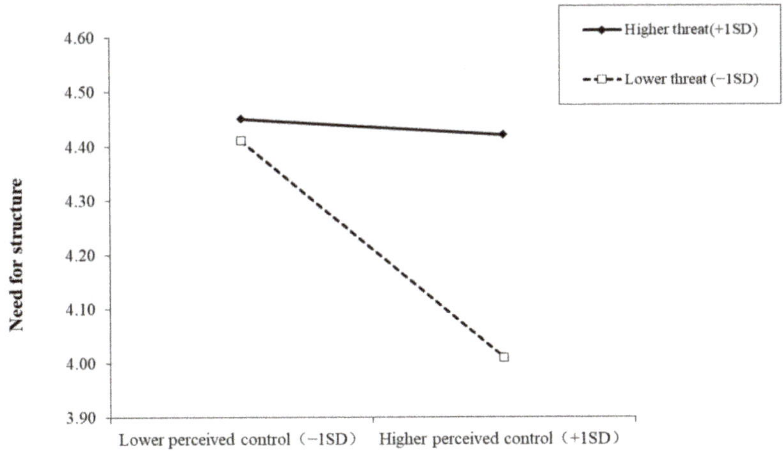

Figure 7. Interactive effect of pandemic threat and perceived control on need for structure. Note: Pandemic threat is graphed for two levels: higher pandemic threat (1 *SD* above the mean) and lower pandemic threat (1 *SD* below the mean).

4. Discussion

Based on the self-reported data in China during the COVID-19 pandemic and the objective risk level of each region given by official authority, this study tested the mediating effect and moderating effect hypotheses mentioned above. The results support all our hypotheses. Firstly, the results suggested that the mediating effect of perceived control on the relationship between social class (both objective and subjective) and need for structure is significant; thus, social class negatively predicted need for structure and this association was partially mediated by perceived control. Specifically, the lower an individual's social class is, the lower his or her sense of control is, and, therefore, the higher his or her need for structure tends to be. Furthermore, the results also showed that pandemic threat moderated the relationship between perceived control and need for structure, and the relationship between social class and need for structure, finally leading to the moderated mediating effect. Under the condition of higher pandemic threat, individuals with higher perceived control increased their need for structure significantly, so the predictive effect of perceived control on need for structure was no longer significant. Similarly, under the condition of higher pandemic threat, individuals of higher social class increased their need for structure significantly, so to the predictive effect of social class on need for structure was no longer significant. Finally, the results showed the moderating effect of pandemic threat on the mediating model of "social class → perceived control → need for structure". Therefore, all the hypotheses of this study were supported.

Previous studies tended to regard the need for structure as an independent variable and to examine its predictive effect on other psychological outcomes [45,46]. Conversely, few studies have taken the need for structure as a dependent variable and focused on the factors influencing it. Although the need for structure can be regarded as a relatively stable personality trait, it can also be influenced by other individual and environmental factors [47,48]. Especially in the context of uncertainty, need for structure can be regarded as the psychological basis of many psychological and behavioral factors, such as conspiracy theory thinking [49] and stereotyping [23]. It is meaningful to pay attention to need for structure and its influencing factors under the pandemic conditions. Accordingly, this study first examined the predictive effect of social class on need for structure, and found that people of lower class tend to develop a higher level of need for structure due to their relatively lower perceived control. This conclusion supports an expansion of previous research. Previous studies have found that social class positively predicts perceived control [21,29], while perceived control negatively predicts need for structure [30,31]. Although a previous study directly investigated the relationship among the three variables [7], it focused only on the student samples and the effect of subjective social class. The present study provides more solid evidence for this mediation model by using a sample of non-student adults from different provinces in China. This result more directly reveals the difference in need for structure among people of different social classes and the psychological mechanism underlining their lack of control. Compensatory control theory proposes that when personal control is threatened, individuals are more inclined to seek structure to compensate for personal control [6,11]. The results of this study show that people of lower class are more likely to feel the lack of control and then develop compensatory control, which has enlightenment value for the development of compensatory control research in the future.

In addition, this study's most important finding is the moderating effect of pandemic threat. This phenomenon suggests that for individuals who generally lack one kind of motivation (e.g., the need for structure), it is more likely for them to be provoked by a threat (e.g., the COVID-19 pandemic) and the particular motivation of them will increases even more significantly. Similar views have been proposed and supported by previous studies [33–35] and the present study supplements the conclusions of this kind of research. At the same time, the results also support the cognitive motivation model of stress. This model suggests that an important aspect of the psychological impact of stress and threat is the increased desire for certainty [32], which is consistent with the conclusions regarding the need for structure made in the present study. We also found that, when faced with the threat of COVID-19, even those from higher classes (and who had a higher sense of control) experienced an increase in their need for structure, order, and certainty (though they did not in their normal state). This showed a cross-group consistency in psychological needs during the pandemic.

Why do individuals who normally deal better with uncertainties (individuals of higher class and with higher perceived control) experience the greater impact of the pandemic threat? We believe that it is necessary to distinguish their demonstration of the general state and the crisis state. In general, individuals of higher social class (and usually with a higher sense of control [21]) command more social resources, which can support them to cope with the challenges of normal life [26]. In contrast, lower-class individuals are less capable to deal with environmental threats due to a lack of resources, and, therefore, are more in need of certainty and order [7]. Under the condition of a new kind of threat (the COVID-19 pandemic), however, the upper-class individuals feel a threat that differs from the ones they face in their daily lives, which leads to a significant increase in their need for structure and avoidance of uncertainty. The threat of the pandemic has a lower impact on lower-class individuals, perhaps because they have been accustomed to threats from various domains. Therefore, instead of saying that the threat of the pandemic affects upper-class individuals more, it can also be interpreted as the unequal distribution of "normal" uncertainties and threats across different classes in daily life.

This study presents three theoretical implications that may provide some insight for the future research. First, the study observed that lower personal control is not the only source of the need for structure. On the contrary, people with a higher sense of control may also have a relatively high need for structure under certain conditions, such as the threat of a pandemic. Therefore, researchers of compensatory control theory need to further investigate the boundary conditions of the compensatory control model. Second, in terms of the need for structure, although this variable is usually regarded as a relatively stable personality trait [42], our study revealed that this basic need fluctuates under certain conditions. We found that the interaction of individual factors (social class, personal control) and environmental factors (pandemic threat) significantly predicted the need for structure. This suggests that future research on the need for structure should focus on the interaction effect between individual and environmental factors to comprehensively reveal the factors influencing this need. Third, this study adopted two operational definitions for the measurement of social class, that is, objective social class and subjective social class, and the effects were shown to be almost identical. Previous studies have found that the two have different effects on the prediction of some dependent variables [50]. For example, some studies found that subjective class positively predicts individual's support for social system, while objective class is negatively correlated with system support [51,52]. In the present study, however, the effect of subjective class was almost the same as that of objective class, and together their effects supported all our assumptions. On the one hand, this reflects the stability of the conclusions of our study. On the other hand, it also shows that the concepts of subjective class and objective class still have a certain commonality and relevance.

In addition, this study also has some practical significance. The COVID-19 outbreak has greatly affected the way we think and live. At the same time, economic inequality, environmental problems, new technology, and many other factors have left the world in a state of uncertainty. The results of this study highlight that when faced with the threat and stress of a pandemic, people prefer to pursue a structured, orderly, and predictable life and do not want to face the random, uncontrollable, and changing physical and social environment. Moreover, even higher social class groups will have more needs and preferences for order and structure in the context of an epidemic or pandemic. Therefore, in the midst of the current pandemic, governments should consider whether their pandemic management policies meet the public's need for structure and aim to maximize citizens' sense of structure and order. Moreover, due to the consistency in the need for structure among the upper and lower social classes in the context of the pandemic, policy makers must also ensure the interests and security of both higher- and lower-class groups without distinction.

Finally, this study has some limitations, which should be investigated in future research to conduct a deeper exploration of the topic. First, the sample was derived only from China and was investigated in the context of small COVID-19 outbreaks in several Chinese provinces in July and August 2021. China's pandemic-prevention policy is relatively stricter [17], and Chinese individuals exhibit higher levels of collectivism when facing the pandemic and the related policy measures [53]. Thus, Chinese individuals' psychological response to COVID-19 may be influenced by certain unique sociocultural factors. Therefore, the behaviors of people in other countries and regions should be investigated in the future to test the conclusions of the present study. Second, since students and individuals who chose the wrong risk level of their residential area were excluded from this study, the representation of the present study findings may be slightly inadequate. Although this may not have affected the main conclusions of the present study, future research should include more representative samples. Third, our study's conclusions rely on cross-sectional data, and the investigation of the relationship between variables was based on the correlation method, which cannot provide strong proof of a causal relationship. Consequently, alternative methods rooted in experimental design should be considered in future research to further verify the model and effects observed in this study, such as implicit-mediation analysis [54]. In addition, implementing longitudinal design is also a feasible way to test the robustness of the conclusions. Fourth, the present study only focused on the moderating effect of the threat of COVID-19. However, threats come from many sources in real life. Do all threats result in this effect? This question should also be examined in more complex studies in the future. Finally, the measurement of the participants' occupation may not accurately describe the reality rank of some participants. Although the problem may be minor, it needs to be acknowledged. Future research can explore more ways to assess an individual's objective social class.

5. Conclusions

Given the multiple psychological and behavioral impacts of the COVID-19 pandemic, we must focus on the common psychological underpinnings behind the typical manifestations of these impacts. The need for structure is one such motivational factor and can predict many psychological and behavioral performances. Despite the general individual differences in the need for structure (to be specific, higher-class individuals exhibit lower need for structure), individuals will demonstrate the same higher preference for structure under the threat of COVID-19 pandemic, regardless of their social class. Therefore, when formulating pandemic-prevention policies, the governments should give more consideration to protect the needs of structure, order, and certainty of individuals from different social classes, races, and groups.

Author Contributions: Conceptualization, T.-T.R., S.-L.Y. and X.Z.; methodology, T.-T.R., S.-L.Y. and X.Z.; formal analysis, T.-T.R. and S.-L.Y.; data curation, T.-T.R. and S.-L.Y.; investigation, T.-T.R. and S.-L.Y.; writing—original draft preparation, T.-T.R. and S.-L.Y.; writing—review and editing, X.Z. All authors have read and agreed to the published version of the manuscript.

Funding: This research was funded by National Natural Science Foundation of China (No. 72001171), Humanity and Social Science Youth foundation of Ministry of Education of China (No. 18YJC190029), and China Postdoctoral Science Foundation (No. 2017M623138).

Institutional Review Board Statement: All procedures performed in studies involving human participants were in accordance with the 1964 Helsinki declaration and approved by the Biomedical Ethics Committee of Health Science Center, Xi'an Jiaotong University (Approval Code: 2021-1549).

Informed Consent Statement: Informed consent was obtained from all subjects involved in the study.

Data Availability Statement: Data will be provided if requested to the authors.

Conflicts of Interest: The authors declare no conflict of interest.

References

1. Pak, A.; Adegboye, O.A.; Adekunle, A.I.; Rahman, K.M.; McBryde, E.S.; Eisen, D.P. Economic Consequences of the COVID-19 Outbreak: The Need for Epidemic Preparedness. *Front. Public Health* **2020**, *8*, 241. [CrossRef] [PubMed]
2. Huang, Y.; Zhao, N. Generalized anxiety disorder, depressive symptoms and sleep quality during COVID-19 outbreak in China: A web-based cross-sectional survey. *Psychiatry Res.* **2020**, *288*, 112954. [CrossRef]
3. Van Bavel, J.J.; Baicker, K.; Boggio, P.S.; Capraro, V.; Cichocka, A.; Cikara, M.; Crockett, M.J.; Crum, A.J.; Douglas, K.M.; Druckman, J.N.; et al. Using social and behavioural science to support COVID-19 pandemic response. *Nat. Hum. Behav.* **2020**, *4*, 460–471. [CrossRef]
4. Kay, A.C.; Laurin, K.; Fitzsimons, G.M.; Landau, M.J. A functional basis for structure-seeking: Exposure to structure promotes willingness to engage in motivated action. *J. Exp. Psychol. Gen.* **2014**, *143*, 486–491. [CrossRef]
5. Friesen, J.P.; Kay, A.C.; Eibach, R.P.; Galinsky, A.D. Seeking structure in social organization: Compensatory control and the psychological advantages of hierarchy. *J. Pers. Soc. Psychol.* **2014**, *106*, 590–609. [CrossRef]
6. Landau, M.J.; Kay, A.C.; Whitson, J.A. Compensatory control and the appeal of a structured world. *Psychol. Bull.* **2015**, *141*, 694–722. [CrossRef] [PubMed]
7. Mao, J.; Yang, S.; Guo, Y. Are individuals from lower social classes more susceptible to conspiracy theories? An explanation from the compensatory control theory. *Asian J. Soc. Psychol.* **2020**, *23*, 372–383. [CrossRef]
8. Ma, A.; Kay, A.C. Compensatory control and ambiguity intolerance. *Organ. Behav. Hum. Decis. Process.* **2017**, *140*, 46–61. [CrossRef]
9. Axt, J.R.; Landau, M.J.; Kay, A.C. The Psychological Appeal of Fake-News Attributions. *Psychol. Sci.* **2020**, *31*, 848–857. [CrossRef] [PubMed]
10. Kay, A.C.; Gaucher, D.; Napier, J.L.; Callan, M.J.; Laurin, K. God and the government: Testing a compensatory control mechanism for the support of external systems. *J. Pers. Soc. Psychol.* **2008**, *95*, 18–35. [CrossRef]
11. Kay, A.C.; Whitson, J.A.; Gaucher, D.; Galinsky, A.D. Compensatory Control. *Curr. Dir. Psychol. Sci.* **2009**, *18*, 264–268. [CrossRef]
12. Sullivan, D.; Landau, M.J.; Rothschild, Z.K. An existential function of enemyship: Evidence that people attribute influence to personal and political enemies to compensate for threats to control. *J. Pers. Soc. Psychol.* **2010**, *98*, 434–449. [CrossRef]
13. Kakkar, H.; Sivanathan, N. When the appeal of a dominant leader is greater than a prestige leader. *Proc. Natl. Acad. Sci. USA* **2017**, *114*, 6734–6739. [CrossRef]
14. Fritsche, I.; Moya, M.; Bukowski, M.; Jugert, P.; De Lemus, S.; Decker, O.; Valor-Segura, I.; Navarro-Carrillo, G. The Great Recession and Group-Based Control: Converting Personal Helplessness into Social Class In-Group Trust and Collective Action. *J. Soc. Issues* **2017**, *73*, 117–137. [CrossRef]
15. Lee, H.; Singh, G.K. Monthly trends in self-reported health status and depression by race/ethnicity and socioeconomic status during the COVID-19 Pandemic, United States, April 2020–May 2021. *Ann. Epidemiol.* **2021**, *63*, 52–62. [CrossRef]
16. Wu, X.; Li, X.; Lu, Y.; Hout, M. Two tales of one city: Unequal vulnerability and resilience to COVID-19 by socioeconomic status in Wuhan, China. *Res. Soc. Strat. Mobil.* **2021**, *72*, 100584. [CrossRef] [PubMed]

17. Zhou, M.; Guo, W. Social factors and worry associated with COVID-19: Evidence from a large survey in China. *Soc. Sci. Med.* **2021**, *277*, 113934. [CrossRef] [PubMed]
18. Brailovskaia, J.; Margraf, J. The relationship between burden caused by coronavirus (Covid-19), addictive social media use, sense of control and anxiety. *Comput. Hum. Behav.* **2021**, *119*, 106720. [CrossRef]
19. Branley-Bell, D.; Talbot, C.V. "It is the only constant in what feels like a completely upside down and scary world": Living with an eating disorder during COVID-19 and the importance of perceived control for recovery and relapse. *Appetite* **2021**, *167*, 105596. [CrossRef]
20. White, H.A. Need for cognitive closure predicts stress and anxiety of college students during COVID-19 pandemic. *Pers. Individ. Differ.* **2021**, *187*, 111393. [CrossRef]
21. Lachman, M.E.; Weaver, S.L. The sense of control as a moderator of social class differences in health and well-being. *J. Pers. Soc. Psychol.* **1998**, *74*, 763–773. [CrossRef] [PubMed]
22. Whitson, J.A.; Galinsky, A.D. Lacking Control Increases Illusory Pattern Perception. *Science* **2008**, *322*, 115–117. [CrossRef] [PubMed]
23. Ma, A.; Axt, J.; Kay, A.C. A control-based account of stereotyping. *J. Exp. Soc. Psychol.* **2019**, *84*, 103819. [CrossRef]
24. Gasiorowska, A.; Zaleskiewicz, T. Trading in search of structure: Market relationships as a compensatory control tool. *J. Pers. Soc. Psychol.* **2021**, *120*, 300–334. [CrossRef]
25. Shepherd, S.; Kay, A.C.; Landau, M.J.; Keefer, L.A. Evidence for the specificity of control motivations in worldview defense: Distinguishing compensatory control from uncertainty management and terror management processes. *J. Exp. Soc. Psychol.* **2011**, *47*, 949–958. [CrossRef]
26. Kraus, M.W.; Piff, P.K.; Mendoza-Denton, R.; Rheinschmidt, M.L.; Keltner, D. Social class, solipsism, and contextualism: How the rich are different from the poor. *Psychol. Rev.* **2012**, *119*, 546–572. [CrossRef]
27. Manstead, A.S.R. The psychology of social class: How socioeconomic status impacts thought, feelings, and behaviour. *Br. J. Soc. Psychol.* **2018**, *57*, 267–291. [CrossRef]
28. Kraus, M.W.; Piff, P.K.; Keltner, D. Social class, sense of control, and social explanation. *J. Pers. Soc. Psychol.* **2009**, *97*, 992–1004. [CrossRef]
29. Gallo, L.C.; Bogart, L.M.; Vranceanu, A.-M.; Matthews, K.A. Socioeconomic Status, Resources, Psychological Experiences, and Emotional Responses: A Test of the Reserve Capacity Model. *J. Pers. Soc. Psychol.* **2005**, *88*, 386–399. [CrossRef]
30. Cutright, K.M. The Beauty of Boundaries: When and Why We Seek Structure in Consumption. *J. Consum. Res.* **2012**, *38*, 775–790. [CrossRef]
31. Cutright, K.M.; Bettman, J.R.; Fitzsimons, G.J. Putting Brands in Their Place: How a Lack of Control Keeps Brands Contained. *J. Mark. Res.* **2013**, *50*, 365–377. [CrossRef]
32. Bar-Tal, Y.; Shrira, A.; Keinan, G. The Effect of Stress on Cognitive Structuring. *Pers. Soc. Psychol. Rev.* **2013**, *17*, 87–99. [CrossRef] [PubMed]
33. Banfield, J.C.; Kay, A.C.; Cutright, K.M.; Wu, E.C.; Fitzsimons, G.J. A Person by Situation Account of Motivated System Defense. *Soc. Psychol. Pers. Sci.* **2011**, *2*, 212–219. [CrossRef]
34. Nail, P.R.; McGregor, I. Conservative Shift among Liberals and Conservatives Following 9/11/01. *Soc. Justice Res.* **2009**, *22*, 231–240. [CrossRef]
35. Nail, P.R.; McGregor, I.; Drinkwater, A.E.; Steele, G.M.; Thompson, A.W. Threat causes liberals to think like conservatives. *J. Exp. Soc. Psychol.* **2009**, *45*, 901–907. [CrossRef]
36. Schönbrodt, F.; Perugini, M. At what sample size do correlations stabilize? *J. Res. Pers.* **2013**, *47*, 609–612. [CrossRef]
37. Richard, F.D.; Bond, C.F.; Stokes-Zoota, J.J.; Bond, J.C.F. One Hundred Years of Social Psychology Quantitatively Described. *Rev. Gen. Psychol.* **2003**, *7*, 331–363. [CrossRef]
38. Shi, B.-G.; Shen, J.-l. The relationships among family SES, intelligence, intrinsic motivation and creativity. *Psycho-Log. Dev. Educ.* **2007**, *23*, 30–34. Available online: http://www.devpsy.com.cn/CN/Y2007/V23/I1/30 (accessed on 10 January 2022). (In Chinese)
39. Xie, X.; Wang, Y.; Wang, P.; Zhao, F.; Lei, L. Basic psychological needs satisfaction and fear of missing out: Friend support moderated the mediating effect of individual relative deprivation. *Psychiatry Res.* **2018**, *268*, 223–228. [CrossRef]
40. Ren, C. Measurement methodology on social economic status index of students. *J. Educ. Stud.* **2010**, *6*, 77–82. Available online: https://t.cnki.net/kcms/detail?v=3uoqIhG8C46NmWw7YpEsKL-WhGHP2RH_WMv_DQNmseEXweKPCrt6MHrQZ7HKZFmsMnp4gafl_-VtXS9dilZzVqe4kTn-5IhJ&uniplatform=NZKPT (accessed on 10 January 2022).
41. Adler, N.E.; Epel, E.S.; Castellazzo, G.; Ickovics, J.R. Relationship of subjective and objective social status with psychological and physiological functioning: Preliminary data in healthy, White women. *Health Psychol.* **2000**, *19*, 586–592. [CrossRef] [PubMed]
42. Neuberg, S.L.; Newsom, J.T. Personal need for structure: Individual differences in the desire for simpler structure. *J. Pers. Soc. Psychol.* **1993**, *65*, 113–131. [CrossRef]
43. Podsakoff, P.M.; MacKenzie, S.B.; Lee, J.Y.; Podsakoff, N.P. Common method biases in behavioral research: A critical review of the literature and recommended remedies. *J. Appl. Psychol.* **2003**, *88*, 879–903. [CrossRef] [PubMed]
44. Hayes, A. *Introduction to Mediation, Moderation, and Conditional Process Analysis: A Regression-Based Approach*; The Guilford Press: New York, NY, USA, 2013.
45. Rietzschel, E.F.; Slijkhuis, J.M.; Van Yperen, N.W. Task structure, need for structure, and creativity. *Eur. J. Soc. Psychol.* **2014**, *44*, 386–399. [CrossRef]

46. Hamtiaux, A.; Houssemand, C. Adaptability, Cognitive Flexibility, Personal Need for Structure, and Rigidity. *J. Psychol. Res.* **2012**, *2*, 563–585. [CrossRef]
47. Quan, P.; Feng, C.; Yang, Q. Lacking Control: Situation Valence, Effects of Perceived Control, and Illusory Pattern Perception. *Soc. Behav. Pers. Int. J.* **2011**, *39*, 1413–1416. [CrossRef]
48. Hess, T.M. Ageing-related influences on personal need for structure. *Int. J. Behav. Dev.* **2001**, *25*, 482–490. [CrossRef]
49. Kofta, M.; Soral, W.; Bilewicz, M. What breeds conspiracy antisemitism? The role of political uncontrollability and uncertainty in the belief in Jewish conspiracy. *J. Pers. Soc. Psychol.* **2020**, *118*, 900–918. [CrossRef]
50. Yang, S.-L.; Xu, B.-X.; Yu, F.; Guo, Y.-Y. Revisiting the status-legitimacy hypothesis: Concepts, boundary conditions, and psychological mechanisms. *J. Pac. Rim Psychol.* **2019**, *13*, e20. [CrossRef]
51. Brandt, M.J. Do the disadvantaged legitimize the social system? A large-scale test of the status–legitimacy hypothesis. *J. Pers. Soc. Psychol.* **2013**, *104*, 765–785. [CrossRef]
52. Li, W.; Yang, Y.; Wu, J.; Kou, Y. Testing the Status-Legitimacy Hypothesis in China: Objective and Subjective Socioeconomic Status Divergently Predict System Justification. *Pers. Soc. Psychol. Bull.* **2020**, *46*, 1044–1058. [CrossRef] [PubMed]
53. Lu, J.G.; Jin, P.; English, A.S. Collectivism predicts mask use during COVID-19. *Proc. Natl. Acad. Sci. USA* **2021**, *118*, 2021793118. [CrossRef] [PubMed]
54. Bullock, J.G.; Green, D.P. The Failings of Conventional Mediation Analysis and a Design-Based Alternative. *Adv. Methods Pract. Psychol. Sci.* **2021**, *4*, 1–18. [CrossRef]

International Journal of
Environmental Research and Public Health

MDPI

Article

Psychological Impact of the COVID-19 Pandemic on Students, Assistants, and Faculty of a Dental Institute of Saudi Arabia

Saqib Ali [1], Saman Tauqir [2], Faraz Ahmed Farooqi [3], Badr Al-Jandan [1], Hawra Al-Janobi [1], Sami Alshehry [1], Adel Ibrahim Abdelhady [1] and Imran Farooq [4,*]

1 Department of Biomedical Dental Sciences, College of Dentistry, Imam Abdulrahman Bin Faisal University, Dammam 31441, Saudi Arabia; drsaqiibali@gmail.com (S.A.); baljandan@iau.edu.sa (B.A.-J.); haaljanobi@iau.edu.sa (H.A.-J.); smalshehri@iau.edu.sa (S.A.); aiabdulhady@iau.edu.sa (A.I.A.)
2 Department of Physiology, Institute of Basic Medical Sciences, Khyber Medical University, Peshawar 25120, Pakistan; samantauqir@gmail.com
3 Department of Dental Education, College of Dentistry, Imam Abdulrahman Bin Faisal University, Dammam 31441, Saudi Arabia; fafarooqi@iau.edu.sa
4 Faculty of Dentistry, University of Toronto, Toronto, ON M5G 1G6, Canada
* Correspondence: imran.farooq@mail.utoronto.ca

Abstract: This study aimed to assess the perceived stress levels in students, assistants, and faculty members of the College of Dentistry, Imam Abdulrahman Bin Faisal, University (IAU), Kingdom of Saudi Arabia (KSA) during the novel coronavirus disease 2019 (COVID-19) pandemic. Using the Cohen's perceived stress scale (PSS) questionnaire (consisting of 14 items, hence called PSS-14), an online observational survey was conducted. The PSS 14 was rated on a 5-point Likert scale ranging from 0 (never) to 4 (very often). The scores ranging from 0–18 represented low stress, 19–37 represented moderate stress, and 38–56 represented high stress. The second-and third-year students were designated as junior year students, while fourth-year onwards were considered senior year students. Out of total 265 participants, 65% (173) were female, and the majority of the participants were dental students 70% (185) with a mean age of 26.71 ± 9.26 years. In the present study, the average PSS score for the participants was computed as 29.89 (range score: 0–56) which shows moderate stress levels among the respondents. The PSS score for the students was 31.03; for the faculty, it was 28, while for the assistants, it was 27.05. Among the three participant groups, the students were found more on the severe stress side (19%) (p-value = 0.002), and among them, the senior year students (6th year) showed significantly higher stress levels compared to the junior year students (p-value = 0.005). Age-wise, the participants below 20 years were most stressed (21%), followed by those 20–30 years old (18%). Female participants were more severely stressed than males (17% vs. 10%, respectively). It was concluded that the students experienced more stress, followed by the faculty members and dental assistants. In addition, younger participants, females, and senior year students were more stressed than their counterparts. Future studies directed at evaluating stress levels of these groups from different dental institutes could provide an opportunity for policymakers to offer various resources to improve their mental health.

Keywords: COVID-19; stress; psychology; dentistry

Citation: Ali, S.; Tauqir, S.; Farooqi, F.A.; Al-Jandan, B.; Al-Janobi, H.; Alshehry, S.; Abdelhady, A.I.; Farooq, I. Psychological Impact of the COVID-19 Pandemic on Students, Assistants, and Faculty of a Dental Institute of Saudi Arabia. *Int. J. Environ. Res. Public Health* **2021**, *18*, 13366. https://doi.org/10.3390/ijerph182413366

Received: 31 October 2021
Accepted: 14 December 2021
Published: 19 December 2021

1. Introduction

The coronavirus disease 2019 (COVID-19) originated as a cluster of inexact pneumonia cases in December 2019 in Wuhan, China [1]. At the present moment, it has become a global pandemic, affecting every nation of the world [2]. Experts have reported that when the COVID-19 virus infects someone, the lesions are not limited to their lungs: the virus causes viremia upon entering the human body, resulting in diverse clinical manifestations including fever, fatigue, diarrhea, and some other nonspecific signs and symptoms [3–5]. The COVID-19 is a highly transmissible disease [3]. Due to a high transmissibility rate, the

Saudi government had to enforce social distancing at a population and individual level [6]. To prevent the rapid transmission of the disease, different measures were introduced around the country including the closure of the educational institutes, avoidance of open gatherings, and nationwide lockdown [6,7]. Due to these sudden closures, educational and professional activities were affected during the COVID-19 pandemic [8]. In fact, globally there are more than 100 countries that have reported suspension of teaching activities during the pandemic [9]. Owing to the severity of the situation, many universities halted campus-based teaching and continued with the online teaching [8]. Unfortunately, stakeholders of the institutions (students and employees) were not ready for this sudden switch, and this led to an increase in their stress levels. During the time of this public health emergency, medical caretakers, doctors, paramedics, nurses and medical students were also exposed to high levels of stress both physically and psychologically causing mental health problems [10,11]. The fear of catching the virus has aggravated psychological pressure and mental illness in the said population, making them vulnerable to high stress [12,13]. The pandemic has caused a "mental health catastrophe" causing psychiatric disorders after the COVID-19 outbreak [14]. All the communities became vulnerable and felt threatened by potential health emergencies [15], and during the time of social distancing, homeschooling, home quarantine, and work closures, people need support [16]. Quarantine has a wide range of psychological impacts on an individual's mind, and its effects are long-lasting [16]. Previously, during the Middle East Respiratory Syndrome (MERS) outbreak, there were high levels of stress seen in the medical students of KSA [17]. Similarly, during the COVID pandemic, perceived stress among school and university students recorded in virtual classrooms was high to moderate [18]. In another study conducted on dental students in Romania, the impact of COIVD-19 was investigated, and findings demonstrated their emotional state being adversely affected [19]. Previously, health care students from the central region of KSA also reported fear and anxiety due to COVID-19 [20]. Depression, anxiety, and fear were reported in a study that was conducted on dental interns in Riyadh, KSA [21]. Considering the importance of mental health, this subject should be investigated further at dental institutions.

Dental schools cater preclinical and clinical students who attend lectures, laboratory sessions, and clinics (treating patients in their senior years). The dental faculty teach and train students both non-clinically and clinically over the period of their course and they all are assisted by dental assistants/ nurses in laboratories and clinics. The authors believe that dental schools are unique in a way that students, faculty, and dental assistants work as a team to learn, train, and treat patients in their clinical practice. Due to the involvement of students, faculty, and assistants with the patients, the fear of contracting COVID-19 is always present, and this issue needs further exploration. COVID-19 caused fear, anxiety, and stress among the academic community specifically those associated with health care [22]. Currently, there are no significant studies on psychological stress levels of dental students, assistants, and faculty after the lockdown and resumption of on-campus educational and clinical activities have begun.

Therefore, it is important to study the effects of such rapidly spreading infectious diseases on the psychological well-being of the current and future frontline warriors. Thus, the goal of the present study was to assess the perceived stress brought by the COVID-19 pandemic amongst students (undergraduates and interns), dental assistants, and the faculty members of the College of Dentistry (COD), Imam Abdulrahman Bin Faisal University (IAU), Dammam, Kingdom of Saudi Arabia (KSA). The findings of this study could help establish measures to improve the psychological well-being, and help identify the most vulnerable group so psychological intervention can be directed towards them. Additionally, the results from this study can be taken as a pathfinder to explore psychological stress among dental schools around the country for the development of effective screening tools and strategies for intervention to revitalize psychological resilience among the current and future frontline warriors.

2. Materials and Methods

The ethics board of the college approved the study (Ref: EA-202155). The research was carried in accordance with the Helsinki Declaration. A cross-sectional web-based observational study was designed and carried out at COD, IAU, KSA from 1 to 31 March 2021. A questionnaire was uploaded online using the website QuestionPro. A consent form was attached with the survey, and confidentiality of the respondent's information was assured. The questionnaire link was shared with the class representatives of various batches of students and with all the faculty and assistants via Email, WhatsApp^{TM}, Facebook^{TM}, and other social media websites, and they were encouraged to share it with their colleagues. Thus, the link was shared through all the primary sources of communication to reach many subjects. The participant recruitment process adapted in our study is shown in Figure 1.

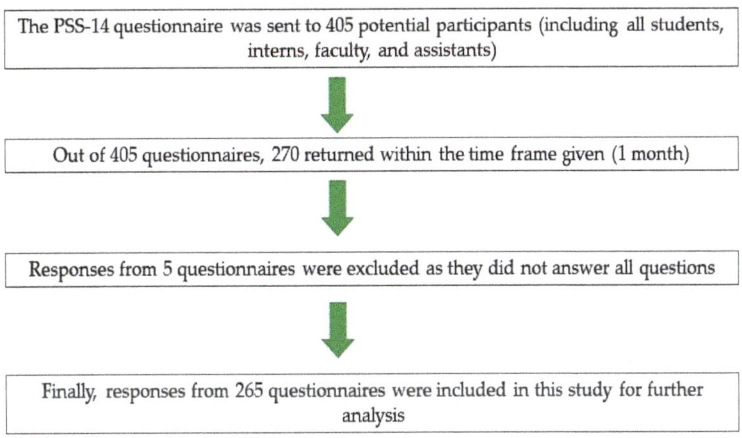

Figure 1. Flow chart showing the participant recruitment process of our study.

Upon clicking the link, the participants were directed to the consent section of the study. After they agreed to the survey, they first filled in the demographic details, which included age, gender, educational level, and residence details (living with family or in a dorm, optional question). After filling in these details, a set of questions appeared in a sequence which the participants had to answer. In the current study, we utilized an Arabic version [23] of the Cohen's perceived stress scale (PSS 14) [24] to assess our participants' stress responses during the COVID-19 pandemic. This stress scale was used during the COVID-19 pandemic and it was shown to be effective in assessing the stress levels of the participants [25,26]. The PSS 14 was rated on a 5-point Likert scale ranging from (0 = never) to (4 = very often). Seven positive items were reverse coded (e.g., 0 = 4, 1 = 3, 2 = 2, etc.), which included items 4, 5, 6, 7, 9, 10, and 13, described as positively stated items in the questionnaire. The total PSS score was obtained by summing all 14 items' scores, and a higher total score indicated higher perceived stress. The scores ranging from 0–18 were considered as low stress, 19–37 were considered as moderate score, and the scores ranging from 38–56 were considered as high stress, as coded earlier by Higgins [27]. The age range was divided into a group of four ranging between 18–20, 21–25, 26–30, and 31 or above. Second- and third-year students were designated as junior year students, while those of fourth-, fifth-, and sixth year, and interns, were considered as senior year students. The inclusion criteria were that the dental students (undergraduate students and interns), faculty, and dental assistants must be studying or working in our university, and the participants voluntarily responded to the survey.

Statistical Analysis

Data were exported to Excel from Google Docs initially and were then transferred to SPSS (version 22, IBM, Chicago, USA) for analysis. Sociodemographic characteristics of the participants were presented in the form of frequencies, percentages, mean, and standard deviation (where appropriate). A chi-square test was performed between demographics and perceived stress categories (low, moderate, and high) to compare them. Mean PSS score was compared for age categories, participants group, and level of education using One Way ANOVA. Logistic regression models were created to evaluate the crude association between PSS Score (dependent) and demographical characteristics (independent variables). Predictors with less than <0.10 were retained for the final regression model. All individual predictors were combined, and an unstandardized B coefficient, 95% CI, was presented. p-values $\leq$ 0.05 were considered significant.

3. Results

Our study had a response rate of 65%. In our study, more than half of the participants were female (65%), and majority of the participants (70%) were dental students with a mean age of 26.71 years. Among the dental students, 19% were junior students (second year), followed by fourth-year students and interns (18% each). Faculty participants were found to be the lowest among the respondents (15%) (Table 1).

Table 1. Showing demographics of the participants in our study.

		Frequency	Percentage
Age (years)	26.71 ± 9.26		
Gender	Male	92	35
	Female	173	65
Participants Group	Faculty	41	15
	Student	185	70
	Dental Assistant	39	15
Academic Year Level	2nd Year	35	19
	3rd Year	26	14
	4th Year	33	18
	5th Year	28	15
	6th Year	29	16
	Interns	34	18
Living in Dorm (optional question)	Yes	66	25
	No	154	58

The majority of participants showed moderate stress, and they were aged >40 years. Participants below 20 years were most stressed (21%), followed by 20–30 years old (18%), and the eldest participant group of the study showed no severe stress levels (0%). Age categories were significantly associated with the level of stress (p-value = 0.043). Female participants were more severely stressed than males (17% vs. 10%, respectively), and the association between gender and level of stress was also statistically significant (p-value = 0.040). Similarly, among the participants' group, the students were found more on the severe stress side (19%) (p-value = 0.002), and among them, the senior year level (6th year) showed significantly higher stress level compared to junior year students (p-value = 0.005) (Table 2).

Table 2. Showing stress levels of the participants involved in our study. Stress levels are presented as mean (SD).

		Low Stress (0–18)	Moderate Stress (19–37)	High Stress (38–56)	p-Value
Age (groups)	Less than 20	2 (4)	35 (75)	10 (21)	0.043 *
	20–30	6 (4)	109 (78)	25 (18)	
	30–40	3 (9)	30 (88)	1 (3)	
	More than 40	3 (12)	22 (88)	0 (0)	
Gender	Male	8 (9)	75 (81)	9 (10)	0.04 *
	Female	7 (4)	137 (79)	29 (17)	
Participants Group	Faculty	6 (15)	33 (80)	2 (5)	0.002 *
	Student	8 (4)	142 (77)	35 (19)	
	Dental Assistant	1 (3)	37 (94)	1 (3)	
Academic Year Level	2nd Year	1 (3)	29 (83)	5 (14)	0.005 *
	3rd Year	0 (0)	21 (81)	5 (19)	
	4th Year	0 (0)	31 (94)	2 (6)	
	5th Year	1 (4)	18 (64)	9 (32)	
	6th Year	1 (3)	17 (59)	11 (38)	
	Interns	5 (15)	27 (79)	2 (6)	

* significant at $p < 0.05$.

In the present study, the average PSS score for the participants was computed as 29.89 (range score: 0–52) which explains the moderate stress level seen in the participants. All the participants' groups when evaluated by age and academic year levels, showed a significant mean difference in PSS score (Table 3). The average PSS score significantly reduced with the increase in age (p-value = 0.001). Stress score was significantly higher among the students as compared to the faculty (31 vs. 28, p-value = 0.001). Among the students, the highest PSS score (34.41) was recorded among the most senior students (6th year) whereas, the lowest score (30) was recorded among the most junior students (2nd year), and the differences were statistically significant (p-value = 0.001).

Table 3. Showing the average PSS scores of the participants involved in our study.

Demographic Variables		Average PSS Score	Standard Deviation	F-Value, p-Value
Age (groups)	Less than 20	31.28 [a]	7.635	6.54, 0.001 *
	20–30	31.04 [b]	6.941	
	30–40	27.74	5.941	
	More than 40	25.4 [ab]	6.198	
Participants Group	Faculty	28 [a]	7.308	7.26, 0.001 *
	Student	31.03 [a]	7.286	
	Dental Assistant	27.05	4.334	
Academic Year Level	2nd Year	30.00	6.593	4.65, 0.001 *
	3rd Year	31.73 [a]	5.943	
	4th Year	31.33 [a]	4.428	
	5th Year	33.04 [a]	7.928	
	6th Year	34.41 [a]	7.771	
	Interns	26.74 [a]	8.28	
Overall PSS Score of Participants		29.89	7.103	

* significant at $p < 0.05$, [a,b] same alphabets show significant difference.

Hosmer and Lameshow test statistics support the model fitness ($X^2 = 6.003$, p-0.199), and small Negelkerke R-square values support the good of fit test ($R^2 = 0.091$). Logistic regression revealed that female students were more likely to have high stress compared to the male participants (OR: 4.89, p-value = 0.027), whereas the increased-age participants were less likely to have stress compared to the younger age group participants (less than 20 years old) (Table 4).

Table 4. Logistic regression analysis associated with factors possibly related to high stress.

Variables in Equation		OR	Lower 95% CL	Upper 95% CL	Wald X^2	p-Value
Gender	Male	1				
	Female	4.195	1.178	14.943	4.89	0.027 *
Age (groups)	Less than 20	1				
	20–30	0.866	0.166	4.258	0.029	0.865
	30–40	0.363	0.055	2.390	1.111	0.929
	More than 40	0.146	0.018	1.151	3.337	0.068

* significant at $p < 0.05$.

4. Discussion

In the present study, the average 14-item PSS score for the participants was computed as 29.89 (range score: 0–52). Our results revealed a comparable stress level when they were compared to a study conducted on medical students in India, where the average PSS scale score was 27.60 [28]. This similarity in both countries indicated that the pandemic had left its effect on the minds of medical students [29]. Another study conducted in Saudi Arabia evaluated stress levels of the university students using the Arabic version of the PSS demonstrated that 86.7% of the participants had moderate- to high-stress levels [30]. Similarly, a Spanish study conducted by Odriozola-González et al. [31] reported moderate to extreme anxiety, depression, and stress scores (21.3%, 34.19%, and 28.14%, respectively) among the university students during the pandemic, which are in line with the stress score of our study. These psychological responses during the time of social distancing might be due to lack of interpersonal communication, the fear of getting infected, and transferring the disease to close family members. Son et al., previously reported increased levels of stress, depressive thoughts, and anxiety in medical students [32]. Our study also reports that most of the participants were moderate to severely stressed due to the pandemic situation. Almost similar stress scores in the above-mentioned studies from different countries in comparison to our study indicate that COVID-19 has affected students around the world similarly. In addition to social distancing, stress can be due to academic, financial, and social difficulties. Coping with the online mode of teaching might also be a challenge for students as they might have faced difficulty in dealing with technology, and faced other problems like absence of stable internet connection, and other online challenges [33]. Our results, when compared with the previously validated studies conducted on healthy populations [31,32,34], showed higher stress, which shows the adverse impact of the pandemic.

In the current study, the mean PSS scores were higher in female participants, with 65% of the female participants showing moderate to severe levels of stress. Another study reported that 73.5% of the females reported moderate to severe stress [35], supporting the current study findings. The female participants of our study were found to be more stressed than males (17% vs. 10%, respectively). A study conducted in South-Western China evaluated stress and anxiety, and the stress scores reported were higher in female quarantined communities during the COVID-19 outbreak when compared with their counterparts [35]. Similarly, another study conducted on undergraduate students in Turkey reported higher stress levels among female students [36]. Earlier studies conducted in Saudi Arabia have reported high-stress scores among different university students, and stress levels were higher among female students [6,17]. The high levels of stress seen in our female participants could possibly be attributed to the fact that males tend to hide their fears due to their conventional gender role [37], which could have led them to report less stress levels in our study. Another plausible reason could be owed to neuroticism (trait of being anxious and emotionally vulnerable), which is found to be more common in females [38], and this could have also resulted in the observation of higher stress levels reported by females in our study. It should also be considered that during the pandemic, mandatory lockdowns were implemented, and females are more at risk of suffering the effects of loneliness on their mental health compared with the males [39], and this could have triggered them to report higher stress levels in our study as well. In addition, in contrast to our study findings, a Chinese study conducted on university students during the COVID-19 outbreak reports no gender-related differences among male and female students regarding stress [40]. In general, medical studies are stressful [41], but a conclusive reason responsible for the different stress levels seen among female and male students could not be determined and requires further investigations.

The COVID-19 has inflicted psychological distress among all population groups [42]. Age-wise, the participants who were less than 20 years old were found to be more stressed, and the PSS score reported in our study decreased linearly with the increasing age of the participants. A previous study has reported that younger people were more vulnerable to depression, stress, and anxiety during the COVID-19 pandemic [43], and our study results are in agreement with that study. Another earlier study reported similar findings and revealed that younger-aged female participants reported more stress levels than all other groups [44]. A probable reason for this finding could be attributed to the fact that younger people worry about their health and academic performance, as shown by an earlier study [45]. On the other hand, older-aged people are better at developing coping strategies to tackle stress [46] and therefore, because of this, they reported lower stress levels in our study.

In the current study, dental assistants/nurses showed the average PSS scores of 27.0, which refers to a moderate stress scale. A Turkish study before the COVID-19 outbreak determined that nursing students face stress levels that could be classified as being above moderate levels [47]. Another study from India indicated moderate levels of PSS scores in nurses with a mean score of 21.88 [48]. Our study also identified moderate levels of stress experienced by the dental assistants/nurses during the pandemic. On the contrary, a study in Norway reported a substantial psychological impact of COVID-19 on dental assistants, causing more stress [49]. The reason for stress seen in this group could be attributed to the fact that dental assistants/nurses have to fulfill their duties even at the time of a pandemic. Lack of personal protective equipment (PPE), discomfort caused by the prolonged usage of PPE, increased workload, along with less experience to deal with the novel virus might have contributed to the stress levels seen in this group [50].

The average PSS score of the faculty in the study indicated the mean score of 28, which indicated that along with the students, the university faculty was equally affected by the pandemic. A study performed in India reported perceived stress to be moderate in dental faculties, which is not in line with our study [51]. However, a study from Norway reported that dental professionals could face increased psychological impacts related to the COVID-19 pandemic [49]. The high-stress score seen in the faculty in our study could be attributed to the fact that dental faculty not only have to be concerned about their own safety, but also for the well-being of their patients, students, and dental assistants as well. They are more vulnerable to infection because of having a close contact with their patients in clinics and while teaching their students during the clinical sessions. A previous study has also reported that dental professionals from all over the world perceive a higher risk of COVID-19 contamination [52]. The lack of knowledge about the controlling of infective virus might have also caused a widespread panic among the faculty in our study. A study conducted in China also reported higher levels of perceived stress in medical staff [53]. It should be noted that psychological stress weakens immunity and makes the person prone to infections [54]; hence, this problem should be tackled as early as possible.

Several countries, including Saudi Arabia, took measures to control the rapidly spreading virus. Citizens were asked to isolate themselves at home and take preventive measures since the advent of the pandemic. Outbreaks like Ebola [55], Severe Acute Respiratory

Syndrome (SARS) [56], and MERS [57] have shown some unique concerns related to the mental health of individuals. The situation of lockdown and missing out on major academic tasks (practical sessions and clinical rotations), might have made students more stressed about their future [58], as seen in our study. The effects of COVID-19 are global [59,60] and our study provides a platform for the institute's policymakers and administrators to provide social assistance to the vulnerable groups.

5. Conclusions

It was concluded that the students experienced more stress, followed by the faculty members and dental assistants. In addition, younger participants, females, and senior year students were more stressed than their counterparts. Identifying abnormal stress levels and their timely management and adequate counseling is crucial. It is suggested that in the future, there should be regular checkups of students' stress levels to evaluate their mental health along with the faculty members and assistants. This could help them to overcome their stresses and address their concerns. Our study results contribute to the literature because our findings highlight that not only students could be stressed, but their teaching faculty members and dental assistants could also be at an increased risk of feeling stressed. We recommend developing the skill of managing distress in a sample of students. We also recommend making a distinction between student risk groups who may not have yet acquired enough skill to manage psychological distress and help them in all possible manners.

Author Contributions: Conceptualization, S.A. (Saqib Ali); methodology, S.A. (Saqib Ali), S.T., F.A.F., B.A.-J., H.A.-J., S.A. (Sami Alshehry), A.I.A., and I.F.; software, S.A. (Saqib Ali), S.T., F.A.F., B.A.-J., H.A.-J., S.A. (Sami Alshehry), A.I.A., and I.F.; validation, S.A. (Saqib Ali), S.T., F.A.F., B.A-J., H.A.-J., S.A. (Sami Alshehry), A.I.A., and I.F.; formal analysis, S.A. (Saqib Ali), S.T., F.A.F., B.A.-J., H.A.-J., S.A. (Sami Alshehry), A.I.A., and I.F.; investigation, S.A. (Saqib Ali), S.T., F.A.F., B.A.-J., H.A.-J., S.A. (Sami Alshehry), A.I.A.,and I.F.; resources, S.A. (Saqib Ali), S.T., F.A.F., B.A.-J., H.A.-J., S.A. (Sami Alshehry), A.I.A., and I.F.; data curation, S.A. (Saqib Ali), S.T., F.A.F., B.A.-J., H.A.-J., S.A. (Sami Alshehry), A.I.A., and I.F.; writing—original draft preparation, S.A. (Saqib Ali), S.T., F.A.F., B.A.-J., H.A.-J., S.A. (Sami Alshehry), A.I.A., and I.F.; writing—review and editing, S.A. (Saqib Ali), S.T., F.A.F., B.A.-J., H.A.-J., S.A. (Sami Alshehry), A.I.A., and I.F.; visualization, S.A. (Saqib Ali), S.T., F.A.F., B.A.-J., H.A.-J., S.A. (Sami Alshehry), A.I.A., and I.F.; supervision, B.A.-J., and I.F.; project administration, S.A. (Saqib Ali), S.T., F.A.F., B.A.-J., H.A.-J., S.A. (Sami Alshehry), A.I.A., and I.F. All authors have read and agreed to the published version of the manuscript.

Funding: This research received no external funding.

Institutional Review Board Statement: The study was conducted according to the guidelines of the Declaration of Helsinki, and approved by the Institutional Review Board (or Ethics Committee) of College of Dentistry, IAU, Dammam, Saudi Arabia (Ref: EA-202155).

Informed Consent Statement: Informed consent was obtained from all subjects involved in the study.

Acknowledgments: We would like to thank the undergraduate students, interns, dental assistants and faculty at our university who voluntarily agreed to participate in the survey.

Conflicts of Interest: The authors declare no conflict of interest.

References

1. Wang, C.; Horby, P.W.; Hayden, F.G.; Gao, G.F. A novel coronavirus outbreak of global health concern. *Lancet* **2020**, *395*, 470–473. [CrossRef]
2. Zu, Z.Y.; Di Jiang, M.; Xu, P.P.; Chen, W.; Ni, Q.Q.; Lu, G.M.; Zhang, L.J. Coronavirus Disease 2019 (COVID-19): A Perspective from China. *Radiology* **2020**, *296*, E15–E25. [CrossRef] [PubMed]
3. Wu, P.; Fang, Y.; Guan, Z.; Fan, B.; Kong, J.; Yao, Z.; Liu, X.; Fuller, C.J.; Susser, E.; Lu, J.; et al. The Psychological Impact of the SARS Epidemic on Hospital Employees in China: Exposure, Risk Perception, and Altruistic Acceptance of Risk. *Can. J. Psychiatry* **2009**, *54*, 302–311. [CrossRef]

4. Ali, S.; Alam, B.F.; Farooqi, F.; Almas, K.; Noreen, S. Dental and Medical Students' Knowledge and Attitude toward COVID-19: A Cross-Sectional Study from Pakistan. *Eur. J. Dent.* **2020**, *14*, S97–S104. [CrossRef]
5. Zhang, W.; Du, R.-H.; Li, B.; Zheng, X.-S.; Yang, X.-L.; Hu, B.; Wang, Y.-Y.; Xiao, G.-F.; Yan, B.; Shi, Z.-L.; et al. Molecular and serological investigation of 2019-nCoV infected patients: Implication of multiple shedding routes. *Emerg. Microbes Infect.* **2020**, *9*, 386–389. [CrossRef]
6. Khalil, R.; Mansour, A.E.; Fadda, W.A.; Almisnid, K.; Aldamegh, M.; Al-Nafeesah, A.; Alkhalifah, A.; Al-Wutayd, O. The sudden transition to synchronized online learning during the COVID-19 pandemic in Saudi Arabia: A qualitative study exploring medical students' perspectives. *BMC Med. Educ.* **2020**, *20*, 1–10. [CrossRef]
7. Ali, S.; Alam, B.F.; Noreen, S.; Anwar, M.; Qazi, S.H.; Hussain, T. Motivation and job satisfaction levels among medical and dental faculty members of Pakistan amidst the COVID-19 outbreak. *Work* **2021**, *69*, 359–366. [CrossRef]
8. Choi, B.; Jegatheeswaran, L.; Minocha, A.; Alhilani, M.; Nakhoul, M.; Mutengesa, E. The impact of the COVID-19 pandemic on final year medical students in the United Kingdom: A national survey. *BMC Med. Educ.* **2020**, *20*, 1–11. [CrossRef] [PubMed]
9. Vergara de la Rosa, E.; Vergara Tam, R.; Alvarez Vargas, M.; Camacho Saavedra, L.; Galvez Olortegui, J. Distance medical education in the times of COVID-19. *Educ. Méd. Super.* **2020**, *34*, 2.
10. Ali, S.; Tauqir, S.; Alam, B.F.; Farooqi, F.; Khan, A.M.; Khabeer, A. COVID-19 knowledge, attitude and awareness among preclinical and clinical dental students: An online-based cross-sectional survey. *J. Oral. Res.* **2021**, *10*, 1–9.
11. Wang, J.; Cheng, Y.; Zhou, Z.; Jiang, A.; Guo, J.; Chen, Z.; Wan, Q. Psychological status of Wuhan medical staff in fighting against COVID-19. *Med. J. Wuhan Univ.* **2020**, *4*, 547–550.
12. Verma, S.; Mythily, S.; Chan, Y.H.; Deslypere, J.P.; Teo, E.K.; Chong, S.A. Post-SARS psychological morbidity and stigma among general practitioners and traditional Chinese medicine practitioners in Singapore. *Ann. Acad. Med. Singap.* **2004**, *33*, 743–748.
13. Kang, L.; Li, Y.; Hu, S.; Chen, M.; Yang, C.; Yang, B.X.; Liu, Z. The mental health of medical workers in Wuhan, China dealing with the 2019 novel coronavirus. *Lancet Psychiatry* **2020**, *7*, e14. [CrossRef]
14. Mak, I.W.C.; Chu, C.M.; Pan, P.C.; Yiu, M.G.C.; Chan, V.L. Long-term psychiatric morbidities among SARS survivors. *Gen. Hosp. Psychiatry* **2009**, *31*, 318–326. [CrossRef]
15. Taylor, M.; Barr, M.; Stevens, G.; Bryson-Taylor, D.; Agho, K.; Jacobs, J.; Raphael, B. Psychosocial stress and strategies for managing adversity: Measuring population resilience in New South Wales, Australia. *Popul. Health Metr.* **2010**, *8*, 1–9. [CrossRef] [PubMed]
16. Brooks, S.K.; Webster, R.K.; Smith, L.E.; Woodland, L.; Wessely, S.; Greenberg, N.; Rubin, G.J. The psychological impact of quarantine and how to reduce it: Rapid review of the evidence. *Lancet* **2020**, *395*, 912–920. [CrossRef]
17. Al-Rabiaah, A.; Temsah, M.H.; Al-Eyadhy, A.A.; Hasan, G.M.; Al-Zamil, F.; Al-Subaie, S.; Somily, A.M. Middle East Respiratory Syndrome-Corona Virus (MERS-CoV) associated stress among medical students at a university teaching hospital in Saudi Arabia. *J. Infect. Public Health* **2020**, *13*, 687–691. [CrossRef] [PubMed]
18. Deemah, A.A.; Sumayah, A.; Dalal, A. Perceived stress among students in virtual classrooms during the COVID-19 outbreak in KSA. *J. Taibah Univ. Med. Sci.* **2020**, *15*, 398–403.
19. Iosif, L.; Ţâncu, A.M.C.; Didilescu, A.C.; Imre, M.; Gălbinașu, B.M.; Ilinca, R. Self-Perceived Impact of COVID-19 Pandemic by Dental Students in Bucharest. *Int. J. Environ. Res. Public Health* **2021**, *18*, 5249. [CrossRef]
20. Shaikh, S.; Mohsin, S.F.; Agwan, M.A.S.; Ali, S.; Alsuwaydani, Z.A.; AlSuwaydani, S.A. COVID-19: Fear and anxiety among healthcare students in Saudi Arabia: A cross-sectional study. *Eur. J. Mol. Clin. Med.* **2021**, *8*, 1638–1647.
21. Khanagar, S.B.; Alfadley, A. Psychological impact of the COVID-19 pandemic on dental interns in Riyadh, Saudi Arabia: A cross-sectional survey. *Int. J. Clin. Pediatr. Dent.* **2020**, *13*, 508. [PubMed]
22. Saddik, B.; Hussein, A.; Sharif-Askari, F.S.; Kheder, W.; Temsah, M.H.; Koutaich, R.A.; Halwani, R. Increased levels of anxiety among medical and non-medical university students during the COVID-19 pandemic in the United Arab Emirates. *Risk. Manag. Healthc. Policy* **2020**, *13*, 2395. [CrossRef] [PubMed]
23. Almadi, T.; Cathers, I.; Hamdan Mansour, A.M.; Chow, C.M. An Arabic version of the perceived stress scale: Translation and validation study. *Int. J. Nurs. Stud.* **2012**, *49*, 84–89. [CrossRef] [PubMed]
24. Cohen, S.; Kamarck, T.; Mermelstein, R. A global measure of perceived stress. *J. Health Soc. Behav.* **1983**, *24*, 385–396. [CrossRef]
25. Şanlıtürk, D. Perceived and sources of occupational stress in intensive care nurses during the COVID-19 pandemic. *Intensiv. Crit. Care Nurs.* **2021**, *67*, 103107. [CrossRef]
26. Sözer, A.K.G.; Güdül, Ö.H.; Yangın, H. Relationship between menopausal symptoms and perceived stress during the COVID-19 pandemic. *J. Women Aging* **2021**, 1–12. [CrossRef] [PubMed]
27. Higgins, M. Perceived Stress Scale. Available online: https://melindahiggins2000.github.io/CHDWBCodebook/pss.html (accessed on 11 December 2021).
28. Muley, P.P.; Muley, P.A.; Meshram, K.A. Effect of COVID-19 Lockdown on Perceived Stress Scale in Medical Students. *Ind. J. Forensic Med. Toxicol.* **2020**, *14*, 6426–6429.
29. Huremović, D. *Psychiatry of Pandemics: A Mental Health Response to Infection Outbreak*; Springer: Berlin/Heidelberg, Germany, 2019.
30. AlHadi, A.N.; Alhuwaydi, A.M. The mental health impact of pandemic COVID-19 crisis on university students in Saudi Arabia and associated factors. *J. Am. Coll. Health* **2021**, *26*, 1–9. [CrossRef] [PubMed]
31. Odriozola-González, P.; Planchuelo-Gómez, Á.; Irurtia, M.J.; de Luis-García, R. Psychological effects of the COVID-19 outbreak and lockdown among students and workers of a Spanish university. *Psychiatry Res.* **2020**, *290*, 113108. [CrossRef] [PubMed]

32. Son, C.; Hegde, S.; Smith, A.; Wang, X.; Sasangohar, F. Effects of COVID-19 on college students' mental health in the United States: Interview survey study. *J. Med. Internet Res.* **2020**, *22*, e21279. [CrossRef]
33. Farooq, I.; Ali, S.; Moheet, I.A.; AlHumaid, J. COVID-19 outbreak, disruption of dental education, and the role of teledentistry. *Pak. J. Med. Sci.* **2020**, *36*, 1726. [CrossRef] [PubMed]
34. Cohen, S. Perceived stress in a probability sample of the United States. In *The Social Psychology of Health*; Spacapan, S., Oskamp, S., Eds.; Sage Publications, Inc.: Newbury Park, CA, USA, 1988; pp. 31–67.
35. Lei, L.; Huang, X.; Zhang, S.; Yang, J.; Yang, L.; Xu, M. Comparison of prevalence and associated factors of anxiety and depression among people affected by versus people unaffected by quarantine during the COVID-19 epidemic in Southwestern China. *Med. Sci. Monit.* **2020**, *26*, e924609-1. [CrossRef]
36. Lippa, R.A. Gender differences in personality and interests: When, where, and why? *Soc. Personal. Psychol. Compass* **2010**, *4*, 1098–1110. [CrossRef]
37. Farooq, I.; Ali, S. A cross sectional study of gender differences in dental anxiety prevailing in the students of a Pakistani dental college. *Saudi J. Dent. Res.* **2015**, *6*, 21–25. [CrossRef]
38. Hernández-García, F.; Gómez, O.G.; González-Velázquez, V.E.; Pedraza-Rodríguez, E.M.; Zamora-Fung, R.; Herrera, L.A.L. Perceived stress by students of the medical sciences in Cuba toward the COVID-19 pandemic: Results of an online survey. *Rev. Colomb. Psiquiatr.* **2021**, *50*, 176–183. [CrossRef]
39. McQuaid, R.J.; Cox, S.M.L.; Ogunlana, A.; Jaworska, N. The burden of loneliness: Implications of the social determinants of health during COVID-19. *Psychiatry Res.* **2021**, *296*, 113648. [CrossRef] [PubMed]
40. Cao, W.; Fang, Z.; Hou, G.; Han, M.; Xu, X.; Dong, J.; Zheng, J. The psychological impact of the COVID-19 epidemic on college students in China. *Psychiatry Res.* **2020**, *287*, 112934. [CrossRef]
41. Dwivedi, D.; Kaur, N.; Shukla, S.; Gandhi, A.; Tripathi, S. Perception of stress among medical undergraduate during coronavirus disease-19 pandemic on exposure to online teaching. *Natl. J. Physiol. Pharm. Pharmacol.* **2020**, *10*, 1. [CrossRef]
42. Qiu, J.; Shen, B.; Zhao, M.; Wang, Z.; Xie, B.; Xu, Y. A nationwide survey of psychological distress among Chinese people in the COVID-19 epidemic: Implications and policy recommendations. *Gen. Psych.* **2020**, *33*, e100213. [CrossRef] [PubMed]
43. Varma, P.; Junge, M.; Meaklim, H.; Jackson, M.L. Younger people are more vulnerable to stress, anxiety and depression during COVID-19 pandemic: A global cross-sectional survey. *Prog. Neuro-Psychopharmacol. Biol. Psychiatry* **2021**, *109*, 110236. [CrossRef]
44. Kowal, M.; Coll-Martín, T.; Ikizer, G.; Rasmussen, J.; Eichel, K.; Studzińska, A.; Koszałkowska, K.; Karwowski, M.; Najmussaqib, A.; Pankowski, D.; et al. Who is the Most Stressed During the COVID-19 Pandemic? Data From 26 Countries and Areas. *Appl. Psychol. Health Well-Being* **2020**, *12*, 946–966. [CrossRef]
45. Mahdy, M.A.A. The Impact of COVID-19 Pandemic on the Academic Performance of Veterinary Medical Students. *Front Vet Sci.* **2020**, *7*, 594261. [CrossRef]
46. Di Crosta, A.; Palumbo, R.; Marchetti, D.; Ceccato, I.; La Malva, P.; Maiella, R.; Cipi, M.; Roma, P.; Mammarella, N.; Verrocchio, M.C.; et al. Individual Differences, Economic Stability, and Fear of Contagion as Risk Factors for PTSD Symptoms in the COVID-19 Emergency. *Front. Psychol.* **2020**, *11*, 567367. [CrossRef] [PubMed]
47. Kılınç, T.; Çelik, A.S. Relationship between the social support and psychological resilience levels perceived by nurses during the COVID-19 pandemic: A study from Turkey. *Perspect. Psychiatr. Care* **2021**, *57*, 1000–1008. [CrossRef] [PubMed]
48. Sheroun, D.; Wankhar, D.D.; Devrani, A.; Lissamma, P.V.; Chatterjee, K. A study to assess the perceived stress and coping strategies among B. Sc. nursing students of selected colleges in Pune during COVID-19 pandemic lockdown. *Int. J. Sci. Healthc. Res.* **2020**, *5*, 280–288.
49. Uhlen, M.M.; Ansteinsson, V.E.; Stangvaltaite-Mouhat, L.; Korzeniewska, L.; Skudutyte-Rysstad, R.; Shabestari, M.; Hovden, E.A.S. Psychological impact of the COVID-19 pandemic on dental health personnel in Norway. *BMC. Health Serv. Res.* **2021**, *21*, 1–11. [CrossRef] [PubMed]
50. Arnetz, J.E.; Goetz, C.M.; Arnetz, B.B.; Arble, E. Nurse reports of stressful situations during the Covid-19 pandemic: Qualitative analysis of survey responses. *Int. J. Environ. Res Public Health* **2020**, *17*, 8126. [CrossRef] [PubMed]
51. Babu, L.S.; Pillai, M.J.; Janardhanan, K.A. Prevalence of Perceived Stress, Due To COVID-19 Among Faculties Of Government Dental Colleges In Kerala, India. *Cogent Psychol.* **2021**, *8*, 1978635. [CrossRef]
52. Gambarini, E.; Galli, M.; Di Nardo, D.; Miccoli, G.; Patil, S.; Bhandi, S.; Giovarruscio, M.; Testarelli, L.; Gambarini, G. A Survey on Perceived COVID-19 Risk in Dentistry and the Possible Use of Rapid Tests. *J. Contemp. Dent. Pract.* **2020**, *21*, 718–722.
53. Li, Z.; Yi, X.; Zhong, M.; Li, Z.; Xiang, W.; Wu, S.; Xiong, Z. Psychological Distress, Social Support, Coping Style, and Perceived Stress Among Medical Staff and Medical Students in the Early Stages of the COVID-19 Epidemic in China. *Front. Psychiatry* **2021**, *12*, 664808. [CrossRef] [PubMed]
54. Cruz-Pereira, J.S.; Rea, K.; Nolan, Y.M.; O'Leary, O.F.; Dinan, T.G.; Cryan, J.F. Depression's unholy trinity: Dysregulated stress, immunity, and the microbiome. *Annu. Rev. Psychol.* **2020**, *71*, 49–78. [CrossRef]
55. Shultz, J.M.; Baingana, F.; Neria, Y. The 2014 Ebola Outbreak and Mental Health: Current Status and Recommended Response. *JAMA* **2015**, *313*, 567–568. [CrossRef]
56. Lung, F.W.; Lu, Y.C.; Chang, Y.Y.; Shu, B.C. Mental symptoms in different health professionals during the SARS attack: A follow-up study. *Psychiatry Q.* **2009**, *80*, 107–116. [CrossRef] [PubMed]
57. Son, H.; Lee, W.J.; Kim, H.S.; Lee, K.S.; You, M. Hospital workers' psychological resilience after the 2015 Middle East respiratory syndrome outbreak. *Soc. Behav. Pers. Int. J.* **2019**, *47*, 1–13. [CrossRef]

58. Feizi, A.; Aliyari, R.; Roohafza, H. Association of perceived stress with stressful life events, lifestyle and sociodemographic factors: A large-scale community-based study using logistic quantile regression. *Comput. Math. Methods Med.* **2012**, *2112*, 151865. [CrossRef] [PubMed]
59. Saadat, S.; Rawtani, D.; Hussain, C.M. Environmental perspective of COVID-19. *Sci. Total Environ.* **2020**, *728*, 138870. [CrossRef] [PubMed]
60. Shrestha, N.; Shad, M.Y.; Ulvi, O.; Khan, M.H.; Karamehic-Muratovic, A.; Nguyen, U.D.T.; Baghbanzadeh, M.; Wardrup, R.; Aghamohammadi, N.; Cervantes, D.; et al. The impact of COVID-19 on globalization. *One Health* **2020**, *11*, 100180. [CrossRef]

International Journal of
Environmental Research and Public Health

MDPI

Article

Undergraduate Students' Online Health Information-Seeking Behavior during the COVID-19 Pandemic

Wan-Chen Hsu

Center for Teaching & Learning Development, National Kaohsiung University of Sciences and Technology, No. 1, University Rd., Yanchao Dist., Kaohsiung City 824, Taiwan; wanchen@nkust.edu.tw;
Tel.: +886-7-3814526 (ext. 31171)

Abstract: As the COVID-19 pandemic has swept across the world, the amount of health-related information available has skyrocketed. Individuals can easily access health information through the internet, which may influence their thoughts or behavior, causing potential technological risks that may affect their lives. This study examined the online health information-seeking behavior of undergraduate students. Taking health issues as a guiding framework, content analysis was adopted to assess participants' online health information-seeking behavior using a computer screen recording software, and coding analysis was conducted. The study was conducted during the COVID-19 pandemic with a formal sample of 101 participants. In terms of online health information-seeking behavior, 59% of the study participants used nouns as keywords, only 27% used Boolean logic retrieval techniques, 81% paid attention to the date of the data, and 85% did not consider the author's professionalism. The results indicate that health information-seeking behavior and outcome judgments may be a missing piece of the puzzle in higher education. Consequently, the development of online health information-seeking skills through programs for undergraduate students is suggested to ensure that online readers have access to appropriate health information.

Keywords: health information; online health information; information-seeking behavior; undergraduate students; COVID-19

Citation: Hsu, W.-C. Undergraduate Students' Online Health Information-Seeking Behavior during the COVID-19 Pandemic. *Int. J. Environ. Res. Public Health* **2021**, *18*, 13250. https://doi.org/10.3390/ijerph182413250

Academic Editors: Paul B. Tchounwou, Paolo Roma, Merylin Monaro and Cristina Mazza

Received: 28 October 2021
Accepted: 13 December 2021
Published: 16 December 2021

1. Introduction

The COVID-19 pandemic, caused by the novel Sars-CoV-2 coronavirus, has caused the death of millions of people and disrupted daily life worldwide. During this pandemic, individuals were restricted from going outside, and physical activities were reduced as a result of its impact. Consequently, people gathered, exchanged information, and entertained themselves via the internet, with online health information becoming an alternative to personal visits to physical hospitals and medical centers. On 19 May 2021, Taiwan's Ministry of Education announced that students at all levels would stop attending schools, fully initiating online instruction. The impact of campus closures and significant social changes brought many challenges to higher education, affecting personal internet use. The COVID-19 pandemic brought into renewed focus the health of students in higher education, which already necessitated concern [1]. In Taiwan, the internet is the source of health-related information for 100% of undergraduate students who avail it on a frequent basis [2]. When these students encounter health-related problems, they often resort to the internet to obtain information as a temporary solution [3].

Online platforms have the potential to provide individuals with useful information, increase their engagement, and potentially revolutionize the patient–physician relationship [4]. Information seeking has become a focus of health communication scholarship, since individuals can now use a variety of platforms, such as the television, newspapers, the internet, and other interpersonal communication channels, to gain knowledge [5]. Chen and Lee [6] noted that people often have limited skills related to retrieving and evaluating the vast amount of information available from a variety of online sources with varying quality. This overwhelming availability of online health information highlights the importance of understanding the status and key influencing factors of its use among individuals.

Health information is defined as information that can assist individuals in promoting their health, making health-related decisions, and participating in the healthcare system [7]. Information seeking can be unintentional, passive, or active [8] and is often purposeful, with individuals seeking information to meet a personal need or goal [9]. Information-seeking behavior is the action of searching for and using information in any way, following an individual's need. In particular, it relates to the behavior arising from an interaction with the information source when one needs information; it can range from passive attention to passive searching, active searching, and ongoing searches, all of which fall within the scope of information-seeking behavior [9]. Online health information-seeking behavior is dominated by active information seeking and passive information acquisition [7]. Health information-seeking behavior is a type of personal health promotion in which individuals obtain expertise from various sources, such as doctors, to inform their decisions, improve their food and nutrition intake, relieve stress, and reduce drug abuse [5]. In sum, online health information-seeking behavior involves individuals' retrieval of health information from the internet, which can be actively or passively motivated, for the purpose of obtaining knowledge for personal health promotion and facilitating decision making.

Regarding health information retrieval and health promotion theories, the social cognitive theory is one of the most widely used theoretical frameworks [10]. Bandura's social cognitive theory provides a structure for interpreting the relevant results of individuals after retrieving information [11,12]. For example, how much confidence an individual has in finding quality health information, i.e., their self-efficacy in searching, is also related to the expected results after retrieval. Self-efficacy can be a powerful predictor of expected results regarding an individual's online health information-seeking behavior [13]. The risk information seeking and processing model (RISP) is one of the representative theoretical models explaining online information seeking. It emphasizes that the behavior of individuals to retrieve online information is triggered by insufficient cognitive data (termed as information insufficiency hereafter); according to the model, a lack of information is the main factor directly driving information seeking, alongside other incidental social and psychological factors, such as emotional response (worry, anxiety) and subjective criticism of information. The RISP model thus provides a framework to explain the key influencing factors that individuals use to seek and process relevant risk information in a more systematic or deliberate manner. Brown, Skelly, and Chew-Graham [14] proposed a model, pointing out that individuals' online health information retrieval is affected by their previous experience, health beliefs, and other personal background factors.

Research on health information-seeking behavior in Taiwan remains in its infancy. Previous studies have focused on the content of health information texts [15,16], the effect of health information on readers' intention to use it [17], health information-seeking experiences [17,18], the relationship between online information seeking and cognitive factors [19], and how post-search emotions affect social cognitive factors and perceptions, indirectly shaping attitudes and behavior [13]. Information literacy, one of the core competencies of eHealth literacy, is an individual's ability to understand how to effectively search for, organize, and use information, for example, by retrieving relevant information using a keyword [20].

Health-related issues, such as health literacy, are more frequently discussed in the context of adult health decision making and health behavior. Although adolescents need to increase their sense of responsibility for maintaining their own health, less research has been conducted among this age group [21]. The present study, therefore, investigated the online health information-seeking behaviors of undergraduate students, using common health problems as a guide. Here, online health information-seeking behavior was defined as individuals retrieving health information through the internet. The specific behavioral items observed were "keyword selection", "information browsing", and "information sources"; suggestions were then devised for a skills development program to shape undergraduate students' online health information-seeking behaviors based on the findings. The academic contributions of this study could enrich our knowledge and theoretical scope of online health information-seeking behavior issues, highlighting their value for students in the COVID-19 era.

2. Materials and Methods

2.1. Study Methods

This study examined undergraduate students' online health information-seeking behavior during the COVID-19 pandemic. In this study, the Delphi method was used for gaining consensus through controlled feedback from a panel—a group made up of experts in the subject. The method is often used when there is limited or conflicting evidence, the participants may be geographically dispersed, and anonymity is desired to control for dominant individuals. The Delphi method consists of panel selection, the development of content surveys, and iterative stages of anonymous responses to gain consensus [22]. The relevance and objectives of Delphi techniques differ among various disciplines. While they are primarily used in the context of technical and natural sciences to analyze future developments, they are also used in health sciences to reach consensus [23].

In the initial stage of this study, test questions on the health issues sought by college students online were developed. The team members tasked with the development of these questions included scholars and experts in the fields of health promotion and hygiene education, education testing, and physicians and nurses with rich experience in medical services. The investigation was continued with the research questions on health problems sought online by college students.

We conducted interview surveys of 101 students from four universities to understand their online health information-seeking behavior. The data were analyzed using both quantitative and qualitative methods. Content analysis is a research tool that is used to determine the presence of certain words, themes, or concepts within qualitative data [24]. In this study, content analysis was used to pre-program health questions and solicit undergraduate students from four universities in south and central Taiwan to participate. Prior to data collection, student participants gave their consent to be profiled in an online retrieval behavior video and were asked to find appropriate answers to health-related questions on the internet. The video data were then coded and analyzed to understand the status of online health information-seeking behaviors demonstrated by undergraduate students.

2.2. Study Participants

The sample consisted of students on campus who voluntarily wished to participate. Data were collected during the COVID-19 pandemic between March and May 2020 from public libraries on the campuses of the four universities. It was ensured that the participants' privacy was protected and that they would not be disturbed during participation. The students agreed to use a browser to search for information pertaining to the preset health questions and have their screens recorded during the process. The final sample comprised 31 students from one university in central Taiwan and 70 students from three universities in southern Taiwan—resulting in a total sample size of 101. A total of 101 valid responses were thus obtained for image content analysis.

2.3. Study Tools

To investigate the online health information-seeking behavior of the undergraduate students, this study referred to the "14 Health Topics of the Health Promotion Administration, Ministry of Health and Welfare (Taiwan)", the "Top 10 Health Education and Teaching Issues in the United States", and the six categories of health information in Liao et al.'s [7] study, as the basis for formulating the example health issues. Liao et al.'s categories included disease treatment, diet and nutrition, exercise and fitness, health and aging prevention, medical consultation and treatment, and preventive health care, being supplemented with health issues of public concern. The health issues of concern to undergraduate students in this study comprised four topics: "balanced diets", "obesity prevention", "health and fitness promotion", and "sleep management", each of which was extended to two questions, for a total of eight questions. The students were asked to select one of the eight questions and provide written answers to it, in order to reveal the status of their online health information-seeking behaviors and actual behaviors. Taking "balanced diet" as an example, the design concept of the health-related questions used in the research is shown in Table 1.

Table 1. Example of the design concept of health-related questions of concern to undergraduate students.

Health Question Design	Reason and Reference for Health Question Design [1]	Correct Answer Reference [1]
The slogan "Five Servings of Fruit and Vegetables a Day" encourages people to eat five servings of fruit and vegetables every day. If you eat five servings of the recommended weight of vegetables in a day, how many grams of vegetables do you think you should eat?	According to the Health Promotion Administration's Health Behavioral Risk Factor Surveillance System (BRFSS) 2016, only 12.9% of adults aged 18 or above (9.4% of men and 16.3% of women) met the recommended daily intake of three servings of vegetables and two servings of fruit, which was less than the recommended number of servings in the Dietary Guidelines. Only 20.7% of the surveyed citizens consumed five servings of fruit and vegetables.	The Health Promotion Administration reminds the public to develop a healthy diet that includes "three servings of vegetables and two servings of fruit", by consuming three servings of vegetables (one serving of cooked vegetables is about half a bowl) and two servings of fruit (one serving of fruit is about the size of a fist) every day, and to select local, seasonal, colorful vegetables and fruits in their original state.

[1] Data source: [25].

2.4. Data Collection and Analysis

The study was ethically reviewed according to the human research ethics governance framework, and participants were asked to complete an informed consent form prior to data collection. An oCam screen recording program was used to record the online health information retrieval behavior of each participant on the computer screen, which was transcribed for coding and analysis following the study's completion. The content analysis framework of the participants' online health information retrieval behavior included "keyword selection", "Boolean logic query", "limited scope for query", "information browsing", and "information source".

The reliability of the content analysis was measured using inter-rater reliability [26], in which higher consistency results indicate higher reliability of the analysis. The reliability coefficients for the coding results were calculated according to the formulae of mutual agreement, mean agreement, and reliability coefficients, as follows

$$\text{Mean agreement} = \frac{2M}{N1 + N2}$$

$$\text{Reliability coefficient} = \frac{n \times Mean\ mutual\ agreement}{1 + (n-1) \times Mean\ agreement}$$

M: The number of variables for which the coding result was fully agreed between two persons.

$N1$: The total number of variables coded by the first coder.

$N2$: The total number of variables coded by the second coder.

n: The number of coders.

Content analysis of the data could only be performed following the determination of the reliability coefficient. Two coders coded 30 samples and calculated a mean agreement of 0.67 and a reliability coefficient of 0.80.

3. Results

In this study, the Delphi method was used to encode the data content of the responses to the survey results, using descriptive statistics to restore the current status of college students' online information retrieval behavior.

3.1. Undergraduate Students' Online Health Information-Seeking Behavior Is Mostly Based on Using Nouns as Keywords, with Few Using Boolean Logic Techniques, and Unlimited Scope for Queries

A skillful use of internet search functions, such as the selection of keywords, application of Boolean logic, and limitation of the query scope, allows users to focus more specifically on the relevant online information during the search process, filtering out unnecessary information. Table 2 shows the status of online health information-seeking behaviors among the undergraduate students surveyed, as well as their actual behaviors. When choosing keywords for their searches, 59% of the participants used nouns as keywords; 43% used nouns, adjectives, and adverbs as common keywords; and 28% used sentences. Regarding the search technique of Boolean logic, only 27% of the participants used the operators "AND", "OR", and "NOT". In terms of limiting the scope of their queries, 12% of the study participants limited the type of data searched, while only 2% limited the date and language of the data retrieved; this indicated a low percentage of users who limit the date, form, and language of information for narrowing down the scope of their searches.

Table 2. Current status of health information retrieval behavior among undergraduate students: Information seeking.

Check Questions about Online Health Information Retrieval Behavior		**Code Type**	
Keyword selection	1. How to use keywords: Nouns as keywords	Used 60 (59%)	Not used 41 (41%)
	2. How to use keywords: Nouns, adjectives, and adverbs as common keywords	Used 43 (43%)	Not used 58 (57%)
	3. How to use keywords: Sentences as keywords	Used 28 (28%)	Not used 73 (72%)
Boolean logic query	How to reduce the scope of data and whether to use the operators "AND", "OR", and "NOT"	Used 27 (27%)	Not used 74(73%)
Unlimited scope for query	1. Whether to limit the scope of the query: Limit the date of the unnamed title	Yes 2 (2%)	No 99 (98%)
	2. Whether to restrict the scope of the query: Limit the data type	Yes 12 (12%)	No 89 (88%)
	3. Whether to limit the scope of the query: Limit the language	Yes 2 (2%)	No 99 (98%)

3.2. Status of Online Health Information-Seeking Behavior among Undergraduate Students: Information Browsing and Information Sources

The results showed that the average number of web pages visited by the study participants to determine the adequacy of the information available on a given health topic was 2.99; their overall browsing time was 5.54 min; and the average time they spent on each web page was 2.39 min. Regarding the information source, 81% of the respondents were concerned about the newness of the information and the year of publication. The information sources consulted were mostly "organization websites" (45%) and magazines or periodicals (40%), while news reports (8%), forums and chat rooms (13%), and personal websites (22%) accounted for a minority of the information sources. However, in terms of the professionalism of the data sources, 22% of the users believed that the authors of the data they retrieved were experts in the related fields, and 42% of the data mentioned the author's affiliation; however, 85% of the users found that the authors of the data were anonymous, or believed that they were unprofessional, as shown in Table 3.

Table 3. Status of health information retrieval behavior among undergraduate students: Information browsing and information sources.

Check Questions about Online Health Information Retrieval Behavior		Code Type	
Information browsing	1. Number of pages viewed	Min. 1, Max. 14, Mean 2.99 (SD = 2.33)	
	2. Overall query time	Min. 1.42 s, Max. 17.43 s, Mean 5.54 s (SD = 3.04)	
	3. Average time on page	Min. 0.65 s, Max. 6.23 min, Mean 2.39 min (SD = 1.31)	
Information source	1. Whether the data source is new or old (year) can be marked in the Word file	Directly expressed in AD year 82 (81%)	No time for data 19 (19%)
	2. Whether there is a source of information: Website of the organization	Yes 45 (45%)	No 56 (55%)
	3. Whether there is a source of information: Magazines or periodicals	Yes 40 (40%)	No 61 (60%)
	4. Whether there is a source of information: News reports	Yes 8 (8%)	No 93 (92%)
	5. Whether there is a source of information: Forums or chat rooms	Yes 13 (13%)	No 88 (87%)
	6. Whether there is a source of information: Related research papers	Yes 0 (0%)	No 101 (100%)
	7. Whether there is a source of information: Personal web pages	Yes 22 (22%)	No 79 (78%)
	8. Professionalism of the information source: The author is a professional, for example, an expert in a related field or a physician	Yes 22 (22%)	No 79 (79%)
	9. Professionalism of the information source: The author is a professional, and their affiliation is mentioned	Yes 42 (42%)	No 59 (58%)
	10. Professionalism of the information source: The author of the data is anonymous or a non-professional	Yes 85 (84%)	No 16 (16%)

4. Discussion

4.1. Is Information Literacy the Missing Part of Health Promotion among Undergraduate Students?

It was found that most of the keywords used by the participants in the search for health information were nouns, although some did use a mixture of nouns, adjectives, and adverbs. Few searched using Boolean logic, and they seldom limited the scope of their queries to narrow down the results, indicating that the undergraduate students had few relevant skills in searching for information.

Information literacy is one of the multiple components of health literacy that adolescents are aware of, encompassing a range of skills and knowledge that are relevant to health behaviors and can reduce health risks [21]. When individuals are familiar with internet search methods, they can easily filter out useful information based on the purpose of the search and the source of the data. Conversely, users who are unfamiliar with these operations are easily distracted by irrelevant information, which affects the accuracy and usefulness of their information judgments. Furthermore, individuals who are exposed to a large amount of online health information and are unable to critique and make good use of this information may suffer negative effects, leading to feelings of anxiety that can cause emotional distress and even severe cyberchondria [27]. Joseph and Fleary [21] explored adolescents' perceptions of health literacy and revealed that they involved more functional than critical literacy. Criticality involves reading, understanding, and acting upon health information, having potential effects and benefits for individuals and society. This highlights the importance of critical skill development and education for the youth in particular.

4.2. What Is the Potential Risk of Self-Diagnosis Due to the Explosion of Health Information during the COVID-19 Pandemic?

This study found that 81% of the participants were concerned about the newness of the information they found and the year of the source. In terms of the professionalism of the source, 22% of the users believed that the author of the information they retrieved was an expert in the field. Meanwhile, 42% of the information retrieved mentioned the author's affiliation. However, 85% of the participants were dubious about the information they found on the internet, as its author was either anonymous, or they believed the author was not a professional. In fact, obtaining health-related information on the internet and diagnosing oneself based on it affects one's health-related behaviors, decisions, and actions. Sturiale et al. [4] found that there was a correlation between those who used the internet for work and those who had knowledge of both symptoms and their likely diagnosis before consultation, among patients. Patients who used the internet daily were more likely to request a consultation within six months of symptom onset. Additionally, those with anorectal diseases were more likely to have knowledge of their disease and symptoms before the visit. Hsu et al. [3] surveyed a sample of undergraduate students to explore their experiences with online health information and found that they retrieved health information related to their needs from the internet in order to prevent or maintain their health conditions. However, the prescriptions they retrieved online only offered reference answers, and sometimes inner doubts still lingered in their minds. Using the flu as an example, Myrick employed a naturalistic experiment to test the emotions of 380 Americans after retrieving information online, exploring the theoretical models that shaped cognition and behavior [13]. It was found that the study participants had difficulty retrieving information when they had a dubious attitude. Myrick further tested how to improve the skills required for the online health information retrieval process, observing that individuals had multiple emotions (fear, hope, satisfaction, interest, and motivation) after retrieving information, and the mediating effect of "social cognitive factors" affected their subsequent attitudes and behaviors. The positive emotions of interest and hope experienced during the online health information-seeking process positively influenced individuals' confidence and behavioral intentions.

The number of medical articles published on the internet increased significantly during the COVID-19 pandemic [28]; however, at the same time, the amount of fake news and disinformation skyrocketed to several dozen times the previous level [29]. As the internet booms and health information spreads, the World Wide Web has become a major source for the public to search for information about medical and health risks. In tandem with this boom, many health and disease-focused websites have emerged to provide the public with more immediate access to health information. Such sites provide information and resources for readers with medical conditions, assisting them with possible self-diagnostic references for certain symptoms and helping them decide whether to self-treat or consult a physician [30]. The use of the internet to retrieve health-related information is a behavioral manifestation of the individuals' search for peace of mind. However, the information available on the internet is not always accurate and reliable; therefore, it is important to promote individuals' online search skills to reduce uncertainty, worries, and anxiety, avoiding incorrect self-diagnosis. As individuals are exposed to the risks of online information technology, it is critical to understand how they use health information when they are inundated with it online [31]. A key strategy for managing health care surge is "forward triage"—the sorting of patients before they arrive at the emergency department (ED). Direct-to-consumer (or on-demand) telemedicine, a 21st-century approach to forward triage that allows individuals to be efficiently screened, is both patient-centered and conducive to self-quarantine, protecting patients, clinicians, and the community from exposure to any infectious disease, such as COVID-19. Furthermore, it allows physicians and patients to communicate using smartphones or webcam-enabled computers, which may be beneficial during situations such as the COVID-19 pandemic [32]. Telemedicine, however, may not always be the go-to approach for physicians in Italy. For example, the utilization of telemedicine for the diagnosis of common proctologic conditions (e.g., hemorrhoidal disease, anal abscess and fistula, anal condylomas, and anal fissure) and functional pelvic floor disorders was generally considered inappropriate. Teleconsultation was instead deemed appropriate only for the diagnosis and management of pilonidal disease, revealing the boundaries of telemedicine in Italy. Therefore, infrastructures, logistics, and legality related to telemedicine need to be standardized [33].

5. Conclusions

This study investigated the online health information-seeking behavior of undergraduate students. The results revealed that most of the keywords used by the study participants when searching for health information were nouns, although some used a mixture of nouns, adjectives, and adverbs. Few participants searched using Boolean logic, and few limited the scope of their queries to narrow down the retrieved data. Almost all the study participants questioned the validity of the information they found, considered the authors of the data to be anonymous or non-professionals, and were dubious about the information available on the internet.

The widespread availability of e-health information has become an important issue for public health gains. From the viewpoint of the reader, individuals are exposed to a large amount of information that is easily accessible for everyone on the internet, suggesting that technological risks are relevant to individuals' lives but are often widely ignored or overlooked. It is suggested that in the future, the online health information retrieval skills needed by adolescents can be appropriately integrated into university curricula in the form of training through relevant information collection skills and expertise, such as clinical understanding, prevention strategies, and navigation of the healthcare system [27]. Students' skills in searching for information and their ability to distinguish between true and false information should also be fostered.

This study had a few limitations. The Delphi method used in the research has its own restriction, such as the identification of "consensus" amongst experts, which appears to be the central motivation for the application of Delphi techniques in health sciences. Nevertheless, there is no general definition for what consensus actually is. As far as the research replicability is concerned, this study was aimed at college students, and there were limitations related to the ecological validity of our research results due to the small sample size. Future studies should, therefore, employ larger research samples, using this article as an introduction for further analysis regarding the process of seeking health information in relation to the COVID-19 pandemic. In terms of the study design, this research asked respondents to answer pre-designed health questions, which may have limited its intrinsic validity, failing to assess the online health information retrieval behavior of individuals when they face personal health problems. In addition to designing a series of health questions to explore the participants' online health information retrieval practices through observational methods, future research could ask participants to describe their online health information retrieval process in a "think aloud" manner to better understand their subjective use.

Funding: This research was funded by the Ministry of Science and Technology, Taiwan, grant number 109-2511-H-992-005-MY2.

Institutional Review Board Statement: The study was conducted according to the guidelines of the Declaration of Helsinki and approved by the Review of Human Research Ethics Committee of National Cheng Kung University (NCKU) (protocol code #108-202 on 19 May 2019).

Informed Consent Statement: Informed consent was obtained from all subjects involved in the study.

Data Availability Statement: Not available.

Conflicts of Interest: The author declares no conflict of interest.

References

1. Son, C.; Hegde, S.; Smith, A.; Wang, X.; Sasangohar, F. Effects of COVID-19 on college students' mental health in the United States: Interview survey study. *J. Med. Internet Res.* **2020**, *22*, e21279. [CrossRef]
2. Taiwan Network Information Center. Taiwan Internet Report. Available online: https://report.twnic.tw/2020/assets/download/TWNIC_TaiwanInternetReport_2020_CH.pdf (accessed on 12 January 2020).
3. Hsu, W.C.; Chen, S.F.; Ho, C.J. Experience of using web health information among undergraduate students: An analysis from the health literacy perspective. *J. Health Promot. Health Educ.* **2011**, *35*, 1–22.
4. Sturiale, A.; Pata, F.; De Simone, V.; Pellino, G.; Campennì, P.; Moggia, E.; Manigrasso, M.; Milone, M.; Rizzo, G.; Morganti, R.; et al. Internet and social media use among patients with colorectal diseases (ISMAEL): A nationwide survey. *Colorectal Dis.* **2020**, *22*, 1724–1733. [CrossRef] [PubMed]
5. Moorman, C.; Matulich, E. A model of consumers' preventive health behavior: The role of health motivation and health ability. *J. Consum. Res.* **1993**, *20*, 208–228. [CrossRef]
6. Chen, W.; Lee, K.H. More than search? Informational and participatory eHealth behavior. *Comput. Hum. Behav.* **2014**, *30*, 103–109. [CrossRef]
7. Liao, W.C.; Chiu, L.A.; Yueh, H.P. A study of rural elderly's health information needs and seeking behavior. *J. Libr. Inf. Stud.* **2012**, *10*, 155–204. [CrossRef]
8. Case, D.O. *Looking for Information: A Survey of Research on Information Seeking, Needs and Behavior*; Academic Press: San Diego, CA, USA, 2002.
9. Wilson, T.D. Human information behavior. *Inf. Sci.* **2000**, *3*, 49–55. [CrossRef]
10. Dawkins-Moultin, M.; Mcdonald, A.; Mckyer, E.L. Integrating the principles of socioecology and critical pedagogy for health promotion health literacy interventions. *J. Health Commun.* **2016**, *21*, 30–35. [CrossRef]
11. Bandura, A. The self system in reciprocal determinism. *Am. Psychol.* **1978**, *33*, 344–358. [CrossRef]
12. Bandura, A. *Self-Efficacy: The Exercise of Control*; W. H. Freeman and Company: New York, NY, USA, 1997.
13. Myrick, J.G. The role of emotions and social cognitive variables in online health information seeking processes and effects. *Comput. Hum. Behav.* **2017**, *68*, 422–433. [CrossRef]
14. Brown, R.J.; Skelly, N.; Chew-Graham, C.A. Online health research and health anxiety: A systematic review and conceptual integration. *Clin. Psychol.* **2019**, *27*, e12299. [CrossRef]
15. Lo, W.L.; Chiu, M.H. A content analysis of internet health rumors. *J. Educ. Media Libr. Sci.* **2015**, *52*, 3–31. [CrossRef]
16. Lu, H.Y. The influence of the perceived importance and credibility of health information in the media on health information-seeking behavior. *Comm. Soc.* **2015**, *34*, 89–115.
17. Liao, C.C.; Kuo, P.Y.; To, P.L.; Chung, Y.C. The study of continuance intention to use health information websites. *Electron. Commer. Stud.* **2012**, *10*, 145–168.
18. Wei, M.H.; Hung, W.C. Health information seeking experiences of adults in urban and remote communities: Results of focus group discussions. *J. Health Promot. Health Educ.* **2010**, *34*, 93–114. [CrossRef]
19. Go, E.; You, K.H. Health-related online information seeking and behavioral outcomes: Fatalism and self-efficacy as mediators. *Soc. Behav. Pers.* **2018**, *46*, 871–880. [CrossRef]
20. Norman, C.D.; Skinner, H.A. eHealth literacy: Essential skills for consumer health in a networked world. *J. Med. Internet Res.* **2006**, *8*, e9. [CrossRef]
21. Joseph, P.; Fleary, S.A. "The way you interpret health": Adolescent definitions and perceptions of health literacy. *J. Sch. Health* **2021**, *91*, 599–607. [CrossRef]
22. Taylor, E. We agree, don't we? The Delphi method for health environments research. *HERD* **2020**, *13*, 11–23. [CrossRef]
23. Niederberger, M.; Spranger, J. Delphi Technique in Health Sciences: A map. *Front. Public Health* **2020**, *8*, 457. [CrossRef]
24. Columbia University Mailman School of Public Health. Content Analysis. Available online: https://www.publichealth.columbia.edu/research/population-health-methods/content-analysis (accessed on 18 January 2020).
25. Healthy Five Fruits and Vegetables. Available online: https://www.hpa.gov.tw/Pages/Detail.aspx?nodeid=543&pid=715 (accessed on 15 January 2020).
26. Ou, Y.S. *Content Analysis*; Taiwan Normal University Press: Taipei, Taiwan, China, 2000.
27. Jokić-Begić, N.; Mikac, U.; Čuržik, D.; Jokić, D.S. The development and validation of the Short Cyberchondria Scale (SCS). *J. Psychopathol. Behav. Assess.* **2019**, *41*, 1–15. [CrossRef]

28. Chrzanowski, J.; Sołek, J.; Fendler, W.; Jemielniak, D. Assessing public interest based on Wikipedia's most visited medical articles during the SARS-CoV-2 outbreak: Search trends analysis. *J. Med. Internet Res.* **2021**, *23*, e26331. [CrossRef]
29. Mangono, T.; Smittenaar, P.; Caplan, Y.; Huang, V.S.; Sutermaster, S.; Kemp, H.; Sgaier, S.K. Information-seeking patterns during the COVID-19 pandemic across the United States: Longitudinal analysis of Google Trends data. *J. Med. Internet Res.* **2021**, *23*, e22933. [CrossRef] [PubMed]
30. Ryan, A.; Wilson, S. Internet healthcare: Do self-diagnosis sites do more harm than good? *Expert Opin. Drug Saf.* **2008**, *7*, 227–229. [CrossRef] [PubMed]
31. Zahnd, W.E.; Scaife, S.L.; Francis, M.L. Health literacy skills in rural and urban populations. *Am. J. Health Behav.* **2009**, *33*, 550–557. [CrossRef] [PubMed]
32. Hollander, J.E.; Carr, B.G. Virtually perfect? Telemedicine for COVID-19. *N. Engl. J. Med.* **2020**, *382*, 1679–1681. [CrossRef] [PubMed]
33. Gallo, G.; Grossi, U.; Sturiale, A.; Di Tanna, G.L.; Picciariello, A.; Pillon, S.; Mascagni, D.; Altomare, D.F.; Naldini, G.; Perinotti, R.; et al. E-consensus on telemedicine in proctology: A RAND/UCLA-modified study. *Surgery* **2021**, *170*, 405–411. [CrossRef] [PubMed]

International Journal of
Environmental Research and Public Health

MDPI

Article

The Relationship among COVID-19 Information Seeking, News Media Use, and Emotional Distress at the Onset of the Pandemic

Juwon Hwang [1,*], Porismita Borah [2], Dhavan Shah [3] and Markus Brauer [4]

[1] School of Media and Strategic Communications, Oklahoma State University, Stillwater, OK 74078, USA
[2] Edward R. Murrow College of Communication, Washington State University, Pullman, WA 99163, USA; p.borah@wsu.edu
[3] School of Journalism and Mass Communication, University of Wisconsin-Madison, Madison, WI 53706, USA; dshah@wisc.edu
[4] Department of Psychology, University of Wisconsin-Madison, Madison, WI 53706, USA; markus.brauer@wisc.edu
* Correspondence: juwon.hwang@okstate.edu

Citation: Hwang, J.; Borah, P.; Shah, D.; Brauer, M. The Relationship among COVID-19 Information Seeking, News Media Use, and Emotional Distress at the Onset of the Pandemic. *Int. J. Environ. Res. Public Health* **2021**, *18*, 13198. https://doi.org/10.3390/ijerph182413198

Academic Editors: Paolo Roma, Merylin Monaro, Cristina Mazza and Pasquale Caponnetto

Received: 16 October 2021
Accepted: 10 December 2021
Published: 14 December 2021

Abstract: Although several theories posit that information seeking is related to better psychological health, this logic may not apply to a pandemic like COVID-19. Given uncertainty inherent to the novel virus, we expect that information seeking about COVID-19 will be positively associated with emotional distress. Additionally, we consider the type of news media from which individuals receive information—television, newspapers, and social media—when examining relationships with emotional distress. Using a U.S. national survey, we examine: (1) the link between information seeking about COVID-19 and emotional distress, (2) the relationship between reliance on television, newspapers, and social media as sources for news and emotional distress, and (3) the interaction between information seeking and use of these news media sources on emotional distress. Our findings show that seeking information about COVID-19 was significantly related to emotional distress. Moreover, even after accounting for COVID-19 information seeking, consuming news via television and social media was tied to increased distress, whereas consuming newspapers was not significantly related to greater distress. Emotional distress was most pronounced among individuals high in information seeking and television news use, whereas the association between information seeking and emotional distress was not moderated by newspapers or social media news use.

Keywords: information seeking; television news use; emotional distress; COVID-19; social media news use

1. Introduction

The COVID-19 pandemic has not only disrupted basic everyday activities, but also fostered emotional distress [1–3]. After isolated cases and clusters started appearing in the early months of 2020, by March the U.S. saw rapidly increasing case counts indicating community transmission [4]. With COVID-19 declared a pandemic by the World Health Organization on 11 March and a national emergency by the Trump administration on 13 March, states implemented shelter-in-place or stay at home orders [5], potentially contributing to unease and mental distress. Research documenting the extent of emotional distress during the COVID-19 pandemic is rapidly emerging (e.g., [1,2,6,7]). This research builds on work showing that there is a significant relationship between the occurrence of infectious disease outbreaks and negative psychological consequences. For example, people are likely to develop greater incidence of depression [8], psychological distress [8,9], and anxiety [10] during pandemics.

Since the COVID-19 outbreak, individuals have sought to understand basic information related to the virus such as its impact, effective treatment, and vaccine development [11]. The lack of predictability, the rising number of confirmed cases and deaths, and changing health guidelines led wide swaths of the public to seek information about the pandemic [12]. In fact, according to a report from the Pew Research Center, 70% of U.S. citizens searched online for information about the coronavirus in the early months of the pandemic [13].

Several theories and empirical findings suggest a positive relationship between information seeking and emotional distress especially during crises. In fact, information seeking about negative events such as natural disasters [14,15], terrorism [16,17], and pandemics [18] is linked to emotional distress. Moreover, following the reliance on heuristics under uncertainty [19,20], an unprecedented amount of information may cause emotional distress. So, when confronted by intense media coverage about COVID-19, people may perceive higher levels of threat, which, in turn, may trigger higher stress. Finally, people might be incapable of avoiding information seeking because of the need-to-know basic information, such as the symptoms of infection.

Information seeking, as a proxy for attention paid to COVID-19 news, may interact with the news source through which information is consumed. Specific combinations of attention and exposure may also be related to emotional distress, with certain types of news sources more likely to spur strong emotions (e.g., [21,22]). Particularly for television, attention must be considered alongside exposure [23,24], especially considering the unique capabilities of video for conveying emotions [17]. This is because news on television features vivid images, motion and sound, whereas newspapers emphasize text and limited use of visuals. Taking into account the medium through which people find news during the COVID-19 pandemic may explain distress mechanisms. Furthermore, the types of media through which individuals find news may moderate the relationship between information seeking and emotional distress. For example, if an individual tends to rely on television as a source for news and is seeking information about COVID-19, the modality of this medium may amplify the association between information seeking and emotional distress beyond the direct relationship of each factor.

Using a U.S. national survey, we examine: (1) the link between information seeking concerning the COVID-19 pandemic and individuals' emotional distress, (2) the relationship between reliance on television, newspapers, and social media as sources for news exposure on emotional distress during the pandemic after accounting for COVID-19 information seeking, and (3) the interaction between information seeking about COVID-19 and use of these news media sources on emotional distress. In doing so, our study attempts to understand the psychological toll of information seeking and news media use during an ongoing pandemic. Understanding these relationships is critical because seeking information via news media has been especially important during the COVID-19 pandemic. However, at the same time, the contentiousness of partisan news and the presentational styles of some media forms about the pandemic could lead to emotional distress. In this study, we attempt to unpack these relationships.

1.1. Information Seeking and Emotional Distress

Information seeking is the process by which individuals "purposefully make an effort to change their state of knowledge" ([25], p. 549; [26]). Both individuals' motivation to seek information and media coverage on the specific topic tend to increase during crises [11,27]. Due to the novel nature of COVID-19 especially, information about COVID-19 has been placed at the forefront of much of the media [28]. The pandemic dominated news content during the first half of 2020 [27,28]. Given its prevalence and potential impact, theories and studies suggest a positive relationship between information seeking and emotional distress during a major pandemic like the one caused by COVID-19.

First, information seeking about certain events using media might be related to negative emotions [14–16,18]. This is particularly evident in studies on information seeking about traumatic events, such as disasters [14,15], terrorism [16,17], and pandemics [18]. When a traumatic event occurs, individuals often attempt to reduce uncertainty about the event by engaging in information seeking. However, efforts to learn more about the traumatic event may be linked with negative emotional reactions to said event [16]. In the case of September 11, people sought to alleviate uncertainty by seeking information about the event, and this behavior was related to a variety of negative emotions [16], due partially to underlying uncertainty about the event [16] and the ways in which media covered it. This same logic can be applied to the global COVID-19 pandemic, as the uncertainty and unpredictability of COVID-19 poses risks to individuals' mental health (e.g., [1,2,6,7]).

Second, the reliance on heuristics under uncertainty [19,20] also helps explain why individuals are stressed with COVID-19 information seeking. Uncertain people tend to refer to heuristics, or mental shortcuts. According to the availability heuristic [19,20], there are situations in which people assess the likelihood of an event by how readily examples come to mind [20]. People may perceive higher levels of threat when the events are salient and memorable, with vivid evidence [20]. Media coverage is one way to make the event available in people's minds, ensuring that people are easily able to retrieve information concerning that event. In the case of COVID-19, there has been a remarkable amount of media coverage, making it available to most people who seek information about the pandemic. This higher availability of information about the global pandemic may cause higher levels of stress.

Finally, under certain circumstances, individuals might choose to avoid information seeking when they perceive that more knowledge might lead to distress [29–31]. However, avoiding information seeking might not always be an option. In the case of the COVID-19 pandemic, an already unprecedented amount of uncertainty has been increased by the spread of conspiracy theories and misinformation [12]. Even if people know consuming information leads to stress, they might not have a choice to avoid it, due to the need to find basic answers like safe ways to get groceries or symptoms of COVID-19 infection. The evolving nature of the pandemic meant critical information frequently changed, requiring active information seeking to keep up with changing facts and guidelines, despite the potential distress.

Since the onset of the COVID-19 pandemic, there has been a growing body of the literature dealing with information seeking and emotional distress (e.g., [32–34]). The previous findings, however, are somewhat inconsistent. While some studies showed that information seeking is significantly related to anxiety [33] or information overload [34], other studies indicated that high levels of information seeking are associated with higher levels of well-being and risk perception [32]. To address the inconsistency in the literature, we examine the relationship between COVID-19 information seeking and emotional distress using a large U.S. national sample. Despite the mixed findings, based on the aforementioned discussion, we propose our first hypothesis as follows:

Hypothesis 1. *A higher level of COVID-19 information seeking is positively related to emotional distress during the COVID-19 pandemic.*

1.2. Information Seeking, General News Media Use, and Emotional Distress

The association between news media use and individuals' emotional distress concerning COVID-19 may depend on the modality of the news medium from which individuals get information. This idea is associated with Marshall McLuhan's [35] early work, which emphasizes the differences in media modalities. Studies in the McLuhan tradition focus on "the differences in the physical modalities of video versus print and offer evidence to show that video is the most effective medium for communicating information" ([36], p. 79). Indeed, audiovisual media such as television have been found to have a greater impact on information recall and counterarguing compared to print media [37,38]. Audiovisual media attract attention and stimulate involvement [39]. By contrast, the presentation of information in print modalities seems to reduce the ability to foster emotional arousal [17]. In line with this research, we consider how consuming news via television, newspapers, and social media may be related to emotional distress beyond information seeking concerning COVID-19. Furthermore, the link between COVID-19 information seeking and emotional distress may not be the same for all news consumers. Instead, the type of media through which individuals find general news may interact with information seeking about COVID-19 to explain emotional distress.

1.3. Television News

Because television news, as an audiovisual medium, may require fewer cognitive skills than print media, it is more likely to capture the attention of people who possess fewer cognitive skills [36]. Its combination of audio and visual tracks, repeated usage of strong imagery, and news anchors' visible displays of emotion may elicit emotional responses in news viewers [40,41]. Indeed, television news is more emotionally arousing than newspaper stories [17]. Previous studies show the strong association between television news consumption and viewers' negative emotional outcomes (e.g., [22,42–46]). However, this association may be due to the kind of thinking television viewers have to do to make sense of a cultural experience [47]. An experimental study showed that exposure to a random newscast triggered increased negative emotions, and manifested in heightened anxiety, total mood disturbance, and decreased positive affect [45]. The emotional distress may be more intense after exposure to televised reports of exceptionally negative events [46]. In addition, a systematic review of literature on disaster news viewing and psychological outcomes linked consumption of televised news with a range of negative emotions [22]. Specifically, television viewing in the context of terrorism was associated with posttraumatic stress (PTS; [43]), stress reactions [44], and negative emotional responses [17]. Given that the technical features of television are particularly appropriate for evoking emotional responses, we propose the following hypothesis:

Hypothesis 2. *Accounting for information seeking about COVID-19, consuming news via television will be related to increased emotional distress.*

Hypothesis 3. *The association between COVID-19 information seeking and emotional distress will be moderated by television news use, with the association between information seeking and emotional distress stronger for individuals with higher television news use.*

1.4. Newspapers

In contrast to television news, newspapers and other print media's lack of visual, motion, and audio cues reduce a reader's sense of presence. Moreover, newspapers and newsmagazines provide in-depth, thematic, and analytic coverage on issues and matters of public interest, with less emotion-laden language compared to television news, which tends to combine an emphasis on emotional content with episodic coverage [17]. These characteristics position newspapers as a less emotionally arousing medium.

Research shows that newspapers evoke weaker emotions in readers when compared with the effect of television news on viewers (e.g., [36]). For example, while people who watched television news experienced stronger emotions related to terrorist attacks, newspaper usage was not a significant factor in explaining individuals' emotional responses [17]. Similarly, according to a systematic review of literature on various forms of disaster media and psychological outcomes [22], none of the reviewed studies showed significant associations between newspaper use and psychological outcomes such as depression, stress, and anxiety. Given that newspaper stories feature fewer emotion-laden visuals, we propose the following hypothesis:

Hypothesis 4. *Accounting for information seeking about COVID-19, consuming news via newspapers will be related to decreased emotional distress.*

Hypothesis 5. *The association between COVID-19 information seeking and emotional distress will be moderated by newspaper use, with the association between information seeking and emotional distress weaker for individuals with higher newspaper use.*

1.5. Social Media News

Finally, with the rise of mobile technology, accessing news and information on social media has become commonplace and frequent [48]. In 2019, 53% of U.S. adults received news from social media, up from 47% in 2018 [48]. While social media share traditional media's ability to provide news to users [49], social media have unique characteristics that are markedly different from traditional forms of media. First, while traditional media are defined as either textual media (e.g., newspapers) or audiovisual media (e.g., television news), social media provide a combination of modality (i.e., both textual and audiovisual mode). Social media users can share dramatic multimedia clips about apparent health risks using video sharing sites such as YouTube [21], many of which are unverified. Second, social media are highly personalized platforms, connecting users with similar interests, often with personal or professional relationships [50]. Social media can reflect a social endorsement from 'people like me' via established social contacts (e.g., Facebook) or through like-minded individuals (e.g., Twitter). This aspect of social media allows for the rapid spread of misinformation [51] because users rely on social endorsement [52] rather than verified information. According to a report from the Pew Research Center, those who get most of their news from social media reported seeing at least some misinformation about the COVID-19 outbreak [53]. These same news consumers said media have exaggerated the threat posed by COVID-19.

All of these features of social media may have caused the discourse on social media concerning COVID-19 to be emotionally arousing and stressful. Prior research shows higher levels of emotional distress among social media news users than other media users. One study showed that individuals who consumed news solely from news feeds, or news feeds plus online news websites, had higher rates of neuroticism (feeling anxious or depressed/worried) compared to participants consuming news exclusively offline [54]. Another study compared post-traumatic stress one month after Hurricane Sandy among those who learned about the disaster through traditional media (television, newspapers, and radio) versus those who learned about it through social media (Facebook, YouTube, and Twitter; [21]). The researchers found that posttraumatic stress was higher in those using social media relative to those using only traditional media. This could be because social media exert direct and personal impact, owing to the type of content being shared, compared to traditional media that provide more 'objective' information.

The modality of social media (i.e., combination of audiovisual and textual information), its endorsement functions (i.e., likes, shares), and the lack of gatekeeping of information sources circulated on social media may strengthen emotional responses in those who rely on this as a source for news. Accordingly, we predict the following hypotheses:

Hypothesis 6. *Accounting for information seeking about COVID-19, consuming news via social media will be related to increased emotional distress.*

Hypothesis 7. *The association between COVID-19 information seeking and emotional distress will be moderated by social media news use, with the association between information seeking and emotional distress stronger for individuals with higher social media news use.*

2. Methods

2.1. Data

Responding to widespread "community transmission" within the U.S. (the virus being transmitted by individuals with no travel history) in mid-March 2020, a survey was rapidly assembled and collected by a cross-disciplinary team of researchers at a large Midwestern university. Data were collected from 26 March to 1 April 2020 using a Qualtrics panel, a representative sample of U.S. residents based on a pre-recruited pool of panelists ($n = 2251$). This sample also contained a probability sub-sample of residents of the Midwestern state in which the sponsoring university is located. Participants had a mean age of 46.6 ($SD = 17.0$), 58.2% were female, and 68.9% were white. In terms of education, 22.4% had some high school education or a high school diploma, 21.4% had some college education but no degree, 35.8% had an associate's or bachelor's degree, and 20.4% had an advanced degree.

2.2. Measures

Emotional distress. Participants indicated the extent to which they experienced the following feelings since they became aware of the COVID-19 outbreak: (1) "Overwhelmed," (2) "Anxious," and (3) "Afraid about what might happen." Responses options ranged on a 5-point scale from 1 = *not at all* to 5 = *very much* ($M = 3.45$, $SD = 1.08$, Cronbach's $\alpha = 0.83$).

COVID-19 information seeking. Participants were asked to answer a single-item about how frequently they had sought news updates about COVID-19 on a 5-point scale from 1 = *never* to 5 = *any time I have the chance* ($M = 3.77$, $SD = 1.12$).

General news media usage. General news media usage separated by media type, was assessed by the question "How often do you get news from the following sources?" rated on a 5-point scale from 1 = *never* to 5 = *every day*. Television news media usage was measured with the item, "National network news, such as ABC, NBC, CBS" ($M = 3.62$, $SD = 1.38$). Newspaper news media usage was measured with the item, "newspaper and news magazines" ($M = 3.00$, $SD = 1.45$). Finally, social media news media usage was assessed with the item, "social media platforms such as Facebook, Twitter, and YouTube" ($M = 3.11$, $SD = 1.53$).

Control variables. Demographic characteristics were also incorporated into the analysis, including age, gender, ethnicity, and education level. We also included additional variables that may be related to emotional distress during the pandemic, such as (a) the likelihood of getting infected with COVID-19 as measured on a 5-point scale from 1 = *very unlikely* to 5 = *very likely* ($M = 2.60$, $SD = 1.11$), (b) whether participants knew someone likely to suffer serious negative consequences if infected with COVID-19 (*yes* = 1275, 58.1%; *no* = 921, 41.9%), and (c) whether they knew someone who has tested positive for COVID-19 (*yes* = 326, 14.8%; *no* = 1870, 85.2%). In addition, a measure of political ideology, measured on a 5-point scale from 1 = *liberal* to 5 = *conservative* ($M = 3.06$, $SD = 1.08$), was included in the analysis. Table 1 presents descriptive statistics and Pearson correlation coefficients among the variables.

Table 1. Descriptive statistics and correlations.

Variables	*M*	*SD*	1	2	3	4	5
1. Emotional distress	3.45	1.08	-				
2. Information seeking about COVID-19	3.77	1.12	0.361 ***	-			
3. Television news	3.62	1.38	0.246 ***	0.359 ***	-		
4. Newspapers	3.00	1.45	0.177 ***	0.292 ***	0.370 ***	-	
5. Social media news	3.11	1.53	0.311 ***	0.210 ***	0.141 ***	0.143 ***	-

Note. *M* denotes mean; *SD* denotes standard deviation. *** $p < 0.001$.

2.3. Analytic Strategy

Hierarchical linear regression analysis was performed to examine the proposed hypotheses. The analysis was conducted in four steps. Emotional distress was entered as a continuous dependent variable; control variables including demographics, likelihood of getting infected, whether participants knew someone likely to suffer serious negative consequences or who has tested positive for the COVID-19 coronavirus, and political ideology were entered in Step 1. Information seeking about COVID-19 was entered in Step 2. The three news media use variables for television, newspapers, and social media were entered in Step 3 (to address possible multicollinearity between our multiple news media use terms, we also tested versions of the same model where we added each news media use variable and each interaction term separately. We confirmed that the results held). Finally, the interactions between information seeking about COVID-19 and the news media use measures were entered in Step 4. All predictors were mean-centered before they were entered in the moderated regression model. The analysis was conducted using SPSS version 26 (SPSS Inc., Armonk, NY, USA).

3. Results

Among the control variables, age and gender were significant predictors of emotional distress. Younger (β = −0.145, $p < 0.001$) females (β = 0.130, $p < 0.001$) were more likely to be emotionally distressed. Higher levels of distress were reported when people perceived higher likelihood of getting infected by COVID-19 (β = 0.178, $p < 0.001$) and if they knew someone who was high risk (β = 0.054, $p < 0.01$). Moreover, people with conservative ideology were less likely to be distressed (β = −0.068, $p < 0.01$).

Regarding H1, results revealed that while accounting for a variety of control variables, the more COVID-19 information individuals sought the more likely they were to be emotionally distressed (β = 0.255, $p < 0.001$; see Table 2). Thus, H1 was supported.

Table 2. Hierarchical regression analysis examining the relationships between COVID-19 information seeking, news media usage, and emotional distress.

	Emotional Distress (β)
Block1: Control variables	
Age	−0.145 ***
Gender (Female = 1)	0.130 ***
Ethnicity (Minority = 1)	0.029
Education	−0.034
Likelihood of getting infected	0.178 ***
Know someone who is in high risk (yes = 1, no = 0)	0.054 **
Know someone who has tested positive (yes = 1, no = 0)	0.004
Political ideology (1 = liberal to 5 = conservative)	−0.068 **
ΔR^2	9.2%
Block2: Information seeking	
COVID-19 Information seeking	0.255 ***
ΔR^2	11.3%
Block3: News media usage	
Television news	0.099 ***
Newspapers	0.032
Social media	0.137 ***
ΔR^2	3.4%
Block4: Interactions	
Information seeking × Television news	0.046 *
Information seeking × Newspapers	−0.002
Information seeking × Social media	0.017
ΔR^2	0.4%
Total R^2	24.3%

Note. All of the coefficients are standardized. Predictors (information seeking and news media usage) are mean-centered. ΔR^2, the R square change, shows the improvement in R-square when the next group of predictors is added. * $p < 0.05$, ** $p < 0.01$, *** $p < 0.001$.

For H2, H4, and H6, even after statistically controlling for several variables, including COVID-19 information seeking, consuming news via television and social media was related to increased emotional distress (β = 0.099, $p < 0.001$ and β = 0.137, $p < 0.001$, respectively), whereas consuming news via newspapers was not (β = 0.032, $p = 0.132$). Thus, H2 and H6 were supported, but H4 was not.

With respect to H3, H5, and H7, findings indicated that emotional distress was significantly higher among those high in COVID-19 information seeking and television news use (β = 0.046, $p = 0.033$). There was no significant interaction between information seeking about COVID-19 and either newspaper use or social media news use (β = −0.002, $p = 0.917$ and β = 0.017, $p = 0.393$, respectively). This result provides support for H3 but not H5 or H7.

To understand the nature of this interaction, we plotted the interactive relationships between COVID-19 information seeking and television news use. These relationships are presented in Figure 1, which shows that the emotional distress experienced by those seeking COVID-19 information was further amplified among television news consumers. Thus, H3 was supported.

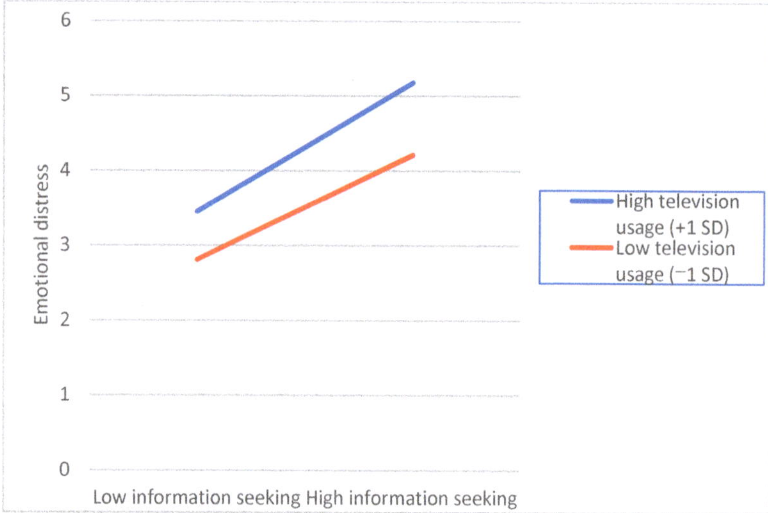

Figure 1. Interaction between information seeking and television news usage on emotional distress.

4. Discussion

The rapid emergence of COVID-19 has caused considerable psychological stress in the global population [2,6,7]. People seek information about the pandemic and follow the news to keep updated. We set out to understand the relationships among information seeking concerning COVID-19, general news media use, and emotional distress during the early stages of the pandemic, with a focus on media modality.

Our primary findings reveal that the more individuals sought COVID-19 information, the more likely they were to be emotionally distressed. Moreover, after accounting for COVID-19 information seeking, consuming news via television and social media was related to increased distress, while consuming newspapers was unrelated to distress. Our moderation analysis revealed that active COVID-19 information seekers who relied on television news were more likely to be emotionally distressed, but the association between COVID-19 information seeking and emotional distress was not amplified by newspaper or social media news use.

These findings contribute to the literature on several fronts. First and foremost, we advanced research on information seeking and emotional response by focusing on information seeking about a novel virus, which has resulted in an unprecedented global burden. The positive association between information seeking and emotional distress during the COVID-19 pandemic is reflective of this unique situation. It is notable that the positive association between information seeking and emotional distress remained significant when the three news sources were added to the model. There could be multiple possible reasons for these findings. First, while information seeking normally reduces uncertainty [55,56], COVID-19 information seeking likely increases uncertainty and anxiety because answers to basic questions, like when the pandemic will end, how the virus is transmitted, and its specific short-term and long-term impact remain unavailable. Although "ignorance may be bliss" from an emotional standpoint, the emotional distress concerning COVID-19 may be adaptive, possibly increasing protective health measures. In late March, the COVID-19 information available was quite limited, and centered on hand washing and social distancing recommendations, the lack of personal protective equipment and other medical equipment, and the increasing number of hospitalizations and deaths.

Next, our findings indicated that consuming news via television was related to increased emotional distress. Moreover, our moderation analysis revealed that people who sought COVID-19 information and viewed more television news tended to be even more emotionally distressed. Television's vivid imagery and sound make it an emotionally arousing medium, so television news users may have a higher likelihood of experiencing distress when COVID-19 information seeking. These findings are consistent with previous research showing a strong association between television news and negative emotions during times of crisis, such as September 11 (e.g., [17]) and natural disasters (e.g., [57]). Our results suggest that the effect of television news on negative emotions can be applied to COVID-19.

In addition, our findings indicate that the more people consumed news from social media, the more likely they were to be emotionally distressed. This again could be due to the modality of social media, given it often combines text, audio, and video. The heightened distress among social media news users could also be due to misinformation and exaggeration of risks [53] and unverified contending opinions about an issue, which may heighten uncertainty [58–60]. The political nature of COVID-19 [61] means there is an immense amount of disagreement on social media platforms, extending to the very existence of the virus [62]. In addition, the fact that we found no interaction effects between information seeking and social media use on emotional distress could imply that the distress caused by social media may not be driven by information seeking but by other types of social media uses such as social interactions.

Finally, while we expected that consuming news via newspapers would be related to lower distress, given the less emotionally arousing modality and lesser partisan reporting style, our results revealed no significant association between newspapers and distress. This result could reflect that news users' heightened stress during this pandemic was not accentuated by print media. Taken together, these results suggest that people who relied on television—and to a lesser extent social media—for news were more likely to experience emotional distress concerning COVID-19.

To sum, our findings show that people should be careful about their information gathering habits. We would recommend moderating media exposure because repeated media usage, especially via television news [22,43–46] may lead to heightened stress. Individuals should also take caution while gathering pandemic news from social media. Of course, the pandemic necessitates that we stay updated with the news for our own safety and the safety of those around us, but thoughtful information gathering and news consumption habits will perhaps facilitate better emotional health.

Limitations and Future Directions

As with all research, our study comes with caveats. Due to the cross-sectional nature of the study, we cannot draw conclusions concerning causal relationships. It is also possible those with more emotional distress are more likely to seek COVID-19 information. Moreover, although we attribute the positive association between information seeking and emotional distress to unique features of COVID-19 information, such as persistent uncertainty, ubiquitous news coverage, and topic unavoidability, it is possible that information seeking could cause higher emotional distress only immediately; in the long-term, the emotional distress could become weak, possibly because people might gain a sense of control. However, prior research shows that in times of crises, information seeking can lead to emotional distress (e.g., [17,21,22,43–46]). Our findings support this phenomenon. Despite our justification, future studies should use longitudinal data to confirm causal relationships.

Related to this, it would be important to statistically control for media use level before the pandemic, since some people might increase their media use at the onset of the pandemic with others' media use remaining static. Similarly, it would be ideal to measure the extent to which emotional distress was changed due to the emergence of the pandemic. Due to the lack of those pre-COVID measures in our dataset, however, we were not able to add those control variables in our model. Future studies should measure pre-pandemic values for primary behavioral variables to understand the dynamics of behaviors caused by the pandemic.

Additionally, our measurement of emotional distress only tracked those feeling overwhelmed, anxious, and afraid about what might happen. Given that emotional distress can also be linked to feeling depressed, worried, and sad, future studies should encompass more specific emotions with valid measurement. Moreover, we measured COVID-19 information seeking with a single item. Although our item clearly captured the extent of information seeking with regard to COVID-19, future studies should check the validity of the variable using a multi-measure approach that attends to exposure and attention in additional to information seeking. Similarly, while newspapers and news magazines may feature different characteristics, we measured them within an item, not differentiating those two. Also, although television news includes a variety of cable channels, including highly partisan outlets, we measured television news with national news networks. Future studies should define television news more broadly with more robust measurement.

5. Conclusions

Since the pandemic began, COVID-19 has dominated the news cycle [27,63]. Moreover, along with the pandemic, there has been another attack on the public, termed the "infodemic" [64] as people have been exposed to an abundance of false information. People are maneuvering this media environment to get information and manage the emotional stress they are feeling. Our study takes a preliminary step toward examining the association between information seeking, use of various types of news media, and emotional health during the early days of the COVID-19 pandemic. Examining emotional health is crucial in this situation, when people were primarily inside their homes and away from friends and family for months on end. The toll of this pandemic will not only be measured in terms of the loss of life, the long-term medical consequences, or the economic impact, but in terms of the emotional toll on the public.

Author Contributions: J.H. conceptualized the study, analyzed the data, and wrote the manuscript; P.B. conceptualized the study and wrote the manuscript; D.S. conceptualized the study and edited the manuscript; M.B. conceptualized the study, collected the data, and edited the manuscript. All authors have read and agreed to the published version of the manuscript.

Funding: This research was partially supported by Grant #AAI9733 from the Vice Chancellor for Research and Graduate Education of the University of Wisconsin-Madison, awarded to Markus Brauer.

Institutional Review Board Statement: The study was approved by the Institutional Review Board of the University of Wisconsin-Madison (IRB# 2020-0368).

Informed Consent Statement: Informed consent was obtained from all subjects involved in the study.

Data Availability Statement: The data presented in this study are available on request from the corresponding author.

Conflicts of Interest: The authors declare no conflict of interest.

References

1. Li, S.; Wang, Y.; Xue, J.; Zhao, N.; Zhu, T. The impact of COVID-19 epidemic declaration on psychological consequences: A study on active Weibo users. *Int. J. Environ. Res. Public Health* **2020**, *17*, 2032. [CrossRef]
2. Park, C.L.; Russell, B.S.; Fendrich, M.; Finkelstein-Fox, L.; Hutchison, M.; Becker, J. Americans' COVID-19 Stress, Coping, and Adherence to CDC Guidelines. *J. Gen. Intern. Med.* **2020**, *35*, 2296–2303. [CrossRef] [PubMed]
3. Restubog, S.L.D.; Ocampo, A.C.G.; Wang, L. Taking control amidst the chaos: Emotion regulation during the COVID-19 pandemic. *J. Vocat. Behav.* **2020**, *119*, 103440. [CrossRef]
4. Schuchat, A.; CDC COVID-19 Response Team. Public health response to the initiation and spread of pandemic COVID-19 in the United States, 24 February–21 April 2020. *Morb. Mortal. Wkly. Rep.* **2020**, *69*, 551. [CrossRef]
5. Marroquín, B.; Vine, V.; Morgan, R. Mental health during the COVID-19 pandemic: Effects of stay-at-home policies, social distancing behavior, and social resources. *Psychiatry Res.* **2020**, *293*, 113419. [CrossRef]

6. Cao, W.; Fang, Z.; Hou, G.; Han, M.; Xu, X.; Dong, J.; Zheng, J. The psychological impact of the COVID-19 epidemic on college students in China. *Psychiatry Res.* **2020**, *287*, 112934. [CrossRef]
7. Huang, Y.; Zhao, N. Generalized anxiety disorder, depressive symptoms and sleep quality during COVID-19 outbreak in China: A web-based cross-sectional survey. *Psychiatry Res.* **2020**, *288*, 112954. [CrossRef]
8. Shultz, J.M.; Baingana, F.; Neria, Y. The 2014 Ebola outbreak and mental health: Current status and recommended response. *JAMA* **2015**, *313*, 567–568. [CrossRef]
9. Thompson, R.R.; Garfin, D.R.; Holman, E.A.; Silver, R.C. Distress, worry, and functioning following a global health crisis: A national study of Americans' responses to Ebola. *Clin. Psychol. Sci.* **2017**, *5*, 513–521. [CrossRef]
10. Bults, M.; Beaujean, D.J.; de Zwart, O.; Kok, G.; van Empelen, P.; van Steenbergen, J.E.; Richardus, J.H.; Voeten, H.A. Perceived risk, anxiety, and behavioural responses of the general public during the early phase of the Influenza A (H1N1) pandemic in the Netherlands: Results of three consecutive online surveys. *BMC Public Health* **2011**, *11*, 2. [CrossRef] [PubMed]
11. Baker, S.; Bloom, N.; Davis, S.; Terry, S. *COVID-Induced Economic Uncertainty*; National Bureau of Economic Research: Cambridge, MA, USA, 2020.
12. O'Sullivan, D. How Covid-19 Misinformation Is Still Going Viral. CNN. Available online: https://www.cnn.com/2020/05/08/tech/covid-viral-misinformation/index.html (accessed on 4 December 2021).
13. Anderson, M.; Vogels, E.A. Americans Turn to Technology during COVID-19 Outbreak, Aay an Outage would Be a Problem. 2020. Available online: https://www.pewresearch.org/fact-tank/2020/03/31/americans-turn-to-technology-during-covid-19-outbreak-say-an-outage-would-be-a-problem/ (accessed on 4 December 2021).
14. Griffin, R.J.; Neuwirth, K.; Dunwoody, S.; Giese, J. Information sufficiency and risk communication. *Media Psychol.* **2004**, *6*, 23–61. [CrossRef]
15. Griffin, R.J.; Yang, Z.; Huurne, E.; Boerner, F.; Ortiz, S.; Dunwoody, S. After the flood: Anger, attribution, and the seeking of information. *Sci. Commun.* **2008**, *29*, 285–315. [CrossRef]
16. Boyle, M.P.; Schmierbach, M.; Armstrong, C.L.; McLeod, D.M.; Shah, D.V.; Pan, Z. Information seeking and emotional reactions to the September 11 terrorist attacks. *J. Mass Commun. Q.* **2004**, *81*, 155–167. [CrossRef]
17. Cho, J.; Boyle, M.P.; Keum, H.; Shevy, M.D.; McLeod, D.M.; Shah, D.V.; Pan, Z. Media, terrorism, and emotionality: Emotional differences in media content and public reactions to the September 11th terrorist attacks. *J. Broadcast. Electron. Media* **2003**, *47*, 309–327. [CrossRef]
18. Kim, H.K.; Niederdeppe, J. The role of emotional response during an H1N1 influenza pandemic on a college campus. *J. Public Relat. Res.* **2013**, *25*, 30–50. [CrossRef]
19. Kahneman, D.; Slovic, P.; Tversky, A. *Judgement under Uncertainty: Heuristics and Biases*; Cambridge University Press: Cambridge, UK, 1982.
20. Tversky, A.; Kahneman, D. Judgement under uncertainty: Heuristics and biases. *Science* **1974**, *185*, 1124–1131. [CrossRef]
21. Goodwin, R.; Palgi, Y.; Hamama-Raz, Y.; Ben-Ezra, M. In the eye of the storm or the bullseye of the media: Social media use during Hurricane Sandy as a predictor of post-traumatic stress. *J. Psychiatr. Res.* **2013**, *47*, 1099–1100. [CrossRef]
22. Pfefferbaum, B.; Newman, E.; Nelson, S.D.; Nitiéma, P.; Pfefferbaum, R.L.; Rahman, A. Disaster media coverage and psychological outcomes: Descriptive findings in the extant research. *Curr. Psychiatry Rep.* **2014**, *16*, 464. [CrossRef]
23. McLeod, J.M.; McDonald, D.G. Beyond simple exposure: Media orientations and their impact on political processes. *Commun. Res.* **1985**, *12*, 3–33. [CrossRef]
24. Shah, D.V.; McLeod, J.M.; Yoon, S.H. Communication, context, and community: An exploration of print, broadcast, and Internet influences. *Commun. Res.* **2001**, *28*, 464–506. [CrossRef]
25. Cho, H.; Lee, J. Collaborative information seeking in intercultural computer-mediated communication groups: Testing the influence of social context using social network analysis. *Commun. Res.* **2008**, *35*, 548–573. [CrossRef]
26. Marchionini, G. *Information Seeking in Electronic Environments*; Cambridge University Press: Cambridge, UK, 1995.
27. Liu, Q.; Zheng, Z.; Zheng, J.; Chen, Q.; Liu, G.; Chen, S.; Chu, B.; Zhu, H.; Akinwunmi, B.; Huang, J.; et al. Health communication through news media during the early stage of the COVID-19 outbreak in china: Digital topic modeling approach. *J. Med. Internet Res.* **2020**, *22*, e19118. [CrossRef] [PubMed]
28. Aslam, F.; Awan, T.M.; Syed, J.H.; Kashif, A.; Parveen, M. Sentiments and emotions evoked by news headlines of coronavirus disease (COVID-19) outbreak. *Humanit. Soc. Sci. Commun.* **2020**, *7*, 23. [CrossRef]
29. Bradac, J.J. Theory comparison: Uncertainty reduction, problematic integration, uncertainty management, and other curious constructs. *J. Commun.* **2001**, *51*, 456–476. [CrossRef]
30. Brashers, D.E. Communication and uncertainty management. *J. Commun.* **2001**, *51*, 477–497. [CrossRef]
31. Brashers, D.E.; Goldsmith, D.J.; Hsieh, E. Information seeking and avoiding in health context. *Hum. Commun. Res.* **2002**, *28*, 258–271. [CrossRef]
32. Capone, V.; Caso, D.; Donizzetti, A.R.; Procentese, F. University student mental well-being during COVID-19 outbreak: What are the relationships between information seeking, perceived risk and personal resources related to the academic context? *Sustainability* **2020**, *12*, 7039. [CrossRef]
33. Ebrahim, A.H.; Saif, Z.Q.; Buheji, M.; AlBasri, N.; Al-Husaini, F.A.; Jahrami, H. COVID-19 information-seeking behavior and anxiety symptoms among parents. *OSP J. Health Care Med.* **2020**, *1*, 1–9.
34. Soroya, S.H.; Farooq, A.; Mahmood, K.; Isoaho, J.; Zara, S.E. From information seeking to information avoidance: Understanding the health information behavior during a global health crisis. *Inf. Process. Manag.* **2021**, *58*, 102440. [CrossRef]

35. McLuhan, M. The medium is the message. In *Crime and Media*; Routledge: London, UK, 1964.
36. Neumann, W.R.; Crigler, A.N.; Just, M.R. *Common Knowledge: News and the Construction of Political Meaning*; University of Chicago: Chicago, IL, USA, 1992.
37. Corston, R.; Colman, A.M. Modality of communication and recall of health-related information. *J. Health Psychol.* **1997**, *2*, 185–194. [CrossRef] [PubMed]
38. Pfau, M.; Holbert, R.L.; Zubric, S.J.; Pasha, N.H.; Lin, W.K. Role and influence of communication modality in the process of resistance to persuasion. *Media Psychol.* **2000**, *2*, 1–33. [CrossRef]
39. Chaiken, S.; Eagly, A.H. Communication modality as a determinant of message persuasiveness and message comprehensibility. *J. Personal. Soc. Psychol.* **1976**, *34*, 605. [CrossRef]
40. Newhagen, J.E. TV news images that induce anger, fear, and disgust: Effects on approach-avoidance and memory. *J. Broadcasting Electron. Media* **1998**, *42*, 265–276. [CrossRef]
41. Potts, R.; Sanchez, D. Television viewing and depression: No news is good news. *J. Broadcasting Electron. Media* **1994**, *38*, 79–90. [CrossRef]
42. Ahern, J.; Galea, S.; Resnick, H.; Kilpatrick, D.; Bucuvalas, M.; Gold, J.; Vlahov, D. Television images and psychological symptoms after the September 11 terrorist attacks. *Psychiatry Interpers. Biol. Process.* **2002**, *65*, 289–300. [CrossRef]
43. Ben-Zur, H.; Gil, S.; Shamshins, Y. The relationship between exposure to terror through the media, coping strategies and resources, and distress and secondary traumatization. *Int. J. Stress Manag.* **2012**, *19*, 132–150. [CrossRef]
44. Holman, E.A.; Garfin, D.R.; Silver, R.C. Media's role in broadcasting acute stress following the Boston Marathon bombings. *Proc. Natl. Acad. Sci. USA* **2014**, *111*, 93–98. [CrossRef] [PubMed]
45. Szabo, A.; Hopkinson, K.L. Negative psychological effects of watching the news in the television: Relaxation or another intervention may be needed to buffer them! *Int. J. Behav. Med.* **2007**, *14*, 57–62. [CrossRef] [PubMed]
46. Propper, R.E.; Stickgold, R.; Keeley, R.; Christman, S.D. Is television traumatic?: Dreams, stress, and media exposure in the aftermath of September 11, 2001. *Psychol. Sci.* **2007**, *18*, 334–340. [CrossRef]
47. Johnson, S. Everything bad is good for you: How today's popular culture is actually making us smarter. *Teach. Coll. Rec.* **2006**, *108*, 187–190.
48. Shearer, E.; Grieco, E. Americans Are Wary of the Role Social Media Sites Play in Delivering the News. 2019. Available online: https://www.journalism.org/2019/10/02/americans-are-wary-of-the-role-social-media-sites-play-in-delivering-the-news/ (accessed on 4 December 2021).
49. Lee, C.S.; Ma, L. News sharing in social media: The effect of gratifications and prior experience. *Comput. Hum. Behav.* **2012**, *28*, 331–339. [CrossRef]
50. Intravia, J.; Wolff, K.T.; Paez, R.; Gibbs, B.R. Investigating the relationship between social media consumption and fear of crime: A partial analysis of mostly young adults. *Comput. Hum. Behav.* **2017**, *77*, 158–168. [CrossRef]
51. Ghenai, A.; Mejova, Y. Fake cures: User-centric modeling of health misinformation in social media. *Proc. ACM Hum. Comput. Interact.* **2018**, *2*, 58. [CrossRef]
52. Borah, P.; Xiao, X. The importance of 'likes': The interplay of message framing, source, and social endorsement on credibility perceptions of health information on Facebook. *J. Health Commun.* **2018**, *23*, 399–411. [CrossRef] [PubMed]
53. Jurkowitz, M.; Mitchell, A. Americans Who Primarily Get News through Social Media Are Least Likely to Follow COVID-19 Coverage, Most Likely to Report Seeing Made-Up News. 2020. Available online: https://www.journalism.org/2020/03/25/americans-who-primarily-get-news-through-social-media-are-least-likely-to-follow-covid-19-coverage-most-likely-to-report-seeing-made-up-news/ (accessed on 4 December 2021).
54. Sindermann, C.; Elhai, J.D.; Moshagen, M.; Montag, C. Age, gender, personality, ideological attitudes and individual differences in a person's news spectrum: How many and who might be prone to "filter bubbles" and "echo chambers" online? *Heliyon* **2020**, *6*, e03214. [CrossRef]
55. Berger, C.R. Communicating under uncertainty. In *Interpersonal Processes: New Directions in Communication Research*; Roloff, M.E., Miller, G.R., Eds.; Sage Publishing: Beverly Hills, CA, USA, 1987; pp. 39–62.
56. Berger, C.; Calabrese, R. Some explorations in initial interaction and beyond: Toward a developmental theory of interpersonal communication. *Hum. Commun. Res.* **1975**, *1*, 99–112. [CrossRef]
57. Houston, J.B.; Pfefferbaum, B.; Rosenholtz, C.E. Disaster news: Framing and frame changing in coverage of major US natural disasters, 2000–2010. *J. Mass Commun. Q.* **2012**, *89*, 606–623. [CrossRef]
58. Hwang, J. Health information sources and the influenza vaccination: The mediating roles of perceived vaccine efficacy and safety. *J. Health Commun.* **2020**, *25*, 727–735. [CrossRef] [PubMed]
59. Lin, W.Y.; Zhang, X.; Song, H.; Omori, K. Health information seeking in the Web 2.0 age: Trust in social media, uncertainty reduction, and self-disclosure. *Comput. Hum. Behav.* **2016**, *56*, 289–294. [CrossRef]
60. Zhao, Y.; Zhang, J. Consumer health information seeking in social media: A literature review. *Health Inf. Libr. J.* **2017**, *34*, 268–283. [CrossRef]
61. Shribman, D. As the U.S. Grapples with COVID-19, It's Clear That the Pandemic Is Political. Available online: https://www.theglobeandmail.com/world/us-politics/article-as-the-us-grapples-with-covid-19-its-clear-that-the-pandemic-is/ (accessed on 4 December 2021).

62. The Associated Press. Video Stitches False Claims Together to Paint COVID-19 as a Political Hoax. 2020. Available online: https://apnews.com/afs:Content:9065413346 (accessed on 4 December 2021).
63. Jurkowitz, M.; Mitchell, A. Cable TV and COVID-19: How Americans Perceive the Outbreak and View Media Coverage Differ by Main News Source. 2020. Available online: https://www.journalism.org/2020/04/01/cable-tv-and-covid-19-how-americans-perceive-the-outbreak-and-view-media-coverage-differ-by-main-news-source/ (accessed on 4 December 2021).
64. World Health Organization. Novel Coronavirus (2019-nCoV). 2020. Available online: https://www.who.int/docs/default-source/coronaviruse/situation-reports/20200202-sitrep-13-ncov-v3.pdf (accessed on 4 December 2021).

International Journal of
Environmental Research and Public Health

MDPI

Article

The Relationships among Anxiety, Subjective Well-Being, Media Consumption, and Safety-Seeking Behaviors during the COVID-19 Epidemic

Yi-Fang Luo [1,2], Heng-Yu Shen [1,*], Shu-Ching Yang [1,*] and Liang-Ching Chen [1,3]

1 The Intelligent Electronic Commerce Research Center, Institute of Education, National Sun Yat-Sen University, Kaohsiung 80424, Taiwan; a0989909301@gmail.com (Y.-F.L.); jokiceman@gmail.com (L.-C.C.)
2 Center for Teaching and Learning Development, National Kaohsiung University of Science and Technology, Kaohsiung 805301, Taiwan
3 Department of Foreign Languages, R.O.C. Military Academy, Kaohsiung 83059, Taiwan
* Correspondence: shy7449@g-mail.nsysu.edu.tw (H.-Y.S.); shyang@mail.nsysu.edu.tw (S.-C.Y.)

Abstract: The COVID-19 epidemic has been confirmed as the largest scale outbreak of atypical pneumonia since the outbreak of severe acute respiratory syndrome (SARS) in 2003 and it has become a public health emergency of international concern. It exacerbated public confusion and anxiety, and the impact of COVID-19 on people needs to be better understood. Indeed, prior studies that conducted meta-analysis of longitudinal cohort research compared mental health before versus during the COVID-19 pandemic and proved that public health polices (e.g., city lockdowns, quarantines, avoiding gatherings, etc.) and COVID-19-related information that circulates on new media platforms directly affected citizen's mental health and well-being. Hence, this research aims to explore Taiwanese people's health status, anxiety, media sources for obtaining COVID-19 information, subjective well-being, and safety-seeking behavior during the COVID-19 epidemic and how they are associated. Online surveys were conducted through new media platforms, and 342 responses were included in the analysis. The research results indicate that the participants experienced different aspects of COVID-19 anxiety, including COVID-19 worry and perceived COVID-19 risk. Among the given media sources, the more participants searched for COVID-19 information on new media, the greater they worried about COVID-19. Furthermore, COVID-19 worry was positively related to safety-seeking behavior, while perceived COVID-19 risk was negatively related to subjective well-being. This paper concludes by offering some suggestions for future studies and pointing out limitations of the present study.

Keywords: COVID-19 epidemic; anxiety; media consumption; subjective well-being; safety-seeking behaviors

Citation: Luo, Y.-F.; Shen, H.-Y.; Yang, S.-C.; Chen, L.-C. The Relationships among Anxiety, Subjective Well-Being, Media Consumption, and Safety-Seeking Behaviors during the COVID-19 Epidemic. *Int. J. Environ. Res. Public Health* **2021**, *18*, 13189. https://doi.org/10.3390/ijerph182413189

Academic Editors: Paolo Roma, Merylin Monaro and Cristina Mazza

Received: 25 October 2021
Accepted: 10 December 2021
Published: 14 December 2021

1. Introduction

In December 2019, a novel coronavirus disease (COVID-19) was discovered and started to spread worldwide [1]. The World Health Organization (WHO) [2] further declared the COVID-19 epidemic to be a public health emergency of international concern on January 30, 2020, which has caused high levels of public concern and fear about the possibility of a pandemic [1]. The media can provide fast and critical guidance regarding the pandemic [2]; however, different types of media may have different effects on coping. While traditional media (e.g., TV, newspapers, and radio) provide formal information about threats, new media (e.g., Internet and social media) has a more direct, personal impact on risk assessment [3]. New media may increase personal stress responses by sharing and viewing uncensored media content [4]. In addition, even new media may become a source of rapid dissemination of misinformation, aggravating public confusion and anxiety (Kim, 2019) [2] and thus negatively affect public health and well-being [5–9].

A meta-analysis of longitudinal cohort studies comparing mental health before versus during the COVID-19 pandemic in 2020 found an overall increase in mental health symptoms—e.g., [10–14]. Canet-Juric et al. (2020) assessed the citizen's emotional impact of the lockdown measures implemented by the Argentinian government to fight the COVID-19 pandemic [15]. They surveyed the Argentinian general population twice (2 days after the mandatory quarantine started (time 1) vs. 2 weeks later (time 2). A total of 6057 people answered the two internet surveys and statistically significant variations were observed between the two time points. Their study suggested that it is necessary to continue monitoring mental health problems on the general population and necessary to create programs aimed at promoting mental health and to distribute information about it. Ramiz et al. (2021) conducted a longitudinal study of mental health, before and during the COVID-19 lockdown, in the French population [16]. They found, overall, people's mental health deteriorated during the lockdown in France amid the 2020 COVID-19 pandemic. Moreover, their self-rated physical health improved but those who experienced a worse physical health were more likely to have mental health issues.

Anxiety is viewed as subsuming fear, panic, and worry, and it can be maladaptive, disrupting performance and interfering with both psychological and physical well-being [17]. Existing research results have shown that anxiety regarding the COVID-19 epidemic has a negative impact on health [18,19]. However, the literature also indicates that anxiety can trigger individual alertness and motivation to engage in safe behaviors that can promote survival and contribute to personal well-being [20,21]. The COVID-19 epidemic is a major public health event that involves the spread of the disease worldwide, and the impact of COVID-19 on people needs to be better understood [22].

Therefore, this research aims to understand Taiwanese people's health status, anxiety about COVID-19, media sources for obtaining COVID-19 information, subjective well-being, and safety-seeking behavior during the COVID-19 epidemic.

1.1. Research Question and Hypothesis 1

The COVID-19 outbreak has caused public anxiety [6,22,23]. Anxiety, including complex emotional responses such as tension, fear, panic, and worry, is a very important concept in personality psychology [24]. Anxiety arises from the evaluation of a high degree of uncertainty about whether impending physical or psychological harm can be avoided [25]. Such an evaluation of uncertainty involves risk judgment, which includes perceived risk and worry [26]. Risk perception is a subjective cognitive assessment that involves the assessment of the probability of a specified negative accident occurring and the severity of consequences [27,28]. Worry is an emotional response, such as "feeling worried" when thinking about a risk source. According to the risk-as-feelings approach [29], cognitive assessment and worry have a reciprocal influence [26]. Therefore, this study intends to understand the anxiety state of participants during the COVID-19 epidemic and propose the following research questions:

Q_1: What is the participant's COVID-19 anxiety, including the perceived risk and worry?

For people with poor health, especially those suffering from certain diseases that have potential risks for infectious diseases due to the nature of the disease, catastrophic thinking about physical symptoms and overestimation of the risk of serious diseases may cause higher anxiety during pandemics [30,31]. The findings reported by Malesza and Kaczmarek (2021) also show that people with chronic diseases and poorer overall health have higher COVID-19 anxiety due to a greater perceived risk of infection [32]. Accordingly, we propose the following hypothesis:

Hypothesis 1 (H1). *Health status negatively predicts COVID-19 anxiety.*

1.2. Research Hypothesis 2 and Hypothesis 3

In public health crises, people believe that as much information as possible can help them understand the severity of the crisis which, in turn, helps them take protective action, reduce anxiety, and promote control over the situation [33]. In practice, however, public anxiety and stress for large-scale health crises may also be created by the media itself, the so-called media panic, which exists in different media sources, including newspapers, TV, radio, and the Internet. [34]. Although different types of media may have different effects on coping, little is known about the relationship between media source preference and audience response to large-scale pandemics [3].

Among many media sources, new media has become a research focus because new media platforms have been considered one of the most commonly used information resources [35]. Existing studies have shown that new media exposure may cause anxiety during a large-scale pandemic [16,36,37]. New media networks provide a new approach for combining and exchanging information [38], making it easy for Internet users, such as official departments, self-media, and netizens, to release and transfer related information on online media, which may lead to (mis)information overload and, in turn, cause individuals' health problems, such as anxiety [6,33,37]. Compared with traditional media, the information quality of new media is out of control. Moreover, the interactive nature of new media is more likely to cause negative "emotional contagion" in disasters, which may cause new media users to experience more negative psychological effects [39]. Accordingly, we explore the relationship between different media sources and COVID-19 anxiety and propose the following hypotheses:

Hypothesis 2 (H2). *Higher anxiety to receive information from new media than traditional media.*

Hypothesis 3 (H3). *New media use frequency positively predicts COVID-19 anxiety.*

1.3. Research Hypothesis 3

Anxiety is associated with worse indicators of well-being [7]. Subjective well-being is a concept designed to evaluate the current life situation of an individual. Individuals with high subjective well-being give positive comments on their life conditions, while people with low subjective well-being give negative comments on their life conditions [8].

Existing studies have demonstrated that anxiety regarding COVID-19 affects individuals' psychological well-being [5,9]. However, well-being is multidimensional [8]. Riediker and Koren (2004) [40] adopted the WHO (1948) definition of health, equating health with well-being [41] and explaining that well-being consists of physical, mental, and social elements. Existing studies mainly focus on the well-being of mental health but lack other dimensions of well-being. This research is expected to explore more comprehensive well-being and propose the following hypothesis:

Hypothesis 4 (H4). *COVID-19 anxiety is negatively related to subjective well-being.*

However, anxiety is also seen as an adaptive function that enables individuals to enhance their readiness for action when faced with ambiguous and unpredictable threats [20]. Therefore, proper anxiety about self-health helps individuals be alert to their own health and seek improvement [42]. In other words, anxiety is not only a result of health problems but also an alert and motivation that drives people to "seek safe behaviors" to effectively reduce threats [21]. Similarly, Li et al. (2020) noted that, in the face of potential disease threats, people tend to develop avoidance behaviors (e.g., avoid contact with people with pneumonia-like symptoms) and strictly follow social norms (e.g., conformity) [19]. Accordingly, we propose the following hypothesis:

Hypothesis 5 (H5). *COVID-19 anxiety is positively related to safety-seeking behaviors to prevent infection.*

The hypotheses that form the framework of this study are shown in Figure 1.

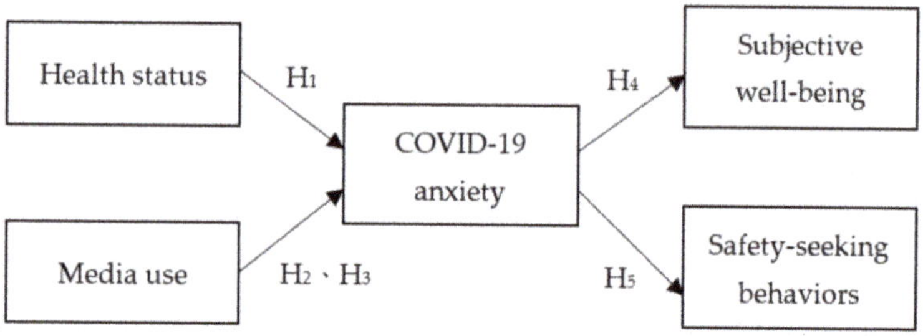

Figure 1. Research hypothesis framework.

2. Methods

2.1. Studied Population

The study was conducted in 2020 and the research group consisted of 342 people. The characteristics of the study sample, including its sociodemographic characteristics, are presented in Table 1. The criteria for inclusion in the study were: age $\geq$ 18 years of age, Taiwan nationality, female or male gender. An anonymous online questionnaire was designed using a Google form in the traditional Chinese language that was accessible from any device with an Internet connection to invite potential respondents. The survey was disseminated via social networks (especially Facebook and Plurk) and respondents were encouraged to pass the survey on to others.

Table 1. Participant demographic characteristics.

Variables	Category	N	%
Gender	Woman	146	42.69%
	Man	196	57.31%
Age	<20	140	40.94%
	21–30	174	50.88%
	>31	28	8.18%
Occupation	Student	284	83.04%
	Non-student	58	16.96%
Education	Associate's degree	21	6.14%
	Bachelor's degree	249	72.81%
	Master or doctoral degree	72	21.05%

According to Taiwan's "Ministry of Science and Technology (MOST) Communication Survey Database (four times in one phase) (2015): Political and Citizen Communication" (2002 interviewees in total), in terms of the frequency of receiving public affairs through traditional media, there is a significant difference between the men and women who are over 60 years old ($t = 4.81$, $p < 0.05$), while there is no significant difference between different sexes under 60 years of age. It can be found that in the younger generation, gender is no longer a factor that affects or limits the citizen's reception of public affairs information. In addition, there is no significant difference in the frequency of using traditional media to receive public affairs among all interviewees of different age groups. In the section of new media, the difference is mainly the frequency of receiving public affairs between the younger and elder generations. Therefore, the population studied in this paper is mainly concentrated on students because they mainly use new media channels to finish the questionnaires [43].

2.2. Survey Instrument

2.2.1. Health Status

Self-rated health status was measured by asking the participants how they felt in terms of their general state of health, and the responses ranged from "very poor" (1) to "very good" (5). This was one of the widely used validated indicators of health in the field of social sciences [44]. In this study, most of the participants rated their level of health as 4 (40.35%) or 5 (39.18%). In other words, the participants' self-rated health tended to be good ($M = 4.17$, $SD = 0.79$).

2.2.2. Media Consumption

The items were modified based on the media exposure measurement of Hong, Kim, and Xiong [45]. "Traditional media consumption" refers to the frequency of reading printed materials (such as newspapers and magazines), listening to the radio, and watching TV to obtain information related to COVID-19 (3 items). "New media consumption" refers to the frequency of obtaining COVID-19-related information from Internet news and social media. Responses were given on a 5-point Likert scale ranging from 1 (never) to 5 (always). The reliability and validity analysis showed that the factor loadings of "traditional media consumption" were, respectively, 0.88, 0.82, and 0.73, the total explained variance was 65.70%, and Cronbach's α was 0.73. In "new media consumption", the factor loads were 0.85 and 0.85, the total explained variance was 72.26%, and Cronbach's α was 0.62.

2.2.3. Subjective Well-Being

Subjective well-being mainly investigates the participants' subjective perceptions of the impact of COVID-19 on their well-being. According to Riediker and Koren's [40] definition of well-being, the study investigated the participants' subjective well-being, namely physical health, mental health, and social relationships (including what do you think is the impact of COVID-19 on your physical health/mental health/social relationship?). The responses were given using a 9-point Likert scale ranging from −4 to 4, where a score of 0 indicates no impact at all, a score of −1 to −4 indicates a negative impact, and a score of 1 to 4 indicates a positive impact; thus, a more negative score indicates a greater negative impact of COVID-19 on well-being and vice versa. The reliability and validity analysis showed that the factor loadings ranged from 0.75 to 0.87, the total explained variance was 68.77%, and Cronbach's α was 0.78.

2.2.4. COVID-19 Anxiety

This study is based on the anxiety classification proposed by Rundmo and Nordfjærn (2017) [26] and references relevant literature (e.g., [42]) to compile this COVID-19 anxiety scale. The items were answered on a 5-point Likert scale ranging from 1 (strongly disagree) to 5 (strongly agree). The exploratory factor analysis (EFA) showed that the Kaiser–Meyer–Olkin (KMO) test value was 0.81 (χ^2 =1416.79, $p < 0.001$) [46], the factor loadings ranged from 0.66 to 0.87, and the total explained variance was 69.75%. The scale was divided into two aspects: COVID-19 worry (e.g., worry individuals themselves or family will become infected with COVID-19, $\alpha = 0.88$) and perceived COVID-19 risk (e.g., a high probability of becoming infected with COVID-19, very likely to be exposed to people with suspected or possible cases of COVID-19, $\alpha = 0.91$).

2.2.5. Safety-Seeking Behavior

Safety-seeking behavior assessed the participants' degree of compliance with the government's recommendations on preventing COVID-19 infection, including avoiding gatherings, maintaining social distance from others, maintaining hygiene habits of frequent hand washing, and wearing masks in indoor public places. The items were developed with reference to related literature—e.g., [1,22]. Responses were given on a 5-point Likert scale ranging from 1 (strongly disagree) to 5 (strongly agree). The reliability and validity analysis showed that the factor loadings were from 0.72 to 0.87, the total explained variance was 65.93%, and Cronbach's α was 0.82.

2.3. Data Analysis

Statistical Product and Service Solutions 22.0 (SPSS) (IBM Corp, Armonk, NY, USA) software was used as a statistical tool in this study. A Kaiser–Meyer–Olkin (KMO) test was used to determine the sampling adequacy of data that were to be used for factor analysis [45]. The principal component analysis method with varimax rotation and eigenvalues >1 for EFA was adopted. Descriptive statistical analysis was performed to obtain a preliminary understanding of the respondents' demographic characteristics and their health-related conditions, attitudes, behaviors, and literacy. A repeated-measures ANOVA or paired t-test and a simple or multiple regression analysis were used to analyze the data of this study.

2.4. Ethical Issues

This study followed the code of research ethics and conformed to the Taiwan government's institutional review board rules for exempt review. We did not collect any relevant identifying information of the humans involved and an anonymous design questionnaire was used in this study. The questionnaire instructions clearly informed the participants of the research purpose and their rights regarding joining or dropping out of this study at any time during online filling-in. Participants were informed and assured that their participation was voluntary, anonymous, and strictly confidential and that they may stop participating in the study at any time without fear of penalty

3. Results

Table 2 provides a summary of descriptive analysis among demographic characteristics.

Table 2. Summary of descriptive analysis among demographic characteristics.

Variables Category	COVID-19 Worry	Perceived COVID-19 Risk	Physical Health	Mental Health	Social Relationship	Safety-Seeking Behavior
Gender						
Woman	3.90 (0.88)	2.99 (0.84)	−0.40 (1.50)	−0.75 (1.54)	−0.07 (1.17)	4.17 (0.63)
Man	3.84 (0.80)	2.92 (0.80)	−0.50 (1.17)	−0.76 (1.12)	−0.31 (0.99)	4.21 (0.63)
Age						
<20	3.88 (0.86)	2.97 (0.90)	−0.39 (1.21)	−0.71 (1.21)	−0.12 (1.04)	4.11 (0.67)
21–30	3.90 (0.85)	2.95 (0.76)	−0.53 (1.40)	−0.84 (1.37)	−0.21 (1.04)	4.25 (0.60)
>31	3.58 (0.63)	2.79 (0.77)	−0.32 (1.33)	−0.43 (1.43)	−0.61 (1.40)	4.29 (0.54)
Occupation						
Student	3.88 (0.85)	2.94 (0.81)	−0.49 (1.30)	−0.80 (1.29)	−0.17 (1.00)	4.16 (0.64)
Non-student	3.81 (0.80)	2.98 (0.87)	−0.28 (1.41)	−0.53 (1.44)	−0.41 (1.38)	4.35 (0.53)
Education						
Associate's	3.77 (0.83)	2.90 (0.68)	−0.10 (1.64)	−0.76(1.34)	−0.24 (0.77)	4.12 (0.73)
Bachelor's	3.89 (0.81)	2.94 (0.84)	−0.51 (1.20)	−0.74 (1.27)	−0.19 (1.08)	4.21 (0.64)
Master's and above	3.82 (0.93)	2.98 (0.81)	−0.39 (1.60)	−0.81 (1.47)	−0.26 (1.14)	4.17 (0.55)

3.1. COVID-19 Anxiety

In response to the first research question, the study adopted a paired t-test, and the results showed that the participants' worry about COVID-19 ($M = 3.87$, $SD = 0.84$) was significantly higher than the perceived risk of COVID-19 ($M = 2.95$, $SD = 0.82$) ($t_{(341)} = 19.57$, $p < 0.001$, Cohen's $d = 1.06$).

3.2. New Media Consumption to Obtain COVID-19 Information

In response to the second research question, the study adopted a paired *t*-test, and the results showed that new media consumption ($M = 4.37$, $SD = 0.62$) was significantly higher than traditional media consumption ($M = 2.35$, $SD = 0.85$) ($t_{(341)} = 37.19$, $p < 0.001$, Cohen's $d = 2.72$).

3.3. Analysis of Health Status and COVID-19 Anxiety

The results of the simple regression analysis showed that the participants' health status significantly negatively predicted their perceived COVID-19 risk (beta = −0.24, $p < 0.001$, $R^2 = 0.06$). However, there was no significant predictive relationship between health status and COVID-19 worry (beta = −0.02, $p = 0.68$). Thus, Research Hypothesis 1, that health status negatively predicts COVID-19 anxiety, was partially supported.

3.4. Analysis of Media Consumption and COVID-19 Anxiety

Table 3 shows that the frequency of new media consumption was significantly positively related to COVID-19 worry (beta = 0.23, $p < 0.001$) but not perceived COVID-19 risk (beta = 0.06, $p = 0.28$). In addition, the frequency of traditional media consumption was non-significantly positively related to COVID-19 worry (beta = 0.09, $p = 0.09$) and perceived COVID-19 risk (beta = 0.07, $p = 0.22$). Thus, Research Hypothesis 2, that new media use frequency positively predicts COVID-19 anxiety, was partially supported.

Table 3. Multiple regression analysis of media consumption.

Variable Media Consumption	COVID-19 Worry		Perceived COVID-19 Risk	
	Beta	*t*	*Beta*	*t*
Traditional media	0.09	1.71	0.07	1.22
New media	0.23	4.26 ***	0.06	1.09
	$R = 0.25$ $R^2 = 0.06$ $F_{(2339)} = 11.17$ ***		$R = 0.09$ $R^2 = 0.01$ $F_{(2339)} = 1.45$	

*** $p < 0.001$. *Beta*: standardized coefficients.

3.5. Analysis of COVID-19 Anxiety and Subjective Well-Being

Table 4 shows that the perceived COVID-19 risk was negatively related to physical health (beta = −0.16, $p < 0.001$) and mental health (beta = −0.21, $p < 0.001$). However, there were no significant predictive relationships between the two aspects of anxiety and social relationships. Thus, Hypothesis 3, which posits that COVID-19 anxiety is negatively related to subjective well-being, was partially supported.

Table 4. Multiple regression analysis of COVID-19 anxiety.

Aspect	Physical Health		Mental Health		Social Relationship		Safety-Seeking Behavior	
	Beta	*t*	*Beta*	*t*	*Beta*	*t*	*Beta*	*t*
COVID-19 worry	−0.06	−0.98	−0.07	−1.26	0.07	1.18	0.37	6.45 ***
Perceived COVID-19 risk	−0.16	−2.63 ***	−0.21	−3.48 ***	−0.04	−0.63	0.01	0.14
	$R = 0.19$ $R^2 = 0.04$ $F(2339) = 6.42$ **		$R = 0.25$ $R^2 = 0.06$ $F_{(2339)} = 11.10$ ***		$R = 0.06$ $R^2 = 0.004$ $F_{(2339)} = 0.70$		$R = 0.37$ $R^2 = 0.14$ $F_{(2339)} = 26.66$ ***	

** $p < 0.01$. *** $p < 0.001$. *Beta*: standardized coefficients.

3.6. Analysis of COVID-19 Anxiety and Safety-Seeking Behavior

Table 2 also shows that COVID-19 worry was significantly positively related to safety-seeking behavior (beta = 0.37, $p < 0.001$). However, perceived COVID-19 risk was not significantly related to safety-seeking behavior (beta = 0.01, p = 0.89). Thus, Research Hypothesis 4, that COVID-19 anxiety is positively related to safety-seeking behaviors to prevent infection, was partially supported.

4. Discussion

This study attempted to investigate Taiwanese people's health status, anxiety, media consumption types, subjective well-being, and safety-seeking behavior during the COVID-19 epidemic. Consistent with previous findings, the study findings showed that new media was the most common source of information about COVID-19 [22]. As Internet and mobile communication technologies have been recently and widely integrated into our daily lives, online resources have become the main way for people to obtain information [47].

However, new media, which is a product of the development of the Internet, may exacerbate anxiety during the epidemic [23]. This study found that the participants experienced different aspects of COVID-19 anxiety and that these different aspects of anxiety had different relationships with media consumption, subjective well-being, and safety-seeking behavior. First, according to previous studies, anxiety arises from the evaluation of uncertainty [25] and includes perceived risk and worry [26]. The results of this study also revealed the complexity of anxiety during the COVID-19 epidemic. In this study, COVID-19-related anxiety was divided into the following two aspects: COVID-19 worry, including worry about the infection of oneself and one's relatives and friends and worry about the outbreak and return of the epidemic; and perceived COVID-19 risk, including the perceived risk of the possibility of infection with COVID-19 and exposure to people with suspected cases and the perceived possible consequences of COVID-19 infection when going out, despite taking preventive measures.

Furthermore, this study found that, although the participants reported a low perceived risk of COVID-19, they had high levels of worry about COVID-19. Emotional responses to risky situations and cognitive assessments of those risks are often inconsistent [29]. Therefore, when faced with extremely undesirable outcomes, people will still have a high level of anxiety, despite the low probability of these outcomes [25]. In other words, when faced with extremely undesirable outcomes, the anxiety caused by the emotional response is more critical than the anxiety caused by the cognitive evaluation.

In addition, when an emotional response to risk diverges from a cognitive evaluation of risk, the emotional response is often the predominant predictor of risk-related behavior [25,29]. Consistent with previous studies, this study found that COVID-19 worry, but not perceived COVID-19 risk, was positively related to safety-seeking behavior. However, this study also found that the frequency of new media consumption was positively related to COVID-19 worry. The relationship between new media and emotional responses may be due to the viral spread of misinformation and false reports about COVID-19 in new media during the epidemic, which has caused unfounded fear among many netizens, with the potential to confuse people and cause anxiety (Kim, 2019) [2]. In addition, many netizens have expressed their negative emotions, such as fear, worry, tension, and anxiety, through new media, which, in turn, has caused negative emotional contagion in the online community [23].

Finally, this study found that the participants' self-rated health status was poorer and their anxiety from perceived COVID-19 risk was higher. In an epidemic, it is common for individuals to feel stressed [48], which leads to anxiety [17]. In particular, people with poor health are more likely to experience anxiety from the stress of the epidemic [22]. According to Lundberg (1998) [49], the degree of stress depends on an individual's cognitive evaluation of danger and potential injury. Therefore, people with poorer overall health tend to consider physical symptoms catastrophically and overestimate the risk of serious diseases, which may cause higher anxiety during pandemics [30–32]. The results also echoed with Robinson et al.'s meta-analysis of longitudinal cohort studies, revealing that when comparing mental health symptoms to pre-pandemic levels, larger rises for depressive symptoms and those with existing poor physical health may have been most affected [14].

The study found that risk was not significantly related to safety-seeking behaviors to prevent infection, only worry was significantly positively related to safety-seeking behavior. The researchers infer that it may be related to the temporal and spatial backgrounds of the pandemic. It was before the COVID-19 outbreak in Taiwan, and therefore citizen's awareness of COVID-19 risk was relatively low. However, through media reports, people began to know the catastrophe that COVID-19 caused in other severely affected areas, and they may have started to worry about the impacts of the virus and whether it would infect themselves and their relatives and friends. This paper suggested that future research can further explore where there exist other intervening variables, for example, whether factors that the health status of participants may cause such differences.

Anxiety may further reduce well-being [7]; that is, anxiety may lead to worse physical and mental health [50]. Existing studies have demonstrated that anxiety regarding COVID-19 affects individuals' psychological well-being [5,9]. This study has similar findings, finding that anxiety from perceived COVID-19 risk has a negative impact on the well-being of physical and mental health.

However, this study found that anxiety has no significant predictive relationship with the well-being of social relationships. This may be because, even though the Taiwanese government implemented some regulations to prevent the spread of COVID-19, including delaying the start of the new semester for schools, restrictions on the number of people at large indoor and outdoor gatherings, social distancing, and wearing masks, there were no stringent restrictions on movement and no local or national lockdown [51]. Furthermore, the development of the Internet makes being online provide opportunities to connect with families, friends, and other people from beyond communities [52]. Therefore, even if COVID-19 causes inconvenience in face-to-face interpersonal relationships, people can still seek online ways to maintain interpersonal relationships. The above reasons may cause people's COVID-19 anxiety to have less impact on the well-being of interpersonal relationships.

5. Conclusions

This study revealed that new media has become the main source of COVID-19 information and the more participants searched for COVID-19 information on new media, the greater they were worried about COVID-19. Therefore, this study suggests that it is necessary to ensure the accuracy of COVID-19-related information that is communicated to the public. In particular, individuals with poor health are more likely to be vulnerable because of anxiety during the epidemic. Therefore, it is necessary to pay more attention to the anxiety of these vulnerable groups during the COVID-19 epidemic. In addition, this study revealed that COVID-19 worry is an emotional response rather than a cognitive assessment and that COVID-19 worry helps people engage in preventive behavior. However, whether anxiety caused by an excessive emotional response will cause undesirable behavior, such as unnecessary visits to emergency departments or the hoarding of face masks [6], needs further exploration.

Future studies may need to further consider participants' demographic information (e.g., socioeconomic status, gender, age groups, occupation), relevant factors (e.g., physical health conditions, resilience, protective factors, psychological adjustment, coping strategy), and mixed methods (e.g., qualitative, longitudinal) in understanding the relationships among examined constructs, and to further examine the change over time and whether the changes are persistent or short lived, and if changes were symptom specific.

This study had some limitations. Although new media, such as search engines, social media apps, online discussion boards, etc., has changed the ways we retrieve and acquire information, fake news and false reports (information) occur frequently and make people panic or cause some mental diseases, especially amid the COVID-19 pandemic. With the advancement of information, communication, and technology (ICT), it is important to explore the impacts of the aforementioned issues. Hence, this paper mainly focused on investigating the citizen who mainly relies on new media channels to obtain information. The survey respondents are mostly young people, as this group of citizens may spend more time on smartphones or computers than other groups and have a high likelihood of accessing and finishing the online surveys of the present study, which is also consistent with the results of the Taiwan MOST Communication Survey Database (2015) [43]. The research results may not be analogized to other population groups (e.g., middle-aged, senior citizens, etc.). Nevertheless, this research only used the new media platforms as the primary survey channel because the researchers valued the social issues of the new media, but the derived problem is that the results may not be widely applicable to non-social media users. Thus, it is suggested that future research can investigate the anxiety, subjective well-being, media consumption, and safety-seeking behaviors amid the COVID-19 epidemic in different population groups through multiple ways.

Because of individual subjectivity, participants' self-reports may not reflect their actual media consumption behavior and safety-seeking behavior. Furthermore, although in a statistical sense, health status and new media use frequency can predict COVID-19 anxiety, and COVID-19 anxiety can predict subjective well-being and safety-seeking behaviors, in a practical sense, these variables are related but not necessarily causally related. Therefore, other diversified research methods can be used in future research to clarify the relationship between these variables. Another limitation of this study was that subjective well-being investigated only physical health, mental health, and social relationships. However, subjective well-being is an individual's evaluation of life conditions, and the life of human beings contains broader aspects. It is suggested that future research should continue to track the impacts of different aspects of COVID-19-related anxiety on broader aspects of life, such as the economy. Although this study had limitations, it is still helpful for understanding the relationship between anxiety and related variables during the COVID-19 epidemic and can be regarded as a basis for subsequent research development.

Author Contributions: Conceptualization, Y.-F.L., H.-Y.S., and S.-C.Y.; methodology, Y.-F.L. and S.-C.Y.; software, Y.-F.L.; validation, H.-Y.S., Y.-F.L., S.-C.Y. and L.-C.C.; formal analysis, H.-Y.S. and L.-C.C.; investigation, H.-Y.S. and S.-C.Y.; resources, Y.-F.L.; data curation, Y.-F.L., H.-Y.S., and S.-C.Y.; writing—original draft preparation, Y.-F.L.; writing—review and editing, Y.-F.L., H.-Y.S., S.-C.Y. and L.-C.C.; visualization, Y.-F.L.; supervision, S.-C.Y.; project administration, H.-Y.S., S.-C.Y. and L.-C.C.; funding acquisition, S.-C.Y. All authors have read and agreed to the published version of the manuscript.

Funding: This research was financially supported by the Intelligent Electronic Commerce Research Center from The Featured Areas Research Center Program within the framework of the Higher Education Sprout Project by the Ministry of Education in Taiwan (10C0701, 2020-2021).

Institutional Review Board Statement: Ethical review and approval were waived for this study due to no relevant identifying information of the humans involved and an anonymous online design questionnaire being used in this study.

Informed Consent Statement: Informed consent was obtained from all subjects involved in the study.

Data Availability Statement: The data presented in this study are available on request from the corresponding author.

Acknowledgments: This work was financially supported by the Intelligent Electronic Commerce Research Center from the Featured Areas Research Center Program within the framework of the Higher Education Sprout Project by the Ministry of Education (MOE) in Taiwan.

Conflicts of Interest: The authors declare that they have no conflict of interest.

References

1. Taghrir, M.H.; Borazjani, R.; Shiraly, R. COVID-19 and Iranian medical students; A survey on their related-knowledge, preventive behaviors and risk perception. *Arch. Iran. Med.* **2020**, *23*, 249–254. [CrossRef] [PubMed]
2. Kim, J.W. Countering Anti-Vaccination Rumors on Twitter (Unpublished Doctoral Dissertation), Syracuse University, Syracuse, NY, USA, August 2019.
3. Levaot, Y.; Greene, T.; Pargi, Y. The associations between media use, peritraumatic distress, anxiety and resilience during the COVID-19 pandemic. *J. Psychiatr. Res.* **2020**. [CrossRef] [PubMed]
4. Hall, B.J.; Xiong, Y.X.; Yip, P.S.Y.; Lao, C.K.; Shi, W.; Sou, E.K.L.; Lam, A.I.F. The association between disaster exposure and media use on post-traumatic stress disorder following Typhoon Hato in Macao, China. *Eur. J. Psychotraumatol.* **2019**, *10*, 1558709. [CrossRef] [PubMed]
5. Haham, L.M.; Youngster, M.; Kuperman Shan, A.; Yee, S.; Ben-Kimhy, R.; Medina-Artom, T.R.; Hourvitz, A.; Kedem, A.; Librach, C. Suspension of fertility treatment during the COVID-19 pandemic: Views, emotional reactions and psychological distress among women undergoing fertility treatment. *Reprod. Biomed. Online* **2021**, *42*, 849–858. [CrossRef] [PubMed]
6. Holmes, E.A.; O'Connor, R.C.; Perry, V.H.; Tracey, I.; Wessely, S.; Arseneault, L.; Ballard, C.; Christensen, H.; Cohen Silver, R.; Everall, I.; et al. Multidisciplinary research priorities for the COVID-19 pandemic: A call for action for mental health science. *Lancet Psychiatry* **2020**, *7*, 547–560. [CrossRef]
7. Juhl, J.; Routledge, C. Putting the terror in terror management theory: Evidence that the awareness of death does cause anxiety and undermine psychological wellbeing. *Curr. Dir. Psychol. Sci.* **2016**, *25*, 99–103. [CrossRef]
8. Marttila, E.; Koivula, A.; Räsänen, P. Does excessive social media use decrease subjective well-being? A longitudinal analysis of the relationship between problematic use, loneliness and life satisfaction. *Telemat. Inform.* **2020**, *59*, 10556. [CrossRef]
9. Silva, W.; Brito, T.; Pereira, C.R. Anxiety associated with COVID-19 and concerns about death: Impacts on psychological well-being. *Pers. Individ. Dif.* **2021**, *176*, 110772. [CrossRef]
10. Kobayashi, L.C.; O'Shea, B.Q.; Kler, J.S.; Nishimura, R.; Palavicino-Maggio, C.B.; Eastman, M.R.; Vinson, Y.R.; Finlay, J.M. Cohort profile: The COVID-19 Coping Study, a longitudinal mixed-methods study of middle-aged and older adults' mental health and well-being during the COVID-19 pandemic in the USA. *BMJ Open* **2021**, *11*, e044965. [CrossRef]
11. Magson, N.R.; Freeman, J.Y.A.; Rapee, R.M.; Richardson, C.E.; Oar, E.L.; Fardouly, J. Risk and protective factors for prospective changes in adolescent mental health during the COVID-19 pandemic. *J. Youth Adolesc.* **2021**, *50*, 44–57. [CrossRef]
12. Newby, J.M.; O'Moore, K.; Tang, S.; Christensen, H.; Faasse, K. Acute mental health responses during the COVID-19 pandemic in Australia. *PLoS ONE* **2020**, *15*, e0236562. [CrossRef]
13. O'Connor, R.C.; Wetherall, K.; Cleare, S.; McClelland, H.; Melson, A.J.; Niedzwiedz, C.L.; O'Carroll, R.E.; O'Connor, D.B.; Platt, S.; Scowcroft, E.; et al. Mental health and well-being during the COVID-19 pandemic: Longitudinal analyses of adults in the UK COVID-19 Mental Health & Wellbeing study. *Br. J. Psychiatry* **2021**, *218*, 326–333. [CrossRef]
14. Robinson, E.; Sutin, A.R.; Daly, M.; Jones, A. A systematic review and meta-analysis of longitudinal cohort studies comparing mental health before versus during the COVID-19 pandemic in 2020. *J. Affect Disord.* **2022**, *296*, 567–576. [CrossRef]
15. Canet-Juric, L.; Andres, M.L.; del Valle, M.; Lopez-Morales, H.; Poo, F.; Galli, J.I.; Yerro, M.; Urquijo, S. A longitudinal study on the emotional impact cause by the COVID-19 pandemic quarantine on general population. *Front. Psychol.* **2020**, *11*, 565688. [CrossRef] [PubMed]
16. Ramiz, L.; Contrand, B.; Rojas Castro, M.Y.; Dupuy, M.; Lu, L.; Sztal-Kutas, C.; Lagarde, E. A longitudinal study of mental health before and during COVID-19 lockdown in the French population. *Global. Health* **2021**, *17*, 29. [CrossRef] [PubMed]
17. Nitschke, J.B.; Heller, W.; Miller, G.A. Anxiety, stress, and cortical brain function. In *The Neuropsychology of Emotion*; Borod, J.C., Ed.; Oxford University Press: New York, NY, USA, 2020; pp. 298–319.
18. Cao, W.; Fang, Z.; Hou, G.; Han, M.; Xu, X.; Dong, J.; Zheng, J. The psychological impact of the COVID-19 epidemic on college students in China. *Psychiatry Res.* **2020**, *287*, 112934. [CrossRef] [PubMed]
19. Li, S.; Wang, Y.; Xue, J.; Zhao, N.; Zhu, T. The impact of COVID-19 epidemic declaration on psychological consequences: A study on active Weibo users. *Int. J. Environ. Res. Public Health* **2020**, *17*, 2032. [CrossRef] [PubMed]
20. Cornwell, B.R.; Mueller, S.C.; Kaplan, R.; Grillon, C.; Ernst, M. Anxiety, a benefit and detriment to cognition: Behavioral and magnetoencephalographic evidence from a mixed-saccade task. *Brain Cogn.* **2012**, *78*, 257–267. [CrossRef]
21. Meulders, A.; van Daele, T.; Volders, S.; Vlaeye, J.W.S. The use of safety-seeking behavior in exposure-based treatments for fear and anxiety: Benefit or burden? A meta-analytic review. *Clin. Psychol. Rev.* **2016**, *45*, 144–156. [CrossRef]
22. Wang, C.; Pan, R.; Wan, X.; Tan, Y.; Xu, L.; Ho, C.S.; Ho, R.C. Immediate psychological responses and associated factors during the initial stage of the 2019 coronavirus disease (COVID-19) epidemic among the general population in China. *Int. J. Environ. Res. Public Health* **2020**, *17*, 1729. [CrossRef] [PubMed]
23. Gao, J.; Zheng, P.; Jia, Y.; Chen, H.; Mao, Y.; Chen, S.; Wang, Y.; Fu, H.; Dai, J. Mental health problems and social media exposure during COVID-19 outbreak. *PLoS ONE* **2020**, *15*, e0231924. [CrossRef]
24. Wang, W.Y.; Wang, K.Y.; Tang, Y.Y. Anxiety: A concept analysis. *Chang Gung Nurs.* **2007**, *18*, 59–67. [CrossRef]
25. Ghassemi, M.; Bernecker, K.; Brandstätter, V. "Take care, honey!": People are more anxious about their significant others' risk behavior than about their own. *J. Exp. Soc. Psychol.* **2020**, *86*, 103879. [CrossRef]
26. Rundmo, T.; Nordfjærn, T. Does risk perception really exist? *Saf. Sci.* **2017**, *93*, 230–240. [CrossRef]

27. Sjöberg, L.; Moen, B.; Rundmo, T. Explaining risk perception. An evaluation of the psychometric paradigm in risk perception research. *Rotunde Publ. Rotunde* **2004**, *84*, 55–76.
28. So, S.H.; Sun, X.; Chan, G.; Chan, I.; Chiu, C.; Chan, S.; Wong, W.; Leung, P.W.; Chen, E. Risk perception in paranoia and anxiety: Two investigations across clinical and nonclinical populations. *Schizophr. Res. Cogn.* **2020**, *21*, 100176. [CrossRef]
29. Loewenstein, G.F.; Weber, E.U.; Hsee, C.K.; Welch, N. Risk as feelings. *Psychol. Bull.* **2001**, *127*, 267–286. [CrossRef]
30. Dilek, T.D.; Boybay, Z.; Kologlu, N.; Tin, O.; Güler, S.; Saltık, S. The impact of SARS-CoV2 on the anxiety levels of subjects and on the anxiety and depression levels of their parents. *Mult. Scler. Relat. Disord.* **2021**, *47*, 102595. [CrossRef]
31. Nikčević, A.V.; Marino, C.; Kolubinski, D.C.; Leach, D.; Spada, M.M. Modeling the contribution of the Big Five personality traits, health anxiety, and COVID-19 psychological distress to generalized anxiety and depressive symptoms during the COVID-19 pandemic. *J. Affect. Disord.* **2021**, *279*, 578–584. [CrossRef]
32. Malesza, M.; Kaczmarek, M.C. Predictors of anxiety during the COVID-19 pandemic in Poland. *Pers. Individ. Dif.* **2021**, *170*, 110419. [CrossRef]
33. Lachlan, K.A.; Hutter, E.; Gilbert, C.; Spence, P.R. From what I have heard, this is bad: An examination of Americans' source preferences and information seeking during the COVID-19 pandemic. *Prog. Disaster Sci.* **2021**, *9*, 100145. [CrossRef]
34. Leach, J. Media Panics. In *Encyclopedia of Language and Linguistics*; Brown, K., Ed.; Elsevier: Amsterdam, The Netherlands, 2006; pp. 607–609.
35. Radwan, E.; Radwan, A.; Radwan, W. The role of social media in spreading panic among primary and secondary school students during the COVID-19 pandemic: An online questionnaire study from the Gaza Strip, Palestine. *Heliyon* **2020**, *6*, e05807. [CrossRef] [PubMed]
36. Lin, C.Y.; Broström, A.; Griffiths, M.D.; Pakpour, A.H. Investigating mediated effects of fear of COVID-19 and COVID-19 misunderstanding in the association between problematic social media use, psychological distress, and insomnia. *Internet Interv.* **2020**, *21*, 100345. [CrossRef]
37. Soroya, S.H.; Farooq, A.; Mahmood, K.; Isoaho, J.; Zara, S. From information seeking to information avoidance: Understanding the health information behavior during a global health crisis. *Inf. Process Manag.* **2021**, *58*, 102440. [CrossRef]
38. Wang, X.; Liu, Z. Online engagement in social media: A cross-cultural comparison. *Comput. Hum. Behav.* **2019**, *97*, 137–150. [CrossRef]
39. Chao, M.; Xue, D.; Liu, T.; Yang, H.; Hall, B.J. Media use and acute psychological outcomes during COVID-19 outbreak in China. *J. Anxiety Disord.* **2020**, *74*, 102248. [CrossRef] [PubMed]
40. Riediker, M.; Koren, H.S. The importance of environmental exposures to physical, mental and social well-being. *Int. J. Hyg. Environ. Health* **2004**, *207*, 193–201. [CrossRef]
41. WHO. *Constitution of the World Health Organization*; World Health Organization: Geneva, Switzerland, 1948.
42. Chiang, M.J.; Teng, M.H. An exploratory investigation on psychometric properties of the short health anxiety inventory Taiwan version. *Arch. Clin. Psychol.* **2014**, *8*, 1–14. [CrossRef]
43. Chang, C.-C. *The 2015 Taiwan Communication Survey (Phase One, Year Four): Political and Civic Communication (D00161)*; Department of Advertising, National Chengchi University: Taipei, Taiwan, 2020. [CrossRef]
44. Chang, Q.; Peng, C.; Guo, Y.; Cai, Z.; Yip, P.S. Mechanisms connecting objective and subjective poverty to mental health: Serial mediation roles of negative life events and social support. *Soc. Sci. Med.* **2020**, *265*, 113308. [CrossRef]
45. Hong, Y.; Kim, J.S.; Xiong, L. Media exposure and individuals' emergency preparedness behaviors for coping with natural and human-made disasters. *J. Enviorn. Psychol.* **2019**, *63*, 82–91. [CrossRef]
46. Kaiser, H.F. An index of factorial simplicity. *Psychometrika* **1974**, *39*, 31–36. [CrossRef]
47. Lomanowska, A.L.; Guitton, M.J. Online intimacy and well-being in the digital age. *Internet Interv.* **2016**, *4*, 138–144. [CrossRef] [PubMed]
48. IASC MHPSS Reference Group. [United Nations]. *Briefing Note on Addressing Mental Health and Psychosocial Aspects of COVID-19 Outbreak*; Version 1.1; OCHA: New York, NY, USA, 2020.
49. Lundberg, A. Environmental change and human health. In *The Environment and Mental Health: A Guide for Clinicians*; Lundberg, A., Ed.; Lawrence Erlbaum: Mahwah, NJ, USA, 1998; pp. 5–23.
50. Stikkelbroek, Y.; Bodden, D.H.; Kleinjan, M.; Reijnders, M.; van Baar, A.L. Adolescent depression and negative life events, the mediating role of cognitive emotion regulation. *PLoS ONE* **2016**, *11*, e0161062. [CrossRef] [PubMed]
51. Summers, J.; Cheng, H.Y.; Lin, H.H.; Barnard, L.T.; Kvalsvig, A.; Wilson, N.; Baker, M.G. Potential lessons from the Taiwan and New Zealand health responses to the COVID-19 pandemic. *Lancet Reg. Health West. Pac.* **2020**, *4*, 100044. [CrossRef] [PubMed]
52. Tiwari, S.; Lane, M.; Alam, K. Do social networking sites build and maintain social capital online in rural communities? *J. Rural. Stud.* **2019**, *66*, 1–10. [CrossRef]

International Journal of
Environmental Research and Public Health

MDPI

Article

Accept Anxiety to Improve Sleep: The Impact of the COVID-19 Lockdown on the Relationships between Mindfulness, Distress, and Sleep Quality

Marco Mirolli [1,*,†], Luca Simione [1], Monica Martoni [2] and Marco Fabbri [3,*,†]

1 Institute of Cognitive Sciences and Technologies, National Research Council (ISTC-CNR), Via San Martino della Battaglia 44, 00185 Rome, Italy; luca.simione@istc.cnr.it
2 Department of Experimental, Diagnostic and Specialized Medicine, St. Orsola-Malpighi Hospital, University of Bologna, Via Massarenti 9, 40138 Bologna, Italy; monica.martoni@unibo.it
3 Department of Psychology, University of Campania Luigi Vanvitelli, Viale Ellittico 31, 81100 Caserta, Italy
* Correspondence: marco.mirolli@istc.cnr.it (M.M.); marco.fabbri@unicampania.it (M.F.)
† These authors contributed equally to the paper.

Citation: Mirolli, M.; Simione, L.; Martoni, M.; Fabbri, M. Accept Anxiety to Improve Sleep: The Impact of the COVID-19 Lockdown on the Relationships between Mindfulness, Distress, and Sleep Quality. *Int. J. Environ. Res. Public Health* **2021**, *18*, 13149. https://doi.org/10.3390/ijerph182413149

Academic Editors: Paolo Roma, Merylin Monaro and Cristina Mazza

Received: 23 October 2021
Accepted: 10 December 2021
Published: 13 December 2021

Publisher's Note: MDPI stays neutral with regard to jurisdictional claims in published maps and institutional affiliations.

Abstract: It has been recently proposed that mindfulness can improve sleep quality through the mediating role on psychological distress and that acceptance may play a pivotal role in mindfulness beneficial effects. The aim of the present work was to understand the effects of the COVID-19 lockdown on dispositional mindfulness, sleep, and distress, and on their relationships. In particular, we wanted to test the hypothesis that the detrimental effects of lockdown on sleep depended on mindfulness and distress (including anxiety and depression) and that the acceptance facet of mindfulness played the leading role. A longitudinal study based on self-report questionnaires was conducted on 39 Italian adults (M age = 35.03, SD = 14.02; 21 men) assessing mindfulness, distress, and sleep quality before (23 December 2019–8 March 2020) and during (27 April 2020–10 May 2020) the first Italian COVID-19 lockdown. Lockdown decreased mindfulness while increasing distress and sleep problems. Path analysis showed that the effects of lockdown on sleep were fully mediated by mindfulness and distress. Furthermore, a more detailed analysis showed that these effects were mainly dependent on the acceptance component of mindfulness working through anxiety. The present study confirms, in the context of the COVID-19 lockdown, a model according to which mindfulness, and specifically acceptance, influences sleep through the mediating role of distress.

Keywords: sleep quality; mindfulness; distress; COVID-19 lockdown; longitudinal study; path analysis

1. Introduction

The spread of COVID-19 resulted in a high prevalence of sleep problems not only in COVID-19 patients, but also in healthcare workers and in the general population [1,2]. In Italy, the first lockdown, which involved home confinement and social distancing for the entire population from 10 March to 3 May 2020, affected both sleep and mental health, with an increase in sleep difficulties, especially in people with a higher level of depression, anxiety, and stress [3,4]. Indeed, both the pandemic itself and the resulting quarantine have been shown to increase stress and stress-related disturbances [1,5–7]. However, little is known about the mechanisms underlying these deleterious effects.

A possible psychological factor that is likely to be relevant is mindfulness, which can be defined as being present in the moment intentionally and with a non-judging attitude [8]. Mindfulness has been associated with better sleep quality [9], greater well-being [10], and lower levels of depression and anxiety [11], and mindfulness-based approaches have been used to improve insomnia, depression, and anxiety symptoms [12]. Importantly, mindfulness has been shown to have a protective effect on sleep during the COVID-19 lockdown [13]. Recently, Simione et al. [14] have shown that the positive relationships between dispositional mindfulness and sleep quality fully depend on the mediational role of stress, which is in accordance with recent models of insomnia such as the stress-diathesis [15] and the metacognitive [16] models.

However, mindfulness is a multidimensional concept [17], and different mindfulness components have different effects on different outcomes [18]. Lindsay and Creswell [19] proposed the Monitoring and Acceptance theory (MAT), according to which mindfulness works through the two mechanisms of attention monitoring and acceptance: while monitoring alone tends to increase affective reactivity, monitoring and acceptance together lead to increased psychophysical well-being. However, Simione et al. [20] have shown that the beneficial effects of mindfulness seem to depend almost entirely on acceptance alone, with monitoring playing a deleterious role in only a few cases, which, interestingly, include sleep problems.

In the present longitudinal study, we assessed dispositional mindfulness, distress symptoms, and sleep problems in the same sample both before and during the first Italian COVID-19 lockdown. While predicting that lockdown would worsen both distress symptoms and sleep problems, we were interested in testing whether mindfulness, and specifically its acceptance component, could play a mediating role in these changes. In particular, on the basis of the reviewed literature, we hypothesized that lockdown may increase sleep problems by reducing mindfulness and increasing psychological distress and that the beneficial effects of mindfulness would depend mainly on acceptance.

2. Materials and Methods

2.1. Participants and Procedure

A convenience sample method was used, recruiting participants from the general population through email and social media (no mindfulness practice nor any particular interest in mindfulness was required for participation). During the period from 23 December 2019 to 8 March 2020, 43 volunteers participated in the survey, after reading the written consent form and explicitly agreeing to take part in the study. In this first period, all questionnaires (see below) were individually administered in paper-and-pencil form. The study protocol was approved by the Ethics Committee of the Department of Psychology at the University of Campania Luigi Vanvitelli and it originally aimed to investigate the relationship between dispositional mindfulness and different psychological and cognitive variables. When home restriction was adopted in Italy in response of the COVID-19 pandemic, the aim of the study was changed in order to assess the effect of lockdown on sleep, mindfulness, and distress. Consequently, we re-contacted all participants and asked them to complete an online survey (using the Google Moduli platform) including the same questionnaires filled in during the first period. Thirty-nine of the 43 volunteers responded and filled the questionnaires from 17 April to 10 May, 2020. We collected the following demographic data for each participant: age, sex, city, educational level, and occupation. The mean age was 35.03 years (SD = 14.02 years), with 21 men. All participants lived in the south of Italy, the educational level ranged from eight grade diploma to PhD title, and the occupational status covered unemployment, student, and workers in both private and public fields.

2.2. Materials

Dispositional mindfulness was measured using the Italian version of the Five Facets Mindfulness Questionnaire (FFMQ [21]), containing 39 items divided in five subscales: observing, describing, acting with awareness, non-judging, and non-reacting. Participants were requested to rate each statement on a 5-point Likert scale. Higher total scores indicate higher dispositional mindfulness. Following the literature on MAT theory [19,20], we considered monitoring as being represented by observing and acceptance as being represented by non-judging and non-reacting. The psychometric properties of this scale are good [21].

The Italian version of the Hospital Anxiety and Depression Scale (HADS [22]) was administered to assess general distress. The HADS consists of 14 items divided in two subscales: anxiety and depression. Participants are requested to rate how they have been feeling in the past week on a 4-point scale. The psychometric properties of the HADS are good [22]. Following Iani et al. [22], the total score was used as a measure of general psychological distress.

In order to detect sleep quality as well as sleep-related wake disorders, the Italian version of the Mini Sleep Questionnaire (MSQ [23]) was used. In this questionnaire, 6 of the 10 items are related to sleep problems while 4 items are related to wake problems. Respondents had to indicate the frequency of occurrence for each statement in the past week on a 7-point scale. Beyond the total score, as suggested by Natale et al. [23], we also calculated the scores of the sleep and wake subscales. The psychometric properties of the MSQ are good [24].

Given that circadian typology has been shown to influence sleep problems [25], in order to control for such a factor, we also administered the Italian version of the reduced Morningness-Eveningness Questionnaire to measure circadian typology (rMEQ [26]). The rMEQ includes 5 items and the total score is obtained by summing up all the items, with higher scores reflecting a morningness preference. The psychometric properties of rMEQ are good [26].

2.3. Data Analysis

First, we checked for the presence of a common method bias in the responses using two tests: the Harman's one-factor test and the correlation matrix test [27]. In the first test we computed the variance explained by a single-factor exploratory model including all the items administered, considering the bias to be present if the proportion of variance explained by this single factor was higher than 50%. In the second test we considered the correlation matrix between all assessed variables, considering the bias to be present if correlations were higher than 0.90. In both tests, for each variable we considered all the observations (i.e., each participant assessed both before and during the lockdown).

Secondly, we assessed the effect of lockdown on the measured variables through a repeated-measures MANOVA followed by a series of one-way repeated-measures ANCOVAs to assess the effect of time on each dependent variable, while controlling for the effects of sex, age, and education level. As a measure of effect size, we used the partial eta squared which is recommended in order to improve the comparability of effect sizes between studies [28].

Then, we tested our hypothesis that lockdown onset impacted mindfulness, which affected psychological distress, in turn influencing sleep problems. To this aim, we tested the indirect effect of mindfulness on the effect of time on distress/sleep by using path analysis with the Huber-White robust standard errors estimator and bias-corrected confidence intervals that test indirect or mediated effects [29]. In particular, we tested two models. In the first one we included the total score for each scale, in order to assess the relationships between mindfulness, general distress, and sleep problems. In the second model, we used the subscale scores of each questionnaire to investigate the differential contribution of each facet or aspect to the considered effects. Regarding mindfulness, following the literature on MAT theory [19,20], we took into account only the variables considered to be related to either monitoring (i.e., observing) or acceptance (i.e., non-judging and non-reacting). In both models, we controlled for the effects of age, sex, education level, and chronotype (rMEQ score).

As both models were fully saturated (i.e., they perfectly fitted the data because they had as many parameters as there were values to be fitted) no goodness of fit scores could be calculated. In order to both obtain interpretable goodness of fit statistics and reduce the number of free parameters so to counterbalance the small numerosity of the sample, we also analyzed simplified versions of the models where all non-significant path (and covariates) were removed. For each model, we calculated the following fitting indexes: $\chi 2$

statistics, comparative fit index (CFI), Tucker–Lewis index (TLI), root mean square error of approximation (RMSEA), and standard root mean square residual (SRMR). Model fit was considered as adequate with the following values: non-significant $\chi 2$, CFI and TLI above 0.95, RMSEA of 0.06 or less, SRMR of 0.08 or less [30]. Raw data are available as Supplementary Materials.

3. Results

Both tests for a common method bias showed that no such bias was present. The variance explained by a single-factor model was only 14.72%, much lower than the threshold of 50% (Harman's one-factor test). Furthermore, all the correlation coefficients between our variables were between 0.01 and 0.65 (absolute value), that is smaller than the threshold value of 0.90 (correlation matrix test).

3.1. Effects of Lockdown

The MANOVA assessing the effect of lockdown on our variables was significant for time, Pillai's Trace = 0.57, $F(7,38) = 6.04$, $p < 0.01$, indicating a significant overall impact of lockdown on the variables. The results of the subsequent one-way repeated-measures ANCOVAs are reported in Table 1 (together with Cronbach's αs of all variables). Two mindfulness facets (i.e., observing and non-judging) and the total mindfulness score changed as a function of time. In particular, observing increased during lockdown while non-judging and total mindfulness decreased. Regarding psychological distress, anxiety did not change, while both depression and HADS total increased. Regarding sleep-related problems, sleep quality (sleep factor) decreased, while daytime sleepiness (wake factor) and MSQ total did not change. Lastly, circadian typology (rMEQ) did not change. Overall, these results showed that lockdown impacted different areas of psychological functioning, including mindfulness, distress, and sleep quality.

Table 1. Reliability, means, standard deviations, and one-way ANCOVA statistics for variables measured before (Time 0) and during (Time 1) lockdown.

Scale	Variable	Cronbach's α	Time 0		Time 1			
			M	SD	M	SD	$F(1,37)$	η^2_p
FFMQ	**Observing**	**0.79**	**27.36**	**6.7**	**29.74**	**4.56**	**6.51 ***	**0.15**
	Non-judging	**0.80**	**27.18**	**5.4**	**22.49**	**5.57**	**16.56 ****	**0.31**
	Non-reacting	0.71	21.49	4.4	22.36	3.54	1.57	0.04
	FFMQ tot	**0.86**	**131.03**	**16.72**	**123.13**	**11.38**	**6.96 ***	**0.16**
HADS	Anxiety	0.76	9.31	2.91	9.77	3.19	0.90	0.02
	Depression	**0.82**	**8.13**	**1.96**	**9.13**	**2.41**	**7.26 ***	**0.16**
	HADS tot	**0.86**	**17.44**	**4.12**	**18.90**	**4.68**	**4.43 ***	**0.11**
MSQ	**Sleep**	**0.75**	**14.26**	**6.05**	**15.74**	**6.04**	**4.58 ***	**0.11**
	Wake	0.84	13.10	5.16	13.28	5.52	0.05	0.01
	MSQ tot	0.85	27.36	10.18	29.03	10.71	1.72	0.04
rMEQ	rMEQ tot	0.51	14.74	3.53	14.13	3.81	1.21	0.03

Note. Sleep = sleep quality, Wake = daytime sleepiness. Time 0 = before lockdown, Time 1 = during lockdown. Cronbach's αs were computed on the Time 0 data. An interpretable measure of effect size is reported as partial eta squared (η^2_p). Variables that changed significantly from Time 0 to Time 1 are reported in boldface. Significant level is indicated as follows: * $p < 0.05$; ** $p < 0.01$.

3.2. From Lockdown to Sleep Problems through Mindfulness and Distress

Table 2 shows the estimated coefficients of the model including the high-level variables (Figure 1). This analysis revealed that lockdown significantly decreased mindfulness, and this, in turn, decreased distress, while distress increased sleep problems. Furthermore, we found three significant indirect effects: from lockdown to distress through mindfulness (b = 0.61, CI = [0.08, 1.64], SE = 0.35, β = 0.07), from lockdown to sleep through both mindfulness and distress (b = 0.51, CI = [0.05, 1.88], SE = 0.36, β = 0.03), and from mindfulness to sleep problems through distress (b = −0.06, CI = [−0.16, −0.01], β = −0.09). All indirect effects represented full mediation, as time did not significantly affect distress or sleep problems, nor did mindfulness directly affect sleep. Testing the model while removing the covariates did not significantly alter any of the considered paths. Hence, we tested the fit of the simplified model containing only significant paths and no covariate. This showed good fit statistics: $\chi 2(3) = 1.04$, $p = 0.79$, CFI = 1.00, TLI = 1.00, RMSEA = 0.01, SRMR = 0.03.

Table 2. SEM estimated coefficients for model 1.

Path			b	CI_{lower}	CI_{upper}	SE	β
Lockdown	→	**FFMQ**	**−7.88 ***	**−14.95**	**−1.42**	**3.45**	**−0.27**
Lockdown	→	HADS	0.85	−1.01	2.82	0.97	0.10
Lockdown	→	MSQ	0.13	−3.99	4.53	2.20	0.01
FFMQ	→	**HADS**	**−0.08 ***	**−0.15**	**−0.01**	**0.04**	**−0.26**
HADS	→	**MSQ**	**0.82 ***	**0.16**	**1.32**	**0.29**	**0.35**
FFMQ	→	MSQ	−0.04	−0.18	0.17	0.08	−0.05

Note. b = unstandardized coefficient, CI_{lower} and CI_{upper} = lower and upper 95% bootstrapped confidence intervals of b, SE = standard error, β = standardized coefficient. Significant paths are reported in boldface. Significant level is indicated as follows: * $p < 0.05$.

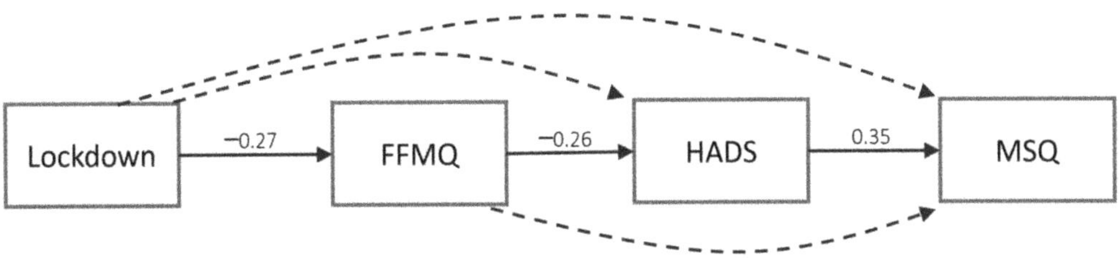

Figure 1. First model including only the total scores. Continuous arrows represent significant paths, while dotted arrows represent non-significant paths. Standardized coefficients are reported only for significant paths.

3.3. *The Effects of Mindfulness Depend on Acceptance*

Table 3 shows the estimated coefficients of the model including the low-level variables (Figure 2). We found a significant effect of lockdown on non-judging but not on observing nor on non-reacting. Anxiety was significantly reduced by both non-judging and non-reacting but was not influenced by observing. Depression was not predicted by observing nor by non-judging, but it was reduced by non-reacting. Lastly, anxiety increased both components of the sleep-wake cycle (sleep and wake), whereas depression did not influence any of them. Regarding indirect effects, we found a significant path from lockdown to anxiety through non-judging (b = 1.01, CI = [0.36, 1.86], SE = 0.37, β = 0.17), two significant paths from non-judging to sleep (b = −0.12, CI = [−0.29, −0.02], SE = 0.07, β = −0.12) and wake (b = −0.17, CI = [−0.34, −0.06], SE = 0.07, β = −0.20) through anxiety, and two significant paths from lockdown to both sleep (b = 0.55, CI = [0.04, 1.47], SE = 0.36, β = 0.05) and wake (b = 0.82, CI = [0.21, 1.81], SE = 0.40, β = 0.08) through non-judging and anxiety. Lockdown had no significant direct effect on anxiety, depression, sleep, or wake. However, both observing and non-judging had a significant direct effect on sleep (the first positive, the second negative). To sum up, this model confirmed that the main direct and indirect effects of time were mostly dependent on acceptance (in particular, on the non-judging facet). Observing had a direct deleterious effect only on sleep, while non-reacting reduced both anxiety and depression; none of these effects, however, were influenced by time. Even in this case, testing the model while removing the covariates did not significantly alter the results. The simplified model including only significant paths and no covariates revealed acceptable fit statistics: $\chi 2(10) = 9.89$, $p = 0.45$, CFI = 1.00, TLI = 1.00, RMSEA = 0.01, SRMR = 0.09.

Table 3. SEM estimated coefficients for model 2.

Path			b	CI_{lower}	CI_{upper}	SE	β
Lockdown	→	Sleep	−0.74	−3.44	2.06	1.43	−0.06
Lockdown	→	Wake	−1.03	−3.19	0.95	1.03	−0.10
Lockdown	→	Anxiety	−0.42	−1.65	0.81	0.61	−0.07
Lockdown	→	Depression	0.76	−0.22	1.66	0.49	0.17
Lockdown	→	Observing	2.19	−0.42	4.65	1.26	0.19
Lockdown	**→**	**Non-judging**	**−4.69 ****	**−7.06**	**−2.23**	**1.24**	**−0.38**
Lockdown	→	Non-reacting	0.76	−1.30	2.61	0.99	0.09
Observing	→	Anxiety	0.01	−0.11	0.12	0.06	0.03
Non-judging	**→**	**Anxiety**	**−0.21 ****	**−0.33**	**−0.10**	**0.06**	**−0.43**
Non-reacting	**→**	**Anxiety**	**−0.15 ***	**−0.28**	**−0.01**	**0.07**	**−0.21**
Observing	→	Depression	−0.01	−0.13	0.08	0.05	−0.04
Non-judging	→	Depression	−0.07	−0.16	0.03	0.05	−0.19
Non-reacting	**→**	**Depression**	**−0.12 ***	**−0.26**	**−0.01**	**0.07**	**−0.23**
Observing	**→**	**Sleep**	**0.21 ***	**0.04**	**0.47**	**0.11**	**0.20**
Non-judging	**→**	**Sleep**	**−0.29 ***	**−0.61**	**−0.02**	**0.14**	**−0.30**
Non-reacting	→	Sleep	0.19	−0.15	0.61	0.19	0.14
Observing	→	Wake	0.12	−0.05	0.33	0.09	0.13
Non-judging	→	Wake	−0.11	−0.35	0.10	0.11	−0.12
Non-reacting	→	Wake	0.04	−0.32	0.39	0.18	0.04
Anxiety	**→**	**Sleep**	**0.55 ***	**0.08**	**1.13**	**0.27**	**0.28**
Depression	→	Sleep	−0.03	−0.74	0.60	0.35	−0.01
Anxiety	**→**	**Wake**	**0.81 ***	**0.40**	**1.16**	**0.20**	**0.47**
Depression	→	Wake	−0.05	−0.57	0.47	0.26	−0.02

Note. b = unstandardized coefficient, CI_{lower} and CI_{upper} = lower and upper 95% bootstrapped confidence intervals of b, SE = standard error, β = standardized coefficient. Significant paths are reported in boldface. Significant level is indicated as follows: * $p < 0.05$, ** $p < 0.01$.

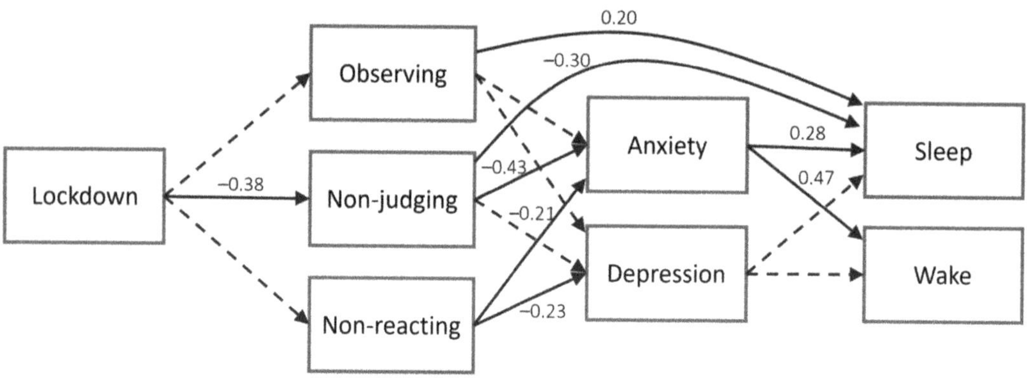

Figure 2. Second model including all the subscale scores. Continuous arrows represent significant paths, while dotted arrows represent non-significant paths. Standardized coefficients are reported only for significant paths. For the sake of clarity, only the direct paths from lower levels to higher levels that were significant are shown: e.g., the paths from lockdown to distress and sleep variables are not shown because they were not significant.

4. Discussion

The present study aimed to explain how the COVID-19 restrictions impacted on the sleep through an analysis of the mediational role of mindfulness and distress. Our results showed that the lockdown resulted in a general decrease in mindfulness (with an increase in observing and a decrease in non-judging), an increase in depression and distress, and an increase in sleep problems. Our first model fully supported our hypothesis that the effect of lockdown on sleep depended on mindfulness and distress. In particular, the model showed that lockdown decreased mindfulness, mindfulness decreased distress, and distress increased sleep problems. Furthermore, indirect pathways showed that mindfulness fully mediated the relationship between lockdown and distress, mindfulness and distress fully mediated the relationship between lockdown and sleep, and distress fully mediated the relationship between mindfulness and sleep. The second model supported the hypothesis that acceptance played the main role in the beneficial effects of mindfulness on sleep. In particular, it showed that: lockdown reduced non-judging; both acceptance facets (i.e., non-judging and non-reacting) decreased anxiety; non-reacting reduced depression; anxiety increased both components of the sleep-wake cycle. The only significant influence of the monitoring factor (i.e., observing) was an increase in sleep problems (which were also decreased by non-judging). Furthermore, indirect effects confirmed both the pivotal role of acceptance (and specifically of non-judging) in the beneficial outcomes of mindfulness and the mediated nature of the effect of lockdown on sleep: non-judging fully mediated the relationship between lockdown and anxiety, anxiety mediated the relationship between non-judging and problems in sleep (partially) and wake (fully), and non-judging and anxiety fully mediated the relationship between lockdown and both sleep and wake problems.

Several lines of research support the view that the effects of lockdown on sleep depend on the mediating role of mindfulness and distress. First, mindfulness is negatively correlated to stress [11,31] and mindfulness interventions have positive effects on stress and stress-related disorders [32]. Second, stress is well-known to have a deleterious effect on sleep [33], which is in accordance with the stress diathesis model of insomnia, according to which sleep problems depend mainly on stressful events and stress-induced cognitive intrusions [15]. Third, the mediational role of stress and stress-related disturbances in the link between mindfulness and sleep is supported by several cross-sectional studies [14,34] and is also in accordance with the meta-cognitive model of insomnia [16]: according to this model mindfulness can improve insomnia by reducing the distress produced by sleep-related worries, which are the main causes of the secondary arousal that contributes to insomnia. Furthermore, Simione et al. [14] have proposed that mindfulness could act on insomnia also by reducing primary arousal through a reduction of the impact of stressful events. Finally, a recent work involving two studies (one in Wuhan, China, and the other in the United Kingdom) demonstrated the protective role of mindfulness in the relationship between COVID-19-related stressors and decreases in sleep duration [13].

As far as mindfulness facets are concerned, the monitoring and acceptance components of mindfulness behaved in an opposite way: while non-judging decreased during lockdown, observing increased, and while acceptance facets (non-judging and non-reacting) jointly had beneficial direct and indirect effects on all distress and sleep variables, the monitoring facet (observing) had a deleterious effect only on sleep problems. The differential effect of lockdown on the two relevant mindfulness facets seems logical. It is reasonable that during the lockdown people tended to be more vigilant with respect to themselves and the surroundings due to the threat of illness, which might explain the higher observing scores. The same heightened perceived risk might also explain the decrease in non-judging, as the judgement of one's thoughts and behaviors was considered to be important (and socially reinforced) for protecting one's safety. Even the effects of these changes in mindfulness aspects on distress and sleep make sense given the pandemic context. Indeed, while these changes might be the result of trying to preserve one's health, they had a detrimental effect on one's well-being: they led to more anxiety (e.g., noticing more things to be worried about, worrying more about the health and well-being of oneself and loved ones), which in turn detrimentally impacted sleep.

Beyond being understandable given the very peculiar pandemic context, these results are also consistent with previous research. For example, acceptance has been associated with many beneficial outcomes including lower stress, anxiety, and depression [35], while a recent meta-analysis showed that observing correlates with a few psychological symptoms, including anxiety [18]. Consistently with the current results, in Simione et al. [20], sleep problems were the only outcomes (apart from general distress) that were predicted by the observing facet. According to the influential MAT theory of mindfulness, monitoring alone tends to increase affective reactivity, which can lead to both more psychological symptoms and a greater level of well-being, while acceptance moderates the effect of monitoring in a such way that together they lead to increased psychological well-being [19]. However, on the basis of both their own data and the available literature, Simione et al. [20] showed that these hypotheses were not well-supported, as monitoring was related to only a few psychological outcomes (mainly negative) while acceptance only rarely moderated monitoring, and, even when it did, it protected against the negative effects of monitoring rather than leading to the best psychological outcomes. For these reasons, the authors proposed an alternative hypothesis according to which acceptance alone is mainly responsible for the benefits of mindfulness, whereas monitoring plays only an ancillary role in developing acceptance, while sometimes providing negative consequences. Even though in the present study we could not test for the interaction between acceptance and monitoring due to our small sample size, our results seem to support this alternative hypothesis, as monitoring (observing) played a very limited deleterious role, while acceptance facets (non-reacting and especially non-judging) were the main drivers of change.

Shallcross et al. [36] proposed that mindfulness improves sleep through the mechanisms of experiential awareness, attentional control, and acceptance, which collectively target all the processes that contribute to sleep disturbance: rumination, primary arousal, secondary arousal, sleep monitoring/selective attention and effort, and distorted perceptions regarding sleep impairment. According to this view, acceptance works only on the last three factors, while the first two are targeted only by experiential awareness and attentional control. However, in our data acceptance alone was responsible for the benefits of mindfulness on sleep, in particular through a mediated effect on anxiety. Indeed, while experiential awareness and attentional control without acceptance may even be detrimental in case the current state is unpleasant and unwanted (e.g., stressful thoughts and lack of sleep), thus increasing rumination and primary arousal, acceptance has been associated with less worry and rumination [37], and with less stress and fewer stress-related disturbances [35]. Hence, it is likely that acceptance alone could act on all the processes that contribute to sleep problems.

Finally, we showed that the lockdown-related sleep problems depended on a decrease in mindfulness traits, and thus the present research adds evidence to the mounting literature recommending the use of mindfulness-based interventions to treat insomnia and sleep disturbances [12,16,36]. Furthermore, by showing the pivotal role of acceptance (non-judging) in linking lockdown and sleep problems, our results suggest that it may be interesting to design mindfulness-based interventions that focus particularly on developing acceptance skills so as to test their capacity to prevent sleep problems, particularly in stressful situations.

An important strength of the present study consists in being one of the few studies with "real" pre-lockdown measures of analyzed variables, thus leading to an authentic longitudinal study assessing the impact of the lockdown. Due to the impossibility of foreseeing the advent of the pandemic and the related restrictions, the majority of the previous studies concerning the effects of the pandemic on sleep had to make important compromises, which inevitably limited the reliability. For example, Cellini et al. [3] asked participants to think about the week before any restriction in Italy, which may introduce memory biases in subjects' responses. Similarly, Salfi et al. [4] longitudinally assessed sleep quality, insomnia symptoms, and general distress (anxiety, depression, and stress) in an Italian sample from the first to the second wave of COVID-19 thus comparing similar situations, as the pandemic was continuously present in Italy between the two waves (with different degrees of risk).

However, the present study has its own limitations. First and foremost, the main limit of the present study lies in the small numerosity of the sample which was due to the fact that when the lockdown began, only a small group of participants had compiled the questionnaires. When evaluating model's generalization, one should consider several factors, including the study design and the strength of path coefficients. Our study uses a longitudinal design, which is far more robust than a cross-sectional one, and our main direct and meditated paths reported medium sized effects (ranging from 0.25 to 0.47). As suggested in [38], to find a reliable medium-sized mediation path in a longitudinal study like our own with bootstrapping coefficients, about 40/50 participants should be sufficient. Moreover, our model could be considered unbiased as we did not face non-convergence and improper solutions problems during model estimation [39]. So, from this point of view, the numerosity of our sample was almost acceptable. However, our two models contained, respectively, 21 and 63 free parameters. Considering the rule of thumb requiring a 10:1 ratio between observations and free parameters [40], the numerosity of our sample was indeed too small. For this reason (and also to get non-identified models for which we could obtain interpretable goodness of fit statistics), we simplified our models by removing all non-significant paths and covariates, as testing both models while removing the covariates did not alter significantly any of the considered paths. In this way, we obtained two models whose paths were supported both by the literature and by the previous 'full' models. These 'simplified' models had, respectively, six and 12 free parameters, and both demonstrated good fit indexes. This makes the numerosity of our observation (78) adequate for the first model, while a bit too low for the second model, which consequently should be considered with more caution. Anyway, we think that the limitation due to the small sample was counterbalanced by the possibility of giving a real picture of the effects of lockdown restrictions on the assessed variables. Furthermore, the fact that our results confirmed both our hypotheses, which were based on the previous literature, suggests that the study power was enough for detecting at least the main true effects. Another limit of the present work depends on the measurement tool used for assessing mindfulness. Even if the FFMQ is the most widely used tool adopted for measuring mindfulness, the acceptance dimension is defined by two distinct measures (non-judging and non-reacting), which could be a source of confusion. Future research should confirm the role of acceptance in protecting from sleep problems using another mindfulness tool such as the Philadelphia Mindfulness Scale (PHLMS [41]), as this includes only one scale for acceptance and one for awareness (which can be considered as a measure of attention monitoring). Finally, our study used only self-report questionnaires, which could limit the reliability and validity of our findings due to well-known problems related to self-report measures, such as limited introspective abilities, problems of interpretation, and response biases such as social desirability. Future studies could improve this aspect by also adopting more objective measures of the assessed variables. From this point of view, the development of behavioral measures of mindfulness represents an important challenge for future research [42].

5. Conclusions

The present longitudinal work showed that the detrimental effect of the first Italian COVID-19 lockdown on sleep was fully mediated by mindfulness and distress and that these effects were dependent on the acceptance component working through anxiety, thus confirming our hypotheses based on previously published cross-sectional results [14,20]. By significantly advancing our knowledge of the mechanisms linking sleep to mindfulness and distress, this work not only adds evidence to the mounting literature recommending the use of mindfulness-based interventions to treat insomnia and sleep disturbances, but it also suggests the possibility to develop novel mindfulness-based interventions that focus particularly on acceptance for preventing sleep problems in stressful situations.

Supplementary Materials: The following are available online at https://www.mdpi.com/article/10.3390/ijerph182413149/s1, Table S1: MirolliEtAl_IJERPH_SupplementaryMaterialS1_Data.csv.

Author Contributions: Conceptualization, M.M. (Marco Mirolli), L.S., M.M. (Monica Martoni) and M.F.; Data curation, M.M. (Marco Mirolli), L.S. and M.F.; Formal analysis, M.M. (Marco Mirolli), L.S. and M.F.; Investigation, M.M. (Monica Martoni) and M.F.; Methodology, M.M. (Marco Mirolli), L.S. and M.F.; Project administration, M.M. (Marco Mirolli) and M.F.; Resources, M.F.; Software, L.S.;

Supervision, M.M. (Marco Mirolli) and M.F.; Validation, L.S.; Visualization, L.S.; Writing—original draft, M.M. (Marco Mirolli) and M.F.; Writing—review & editing, L.S. and M.M. (Monica Martoni). All authors have read and agreed to the published version of the manuscript.

Funding: This research received no external funding.

Institutional Review Board Statement: The study was conducted according to the guidelines of the Declaration of Helsinki, and approved by the Ethics Committee of the Department of Psychology at the University of Campania Luigi Vanvitelli (protocol code Fabbri_5/2020).

Informed Consent Statement: Informed consent was obtained from all subjects involved in the study.

Data Availability Statement: The data presented in this study are available in Table S1.

Conflicts of Interest: The authors declare no conflict of interest.

References

1. Morin, C.M.; Bjorvatn, B.; Chung, F.; Holzinger, B.; Partinen, M.; Penzel, T.; Ivers, H.; Wing, Y.K.; Chan, N.Y.; Merikanto, I.; et al. Insomnia, anxiety, and depression during the COVID-19 pandemic: An international collaborative study. *Sleep Med.* **2021**, *87*, 38–45. [CrossRef] [PubMed]
2. Jahrami, H.; BaHammam, A.S.; Bragazzi, N.L.; Saif, Z.; Faris, M.; Vitiello, M.V. Sleep problems during the COVID-19 pandemic by population: A systematic review and meta-analysis. *J. Clin. Sleep Med.* **2021**, *17*, 299–313. [CrossRef] [PubMed]
3. Cellini, N.; Canale, N.; Mioni, G.; Costa, S. Changes in sleep pattern, sense of time and digital media use during COVID-19 lockdown in Italy. *J. Sleep Res.* **2020**, *29*, e13074. [CrossRef] [PubMed]
4. Salfi, F.; D'Atri, A.; Tempesta, D.; Ferrara, M. Sleeping under the waves: A longitudinal study across the contagion peaks of the COVID-19 pandemic in Italy. *J. Sleep Res.* **2021**, *30*, e13313. [CrossRef] [PubMed]
5. Brooks, S.K.; Webster, R.K.; Smith, L.E.; Woodland, L.; Wessely, S.; Greenberg, N.; Rubin, G.J. The psychological impact of quarantine and how to reduce it: Rapid review of the evidence. *Lancet* **2020**, *395*, 912–920. [CrossRef]
6. Ozamiz-Etxebarria, N.; Idoiaga Mondragon, N.; Dosil Santamaría, M.; Picaza Gorrotxategi, M. Psychological Symptoms during the Two Stages of Lockdown in Response to the COVID-19 Outbreak: An Investigation in a Sample of Citizens in Northern Spain. *Front. Psychol.* **2020**, *11*, 1491. [CrossRef]
7. Vindegaard, N.; Benros, M.E. COVID-19 pandemic and mental health consequences: Systematic review of the current evidence. Brain, Behavior, and Immunity. *Brain Behav. Immun.* **2020**, *89*, 531–542. [CrossRef]
8. Kabat-Zinn, J. *Wherever You Go, There You Are: Mindfulness Meditation in Everyday Life*; Hyperion Books: New York, NY, USA, 1994.
9. Howell, A.J.; Digdon, N.L.; Buro, K.; Sheptycki, A.R. Relations among mindfulness, well-being, and sleep. *Personal. Individ. Differ.* **2008**, *45*, 773–777. [CrossRef]
10. Brown, K.W.; Ryan, R.M. The benefits of being present: Mindfulness and its role in psychological well-being. *J. Personal. Soc. Psychol.* **2003**, *84*, 822–848. [CrossRef]
11. Mayer, B.; Polak, M.G.; Remmerswaal, D. Mindfulness, Interpretation Bias, and Levels of Anxiety and Depression: Two Mediation Studies. *Mindfulness* **2019**, *10*, 55–65. [CrossRef]
12. Ong, J.C.; Moore, C. What do we really know about mindfulness and sleep health? *Curr. Opin. Psychol.* **2020**, *34*, 18–22. [CrossRef]
13. Zheng, M.X.; Masters-Waage, T.C.; Yao, J.; Lu, Y.; Tan, N.; Narayanan, J. Stay Mindful and Carry on: Mindfulness Neutralizes COVID-19 Stressors on Work Engagement via Sleep Duration. *Front. Psychol.* **2020**, *11*, 610156. [CrossRef]
14. Simione, L.; Raffone, A.; Mirolli, M. Stress as the Missing Link between Mindfulness, Sleep Quality, and Well-being: A Cross-sectional Study. *Mindfulness* **2020**, *11*, 439–451. [CrossRef]
15. Drake, C.L.; Pillai, V.; Roth, T. Stress and Sleep Reactivity: A Prospective Investigation of the Stress-Diathesis Model of Insomnia. *Sleep* **2014**, *37*, 1295–1304. [CrossRef]
16. Ong, J.C.; Ulmer, C.S.; Manber, R. Improving sleep with mindfulness and acceptance: A metacognitive model of insomnia. *Behav. Res. Ther.* **2012**, *50*, 651–660. [CrossRef]
17. Sauer, S.; Walach, H.; Schmidt, S.; Hinterberger, T.; Lynch, S.; Büssing, A.; Kohls, N. Assessment of Mindfulness: Review on State of the Art. *Mindfulness* **2013**, *4*, 3–17. [CrossRef]
18. Carpenter, J.K.; Conroy, K.; Gomez, A.F.; Curren, L.C.; Hofmann, S.G. The relationship between trait mindfulness and affective symptoms: A meta-analysis of the Five Facet Mindfulness Questionnaire (FFMQ). *Clin. Psychol. Rev.* **2019**, *74*, 101785. [CrossRef]
19. Lindsay, E.K.; Creswell, J.D. Mechanisms of mindfulness training: Monitor and Acceptance Theory (MAT). *Clin. Psychol. Rev.* **2017**, *51*, 48–59. [CrossRef]
20. Simione, L.; Raffone, A.; Mirolli, M. Acceptance, and Not Its Interaction with Attention Monitoring, Increases Psychological Well-Being: Testing the Monitor and Acceptance Theory of Mindfulness. *Mindfulness* **2021**, *12*, 1398–1411. [CrossRef]
21. Giovannini, C.; Giromini, L.; Bonalume, L.; Tagini, A.; Lang, M.; Amadei, G. The Italian Five Facet Mindfulness Questionnaire: A Contribution to its Validity and Reliability. *J. Psychopathol. Behav. Assess* **2014**, *36*, 415–423. [CrossRef]

22. Iani, L.; Lauriola, M.; Costantini, M. A confirmatory bifactor analysis of the hospital anxiety and depression scale in an Italian community sample. *Health Qual. Life Outcomes* **2014**, *12*, 84. [CrossRef] [PubMed]
23. Natale, V.; Fabbri, M.; Tonetti, L.; Martoni, M. Psychometric goodness of the Mini Sleep Questionnaire. *Psychiatry Clin. Neurosci.* **2014**, *68*, 568–573. [CrossRef] [PubMed]
24. Fabbri, M.; Beracci, A.; Martoni, M.; Meneo, D.; Tonetti, L.; Natale, V. Measuring Subjective Sleep Quality: A Review. *Int. J. Environ. Res. Public Health* **2021**, *18*, 1082. [CrossRef] [PubMed]
25. Adan, A.; Fabbri, M.; Natale, V.; Prat, G. Sleep Beliefs Scale (SBS) and circadian typology. *J. Sleep Res.* **2006**, *15*, 125–132. [CrossRef]
26. Natale, V.; Esposito, M.J.; Martoni, M.; Fabbri, M. Validity of the reduced version of the Morningness-Eveningness Questionnaire. *Sleep Biol. Rhythm.* **2006**, *4*, 72–74. [CrossRef]
27. Tehseen, S.; Ramayah, T.; Sajilan, S. Testing and Controlling for Common Method Variance: A Review of Available Methods. *J. Manag. Sci.* **2017**, *4*, 146–175. [CrossRef]
28. Lakens, D. Calculating and reporting effect sizes to facilitate cumulative science: A practical primer for t-tests and ANOVAs. *Front. Psychol.* **2013**, *4*, 863. [CrossRef]
29. Lai, K. Estimating Standardized SEM Parameters Given Nonnormal Data and Incorrect Model: Methods and Comparison. *Struct. Equ. Model.* **2018**, *25*, 600–620. [CrossRef]
30. Hu, L.-T.; Bentler, P.M. Cutoff criteria for fit indexes in covariance structure analysis: Conventional criteria versus new alternatives. *Struct. Equ. Model. Multidiscip. J.* **1999**, *6*, 1–55. [CrossRef]
31. Tomlinson, E.R.; Yousaf, O.; Vittersø, A.D.; Jones, L. Dispositional Mindfulness and Psychological Health: A Systematic Review. *Mindfulness* **2018**, *9*, 23–43. [CrossRef]
32. Sedlmeier, P.; Loße, C.; Quasten, L.C. Psychological Effects of Meditation for Healthy Practitioners: An Update. *Mindfulness* **2018**, *9*, 371–387. [CrossRef]
33. Linton, S.J.; Kecklund, G.; Franklin, K.A.; Leissner, L.C.; Sivertsen, B.; Lindberg, E.; Svensson, A.C.; Hansson, S.O.; Sundin, Ö.; Hetta, J.; et al. The effect of the work environment on future sleep disturbances: A systematic review. *Sleep Med. Rev.* **2015**, *23*, 10–19. [CrossRef]
34. Lau, W.K.W.; Leung, M.-K.; Wing, Y.-K.; Lee, T.M.C. Potential Mechanisms of Mindfulness in Improving Sleep and Distress. *Mindfulness* **2018**, *9*, 547–555. [CrossRef]
35. Cash, M.; Whittingham, K. What Facets of Mindfulness Contribute to Psychological Well-being and Depressive, Anxious, and Stress-related Symptomatology? *Mindfulness* **2010**, *1*, 177–182. [CrossRef]
36. Shallcross, A.J. Waking up to the problem of sleep: Can mindfulness help? A review of theory and evidence for the effects of mindfulness for sleep. *Curr. Opin. Psychol.* **2019**, *13*, 37–41. [CrossRef]
37. Paul, N.A.; Stanton, S.J.; Greeson, J.M.; Smoski, M.J.; Wang, L. Psychological and neural mechanisms of trait mindfulness in reducing depression vulnerability. *Soc. Cogn. Affect. Neurosci.* **2013**, *8*, 56–64. [CrossRef]
38. Chen, F.; Bollen, K.A.; Paxton, P.; Curran, P.J.; Kirby, J.B. Improper Solutions in Structural Equation Models: Causes, Consequences, and Strategies. *Sociol. Methods Res.* **2001**, *29*, 468–508. [CrossRef]
39. Pan, H.; Liu, S.; Miao, D.; Yuan, Y. Sample Size Determination for Mediation Analysis of Longitudinal Data. *BMC Med. Res. Methodol.* **2018**, *18*, 32. [CrossRef]
40. Kline, R.B. *Principles and Practice of Structural Equation Modeling*; The Guilford Press: New York, NY, USA, 2016.
41. Cardaciotto, L.; Herbert, J.D.; Forman, E.M.; Moitra, E.; Farrow, V. The Assessment of Present-Moment Awareness and Acceptance: The Philadelphia Mindfulness Scale. *Assessment* **2008**, *15*, 204–223. [CrossRef]
42. Hadash, Y.; Bernstein, A. Behavioral assessment of mindfulness: Defining features, organizing framework, and review of emerging methods. *Curr. Opin. Psychol.* **2019**, *28*, 229–237. [CrossRef]

International Journal of
Environmental Research and Public Health

MDPI

Article

Public Perception of SARS-CoV-2 Vaccinations on Social Media: Questionnaire and Sentiment Analysis

Charlotte Roe [1], Madison Lowe [1], Benjamin Williams [2] and Clare Miller [1,*]

1 School of Life Sciences, University of Lincoln, Lincoln LN6 7TS, UK; 15568465@students.lincoln.ac.uk (C.R.); 16655259@students.lincoln.ac.uk (M.L.)
2 School of Computer Science, University of Lincoln, Lincoln LN6 7TS, UK; bWilliams@lincoln.ac.uk
* Correspondence: cmiller@lincoln.ac.uk; Tel.: +44-(0)1522-837364

Abstract: Vaccine hesitancy is an ongoing concern, presenting a major threat to global health. SARS-CoV-2 COVID-19 vaccinations are no exception as misinformation began to circulate on social media early in their development. Twitter's Application Programming Interface (API) for Python was used to collect 137,781 tweets between 1 July 2021 and 21 July 2021 using 43 search terms relating to COVID-19 vaccines. Tweets were analysed for sentiment using Microsoft Azure (a machine learning approach) and the VADER sentiment analysis model (a lexicon-based approach), where the Natural Language Processing Toolkit (NLTK) assessed whether tweets represented positive, negative or neutral opinions. The majority of tweets were found to be negative in sentiment (53,899), followed by positive (53,071) and neutral (30,811). The negative tweets displayed a higher intensity of sentiment than positive tweets. A questionnaire was distributed and analysis found that individuals with full vaccination histories were less concerned about receiving and were more likely to accept the vaccine. Overall, we determined that this sentiment-based approach is useful to establish levels of vaccine hesitancy in the general public and, alongside the questionnaire, suggests strategies to combat specific concerns and misinformation.

Keywords: SARS-CoV-2; COVID-19; vaccinations; sentiment analysis; Twitter; anti-vax; vaccine hesitancy; Python; VADER; NLTK

Citation: Roe, C.; Lowe, M.; Williams, B.; Miller, C. Public Perception of SARS-CoV-2 Vaccinations on Social Media: Questionnaire and Sentiment Analysis. *Int. J. Environ. Res. Public Health* **2021**, *18*, 13028. https://doi.org/10.3390/ijerph182413028

Academic Editors: Paolo Roma, Merylin Monaro, Cristina Mazza and Anthony R. Mawson

Received: 24 September 2021
Accepted: 7 December 2021
Published: 10 December 2021

Publisher's Note: MDPI stays neutral with regard to jurisdictional claims in published maps and institutional affiliations.

1. Introduction

1.1. Coronavirus Disease 2019 in the UK and Vaccination Uptake

Coronavirus disease 2019 (COVID-19), caused by novel severe acute respiratory Coronavirus 2 (SARS-CoV-2), was first reported in Wuhan, China in December 2019. As has already been well reported, COVID-19spread rapidly across the globe and was declared a pandemic by the World Health Organisation (WHO) in March 2020. In late January 2020, the first case was reported in the United Kingdom (UK) and by the end of March 2020, 6650 cases had been recorded in the UK and a nationwide lockdown had begun [1].

On 8 December 2020, the UK became the first country to rollout a COVID-19 vaccination programme; and by 15 August 2021, an estimated 87.1% of the adult population in the UK had received one dose of either the Oxford/AstraZeneca, Moderna or Pfizer-BioNTech vaccine and 74.9% were fully vaccinated with two doses [2]. Even before the first dose was administered, false rumours and misinformation had begun to circulate on social media, at times fuelled by the idea that emergency regulatory approval of these vaccines was linked to unreliability or safety concerns, threatening to diminish public confidence in the vaccination programme [3]. By 15 August 2021, the cumulative total of deaths in the UK where the death certificate mentioned COVID-19 as one of the causes was 157,361. The cumulative total number of doses of vaccinations administered in the UK on the same date was 88,037,283 [2].

1.2. Anti-Vaccination Movement

Since their introduction, vaccinations have revolutionised health care whilst at the same time persistently facing opposition [4,5] from hesitant individuals who perceive them as unnecessary or dangerous [6]. 'Anti-vaccinators' or 'anti-vaxxers' may reject vaccinations in the belief that they contain toxins and cause serious adverse effects [7]. More extreme conspiracy theories accuse pharmaceutical companies of producing fake vaccine data, concealing harmful vaccine side effects and exaggerating vaccine efficacy statistics [8].

Hesitancy is typically associated with a lack of trust in the health-care system [9] and unfamiliarity with vaccine-preventable diseases [10]. For example, in 1974, it was reported that an antigen in the pertussis vaccine was responsible for 36 neurological complications including convulsions and intellectual developmental disorders in previously healthy children. Despite the study concluding that these complications were extremely rare and the risks of immunisation outweighed the risks of disease [9], many parents in Britain refused to vaccinate their children against pertussis throughout the 1970s and 1980s. Between 1971 and 1974, vaccination rates dropped significantly from 78.5% to 37% [11], leading to severe strain on the NHS [12,13].

The measles, mumps, and rubella (MMR) controversy was the result of a now discredited paper linking the MMR vaccine to autism in children [8,14], which led to a reduction in MMR uptake after its publication in 1998 and the debate still rumbles on. Although MMR vaccination uptake has improved since 2004, according to the WHO, it is still under the 95% threshold to ensure herd immunity; and in 2017, an estimated 142,000 people died from measles unnecessarily [6,15,16], leading the WHO to declare vaccine hesitancy as an official threat to global health in 2019 [17] and highlighting the need for medical professionals to address vaccine safety concerns to encourage uptake.

1.3. Social Media and Vaccine Hesitancy

Web 2.0 has made discovering and sharing information online more convenient than ever with the move from passive consumption to active generation of content, leading to Health 2.0, where social media users share advice and experiences relating to health care [18]. However, despite social media being readily utilised to promote public health, and increasing numbers of people using social media to research vaccinations [17,19], health-care professionals remain a key source of vaccine information [20]. Media and celebrity opinion on social media is known to contribute to anti-vaccine beliefs [21] and the way in which research is interpreted by the media can have a profound effect on influencing public perception [22,23]. Scientists regularly challenge inaccurate information on social media and one high-profile example of this occurred in September 2021, when Professor Chris Whitty, the Chief Medical Officer for England and Chief Medical Advisor for the UK Government, was asked at a televised press conference about a tweet by rapper Nicki Minaj which claimed that her cousin's friend was rendered impotent after taking a Coronavirus vaccine which caused swelling in his testicles. Prof Whitty said that these "myths ... untrue ... designed to scare ... they should be ashamed", leading to a conversation which continued afterwards in the media, including on social media. Despite progress being made to combat false reporting of science [23], understanding reasons behind vaccine hesitation will allow insight into how these beliefs may be counteracted effectively. Analysis of tweets during a 2013 measles outbreak [24] noted users informing each other about the importance of vaccination in light of the outbreak, illustrating a positive application of social media to educate others regarding the importance of vaccines to prevent outbreaks of disease.

However, the echo-chamber effect described by Piedrahita-Valdés et al. (2021), explains how users with differing beliefs consume homogeneously polarised content regarding vaccines and form opposing groups who rarely communicate with one another positively [25]. Hence, debate regarding vaccines may have little positive outcome, as prior personal beliefs are only reinforced in this environment. Efforts by health professionals to promote vaccination through social media have not always received a positive response;

and in extreme cases, health-care professionals have been threatened after posting videos online encouraging vaccination [26].

During the UK national lockdowns in 2020 and 2021, much of the conversation regarding COVID-19 took place on social media platforms including Twitter, which has approximately 300 million monthly users [27,28]. Social media has become a common platform for individuals to voice their concern and share their thoughts with others during times of crisis [29]; but whilst these platforms allow the rapid dissemination of information, there is no guarantee that the information is correct, reliable or accurate [30] and the majority of anti-vaccination communication and conversation takes place over the internet [31]. Google search interest for the term 'vaccine' has greatly increased since March 2020, peaking in March 2021 [32].

In a July 2020 UK survey, 16% of participants stated that they would be unlikely to accept a COVID-19 vaccine [33]; and between September and October 2020, 12% and 17% of individuals were strongly hesitant or very unsure, respectively [34]. The likelihood of refusal of the COVID-19 vaccine was also found to be higher among young adults who are indifferent about COVID-19 and lack trust in scientists [33].

1.4. Sentiment Analysis and Data Mining

Natural language processing (NLP) research topics rely heavily on the use of sentiment analysis and opinion mining, where sentiment analysis is the study of opinions, feelings and attitudes towards a product, organisation or event [35–37]. Opinion—or text—mining involves extracting knowledge and information from online text, usually focusing on a certain topic and categorising it as positive, negative or neutral [38,39].

Python is a versatile computer programming language which can manage large datasets, making it ideal for use in complex projects [40–42]. It can be used to retrieve tweets that contain chosen search terms and store them via a designated database engine, such as SQLite. Valance Aware Dictionary and sEntiment Reasoner (VADER) is one of many tools found within the popular Natural Language Toolkit (NLTK), with an excess of 9000 lexicon features and the ability to analyse sentiments extracted from social media sources. It produces a gold-standard sentiment lexicon by combining quantitative and qualitative methods [43]. Sentiment lexicons contain lists with initial lexical capabilities (words) categorised to a semantic orientation (i.e., positive or negative) [38,44]. The VADER lexicon is a collection of predefined words with an associated polarity score—analysing the positive and negative aspects of text and determining overall polarity. Typically, neutral sentiments have a polarity score of 0 due to unidentifiable sentiment in the text. Negative and positive sentiments are assigned polarity scores of less than and greater than 0, respectively [45]. According to Satter et al. (2021), it is one of the easiest approaches to sentiment classification [28] with VADER based on a gold-standard sentiment lexicon with an ability to process acronyms and slang words [46], making it highly sensitive to sentiment expressions when applied to social media contexts. Hutto and Gilbert (2014) determined that VADER analysis performed better in comparison to eleven other highly regarded sentiment models and interestingly the accuracy of VADER has been determined to outperform individual human analysers at correctly classifying the sentiment of tweets [47]. In the majority of machine learning approaches to sentiment classification, for example, Microsoft Azure's Text Analytics suite, a labelled dataset is required, whereby the polarity of text is predefined. Whilst Azure's graphical interface can be utilised by individuals with little to no formal computer programming experience, making it an ideal software to use for novices, VADER, on the other hand, requires domain-specific knowledge of computing to use.

1.5. Sentiment Analysis of Vaccine Hesitance

Vaccine hesitancy is a fluid and ever-changing phenomenon [47]. Previous studies have typically focused on vaccine hesitance in general rather than being directed at specific vaccines and have revealed different trends across time [25,48]. Rahim et al. (2020) analysed approximately 100,000 tweets about vaccinations between October 2019 and March 2020 and determined that the majority (41%) were positive in sentiment, closely followed by neutral sentiment (39%) and 20% were negative [48]. COVID-19-specific vaccine hesitancy has also been investigated: in May 2020, vaccine hesitancy rates were low (20–25%) in American and Canadian adults [49], whereas, in Italy, the rates of COVID-19 vaccine hesitancy were 41% [50] and 26% in France [51].

1.6. Research Involving Questionnaires

Before the explosion of online sentiment mining, researchers solely used qualitative data collection methods in the form of surveys and particularly questionnaires [52]. Online questionnaires have many advantages, including increased collection of data, decreased cost and time to collect data and readily exportable formats for analytical simplicity [53,54]. To establish trends, attitudes and patterns, questionnaires are usually incorporated into mixed-method research and often yield information that computer-based programs may not identify. For example, questionnaires can extract demographic information and include questions exploring the reasoning behind opinions [54].

1.7. Aims and Objectives

The overall aim of this study was to determine the sentiment of public opinion regarding COVID-19 vaccinations. This was carried out via sentiment analysis of English language tweets on Twitter and followed up with a questionnaire which was distributed from the UK. The goal of the questionnaire was to explore attitudes to the expression of any particular sentiment, rather than to find any specific correlation between the two. Specifically, we aimed to determine the following:

1. Whether negative opinion regarding COVID-19 vaccines exists on Twitter.
2. Whether lexicon-based (PYTHON/VADER) and machine learning (Microsoft Azure) approaches to sentiment classification yield different sentiment results.
3. Whether low levels of concern about COVID-19 vaccines lead to high acceptance of the vaccine.
4. Whether public opinion towards COVID-19 vaccinations becomes more positive over time.

2. Materials and Methods

2.1. Data Collection

In order to share information on Twitter as widely as possible, Twitter provides broad access to public Twitter data via their own Application Programming Interface (API). In this study, Twitter's official API was used to collect tweets in real time between 1 July 2021 and 21 July 2021. The language filter arguments "EN" and "RT" were applied to only select English tweets and filter out re-tweets. Tweet scraping was conducted using 43 search terms relating to COVID-19 vaccinations (Table 1) on Twitter's asymmetric cryptography (OAuth2) process and saved into an SQLite database. Following a small pilot study to establish which key words would be most useful to investigate, key words were selected based on the COVID-19 vaccines available in the UK at the time of data collection and also to avoid collecting a large number of tweets that would have discussed vaccines in general rather than being specifically related to COVID.

A total of 137,781 tweets were collected and stored in a database. Data collected included the user's display name, twitter handle, tweet text and date/time the tweet was published.

Table 1. Text mining parameter details.

Parameters	Details
Search terms	Vaccineforall, Vaccine, Antivaccine, Vaccinationcovid, Covid19, AstraZeneca, Astrazenecavaccine, Pfizer, Pfizervaccine, UKvaccinerollout, Covidvaccine, Covidvaccination, Covid19vaccine, Covid19vaccination, Modernavaccine, Oxfordvaccine, UKvaccine, AZvaccine, vaccinesideeffects, Antivax, Antivaxxer, Antivaxxers, OxfordAZvaccine, Moderna, Modernasideffects, Astrazenecasideffects, Pfizersideffects, Oxfordsideffects, seconddose, firstdose, Vaccineconspiracy, UKfightscorona, Covid19UK, Covidenier, vaccinehesitancy, AZvax, modernavax, anti-vaccination, anti-vax, anti-vaxxers, pro-vax, covid19jab

2.2. Sentiment Data Analysis—Machine Learning Approach (MLP)

Primary sentiment analysis was conducted on the dataset using Azure on Microsoft Excel. The software yielded the results as 'positive', 'negative' or 'neutral' and scored the confidence of the analysis, with a score of 1 being most confident with the analysis and 0 being least confident.

2.3. Sentiment Data Analysis—Lexicon-Based Approach

A Python-based API for Twitter was used to collect live tweets, which were recorded into a relational database using SQLite. Sentiment analysis was performed post-collection using the VADER algorithm, as part of the NLTK Python package. It is worth noting that Python version 3.9.0 was used throughout this process. Custom-made software built with Python 3.9.0 was used to perform the word frequency analysis. NLTK was used in the pre-processing of tweets—to remove stop words—prior to the word frequency analysis.

The provided sentiment compound—or sentiment score—calculated from the sum of lexicon ratings, was normalised between −1 (extreme negative) and +1 (extreme positive). This technique determined the polarity—or positivity and negativity—and the intensity of the expressed emotion. The intensity of emotion of each tweet is divided into the quantity of positive, negative and neutral elements the tweet contained—adding to a total value of 1. Each tweet was classified as positive, negative or neutral according to its compound score. Compound scores less than 0.05 were considered negative, scores between −0.05 and 0.05 were considered neutral and scores above 0.05 were classified as positive [41,55].

2.4. Statistical Analysis

Descriptive statistics analysed differences between the program outputs and to test for significance between approaches, sentiment frequency, and sentiment against time. Questionnaire results were analysed on JISC (www.jisc.ac.uk, (accessed on 12 August 2021)) [56] automatically. Chi-square tests, two-way ANOVA and descriptive statistics were performed on Microsoft Excel and Statistics Kingdom (www.Statskingdom.com, (accessed on 14 August 2021)) [57] and Welch's and two-sample *t*-tests were performed using Python 3.9.0 and MATLAB.

2.5. Questionnaire

Using the JISC software to design, distribute and record the results, the questionnaire (Table A1)—composed of 22 questions—was distributed to anonymous adult participants (n = 182). The questionnaire was designed to investigate attitudes towards COVID-19 disease and COVID-19 vaccinations with the aim to determine personal knowledge and opinion of vaccinations as well as identifying factors that may influence vaccine hesitancy. Demographic data including age (18–29, 30–39, 40–49, 50–59, 60–69, and 70+) and parenthood status were recorded by the respondents. Questions including whether participants have previously received vaccinations for themselves or their children and whether they have accepted or will accept a COVID-19 vaccination were posed. Free-text opportunities to elaborate on the reasons for declining vaccinations for themselves or their children were provided. The participants were also asked agree/disagree-style questions relating to COVID-19 vaccinations and their general knowledge surrounding vaccinations. The questionnaire was distributed via email and social media platforms including Twitter and Facebook. Incomplete responses were excluded from this study.

3. Results

3.1. Python Sentiment Analysis

3.1.1. Tweet Sentiment Scores

The VADER algorithm is the gold standard used among sentiment researchers [47]. Due to its wider term coverage [58], quick application [41] and high classification accuracy [59], we opted to use the results from this approach for the rest of this study. Between 1 July 2021 and 21 July 2021, Python scraped a total of 137,781 tweets relating to the chosen search terms. The compound scores were plotted against time (Figure 1). There was no obvious trend from the graphical representation, and therefore sentiment groups were investigated individually.

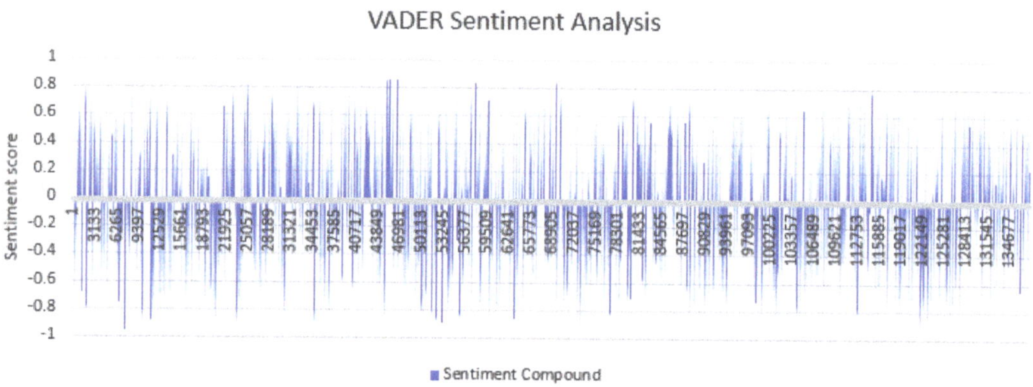

Figure 1. VADER sentiment scores for each tweet. Values greater than 0.05 are displayed as positive, values between −0.05 and 0.05 are neutral and values less than 0.05 are negative tweets. The lengths of the peaks represent the intensity of negativity or positivity. Values represent the tweet number. The horizontal axis shows the tweets in order, ranging from 1 July 2021 (**left** of graph) to 21 July 2021 (**right** of graph).

3.1.2. Word Frequency

The word count (Figure 2) shows the most frequently identified term was clearly '#covid19' with other terms such as 'people', 'get' and 'vaccine' also frequently used. There was no mention of specific groups such as 'children' or 'parents', only the collective term 'people'.

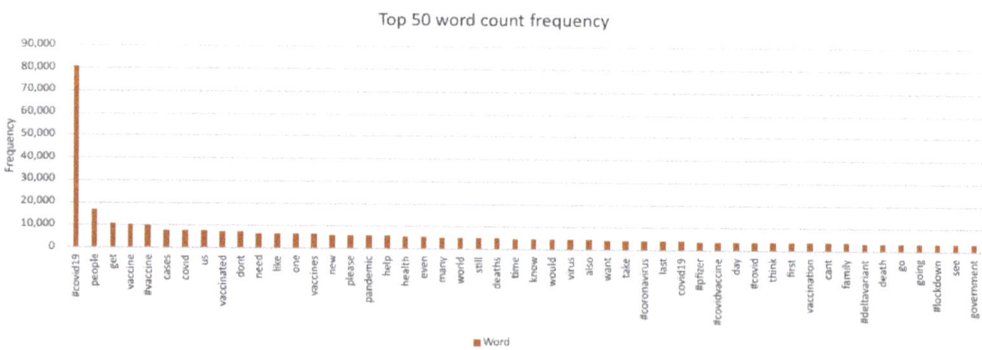

Figure 2. Top 50 frequently recurring words.

A word cloud (Figure 3a) displays the most frequently used words in size descending order. The larger-sized words depict a higher frequency of the word. To further understand the relationship between words and their frequency, analysis into the most prevalent words was conducted from the separate positive, negative and neutral groups.

In the positive category (Figure 3b), the most commonly recurring words were '#covid19' (29,661), 'people' (5313) and 'please' (4455). In the neutral category (Figure 3c), the most commonly used words were '#covid19' (14,399), 'people' (2469) and '#vaccine' (2322). In the negative category (Figure 3d), the most commonly used words were '#covid19' (31,725), 'people' (7925) and 'get' (4282). Noticeable words in this category include 'don't', 'get', 'vaccinated' and 'death', which could suggest that users are advising others not to receive the vaccinations.

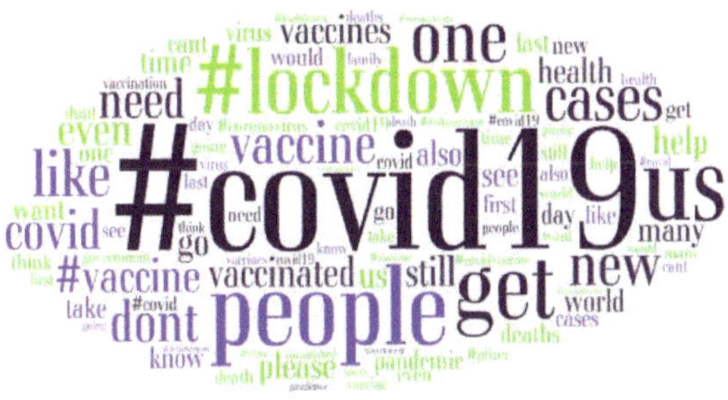

(a)

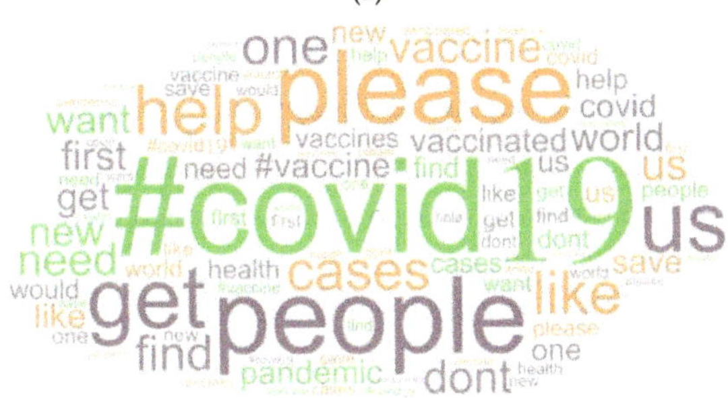

(b)

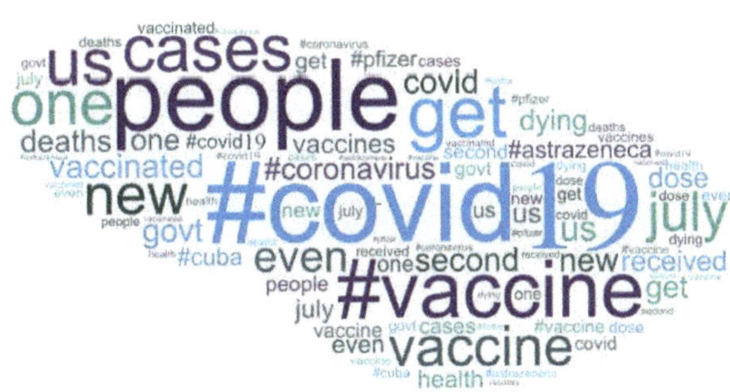

(c)

Figure 3. *Cont.*

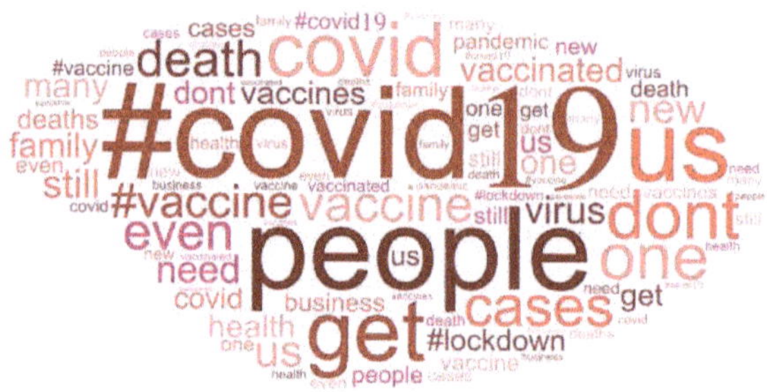

(d)

Figure 3. (**a**) Word cloud of the top fifty repeated words (https://wordart.com/, (accessed on 15 August 2021)); (**b**) word cloud of the top twenty-five most repeated words in the positive category; (**c**) word cloud of the top twenty-five most repeated words in the neutral category; (**d**). word cloud of the top twenty-five most repeated words in the negative category.

The frequency and percentage (Table 2) of the sentiment of tweets in each week were determined to establish whether there was a trend across time between the groups.

Table 2. Frequency and percentages of tweets collected for each week.

Week	Negative Tweets		Positive Tweets		Neutral Tweets		Total Frequency
	Frequency	Percentage (%)	Frequency	Percentage (%)	Frequency	Percentage (%)	
1	13,900	37.9	14,305	39.0	8398	22.9	36,603
2	19,691	39.0	19,394	38.4	11,352	22.5	50,437
3	20,308	40.0	19,372	38.1	11,061	21.7	50,741
Total	53,899		53,071		30,811		

During week 1, positive tweets were the most frequent (14,305; 39.0%) compared to negative (13,900; 37.9%) and neutral (8398; 22.9%). By week 2 and week 3, negative tweets (19,691; 39.0% and 20,308; 40.0%, respectively) were most frequent compared to positive (19,394; 38.4% and 19,372; 38.1%) and neutral (11,352; 22.5% and 11,061; 21.7%) (Table 2, Figure 4).

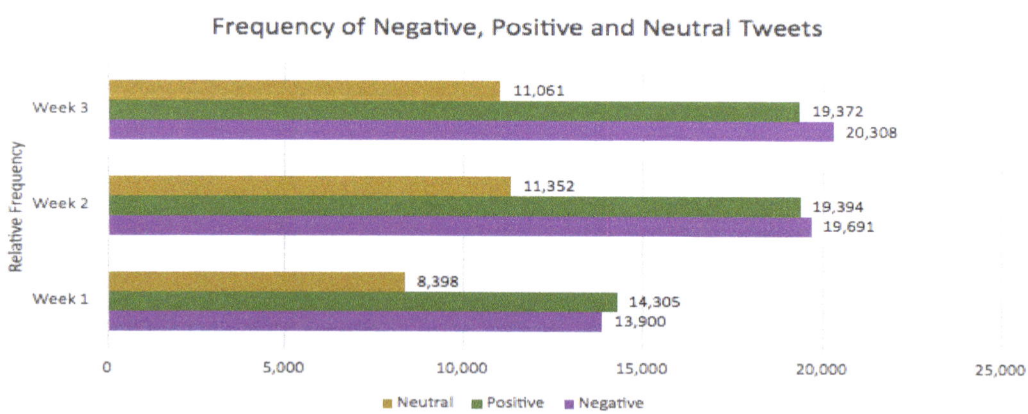

Figure 4. Frequency of negative, positive and neutral tweets over a 3 week period. The frequency of all sentiment groups increased in week 2 compared to week 1. The frequency of negative tweets continued to increase into week 3, whereas positive and neutral tweets slightly decreased.

To determine whether there was a significant difference between the frequency of positive, negative and neutral scores, mean values were established for each week of data collection (Figure 5).

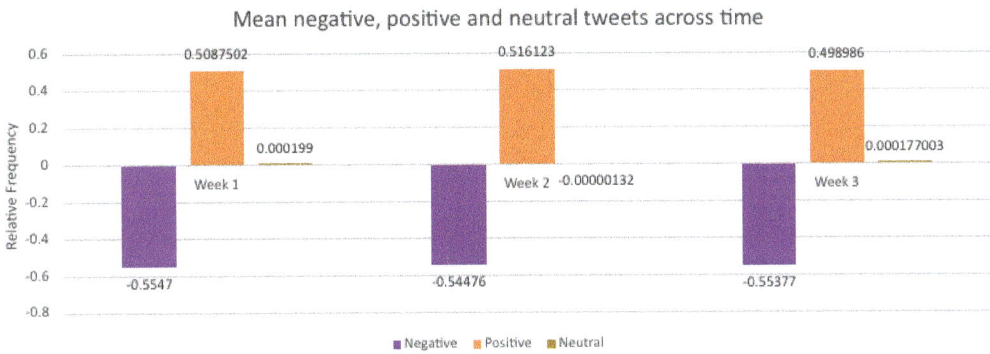

Figure 5. Average values of negative, positive and neutral scores displayed over time. During week 2, the mean values for neutral tweets are lower (>−0.01) than the previous and following week.

A two-sample *t*-test with equal standard deviation was performed between the first and final week of each sentiment group to investigate difference over time. The positive average (0.508; SD = 0.511) during week 1 was found to be equal to the positive average in week 3 (0.498; $p = 0.110$). The Test statistic ($t = 1.597$) was found in the 95% critical value accepted range. The negative average (−0.554; SD = 0.511) values during week 1 were found to be equal to the negative average in week 3 (−0.553; $p = 0.858$). The Test statistic ($t = -0.177$) was in the 95% critical value accepted range. The neutral average (0.00019; SD = 0.511) values during week 1 were found to be equal to the negative average in week 3 (0.00017; $p = 0.997$). The Test statistic ($t = 0.003$) was in the 95% critical value accepted range.

3.1.3. Intensity of Sentiment

Week 1 (−0.345, 0.508, 0.00019) and week 3 (−0.358, 0.499, 0.00017) displayed similar trends of negative, positive and neutral tweets, respectively (Figure 5). During week 2, neutral tweets displayed more negativity than positivity (−1.322).

The means of tweets were subjected to a two-way ANOVA (Table 3). The difference between weeks is not statistically significant ($p = 0.1951$), which is indicative of no significant change in mean values between weeks. The difference between averages of the sentiment results (i.e., negative mean value against positive mean value against neutral mean value) is statistically significant ($p < 0.0001$).

Table 3. Descriptive statistics of two-way ANOVA of the mean values of sentiment groups.

Source	DF	Sum of Square (SS)	Mean Square (MS)	F Statistic ($df_1 df_2$)	*p*-Value
Week	2	0.0001162	0.00005809	2.528 (2,4)	0.1951
Sentiment Groups	2	1.6833	0.8416	36,625.9271 (2,4)	<0.001
Error	4	0.00009192	0.00002298		
Total	8	1.6835	0.2104		

Negative tweets had a higher mean value (0.52706) than positive (0.48196) and neutral (0.50119) tweets (Table 4). To compare the means between the groups, Welch's *t*-test (two-sample *t*-test) was performed (due to unequal variance and differing *n*) using MATLAB. Firstly, the values were normalised by mapping to the range of 0–1, where 0 is the "least" and 1 is the "most", i.e., negative tweets were mapped from [−1, −0.05] to [0, 1], where 0 is least negative (−0.05) and 1 is most negative (−1). This was achieved using an inverse interpolation function (t−a)/(b−a), where t is the value, a is the lower bound and b is the upper bound.

Table 4. Descriptive statistics of collected data, post-normalisation.

Category	n [1]	Mean	Std. dev [2]
Positive	53,071	0.48196	0.246031
Negative	53,899	0.52706	0.258930
Neutral	30,812	0.50119	0.066879

[1] Sample size; [2] standard deviation.

Welch's *t*-test demonstrated that positive vs. negative ($p < 0.001$), positive vs. neutral ($p < 0.001$) and negative vs. neutral ($p < 0.001$) groups show statistical significance between the means. This suggests that sentiment across our dataset displays a larger intensity of negative sentiment compared to positive or neutral., i.e., the negative tweets are "more" negative than the positivity in positive tweets.

3.2. *Machine Learning vs. Lexicon Based: A Comparison of Negative, Positive and Neutral Tweets*

The Natural Language Toolkit (or NLTK) (https://www.nltk.org/, (accessed on 21 July 2021)) [60] was used for the VADER sentiment analysis and scored 53,899 tweets as negative, 53,071 as positive and 30,811 as neutral, whereas Azure determined the frequency of the categories as 67,538, 45,282 and 24,961, respectively. They reveal similar trends whereby most tweets were negative, followed by positive and neutral tweets being least prevalent (Table 5).

Table 5. Comparison between Python-based VADER and Microsoft Azure sentiment analysis approaches.

Parameters	VADER	Azure
Positive	53,071	45,282
Negative	53,899	67,538
Neutral	30,811	24,961
Median	0	0.459178
Mean	−0.01978	0.445796
Variance	0.262321	0.071255
Skewness	−0.04129	0.00218
SD [1]	0.512173	0.266937
Total	137,781	137,781

[1] Standard deviation.

The lexicon-based (VADER) and machine learning (Microsoft Azure) approaches to classify sentiment were compared (Table 5, Figure 6). A total of 39.11% of tweets were scored as negative by VADER and 49.01% were scored as negative by Azure. The percentage of tweets scored by VADER and Azure as positive were 38.51% and 32.86%, respectively. A total of 22.36% and 18.11% were considered neutral.

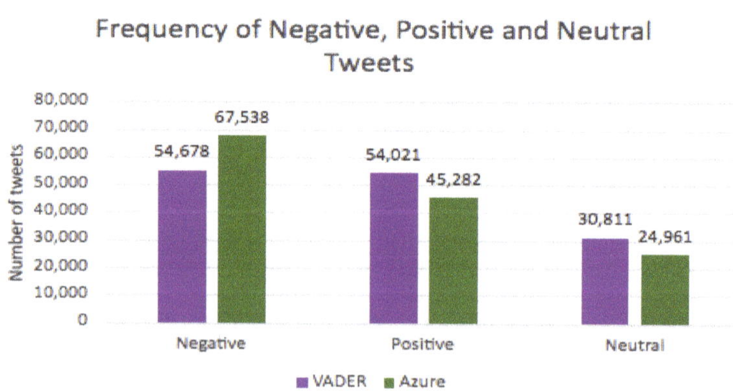

Figure 6. Total number of negative, positive and neutral tweets as determined by Microsoft Azure and VADER.

3.3. Questionnaire

The questionnaire collected a total of 188 responses. A total of 6 responses were excluded due to the participants not meeting the requirements for this study or not agreeing to their data being shared and so we used the complete 182 responses in the analysis (Table A1).

A total of 31.9% of participants were between 18 and 29 years (the largest age group of participants), with 90.1% stating they had previously searched for information regarding COVID-19 online (e.g., Google). The most common length of time spent on social media was recorded as 'daily' (64.3%). Most of the participants (85.7%) had previously accepted all vaccines they had been offered), 73.8% were not concerned about receiving a COVID-19 vaccination, 17.1% were slightly concerned, 4.3% were very concerned and 4.3% stated that they were impartial.

We asked whether participants had accepted—or will accept—a COVID-19 vaccine. Of the 182 participants, 8.2% have not/will not accept the vaccine, 1.6% said they did not know, and the majority (90.1%) stated that they had already or would accept a vaccine. The most likely reason (40.2%) for accepting a COVID-19 vaccine was 'I want the world to go back to how it used to be before the COVID-19 pandemic', whereas the most common reason for not accepting the COVID-19 vaccine was 'I have done my own research and do not believe them to be safe' (52.9%).

In response to whether the participants would allow their child under the age of 18 to have a COVID-19 vaccination if they were offered them in the future, 26.8% would not vaccinate and 5.4% probably would not vaccinate their children against COVID-19. A total of 17.9% were unsure whether they would vaccinate their children, 8.9% probably would and 41.1% said yes, they would vaccinate their children. Participants with adult children (18 or older) or without children automatically skipped this question. We compared level of concern to vaccination acceptance or rejection (Figure 7). Out of 52 participants showing some level of concern, 15 of these participants rejected the vaccine.

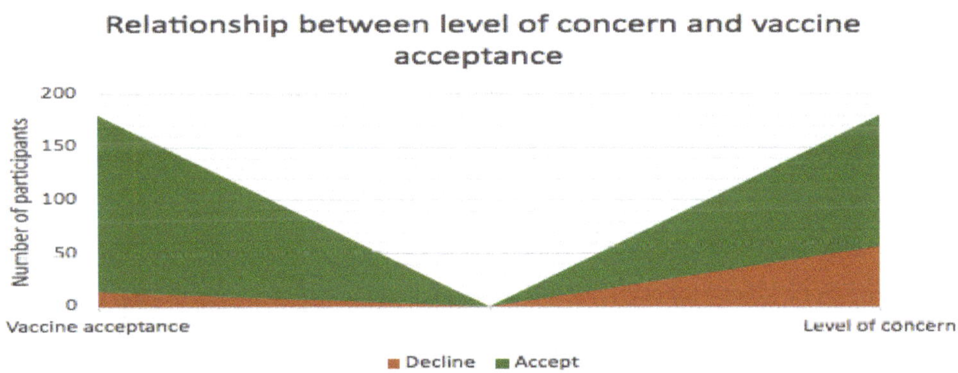

Figure 7. The relationship between level of concern and acceptance and rejection of a COVID-19 vaccine.

We asked how the participants would consider their current depth of knowledge regarding vaccinations generally. Knowledge scores ranged from 0 (no knowledge) to 5 (deep/thorough knowledge). Overall, 2.2% stated that they had no understanding, 74.2% felt they had some understanding, and 23.6% had a deep understanding.

Several chi-square tests (significance level, alpha, of 0.05) were performed to determine whether there was an association between certain vaccine refusal prediction factors (Table 6). The results show that the uptake of COVID-19 vaccines was dependent on previous vaccine history ($p < 0.001$) and an individuals' level of concern ($p < 0.001$). However, vaccination understanding ($p = 0.949491$), age ($p = 0.057899$) and time spent on social media ($p = 0.925771$) did not influence the acceptance of COVID-19 vaccinations. Chi-square analysis was also performed between responses of the statement 'Vaccine safety and effectiveness data are often false' and intensity of concern and found a significant relationship ($p < 0.001$) (Table 6). The majority of respondents who were not concerned about receiving a COVID-19 vaccine 'strongly disagreed' with the statement (52.89%), whereas those who were most concerned stated that they 'don't know' (42.86%).

Table 6. Chi-square statistical analysis to determine a dependent association between accepting a COVID-19 and the variables in the table. Vaccine safety (far right column) was analysed against how concerned the participant was.

Parameters	Vaccine Knowledge	Age	Time on Social Media	Vaccine History	Level of Concern	Vaccine Safety
Chi-Square (Observed value)	2.14521	14.25356	3.421087	56.18451	116.8076	54.87902
Chi-Square (Critical value)	9.487729	18.30704	15.50731	9.487729	12.59159	9.487729
DF	6	10	8	4	6	15
p-value	0.905871	0.161737	0.905227	<0.001	<0.001	<0.001

4. Discussion

4.1. Machine Learning vs. Lexicon-Based Approaches

Sentiment analysis research has become popular over the past two decades [40,61,62]; as more efficient sentiment classification models are devised [63] and studies have compared automated analysis of conversations on social media with manual approaches [64].

Prior studies have compared machine learning methods of text analysis (i.e., SVM) with lexicon-based approaches [28,65,66] and often conclude the machine learning methods are more effective. For example, Sattar et al. (2021) concluded that VADER was less accurate than machine learning applications and used TextBlob in their study [28]. However, Dhaoui et al. (2015) determined that both approaches performed similarly when analysing Facebook reviews for both positive and negative classification [67]. Much of the literature on this is contradictory and highlights the need for continued research in this area of comparing the accuracy and precision of the machine and lexicon methods. For example, Nguyen et al. (2018) stated that SVM displayed 89% accuracy and 90% precision in comparison to VADER (83% and 90%, respectively) [68], whereas in a different study, SVM's accuracy and precision were different (71.8% and 66.8% and, respectively) as were that of lexicon-based approaches (71.1% and 65.1% and, respectively) [69]. Despite much of the literature claiming the inferiority of lexicon-based approaches, our research required classification of how positive and negative online sentiment was: one advantage of the VADER model [41].

In other studies, Microsoft Azure has been found to yield better results when compared to other analyser tools such as Stanford NLP [64], IBM Watson Natural Language Understanding, OpinionFinder 2.0 and Sentistrength [70]. However, as Azure only identifies polarity, it is a less accurate method of measuring an individual's opinion towards a topic compared to other approaches such as VADER [71] and so part of this study compared the sentiment analysis approaches of Microsoft Azure and VADER.

Previous studies have explored sentiment surrounding COVID-19 vaccinations on Twitter [72,73]. Xue et al. (2020) used Latent Dirichlet Allocation (LDA)—a machine learning approach—and collected four million tweets on COVID-19 using 25 search words. Their aim was to identify popular themes, sentiment, bigrams and unigrams. The NRC Emotion Lexicon classified sentiments into several emotions including anger, fear, surprise, sadness, disgust, joy, trust and anticipation and revealed that Twitter users display 'fear' when discussing new cases of COVID-19, as opposed to 'trust' [74]. Bhagat et al. (2020) used TextBlob to perform sentiment analysis and scraped 154 articles from blogging and news websites. Over 90% of the articles were positive and blogs were found to be more positive than newspaper articles [75]. Sattar et al. (2021) adopted a similar approach to the present study, analysing COVID-19 vaccine sentiment using a large number of tweets ($n = \sim 1.2$ million) using a lexicon-based classifier, namely VADER and TextBlob. They also defined their neutral sentiments between -0.05 and 0.05 and determined that public sentiment was more positive than negative.

4.2. Word Identification and Word Frequency

The results confirm that negativity towards the COVID-19 vaccines is present on Twitter alongside tweets that are positive and neutral in sentiment. Similar studies corroborate these results [10,49,76], with suggestions that development speed and safety concerns are some of the reasons why hesitancy is expressed [77]. Chandrasekaran et al. examined the trends of sentiment of several topics associated with COVID-19 between January 2020 and May 2020 and found that although Twitter users expressed negativity about the spread and symptoms of COVID-19, they determined that positive feelings were expressed when sharing information on drugs and new therapies [55]. In the present study, the commonly used term 'people' suggests that concerns do not specifically relate to children, elderly or any other specific group. Although the hashtag '#covid19' was the most frequently occurring word in all three sentiment groups, analysis found that a higher number of negative tweets contained the hashtag (31,725) in comparison to positive (29,661) and neutral (14,399) tweets.

A study on the sentiment surrounding human papillomavirus vaccines found different keywords associated within their word clusters. The authors suggested that 'HPV' was associated with personal words including 'I' and 'me' and '#HPV' was associated with words such as 'learn' and 'prevent'. The authors considered these 'awareness-raising words' [78]. Our findings show similar results; 'people', 'don't', 'health', 'vaccines', and 'death' were noticeable in the negative groups. This could also be indicative of concerns about the risks of accepting the vaccine [79]. Words including 'people', 'please', 'help' 'vaccine' 'first' and 'need' were found to be frequently occurring in the positive group. These terms suggest that discourse leans towards promotion and encouragement of vaccinating, with similar key words found in previous studies [79]. The only similarities of the word frequencies performed by Sattar et al. (2021) and this study were 'death' and 'people' in the negative category, 'vaccine' in the positive category and 'help' and 'first' in both the positive and neutral categories. They also identified words that were not found in our study including 'party,' 'happy' and 'thank' [28].

Previous research suggests that social media users tend to interact with others who share common beliefs and ignore or argue with individuals who have opposite views [80,81], creating an echo chamber. Due to this, it has been suggested that public health interventions could reinforce vaccine hesitancy [81–83] and identifying keywords or hashtags that hesitant individuals commonly use would be a more effective strategy [84] to countering the problem. This study has identified several keywords and hashtags to assist in this process.

4.3. Relative Frequency of Tweets

We observed the frequency and relative frequency of tweets in each week of this study. Despite most of the tweets in the dataset being negative, positive tweets (14,305; 39.0%) were the most predominant during the first week of data collection between 1 July 2021 and 7 July 2021 whereas, in the final two weeks, between 8 July 2021 and 21 July 2021, negative tweets (19,691; 39.0% and 20,308; 40%) were most common. Neutral tweets were significantly lower than both negative and positive tweets throughout the entire time of collection (22.9%, 22.5% and 21.7%). Piedrahita-Valdes et al. (2021) performed sentiment analysis on vaccine-hesitant tweets between June 2011 and April 2019 and found neutral tweets were predominant throughout the study, in contrast to the present study. They also found that negative tweets peaked at times and noted that at least one of these peaks coincided with a documentary linking autism to vaccines. Similarly, they identified positive-related peaks occurring in April which coincided with World Immunisation week [25]. Furthermore, a noticeable increase in anti-vaccine discourse was experienced on Twitter in 2015, coinciding with a measles outbreak (2014–2015), a newly released film "Vaxxed" and the publication of the book "Vaccine Whistleblower" [17], supporting the idea that conversations relating to vaccine hesitancy fluctuate over time.

The mean of neutral tweets displayed a negative sentiment compound (−0.00000132) during week 2 of the investigation, whereas, in weeks 1 and 3, neutral tweets were positive

(0.000199 and 0.000177, respectively). This is suggestive of concurrent events that the general public are exposed to [17] such as case numbers, the reporting of daily hospitalisation and death figures, the pace of the UK vaccination programme and the expansion of testing capability in addition to wider political factors including legislated social distancing, lockdowns, working from home mandates and face mask wearing. For example, on 5 July 2021 plans to remove the mandated wearing of facemasks from 19 July 2021 were announced in England. This announcement could have been a key factor in the high positive sentiment we detected in this study in week 1. By 7 July 2021, however, the UK's weekly COVID-19 cases had doubled in comparison to the week prior; and between 8 and 14 July (corresponding to week 2 in this study), cases continued to rise in the UK, with over 50,000 new cases reported on 17 July 2021 [85]. As these events unfolded, 1200 scientists formally challenged the easing of lockdown restrictions in England [86], a discussion that is likely to have added to the negative sentiment at the time. Public opinion remained polarised and by week 3 of our study, we found the highest frequency of tweets which reflected negative sentiment at the same time as the number of tweets that were positive in sentiment increased from week 2 (38.4%) to week 3 (47.6%). Whilst previous research has identified vaccine hesitancy fluctuating over time [17], it would be interesting to compare the dates of specific announcements and wider discussions with daily sentiment analysis to determine whether there is a relationship between the two.

4.4. *Questionnaire: Vaccine Hesitancy towards COVID-19 Vaccinations*

Our study is the only one to date to incorporate a questionnaire alongside the exploration of sentiment analysis on Twitter towards COVID-19 vaccinations. Most respondents (90.1%) had or would accept a COVID-19 vaccine, a view that is in line with conclusions drawn by other studies [87,88] whilst others have reported less public support for COVID-19 vaccinations [89].

The identification of factors that might predict hesitancy towards COVID-19 vaccines was investigated. A positive correlation between intensity of concern regarding vaccines and their uptake was established, suggesting that participants with higher levels of (or more intense) concern are less likely to accept the vaccine, whereas those with low levels (less intense) or no concern are more likely to accept the COVID-19 vaccine.

Additional predictors of vaccine hesitancy were explored by considering whether age, vaccine history, level of vaccine understanding and usage of social media were likely to influence an individual's decision to take a COVID-19 vaccination. No association was established between vaccine refusal and age, despite the Pew Research Group (2017) finding younger adults (<30 years) were less likely to consider beneficial aspects of the MMR vaccine outweighed the risks, compared to older age groups [90]. The same study found individuals with higher levels of understanding considered the risk of vaccine side effects as low, whereas there was no association found between vaccination understanding and vaccination uptake in our study. Survey research on COVID-19 vaccine hesitancy corroborated our results by also finding no association between age and vaccine refusal [91] although Bendau et al. (2021) did establish an association between vaccine hesitance and concern [92]. Interestingly, 17.2% of respondents in the present study somewhat or strongly agreed that "vaccine safety and effectiveness data are often false", suggesting a significant proportion of the general public have concerns trusting this information as evidenced previously [9]. Anecdotal evidence from the questionnaire suggests that participants are more likely to write negative comments. This view is supported by the literature where it is understood that negative emotions (such as anger, frustration, sadness and disappointment) motivate individuals to articulate their views [93,94].

Reports suggest that the acceptance of vaccines in emergency situations (such as a pandemic) differs to that of routinely administered vaccines in non-crisis situations [87]. However, contrastingly, public concerns surrounding safety are higher with the uncertainties that come with novel vaccines and new emerging infectious diseases [87,95–97]. For example, in the UK, France, Greece, America and Australia, only 17% to 67% of the general public was willing to accept the vaccine for the H1N1 pandemic in 2009 [95–102], highlighting public concern in this area and also likely variable uptake figures. Chaudhri et al. (2021) established the public had a weakly positive sentiment towards receiving a COVID-19 vaccine [73]. Vaccination history has previously been identified as a major predictor of vaccine uptake [95,98,101,103], a view also identified in the present study which established an association between vaccine history and acceptance. Individuals with full previous vaccination history were more likely to accept a COVID-19 vaccine, further confirming the idea of the echo chamber effect.

The present study has confirmed the idea that vaccine compliance remains inconsistent with negative opinions and hesitancy still widespread [91,92] and the inclusion of a questionnaire provided a greater picture of overall sentiment towards vaccines. The questionnaire revealed generally positive sentiment, whereas more negative sentiment was found online, alongside positive and neutral views. The questionnaire revealed that concerns about vaccines typically centred around trust in safety and effectiveness.

4.5. Limitations and Further Work

As part of the pilot work for the present study, we manually categorised the sources (Twitter accounts) as 'personal', 'accredited medical', 'news' or 'government/public health'. It would have been helpful if we could have extended this into the main study to facilitate a better understanding of the most common sources of misinformation. However, with the large dataset in the main study, this was unrealistic, and we seek an automated approach to this for future studies.

The data were collected over a short period in July 2021 and so it would be interesting to extend this study to look at historical and future tweets to further understand whether public opinion regarding COVID-19 vaccinations changed during the course of the pandemic. It would also be interesting to compare the dates of specific events in the media with daily sentiment analysis to determine whether they are closely related.

The questionnaire was distributed via social media and so responses were limited to people with access and were typically in the authors' extended networks. Future studies should endeavour to distribute the questionnaire more widely and in particular to reach public without access to social media. Concern exists in the UK that certain groups are more susceptible to vaccine misinformation and we would like to reach those communities with future research. This is also the case with the sentiment analysis which only collected tweets in English and therefore had the potential to miss the view of non-English speaking groups in the UK.

A simplified interface would benefit this research as the low accuracy of Microsoft Azure and the complexity of using data mining and analysis tools such as Python requires specific computing expertise. Thus, a simplified graphical interface is in development that would benefit future projects seeking to collect datasets for analysis without a need for an understanding of Python or the VADER algorithm.

Sentiment analysis is a popular and rapidly developing area. An interesting avenue for further research would be to compare our approach using VADER to other language-encoder-based approaches (such as using Bert or GPT), in particular exploring whether these could be useful developments that would work with NLTK.

5. Conclusions

This study established that machine learning and lexicon-based sentiment analysis methods yielded different frequencies of sentiment results. Negative sentiment was found to be most frequent online, with a higher intensity of negativity within the neutral tweets. There was no significant change in sentiment towards COVID-19 across the three-week data collection period. Positive correlations were established between COVID-19 vaccine acceptance with full vaccination history and low levels of concern.

Sentiment analysis provides evidence to assess public perception about various topics [104], allowing officials in charge of managing the impact of COVID-19 and health policy makers insight into how the public feel about vaccination safety and efficacy so they can identify areas and misconceptions that need to be addressed [93,94].

The identification of frequently occurring negative terms and of predictors that influence vaccine hesitancy can be utilised to deploy effective strategies such as educational campaigns to increase public confidence in the COVID-19 vaccines and improve vaccine uptake. To ensure vaccination uptake targets are met, this requires continued attention.

Author Contributions: Conceptualisation, C.M., M.L. and C.R.; methodology, C.M., M.L., C.R. and B.W.; analysis, C.M., C.R. and B.W.; writing—original draft preparation, M.L. and C.R.; writing—review and editing, C.M., C.R. and B.W.; supervision, C.M. All authors have read and agreed to the published version of the manuscript.

Funding: This research received no external funding.

Institutional Review Board Statement: The study was conducted according to the guidelines of the Declaration of Helsinki, and approved by the Institutional Review Board (or Ethics Committee) of the School of Life Sciences, University of Lincoln. Reference: BGY9013M15568465, 17 June 2021.

Informed Consent Statement: Informed consent was obtained from all subjects involved in the study.

Data Availability Statement: Data available on request due to ethical restrictions. The data presented in this study are available on request from the corresponding author. The data are not publicly available due to conditions of ethical approval.

Acknowledgments: The authors would like to thank Jonathan Roe and Jamie Smith.

Conflicts of Interest: The authors declare no conflict of interest.

Appendix A

Table A1. Summary of the raw data from participants' answers ($n = 182$). Due to the different nature of written response options to certain questions, these have been distinguished with quotation marks.

	Question	Responses (%)					
1	What is your age?	18–29 (31.9)	30–39 (17.6)	40–49 (12.1)	50–59 (20.9)	60–69 (13.2)	70+ (4.4)
2	Have you used a search engine (e.g., Google) since January 2020 to search for information about Coronavirus or COVID-19?	Yes (90.1)		No (9.4)		Don't know (0.6)	
3	How often do you use social media (e.g., Twitter, Instagram, Facebook and Snapchat)	Never (2.7)	Rarely (2.2)	Monthly (0.0)	Weekly (3.8)	Daily (64.3)	More frequently than daily (26.9)
4	Do you believe that information on social media is reliable?	Always reliable (1.1)	Sometimes reliable (70.9)	Rarely reliable (24.2)	Never reliable (2.7)	Don't know (1.1)	
5	Have you ever tested positive for COVID-19?	Yes (7.7)		No (92.3)		Don't know (0.0)	
6	As far as you are aware, have you accepted all of the vaccinations you have been invited to (excluding COVID-19) since the age of 18?	Yes I have had all vaccinations I have been invited to (85.7)	I have had some of my vaccinations (8.2)	I have not had any of my vaccinations (2.7)	I have not had vaccinations due to an underlying cause (0.5)	I have decided to opt out of vaccinations (2.7)	Don't know (0.0)
7	Have you already or are you going to accept a vaccine against COVID-19?	Yes (90.1)		No (8.2)		Don't know (1.6)	
7a	If you selected don't know, please specify: (optional)	Response 1: "Too early to be sure of safety." Response 2: "Not sure if I will have my second vaccine." Response 3: "I would like to know more long term side effects before committing to being vaccinated."					
8	Have you received a vaccination to protect you against COVID-19	Yes (98.2)		No (1.8)		Don't know (0.0)	
9	Which vaccine did you receive?	Pfizer (49.1)	Oxford Astra Zeneca (48.4)	Modern (1.9)	Janssen (Johnson & Johnson) (0.0)	Don't know (0.6)	Other (0.0)
10	Are you concerned about accepting the COVID-19 vaccine/did you have concerns before receiving the vaccine?	I am not/was not concerned (73.8)	I feel/felt impartial (4.3)	I am/was slightly concerned (17.1)	I am/was very concerned (4.3)	Other (0.6)	
10a	If you selected other, please specify: (optional)	Response 1: "I'm informed about side effects and don't believe what you see in the news without looking at the actual data. So initially concerned but not after looking into the clotting issue."					

Table A1. *Cont.*

	Question	Responses (%)					
11	Why did (or why will) you accept the COVID-19 vaccine? (Please select the most likely reason)	I have done my own research and I believe them to be safe (20.7)	I want the world to go back to how it used to be before the COVID-19 pandemic (40.2)	I know of or have lost someone to COVID-19 who did not receive the vaccination in time (5.5)	For protection for myself (27.4)	Other (6.1)	
11a	If you selected other, please specify: (optional)	Response 1: "Mainly to protect others." Response 2: "For protection of the weak and vulnerable as well as myself." Response 3: "Family member I care for is vulnerable otherwise I may have declined." Response 4: "NHS worker." Response 5: "Protection for my high risk family (mother and father)."					
12	Why did (or why will) you not accept the COVID-19 vaccine? (tick all that apply)	I worry I might get COVID019 (0.0)	I have done my own research and I do not believe them to be safe (52.9)	I worry about the adverse reactions (23.5)	I do not believe the trials have been long enough to ensure accurate results (64.7)	Other (23.5)	
12a	If you selected other, please specify: (optional)	Response 1: "I have had both vaccine doses." Response 2: "I have an immune system. The majority of people do not need a vaccine for covid 19 . . . . In my opinion. My mother also had a severe adverse reaction to the Astra Zeneca jab and is now suffering high blood pressure." Response 3: "I've had the flu jab—that's all I needed!" Response 4: "I keep myself fit and healthy, I do not have any medical conditions, I ensure I eat a balanced diet and maintain a normal BMI, I exercise frequently and take my general health very seriously thus I did not feel it necessary to have the vaccine. I felt that pressure from colleagues, family and social media made me feel like I didn't have a choice. I work in an nhs hospital."					
13	If you have children, what age are they? (If you have multiple children, please select the age of the youngest)	0–4 years (16.3)	5–10 years (7.6)	11–15 years (4.1)	16–17 years (1.2)	18 years + (32.6)	I do not have children (38.4)
14	As of 1 July 2021 in the UK, children under the age of 18 are not routinely offered a COVID-19 vaccine. If this changed and children were offered the vaccine, would you give permission for your child/children to have the vaccine?	Yes (41.1)	Probably (8.9)	Don't know (17.9)	Probably not (5.4)	No (26.8)	
15	If you selected no/probably not to the previous question, please tick the most relevant box	They have an underlying disorder that prevents them from having vaccinations (0.0)	I do not trust what is in the vaccine (22.2)	I do not believe that they work (0.0)	I do not want them to suffer possible long term adverse reactions (50.0)	Other (27.8)	
15a	If you selected other, please specify: (optional)	Response 1: "Given that the effects on children of the virus is known and proven to be low on children on balance I don't think any benefits outweigh the negatives as the vaccine has not been out for long." Response 2: "Children were never in the at risk group. I believe this experimental poison that's only approved for EMERGENCY use (e.g., not approved like measles/chicken pox/meningitis) will cause life changing side effects or even death. How many dead children from this vaccine are acceptable? 1? 10? 100? We are vaccinating a population over a disease with a 99.7% survival rate-oh and it's not even 100% effective!" Response 3: "Covid 19 does not affect children . . . why would anyone vaccinate a child against something that wouldn't cause them any harm in the first place?" Response 4: "I would like to see more long term data on infants receiving a vaccine before making my mind."					
16	Have/would you use Twitter to find out information about COVID-19 or Coronavirus?	Yes (11.5)		No (83.5)		Don't know (4.9)	
17	I would describe my attitude towards receiving a COVID-19 vaccine as:	Very interested (52.7)	Interested (19.2)	Neutral (12.1)	Uneasy (8.8)	Against it (7.1)	Don't know (0.0)
18	If friends or family were offered a COVID-19 vaccine I would:	Strongly encourage them (61.0)	Encourage them (19.8)	Not say anything (12.1)	Discourage them (1.6)	Strongly discourage them (3.3)	Don't know (2.2)
19	Taking a COVID-19 vaccination is:	Extremely important (64.6)	Important (21.5)	Neither important nor unimportant (6.1)	Unimportant (2.2)	Extremely unimpor-tant (2.8)	Don't know (2.8)
20	Do you consider the COVID-19 vaccine more dangerous than the COVID-19 disease?	Strongly agree (6.6)	Somewhat agree (6.6)	Neither agree nor disagree (7.7)	Somewhat disagree (12.1)	Strongly disagree (64.3)	Don't know (2.7)
21	Vaccine safety and effectiveness data are often false	Strongly agree (5.0)	Somewhat agree (12.2)	Neither agree nor disagree (16.0)	Somewhat disagree (20.4)	Strongly disagree (40.3)	Don't know (6.1)
22	How would you describe your general knowledge of vaccinations?	Deep/thorough understanding (23.6)	Some understanding (74.2)	No understanding (2.2)		Don't know (0.0)	

References

1. Chadeau-Hyam, M.; Bodinier, B.; Elliot, J.; Whitaker, M.D.; Tzoulaki, I.; Vermeulen, R.; Kelly-Irving, M.; Delpierre, C.; Elliot, P. Risk factors for positive and negative COVID-19 tests: A cautious and in-depth analysis of UK biobank data. *Int. J. Epidemiol.* **2020**, *49*, 1454–1467. [CrossRef]
2. Public Health England, Coronavirus (COVID-19) in the UK. 2021. Available online: https://coronavirus.data.gov.uk (accessed on 8 July 2021).
3. Puri, N.; Coomes, E.A.; Haghbayan, H.; Gunaratne, K. Social media and vaccine hesitancy: New updates for the era of COVID-19 and globalized infectious diseases. *Hum. Vaccine Immunother.* **2020**, *16*, 2586–2593. [CrossRef] [PubMed]
4. Kata, A. Anti-vaccine activists, Web 2.0, and the postmodern paradigm—An overview of tactics and tropes used online by the anti-vaccination movement. *Vaccine* **2012**, *30*, 3778–3789. [CrossRef] [PubMed]
5. Jacobson, R.M.; St Sauver, J.L.; Finney Rutten, L.J. Vaccine Hesitancy. *Mayo Clin. Proc.* **2015**, *90*, 1562–1568. [CrossRef]
6. Cacciatore, M.A.; Nowak, G.J.; Evans, N.J. It's complicated: The 2014–2015 US measles outbreak and parents' vaccination beliefs, confidence, and intentions. *Risk Anal.* **2018**, *38*, 2178–2192. [CrossRef] [PubMed]
7. Smith, N.; Graham, T. Mapping the anti-vaccine movement on Facebook. *Inf. Commun. Soc.* **2017**, *22*, 1310–1327. [CrossRef]
8. Taylor, B.; Miller, E.; Farrington, C.P.; Petropoulos, M.C.; Favot-Mayaud, I.; Li, J.; Waight, P.A. Autism and measles, mumps, and rubella vaccine: No epidemiological evidence for a causal association. *Lancet* **1999**, *353*, 2026–2029. [CrossRef]
9. Kulenkampff, M.; Schwartzman, J.S.; Wilson, J. Neurological complications of pertussis inoculation. *Arch. Dis. Child.* **1974**, *49*, 46–49. [CrossRef]
10. Salmon, D.A.; Dudley, M.Z.; Glanz, J.M.; Omer, S.B. Vaccine hesitancy: Causes, consequences, and a call to action. *Vaccine* **2015**, *33*, 66–71. [CrossRef]
11. Swansea Research Unit of the Royal College of General Practitioners. Effect of a low pertussis vaccination take-up on a large community. *Br. Med. J. (Clin. Res. Ed.)* **1981**, *282*, 23–26. [CrossRef]
12. Begg, N.; White, J.; Bozoky, Z. Media dents confidence in MMR vaccine. *Br. Med. J.* **1998**, *316*, 561. [CrossRef]
13. Gangarosa, E.; Galazka, A.M.; Wolfe, C.R.; Philips, L.M.; Gangarosa, R.E.; Miller, E.; Chen, R.T. Impact of anti-vaccine movements on pertussis control: The untold story. *Lancet* **1998**, *351*, 356–361. [CrossRef]
14. Hansen, N.D.; Mølbak, K.; Cox, I.J.; Lioma, C. Relationship between Media Coverage and Measles-Mumps-Rubella (MMR) vaccination Uptake in Denmark: Retrospective Study. *JMIR Pub. Health Surveill.* **2019**, *5*, e9544. [CrossRef] [PubMed]
15. World Health Organisation. News Updates. 2021. Available online: https://www.who.int/news-room/news-updates (accessed on 14 August 2021).
16. Kupferschmidt, K. Study pushes emergence of measles back to antiquity. *Science* **2020**, *367*, 11–12. [CrossRef] [PubMed]
17. Gunaratne, K.; Coomes, E.A.; Haghbayan, H. Temporal trends in anti-vaccine discourse on Twitter. *Vaccine* **2019**, *37*, 4867–4871. [CrossRef]
18. Scanfeld, D.; Scanfeld, V.; Larson, E.L. Dissemination of health information through social networks: Twitter and antibiotics. *Am. J. Infect. Control* **2010**, *38*, 182–188. [CrossRef]
19. Betsch, C.; Brewer, N.T.; Brocard, P.; Davies, P.; Gaissmaier, W.; Haase, N.; Leask, J.; Renkewitz, F.; Renner, B.; Reyna, V.F.; et al. Opportunities and challenges of Web 2.0 for vaccine decisions. *Vaccine* **2012**, *30*, 3727–3733. [CrossRef] [PubMed]
20. Ortiz-Sánchez, E.; Velando-Soriano, A.; Pradas-Hernández, L.; Vargas-Román, K.; Gómez-Urquiza, J.L.; Cañdas-De la Fuente, G.; Albendín-García, L. Analysis of the Anti-Vaccine Movement in Social Networks: A Systematic Review. *Int. J. Environ. Res. Public Health* **2020**, *17*, 5394. [CrossRef] [PubMed]
21. Anderson, P. Another media scare about MMR vaccine hits Britain. *Br. Med. J.* **1999**, *318*, 1578. [CrossRef]
22. Diresta, R.; Lotan, G. Anti-Vaxxers Using Twitter to Manipulate a Vaccine Bill. 2015. Available online: https://cran.rproject.org/web/packages/SocialMediaLab/SocialMediaLab.pdf (accessed on 19 July 2021).
23. Sense about Science. 2021. Available online: https://senseaboutscience.org (accessed on 11 August 2021).
24. Mollema, L.; Harmsen, I.A.; Broekhuizen, E.; Clijnk, R.; Melker, H.D.; Paulussen, T.; Kok, G.; Ruiter, R.; Das, E. Disease Detection or Public Opinion Reflection? Content Analysis of Tweets, Other Social Media, and Online Newspapers During the Measles Outbreak in the Netherlands in 2013. *J. Med. Internet Res.* **2015**, *17*, e128. [CrossRef]
25. Piedrahita-Valdes, H.; Piedrahita-Castillo, D.; Bermejo-Higuera, J.; Guillem-Saiz, P.; Bermejo-Higuera, J.R.; Guillem-Saiz, J.; Sicilia-Montalvo, J.A.; Machio-Regidor, F. Vaccine hesitancy on social media: Sentiment analysis from June 2011 to April 2019. *Vaccines* **2021**, *9*, 28. [CrossRef] [PubMed]
26. Kullar, R.; Goff, D.A.; Gauthier, T.P.; Smith, T.C. To Tweet or Not to Tweet—A Review of the Viral Power of Twitter for Infectious Diseases. *Technol. Infect. Dis.* **2020**, *22*, 14. [CrossRef]
27. Twitter Revenue and Usage Statistics. 2021. Available online: https://www.businessofapps.com/data/twitter-statistics/ (accessed on 14 August 2021).
28. Sattar, N.S.; Arifuzzaman, S. COVID-19 Vaccination awareness and aftermath: Public sentiment analysis on Twitter data and vaccinated population prediction in the USA. *Appl. Sci.* **2021**, *11*, 6128. [CrossRef]
29. Neubaum, G.; Rosner, L.; Rosenthal-von der Putten, A.; Kramer, N.C. Psychosocial functions of social media usage in a disaster situation: A multi-methodological approach. *Comput. Hum. Behav.* **2014**, *34*, 28–38. [CrossRef]
30. Skinner, G. Who's least likely to say they'll get a COVID-19 vaccine? *Ipsos Mori.* **2020**. Available online: https://www.ipsos.com/en-uk/whos-least-likely-say-they\T1\textquoterightll-get-covid-19-vaccine (accessed on 17 August 2021).

31. Freeman, D.; Loe, B.S.; Chadwick, A.; Vaccari, C.; Waite, F.; Rosebrock, L.; Jenner, L.; Petit, A.; Lewandowsky, S.; Vanderslott, S.; et al. COVID-19 vaccine hesitancy in the UK: The Oxford coronavirus explanations, attitudes, and narratives survey (Oceans) II. *Psychol. Med.* **2020**, 1–15. [CrossRef]
32. Google Trends. 2021. Available online: www.trends.google.com (accessed on 19 July 2021).
33. Kaur, C.; Sharma, A. Twitter Sentiment Analysis on Coronavirus using Textblob. *EasyChair Prepr.* **2020**, *2974*, 1–10.
34. Tholana, V.S.S.A. Literature Review on Sentiment Analysis. *Int. J. Adv. Res. Ideas Innov. Technol.* **2017**, *3*, 5.
35. Li, N.; Wu, D.D. Using text mining and sentiment analysis for online forums hotspot detection and forecast. *Decis. Support Syst.* **2010**, *48*, 354–368. [CrossRef]
36. Bari, M.D.; Sharoff, S.; Thomas, M. Sentiml: Functional annotation for multilingual sentiment analysis. *ICPS Proc.* **2013**, *15*, 1–7. [CrossRef]
37. Ghassi, M.; Skinner, J.; Zimbra, D. Twitter brand sentiment analysis: A hybrid system using n-gram analysis and dynamic artificial neural network. *Expert Syst. Appl.* **2013**, *40*, 6266–6282. [CrossRef]
38. Tane, J.; Schmitz, C.; Stumme, G. Semantic resource management for the web: An e-learning application. In Proceedings of the 13th International World Wide Web conference on Alternate Track Papers and Posters, New York, NY, USA, 19–21 May 2004; pp. 1–10. [CrossRef]
39. Raghupathi, V.; Ren, J.; Raghupathi, W. Studying public perception about vaccination: A sentiment analysis of Tweets. *Int. J. Environ. Res. Public Health* **2020**, *17*, 3464. [CrossRef] [PubMed]
40. Cieliebak, M.; Durr, O.; Uzdilli, F. *Potential and Limitations of Commercial Sentiment Detection Tools*; Zurich University of Applied Sciences: Winterthur, Switzerland, 2013.
41. Bonta, V.; Janardhan, N.K.N. A Comprehensive Study on Lexicon Based Approaches for Sentiment Analysis. *Asian J. Comput. Sci. Technol.* **2019**, *8*, 1–6. [CrossRef]
42. Shelar, A.; Huang, C.-Y. Sentiment Analysis of Twitter Data. In Proceedings of the International Conference on Computational Science and Computational Intelligence, Las Vegas, NV, USA, 12–14 December 2018; pp. 1301–1302. [CrossRef]
43. Amin, A.; Hossain, I.; Akther, A.; Alam, K.M. Bengali VADER: A sentiment analysis approach using modified VADER. In Proceedings of the 2019 International Conference on Electrical, Computer and Communication Engineering (ECCE), Cox'sBazar, Bangladesh, 7–9 February 2019; pp. 1–6. [CrossRef]
44. Hatzivassiloglou, V.; McKeown, K.R. Predicting the semantic orientation of adjectives. In Proceedings of the 35th Annual Meeting of the Association for Computational Linguistics and Eighth Conference of the European Chapter of the Association for Computational Linguistics, Madrid, Spain, 7–12 July 1997; pp. 174–181.
45. Sarker, D.; Bali, R.; Sahrma, T. Analyzing movie reviews sentiment. In *Practical Machine Learning with Python: A Problem-Solver's Guide to Building Real-World Intelligent Systems*; Apress: Berkley, CA, USA, 2018; pp. 246–342.
46. Ao, S.; Chan, A.S.; Castillo, O.; Kim, H.; Katagiri, H. *Transactions on Engineering Sciences: Special Issue for the International Association of Engineers Conferences 2019, IAENG*; World Scientific Publishing Pte: Singapore, 2020; pp. 72–73.
47. Hutto, C.; Gilbert, E. *VADER: A Parsimonious Rule-Based Model for Sentiment Analysis of Social Media Text [Scholarly Project]*; Comp. Social Lab: Atlanta, GA, USA, 2014; Available online: http://comp.social.gatech.edu/papers/icwsm14.vader.pdf (accessed on 1 August 2021).
48. Rahim, N.H.A.; Rafie, S.H.M. Sentiment analysis of social media data in vaccination. *Int. J. Emerg. Trends Eng. Res.* **2020**, *8*, 5259–5264. [CrossRef]
49. Taylor, S.; Landry, C.A.; Paluszek, M.M.; Groenewoud, R.; Rachoe, G.S.; Asmundson, G.J.G. A proactive Approach for Managing COVID-19: The importance of Understanding the Motivational Roots of Vaccination Hesitancy for SARS-CoV-2. *Front. Psychol.* **2020**, *11*, 575950. [CrossRef]
50. Graffigna, G.; Palamenghi, L.; Boccia, S.; Barello, S. Relationship between Citizens' Health Engagement and Intention to Take the COVID-19 Vaccine in Italy: A Mediation Analysis. *Vaccines* **2020**, *8*, 576. [CrossRef]
51. Group, C. A future vaccination campaign against COVID-19 at risk of vaccine hesitancy and politicization. *Lancet Infect. Dis.* **2020**, *20*, 769–770.
52. Zucco, C.; Paglia, C.; Graziano, S.; Bella, S.; Cannataro, M. Sentiment analysis and text mining of questionnaires to support telemonitoring programs. *Information* **2020**, *11*, 550. [CrossRef]
53. Allery, L.A. Design and use questionnaires for research in medical education. *Educ. Prim. Care* **2016**, *27*, 234–238. [CrossRef]
54. McGuirk, P.M.; O'Neill, P. Using Questionnaires in Qualitative Human Geography. Faculty of Social Sciences—Papers. 2016, Volume 2518, pp. 246–273. Available online: https://ro.uow.edu.au/sspapers/2518 (accessed on 16 August 2021).
55. Chandrasekaran, R.; Mehta, V.; Valkunde, T.; Moustakas, E. Topics, Trends, and Sentiments of Tweets About the COVID-19 Pandemic: Temporal Infoveillance Study. *J. Med. Internet Res.* **2020**, *22*, e22624. [CrossRef]
56. JISC Online Surveys. 2021. Available online: www.JISC.ac.uk (accessed on 1 July 2021).
57. StatsKingdom. 2021. Available online: www.statskingdom.com (accessed on 13 August 2021).
58. D'Andrea, A.; Ferri, F.; Grifoni, P.; Guzzo, T. Approaches, Tools and Applications for Sentiment Analysis Implementation. *Int. J. Comput. Appl.* **2015**, *125*, 0975–8887. [CrossRef]
59. Hutto, C.J.; Gilbert, E. VADER: A Parsimonious Rule-based Model for Sentiment Analysis of Social Media Test. *Assoc. Adv. Artif. Intell.* 2015. Available online: https://www.researchgate.net/publication/275828927_VADER_A_Parsimonious_Rule-based_Model_for_Sentiment_Analysis_of_Social_Media_Text (accessed on 12 August 2021).

60. NLTK. 2021. Available online: https://www.nltk.org/ (accessed on 1 July 2021).
61. Karn, A.; Shrestha, A.; Pudasaini, A.; Mahara, B.; Jaiswal, A. Statistic based Sentiment Analysis of Social Media Data. *Int. Res. J. Innov. Eng. Technol.* **2018**, *2*, 28–32.
62. Mantyla, M.V.; Graziotin, D.; Kuutila, M. The evolution of Sentiment Analysis—A review of research topics, venues and top cited papers. *Comput. Sci. Rev.* **2018**, *27*, 16–32. [CrossRef]
63. Abdelwahab, O.; Bahgat, M.; Lowrance, C.J.; Elmaghraby, A. Effect of training set size on SVM and Naïve Bayes for Twitter sentiment analysis. In Proceedings of the 2015 IEEE International Symposium on Signal Processing and Information Technology (ISSPIT), Abu Dhabi, United Arab Emirates, 7–10 December 2015; pp. 46–51.
64. Canhoto, A.I.; Padmanabhan, Y. 'We (don't) know how you feel'—A comparative study of automated vs. manual analysis of social media conversations. *J. Mark. Manag.* **2015**, *13*, 1141–1157. [CrossRef]
65. Chaovalit, P.; Zhou, L. Movie review mining: A comparison between supervised and unsupervised classification approaches. In *System Sciences, Proceedings of the 38th Annual Hawaii International Conference HICSS'05, Big Island, HI, USA, 3–6 January 2005*; IEEE: Piscataway, NJ, USA, 2005; pp. 1–9.
66. Kolchyna, O.; Souza, T.T.P.; Treleaven, P.C.; Aste, T. Twitter sentiment analysis: Lexicon method, machine learning method and their combination. *arXiv* **2015**, arXiv:1507.00955.
67. Dhaoui, C.; Webster, C.M.; Tan, L.P. Social media sentiment analysis: Lexicon versus machine learning. *J. Consum. Mark.* **2017**, *34*, 480–488. [CrossRef]
68. Nguyen, H.; Veluchamy, A.; Diop, M.; Iqbal, R. Comparative study of sentiment analysis with product reviews using machine learning and lexicon based approaches. *Data Sci. Rev.* **2018**, *1*, 4–7.
69. Lu, B.; Tsou, B.K. Combining a large sentiment lexicon and machine learning for subjectivity classification. In Proceedings of the 2010 International Conference on Machine Learning and Cybernetics, Qingdao, China, 11–14 July 2010; pp. 3311–3316. [CrossRef]
70. Dolianiti, F.S.; Iakovakis, D.; Dias, S.B.; Hadjileontiadou, S.J.; Diniz, J.A.; Natsiou, G.; Tsitoiuridou, M.; Bamidis, P.D.; Hadjileontiadis, L.J. Sentiment analysis on educational datasets: A comparative evaluation of commercial tools. *Educ. J. Univ. Patras UNESCO Chair* **2019**, *6*, 262–273.
71. Sweigart, A. Invent Your Own Computer Games with Python. 2nd Edition. 2012. Available online: https://inventwithpython.com/ (accessed on 19 July 2021).
72. Villavicencio, C.; Macrohon, J.J.; Inbaraj, X.A.; Jeng, J.H.; Hsieh, J.G. Twitter Sentiment Analysis towards COVID-19 Vaccines in the Philippines Using Naïve Bayes. *Information* **2021**, *12*, 204. [CrossRef]
73. Chaudhri, A.A.; Saranya, S.; Dubey, S. Implementation Paper on Analyzing COVID-18 Vaccines on Twitter Dataset Using Tweepy and Text Blob. *Ann. Rom. Soc. Cell Biol.* **2021**, *25*, 8393–8396.
74. Xue, J.; Chen, J.; Hu, R.; Chen, C.; Zheng, C.; Liu, X.; Zhu, T. Twitter discussions and emotions and COVID-19 pandemic: A machine learning approach (2020). *arXiv* **2020**, arXiv:2005.12830.
75. Baghat, K.K.; Mishra, S.; Dixit, A.; Chang, C.Y. Public Opinions about online learning during COVID-19: A sentiment analysis approach. *Sustainability* **2021**, *13*, 3364. [CrossRef]
76. Del Vicario, M.; Bessi, A.; Zollo, F.; Petroni, F.; Scala, A.; Caldarelli, G.; Quattrociocchi, W. The spreading of misinformation online. *Proc. Natl. Acad. Sci. USA* **2016**, *113*, 554–559. [CrossRef] [PubMed]
77. Dredze, M.; Broniatowski, D.A.; Hilyard, K.M. Zika vaccine misconception: A social media analysis. *Vaccine* **2016**, *34*, 3441. [CrossRef] [PubMed]
78. Massey, P.M.; Leader, A.; Yom-Tov, E.; Budena, A.; Fisher, K.; Klasse, A.C. Applying multiple data collection tools to quantify Human Papillomavirus vaccine communication on Twitter. *J. Med. Internet Res.* **2016**, *18*, 12. [CrossRef]
79. Mahajan, R.; Romine, W.; Miller, M.; Banerjee, T. Analyzing public outlook towards vaccination using Twitter. In Proceedings of the 2019 IEEE International Conference on Big Data (Big Data), Los Angeles, CA, USA, 9–12 December 2019; pp. 2763–2772. [CrossRef]
80. Yuan, X.; Schuchard, R.J.; Crooks, A.T. Examining emergent communities and social bots within the polarized online vaccination debate in Twitter. *Soc. Media+ Soc.* **2019**, *5*, 20563051198546. [CrossRef]
81. Meyer, S.B.; Violette, R.; Aggarwal, R.; Simeoni, M.; MacDoughall, H.; Waite, N. Vaccine hesitancy and Web 2.0: Exploring how attitudes and beliefs about influenza vaccination are exchanged in online threaded user comments. *Vaccine* **2019**, *37*, 1769–1774. [CrossRef]
82. Nyhan, B.; Reifler, J.; Richey, S.; Freed, G.L. Effective messages in vaccine promotion: A randomized trial. *Pediatrics* **2014**, *133*, e835–e842. [CrossRef]
83. Nyhan, B.; Reifler, J. Does correcting myths about the flu vaccine work? An experimental evaluation of the effects of corrective information. *Vaccine* **2015**, *33*, 459–464. [CrossRef]
84. Massey, P.M.; Budenz, A.; Leader, A.; Fisher, K.; Klassen, A.C.; Yom-Tov, E. What drives heath professionals to tweet about # HPV vaccine? Identifying strategies for effective communication. *Prev. Chronic Dis.* **2018**, *15*, 15. [CrossRef]
85. Medicines & Healthcare Products Regulatory Agency, MHRA Guidance on Coronavirus (COVID-19). 2021. Available online: https://www.gov.uk/government/collections/mhra-guidance-on-coronavirus-covid-19 (accessed on 13 July 2021).
86. British Foreign Policy Group. COVID-19 Timeline. 2021. Available online: https://bfpg.co.uk/2020/04/covid-19-timeline/ (accessed on 14 August 2021).

87. Huang, C.; Wang, Y.; Li, X.; Ren, L.; Zhao, J.; Hu, Y.; Zhang, L.; Fan, G.; Xu, J.; Gu, X.; et al. Clinical features of patients infected with 2019 novel coronavirus in Wuhan, China. *Lancet* **2020**, *395*, 497–506. [CrossRef]
88. Dodd, R.H.; Pickles, K.; Nickel, B.; Cvejic, E.; Ayre, J.; Batcup, C.; Bonner, C.; Copp, T.; Cornell, S.; Dakin, T.; et al. Concerns and motivations about COVID-19 vaccination. *Lancet Infect. Dis.* **2021**, *21*, 163–191. [CrossRef]
89. Chowdhury, A.A.; Das, A.; Saha, S.K.; Rahman, M.; Hasan, K.T. Sentiment Analysis of COVID-19 Vaccination from Survey Responses in Bangladesh. Researchsquare Preprint. 2021. Available online: https://assets.researchsquare.com/files/rs-482293/v1_stamped.pdf?c=1620421587 (accessed on 16 August 2021).
90. Pew Research Centre. *Parents of Young Children Are More 'Vaccine Hesitant'*; Pew Research Centre: Washington, DC, USA, 2017; Available online: https://www.pewresearch.org/fact-tank/2017/02/06/parents-of-young-children-are-more-vaccine-hesitant/ (accessed on 13 August 2021).
91. Dror, A.A.; Eisenbach, N.; Taiber, S.; Morozov, N.G.; Mizrachi, M.; Zigron, A.; Srouji, S.; Sela, E. Vaccine hesitancy: The next challenge in the fight against COVID-19. *Eur. J. Epidemiol.* **2020**, *35*, 775–779. [CrossRef]
92. Bendau, A.; Plag, J.; Petzold, M.B.; Strohle, A. COVID-19 vaccine hesitancy and related fears and anxiety. *Int. Immunopharmacol.* **2021**, *97*, 107724. [CrossRef]
93. Alicke, M.D.; Braun, J.C.; Glor, J.E.; Klotz, K.L.; Magee, J.; Sederholm, H.; Siegel, R. Complaining Behaviour in social interactions. *Personal. Soc. Psychol. Bull.* **1992**, *18*, 286–295. [CrossRef]
94. You, K.H.; Gretzel, U. What motivates consumers to write online travel reviews? *Fac. Commer.* **2008**, *1*, 282–296. [CrossRef]
95. Eastwood, K.; Durrheim, D.N.; Jones, A.; Butler, M. Acceptance of pandemic (H1N1) 2009 influenza vaccination by the Australian public. *Med. J. Aust.* **2010**, *192*, 33–36. [CrossRef]
96. Raude, J.; Caille-Brillet, A.-L.; Setbon, M. The 2009 pandemic H1N1 influenza vaccination in France: Who accepted to receive the vaccine and why? *PLoS Curr.* **2010**, *2*. [CrossRef] [PubMed]
97. Maurer, J.; Harris, K.M.; Parker, A.M.; Lurie, N. Does receipt of seasonal influenza vaccine predict intention to receive novel H1N1 vaccine: Evidence from a nationally representative survey of U.S. adults. *Vaccine* **2009**, *27*, 5732–5734. [CrossRef]
98. Maurer, J.; Uscher-Pines, L.; Harris, K.M. Perceived seriousness of seasonal and A(H1N1) influenzas, attitudes toward vaccination, and vaccine uptake among U.S. adults: Does the source of information matter? *Prev. Med.* **2010**, *51*, 185–187. [CrossRef] [PubMed]
99. Schwarzinger, M.; Flicoteaux, R.; Cortarenoda, S.; Obadia, Y.; Moatti, J.-P. Low Acceptability of A/H1N1 Pandemic Vaccination in French Adult Population: Did Public Health Policy Fuel Public Dissonance? *PLoS ONE* **2010**, *5*, 4. [CrossRef] [PubMed]
100. Sypsa, V.; Livanios, T.; Psichogiou, M.; Malliori, M.; Tsiodras, S.; Nikolakopoulos, I.; Hatzakis, A. Public perceptions in relation to intention to receive pandemic influenza vaccination in a random population sample: Evidence from a cross-sectional telephone survey. *Eurosurveillance* **2009**, *14*, 19437. [CrossRef] [PubMed]
101. Rubin, G.J.; Potts, H.; Michie, S. The impact of communications about swine flu (influenza A H1N1v) on public responses to the outbreak: Results from 36 national telephone surveys in the UK. *Health Technol. Assess.* **2010**, *14*, 183–266. [CrossRef] [PubMed]
102. Seale, H.; Heywood, A.E.; McLaws, M.; Ward, K.F.; Lowbridge, C.P.; Van, D.; MacIntyre, C.R. Why do I need it? I am not at risk! Public perceptions towards the pandemic (H1N1) 2009 vaccine. *BMC Infect. Dis.* **2010**, *10*, 99. [CrossRef]
103. Nguyen, T.; Henningsen, K.H.; Brehaut, J.C.; Hoe, E.; Wilson, K. Acceptance of a pandemic influenza vaccine: A systematic review of surveys of the general public. *Infect. Drug Resist.* **2011**, *4*, 197–207. [PubMed]
104. Soni, R.; Mathai, J. Improved Twitter Sentiment Prediction through 'Cluster-then-Predict Model. *Int. J. Comput. Sci. Netw.* **2015**, *4*, 2277–5420.

International Journal of
Environmental Research and Public Health

MDPI

Article

What about the Consequences of the Use of Distance Learning during the COVID-19 Pandemic? A Survey on the Psychological Effects in Both Children and Parents

Maria Grazia Maggio [1], Maria Chiara Stagnitti [2], Patrizia Calatozzo [2], Antonino Cannavò [3], Daniele Bruschetta [3], Marilena Foti Cuzzola [2], Alfredo Manuli [3], Giovanni Pioggia [4] and Rocco Salvatore Calabrò [5,*]

1 Department of Biomedical and Biotechnological Science, The University of Catania, 95123 Catania, Italy; mariagraziamay@gmail.com
2 Studio di Psicoterapia Relazionale e Riabilitazione Cognitiva, 98124 Messina, Italy; mariachiara.stagnitti@gmail.com (M.C.S.); patrizia.calatozzo@gmail.com (P.C.); marilenafoti@yahoo.it (M.F.C.)
3 AOU Policlinico "G. Martino", 98125 Messina, Italy; antonino.cannavo.85@gmail.com (A.C.); d.bruschetta@unime.it (D.B.); manulialfredo@gmail.com (A.M.)
4 Institute for Biomedical Research and Innovation, National Research Council of Italy (IRIB-CNR), 98164 Messina, Italy; giovanni.pioggia@irib.cnr.it
5 IRCCS Centro Neurolesi "Bonino Pulejo", 98121 Messina, Italy
* Correspondence: salbro77@tiscali.it

Citation: Maggio, M.G.; Stagnitti, M.C.; Calatozzo, P.; Cannavò, A.; Bruschetta, D.; Foti Cuzzola, M.; Manuli, A.; Pioggia, G.; Calabrò, R.S. What about the Consequences of the Use of Distance Learning during the COVID-19 Pandemic? A Survey on the Psychological Effects in Both Children and Parents. *Int. J. Environ. Res. Public Health* **2021**, *18*, 12641. https://doi.org/10.3390/ijerph182312641

Academic Editors: Paolo Roma, Merylin Monaro, Cristina Mazza and Paul B. Tchounwou

Received: 15 October 2021
Accepted: 29 November 2021
Published: 30 November 2021

Publisher's Note: MDPI stays neutral with regard to jurisdictional claims in published maps and institutional affiliations.

Abstract: Background: The COVID-19 pandemic implicated many social restrictions, including the use of distance learning (DL). Indeed, parents were obligated to support their children in online lessons and schoolwork. The aim of this study was to investigate the psycho-emotional impact of the COVID-19 pandemic on parents and children submitted to DL. Methods: One hundred and ninety-two participants (96 parents and 96 children) were enrolled in this study. Parents and children completed an online questionnaire, structured in four sections. Results: The results showed that parents had higher levels of stress and anxiety. In particular, the stress for DL was positively correlated with depression and anxiety. Parents' jobs were negatively correlated with their levels of anxiety and stress. On the other hand, children reported higher levels of depressive symptoms and event-related anxiety, which increased as children got older. The stress and the anxiety in parents were positively correlated with the mood depression and anxiety of their children. Conclusions: The COVID-19 pandemic had a negative impact on the psychological well-being of children and parents who used DL. Although DL could be an alternative teaching method during pandemics, face-to-face teaching is fundamental and irreplaceable as it encourages dialogue, involvement, and human contact.

Keywords: COVID-19; distance learning; psycho-emotional impact

1. Introduction

The COVID-19 pandemic, an infectious disease caused by the new coronavirus SARS-CoV-2, is a global health problem that has affected millions of people since January 2020 [1]. To limit COVID-19 transmission, national governments took precautionary actions, such as adopting careful personal hygiene, wearing masks and gloves, and implementing social distancing [2]. In particular, the Italian government adopted measures aimed at limiting social contacts, including the closure of public places (i.e., schools, offices, theatres, restaurants, bars, parts of public transport) and exhorting people to stay at home [3]. These measures of social distancing caused substantial changes in daily social life, affecting children's, adolescents', and parents' lifestyles. The use of smart-working and distance learning (DL) forced children and parents to spend a lot of time at home, in front of their computer and smartphone screens [3,4]. Moreover, the COVID-19 pandemic caused a socio-economic crisis with job losses, financial insecurity, mental health problems, and lack of care services, including childcare services [5]. All these stressors had negative effects on the mental well-being of each family member [3]. In more detail, about one in four parents reported worsening mental health, and one in seven parents had worsening behavioral health for their children since the pandemic began. Of note, the worsening of parental mental health and children's behavioral health were at times intertwined, with nearly 1 in 10 families reporting worsening of both. This resulted in loss of childcare, delays in health care visits, and worsened food security.

The United Nations Educational, Scientific, and Cultural Organization estimated that during the pandemic, 1.38 billion children have been out of school or childcare, without access to group activities, team sports, or playgrounds [6]. The closing of schools and lack of childcare services obligated parents to take greater responsibilities for their children's care and home education, supporting them during distance learning (DL) with online lessons and schoolwork [7–9], leading to negative impacts on the well-being of children and parents [4,5,7,8,10,11]. In more detail, it has been shown that the negative impact of the pandemic depends on how parents are able to adapt. According to Fegert et al., more flexible parents tend to see pandemic limitations in a positive way, due to the opportunity to spend more time in the family; on the other hand, for others, the pandemic represents a threat to family well-being and personnel, eliciting unresolved conflicts [12]. Indeed, there has been an increase in family violence, child abuse, and neglect during the pandemic [5,7–9,13]. What is more, parental emotional and physical burnout can be linked to other factors, such as the type of daily activities that involve children, and chronic and critical stresses, such as the presence of diseases [4,5,7]. Excessive parental exhaustion could cause a sense of fatigue in parenting activities with little emotional involvement and/or estrangement from children, which significantly affects the mental well-being of children [5,14]. Additionally, a survey found that another concern for parents is their children's mental and emotional health. Some authors have shown that closing school and home daily routines can be harmful to children, especially if they have a behavioral disorder [8,9,15]. Furthermore, children's cognitive and emotional regulation systems are immature and can be vulnerable to the psychological effects of the pandemic with negative outcomes. Some recent studies have found higher rates of anxiety and depression in children than adults [8–11,16]. DL could allow the maintenance of school routines and contact with peers, offering parents a chance to receive help from teachers. It uses technology to enable students to learn without being physically present in the classroom, thus individualizing the learning process [17]. However, few studies have investigated the psychological effects of the pandemic on parents and children while also considering the effect of DL.

Thus, the present study sought to investigate whether and to what extent the use of DL during the COVID-19 pandemic has affected the psychological well-being of a sample of Italian children and their parents.

2. Materials and Methods

2.1. Participants and Settings

We used a cross-sectional survey design to assess the psychological effects of the lockdown due to the COVID-19 pandemic on both parents and children, using an anonymous online questionnaire. The online survey was administered using some common tools found on smartphones (e.g., WhatsApp, Facebook) or e-mail. Potential study participants were identified through school records of the main primary and secondary schools in the province of Messina, Sicily, after a previous contact with the principal, who informed teachers and parents about our research.

Inclusion criteria for parents were: (i) to live in Messina, and (ii) to be the main person responsible for the DL of the children. To be included in the study, children had to attend compulsory education with an age range of 5–16 years.

The final sample consisted of 96 parents (94.8% women; mean age in years 44.62 ± 5.30) and 96 children (51% females; mean age in years 11.81 ± 3.23).

2.2. Procedures

Participants were interviewed online, as it was not possible to administer tests using face-to-face modalities, due to the restrictive measures of the COVID-19 pandemic. They filled out the questionnaires in Italian, through an online survey platform, reached by a simple link (Table 1). The data collection was performed from 17 March 2020 to 2 May 2021.

Table 1. Descriptive analysis of children's and caregivers' characteristics.

	Children	
Age		11.81 ± 3.23
Gender		
	Male	47 (48.9%)
	Female	49 (51.1%)
	Caregivers	
Age (years)		44.62 ± 5.30
Gender		
	Male	5 (5.2%)
	Female	91 (94.8%)
Professions		
	Freelancer	22 (22.9%)
	Employee	23 (24.0%)
	Housewife	10 (10.4%)
	Doctor	9 (9.4%)
	Healthcare staff	9 (9.4%)
	Teacher	10 (10.4%)
	Unemployed	6 (6.2%)
		7 (7.3%)

Mean ± standard deviation are used to describe continuous variables; proportions (numbers and percentages) are used to describe categorical variables.

This study complies with the principles contained in the Declaration of Helsinki and all participants provided informed consent. Anonymity was guaranteed by the online form, in which the data were password-protected and managed only by those responsible for the research.

2.3. Outcome Measures

The survey consisted of several sections. The first part consisted of a structured interview on the socio-demographic data (gender, age, education, schooling, city of birth, profession) of both the caregiver and child/student who used DL. The second part presented a series of psychological scales for assessing the psychological impact of DL on parents.

The psychological battery included:

- The Depression Anxiety Stress Scales (DASS-21), a questionnaire validated on the Italian population and composed of 21 items on a 4-point Likert scale that measures anxiety, stress, and depression. Regarding internal consistency, Cronbach's alpha coefficient is 0.87 for depression, 0.80 for anxiety, 0.89 for stress [18,19].

- The Stress for Distance learning in the COVID-19 era (SDC-Q) is a questionnaire of 6 questions on a 4-point Likert scale. This questionnaire examines the perception of stress in the family's management caused by the use of DL.

The third part included tests that children and adolescents had to fill in via self-assessment with parental support:

- The Children Depression Inventory (CDI) is a self-assessment scale validated on the Italian population for depression that can be used with children between the ages of 8 and 17. The test consists of 27 items; each item has three possible answers with a score from 0 to 2. The psychometric characteristics of CDI have been reported in many studies. Researchers typically report internal coherence reliability coefficients around 0.80 [20,21]; and test-retest reliability coefficients ranging around 0.87 [21,22].

- The State-Trait Anxiety Inventory for Children (S.T.A.I.C.) is a tool for measuring anxiety with upper-elementary- or junior-high-school-aged children and consists of two twenty-item scales. The Cronbach's alpha coefficient of the STAI is 0.82 [23,24].

Finally, both groups were administered the System Usability Scale (SUS) to evaluate the usability of DL. The system usability scale (SUS) is a Likert scale with ten items that provides a global view of subjective usability assessments. SUS requires only one evaluation at the end of the treatment; scores above 50.0 indicate good usability of the device [25].

2.4. Statistical Analysis

Statistical analysis was performed using SPSS Statistic 16.0 (IBM SPSS Statistics, New York, NY, USA). The descriptive statistics were analyzed and expressed as mean ± standard deviation or as median ± first third quartile for continuous variables, as appropriate; frequencies (%) were used for categorical variables. Clinical scale scores were expressed as a mean and standard deviation; the perception of usability of the questionnaire was expressed in percentages. We used linear regressions to calculate the univariate associations between two categorical variables. All tests were two-tailed, with a significance level of $p < 0.05$.

3. Results

One hundred and ninety-two participants (96 parents: mean age ± SD: 44.62 ± 5.30 years; and 96 children: mean age ± SD: 11.81 ± 3.23) were included in the study. A more detailed description of the sample is reported in Table 1. All of the participants completed the online questionnaire, with good usability of the tool and without reporting excessive difficulties. In fact, both parents (89%) and children (94%) indicated that the questionnaire was easy to fill out.

As shown in Table 2, parents had higher levels of stress (SDC Questionnaire: 4.41 ± 4.1; DASS-21 S: 10.66 ± 4.3) and anxiety (DASS-21 A: 9.03 ± 4.1). The children reported higher mood depression (CDI: 24.04 ± 3.3) and anxiety (S.T.A.I.C. 1: 41.81 ± 4.9).

Table 2. Average of the clinical scale of caregivers.

Test/Scale	Mean ± SD	Cut-Off
DASS-21 S	**10.66 ± 4.3**	>10
DASS-21 A	**9.03 ± 4.1**	>6
DASS-21 D	8.60 ± 4.7	>10
SDC Q	**4.41 ± 4.1**	>2
SUS Parents	**70.47 ± 19.9**	<50
CDI	**24.04 ± 3.3**	>15
S.T.A.I.C. 1	**41.81 ± 4.9**	>40
S.T.A.I.C. 2	14.23 ± 9.3	>40
SUS Children	**70.46 ± 19.9**	<50

Legend: DASS-21 S = Depression Anxiety Stress Scales—Stress; DASS-21 A = Depression Anxiety Stress Scales—Anxiety; DASS-21 D = Depression Anxiety Stress Scales—Depression; SDC Q= Stress for Distance learning in COVID-19 era Questionnaire; SUS Parents = System Usability Scale; CDI = Children Depression Inventory; S.T.A.I.C. 1 = State-Trait Anxiety Inventory for Children—State; S.T.A.I.C. 2 = State-Trait Anxiety Inventory for Children—Trait; SUS Children = System Usability Scale. Significant mean ± standard deviations are in bold.

Following linear regression analysis, there were no statistically significant differences in sex and age of the children, or in levels of anxiety ($p = 0.621$), stress ($p = 0.116$), depression ($p = 0.756$), or stress for DL ($p = 0.324$) in the parent group.

Parental stress was positively correlated with anxiety ($p < 0.001$), depressive symptoms ($p < 0.001$), and stress for DL ($p = 0.004$), whereas in children/adolescents, depression correlated with their anxious status ($p < 0.001$ for both tests). Furthermore, as the children got older, their depressive and anxious symptoms increased.

Parental depression symptoms were correlated with their children's anxiety symptoms ($p = 0.03$ for both tests). Moreover, parents' anxiety and stress were correlated with anxiety and depressive symptoms of their children ($p < 0.01$ for both tests). The stress for DL during COVID-19 in parents was associated with trait anxiety of their children/adolescents ($p < 0.001$).

Children's depression symptoms correlated with their parent's anxiety levels ($p < 0.001$) and stress ($p = 0.01$). A higher level of anxiety in children/adolescents was also positively correlated with parental stress ($p = 0.003$).

Finally, we observed that 61.5% of children/adolescents liked to use the DL system and would like to employ it in the future (54.2%), but they believed that this system was not the same as face-to-face lessons (60.4%).

As regards acceptance of the DL, we found high usability, as parents obtained an average score of 70.47 (SD 19.9) and children of 70.46 (SD 19.9).

4. Discussion

In our study, we evaluated the psychological impact of COVID-19 on Italian children aged 5–16 and their parents, with regard to the use of DL. Our results showed that lockdown measures due to the COVID-19 have negatively affected the behavioral and emotional aspects of both children and parents. Regarding the well-being of children during the quarantine, our results underlined high levels of depressive symptoms and event-related anxiety, compared to the general population. This finding is in line with previous reports, which highlight an increase in emotional symptoms in children during periods of lockdown [6,9]. Moreover, our sample showed high levels of parents' anxiety and stress, as compared to the general population. The data are in line with previous studies [7–10], which have also been carried out in other countries [26,27]. Finally, the parental symptoms are related to the psychological symptoms of the children. Given that the presence of higher levels of stress and the onset of psychological problems in parents can adversely affect the psychological well-being of children [10–16], cooperation between parents and teachers is essential not only for educational purposes but also in the support of children [9,10]. For this reason, DL could be a good education tool in the lockdown phase, also considering that most of the children/adolescents liked the DL system and would like to use it in the future. Furthermore, both children and parents have declared high usability and acceptance of the DL.

To the best of our knowledge, few studies have been carried out to evaluate well-being in the parent–child dyad [5,7–10,28,29] during the pandemic, especially investigating the correlation between emotional symptoms (anxiety, depression, stress) of parents and children. However, the COVID-19 pandemic has significantly affected family daily life by changing established routines and presenting new educational challenges for parents and children. In particular, the restrictions on going out and the need to use DL have forced parents to spend many hours managing their children and the psychological problems deriving from the reduction of social activities. Parents and children faced an unknown situation with a highly stressful value, amplified by the media hype and by the uncertainty and fear of the virus [6]. Orgilés et al. [10] observed that 85.7% of parents perceived changes in their children's emotional state and behaviors during the quarantine. Moreover, parents had higher levels of anxiety and psychological distress, and lower levels of perceived self-control and psychological well-being [4,5,7,8,11]. In particular, the risk of psychological distress is higher in parents of children with pre-existing psychological and behavioral difficulties, who require personalized teaching because of their special needs [4,7,30]. This aspect is particularly important in DL, where the presence of remote teaching can reduce the active involvement of the child, who also needs the parent to solve the technical problems of the DL platforms [31]. This is why parents of children with intellectual disabilities present with a higher burden and stress.

Notably, in our study, nearly all parents responding to the questionnaire were females. These data are in line with the literature [7], demonstrating that the pandemic had a negative psychological impact on Italian mothers, who are mainly responsible for the child's management, especially regarding DL. Indeed, it has been shown that quarantine and COVID-19 restrictions can be perceived as an uncertain and threatening situation, capable of triggering symptoms of anxiety [32] and stress [33].

Furthermore, as observed by Cusinato et al. [7], our study shows that some socio-demographic and contextual variables can influence parental well-being. Particularly, the type of profession, such as freelancer or unemployment, is related to greater stress and anxiety. This is probably due to the economic uncertainties of these jobs that prevent them from finding the right strategies to deal with it.

According to our results, there is a positive association between the emotional symptoms of the parents (in particular the DL-related stress experienced in the COVID-19 period) and the depressive and anxious symptoms of the children. This further supports the idea that, in the parent–child dyad, there is a reciprocal enhancement of negative symptoms, which can affect the quality of life. Moreover, these data underline the mutual influence between the psychological health of children and parents [7].

It is, therefore, essential that both parents and children are considered in planning interventions in the family environment, avoiding isolated approaches. In fact, it has been shown that parents who have a better psychological adaptation can experience fewer difficulties in their parental role, and this in turn can positively affect the well-being of their children [7]. To this aim, the family should be considered from a systemic perspective, in which all family members mutually influence each other's adaptation, favoring the development of new resources that promote well-being even in difficult times, including pandemics [1,34]. This important approach may be of help when dealing with DL, which has revolutionized the way children learn and study, involving parents more than in previous times.

We believe that it is important to deepen these issues, as remote school and teleconferencing could be a useful resource when integrated with normal teaching, also considering their impact on the family context [1].

Another important result of our study is that we did not find statistically significant relationships between the child's age and sex and the levels of anxiety, stress, depression, and stress of their parents. However, it would be useful to explore this aspect in larger samples involving more male parents to confirm these results.

Despite the interesting results, our study has some limitations. First of all is the online modality to assess the participants. In fact, although it allowed us to reach a fair sample during the lockdown, it did not allow us to control for some contextual variables (such as noise or other distractions) or verify if the participants completed the questionnaire accurately. These potential biases due to the online survey indicate the need for some caution in interpreting the results. Our sample is not representative of fathers, because only 5.2% of the enrolled parents were males. Moreover, most participants had a median/high education, and this could represent a sample bias, as parents with lower education and incomes could have had worse outcomes. Finally, although the study confirmed a correlation between children's behavior and parents' well-being, we did not properly address the effects of confinement on parent–child relationships. Future surveys should address these important concerns.

5. Conclusions

In conclusion, our study pointed out that the COVID-19 pandemic had a negative impact on the psychological well-being of both children and parents who used DL. This suggests that, although DL could be a valid alternative tool, face-to-face teaching is fundamental, especially at a young age. Indeed, differently from DL, normal teaching encourages dialogue, involvement, and human contact, and builds a better environment in which children may train their skills, including the soft ones.

Author Contributions: Conceptualization, M.G.M., M.F.C. and M.C.S.; methodology, M.G.M., P.C. and A.C.; software, M.G.M.; validation, M.G.M. and R.S.C.; formal analysis, M.G.M., M.C.S. and R.S.C.; investigation, M.F.C. and A.M.; resources, M.G.M., M.F.C., A.C. and A.M.; data curation, M.G.M. and R.S.C.; writing—original draft preparation, M.G.M., M.C.S. and P.C; writing—review and editing, M.G.M. and R.S.C.; supervision, R.S.C.; project administration, M.G.M.; resources and supervision, D.B. and G.P. All authors have contributed to the project development. All authors have read and agreed to the published version of the manuscript.

Funding: This research received no external funding.

Institutional Review Board Statement: The study was conducted according to the guidelines of the Declaration of Helsinki, and approved by the Local Institutional Review Board (UNIME 141/20/P).

Informed Consent Statement: Informed consent was obtained from all subjects involved in the study.

Data Availability Statement: Data could be available on demand to the corresponding author.

Conflicts of Interest: The authors declare no conflict of interest.

References

1. Calabrò, R.S.; Maggio, M.G. Telepsychology: A new way to deal with relational problems associated with the COVID-19 epidemic. *Acta Biomed.* **2020**, *91*, e2020140. [CrossRef]
2. Maggio, M.G.; De Luca, R.; Manuli, A.; Calabrò, R.S. The five 'W' of cognitive telerehabilitation in the COVID-19 era. *Expert Rev. Med. Devices* **2020**, *17*, 473–475. [CrossRef]
3. Janssen, L.H.C.; Kullberg, M.-L.J.; Verkuil, B.; Van Zwieten, N.; Wever, M.C.M.; Van Houtum, L.A.E.M.; Wentholt, W.G.M.; Elzinga, B.M. Does the COVID-19 pandemic impact parents' and adolescents' well-being? An EMA-study on daily affect and parenting. *PLoS ONE* **2020**, *15*, e0240962. [CrossRef] [PubMed]
4. Marchetti, D.; Fontanesi, L.; Mazza, C.; Di Giandomenico, S.; Roma, P.; Verrocchio, M.C. Parenting-Related Exhaustion during the Italian COVID-19 Lockdown. *J. Pediatr. Psychol.* **2020**, *45*, 1114–1123. [CrossRef] [PubMed]
5. Patrick, S.W.; Henkhaus, L.E.; Zickafoose, J.S.; Lovell, K.; Halvorson, A.; Loch, S.; Letterie, M.; Davis, M.M. Well-being of Parents and Children during the COVID-19 Pandemic: A National Survey. *Pediatrics* **2020**, *146*, e2020016824. [CrossRef] [PubMed]
6. Cluver, L.; Lachman, J.M.; Sherr, L.; Wessels, I.; Krug, E.; Rakotomalala, S.; Blight, S.; Hillis, S.; Bachman, G.; Green, O.; et al. Parenting in a time of COVID-19. *Lancet* **2020**, *395*, e64. [CrossRef]
7. Cusinato, M.; Iannattone, S.; Spoto, A.; Poli, M.; Moretti, C.; Gatta, M.; Miscioscia, M. Stress, Resilience, and Well-Being in Italian Children and Their Parents during the COVID-19 Pandemic. *Int. J. Environ. Res. Public Health* **2020**, *17*, 8297. [CrossRef] [PubMed]
8. Russell, B.S.; Hutchison, M.; Tambling, R.; Tomkunas, A.J.; Horton, A.L. Initial Challenges of Caregiving during COVID-19: Caregiver Burden, Mental Health, and the Parent–Child Relationship. *Child Psychiatry Hum. Dev.* **2020**, *51*, 671–682. [CrossRef]
9. Spinelli, M.; Lionetti, F.; Pastore, M.; Fasolo, M. Parents' Stress and Children's Psychological Problems in Families Facing the COVID-19 Outbreak in Italy. *Front. Psychol.* **2020**, *11*, 1713. [CrossRef] [PubMed]
10. Orgilés, M.; Morales, A.; DelVecchio, E.; Mazzeschi, C.; Espada, J.P. Immediate Psychological Effects of the COVID-19 Quarantine in Youth from Italy and Spain. *Front. Psychol.* **2020**, *11*, 579038. [CrossRef]
11. Zhao, Y.; Guo, Y.; Xiao, Y.; Zhu, R.; Sun, W.; Huang, W.; Liang, D.; Tang, L.; Zhang, F.; Zhu, D.; et al. The Effects of Online Homeschooling on Children, Parents, and Teachers of Grades 1–9 during the COVID-19 Pandemic. *Med. Sci. Mon. Int. Med. J. Exp. Clin. Res.* **2020**, *26*, e925591-1–e925591-10. [CrossRef] [PubMed]
12. Fegert, J.M.; Vitiello, B.; Plener, P.L.; Clemens, V. Challenges and burden of the Coronavirus 2019 (COVID-19) pandemic for child and adolescent mental health: A narrative review to highlight clinical and research needs in the acute phase and the long return to normality. *Child Adolesc. Psychiatry Ment. Health* **2020**, *14*, 20. [CrossRef] [PubMed]
13. Roje Đapić, M.; Buljan Flander, G.; Prijatelj, K. Children behind closed doors due to COVID-19 isolation: Abuse, neglect and domestic violence. *Arch. Psych. Res.* **2020**, *56*, 181–192. [CrossRef]
14. Mikolajczak, M.; Gross, J.J.; Roskam, I. Parental Burnout: What Is It, and Why Does It Matter? *Clin. Psychol. Sci.* **2019**, *7*, 1319–1329. [CrossRef]
15. Lee, J. Mental health effects of school closures during COVID-19. *Lancet Child Adolesc. Health* **2020**, *4*, 421. [CrossRef]
16. Zhou, X. Managing psychological distress in children and adolescents following the COVID-19 epidemic: A cooperative approach. *Psychol. Trauma* **2020**, *12*, S76–S78. [CrossRef] [PubMed]
17. Farahmand, S.; Jalili, E.; Arbab, M.; Sedaghat, M.; Shirazi, M.; Keshmiri, F.; Azizpour, A.; Valadkhani, S.; Bagheri-Hariri, S. Distance learning can be as effective as traditional learning for medical students in the initial assessment of trauma patients. *Acta Med. Iran.* **2016**, *54*, 600–604. [PubMed]

18. Osman, A.; Wong, J.L.; Bagge, C.L.; Freedenthal, S.; Gutierrez, P.M.; Lozano, G. The Depression Anxiety Stress Scales-21 (DASS-21): Further Examination of Dimensions, Scale Reliability, and Correlates. *J. Clin. Psychol.* **2012**, *68*, 1322–1338. [CrossRef]
19. Bottesi, G.; Ghisi, M.; Altoè, G.; Conforti, E.; Melli, G.; Sica, C. The Italian Version of the Depression Anxiety Stress Scales-21: Factor Structure and Psychometric Properties on Community and Clinical Samples. *Compr. Psychiatry* **2015**, *60*, 170–181. [CrossRef]
20. Cole, D.A.; Carpentieri, S. Social status and the comorbidity of child depression and conduct disorder. *J. Consult. Clin. Psychol.* **1990**, *58*, 748–757. [CrossRef]
21. Kovacs, M. *The Children's Depression Inventory: A Self-Rated Depression Scale for School-Aged Youngsters*; University of Pittsburgh School of Medicine: Pittsburgh, PA, USA, 1983.
22. Camuffo, M.; Cerutti, R.; Lucarelli, L.; Mayer, R.C.D.I. *Children's Depression Inventory—Questionario di Autovalutazione di Maria Kovacs—Manuale*; Organizzazioni Speciali: Firenze, Italy, 1988.
23. Nilsson, S.; Buchholz, M.; Thunberg, G. Assessing Children's Anxiety Using the Modified Short State-Trait Anxiety Inventory and Talking Mats: A Pilot Study. *Nurs. Res. Pract.* **2012**, *2012*, 932570. [CrossRef]
24. Delvecchio, E.; Cavallina, C.; DI Riso, D.; Mazzeschi, C. Early Evidence of the Italian Validation of the Trait Anxiety Scale of the State-Trait Anxiety Inventory for Children. *Eur. J. Dev. Psychol.* **2017**, *15*, 214–223. [CrossRef]
25. Lewis, J.R. The system usability scale: Past, present, and future. *Int. J. Hum. Comput. Interact.* **2018**, *34*, 577–590. [CrossRef]
26. Kavčič, T.; Avsec, A.; Kocjan, G.Z. Psychological Functioning of Slovene Adults during the COVID-19 Pandemic: Does Resilience Matter? *Psychiatr. Q.* **2020**, *92*, 207–216. [CrossRef] [PubMed]
27. Wang, G.; Zhang, Y.; Zhao, J.; Zhang, J.; Jiang, F. Mitigate the effects of home confinement on children during the COVID-19 outbreak. *Lancet* **2020**, *395*, 945–947. [CrossRef]
28. Di Giorgio, E.; Di Riso, D.; Mioni, G.; Cellini, N. The interplay between mothers' and children behavioral and psychological factors during COVID-19: An Italian study. *Eur. Child Adolesc. Psychiatry* **2021**, *30*, 1401–1412, Advance Online Publication. [CrossRef]
29. Gassman-Pines, A.; Ananat, E.O.; Fitz-Henley, J. COVID-19 and Parent-Child Psychological Well-being. *Pediatrics* **2020**, *146*, e2020007294. [CrossRef]
30. Colizzi, M.; Sironi, E.; Antonini, F.; Ciceri, M.L.; Bovo, C.; Zoccante, L. Psychosocial and Behavioral Impact of COVID-19 in Autism Spectrum Disorder: An Online Parent Survey. *Brain Sci.* **2020**, *10*, 341. [CrossRef] [PubMed]
31. Saurabh, K.; Ranjan, S. Compliance and Psychological Impact of Quarantine in Children and Adolescents due to COVID-19 Pandemic. *Indian J. Pediatr.* **2020**, *87*, 532–536. [CrossRef]
32. Freeston, M.; Tiplady, A.; Mawn, L.; Bottesi, G.; Thwaites, S. Towards a model of uncertainty distress in the context of Coronavirus (COVID-19). *Cogn. Behav. Ther.* **2020**, *13*, e31. [CrossRef]
33. Amin, S. The psychology of coronavirus fear: Are healthcare professionals suffering from corona-phobia? *Int. J. Health Manag.* **2020**, *13*, 249–256. [CrossRef]
34. Maggio, M.G.; De Luca, R.; Torrisi, M.; De Cola, M.C.; Buda, A.; Rosano, M.; Visani, E.; Pidalà, A.; Bramanti, P.; Calabrò, R.S. Is there a correlation between family functioning and functional recovery in patients with acquired brain injury? An exploratory study. *Appl. Nurs. Res.* **2018**, *41*, 11–14. [CrossRef] [PubMed]

International Journal of
Environmental Research and Public Health

MDPI

Article

Quality of Life, Insomnia and Coping Strategies during COVID-19 Pandemic in Hospital Workers. A Cross-Sectional Study

Sebastiano Italia [1], Chiara Costa [2], Giusi Briguglio [1], Carmela Mento [3], Maria Rosaria Anna Muscatello [4], Angela Alibrandi [5], Francesca Larese Filon [6], Giovanna Spatari [1], Michele Teodoro [1,*] and Concettina Fenga [1]

1 Department of Biomedical and Dental Sciences and Morphofunctional Imaging, Occupational Medicine Section, University of Messina, 98125 Messina, Italy; sebastos87@hotmail.it (S.I.); giusi.briguglio@hotmail.it (G.B.); gspatari@unime.it (G.S.); cfenga@unime.it (C.F.)
2 Clinical and Experimental Medicine Department, University of Messina, 98125 Messina, Italy; ccosta@unime.it
3 Department of Biomedical and Dental Sciences and Morphofunctional Imaging, Clinical Psychology, Psychiatric Unit, University of Messina, 98125 Messina, Italy; carmela.mento@unime.it
4 Department of Biomedical and Dental Sciences and Morphofunctional Imaging, Psychiatric Unit, University of Messina, 98125 Messina, Italy; maria.muscatello@unime.it
5 Department of Economics, University of Messina, 98125 Messina, Italy; angela.alibrandi@unime.it
6 Department of Medical Sciences, Clinical Unit of Occupational Medicine, University of Trieste, 34100 Trieste, Italy; larese@units.it
* Correspondence: michele.teodoro@unime.it; Tel.: +39-090-221-2061

Citation: Italia, S.; Costa, C.; Briguglio, G.; Mento, C.; Muscatello, M.R.A.; Alibrandi, A.; Larese Filon, F.; Spatari, G.; Teodoro, M.; Fenga, C. Quality of Life, Insomnia and Coping Strategies during COVID-19 Pandemic in Hospital Workers. A Cross-Sectional Study. *Int. J. Environ. Res. Public Health* **2021**, *18*, 12466. https://doi.org/10.3390/ijerph182312466

Academic Editors: Paolo Roma, Merylin Monaro and Cristina Mazza

Received: 22 October 2021
Accepted: 25 November 2021
Published: 26 November 2021

Abstract: COVID-19 became a pandemic in a few months, leading to adverse health outcomes, reducing the quality of life, affecting the sleep/wake cycle, and altering coping strategies, especially among hospital personnel. Life quality, insomnia, and coping strategies were thus assessed among hospital personnel during the first wave of the COVID-19 pandemic in Italy. This cross-sectional study was conducted from May to November 2020 through an online survey. There were 558 participants (28.5% males and 71.5% females) enrolled in two different metropolitan areas (in North and South of Italy, respectively). Three standardized questionnaires were administered: European Quality of life–5 Dimensions (EQ-5D), Athens Insomnia Scale (AIS), and Brief COPE. Differences in sociodemographic characteristics and work-related factors were also investigated in order to identify possible predictors through a generalized linear model and logistic regression analysis. Results showed good perceived life quality and high insomnia prevalence. After sample stratification, the statistical analysis highlighted that personal (gender, age, educational level) and work-related factors (employment in COVID wards, remote working) played different roles in predicting quality of life, insomnia, and coping attitude. Active, Planning, and Acceptance were the most frequently adopted coping strategies. Despite women confirming their attitude in reacting to the difficulties, adopting emotion-focused coping strategies, they showed a higher probability to develop insomnia, so a gender perspective should be considered in the health protection of this working category. An integrated approach should be implemented at individual, interpersonal and organizational levels aiming to monitor psychological distress, favor regular sharing and communication between peers, and also allow conciliation of work with family life. At the organizational level, preventive and protective measures adequate to work-related risk to COVID-19 should be adopted.

Keywords: COVID-19; hospital workers; quality of life; coping strategy; insomnia

1. Introduction

Coronavirus disease (COVID-19), which started in Wuhan, China, in December 2019, became a pandemic in a few months, leading to extraordinary risks to human beings [1]. Despite the majority of infected subjects having a moderate illness and about 10–15% of patients developing grave complications [2], until 21 October 2021, about 4.9 million deaths were declared, with over 241 million cases confirmed globally [3].

In Italy, the epidemiological situation during the first wave, since February 2020, differently concerned the country with a significant burden of disease in the North rather than the South; in particular, Lombardy, Piedmont, Emilia Romagna, and Veneto were the most affected northern regions [4]. The Italian government handled this critical situation by implementing preventive measures and adopting a national lockdown on 10 March 2020 [5]. Consequently, Italians lived in social isolation for about two months; only indispensable activities were allowed and leaving home was consented to only for health reasons, purchasing vital products, and reaching the workplace, when permitted [6]. The pandemic altered everybody's lives and work behaviors, particularly those healthcare workers (HCWs) who were involved on the frontline with increased exposure to SARS-CoV-2 infection, lack of validated guidelines, and shortage of resources including personal protective equipment [7]. In addition, these workers have often decided to live far from their loved ones to keep them safe from an additional risk of contagion [8].

In previous research, outbreaks of other contagious diseases led to adverse health outcomes in HCWs impacting physical, social, emotional, or spiritual wellbeing, globally reducing the quality of life [9–11]. Despite life quality being a broad-range concept, the WHO defines it as the subjective perception of own position in life in the specific cultural context and in relation to personal expectations, standards, and concerns [12]. The literature describes five dimensions that define life quality in terms of mobility, self-care, usual activities, pain/discomfort, and anxiety/depression [13]. The current COVID-19 pandemic has created circumstances with overwhelming stressors on HCWs, through increased working loads, high risk of exposure to SARS-CoV-2, and overall disruptions of daily life, leading to increased anxiety, stress, depression, burnout and sleep disorders [14], especially insomnia [15], and to a drastic reduction in the perceived quality of life [16,17].

The considerable psychological impact of the COVID-19 pandemic has undoubtedly influenced feelings and behaviors [18,19], requiring the adoption of coping strategies to play a buffering role on stress and have a preventive effect on mental health [20]. Different coping strategies are used depending on external factors (such as cultural and workplace context or geographical area) [21] and individual components (e.g., rage, terror, or sadness) [22].

Though it has been demonstrated that the trend of contagion has differently affected the mental health status of HCWs working in areas with dissimilar incidences of COVID-19 cases [23,24], it is also true that regional differences in stress perception and coping strategies also depend on cultural factors, home/work interface, social support, and economic environment [25,26]. In a Chinese study, comparing subjects coming from Hubei and from non-endemic provinces, health workers in the endemic region showed lower anxiety levels about the COVID-19 epidemic [23]. In a multicentre prospective cohort epidemiological study, the regional origin explained a small fraction of differences in perceived job stress [27], while other factors seem to play major roles in affecting this aspect. For example, family is a fundamental source of support, particularly in developing areas where social services are scarce [28]. Under these premises, we mainly aimed to assess the quality of life, insomnia, and analyze the different coping strategies adopted among hospital personnel during the first wave of the COVID-19 pandemic in Italy. More specifically, we examined the differences in sociodemographic characteristics and work-related factors in two different Italian metropolitan areas with similar epidemiological trends, located in the North and in the South of Italy, respectively. We intended to identify eventual work-related and sociodemographic predictors of worse outcomes, suggesting insights on the best tailored preventive and organizational measures in the workplace.

2. Materials and Methods

2.1. Study Design and Population

This cross-sectional study was conducted from May to November 2020 through an online survey. Participants were enrolled among hospital personnel working in different medical treatment facilities and included physicians, nurses, and other employees (such as biologists, pharmacists, laboratory technicians, and office workers). According to Italian legislation, in order to reduce the number of SARS-CoV-2 infections in the workplaces, employers had the possibility, when applicable, to guarantee working from home for the most vulnerable subjects. Consequently, some office workers enrolled in the present investigation performed remote work.

Study subjects were recruited in two Italian metropolitan areas, namely Trieste (group N) in the North and Messina (group S) in the South of Italy.

Data were collected through an online platform recruiting subjects by spreading an invitation link. In order to increase the diffusion and validity of this sampling method, the invitation for the survey was sent to directors and coordinators, requesting them to spread it to their teams in a hierarchical line.

2.2. Procedures and Measures

The self-administered questionnaire was composed of two sections and took no more than twenty minutes to be completed. The first section investigated the sample's sociodemographic characteristics and work-related factors: gender, age, educational degree, marital status, number of children, profession, employment in COVID wards, number of contacts per week with COVID patients, remote working, and seniority. The second one comprised three standardized questionnaires: European Quality of life–5 Dimensions (EQ-5D), Athens Insomnia Scale (AIS), and Brief COPE.

The European Quality of life–5 Dimensions (EQ-5D) is a broadly used questionnaire developed in Europe to evaluate the essential quality of life components. This tool measures mobility, self-care, usual activities, pain/discomfort, and anxiety/depression through one question for each of the five dimensions. Throughout an algorithm, the given answers permit the calculation of the EQ-5D index, in which 0 is death and 1 represents perfect health. The EQ-5D questionnaire also comprises a Visual Analog Scale (VAS), measuring respondents' perceived health status, ranging from 0 (the worst thinkable wellbeing) to 100 (the best thinkable wellbeing) [29]. Specifically, the EQ-5D index value describes the health state, while the EQ-VAS gives information about individual health perception [30,31].

The Athens Insomnia Scale (AIS) is an eight-item questionnaire that reveals insomnia. The first five questions report the subject's nocturnal symptoms, while the last three items investigate the daytime impact due to sleep disorders. Each item is assigned a score from 0 to 3 according to a 4-point Likert scale (with 0 equivalent to "no problem" and 3 to a "severe problem"). The maximum total score is 24, which indicates the most severe insomnia symptoms. A cut-off of $\geq$6 represents the criterion for confirming insomnia symptoms [32].

The Brief COPE evaluates different coping strategies, both adaptation and maladaptation approaches. We used this tool to evaluate the stress response in a recent period ("situational-actual" version). The questionnaire includes 28 items, each assigned a score from 1 to 4 according to a 4-point Likert scale, divided into 14 factors, each consisting of two items. The 14 factors are Self-Distraction; Active Coping; Denial; Substance Use; Emotional Support; Instrumental Support; Behavioral Disengagement; Venting; Positive Reframing; Planning; Humor; Acceptance; Religion and Self-Blame [33].

2.3. Ethical Issues

This study was carried out in accordance with the Declaration of Helsinki's ethical standards. The study needed no formal approval by the local Ethics Committee, though a formal communication of study beginning was given (notification with request for acknowledgement). All the subjects who accepted voluntary participation in the survey provided informed consent. Participation was voluntary and without compensation.

2.4. Statistical Analysis

Descriptive analyses were performed for all variables; in particular, categorical variables were expressed as frequency and proportion, whilst continuous variables were expressed as mean and standard deviation. To determine differences between groups in categorical variables, we used chi-square tests and Fisher's exact tests, as appropriate. After applying the Kolmogorov-Smirnov test and verifying the non-Gaussian distribution in most continuous variables, the differences between groups were evaluated using the Mann—Whitney U test. The reliability of the three standardized questionnaires was evaluated by assessing their internal consistency through the computation of Chronbach's alpha. Furthermore, in order to identify possible predictors of outcomes considered in the current investigation, we adopted different models: we used the generalized linear models for EQ-5D-Index, for EQ-VAS, and for each one of the 14 coping strategies of Brief-COPE; in addition, we estimated univariate and multivariate logistic regression models for Athens Insomnia Scale (dichotomized variable in according to previously described criterion). p values < 0.05 were considered statistically significant and reported in bold characters in the Tables. Statistical analysis was performed using IBM SPSS Statistics 23 (IBM Corp, Armonk, NY, USA).

3. Results

A total of 558 respondents, 347 participants in group N and 211 in group S, accepted to participate in the study and completed the survey. A detailed description of the study population is summarized in Table 1.

Table 1. Description of study population: sociodemographic characteristics and work-related factors.

		Total *n* (%)	**Group N** *n* (%)	**Group S** *n* (%)	*p*-**Value**
SOCIODEMOGRAPHIC FACTORS					
Total		558 (100)	347 (62.2)	211 (37.8)	
Gender					
	Male	159 (28.5)	86 (24.8)	73 (34.6)	**0.013**
	Female	399 (71.5)	261 (75.2)	138 (65.4)	
Age					
	<40 y	215 (38.5)	95 (27.4)	120 (56.9)	**<0.001**
	>40 y	343 (61.5)	252 (72.6)	91 (43.1)	
Education					
	Middle school	14 (2.5)	13 (3.7)	1 (0.2)	**<0.001**
	High School	108 (19.4)	83 (23.9)	25 (11.8)	
	Graduation	247 (44.3)	131 (37.8)	116 (55.0)	
	Post-graduation	189 (33.9)	120 (34.6)	69 (32.7)	
Marital status					
	Not married	135 (24.2)	62 (17.9)	73 (34.6)	**<0.001**
	Unmarried partners	117 (21.0)	86 (24.8)	31 (14.7)	
	Married	258 (46.2)	166 (47.8)	92 (43.6)	
	Divorced	48 (8.6)	33 (9.5)	15 (7.1)	
Parenthood					
	No	255 (45.7)	140 (40.3)	115 (54.5)	**0.001**
	Yes	303 (54.3)	207 (59.7)	96 (45.5)	
Number of children					
	Mean ± SD	0.96 ± 1.06	1.04 ± 1.03	0.82 ± 1.11	**0.003**

Table 1. *Cont.*

		Total *n* (%)	Group N *n* (%)	Group S *n* (%)	*p*-Value
WORK-RELATED FACTORS					
Profession					
	Physician	184 (33.0)	67 (19.3)	117 (55.5)	**<0.001**
	Nurse	212 (38.0)	154 (44.4)	58 (27.5)	
	Others	162 (29.0)	126 (36.3)	36 (17.1)	
COVID Ward					
	No	450 (80.6)	282 (81.3)	168 (79.6)	0.633
	Yes	108 (19.4)	65 (18.7)	43 (20.4)	
Number of contacts per week with COVID patients					
	None	269 (48.2)	160 (46.1)	109 (51.7)	0.471
	One	81 (14.5)	49 (14.1)	32 (15.2)	
	Five	139 (24.9)	93 (26.8)	46 (21.8)	
	Exclusive	69 (12.4)	45 (13.0)	24 (11.4)	
Remote working					
	No	490 (87.8)	321 (92.5)	169 (80.1)	**<0.001**
	Yes	68 (12.2)	26 (7.5)	42 (19.9)	
Seniority (years)					
	Mean ± SD	16.17 ± 12.62	18.97 ± 12.75	11.56 ± 10.96	**<0.001**

The study population consisted of 399 women (71.5%) and 159 men (28.5%) aged 18–65 years. We found statistically significant differences between the two groups in all the considered sociodemographic characteristics: the number of women in group N was higher than in group S (75.2% and 65.4%, respectively); less than one-third of subjects in group N (27.4%) and the majority in group S (56.9%) were aged under 40 years; most participants in group S were graduated (55%), while in group N the percentages were more equally distributed among the different educational degree. Regarding marital status, in group S, single (not married and divorced) and in pairs (married and unmarried partners) were similarly represented, whilst in group N, the majority had a partner (72.6%) and parenthood was more frequent in group N than in group S (59.7% and 45.5% had children, respectively).

Considering work-related factors, most of the participants were nurses in group N and doctors in group S; in both groups, there were no statistical differences in relation to the employment in COVID wards and the number of contacts per week with COVID patients. Moreover, 68 subjects (42 in group S and 26 in group N) were employed in remote working during the pandemic. In addition, we observed a higher length of employment in group N than in group S, with a statistically significant difference.

European Quality of life–5 Dimensions (Index and VAS), Athens Insomnia Scale and Brief COPE scores are reported in Table 2. The reliability assessment showed the following Chronbach's alpha: EQ–5 D Index 0.59; Athens Insomnia Scale 0.86; while for the different coping strategies we found Active 0.70; Planning 0.74; Positive Reframing 0.70; Acceptance 0.54; Humor 0.65; Religion 0.88; Emotional Support 0.81; Instrumental Support 0.79; Self Distraction 0.50; Denial 0.55; Venting 0.58; Substance Use 0.89; Disengagement 0.50; Self Blame 0.42.

Despite the two groups showing high values of self-reported quality of life, group S showed better scores than group N both in Index and VAS of EQ-5D questionnaire with statistically significant differences. Moreover, we stratified the sample into different subgroups according to sociodemographic and work-related variables, comparing the two groups. Subsequently, we found the highest values of EQ-5D-Index in the stratified group S, with statistically significant differences among women, graduated subjects, participants with no children, workers not employed in COVID wards. Moreover, a similar trend was observed in EQ-VAS, except for gender, for which statistical significance was found among men but not among women. Furthermore, in order to identify possible predictors of better scores, we used a generalized linear model for EQ-5D-Index as reported in Table 3.

Table 2. Mean scores of validated questionnaires assessing health-related and perceived quality of life, insomnia, and coping strategies in healthcare personnel during the first wave of COVID-19 pandemic (n = 558).

	Total Mean ± SD	Group N Mean ± SD	Group S Mean ± SD	p-Value
EQ-5D-Index	0.785 ± 0.230	0.764 ± 0.226	0.821 ± 0.232	**<0.001**
EQ-VAS	75.70 ± 17.51	74.50 ± 17.07	77.68 ± 18.18	**0.004**
Athens Insomnia Scale				
Mean ± SD	5.76 ± 3.96	5.87 ± 3.92	5.57 ± 4.02	0.252
≥6 (%)	253 (45.3)	162 (46.7)	91 (43.1)	0.413
Brief-COPE				
Active	6.53 ± 1.37	6.57 ± 1.29	6.47 ± 1.51	0.877
Planning	6.56 ± 1.32	6.57 ± 1.24	6.55 ± 1.45	0.578
Positive Reframing	5.51 ± 1.58	5.55 ± 1.55	5.43 ± 1.62	0.396
Acceptance	6.11 ± 1.32	6.14 ± 1.22	6.05 ± 1.48	0.943
Humor	3.72 ± 1.46	3.61 ± 1.40	3.91 ± 1.55	**0.029**
Religion	3.66 ± 1.87	3.40 ± 1.81	4.09 ± 1.89	**<0.001**
Emotional Support	4.49 ± 1.67	4.51 ± 1.64	4.47 ± 1.71	0.697
Instrumental Support	4.91 ± 1.64	4.98 ± 1.53	4.78 ± 1.80	0.116
Self Distraction	5.24 ± 1.59	5.22 ± 1.59	5.26 ± 1.60	0.913
Denial	2.78 ± 1.19	2.63 ± 1.06	3.01 ± 1.34	**0.001**
Venting	4.45 ± 1.50	4.53 ± 1.47	4.32 ± 1.55	0.111
Substance Use	2.25 ± 0.83	2.22 ± 0.76	2.31 ± 0.94	0.426
Disengagement	2.82 ± 1.15	2.80 ± 1.08	2.86 ± 1.26	0.993
Self Blame	5.03 ± 1.44	4.89 ± 1.35	5.25 ± 1.56	**0.009**

Table 3. Generalized linear model for EQ-5D-Index, assessing quality of life in healthcare workers during the first wave of COVID-19 pandemic (n = 558).

	Independent Variables	B-Value	95% CI	p-Value
	Total			
	Sex (male)	0.08	0.04–0.12	**<0.001**
	Age (>40 y)	−0.02	−0.08–0.04	0.570
	Education	0.03	0.01–0.05	**0.029**
	Marital status (married)	0.03	−0.01–0.07	0.128
	Parenthood	−0.02	−0.07–0.02	0.294
	Region (south)	0.02	−0.02–0.06	0.429
	Profession (nurse)	0.01	−0.01–0.01	0.824
	COVID ward (yes)	−0.01	−0.06–0.05	0.841
	N° contacts with COVID patients per week	−0.01	−0.03–0.01	0.329
	Remote working (yes)	0.01	−0.05–0.07	0.732
	Seniority (years)	−0.01	−0.02–−0.01	**0.007**
Group N				
	Sex (male)	0.09	0.04–0.14	**0.001**
	Age (>40 y)	−0.03	−0.11–0.04	0.367
	Education	0.03	0.01–0.05	0.069
	Marital status (married)	0.06	0.01–0.11	**0.036**
	Parenthood	−0.01	−0.06–0.04	0.717
	Profession (nurse)	0.01	−0.01–0.01	0.668
	COVID ward (yes)	0.01	−0.07–0.06	0.911
	N° contacts with COVID patients per week	0.01	−0.02–0.03	0.975
	Remote working (yes)	−0.01	−0.10–0.08	0.782
	Seniority (years)	0.01	−0.01–0.01	0.238
Group S				
	Sex (male)	0.09	0.02–0.15	**0.007**
	Age (>40 y)	0.07	−0.03–0.18	0.166
	Education	0.04	−0.01–0.08	0.130
	Marital status (married)	−0.01	−0.08–0.05	0.686
	Parenthood	−0.02	−0.10–0.06	0.653
	Profession (nurse)	0.01	−0.01–0.01	0.558
	COVID ward (yes)	−0.02	−0.05–0.01	0.907
	N° contacts with COVID patients per week	−0.02	−0.05–0.01	0.126
	Remote working (yes)	0.01	−0.08–0.08	0.973
	Seniority (years)	−0.01	−0.02–−0.01	**<0.001**

In the total sample, male gender, high education levels, and lower seniority were positive predictors of a better perceived quality of life according to EQ-5D-Index. Having a partner and lower seniority were considered predictors of a better quality of life respectively in group N and group S. For EQ-VAS (Table 4), male gender and high education levels in the total sample represented significant predictors of better perceived quality of life. High education degree was identified as a positive predictor both in group N and S; while in group S male gender and lower seniority were considered predictors of more excellent scores in the European Quality of life questionnaire.

Table 4. Generalized linear model for EQ-VAS, assessing perceived wellbeing in healthcare workers during the first wave of COVID-19 pandemic (n = 558).

	Independent Variables	B-Value	95% CI	*p*-Value
	Total			
	Sex (male)	3.36	0.16–6.55	**0.039**
	Age (>40 y)	−3.42	−8.06–1.21	0.148
	Education	2.59	0.74–4.44	**0.006**
	Marital status (married)	1.44	−1.84–4.72	0.390
	Parenthood	−1.84	−5.35–1.67	0.303
	Region (south)	−0.17	−3.35–3.02	0.919
	Profession (nurse)	0.01	−0.01–0.01	0.145
	COVID ward (yes)	−1.65	−5.69–2.40	0.425
	N° contacts with COVID patients per week	0.78	−0.73–2.28	0.312
	Remote working (yes)	2.49	−2.08–7.06	0.285
	Seniority (years)	−0.12	−0.29–0.05	0.180
Group N				
	Sex (male)	0.97	−3.21–5.15	0.649
	Age (>40 y)	−5.57	−11.36–0.23	0.060
	Education	2.46	0.27–4.64	**0.028**
	Marital status (married)	1.49	−2.73–5.71	0.488
	Parenthood	−0.03	−4.29–4.23	0.989
	Profession (nurse)	0.01	−0.01–0.01	0.232
	COVID ward (yes)	1.88	−.34–7.22	0.488
	N° contacts with COVID patients per week	0.17	−1.77–2.12	0.862
	Remote working (yes)	−0.35	−7.43–6.73	0.922
	Seniority (years)	0.02	−0.17–0.22	0.833
Group S				
	Sex (male)	7.50	2.52–12.48	**0.003**
	Age (>40 y)	4.95	−3.14–13.03	0.229
	Education	3.57	0.02–7.11	**0.048**
	Marital status (married)	1.90	−3.34–7.15	0.475
	Parenthood	−3.56	−9.76–2.65	0.260
	Profession (nurse)	0.01	0.00–0.01	0.478
	COVID ward (yes)	−6.93	−13.18–−0.67	**0.030**
	N° contacts with COVID patients per week	1.95	−0.43–4.33	0.108
	Remote working (yes)	2.00	−4.06–8.06	0.515
	Seniority (years)	−0.66	−1.03–−0.29	**<0.001**

Differently, the Athens Insomnia Scale questionnaire revealed insomnia in 162 out of 247 subjects (46.7% in group N) and 91 out of 211 (43.1% in group S), without statistically significant differences. Nevertheless, after stratifying the sample as described above, we found statistically significant differences among not married subjects and participants with no children, showing worse outcomes in group N after stratification. Moreover, in the distribution of the Athens Insomnia Scale, we considered the score 6 as pathological cut-off (such as proposed by Soldatos et al. [32]); consequently, we used univariate and multivariate logistic regression (Table 5) in order to individuate significant predictors of insomnia symptoms.

Accordingly with univariate logistic regression, female subjects (OR 2.09, 95% CI 1.42–3.07) and nurses (OR 1.62, 95% CI 1.09–2.42), both male and female, showed a high risk of suffering from insomnia in the total sample, while multivariate approach showed only women as the category at high risk (OR 2.20, 95% CI 1.48–3.28), in the overall sample as well as in both groups N and S. In group N, single subjects (not married and divorced) showed a higher risk of suffering from insomnia (OR 1.76, 95% CI 1.09–2.83) in univariate regression. In group S univariate approach showed that the number of contacts per week with COVID patients was also a work-related factor determining a high risk of insomnia (OR 1.29, 95% CI 1.00–1.66); moreover, in the multivariate logistic regression, nurses showed a lower risk of insomnia when compared to physicians (OR 0.99, 95% CI 0.98–0.99).

Table 5. Univariate and multivariate logistic regression for Athens Insomnia Scale in healthcare workers during the first wave of COVID-19 pandemic (n = 558).

		UNIVARIATE			MULTIVARIATE	
Independent Variables	**OR**	**95% CI**	***p*-Value**	**OR**	**95% CI**	***p*-Value**
Total						
Sex (female)	2.09	1.42–3.07	**<0.001**	2.20	1.48–3.28	**<0.001**
Age (>40 y)	1.15	0.81–1.62	0.434	1.46	0.65–2.01	0.636
Education	0.89	0.72–1.10	0.281	0.91	0.73–1.13	0.391
Marital status (married)	0.82	0.58–1.17	0.275	0.81	0.55–1.21	0.304
Parenthood	0.96	0.69–1.34	0.814	0.94	0.61–1.43	0.761
Region (south)	0.87	0.61–1.22	0.413	0.99	0.68–1.46	0.975
Profession (nurse)	1.62	1.09–2.42	**0.018**	1.00	1.00–1.01	0.674
COVID ward (yes)	1.15	0.76–1.75	0.514	0.91	0.56–1.48	0.705
N° contacts with COVID patients per week	1.30	0.93–1.81	0.127	1.20	1.00–1.44	0.057
Remote working (yes)	0.72	0.43–1.21	0.211	0.77	0.44–1.35	0.771
Seniority (years)	1.00	0.99–1.02	0.624	1.00	0.98–1.02	0.997
Group N						
Sex (female)	2.19	1.31–3.65	**0.003**	2.27	1.34–3.85	**0.002**
Age (>40 y)	1.08	0.67–1.74	0.744	1.36	0.67–2.78	0.393
Education	0.89	0.70–1.14	0.371	0.91	0.70–1.18	0.470
Marital status (married)	0.57	0.35–0.92	**0.021**	0.62	0.37–1.03	0.065
Parenthood	0.76	0.50–1.17	0.216	0.77	0.46–1.30	0.324
Profession (nurse)	1.00	1.00–1.01	0.247	1.00	1.00–1.01	0.128
COVID ward (yes)	1.05	0.61–1.80	0.857	0.96	0.50–1.84	0.895
N° contacts with COVID patients per week	1.05	0.87–1.27	0.612	1.14	0.90–1.45	0.281
Remote working (yes)	0.83	0.37–1.85	0.642	0.78	0.33–1.85	0.569
Seniority (years)	0.99	0.98–1.02	0.885	0.99	0.97–1.02	0.635
Group S						
Sex (female)	1.93	1.07–3.48	**0.030**	2.81	1.46–5.38	**0.002**
Age (>40 y)	1.15	0.66–1.99	0.623	0.76	0.27–2.16	0.607
Education	0.91	0.60–1.38	0.652	0.98	0.63–1.54	0.932
Marital status (married)	0.79	0.45–1.38	0.406	1.30	0.66–2.55	0.446
Parenthood	1.32	0.77–2.29	0.316	1.22	0.55–2.72	0.626
Profession (nurse)	0.99	0.99–1.00	0.099	0.99	0.98–0.99	**0.033**
COVID ward (yes)	1.34	0.68–2.62	0.398	0.94	0.42–2.10	0.883
N° contacts with COVID patients per week	1.29	1.00–1.66	**0.050**	1.34	0.99–1.83	0.058
Remote working (yes)	0.68	0.34–1.37	0.280	0.96	0.44–2.10	0.914
Seniority (years)	1.01	0.98–1.03	0.484	1.01	0.96–1.06	0.649

Considering the mean scores of the Brief COPE questionnaire (Table 2), the coping strategies with the highest values were Active, Planning and Acceptance, while Substance Use and Disengagement reported the lowest scores in both groups. Moreover, group S reported higher values than group N in Humor, Religion, Denial, and Self-blame, showing statistically significant differences. Additionally, we applied a generalized linear model for each one of the 14 coping strategies. In the overall sample, we found different predictive variables as illustrated in Table 6A,B, for sociodemographic and work-related features of the study population, respectively. Male gender was revealed to be the most frequently described negative predictor in our statistical models, showing that being a woman is related to almost all the analyzed coping strategies. An age of >40 y acted as a predictor of Acceptance and Religion; education positively predicted Emotional Support, while a lower educational level was in relation with Denial and Venting. Being part of group S predicted Religion and Denial, while group N participants were related to Instrumental Support. As regards work-related factors, the employment in COVID wards was related to Emotional and Instrumental Support. On the other hand, remote working predicted Religion, Denial, and Disengagement. No predictive variables were found for the coping strategies Positive reframing, Humor, and Substance use. While Disengagement was not predicted from any sociodemographic characteristics, no work-related variables were found as predictors of Acceptance, Self-distraction, Venting, and Self-blame.

Table 6. (**A**). Generalized linear model for Brief-COPE in relation to sociodemographic predictors in healthcare workers (n = 558). (**B**). Generalized linear model for Brief-COPE in relation to work-related predictors in healthcare workers (n = 558).

(A)

	Sociodemographic Characteristics					
Coping Strategies	**Male**	**Age > 40 y**	**Education**	**Married**	**Parenthood**	**Southern Area**
Active	−0.38 *T (−0.68 to −0.07); −0.50 *S (−0.97 to −0.04)					
Planning	−0.35 *T (−0.64 to −0.05)					
Acceptance		0.64 *N (0.12 to 1.15)				
Religion	−0.39 *T (−0.78 to −0.01); −0.61 *N (−1.15 to −0.07)	0.71 *T (0.09 to 1.32) 1.57 **S (0.52 to 2.63)				0.88 ***T (0.47 to 1.29)
Emotional Support	−0.76 ***T (−1.12 to −0.40); −0.98 ***N (−1.47 to −0.49)		0.45 *S (0.01 to 0.89)			
Instrumental Support	−0.67 ***T (−1.03 to −0.32); −0.72 **N (−1.18 to −0.26)					−0.44*T (−0.81 to −0.06)
Self Distraction	−0.40 *T (−0.73 to −0.06)				−0.48 *T (−0.88 to −0.09)	
Denial	−0.39 *N (−0.74 to −0.04)		−0.29 *N (−0.55 to −0.03)			0.53 ***T (0.25 to 0.81)
Venting	−0.58 ***T (−0.91 to −0.25); −0.85 ***N (−1.30 to −0.40)		−0.22 *N (−0.42 to −0.01)			
Self Blame	−0.45 **T (−0.75 to −0.15); −0.53 *S (−0.97 to −0.09)					

(B)

	Work-Related Factors				
Coping Strategies	Nurse	COVID Ward	COVID Patients	Remote Work	Seniority
Active	−0.41 *T (−0.78 to −0.41)				
Planning			0.27 *S (0.04 to 0.50)		
Religion			0.26 *N (0.02 to 0.50)	0.81 *T (0.17 to 1.45); 0.80 *S (0.04 to 1.56)	
Emotional Support		0.61 **T (0.16 to 1.06); 0.79 **N (0.24 to 1.34)			−0.03 *T (−0.05 to −0.01); −0.03 *N (−0.05 to −0.01)
Instrumental Support		0.98 *S (0.19 to 1.78)			
Denial	0.5 6 *S (0.01 to 1.12)			0.47 *T (0.02 to 0.91); 0.65 *S (0.10 to 1.20)	0.04 *S (0.01 to 0.07)
Disengagement				0.45 *T (0.02 to 0.89); 0.64 *S (0.10 to 1.18)	

Table reports B-values; 95% CI (in brackets); T = Total sample; N = Group N; S = Group S; * = p-value < 0.05; ** = p-value < 0.01; *** = p-value < 0.001. No predictive variables were found for the coping strategies Positive reframing, Humor, Substance use and Disengagement. Acceptance, Humor, Self-distraction, Venting, Substance use and Self-blame.

4. Discussion

This study investigated the quality of life and insomnia among hospital personnel during the first wave of the COVID-19 pandemic in Italy. The adoption of different coping strategies was also analyzed. In particular, we investigated the differences in sociodemographic characteristics and work-related factors in two different Italian metropolitan areas, located in Northern and Southern Italy (group N and group S, respectively). We also identified work-related and sociodemographic predictors of specific outcomes.

Our results showed an overall good perceived quality of life despite a high prevalence of insomnia among the participants in both groups. The Brief-COPE questionnaire revealed that the subjects experienced adequate adaptive mechanisms, demonstrating that Active, Planning, and Acceptance were the most frequently adopted coping strategies in both groups.

The EQ-5D and EQ-VAS questionnaires showed good health status and perceived quality of life in both groups. We can hypothesize that this finding might be explained by different possible factors: low incidence of COVID-19 cases in the two metropolitan areas may have been adequately managed. Furthermore, since the survey was conducted during the first wave, the interviewed subjects may have underestimated the magnitude of the pandemic; another explanation might be found in a good level of organizational support with adequate provision of medical equipment and PPE (personal protective equipment). In particular, group S participants reported higher scores which their sociodemographic characteristics may explain: the majority of subjects was <40 y (56.9% vs. 27.4% in group N), the percentage of male participants was higher than group N (34.6% vs. 24.8%, respectively) and most of the interviewees were graduated (55% vs. 37.8% in group N). In fact, aging is associated with an increased burden of disease, and a higher education level is reported to confer knowledge and consciousness regarding the risk of infection and correct preventive measures, particularly in the COVID-19 pandemic [34–38].

Moreover, regarding work-related features, it can be highlighted that only in group S did high seniority act as a predictor of worse overall life quality, whereas working in COVID wards predicted its perception. This relation was not present in group N: probably, the organization of the healthcare system with a higher readiness level in the working context of this group may have played a role in buffering the negative impact of the pandemic on mental health and social life on HCWs [39,40]. In fact, the investigated northern metropolitan area was in proximity to the most affected Italian regions during the first pandemic wave.

As demonstrated in other research, in frontline hospital workers, working conditions increased the perception of personal threat, increasing stress levels with an inevitable worsening of the perception of health status and quality of life [41,42]. In contrast, another study on nurses reported that the social domain of quality of life had a significant positive association with working experience [43].

In our total sample, we found that high education level was a predictor of better perceived health status in the two study groups, in accordance with the existing literature [34–36]. In fact, as mentioned above, an elevated level of education generally corresponds to higher career profiles with greater earnings and a better perception of life quality as well as more robust mechanisms to face situations of initial disability or deterioration in health status. Moreover, male gender was related to better life quality, both overall ($p < 0.001$) and perceived ($p < 0.05$), confirming that men are more likely to report good scores when compared with women [37]; during this period of a whole disruption concerning many organizational aspects in daily life, the social pressure exerted by family may have negatively impacted the quality of life, especially in women.

As is well known, the new living arrangement, mainly due to social distancing, has led to unprecedented social experiences, resulting in an increase of anxiety, stress, depression, burnout, and sleep disorders [14]. In particular, insomnia was revealed to be one of the most frequent disturbances [15]. In accordance with other research [44,45] and a recent meta-analysis [46], we found a high prevalence of insomnia in our study population, with almost half of participants reporting insomnia symptoms in both groups. Our data revealed that different factors in the two groups could represent a risk to the onset of insomnia. In group S, subjects with a higher number of contacts per week with COVID patients had a greater risk of insomnia. Literature suggests that working conditions linked to an elevated number of contacts with COVID-19 patients may justify the higher levels of distress, resulting in sleep problems [47–49].

The stratification of the study population by gender and professional category highlighted an increased risk of insomnia among women (OR 2.09, $p < 0.001$) and nursing personnel (OR 1.62, $p = 0.018$), similarly to other studies [48,49]. Evidence suggests that women are more susceptible to sleep disorders, also due to a double burden of work hanging on them [50]. Since women are more disposed to suffer from psychological symptoms, including mood disorders [51,52], subsequently to stressful events, the COVID-19 pandemic represented a traumatic component that may have revealed this greater vulnerability. These conditions may negatively influence sleep quality [53]. Though explaining this gender difference is not straightforward, individual features (e.g., genetics, hormones) and social disparities might represent the possible causes [54]. Additionally, the literature suggests that nurses are more exposed to the pandemic burden [49].

The female gender was also a predictor of higher scores in almost all coping strategies encountered by the Brief-COPE questionnaire, especially those related to support.

In general, women showed a more intense effort in their attempt to cope with the difficulties linked to the pandemic situation and were confirmed to be more likely to use emotion-focused coping strategies, while men tend to rely more on problem-focused strategies [55].

Concerning the capacity to handle stressful situations, the most commonly used strategies, equally adopted in both study groups, were those with a positive attitude towards the workplace (Active, Planning, and Acceptance), similar to previous studies on HCWs [56,57]. The functional coping strategies permit to favorably decode adverse circumstances, positively affecting mental wellbeing and life quality [58]. Following the application of the statistical model, in group N we only found a sociodemographic characteristic, age > 40 y, as a predictor of Acceptance; in fact, age could be considered as a protective characteristic against the development of stress and a greater individual experience may orientate coping to the adoption of positive strategies in this working population [59]. Differently, in group S data showed that a work-related factor, the number of contacts per week with COVID-19 patients, played a role in predicting Planning attitude. Contrary to other research in which greater exposure to SARS-CoV-2 infection has led HCWs to adopt maladaptive behaviors [58], this work-related factor in our Southern population acted as a positive stimulus in adopting a more functional coping strategy. We can hypothesize that there are not only demographic features but also cultural and environmental factors that can influence the use of this strategy, so a higher workload with challenging tasks seems to correspond to more significant planning activity.

Moreover, the national lockdown and government restrictive preventive measures limited social relationships also outside the work environment, with a consequent impact on coping strategies involving social support (emotional and instrumental support). Notwithstanding, our study population demonstrated to rely on social interactions, confirming other data in the literature [60,61]. In particular, being part of group N acted as a predictor of the Instrumental Support strategy, which is a problem-focused strategy whereby subjects seek information, advice, and assistance [62]. Considering the higher prevalence of the pandemic in most regions of Northern Italy, these subjects may have been more afraid to infect their families, leading them to the choice to live far from their loved ones [7], resulting in a greater search for social support, especially counseling and enlightenment.

Furthermore, our results showed a significant difference between the two groups: religion was a frequent mechanism in group S, particularly in older subjects and those working remotely; whereas in group N females and more COVID-exposed participants tended to practice their spirituality in critical situations [63]. Some people have shown a significant attitude to draw resources from their religious feelings in the current pandemic [64], although explaining individual motivations is not straightforward.

Working from home has resulted in being predictive of relying not only on religion but also on maladaptive coping strategies, particularly in group S of this population (Table 6B). The strategies aiming to avoidant behaviors (Self-distraction, Denial, and Disengagement) constitute a risk factor for elevated distress levels, in fact, they are categorized among dis-functional reactions to stressful situations [65,66]. Despite our investigation showing low scores in most of these strategies, group S was related to Denial, pretending that the situation was not real [67]. It is possible that due to cultural and environmental characteristics, these subjects tended to minimize the threat, keep feelings to themselves and avoid mental distress by making an effort to forget.

Overall, our data underline that dissimilar variables play distinct roles in affecting coping tactics in the two geographical areas. Actually, as predictors for psychological distress depend on the specific context, also the consequent coping strategies are not absolute and depend on a multiplicity of variables.

The first limitation of this study is the cross-sectional design that does not permit to define the direction of causality. Second, despite the fact that we used all validated questionnaires, the online administration of a survey could be affected by a responder bias: the sample was recruited through network invitation, so enrolled subjects had to be able to use web resources. Finally, due to the self-administration of questionnaires, we cannot generalize our findings because of the risk of overestimating psychological disturbs and insomnia.

In spite of these limitations, the strength of this survey has been to evaluate the quality of life, insomnia, and coping strategies in facing COVID-19 physical and emotional burden, through the comparison of two groups residing in distinct Italian metropolitan areas with matching low SARS-CoV-2 incidence rate but dissimilar sociodemographic features and work-related factors. Only a few Italian investigations were conducted among different regions, assessing the impact of COVID-19 on HCWs, in terms of psychological safety and workload [57,68–71]. This kind of comparison has permitted us to achieve new insights on how sociodemographic characteristics and work-related factors may have played different roles depending on different organizational settings, in a preventive perspective.

Since the first year of this ongoing pandemic, the lesson learned is that, for a future similar emergency, public health authorities should implement support programs dedicated explicitly to more vulnerable personnel between HCWs. Given the gender-linked mental health challenges and coping attitudes, women would particularly benefit from psychosocial support delivered according to their work schedules to avoid interference with parental tasks.

A multilevel integrated approach should be implemented on the individual HCW aiming to monitor psychological distress and help in accepting negative emotions; at the interpersonal dimension, to favor regular sharing and communication between peers, also to allow conciliation of work with family life; in particular, for remote workers, the organization of frequent online meetings could help in maintaining contact between co-workers and avoid disengagement. Moreover, at the organizational level, preventive and protective measures adequate to work-related risk to COVID-19 [72] should be adopted, allowing timely availability of clear information, guidelines, and protective equipment.

5. Conclusions

Globally, our study population reported good perceived quality of life and self-reported health status, despite the pandemic situation.

Women confirmed their attitude to positively react to the difficulties linked to the pandemic, adopting emotion-focused and support-related coping strategies.

A high prevalence of insomnia was reported, particularly by women and nurses. Considering the high feminization of healthcare professions in western countries, as well as the higher probability for women to develop mental health disturbs, gender perspective should be considered at the organizational level; we suggest enhancing health protection actions dedicated to these more vulnerable categories, through prevention and intervention programs oriented towards psychosocial support to mitigate the impact of stressful events, such as the COVID-19 pandemic.

Author Contributions: Conceptualization, C.F., C.C. and S.I.; methodology, C.M., M.R.A.M., C.F., C.C.; software and data curation, A.A., S.I.; validation, G.B.; formal analysis, A.A. and S.I.; investigation, M.T.; resources, G.S. and F.L.F.; writing—original draft preparation, S.I., M.T.; writing—review and editing, C.F., C.C., S.I.; supervision, C.C., C.F.; project administration, C.F.; funding acquisition, C.F. All authors have read and agreed to the published version of the manuscript.

Funding: This research received no external funding.

Institutional Review Board Statement: This study was carried out in accordance with the Declaration of Helsinki's ethical standards. The study needed no formal approval by the local Ethics Committee.

Informed Consent Statement: Informed consent was obtained from all subjects involved in the study.

Data Availability Statement: The datasets generated and analyzed during the current study are available from the corresponding author on reasonable request.

Conflicts of Interest: The authors declare no conflict of interest.

References

1. Konetzka, R.T.; White, E.M.; Pralea, A.; Grabowski, D.C.; Mor, V. A systematic review of long-term care facility characteristics associated with COVID -19 outcomes. *J. Am. Geriatr. Soc.* **2021**, *69*, 2766–2777. [CrossRef] [PubMed]
2. Wu, Z.; McGoogan, J.M. Characteristics of and Important Lessons from the Coronavirus Disease 2019 (COVID-19) Outbreak in China: Summary of a Report of 72,314 Cases from the Chinese Center for Disease Control and Prevention. *JAMA* **2020**, *323*, 1239–1242. [CrossRef]
3. World Health Organization. Situation by Country, Territory & Area. Available online: https://covid19.who.int (accessed on 27 September 2021).
4. Epicentro. Instituto Superiore Di Sanità. Available online: https://www.epicentro.iss.it/coronavirus/sars-cov-2-dashboard (accessed on 17 June 2021).
5. Barchielli, B.; Baldi, M.; Paoli, E.; Roma, P.; Ferracuti, S.; Napoli, C.; Giannini, A.M.; Lausi, G. When "Stay at Home" Can Be Dangerous: Data on Domestic Violence in Italy during COVID-19 Lockdown. *Int. J. Environ. Res. Public Health* **2021**, *18*, 8948. [CrossRef]
6. Marelli, S.; Castelnuovo, A.; Somma, A.; Castronovo, V.; Mombelli, S.; Bottoni, D.; Leitner, C.; Fossati, A.; Ferini-Strambi, L. Impact of COVID-19 lockdown on sleep quality in university students and administration staff. *J. Neurol.* **2020**, *268*, 8–15. [CrossRef] [PubMed]
7. Wu, P.E.; Styra, R.; Gold, W.L. Mitigating the psychological effects of COVID-19 on health care workers. *Can. Med. Assoc. J.* **2020**, *192*, E459–E460. [CrossRef]
8. Trumello, C.; Bramanti, S.M.; Ballarotto, G.; Candelori, C.; Cerniglia, L.; Cimino, S.; Crudele, M.; Lombardi, L.; Pignataro, S.; Viceconti, M.L.; et al. Psychological Adjustment of Healthcare Workers in Italy during the COVID-19 Pandemic: Differences in Stress, Anxiety, Depression, Burnout, Secondary Trauma, and Compassion Satisfaction between Frontline and Non-Frontline Professionals. *Int. J. Environ. Res. Public Health* **2020**, *17*, 8358. [CrossRef] [PubMed]
9. Gu, J.; Zhong, Y.; Hao, Y.; Zhou, D.; Tsui, H.; Hao, C.; Gao, Q.; Ling, W.; Lau, J.T.F. Preventive Behaviors and Mental Distress in Response to H1N1 Among University Students in Guangzhou, China. *Asia Pac. J. Public Health* **2015**, *27*, NP1867–NP1879. [CrossRef] [PubMed]
10. Schreiber, M.; Cates, D.; Formanski, S.; King, M. Maximizing the Resilience of Healthcare Workers in Multi-hazard Events: Lessons from the 2014–2015 Ebola Response in Africa. *Mil. Med.* **2019**, *184*, 114–120. [CrossRef] [PubMed]
11. Lee, S.M.; Kang, W.S.; Cho, A.-R.; Kim, T.; Park, J.K. Psychological impact of the 2015 MERS outbreak on hospital workers and quarantined hemodialysis patients. *Compr. Psychiatry* **2018**, *87*, 123–127. [CrossRef] [PubMed]
12. World Health Organization. Available online: https://www.who.int/tools/whoqol (accessed on 4 October 2021).
13. Rabin, R.; De Charro, F. EQ-SD: A measure of health status from the EuroQol Group. *Ann. Med.* **2001**, *33*, 337–343. [CrossRef]
14. Danet, A.D. Psychological impact of COVID-19 pandemic in Western frontline healthcare professionals. A systematic review. *Med. Clín.* **2021**, *156*, 449–458. [CrossRef]
15. Dutta, A.; Sharma, A.; Torres-Castro, R.; Pachori, H.; Mishra, S. Mental health outcomes among health-care workers dealing with COVID-19/severe acute respiratory syndrome coronavirus 2 pandemic: A systematic review and meta-analysis. *Indian J. Psychiatry* **2021**, *63*, 335. [CrossRef]
16. Rose, S.; Hartnett, J.; Pillai, S. Healthcare worker's emotions, perceived stressors and coping mechanisms during the COVID-19 pandemic. *PLoS ONE* **2021**, *16*, e0254252. [CrossRef] [PubMed]

17. Suryavanshi, N.; Kadam, A.; Dhumal, G.; Nimkar, S.; Mave, V.; Gupta, A.; Cox, S.R.; Gupte, N. Mental health and quality of life among healthcare professionals during the COVID-19 pandemic in India. *Brain Behav.* **2020**, *10*, e01837. [CrossRef] [PubMed]
18. Huang, L.; Lei, W.; Xu, F.; Liu, H.; Yu, L. Emotional responses and coping strategies in nurses and nursing students during Covid-19 outbreak: A comparative study. *PLoS ONE* **2020**, *15*, e0237303. [CrossRef]
19. Costa, C.; Teodoro, M.; Briguglio, G.; Vitale, E.; Giambò, F.; Indelicato, G.; Micali, E.; Italia, S.; Fenga, C. Sleep Quality and Mood State in Resident Physicians during COVID-19 Pandemic. *Int. J. Environ. Res. Public Health* **2021**, *18*, 8023. [CrossRef] [PubMed]
20. Singh, S.; Gupta, B.; Mishra, P. Coping strategies and social support as moderators of occupational stress and mental health link among police personnel. *Ind. Psychiatry J.* **2021**, *30*, 67. [CrossRef]
21. Richter, A.; Näswall, K.; de Cuyper, N.; Sverke, M.; De Witte, H.; Hellgren, J. Coping with job insecurity. *Career Dev. Int.* **2013**, *18*, 484–502. [CrossRef]
22. Jauregui, P.; Onaindia, J.; Estévez, A. Adaptive and Maladaptive Coping Strategies in Adult Pathological Gamblers and Their Mediating Role with Anxious-Depressive Symptomatology. *J. Gambl. Stud.* **2017**, *33*, 1081–1097. [CrossRef] [PubMed]
23. Yuan, S.; Liao, Z.; Huang, H.; Jiang, B.; Zhang, X.; Wang, Y.; Zhao, M. Comparison of the Indicators of Psychological Stress in the Population of Hubei Province and Non-Endemic Provinces in China During Two Weeks During the Coronavirus Disease 2019 (COVID-19) Outbreak in February 2020. *Med. Sci. Monit.* **2020**, *26*, e923767. [CrossRef]
24. Uphoff, E.P.; Lombardo, C.; Johnston, G.; Weeks, L.; Rodgers, M.; Dawson, S.; Seymour, C.; Kousoulis, A.A.; Churchill, R. Mental health among healthcare workers and other vulnerable groups during the COVID-19 pandemic and other coronavirus outbreaks: A rapid systematic review. *PLOS ONE* **2021**, *16*, e0254821. [CrossRef] [PubMed]
25. Costa, C.; Briguglio, G.; Mondello, S.; Teodoro, M.; Pollicino, M.; Canalella, A.; Verduci, F.; Italia, S.; Fenga, C. Perceived Stress in a Gender Perspective: A Survey in a Population of Unemployed Subjects of Southern Italy. *Front. Public Health* **2021**, *9*, 640454. [CrossRef] [PubMed]
26. Briguglio, G.; Teodoro, M.; Italia, S.; Verduci, F.; Pollicino, M.; Coco, M.; De Vita, A.; Micali, E.; Alibrandi, A.; Lembo, G.; et al. Salivary Biomarkers and Work-Related Stress in Night Shift Workers. *Int. J. Environ. Res. Public Health* **2021**, *18*, 1–12. [CrossRef]
27. De Smet, P.; Sans, S.; Dramaix, M.; Boulenguez, C.; de Backer, G.; Ferrario, M.M.; Cesana, G.; Houtman, I.; Isacsson, S.O.; Kittel, F.; et al. Gender and regional differences in perceived job stress across Europe. *Eur. J. Public Health* **2005**, *15*, 536–545. [CrossRef] [PubMed]
28. Song, Y.; Sörensen, S.; Yan, E.C.W. Family Support and Preparation for Future Care Needs Among Urban Chinese Baby Boomers. *J. Gerontol. Ser. B* **2016**, *73*, gbw062-1076. [CrossRef] [PubMed]
29. Balestroni, G.; Bertolotti, G. EuroQol-5D (EQ-5D): An instrument for measuring quality of life. *Monaldi Arch. Chest Dis.* **2012**, *78*, 155–159. [CrossRef] [PubMed]
30. Golicki, D.; Niewada, M.; Karlińska, A.; Buczek, J.; Kobayashi, A.; Janssen, M.F.; Pickard, A.S. Comparing responsiveness of the EQ-5D-5L, EQ-5D-3L and EQ VAS in stroke patients. *Qual. Life Res.* **2015**, *24*, 1555–1563. [CrossRef] [PubMed]
31. Młyńczak, K.; Golicki, D. Validity of the EQ-5D-5L questionnaire among the general population of Poland. *Qual. Life Res.* **2021**, *30*, 817–829. [CrossRef]
32. Soldatos, C.R.; Dikeos, D.G.; Paparrigopoulos, T.J. Athens Insomnia Scale: Validation of an instrument based on ICD-10 criteria. *J. Psychosom. Res.* **2000**, *48*, 555–560. [CrossRef]
33. Carver, C.S. You want to measure coping but your protocol' too long: Consider the brief cope. *Int. J. Behav. Med.* **1997**, *4*, 1–166. [CrossRef]
34. Kang, L.; Ma, S.; Chen, M.; Yang, J.; Wang, Y.; Li, R.; Yao, L.; Bai, H.; Cai, Z.; Yang, B.X.; et al. Impact on mental health and perceptions of psychological care among medical and nursing staff in Wuhan during the 2019 novel coronavirus disease outbreak: A cross-sectional study. *Brain, Behav. Immun.* **2020**, *87*, 11–17. [CrossRef]
35. Cheung, T.; Fong, T.K.; Bressington, D. COVID-19 under the SARS Cloud: Mental Health Nursing during the Pandemic in Hong Kong. *J. Psychiatr. Ment. Health Nurs.* **2021**, *28*, 115–117. [CrossRef] [PubMed]
36. Ping, W.; Zheng, J.; Niu, X.; Guo, C.; Zhang, J.; Yang, H.; Shi, Y. Evaluation of health-related quality of life using EQ-5D in China during the COVID-19 pandemic. *PLoS ONE* **2020**, *15*, e0234850. [CrossRef] [PubMed]
37. Tran, T.V.; Nguyen, H.C.; Pham, L.V.; Nguyen, M.H.; Nguyen, H.C.; Ha, T.H.; Phan, D.T.; Dao, H.K.; Nguyen, P.B.; Trinh, M.V.; et al. Impacts and interactions of COVID-19 response involvement, health-related behaviours, health literacy on anxiety, depression and health-related quality of life among healthcare workers: A cross-sectional study. *BMJ Open* **2020**, *10*, e041394. [CrossRef]
38. Ma, C.; Ma, L.; Helwan, A.; Ma'Aitah, M.K.S.; Jami, S.A.; Al Mobarak, S.; Das, N.K.; Haque, A. An online survey and review about the awareness, coping style, and exercise behavior during the "COVID-19 pandemic situation" by implementing the cloud-based medical treatment technology system in China among the public. *Sci. Prog.* **2021**, *104*. [CrossRef] [PubMed]
39. Cai, Z.; Cui, Q.; Liu, Z.; Li, J.; Gong, X.; Liu, J.; Wan, Z.; Yuan, X.; Li, X.; Chen, C.; et al. Nurses endured high risks of psychological problems under the epidemic of COVID-19 in a longitudinal study in Wuhan China. *J. Psychiatr. Res.* **2020**, *131*, 132–137. [CrossRef] [PubMed]
40. Van Steenkiste, E.; Schoofs, J.; Gilis, S.; Messiaen, P. Mental health impact of COVID-19 in frontline healthcare workers in a Belgian Tertiary care hospital: A prospective longitudinal study. *Acta Clin. Belg.* **2021**, 1. [CrossRef] [PubMed]
41. Lai, J.; Ma, S.; Wang, Y.; Cai, Z.; Hu, J.; Wei, N.; Wu, J.; Du, H.; Chen, T.; Li, R.; et al. Factors associated with mental health outcomes among health care workers exposed to coronavirus disease 2019. *JAMA Netw. Open* **2020**, *3*, e203976. [CrossRef]

42. Kang, L.; Li, Y.; Hu, S.; Chen, M.; Yang, C.; Yang, B.X.; Wang, Y.; Hu, J.; Lai, J.; Ma, X.; et al. The mental health of medical workers in Wuhan, China dealing with the 2019 novel coronavirus. *Lancet Psychiatry* **2020**, *7*, e14. [CrossRef]
43. Sharma, S.K.; Mudgal, S.K.; Thakur, K.; Parihar, A.; Chundawat, D.S.; Joshi, J. Anxiety, depression and quality of life (QOL) related to COVID-19 among frontline health care professionals: A multicentric cross-sectional survey. *J. Fam. Med. Prim. Care* **2021**, *10*, 1383–1389. [CrossRef]
44. Idrissi, A.J.; Lamkaddem, A.; Benouajjit, A.; Ben El Bouaazzaoui, M.; El Houari, F.; Alami, M.; Labyad, S.; Chahidi, A.; Benjelloun, M.; Rabhi, S.; et al. Sleep quality and mental health in the context of COVID-19 pandemic and lockdown in Morocco. *Sleep Med.* **2020**, *74*, 248–253. [CrossRef] [PubMed]
45. Fiorillo, A.; Gorwood, P. The consequences of the COVID-19 pandemic on mental health and implications for clinical practice. *Eur. Psychiatry* **2020**, *63*, e32. [CrossRef] [PubMed]
46. Al Maqbali, M.; Al Sinani, M.; Al-Lenjawi, B. Prevalence of stress, depression, anxiety and sleep disturbance among nurses during the COVID-19 pandemic: A systematic review and meta-analysis. *J. Psychosom. Res.* **2021**, *141*, 110343. [CrossRef]
47. Klimkiewicz, A.; Schmalenberg, A.; Klimkiewicz, J.; Jasińska, A.; Jasionowska, J.; Machura, W.; Wojnar, M. COVID-19 Pandemic Influence on Healthcare Professionals. *J. Clin. Med.* **2021**, *10*, 1280. [CrossRef]
48. Voitsidis, P.; Gliatas, I.; Bairachtari, V.; Papadopoulou, K.; Papageorgiou, G.; Parlapani, E.; Syngelakis, M.; Holeva, V.; Diakogiannis, I. Insomnia during the COVID-19 pandemic in a Greek population. *Psychiatry Res.* **2020**, *289*, 113076. [CrossRef] [PubMed]
49. Tselebis, A.; Lekka, D.; Sikaras, C.; Tsomaka, E.; Tassopoulos, A.; Ilias, I.; Bratis, D.; Pachi, A. Insomnia, Perceived Stress, and Family Support among Nursing Staff during the Pandemic Crisis. *Healthcare* **2020**, *8*, 434. [CrossRef] [PubMed]
50. Sato, S.; Liu, Y.; Ikeda, A.; Filomeno, R.; Suzuki, Y.; Maruyama, K.; Tomooka, K.; Wada, H.; Koyama, Y.; Tanigawa, T. Work-family conflict and insomnia symptoms among women working in aged care services in Japan. *Sleep Med.* **2021**, *82*, 155–158. [CrossRef]
51. Li, S.H.; Graham, B.M. Why are women so vulnerable to anxiety, trauma-related and stress-related disorders? The potential role of sex hormones. *Lancet Psychiatry* **2016**, *4*, 73–82. [CrossRef]
52. Costa, C.; Mondello, S.; Micali, E.; Indelicato, G.; Licciardello, A.A.; Vitale, E.; Briguglio, G.; Teodoro, M.; Fenga, C. Night shift work in resident physicians: Does it affect mood states and cognitive levels? *J. Affect. Disord.* **2020**, *272*, 289–294. [CrossRef]
53. Griffin, S.C.; Williams, A.; Mladen, S.N.; Perrin, P.B.; Dzierzewski, J.M.; Rybarczyk, B.D. Reciprocal Effects Between Loneliness and Sleep Disturbance in Older Americans. *J. Aging Health* **2020**, *32*, 1156–1164. [CrossRef]
54. Kolakowsky-Hayner, S.; Goldin, Y.; Kingsley, K.; Alzueta, E.; Arango-Lasprilla, J.; Perrin, P.; Baker, F.; Ramos-Usuga, D.; Constantinidou, F. Psychosocial Impacts of the COVID-19 Quarantine: A Study of Gender Differences in 59 Countries. *Medicina* **2021**, *57*, 789. [CrossRef]
55. Laufer, A.; Bitton, M.S. Gender differences in the reaction to COVID-19. *Women Health* **2021**, *61*, 800–810. [CrossRef] [PubMed]
56. Wong, T.W.; Yau, J.K.; Chan, C.L.; Kwong, R.S.; Ho, S.M.; Lau, C.C.; Lau, F.L.; Lit, C.H. The psychological impact of severe acute respiratory syndrome outbreak on healthcare workers in emergency departments and how they cope. *Eur. J. Emerg. Med.* **2005**, *12*, 13–18. [CrossRef] [PubMed]
57. Babore, A.; Lombardi, L.; Viceconti, M.L.; Pignataro, S.; Marino, V.; Crudele, M.; Candelori, C.; Bramanti, S.M.; Trumello, C. Psychological effects of the COVID-2019 pandemic: Perceived stress and coping strategies among healthcare professionals. *Psychiatry Res.* **2020**, *293*, 113366. [CrossRef]
58. Flesia, L.; Monaro, M.; Mazza, C.; Fietta, V.; Colicino, E.; Segatto, B.; Roma, P. Predicting Perceived Stress Related to the Covid-19 Outbreak through Stable Psychological Traits and Machine Learning Models. *J. Clin. Med.* **2020**, *9*, 3350. [CrossRef] [PubMed]
59. Park, C.L.; Russell, B.S.; Fendrich, M.; Finkelstein-Fox, L.; Hutchison, M.; Becker, J. Americans' COVID-19 Stress, Coping, and Adherence to CDC Guidelines. *J. Gen. Intern. Med.* **2020**, *35*, 2296–2303. [CrossRef] [PubMed]
60. Nashwan, A.J.; Villar, R.C.; Al-Qudimat, A.R.; Kader, N.; Alabdulla, M.; Abujaber, A.A.; Al-Jabry, M.M.; Harkous, M.; Philip, A.; Ali, R.; et al. Quality of Life, Sleep Quality, Depression, Anxiety, Stress, Eating Habits, and Social Bounds in Nurses during the Coronavirus Disease 2019 Pandemic in Qatar (The PROTECTOR Study): A Cross-Sectional, Comparative Study. *J. Pers. Med.* **2021**, *11*, 918. [CrossRef]
61. Vagni, M.; Maiorano, T.; Giostra, V.; Pajardi, D. Coping With COVID-19: Emergency Stress, Secondary Trauma and Self-Efficacy in Healthcare and Emergency Workers in Italy. *Front. Psychol.* **2020**, *11*, 566912. [CrossRef] [PubMed]
62. Collado, A.; Hainaut, J.-P.; Monfort, V.; Bolmont, B. Sensation Seeking and Adaptation in Parabonauts. *Front. Psychol.* **2018**, *9*, 296. [CrossRef] [PubMed]
63. Ano, G.G.; Vasconcelles, E.B. Religious coping and psychological adjustment to stress: A meta-analysis. *J. Clin. Psychol.* **2005**, *61*, 461–480. [CrossRef]
64. Abdullah, I.; Parveen, S.; Khan, N.S.; Abdullah, D. Anxiety, OCD, delusions, and religiosity among the general public during the COVID-19 pandemic. *Int. Soc. Sci. J.* **2021**, *71*, 163–178. [CrossRef] [PubMed]
65. Phua, D. Coping Responses of Emergency Physicians and Nurses to the 2003 Severe Acute Respiratory Syndrome Outbreak. *Acad. Emerg. Med.* **2005**, *12*, 322–328. [CrossRef] [PubMed]
66. Teasdale, E.; Yardley, L.; Schlotz, W.; Michie, S. The importance of coping appraisal in behavioural responses to pandemic flu. *Br. J. Health Psychol.* **2012**, *17*, 44–59. [CrossRef]
67. Csigó, K.; Ritzl, A. First Reactions and Attitudes of Psychiatric Workers in Budapest Psychiatric Care Units Regarding the COVID-19 Pandemic. *Prim. Care Companion CNS Disord.* **2021**, *23*, 20m02850. [CrossRef]

68. Felice, C.; Di Tanna, G.L.; Zanus, G.; Grossi, U. Impact of COVID-19 Outbreak on Healthcare Workers in Italy: Results from a National E-Survey. *J. Community Health* **2020**, *45*, 675–683. [CrossRef] [PubMed]
69. Conti, C.; Fontanesi, L.; Lanzara, R.; Rosa, I.; Porcelli, P. Fragile heroes. The psychological impact of the COVID-19 pandemic on health-care workers in Italy. *PLoS ONE* **2020**, *15*, e0242538. [CrossRef]
70. Cerami, C.; Santi, G.C.; Galandra, C.; Dodich, A.; Cappa, S.F.; Vecchi, T.; Crespi, C. Covid-19 Outbreak in Italy: Are We Ready for the Psychosocial and the Economic Crisis? Baseline Findings from the PsyCovid Study. *Front. Psychiatry* **2020**, *11*, 556. [CrossRef]
71. Toia, F.; Romeo, M.; Abate, M.; Avarotti, E.; Battiston, B.; Bruno, G.; Cannavo, F.; Casamichele, C.; Colonna, M.; Catena, N.; et al. Impact of COVID-19 on hand surgery in Italy: A comparison between the Northern and the Southern regions. *Hand Surg. Rehabilit.* **2021**, *40*, 139–144. [CrossRef]
72. World Health Organization. COVID-19: Occupational Health and Safety for Health Workers: Interim Guidance. Available online: https://apps.who.int/iris/handle/10665/339151 (accessed on 19 October 2021).

International Journal of
Environmental Research and Public Health

MDPI

Article

Sustained Effects of Government Response on the COVID-19 Infection Rate in China: A Multiple Mediation Analysis

Taixiang Duan [1], Zhonggen Sun [2] and Guoqing Shi [3,*]

1 Department of Sociology, Hohai University, Nanjing 211100, China; duantaixiang@163.com
2 School of Public Administration, Hohai University, Nanjing 211100, China; sunzhonggen@hhu.edu.cn
3 Asian Research Center, Hohai University, 8 Focheng West Road, Jinagning District, Nanjing 211100, China
* Correspondence: gshi@hhu.edu.cn; Tel.: +86-25-83786235

Abstract: Many scholars have considered the relationship between the government response to COVID-19, an important social intervention strategy, and the COVID-19 infection rate. However, few have examined the sustained impact of an early government response on the COVID-19 infection rate. The current paper fills this gap by investigating a national survey performed in February 2020 and infection data from Chinese cities surveyed 1.5 years after the outbreak of COVID-19. The results suggest that the Chinese government's early response to COVID-19 significantly and sustainedly reduced China's COVID-19 infection rate, and that this impact worked through risk perception, the adoption of protective action recommendations (PARs), and the chain-mediating effects of risk perception and the adoption of PARs, respectively. These findings have important practical value. In demonstrating how government response and infection rate at the macro level are connected to the behaviour of individuals at the micro level, they suggest feasible directions for curbing the spread of diseases such as COVID-19. When facing such public health emergencies, the focus should be on increasing the public's risk perception and adoption of PARs.

Keywords: sustained effects; government response; infection rate; risk perception; adoption of PARs; COVID-19; China

Citation: Duan, T.; Sun, Z.; Shi, G. Sustained Effects of Government Response on the COVID-19 Infection Rate in China: A Multiple Mediation Analysis. *Int. J. Environ. Res. Public Health* **2021**, *18*, 12422. https://doi.org/10.3390/ijerph182312422

Academic Editors: Paolo Roma, Merylin Monaro and Cristina Mazza

Received: 17 October 2021
Accepted: 23 November 2021
Published: 25 November 2021

1. Introduction

COVID-19 is caused by a novel coronavirus even more infectious than the virus responsible for the 2002–2004 SARS outbreak. COVID-19 was classified by the World Health Organization as a pandemic on March 11, 2020 [1]. By August 5, 2021, 200 million confirmed cases and 4.26 million deaths had been reported worldwide. However, China had reported only 121,326 confirmed cases and 5651 deaths [2]. These figures are surprisingly low, given our limited understanding of the virus and the absence of effective drug treatments. At the time of writing, only 36,798 new cases of infection have been reported in China in the last year. Why are the numbers of infections and deaths in China so much lower than those in other countries? A research team from the University of Oxford shed light on this question by reporting a link between government response and the spread of COVID-19, with strong early intervention by the Chinese government playing a crucial role in limiting the spread of the disease [3]. Scholars have generally agreed that the Chinese government's early intervention was very effective [4–11]. However, the government relaxed its intervention efforts in May 2020, when the world considered China to be at the highest risk of experiencing a sustained COVID-19 epidemic, and there have since been no major COVID-19 spikes in China. Did the government's early intervention thus have a sustained impact on COVID-19 infection, limiting the later spread of the disease? If so, what was the mechanism of this impact? These questions have not been explored in previous studies, but answering them may help to curb the future spread of a pandemic such as COVID-19. In the current paper, we attempt to fill this research gap.

2. The Effect of Government Response on the Infection Rate

2.1. Immediate Effects of Government Response on the Infection Rate

Studies have shown that social interventions are needed to control the spread of epidemic diseases. Bauch and Galvani point out thatcontrol of the SARS coronavirus depended partly on the degree of acceptance of quarantine and isolation among the population; such acceptance is often determined by social norms [12]. In the book *The Rules of Contagion: Why Things Spread and Why They Stop*, Kucharski concluded that the factors that influence the reproduction number of an epidemic disease include duration, opportunities, transmission, and susceptibility [13]. In his view, curing a patient reduces the duration of infection, isolating a patient reduces the opportunities for infection, wearing a condom or mask reduces contagion, and vaccination reduces population susceptibility. Government response to COVID-19 consists of social interventions implemented to curb the spread of the disease. COVID-19 intervention policies are complex and vary between countries, but they can be broadly categorised into five major areas, namely, containment and closure, economic responses, health systems, vaccine policies, and miscellaneous policies [3]. Many studies have attempted to determine the most effective intervention policies. For example, Richard et al. examined the effects of four types of government response—event bans, school closures, bar and pub closures, and lockdown—and discovered that event bans and school closures directly reduced virus transmission, while the influence of a full lockdown was slightly delayed [14]. Scholars have used epidemiological data on COVID-19 and anonymised migration data to simulate outbreaks and intervention effects across China. A comparison of infections in Wuhan, Hubei province, with those in other cities in Hubei and cities in other provinces revealed that early detection and isolation were more effective than travel restrictions. Reducing social contact curbed the spread of COVID-19 and prevented or delayed the arrival of a second wave of the outbreak. The authors also found that although travel restrictions had not prevented the virus from spreading from Wuhan, they had prevented its wider geographical spread [4].

The degree of policy implementation is also an important predictor of the COVID-19 infection rate. An international comparative study using data from China, Italy, Brazil, Canada, the United Kingdom, and the United States found that the stringency of intervention policy implementation was negatively associated with the number of new cases. This study also found that the Chinese government had maintained strong prevention and control measures for the first 100 days of the outbreak, during which China had experienced a dramatic decrease in infections [3]. When the virus was first detected in Guangdong province, the province's health commission quickly activated a Level I emergency response and implemented a series of public interventions, including traffic restrictions, social distancing, home and centralised quarantines, medical resource mobilisation, and other prevention and control measures, which significantly restrained the local spread of the disease [15]. Differences in the degree of policy implementation may stem from differing individual responses to government policies or from differences in national policy environments, such as social norms, cultural traditions, the political atmosphere, and other macro-level factors that interact with government response [16,17]. In general, policies that are strictly enforced tend to bring about better results, especially in the early stages [3,4,6,14–16].

The timing of policy initiation is another important predictor of the effectiveness of government response to COVID-19. Take social distancing as an example. A series of studies found that isolating infected people decreased and delayed transmission as well as reducing the epidemic's peak [4,8,18–20]. Using counterfactual simulations, another study discovered that if the same restrictions on mobility had been implemented just one to two weeks earlier, a substantial number of cases and deaths would have been avoided. Specifically, 61.6% of the infections and 55% of the deaths reported nationwide by May 3, 2020 could have been avoided if these preventive and control measures had been implemented just one week earlier [4]. A study of the relationship between the first emergency quarantine policy in Portugal from 18 March to 2 May 2020 and the public's health behaviour showed that 79.8% of the participants, whose physical activity took place indoors, complied with the government quarantine measures and adapted their health behaviour [21]. Therefore, early social distancing plays a key role in relieving pressure on healthcare facilities and ensuring a sustained supply of healthcare resources. At this level, the timing of social distancing implementation is crucial to controlling large-scale outbreaks. Social distancing has been shown to reduce not only new cases but also cumulative cases. This implies that early government intervention may have some sustained effects, in that people became more aware of the virus during home isolation and were more likely to adopt protective action recommendations (PARs) after home isolation, thereby reducing their own infection rates.

2.2. *Sustained Effects of Government Response on Infection Rate*

The findings of the aforementioned studies demonstrate the immediate inhibitory impact of government response on the spread of COVID-19. However, little is known about the sustained effects of an early government response on the COVID-19 infection rate. We propose that there are two ways in which government response can exert a sustained impact on the spread of infection: one is by influencing individuals psychologically, such as through risk perception, precautionary awareness, emotions, and confidence; and the other is by directly influencing individuals' protective behaviours, such as mask-wearing and social distancing.

2.2.1. The Mediating Role of Risk Perception

Risk perception, a core concept of the risk society, has received much attention from researchers, especially in the context of the COVID-19 pandemic [22–24]. Risk perception is an individual's subjective judgement of the characteristics and severity of risk, and it influences their decision-making when faced with an unexpected, uncontrollable, unknown, and potentially fatal public crisis such as COVID-19 [22]. A large body of research suggests that risk perception can be a powerful mediator of the relationship between social intervention measures and the spread of disease [22,25,26].

First, government response has a significant impact on individuals' risk perception. Studies have established that providing detailed information on government response to COVID-19, especially positive messages about infection risk prevention and control [22,26–33], such as news of the construction of the Fangcang shelter hospital and the preventative efforts and achievements of health workers and volunteers, as well as protection guidelines and other information about COVID-19, can influence people's perception of risk and promote their cooperation with epidemic prevention, thereby reducing the COVID-19 infection rate.

Second, government response can alleviate the impact of negative emotions on the COVID-19 infection rate by altering risk perception. In the early stages of an epidemic, the public may hold conflicting attitudes towards and perceptions of the severity of the threat posed by the unknown disease; some may be positive and optimistic, while others may be negative and pessimistic. Research has found that risk perceptions based on positive emotions, such as gratitude and hope, are critical to government efforts to promote cooperation to prevent the spread of an infectious disease [34]. Conversely, risk perceptions based on negative emotions, such as anxiety and fear, can reduce individuals' cooperation with government efforts [35]. Health anxiety, measured on a continuum from no health anxiety to pathological health anxiety, can also influence individuals' cooperation with the government to prevent the spread of an epidemic [36,37]. Studies have shown that information and advice released by the government can lead to the formation of appropriate risk perceptions [22,26], which can alleviate negative emotions [29,38–40]. Therefore, we can infer that risk perception mediates the impact of government response on infection rate

2.2.2. The Mediating Role of PAR Adoption

During a pandemic, even when governments have developed early intervention policies, the cooperation of individuals is necessary to stop the spread of the disease. Studies have found that PAR adoption by individuals is an extremely important strategy for interrupting the spread of the COVID-19 pandemic [22]. Government response can influence whether individuals adopt PARs. When people see the authorities taking swift action, they are more likely to take the threat seriously and thus to comply with prevention measures. In addition, legal disciplinary mechanisms, cultural norms, and public opinion can lead individuals to comply passively with PARs to avoid possible punishment and/or public condemnation, thus reducing their likelihood of being infected. During the Chinese New Year festival in 2020, the Chinese government called for strict home isolation for all residents to stop the spread of COVID-19, which to some extent created a new social norm. The policy was conveyed to communities through announcements and brochures on the importance of home isolation. Volunteers and property staff monitored residents' observance of the policy, which directly increased their awareness of and compliance with PARs. As a result, the spread of COVID-19 was effectively controlled [22].

However, the effectiveness of government response in reducing infection rate through individuals' adoption of PARs can vary between individuals. For example, some scholars have found that people with higher levels of perceived distress during the outbreak have more public health knowledge and are therefore more likely to adopt PARs, while people with lower levels of perceived distress know less about public health and are thus less likely to adopt PARs [40–42]. Scholars have also found a correlation between an individual's perception of the probability of infection and their adoption of PARs during a pandemic; when individuals perceive the probability to be higher, they are more likely to adopt PARs to reduce the risk of infection or prevent its occurrence [40,41,43,44]. Using a protective action decision model, Lindell and Perry found that individuals' psychological risk perception and protective behaviours were shaped by their attention to the information disclosed by society and the environment [45]. Although strict interventions lock down local communities and disrupt normal social interactions, they also enhance people's sense of efficacy in preventing infection in their communities. People with higher levels of efficacy, such as healthcare professionals, are more likely to adopt PARs and cooperate with the government's intervention policies. In contrast, people with lower levels of efficacy, such as those who perceive the government's response to be ineffective, are less inclined to cooperate, thus doing little to limit the spread of the pandemic [22,38].

2.2.3. The Multiple Mediating Effects of Risk Perception and PAR Adoption

Studies have found that risk perception is an important factor in the decision to adopt PARs [22,26]. Individuals with lower levels of risk perception tend to be less vigilant in guarding against infection, which may reduce their likelihood of PAR adoption and in turn increase the infection rate [46]. Two characteristics of COVID-19 risk perception, perceptions of the pandemic's severity and feelings of anxiety, are significantly associated with individuals' COVID-19 PAR adoption. Researchers have found that people who perceive the pandemic as more severe are more likely to collect information about it and follow various government protection strategies, increasing their confidence in adopting and thus their likelihood of adopting PARs. Conversely, individuals who perceive the pandemic as less threatening and feel less anxious about it are less likely to take protective measures [36–39,47,48].

The social amplification of risk framework proposed by Kasperson and colleagues argues that the social context in which government intervention is implemented, including the interaction effects between crisis events and individual psychology, institutional culture, and social norms, can impact individual risk perceptions [49]. For example, government policies and social norms supporting public mask-wearing and international travel control can influence individual risk perceptions and effectively reduce COVID-19 mortality. Therefore, the government, as the main body responsible for pandemic management, formulates and implements intervention policies, including various public initiatives such as government-organised rescue and treatment, publicity, and prevention and control, which change the social environment, affect people's risk perceptions, and subsequently influence their PAR adoption decisions [22]. Researchers have found that per capita COVID-19 mortality is lower in countries with cultural norms or government policies supporting public mask-wearing [17]. Studies have examined the relationship between government response, risk perception, and PAR adoption and determined that risk perception is an important mediator between government response and PAR adoption [22]. Thus, risk perception and PAR adoption are not independent factors affecting infection rate. Government response may affect infection rate by influencing the public's risk perception and therefore promoting public compliance with protective behaviours.

Therefore, this study investigates the sustained effects of government response on the COVID-19 infection rate in China. We propose a conceptual model of government response, risk perception, PAR adoption, and infection rate based on the literature, as shown in Figure 1, to examine the mediational pathway between government response and infection rate. We posit the following three hypotheses:

Hypothesis 1 (H1). *Risk perception mediates the association between government response and infection rate.*

Hypothesis 2 (H2). *PAR adoption mediates the association between government response and infection rate.*

Hypothesis 3 (H3). *The relationship between government response and infection rate is sequentially mediated by risk perception and PAR adoption.*

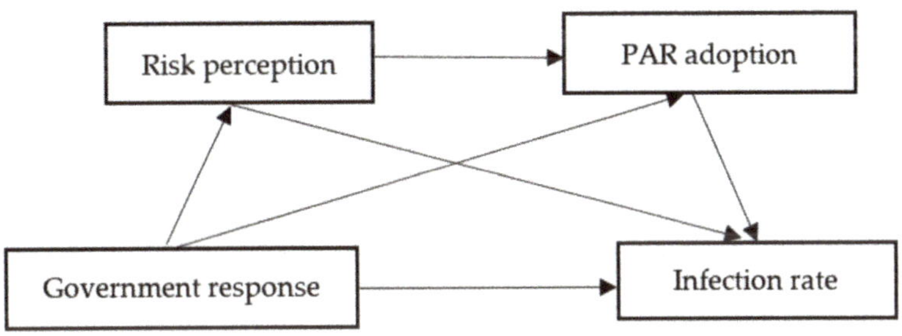

Figure 1. Conceptual model.

3. Materials and Methods

3.1. Participants and Procedure

The data for the present study were drawn from a large-scale research project conducted between 11 and 18 February 2020 by the School of Public Administration of Hohai University that investigated the psychosocial impact of COVID-19 on the public in China. The project distributed questionnaires via the Internet and conducted a survey using quota sampling. It collected 8000 questionnaires in 13 prefecture-level cities in Jiangsu province and another 30 provincial capitals in mainland China. Before beginning the survey, the participants were informed that their participation was voluntary and could be discontinued at any time. They were also informed that no personal information would be collected; their survey responses would remain anonymous and have no bearing on their academic standing. The project was approved by the Human Subjects Ethics Sub-Committee at the university with which the corresponding author is affiliated.

Originally, 8138 people completed the survey. After eliminating the survey responses of participants younger than 18 and questionnaires with many missing values, a total of 7092 valid samples were ultimately obtained. Infection rate was calculated based on the numbers of confirmed cases published by local health committees and the official 2020 population data for the cities surveyed.

3.2. Measures

Infection rate: 'Infection rate' refers to the number of confirmed cases over the past year per 100,000 population. We collected the number of confirmed COVID-19 cases announced by the health commission of each surveyed city between February 2020 and February 2021 and the permanent population data in the statistical yearbooks of each city for 2020. We then calculated each city's infection rate based on these data.

Government response: 'Government response' refers to the actions taken by the government to advise or mandate that the public and private sectors take certain measures to restrict the severity or spread of the pandemic. Based on the 'Level I Response Measures for Pneumonia Outbreak in Response to Novel Coronavirus Infection' issued by each province, the research team compiled a list of 20 common prevention and control measures (see Table 1). The respondents were asked in the questionnaire whether their local governments had adopted these measures. If a measure had been adopted, the response was recorded as '1' and '0' otherwise. The sum was divided by 20 to calculate the government response index.

Table 1. Measures of government response.

Type	Measure(s)	Options
Infection source management	Screen for fever and suspected patients Isolation of people returning from areas with serious outbreaks	1. Yes 0. No
Medical treatment	Set up a designated treatment hospital Psychological service hotline launched	
Surveillance of public places	Detect passengers' body temperature on public transportation Implement vehicle and personnel control at the borders Disinfection of public areas Mandatory wearing of masks in public places Enclosed neighbourhoods and villages Suspend operation of medium-sized and large commercial facilities Closure of entertainment venues Suspension of large public gatherings	
Publicity and education	Distribution of brochures on COVID-19 prevention Broadcast information on COVID-19 over the radio	
Information release	Timely publication of local infection information	
Material security	Distribution of masks, disinfectant, and other supplies to local residents Limit the number of people per household allowed outside to purchase supplies each day	
Joint prevention and control	Monitoring people's return home from other provinces Mobility to other provinces requires proof from the local committee Suspension of group tours and other activities	

Risk perception: Public conceptions of risk are complex and influenced by qualitative factors [50], including the extent to which a given risk is viewed as fatal, uncontrollable, and unknown. We adopted the measurement method of Liu et al. [51] and measured these factors using three items rated on a 5-point Likert-type scale. A sample item is 'How seriously do you take the COVID-19 epidemic in mainland China?' We conducted factor analysis of the results to generate a three-item risk perception scale. The Cronbach's alpha coefficient for the three items on this scale was 0.764, indicating acceptable internal consistency. The response distribution was linearly transformed to range from 0 to 100, with 100 indicating the highest level of risk perception.

PAR adoption: Four items from the Guidelines for the Public's Protective Behaviour for COVID-19, produced by the Chinese Centre for Disease Control and Prevention [52], were adopted to measure the protective behaviours undertaken by the respondents [22]. A sample item is, 'Have you taken the recommended protective action of wearing a mask when going out in the past two weeks?' For each of the recommended protective behaviours, the respondents indicated whether they had complied or not complied. If the respondent had adopted all four recommended protective behaviours over the preceding two weeks, he or she was considered to be a good adopter of the recommended protective behaviour and assigned a value of 4. If the respondent had not adopted all four recommended protective behaviours over the preceding two weeks, he or she was assigned a value of 0.

We controlled for the demographic characteristics of gender, age, household registration, years of schooling, health status, urbanisation rate, and region. The descriptive statistics for each variable are presented in Table 2.

Table 2. Descriptive statistics for the main variables.

Variable	Mean	SD	Min	Max
Infection rate (per 100,000 population)	1.095	6.465	0.023	45.43
Risk perception	92.45	10.34	0	100
PAR adoption	3.920	0.350	0	4
Government response	0.846	0.187	0	1
Gender (0 = male)	0.588	0.492	0	1
Age group (0 = more than 60 years old)				
40–60	0.297	0.457	0	1
18–40	0.690	0.463	0	1
Household registration (0 = rural household)	0.580	0.494	0	1
Years of schooling	15.04	3.364	6	19
Health status (0 = bad)	0.938	0.241	0	1
Urbanisation rate	0.604	0.100	0.418	0.881
Region (0 = eastern China)				
Central China	0.263	0.440	0	1
Western China	0.163	0.370	0	1

3.3. Analytical Strategy

First, the Statistical Package for the Social Sciences (SPSS) 23.0 was used to obtain descriptive statistics and correlations between the main variables. Second, we conducted mediation analysis using the stepwise regression method proposed by Mackinnon et al. [53] to examine the multiple mediating roles of risk perception and PAR adoption in the relationship between government response and infection rate. In the first step, we tested the effect of government response on risk perception and PAR adoption. Next, we used stepwise regression to compare the changes in the magnitude of the coefficients of the main explanatory variables in the model before and after the addition of the mediating variables, and make a preliminary determination of the possible mediating variables. We used the following regression model:

$$Y = \alpha + \beta X + \delta C + \varepsilon \quad (1)$$

$$M1 = \alpha + \beta X + \delta C + \varepsilon \quad (2)$$

$$M2 = \alpha + \beta X + \gamma M1 + \delta C + \varepsilon \quad (3)$$

$$Y = \alpha + \beta X + \gamma M1 + \lambda M2 + \delta C + \varepsilon \quad (4)$$

where Y is the dependent variable (infection rate), X is the independent variable (government response), M1 is a possible mediating variable (risk perception), M2 is another possible mediating variable (PAR adoption), and C is a set of control variables including gender, age, household registration, years of schooling, health status, urbanisation rate, and region.

Finally, the PROCESS macro was used to examine the multiple mediating roles of risk perception and PAR adoption in the relationship between government response and infection rate. Model 6 from the PROCESS macro in SPSS, as developed by Hayes [54], was used to conduct a multiple mediation analysis and the bootstrapping method (sampling repeated 1000 times) was used to construct a 95% confidence interval.

4. Results

4.1. Descriptive Statistics

Table 3 presents the correlation matrix of the key variables. The results indicated that government response was significantly negatively associated with infection rate and significantly positively associated with risk perception and PAR adoption. Risk perception was significantly negatively associated with infection rate and significantly positively associated with PAR adoption. PAR adoption was significantly negatively associated with infection rate.

Table 3. Correlations between infection rate, government response, risk perception, and PAR adoption.

	1	2	3	4
1. Infection rate	1			
2. Government response	−0.035 **	1		
3. Risk perception	−0.028 *	0.131 ***	1	
4. PAR adoption	−0.041 **	0.150 ***	0.169 ***	1

Note: * $p < 0.05$, ** $p < 0.01$, *** $p < 0.001$.

4.2. Mediation Effect Testing

The PROCESS macro was used to examine the multiple mediating roles of risk perception and PAR adoption in the relationship between government response and infection rate. We included the participants' gender, age, household registration, years of schooling, health status, urbanisation rate, and region as covariates. Table 4 shows that government response was positively associated with risk perception (b = 7.452, $p < 0.001$), whereas risk perception was negatively related to infection rate (b = −0.028, $p < 0.01$). Government response was positively associated with PAR adoption (b = 0.255, $p < 0.001$) and negatively related to infection rate (b = −0.859, $p < 0.01$). Risk perception showed a positive association with PAR adoption (b = 0.030, $p < 0.001$) and government response was negatively related to infection rate (b = −1.688, $p < 0.05$).

Table 4. Effects of government response on risk perception, PAR adoption, and infection rate.

	(1) Risk Perception	(2) PAR Adoption	(3) Infection Rate	(4) Infection Rate
Government response	7.452 ***	0.255 ***	−2.308 ***	−1.688 *
	(1.139)	(0.035)	(0.734)	(0.739)
Risk perception		0.030 ***		−0.028 **
		(0.000)		(0.009)
PAR adoption				−0.859 **
				(0.287)
Gender (0 = Male)	0.060	−0.001	−0.349 *	−0.351 *
	(0.275)	(0.008)	(0.176)	(0.175)
Age group (0 = more than 60 years old)				
40–60	−0.588	−0.052	0.862	0.829
	(1.117)	(0.035)	(0.708)	(0.707)
18–40	−1.384	−0.058	0.513	0.495
	(1.110)	(0.034)	(0.704)	(0.703)
Household registration (0 = rural household)	0.145	0.051 ***	0.406 *	0.440 *
	(0.305)	(0.009)	(0.197)	(0.197)
Years of schooling	−0.300 ***	−0.004 *	−0.071 *	−0.065 *
	(0.047)	(0.001)	(0.030)	(0.030)
Health status (0 = bad)	4.168 ***	0.059 ***	0.493	0.439
	(0.563)	(0.017)	(0.360)	(0.361)

Table 4. *Cont.*

	(1) Risk Perception	(2) PAR Adoption	(3) Infection Rate	(4) Infection Rate
Urbanisation rate	−6.142 ***	−0.047	15.225 ***	15.302 ***
	(1.464)	(0.045)	(0.967)	(0.967)
Region (0 = eastern China)				
Central China	−1.462 ***	−0.013	5.721 ***	5.743 ***
	(0.362)	(0.011)	(0.234)	(0.234)
Western China	−0.723	−0.021	0.075	0.087
	(0.417)	(0.013)	(0.277)	(0.276)
Constant	94.455 ***	3.543 ***	−9.773 ***	−9.071 ***
	(1.714)	(0.066)	(1.102)	(1.714)
N	7092	7092	7092	7092
R^2	0.046	0.036	0.136	0.139

Note: (1) Standard errors appear in parentheses; (2) * $p < 0.05$, ** $p < 0.01$, *** $p < 0.001$.

The results of the bootstrap analysis are shown in Table 5. None of the 95% confidence intervals for the path coefficients included zero, suggesting that the total effects, direct effects, and indirect effects were all significant (−2.308, −1.688, and −0.62, respectively). The mediating effects accounted for 26.87% of the total effects. Specifically, the effect of the path 'government response → risk perception → infection rate' was −0.209, accounting for 9.06% of the total effects; the effect of the path 'government response → PAR adoption → infection rate' was −0.219, accounting for 9.49% of the total effects; and the effect of the path 'government response → risk perception → PAR adoption → infection rate' was −0.192, accounting for 8.32% of the total effects. Thus, risk perception and PAR adoption mediated the relationship between government response and infection rate not only in parallel but also sequentially.

Table 5. Bootstrap analysis of multiple mediation effects.

	Effect Size	SE	95% CIs of Indirect Effect		Percentage of Total Effects
			Lower Bound	Upper Bound	
Indirect effects	−0.620	0.106	−3.237	−0.339	26.87%
X->M1->Y	−0.209	0.072	−0.327	−0.046	9.06%
X->M2->Y	−0.219	0.082	−0.369	−0.047	9.49%
X->M1->M2->Y	−0.192	0.056	−0.425	−0.012	8.32%

Note: (1) N = 7092; (2) Covariates: gender, age, household registration, years of schooling, health status, urbanisation rate, and region; (3) X = government response, M1 = risk perception, M2 = PAR adoption, Y = infection rate; (4) bootstrap sample size = 1000.

5. Discussion

Based on data from a nationwide survey conducted by a research group in mainland China in February 2020 and data on infection cases in selected cities in the 1.5 years following the outbreak of COVID-19 in December 2019, this study investigated the sustained effect of an early government response to the pandemic (i.e., the relationship between an early government response and the COVID-19 infection rate after 1.5 years). The contributions of the study are as follows. It offers novel insights into the effects of the government's implementation of a single policy and the multiple effects of prevention measures by comprehensively sorting out various government responses and evaluating the persistent effects of early intervention policies on the COVID-19 infection rate. In addition, this study reveals multiple mediating effects of an early government response on the COVID-19 infection rate. It confirms the role of social intervention in preventing the spread of epidemics, from a perspective that differs substantially from those of environmental science [55] and epidemiology [56].

First, this study carefully combed through the various epidemic prevention initiatives in the surveyed cities to construct a composite indicator to measure early intervention by the Chinese government and found that the government's early response was significantly negatively associated with infection rate. By collating the COVID-19 prevention and control announcements released on the Chinese government's official website, we summarised the initiatives implemented in the early stages of the COVID-19 outbreak, including 20 different intervention strategies, which can be classified into six categories that each point to a different issue in the outbreak prevention and control process. The rigorous government interventions implemented in the early stages and the rapid and active implementation of these measures are what prevented China, a country with a large population and one of the earliest COVID-19 outbreaks, from developing more COVID-19 infections and deaths than other countries [3]. This suggests that China's aggressive and multifaceted response may have prevented a worst-case scenario, inhibited the global spread of COVID-19, and mitigated the global impact of the virus [4]. Thus, the Chinese government's early COVID-19 interventions and their effects deserve to be noted.

This study's findings have important implications for future efforts to contain the spread of the epidemic. It reveals that the government's response to COVID-19 and other pandemics should not be reactive but proactive, and should not involve a single initiative but a complete set of action strategies. The six categories of measures provide a more detailed picture of the Chinese government's response to a pandemic and can serve as a set of action strategies to prevent the spread of COVID-19. This empirical study also shows that government response should be more comprehensive, scientific, and equitable, including disease detection, and combined with that, Professor Jing Jun advocated to build an epidemic preparedness and response system including incident verification, isolation of the source of infection, public communication, travel warnings, prevention of systemic breakdown, protection of human rights, the right to health of the whole community and control of social fears" [57]. Some studies have also found that a government's response explains differences in prevention and control effectiveness across countries [3], and the findings in this paper provide theoretical and practical insights into the response to epidemics in countries with the same social context.

Subsequently, this study determined that China's early government response had a sustained impact on the COVID-19 infection rate. Although previous studies are consistent with the findings of Post et al. that the point of change in the daily effective contact rate overlapped with the moment of government response [14], Lai et al. found that if the government's response had been implemented earlier, the number of COVID-19 cases could have been reduced [4]. Other scholars have analysed the impact of strict quarantine measures versus reopening public places on the early spread of COVID-19 [58], including COVID-19 infection and mortality rates [17,19,58–62]. Although many studies have shown that both early and severe prevention and control policies, as well as later, lenient intervention strategies, inhibited the spread of COVID-19, they have neglected the possibility that an early government response may also have had a sustained effect on the COVID-19 infection rate in later stages. Meanwhile these studies, in highlighting the impact of an early government response on the infection rate of the epidemic, have emphasised that the lag in response may lead to a delayed reduction in the infection rate. In contrast, this paper emphasises the sustained reduction in the infection rate that occurs as a result of the sustained effect of the government response. The present study established a negative association between an early government response and COVID-19 infection rates over the past year and a half, suggesting that early and severe interventions have a lasting effect on the spread of the epidemic.

This study also delved into the mechanisms underlying the impact of an early government response on the prevalence of an epidemic (i.e., why does an early government response have a sustained impact on the COVID-19 infection rate?) Two mechanisms of action were identified. The first is that an early government response affects the COVID-19 infection rate vis-à-vis its influence on people's risk perception. Numerous studies have proven the role of scientific, transparent information in risk perception during an epidemic, including 'the information release' and 'publicity and education' measures, which enable people to form an objective assessment of the outbreak and foster an appropriate risk perception. Government information on public emergencies indirectly influences protective behaviour through individual factors such as risk perception, because of detailed outbreak information and positive risk communication. Statistical information on the outbreak and detailed information on the trajectory of confirmed cases make individuals aware of the seriousness of the pandemic, and detailed information enhances individual risk assessment [38]. At the same time, this poses a challenge for governments attempting to reduce the impact of fake news in the information age and in social media. In terms of the response process, both the relevant Supreme Court directive and the 'Rumours exposed website' created by Tencent (the parent company of WeChat) helped reduce the spread of confusion and panic [63]. The impact of government response on public perception of risk is therefore not achieved by a single measure but rather by a combination of them. When faced with a rapidly spreading pandemic such as COVID-19, a drastic and strict government response effectively increase people's perception of the risk of infection, resulting in more cooperative behaviour that inhibits the spread of the virus and reduces its infection rate. Studies have pointed out that increasing people's risk perception contributes to superior suppression of virus transmission.

The second mechanism is that an early government response affects the COVID-19 infection rate by increasing the public's adoption of PARs. Scholars have found that an early government response, such as swiftly disseminating COVID-19 knowledge, monitoring infected cases, and restricting population movement and interpersonal contact, including lockdowns, travel restrictions, and shutting down public places, have a direct contribution to public's adoption of PARs. Therefore, government response in the early stages of COVID-19 outbreak will control the spread of disease by influencing individuals' protective behaviours. While risk perception and the public's adoption of PARs have also been the focus of previous studies, this study identified risk perception as an important mediating factor between government response and the public's adoption of PARs. People's compliance with recommended protective behaviours is not the ultimate goal of government response to COVID-19, reducing infection and mortality rates is the real goal. Studies have rarely explored the relationship between the public's adoption of PARs and infection rates. This paper extends the evaluation of the effectiveness of government response in reducing the COVID-19 infection rate by analysing the relationship between early government response, risk perception, the public's adoption of PARs, and COVID-19 infection rate.

In addition, this study found a correlation between risk perception and the public's adoption of PARs, and showed that the effect of an early government response on the COVID-19 infection rate may exert multiple mediating effects through risk perception and the public's adoption of PARs. That is, an early government response may influence people's risk perception, which in turn promotes their adherence to recommended protective behaviours and ultimately suppresses the COVID-19 infection rate. In the past year, repeated outbreaks of COVID-19 in Xinjiang, Beijing, Guangzhou, Nanjing, Xiamen, and other provinces in China have been quickly contained rather than spreading to multiple provinces across the country, as was the case with the initial Wuhan outbreak. A major reason for this success is that the Chinese population developed an adequate level of risk perception after the Wuhan outbreak, and when confronted with subsequent COVID-19 outbreaks, they were able to quickly adopt recommended protective behaviours to protect themselves and contain the spread. These are strong indications that an early government response has a sustained and important impact on later prevention and control. This shows how government response and infection rate at the macro level are connected to individuals at the micro level. These findings not only enrich the literature but also provide important practical insights.

In practice, it would be undesirable to relax outbreak control, because we are still in the midst of the pandemic and far from being completely victorious over COVID-19. However, persisting with strict prevention and control in countries where the outbreak is under better control is not advisable; this study reveals that instead, increasing risk perception and promoting the public's adoption of PARs are feasible practical strategies. People's risk perceptions should be continuously cultivated. In the post-pandemic era, it will be important to continue providing the public with scientific information on COVID-19 and how to protect themselves and others. This will foster the formation of health beliefs that will enable COVID-19 to be defeated with ease and increase cooperation between the public and the government. This will not only effectively reduce the administrative costs of epidemic invention for the government but also encourage the public to respond to COVID-19 variants with flexibility. Adopting PARs can enable individuals to protect themselves and interrupt the chain of epidemic transmission. Studies in the field of infectious diseases have demonstrated that individual health behaviours play a direct role in overcoming diseases. Why was the Chinese government able to effectively control the spread of the virus during the COVID-19 pandemic? The answer lies in the public's adoption of PARs such as physical distancing, mask-wearing, and handwashing. The multiple mediating roles of risk perception and PAR adoption remind us that in the post-pandemic era, inducing people to adopt recommended protective behaviours can intervene in their risk perception, and vice versa. Once a reasonable level of risk perception has been developed, it can continuously guide people to adjust their health behaviours in response to a health crisis and eventually help to overcome the crisis.

Therefore, our findings prompt us to further consider that, first, government response to pandemics should not be reactive but proactive, and should consider the cultivation of public health behaviours and health beliefs. Second, the response should not be singular but systemic and comprehensive, and should consider the effectiveness of the interactions between the various measures. Third, it should not only emphasise 'just-in-time' and 'short-term' effects but should also focus on long-term and sustained effects. We suggest that in the face of an unknown pandemic, the emphasis should be on predictive awareness of the epidemic, the construction of 'an epidemic preparedness and response system', and the establishment of a multi-source early warning system for infectious diseases that incorporates the public, companies, research institutions, public participation in in-hospital reporting, and other data sources.

6. Limitations and Avenues for Future Research

Although our study contributes to both the literature and anti-epidemic practice, several limitations should be noted. First, the data on both risk perception and the public's adoption of PARs were based on the results of a 2020 survey conducted at the outset of the COVID-19 outbreak, when people's understanding of the disease was much more limited than it is now. With a greater understanding of COVID-19, people's risk perceptions are likely to change and they are more likely to comply with recommended protective behaviours for self-protection. Second, risk perception and the public's adoption of PARs may be influenced by several factors aside from government response, such as the severity of COVID-19. There may be regional and group differences in risk perception and the public's PAR adoption depending on regional and group differences in the severity of COVID-19 [64]. Such regional differences should be considered in future research. Third, multiple mechanisms may underlie the sustained impact of an early government response on the rate of COVID-19 infection, only one of which is revealed in this paper. Future studies should explore other potential mechanisms underlying this impact.

In addition, when we look at the international situation, we see both the differences in the health care base and the historical characteristics of each country's health care system, leading to differences in each country's response capacity. Russia has a massive government sanitary epidemiology service (Rospotrebnadzor), which is unique in the world for historical reasons, which has effectively prevented the importation of the epidemic [65].

However, there was not enough time to respond before COVID-19 swept through Brazil. The epidemic hit the country's economy hard, with significant regional disparities in health care capacity and the spread of the virus to poorer areas with less capacity [66]. Due to its low government spending on health care and lack of health care infrastructure, India leapt to the forefront of the world's epidemic [67]. Therefore, it remains an open question whether our findings shed light on how other countries' government response affects the infection rate, and whether this pathway still exists.

7. Conclusions

This paper investigates the sustained effect of an early government response on the rate of COVID-19 infection based on national survey data and infection data on Chinese cities. The results indicate that the early response of China's government significantly reduced the country's COVID-19 infection rate and that this this impact worked through risk perception, through the public's adoption of PARs, and through risk perception and the public's PAR adoption in a chain-mediated manner. These findings have great practical value. In showing how government response and infection rate at the macro level are connected to the behaviour of individuals at the micro level, they provide viable directions for curbing the spread of infectious diseases like COVID-19.

Author Contributions: Conceptualisation, T.D. and G.S.; methodology, T.D.; software, T.D.; validation, Z.S. and G.S.; formal analysis, T.D.; investigation, G.S., Z.S. and T.D.; resources, T.D. and G.S.; data curation, T.D.; writing—original draft preparation, T.D.; writing—review and editing, G.S. and Z.S.; visualisation, G.S. and Z.S. and T.D.; supervision, G.S.; project administration, Z.S. and T.D.; funding acquisition, G.S. All authors have read and agreed to the published version of the manuscript.

Funding: This study was supported by grants titled *Social mentality and prevention and control in response to major public health emergencies* (B200203041 and B200207033) from Hohai University's Central University Basic Scientific Research Business Expenses Project Funding and Population Research Fund of Jiangsu Province JSPA9002.

Institutional Review Board Statement: The study was conducted according to the guidelines of the Declaration of Helsinki, and approved by the Institutional Review Board of School of Public Administration of Hohai University (protocol code 2021006 and 8 October 2021).

Informed Consent Statement: Informed consent was obtained from all subjects involved in the study.

Data Availability Statement: The data are not publicly available, following the decision of the ethics committee on how to conduct this study.

Acknowledgments: Thanks to Huicong Liu, Qi Yang, Lin Zhu, Junzhuo Xu, Xiaocheng Zhang, Likun Gu, and You He for their help in collecting data.

Conflicts of Interest: The authors declare no conflict of interest.

References

1. World Health Organization. Timeline of WHO's Response to the COVID-19 Outbreak. Available online: https://www.who.int/zh/news/item/29-06-2020-covidtimeline (accessed on 5 August 2021).
2. National Health Commission of the People's Republic of China. The Latest Situation of the New Coronavirus Pneumonia Epidemic Situation as of 24:00 on March 9. Available online: http://www.nhc.gov.cn/xcs/yqtb/202108/b27926ccc526497cbe06c7ce2fcb1834.shtml (accessed on 5 August 2021).
3. Petherick, A.; Kira, B.; Cameron-Blake, E.; Tatlow, H.; Hallas, L.; Hale, H.; Phillips, B.; Zhang, Y.; Webster, S.; Anania, J.; et al. Variation in Government Responses to COVID-19. Available online: https://www.bsg.ox.ac.uk/research/publications/variation-government-responses-covid-19 (accessed on 11 June 2021). This Working Paper Is Updated Frequently.
4. Lai, S.; Ruktanonchai, N.; Zhou, L.; Prosper, O.; Floyd, J.; Wesolowski, A.; Santillana, M.; Zhang, C.; Du, X.; Yu, H.; et al. Effect of non-pharmaceutical interventions to contain COVID-19 in China. *Nature* **2020**, *585*, 410–413. [CrossRef] [PubMed]
5. Ding, D.; Cheng, M.; Del Pozo Cruz, B.; Lin, T.; Sun, S.; Zhang, L.; Yang, Q.; Ma, Z.; Wang, J.; Jia, Y.; et al. How COVID-19 lockdown and reopening affected daily steps: Evidence based on 164,630 person-days of prospectively collected data from Shanghai, China. *Int. J. Behav. Nutr. Phy.* **2021**, *18*, 40. [CrossRef] [PubMed]

6. Zhao, X.M.; Li, X.H.; Nie, C.H. Backtracking transmission of COVID-19 in China: Based on big data source, and effect of strict pandemic control policy. *Bull. Chin. Acad. Sci.* **2020**, *35*, 248–255.
7. Lai, S.; Bogoch, I.I.; Ruktanonchai, N.W.; Watts, A.; Lu, X.; Yang, W.; Yu, H.; Khan, K.; Tatem, A.J. Assessing spread risk of Wuhan novel coronavirus within and beyond China, January–April 2020: A travel network-based modelling study. *MedRxiv* **2020**. [CrossRef]
8. Fong, M.; Gao, H.; Wong, J.; Xiao, J.; Shiu, E.; Ryu, S.; Cowling, B. Nonpharmaceutical measures for pandemic influenza in nonhealthcare settings—Social distancing measures. *Emerg. Infect. Dis.* **2020**, *26*, 976–984. [CrossRef] [PubMed]
9. Ryu, S.; Gao, H.; Wong, J.Y.; Shiu, E.Y.; Xiao, J.; Fong, M.W.; Cowling, B.J. Nonpharmaceutical measures for pandemic influenza in nonhealthcare settings—International travel-related measures. *Emerg. Infect. Dis.* **2020**, *26*, 961–966. [CrossRef] [PubMed]
10. Xiao, J.; Shiu, E.; Gao, H.; Wong, J.; Fong, M.; Ryu, S.; Cowling, B. Nonpharmaceutical measures for pandemic influenza in nonhealthcare settings—Personal protective and environmental measures. *Emerg. Infect. Dis.* **2020**, *26*, 967–975. [CrossRef] [PubMed]
11. Chen, W.; Wang, Q.; Li, Y.; Yu, H.; Xia, Y.; Zhang, M.; Qin, Y.; Zhang, T.; Peng, Z.; Zhang, R.; et al. Early containment strategies and core measures for prevention and control of novel coronavirus pneumonia in China. *Chin. Prev. Med.* **2020**, *54*, 239–244.
12. Bauch, C.; Galvani, A. Social Factors in Epidemiology. *Science* **2013**, *342*, 47–49. [CrossRef] [PubMed]
13. Kucharski, A. *The Rules of Contagion: Why Things Spread—and Why They Stop*; Wellcome Collection: London, UK, 2020; pp. 165–195.
14. Post, R.; Regis, M.; Zhan, Z.; van den Heuvel, E. How did governmental interventions affect the spread of COVID-19 in European countries? *BMC Public Health* **2021**, *21*. [CrossRef]
15. Xiao, J.; Hu, J.; He, G.; Liu, T.; Kang, M.; Rong, Z.; Lin, L.; Zhong, H.; Huang, Q.; Deng, A.; et al. The time-varying transmission dynamics of COVID-19 and synchronous actions in China. *Int. J. Infect. Dis.* **2020**, *103*, 617–623. [CrossRef] [PubMed]
16. Wang, Y. Government Policies, National Culture and Social Distancing during the First Wave of the COVID-19 Pandemic: International Evidence. *Saf. Sci.* **2020**, *135*, 105138. [CrossRef]
17. Leffler, C.T.; Ing, E.; Lykins, J.D.; Hogan, M.; McKeown, C.A.; Grzybowski, A. Association of country-wide coronavirus mortality with demographics, testing, lockdowns, and public wearing of masks. *Am. J. Trop. Med. Hygiene* **2020**, *103*, 2400–2411. [CrossRef]
18. Cowling, B.; Ali, S.; Ng, T.; Tsang, T.; Li, J.; Fong, M.; Liao, Q.; Kwan, M.; Lee, S.; Chiu, S.; et al. Impact assessment of non-pharmaceutical interventions against coronavirus disease 2019 and influenza in Hong Kong: An observational study. *Lancet Public Health* **2020**, *5*, e279–e288. [CrossRef]
19. Meo, S.A.; Abukhalaf, A.A.; Alomar, A.A.; AlMutairi, F.; Usmani, A.; Klonoff, D. Impact of lockdown on COVID-19 prevalence and mortality during 2020 pandemic: Observational analysis of 27 countries. *Eur. J. Med Res.* **2020**, *25*, 1–7. [CrossRef]
20. Guo, S.; An, R.; Mcbride, T.D.; Yu, D.; Yang, Y. Mitigation interventions in the United States: An exploratory investigation of determinants and impacts. *Res. Soc. Work Pract.* **2021**, *31*, 26–41. [CrossRef]
21. Forte, T.; Santinha, G.; Carvalho, S.A. The COVID-19 pandemic strain: Teleworking and health behavior changes in the Portuguese context. *Healthcare* **2021**, *9*, 1151. [CrossRef] [PubMed]
22. Duan, T.X.; Jiang, H.; Deng, X.; Zhang, Q.; Wang, F. Government intervention, risk perception, and the adoption of protective action recommendations: Evidence from the COVID-19 prevention and control experience of China. *Int. J. Env. Res. Pub. Health* **2020**, *17*, 3387. [CrossRef]
23. Sun, Z.G.; Yang, B.Q.; Zhang, R.L.; Cheng, X. Influencing factors of understanding COVID-19 risks and coping behaviors among the elderly population. *Int. J. Env. Res. Pub. Health* **2020**, *17*, 5889. [CrossRef]
24. Dryhurst., S.; Schneider, C.; Kerr, J.; Freeman, A.; Linden, S. Risk perceptions of COVID-19 around the world. *J. Risk Res.* **2020**. [CrossRef]
25. Leppin, A.; Aro, A. Risk perceptions related to SARS and avian influenza: Theoretical foundations of current empirical research. *Int. J. Behav. Med.* **2009**, *16*, 7–29. [CrossRef] [PubMed]
26. Wang, F.; Wei, J.; Shi, X. Compliance with recommended protective actions during an H7N9 emergency: A risk perception perspective. *Disasters* **2018**, *42*, 207–232. [CrossRef] [PubMed]
27. Porumbescu, G. Using Transparency to Enhance Responsiveness and Trust in Local Government: Can It Work? *State Local Gov. Review* **2015**, *47*, 205–213. [CrossRef]
28. Qazi, A.; Qazi, J.; Naseer, K.; Zeeshan, M.; Hardaker, G.; Maitama, J.Z.; Haruna, K. Analyzing situational awareness through public opinion to predict adoption of social distancing amid pandemic COVID-19. *J. Med Virol.* **2020**, *92*, 849–855. [CrossRef] [PubMed]
29. Shlomo, M.; Eran, V.G.; Nissim, C. How well do they manage a crisis? The government's effectiveness during the COVID-19 pandemic. *Public Adm. Rev.* **2021**. [CrossRef]
30. DiFonzo, N.; Prashant, B. Rumors influence: Toward a dynamic social impact theory of rumor. In *The Science of Social Influence: Advances and Future Progress*; Pratkanis, A.R., Ed.; Psychology Press: Hove, UK, 2007; pp. 271–295.
31. Michelle Driedger, S.; Ryan, M.; Cindy, J. "Damned if you do, and damned if you don't": Communicating about uncertainty and evolving science during the H1N1 influenza pandemic. *J. Risk Res.* **2018**, *24*, 574–592. [CrossRef]
32. Siegrist, M.; Zingg, A. The role of public trust during pandemics. *Eur. Psychol.* **2013**, *19*, 23–32. [CrossRef]
33. Vaughan, E.; Timothy, T. Effective health risk communication about pandemic influenza for vulnerable populations. *Am. J. Infect. Control* **2009**, *99*, S324–S332. [CrossRef]

34. Kim, H.K.; Jeff, N. The role of emotional response during an H1N1 influenza pandemic on a college campus. *J. Public Relat. Res.* **2013**, *25*, 30–50. [CrossRef]
35. Zhou, M.; Guo, W. Social factors and worry associated with COVID-19: Evidence from a large survey in China. *Soc. Sci. Med.* **2021**, *277*, 113934. [CrossRef]
36. Jungmann, S.M.; Witthft, M. Health anxiety, cyberchondria, and coping in the current COVID-19 pandemic: Which factors are related to coronavirus anxiety? *J. Anxiety Disord.* **2020**, *73*, 102239. [CrossRef]
37. Fullana, M.A.; Hidalgo-Mazzei, D.; Vieta, E.; Radua, J. Coping behaviors associated with decreased anxiety and depressive symptoms during the COVID-19 pandemic and lockdown. *J. Affect. Disord.* **2020**, *275*, 80–81. [CrossRef] [PubMed]
38. Dai, B.; Fu, D.; Zheng, Y.; Liu, B.; Li, Q.; Liu, X. The effects of governmental and individual predictors on COVID-19 protective behaviors in China: A path analysis model. *Public Adm. Rev.* **2020**, *80*, 797–804. [CrossRef] [PubMed]
39. Zheng, L.; Miao, M.; Lim, J.Y.; Li, M.; Zhang, X. Is lockdown bad for social anxiety in COVID-19 regions?: A national study in the SOR perspective. *Int. J. Environ. Res. Public Health* **2020**, *17*, 4561. [CrossRef] [PubMed]
40. Matovu, J.; Kabwama, S.; Ssekamatte, T.; Ssenkusu, J.; Wanyenze, R. COVID-19 awareness, adoption of COVID-19 preventive measures, and effects of COVID-19 lockdown among adolescent boys and young men in Kampala, Uganda. *J. Community Health* **2021**, *46*, 1–12. [CrossRef]
41. Folkman, S.; Moskowitz, J.T. Stress, positive emotion, and coping. *Curr. Dir. Psychol. Sci.* **2016**, *9*, 115–118. [CrossRef]
42. Fredrickson, B.; Tugade, M.; Waugh, C.; Larkin, G. What good are positive emotions in crisis? A prospective study of resilience and emotions following the terrorist attacks on the United States on September 11th, 2001. *J. Pers. Soc. Psychol.* **2003**, *84*, 365–376. [CrossRef]
43. Stangier, U.; Kananian, S.; Schüller, J. Perceived vulnerability to disease, knowledge about COVID-19, and changes in preventive behavior during lockdown in a German convenience sample. *Curr. Psychol.* **2021**, *26*, 1–9. [CrossRef]
44. French, P.E. Enhancing the legitimacy of local government pandemic influenza planning through transparency and public engagement. *Public Adm. Rev.* **2011**, *71*, 253–264. [CrossRef]
45. Lindell, M.K.; Perry, R.W. The protective action decision model: Theoretical modifications and additional evidence. *Risk Anal.* **2012**, *32*, 616–632. [CrossRef]
46. Kim, Y.; Zhong, W.; Megan, J.; Lauren, W. Public risk perceptions and preventive behaviors during the 2009 H1N1 influenza pandemic. *Disaster Med. Public Health Prep.* **2015**, *9*, 145–154. [CrossRef]
47. Iorfa, S.; Ottu, I.; Oguntayo, R.; Ayandele, O.; Kolawole, S.; Gandi, J.; Dangiwa, A.; Olapegba, P. COVID-19 knowledge, risk perception, and precautionary behavior among Nigerians: A moderated mediation approach. *Front. Psychol.* **2020**, *11*, 566773. [CrossRef] [PubMed]
48. Chon, M.G.; Hyojung, P. Predicting public support for government actions in a public health crisis: Testing fear, organization-public relationship, and behavioral intention in the framework of the situational theory of problem solving. *Health Commun.* **2021**, *36*, 476–486. [CrossRef] [PubMed]
49. Kasperson, R.; Renn, O.; Slovic, P.; Brown, H.; Emel, J.; Goble, R.; Kasperson, J.; Ratick, S. The social amplification of risk: A conceptual framework. *Risk Anal.* **1988**, *8*, 177–187. [CrossRef]
50. Slovic, P. Perception of risk. *Science* **1987**, *236*, 280–285. [CrossRef]
51. Liu, J.T.; Hammitt, J.K.; Wang, J.D.; Tsou, M.W. Valuation of the risk of SARS in Taiwan. *Health Econ.* **2005**, *14*, 83–91. [CrossRef]
52. National Health Commission of the People's Republic of China. The Guidelines for the Public's Protective Behavior of COVID-19. Available online: http://www.nhc.gov.cn/xcs/fkdt/202001/bc661e49b5bc487dba182f5c49ac445b.shtml (accessed on 31 January 2020).
53. MacKinnon, D.P.; Lockwood, C.M.; Williams, J. Confidence limits for the indirect effect: Distribution of the product and resampling methods. *Multivar. Behav. Res.* **2004**, *39*, 99–128. [CrossRef]
54. Hayes, A. Introduction to mediation, moderation, and conditional process analysis. *J. Educ. Meas.* **2013**, *51*, 335–337.
55. Al-Rousan, N.; Al-Najjar, H. The correlation between the spread of COVID-19 infections and weather variables in 30 Chinese provinces and the impact of Chinese government mitigation plans. *Eur. Rev. Med. Pharmacol. Sci.* **2020**, *24*, 4565–4571.
56. Qi, A.; Shi, Z.; Dg, D.; Lou, Y.; Yang, S.; Musa, S.; Wang, M.; Cai, Y.; Wang, W.; Yang, L.; et al. A conceptual model for the coronavirus disease 2019 (COVID-19) outbreak in Wuhan, China with individual reaction and governmental action. *Int. J. Infect. Dis.* **2020**, *93*, 211–216.
57. Jun, J. The Social Component of Early Warning of New Infectious Diseases. Available online: https://baijiahao.baidu.com/s?id=1663240806042498388&wfr=spider&for=pc (accessed on 7 April 2020).
58. Mati, S. Do as your neighbours do? Assessing the impact of lockdown and reopening on the active COVID-19 cases in Nigeria. *Social Sci. Med.* **2020**, *270*, 113645. [CrossRef] [PubMed]
59. Flaxman, S.; Mishra, S.; Gandy, A.; Unwin, H.; Walker, P. Estimating the effects of non-pharmaceutical interventions on COVID-19 in Europe Mélodie Monod, Imperial college COVID-19 response team. *Azra C Nat.* **2020**, *584*, 257–261.
60. Pan, A.; Liu, L.; Wang, C.; Guo, H.; Hao, X.; Wang, Q.; Huang, J.; He, N.; Yu, H.; Lin, X. Association of public health interventions with the epidemiology of the COVID-19 outbreak in Wuhan, China. *Jama* **2020**, *323*, 1915–1923. [CrossRef] [PubMed]
61. Banholzer, N.; Eva van, W.; Kratzwald, B.; Seeliger, A.; Tschernutter, D.; Bottrighi, P.; Cenedese, A.; Salles, G.; Vach, W.; Feuerriegel, S. The estimated impact of non-pharmaceutical interventions on documented cases of COVID-19: A cross-country analysis. *MedRxiv* **2020**. [CrossRef]

62. Dehning, J.; Zierenberg, J.; Spitzner, F.P.; Wibral, M.; Neto, J.P. Wcs in the spread of COVID-19 reveals the effectiveness of interventions. *Science* **2020**, *369*, eabb9789. [CrossRef]
63. Hua, J.; Shaw, R. Corona virus (COVID-19) "infodemic" and emerging issues through a data lens: The case of China. *Int. J. Environ. Res. Public Health* **2020**, *17*, 2309. [CrossRef] [PubMed]
64. Sohel, S.; Hossain, B.; Alam, K.; Shi, G.Q.; Shabbir, R.; Sifullah, M.; Mamy, M. COVID-19 induced impact on informal migrants in Bangladesh: A qualitative study. *Int. J. Sociol. Soc. Policy* **2021**. [CrossRef]
65. Reshetnikov, V.; Mitrokhin, O.; Shepetovskaya, N.; Belova, E.; Jakovljevic, M. Organizational measures aiming to combat COVID-19 in the Russian Federation: The first experience. *Expert Rev. Pharm. Outcomes Res.* **2020**, *20*, 571–577. [CrossRef]
66. The World Bank. Covid-19 in Brazil: Impacts and Policy Responses. Available online: https://www.worldbank.org/en/country/brazil/publication/covid-19-in-brazil-impacts-policy-responses (accessed on 7 July 2020).
67. Gauttam, P.; Patel, N.; Singh, B.; Jaspal, K.; Chattu, V.; Mihajlo, J. Public health policy of India and COVID-19: Diagnosis and prognosis of the combating response. *Sustainability* **2021**, *13*, 1–18.

International Journal of
Environmental Research and Public Health

MDPI

Article

Behavioral Factors Associated with COVID-19 Risk: A Cross-Sectional Survey in Japan

Sae Ochi [1,*], Mirai So [2], Sora Hashimoto [3], Kenzo Denda [4] and Yoichi Sekizawa [5]

1 Department of Laboratory Medicine, The Jikei University School of Medicine, Tokyo 105-0003, Japan
2 Department of Psychiatry, Tokyo Dental College, Tokyo 101-0061, Japan; somirai@tdc.ac.jp
3 United Health Communication Co., Ltd., Tokyo 103-0006, Japan; hashimoto@uhc.jp
4 Hiramatsu Memorial Hospital, Sapporo 064-8536, Japan; denda_kenzo_0330@yahoo.co.jp
5 Research Department, Research Institute of Economy, Trade and Industry, Tokyo 100-8901, Japan; sekizawa-yoichi@rieti.go.jp
* Correspondence: ochisae1024@jikei.ac.jp

Abstract: Background: Behaviors to avoid infection are key to minimizing casualties of the COVID-19 pandemic, as well as to avoid excessive interventions that are less effective. This study aims to identify behavioral patterns associated with SARS-CoV-2 infection in the real world. Methods: A questionnaire-based cross-sectional study was conducted targeting a research panel of NTTCom Online Marketing Solutions Corporation or its affiliates. Data were extracted so that their demographic composition ratios matched the population estimates. Individuals who answered with consistency to have been diagnosed with SARS-CoV-2 at a medical facility were categorized into a SARS-CoV-2 group. Differences in lifestyles were compared using multiple regression and inverse probability weighing. Results: In total 13,277 participants were included, of whom 44 (0.33%) were categorized as the SARS-CoV-2 group. Diagnosis of SARS-CoV-2 was negatively correlated with crowd avoidance, mask wearing, and hand-washing behavior. On the contrary, the diagnosis was positively correlated with some behaviors that appear to be preventive actions against the infection, such as changing clothes frequently, sanitizing belongings, and remote working. Conclusions: It is important to conduct evidence-based intervention on people's behaviors and to avoid excessive interventions that are less effective, so that people can minimize the indirect harm, such as exhaustion and economic loss.

Keywords: COVID-19; SARS-CoV-2; behavioral change; remote work; exercise

Citation: Ochi, S.; So, M.; Hashimoto, S.; Denda, K.; Sekizawa, Y. Behavioral Factors Associated with COVID-19 Risk: A Cross-Sectional Survey in Japan. *Int. J. Environ. Res. Public Health* **2021**, *18*, 12184. https://doi.org/10.3390/ijerph182212184

Academic Editors: Paolo Roma, Merylin Monaro and Cristina Mazza

Received: 17 October 2021
Accepted: 16 November 2021
Published: 20 November 2021

1. Introduction

COVID-19, a syndrome caused by SARS-CoV-2, has dramatically changed the lifestyles of people all over the world. Although a sense of normalcy is beginning to return in some countries due to vaccine development and introduction, there are cases of 'breakthrough infection' among those who are fully vaccinated [1]. Therefore, it is expected to take some time before the infection becomes under control. Therefore, traditional public health measures, including infection-avoidance behavior of each individual, are still highly important to minimize casualties of the infection [2].

Even so, many people feel fatigued by large-scale restrictions on their movements, including lockdowns and curfews. Excessive regulations can greatly and negatively affect people's physical and mental health [3], as well as economic status [4,5]. A systematic review suggested deterioration of mental health might be a global health problem [6]. There is also a concern about increase in domestic violence and substance abuse [7]. Particularly in Japan, an increase in the suicide rate among women in Japan has been reported [8], which is attributed to anxiety about their children's health, increase in domestic violence, and high frequency of lay-offs. Not only population health, but also the healthcare system itself, might be affected by austerity measures [9]. To minimize such indirect negative impacts of the pandemic on public health, prevention measures should not only be effective, but also be lean so that people are not exhausted by the long-term excessive restrictions of their behaviors.

SARS-CoV-2 has only two simple transmission routes: via inhalation of droplets scattered by an infected person's coughing or talking, or via touching one's eyes, nose, or mouth with a contaminated hand [10]. General measures for individuals include mask use, hand washing, ventilation of a space, and distancing from other people [11]. In addition to these, there are often governmental interventions such as lockdowns, curfews, and induction of remote works. All of these measures are effective in many cases, but the effectiveness of each measure differs by region and culture. For example, "social distancing" can be a priority in Europe and the U.S., where there is a custom of hugging and handshaking. This measure may not necessarily be a priority in Asian countries where people bow when greeting each other. On the other hand, hand washing might be more important in many Asian countries where there is a custom of eating with one's hands [12]. Thus, it is necessary to prioritize behavioral interventions based on epidemiological evidence to reduce the infection risk at a regional level.

In this study, behavioral patterns associated with a COVID-19 diagnosis were analyzed based on the results of a large-scale questionnaire survey in Japan. By identifying effective preventive measures in the real world, this research will contribute to prioritizing protective measures that are both effective and sustainable.

2. Materials and Methods

2.1. Patient and Public Involvement

Data were collected as part of the research project, "Basic research for exploring the ideal medical intervention after the advent of the new coronavirus", of the Research Institute of Economy, Trade, and Industry (RIETI). The online survey was called, "the 2020 Continuing survey on mental and physical health during the COVID-19 pandemic" (hereinafter RIETI questionnaire survey), and NTTCom Online Marketing Solutions Corporation was commissioned to conduct it. The data used in our study were microdata of the first survey conducted during the period 27 October–6 November 2020. The content of the questions is presented in Supplementary Table S1.

2.2. Data Collection

The surveyed subjects were men and women Japan-wide aged 18–74 years and were members of a research panel of NTTCom Online Marketing Solutions Corporation or its affiliates. They were extracted so that their demographic composition ratios of sex, age, and distribution of prefectures matched the population estimates of the Statistics Bureau of Japan (final estimates, May 2020). The final number of respondents was targeted to be approximately 15,000.

Data were excluded when: individuals provided non-existent zip codes; zip codes did not match the given prefectures; there were extreme outlying values for height and weight (200 cm or more for height, and less than 35 kg or 100 kg or more for weight, which is abnormal in Japan); age differed by 2 years or more from that previously given in the survey company's registration; or response time was very short (less than 5 min) or very long (10 h or more). The remaining individuals were recognized as valid respondents.

2.3. Statistical Analysis

2.3.1. Outcome Variables

The outcome index used in this study was the SARS-CoV-2 diagnosis status. If an individual chose the answer, "I have been diagnosed as SARS-CoV-2 infection at a medical facility and am currently under treatment" or "I was diagnosed as SARS-CoV-2 infection at a medical facility and have already recovered", then he/she was categorized into a SARS-CoV-2 group and the presence of diagnosis was used as the primary outcome variable.

This study established that the subjects "experienced SARS-CoV-2 infection" only if they were diagnosed with it at a medical facility.

The questionnaire was conducted 3 times: in October 2020, January 2021, and May 2021. If there was a discrepancy between the answer about SARS-CoV-2 diagnosis (e.g., a participant answered,"I was diagnosed as SARS-CoV-2 infection" in the first questionnaire and "Not diagnosed" in the second one), the data were omitted.

2.3.2. Explanatory Variables

In addition to the SARS-CoV-2 diagnosis status, this survey asked the questions below regarding underlying disease and behavior. The detail of each question is shown in Table S1.

- Pre-existing diseases;
- Behaviors to avoid contracting SARS-CoV-2;
- Average days and hours of exercise in a week;
- Main exercise type;
- Change in the amount of exercise compared with the same time last year;
- Frequency of going out;
- Frequency of working from home in the past one month.

2.3.3. Comparison of the Two Groups

To compare the two groups, Wilcoxon's rank sum test and chi-square test were used for continuous variables and categorical variables, respectively.

2.3.4. Multivariate Analysis

Logistic regression analysis was performed to assess the relationship between outcome and explanatory variables after adjustment for age, sex, and body mass index (BMI). To minimize the effects of outliers, a robust method was applied for the following regression tests.

The proportion of patients diagnosed as SARS-CoV-2 infection was very low. Thus, this study also used inverse probability weighting (IPW) to estimate the average treatment effect (ATE) of each item on SARS-CoV-2 infection and on the risk of infection symptom occurrence. In IPW, a propensity score is used to weigh each observed value in the sample. Two types of expected values are then estimated: the expected value of the outcome if the treatment is used for the overall sample (in this analysis, if individuals had travelled) and the expected value of the outcome if the treatment is not used. The ATE is estimated from the difference between these values.

Specifically, the inverse of the estimated propensity score $(1/\partial)$ is used for weighting. The inverse of a propensity score increases as the propensity score decreases. Therefore, a smaller weight is given to an observed value with a larger propensity score in the treated group, and a larger weight is given to an observed value with a larger propensity score in the control group. In other words, calculation is done with more weighting for an observed value that is rarer or accounts for a smaller proportion of the sample for each of the treated group and control group.

The statistical analyses were carried out using Stata/SE 16.0 (StataCorp LLC, College Station, TX, USA).

2.3.5. Sensitivity Analysis

Sensitivity analysis was conducted targeting the participants who answered to have been diagnosed as SARS-CoV-2 in the survey in May 2021 only.

2.3.6. Ethical Considerations

All individuals who participated in this study consented to their participation. This study was conducted with the approval of the ethics committee of Hiramatsu Memorial Hospital affiliated with Specified Jisoukai Medical Corporation (ID of approval: 20200925).

3. Results

3.1. Background of the Responders

There was a total of 19,340 respondents during the survey period, of whom 6063 were excluded because the reliability of their responses could not be fully ensured. As a result, the number of analyzed subjects was 13,277 (6582 males and 6739 females), of whom 44 (0.33%) were validated as the SARS-CoV-2 group and 13,277 were in the control group.

Table 1 shows the background factors of the two groups. The SARS-CoV-2 group included a higher proportion of younger people compared with the control group. The proportion of coexistence of heart disease was also higher in the SARS-CoV-2 group (11.4% in the SARS-CoV-2 group vs. 2.3% in the control group).

For lifestyle factors, a lower proportion of the SARS-CoV-2 group avoided crowded places (65.9% in the SARS-CoV-2 group vs. 87.1% in the control group), wore a mask (84.1% vs. 97.3%), and washed hands (77.3% vs. 96.5%). On the contrary, a higher proportion of the SARS-CoV-2 group changed clothes frequently (50.0% vs. 21.2%) and disinfected their belongings (54.5% vs. 28.2%). The proportion of those who worked from home largely all of the time was higher among the SARS-CoV-2 group than the control group (68.2% vs. 60.9%).

Table 1. Background of the participants. Difference between the SARS-CoV-2 group and the control group were calculated by chi-squared test.

Variables	Categories	SARS-CoV-2 Group (N = 44)		Control Group (N = 13,277)		*p*
		N	%	N	%	
Age group	18–19	2	4.5	297	2.2	<0.01
	20–29	12	27.3	1270	9.6	
	30–39	8	18.2	1479	11.1	
	40–49	10	22.7	2698	20.3	
	50–59	7	15.9	2863	21.6	
	60–69	3	6.8	3076	23.2	
	70–74	2	4.5	1594	12.0	
Gender	Female	16	36.4	6566	49.5	0.09
	Male	28	63.6	6711	50.5	
BMI	<18.5	3	6.8	1736	13.1	0.39
	18.5–25	31	70.5	9044	68.1	
	25–30	9	20.5	2097	15.8	
	≥30	1	2.3	400	3.0	
Pre-existing condition	High blood pressure	11	25.0	2179	16.4	0.13
	Lipid abnormalities	5	11.4	1242	9.4	0.65
	Diabetes	5	11.4	671	5.1	0.06
	Heart disease	5	11.4	299	2.3	<0.01
	Renal disease	1	2.3	102	0.8	0.26
	Cancer	1	2.3	201	1.5	0.68
	Lung or respiratory disease	1	2.3	299	2.3	0.99
	Other condition *	2	4.5	184	1.4	0.08

Table 1. *Cont.*

Variables	Categories	SARS-CoV-2 Group (N = 44)		Control Group (N = 13,277)		p
		N	%	N	%	
Lifestyle	Avoid poorly ventilated places	36	81.8	11,348	85.5	0.49
	Avoid places where many people gather	29	65.9	11,570	87.1	<0.01
	Avoid talking or projecting voice near someone	31	70.5	10,664	80.3	0.10
	Wear a mask	37	84.1	12,915	97.3	<0.01
	Wash hands	34	77.3	12,808	96.5	<0.01
	Disinfect hands	36	81.8	11,848	89.2	0.11
	Change clothes frequently	22	50.0	2820	21.2	<0.01
	Gargle	28	63.6	9122	68.7	0.47
	Disinfect belongings	24	54.5	3743	28.2	<0.01
	Keep distance from others when going out	30	68.2	10,937	82.4	0.01
	Refrain from visiting hospitals and clinics as much as possible	22	50.0	6572	49.5	0.59
	Try to go out as seldom as possible	30	68.2	8082	60.9	0.32
Frequency of working from home	Largely all of the time	6	13.6	900	6.8	<0.01
	Half or more of the time	5	11.4	359	2.7	
	Less than half or more of the time	3	6.8	533	4.0	
	Almost never	18	40.9	5952	44.8	

N.A.: not applicable. * Disease due to which you were prohibited by a doctor from exercising, or disease or injury due to which you have major difficulties in walking (e.g., rheumatoid arthritis and bone fracture).

3.2. Multivariate Logistic Regression Analysis

Multivariate logistic regression analysis was conducted (Table 2, left column and Figure 1).

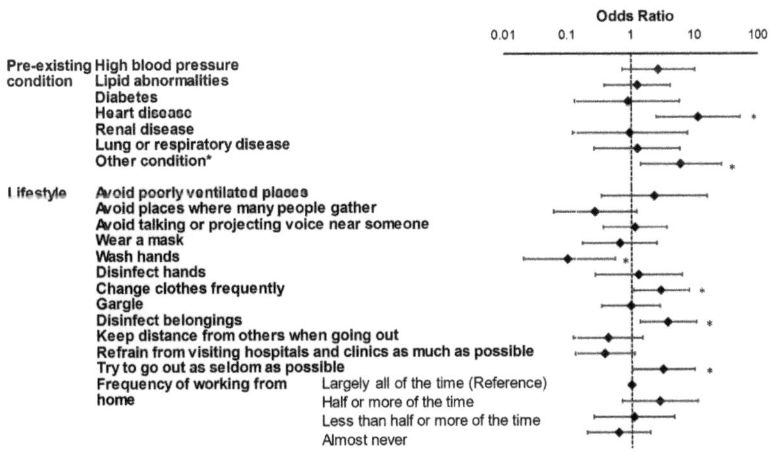

Figure 1. Odds ratio of COVID-19 infection by multivariate logistic regression for pre-existing conditions and lifestyle factors. * $p < 0.05$.

Table 2. Comparisons of COVID-19 and control groups using two statistical methods. Multiple logistic regression (left column) and inverse-probability weighing method (IPW, right column) were conducted. IPW was controlled for age and coexistence with heart disease. Odds ratio and average treatment effects of being in the COVID-19 group are shown.

Variables	Multiple Regression				IPW			
	OR	95%CI		p	ATE (%change)	95%CI		p
Age	0.94	0.91	0.98	<0.01	N.A.			
Male gender	0.96	0.87	1.06	0.47				
BMI	0.91	0.43	1.92	0.81				
Pre-existing condition								
High blood pressure	2.72	0.73	10.15	0.14	195.0	−78.7	468.6	0.16
Lipid abnormalities	1.27	0.38	4.25	0.69	107.2	−118.3	332.7	0.35
Diabetes	0.89	0.13	5.86	0.90	194.8	−107.6	497.2	0.21
Heart disease	11.33	2.50	51.25	<0.01	2704.4	−918.2	6327.0	0.14
Renal disease	0.95	0.12	7.78	0.96	912.9	−964.4	2790.2	0.34
Lung or respiratory disease	1.26	0.26	5.99	0.77	−62.1	−140.8	16.5	0.12
Other condition *	6.03	1.41	25.77	0.02	152.4	−336.5	641.3	0.54
Lifestyle								
Avoid poorly ventilated places	2.31	0.34	15.56	0.39	443.6	−324.1	1211.2	0.26
Avoid places where many people gather	0.27	0.06	1.22	0.09	−62.2	−115.6	−8.7	0.02
Avoid talking or projecting voice near someone	1.15	0.36	3.67	0.81	−19.0	−81.0	43.1	0.55
Wear a mask	0.66	0.17	2.55	0.54	−86.4	−175.4	2.6	0.06
Wash hands	0.10	0.02	0.56	0.01	−84.8	−155.8	−13.7	0.02
Disinfect hands	1.30	0.27	6.38	0.74	−44.0	−117.8	29.9	0.24
Change clothes frequently	2.96	1.08	8.15	0.04	274.4	113.2	435.6	<0.01
Gargle	0.98	0.34	2.85	0.97	−16.3	−74.3	41.7	0.58
Disinfect belongings	3.78	1.37	10.44	0.01	100.0	55.9	144.1	<0.01
Keep distance from others when going out	0.43	0.12	1.51	0.19	−43.8	−102.4	14.8	0.14
Refrain from visiting hospitals and clinics as much as possible	0.38	0.13	1.12	0.08	2.1	−59.5	63.7	0.95
Try to go out as seldom as possible	3.20	1.03	9.88	0.04	45.2	−28.6	119.0	0.23
Frequency of working from home								
Largely all of the time	1 (Reference)				0 (Reference)			
Half or more of the time	2.79	0.71	10.97	0.14	15.1	−96.8	1.8	0.79
Less than half or more of the time	1.09	0.25	4.78	0.91	−67.8	−142.6	0.1	0.08
Almost never	0.62	0.20	1.97	0.42	−77.1	−143.4	−0.2	0.02

IPW: inverse probability weighting analysis, OR: odds ratio; CI: confidence interval; N.A.: not applicable, ATE: average treatment effect. * Disease due to which you were prohibited by a doctor from exercising, or disease or injury due to which you have major difficulties in walking (e.g., rheumatoid arthritis and bone fracture).

Age was negatively correlated with diagnosis (odds ratio (OR) 0.94 per year, 95% confidence interval (CI) 0.91–0.98, $p < 0.01$ in multiple regression), while coexistence of heart disease (OR 11.33, 95%CI 2.50 to 51.25, $p < 0.01$) and other conditions (OR 6.03, 95%CI 1.41 to 25.77, $p = 0.02$) were positively associated with SARS-CoV-2 infection. As for lifestyle factors, washing hands (OR 0.10, 95%CI 0.02 to 0.56, $p = 0.01$) was negatively associated with infection. Interestingly, the diagnosis was significantly and positively correlated with changing clothes frequently (OR 2.96, 95%CI 1.08 to 8.15, $p = 0.04$), sanitizing belongings (OR 3.78, 95%CI 1.37 to 10.44, $p = 0.01$), and avoiding outings (OR 3.20, 95%CI 1.03 to 9.88, $p = 0.04$).

3.3. Analysis Using Inverse Probability Weighting Method

As sample size of the SARS-CoV-2 group was small, an IPW analysis was also conducted, controlling for background factors that showed significant differences in multiple regression, that is, age and coexistence of heart disease (Table 2, right column).

Habit of crowd avoidance (ATE −62.2, 95%CI −115.6 to −8.7, $p = 0.02$) and hand washing (ATE −84.8, 95%CI −155.8 to −13.7, $p = 0.02$) were negatively correlated with SARS-CoV-2 infection. In contrast, habits of changing clothes frequently (ATE 274.4, 95%CI 113.2 to 435.6, $p < 0.01$) and sanitizing their belongings (ATE 100.0, 95%CI 55.9 to 144.1, $p < 0.01$) were positively associated with the infection, which was consistent with the results of the logistic regression. In addition, no or rare remote work (ATE −77.1, 95%CI −143.4 to −0.2, $p = 0.02$) were negatively correlated with infection compared with almost daily remote work, which was contrary to the common thinking that remote working is effective in infection prevention.

3.4. Sensitivity Analysis

For sensitivity analysis, the same analysis in Table 2 was conducted among those who responded as being diagnosed as SARS-CoV-2 in the third survey (thus, their answers were not fully validated). In total, 110 were included in the SARS-CoV-2 group and 16,365 in the control group. In this analysis, habit of changing clothes frequently and sanitizing their belongings were consistently and positively associated with SARS-CoV-2 infection in IPW analysis (Table S2).

4. Discussion

This study is the first Japan-wide study that analyzed behavioral factors associating with SARS-CoV-2 infection in detail. It reconfirmed the effectiveness of mask wearing and hand washing in risk reduction. At least for infection prevention, the study did not show effectiveness of excessive behavior, such as frequent changing of clothes and extreme reduction of outings.

The most notable finding is that remote working and restrictions on outings did not always reduce the risk of COVID-19. Instead, these actions even appeared to increase the risk of the infection. This is contrary to previous analysis that showed effectiveness of lockdown [13,14]. There could be several reasons for this result. One possibility is that remote working and restrictions on outings gave a false sense of security and individuals began to neglect hand washing and mask wearing. A study of one Massachusetts city examined the genetic material of SARS-CoV-2 attached to surfaces to investigate the virus in the environment. PCR was positive in approximately 8% of the samples taken from environmental surfaces, and a particularly high level of virus was attached to the surfaces of trash cans [15]. Thus, even if outings are restricted, individuals cannot completely avoid their contact with environmental surfaces. Therefore, the infection risk could increase, especially if there is inadequate hand washing. Another possibility is that, even if individuals work remotely, they could be engaging in other high-risk behavior such as eating out with multiple individuals.

Our research also revealed that frequent changing of clothes and sanitizing belongings were significantly and positively associated with the infection risk. The result, however, does not mean that wearing and removing clothes increase the infection risk. It instead suggests that individuals who engage in such behavior might have limited knowledge of infection—they could be implementing ineffective preventive measures while neglecting the practice of highly effective ones. It is also possible that frequent changing of clothes could be a sign of mental disorder triggered by anxiety of infection, which has been reported to increase the COVID-19 risk [16].

In general, a moderate level of exercise is necessary for reduction of health risk. Our study showed walking may have a preventive effect of infection. However, our research also indicated that a high infection risk was correlated with 4 or more days of exercise, 30 min^{-1} h duration, and running was associated with a higher proportion of infection. The result suggests that individuals might have increased their contact with the virus by going out to exercise or by the use of a gym. Even so, a moderate level of exercise decreased the risk of severe illness from infection. It also has a preventive effect on other conditions (including diabetes, obesity, and hypertension) which increases the risk of severe illness from infection. Therefore, individuals should not unnecessarily avoid exercising.

The findings of this study strongly suggest that we may need a strategy other than legislation to change behaviors of populations. Epistemic communities, defined as "a network of professionals with recognized expertise and competence in a particular domain and an authoritative claim to policy-relevant knowledge in that domain or issue area [17]", may play an important role in nudging the public to take effective and efficient actions without legislation [18]. This epistemic community may also help citizens act according to expectations independently and voluntarily and may reduce the needs of aggressive interventions by the government. Although there is a study that suggests the efficacy of such a strategy in a specific field [19], further research is needed to elucidate the effective ways to achieve population health in disaster settings.

This study has several limitations. The first limitation is that the study relied only on participant responses to determine whether or not they "experienced COVID-19 infection", which was the primary outcome variable. As of 1 November 2020, there was a cumulative total of 101,368 people who tested positive by PCR test according to the Japanese Ministry of Health, Labour and Welfare. It translates to only 0.1% of the entire population of Japan testing positive. In our study, 0.48% of the total valid respondents said that they had been diagnosed as having COVID-19 infection, which is about three times more than that of the Japanese ministry's. Thus, it is highly likely that there was an upward bias in our study. For example, individuals with an infection experience could have more actively sought to participate in our study because of their increased interest in the significance and content of this online survey, causing an upward bias in participation of this type of subject. The RIETI questionnaire survey used self-reported information on their SARS-CoV-2 diagnosis at a medical facility to establish the presence or absence of SARS-CoV-2 infection experience. The study, therefore, does not include information on individuals who could have had SARS-CoV-2. These individuals might not have received the diagnosis because they were asymptomatic or only had mild infection and recovered without medical intervention. If the individuals with a diagnosis differed from asymptomatic or mild cases in their behavioral pattern or individual characteristics, such differences could have introduced a constant bias into the analysis results.

The second limitation is that the study was cross sectional. Therefore, a causal relationship cannot be determined between infection and behavior: individuals with a SARS-CoV-2 diagnosis could have been more careful in their daily lives. This possibility is supported by our result that the SARS-CoV-2 group had only a few individuals who had an exercise habit. This habit seems to increase the infection risk, as previously mentioned. Considering the likelihood of such bias, interpretation of estimates should be carefully examined (such as the average treatment effect), particularly the interpretation of the level of effect size. The RIETI questionnaire survey is a panel survey. Even if there were biases from active participation of the aforementioned type of individuals, the data might not show newly confirmed SARS-CoV-2 cases in second and later surveys conducted at our scale. Therefore, second and later surveys should also be analyzed in the same way.

Given these considerations of limitation, infection was still more strongly and negatively correlated with hand washing and mask wearing compared with other behaviors. This result is important in devising effective and sustainable infection control in the future.

5. Conclusions

This study analyzed correlation of behavioral factors and diagnosis of SARS-CoV-2 infection in Japan. Our findings suggested that curfews and remote working might not necessarily lead to sufficient reduction of the infection risk of the entire society, at least in Japanese society. Instead, appropriate preventive actions such as hand sanitizing and mask wearing are the first priorities. For long-term infection control, it is important to utilize efficient behavioral intervention. At the same time, it is important to avoid excessive interventions that are less effective, so that people can minimize the indirect harm and economic loss due to curfews and other restrictions.

Supplementary Materials: The following are available online at https://www.mdpi.com/article/10.3390/ijerph182212184/s1, Table S1: Contents of questionnaire; Table S2, Results of sensitivity analysis.

Author Contributions: Conceptualization, S.O., M.S., S.H., and Y.S.; Methodology, S.O.; validation, M.S., S.H., K.D., and Y.S.; Formal analysis, S.O. and Y.S.; Investigation, S.O., M.S., S.H., K.D., and Y.S.; Data curation, Y.S.; Writing—original draft preparation, S.O.; Writing—review and editing, M.S., S.H., and Y.S.; Supervision, Y.S.; Project administration, S.O., M.S., S.H., K.D., and Y.S.; funding acquisition, S.O. and Y.S. All authors have read and agreed to the published version of the manuscript.

Funding: The present study was funded by the RIETI, Japan and was supported by the Joint Usage/Research project of the International Research Institute of Disaster Science (IRIDeS), Mishima Kaiun Memorial Foundation, and Tohoku University (No. 20-06).

Institutional Review Board Statement: This study was conducted with the approval of the ethics committee of Hiramatsu Memorial Hospital affiliated with Specified Jisoukai Medical Corporation (ID of approval: 20200925).

Informed Consent Statement: All individuals who participated in this study consented to their participation.

Data Availability Statement: Data was obtained by NTTCom Online Marketing Solutions Corporation and are not publicly available.

Conflicts of Interest: The funders had no role in the design of the study; in the collection, analyses, or interpretation of data; in the writing of the manuscript; or in the decision to publish the results.

References

1. CDC. The Possibility of COVID-19 after Vaccination: Breakthrough Infections. 9 November 2021. Available online: https://www.cdc.gov/coronavirus/2019-ncov/vaccines/effectiveness/why-measure-effectiveness/breakthrough-cases.html (accessed on 13 November 2021).
2. Godlee, F. Covid-19: Vaccine woes highlight vital role of traditional public health. *BMJ* **2021**, *373*, n968. [CrossRef]
3. Ganesan, B.; Al-Jumaily, A.; Fong, K.N.K.; Prasad, P.; Meena, S.K.; Tong, R.K. Impact of Coronavirus Disease 2019 (COVID-19) Outbreak Quarantine, Isolation, and Lockdown Policies on Mental Health and Suicide. *Front. Psychiatry* **2021**, *12*, 565190. [CrossRef] [PubMed]
4. Mulugeta, T.; Tadesse, E.; Shegute, T.; Desta, T.T. COVID-19: Socio-economic impacts and challenges in the working group. *Heliyon* **2021**, *7*, e07307. [CrossRef] [PubMed]
5. Kithiia, J.; Wanyonyi, I.; Maina, J.; Jefwa, T.; Gamoyo, M. The socio-economic impacts of Covid-19 restrictions: Data from the coastal city of Mombasa, Kenya. *Data Brief* **2020**, *33*, 106317. [CrossRef] [PubMed]
6. Vindegaard, N.; Benros, M.E. COVID-19 pandemic and mental health consequences: Systematic review of the current evidence. *Brain Behav. Immun.* **2020**, *89*, 531–542. [CrossRef] [PubMed]
7. Abdo, C.; Miranda, E.P.; Santos, C.S.; Junior, J.B.; Bernardo, W.M. Domestic violence and substance abuse during COVID19: A systematic review. *Indian J. Psychiatry* **2020**, *62*, S337–S342. [CrossRef] [PubMed]
8. Wingfield-Hayes, R. Covid and Suicide: Japan's Rise a Warning to the World? *BBC News*. 18 February 2021. Available online: https://www.bbc.com/news/world-asia-55837160 (accessed on 13 November 2021).
9. Stuckler, D.; Reeves, A.; Loopstra, R.; Karanikolos, M.; McKee, M. Austerity and health: The impact in the UK and Europe. *Eur. J. Public Health* **2017**, *27*, 18–21. [CrossRef] [PubMed]
10. WHO. Transmission of SARS-CoV-2: Implications for Infection Prevention Precautions. 9 July 2020. Available online: https://www.who.int/news-room/commentaries/detail/transmission-of-sars-cov-2-implications-for-infection-prevention-precautions (accessed on 13 November 2021).

11. Zhou, L.; Ayeh, S.K.; Chidambaram, V.; Karakousis, P.C. Modes of transmission of SARS-CoV-2 and evidence for preventive behavioral interventions. *BMC Infect. Dis.* **2021**, *21*, 496. [CrossRef] [PubMed]
12. Ikeda, N.; Saito, E.; Kondo, N.; Inoue, M.; Ikeda, S.; Satoh, T.; Wada, K.; Stickley, A.; Katanoda, K.; Mizoue, T.; et al. What has made the population of Japan healthy? *Lancet* **2011**, *378*, 1094–1105. [CrossRef]
13. Alfano, V.; Ercolano, S. The Efficacy of Lockdown Against COVID-19: A Cross-Country Panel Analysis. *Appl. Health Econ. Health Policy* **2020**, *18*, 509–517. [CrossRef] [PubMed]
14. Lau, H.; Khosrawipour, V.; Kocbach, P.; Mikolajczyk, A.; Schubert, J.; Bania, J.; Khosrawipour, T. The positive impact of lockdown in Wuhan on containing the COVID-19 outbreak in China. *J. Travel. Med.* **2020**, *27*. [CrossRef] [PubMed]
15. Harvey, A.P.; Fuhrmeister, E.R.; Cantrell, M.E.; Pitol, A.K.; Swarthout, J.M.; Powers, J.E.; Nadimpalli, M.L.; Julian, T.R.; Pickering, A.J. Longitudinal Monitoring of SARS-CoV-2 RNA on High-Touch Surfaces in a Community Setting. *Environ. Sci. Technol. Lett.* **2021**, *8*, 168–175. [CrossRef] [PubMed]
16. Li, L.; Li, F.; Fortunati, F.; Krystal, J.H. Association of a Prior Psychiatric Diagnosis with Mortality among Hospitalized Patients with Coronavirus Disease 2019 (COVID-19) Infection. *JAMA Netw. Open* **2020**, *3*, e2023282. [CrossRef] [PubMed]
17. Haas, P.M. Introduction: Epistemic communities and international policy coordination. *Int. Organ.* **2009**, *46*, 1–35. [CrossRef]
18. Eyles, J.; Robinson, K.; Elliott, S. An epistemic community comes and goes? Local and national expressions of heart health promotion in Canada. *BMC Health Serv. Res.* **2009**, *9*, 35. [CrossRef] [PubMed]
19. Lebel, U. The immunized integration of Religious-Zionists within Israeli society: The pre-military academy as an institutional model. *Soc. Identities* **2016**, *22*, 642–660. [CrossRef]

International Journal of
Environmental Research and Public Health

MDPI

Article

Predictors of Positive and Negative Emotions Experienced by Poles during the Second Wave of the COVID-19 Pandemic

Estera Twardowska-Staszek *, Irmina Rostek, Krzysztof Biel and Anna Seredyńska

Institute of Educational Sciences, Jesuit University Ignatianum in Krakow, 31-501 Cracow, Poland; irmina.rostek@ignatianum.edu.pl (I.R.); krzysztof.biel@ignatianum.edu.pl (K.B.); anna.seredynska@ignatianum.edu.pl (A.S.)
* Correspondence: estera.twardowska-staszek@ignatianum.edu.pl

Abstract: The objective of the research was to specify the predictors of positive and negative emotions experienced by Poles during the second wave of the COVID-19 pandemic. The researchers used the following standardized measurement tools: emotions (PANAS), mood (UMACL), satisfaction with life (SWLS), optimism (LOT-R), and coping with stress (CISS). They also used a questionnaire to collect sociodemographic information and data concerning COVID-19 infections. In total, 595 participants (80.50% women) aged 18–75 participated in the research. It was concluded that the predictors of positive emotions included a task-oriented coping style, level of satisfaction with life, being a man, hedonic tone in the description of mood, and being an employed student. The negative predictors of positive emotions included emotion-oriented coping and the level of energetic arousal in the description of mood. The predictors of negative emotions were tense arousal in the description of mood, emotion-oriented coping, being over 60 years of age, and changes in respondents' standard of living. The negative predictors of negative emotions included living in a medium-sized town or in a village. The research conclusions encourage us to pay special attention to possible at-risk groups threatened with mental health disorders and to factors that protect people against negative psychological consequences of the COVID-19 pandemic.

Keywords: pandemic; COVID-19; mental health; emotions; optimism; satisfaction with life; coping with stress

Citation: Twardowska-Staszek, E.; Rostek, I.; Biel, K.; Seredyńska, A. Predictors of Positive and Negative Emotions Experienced by Poles during the Second Wave of the COVID-19 Pandemic. *Int. J. Environ. Res. Public Health* **2021**, *18*, 11993. https://doi.org/10.3390/ijerph182211993

Academic Editors: Paolo Roma, Merylin Monaro and Cristina Mazza

Received: 20 October 2021
Accepted: 12 November 2021
Published: 15 November 2021

1. Introduction

The SARS-CoV-2 coronavirus, which was first diagnosed in Wuhan, China, in December 2019, was first recognized in a Polish patient on 4 March 2020 [1]. This day is the beginning of the first wave of the epidemic in Poland. Over the following 2 months, the government implemented various preventive measures. First, mass events were cancelled, followed by severe restrictions on international travel to and from Poland. Within the following few weeks, educational institutions at all levels were closed, and then switched from teaching and learning on-site to teaching and learning online. Serious limitations in movement were introduced (parks, beaches, boulevards, and, finally, forests were closed), along with fines for breaches of those restrictions. In addition, the obligation to cover one's mouth and nose in public spaces was implemented [1].

The first analyses concerning the psychological consequences of the epidemic were performed in China as early as the beginning of 2020 [2]. The first reviews of research results [3], which were published in April, summed up the information from Chinese observations and articles describing the possible influence of the pandemic on mental health. In additiom, publications prepared in many other countries (e.g., Brazil, Canada, Iran, Iraq) suggested that the epidemic may decrease people's level of functioning in a subjective dimension, e.g., by increasing one's sense of insecurity, loneliness, anxiety, and stress, and in an objective dimension, e.g., through a worsening in the economic situation of both individuals and whole countries. In addition, the first pandemic reports attempted to indicate groups at risk of not coping well with the situation. Such groups included people infected with COVID-19, their families, people who had pre-existing conditions before the pandemic, and health service employees [3].

The fear of becoming infected with the virus affected people all over the world. A Gallup poll conducted in March in 19 countries indicated that more than half of respondents were afraid of becoming infected or worried about their family members who may become infected with the coronavirus. The most apprehensive respondents were the Italians, among which 90% expressed anxiety, while the least worried were the Japanese and the American respondents—52% of respondents in those countries were fearful of the coronavirus infection. Interestingly, the relatively lowest levels of anxiety among the Japanese and Americans had nothing to do with their evaluation of both the current and future situation in their countries. Only 23% of the Japanese and 42% of the American respondents believed that their governments had coped with the pandemic very well. In addition, when asked about the predicted end of the pandemic, the citizens of those countries expressed poor optimism: only 11% of Japanese and 28% of Americans believed that life would return to normal by the end of 2020 [4].

The first analyses concerning the mental state of Poles during the pandemic were performed in March (e.g., [5–8] and April 2020 (e.g., [9–12]). The research conducted in March [4] showed that, at first, Poles' emotional reactions were not dominated by negative emotions. The people researched who kept personal diaries experienced happiness and relaxation twice as often as anger, anxiety, or sadness. Later, a repeated cross-sectional survey was conducted among students of Polish universities in March and April (using the Depression Anxiety Stress Scales, DASS) [6], which revealed that depression indices increased in a significant manner, while anxiety and stress indices increased in a statistically insignificant manner. In other studies among students [7], which were conducted in March and April (with the use of the Generalized Anxiety Disorder scale, GAD-7), researchers found that 65% of students experienced fear, while 14% reported a severe anxiety disorder. In addition, 56% of the students who participated in the survey experienced a high or very high level of stress (measured with the Perceived Stress Scale, PSS-10.

The research conducted in March on a representative sample of Poles [8] indicated a high level of nervousness in the general population (in the self-evaluation of nervousness due to the pandemic on a scale from 1 to 100, M = 63.44). Most stress factors were related to other people: strangers as potential and irresponsible virus spreaders (75% of the people researched identified with this fear), as well as family members as possible victims of the virus (72%). People's fear of contracting the virus was less intensive (59%). In addition, the level of stress was measured during this study (with the use of a tool prepared on the basis of GAD-7 and Patient Health Questionnaire, PHQ-9) (in the evaluation of the scale from 1 to 5, M = 2.76). In April, the level of nervousness decreased by a small, but statistically significant degree (M = 60.20), while people's fears mainly related to the financial crisis (80%) and to the inefficiency of the health care system (79%). The fear of becoming infected with the virus was still lower than fear about the health of family members. The level of stress decreased slightly, but in a statistically significant manner (M = 2.70).

The research conducted among the general population of Poland in April [9] indicated that 77% people were afraid of becoming infected, and 71% reported anxiety at different levels of intensity (44% of the results might suggest the occurrence of general anxiety disorder). Retrospectively, the people surveyed (85%) indicated feeling nervousness, anxiety, and tension within 14 days preceding the survey (utilizing the GAD-7). Other studies of a similar nature [10] showed a similar picture: 52.82% of the people surveyed using the GHQ–28 (General Health Questionnaire-28) obtained a sten score of 7 or more, while 26.18% obtained sten scores at level 9 or 10 (which suggests the occurrence of serious mental health problems). The results concerning stress were similar (research was conducted utilizing the PSS-10): 53% of those surveyed obtained a sten score of 7 or higher (which confirms the high level of stress they experienced). The results obtained using the same scale (PSS-10) in other studies [11] indicated a moderate level of stress in 57% of people, while a high level of stress was found among 29% of respondents.

The first weeks of the pandemic were characterized by a large fluctuation of emotions: in the abovementioned studies conducted by Gallup [4], which were conducted between the end of March and the beginning of April. In 9 out of 13 countries, the number of people afraid of contracting the coronavirus increased, while between the beginning of April and the beginning of June, in 9 out of 13 countries, the number of such people decreased.

In the last week of April, the process of removing restrictions began in Poland, which was primarily motivated by economic factors. Despite the increase in the number of infections, the Polish prime minister, Mateusz Morawiecki, announced that the pandemic was "in retreat", which was reflected in the emotions experienced by Poles. At the turn of May and June, the level of nervousness due to the epidemic dropped (M = 52.8). Furthermore, specific symptoms of such nervousness changed, the most intensive of them being uncertainty related to a possible economic crisis (63%). In total, 45% of Poles were afraid of contracting COVID-19, while 60% were afraid that their family members would fall ill [8]. Compared to May, in July the intensity of depression and general anxiety disorder symptoms decreased (analyzed using the GAD-7 and PHQ-9) [13].

Inasmuch as in the first phase of the pandemic. the occurrence of three basic approaches to the situation among those surveyed could be noticed [14]: the involved approach, which constituted almost half of people in the researched group; and the cautious and indifferent approaches, which each constituted a quarter of respondents. The improvement in the emotional state of Poles in the summer was accompanied by a kind of denial of the pandemic problem. Such denial was confirmed by the results of a large survey conducted by Ipsos [15] in different countries, the results of which were published in September. In the question concerning the willingness to be vaccinated against COVID-19, Poland (in the group of 27 countries) placed second to last (just before Russia), with only 54% people prepared to be vaccinated. Moreover, while 45% of respondents from the 27 countries surveyed in September (also by Ipsos) [16] declared that, at that moment, the biggest problem in their countries was COVID-19, in Poland, the percentage was only 38%. The most serious concerns (after the pandemic) of the world's population included unemployment, poverty, inequalities, crime, and violence, but Poles were not afraid of these. Polish people were not worried about losing a job (the second to last position, with 19%; 39% being the mean for all the analyzed countries); they were the least worried about poverty and social inequalities (17%, with 30% being the average result for all the countries); and they were not afraid of crime and violence (6% compared to a 27% average for the other countries). The Poles' most serious problems (which were largely influenced by the political and economic situation in the country) included those related to the functioning of the health service (45%—the second position among all the countries, the mean being 21%) and corruption (35%—the eighth position, with a mean of 27%). In addition, Poles' worries that were greater than the world's mean were connected with financial assistance provided by the state, e.g., measures related to taxation or inflation.

Along with the second wave of the pandemic in October, due to a high increase in the number of infections, educational, cultural, sport institutions, and restaurants were again closed. Following an increase in infections in November amounting to around 20 thousand cases per day and a record-breaking number of deaths (more than 600 people a day), in the middle of December, a national lockdown was introduced. This resulted in the closure of hotels, shopping centers, ski resorts, limitations in the number of people meeting in family houses during Christmas, as well as a ban on movement from one place to another on New Year's Eve. Moreover, at the end of October, women's protests against a toughening of the abortion laws began. In the second half of December, the number of infections decreased, and the first COVID-19 vaccination was administered.

Longitudinal studies revealed that, at the end of the year, people's nervousness related to the pandemic had returned to levels observed the previous April, but the main object of their worries changed (69% of the surveyed people were mainly worried about limited access to health services, 61% were worried about the country's financial situation) [8]. Comparing to July, the number of people from the high-risk group of patients with a clinically important intensification of depression symptoms (29% for women and 24% for men) and anxiety symptoms (31% for women and 26% for men) increased significantly [13]. In cross-sectional studies, the average level of anxiety (analyzed using the Hospital Anxiety and Depression Scale, HADS) had increased, with anxiety disorders occurring among 32.69% of the people surveyed. Similar to the longitudinal studies, 23.14% of respondents revealed depression symptoms, and the average level of stress (measured with PSS) was high [17]. In the case of 59.2% participants, the mean result of the GHQ-28 indicated the occurrence of minor mental disorders [18].

The Ipsos research that was conducted at that time showed that, in November, the primary concern of Poles was the coronavirus (55% of respondents indicated the pandemic as one of the three most important problems in the country). In addition, compared to September, the level of anxiety related to the functioning of the health service increased (53%) [19]. In December, the level of people's anxiety about the coronavirus decreased (to 42%), while the condition of the Polish health service was, again, the main concern of respondents (53%). When asked whether they believe that the situation in the country was moving in the right direction, 82% of Poles declared "no." This was the highest percentage in all the 27 countries surveyed [20].

Three conclusions can be drawn from the above results. First, due to a high dynamic of change, it is necessary to conduct further research (both cross-sectional and longitudinal) in the following weeks and months of the pandemic. Second, because of significant cultural differences in experiencing pandemic stress, it is necessary to consider the elements that go beyond the virus threat in diagnosing the mental condition of Poles. Third, it is necessary to carefully analyze people's mental health and well-being, considering not only the most common aspects such as anxiety, stress, and depression, which were noticeable at the very beginning of the pandemic, but also more subtle issues related to a person's emotional functioning.

The research described in this article constitutes the first stage of a broader research project which, in its assumptions, aims to look for predictors of emotional wellbeing in the context of such variables as sociodemographic data, satisfaction with life, optimism, and styles of coping with stress. According to pre-pandemic surveys, experiencing positive emotions was related to good mental health and social adjustment, as well as rare episodes of anxiety, while experiencing negative emotions may be connected with decreased psychosocial functioning [21]. Thus, the objective of our research was to learn about the predictors of the positive and negative emotions of adult Poles during the second wave of the COVID-19 pandemic. It is assumed that the research results will be the basis for introducing psychological interventions, the aims of which are to prevent and reduce negative consequences for people's mental health.

2. Materials and Methods

2.1. Participants

Due to the epidemiological situation, the research was conducted online with participants who were asked to complete an online survey shared through personal contacts (text messages and e-mail) and on social media (Facebook). To be included in the survey, participants had to be over 18 years of age and a resident of Poland.

2.2. Measures

Sociodemographic variables and data related to COVID-19 infection were collected using an ad hoc self-made questionnaire. The questionnaire comprised 7 sections, including standard sociodemographic variables (sex, age, marital status, children, place of residence, level of education, employment), and an additional question concerning changes in economic conditions as a result of the pandemic. The variables related to the

COVID-19 infection related to current or past COVID-19 infection among participants or their family members.

In a further part of the survey, 5 standardized psychometric tools were used:

2.2.1. Positive and Negative Affect Schedule

In our study, a Polish adaptation (Skala Uczuć Pozytywnych i Negatywnych, SUPIN) [21] of the Positive and Negative Affect Schedule (PANAS) [22] was used. The PANAS consists of 20 items—adjectives describing positive and negative emotions. The items are rated by subjects on a 5-point scale (1 = "very slightly" or "not at all", 2 = "a little", 3 = "moderately", 4 = "quite a bit", 5 = "extremely") in order to assess the intensity of each affect. As a result, two 10-item subscales are created that measure the positive affect (PA) and negative affect (NA). Cronbach's α reliability indices for the scale ranged from 0.86 (PA) to 0.95 (NA).

2.2.2. Mood

Mood was assessed with a Polish adaptation (Przymiotnikowa Skala Nastroju UMACL) [23] of the UWIST Mood Adjective Checklist (UMACL) [24]. The UMACL scale consists of 29 items in the form of adjectives describing mood. The surveyed people choose an answer from a 4-point scale ("definitely", "slightly", "slightly not", "definitely not"), rating the applicability of each adjective to their current mood. The UMACL measures three dimensions of mood: hedonic tone (HT), tense arousal (TA) and energetic arousal (EA). The Hedonic Tone (HT) (pleasure–displeasure) scale consists of 10 items. The Tense Arousal (TA) (nervous–relaxed) scale consists of 9 items. The Energetic Arousal (EA) (energy to act) scale consists of 10 items. Cronbach's α reliability indices for the scale ranged from 0.79 to 0.92 for the individual subscales.

2.2.3. Satisfaction with Life

Satisfaction with life was assessed with a Polish adaptation (Skala Satysfakcji z Życia) [25] of the Satisfaction with Life Scale (SWLS) [26]. The SWLS contains five statements regarding one's life. The participants are asked to rate each provided statement on a 7-point scale (1 = "strongly disagree", 7 = "strongly agree"). Higher scores denote greater satisfaction with life. The Cronbach's α coefficient was 0.81.

2.2.4. Optimism

Optimism was measured using a Polish adaptation (Test Orientacji Życiowej) [27] of the Life Orientation Test-Revised (LOT-R) [28]. The scale consists of 10 items. The respondents are asked to rate the extent to which they agree with each item on a 5-point scale (from 0 = "strongly disagree" to 4 = "strongly agree"). The total score is calculated by adding the points from 6 diagnostic statements, ranging from 0 to 24 points, with higher scores denoting more optimism. The Cronbach's α coefficient was 0.76.

2.2.5. Coping with Stress

To measure coping with stress, the Polish adaptation (Kwestionariusz Radzenia sobie w Sytuacjach Stresowych) [29] of the Coping Inventory for Stressful Situations (CISS) [30] was used. The CISS contains 48 items describing various behaviors in stressful situations. The respondents are asked to rate the frequency of engaging in a given behavior in a stressful situation on a 5-point scale (from 1 = "never" to 5 = "very often"). The results are described in terms of three styles of coping with stress: task-oriented coping (TOC), emotion-oriented coping (EOC), and avoidance-oriented coping (AOC). The latter style may take the form of distraction (D) or social diversion (SD). The Cronbach's α reliability indices for the scale ranged from 0.82 to 0.89 for the individual subscales.

2.3. Design and Procedure

Our research was an ex post-facto cross-sectional study conducted using an online survey questionnaire. The ethics approval was obtained from the Ethics Committee of the

Jesuit University Ignatianum in Krakow in accordance with the principles embodied in the Declaration of Helsinki. The participants explicitly expressed their consent by checking a box after reading the instruction which explained the aims of the study, data processing, and data anonymity.

First, a survey questionnaire was developed in Google Forms, which consisted of two parts. The first one included sociodemographic variables and data related to COVID-19 infection. The second part contained standardized research tools. The study was conducted using the "snowball" method (via social media). Participation in the study was voluntary and anonymous, and the participants could resign from filling in and submitting their responses at any time. Filling in the survey took approximately 20 min.

The study was conducted from 1 December 2020 to 1 January 2021. It was a special month, because at that time, the number of new coronavirus cases and COVID-related deaths in Poland was very high (9.105 new infections and 449 deaths were recorded on 1 December 2020) [31], which resulted in tightened government restrictions. It should also be underlined that, for many Poles, December is a month of spiritual preparation for Christmas, and that restrictions limited both family contacts and active participation in religious ceremonies.

2.4. Data Analysis

The statistical analysis was performed with the R software, version 4.0.3 [32]. The analysis of qualitative (i.e., non-numeric) variables was performed by calculating the number and percentage of occurrences of each value. The analysis of quantitative variables (i.e., expressed in number) was performed by calculating the mean, standard deviation, median, and quartiles. The multivariate analysis of the influence of many variables on the quantitative variable was performed using the linear regression method. The results are presented as the values of the regression model parameters with a 95% confidence interval. A significance level of 0.05 was adopted in the analysis. Thus, all p values below 0.05 were interpreted as showing significant relationships.

3. Results

3.1. Participants

There were 595 respondents who participated in the research: 476 women (80.50%) and 116 men (19.50%). The respondents' age range was from 18 to 75 years of age (M = 35.95, SD = 13.32). Table 1 shows characteristics of the sample, both in terms of the sociodemographic and COVID-related variables.

Table 1. Characteristics of the sample: sociodemographic and COVID-19-related variables.

Sociodemographic and COVID-Related Variables		*n*	%
Sex	Female	476	80.50
	Male	116	19.50
Age	Under 22	124	20.84
	23–34 years of age	156	26.22
	35–60 years of age	280	47.06
	Over 60 years of age	35	5.88
Marital status	Single	259	43.52
	Married	297	49.92
	Others	39	6.56
Children	No	285	47.90
	Yes	310	52.10
Place of residence	Big city	277	46.55
	Medium-sized city	86	14.45
	Small city	62	10.42
	Village	170	28.57

Table 1. *Cont.*

Sociodemographic and COVID-Related Variables		*n*	%
Education	Higher	353	59.33
	Secondary	64	10.76
	Other	178	29.92
Employment	Student	114	19.16
	Employed	320	53.78
	Not employed	63	10.59
	Employed student	98	16.47
Economic conditions	Not changed	357	60.00
	Decreased	185	31.09
	Improved	53	8.91
Have you had COVID 19?	No	462	77.65
	Yes	133	22.35
Has anyone in your family had COVID 19?	No	306	51.43
	Yes	289	48.57

The study participants were mostly women, middle-aged, big city dwellers, with higher education, employed, and whose economic situation has not changed during pandemic. The variables related to marital status and children were evenly distributed.

3.1.1. Emotions

The PANAS scale is useful for diagnosing the sign and intensity of emotions experienced by people. The scale result makes it possible to evaluate the current positive and negative emotions. The results of the PANAS are presented in Table 2.

Table 2. The characteristics of the study participants regarding the level of positive and negative affect.

Level	PANAS	
	PA [1]	NA [2]
Low	227 (38.15%)	65 (10.92%)
Medium	180 (30.25%)	173 (29.08%)
High	188 (31.60%)	357 (60.00%)

[1] PA—Positive Affect, [2] NA—Negative Affect.

It is assumed that people who obtain higher results in the subscale of positive affect (PA) are generally mentally healthy and socially adjusted, and they experience anxiety less frequently. In turn, people who obtain higher results in the subscale of negative affect are characterized by worse psychosocial functioning [21]. Whereas the sample was heterogenous in terms of experiencing positive emotions, more than half of the respondents displayed negative emotions in a pandemic situation. Therefore, feelings such as anxiety, fear, nervousness, and worry were common in the research group.

3.1.2. Mood

In the Polish adaptation of the UMACL scale, mood is defined as "an affective experience with a moderate time of duration (at least several minutes), unrelated to an object or related to a quasi-object, which includes three dimensions of the essential affect: tense arousal, energetic arousal and hedonic tone" [23]. The results of the UMACL are presented in Table 3.

Table 3. The characteristics of the study participants regarding the level of mood dimensions.

Level	UMACL		
	HT [1]	TA [2]	EA [3]
Low	558 (93.78%)	11 (1.85%)	548 (92.10%)
Medium	37 (6.22%)	143 (24.03%)	40 (6.72%)
High	0 (0.00%)	441 (74.12%)	7 (1.18%)

[1] HT—Hedonic Tone, [2] TA—Tense Arousal, [3] EA—Energetic Arousal.

Positive mood is expressed in a high result in HT and EA, and a low result in TA. The reverse, i.e., a low level of hedonic tone, a low level of energetic arousal, and a high level of tense arousal, indicates a negative mood. The study showed a decrease in mood in the research group, as evidenced by the low level of hedonic tone (HT), which refers to pleasant-unpleasant feelings; low level of energetic arousal (EA), which refers to the energy to act; and high level of tense arousal (TA), which refers to anxiety.

3.1.3. Satisfaction with Life

Apart from experiencing positive emotions and the lack of negative emotions, satisfaction with life is an element of good mood. The results of the SWLS are presented in Table 4.

Table 4. The characteristics of the study participants regarding the level of satisfaction with life.

	SWLS
Level	
Low	194 (32.61%)
Medium	186 (31.26%)
High	215 (36.13%)

No difference was observed in the number of people with low, medium, and high levels of satisfaction with life.

3.1.4. Optimism

Dispositional optimism is a generalized tendency to expect good outcomes in future. Research shows that such optimism is an important predictor of a person's wellbeing and that it facilitates success and resistance to stressful life situations, e.g., the pandemic [27]. The results of the LOT-R are presented in Table 5.

Table 5. The characteristics of the study participants regarding life orientation.

Life Orientation	LOT-R
Pessimistic	195 (32.77%)
Neutral	171 (28.74%)
Optimistic	229 (38.49%)

The optimistic orientation was most common among the respondents, while the pessimistic one was the second most common and the neutral one was the least frequent.

3.1.5. Styles of Coping with Stressful Situations

In psychological literature, different definitions of "stress" and "coping with stress" can be found. In this research, the authors assumed that stress results from the lack of balance between demands and abilities to cope with them. Coping with stress, in turn, includes "constantly changing cognitive and behavioural efforts to manage specific external and/or internal demands that are appraised as taxing or exceeding the resources of the person" [33] (p. 141). The results obtained by the research participants in terms of their coping with stress styles are presented in Table 6.

Table 6. The characteristics of the study participants regarding styles of coping with stress.

Level	CISS				
	TOC [1]	EOC [2]	AOC [3]	D [4]	SD [5]
Low	174 (29.24%)	139 (23.36%)	119 (20.00%)	89 (14.96%)	165 (27.73%)
Medium	226 (37.98%)	233 (39.16%)	241 (40.50%)	284 (47.73%)	236 (39.66%)
High	195 (32.77%)	223 (37.48%)	235 (39.50%)	222 (37.31%)	194 (32.61%)

[1] TOC—task-oriented coping, [2] EOC—emotion-oriented coping, [3] AOC—avoidance-oriented coping, [4] D—distraction, [5] SD—social diversion.

The avoidance-oriented style was slightly dominant among the participants. Avoidance-oriented coping may take the form of distraction and social diversion. Both forms are aimed at avoiding a stressful situation [29]. Of the two forms, distraction is more often chosen. The second most frequently indicated is an emotion-oriented coping style, which includes focusing on one's emotions and taking up actions aimed at lowering emotional tension. The least frequently chosen style is task-oriented coping (which includes taking actions aimed at solving a problem (e.g., through planning or taking up particular activities).

3.2. Predictors of Positive and Negative Emotions

Another issue that was analyzed was the influence of demographical variables, health situation related to COVID-19, mood, optimism, satisfaction with life, as well as styles of coping with stress, on experiencing positive and negative emotions.

The results of the analyses are presented in the Table 7.

Table 7. Predictors of positive and negative emotions—linear regression results.

Variable		PA [1]				NA [2]			
		Parameter	95% CI		*p*	Parameter	95% CI		*p*
Sex	Female	ref.				ref.			
	Male	1.935	0.692	3.179	0.002 *	−0.234	−1.407	0.939	0.696
Age	Up to 22	ref.				ref.			
	23–34	0.666	−1.174	2.506	0.479	1.063	−0.673	2.799	0.231
	35–60	−0.951	−3.565	1.663	0.476	1.189	−1.277	3.655	0.345
	Over 60	−1.265	−4.688	2.159	0.469	3.282	0.052	6.512	0.047 *
Marital status	Single/in informal relationships	ref.				ref.			
	Married	−0.566	−2.237	1.105	0.507	0.557	−1.019	2.134	0.489
	Other	1.231	−1.157	3.618	0.313	0.738	−1.514	2.99	0.521
Children	No	ref.				ref.			
	Yes	0.18	−1.536	1.896	0.837	−0.468	−2.087	1.151	0.571
Place of residence	Big city	ref.				ref.			
	Medium-sized city	−0.898	−2.35	0.553	0.226	−1.606	−2.975	−0.237	0.022 *
	Small city	1.264	−0.367	2.895	0.129	0.375	−1.164	1.913	0.633
	Village	0.087	−1.059	1.234	0.882	−1.37	−2.452	−0.289	0.013 *
Education	Higher education	ref.				ref.			
	Secondary education	−1.019	−2.666	0.628	0.226	−0.009	−1.563	1.545	0.991
	Other	0.41	−1.12	1.939	0.6	−0.728	−2.171	0.715	0.323
Employment	Student	ref.				ref.			
	Employed	1.852	−0.456	4.16	0.116	−0.117	−2.294	2.061	0.916
	Not employed	1.74	−0.922	4.401	0.201	−0.088	−2.599	2.422	0.945
	Employed student	2.198	0.419	3.977	0.016 *	0.698	−0.98	2.376	0.415

Table 7. *Cont.*

Variable		PA [1]				NA [2]			
		Parameter	95% CI		p	Parameter	95% CI		p
Economic conditions	Not changed	ref.				ref.			
	Decreased	−0.096	−1.202	1.009	0.864	1.452	0.409	2.495	0.007 *
	Improved	−0.787	−2.549	0.975	0.382	2.314	0.652	3.976	0.007 *
Have you had COVID 19?	No	ref.				ref.			
	Yes	−0.881	−2.106	0.345	0.16	0.407	−0.749	1.564	0.49
Has anyone in your family had COVID 19?	No	ref.				ref.			
	Yes	−0.243	−1.259	0.773	0.64	−0.2	−1.159	0.758	0.682
UMACL: HT [3]		0.357	0.096	0.618	0.008 *	0.028	−0.218	0.275	0.821
UMACL: TA [4]		−0.144	−0.331	0.042	0.13	1.545	1.369	1.721	<0.001 *
UMACL: EA [5]		−0.8	−0.965	−0.634	<0.001 *	0.138	−0.018	0.294	0.083
SWLS		0.235	0.131	0.338	<0.001 *	−0.038	−0.136	0.06	0.442
LOT-R		−0.019	−0.152	0.113	0.774	−0.089	−0.214	0.036	0.165
CISS: TOC [6]		0.18	0.114	0.247	<0.001 *	0.032	−0.031	0.096	0.313
CISS: EOC [7]		−0.104	−0.165	−0.043	0.001 *	0.103	0.045	0.161	<0.001 *
CISS: AOC [8]		0.009	−0.293	0.312	0.952	−0.163	−0.448	0.123	0.264
CISS: D [9]		0.013	−0.34	0.365	0.944	0.213	−0.119	0.545	0.21
CISS: SD [10]		0.154	−0.234	0.541	0.437	0.156	−0.21	0.521	0.405

* p—values below 0.05; [1] PA—Positive Affect, [2] NA—Negative Affect, [3] HT—Hedonic Tone, [4] TA—Tense Arousal, [5] EA—Energetic Arousal, [6] TOC—task-oriented coping, [7] EOC—emotion-oriented coping, [8] AOC—avoidance-oriented coping, [9] D—distraction, [10] SD—social diversion.

3.2.1. Predictors of Positive Emotions (PA)

The multivariate model of linear regression confirmed that significant ($p < 0.05$) independent predictors of PA included: an emotion-oriented style of coping with stress (beta = −0.104; $p = 0.001$) and task-oriented coping (beta = 0.18; $p < 0.001$), level of satisfaction with life (beta = 0.235; $p < 0.001$), and level of energetic arousal in the description of mood (beta = −0.8; $p < 0.001$). A weaker predictor of experiencing positive emotions was being a man (beta = 1.935; $p = 0.002$), hedonic tone in the description of mood (beta = 0.357; $p = 0.008$), and being an employed student (beta = 2.198; $p = 0.016$). The R^2 coefficient for this model (PE) was 54.57%, which means that 54.57% of PA variability was explained by the variables used in the model. The remaining 45.43% depends on the variables that were not taken into account in the model and accidental factors.

3.2.2. Predictors of Positive of Negative Emotions (NA)

The multivariate model of linear regression confirmed that the significant ($p < 0.05$) independent predictors of NA were: tense arousal in the description of mood (beta = 1.545; $p < 0.001$) and an emotion-oriented coping with stress (beta = 0.103; $p < 0.001$). Other significant predictors included being over 60 years old (beta = 3.282; $p = 0.047$), living in a medium-sized city (beta = −1.606; 0.022), living in a village (beta = −1.37; $p = 0.013$), as well as decreased (beta = 1.452; $p = 0.007$) and increased (beta = 2.314; $p = 0.007$) level of life in the recent time. The R^2 coefficient for this model was 63.42%, which means that 63.42% of NA variability was explained by the variables used in the model. The remaining 36.58% depends on the variables that were not taken into account in the model and accidental factors.

4. Discussion

Experiencing negative emotions during the pandemic is a fully understandable phenomenon. In the case of 60% of respondents, the intensification of negative emotions reached a high level. Such emotions may result from a variety of factors, the importance of which may be different in various cultural contexts. In the case of the Polish respondents, this may include the following factors: the threat to one's health and to the health of family members; isolation and, at the same time, the inability to distance oneself from people with whom we live; and economic uncertainty, together with a simultaneous crisis of trust in public institutions [8]. The objective of this research was to search for predictors of the experience of positive and negative emotions of Polish respondents during the second wave of the COVID-19 pandemic in the hope that the diagnosis of their mental condition will help design actions that might prevent negative consequences for their mental health.

Referring to the research that was conducted earlier, it is worth analyzing the key social and demographical variables. Whereas sex was not an important predictor of experiencing negative emotions, being a man was a predictor of experiencing positive emotions. In the majority of Polish analyses that were conducted earlier and that considered the sex variable, women's results were worse as far as mental wellbeing was concerned (e.g., anxiety, stress, or depression) [6,7,9,10,17,18]. Only in one study was the difference between the sexes statistically insignificant in some measurements [13]. Women stand on the frontline in the fight against the coronavirus. In a UN report published in April 2020, a strong thesis was formulated: "The COVID-19 global crisis has made starkly visible the fact that the world's formal economies and the maintenance of our daily lives are built on the invisible and unpaid labor of women and girls" [34]. In this situation, in which responsibility for caring for children, for the ill, and for the elderly was largely moved from the state to individuals and families, in most cases, women became the ones who had to take responsibility for it. This also limited women's ability to work the well-paid jobs they had before the pandemic, and from a long-term perspective, it may constitute a serious obstacle on their career path [35]. Moreover, jobs performed by women are often jobs with a high risk of becoming infected with the virus (medical staff, teachers, office workers) [34]. Finally, in December, apart from the above-mentioned factors, women were burdened with preparations for Christmas which, in traditional Polish families, are mainly the responsibility of women. Thus, on the one hand, negative emotions experienced by women at that time could be based on culturally determined tasks related to unpaid and unappreciated work that involves caring for others' needs. On the other hand, women's negative feelings could be based on stronger social approval of experiencing such emotions by women rather than by men. However, such a trend was not confirmed by our research. Emotional costs take the form of a ricochet: a higher probability of a higher level of positive emotions among the men than among the women participating in our research.

Many analyses performed in different parts of the world have shown that the emotional distress experienced during the pandemic mainly influenced people from younger age groups. A meta-analysis of the research on emotional well-being of young people during the pandemic [36] showed that they are much more threatened with the risk of experiencing anxiety, stress, and depression than older people. In addition, young people experienced problems with sleeping [37], somatization disorders, and obsessive-compulsive disorders [38]. Stronger symptoms of emotional disorders among young people may be explained by lower psychological resilience resulting from, e.g., shorter life experience or a more drastic change in the lifestyle they led [13]. Nevertheless, in our research, the only age-related predictor of emotions was being over 60 years old, which was a predictor of negative emotions. The pandemic negatively influenced the way in which older people function because they lost the opportunity to move around, they became lonelier, and they experienced more conflicts within their families [39]. Another source of negative emotions in this age group might be older people's increased susceptibility to contracting the virus and being more seriously affected than younger people [40]. Moreover, considering the fact that the greatest source of stress for Poles is the state of the health service [16,20], which older people use most frequently, a higher risk of experiencing negative emotions among them is perfectly understandable. Finally, for older people, isolation bears different connotations than for younger people. Older people have lower technological competences, and they often fear using new forms of media communication, which makes them feel much more isolated than young people [41].

In contrast, one of the predictors of positive emotions was combining work with studies. On the one hand, the simultaneous fulfillment of two tasks is a great challenge, especially due to the risk of losing a job to which young people working in services are often exposed, and due to dynamic changes in the system of education (the necessity to deal with the requirements of online education) [36]. On the other hand, the necessity to fulfil tasks in two social contexts at the same time increases the probability of maintaining social relationships and weakens the sense of isolation, which is one of the sources of anxiety and other disorders [42,43].

From the research, the authors have concluded that research participants living in villages and medium-sized cities experience negative emotions to a lesser degree. Living in a big city increases the risk of contracting the virus, makes it more difficult to maintain social distance, and limits the opportunity to engage in outdoor activities [19]. Furthermore, the pandemic limited people's access to the biggest attractions connected with living in a city (access to cultural institutions and to a variety of attractive services). Other factors that increase the possibility of experiencing negative emotions may include limited and closed spaces, the necessity to maintain contact with strangers, and the sense of greater anonymity.

The strongest predictors of emotions included the styles of coping with stress. A predictor of positive emotions was a task-oriented style, while in the case of negative emotions, an emotion-oriented way of coping was a predictor. The latter style also lowered the opportunity to experience positive emotions. Task-oriented coping relates to an important element of constructive coping with pandemic stress: control over one's surrounding reality [44]. This style involves reformulating the evaluation of the situation from a threat to a challenge or a task to be fulfilled. In the context of the pandemic, the style may be reflected in behaviors that reduce the risk of becoming infected with the virus, as well as actions such as planning everyday routines, looking for reliable information about the virus, etc.

In our research, emotion-oriented coping was a predictor of negative emotions and the original affect dimension related to lower mood (tense arousal). The adaptive way of dealing with negative emotions involves recognizing, naming, and accepting emotions that accompany difficult situations. The emotion-oriented style of coping with stress, the essence of which is focusing on one's own emotions and taking up actions aimed at reducing emotional tension, seems to be a non-adaptive solution, especially because, in the case of uncertain and uncontrollable conditions, these actions are doomed to failure. Continuous tense arousal and energetic arousal related to our body's preparation to respond to threats results in exhaustion. However, an important predictor of positive emotions was hedonic tone.

Similar to other analyses [45,46], our research has confirmed the relationship between mental wellbeing and satisfaction with life. Comparing this conclusion with the statement that an increased or decreased standard of living within the last 10 months is an important predictor of negative emotions, it could be noticed that one of the protective factors is the opportunity to use the resources gathered during the pandemic and to maintain a sense of stability/unchangeability in a changing world.

5. Conclusions

Surveys that diagnose the mental state of people in different countries are very useful in preventing negative consequences for their inhabitants' mental health. Such a diagnosis should take into account the high dynamic of changes people face during a pandemic, as well as different ways of experiencing and interpreting pandemic stress by people from a variety of cultural contexts. In the Polish reality, people are not worried about their own illness or death to a high degree, but they are concerned about their family members' health and about the crisis of trust in governmental institutions during the pandemic.

In the presented research, which was conducted during the second wave of the pandemic (December 2020), 60% of the participants revealed a high level of negative emotions. Due to the possible connection between the high intensity of negative emotions and negative consequences for one's mental health, it is important for researchers to look for factors that increase the risk of experiencing negative feelings. Significant predictors of negative emotions include mood-related tense arousal in the description of mood and an emotion-oriented style of coping with stress. On the other hand, important predictors of positive emotions are a task-oriented style of coping with stress, level of satisfaction with life, and hedonic tone in the description of mood. These aspects may become the basic indicators for specialists who will work on preventive actions and psychological care.

In addition, it is worth focusing on supporting particular at-risk groups, i.e., people over 60 years old (e.g., through increasing their online activities) or women (through increasing their chances to experience good emotions by appreciating the value of their unpaid work).

It should be emphasized that these results must be considered in the light of numerous limitations. Adults of different ages (i.e., over 18 years old) were recruited for the research. However, because of our recruitment method (i.e., snowball sampling), both men, people with primary/middle school and vocational education, and older people were underrepresented in the research sample. Another limitation is related to the type of the research. A better solution would be longitudinal research, which would allow to make reliable conclusions about the change and its dynamics in the psychological wellbeing of the sample. Finally, the research was conducted mainly by means of the Internet to provide comfort and safety to the participants. As a result, the sample consisted primarily of people who have access to the Internet. The abovementioned limitations make it impossible to generalize the research results as representative of the population as a whole.

Despite the limitations, the research results obtained shed some light on the emotional wellbeing of adult Poles during the second wave of the COVID-19 pandemic. These findings are important because the intensification of negative emotions can contribute to problems not only in mental health, but also in everyday activities, such as study, work, social relations, or sexual contacts. The authors are aware that further research should be conducted to increase the number of participants in each age group, from children to seniors.

In the context of an unpredictable future, researchers face the task of monitoring the emotional condition of the general population and of particular at-risk groups in order to inspire practical preventive and therapeutic actions, as well as social initiatives that reinforce solidarity, mutual care, and responsibility.

Author Contributions: Conceptualization, E.T.-S.; methodology, E.T.-S.; validation, I.R., K.B. and A.S.; formal analysis, E.T.-S. and I.R.; investigation, E.T.-S.; resources, E.T.-S. and I.R.; data curation, E.T.-S.; writing—original draft preparation, E.T.-S. and I.R.; writing—review and editing, A.S. and K.B.; visualization, E.T.-S. and I.R. All authors have read and agreed to the published version of the manuscript.

Funding: This research received no external funding.

Institutional Review Board Statement: The study was conducted according to the guidelines of the Declaration of Helsinki and approved by the Ethics Committee of Jesuit University Ignatianum in Krakow (15 June 2021).

Informed Consent Statement: Informed consent was obtained from all subjects involved in the study.

Data Availability Statement: The data presented in this study are available on request from the corresponding author.

Conflicts of Interest: The authors declare no conflict of interest.

References

1. Fundacja Aflofarm. Ogólnopolskie Badania. Polacy Rok po Wybuchu Pandemii SARS-CoV-2. Available online: https://www.aflofarm.com.pl/media/filer_public/62/df/62df6272-14e6-49be-822a-91ea15445bc1/polacy_rok_po_wybuchu_pandemii_sars-cov-2_-_raport_fundacji_aflofarm.pdf (accessed on 2 July 2021).
2. Wang, C.; Pan, R.; Wan, X.; Tan, Y.; Xu, L.; Ho, C.S.; Ho, R.C. Immediate Psychological Responses and Associated Factors during the Initial Stage of the 2019 Coronavirus Disease (COVID-19) Epidemic among the General Population in China. *Int. J. Environ. Res. Public Health* **2020**, *17*, 1729. [CrossRef]
3. Rajkumar, R.P. COVID-19 and Mental Health: A Review of the Existing Literature. *Asian J. Psychiatry* **2020**, *52*, 102066. [CrossRef] [PubMed]
4. Gallup International Association. 3rd Wave of the Gallup International Survey on the Corona Crisis. Available online: https://www.gallup-international.com/survey-results/survey-result/3rd-wave-of-the-gallup-international-survey-on-the-corona-crisis (accessed on 1 July 2021).
5. Moroń, M.; Biolik-Moroń, M. Trait Emotional Intelligence and Emotional Experiences during the COVID-19 Pandemic Outbreak in Poland: A Daily Diary Study. *Pers. Individ.* **2021**, *168*, 110348. [CrossRef] [PubMed]
6. Debowska, A.; Horeczy, B.; Boduszek, D.; Dolinski, D. A Repeated Cross-sectional Survey Assessing University Students' Stress, Depression, Anxiety, and Suicidality in the Early Stages of the COVID-19 Pandemic in Poland. *Psychol. Med.* **2020**, 1–4. [CrossRef]
7. Rogowska, A.M.; Kuśnierz, C.; Bokszczanin, A. Examining Anxiety, Life Satisfaction, General Health, Stress and Coping Styles During COVID-19 Pandemic in Polish Sample of University Students. *Psychol. Res. Behav. Manag.* **2020**, *13*, 797–811. [CrossRef]
8. Hamer, K.; Baran, M. Wpływ Pandemii COVID-19 na Zachowania, Postawy i Dobrostan Polaków. Raport z Badań. Available online: https://covid19psychologia.com/2021/02/22/podsumowanie-wplyw-pandemii-na-zachowania-postawy-i-dobrostan-polakow-w-2020-roku/ (accessed on 1 July 2021).
9. Babicki, M.; Mastalerz-Migas, A. Występowanie zaburzeń lękowych wśród Polaków w dobie pandemii COVID–19. *Psychiatria Polska* **2020**, *188*, 1. [CrossRef]
10. Talarowska, M.; Chodkiewicz, J.; Nawrocka, N.; Miniszewska, J.; Biliński, P. Mental Health and the SARS-COV-2 Epidemic—Polish Research Study. *Int. J. Environ. Res. Public Health* **2020**, *17*, 7015. [CrossRef] [PubMed]
11. Lipert, A.; Kozłowski, R.; Timler, D.; Marczak, M.; Musiał, K.; Rasmus, P.; Kamecka, K.; Jegier, A. Physical Activity as a Predictor of the Level of Stress and Quality of Sleep during COVID-19 Lockdown. *Int. J. Environ. Res. Public Health* **2021**, *18*, 5811. [CrossRef]
12. Golińska, P.B.; Cieślak, M.; Hubert, O.; Bidzan, M. Mental Health and the Symptoms of PTSD in People with Depression and Anxiety Disorders during the COVID-19 Pandemic. *Int. J. Environ. Res. Public Health* **2021**, *18*, 5542. [CrossRef] [PubMed]
13. Gambin, M.; Sękowski, M.; Woźniak-Prus, M.; Pisula, E.; Hansen, K.; Kmita, G.; Kubicka, K.; Gorgol, J.; Huflejt-Łukasik, M.; Holas, P.; et al. Objawy Depresji i Lęku Wśród Polaków w Trakcie Epidemii COVID-19. Raport z Badań Podłużnych. Available online: http://psych.uw.edu.pl/wpcontent/uploads/sites/98/2021/01/Raport_objawy_depresji_leku_IV_fale.pdf (accessed on 1 July 2021).
14. Boguszewski, R.; Makowska, M.; Podkowińska, M.A. Typology of Poles' Attitudes toward COVID-19 during the First Wave of the Pandemic. *Int. J. Environ. Res. Public Health* **2021**, *18*, 2002. [CrossRef]
15. Ipsos. Three in Four Adults Globally Say They'd Get a Vaccine for COVID-19. Available online: https://www.ipsos.com/en/three-four-adults-globally-say-theyd-get-vaccine-covid-19 (accessed on 1 July 2021).
16. Ipsos. What Worries the World? September 2020. Available online: https://www.ipsos.com/sites/default/files/ct/news/documents/2020-09/www-report-september-2020-ipsos.pdf (accessed on 1 July 2021).
17. Chodkiewicz, J.; Miniszewska, J.; Krajewska, E.; Biliński, P. Mental Health during the Second Wave of the COVID-19 Pandemic—Polish Studies. *Int. J. Environ. Res. Public Health* **2021**, *18*, 3423. [CrossRef]
18. Babicki, M.; Szewczykowska, I.; Mastalerz-Migas, A. Mental Health in the Era of the Second Wave of SARS-CoV-2: A Cross-Sectional Study Based on an Online Survey among Online Respondents in Poland. *Int. J. Environ. Res. Public Health* **2021**, *18*, 2522. [CrossRef]
19. Ipsos. COVID-19 and World Worries. November 2020. Available online: https://www.ipsos.com/sites/default/files/ct/news/documents/2020-11/covid-19-and-world-worries-november-2020-ipsos.pdf (accessed on 2 July 2021).
20. Ipsos. COVID-19 and World Worries. December 2020. Available online: https://www.ipsos.com/sites/default/files/ct/news/documents/2020-12/covid-19-and-world-worries-december-2020-ipsos.pdf (accessed on 2 July 2021).
21. Brzozowski, P. *Skala Uczuć Pozytywnych i Negatywnych SUPIN: Polska Adaptacja Skali PANAS Davida Watsona i Lee Anny Clark*; Pracownia Testów Psychologicznych Polskiego Towarzystwa Psychologicznego: Warszawa, Polska, 2010.
22. Watson, D.; Clark, L.A.; Tellegen, A. Development and Validation of Brief Measures of Positive and Negative Affect: The PANAS Scales. *J. Pers. Soc. Psychol.* **1988**, *54*, 1063–1070. [CrossRef]
23. Goryńska, E. *Przymiotnikowa Skala Nastroju UMACL Geralda Matthewsa, A. Grahama Chamberlaina, Dylana M. Jonesa*; Pracownia Testów Psychologicznych Polskiego Towarzystwa Psychologicznego: Warszawa, Polska, 2005.
24. Matthews, G.; Jones, D.M.; Chamberlain, A.G. Refining the Measurement of Mood: The UWIST Mood Adjective Checklist. *Br. J. Psychol.* **1990**, *81*, 17–42. [CrossRef]
25. Juczyński, Z. *Narzędzia Pomiaru Stresu i Radzenia Sobie ze Stresem*; Pracownia Testów Psychologicznych Polskiego Towarzystwa Psychologicznego: Warszawa, Polska, 2009.

26. Diener, E.; Emmons, R.A.; Larsen, R.J.; Griffin, S. The Satisfaction with Life Scale. *J. Pers. Assess.* **1985**, *49*, 71–75. [CrossRef] [PubMed]
27. Poprawa, R. Zasoby Osobiste w Radzeniu Sobie ze Stresem. In *Elementy Psychologii Zdrowia*; Dolińska-Zygmunt, G., Ed.; Wydawnictwo Uniwersytetu Wrocławskiego: Wrocław, Polska, 1996; pp. 101–136.
28. Scheier, M.F.; Carver, C.S.; Bridges, M.W. Distinguishing Optimism from Neuroticism (and Trait Anxiety, Self-mastery, and Self-esteem): A Reevaluation of the Life Orientation Test. *J. Pers. Soc. Psychol.* **1994**, *67*, 1063–1078. [CrossRef] [PubMed]
29. Strelau, J.; Jaworska, A.; Wrześniewski, K.; Szczepaniak, P. *Kwestionariusz Radzenia Sobie w Sytuacjach Stresowych*; Pracownia Testów Psychologicznych Polskiego Towarzystwa Psychologicznego: Warszawa, Polska, 2005.
30. Endler, N.; Parker, J.D. *Coping Inventory for Stressful Situations*; Multi-Health Systems: Toronto, ON, Canada, 1990.
31. Ministerstwo Zdrowia. Oficjalny Profil Ministerstwa Zdrowia (Official Profile of the Ministry of Health). Available online: https://twitter.com/MZ_GOV_PL (accessed on 2 July 2021).
32. R Core Team. *A Language and Environment for Statistical Computing*; R Foundation for Statistical Computing: Vienna, Austria, 2020; Available online: https://www.R-project.org/ (accessed on 2 July 2021).
33. Lazarus, R.S.; Folkman, S. *Stress, Appraisal, and Coping*; Springer: New York, NY, USA, 1984.
34. United Nations. UN Policy Brief: The Impact of COVID-19 on Women. 9 April 2020. Available online: https://www.un.org/sexualviolenceinconflict/wp-content/uploads/2020/06/report/policy-brief-the-impact-of-covid-19-on-women/policy-brief-the-impact-of-covid-19-on-women-en-1.pdf (accessed on 1 July 2021).
35. Power, K. The COVID-19 Pandemic has Increased the Care Burden of Women and Families. *Sustain. Sci. Pract. Policy* **2020**, *16*, 67–73. [CrossRef]
36. Cielo, F.; Ulberg, R.; Di Giacomo, D. Psychological Impact of the COVID-19 Outbreak on Mental Health Outcomes among Youth: A Rapid Narrative Review. *Int. J. Environ. Res. Public Health* **2021**, *18*, 6067. [CrossRef]
37. Cellini, N.; Canale, N.; Mioni, G.; Costa, S. Changes in Sleep Pattern, Sense of Time and Digital Media Use during COVID-19 Lockdown in Italy. *J. Sleep Res.* **2020**, *29*, e13074. [CrossRef]
38. Jiang, R. Knowledge, Attitudes and Mental Health of University Students during the COVID-19 Pandemic in China. *Child Youth Serv. Rev.* **2020**, *119*, 105494. [CrossRef] [PubMed]
39. Llorente-Barroso, C.; Kolotouchkina, O.; Mañas-Viniegra, L. The Enabling Role of Ict to Mitigate the Negative Effects of Emotional and Social Loneliness of the Elderly during COVID-19 Pandemic. *Int. J. Environ. Res. Public Health* **2021**, *18*, 3923. [CrossRef] [PubMed]
40. Lithander, F.E.; Neumann, S.; Tenison, E.; Lloyd, K.; Welsh, T.J.; Rodrigues, J.C.L.; Higgins, J.P.T.; Scourfield, L.; Christensen, H.; Haunton, V.J.; et al. COVID-19 in Older People: A Rapid Clinical Review. *Age Ageing* **2020**, *49*, 501–515. [CrossRef]
41. Lee, C.-J.; Hsu, Y. Promoting the Quality of Life of Elderly during the COVID-19 Pandemic. *Int. J. Environ. Res. Public Health* **2021**, *18*, 6813. [CrossRef] [PubMed]
42. Bhardwaj, T.; Bhardwaj, S. Emotional Concerns of the Elderly During Coronavirus Pandemic in India. *Indian J. Gerontol.* **2021**, *35*, 257–275.
43. Raval, N. Mental Health Implications of COVID-19 in India. *Indian J. Health Well-Being* **2020**, *11*, 276–281.
44. Polizzi, C.; Lynn, S.J.; Perry, A. Stress and Coping in the Time of COVID-19: Pathways to Resilience and Recovery. *Clin. Neuropsychiatry* **2020**, *17*, 59–62. [CrossRef]
45. Trzebiński, J.; Cabański, M.; Czarnecka, J.Z. Reaction to the COVID-19 Pandemic: The Influence of Meaning in Life, Life Satisfaction, and Assumptions on World Orderliness and Positivity. *J. Loss Trauma* **2020**, *25*, 544–557. [CrossRef]
46. Karataş, Z.; Tagay, Ö. The Relationships between Resilience of the Adults Affected by the Covid Pandemic in Turkey and Covid-19 Fear, Meaning in Life, Life Satisfaction, Intolerance of Uncertainty and Hope. *Pers. Individ. Differ.* **2021**, *172*, 110592. [CrossRef]

International Journal of
Environmental Research and Public Health

MDPI

Article

Fear of Infection and the Common Good: COVID-19 and the First Italian Lockdown

Lloyd Balbuena [1,*] and Merylin Monaro [2,*]

[1] Department of Psychiatry, University of Saskatchewan, Saskatoon, SK S7N 0W8, Canada
[2] Department of General Psychology, University of Padova, 35151 Padua, Italy
* Correspondence: lloyd.balbuena@gmail.com (L.B.); merylinmonaro@gmail.com (M.M.)

Abstract: In the first quarter of 2020, Italy became one of the earliest hotspots of COVID-19 infection, and the government imposed a lockdown. During the lockdown, an online survey of 2053 adults was conducted that asked about health behaviors and about the psychological and overall impact of COVID-19. The present study is a secondary analysis of that data. We hypothesized that self-control, higher socio-economic status, existing health conditions, and fear of infection were all inversely related to actions (or intentions) that violated the lockdown (i.e., infractions). Using partial least squares structural equation modeling (PLS-SEM), we found that only the fear of infection significantly dissuaded people from violating lockdown rules. Since it is not practical or ethical to sow a fear of infection, our study indicates that enacting rules and enforcing them firmly and fairly are important tools for containing the infection. This may become more important as vaccines become more widely available and people lose their fear of infection.

Keywords: social dilemma; fear of infection; safety measures; collective behavior; pathogens; self-control

Citation: Balbuena, L.; Monaro, M. Fear of Infection and the Common Good: COVID-19 and the First Italian Lockdown. *Int. J. Environ. Res. Public Health* **2021**, *18*, 11341. https://doi.org/10.3390/ijerph182111341

Academic Editor: Paul B. Tchounwou

Received: 23 September 2021
Accepted: 26 October 2021
Published: 28 October 2021

1. Introduction

In June 2020, more than 9 million people worldwide had been diagnosed with COVID-19, which resulted in 472,856 deaths [1]. Italy was an early hotspot, with infections increasing exponentially ($R_0 > 2.5$) from mid-February to early March 2020 [2]. The Italian government imposed a nationwide lockdown in early March [3]. With the help of this lockdown, Italy flattened the infection curve dramatically [4].

Lockdowns have reduced the number of infections by an estimated 81 percent and have saved more than 3 million lives in 11 European countries from February to May 2020 [5]. The same report concluded that lockdowns have been the most effective government intervention by a large margin, when compared to school closures, social distancing, social isolation, and the cancelling of public events [5]. Unfortunately, lockdowns are unsustainable, and have led to the loss of millions of jobs, and economic uncertainty [6]. Lockdowns also have detrimental psychological effects, including loneliness, anxiety, depression, sleep problems, and suicidal ideation [7–10]. Feelings of isolation may have contributed to lockdown violations in both overt and covert ways.

In this work, we used the rational agent theory, studied in neoclassical economics, as a framework for understanding lockdown violations. This theory posits that individual actions are governed by the desire to satisfy needs or wants. Whatever is believed to provide the greatest satisfaction (or value) is likely to be carried out [11]. Consider somebody who is of two minds about getting a small car (which is good for the environment) and a luxury SUV (for comfort and status). Assuming that price is not a concern, the person might reason as follows: the harm to the environment is a cost that is shared by many people, while the benefit of the SUV is enjoyed solely by oneself. The person decides to buy the SUV.A COVID-19 lockdown can be viewed as a dilemma in which the common good is served by everyone's compliance, but personal interests are maximized if everyone else complied except oneself. This is an instance of the so-called tragedy of the commons [12].

A person who shops unnecessarily gains temporary relief from confinement. Since it is impossible to police shoppers if their grocery trips are truly necessary, the common good can be undermined by self-serving actions.

We can extend the SUV vs. small car analogy to consider the role of fear. Suppose that the SUV only comes in a self-driving mode, i.e., it does not allow the person to take control of the vehicle. Although generally safe, self-driving features have been shown to fail in rare occasions, resulting in death. In this modified scenario, the imagined benefits of the SUV are tempered by the small chance of dying in an accident. It would be reasonable to infer that more risk-averse people would opt for the small car with no self-driving features. This situation mirrors the COVID-19 lockdown in which an unnecessary trip to the grocery provides relief from isolation but carries a small risk of catching the virus. People with higher anxiety are probably less likely to make unnecessary grocery trips.

We hypothesized that adherence to the lockdown was influenced by psychological traits, socio-economic status, health conditions making one more susceptible to infection, and the fear of infection. Our specific hypotheses were:

1. *Higher self-control is inversely related to lockdown violations.* Self-control is defined as the ability to restrain impulses, and overall self-discipline [13].
2. *Higher socio-economic status (SES) is inversely related to lockdown violations.* This was based in part on a German study that reported a positive association of higher education and engaging in COVID-19 protective measures [14].
3. *Having health conditions is inversely related to lockdown violations.*
4. *Greater fear of infection is inversely related to lockdown violations.*

2. Materials and Methods

2.1. Participants and Data

This is a secondary data analysis of 2053 Italian adults who responded to an online survey administered in March 2020, coinciding with the first wave of the pandemic [3]. Most participants were female (n = 1555), 480 were male and 18 reported "other". The respondents had a mean age (SD) of 35.81 (13.19). Please refer to the paper by Flesia et al. [3] for a complete description of the study. The materials are available on Zenodo (10.5281/zenodo.5523260). The present work did not require ethics approval, however the original study was approved by the University of Padova Ethics Committee for Psychological Research (protocol 3576, unique code 189B46FE116994F1A8D1077B835D83BB).

We calculated the adequacy of the sample size using Kock and Hadaya's inverse square root formula [15]. A minimum of 316 people was necessary to achieve 80 percent power, at an alpha of 0.05.

2.2. Measures

Self-control was assessed using the 13-item Brief Self-Control Scale [16]. Linder et.al. compared unidimensional and two-factor solutions and recommended that the total score be used [17]. The internal reliability of the BSCS in this sample (Cronbach's alpha = 0.84) was identical to that of previous studies.

Socio-economic status (SES) was assessed using participants' typical income, their highest level of education, and how they continued to earn money during the pandemic (i.e., salary or governmental support). These indicators were based on Green's three-item measure of socio-economic status [18]. This was chosen because of its relevance to health-related behavior and its parsimony. Since we did not have the exact job titles of respondents, we added a student status. This distinguished established workers and students from having the same attainments. This was necessary because approximately one-fourth of the respondents were students.

The fear of infection was assessed with the questions: (1) How much do you feel in danger of COVID 19 infection? (2) In the last period, are you paying more attention than usual to your physical symptoms? (3) Are you actively searching for information on the progress of the pandemic? These were Likert-type questions with five levels for the first two questions and six levels for the third. The questions were similar in content to "afraid of losing life", "hands getting clammy", "anxiety when watching COVID-19 news in social media" in the Fear of COVID-19 Scale [19]. The survey contained the question, *Do you currently suffer from any of the following diseases?* The available choices were: *immunosuppression, cardiovascular disease, pulmonary disease, cancer, diabetes*, and *none of the above*.

Our dependent variable was a composite of risky behaviors or intentions to disregard restrictions, which we called infractions. This was assessed with six yes-or-no questions: *(1) I respect loyally the rules imposed by ministerial ordinances, (2) I go out regularly in defiance of the ban, (3) I only go out when necessary, (4) I happened to go out for a walk in defiance of the ban, (5) I happened to go to the grocery store without real necessity, (6) I am looking for tricks to bypass the ordinances.* Questions 1 and 3 were reverse-coded to conform to the rest.

We considered self-control, SES, fear of infection and infractions as latent variables, and their respective items as indicators.

2.3. Analysis

We chose partial least squares structural equation modeling (PLS-SEM) to examine if infractions could be predicted by self-control, health conditions, SES, or a fear of infection. PLS-SEM was chosen because health conditions and socioeconomic status (SES) are more appropriately treated as formative variables instead of reflective variables. Reflective variables are latent constructs that are manifested by empirically measured indicators (or item responses) [20]. Covariance-based SEM (which is usually called SEM) considers underlying constructs as causes. In contrast, formative variables are defined by indicators that are assumed to be the causes of the latent variable [21]. Furthermore, covariance-based SEM requires that the indicators represent a normally distributed latent variable (or be categorized versions thereof) [22,23]. However, using polychoric correlations for ordinal indicators, for example, may still result in biased estimates and standard errors [24]. In contrast, PLS-SEM is a non-parametric method that handles non-normally distributed data, and both reflective and formative indicators [25].

To test hypotheses one to four, we regressed infractions against the four latent variables as shown in Model 1 (Figure 1). To examine if the presence of health conditions indirectly inhibited infractions by increasing the fear of infection, we added a path from health conditions to fear of infection in Model 2 (Figure 2). Confidence intervals and p values were calculated based on 5000 bootstrap replicates.

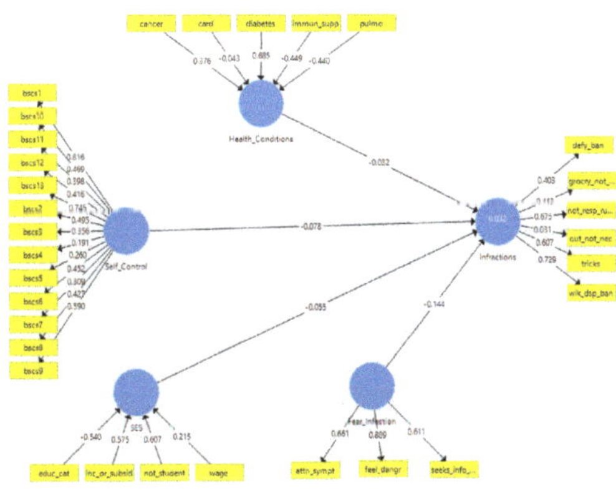

Figure 1. *Model 1*: Direct effects only. Please refer to Appendix A Table A1 for the exact wording of indicators. The outcome (infractions) is predicted by four latent variables indicated by circles (self-control, health conditions, SES, and fear of infection). Rectangles are the observed variables. Arrows terminating in infractions are regression coefficients. Arrows originating from a latent variable (reflective) and terminating in a rectangle represent loading. Arrows originating from a rectangle and ending in a latent variable (formative) represent weights.

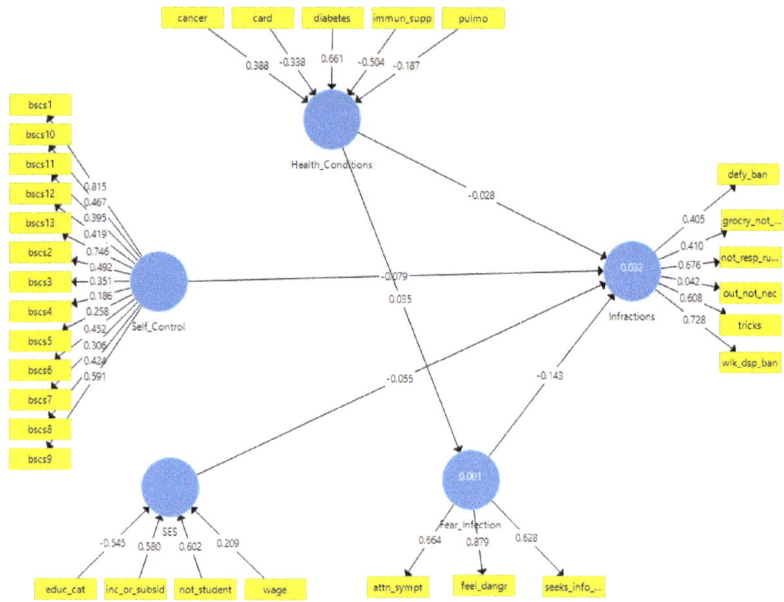

Figure 2. *Model 2:* Direct Effects + 1 indirect Effect. The same as Model 1 except for an added path (regression coefficient) from health conditions to fear of infection. The indirect effect of health conditions on infractions is not significant.

Appendix B Models 1 and 2 were implemented in the Stata package plssem [24] and the results were visualized, assessed for quality, and checked for consistency with SmartPLS 3 [25] and ADANCO 2.0 [26]. All three programs produced identical results.

3. Results

The direct effects model (Table 1 and Figure 1) shows that only fear of infection had a significant, inverse association with infractions. The other variables had an inverse association with the outcome but were not statistically significant. The indirect effect of health conditions through a fear of infection (0.04 × −0.14) was not significant (Table 2 and Figure 2). Both models had poor predictive value for infractions (R^2 = 3.2%)

Table 1. Model 1: Direct Effects Only.

Variable	Beta	Bootstrapped 95% CI	t	*p*
Fear of Infection	−0.14	−0.19–−0.11	−6.88	<0.001
Health Conditions	−0.03	−0.07–0.09	−0.60	0.54
SES	−0.06	−0.12–0.09	−0.80	0.43
Self-Control	−0.08	−0.15–0.12	−1.16	0.25

The overall fit of our two models were assessed using the standardized root mean squared residual (SRMR) [27]. SRMR quantifies the discrepancy between the correlations implied our models and the observed data [28], therefore lower values are better. The SRMRs for Models 1 and 2 were 0.69 and 0.70, respectively. These were both within the suggested cut-off value of 0.80 [29]. However, the direct-effects-only model (Model 1) was more parsimonious.

Table 2. Model 2: Direct Effects + 1 Indirect Effect.

Variable	Beta	Bootstrapped 95% CI	t	p
Direct Effects on Infractions				
Fear of Infection	−0.14	−0.19–−0.10	−6.63	<0.001
Health Conditions	−0.03	−0.06–0.09	−0.65	0.51
SES	−0.06	−0.12–0.09	−0.79	0.43
Self-Control	−0.08	−0.15–0.12	−1.17	0.24
Indirect Effect through Fear of Infection				
Health Conditions	−0.01	−0.01–0.00	−0.57	0.57

The quality of our measured constructs was assessed by inspecting the composite reliability (CR), the average variance extracted (AVE), and the possible multicollinearity. These indices were applicable only for the reflective latent variables (self-control, fear of infection, and infractions). CR is a measure of internal consistency (similar to Cronbach's alpha) but does not require equal loading of the indicators [25]. CR values above 0.7 are preferable, although 0.60 and above are acceptable for exploratory research [25]. AVE is the mean of indicator reliabilities for a construct and should be above 0.5 [21]. (Table 3) Compared to the Fear of COVID-19 Scale which had values of 0.88 and 0.51 for CR and AVE respectively, *fear of infection* had 0.77 and 0.54. Multicollinearity is indicated by a variance inflation factor (VIF) exceeding 3.0 [21]. None of our indicators (items) were collinear, with a VIF which ranged from 1.00 to 1.76 (Appendix A Table A1).

Table 3. Reliability of Reflective Latent Variables.

Variable	Composite Reliability	Average Variance Extracted (AVE)
Fear of Infection	0.77	0.54
Self-Control	0.78	0.24
Infractions	0.66	0.28

4. Discussion

In a large sample of adults surveyed during the first COVID-19 lockdown in Italy, we found that only the fear of infection was inversely related to actions (or intentions) which violated government restrictions. Contrary to Hypotheses 1–3, self-control, SES, and the presence of health conditions were not related to infractions. Our results suggest that the fear of infection had a positive aspect: it dissuaded people from violating lockdown rules. Despite this, fear of infection only accounted for a minuscule amount of the outcome, so there are probably more important reasons and causes.

From the perspective of evolutionary theory, fear is an adaptive response by an organism to an external threat [30]. Avoidance is an aspect of fear that confers protection from pathogens, and can be triggered by cues such as sneezing and coughing [30]. However, it is argued that epidemics arose only when people started living in settlements [31], so there may not be an innate fear of pathogens in contrast to an innate fear of snakes [32]. This may explain why mass gatherings continued even though COVID-19 deaths and infections were constantly in the news [33]. The finding that the fear of infection promoted lockdown compliance may not have direct practical importance. Worldwide, levels of anxiety are already elevated [34], so inducing fear may simply increase psychological distress and mental health problems. Instilling a fear of infection is also ethically dubious and lacking in a theoretical basis. Clear communication of "hard truths" by the government without fear-mongering may win public trust in the long run [35]. From a policy perspective, it may be more realistic to legislate penalties appropriate to particular violations. For example, a comparison of German counties that both imposed and did not impose fines showed that fines were inversely associated with COVID-19 infection rates [36]. In effect, fines may deter rule violations. As people become accustomed to living with COVID-19, fear of infection diminishes, so financial penalties may become more relevant for health behaviors.

That greater self-control was not inversely associated with infractions is surprising. Self-control is a central concept in explaining deviant behavior. Gottfredson and Hirch postulated that criminal acts are simple, easy, and provide immediate gratification [37]. This definition of criminal acts is particularly apt for the indicators *going for a walk* and *unnecessary trip to the grocery*. According to Gottfredson and Hirch, criminals (rule violators) seek pleasure and avoid pain. People with lower levels of self-control will violate a rule when the perceived benefit exceeds the perceived cost. There is substantial (but not unequivocal) evidence that greater self-control is associated with the observance of rules, superior health, and better social adjustment [16,38]. Hence, the non-significant effect of self-control on infractions demands an explanation.

We offer three possibilities. Firstly, it is possible that the risks of COVID-19 infection may have been judged too high relative to the infractions' rewards. This cognitive appraisal may have been influenced by the fear of infection. Although there have been previous virus outbreaks (i.e., H1N1), no previous outbreak in modern times has come close to the impact that COVID-19 has had. Secondly, a sense of solidarity (i.e., "we are all in this together ") may have also dampened self-seeking behaviors. When survival is threatened by a disaster, there can be a feeling of a shared humanity that transcends class distinctions [39]. In spite of the lockdown, people in Italy used digital resources to stay connected, and this promoted a greater sense of belonging [40]. Third, self-control during a pandemic may manifest itself more prominently in thoughts instead of actions. A Slovakian study reported that feelings of a lack of control significantly predicted the endorsement of COVID-19 conspiracy theories [41].

The nonsignificant effect of SES on infractions was also surprising. Health behaviors are influenced by personal knowledge and beliefs. A US study reported that people with a high school education (vs. a higher attainment) were less likely to intend to get vaccinated, to engage in hand-washing and masking, and to support social distancing requirements [42]. It is possible that different components of SES diverge in their relation to COVID-19 beliefs and actions. For example, among university students in Jordan, those who scored lower in a knowledge test about COVID-19 were more likely to believe in conspiracy theories [42]. Surprisingly, postgraduate students, who scored higher in the knowledge test compared to undergraduates, were more likely to violate quarantine rules [43].

The present study had several limitations. As a secondary analysis, the present study inherits the online design of the original work and its limitations [3]. Notably, older people, those with less education and with a lower SES, and men were underrepresented. With a cross-sectional design, our study cannot conclude that fear of infection causes fewer infractions. Although this is our preferred interpretation, we cannot rule out the possibility that those who had higher infractions became less afraid of infection. Among our reflective variables, *self-control* did not achieve a satisfactory AVE (Table 2). For self-control to have an AVE greater than or equal to 0.5, its indicators should have a loading of at least 0.70 [25]. Model 1 shows that only two items had at least that magnitude. One possibility is that the Brief Self-Control Scale should be divided into two factors [17]. We did not do so because these factors may represent wording effects (negative vs. positively worded items) [13]. Similarly to *self-control, infractions* also had unsatisfactory AVE. Importantly, *health conditions* and *infractions* were self-reported. The sensitive nature of this information may have influenced the responses obtained. Bearing these limitations in mind, our results indicate that the fear of infection served a useful purpose.

5. Conclusions

A higher fear of infection, but not self-control, presence of health conditions, and SES, was inversely related to self-reported violations of lockdown rules. Health conditions were not associated with fear of infection. With the increasing availability of vaccines and lockdown fatigue, the enactment of laws and their fair and firm enforcement may be needed to contain future outbreaks.

Author Contributions: Conceptualization, L.B. and M.M.; methodology, L.B.; formal analysis, L.B.; resources, M.M.; data curation, M.M.; writing—original draft preparation, L.B.; writing—review and editing, M.M.; visualization, L.B. All authors have read and agreed to the published version of the manuscript.

Funding: This research received no external funding.

Institutional Review Board Statement: Not applicable. This was a secondary analysis of publicly available data.

Informed Consent Statement: Not applicable.

Data Availability Statement: The data are available from Zenodo (10.5281/zenodo.5523260).

Acknowledgments: We are grateful to Merylin Monaro and colleagues for making the data in their paper publicly available (Reference #3). For this study, we used a subset of the variables collected in their work. We thank Sergio Venturini for guidance in using the Stata plssem package.

Conflicts of Interest: The authors declare no conflict of interest.

Appendix A

Table A1. Variable names, Descriptions and Variance Inflation Factor.

Latent Variable/Indicator	Description	VIF
Brief Self-Control Scale		
bscs1	I am good at resisting temptation	1.423
bscs2	I have a hard time breaking bad habits	1.473
bscs3	I am lazy	1.323
bscs4	I say inappropriate things	1.299
bscs5	I do certain things that are bad for me, if they are fun	1.707
bscs6	I refuse things that are bad for me	1.564
bscs7	I wish I had more discipline	1.546
bscs8	People would say that I have iron self-discipline	1.600
bscs9	Pleasure and fun sometimes keep me from getting work done	1.328
bscs10	I have trouble concentrating	1.761
bscs11	I am able to work effectively toward long-term goals	1.290
bscs12	Sometimes I can't stop myself from doing something, even if I know it is wrong	1.287
bscs13	I often act without thinking through all the alternatives	1.697
Health_ Conditions		
diabetes	Do you currently suffer from diabetes?	1.001
cancer	Do you currently suffer from cancer?	1.003
immun_supp	Do you currently suffer from immunosuppression?	1.007
pulmo	Do you currently suffer from pulmonary diseases?	1.009
card	Do you currently suffer from cardiovascular diseases?	1.013
SES		
not_student	Employment condition: student (reversed)	1.119

Table A1. *Cont.*

Latent Variable/Indicator	Description	VIF
wage	Monthly income of your cohabitation (euros): (<500, 500–1000, 1000–2000, 2000–3000, 3000–4000, >4000)	1.044
educ_cat	Educational level (elementary school, secondary school, high school, three-year degree, master's degree, Master/Doctorate/Specialization)	1.092
inc_or_subsid	Earning income or stopped working but getting paid	1.145
Fear_Infection		
seeks_info_ascend	Are you actively searching for information on the progress of the epidemic? (number of positive people, number of deaths, containment policies, etc.)	1.118
feel_dangr	How much do you feel in danger of COVID-19 infection?	1.258
attn_sympt	In the last period, are you paying more attention than usual to your physical symptoms?	1.266
Infraction		
out_not_nec	I only go out when necessary (reversed)	1.005
defy_ban	I go out regularly in defiance of the ban	1.048
wlk_dsp_ban	I happened to go out for a walk indefiance of the ban	1.097
grocry_not_nec	I happened to go to the grocery store without real necessity	1.056
tricks	I am looking for tricks to bypass the ordinances (e.g., I go daily working even if not necessary because I could work from home, I walk around with the dog more times than necessary, I go jogging)	1.183
not_resp_rules	I respect loyally the rules imposed by ministerial ordinances (reversed)	1.206

Appendix B. Stata Code for Models 1 and 2

The following code requires that the plssem package is installed. The data are available from Zenodo (10.5281/zenodo.5523260).

Model 1:

```
plssem (SC > bscs1-bscs13)///
(HealthConds < immun_supp card pulmo cancer diabetes)///
(SES < wage inc_or_subsid educ_cat not_student)///
(Fearinfect > feel_dangr attn_sympt seeks_info_ascend)///
(Infrac > not_resp_rules defy_ban out_not_nec wlk_dsp_ban grocry_not_nec tricks),///
structural(Infrac SC Fearinfect SES HealthConds)///
boot(5000) seed(919) stats maxiter(100)
estat total
```

Model 2:

```
plssem (SC > bscs1-bscs13)///
(HealthConds < immun_supp card pulmo cancer diabetes)///
(SES < wage inc_or_subsid educ_cat not_student)///
(Fearinfect > feel_dangr attn_sympt seeks_info_ascend)///
(Infrac > not_resp_rules defy_ban out_not_nec wlk_dsp_ban grocry_not_nec tricks),///
structural(Infrac SC Fearinfect SES HealthConds,///
Fearinfect HealthConds)///
boot(5000) seed(919) stats maxiter(100)
estat indirect, effects(Infrac Fearinfect HealthConds)///
boot(500) seed(919)
```

References

1. Dong, E.; Du, H.; Gardner, L. An interactive web-based dashboard to track COVID-19 in real time. *Lancet Infect Dis.* **2020**, *20*, 533–534. [CrossRef]
2. Remuzzi, A.; Remuzzi, G. COVID-19 and Italy: What next? *Lancet* **2020**, *395*, 1225–1228. [CrossRef]
3. Flesia, L.; Monaro, M.; Mazza, C.; Fietta, V.; Colicino, E.; Segatto, B.; Roma, P. Predicting Perceived Stress Related to the Covid-19 Outbreak through Stable Psychological Traits and Machine Learning Models. *J. Clin. Med.* **2020**, *9*, 3350. [CrossRef] [PubMed]
4. BBC News. Coronavirus: Italy Takes 'Calculated Risk' in Easing Restrictions—PM: BBC. 2020. Available online: https://www.bbc.com/news/world-europe-52687448 (accessed on 11 June 2020).
5. Flaxman, S.; Mishra, S.; Gandy, A.; Unwin, H.J.T.; Mellan, T.A.; Coupland, H.; Whittaker, C.; Zhu, H.; Berah, T.; Eaton, J.W.; et al. Estimating the effects of non-pharmaceutical interventions on COVID-19 in Europe. *Nature* **2020**, *584*, 257–261. [CrossRef] [PubMed]
6. Baker, S.; Bloom, N.; Davis, S.; Terry, S. *COVID-Induced Economic Uncertainty*; Working Paper 26983; National Bureau of Economic Research: Cambridge, MA, USA, 2020.
7. Killgore, W.D.S.; Cloonan, S.A.; Taylor, E.C.; Dailey, N.S. Loneliness: A signature mental health concern in the era of COVID-19. *Psychiatry Res.* **2020**, *290*, 113117. [CrossRef] [PubMed]
8. Killgore, W.D.S.; Cloonan, S.A.; Taylor, E.C.; Fernandez, F.; Grandner, M.A.; Dailey, N.S. Suicidal ideation during the COVID-19 pandemic: The role of insomnia. *Psychiatry Res.* **2020**, *290*, 113134. [CrossRef] [PubMed]
9. Odriozola-Gonzalez, P.; Planchuelo-Gomez, A.; Irurtia, M.J.; de Luis-Garcia, R. Psychological effects of the COVID-19 outbreak and lockdown among students and workers of a Spanish university. *Psychiatry Res.* **2020**, *290*, 113108. [CrossRef]
10. Pappa, S.; Ntella, V.; Giannakas, T.; Giannakoulis, V.G.; Papoutsi, E.; Katsaounou, P. Prevalence of depression, anxiety, and insomnia among healthcare workers during the COVID-19 pandemic: A systematic review and meta-analysis. *Brain Behav. Immun.* **2020**, *88*, 901–907. [CrossRef] [PubMed]
11. Lowenberg, A.D. Neoclassical Economics as a Theory of Politics and Institutions. *Cato J.* **1990**, *9*, 619–639.
12. Hardin, G. The tragedy of the commons. The population problem has no technical solution; it requires a fundamental extension in morality. *Science* **1968**, *162*, 1243–1248. [CrossRef]
13. Ferrari, J.R.; Stevens, E.B.; Jason, L.A. The Relationship of Self-Control and Abstinence Maintenance: An Exploratory Analysis of Self-Regulation. *J. Groups Addict. Recover.* **2009**, *4*, 32–41. [CrossRef]
14. Lüdecke, D.; von dem Knesebeck, O. Protective behavior in course of the COVID-19 outbreak–survey results from Germany. *Front Public Health.* **2020**, *8*, 1–8. [CrossRef] [PubMed]
15. Kock, N.; Hadaya, P. Minimum sample size estimation in PLS-SEM: The inverse square root and gamma-exponential methods. *Inform. Syst. J.* **2018**, *28*, 227–261. [CrossRef]
16. Tangney, J.P.; Baumeister, R.F.; Boone, A.L. High self-control predicts good adjustment, less pathology, better grades, and interpersonal success. *J. Personal.* **2004**, *72*, 271–324. [CrossRef] [PubMed]
17. Lindner, C.; Nagy, G.; Retelsdorf, J. The dimensionality of the Brief Self-Control Scale-An evaluation of unidimensional and multidimensional applications. *Pers. Indiv. Differ.* **2015**, *86*, 465–473. [CrossRef]
18. Green, L.W. Manual for Scoring Socioeconomic Status for Research on Health Behavior. *Public Health Rep.* **1970**, *85*, 815–827. [CrossRef]
19. Ahorsu, D.K.; Lin, C.Y.; Imani, V.; Saffari, M.; Griffiths, M.D.; Pakpour, A.H. The Fear of COVID-19 Scale: Development and Initial Validation. *Int. J. Ment. Health Addict.* **2020**, 1–9. [CrossRef]
20. Bollen, K.A. Latent variables in psychology and the social sciences. *Annu. Rev. Psychol.* **2002**, *53*, 605–634. [CrossRef] [PubMed]
21. Hair, J.F.; Howard, M.C.; Nitzl, C. Assessing measurement model quality in PLS-SEM using confirmatory composite analysis. *J. Bus. Res.* **2020**, *109*, 101–110. [CrossRef]
22. Bollen, K.A. *Structural Equations with Latent Variables*; Wiley: New York, NY, USA, 1989; Volume XIV, 514p.
23. Rhemtulla, M.; Brosseau-Liard, P.E.; Savalei, V. When Can Categorical Variables Be Treated as Continuous? A Comparison of Robust Continuous and Categorical SEM Estimation Methods Under Suboptimal Conditions. *Psychol. Methods.* **2012**, *17*, 354–373. [CrossRef]
24. Foldnes, N.; Gronneberg, S. Pernicious Polychorics: The Impact and Detection of Underlying Non-normality. *Struct. Equ. Modeling* **2020**, *27*, 525–543. [CrossRef]
25. Hair, J.F.; Hult, G.T.M.; Ringle, C.M.; Sarstedt, M. *A Primer on Partial Least Squares Structural Equation Modeling (PLS-SEM)*, 3rd ed.; SAGE: Los Angeles, CA, USA, 2014.
26. Henseler, J., Jr.; Dijkstra, T. *ADANCO 2.0.*; Composite Modeling: Kleve, Germany, 2015.
27. Hu, L.T.; Bentler, P.M. Fit indices in covariance structure modeling: Sensitivity to underparameterized model misspecification. *Psychol. Methods* **1998**, *3*, 424–453. [CrossRef]
28. Henseler, J., Jr. *Composite-Based Structural Equation Modeling: Analyzing Latent and Emergent Variables*; The Guilford Press: New York, NY, USA, 2021.
29. Hu, L.T.; Bentler, P.M. Cutoff Criteria for Fit Indexes in Covariance Structure Analysis: Conventional Criteria Versus New Alternatives. *Struct. Equ. Modeling* **1999**, *6*, 1–55. [CrossRef]
30. Marks, I.M.; Nesse, R.M. Fear and Fitness—An Evolutionary Analysis of Anxiety Disorders. *Ethol. Sociobiol.* **1994**, *15*, 247–261. [CrossRef]

31. Ackerman, J.M.; Tybur, J.M.; Blackwell, A.D. What Role Does Pathogen-Avoidance Psychology Play in Pandemics? *Trends Cogn. Sci.* **2021**, *25*, 177–186. [CrossRef] [PubMed]
32. Headland, T.N.; Greene, H.W. Hunter-gatherers and other primates as prey, predators, and competitors of snakes. *Proc. Natl. Acad. Sci. USA* **2011**, *108*, E1470–E1474. [CrossRef]
33. Ebrahim, S.H.; Memish, Z.A. COVID-19—the role of mass gatherings. *Travel Med. Infect. Dis.* **2020**, *34*, 101617. [CrossRef]
34. Sit, S.M.; Lam, T.H.; Lai, A.Y.; Wong, B.Y.; Wang, M.P.; Ho, S.Y. Fear of COVID-19 and its associations with perceived personal and family benefits and harms in Hong Kong. *Transl. Behav. Med.* **2021**, *11*, 793–801. [CrossRef]
35. Petersen, M.B. COVID lesson: Trust the public with hard truths. *Nature* **2021**, *598*, 237. [CrossRef] [PubMed]
36. Chae, S.H.; Park, H.J. Effectiveness of Penalties for Lockdown Violations During the COVID-19 Pandemic in Germany. *Am. J. Public Health* **2020**, *110*, 1844–1849. [CrossRef]
37. Gottfredson, M.R.; Hirschi, T. *A General Theory of Crime*; Stanford University Press: Stanford, CA, USA, 1990; Volume XVI, 297p.
38. Moffitt, T.E.; Arseneault, L.; Belsky, D.; Dickson, N.; Hancox, R.J.; Harrington, H.; Houts, R.; Poulton, R.; Roberts, B.W.; Ross, S.; et al. A gradient of childhood self-control predicts health, wealth, and public safety. *Proc. Natl. Acad. Sci. USA* **2011**, *108*, 2693–2698. [CrossRef] [PubMed]
39. Fritz, C.E.; Williams, H.B. The Human Being in Disasters—A Research Perspective. *Ann. Am. Acad. Polit. Soc. Sci.* **1957**, *309*, 42–51. [CrossRef]
40. Gabbiadini, A.; Baldissarri, C.; Durante, F.; Valtorta, R.R.; De Rosa, M.; Gallucci, M. Together Apart: The Mitigating Role of Digital Communication Technologies on Negative Affect During the COVID-19 Outbreak in Italy. *Front. Psychol.* **2020**, *11*, 2763. [CrossRef] [PubMed]
41. Srol, J.; Mikuskova, E.B.; Cavojova, V. When we are worried, what are we thinking? Anxiety, lack of control, and conspiracy beliefs amidst the COVID-19 pandemic. *Appl. Cogn. Psych.* **2021**, *35*, 720–729. [CrossRef] [PubMed]
42. Earnshaw, V.A.; Eaton, L.A.; Kalichman, S.C.; Brousseau, N.M.; Hill, E.C.; Fox, A.B. COVID-19 conspiracy beliefs, health behaviors, and policy support. *Transl. Behav. Med.* **2020**, *10*, 850–856. [CrossRef] [PubMed]
43. Sallam, M.; Dababseh, D.; Yaseen, A.; Al-Haidar, A.; Ababneh, N.A.; Bakri, F.G.; Mahafzah, A. Conspiracy Beliefs Are Associated with Lower Knowledge and Higher Anxiety Levels Regarding COVID-19 among Students at the University of Jordan. *Int. J. Environ. Res. Public Health* **2020**, *17*, 4915. [CrossRef] [PubMed]

International Journal of
Environmental Research and Public Health

MDPI

Article

Generalized Anxiety as a Risk Factor for Dysfunctional Eating Behavior after Obesity Surgery during the COVID-19 Pandemic

Corinna Pfeiffer [1,*], Adam Schweda [1], Lynik Chantal Schüren [2], Marco Niedergethmann [2], Jasmin Steinbach [1], Vanessa Rentrop [1], Anita Robitzsch [1], Nora Dörrie [1], Alexander Bäuerle [1], Martin Teufel [1], Eva-Maria Skoda [1,†] and Benjamin Weismüller [1,†]

1 Clinic for Psychosomatic Medicine and Psychotherapy, LVR-University Hospital Essen, University of Duisburg-Essen, 45147 Essen, Germany; adam.schweda@lvr.de (A.S.); jasmin.steinbach@lvr.de (J.S.); vanessa.rentrop@lvr.de (V.R.); anita.robitzsch@lvr.de (A.R.); nora.doerrie@lvr.de (N.D.); alexander.baeuerle@uni-due.de (A.B.); martin.teufel@uni-due.de (M.T.); eva-maria.skoda@uni-due.de (E.-M.S.); benjaminmaurice.weismueller@lvr.de (B.W.)
2 Department of Surgery, Alfried-Krupp Hospital Essen, 45131 Essen, Germany; lynik.schueren@krupp-krankenhaus.de (L.C.S.); marco.niedergethmann@krupp-krankenhaus.de (M.N.)
* Correspondence: corinna.pfeiffer@uni-due.de
† These authors contributed equally to this study.

Abstract: Purpose: The present study investigates the impact of obesity surgery on mental health (i.e., eating behavior and distress) during the COVID-19 pandemic. **Methods:** Two hundred fifty-four participants were recruited via social media. One hundred fourteen (44.53%) of them were surgery candidates (waiting for obesity surgery), while 142 (55.46%) had already undergone surgery. Participants who underwent surgery were compared to participants that did not yet undergo surgery in terms of mental burden (depression and anxiety), as well as safety and eating behavior. Further moderation analyses attempted to identify risk factors for increased COVID-19-related dysfunctional eating behavior after surgery. **Results:** Participants who underwent surgery showed generally lower levels of depression and general anxiety on a trend level. Moderation analyses suggested that people with high levels of generalized anxiety actually show more dysfunctional COVID-19-specific eating behavior after obesity surgery. **Conclusion:** On a trend level, obesity surgery appears to attenuate symptoms of generalized anxiety and depression. Yet, surgery patients with high levels of generalized anxiety exhibit even higher levels of dysfunctional eating during the COVID-19 pandemic. It is therefore particularly important to support people at risk.

Keywords: anxiety; obesity; eating disorder; obesity surgery; COVID-19; mental health

Citation: Pfeiffer, C.; Schweda, A.; Schüren, L.C.; Niedergethmann, M.; Steinbach, J.; Rentrop, V.; Robitzsch, A.; Dörrie, N.; Bäuerle, A.; Teufel, M.; et al. Generalized Anxiety as a Risk Factor for Dysfunctional Eating Behavior after Obesity Surgery during the COVID-19 Pandemic. *Int. J. Environ. Res. Public Health* **2021**, *18*, 10890. https://doi.org/10.3390/ijerph182010890

Academic Editors: Paolo Roma, Merylin Monaro and Cristina Mazza

Received: 17 September 2021
Accepted: 11 October 2021
Published: 16 October 2021

1. Introduction

In March 2020, the World Health Organization declared the spread of the novel coronavirus a worldwide pandemic [1]. Until then, obesity had long been named the worst pandemic of the 21st century and caused more deaths than being underweight worldwide [2]. Since 1975, the prevalence of obesity nearly tripled [2]. Six hundred fifty-nine million adults (18 years and older) were obese in 2017, leading to over 4 million overweight-related deaths, according to the global burden of disease report [3]. Recent studies on COVID-19 showed that obesity worsens the outcome from COVID-19 [4] and that mortality increases as a function of the body mass index (BMI) [5–8], thus making people suffering from obesity highly at risk for a severe course of disease.

Obese individuals are known to suffer more often than normal-weight controls from a variety of mental comorbidities such as depression, anxiety disorders or eating disorders, and reduced health-related quality of life [9–12]. A bi-directional link of obesity and depression can be found throughout various studies, showing that obese patients are more depressed and vice versa [13]. Emotional distress and impaired self-management may lead to a loss of structure and a relapse into old behavioral patterns, eventually resulting in weight gain [14]. Additionally, heightened mental stress and problems in emotion regulation trigger impulsive eating symptoms such as binge eating and purging behavior [15,16]. This makes the group of patients suffering from obesity at high risk for elevated levels of psychological burden. Recent studies show the COVID-19 pandemic put a high mental strain not only on the general population but even more so on already psychologically burdened individuals. Patients suffering from obesity seem to be even more at risk for COVID-19-associated psychological burden [17,18]. A retrospective medical chart review showed that since stay-at-home orders were initiated because of the COVID-19 pandemic, patients with obesity reported increased anxiety and depression regardless of infection status [19]. Another study showed that people with obesity had a significant increase in weight, BMI, and changes in the eating psychopathology during the COVID-19 pandemic [20]. These findings not only underlined obese individuals' risk of various somatic and psychological comorbidities, but also suggested a high-risk status in the current COVID-19-pandemic.

In Western countries, obesity surgery is the most common treatment for patients with BMI ≥ 40 kg/m^2 or BMI ≥ 35 kg/m^2 who also suffer from obesity-related comorbidities and did not respond to behavioral treatment, exercises, and nutritional treatment [21,22]. A recent RCT found that obesity surgery candidates seem to suffer from equally elevated levels of depression as psychotherapy inpatients, making this group also prone to heightened psychological strain during the current pandemic [23]. Findings from before the COVID-19 pandemic showed that for most of these patients, mental health improves after obesity surgery even if the mechanism and the psychological factors remain unclear [24,25]. Although dysfunctional eating behaviors decreased directly after obesity surgery between the first and third year after the intervention, dysfunctional eating behavior significantly increases again [26]. Weight loss as a result of obesity surgery does not mean an improvement in mental health at the same time, as the expectations of a life-changing measure can be exaggerated and frustrating [27].

Literature is lacking on the impact of obesity surgery in obese individuals concerning eating behavior and the psychological distress during the COVID-19 pandemic. Restrictions in social life due to quarantine measures, physical distancing, and COVID-19-related fear may pose a special burden for this vulnerable patient group. The aim of the current study was to investigate to what extent obesity surgery affects COVID-19-related eating behavior, generalized anxiety, depression, and psychological distress. It is hypothesized that obesity surgery significantly affects dysfunctional eating behavior, bulimic eating behavior, anxiety, and depression during the current COVID-19 pandemic. More precisely, patients probably suffer less from dysfunctional COVID-19-specific eating behaviors, anxiety, and depression after they obtained an obesity surgery compared to a group of obese people that are still awaiting such a surgical measure.

2. Method

2.1. Participants and Procedure

Participants were recruited online from a German obesity center of excellence and via social media from 10 May to 7 July 2020. Two hundred fifty-four participants (223 female, 31 male) completed the study: 114 participants (99 female, 15 male) did not (yet) have an obesity surgery, while 140 (124 female, 16 male) did already undergo obesity surgery. Mann–Whitney tests did not reveal significant gender differences between the with and without surgery groups ($U = 8070.00$, $p = 0.944$), but difference in age between surgery groups was significant ($U = 6764.50$, $p = 0.019$). Table 1 lists all sociodemographic and medical data, including age and gender distributions of both groups. Electronic informed consent was given and confirmed by all participants. Participation was voluntary and anonymous, and participants could withdraw from the study at any time. The proposed study was conducted in accordance with the Declaration of Helsinki, and the local Ethics Committee of the Medical Faculty approved this study (20-9307-BO).

Table 1. Sociodemographic characteristics separately for both groups (with and without surgery).

	Without Surgery		With Surgery		
	N	%	N	%	p-Value
Sex					
Female	99	86.8	124	87.3	
Male	15	13.2	16	11.3	0.821
Age					
18–24 years	5	4.4	1	0.7	
25–34 years	26	22.8	27	19	
35–44 years	45	39.5	52	36.6	
45–54 years	26	22.8	30	21.1	
55–64 years	11	9.6	25	17.6	
65–74 years	1	0.9	5	3.5	
≥75 years	0	0	2	1.4	0.100
Marital status					
Single	24	21.1	30	21.1	
Married	61	53.5	70	49.3	
In a relationship	16	14	27	19	
Divorced/separated	12	10.5	8	5.6	
Widowed	1	0.9	4	2.8	0.371
Educational level					
University education	12	10.5	20	14.1	
Higher education entrance qualification	33	28.9	32	22.5	
Higher secondary education	42	36.8	63	44.4	
Lower secondary education	22	19.3	25	17.6	0.460
Employment					
Employed	63	55.3	98	69	
Not employed	37	32.5	44	31	0.402
City size (Population)					
100,000 residents	65	57	85	59.9	
20,000 residents	21	18.4	25	17.6	
5000 residents	18	15.8	14	9.9	
<5000 residents	10	8.8	18	12.7	0.428
Mental illness					
yes	34	29.8	42	29.6	
no	80	70.2	100	70.4	1.000
Somatic illness					
none	15	13.2	29	20.4	0.172
Cardiovascular disease	11	9.6	6	4.2	0.271
Diabetes mellitus	23	20.2	28	19.7	1.000
Chronic respiratory disease	24	21.1	26	18.3	0.695
Hypertension	56	49.1	47	33.1	0.014
Intermittent claudication	1	0.9	3	2.1	0.776
Sleep apnea	21	18.4	25	17.6	0.996
Lip-metabolic disorder	12	10.5	14	9.9	1.000
Articular gout	11	9.6	13	3.2	1.000
Hypothyroidism	35	30.7	44	31	0.142
Polycystic ovary syndrome	8	7	11	7.7	1.000
Arthropathy	41	36	49	34.5	0.912
other	18	15.8	26	18.3	0.715
Total	114	100	142	100	

2.2. Measures

Demographic information such as the participant's age (see above), gender (male; female; other), community size, education, and their current occupation were assessed. Then, validated instruments and self-generated scales assessed psychological states and psychological reactions to COVID-19. Weight and height were also assessed. Mental burdens during the previous two weeks were measured using the Patient Health Questionnaire-2 (PHQ-8, measuring depression symptoms with two items on a four-point Likert Scale [28,29]) and the Generalized Anxiety Disorder-7 (GAD-7, measuring generalized anxiety using seven items on a four-point Likert Scale [30,31]). To measure specific COVID-19-related fear, one single seven-point Likert-scaled item was used (for further information see [32]). Additionally, participants were asked about changes in their general eating behavior since the start of the COVID-19 pandemic in Europe. In 10 self-generated items, participants indicated whether they observed themselves eating more or less, shopping for more groceries, eating more fast food, and eating larger portions on a seven-point Likert Scale (see Supplementary Material for specific wording and factorial analyses). These items were then summarized in one scale indicating dysfunctional COVID-19-specific eating behavior (DCSEB).

2.3. Data Analysis

To assess normality, distributions of all analyzed variables were visually assessed and tested using Kolmogorov–Smirnov tests. Indeed, this approach revealed that all of the tested variables significantly deviated from the normal distribution in both sample groups (all *ps* < 0.007). Accordingly, predominantly non-parametric as well as robust approaches were applied throughout the entire analysis. In order to extract a meaningful scale to express a rise in increased and more unhealthy food intake during the COVID-19 pandemic, a factorial analysis was applied to the 10 items measuring COVID-19-specific eating behavior (DCSEB). Self-generated items for *dysfunctional safety behavior* have been intensively discussed in previous studies by our group (please see [33]). Cronbach's α for *dysfunctional safety behavior* in the current sample was 0.794.

To test univariate associations between COVID-19-related variables—*generalized anxiety, depression, dysfunctional COVID-19-related eating behavior*, and *dysfunctional safety behavior*—Spearman correlation coefficients were computed. To further explore whether obesity surgery had an influence on the respective psychopathological dimension (PHQ-8, GAD-7), COVID-19-related fear, and dysfunctional COVID-19-related eating behavior (DCSEB), group differences (with vs. without surgery) were assessed via Mann–Whitney U tests. Separate robust regression analyses—as implemented in the R package *robustbase* [34]—were then computed to assess whether the associations between *DCSEB* and COVID-19-related fear, depression, and anxiety symptoms (PHQ-8 and GAD-7) are moderated by obesity surgery. To do so, the respective psychological variable, the group variable (*with* and *without* obesity surgery), as well as their interaction coefficients were regressed on *DCSEB*. A full summary of regression coefficients is provided in the Supplemental Materials. The data were analyzed using IBM Statistics SPSS 26 (New York, NY, USA) and R (3.6.3).

3. Results

First, a factorial analysis was performed to extract an interpretable measure of increased and more unhealthy food intake during the COVID-19 pandemic ("dysfunctional COVID-19-specific eating behavior", DCSEB). A parallel analysis, as well as Velicer's minimum average partial (Velicer, 1976), were applied to extract the optimal number of factors. Both analyses convergingly indicated the existence of one factor. Within this one factor (proportion of explained variance = 36%), four items reached standardized factor loadings of above 0.6 (Awang, 2014, Hair, 2008; see Supplemental Material). These items assess whether the individual started to eat larger portions more frequently in an unhealthier fashion, and whether they fell back into old eating patterns. Kaiser–Meyer–Olkin measures of sampling adequacy indicate values of above 0.8 for each item; sum scores were applied to subsequently summarize the scale.

Spearman correlation analyses revealed significant associations between *DCSEB* and *COVID-19-related fear* ($r = 0.167$; $p = 0.008$), *DCSEB* and *generalized anxiety* ($r = 0.396$; $p < 0.001$), and *DCSEB* and depression symptoms ($r = 0.496$; $p < 0.001$). For an overview of all correlation coefficients, see Tables S1 and S2 in the supplementary online material. To explore possible effects of obesity surgery on the psychopathological states and eating behavior, Mann–Whitney U tests were computed to identify differences between groups (*with* and *without* surgery) in each of the psychometric scales mentioned above. These Mann–Whitney U tests revealed no significant differences in the tested variables: *COVID-19-related fear* ($W = 8288$, $p = 0.739$), *dysfunctional safety behavior* ($W = 8695.5$, $p = 0.305$), and *DCSEB* ($W = 8431.5$, $p = 0.566$). However, *p*-values approached significance at $\alpha = 0.05$ for the comparisons between participants with and without obesity surgery in *generalized anxiety* ($W = 9180$, $p = 0.064$) *and depression symptoms* ($W = 9186$, $p = 0.057$), and participants who underwent obesity surgery exhibited lower levels in each of these dimensions. Table 2 lists the psychometric data for the obesity patients *with* and *without* obesity-specific surgery.

Table 2. Psychometric data for the obesity patients with and without an obesity-specific surgery. Mean sum scores and standard deviations (in parentheses) are listed.

	Without Surgery	With Surgery
N	114	142
Weight	132.72 (31.57)	101.43 (22.26)
Body Mass	45.59 (10.49)	35.49 (8.96)
COVID-19-related fear	4.21 (1.95)	4.14 (1.89)
Generalized anxiety (GAD-7)	7.21 (5.19)	6.37 (6.00)
Depression symptoms (PHQ-8)	9.02 (5.19)	8.00 (6.58)
Dysfunctional safety behavior	3.27 (1.57)	3.11 (1.61)
Dysfunctional COVID-19-specific eating behavior (DCSEB)	14.69 (6.23)	14.22 (7.50)

Note: Generalized anxiety was measured by GAD-7 (7 items, 4-point Likert scale, cut-off mild = 5, cut-off moderate = 10); depression symptoms were measured by PHQ-8 (8 items, 4-point Likert scale, cut-off ≥ 10), COVID-19-related fear, dysfunctional safety behavior, Dysfunctional COVID-19-specific eating behavior (DCSEB, see Supplementary online Material). Body mass was computed using the formula weight in kg/(height in m)^2.

To assess whether obesity surgery moderates the relationship between the above-described psychological dimensions and *DSCEB*, robust regression analyses were conducted for each possible predictor, using *group* (*with* vs. *without* surgery) as a moderator and *DCSEB* as the dependent variable. The strongest interest was to reveal unconditional relationships so that one regression model was computed for each predictor.

This moderator analysis revealed a significant interaction between the predictors *generalized anxiety* and group (with vs. without surgery, $b = 0.289$; $p = 0.028$, see supplemental material for illustration of the marginal effects) on *DCSEB*. The regression coefficient for generalized anxiety turned out significant ($b = 0.227$, $p = 0.025$). No differences occurred in the direct comparison between patients with and without surgery ($b = -0.003$, $p = 0.983$). The regression model accounted for 16.6% of variance. This pattern—and particularly the interaction between group and generalized anxiety—remained robust after conditioning on age, gender, and education. No other significant interaction appeared in these regression models (see supplemental online material). To further illustrate this effect, participants were divided according to common cutoffs for the GAD-7, namely participants who show no anxiety (GAD-7 score below five), people who exhibit mild anxiety (GAD-7 scores from five to nine), and participants who report moderate to severe anxiety (GAD-7 scores from 10 to 21, see [35]). The moderating effect of generalized anxiety on DCSEB before and after surgery is shown in Figure 1. Corroboratory results from a further robust regression analysis that included the categorized GAD-7 values (no anxiety vs. mild anxiety vs. moderate to severe anxiety), the group variable (with vs. without surgery), and their interaction term also indicated that while levels of DCSEB remained unchanged for individuals with surgery compared to individuals without surgery in participants with low and mild anxiety levels, participants with high anxiety showed even more DCSEB after surgery (interaction term between surgery [reference: without surgery] and GAD-7 [dummy: mild anxiety with reference: no anxiety]: $b = 0.049$, $se = 0.286$, t (250) = 0.170, $p = 0.865$; interaction term between surgery [reference: without surgery] and GAD-7 [dummy: moderate and severe anxiety with reference: no anxiety]).

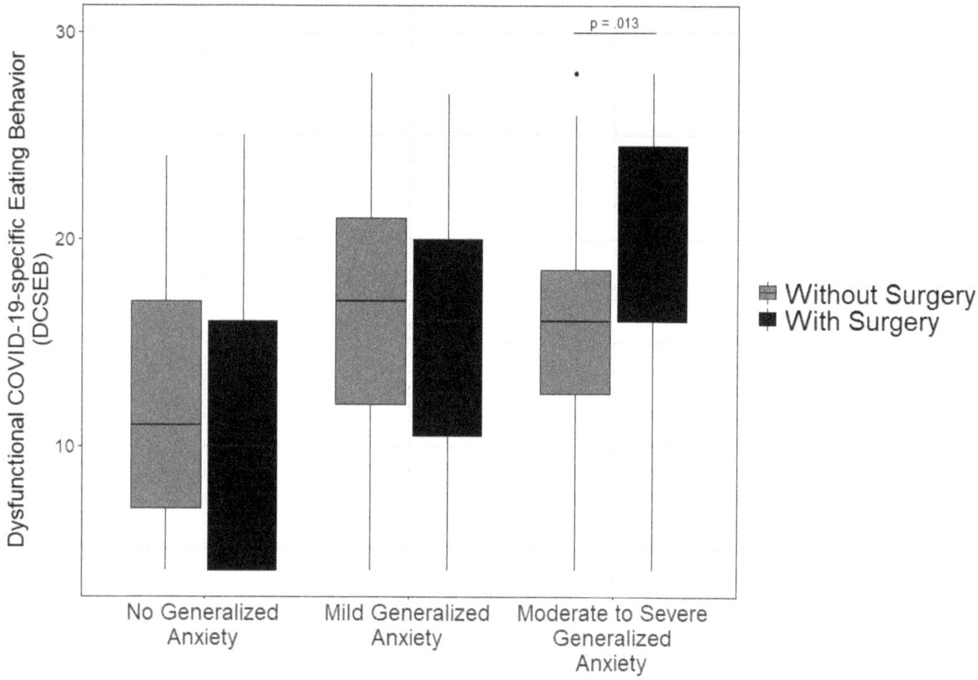

Figure 1. Generalized anxiety as a risk factor for increased levels of dysfunctional COVID-19-specific eating after obesity surgery. Group-wise box-plots indicate medians and interquartile ranges (see supplemental material for illustration of non-splitted continuous data). While for participants with no or mild manifestations of generalized anxiety (GAD-17 scores of 0 to 4, or 5 to 9, respectively), no increase in DCSEB is notable, and individuals with moderate to severe levels of anxiety (GAD-7 > 9) show increased DCSEB after obesity surgery. Whiskers extend to the most extreme data point unless there are data 1.5 inter-quartile-ranges away from the first or the third quartile, respectively. Data points beyond that are shown as a black dot.

4. Discussion

The present study is, to our knowledge, one of the first to investigate the influence of obesity surgery on psychological burden in patients with obesity. We analyzed possible effects of obesity surgery during the COVID-19 pandemic on mental health burden (PHQ-8, GAD-7, COVID-19-related fear, DCSEB) by comparing patients *with* and *without* obesity surgery. In general, group comparisons showed no differences between these groups, suggesting that the surgery did not affect any psychological state. The two groups only differ at a trend level in generalized anxiety and depressive symptoms, suggesting a slightly increased burden in individuals without surgery. More precisely, in individuals that do not suffer (much) from generalized anxiety, DCSEB does not differ across obesity surgery groups (*with* or *without*). In contrast, people that do suffer from generalized anxiety differ in their DCSEB depending on their obesity surgery status (*with* or *without*), with more DCSEB in people with a surgery. Accordingly, generalized anxiety moderates DCSEB after obesity surgery. The interaction between generalized anxiety and history of obesity surgery shows that people with obesity already suffering from generalized anxiety symptoms and/or bulimic eating seem to suffer even more compared to people who already underwent the surgery during the pandemic. Thus, generalized anxiety seems to be a risk factor for dysfunctional eating behavior after obesity surgery during the COVID-19 pandemic.

The COVID-19 pandemic still has a deep impact on our social life, quality of life, and mental health [18,36]. COVID-19-related fear and generalized anxiety, particularly for vulnerable individuals, play decisive roles in mental health during the pandemic [17,32,37,38].

Meanwhile, anxiety is linked to all types of eating disorders [39,40] and is the most prevalent emotion obese people with a binge eating disorder experience prior to a binge [41]. The frequency of binge eating episodes is higher in patients with higher anxiety scores than in grade III obesity patients [42–44]. Thus, negative emotions seem to be controlled and regulated by activating the neuronal reward system during the consumption of palatable foods [45,46].

In times of increased mental distress caused by the COVID-19 pandemic, the access to protective resources could be difficult so that people may fall back into old behaviors using the same emotion regulation strategies as before the pandemic. This means that, on one hand, obesity surgery does not offer an increased stress resilience during the COVID-19 pandemic and, on the other hand, mentally stable people who underwent obesity surgery will continue to do so even in times of crisis. For those who already suffer from mental illnesses or instability, mental decompensation can occur more quickly in times of mental distress because of the COVID-19 pandemic. Thus, psychosocial evaluation and support is of particular importance for obesity patients prior to surgery in order to avoid possible dysfunctional stress regulation, consecutive weight gain, and eventually the deterioration of long-term results [47,48]. Before the pandemic, studies showed that in most patients, mental health improved after obesity surgery even in patients with previous psychiatric illnesses. However, underlying mechanisms and psychological factors remain unclear [24,25,49]. Individual psychological resources seem to be one important protective factor for mental health in people suffering from obesity [50].

These results once again underline the need and importance for structured interdisciplinary aftercare in the group of obesity surgical patients suffering from psychological distress during the COVID-19 pandemic, including psychotherapeutic and psychosocial support. Low-threshold support services are required, such as evidence-based cognitive behavioral emotion regulation skills like stress management, meditation, physical exercise, stimulus control, etc. These could increase the likelihood that mental illnesses will turn chronic [51]. Emerging E-mental health interventions could be a helpful tool and an addition to support people with psychological burden [52]. Special consideration should be given to find tailor-made interventions and aftercare support towards patients who continue to show compensatory eating behavior postoperatively in the context of psychological distress.

4.1. Limitations

First, this study was a cross-sectional study, not a repeated-measurements design, so no causality can be directly inferred from the data regarding obesity surgery. However, as many other relevant variables have been measured and controlled across both groups, moderation effects of the surgery in the present sample can still be interpreted. Then, the presented data were collected by an online questionnaire, which necessarily holds some limitations. For instance, participant response rates cannot be controlled so that a participant bias seems plausible. In consequence, this lack of participant control may influence the results' generalizability. Furthermore, the possibility of selection bias should be considered.

Last, psychological COVID-19-specific traits reported here were not measured by validated instruments, simply because none existed to that date. Ahorsu et al. [53] created the first questionnaire to assess COVID-19-related fear after the present survey had been launched—the Preventive COVID-19 Behavior Scale (PCV-19BS, see [53,54]). Thus, COVID-

19-related fear and DSCED were self-generated items or at least adapted to assess COVID-19-specific traits. As can be seen in previous studies [17,18,33,54], however, this COVID-19-related fear item qualifies relatively well to assess fear, but not generalized anxiety, at the time of the pandemic. Despite being the first study on the influence of obesity surgery on COVID-19 distress, the study is limited in terms of gender differences. Of course, additional factors such as the connection to an obesity center should be considered.

4.2. Conclusions

After obesity surgery, patients can be at risk to be additionally challenged by the pandemic. Psychosocial support is of particular importance for people who already suffer from mental illness to achieve stress resistance, mental health, and weight goals and not to relapse in overcome behaviors. Therefore, it is important to ensure medical, psychological, and surgical care and support for patients with obesity during the COVID-19 pandemic to assure equal opportunities regarding upcoming health challenges.

Supplementary Materials: The following are available online at https://www.mdpi.com/article/10.3390/ijerph182010890/s1, Table S1: The full reports of our regression analyses, Table S2: Correlation Matrix.

Author Contributions: C.P. planning, data collection, study design, data analysis and interpretation, and manuscript writing. A.S. data analysis and interpretation, data interpretation and editing. L.C.S. was co-responsible for the recruitment of the participants. M.N., J.S., V.R., A.R., N.D., A.B. and M.T. data interpretation review and editing. E.-M.S. and B.W. planning, study design, and supervision. All authors contributed to the article and approved the submitted version. All authors have read and agreed to the published version of the manuscript.

Funding: The Open Access Fund of the University of Duisburg-Essen funded the publication of the study. The funder had no role in the design and conduct of the study; management, collection, analysis, and interpretation of the data; preparation, review, or approval of the manuscript and decision to submit the manuscript for publication.

Institutional Review Board Statement: The study was conducted according to the guidelines of the Declaration of Helsinki and approved by the Ethics Committee of the Medical Faculty of Duisburg-Essen (20-9307-BO).

Informed Consent Statement: Informed consent was obtained from all subjects involved in the study.

Data Availability Statement: The raw data will be made available upon reasonable request to the correspondent author.

Conflicts of Interest: The authors declare no conflict of interest.

References

1. World Health Organization. WHO Director-General's Remarks at the Media Briefing on 2019-nCoV on 11 February 2020. Available online: https://www.who.int/dg/speeches/detail/who-director-general-s-remarks-at-the-media-briefing-on-2019-ncov-on-11-february-2020 (accessed on 23 June 2021).
2. World Health Organization. Obesity and Overweight. Available online: https://www.who.int/news-room/fact-sheets/detail/obesity-and-overweight (accessed on 23 June 2021).
3. Afshin, A.; Forouzanfar, M.H.; Reitsma, M.B.; Sur, P.; Estep, K.; Lee, A.; Marczak, L.; Mokdad, A.H.; Moradi-Lakeh, M.; Naghavi, M.; et al. Health Effects of Overweight and Obesity in 195 Countries over 25 Years. *N. Engl. J. Med.* **2017**, *377*, 13–27. [CrossRef] [PubMed]
4. Dietz, W.; Santos-Burgoa, C. Obesity and its implications for COVID-19 mortality. *Obesity* **2020**, *28*, 1005. [CrossRef] [PubMed]
5. Capelo, A.; Da Fonseca, V.; Peixoto, M.; de Carvalho, S.; Azevedo, C.; Elsas, M.; Marques, B. Visceral adiposity is associated with cytokines and decrease in lung function in women with persistent asthma. *Rev. Port. Pneumol.* **2016**, *22*, 255–261. [CrossRef] [PubMed]
6. Muniyappa, R.; Gubbi, S. COVID-19 pandemic, coronaviruses, and diabetes mellitus. *Am. J. Physiol.-Endocrinol. Metab.* **2020**, *318*, E736–E741. [CrossRef] [PubMed]
7. Simonnet, A.; Chetboun, M.; Poissy, J.; Raverdy, V.; Noulette, J.; Duhamel, A.; Labreuche, J.; Mathieu, D.; Pattou, F.; Jourdain, M. High prevalence of obesity in severe acute respiratory syndrome coronavirus-2 (SARS-CoV-2) requiring invasive mechanical ventilation. *Obesity* **2020**, *28*, 1195–1199. [CrossRef] [PubMed]

8. Tartof, S.Y.; Qian, L.; Hong, V.; Wei, R.; Nadjafi, R.F.; Fischer, H.; Li, Z.; Shaw, S.F.; Caparosa, S.L.; Nau, C.L. Obesity and mortality among patients diagnosed with COVID-19: Results from an integrated health care organization. *Ann. Intern. Med.* **2020**, *173*, 773–781. [CrossRef]
9. Mack, I.; Olschlager, S.; Sauer, H.; von Feilitzsch, M.; Weimer, K.; Junne, F.; Peeraully, R.; Enck, P.; Zipfel, S.; Teufel, M. Does Laparoscopic Sleeve Gastrectomy Improve Depression, Stress and Eating Behaviour? A 4-Year Follow-up Study. *Obes. Surg.* **2016**, *26*, 2967–2973. [CrossRef]
10. Rajan, T.; Menon, V. Psychiatric disorders and obesity: A review of association studies. *J. Postgrad. Med.* **2017**, *63*, 182.
11. Sheehan, D.V.; Herman, B.K. The Psychological and Medical Factors Associated With Untreated Binge Eating Disorder. *Prim. Care Companion. CNS Disord.* **2015**. [CrossRef]
12. Simon, G.E.; Von Korff, M.; Saunders, K.; Miglioretti, D.L.; Crane, P.K.; van Belle, G.; Kessler, R.C. Association between obesity and psychiatric disorders in the US adult population. *Arch. Gen. Psychiatry* **2006**, *63*, 824–830. [CrossRef]
13. Luppino, F.S.; de Wit, L.M.; Bouvy, P.F.; Stijnen, T.; Cuijpers, P.; Penninx, B.W.; Zitman, F.G. Overweight, obesity, and depression: A systematic review and meta-analysis of longitudinal studies. *Arch. Gen. Psychiatry* **2010**, *67*, 220–229. [CrossRef]
14. Sockalingam, S.; Leung, S.E.; Cassin, S.E. The impact of coronavirus disease 2019 on bariatric surgery: Redefining psychosocial care. *Obesity* **2020**, *28*, 1010–1012. [CrossRef]
15. Braden, A.; Musher-Eizenman, D.; Watford, T.; Emley, E. Eating when depressed, anxious, bored, or happy: Are emotional eating types associated with unique psychological and physical health correlates? *Appetite* **2018**, *125*, 410–417. [CrossRef]
16. Kelly, N.R.; Tanofsky-Kraff, M.; Vannucci, A.; Ranzenhofer, L.M.; Altschul, A.M.; Schvey, N.A.; Shank, L.M.; Brady, S.M.; Galescu, O.; Kozlosky, M. Emotion dysregulation and loss-of-control eating in children and adolescents. *Health Psychol.* **2016**, *35*, 1110. [CrossRef]
17. Bäuerle, A.; Teufel, M.; Musche, V.; Weismüller, B.; Kohler, H.; Hetkamp, M.; Dörrie, N.; Schweda, A.; Skoda, E.-M. Increased generalized anxiety, depression and distress during the COVID-19 pandemic: A cross-sectional study in Germany. *J. Public Health* **2020**, *42*, 672–678. [CrossRef] [PubMed]
18. Skoda, E.-M.; Bäuerle, A.; Schweda, A.; Dörrie, N.; Musche, V.; Hetkamp, M.; Kohler, H.; Teufel, M.; Weismüller, B. Severely increased generalized anxiety, but not COVID-19-related fear in individuals with mental illnesses: A population based cross-sectional study in Germany. *Int. J. Soc. Psychiatry* **2020**, *67*, 0020764020960773. [CrossRef]
19. Almandoz, J.P.; Xie, L.; Schellinger, J.N.; Mathew, M.S.; Gazda, C.; Ofori, A.; Kukreja, S.; Messiah, S.E. Impact of COVID-19 stay-at-home orders on weight-related behaviours among patients with obesity. *Clin. Obes.* **2020**, *10*, e12386. [CrossRef] [PubMed]
20. Fernández-Aranda, F.; Munguía, L.; Mestre-Bach, G.; Steward, T.; Etxandi, M.; Baenas, I.; Granero, R.; Sánchez, I.; Ortega, E.; Andreu, A. COVID Isolation Eating Scale (CIES): Analysis of the impact of confinement in eating disorders and obesity—A collaborative international study. *Eur. Eat. Disord. Rev.* **2020**, *28*, 871–883. [CrossRef] [PubMed]
21. Nguyen, N.T.; Varela, J.E. Bariatric surgery for obesity and metabolic disorders: State of the art. *Nat. Rev. Gastroenterol. Hepatol.* **2017**, *14*, 160. [CrossRef] [PubMed]
22. Deutsche Gesellschaft für Allgemein- und Viszeralchirurgie. S3-Leitlinie: Chirurgie der Adipositas und metabolischer Erkrankungen. Available online: https://www.awmf.org/uploads/tx_szleitlinien/088-001l_S3_Chirurgie-Adipositasmetabolische-Erkrankungen_2018-02.pdf (accessed on 23 June 2021).
23. Osterhues, A.; von Lengerke, T.; Mall, J.W.; de Zwaan, M.; Müller, A. Health-Related Quality of Life, Anxiety, and Depression in Bariatric Surgery Candidates Compared to Patients from a Psychosomatic Inpatient Hospital. *Obes. Surg.* **2017**, *27*, 2378–2387. [CrossRef] [PubMed]
24. Behrens, S.C.; Lenhard, K.; Junne, F.; Ziser, K.; Lange, J.; Zipfel, S.; Giel, K.E.; Teufel, M.; Mack, I. Effects of Bariatric Surgery on Depression: Role of Body Image. *Obes. Surg.* **2021**, *31*, 1864–1868. [CrossRef]
25. Wimmelmann, C.L.; Dela, F.; Mortensen, E.L. Psychological predictors of mental health and health-related quality of life after bariatric surgery: A review of the recent research. *Obes. Res. Clin. Pract.* **2014**, *8*, e314–e324. [CrossRef]
26. Nasirzadeh, Y.; Kantarovich, K.; Wnuk, S.; Okrainec, A.; Cassin, S.E.; Hawa, R.; Sockalingam, S. Binge Eating, Loss of Control over Eating, Emotional Eating, and Night Eating After Bariatric Surgery: Results from the To-ronto Bari-PSYCH Cohort Study. *Obes. Surg.* **2018**, *28*, 2032–2039. [CrossRef]
27. Kubik, J.F.; Gill, R.S.; Laffin, M.; Karmali, S. The impact of bariatric surgery on psychological health. *J. Obes.* **2013**, *2013*, 837989. [CrossRef]
28. Arroll, B.; Goodyear-Smith, F.; Crengle, S.; Gunn, J.; Kerse, N.; Fishman, T.; Falloon, K.; Hatcher, S. Validation of PHQ-2 and PHQ-9 to screen for major depression in the primary care population. *Ann. Fam. Med.* **2010**, *8*, 348–353. [CrossRef] [PubMed]
29. Kroenke, K.; Spitzer, R.L.; Williams, J.B. The Patient Health Questionnaire-2: Validity of a two-item depression screener. *Med. Care* **2003**, *41*, 1284–1292. [CrossRef] [PubMed]
30. Kertz, S.; Bigda-Peyton, J.; Bjorgvinsson, T. Validity of the Generalized Anxiety Disorder-7 Scale in an acute psychiatric sample. *Clin. Psychol. Psychother.* **2013**, *20*, 456–464. [CrossRef] [PubMed]
31. Löwe, B.; Decker, O.; Müller, S.; Brähler, E.; Schellberg, D.; Herzog, W.; Herzberg, P.Y. Validation and standardization of the Generalized Anxiety Disorder Screener (GAD-7) in the general population. *Med. Care* **2008**, *46*, 266–274. [CrossRef]
32. Bäuerle, A.; Steinbach, J.; Schweda, A.; Beckord, J.; Hetkamp, M.; Weismüller, B.; Kohler, H.; Musche, V.; Dörrie, N.; Teufel, M. Mental health burden of the COVID-19 outbreak in germany: Predictors of mental health impairment. *J. Prim. Care Community Health* **2020**, *11*, 2150132720953682. [CrossRef] [PubMed]

33. Weismüller, B.; Schweda, A.; Dörrie, N.; Musche, V.; Fink, M.; Kohler, H.; Skoda, E.M.; Teufel, M.; Bäuerle, A. Different Correlates of COVID-19-Related Adherent and Dysfunctional Safety Behavior. *Front. Public Health* **2020**, *8*, 625664. [CrossRef]
34. Maechler, M.; Rousseeuw, P.; Croux, C.; Todorov, V.; Ruckstuhl, A.; Salibian-Barrera, M.; Verbeke, T.; Koller, M.; Conceicao, E.L.; di Palma, M.A. Package 'robustbase'. Basic Robust Stat. Available online: https://cran.r-project.org/web/packages/robustbase/index.html (accessed on 10 October 2021).
35. Spitzer, R.L.; Kroenke, K.; Williams, J.B.; Lowe, B. A brief measure for assessing generalized anxiety disorder: The GAD-7. *Arch. Intern. Med.* **2006**, *166*, 1092–1097. [CrossRef]
36. Ravens-Sieberer, U.; Kaman, A.; Erhart, M.; Devine, J.; Schlack, R.; Otto, C. Impact of the COVID-19 pandemic on quality of life and mental health in children and adolescents in Germany. *Eur. Child. Adolesc. Psychiatry* **2021**, *25*, 1–11.
37. Montemurro, N. The emotional impact of COVID-19: From medical staff to common people. *BrainBehav. Immun.* **2020**, *87*, 23–24. [CrossRef]
38. Rajkumar, R.P. COVID-19 and mental health: A review of the existing literature. *Asian J. Psychiatry* **2020**, *52*, 102066. [CrossRef]
39. Bulik, C.M.; Sullivan, P.F.; Fear, J.; Joyce, P.R. Eating disorders and antecedent anxiety disorders: A controlled study. *Acta Psychiatr. Scand.* **1997**, *96*, 101–107. [CrossRef]
40. Kaye, W.; Bulik, C.; Thornton, L.; Barbarich, N.; Masters, K.; Group PFC. Comorbidity of anxiety disorders with anorexia and bulimia nervosa. *Am. J. Psychiatry* **2004**, *161*, 2215–2221. [CrossRef] [PubMed]
41. Dingemans, A.; Danner, U.; Parks, M. Emotion regulation in binge eating disorder: A review. *Nutrients* **2017**, *9*, 1274. [CrossRef] [PubMed]
42. Buckner, J.D.; Silgado, J.; Lewinsohn, P.M. Delineation of differential temporal relations between specific eating and anxiety disorders. *J. Psychiatr. Res.* **2010**, *44*, 781–787. [CrossRef] [PubMed]
43. Matos, M.I.R.; Aranha, L.S.; Faria, A.N.; Ferreira, S.R.; Bacaltchuck, J.; Zanella, M.T. Binge eating disorder, anxiety, depression and body image in grade III obesity patients. *Braz. J. Psychiatry* **2002**, *24*, 165–169. [CrossRef]
44. Wonderlich-Tierney, A.L.; Vander Wal, J.S. The effects of social support and coping on the relationship between social anxiety and eating disorders. *Eat. Behav.* **2010**, *11*, 85–91. [CrossRef] [PubMed]
45. Kate, P.; Deshmukh, G.; Datir, R.; Rao, J. Good mood foods. *J. Nutr. Health Food Eng.* **2017**, *7*, 345–351.
46. Volkow, N.; Wang, G.; Fowler, J.; Tomasi, D.; Baler, R. Food and drug reward: Overlapping circuits in human obesity and addiction. *Brain Imaging Behav. Neurosci.* **2011**, *11*, 1–24.
47. Walędziak, M.; Różańska-Walędziak, A.; Pędziwiatr, M.; Szeliga, J.; Proczko-Stepaniak, M.; Wysocki, M.; Stefura, T.; Major, P. Bariatric surgery during COVID-19 pandemic from patients' point of view—The results of a national survey. *J. Clin. Med.* **2020**, *9*, 1697. [CrossRef] [PubMed]
48. Wild, B.; Hunnemeyer, K.; Sauer, H.; Schellberg, D.; Muller-Stich, B.P.; Konigsrainer, A.; Weiner, R.; Zipfel, S.; Herzog, W.; Teufel, M. Sustained effects of a psychoeducational group intervention following bariatric surgery: Follow-up of the randomized controlled BaSE study. *Surg. Obes. Relat. Dis.* **2017**, *13*, 1612–1618. [CrossRef] [PubMed]
49. Archid, R.; Archid, N.; Meile, T.; Hoffmann, J.; Hilbert, J.; Wulff, D.; Teufel, M.; Muthig, M.; Quante, M.; Konigsrainer, A.; et al. Patients with Schizophrenia Do Not Demonstrate Worse Outcome After Sleeve Gastrectomy: A Short-Term Cohort Study. *Obes. Surg.* **2019**, *29*, 506–510. [CrossRef] [PubMed]
50. Robitzsch, A.; Schweda, A.; Hetkamp, M.; Niedergethmann, M.; Dörrie, N.; Herpertz, S.; Hasenberg, T.; Tagay, S.; Teufel, M.; Skoda, E.-M. The Impact of Psychological Resources on Body Mass Index in Obesity Surgery Candidates. *Front. Psychiatry* **2020**, *11*, 649. [CrossRef] [PubMed]
51. Sanderson, W.C.; Arunagiri, V.; Funk, A.P.; Ginsburg, K.L.; Krychiw, J.K.; Limowski, A.R.; Olesnycky, O.S.; Stout, Z. The nature and treatment of pandemic-related psychological distress. *J. Contemp. Psychother.* **2020**, *50*, 251–263. [CrossRef]
52. Bäuerle, A.; Graf, J.; Jansen, C.; Dörrie, N.; Junne, F.; Teufel, M.; Skoda, E.-M. An e-mental health intervention to support burdened people in times of the COVID-19 pandemic: CoPE It. *J. Public Health* **2020**, *42*, 647–648. [CrossRef] [PubMed]
53. Ahorsu, D.K.; Lin, C.Y.; Imani, V.; Saffari, M.; Griffiths, M.D.; Pakpour, A.H. The Fear of COVID-19 Scale: Development and Initial Validation. *Int. J. Ment. Health Addict.* **2020**, 1–9. [CrossRef]
54. Schweda, A.; Weismüller, B.; Bäuerle, A.; Dörrie, N.; Musche, V.; Fink, M.; Kohler, H.; Teufel, M.; Skoda, E.-M. Phenotyping mental health: Age, community size, and depression differently modulate COVID-19-related fear and generalized anxiety. *Compr. Psychiatry* **2021**, *104*, 152218. [CrossRef]

International Journal of
Environmental Research and Public Health

MDPI

Article

Consequences of the COVID-19 Lockdown in Germany: Effects of Changes in Daily Life on Musical Engagement and Functions of Music

Natalie Alexa Roese [1] and Julia Merrill [1,2,*]

[1] Institute of Music, University of Kassel, Mönchebergstr. 1, 34125 Kassel, Germany; natalie.roese@mail.de
[2] Max Planck Institute for Empirical Aesthetics, Grüneburgweg 14, 60322 Frankfurt am Main, Germany
* Correspondence: julia.merrill@ae.mpg.de

Abstract: The current study investigated how music has been used during the COVID-19 pandemic and how personal factors have affected music-listening behavior. During the shutdown in Spring 2020 in Germany, 539 participants took part in an online survey reporting on functions of music listening, attributes of listened music, and active engagement with music, retrospectively before and during the pandemic. Next to these implicit questions, participants were asked to describe the changes they explicitly noticed in handling music during COVID-19, their current worries, and their new everyday life during the pandemic as well as personality traits and stress reactivity. A logistic regression model was fitted, showing that people reduced their active engagement with music during the lockdown, and the function of killing time and overcoming loneliness became more important, reflecting the need for distraction and filling the silence. Before the lockdown, music was listened to for the function of motor synchronization and enhanced well-being, which reflects how people have lost both their musical and activity routines during the lockdown. The importance of in-person engagement with music in people's lives became particularly evident in the connection between worries about further restrictions and the need for live music.

Keywords: music listening; pandemic; coronavirus; social distance; worries; killing time

Citation: Roese, N.A.; Merrill, J. Consequences of the COVID-19 Lockdown in Germany: Effects of Changes in Daily Life on Musical Engagement and Functions of Music. *Int. J. Environ. Res. Public Health* **2021**, *18*, 10463. https://doi.org/10.3390/ijerph181910463

Academic Editors: Paolo Roma, Merylin Monaro, Cristina Mazza and Paul Tchounwou

Received: 11 August 2021
Accepted: 2 October 2021
Published: 5 October 2021

1. Introduction

The coronavirus disease 2019 (COVID-19) has brought new challenges to modern life. Through the influence of the media, without precedent, we have been able to follow the daily development and the impact of the virus on people's lives. Every single person can probably tell in some way or another how the virus has affected their lives. With the current study, we investigated the role of music in these challenging times with a specific focus on retrospectively assessed changes from before and during the first lockdown in Germany. Hence, we took into account the particular situation in this country during the lockdown and related it to known music listening habits and functions of music in daily life.

1.1. The Situation in Germany at the Start of the Pandemic

When lockdown in Germany started on 13 March 2020, stores, restaurants, bars, and discos had to close. Parties and (sporting, music) events had to be cancelled, and schools and universities had to change to online lessons and homeschooling. Many people had to work from home and reduce their working hours, and some lost their jobs. The unemployment rate in Germany rose by 0.7% from March to April, and there were 10.1 million applications from employers to temporarily reduce employee working hours between March to April. Therefore, the number of people working fewer hours increased to an unprecedented level in Germany during this time [1].

From 13 March until 5 June 2020, people were only allowed to meet people from one other household. Between March and May, there were 181,482 infected people in

Germany, and 8500 people had died of SARS-CoV-2 [2]. Through the media, the people in Germany were confronted with the possibility of an increase in the development of the COVID-19 pandemic comparable to other, strongly affected regions in the world. Based on the proportion of infected people and number of ICU stations, the German government justified the lockdown (and has ever since) to reduce the risk as much as possible of being in a position where the healthcare system has to make ethical judgements about whom to grant intensive care.

There is mixed evidence of the effect of consequences due to COVID-19 on the mental health of the German population. Entringer and Kröger (2020) [3] reported an increase in subjective loneliness during the first months of the restrictions in Germany, which was described as a discrepancy between desired and existing social relationships. Otherwise, the authors report that life satisfaction, emotional well-being, and symptoms of depression and anxiety were, interestingly, unchanged. People were even more satisfied with their health, which was probably because of the contrast to people who were infected with COVID-19 and suffered from health problems of SARS-CoV-2.

In a study by Bäuerle et al. (2020) [4], a high prevalence of generalized anxiety symptoms, depression symptoms, psychological distress, and COVID-19 related worries were seen from March until May, which shows that there was an increased mental health burden during the lockdown (although with a lower prevalence compared to China, which was also investigated). While in times before the pandemic, healthy people were shown to spend 28–55 min worrying [5,6], during the lockdown, people indicate on average spending 4.45 h per day thinking about COVID-19 and its effects [7]. The reported worries were more related to social than to personal aspects; that is, people were more concerned about social consequences than about getting infected or dealing with changes in their daily lives. Additionally, social consequences weighed more than the fear of economic consequences, and people indicated that anxiety due to the pandemic impacted their lives [7].

1.2. Music Use and Functions in Daily Life

That changes in daily life and music listening behavior go hand in hand has been shown in previous work. Music in general can take on an important role in everyday life, or at least as important as other domains, such as hobbies or food preferences [8]. In comparison to other leisure activities, music listening is the most preferred activity compared to sports, TV, books, movies, radio, and magazines or newspapers (e.g., people spend more money on music than on other activities; [9]). Music is often used simultaneously with other activities in daily routine [8,10–14], many of which have been missing during the COVID-19 pandemic [15].

Music in particular is known to be able to regulate mood and arousal [9,16], to cope with negative feelings [11,14,17], to express emotions [16], and to trigger memories and emotions [14,18,19]. Next to talking to friends, music is the second most important strategy for affect regulation [14]. These functions of music listening seem to come into play particularly when people want to change a negative mood or stress [11,14], because then, mood regulation is more important [20]. Certainly, music affects people differently, for example, depending on trait aspects such as personality, where people higher in openness and (slightly) extraversion are also higher in musical sophistication [21,22], but also depending on personal distress, where music can lead to a reduction of arousal and therefore, having a positive effect on fear, anxiety (e.g., [23] Daniel, 2016; [24] Knight and Rickard, 2001), and stress (e.g., [25] Hodges, 2010; [26] Kreutz et al., 2013).

Based on these primarily positive effects, it can be assumed that people use music to counteract the predominantly negative effects of the lockdown (see [3,4,7]). Music might be listened to because of its transformative power, that is to change cognitive, bodily, and self-conceptual states as well as one's energy level [27,28].

1.3. Current Studies on Musical Behavior during the COVID-19 Pandemic

As shown, musical behavior is closely tied to habits and routines in everyday life. Fitting to this, a growing body of research in the past few months has given rise to the idea that music listening and making have changed together with changing habits and routines and adapted to the new way of living during the pandemic.

On the one hand, current studies have shown that music streaming volume decreased in several countries after the start of the lockdown [29], or more generally, by 12.5% after the WHO's pandemic declaration [30]. The decline in music consumption was related to an increasing number of COVID-19 cases; in countries which recovered quickly, the consumption of music grew again [30].

On the other hand, Fink et al. (2021) [31] queried representative samples from six countries about musical behavior during the first lockdown (April–May 2020) and found that particularly the functions of music play an important role in socio-emotional coping during the lockdown as well as music selection behavior toward the so-called "coronamusic." The most important functions of music listening during the lockdown were, after "interest in others' coronamusic behavior," "makes feel like having company," and "reduces loneliness." Some leisure activities ranked higher than music listening (which was ranked 6th), such as calling people, reading/watching news and movies/series, cleaning and cooking. Between 34% and 57% of the participants report about adapted musical behavior during the lockdown.

Mas-Herrero et al. (2020) [32] queried people from mainly three (Western) countries and found that music listening was the major coping strategy for regulating distress during the pandemic, and depression symptoms (The Depression Anxiety Stress Scale; DASS-21) decreased with the amount of music listening.

In another extensive study from eleven countries during the lockdown [33], music was found to be very efficient at attaining the goals (or functions) of enjoyment and maintaining a good mood, reducing loneliness, and creating a sense of togetherness (only socializing was higher, hobbies were equally good), releasing and venting negative emotions, connecting with oneself and detaching from the surroundings, and diversion from the crisis (note that entertainment media were equally efficient). Here, people scoring higher in the DASS-21 chose music more often, which was associated with nostalgia.

Investigating Spanish citizens in their musical behavior during the lockdown [34], another study observed a perceived increase in time spent on musical activities (making and listening) and how music was perceived to help coping for confinement: that is, to relax, escape, raise their mood, or keep them company. While these findings were based on descriptive statistics, inferential statistics were used to show that the employment situation had an impact on the perception of value of music, which was lowest for the retirees as compared to the other groups.

In light of the methods applied in the present study, it is of interest to note the methodological strategies used in these studies to investigate changes in musical behavior from before to during the lockdown. All four studies assessed changes by indirectly asking for perceived changes, e.g., "Since corona crisis measures were introduced, do you now listen to more or less music?" [31] or "How much time did you spend on listening to music during lockdown as compared to the time before the crisis? (much less–much more)" [33,34]. While Mas-Herrero et al. (2020) [32] used the same approach for the majority of the questions, one difference was seen with regard to a question on listening time, which was asked twice: once regarding before and once during the lockdown (note, comparisons were not made between these two points of measurement but only within).

Therefore, the changes between before and during the lockdown have been investigated rather indirectly with one question asking about perceived changes. Since a comparison between both time points is not possible (unless data were collected right before the lockdown), the only other possibility is to query the behavior from before the lockdown retrospectively and then compare the ratings to the same questions asked about the situation during the lockdown. This would allow for the comparison of the same questionnaires assessed for two different time points.

1.4. The Present Study

With the current study, we take an exploratory approach to examine music-listening behavior during the COVID-19 lockdown in Germany via an online survey. The primary goal was to compare the self-reported music listening behavior before and during the lockdown. Therefore, the active engagement with music (Goldsmiths Musical Sophistication Index, Gold-MSI; [35]), functions of music [10], and attributes of music [36] were assessed, once retrospectively before the pandemic and once during the lockdown.

First, changes in functions of music and in active engagement with music were to be expected due to changes in habits and routines during the lockdown. With the choice in assessments, a form of active engagement was investigated that goes beyond just time spent on music listening but includes aspects on seeking music-related information. The functions investigated in the present study covered a wide range including killing time and overcoming loneliness, mind wandering and emotional involvement, motor synchronization and enhanced well-being, and intellectual stimulation.

Second, because music with distinct attributes is often selected for its capacity to affect one's mood, it was expected that changes in overall emotional states affect music selection criteria. The investigated attributes in the current study displayed three categories related to positive valence/joy, arousal/stimulative, and 'depth' (reflective, clever, emotional; see [36]).

Third, the observed changes in musical behavior were to be investigated depending on the personal situation. Therefore, aspects of changes in daily life and the worries related to the lockdown measures were collected. Items were based on daily topics that moved people in Germany at the time in April 2020 covered by the media and taken from statistical reports by the German government. Trait aspects were of interest that indicate how people deal with stress (prolonged stress reactivity and reactivity to work overload) [32,33], and personality dimensions previously reported to be related to musical behavior, that is openness and extraversion [21,22], and negative emotionality, which represents aspects of anxiety, depression, and emotional volatility [37].

To conclude, the present study covers aspects comparable to other studies, but with a major difference in the methodological approach: that is, the retrospective assessment of the behavior from before the lockdown, which allows for an implicit comparison of changes in musical behavior.

2. Materials and Methods

2.1. Ethics Statement

All experimental procedures were approved by the Ethics Council of the Max Planck Society and were undertaken with written informed consent of each participant.

2.2. Participants

Five hundred and thirty-nine participants (55.1% female, 44.3% male, 0.6% non-binary, mean age = 33.18, *SD* = 13.81 years) finished the online survey. The sample was a convenience sample with participants aged 18 years and older. Participants who did not finish the survey (*N* = 168) were not considered further. Most of the participants (44.5%) had as the highest degree a college diploma, while 39.1% had a high school diploma. Almost half of the sample were students (43.8%), 31.2% were employees, 14.5% were self-employed or similar, 4.5% were retired, and 2.2% were unemployed.

2.3. Procedure

Participants were recruited via social media (mainly Facebook), the website of the affiliated university, and with a newspaper article in the local press. The survey was created with LimeSurvey. Data were collected between 6 April and 15 May 2020, which overlaps with the (first) shut down in Germany. The survey lasted about 20 min. There was no monetary compensation for participation.

2.4. Questionnaires

Participants gave information on their demographics (age, gender, education, profession), the number of people in their household, living situation (living alone, with family, partner, in a shared apartment) and the date of the beginning of the lockdown in their area.

2.5. Perceived Changes in Music-Listening Behavior

A custom questionnaire was developed that included twelve items, which evaluated how the participants perceived the changes before the lockdown versus during the lockdown with regard to various aspects of music-listening behavior on a 5-point Likert scale from strongly disagree (1) to strongly agree (5). These aspects included changes arising from the restrictions in place and resulting changes in daily routines during the lockdown: that is, media usage, missing live events, social distancing, and situations and reasons for listening to music. The items and the content was similar to other current studies on music and COVID-19 [31,34], i.e., asking indirectly whether a behavior was higher or lower during the lockdown than before.

2.6. Active Musical Engagement

This and the following two questionnaires were presented in two blocks, firstly with regard to the situation before the lockdown and then during the lockdown. The factor on 'active engagement' from the Gold-MSI [35,38] comprises nine items, measuring free time spent on musical activities, writing and reading about music, income spent on music, keeping track of new music, and openness to unfamiliar music as well as visited music events. Items were evaluated on a 7-point Likert scale from strongly disagree (1) to strongly agree (7). That means that this factor is built on a broad concept of being engaged with music not only focusing on music listening but excluding music making. Note that the question on visited live events was only evaluated in the questionnaire regarding before the lockdown. This was followed by a list of musical styles, asking the participants to choose the styles they normally/currently listen to.

2.7. Attributes of Chosen Music

Items were chosen from the three factors of (ascribed) musical emotions and attributes of music from Fricke and Herzberg (2017) [36]. From the first factor, the attributes reflective, emotional, and clever were chosen ("depth"). From the second factor, the attributes fast, energetic, and voice were chosen ("stimulative"). From the third factor, the attributes uplifting, cheerful/happy, rhythmical, and relaxing were chosen ("joy"). The attributes were evaluated on a 5-point Likert scale from disagree (1) to agree (5).

2.8. Functions of Music Listening

From the original five factors in Greb et al. (2018) [10], four factors were of interest for the current study from which items were chosen that did not show cross-loadings on other factors in the original study. One item described if music is used for 'intellectual stimulation' (all others had cross-loadings). The factor 'mind wandering/emotional involvement' (six items) included items on music triggering imagination, emotions, and goosebumps, and creating a situation to understand, forget, or remember situations. The factor 'motor synchronization/enhanced well-being' (six items) consisted of how music triggers movement, enhances the mood, and enables listeners to feel fit, blow off steam, and sing along. The last factor 'killing time/overcoming loneliness' (three items) consisted of dealing with boredom and loneliness, and in connection with that, having music playing in the background. Since the factor 'updating one's musical knowledge' showed overlap with the above Gold-MSI factor, it was left out. Items were evaluated on a 5-point Likert scale from does not apply (1) to fully applies (5).

2.9. Traits

After the music-related questionnaires, personality traits were assessed with the facets of open-mindedness, extraversion, and negative emotionality from the BFI-2 [39]. From the Perceived Stress Reactivity Scale [40], the factors 'prolonged reactivity' and 'reactivity to work overload' were selected.

2.10. Worries and Changes in Everyday Life

One custom questionnaire evaluated possible worries in relation to the impact of the lockdown (ten items), and another evaluated the changes in everyday life (14 items), which were evaluated on a 5-point Likert scale from does not apply (1) to fully applies (5). They were created based on daily topics that moved people in Germany at the time in April 2020 covered by the media and taken from statistical reports by the German Federal Statistics Office (www.destatis.de; accessed on 10 August 2021), and the platform www.statista.de (accessed on 10 August 2021).

Finally, participants were asked whether the impact of the lockdown had a pleasant effect on their work life (yes/no) and if they were working from home (yes/no/partly), if they were happy about that, and if they had more free time due to working from home (5-point Likert scale from does not apply (1) to fully applies (5)). Questions followed on supervised children, i.e., how many (0, 1, 2, 3, 4, 5, and more), and at which times (in the morning, the afternoon, the evening, the whole day), and if participants actually followed the instruction to stay at home if possible (yes/no).

2.11. Preprocessing and Factor Analyses

For active engagement, attributes, and functions, mean scores of the original factors were computed twice per person: once for the questionnaires describing the situation before and once during the lockdown. All analyses were performed using R Statistics 3.5.1.

The factor structure of the other questionnaires was determined with a factor analysis using oblimin rotation. Parallel analysis was used to determine the number of factors to keep in the factor analysis. Items with loadings $< |0.3|$ were excluded (three items) as well as one factor that did not explain much of the variance and consisted of the two items on social contacts which only applied to a small percentage of the participants. After repeating the factor analysis without these items, factor scores were extracted, and latent variables were created to be used in the statistical models. Descriptive statistics, the details of the factor analysis, and the correlations of all latent variables can be found in the Supplementary Materials. The multicollinearity of each model was checked with variance inflation factors (VIF), the vif() function, accepting VIFs < 3.

2.12. Perceived Changes in Music-Listening Behavior

The first factor 'music use' combines items that describe the different listening situations, media use, and reasons for listening to music. The second factor 'value of music' comprises items about the importance of music in general and having more time to engage with music. The factor 'live music' contains the two items on missing live music and listening more to recorded music (Table 1).

Table 1. Factor solution of the items on perceived changes in music-listening behavior.

Item	Music Use	Value of Music	Live Music
Proportion variance explained	0.41	0.40	0.19
I listen to music in different situations than before.	0.98		
I use other media to listen to music than before.	0.87		
I listen to music for different reasons than before.	0.51		
I miss situations in everyday life, in which I would otherwise listen to music.	0.25		
Music is more important to me.		0.77	
I am happy to have time to listen to music.		0.62	
I listen to music I am familiar with more than before.		0.55	
I listen to music to compensate for missing everyday activities.		0.52	
I use media more often than before.		0.43	
I listen to different music than before.	0.30	0.35	
I miss listening to live music.			0.80
I use recordings more often because I cannot listen to live music.		0.35	0.51

For better readability, factor loadings < |0.3| are omitted. One item in the factor 'music use' with a loading < |0.3| was kept in order to prevent a loading of 1 on this factor.

2.13. Worries

The four factors describe uncertainties about the future, worry of subsistence, further restrictions, and of becoming infected with COVID-19 (Table 2).

Table 2. Factor solution of the items of the questionnaire on worries.

Item	Uncertainty	Subsistence	Restrictions	Sickness
Proportion variance explained	0.31	0.28	0.26	0.15
I am worried about my personal future.	0.82			
I am afraid of professional changes.	0.51			
I am afraid of uncertainties about the future.	0.44			
I am afraid of financial losses.		0.95		
I have existential fear.		0.49		
The restrictions of public life seem threatening to me.			0.80	
I am afraid of further restrictions.			0.66	
I am afraid of falling ill.				0.65
I am afraid that a relative or acquaintance will fall ill.				0.49

2.14. Everyday Life

The two factors describe work-related changes (having more to do and the professional life becoming more stressful) as well as changes in private life (such as being alone, bored, or spending more time for oneself or the family) (Table 3).

Table 3. Factor solution of the items on everyday life.

Item	Work	Private
Proportion variance explained	0.51	0.49
I have more to do than before the corona crisis.	0.84	
My professional life has become more stressful.	0.67	
I am more often alone.		0.44
I spend more time with people in my household.		0.43
I am bored more often.		0.43
I have more contact with friends and family.		0.35
I have more time for myself.		0.35
My everyday family life has become more stressful.		0.34
I find the current restrictions decelerating.		0.32
I can no longer pursue my hobbies.		0.30

2.15. Statistical Analysis

A logistic regression model was fitted predicting behavior from before (0) or during the lockdown (1) with the factors of active engagement, functions of music listening, and attributes of chosen music. For further analyses, a change score for each of these factors was created by subtracting the values from before the lockdown from the ones during the lockdown. Then, eight linear models were fitted with the factors of everyday life, worries, personality, and stress reactivity, predicting each of these change scores. The results are to be interpreted as changes in behavior from before to during the lockdown: In case of a positive estimate, the behavior is currently higher than normal. In case of a negative estimate, the behavior is currently lower than normal.

Similarly, three further linear models were fitted predicting the factors of perceived changes in musical behavior (music value, music use, live music) with the factors of everyday life, worries, personality, and stress reactivity.

3. Results

3.1. Descriptive Statistics

In different sections of the questionnaire, participants had to describe effects of the lockdown on their daily lives (job and living situation, changes in everyday life, worries) and on their music-listening behavior.

3.1.1. Overall Living and Job Situation during the Lockdown

The vast majority of participants reported staying mainly at home (92.4%), and most did not have to take care of children (87.4%). Regarding living arrangements, 17.1% lived alone, 30.9% with their partner, 41.3% lived together with their family, 6.7% lived together with friends, and 3% lived in a flat-sharing community. Many participants perceived the impact of the lockdown on their work situation as unpleasant (73.7%), 64.6% were at least partly working from home during the lockdown, 75% reported being glad to have the opportunity to work from home, and 62% reported having at least partly more free time because of their job situation.

3.1.2. Reported Changes in Everyday Life

Half of the participants are at least partly more often alone (52.9%) and have more time for themselves than before the lockdown (60.1%); 52.4% can at least partly not pursue their hobbies and 68.8% find the current restrictions somewhat decelerating. The family life and the professional life has at least partly become more stressful for 51% and 48.6% of the participants, respectively, and 51.9% report having more to do now than before the lockdown. Nonetheless, half of the participants report only slightly missing social contacts or having less contact with people who are important to them (51.9% and 56.6%, respectively; Table 4).

Table 4. Reported changes in everyday life.

Item	Does Not Apply (in %)	Slightly Applies (in %)	Partially Applies (in %)	Strongly Applies (in %)	Fully Applies (in %)
I spend more time with people in my household.	15.8	46.9	21.7	8.0	7.6
My professional life has become more stressful.	41.9	9.5	9.6	15.6	23.4
I have more to do than before the corona crisis.	40.3	7.8	14.1	15	22.8
I have more time for myself.	13.4	26.5	29.7	15.6	14.8
I have less contact with people who are important to me.	3.2	56.6	24.3	10.2	5.8
I miss social contacts.	3.2	51.9	26.2	14.1	4.6
I find the current restrictions decelerating.	8.0	23.2	29.1	29.9	9.8
My everyday family life has become more stressful.	41.6	7.4	12.2	14.3	24.5
I have more contact with friends and family.	29.9	5.4	10.0	26.7	28.0
I am more often alone.	28.0	19.1	20.4	14.3	18.2
I can no longer pursue my hobbies.	15.6	32.1	20.8	18.6	13.0
I find the current reporting threatening.	21.2	5.8	13.5	30.2	29.3
I feel well informed.	4.5	22.6	40.6	24.9	7.4
I am bored more often.	38.0	9.5	15.4	16.3	20.8

3.1.3. Reported Worries during the Lockdown

Worries due to the COVID-19 pandemic are overall small to moderate with a median of 2 and an interquartile range (IQR) of 1–3 on the 5-point Likert scale (see Supplementary Materials). Most (89.6%) of the participants do not or only partly have existential fear. A similar percentage (83.3%) is seen for financial worries ("I am afraid of financial losses"). The fear of professional changes is low: 75.2% are not or only partly afraid of professional changes. Most of the participants do not or only partly worry about the personal future (77.4%) and about uncertainties about the future (72.7%). Worries about restrictions are rare in our sample with 80.7% ("I am afraid of further restrictions") and 84.4% ("The restrictions of public life seem threatening"). Most (80.9%) of the participants are not or only partly afraid of falling ill themselves, but 82.9% are at least partly afraid that a relative or acquaintance will become infected with COVID-19, representing the most prominent worry (Table 5).

Table 5. Reported worries during the lockdown.

Item	Does Not Apply (in %)	Slightly Applies (in %)	Partially Applies (in %)	Strongly Applies (in %)	Fully Applies (in %)
I am afraid of falling ill.	27.8	33.8	19.3	5.4	13.7
I am afraid that my relatives or aquaintances will fall ill.	4.1	13.0	17.4	28.8	36.7
I am afraid of professional changes.	31.9	26.2	17.1	8.9	16.0
I have existential fears.	52.3	28.0	9.3	3.7	6.7
I am afraid of financial losses.	41.2	29.5	12.6	6.5	10.2
I am afraid of supply shortages.	56.4	30.6	8.3	1.1	3.5
I am worried about my personal future.	32.3	24.7	20.4	9.6	13.0
I am afraid of further restrictions.	32.3	30.4	18.0	6.5	12.8
I am afraid of uncertainties about the future.	21.5	28.4	22.8	9.8	17.4
The restrictions of public life seem threatening.	37.5	31.7	15.2	5.2	10.4

3.1.4. Perceived Differences in Music-Listening Behavior

There are perceived changes concerning music-listening behavior during the lockdown: 44.4% perceived to at least partly listen to music in other situations and 36.9% for other reasons than before. The most extreme categories ("I listen to music in other situations") were chosen by 26.5% ("does not apply") and 5.8% ("fully applies"). Similar results were seen for reasons for music listening ("I listen to music for other reasons"). Only 2.8% indicate to agree; however, 31.4% disagree. Less than half (41.8%) indicate using other entertainment media to listen to music than before the lockdown and 54.8% indicate missing situations in which they typically listen to music.

Furthermore, there are perceived changes that describe the value of music during the lockdown: for 66.6% of the participants, music is more or at least partly more important during the lockdown. Most (75.9%) indicate that they are at least partly happy to have more time to listen to music; 24.3% totally agree and only 8.3% totally disagree. Half of the participants (53.5%) listen more often or at least partly more often to familiar music, but the most extreme category ("fully applies") is only chosen by 5% in contrast to 19.9% ("does not apply"). More than one-third (36.9%) listen at least partly to music to compensate for missing daily activities. Here again, the most extreme category ("fully applies") is only chosen by 5%. Most (82.6%) of the participants use entertainment media more often than before the lockdown. Different music is at least partly listened to by 30%.

The absence of live music seems to be a strong change in the participants' lives: 68.6% miss live music at least partly during the times of confinement; 35.4% strongly agree. Half of the participants (53%) at least partly agree with the statements that they use records to compensate for missing live events (Table 6).

Table 6. Perceived differences in music-listening behavior.

Item	Does Not Apply (in %)	Slightly Applies (in %)	Partially Applies (in %)	Strongly Applies (in %)	Fully Applies (in %)
Music is more important to me than before.	10.9	22.4	28.2	27.6	10.8
I am happy to have more time listening to music.	8.3	15.8	19.5	32.1	24.3
I miss live music.	17.6	13.7	11.5	21.7	35.4
I use records more often to compensate for missing live events.	23.9	23.0	16.5	22.4	14.1
I listen to different music than before.	38.6	31.4	17.4	10.0	2.6
I listen more often to familiar music than before.	19.9	26.7	24.9	23.6	5.0
I listen to music for other reasons than before.	31.4	31.7	16.1	18.0	2.8
I listen to music in other situations than before.	26.5	29.1	13.7	24.9	5.8
I miss situations in which I usually listen to music.	24.5	20.8	11.7	23.2	19.9
I listen to music to compensate for missing daily activities.	31.0	32.1	14.5	17.4	5.0
I use media more often than before.	7.4	10.0	10.0	38.6	34.0
I use other media to listen to music than before.	28.0	30.2	13.4	22.8	5.6

To summarize these findings, we see that between 40% and 50% of the participants report about changes in their everyday lives. Even though the participants in our sample do not suffer from major worries except for worrying that family members or acquaintances might get infected with COVID-19, the impact of the lockdown on daily lives is noticeable. Participants report about changes such as being more often alone or not being able to pursue their hobbies as well as professional changes such as working from home and having more to do than before the lockdown.

Changes in music behavior can be seen regarding media usage, now that live music has become astray, which is missed by many participants. In addition, participants show an adapted music-listening behavior, i.e., concerning situations in which they listen to music and reasons why they do. More than half of the participants indicate missing situations in which they usually listen to music. This rather reflects the consequences of changes in everyday life (routines and habits as well as getting used to a "new normal") than worries that were caused by COVID 19.

3.2. *Inferential Statistics*

3.2.1. Factors Predicting Changes in Musical Behavior before and during the Lockdown

The logistic regression models predicting music-related behavior before and during the lockdown showed a significant effect of active engagement (Gold-MSI) revealing that participants were less musically engaged during the lockdown (Odds Ratio = 0.85, *CI* = 0.75–0.95, p = 0.005, Tjur's R^2 = 0.034). Furthermore, during the lockdown, music was used more to kill time and to overcome loneliness (Odds Ratio = 1.25, *CI* = 1.08–1.45, p = 0.003), while before the lockdown, participants listened to music for motor synchronization and to enhance their well-being (Odds Ratio = 0.75, *CI* = 0.61–0.92, p = 0.006). Musical attributes did not predict changes in behavior.

To be comparable to other studies, it is of note that 30.6% of the participants listened to music for more than two hours every day during the lockdown, while only 23.6% of the participants listened to music for that long before the lockdown. Hence, music listening time alone slightly increased during the lockdown (see Supplementary Materials).

3.2.2. Effects of Worries, Everyday Life, Personality, and Stress Reactivity on Listening Behavior

The fitted linear models predicting attributes of music showed that depth is positively predicted by the factors 'private' and open-mindedness and negatively by the factors 'uncertainty' and 'work' (Table 7). The models predicting changes in functions of music from before to during the lockdown showed a very low explained variance and could not be interpreted any further (R^2 adjusted between −0.003 and 0.010, see Supplementary Materials). Active engagement is not predicted by any factors (R^2 adjusted = −0.005, see Supplementary Materials). The models predicting perceived changes in musical behavior showed that extraversion predicts music use, 'uncertainty' predicts the value of music, and 'restrictions' and open-mindedness predict live music (Table 8). Stress reactivity did not become a significant predictor in any model.

Table 7. Results of the linear models predicting changes in musical attributes.

	Joy			Depth			Stimulative		
Predictors	**Estimates**	*CI*	*p*	**Estimates**	*CI*	*p*	**Estimates**	*CI*	*p*
(Intercept)	−0.40	−0.90–0.10	0.121	−0.96	−1.50–−0.41	**0.001**	−0.13	−0.60–0.34	0.580
subsistence	0.03	−0.03–0.10	0.349	0.05	−0.03–0.12	0.221	0.04	−0.02–0.11	0.177
uncertainty	−0.05	−0.14–0.05	0.343	−0.14	−0.24–−0.03	**0.011**	−0.01	−0.10–0.08	0.770
restrictions	0.01	−0.06–0.08	0.707	0.03	−0.05–0.10	0.503	−0.02	−0.09–0.04	0.490
sickness	0.02	−0.07–0.10	0.709	0.00	−0.09–0.09	0.991	0.00	−0.08–0.08	0.996
work	−0.03	−0.10–0.04	0.419	−0.13	−0.21–−0.06	**0.001**	−0.02	−0.09–0.04	0.457
private	0.07	−0.01–0.15	0.079	0.14	0.06–0.23	**0.001**	0.02	−0.05–0.10	0.537
open-mindedness	0.02	−0.06–0.11	0.581	0.13	0.04–0.23	**0.006**	0.05	−0.03–0.13	0.259
extraversion	0.08	−0.01–0.17	0.073	−0.00	−0.10–0.09	0.955	0.02	−0.06–0.11	0.566
negativity	0.03	−0.07–0.12	0.598	0.05	−0.05–0.16	0.294	−0.02	−0.11–0.06	0.582
stress reactivity	0.02	−0.01–0.06	0.207	0.03	−0.01–0.07	0.129	−0.02	−0.06–0.01	0.176
stress workload	−0.01	−0.04–0.03	0.622	0.01	−0.03–0.05	0.528	0.01	−0.03–0.04	0.672
Observations		539			539			539	
R^2 / R^2 adjusted		0.018/−0.003			0.052/0.033			0.017/−0.004	

Significant *p*-values are indicated in bold.

Table 8. Results of the linear models predicting perceived changes in musical behavior.

	Music Use			Value of Music			Live Music		
Predictors	**Estimates**	*CI*	*p*	**Estimates**	*CI*	*p*	**Estimates**	*CI*	*p*
(Intercept)	−0.81	−1.62–0.00	0.051	−0.59	−1.33–0.15	0.120	−1.07	−1.78–−0.36	**0.003**
subsistence	0.00	−0.11–0.11	0.967	−0.06	−0.16–0.04	0.212	0.02	−0.07–0.12	0.627
uncertainty	0.05	−0.10–0.21	0.515	0.16	0.02–0.30	**0.030**	0.00	−0.14–0.14	0.997
restrictions	0.09	−0.02–0.20	0.125	0.09	−0.01–0.20	0.078	0.16	0.06–0.26	**0.002**
sickness	0.02	−0.11–0.16	0.721	−0.07	−0.19–0.06	0.284	0.01	−0.11–0.13	0.901
work	0.06	−0.05–0.17	0.293	−0.08	−0.18–0.02	0.124	−0.04	−0.14–0.06	0.401
private	−0.03	−0.16–0.10	0.661	0.09	−0.02–0.21	0.118	0.10	−0.01–0.21	0.085
open-mindedness	−0.02	−0.16–0.12	0.736	0.05	−0.08–0.18	0.471	0.29	0.17–0.41	**<0.001**
extraversion	0.23	0.09–0.37	**0.001**	0.09	−0.04–0.21	0.194	0.07	−0.05–0.20	0.254
negativity	0.07	−0.09–0.22	0.395	0.06	−0.08–0.20	0.366	0.00	−0.13–0.14	0.966
stress reactivity	0.00	−0.06–0.06	0.950	0.02	−0.04–0.08	0.459	−0.03	−0.09–0.02	0.246

Table 8. *Cont.*

	Music Use			Value of Music			Live Music		
Predictors	**Estimates**	***CI***	***p***	**Estimates**	***CI***	***p***	**Estimates**	***CI***	***p***
stress workload	−0.02	−0.07–0.04	0.566	−0.03	−0.08–0.02	0.208	−0.04	−0.09–0.01	0.132
Observations	539			539			539		
R^2/R^2 adjusted	0.038/0.018			0.044/0.024			0.085/0.066		

Significant *p*-values are indicated in bold.

4. Discussion

This study investigated music-listening behavior during the lockdown due to the COVID-19 pandemic from April to May 2020 in Germany. In the current study, we put the emphasis on the direct comparison between aspects of music-listening behavior (active musical engagement, functions of music listening, attributes of chosen music) from before and during the lockdown. The current study shows how music-listening behavior adapts to changed daily routines and habits as well as to the burdens of the lockdown. A summary of the results is depicted in Figure 1.

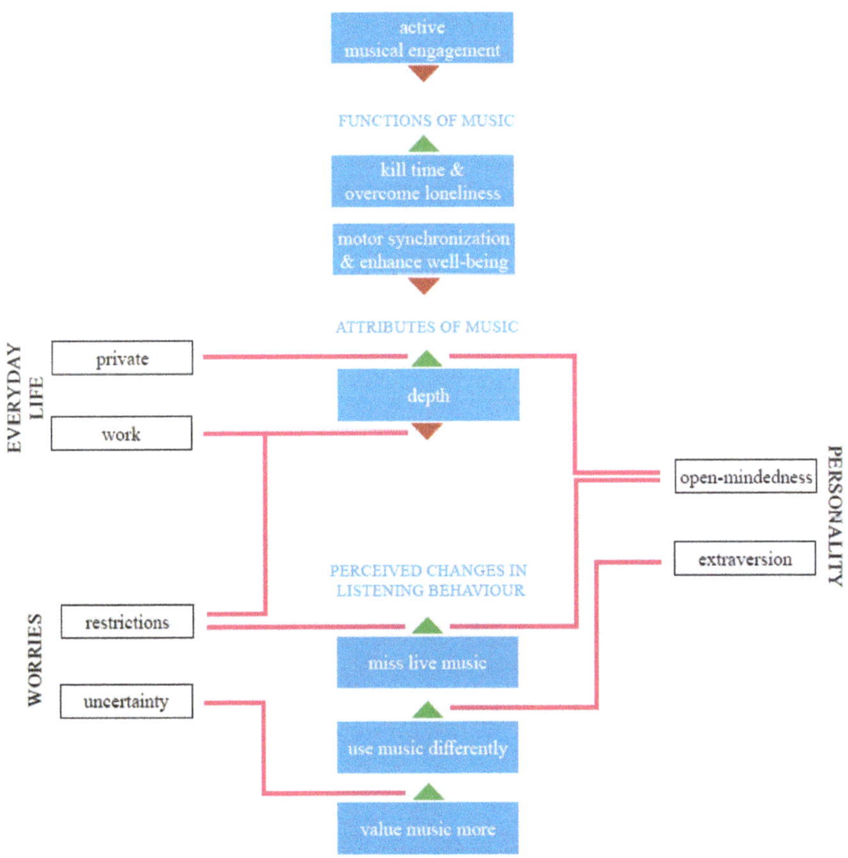

Figure 1. Changes in musical behavior during the lockdown and effects of worries, everyday life, and personality.

The figure shows factors significantly predicting changes in musical behavior from before to during the lockdown (top three boxes) and effects of worries, aspects of everyday life, and personality dimensions on music listening behavior (bottom boxes, pink lines). Green arrows show an increase during the lockdown, red arrows a decrease during the lockdown.

4.1. Decrease in Active Musical Engagement and Changes in Functions of Music Listening

Active engagement was investigated with a broad concept of being engaged with music, such as time spent on musical activities, including writing and reading about music, but excluding music making (Gold-MSI; [35,38]). We saw an overall decrease in active engagement with music during the lockdown compared to before.

If current behavioral studies report on changes in musical behavior before and during the lockdown, they have shown that the majority of participants listened to music as much or more than before restrictions [34] or show a perceived increase in musical activity [31,32], i.e., between 34% and 57% of the participants reported about adapted musical behavior during the lockdown. This is comparable to the current study, where participants report about changes in musical behavior related to different listening situations (30%) and reasons for music listening (37.6%), and missing situations in which they otherwise listen to music (54.8%). However, when comparing these results between the studies, the different assessments of musical activity need to be taken into account, as, for example, the pure listening time also slightly increased in the current study but not the overall engagement with music as measured with the Gold-MSI. By assessing active musical engagement with this standardized measure, it is investigated as a broad phenomenon and not reduced to music listening time. As no other study used this particular factor of an otherwise often cited assessment of musical sophistication, and the current study design differed from previous studies (retrospective assessment of behavior from before the lockdown), comparisons are not entirely valid.

However, the decrease in active engagement in music reflects other findings in relation to the lockdown such as a decrease in music streaming [29,30] and might be explained by the finding that people in Germany spent on average over four hours per day thinking about COVID-19 [7], indicating a permanent distraction that leaves little time and space for musical engagement.

Therefore, the reported changes in everyday life in the present study, such as missing the possibilities to pursue hobbies (52%) and changes in the working situation (64.6% working at least partly from home), have affected daily routines and habits, i.e., activities that have been shown to be tightly connected with music listening (e.g., [8,10,14]). Hence, these constraints have obviously affected music-listening routines, which need a new adjustment over time. Some adjustments could be seen in the current study, which comprise two important functions of music listening.

First, people listen to music more for the function of killing time and overcoming loneliness. Music being used to cope with negative feelings [9,16], for distraction, for filling the silence, and overcoming loneliness [9,10] are well-known functions of music listening, which were also found to be important in other recent investigations on the COVID-19 pandemic (e.g., [31,33]). Although our sample is not that strongly affected by worries concerning COVID-19, concern about changes in daily life as well as worrying that relatives and acquaintances will become infected show that participants had to deal with major constraints in their lives. Changes in private life concerning spatial distancing such as being bored (here, 52.4%) and often alone (52.9%) show moreover that people had to adapt to a "new normal". Additionally, the current study shows that for 66.6% of the participants, music is more important, which fits with the results of Fink et al. (2021) [31] and Mas-Herrero (2020) [32], who show that music is used to deal with the consequences of the pandemic and may reflect the role of music serving as a socio-emotional and distress-regulating coping strategy during troubling times.

Second, in contrast to before the lockdown, music was listened to for the function of motor synchronization and enhanced well-being during the lockdown (i.e., how music triggers movement, enhances the mood, and enables listeners to feel fit, let off steam, and sing along). Even though it was previously shown that music, in comparison to other activities such as entertainment media, was found to be the most effective activity for three out of five well-being goals, that is enjoyment, venting negative emotions, and self-connection [33], the current results show how some of these goals have changed from before to during the lockdown. Furthermore, the function used in the current study connects well-being to certain situations in which music activates people (e.g., at parties and musical events, or at the gym). As about half of the current participants miss situations in which they usually listen to music and about a third indicate listening to music in different situations and for other reasons than before, this finding contributes to the assumption that people have lost their musical as well as their activity routines during the lockdown [15]. Findings by Fink et al. (2021) [31] also show that music-listening situations changed for 42% of the participants to the extent that private music listening sessions became more likely compared to social music listening events.

4.2. Changes in Musical Behavior Depending on Personal Situation

The current results show only a few significant effects of the personal situation on music-listening behavior. Interestingly, the attribute of depth in music was one of the few significantly predicted changes: Music with depth was chosen by people who reported about changes in private life and those higher in open-mindedness. Similarly, people higher in open-mindedness and those with higher fear of further restrictions also miss live music more than others. Previous research has shown that people higher in openness were linked to self-reported musical sophistication and are known for their higher engagement and interest in music and the arts [21,22]. Granot et al. (2021) [33] also found that because music is more important for people higher in openness, the music's efficiency is also higher during the lockdown. Hence, these are the ones in the current study who miss the possibility of a higher engagement with music more strongly (such as live events), and listen to music with depth (reflective, emotional, clever music), reflecting their perceptiveness of emotion expression in music (e.g., [41], in the context of sad music).

On the other hand, people being worried by uncertainties about the future and reported changes in work life listened less to music with depth than before the lockdown. Being occupied with work or worries about the future has the effect that these people do not have the mental capacity to engage in a content-related confrontation with music (see [42,43]). Nonetheless, people who worry about the future value music more in general during the lockdown. Since private music listening provides one of the possibilities to engage with music during the lockdown, it can be used to convey some sort of normalcy and familiarity (e.g., half of the participants report listening to more familiar music during the lockdown). Particularly these people who fear an uncertain future possibly seek security or distraction by musical engagement without deeper confrontation (and therefore avoid music with depth).

Furthermore, people higher in extraversion, i.e., higher in sociability, energy level, and assertiveness [37], perceived using music differently during the lockdown. These results reflect the changes in daily life related to missing social (music listening) events and the resulting need to adapt music listening routines, as well as the need to compensate with different activities.

Overall, the small differences between differently affected groups can be explained with the current sample, which overall did not seem to be that worried by existential changes due to COVID-19 during the first lockdown in Germany. For example, while changes in the job situation are rated as unpleasant, people are still glad to have the possibility to work from home (probably to protect themselves from getting infected). Participants only partly suffer from more stress in daily family life compared to before the lockdown, which can be explained by most participants not having to take care of children and to being confronted with the balance between work and homeschooling. Furthermore, Giordano et al. (2020) [44] shows that for achieving well-being goals such as reducing tiredness, sadness, fear, and worries of clinical staff during the pandemic, the direct use of music (self-administration) is not effective compared to receptive music therapy. Hence, music listening without intervention might not be a useful strategy to deal with worries and changes in daily life in the current sample.

4.3. Limitations

The current study used a convenience sample typical for online surveys with well-educated participants and almost half being students. Only about 13% of the participants had to take care of children (note that in the representative sample of Fink et al. (2021) [31], about 31% lived with child(ren) and 11% had to do homeschooling), and most participants did not report having to face existential changes, which might partly explain why the worries were somewhat low in the current study. Nonetheless, changes in daily life were reported, which shows that the lockdown affected the people in the current study, presenting an important target to be investigated.

In general, using questionnaires to ask about music use and the time spent on music listening may lead to inaccurate responses, which is a limitation that has already been discussed in other COVID-19 and music-related studies (see, [12,34]), particularly when assessing musical behavior retrospectively as in the current study. Even though care was taken that the three questionnaires were assessed first on the retrospective view and then on the current view (and not the same one twice in a row), the responses might have been similar just because the participants remembered what they answered the first time. Still, it also means that participants had to become aware of their changes in behavior and directly compare them with before. Being aware of the strengths and limitations of this investigation, we have taken a unique approach to compare the behavior before and during the lockdown, which makes a valuable addition to other current investigations on this research topic.

The questionnaires on worries, everyday behavior, and perceived changes in music-listening behavior in the current study could not be validated beforehand due to the shortness of time (which is a typical problem in COVID-19 related studies, as discussed in Bäuerle et al. (2020) [4]). Care was taken that the items chosen covered daily topics present in the media and statistical reports of official channels in April 2020. Seeing strong overlap with other current approaches to music and COVID-19 [31–33] assured us that the selection was adequate.

5. Conclusions

Research has provided ample evidence on how various levels of music affect people's everyday lives, but studies about musical engagement in exceptional and troubling times are rare. The study of the COVID-19 pandemic has given us a sad but unique opportunity to start filling in this gap: With the current study, we focused on changes from before and during the lockdown in Germany and on trying to find the connection between the restrictions applied and the changes in music-listening behavior. Overall, we see a decrease in musical engagement in the current sample, reflecting changes in daily routines and a lower capacity to engage with music due to the new challenges. Adjustments of music listening to the lockdown situation include music being used more to kill time and overcome loneliness and less for motor synchronization and enhanced well-being, reflecting a change in musical functions toward coping with loneliness and fewer possibilities to actively engage with music together with other people. In the same vein, many people report missing live music, particularly those worrying about further restrictions, showing the valuable effect of in-person engagement with music.

Finally, the results of the present study can give insights into how people use music during other exceptional circumstances such as death, illness, unemployment, or separation, in which people have to deal with similar worries and changes in daily life.

Supplementary Materials: The following are available online at https://www.mdpi.com/article/10.3390/ijerph181910463/s1, Supporting Information, Data, Questionnaire.

Author Contributions: N.A.R. and J.M. designed the research, N.A.R. collected the data, J.M. and N.A.R. analyzed the data, N.A.R. and J.M. wrote the manuscript. All authors have read and agreed to the published version of the manuscript.

Funding: This research received no external funding.

Institutional Review Board Statement: All experimental procedures were approved by the Ethics Council of the Max Planck Society, and were undertaken with written informed consent of each participant.

Informed Consent Statement: Informed consent was obtained from all participants involved in the study.

Data Availability Statement: The data are included as Supplementary Materials.

Acknowledgments: We would like to thank Katja Rudolph for help with recruiting participants.

Conflicts of Interest: The authors declare no conflict of interest.

References

1. Bundesagentur für Arbeit. Entwicklung des Arbeitsmarkts 2020 in Deutschland. Available online: https://www.arbeitsagentur.de/news/arbeitsmarkt-2020 (accessed on 22 November 2020).
2. Robert Koch Institut. März 2020: Archiv der Situationsberichte des Robert Koch-Instituts zu COVID-19 (ab 4.3.2020). Available online: https://www.rki.de/DE/Content/InfAZ/N/Neuartiges_Coronavirus/Situationsberichte/Archiv_M%C3%A4rz.html (accessed on 22 November 2020).
3. Entringer, T.M.; Kröger, H. Einsam, aber Resilient: Die Menschen haben den Lockdown besser verkraftet als vermutet. Available online: http://hdl.handle.net/10419/222876 (accessed on 22 November 2020).
4. Bäuerle, A.; Teufel, M.; Musche, V.; Weismüller, B.; Kohler, H.; Hetkamp, M.; Dörrie, N.; Schweda, A.; Skoda, E.-M. Increased generalized anxiety, depression and distress during the COVID-19 pandemic: A cross-sectional study in Germany. *J. Public Health* **2020**, *42*, 672–678. [CrossRef]
5. Dupuy, J.-B.; Beaudoin, S.; Rhéaume, J.; Ladouceur, R.; Dugas, M. Worry: Daily self-report in clinical and non-clinical populations. *Behav. Res. Ther.* **2001**, *39*, 1249–1255. [CrossRef]
6. Verkuil, B.; Brosschot, J.F.; Gebhardt, W.A.; Thayer, J.F. When Worries Make you Sick: A Review of Perseverative Cognition, the Default Stress Response and Somatic Health. *J. Exp. Psychopathol.* **2010**, *1*, jep.009110. [CrossRef]
7. Petzold, M.B.; Bendau, A.; Plag, J.; Pyrkosch, L.; Mascarell Maricic, L.; Betzler, F.; Rogoll, J.; Große, J.; Ströhle, A. Risk, resilience, psychological distress, and anxiety at the beginning of the COVID-19 pandemic in Germany. *Brain Behav.* **2020**, *10*, e01745. [CrossRef]
8. Rentfrow, P.J.; Gosling, S.D. The do re mi's of everyday life: The structure and personality correlates of music preferences. *J. Personal. Soc. Psychol.* **2003**, *84*, 1236–1256. [CrossRef] [PubMed]
9. Lonsdale, A.J.; North, A.C. Why do we listen to music? A uses and gratifications analysis. *Br. J. Psychol.* **2011**, *102*, 108–134. [CrossRef] [PubMed]
10. Greb, F.; Schlotz, W.; Steffens, J. Personal and situational influences on the functions of music listening. *Psychol. Music* **2018**, *46*, 763–794. [CrossRef]
11. Juslin, P.N.; Liljeström, S.; Västfjäll, D.; Barradas, G.; Silva, A. An experience sampling study of emotional reactions to music: Listener, music, and situation. *Emotion* **2008**, *8*, 668–683. [CrossRef] [PubMed]
12. North, A.C.; Hargreaves, D.J.; Hargreaves, J.J. Uses of Music in Everyday Life. *Music Perception* **2004**, *22*, 41–77. [CrossRef]
13. Sloboda, J.A.; O'Neill, S.A.; Ivaldi, A. Functions of Music in Everyday Life: An Exploratory Study Using the Experience Sampling Method. *Musicae Sci.* **2001**, *5*, 9–32. [CrossRef]
14. van Goethem, A.; Sloboda, J. The functions of music for affect regulation. *Musicae Sci.* **2011**, *15*, 208–228. [CrossRef]
15. Jaspal, R.; Nerlich, B. Social representations, identity threat, and coping amid COVID-19. *Psychol. Trauma Theory Res. Pract. Policy* **2020**, *12*, S249–S251. [CrossRef] [PubMed]
16. DeNora, T. Music as a technology of the self. *Poetics* **1999**, *27*, 31–56. [CrossRef]
17. Sloboda, J.A. Music in everyday life: The role of emotions. In *Handbook of Music and Emotion: Theory, Research, and Applications*; Juslin, P.N., Sloboda, J.A., Eds.; Oxford University Press: Oxford, UK; New York, NY, USA, 2010; pp. 493–515.
18. Groarke, J.M.; Hogan, M.J. Enhancing wellbeing: An emerging model of the adaptive functions of music listening. *Psychol. Music* **2016**, *44*, 769–791. [CrossRef]
19. van den Tol, A.J.; Edwards, J. Listening to sad music in adverse situations: How music selection strategies relate to self-regulatory goals, listening effects, and mood enhancement. *Psychol. Music* **2015**, *43*, 473–494. [CrossRef]
20. Randall, W.M.; Rickard, N.S. Reasons for personal music listening: A mobile experience sampling study of emotional outcomes. *Psychol. Music* **2017**, *45*, 479–495. [CrossRef]

21. Greenberg, D.M.; Müllensiefen, D.; Lamb, M.E.; Rentfrow, P.J. Personality predicts musical sophistication. *J. Res. Personal.* **2015**, *58*, 154–158. [CrossRef]
22. Nave, G.; Minxha, J.; Greenberg, D.M.; Kosinski, M.; Stillwell, D.; Rentfrow, J. Musical Preferences Predict Personality: Evidence From Active Listening and Facebook Likes. *Psychol. Sci.* **2018**, *29*, 1145–1158. [CrossRef]
23. Daniel, E. Music used as anti-anxiety intervention for patients during outpatient procedures: A review of the literature. *Complementary Ther. Clin. Pract.* **2016**, *22*, 21–23. [CrossRef]
24. Knight, W.E.; Rickard, N.S. Relaxing music prevents stress-induced increases in subjective anxiety, systolic blood pressure, and heart rate in healthy males and females. *J. Music. Ther.* **2001**, *38*, 254–272. [CrossRef]
25. Hodges, D.A. Psychophysiological Measures. In *Handbook of Music and Emotion: Theory, Research, and Applications*; Juslin, P.N., Sloboda, J.A., Eds.; Oxford University Press: Oxford, UK; New York, NY, USA, 2010; pp. 279–311.
26. Kreutz, G.; Murcia, C.Q.; Bongard, S. Psychoneuroendocrine Research on Music and Health: An Overview. In *Music, Health, and Wellbeing*; Kreutz, G., MacDonald, R.A., Mitchell, L., Eds.; Oxford University Press: Oxford, UK, 2013; pp. 457–476.
27. DeNora, T. *Music in Everyday Life*, 9th ed.; Cambridge University Press: Cambridge, UK, 2010.
28. Gabrielsson, A. *Strong Experiences with Music: Music Is Much More Than Just Music*; Oxford University Press: Oxford, UK, 2011.
29. Yeung, T.Y.-C. Did the COVID-19 Pandemic Trigger Nostalgia? Evidence of Music Consumption on Spotify. *SSRN J.* **2020**. [CrossRef]
30. Sim, J.; Cho, D.; Hwang, Y.; Telang, R. Virus Shook the Streaming Star: Estimating the COVID-19 Impact on Music Consumption. *SSRN J.* **2020**, *44*, 154–185. [CrossRef]
31. Fink, L.; Warrenburg, L.A.; Howlin, C.; Randall, W.M.; Hansen, N.C.; Wald-Fuhrmann, M. Viral Tunes: Changes in musical behaviours and interest in coronamusic predict socio-emotional coping during COVID-19 lockdown. *Humanit. Soc. Sci. Commun.* **2021**, *8*, 180. [CrossRef]
32. Mas-Herrero, E.; Singer, N.; Ferreri, L.; McPhee, M.; Zatorre, R.; Ripolles, P. Rock 'n' Roll but not Sex or Drugs: Music is negatively correlated to depressive symptoms during the COVID-19 pandemic via reward-related mechanisms. *PsyArXiv* **2020**. [CrossRef]
33. Granot, R.; Spitz, D.; Cherki, B.; Loui, P.; Timmers, R.; Schaefer, R.; Vuoskoski, J.K.; Soares-Quadros, J.; Cardenas-Soler, R.; Li, S.; et al. "Help! I Need Somebody": Music as a Global Resource for Obtaining Wellbeing Goals in Times of Crisis. *Front. Psychol.* **2021**, *12*, 1038. [CrossRef] [PubMed]
34. Cabedo-Mas, A.; Arriaga-Sanz, C.; Moliner-Miravet, L. Uses and Perceptions of Music in Times of COVID-19: A Spanish Population Survey. *Front. Psychol.* **2020**, *11*, 606180. [CrossRef] [PubMed]
35. Müllensiefen, D.; Gingras, B.; Musil, J.; Stewart, L. The musicality of non-musicians: An index for assessing musical sophistication in the general population. *PLoS ONE* **2014**, *9*, e89642.
36. Fricke, K.R.; Herzberg, P.Y. Personality and self-reported preference for music genres and attributes in a German-speaking sample. *J. Res. Personal.* **2017**, *68*, 114–123. [CrossRef]
37. Soto, C.J.; John, O.P. The next Big Five Inventory (BFI-2): Developing and assessing a hierarchical model with 15 facets to enhance bandwidth, fidelity, and predictive power. *J. Personal. Soc. Psychol.* **2017**, *113*, 117–143. [CrossRef]
38. Schaal, N.K.; Bauer, A.-K.R.; Müllensiefen, D. Der Gold-MSI: Replikation und Validierung eines Fragebogeninstrumentes zur Messung Musikalischer Erfahrenheit anhand einer deutschen Stichprobe. *Musicae Sci.* **2014**, *18*, 423–447. [CrossRef]
39. Danner, D.; Rammstedt, B.; Bluemke, M.; Treiber, L.; Berres, S.; Soto, C.; John, O. *Die Deutsche Version des Big Five Inventory 2 (BFI-2)*; Zusammenstellung sozialwissenschaftlicher Items und Skalen (ZIS), 2016. [CrossRef]
40. Schlotz, W.; Yim, I.S.; Zoccola, P.M.; Jansen, L.; Schulz, P. The Perceived Stress Reactivity Scale: Measurement invariance, stability, and validity in three countries. *Psychol. Assess.* **2011**, *23*, 80–94. [CrossRef]
41. Vuoskoski, J.K.; Thompson, W.F.; McIlwain, D.; Eerola, T. Who Enjoys Listening to Sad Music and Why? *Music Percept.* **2012**, *29*, 311–317. [CrossRef]
42. McIntosh, W.D.; Schwegler, A.F.; Terry-Murray, R.M. Threat and Television Viewing in the United States, 1960–1990. *Media Psychol.* **2000**, *2*, 35–46. [CrossRef]
43. Pettijohn, T.F.; Sacco, D.F. Tough times, meaningful music, mature performers: Popular Billboard songs and performer preferences across social and economic conditions in the USA. *Psychol. Music* **2009**, *37*, 155–179. [CrossRef]
44. Giordano, F.; Scarlata, E.; Baroni, M.; Gentile, E.; Puntillo, F.; Brienza, N.; Gesualdo, L. Receptive music therapy to reduce stress and improve wellbeing in Italian clinical staff involved in COVID-19 pandemic: A preliminary study. *Arts Psychother.* **2020**, *70*, 101688. [CrossRef] [PubMed]

International Journal of
Environmental Research and Public Health

MDPI

Article

The Impact of COVID-19 Pandemic on Italian University Students' Mental Health: Changes across the Waves

Micaela Di Consiglio, Sheila Merola, Tiziana Pascucci, Cristiano Violani and Alessandro Couyoumdjian *

Department of Psychology, Sapienza University of Rome, 00185 Rome, Italy; micaela.diconsiglio@uniroma1.it (M.D.C.); sheila.merola@uniroma1.it (S.M.); tiziana.pascucci@uniroma1.it (T.P.); cristiano.violani@uniroma1.it (C.V.)
* Correspondence: alessandro.couyoumdjian@uniroma1.it

Abstract: To reduce the spread of COVID-19, the Italian government imposed a rigid lockdown and, for a whole year, continued to declare stringent rules to curb the community spread. This study provides an overview of university students' symptomatology and help-seeking behaviour before and during the pandemic. It aims to evaluate the impact of the different phases of the pandemic on students' mental health. We collected data in four-time points between March 2019 and March 2021. A total of 454 students (F = 85; M = 15) were included in the study. Students answered a socio-demographic and a standardized questionnaire (i.e., SCL-90-R) to evaluate a broad range of symptomatology. The results suggest that students experienced moderate to severe levels of depressive, obsessive-compulsive and anxiety symptomatology. About 14% of the sample met the criteria for at least one mental health disorder, but most were not receiving mental health care. During the lockdown, compared with other phases, female students reported worse symptoms in the obsessive-compulsive, interpersonal sensitivity, depression, paranoid ideation, and psychoticism dimensions. The increasing symptomatology disappeared after the lifting of the lockdown. The results showed no difference in the male groups. Preventive and support strategies should be improved in the university context.

Keywords: COVID-19; university students; mental health; psychological distress; help-seeking behavior

Citation: Di Consiglio, M.; Merola, S.; Pascucci, T.; Violani, C.; Couyoumdjian, A. The Impact of COVID-19 Pandemic on Italian University Students' Mental Health: Changes across the Waves. *Int. J. Environ. Res. Public Health* **2021**, *18*, 9897. https://doi.org/10.3390/ijerph18189897

Academic Editor: Paul B. Tchounwou

Received: 24 August 2021
Accepted: 17 September 2021
Published: 20 September 2021

1. Introduction

On 5 January 2020, the World Health Organization (WHO) issued the first disease outbreak news report about a severe acute respiratory syndrome cluster of unknown causes. Later, the WHO assessed that this disease, named COVID-19 and caused by coronavirus SARS-CoV-2, constituted a public health emergency of international concern, and could be characterized as a pandemic. As of March 2020, Italy was the second country globally in terms of registered cases and the first in terms of victims. To combat the rapid escalation of cases in Italy and curb the community spread, Italy's government declared a state of emergency. The first and most rigid containment measure imposed was a national quarantine or lockdown, restricting the movement of the population except for necessity and health circumstances. Italy was the first state in Europe to follow such lockdown measures: attending school and going to work was not allowed, except for well-grounded work-related reasons, and public gatherings were prohibited. The decree also provided the obligation to stay isolated at home for anyone infected [1].

The lockdown caused a sudden change in the population's habits and free movements. Consequently, mental health problems, including anxiety, fear, depressive symptoms, loneliness, and sleep problems, increased to some degree [2–4]. For example, a literature review that evaluated the effects of the COVID-19 pandemic on the population's mental health showed high rates of different symptomatology such as anxiety (ranging from 6.33% to 50.9%), depression (ranging from 14.6% to 48.3%) and posttraumatic stress disorder (ranging from 7% to 53.8%). Moreover, the prevalence of psychological distress ranged from 34.43% to 38% [5]. Studies conducted on the potential psychological impact on the Italian general public have showed that, during the lockdown, a high prevalence of individuals presented anxiety and depressive symptoms, posttraumatic stress symptomatology and sleep disturbances [6–8]. Furthermore, some non-governmental organizations registered an alarming rise in the death rate by suicide; between March and November 2020, 100 out of 200 suicides and suicide attempts in Italy were correlated with COVID-19 [9]. Hence, in the last year, a number of studies were conducted to explore the effect of the lockdown on mental health, suggesting a significant negative impact on individuals' health. However, even if the most stringent lockdown lasted some months, the Italian government continued to declare a series of containment measures to curb the community spread (Table 1). These measures changed quickly based on different indexes regarding the incidence rate, transmission numbers, hospital occupancy and other factors to assess the risk level in each region. Regions were classified into three areas —red, orange, or yellow—corresponding to three risk scenarios, for which specific restrictive measures were foreseen. Besides the three areas, the nation as a whole had to observe a night curfew (from 10 p.m. to 5 a.m.) and people were constantly obliged to wear a mask, including outdoors, and maintain a distance of at least one meter from other people [10]. To the best of our knowledge, less is known about the impact of such restrictions on individuals' mental health.

Table 1. Containment measures in Italy.

Phase	Date	Decree
Quarantine Phase (March–May)	9 March 2020	National lockdown (at-home quarantine, closure of non-essential businesses, schools, and universities).
	4 May 2020	People were allowed to visit their relatives.
	18 May 2020	Reopening of bars, restaurants, beauty centres and other commercial and non-essential businesses.
Second Phase (October–December)	8 October 2020	Mandatory use of masks.
	13 October 2020	Limits on gatherings.
	26 October 2020	Closure of sports centres, cinemas, theatres, museums, and other public spaces and gathering places.
	6 November 2020	Imposition of nationwide night curfew and classification of regions into three areas—red, orange, and yellow—corresponding to three risk scenarios, for which specific restrictive measures were foreseen.
	24–27 December 2020	National red zone.
Third Phase (January–March)	1–3 January 2021	National red zone.
	5–6 January 2021	National red zone.
	7 January 2021	Specific restrictive measures in every region based on the risk scenarios.

Source: https://www.gazzettaufficiale.it/ (accessed on 12 July 2021).

1.1. Mental Health among University Students

The COVID-19 outbreak has impacted almost all sectors of society, including higher education. Indeed, all classes were suspended because of social distancing, and students had to follow lessons using online platforms during the lockdown [11]. These changes had a significant impact on students' lifestyle, academic performance, and mental health. Most students have negative perceptions about e-learning and believe that it does not greatly impact their learning [12]. Approximately 50% of students reported a decrease in study hours and their academic performance, over 10% of students delayed graduation or dropped out from classes, about 40% of working students lost their job [13], and approximately 55% of students reported increasing concern about the exam outcomes [14]. Regarding mental health issues, students reported an increased level of stress, anxiety, and depression during the COVID-19 pandemic [15–17] and an increase in suicidal thoughts [18]. Moreover, students reported difficulty concentrating on academic work and negative changes in their sleep and dietary patterns [17]. Some studies found significant sex differences: female students showed more anxiety than male students [19], and they were at more risk of developing depression in comparison to males. Moreover, females reported more sleep and sexual problems [18]. Some factors contributed to increased stress, anxiety, and depression among university students, such as worry about health, disruption of the daily routine, decreased social interaction [17], and a history of self-injury and suicidal attempts [18]. These results are particularly relevant if we consider that, even before the pandemic, mental health problems were widespread among university students. Anxiety disorders (i.e., panic disorder, generalized anxiety disorders, and social phobia), mood disorders, and substance disorders are the most prevalent disorders among university students [20]. Even if it is not a specific diagnosis, suicide is a significant problem among university students: 6.7% of students have suicidal ideation [21]. Moreover, mental health problems were associated with role impairment in different domains [22] and university career problems [23]. Often, students do not ask for psychological help despite feeling the need for it. Young people prefer to ask for help from friends or family rather than doctors or psychologists [24]. The general misinformation about mental health and the fear of being stigmatized frequently prevent help-seeking behaviour [25,26].

1.2. The Study: Aims and Scope

Such evidence suggests the need to prioritize students' mental health [27] and that the psychological health of university students impacted by the pandemic should be taken seriously. Sapienza University of Rome has offered online psychological support to its students in the wake of this emergency. Online therapy represents the best way to help students facing psychological and emotional problems due to the pandemic and the consequence of routine disruption [28]. In addition to a counselling service, students could also join the NoiBene program. NoiBene is a web-based intervention to promote psychological well-being and prevent psychological distress by developing a series of competencies (i.e., life skills) and reducing dysfunctional coping strategies. Before the pandemic, NoiBene had already been used, and analyses showed its effectiveness in promoting psychological well-being and reducing dysfunctional coping strategies among university students [29]. To deal with COVID-19-related stress, modules about loneliness, relaxation techniques, breathing exercises, and mindfulness were added. Moreover, the intervention included individual weekly meetings with a tutor, a psychologist that supervised the program. The tutor aimed to monitor the online program's progress, provide answers to any questions that the students might have about the exercises, and give support for any issues concerning the quarantine.

The present study aims to provide an explorative and descriptive overview of the symptomatology and help-seeking behaviour of students included in NoiBene between March 2019 and March 2021. The Ethical Committee of the Department of Psychology, Sapienza University of Rome, approved the NoiBene protocol. We hypothesized that the following restrictions had impacted the individuals' psychological health as well as the first quarantine. We divided students into three phases: (a) March 2020–May 2020 (Quarantine Phase); (b) October 2020–December 2020 (Second Phase); (c) January 2021–March 2021 (Third Phase). The quarantine phase was characterized by the most stringent lockdown and by a gradual reopening. During the second phase, after an increase in transmission, the government imposed new restrictive measures such as the mandatory use of masks (including outdoors), the prohibition of gatherings of more than a certain number of people, and a nationwide night curfew. Moreover, the government classified regions into three areas corresponding to three risk scenarios. Lastly, during the third phase, besides previous rules that were maintained, a specific national quarantine was imposed during the national holidays (Table 1). Therefore, we compared clinical symptomatology between students Before COVID with students gathered in the three phases (Quarantine Phase, Second Phase, Third Phase). We formulated a series of research hypotheses based on the specific restriction measures in the different phases, the evolution of the pandemic, and the increasing knowledge about COVID-19 (including the origin of the virus, its transmission, and the mechanisms to stop its spread).

Considering that the COVID-19 quarantine significantly limited social interaction, thereby increasing feelings of loneliness [30,31], we expected that students' depressive symptomatology and relational problems during the first quarantine were higher than those of students in the other groups. Moreover, considering the high level of uncertainty regarding health and economic issues during the quarantine and the uncertainty about the evolution of the pandemic, we expected that anxiety symptomatology during the first quarantine was higher than anxiety symptomatology during the other phases [32]. Lastly, we expected that students' distress was higher than the Second Phase but lower than the Quarantine Phase during the Third Phase. Indeed, in the Third Phase, people brought with them a year of restriction and suffering. Moreover, the beginning of the vaccination campaign promoted hope and a more positive perspective of change but, on the other hand, was associated with fear and uncertainty regarding its efficacy [33,34].

2. Materials and Methods

2.1. Participants

NoiBene was publicized through the official Sapienza website on a page devoted to promoting well-being services. Participation was voluntary and free of charge. NoiBene was presented as a guided self-help program to develop some useful skills to cope with the well-being challenges brought about by the pandemic. Informed consent about the research protocol was presented to every student that asked to follow the program. Twenty-one students did not accept to be included in the study, so they used the program, but their data were excluded from the analysis. The final sample was composed of four-hundred-and-fifty-four (n = 454) students, aged from 19 to 54 (M = 24.80; SD = 4.10), with a majority being female (M = 68; F = 386). Most of the students live with their parents (63.1%), with flatmates (25.3%) and a minority with their partners (5.7%), alone (3.7%) or with a brother or sister (1.1%). The majority of participants (61.7%) were enrolled in the Faculty of Medicine and Psychology and were completing a Master's degree course (59%). About 35.9% of the students never sought psychological help, 15.9% had accessed mental health treatment in the past, and 6.8% were in ongoing therapy. About 41.4% did not give this information.

2.2. Measures

To assess psychological distress, we administered, to every student, the Symptom Checklist-90-Revised, SCL-90-R [35,36], a multidimensional self-report inventory covering nine dimensions of psychological distress: somatization (SOM—distress arising from bodily perceptions), obsessive-compulsive (OC—thoughts, impulses, and actions that are experienced as irresistible), interpersonal sensitivity (IS—feelings of personal inadequacy and inferiority, and distress during interpersonal interactions), depression (DEP—symptoms of depressive syndromes), anxiety (ANX—symptoms that are associated with manifest anxiety), hostility (HOS—thoughts and feelings of anger, irritability, and resentment), phobic anxiety (PHOB—persistent fear response to a specific person, place, object, or situation that leads to avoidance or escape behaviour), paranoid ideation (PAR—projective thinking, hostility, suspiciousness, and centrality), and psychoticism (PSY—withdrawal, isolation, and schizoid lifestyle). It also included three global indices of psychological distress: the Global Severity Index (GSI—index of overall psychological distress), the Positive Symptom Distress Index (PSDI—index of the intensity of symptoms), and the Positive Symptoms

Total (PST—number of self-reported symptoms). The scores were converted to standard T-scores using the norm group appropriate for the participants. T-scores between 55 and 65 suggested moderate to elevated symptomatology; T-scores above 65 suggested elevated symptoms. The Symptom Checklist-90-Revised is an established instrument and has several studies supporting its reliability and validity. Its test-retest reliability has been reported at 0.80 to 0.90 with a time interval of one week. All nine primary subscales correlate with other broad-range inventories [35]. The Italian translation and validation showed Cronbach α values from 0.68 to 0.87 for the nine dimensions [36]. In our study, the Cronbach α ranged from 0.77 to 0.91 for the nine dimensions.

Moreover, every student completed an ad hoc questionnaire to collect demographic data (i.e., age, occupation, residence) and information about their academic status (i.e., faculty, degree course).

2.3. Procedure

Every student that asked to participate received a personal account on NoiBene [29] and provided informed consent about data protection and privacy according to the General Data Protection Regulation (GDPR; EU 2016/679). Then, they answered the SCL-90-R questionnaire. Students with elevated levels of symptomatology were contacted for a diagnostic interview. If severe ongoing clinical conditions (e.g., mood disorders, psychotic disorders) or suicidal ideation were confirmed, the student received feedback about their symptomatology and was directed towards the treatment suited to their needs. In this case, NoiBene was used as a support for their therapy. Otherwise, each student was contacted by a tutor. An experienced psychotherapist supervised the activity of the tutors during the duration of the program. Students could meet the tutor once a week; the meetings were held on video-call platforms, guaranteeing a private space. Every meeting started with a mood check. Then, the tutor introduced specific contents regarding psychological well-being or cognitive vulnerability and discussed any issues with the students. Between meetings, every student was asked to complete the module regarding the topic discussed previously. Indeed, except for the first one, every meeting included a revision about homework (see Table S1 in Supplementary Materials for more details).

3. Statistical Analyses

Statistical analyses were performed using SPSS version 27.0 for Windows (IBM Corp., Armonk, NY, USA). A series of descriptive analyses were conducted on participant characteristics (i.e., demographic variables, academic data, symptomatology, and help-seeking behaviour). A Chi-Squared Test was run to examine whether there was a difference between groups in the proportion of male and female participants. It showed a significantly different distribution of males and females across groups. For this reason, group comparison analyses were conducted considering males and females differently. A series of one-way analysis of variances (ANOVAs) were conducted to investigate differences between four female groups (BeforeCOVID vs. Quarantine vs. SecondPhase vs. ThirdPhase). Considering that the males' symptomatology rating was non-normally distributed, as measured by the Shapiro–Wilk test (p values ranged from <0.001 to 0.02), a series of non-parametric Kruskal–Wallis analyses were conducted to investigate differences between four male groups (BeforeCOVID vs. Quarantine vs. SecondPhase vs. ThirdPhase). The level of significance was set at $p < 0.05$. Effect sizes were calculated using partial eta squared (partial-η^2) for ANOVAs and eta squared (η^2) for Kruskal–Wallis analyses. Both were interpreted based on benchmarks suggested by Cohen [37]: $\eta^2 = 0.01$, small effect size; $\eta^2 = 0.06$, medium effect size; $\eta^2 = 0.14$, large effect size. The post hoc analyses of significant interactions were conducted using the Fisher LSD post hoc test.

4. Results

4.1. Preliminary Analyses

To investigate any differences between groups in terms of the age and gender variables, we conducted a one-way ANOVA and a Chi-Squared test, respectively. No significant differences were found for the age variable ($F(3, 453) = 0.58$, $p = 0.63$). A Chi-Squared test showed a gender difference between groups (χ^2 (23, $N = 454$) = 12.8, $p = 0.005$). In particular, the Adjusted Standardized Residual (ASR), an index based on the difference between the observed counts and expected counts, suggests a significant number of males in the Quarantine group (ASR = 2.8) and a significant number of females in the Third group (ASR = 2.4). Considering the different distribution of male and females across groups (Table 2), we decided to conduct group comparison analyses differently for the male and female groups.

Table 2. Gender by group.

Gender	Before COVID (n = 153)	Quarantine (n = 74)	Second Phase (n = 98)	Third Phase (n = 129)	Total (n = 454)
F	82.4%	74.3%	88.8%	91.5%	85.02%
M	17.6%	25.7%	11.2%	8.5%	14.98%

4.2. Symptomatology

As shown in Table 3, students' mean scores were below the pathological cut-off in every clinical dimension. However, it is noteworthy that the percentage of students who scored above the cut-off was considerable. For example, about 35.2% of students reported an elevated level of depressive symptomatology, and 32.5% of students reported obsessive-compulsive symptomatology. Moreover, about 28.6% of students presented an elevated level of psychological distress and 32.8% of students reported intensive symptomatology.

Table 3. Mean scores (*SD*) of SCL-90-R and percentage of pathological students.

Variable	*M (SD)*	$55 \leq T < 65$ (%)	$T \geq 65$ (%)	Total (%)
SCL-90-R				
Somatization	48.84 (10.77)	12.6	11.0	23.6
Obsessive-compulsive	50.09 (11.39)	17.6	14.5	32.5
Interpersonal sensitivity	48.03 (9.94)	16.5	7.3	23.8
Depression	52.35 (12.27)	16.7	18.5	35.2
Anxiety	50.38 (10.72)	17.0	11.7	28.6
Anger-hostility	47.59 (8.65)	13.0	4.8	17.8
Phobic anxiety	50.14 (10.35)	12.6	8.6	21.1
Paranoid ideation	44.10 (8.47)	8.1	3.7	11.9
Psychoticism	49.95 (9.43)	14.1	9.7	23.8
GSI	49.66 (10.80)	16.7	11.9	28.6
PSDI	51.24 (9.77)	21.6	11.2	32.8
PST	48.18 (11.45)	18.5	11.2	29.7

SCL-90-R = Symptom Checklist-90-Revised; GSI = Global Severity Index; PSDI = Positive Symptom Distress Index; PST = Positive Symptom.

4.3. Group Comparison

A series of one-way ANOVAs were conducted to investigate differences between four female groups: BeforeCOVID vs. Quarantine vs. SecondPhase vs. ThirdPhase. As shown in Table 4, one-way ANOVA showed a significant difference between groups on obsessive-compulsive symptomatology ($F(3, 385) = 3.51$, $p = 0.015$, partial-$\eta^2 = 0.03$). A further post hoc test found that participants in the Quarantine group scored higher than participants in BeforeCOVID group ($p = 0.005$), in the SecondPhase group ($p = 0.002$) and in ThirdPhase group ($p = 0.014$). Results indicated a significant difference between groups in interpersonal sensitivity symptoms ($F(3, 385) = 5.11$, $p = 0.002$, partial-$\eta^2 = 0.04$). A further post hoc test found that feelings of personal inadequacy and inferiority were significantly higher in the Quarantine group than in BeforeCOVID group ($p < 0.001$), in the SecondPhase group ($p < 0.001$) and in ThirdPhase group ($p < 0.001$). Analyses showed a significant difference between groups on depression symptomatology ($F(3, 385) = 4.20$, $p = 0.006$, partial-$\eta^2 = 0.03$). Post hoc analyses suggest that the level of depression in the Quarantine group was statistically higher than the BeforeCOVID group ($p < 0.001$), SecondPhase group ($p = 0.006$) and higher than the ThirdPhase group ($p = 0.004$). There was a statistically significant difference between groups in the paranoid ideation dimension as determined by one-way ANOVA ($F(3, 385) = 3.76$, $p = 0.011$, partial-$\eta^2 = 0.03$). Post hoc analyses suggest that hostility and suspiciousness thoughts in the Quarantine group were statistically higher than BeforeCOVID group ($p = 0.014$), SecondPhase group ($p = 0.002$) and statistically higher than ThirdPhase group ($p = 0.003$). Moreover, analysis showed significant differences in the psychoticism dimension ($F(3, 385) = 3.96$; $p = 0.008$, partial-$\eta^2 = 0.03$). A post hoc test revealed that withdrawal and isolation behaviours, in the Quarantine group were statistically higher than the BeforeCOVID group ($p = 0.01$), the SecondPhase group ($p = 0.005$) and statistically higher than the ThirdPhase group ($p < 0.001$). One-way-ANOVA showed a significant difference between groups on the level of psychological distress ($F(3, 385) = 3.65$, $p = 0.013$, partial-$\eta^2 = 0.03$). Post hoc analysis indicated that the level of overall psychological distress in the Quarantine group was significantly higher than the BeforeCOVID group ($p = 0.004$), SecondPhase group ($p = 0.004$) and ThirdPhase group ($p = 0.004$). Lastly, analysis showed a significant difference between groups on the number of self-reported symptoms ($F(3, 385) = 4.41$, $p = 0.005$, partial-$\eta^2 = 0.03$). Post hoc analyses indicate that the number of self-reported symptoms in the Quarantine group was statistically higher than the BeforeCOVID group ($p < 0.001$), SecondPhase group ($p = 0.003$) and statistically higher than the ThirdPhase group ($p = 0.002$). There were no statistically significant differences between group means as determined by one-way ANOVA in the other dimensions. See Figure S1 in Supplementary Materials for a graphic representation of descriptive analyses.

Table 1. Mean (*SD*) score by female groups; ANOVA analysis.

	Groups						
	Before COVID ($n = 126$)	**Quarantine** ($n = 55$)	**Second Phase** ($n = 87$)	**Third Phase** ($n = 118$)	F ($df = 3$)	p	**Partial-η^2**
SCL-90-R							
Somatization	48.82 (10.89)	51.44 (9.75)	48.02 (11.22)	48.29 (10.74)	1.34	0.262	0.010
Obsessive-compulsive	48.70 (11.62)	53.74 (11.75)	47.97 (10.01)	49.31 (10.65)	3.51	0.015	0.027
Interpersonal sensitivity	47.10 (9.76)	52.37 (11.55)	46.64 (9.62)	46.72 (8.86)	5.11	0.002	0.038
Depression	50.34 (12.59)	57.01 (11.86)	51.37 (11.84)	51.37 (11.36)	4.20	0.006	0.032
Anxiety	49.49 (11.80)	52.28 (10.73)	49.07 (9.20)	49.84 (9.42)	1.21	0.305	0.001
Anger-hostility	47.25 (8.72)	49.67 (10.43)	47.25 (8.19)	47.24 (8.07)	1.23	0.300	0.010
Phobic anxiety	49.11 (9.53)	52.29 (13.68)	51.55 (11.49)	48.84 (7.33)	2.46	0.062	0.019
Paranoid ideation	43.63 (8.88)	46.91 (9.15)	42.55 (6.79)	42.86 (8.01)	3.76	0.011	0.029
Psychoticism	49.31 (9.87)	53.05 (10.95)	48.75 (7.89)	48.20 (7.27)	3.96	0.008	0.030
GSI	48.49 (11.65)	53.45 (10.58)	48.21 (9.88)	48.46 (9.53)	3.65	0.013	0.028
PSDI	46.46 (11.98)	52.56 (10.11)	46.89 (10.54)	46.94 (10.76)	2.20	0.088	0.017
PST	50.22 (10.20)	54.01 (9.45)	50.28 (10.11)	50.86 (8.95)	4.41	0.005	0.033

SCL-90-R = Symptom Checklist-90-Revised; GSI = Global Severity Index; PSDI = Positive Symptom Distress Index; PST = Positive Symptom.

A series of Kruskal–Wallis analyses were conducted to investigate differences between four male groups: BeforeCOVID vs. Quarantine vs. SecondPhase vs. ThirdPhase. As shown in Table 5, the results showed no significant differences between the male groups. See Figure S2 in Supplementary Materials for a graphic representation of descriptive analyses.

Table 5. Mean (*SD*) score by male groups; Kruskal–Wallis analysis.

	Before COVID (*n* = 27)		Quarantine (*n* = 19)		Second Phase (*n* = 11)		Third Phase (*n* = 11)		Kruskal–Wallis		
	M (*SD*)	Mean Rank	*M* (*SD*)	Mean Rank	*M* (*SD*)	Mean Rank	*M* (*SD*)	Mean Rank	X^2 (*df* = 3)	*p* Values	η^2
SCL-90-R											
Somatization	48.98 (10.91)	34.96	44.69 (6.19)	28.11	52.91 (19.69)	41.73	51.09 (11.23)	37.18	3.70	0.296	0.011
Obsessive-compulsive	52.07 (13.46)	30.96	50.69 (10.80)	29.76	56.82 (10.76)	40.55	60.45 (11.61)	45.32	6.29	0.098	0.051
Interpersonal sensitivity	51.33 (12.01)	35.02	48.89 (9.26)	31.71	48.55 (8.39)	32.14	51.73 (7.17)	40.41	1.54	0.672	0.023
Depression	54.11 (13.59)	32.72	53.13 (12.14)	31.18	55.55 (10.90)	35.50	61.27 (13.94)	43.59	3.11	0.374	0.002
Anxiety	52.52 (12.92)	31.94	49.66 (7.06)	31.45	52.82 (13.70)	33.36	60.82 (13.17)	47.18	5.50	0.139	0.040
Anger-hostility	47.22 (7.93)	33.89	47.92 (10.16)	34.21	45.09 (6.19)	28.68	50.36 (8.96)	42.32	2.73	0.434	0.004
Phobic anxiety	49.80 (11.31)	30.78	48.77 (7.92)	33.26	51.36 (9.07)	36.95	55.91 (17.10)	43.32	3.71	0.294	0.011
Paranoid ideation	48.72 (9.90)	38.07	44.08 (7.30)	28.53	43.55 (8.50)	26.55	50.09 (7.82)	44.00	7.01	0.072	0.063
Psychoticism	52.85 (12.82)	32.81	51.92 (8.35)	33.87	54.27 (14.43)	34.50	55.09 (9.18)	39.73	0.99	0.803	0.031
GSI	52.63 (13.57)	33.04	49.44 (8.59)	30.24	53.18 (11.38)	35.36	57.82 (9.57)	44.59	3.92	0.270	0.014
PSDI	51.61 (11.01)	30.83	48.38 (10.84)	34.39	50.77 (11.36)	39.77	58.05 (10.26)	38.41	2.14	0.543	0.013
PST	51.24 (11.28)	33.50	52.81 (8.71)	29.89	55.27 (10.60)	33.77	54.05 (7.11)	45.64	4.61	0.203	0.025

SCL-90-R = Symptom Checklist-90-Revised; GSI = Global Severity Index; PSDI = Positive Symptom Distress Index; PST = Positive Symptom.

5. Discussion

The present study aims to provide an explorative and descriptive overview regarding the psychological distress and symptomatology of students included in NoiBene between March 2019 and March 2021. Moreover, we investigated whether the different phases of the COVID-19 restrictions impacted students' mental health differently.

5.1. Participant Characteristics

Most of the sample was composed of females. These data were consistent with the percentage of females usually included in web-based interventions [38] and with data suggesting that males are less disposed to seek mental help than women [39]. Interestingly, more males asked to participate in NoiBene during the lockdown compared with other phases. From the beginning of the pandemic, it was immediately apparent that, apart from physical health, mental health needed to be seriously taken into consideration. For this reason, psychologists and non-governmental services increased and strengthened online counselling therapy, or e-therapy [40]. It is possible to hypothesize that the increased attention to mental health has normalized the need to ask for help. Considering that the perceptions of normativeness influence help-seeking behaviour [41], this could be the reason why a significant number of males asked for help during the quarantine.

5.2. Symptomatology and Help-Seeking Behavior

Our data revealed that many students experienced moderate to severe levels of depression symptomatology, obsessive-compulsive symptomatology, and anxiety symptomatology. After completing the first screening, one-hundred-and-thirty-two students (29.07% of the total sample size) were contacted for a psychodiagnostic interview due to the high scores obtained. Of the 132 students, 24.2% students refused the interview. A broad range of evidence identified a series of barriers to treatment such as low perceived need, the desire to handle the problem on one's own, attitudinal and structural barriers [42] and internalized and treatment stigma [43]. Considering that these students decided to participate in NoiBene, we can hypothesize that they perceived a need, but they wanted to handle the problem independently. Indeed, young people often use self-help programs, such as NoiBene, to deal with their mental health problems [24]. One hundred students accepted the interview. Of the 100 students, 64% students met the criteria for at least one mental disorder according to The Diagnostic and Statistical Manual of Mental Disorders, DSM-5 [44]. Of these students, eleven (n = 11) were already receiving mental health care, so they were included in the NoiBene program. In contrast, after the interview, fifty-three students (n = 53) were directed toward psychotherapy. Of the 53 students, about 55% of students decided to start psychotherapy, but twenty-three (n = 24) did not accept. This is a remarkable outcome: thanks to the individual meeting that we conducted, we had the opportunity to give personalized feedback about the individual's symptomatology and inform students about how and where to find help in the area. According to the high percentage of students that accepted psychological therapy, it seems to be an efficacious strategy [45]. Regarding students that did not accept, we had the opportunity to explore individual barriers to help-seeking during the interview. The main reasons for refusing were the low perceived need, the fear of being misunderstood by other relevant people, or the idea that talking with a psychologist would exacerbate their problems. Besides the low perceived need, the students' choices were influenced by the treatment stigma, that is, the stigma associated with treatment for mental health, and the anticipated stigma, in other words, the fear of being perceived unfairly by others [43]. Nevertheless, these students asked for access at NoiBene, suggesting that NoiBene reached people who would otherwise not ask for help. Future research should use this advantage and focus on developing a strategy to reduce the stigma among students who are reluctant to start psychotherapy.

5.3. Group Comparison

Our findings partially supported the first hypothesis of our study: only female students showed an increase in depression and anxiety symptomatology and increasing feelings of inadequacy, inferiority, hostility, suspiciousness, and isolated lifestyle. Despite the significant effect, the effect size ranged from a small to medium, suggesting that these differences are not robust. For this reason, the results should be carefully interpreted. As a pandemic is an extraordinary event that cannot be replicated, in interpreting this finding, we should consider that other additional factors could explain the differences found between groups. For example, we have to keep in mind that every group is composed of different students asking to participate at different times of the year. For this reason, we should consider both variables related to students' university commitments, such as exams and examination sessions, and other variables, such as coping strategies to deal with the different containment measures. Even if only tentative interpretations can be suggested given the small to medium effect size, it is possible to hypothesize, looking at the results as a whole, that during the quarantine, the most affected areas were related to mood and the quality of interpersonal relations. Indeed, this pattern of symptomatology is recurring in patients with major depression [46]. Moreover, it is possible to hypothesize that social distancing contributed to the arising of interpersonal relation uncertainties and the presence of negative expectations about interpersonal relationships. In addition, since COVID-19 spreads mainly between people who are in close contact with each other, it could have contributed to raising the perception of the other as a risk for one's health, resulting in hostility or paranoid behaviour. Previous studies, which focused mainly on intimate relationships during the lockdown, indicated that high-stress levels were associated with a decline in intimate relationships [47]. Moreover, the attachment style of partners predicts interpersonal problems and the efficacy of problem-solving strategies [48]. Other studies suggested that working at home can exacerbate familial conflict [49] and that living with others contributed to increased psychological distress [50]. Interestingly, it seems that quarantine did not have an influence on male students. The results showed no significant differences between male groups. These data are consistent with other studies suggesting that COVID-19 had a more negative impact on females than males [51]. Some evidence suggested that during the lockdown, females reported higher levels of stress [50] and anxiety [19] than males and that they were at more risk of developing depression compared to males [18]. Lastly, our findings did not support our second hypothesis. The results did not show a significant increase in psychological distress in the Third Phase. However, despite the non-significant difference between groups, the males' descriptive statistics show that students reported more anxiety and depressive symptoms, hostility and suspiciousness, and overall psychological distress during the Third Phase. Furthermore, even though the difference was not statistically significant, the effect size ranged from small to medium. The small male sample size may have prevented sufficient power to detect differences between groups. Therefore, the findings observed in this study need to be clarified by increasing our sample size. Moreover, to the best of our knowledge, less is known about the longitudinal changes in males' mental health since most studies focused on the gender differences in relation to mental health during COVID-19. Future studies should investigate variables that could affect the different mental health trajectories across the pandemic between males and females.

5.4. Limitations and Future Directions

The study has some limits. First, most of the participants were female. For this reason, we decided to run an analysis for males and females separately. However, the tiny male sample size could have increased the occurrence of Type II Errors, reducing the chance of identifying a significant difference that could exist. Future studies should focus on a strategy to bring males closer to the topic of mental health. Second, our sample recruitment was not totally random: students decided spontaneously to participate in the NoiBene program, which could suggest that they have a particular interest in improving their mental health or that they perceive a need for help. This could have contributed both to the high percentage of psychopathological students and to the heterogeneity of our samples. Even if these limits could have contributed to reducing the study's generalizability, the different flow of students that asked to be included in NoiBene at different moments represent an essential indicator of help-seeking behaviour. Lastly, the four groups that we considered in our analysis were composed of different participants, so we did not have the opportunity to examine any changes over time. However, we had the opportunity to compare psychopathological dimensions between groups to understand how different phases of the COVID-19 restrictions impacted the individual's psychological health. It would be interesting in future studies to differentiate between students living in different regions with different risk scenarios, or to take into account risk and protective factors that underly the psychopathology that occurred during the pandemic.

Besides these limitations, the study has different strengths: we had the chance to assess students before and during the pandemic. This allowed us to observe any change that was associated with the quarantine and the following restrictive rules. Moreover, we conducted individual interviews with every student reporting a high level of psychological distress: this had a fundamental impact in terms of helping students to understand the best treatment according to their needs [45]. In addition, self-report questionnaires can yield much valuable and diagnostic information, but they cannot be used to define a diagnosis. Conducting individual interviews allowed us to go beyond this limit and be sure about students' symptomatology.

6. Conclusions

This study indicates that the lockdown had a significant negative impact on female mental health. Despite the increasing symptomatology during the quarantine among female students, the results suggest that it quickly disappeared after the lifting of the quarantine. Overall, the present study provides new insights into the impact of the pandemic on students' mental health and supports data about psychological distress among university students. Moreover, it gives new perspectives in the field of help-seeking behaviour. Awareness of these topics can be helpful to encourage universities to integrate mental health into their culture and implement preventive and support interventions.

Supplementary Materials: The following are available online at https://www.mdpi.com/article/10.3390/ijerph18189897/s1, Table S1: Protocol of intervention, Figure S1: Mean (SD) score by female groups, Figure S2: Mean (SD) score by male groups.

Author Contributions: Conceptualization, M.D.C. and A.C.; Data curation, M.D.C.; Formal analysis, M.D.C., S.M. and A.C.; Investigation, M.D.C., S.M. and A.C.; Methodology, M.D.C., S.M., T.P., C.V. and A.C.; Supervision, A.C.; Writing—original draft, M.D.C. and A.C.; Writing—review and editing, M.D.C., S.M., T.P., C.V. and A.C. All authors have read and agreed to the published version of the manuscript.

Funding: This research received no external funding.

Institutional Review Board Statement: The study was conducted according to the guidelines of the Declaration of Helsinki. NoiBene protocol was approved by the local Ethical Committee of the Department of Psychology, Sapienza University of Rome (protocol code n. 0000513).

Informed Consent Statement: All participants signed an informed consent form regarding the research protocol, data protection and privacy according to the General Data Protection Regulation (GDPR; EU 2016/679).

Data Availability Statement: Group-level information about the data is available from the corresponding author on reasonable request.

Conflicts of Interest: M.D.C., S.M. and A.C. are members of the NoiBene Team and contributed to the development of NoiBene. A.C. is the scientific director of NoiBene. Other authors declare that there is no conflict of interest.

References

1. Rezza, G.; Bella, A.; Riccardo, F.; Pezzotti, P.; D'Ancona, F.; Siddu, A. Pandemia di COVID-19. Available online: https://www.epicentro.iss.it/coronavirus/sars-cov-2 (accessed on 9 October 2020).
2. Jahrami, H.; BaHammam, A.S.; Bragazzi, N.L.; Saif, Z.; Faris, M.; Vitiello, M.V. Sleep problems during the COVID-19 pandemic by population: A systematic review and meta-analysis. *J. Clin. Sleep Med.* **2021**, *17*, 299–313. [CrossRef]
3. Killgore, W.D.; Cloonan, S.A.; Taylor, E.C.; Dailey, N.S. Loneliness: A signature mental health concern in the era of COVID-19. *Psychiatr. Res.* **2020**, *290*, 113117. [CrossRef] [PubMed]
4. Wu, T.; Jia, X.; Shi, H.; Niu, J.; Yin, X.; Xie, J.; Wang, X. Prevalence of mental health problems during the COVID-19 pandemic: A systematic review and meta-analysis. *J. Affect. Disord.* **2020**, *281*, 91–98. [CrossRef] [PubMed]
5. Xiong, J.; Lipsitz, O.; Nasri, F.; Lui, L.M.; Gill, H.; Phan, L.; Chen-Li, D.; Iacobucci, M.; Ho, R.; Majeed, A.; et al. Impact of COVID-19 pandemic on mental health in the general population: A systematic review. *J. Affect. Disord.* **2020**, *277*, 55–64. [CrossRef] [PubMed]
6. Gualano, M.R.; Lo Moro, G.; Voglino, G.; Bert, F.; Siliquini, R. Effects of COVID-19 lockdown on mental health and sleep disturbances in Italy. *Int. J. Environ. Res. Public Health* **2020**, *17*, 4779. [CrossRef] [PubMed]
7. Mazza, C.; Ricci, E.; Biondi, S.; Colasanti, M.; Ferracuti, S.; Napoli, C.; Roma, P. A nationwide survey of psychological distress among Italian people during the COVID-19 pandemic: Immediate psychological responses and associated factors. *Int. J. Environ. Res. Public Health* **2020**, *17*, 3165. [CrossRef] [PubMed]
8. Rossi, R.; Socci, V.; Talevi, D.; Mensi, S.; Niolu, C.; Pacitti, F.; Di Marco, A.; Rossi, A.; Siracusano, A.; Di Lorenzo, G. COVID-19 pandemic and lockdown measures impact on mental health among the general population in Italy. *Front. Psychiatry* **2020**, *11*, 790. [CrossRef] [PubMed]
9. Foundation BRF. Osservatorio Suicidi COVID. Available online: https://www.fondazionebrf.org/osservatorio-suicidi-COVID-19/ (accessed on 9 October 2020).
10. Ministero Della Salute. FAQ—COVID-19, Questions and Answers. Available online: https://www.salute.gov.it/portale/nuovocoronavirus/homeNuovoCoronavirus.jsp (accessed on 1 June 2021).
11. Aristovnik, A.; Keržič, D.; Ravšelj, D.; Tomaževič, N.; Umek, L. Impacts of the COVID-19 pandemic on life of higher education students: A global perspective. *Sustainability* **2020**, *12*, 8438. [CrossRef]
12. Abbasi, S.; Ayoob, T.; Malik, A.; Memon, S.I. Perceptions of students regarding E-learning during COVID-19 at a private medical college. *Pak. J. Med. Sci.* **2020**, *36*, S57. [CrossRef]

13. Aucejo, E.M.; French, J.; Araya, M.P.U.; Zafar, B. The impact of COVID-19 on student experiences and expectations: Evidence from a survey. *J. Public Econ.* **2020**, *191*, 104271. [CrossRef]
14. Quintiliani, L.; Sisto, A.; Vicinanza, F.; Curcio, G.; Tambone, V. Resilience and psychological impact on Italian university students during COVID-19 pandemic. Distance learning and health. *Psychol. Health Med.* **2021**, 1–12. [CrossRef]
15. Husky, M.M.; Kovess-Masfety, V.; Swendsen, J.D. Stress and anxiety among university students in France during COVID-19 mandatory confinement. *Compr. Psychiat.* **2020**, *102*, 152191. [CrossRef]
16. Liu, X.; Liu, J.; Zhong, X. Psychological state of college students during COVID-19 epidemic. *SSRN* **2020**, *3552814*. [CrossRef]
17. Son, C.; Hegde, S.; Smith, A.; Wang, X.; Sasangohar, F. Effects of COVID-19 on college students' mental health in the United States: Interview survey study. *J. Med. Internet Res.* **2020**, *22*, e21279. [CrossRef]
18. Patsali, M.E.; Mousa, D.P.V.; Papadopoulou, E.V.; Papadopoulou, K.K.; Kaparounaki, C.K.; Diakogiannis, I.; Fountoulakis, K.N. University students' changes in mental health status and determinants of behavior during the COVID-19 lockdown in Greece. *Psychiat. Res.* **2020**, *292*, 113298. [CrossRef]
19. Wang, C.; Zhao, H. The impact of COVID-19 on anxiety in Chinese university students. *Front. Psychol.* **2020**, *11*, 1168. [CrossRef] [PubMed]
20. Auerbach, R.P.; Mortier, P.; Bruffaerts, R.; Alonso, J.; Benjet, C.; Cuijpers, P.; Demyttenaere, K.; Ebert, D.D.; Green, J.G. WHO World Mental Health Surveys International College Student Project: Prevalence and distribution of mental disorders. *J. Abnorm. Psychol.* **2018**, *127*, 623–638. [CrossRef] [PubMed]
21. Downs, M.F.; Eisenberg, D. Help seeking and treatment use among suicidal college students. *J. Am. Coll. Health* **2012**, *60*, 104–114. [CrossRef] [PubMed]
22. Alonso, J.; Mortier, P.; Auerbach, R.P.; Bruffaerts, R.; Vilagut, G.; Cuijpers, P.; Demyttenaere, K.; Ebert, D.D.; Ennis, E.; Gutiérrez-García, R.A.; et al. Severe role impairment associated with mental disorders: Results of the WHO world mental health surveys international college student project. *Depress. Anxiety* **2018**, *35*, 802–814. [CrossRef] [PubMed]
23. Pace, D.; Quinn, L. Empirical support of the overlap between career and mental health counseling of university students. *J. Coll. Stud. Psychother.* **2000**, *14*, 41–50. [CrossRef]
24. Rickwood, D.J.; Deane, F.P.; Wilson, C.J. When and how do young people seek professional help for mental health problems? *Med. J. Australia* **2007**, *187*, S35–S39. [CrossRef] [PubMed]
25. Eisenberg, D.; Golberstein, E.; Gollust, S. Help-Seeking and Access to Mental Health Care in a University Student Population. *Med. Care* **2007**, *45*, 594–601. Available online: http://www.jstor.org/stable/40221479 (accessed on 30 July 2021). [CrossRef] [PubMed]
26. Eisenberg, D.; Downs, M.F.; Golberstein, E.; Zivin, K. Stigma and help seeking for mental health among college students. *Med. Care Res. Rev.* **2009**, *66*, 522–541. [CrossRef]
27. Cuijpers, P.; Auerbach, R.P.; Benjet, C.; Bruffaerts, R.; Ebert, D.; Karyotaki, E.; Kessler, R.C. Introduction to the special issue: The who world mental health international college student (wmh-ics) initiative. *Int. J. Methods Psychiatr. Res.* **2019**, *28*, e1762. [CrossRef]
28. Li, T.M.; Leung, C.S. Exploring student mental health and intention to use online counselling in Hong Kong during the COVID-19 pandemic. *Psychiatr. Clin. Neurosci.* **2020**, *74*, 564–565. [CrossRef]
29. Di Consiglio, M.; Fabrizi, G.; Conversi, D.; La Torre, G.; Pascucci, T.; Lombardo, C.; Violani, C.; Couyoumdjian, A. Effectiveness of NoiBene: A Web-based programme to promote psychological well-being and prevent psychological distress in university students. *Appl. Psychol. Heal. Well-Being* **2021**, *13*, 317–340. [CrossRef]
30. Banerjee, D.; Rai, M. Social isolation in COVID-19: The impact of loneliness. *Int. J. Soc. Psychiatr.* **2020**, *66*, 525–527. [CrossRef]
31. Killgore, W.D.; Cloonan, S.A.; Taylor, E.C.; Lucas, D.A.; Dailey, N.S. Loneliness during the first half-year of COVID-19 Lockdowns. *Psychiatr. Res.* **2020**, *294*, 113551. [CrossRef]
32. Del Valle, M.; Andrés, M.L.; Urquijo, S.; Yerro Avincetto, M.M.; López Morales, H.; Canet Juric, L. Intolerance of uncertainty over COVID-19 pandemic and its effect on anxiety and depressive symptoms. *Rev. Interam. Psicol.* **2020**, *54*, e1335. [CrossRef]
33. Akarsu, B.; Canbay Özdemir, D.; Ayhan Baser, D.; Aksoy, H.; Fidancı, İ.; Cankurtaran, M. While studies on COVID-19 vaccine is ongoing, the public's thoughts and attitudes to the future COVID-19 vaccine. *Int. J. Clin. Pract.* **2021**, *75*, e13891. [CrossRef] [PubMed]
34. Moccia, G.; Carpinelli, L.; Savarese, G.; Borrelli, A.; Boccia, G.; Motta, O.; Capunzo, M.; De Caro, F. Perception of Health, Mistrust, Anxiety, and Indecision in a Group of Italians Vaccinated against COVID-19. *Vaccines* **2021**, *9*, 612. [CrossRef] [PubMed]
35. Derogatis, L.R. *SCL-90-R: Administration, Scoring and Procedures Manual I*; Johns Hopkins: Baltimore, MD, USA, 1977.
36. Sarno, I.; Preti, E.; Prunas, A.; Madeddu, F. *SCL-90-R Symptom Checklist-90-R Adattamento Italiano*; Giunti, Organizzazioni Speciali: Florence, Italy, 2011.
37. Cohen, J. *Statistical Power Analysis for the Behavioral Sciences*; Academic Press: New York, NY, USA, 2013.
38. Davies, E.B.; Morriss, R.; Glazebrook, C. Computer-delivered and web-based interventions to improve depression, anxiety, and psychological well-being of university students: A systematic review and meta-analysis. *J. Med. Internet Res.* **2014**, *16*, e130. [CrossRef] [PubMed]
39. Oliver, M.I.; Pearson, N.; Coe, N.; Gunnell, D. Help-seeking behaviour in men and women with common mental health problems: Cross-sectional study. *Br. J. Psychiatry* **2005**, *186*, 297–301. [CrossRef] [PubMed]

40. Barak, A.; Grohol, J.M. Current and future trends in internet-supported mental health interventions. *J. Technol. Hum. Serv.* **2011**, *29*, 155–196. [CrossRef]
41. Nadler, A. Help-seeking behavior as a coping resource. In *Learned Resourcefulness: On Coping Skills, Self-Control, and Adaptive Behavior*; Rosenbaum, M., Ed.; Springer: New York, NY, USA, 1990; pp. 127–162.
42. Andrade, L.H.; Alonso, J.; Mneimneh, Z.; Wells, J.E.; Al-Hamzawi, A.; Borges, G.; Bromet, E.; Bruffaerts, R.; de Girolamo, G.; De Graaf, R.; et al. Barriers to mental health treatment: Results from the WHO World Mental Health (WMH) Surveys. *Psychol. Med.* **2014**, *44*, 1303. [CrossRef]
43. Clement, S.; Schauman, O.; Graham, T.; Maggioni, F.; Evans-Lacko, S.; Bezborodovs, N.; Morgan, C.; Rüsch, N.; Brown, J.S.L.; Thornicroft, G. What is the impact of mental health-related stigma on help-seeking? A systematic review of quantitative and qualitative studies. *Psychol. Med.* **2015**, *45*, 11–27. [CrossRef]
44. American Psychiatric Association. *Diagnostic and Statistical Manual of Mental Disorders (DSM-5®)*; American Psychiatric Pub.: Washington, DC, USA, 2013.
45. Gulliver, A.; Griffiths, K.M.; Christensen, H.; Brewer, J.L. A systematic review of help-seeking interventions for depression, anxiety and general psychological distress. *BMC Psychiatry* **2012**, *12*, 81. [CrossRef]
46. Kennedy, B.L.; Morris, R.L.; Pedley, L.L.; Schwab, J.J. The ability of the Symptom Checklist SCL-90 to differentiate various anxiety and depressive disorders. *Psychiatr. Q.* **2001**, *72*, 277–288. [CrossRef]
47. Goodwin, R.; Hou, W.K.; Sun, S.; Ben-Ezra, M. Quarantine, distress and interpersonal relationships during COVID-19. *Gen. Psychiatry* **2020**, *33*, e100385. [CrossRef]
48. Overall, N.C.; Chang, V.T.; Pietromonaco, P.R.; Low, R.S.; Henderson, A.M. Partners' attachment insecurity and stress predict poorer relationship functioning during COVID-19 quarantines. *Soc. Psychol. Personal. Sci.* **2021**. [CrossRef]
49. Dockery, M.; Bawa, S. Working from Home in the COVID-19 Lockdown. BCEC, 19, 1–5. Available online: https://bcec.edu.au/assets/2020/05/BCEC-COVID19-Brief-4_Working-from-home.pdf (accessed on 30 July 2021).
50. Flesia, L.; Monaro, M.; Mazza, C.; Fietta, V.; Colicino, E.; Segatto, B.; Roma, P. Predicting perceived stress related to the COVID-19 outbreak through stable psychological traits and machine learning models. *J. Clin. Med.* **2020**, *9*, 3350. [CrossRef]
51. Prowse, R.; Sherratt, F.; Abizaid, A.; Gabrys, R.L.; Hellemans, K.G.; Patterson, Z.R.; McQuaid, R.J. Coping With the COVID-19 Pandemic: Examining Gender Differences in Stress and Mental Health Among University Students. *Front. Psychiatry* **2021**, *12*, 439. [CrossRef]

International Journal of
Environmental Research and Public Health

MDPI

Article

Fear of COVID-19 in Patients with Acute Myocardial Infarction

Marco Marotta [1], Francesca Gorini [2], Alessandra Parlanti [1], Kyriazoula Chatzianagnostou [1], Annamaria Mazzone [1], Sergio Berti [1] and Cristina Vassalle [3,*]

[1] Fondazione CNR-Regione Toscana G. Monasterio, 54100 Massa, Italy; marco.marotta@ftgm.it (M.M.); alessandra.parlanti@ftgm.it (A.P.); zulachat@ftgm.it (K.C.); annamaria.mazzone@ftgm.it (A.M.); berti@ftgm.it (S.B.)
[2] Institute of Clinical Physiology, National Research Council, 56124 Pisa, Italy; fgorini@ifc.cnr.it
[3] Fondazione CNR-Regione Toscana G. Monasterio, Via Moruzzi 1, 56124 Pisa, Italy
* Correspondence: cristina.vassalle@ftgm.it

Abstract: A marked decline in myocardial infarction (AMI) hospitalizations was observed worldwide during the COVID-19 outbreak. The pandemic may have generated fear and adverse psychological consequences in these patients, delaying hospital access. The main objective of the study was to assess COVID fear through the FCV-19S questionnaire (a self-report measure of seven items) in 69 AMI patients (65 ± 11 years, mean ± SD; 59 males). Females presented higher values of each FCV-19S item than males. Older subjects (>57 years, 25th percentile) showed a higher total score with respect to those in the first quartile. The percentage of patients who responded "agree" and "strongly agree" in item 4 ("I am afraid of losing my life because of the coronavirus") and 3 ("My hands become clammy when I think about the coronavirus") was significantly greater in the elderly than in younger patients. When cardiovascular (CV) patients were compared to a previously published general Italian population, patients with CV disease exhibited higher values for items 3 and 4. Measures should be put in place to assist vulnerable and high CV risk patients, possibly adding psychologists to the cardiology team.

Keywords: COVID-19; fear; acute myocardial infarction; distress questionnaires

Citation: Marotta, M.; Gorini, F.; Parlanti, A.; Chatzianagnostou, K.; Mazzone, A.; Berti, S.; Vassalle, C. Fear of COVID-19 in Patients with Acute Myocardial Infarction. *Int. J. Environ. Res. Public Health* **2021**, *18*, 9847. https://doi.org/10.3390/ijerph18189847

Academic Editors: Paolo Roma, Merylin Monaro and Cristina Mazza

Received: 26 July 2021
Accepted: 16 September 2021
Published: 18 September 2021

1. Introduction

Attention to the COVID-19 pandemic has strained the health care system globally, making it difficult to care for patients, especially the most vulnerable subgroups, such as people with acute diseases, including acute myocardial infarction (AMI). In particular, during the COVID-19 outbreak, AMI hospitalizations experienced a "drop" compared to pre-pandemic admission rates, a phenomenon observed worldwide [1,2].

The reasons for this finding are not entirely clear. For example, the decrease in air pollution levels due to quarantine measures may have played a role, although a true decrease in acute cardiac events appears very unlikely [1,2]. Instead, greater patient concern about a referral to hospital emergency departments was suggested as a critical reason for the decline in AMI admissions [1,2]. Of note, AMI patients may present a delayed time from the onset of symptoms to the first medical contact due to the fear of a possible in-hospital infection, as found in Italian and Chinese patients by us and by other researchers [2,3]. As a result, these patients may have a more severe infarction and more complications.

During the COVID-19 outbreak, specific psychometric tools were developed and validated to assess COVID-19 fear [4,5]. In particular, the Fear of COVID-19 Scale (FCV-19S), obtained from a seven-item questionnaire (total score between 7 and 35, a higher sum score indicating greater fear of COVID-19), was validated and applied in different general populations (both Asian and European), and showed significant associations of fear with stress, anxiety, and depression, as assessed by specific validated questionnaires (e.g., Hospital

Anxiety and Depression Scale, Perceived Vulnerability to Disease Scale) [4,6,7]. As for the Italian population, the FCV-19S was previously validated in a cohort of 249 participants (age 18 to 76 years), showing significant and positive correlations with the Hospital Anxiety and Depression Scale (HADS, r = 0.649) and Severity Measure for Specific Phobia—Adult (SMSP-A, r = 0.703) [8]. A study in a large Chinese general population found an elevated level of stress, anxiety, and depression (8.1%, 28.8%, and 16.5%, respectively) during the COVID-19 epidemic, and it remained unchanged at the outbreak peak, four weeks later [9]. Likewise, approximately 25% of 7,143 Chinese students experienced anxiety during the COVID-19 outbreak [10]. As FCV-19S was administered almost exclusively in general populations, it is interesting to study its results in patients, especially CV individuals, where mood alterations and/or lockdown can worsen lifestyle habits, cause poor adherence to therapy, avoidance of regular checks for stable CVD patients, and delays in hospital access in case of acute events [11]. Accordingly, we previously reported preliminary data obtained through the administration of the FCV-19S questionnaire in CV outpatients during the first pandemic wave, comparing their results with those published relatively to the general Italian population, evidencing higher scores in CV risk patients for both emotional (item 4) and symptomatic fear expression (items 3 and 6) [2,8].The main aim of this study was to evaluate the effect of the COVID pandemic on fear of COVID in patients with AMI through the administration of FCV-19S. Moreover, to identify possible differences between stable and acute patients, FCV-19S scores were evaluated in CV outpatients and in AMI patients.

2. Materials and Methods

2.1. Population Characteristics

A total of 69 consecutive Italian patients with ST-elevation myocardial infarction (STEMI) (65 ± 11 years, mean ± SD; 59 males) were enrolled at the Ospedale del Cuore G. Pasquinucci—Clinical Cardiology Department (Massa, a city in *Tuscany, which* is a region in *central Italy*) in the period November 2020–May 2021, interspersed with more or less rigid lockdown periods. From January 2021, access to vaccinations was possible, first for healthcare personnel, then progressively for other worker categories (e.g., schoolteachers, etc.). In this time period, lockdown included variable and progressive limitations, which often targeted the restricted territory of the region in which infections were higher, differently from the strict nationwide lockdown during the first wave. In addition, 30 CV subjects afferent to the cardiology outpatient clinic in the period November 2020–May 2021 (62 ± 6 years) and 30 CV outpatients (64 ± 8 years) afferent to the cardiology outpatients clinic of the Ospedale del Cuore G. Pasquinucci during the first COVID-19 wave for the regular periodic check were also evaluated [2].

The definition of STEMI follows the published SC/ACCF/AHA/WHF guidelines for STEMI criteria and management [12].

Standard therapy (e.g., aspirin, beta-blockers, angiotensin-converting enzyme inhibitors, diuretics, statins) was administered to all eligible patients.

2.2. Criteria of Patient Eligibility

Patients were considered eligible to be enrolled in the study on the basis of the following inclusion criteria: (1) Adult male and female patients, admitted to the coronary care unit (CCU) for chest pain and subsequently ascertained STEMI. Exclusion criteria were as follows: (1) Severe systemic diseases; (2) Systemic inflammatory disease; (3) Patients refusing or unable to supply written informed consent.

2.3. Fear of COVID-19 Scale

The FCV-19S is a self-report measure aimed at assessing fear of COVID-19, and the scale is made up of seven items related to emotional (Items 1, 2, 4, 5) and symptomatic (Items 3, 6, 7) fear reactions to the pandemic [4].

Specifically, patients were asked to answer the following items:

1. I am most afraid of coronavirus;

2. It makes me uncomfortable to think about coronavirus;
3. My hands become clammy when I think about coronavirus;
4. I am afraid of losing my life because of coronavirus;
5. When I watch news and stories about coronavirus on social media, I become nervous or anxious;
6. I cannot sleep because I'm worrying about getting coronavirus;
7. My heart races or palpitates when I think about getting coronavirus.

Participants were asked to respond on a five-item Likert-type scale ranging from 1 (strongly disagree) to 5 (strongly agree), with responses including "strongly disagree" (1), "disagree" (2) "neutral" (3), "agree" (4) and "strongly agree" (5). The minimum possible score for each question is 1, and the maximum is 5. The total score ranges between 7 and 35, with a higher sum score indicating greater fear of COVID-19. The measure showed appropriate internal validity (Cronbach's alpha of 0.82) and was also found to correlate with anxiety and depression, as assessed by the Hospital Anxiety and Depression Scale and the Perceived Vulnerability to Disease Scale. Previous studies [4–8] reported FCV-19\$5 validation in different general population cohorts.

In order to assess anxiety and depression for COVID-19, all enrolled patients completed a COVID fear questionnaire at hospital admission as part of routine clinical practice. The survey took around 10–15 min to complete.

Informed consent was obtained from each patient (or their relatives where necessary), and the study was approved by the local Ethics Committee (number 19214, 11 February 2021).

2.4. Statistical Analysis

Data are expressed as the mean ± standard deviation. Statistical analyses included Student's t-test (to determine the significance of the difference between the means of two data sets, sample size n-1 gives degrees of freedom to estimate variability), χ^2 test (to verify any significant difference between the expected frequencies and the observed frequencies in one or more categories of a contingency table), and linear regression (to evaluate whether there is a relationship between the variables of interest). A comparison between the three groups for total score and items was tested by using ANOVA analysis and a Scheffe's post hoc test.

A p-value of 0.05 was considered statistically significant. Analyses were performed using Statview statistical software version 5.0.1 procedures (Abacus Concepts, Berkeley, CA, USA).

3. Results

3.1. Total FCV-19S Score

The COVID fear questionnaire was administered to a total of 69 STEMI patients admitted at the period of the beginning of November 2020–end of May 2021 in the coronary care unit (CCU) of the Ospedale del Cuore G. Pasquinucci—Clinical Cardiology Department (Massa, Italy).

No significant differences were observed in the total score values according to gender (Table 1). On the other hand, there was a significant correlation between age and total FCV-19S score ($r = 0.2$, $p \leq 0.05$) in the overall STEMI population. When the STEMI population was divided by the 25th percentile of age corresponding to 57 years ($n = 52$ older *versus* $n = 17$ younger patients), the total FCV-19S score resulted in 19 ± 7 and 16 ± 5 in older and younger patients, respectively ($p = 0.08$).

Table 1. Descriptive analysis of the Fear of COVID-19 items by gender.

	Overall Population				Women				Men			
	Mean	Standard Deviation	Skewness	Kurtosis	Mean	Standard Deviation	Skewness	Kurtosis	Mean	Standard Deviation	Skewness	Kurtosis
Item 1	3.7	1.1	−0.5	−0.6	4	1	−0.8	−0.2	3.6	1.2	−0.4	−0.6
Item 2	3.6	1.1	−0.4	−0.6	3.8	0.97	−0.4	−0.6	3.2	1.1	−0.1	−0.7
Item 3	2	1.2	0.5	−0.5	2.4	1.3	0.46	−0.5	1.9	1.1	1.2	0.5
Item 4	2.9	1.4	0.1	−1.4	3.1	1.3	−0.2	−1	2.9	1.4	0.2	−1.4
Item 5	2.8	1.3	0.1	−1.1	3	1.6	0.1	−1	2.8	1.3	0.1	−1
Item 6	1.8	0.9	1.3	1.6	2	1.2	1.7	2.2	1.7	0.9	1	0,3
Item 7	2.1	1.2	1	0.2	2.6	1.6	0.6	−1	2	1	1.1	0.4
Total score	18.5	6.6	0.4	−0.4	20.7	7.4	0.5	−0.4	18.2	6.5	0.4	−0.5

The total FCV-19S score did not significantly differ between the two groups of CV patients taken in the different periods and in STEMI Patients (Table 2).

Table 2. Mean (± standard deviation) of the 7 items of the Italian Fear of COVID-19 score in CV outpatients during the first epidemic wave and the period of November 2020–May 2021.

	First Wave CV Outpatients	November 2020–May 2021 CV Outpatients	November 2020–May 2021 STEMI Patients
Emotional fear reactions			
1. I am most afraid of the coronavirus	3.5 (1.3)	3.8 (1.3)	3.7 (1.1)
2. It makes me uncomfortable to think about the coronavirus	3.2 (1.6)	3.0 (1.2)	3.3 (1.1)
4. I am afraid of losing my life because of the coronavirus	2.9 (1.6)	2.7 (1.2)	2.9 (1.4)
5. When watching news and stories about the coronavirus on social media, I become nervous or anxious	3.0 (1.8)	2.4 (1.3)	2.8 (1.3)
Symptomatic expression of fear			
3. My hands become clammy when I think about the coronavirus	2.1 (0.7)	1.9 (0.9)	2.0 (1.2)
6. I cannot sleep because I'm worrying about getting the coronavirus	2.2 (0.8)	1.4 (0.3) **	1.8 (0.9) *
7. My heart rates or palpitates when I think about getting the coronavirus	2.4 (1.0)	1.6 (0.4) *	2.1 (1.2)
Total mean	2.8 (1.0)	2.4 (0.7)	2.6 (1.0)
Total score	19.5 (6.7)	16.7 (5.1)	18.5 (6.6)

* $p < 0.1$, ** $p < 0.05$ vs. first wave CV outpatients.

3.2. FCV-19S Items

Histograms of the seven items of the Fear of COVID questionnaire in the overall population are shown in Figure 1. Most of the items were distributed asymmetrically, with the lowest frequencies in the higher value categories.

No significant differences were observed when considering each item's values according to gender (Table 1). The percentage of answers corresponding to score 1 and 2 ("strongly disagree" or "disagree"), 3 ("neutral"), or 4 and 5 ("agree" and "strongly agree") in both sexes are reported in Figure 2.

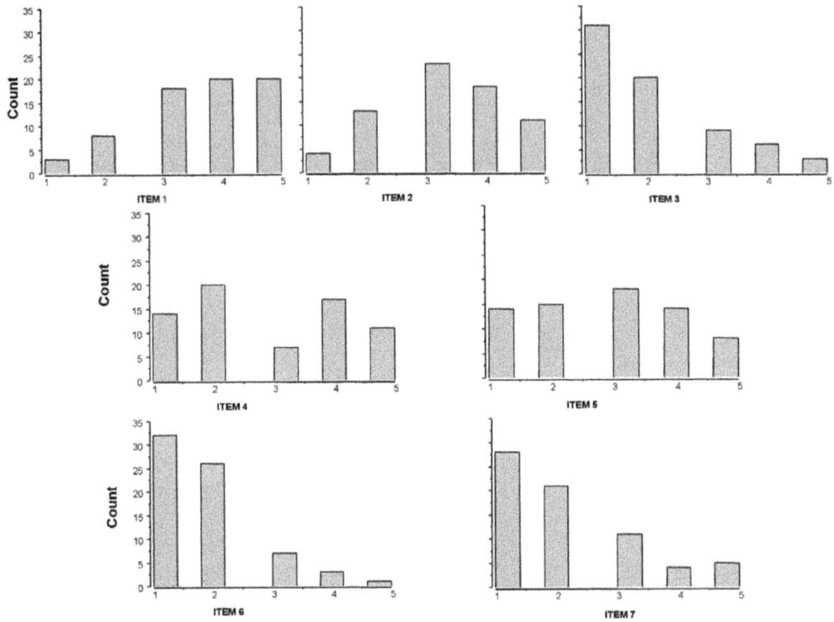

Figure 1. Histograms of the seven items of the Fear of COVID questionnaire in the overall STEMI population.

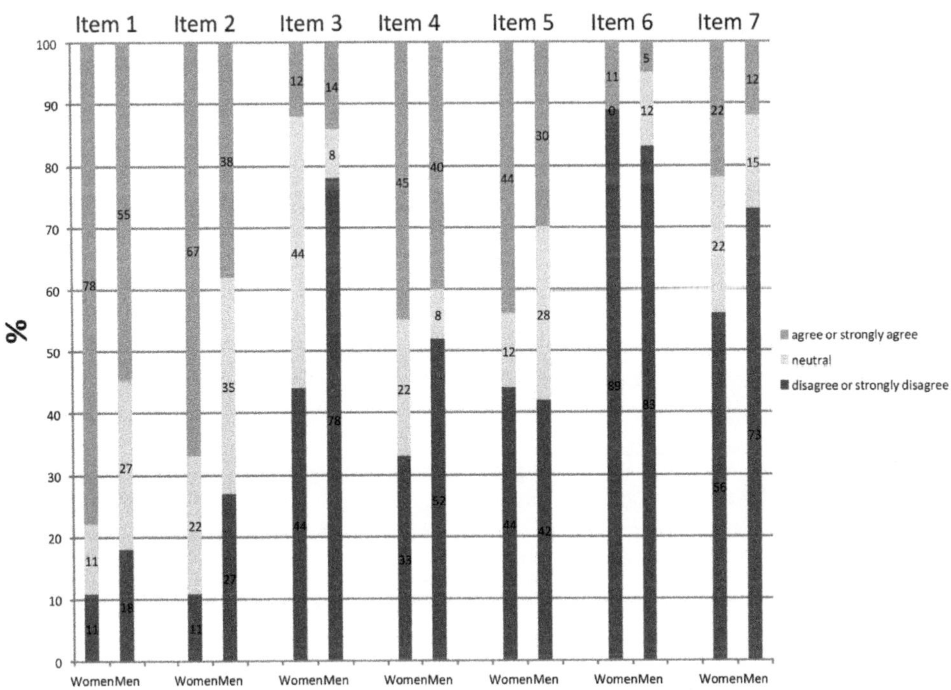

Figure 2. Histograms reporting the % answers corresponding to score 1 and 2 ("strongly disagree" or "disagree"), 3 ("neutral"), or 4 and 5 ("agree" and "strongly agree") in STEMI female and male patients.

There was a significant correlation between age and item 4 ("I am afraid of losing my life because of the coronavirus") (r = 0.3, $p < 0.05$) in the overall STEMI population. Moreover, when the STEMI population was divided by the 25th percentile of age corresponding to 57 years, the percentage of subjects who responded positively ("agree" or "strongly agree") compared to those who responded negatively ("disagree" or "strongly disagree") to item 4 ("I am afraid of losing my life because of the coronavirus", belonging to emotional fear reactions, $p < 0.05$) and 3 ("My hands become clammy when I think about the coronavirus", belonging to the symptomatic expression of fear, $p \leq 0.05$) was significantly higher in the STEMI elderly patient group (Figure 3).

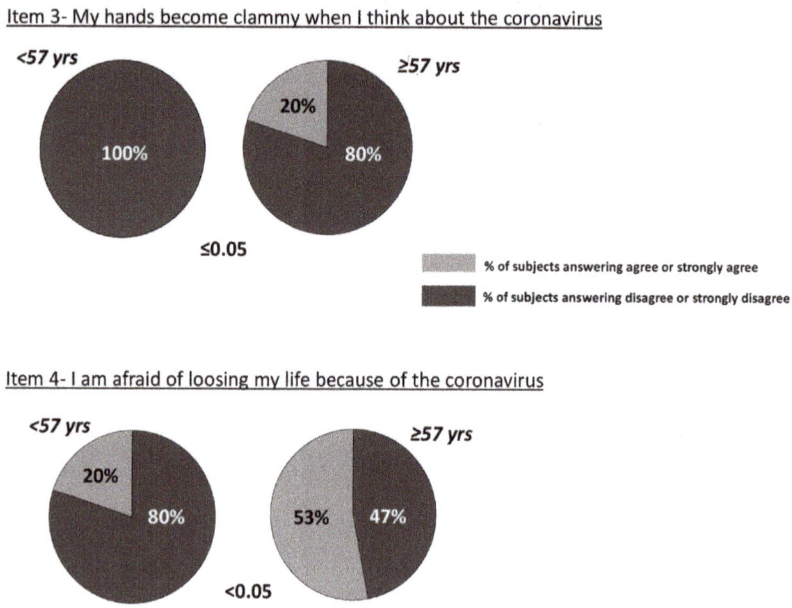

Figure 3. Percentage of STEMI patients answering positively "agree" or "strongly agree" or negatively "disagree" or "strongly disagree" to items 4 and 3 in the groups rated according to the 25th percentile of age (corresponding to 57 years). (Answers reporting "neutral" were excluded by the analysis.) Values are reported as n (%).

When CV patients referred to the outpatient department during the first period of the COVID-19 outbreak (2) were compared to 30 CV outpatients examined in the period November 2020–May 2021, item 6 ("I cannot sleep because I'm worrying about getting the coronavirus") and 7 ("My heart races or palpitates when I think about getting the coronavirus"), belonging to the category of symptomatic expression of fear, resulted lower as the pandemic progressed (Table 2). STEMI patients also exhibited lower levels for item 6 than CV outpatients tested during the first wave of COVID-19 (Table 2). Furthermore, when CV patients were compared with published FCV-19S scores from an Italian general population previously tested in the first wave of COVID-19 [11], both CV outpatients and AMI patients subsequently tested showed higher values for both emotional (item 4—"I am afraid of losing my life because of the coronavirus", corresponding to a value of 2 in the general Italian population) and symptomatic fear expression (item 3—"My hands become clammy when I think about the coronavirus", corresponding to a value of 1.5 in the general Italian population).

4. Discussion

To the best of our knowledge, this is the first report to evaluate FCV-19S in patients with STEMI. This is particularly important, as many data have reported a marked reduction in AMI hospitalizations during the first wave of the worldwide pandemic [2,12–15]. Common international lockdown measures, contradictory and ambiguous information, and inaccurate communications from the media may have fueled fear of possible in-hospital contagion, which may have contributed to the decline in access to the CCU [2]. Clearly, other determinants may have played a role, such as the healthcare focus on COVID patients and the reduction in resources available for other acute emergencies because all efforts directed towards COVID-19, or the decrease in air pollution with the establishment of lockdown measures and consequently its diminished role as potential trigger of acute coronary artery disease, and others [2]. In any case, it is important to consider that STEMI care is strictly time-dependent; thus, any delay in reaching coronary emergency units can increase morbidity and mortality. In fact, the earlier the diagnosis and treatment, the more effective the STEMI treatment, in terms of infarct size and AMI-related complications.

In this context, these are the first data to estimate psychological distress using FCV-19S in CV patients. The values reported for CV outpatients, both in the first wave and in the following period, and in STEMI patients were higher for item 4 ("I am afraid of losing my life because of the coronavirus") and item 3 ("My hands become clammy when I think about the coronavirus"), compared to those observed in an Italian general population subjected to FCV-19S during the first pandemic wave (corresponding to the values of 2 and 1.5, respectively), indicating a greater emotional and symptomatic fear expression in all CV patients [8]. Certainly, in these types of studies, it must be considered that patients with acute or stable coronary artery disease may have high underlying rates of anxiety and depression that may influence the FCV-19S if compared to the general population [16,17]. However, based on our results when comparing patients in the different time periods (see Table 2), the differences in the FCV-19S response seem more related to the characteristics of the lockdown periods (e.g., information from the media, level of constraints imposed) than to the type of patients (acute *versus* stable), with adverse repercussions for all patients (e.g., lack of checks for stable CV patients, and delays in hospital admission in case of AMI).

For this reason, the analysis of data related to the so-called "Total ischemic time" (a term coined to indicate the time from the onset of chest pain to the first medical contact, arrival at the hospital, and balloon inflation during primary percutaneous coronary intervention) is essential in the interpretation of the present results. Indeed, the uncertainty in recognizing the severity of the symptoms and in reaching the emergency department introduces a "COVID-19-related delay" in the "Total ischemic time". This is especially true for the "symptom-onset-to-first medical-contact time" that was significantly longer during the pandemic period than in the pre-pandemic period, as other researchers and we observed in the CCU [2,3,18]. This finding suggests patients' reluctance to promptly contact healthcare personnel who may intervene with the first treatment, go to the hospital or even not seek care at all, even though this attitude could have a detrimental impact on their outcomes. Noteworthy, "Door-to-hospital-arrival-time" and "Hospital-arrival-to-insufflation-time" did not vary significantly in the pre-COVID or during the pre-pandemic and pandemic periods in all evaluated clinical settings [2,3,18] suggesting a good functioning of the healthcare system, and also giving a major role to the patient's fear and reluctance for the reduction in AMI.

Regarding gender, we did not find any significant difference in the level of fear, although female patients presented slightly higher values for each item. This result is absolutely preliminary and limited by the low number of women in our cohort (13%) and certainly needs further deepening. In the literature, other data suggested that higher rates of fear among women can be associated with different emotional distress vulnerabilities depending on gender. Women seem more prone to stress, as well as to an increased risk of developing post-traumatic stress disorders [19]. A 2020 WHO report highlighted that women represent a population with specific concerns, as a significantly higher percentage of women reported being stressed than men during the COVID-19 outbreak, evidencing a greater vulnerability of women to the negative impact of the COVID-19 in terms of mental health and wellbeing [20]. Interestingly, data on FCV-19S in different general ethnic populations (Bangladeshi, British, Brazilian, Taiwanese, Italian, New Zealander, Iranian, Cuban, Pakistani, Japanese, and French) showed that females had a greater fear of COVID-19 than males [21].

In addition, a study specifically designed to evaluate gender differences in fear of COVID-19 suggested greater psychological vulnerability in Cuban women during the pandemic, and that gender significantly predicted COVID-19 fear [22].

Accordingly, in the cardiovascular setting where FCV-19S evaluation had not still been performed, a greater reduction in STEMI admissions was observed comparing women *versus* men (41.2%; $p = 0.011$, and 17.8%; $p = 0.191$, respectively) during the COVID-19 pandemic, which may reflect increased fear in female patients [12].

Since COVID-19 and the highest mortality and complication rate were found in elderly subjects during the outbreak, it is not surprising that older CV patients are more likely to be psychologically affected, as reported in several general populations [23–27]. However, some studies reported lower levels of COVID-19 fear in older subjects than in young to middle-aged adults [21].

Nonetheless, patients with CV disease and comorbidities may feel more vulnerable to death and disability due to COVID-19 than their younger counterparts, likely thinking that the treatments for COVID-19 are somewhat limited and become more fearful of being infected from the virus [28,29].

Notably, "fear" may be a physiological and functional response, which represents a positive reaction towards more adaptive functions aimed at keeping oneself safe from risky situations [30]. However, many of the items in the FCV-19S scale are related to anxiety, a negative emotional state with adverse repercussions [30]. Moreover, loneliness is a strong determinant for all-cause mortality in aged people [31].

It is also noteworthy that CV outpatients examined in the period of November 2020–May 2021 showed significantly lower values for item 6 ("I cannot sleep because I'm worrying about getting the coronavirus") and 7 ("My heart races or palpitates when I think about getting the coronavirus") than those tested with FCV-19S in the first wave, indicating some kind of addiction to stressful conditions.

Indeed, as it is known in the field of stress neurobiology, a stress, always of the same nature, which repeatedly manifests over time (homotypic stress), typically leads to the habituation of stress-sensitive systems, including those affecting the hypothalamic–pituitary–adrenal axis, and unlike a heterotypic unpredictable and variable stress [32,33].

In fact, if biological responses give our body the strength to facilitate survival and face immediate danger, long-lasting stress can cause problems, potentially compromising the functions of the whole organism [34,35]. Therefore, homotypic stress addiction can reduce the overall burden. Further studies are warranted to understand whether biological responses to COVID-19 also fit into this context, as well as to clarify whether these biological responses can influence psychosocial behaviors.

Strengths and Limitations

The main strength of this study is that for the first time, the FCV-19S was administered in CV patients, suggesting that COVID-19 fear may contribute to the delay in regular checks and hospital admissions for stable and acute CV patients.

Due to the limited number of participants, it was difficult to conduct subgroup analyses. For example, the gender analysis included only a small number of female patients. However, this fact is representative of the clinical AMI reality, where there is a male:female event ratio of 5:1 [36]. However, despite the lower incidence of acute coronary artery disease in females, women have worse short- and long-term outcomes than men [37,38]. Moreover, the pre-hospital delay from symptom onset to admission is generally significantly longer for women also ordinarily [39].

These aspects, in addition to an overall greater fear of COVID-19 for women compared to males [40], may result in a further delay in hospital access in the case of AMI for women due to the COVID-19 fear, which could worsen their outcomes. Our preliminary results are in agreement with studies conducted in cohorts of general subjects in different parts of the world [21], suggesting that the female gender may represent a critical predictor for psychological distress. Therefore, although limited in sample size, this study can broaden the knowledge and improve understanding of the factors associated with short-term outcomes after AMI hospitalization by being, to the best of our knowledge, the first to assess fear of COVID-19 in AMI patients.

Unfortunately, we did not enroll AMI patients during the first pandemic wave. Nonetheless, in light of the data collected in the period November 2020–May 2020, the differences observed in the items might be attributable more to the characteristics of the lockdown (e.g., more rigorous lockdown measures) than to the differences between stable and acute CV disease.

Of note, all patients belong to Italian nationality, whereas it was reported that migrants and other similar groups showed a particular fear of COVID and may represent an interesting cohort to study also in the CV setting [41].

5. Conclusions

The COVID-19 pandemic has an impact not only on the rate but also on the timing of AMI hospital admissions. Since the symptom-onset-to-first-medical-contact time plays a crucial role in a longer delay, and patients presented with higher levels of emotional and symptomatic fear expressions than the general population, a major cause of this delayed presentation could be attributable to changes in patient behavior and risk perception, which arouses reluctance to come to the hospital for fear of contracting COVID-19, as confirmed by the patients themselves in previously published reports [42,43]. Interestingly, recent data have not confirmed the association between a decrease in hospital admissions for acute coronary syndrome and a decrease in air pollution due to lockdown containment measures, indirectly giving strength to other hypotheses for the drop observed in AMI procedures [44].

While it is true that patients may develop some sort of addiction to the fear of COVID-19, measures should be put in place to assist high CV risk and more vulnerable patients and (e.g., women, elderly, frail subjects), along with correct information to patients on the pandemic course and on the risks of delayed access to the hospital in case of acute events. In addition, a multidisciplinary team should be implemented when possible, including not only cardiologists and hemodynamics but also psychologists (to provide psychological support to CV patients and reduce distress and subsequent mental problems), in order to avoid patients who have presented too late and are hemodynamically unstable for COVID fear as well as AMI complications.

Author Contributions: Conceptualization, C.V. and M.M.; methodology, M.M.; data validation, M.M.; formal analysis, C.V.; writing—original draft preparation, C.V.; writing—review and editing, M.M., F.G., A.P., K.C., A.M. and S.B.; project administration, A.P. All authors have read and agreed to the published version of the manuscript.

Funding: This research received no external funding.

Institutional Review Board Statement: The study was conducted according to the guidelines of the Declaration of Helsinki and approved by the Institutional Review Board of PISA (protocol code number 19214, 11 February 2021).

Informed Consent Statement: Informed consent was obtained from all subjects involved in the study.

Data Availability Statement: Data available on request from the authors.

Conflicts of Interest: The authors declare no conflict of interest.

References

1. Helal, A.; Shahin, L.; Abdelsalam, M.; Ibrahim, M. Global effect of COVID-19 pandemic on the rate of acute coronary syndrome admissions: A comprehensive review of published literature. *Open Heart* **2021**, *8*, e001645. [CrossRef] [PubMed]
2. Gorini, F.; Chatzianagnostou, K.; Mazzone, A.; Bustaffa, E.; Esposito, A.; Berti, S.; Bianchi, F.; Vassalle, C. "Acute Myocardial Infarction in the Time of COVID-19": A Review of Biological, Environmental, and Psychosocial Contributors. *Int. J. Environ. Res. Public Health* **2020**, *17*, 7371. [CrossRef]
3. Tam, C.F.; Cheung, K.S.; Lam, S.; Wong, A.; Yung, A.; Sze, M.; Lam, Y.M.; Chan, C.; Tsang, T.C.; Tsui, M.; et al. Impact of Coronavirus Disease 2019 (COVID-19) Outbreak on ST-Segment-Elevation Myocardial Infarction Care in Hong Kong, China. *Circ. Cardiovasc. Qual. Outcomes* **2020**, *13*, e006631. [CrossRef] [PubMed]
4. Ahorsu, D.K.; Lin, C.Y.; Imani, V.; Saffari, M.; Griffiths, M.D.; Pakpour, A.H. The Fear of COVID-19 Scale: Development and Initial Validation. *Int. J. Ment. Health Addict.* **2020**, *27*, 1–9. [CrossRef]
5. Taylor, S.; Landry, C.A.; Paluszek, M.M.; Fergus, T.A.; McKay, D.; Asmundson, G.J.G. Development and initial validation of the COVID Stress Scales. *J. Anxiety Disord.* **2020**, *72*, 102232. [CrossRef] [PubMed]
6. Sakib, N.; Bhuiyan, A.K.M.I.; Hossain, S.; Al Mamun, F.; Hosen, I.; Abdullah, A.H.; Sarker, M.A.; Mohiuddin, M.S.; Rayhan, I.; Hossain, M.; et al. Psychometric Validation of the Bangla Fear of COVID-19 Scale: Confirmatory Factor Analysis and Rasch Analysis. *Int. J. Ment. Health Addict.* **2020**, *11*, 1–12. [CrossRef]
7. Reznik, A.; Gritsenko, V.; Konstantinov, V.; Khamenka, N.; Isralowitz, R. COVID-19 Fear in Eastern Europe: Validation of the Fear of COVID-19 Scale. *Int. J. Ment. Health Addict.* **2020**, 1–6. [CrossRef] [PubMed]
8. Soraci, P.; Ferrari, A.; Abbiati, F.A.; Del Fante, E.; De Pace, R.; Urso, A.; Griffiths, M.D. Validation and Psychometric Evaluation of the Italian Version of the Fear of COVID-19 Scale. *Int. J. Ment. Health Addict.* **2020**, 1–10. [CrossRef]
9. Wang, C.; Pan, R.; Wan, X.; Tan, Y.; Xu, L.; McIntyre, R.S.; Choo, F.N.; Tran, B.; Ho, R.; Sharma, V.K.; et al. A longitudinal study on the mental health of general population during the COVID-19 epidemic in China. *Brain Behav. Immun.* **2020**, *87*, 40–48. [CrossRef]
10. Cao, W.; Fang, Z.; Hou, G.; Han, M.; Xu, X.; Dong, J.; Zheng, J. The psychological impact of the COVID-19 epidemic on college students in China. *Psychiatry Res.* **2020**, *287*, 112934. [CrossRef]
11. Finset, A.; Bosworth, H.; Butow, P.; Gulbrandsen, P.; Hulsman, R.L.; Pieterse, A.H.; Street, R.; Tschoetschel, R.; van Weert, J. Effective health communication—A key factor in fighting the COVID-19 pandemic. *Patient Educ. Couns.* **2020**, *103*, 873–876. [CrossRef]
12. De Rosa, S.; Spaccarotella, C.; Basso, C.; Calabrò, M.P.; Curcio, A.; Filardi, P.P.; Mancone, M.; Mercuro, G.; Muscoli, S.; Nodari, S.; et al. Reduction of hospitalizations for myocardial infarction in Italy in the COVID-19 era. *Eur. Heart J.* **2020**, *41*, 2083–2088, Erratum in *Eur. Heart J.* **2021**, *42*, 683. Erratum in *Eur. Heart J.* **2021**, *42*, 322. [CrossRef]
13. Matsushita, K.; Hess, S.; Marchandot, B.; Sato, C.; Truong, D.P.; Kim, N.T.; Weiss, A.; Jesel, L.; Ohlmann, P.; Morel, O. Clinical features of patients with acute coronary syndrome during the COVID-19 pandemic. *J. Thromb. Thrombolysis* **2020**, 1–10. [CrossRef] [PubMed]
14. Sung, H.K.; Paik, J.H.; Lee, Y.J.; Kang, S. Impact of the COVID-19 Outbreak on Emergency Care Utilization in Patients with Acute Myocardial Infarction: A Nationwide Population-based Study. *J. Korean Med. Sci.* **2021**, *36*, e111. [CrossRef] [PubMed]
15. Pessoa-Amorim, G.; Camm, C.F.; Gajendragadkar, P.; De Maria, G.L.; Arsac, C.; Laroche, C.; Zamorano, J.L.; Weidinger, F.; Achenbach, S.; Maggioni, A.P.; et al. Admission of patients with STEMI since the outbreak of the COVID-19 pandemic: A survey by the European Society of Cardiology. *Eur. Heart J. Qual. Care Clin. Outcomes* **2020**, *6*, 210–216. [CrossRef]
16. Miličić, D.; Brajković, L.; Maček, J.L.; Andrić, A.; Ardalić, Ž.; Buratović, T.; Marčinko, D. Type a Personality, Stress, Anxiety and Health Locus of Control in Patients with Acute Myocardial Infarction. *Psychiatr. Danub.* **2016**, *28*, 409–414. [PubMed]
17. Khan, M.A.; Karamat, M.; Hafizullah, M.; Nazar, Z.; Fahim, M.; Gul, A.M. Frequency of anxiety and psychosocial stressful events in patients with acute myocardial infraction. *J. Ayub. Med. Coll. Abbottabad.* **2010**, *22*, 32–35. [PubMed]
18. Aldujeli, A.; Hamadeh, A.; Briedis, K.; Tecson, K.M.; Rutland, J.; Krivickas, Z.; Stiklioraitis, S.; Briede, K.; Aldujeili, M.; Unikas, R.; et al. Delays in Presentation in Patients with Acute Myocardial Infarction During the COVID-19 Pandemic. *Cardiol. Res.* **2020**, *11*, 386–391. [CrossRef] [PubMed]
19. Sareen, J.; Erickson, J.; Medved, M.I.; Asmundson, G.J.; Enns, M.W.; Stein, M.; Leslie, W.; Doupe, M.; Logsetty, S. Risk factors for post-injury mental health problems. *Depress. Anxiety* **2013**, *30*, 321–327. [CrossRef] [PubMed]
20. United Nations. Policy Brief: COVID-19 and the Need for Action on Mental Health. Available online: https://unsdg.un.org/sites/default/files/2020-05/UN-Policy-Brief-COVID-19-and-mental-health.pdf (accessed on 25 June 2021).
21. Chang, K.C.; Kuo, Y.J.; Soraci, P.; Scarf, D.; Broström, A.; Griffiths, M.D.; Pakpour, A.H. Fear of COVID-19 Scale (FCV-19S) across countries: Measurement invariance issues. *Nurs. Open* **2021**, *8*, 1892–1908. [CrossRef]
22. Broche-Pérez, Y.; Fernández-Fleites, Z.; Jiménez-Puig, E.; Fernández-Castillo, E.; Rodríguez-Martin, B.C. Gender and Fear of COVID-19 in a Cuban Population Sample. *Int. J. Ment. Health Addict.* **2020**, 1–9. [CrossRef] [PubMed]
23. Długosz, P. Predictors of Mental Health after the First Wave of the COVID-19 Pandemic in Poland. *Brain Sci.* **2021**, *11*, 544. [CrossRef]
24. Orrù, G.; Bertelloni, D.; Diolaiuti, F.; Conversano, C.; Ciacchini, R.; Gemignani, A. A Psychometric Examination of the Coronavirus Anxiety Scale and the Fear of Coronavirus Disease 2019 Scale in the Italian Population. *Front. Psychol.* **2021**, *12*, 669384. [CrossRef]

25. Hossain, M.A.; Jahid, M.I.K.; Hossain, K.M.A.; Walton, L.M.; Uddin, Z.; Haque, M.O.; Kabir, M.F.; Arafat, S.M.Y.; Sakel, M.; Faruqui, R.; et al. Knowledge, attitudes, and fear of COVID-19 during the Rapid Rise Period in Bangladesh. *PLoS ONE* **2020**, *15*, e0239646. [CrossRef]
26. Chi, X.; Chen, S.; Chen, Y.; Chen, D.; Yu, Q.; Guo, T.; Cao, Q.; Zheng, X.; Huang, S.; Hossain, M.M.; et al. Psychometric Evaluation of the Fear of COVID-19 Scale Among Chinese Population. *Int. J. Ment. Health Addict.* **2021**, 1–16. [CrossRef]
27. Yadav, U.N.; Yadav, O.P.; Singh, D.R.; Ghimire, S.; Rayamajhee, B.; Kanti Mistry, S.; Rawal, L.B.; Ali, A.M.; Kumar Tamang, M.; Mehta, S. Perceived fear of COVID-19 and its associated factors among Nepalese older adults in eastern Nepal: A cross-sectional study. *PLoS ONE* **2021**, *16*, e0254825. [CrossRef]
28. Parlapani, E.; Holeva, V.; Nikopoulou, V.A.; Sereslis, K.; Athanasiadou, M.; Godosidis, A.; Stephanou, T.; Diakogiannis, I. Intolerance of Uncertainty and Loneliness in Older Adults During the COVID-19 Pandemic. *Front. Psychiatry* **2020**, *11*, 842. [CrossRef]
29. Powell, T.; Bellin, E.; Ehrlich, A.R. Older adults and Covid-19: The most vulnerable, the hardest hit. *Hast. Cent. Rep.* **2020**, *50*, 61–63. [CrossRef] [PubMed]
30. Harper, C.A.; Satchell, L.P.; Fido, D.; Latzman, R.D. Functional Fear Predicts Public Health Compliance in the COVID-19 Pandemic. *Int. J. Ment. Health Addict.* **2020**, 1–14. [CrossRef]
31. Rico-Uribe, L.A.; Caballero, F.F.; Martín-María, N.; Cabello, M.; Ayuso-Mateos, J.L.; Miret, M. Association of loneliness with all-cause mortality: A meta-analysis. *PLoS ONE* **2018**, *13*, e0190033. [CrossRef]
32. Aguilera, G. Corticotropin releasing hormone, receptor regulation and the stress response. *Trends Endocrinol. Metab.* **1998**, *9*, 329–336. [CrossRef]
33. Herman, J.P.; Adams, D.; Prewitt, C. Regulatory changes in neuroendocrine stress-integrative circuitry produced by a variable stress paradigm. *Neuroendocrinology* **1995**, *61*, 180–190. [CrossRef] [PubMed]
34. Hill, M.N.; McLaughlin, R.J.; Bingham, B.; Shrestha, L.; Lee, T.T.; Gray, J.M.; Hillard, C.J.; Gorzalka, B.B.; Viau, V. Endogenous cannabinoid signaling is essential for stress adaptation. *Proc. Natl. Acad. Sci. USA* **2010**, *107*, 9406–9411. [CrossRef]
35. Gonçalves de Andrade, E.; Šimončičová, E.; Carrier, M.; Vecchiarelli, H.A.; Robert, M.È.; Tremblay, M.È. Microglia Fighting for Neurological and Mental Health: On the Central Nervous System Frontline of COVID-19 Pandemic. *Front. Cell Neurosci.* **2021**, *15*, 647378. [CrossRef]
36. Lundblad, D.; Holmgren, L.; Jansson, J.H.; Näslund, U.; Eliasson, M. Gender differences in trends of acute myocardial infarction events: The Northern Sweden MONICA study 1985–2004. *BMC Cardiovasc. Disord.* **2008**, *8*, 17. [CrossRef] [PubMed]
37. de Miguel-Yanes, J.M.; Jiménez-García, R.; Hernandez-Barrera, V.; de Miguel-Díez, J.; Muñoz-Rivas, N.; Méndez-Bailón, M.; Pérez-Farinós, N.; López-Herranz, M.; Lopez-de-Andres, A. Sex Differences in the Incidence and Outcomes of Acute Myocardial Infarction in Spain, 2016–2018: A Matched-Pair Analysis. *J. Clin. Med.* **2021**, *10*, 1795. [CrossRef]
38. Chang, S.S.; Lin, S.Y.; Lai, J.N.; Chen, K.W.; Lu, C.R.; Chang, K.C.; Chiu, L.T.; Kao, C.H. Sex differences in long-term cardiovascular outcomes among patients with acute myocardial infarction: A population-based retrospective cohort study. *Int. J. Clin. Pract.* **2021**, *75*, e14066. [CrossRef] [PubMed]
39. Zimmermann, S.; Ruthrof, S.; Nowak, K.; Alff, A.; Klinghammer, L.; Schneider, R.; Ludwig, J.; Pfahlberg, A.B.; Daniel, W.G.; Flachskampf, F.A. Short-term prognosis of contemporary interventional therapy of ST-elevation myocardial infarction: Does gender matter? *Clin. Res. Cardiol.* **2009**, *98*, 709–715. [CrossRef] [PubMed]
40. Tzur Bitan, D.; Grossman-Giron, A.; Bloch, Y.; Mayer, Y.; Shiffman, N.; Mendlovic, S. Fear of COVID-19 scale: Psychometric characteristics, reliability and validity in the Israeli population. *Psychiatry Res.* **2020**, *289*, 113100. [CrossRef] [PubMed]
41. Finell, E.; Tiilikainen, M.; Jasinskaja-Lahti, I.; Hasan, N.; Muthana, F. Lived Experience Related to the COVID-19 Pandemic among Arabic-, Russian- and Somali-Speaking Migrants in Finland. *Int. J. Environ. Res. Public Health* **2021**, *18*, 2601. [CrossRef]
42. Tan, J.H.; Tong, J.; Ho, H.H. Delayed presentation of acute coronary syndrome with mechanical complication during COVID-19 pandemic: A case report. *Eur. Heart J. Case Rep.* **2020**, *5*, ytaa506. [CrossRef] [PubMed]
43. Rosenbaum, L. The Untold Toll—The Pandemic's Effects on Patients without Covid-19. *N. Engl. J. Med.* **2020**, *382*, 2368–2371. [CrossRef] [PubMed]
44. Arrivi, A.; Dominici, M.; Bier, N.; Truglio, M.; Vaudo, G.; Pucci, G. Association Between Air Pollution and Acute Coronary Syndromes During Lockdown for COVID-19: Results from the Terni Hub Center. *Front. Public Health.* **2021**, *9*, 683683. [CrossRef] [PubMed]

International Journal of
Environmental Research and Public Health

MDPI

Article

Longitudinal Distress among Brazilian University Workers during Pandemics

Murilo Ricardo Zibetti [1,*], Fernanda Barcellos Serralta [1] and Chris Evans [2]

[1] Post Graduate Program in Psychology, Universidade do Vale do Rio dos Sinos—UNISINOS, São Leopoldo 93022-970, Brazil; fernandaserralta@gmail.com
[2] Department of Psychology, The University of Sheffield, Sheffield S1 1HD, UK; chris@psyctc.org
* Correspondence: murilozibetti@unisinos.br

Abstract: The present study aimed to examine changes in mental distress in Brazilian university workers during the pandemic. All workers ($n \simeq 1850$) of an institution were invited to respond to a survey that took place in three stages, with collections in May (n = 407), June/July (n = 258), and August (n = 207) 2020, and included questions on demographic, health, general and psychological support, and psychometric assessment of mental distress (Clinical Outcome Routine Evaluation-CORE-OM) combined with an open question about major concerns. The results of the Multilevel Modeling analysis pointed to the absence of significant differences across the repeated measures of distress. The only variable associated with increased psychological distress over time was a lower level of support for household chores. Qualitative analysis of the reported major concerns was carried out with a sub-sample who showed reliable deterioration in CORE-OM across time (n = 17). The diversity of concerns reported by this group reinforced that work–life imbalance contributes to mental distress of university workers during the pandemic. Low response rate, although not unexpected due to the circumstances, limits the generalization of findings. The present data suggest that in addition to issues related to contagion and specific restricted measures to contain the spread of the disease, the personal reorganization of life required to maintain activities at home and work can be an important contributor to pandemic-related psychological distress.

Keywords: COVID-19; pandemics; quarantine; psychological distress; longitudinal studies

Citation: Zibetti, M.R.; Serralta, F.B.; Evans, C. Longitudinal Distress among Brazilian University Workers during Pandemics. *Int. J. Environ. Res. Public Health* **2021**, *18*, 9072. https://doi.org/10.3390/ijerph18179072

Academic Editors: Paolo Roma, Merylin Monaro and Cristina Mazza

Received: 24 July 2021
Accepted: 23 August 2021
Published: 27 August 2021

1. Introduction

In March 2020, the World Health Organization (WHO), declared the spread of the SARS-CoV-2 virus had reached pandemic levels. The circulation of a highly transmissible virus, potentially lethal and untreated, resulted in the imposition of behavioral norms to avoid contagion [1]. The main one involved social distancing that resulted in extensive home confinement [2]. Although it has varied locally, from instructions to stay at home to compulsory isolation, guidelines for social distancing were adopted by several countries.

It was quickly realized that COVID-19 and the measures to contain it were significant psychological stressors [2]. In addition to the possibility of contagion and the isolation, economic losses, changes in routine, and loss of social support also contributed to increased mental struggle [3]. Therefore, since the beginning of the pandemic, researchers have warned of the impacts on mental health and warned that health systems should be prepared to provide psychosocial support to the general population [2–4].

International and national survey studies corroborated these expectations by demonstrating the immediate impacts of the pandemic on mental health in the general population [5]. High rates of mental distress have been identified in cross-sectional studies conducted in countries such as China [6], Italy [7], the United States [8], and Brazil [9,10]. Worsening symptoms such as sadness, anxiety, sleep difficulties, and even suicidal ideation have been reported [6]. A relative consensus was established that belonging to the female gender, being younger, and having history of mental disorder, were risk factors for greater mental distress in this period [6,10,11].

In addition to the immediate mental health effects of the pandemic on the population, some studies have made comparisons before and after social distancing measures. For example, a study conducted in the United Kingdom indicated that the percentage of people classified as suffering from mental illness rose from 19.4% between the years 2017 and 2019 to 30.6% in the first month of isolation [12]. Similar data on deterioration, when compared to those before isolation measures, were obtained in other studies and stages of the pandemic in the United Kingdom [11]. A cross-sectional study conducted in the United States indicated that each day more during the early months of the pandemic predicted an increase of 11% in the odds to change to a higher category of mental distress [8]. These before versus during the pandemic between-group comparison studies presented a picture of psychological deterioration [13]. However, the absence of within-participant follow-up studies creates biases, making conclusions about the evolution of mental health indicators uncertain.

Longitudinal studies of the change in mental health indicators during the pandemic are emerging. A study conducted in China, with an interval of 30 days between the two collections during the pandemic, detected levels of stabilization of mental health indicators at levels below expectations [13]. In Latin America, data collected in Argentina in the first two weeks of the lockdown indicated changes with a small effect size in the indicators of depression, anxiety, and affection [14]. On the other hand, a study conducted in India reported worsening levels of stress, depression, and anxiety over the first two months of lockdown [15]. In Spain, a study carried out between the second and the fifth week of the pandemic indicated complex effects with worsening depression and stabilization of anxiety and post-traumatic stress [16].

Previous studies demonstrate the complexity of the pandemic effects and isolation measures on the general population's mental health. There are three obvious possibilities: (1) deterioration of mental health with aggravation of stressors over time; (2) stabilization of levels of distress due to the maintenance of conditions; (3) recovery of the initial impact due to the reorganization of the routine, individual resilience, and identification of support networks. A meta-analysis of longitudinal studies demonstrated modest effects on depression and anxiety and the absence of longitudinal effects on most of the investigated psychological variables [17]. This study also noted the great variability of effects reported in these studies. The different results are possibly associated with the different methods (sampling, measurement), forms and needs of fulfilling social isolation [17], personal differences in wealth and resources to survive [18], and the different governmental responses to the containment of the pandemic [19].

Longitudinal data on mental health during the pandemic in Brazil is scarce. The objective of the present study was to describe changing mental struggles during the pandemic in a specific group of Brazilian university workers. Few studies have been conducted with university workers, though they are interesting, having access to scientific information and often being able to move work activities to home. Cross-sectional studies conducted in Italy [20] and Spain [21] have reported high levels of anxiety and depression in the population. In addition to the stressors affecting the general population, university workers have found themselves under a particular pressure to keep up their teaching work and supporting their students, but at a distance [22]. In a previous study, we identified that the concern most mentioned by these professionals involved issues related to work, from the quality of the services provided to the pervasive pressures of remote office working [23]. In the same study, we identified that 98% of these professionals reported complying with the social distance measures.

The present study aimed to build on the earlier report by examining possible changes in psychological distress reported by university workers during the initial period of the pandemic, examining the effect of social isolation measures on this population. Secondary objectives were to verify the variables associated with the increase or decrease in suffering and to identify the concerns of people with a worsening mental health status.

2. Materials and Methods

2.1. Study Design

It was a longitudinal and mixed design (quantitative and qualitative). The study's approach was pragmatic as the primary intention of the survey was to provide support to the university community through screening for mental distress and the provision of support measures to these people (remote psychological first aid and referrals). The study used longitudinal data from the three months of the intervention project. This interval was designed based on the evolution of the pandemic's first wave and the end of the first semester of classes.

2.2. Participants

Approximately 1850 university employees or service providers were potentially eligible for research and were invited to participate in the online survey. No inclusion criteria other than working for the university were imposed and there were no exclusion criteria. In the first data collection, in May 2020, 407 responses were received. The participants had a mean age of 37.5 years, and the majority were female (68%) and had been, on average, social distancing for 59 days. In the second stage of data collection, in June, 258 responses were received. These participants had a mean age of 40.9, 72% were female, and they had a mean time in social isolation of 92 days. Finally, 207 participants responded to the third stage in August, who had a mean age of 41 years, 72% were female, and had a mean of 130 days in isolation. Except for the time in isolation, which predictably increased, there were no statistically significant differences ($p > 0.05$) between the proportion by gender and the average age of the participants in the three stages.

The selection criterion for inclusion in this analysis of change was having responded to at least two stages of data collection ($n = 256$). Only 36 participants responded in all three stages, 87 participated in the first and second stages, 70 in the second and third stages, and 63 participants in the first and third stages.

2.3. Instruments

An electronic survey was developed for online completion by the participants. The data on this form can be grouped as follows:

General demographic items: mainly focused on the description of the sample, including issues such as age, gender, and position in the institution.

Demographic and self-care items related to the pandemic: developed to assess factors potentially related to mental and physical health in the pandemic. These included the time of isolation, belonging to a risk group for COVID-19, living or being a worker in essential areas, support received, and health habits (food, alcohol consumption, relaxing activities, and exercise) during pandemics. The questionnaire also contained an open question about the main current concerns of the participants. A very detailed description of the measures, used for each of these variables, was presented in a previous publication [23]. In this study, only the significant variables in that previous study were included as predictors of mental health, namely exercise, support for daily household activities and availability of people to listen, and psychological and psychiatric support.

Clinical Outcomes in Routine Evaluation—Outcome Monitoring (CORE-OM) [24–26]: this is a self-report questionnaire developed in the United Kingdom for monitoring treatment outcomes in mental health. The original version has 34 items answered in a Likert scale format. The questions of the instrument can be grouped as risk scores (6 items) and non-risk (NR) (28 items). For the present study, we chose to use the non-risk items as this set constitutes an indicator of mental distress. In the original study, the NR scale had excellent indicators of internal consistency (Cronbach's $\alpha = 0.94$) [24]. It was used for the present study, the Brazilian Portuguese version adapted by Santana et al. (2015) [27] following the guidance of the CORE System Trust (www.coresystemtrust.org.uk/cst-translation-policy accessed on 12 January 2021). The internal consistency (Cronbach alpha) of the NR was 0.94 for the May stage and 0.93 for both the June/July and August stages.

2.4. Procedures

The study was carried out at a university in southern Brazil after an agreement between the researchers and the university managers, specifically from the committee responsible for the pandemic contingency plan. Participation was invited through an institutional email sent to all employees and service providers in the institution. This email contained a link with access to an online form that took about 30 min. The form remained open for approximately 10 days from the invitation and further e-mails encouraging participation were sent during this period.

Data collection was carried out three times between May and August 2020, maintaining an interval of at least 4 weeks between the end of a collection and the beginning of the subsequent one. The first collection took place between the 9th and 10th week after the interruption of on-site activities at the University. The classes and other university activities remained remote throughout the data collection period.

Pseudonymous linkage of repeat completions was based on a code generated by the participant, maintained in the three collections. Participants who allowed further contact on the form received feedback of results from the survey between the stages.

2.5. Data Analysis

Firstly, analyses described the sample and checked the internal consistency of the CORE-OM instrument. Then, inferential analyses were performed to ascertain the effect on the mental distress indicator over time. For this analysis, the direct effect of time and, separately, the interaction of the effects with predictors were tested.

To evaluate the effect of time, repeated measures were considered, accounting for the variation between subjects through the Multilevel Modeling (MLM) analysis [28–30]. Each of the study stages was categorized as a level, regardless of the time interval between them (i.e., stages one, two, and three). MLM handles non-participation across the three stages by estimating a linear path of any two scores completed. Slope against time was first treated as fixed (stable among participants) then a random effect of time, i.e., different score slopes per participant, were also allowed.

After the identification of changes over time in the NR score, analyses were performed to find out predictors of this change. Stable (gender and age) and time-varying predictors (exercise practice, support in domestic activities, people available to talk, psychological and psychiatric follow-up) were tested separately. Though the latter are time-varying predictors, moderate and high levels of correlation between repeated measures were found (τb coefficient varying from 0.371 to 0.694) and only levels at the first participation were entered. Separate MLM analyses were performed for each of the potential predictors of change. Finally, score changes for participants who answered at least twice were evaluated using the Reliable Change Index (RCI), which indicates, for each participant, whether changes were larger than would be expected 5% of the time based on the reliability of the measure [31,32]. For each of the two time periods, the RCI allowed participants to be categorized as deteriorating, not reliably changing, or improving.. These proportions were compared across the two time periods, and we used this to find participants with deterioration and to inspect qualitative responses provided in the open question about concerns during the pandemic. For this simple analysis, we used the categories previously reported [23] that were identified using the Consensual Qualitative Research for simple qualitative data method—CQR m [33]—in the first stage of study.

2.6. Ethical Considerations

The study was designed in compliance with the guidelines on research with human beings in Resolution 466/2012 and in 510/2016 of the National Health Council (Brazil, 2012;

2016) and Resolution 016/200 of the Federal Council of Psychology (2000). The project was approved by the Ethics Committee of the university where the research was carried out (CAAE: 31225520.0.0000.5344). All participants expressed their consent to participate in the research by accepting an informed consent form available online. At the end of the research, all participants received information about the maintenance of mental health during the pandemic and, when necessary, assistance with remote psychological first aid and referrals, as previewed in the original research–intervention protocol.

3. Results

3.1. Longitudinal Change in NR Scores

The first analyses checked for change in participants who answered at least two stages. This showed mean score changes of −0.009 (95% CI = −0.071 to 0.047) between the first and second collections and −0.013 (95% CI = −0.070 to 0.053) between the second and third collections. That the confidence intervals cover no change, and that each includes the mean for the other change, indicates that, despite the small drop in score at each stage, this was neither an important nor statistically significant change.

In addition to the longitudinal effect, the variability of the change between the stages was evaluated. The mean square changes between the first and the second stages was 0.15 (95% CI = −0.011 to 0.019) and between the second and third stages, it was 0.047 (95% CI = −0.027 to 0.077). In contrast to the absence of a longitudinal effect on NR scores, there was lower variability in change between the second and third stages than between the first and second. This may indicate that people with greater mental health problems or distress were less willing to complete the last two stages of the study. These data also indicate probable distinctions between the change across participants. This result justifies subsequent exploration of effects of potential change predictors and, subsequently, the categorization of individual change using the RCI.

3.2. Testing Potential Predictors of NR Scores Evolution

Neither gender nor age showed a significant effect on change. Gender was related to baseline NR scores, but not to change. After evaluating these demographic predictors, potential predictors of physical exercise, home support, and professional mental health monitoring were explored.

The first variable tested was daily exercise in the baseline of the study. The data showed that the practice of exercise was significantly associated with the NR score ($p = 0.0005$) but did not significantly affect its evolution ($p = 0.47$). The data indicate that the participants who did not exercise daily had higher rates of mental distress in the first stage of the research and kept this elevated level over time.

Two potential predictors addressed support received at home at baseline. Having people at home available to listen and talk was related to the general NR scores ($p = 0.0006$), but not to their longitudinal change ($p = 0.26$). On the other hand, the perceived support for domestic activities was not directly related to the baseline scores distresses ($p = 0.40$) but was related to the evolution across time ($p = 0.001$) (Figure 1).

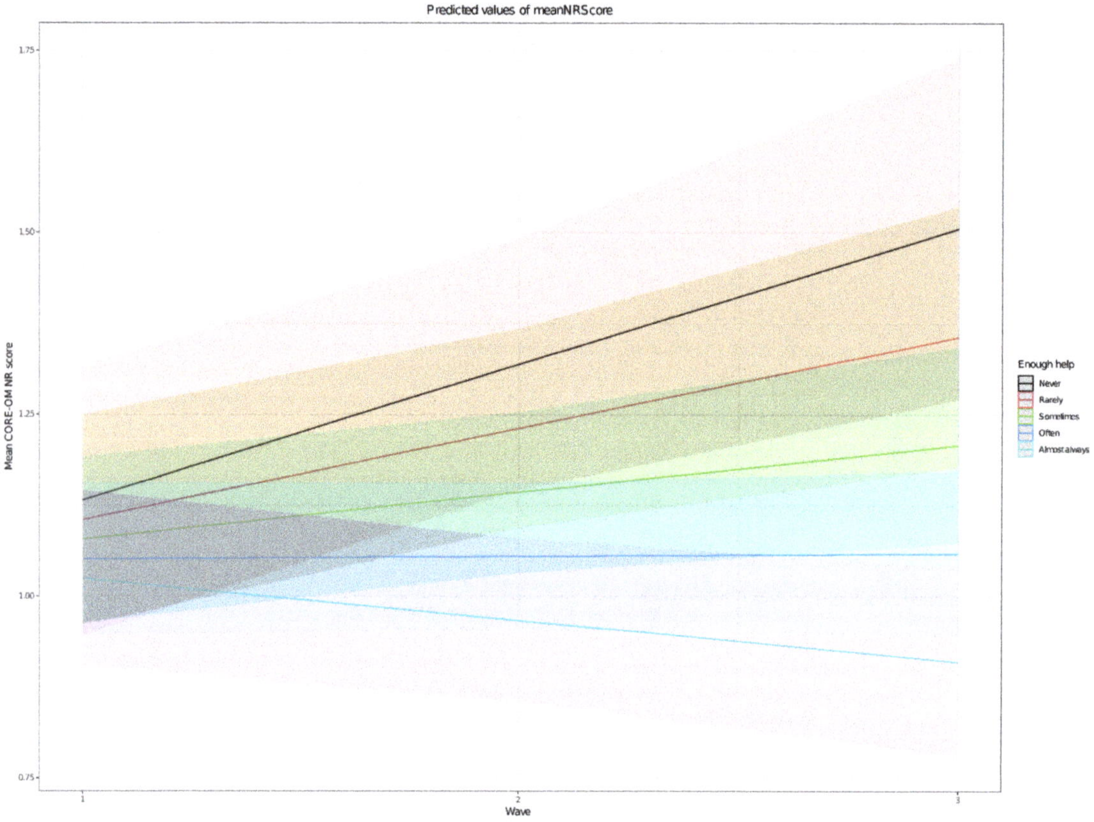

Figure 1. Differential effect of perceived support with household chores on change in CORE-OM NR score.

Finally, indicators related to mental health and their association with NR scores were tested. The results of the MLM indicate that being in counseling is associated neither with mental distress in the first data collection ($p = 0.53$) nor with longitudinal change ($p = 0.28$). Very similar results were identified for psychiatric support for the NR score ($p = 0.73$) and its evolution ($p = 0.16$). The next step in the evaluation was to identify the trajectories of specific subjects and analyze some of their qualitative issues.

3.3. Assessment of Individual Evolution

For this analysis, only respondents from more than one stage were included, comparing them with themselves. It was considered a significant change when the participant's data showed reliable changes in the NR. In this sense, Table 1 shows the evolution data of the participants.

From this data, it is possible to see that a similar proportion of participants showed deterioration, stability, and improvement in each of the stages. To deepen our understanding of these findings, we looked at the participants' individual responses to the qualitative question about their main concerns. These responses were grouped into six domains: work, health, social isolation, life and personal routine, social environment, and future [23]. Many responses were complex; that is, they involved multiple domains. Some examples are presented in Table 2.

Table 1. Evolution of participants in the mental health indicator considering longitudinal monitoring Reliable Change Index.

Time	Total of Participants	Deterioration N (%)	No Reliable Change N (%)	Improvement N (%)
Change wave 1 to 2	87	8 (9.2%)	70 (80.5%)	9 (10.3%)
Change wave 2 to 3	70	3 (4.3%)	62 (88.6%)	5 (7.1%)
Change wave 1 to 3	62	6 (9.7%)	48 (77.4%)	8 (12.9%)

Table 2. Concerns of participants who deteriorated during the 3 months of social isolation.

Vignette	Reported Concern
Vignette 1	*"The lack of direct contact with society, the difficulty in maintaining physical care routine and the distance from cultural activities, travel and entertainment."* (Domains: social isolation; life and personal routine)
Vignette 2	*"Household chores and the uncertainty of what is to come."* (Domains: life and personal routine and future)
Vignette 3	*"Not being able to maintain physical proximity to friends, relatives. The uncertainty about COVID, work, personal life. Suspension of some personal care, for fear of exposing myself."* (Domains: social isolation; future; health)
Vignette 4	*"Feeling of not being able to cope with the demands; feeling of loneliness; emotional and work overload; economic situation of family members."* (Domains: health; work; social isolation; social environment)
Vignette 5	*"Too much time in front of the PC screen."* (Domain: work)
Vignette 6	*"Government of the country; The uncertainty about the future."* (Domains: social environment and future)

The themes included fear of contagion, problems associated with living together due to isolation, excessive domestic and work activities, and broad issues related to the economy, governmental responses, and the future. Perhaps not surprisingly, in view of the small numbers showing reliable deterioration, the qualitative categories of their comments were not very different from those obtained in our previous study with the entire group [21].

4. Discussion

The objective of this article was to investigate in Brazilian university workers within-participant changes in mental health during the pandemic, and the measures for their containment. The data were from three collections between the 9th and 21st weeks of the pandemic in Brazil. The response rate to the first collection was 22%, and dropped to 13.94% and 11.19%, respectively, in the second and third collections. During this period, most respondents worked remotely and voluntarily complied with the measures of social distancing so the effects of the containment measures cannot be separated from the effect of the pandemic itself, as so few did not comply with the measures. Although the rate response is lower than the ideal, this is not unexpected from a voluntary survey with no rewards for participation in very stressful times. Low response rates do not necessarily lead to response bias but happen when the variable of interest affects the decision to participate or not [34]. We acknowledge that this might be the case. Therefore, we recommend caution in interpreting and generalizing these survey results. The quantitative results showed relative stability in the levels of mental distress across the period. Despite similarity in terms of time and stage of the pandemic, the results are different from those obtained in India, which showed a great increase in mental suffering in a longitudinal study [15]. The results were also divergent from the study conducted by Canet-Juric et al. (2020) [14] in

Argentina that showed small effects on indicators of depression and anxiety, and a negative effect during two weeks of lockdown. However, our findings are similar to those obtained in China [13]. In this sense, it is possible that the stability found in both studies occurs due to the balance between the advance of pandemic stressors and resilience adjustments. It is not possible to identify specific issues that justify the similarity of results between our study and the one conducted in China [13], and not with those conducted in Argentina [14] and India [15]. However, methodological (e.g., an instrument used, time of follow-up) and contextual (e.g., stage of the pandemic, the severity of distance measures, economic impact) differences may have influenced the great variability in the results of longitudinal studies during the pandemic [17].

It is noteworthy that the absence of longitudinal effects in the present study is congruent with a meta-analysis published by Prati and Mancini [17]. In this review, no significant impacts were observed during the pandemic for most mental health variables, including psychological distress. In the present study, the data collection was during the course of the pandemic, with no pre-pandemic measures; therefore, we cannot know if psychological health was or was not affected initially in the face of stressors related to the pandemic and the measures for containing it. However, the idea that the pandemic may have caused a rise in distress is suggested by the finding that mean scores in the present study are above the cut-off points for clinical groups obtained before the pandemic in the English and Spanish versions of the instrument [24,35,36].

Whatever the initial effect of the pandemic and restrictions, our findings suggest there was relative stability of the high levels of mental distress across the evaluated period. This possibility would be in line with the observation of Wang et al. (2020) [13] on the stabilization at high levels of suffering, and with the data obtained in the United Kingdom that demonstrated the effects of worsening mental struggle, comparing periods before and during the pandemic, denoting the chronicity of the response to the multiple stressors [11,12]

Despite the absence of a longitudinal effect on mental distress, the results of this study indicate a significant reduction in the variability of the level of distress of the participants in each of the moments of the study. This homogenization may also indicate a bias in which extreme participants (with positive and negative outcomes) tend not to follow all stages of the study. This issue of attrition in longitudinal studies has been little explored in the pandemic mental health literature and might be a contributor to the heterogeneity of the results of pandemic longitudinal studies [17].

A secondary objective of the study was to evaluate predictors of the longitudinal evolution of mental distress during the pandemic. The results indicate that the only variable significantly associated with the evolution of mental suffering in this period was the help received in domestic activities. This is particularly important considering the overload of these professionals who, almost all, now performed both work and domestic activities from their homes. In this sense, adjustments in work to carry out online activities and the greater support required by students may be associated with the greater overload of university workers in the period of the pandemic than for some other professions and occupations [22]. Additionally, with the loss of social support, there has been an increase in domestic and family demands that make it difficult to maintain the balance between life and work in academic contexts [37]. The demands of the pandemic have led to an increase in life–work conflicts, particularly in families with younger children [38], and this variable has been considered a predictor of disagreement and stress in family systems [39]. The qualitative stage of this study reinforces this hypothesis: participants showing reliable, psychological deterioration, like most participants, were concerned with issues beyond contagion and isolation, including other dimensions of the experience of living and working in the context of the pandemic and social detachment.

Stable predictors such as gender, age, and history of mental disorder were not related to the course of mental health in the pandemic. These variables have been reported as predictors of psychological distress during the pandemic in cross-sectional studies conducted in Brazil [9,10] and in several other countries [6,8]. Except for gender, these predictors were also associated with the level of mental distress when examined in the first stage of the present study [23]. Predictors of the evolution of mental distress in longitudinal studies are occasionally different from those identified in cross-sectional studies. This disagreement possibly occurs due to the fact that cross-sectional studies capture greater vulnerability of certain demographic groups to the emergence of psychopathology, even in periods before the pandemic (e.g., [40,41]). Additionally, there are likely differences between the immediate impact of the pandemic and its long-term effects, reinforcing the need for more longitudinal studies in many countries and different social groups.

Non-stable predictors such as exercise, people available to talk, and psychological and psychiatric consultation were not associated with the evolution of mental distress. In general, these variables had effects on mental distress in the first moment that was maintained in the other follow-up measures. Like the stable predictors, most of these variables were associated with mental distress in the cross-sectional analysis from first data collection [23]. The findings about the (psychological or psychiatric) support variable should be interpreted cautiously and in the context of the study, which carried out the data collection with the provision of mental health support to those with greater distress. That the participants knew this may have affected willingness to disclose sometimes stigmatized access to support. Hence, though the relationship found here should generalize to other surveys linked with offers of support, whether the same would be found where no support is offered cannot be known.

This study has many limitations, the main ones being sample size and unknown biases of non-participation. The sample size, though not small, reduces the precision of estimation of effects and reduces the power to detect weak effects and interactions between the predictors. As ever, non-significant effects must be interpreted with caution. Perhaps more important, is that possible biases arising from selective non-participation can, as always, not be known. Responders plus the data suggest a reduction in the variability in the response profile. However, the qualitative data of the participants' concerns complement the conclusions of the study.

Finally, our results, both quantitative and qualitative, indicate that university workers, as presumedly most of the population, faced dramatic changes in their work–life balance during the pandemic. It is possible that the mental overload resulting from these changes, together with the fear of contagion, previous vulnerabilities, and other variables, results in further deterioration of mental health. In this sense, it is quite plausible that the support received for these additional activities (domestic) positively impacts mental health, avoiding this kind of burden.

5. Conclusions

This study provides important results regarding university workers, fulfilling social isolation, during the beginning of the pandemic and is supported by longitudinal, quantitative, and qualitative data. The results suggest that, after an initial negative impact, there was a relative stability of mental distress and that the support received in domestic activities minimizes psychological deterioration. New and more specific studies in this direction can provide data to assist government officials in the planning of public health actions, as well as managers with a review of possible work demands to avoid an increase in psychopathological conditions during pandemics and similar situations.

Author Contributions: Conceptualization: F.B.S. and M.R.Z.; Project administration: F.B.S. and M.R.Z.; Manuscript writing: F.B.S. and M.R.Z.; Methodology: F.B.S., M.R.Z. and C.E.; Quantitative data analysis: C.E.; Qualitative data analysis: F.B.S. and M.R.Z.; Manuscript revision: F.B.S., M.R.Z. and C.E. All authors have read and agreed to the published version of the manuscript.

Funding: This research received no external funding.

Institutional Review Board Statement: The study was conducted according to the guidelines of the Declaration of Helsinki and was approved by the Institutional Ethics Committee of the University of Bell´s River Valley (Universidade do Vale do Rio dos Sinos—UNISINOS), Brazil (protocol code: 31225520.0.0000.5344 approved on 29 May 2020).

Informed Consent Statement: Digital informed consent was obtained from all participants involved in the study.

Data Availability Statement: Research data are available on request from the corresponding author. Data is not public due to confidentiality.

Acknowledgments: We thank Ana Karina Fredrel for the logistical support in data collection.

Conflicts of Interest: The authors declare no conflict of interest.

References

1. Advice for the Public on COVID-19—World Health Organization. Available online: https://www.who.int/emergencies/diseases/novel-coronavirus-2019/advice-for-public (accessed on 12 January 2021).
2. Pfefferbaum, B.; North, C.S. Mental Health and the Covid-19 Pandemic. *N. Engl. J. Med.* **2020**, *383*, 510–512. [CrossRef]
3. Ornell, F.; Schuch, J.B.; Sordi, A.O.; Kessler, F.H.P.; Ornell, F.; Schuch, J.B.; Sordi, A.O.; Kessler, F.H.P. "Pandemic Fear" and COVID-19: Mental Health Burden and Strategies. *Braz. J. Psychiatry* **2020**, *42*, 232–235. [CrossRef]
4. Keep Mental Health in Mind. *Nat. Med.* **2020**, *26*, 631. [CrossRef] [PubMed]
5. Xiong, J.; Lipsitz, O.; Nasri, F.; Lui, L.M.W.; Gill, H.; Phan, L.; Chen-Li, D.; Iacobucci, M.; Ho, R.; Majeed, A.; et al. Impact of COVID-19 Pandemic on Mental Health in the General Population: A Systematic Review. *J. Affect. Disord.* **2020**, *277*, 55–64. [CrossRef]
6. Wang, C.; Pan, R.; Wan, X.; Tan, Y.; Xu, L.; Ho, C.S.; Ho, R.C. Immediate Psychological Responses and Associated Factors during the Initial Stage of the 2019 Coronavirus Disease (COVID-19) Epidemic among the General Population in China. *Int. J. Environ. Res. Public. Health* **2020**, *17*, 1729. [CrossRef]
7. Gualano, M.R.; Lo Moro, G.; Voglino, G.; Bert, F.; Siliquini, R. Effects of Covid-19 Lockdown on Mental Health and Sleep Disturbances in Italy. *Int. J. Environ. Res. Public. Health* **2020**, *17*, 4779. [CrossRef] [PubMed]
8. Holingue, C.; Kalb, L.G.; Riehm, K.E.; Bennett, D.; Kapteyn, A.; Veldhuis, C.B.; Johnson, R.M.; Fallin, M.D.; Kreuter, F.; Stuart, E.A.; et al. Mental Distress in the United States at the Beginning of the COVID-19 Pandemic. *Am. J. Public Health* **2020**, *110*, 1628–1634. [CrossRef]
9. Barros, M.B.; Lima, M.G.; Malta, D.C.; Szwarcwald, C.L.; Azevedo, R.C.; Romero, D.; Souza Júnior, P.R.; Azevedo, L.O.; Machado, Í.E.; Damacena, G.N.; et al. Relato de Tristeza/Depressão, Nervosismo/Ansiedade e Problemas de Sono Na População Adulta Brasileira Durante a Pandemia de COVID-19. *Epidemiol. E Serviços Saúde* **2020**, *29*, e2020427. [CrossRef] [PubMed]
10. De Quadros Duarte, M.; da Silva Santo, M.A.; Lima, C.P.; Giordani, J.P.; Trentini, C.M.; Duarte, M.D.Q.; Santo, M.A.D.S.; Lima, C.P.; Giordani, J.P.; Trentini, C.M. COVID-19 e os impactos na saúde mental: Uma amostra do Rio Grande do Sul, Brasil. *Ciênc. Amp Saúde Coletiva* **2020**, *25*, 3401–3411. [CrossRef] [PubMed]
11. Niedzwiedz, C.L.; Green, M.J.; Benzeval, M.; Campbell, D.; Craig, P.; Demou, E.; Leyland, A.; Pearce, A.; Thomson, R.; Whitley, E.; et al. Mental Health and Health Behaviours before and during the Initial Phase of the COVID-19 Lockdown: Longitudinal Analyses of the UK Household Longitudinal Study. *J. Epidemiol. Community Health* **2020**, *75*, 224–231. [CrossRef] [PubMed]
12. Pierce, M.; Hope, H.; Ford, T.; Hatch, S.; Hotopf, M.; John, A.; Kontopantelis, E.; Webb, R.; Wessely, S.; McManus, S.; et al. Mental Health before and during the COVID-19 Pandemic: A Longitudinal Probability Sample Survey of the UK Population. *Lancet Psychiatry* **2020**, *7*, 883–892. [CrossRef]
13. Wang, C.; Pan, R.; Wan, X.; Tan, Y.; Xu, L.; McIntyre, R.S.; Choo, F.N.; Tran, B.; Ho, R.; Sharma, V.K.; et al. A Longitudinal Study on the Mental Health of General Population during the COVID-19 Epidemic in China. *Brain. Behav. Immun.* **2020**, *87*, 40–48. [CrossRef] [PubMed]
14. Canet-Juric, L.; Andrés, M.L.; del Valle, M.; López-Morales, H.; Poó, F.; Galli, J.I.; Yerro, M.; Urquijo, S. A Longitudinal Study on the Emotional Impact Cause by the COVID-19 Pandemic Quarantine on General Population. *Front. Psychol.* **2020**, *11*, 565688. [CrossRef] [PubMed]
15. Gopal, A.; Sharma, A.J.; Subramanyam, M.A. Dynamics of Psychological Responses to COVID-19 in India: A Longitudinal Study. *PLoS ONE* **2020**, *15*, e0240650. [CrossRef] [PubMed]
16. González-Sanguino, C.; Ausín, B.; Castellanos, M.Á.; Saiz, J.; López-Gómez, A.; Ugidos, C.; Muñoz, M. Mental Health Consequences of the Coronavirus 2020 Pandemic (COVID-19) in Spain. A Longitudinal Study. *Front. Psychiatry* **2020**, *11*, 565474. [CrossRef]
17. Prati, G.; Mancini, A.D. The Psychological Impact of COVID-19 Pandemic Lockdowns: A Review and Meta-Analysis of Longitudinal Studies and Natural Experiments. *Psychol. Med.* **2021**, *51*, 201–211. [CrossRef] [PubMed]
18. Gibson, B.; Schneider, J.; Talamonti, D.; Forshaw, M. The Impact of Inequality on Mental Health Outcomes during the COVID-19 Pandemic: A Systematic Review. *Can. Psychol. Can.* **2021**, *62*, 101–126. [CrossRef]

19. Arendt, F.; Markiewitz, A.; Mestas, M.; Scherr, S. COVID-19 Pandemic, Government Responses, and Public Mental Health: Investigating Consequences through Crisis Hotline Calls in Two Countries. *Soc. Sci. Med.* **2020**, *265*, 113532. [CrossRef]
20. Marelli, S.; Castelnuovo, A.; Somma, A.; Castronovo, V.; Mombelli, S.; Bottoni, D.; Leitner, C.; Fossati, A.; Ferini-Strambi, L. Impact of COVID-19 Lockdown on Sleep Quality in University Students and Administration Staff. *J. Neurol.* **2020**. [CrossRef]
21. Odriozola-González, P.; Planchuelo-Gómez, Á.; Irurtia, M.J.; de Luis-García, R. Psychological Effects of the COVID-19 Outbreak and Lockdown among Students and Workers of a Spanish University. *Psychiatry Res.* **2020**, *290*, 113108. [CrossRef]
22. Sahu, P. Closure of Universities Due to Coronavirus Disease 2019 (COVID-19): Impact on Education and Mental Health of Students and Academic Staff. *Cureus* **2020**, *12*, e7541. [CrossRef]
23. Serralta, F.B.; Zibetti, M.R.; Evans, C. Psychological Distress of University Workers during COVID-19 Pandemic in Brazil. *Int. J. Environ. Res. Public. Health* **2020**, *17*, 8520. [CrossRef] [PubMed]
24. Evans, C.; Connell, J.; Barkham, M.; Margison, F.; McGrath, G.; Mellor-Clark, J.; Audin, K. Towards a Standardised Brief Outcome Measure: Psychometric Properties and Utility of the CORE–OM. *Br. J. Psychiatry* **2002**, *180*, 51–60. [CrossRef] [PubMed]
25. Evans, Chris The CORE-OM (Clinical Outcomes in Routine Evaluation) and Its Derivatives. *Integr. Sci. Pract.* **2012**, *2*, 12–14.
26. Evans, V.; Mellor-Clark, J.; Margison, F. CORE: Clinical Outcomes in Routine Evaluation. *J. Ment Health* **2000**, *9*, 247–255. [CrossRef]
27. Santana, M.R.M.; da Silva, M.M.; Moraes, D.S.D.; Fukuda, C.C.; Freitas, L.H.; Ramos, M.E.C.; Fleury, H.J.; Evans, C.; Santana, M.R.M.; Da Silva, M.M.; et al. Brazilian Portuguese Version of the CORE-OM: Cross-Cultural Adaptation of an Instrument to Assess the Efficacy and Effectiveness of Psychotherapy. *Trends Psychiatry Psychother.* **2015**, *37*, 227–231. [CrossRef]
28. Bates, D.; Mächler, M.; Bolker, B.; Walker, S. Fitting Linear Mixed-Effects Models Using Lme4. *J. Stat. Softw.* **2015**, *67*. [CrossRef]
29. Kuznetsova, A.; Brockhoff, P.B.; Christensen, R.H.B. LmerTest Package: Tests in Linear Mixed Effects Models. *J. Stat. Softw.* **2017**, *82*, 1–26. [CrossRef]
30. Gelman, A.; Hill, J. *Data Analysis Using Regression and Multilevel/Hierarchical Models*; Analytical methods for social research; Cambridge University Press: New York, NY, USA, 2007; ISBN 978-0-521-86706-1.
31. Evans, C.; Margison, F.; Barkham, M. The Contribution of Reliable and Clinically Significant Change Methods to Evidence-Based Mental Health. *Evid. Based Ment. Health* **1998**, *1*, 70–72. [CrossRef]
32. Jacobson, N.S.; Truax, P. Clinical Significance: A Statistical Approach to Defining Meaningful Change in Psychotherapy Research. *J. Consult. Clin. Psychol.* **1991**, *59*, 12–19. [CrossRef]
33. Spangler, P.T.; Liu, J.; Hill, C.E. Consensual qualitative research for simple qualitative data: An introduction to CQR-M. In *Consensual Qualitative Research: A practical Resource for Investigating Social Science Phenomena*; American Psychological Association: Washington, DC, USA, 2012; pp. 269–283. ISBN 1-4338-1007-7.
34. Stedman, R.C.; Connelly, N.A.; Heberlein, T.A.; Decker, D.J.; Allred, S.B. The End of the (Research) World As We Know It? Understanding and Coping With Declining Response Rates to Mail Surveys. *Soc. Nat. Resour.* **2019**, *32*, 1139–1154. [CrossRef]
35. Feixas, G.; Trujillo, A.; Bados, A.; Garcia-Grau, E.; Salla, M.; Medina, J.C.; Montesano, A.; Soriano, J.; Medeiros-Ferreira, L.; Canete, J.; et al. Psychometric properties of the spanish version of the clinical outcomes in routine evaluation–outcome measure. Neuropsychiatric Disease and Treatment. *Neuropsychiatr. Dis. Treat.* **2016**, *12*, 1457. [CrossRef] [PubMed]
36. Paz, C.; Evans, C. The Clinical Outcomes in Routine Evaluation-Outcome Measure: A Useful Option for Routine Outcome Monitoring in Latin America. *Rev. Bras. Psicodrama* **2019**, *27*, 226–230. [CrossRef]
37. Anwer, M. Academic Labor and the Global Pandemic: Revisiting Life-Work Balance under COVID-19. *Susan Bulkeley Butl. Cent. Leadersh. Excell. Adv. Work. Pap. Ser.* **2020**, *3*, 5–13.
38. Schieman, S.; Badawy, P.J.; Milkie, M.A.; Bierman, A. Work-Life Conflict during the COVID-19 Pandemic. *Socius Sociol. Res. Dyn. World* **2021**, *7*. [CrossRef]
39. Daks, J.S.; Peltz, J.S.; Rogge, R.D. Psychological Flexibility and Inflexibility as Sources of Resiliency and Risk during a Pandemic: Modeling the Cascade of COVID-19 Stress on Family Systems with a Contextual Behavioral Science Lens. *J. Context. Behav. Sci.* **2020**, *18*, 16–27. [CrossRef] [PubMed]
40. Baumeister, H.; Härter, M. Prevalence of Mental Disorders Based on General Population Surveys. *Soc. Psychiatry Psychiatr. Epidemiol.* **2007**, *42*, 537–546. [CrossRef] [PubMed]
41. McDonough, P.; Strohschein, L. Age and the Gender Gap in Distress. *Women Health* **2003**, *38*, 1–20. [CrossRef]

International Journal of
Environmental Research and Public Health

MDPI

Article

Factors Affecting COVID-19 Preventive Behaviors among University Students in Beijing, China: An Empirical Study Based on the Extended Theory of Planned Behavior

Jiabin Li [1,†], Xianwei Liu [2,*,†], Yang Zou [3], Yichu Deng [4], Meng Zhang [5], Miaomiao Yu [6], Dongjiao Wu [7], Hao Zheng [8] and Xinliang Zhao [9]

1 Advising Center for Student Development, Beijing University of Technology, Beijing 100124, China; lijiabin@bjut.edu.cn
2 Institute of Higher Education, Research Centre for Capital Engineering Education Development, Beijing University of Technology, Beijing 100124, China
3 College of Business Administration, Capital University of Economics and Business, Beijing 100070, China; zouyang@cueb.edu.cn
4 Publicity Department, Beijing University of Technology, Beijing 100124, China; dengyichu@bjut.edu.cn
5 School of Civil and Transportation Engineering, Beijing University of Civil Engineering and Architecture, Beijing 102616, China; zhangmeng1@bucea.edu.cn
6 Institute of Education Economics and Management, University of Science and Technology Beijing, Beijing 100083, China; yumiaomiao@ustb.edu.cn
7 School of Marxism, Beihang University, Beijing 100191, China; wudongjiao@buaa.edu.cn
8 China Youth & Children Research Center, Beijing 100089, China; zhenghao@buaa.edu.cn
9 Beijing Academy of Educational Sciences, Beijing 100045, China; xlzhao@ciefr.pku.edu.cn
* Correspondence: liuxianwei@bjut.edu.cn; Tel.: +86-010-6739-2673
† The authors contributed equally to the study.

Citation: Li, J.; Liu, X.; Zou, Y.; Deng, Y.; Zhang, M.; Yu, M.; Wu, D.; Zheng, H.; Zhao, X. Factors Affecting COVID-19 Preventive Behaviors among University Students in Beijing, China: An Empirical Study Based on the Extended Theory of Planned Behavior. *Int. J. Environ. Res. Public Health* **2021**, *18*, 7009. https://doi.org/10.3390/ijerph18137009

Academic Editors: Cristina Mazza, Paolo Roma and Merylin Monaro

Received: 28 May 2021
Accepted: 28 June 2021
Published: 30 June 2021

Abstract: Higher education institutions (HEIs), among other social systems, have an irreplaceable role in combating COVID-19. However, we know little about institutional and individual factors that might facilitate university students' beliefs and behaviors toward preventive behaviors for COVID-19 within the higher education context. Our study applies an extended theory of planned behavior (TPB) model to investigate the structural relationships among the institutional climate, attitudes, subjective norms, perceived behavioral control and preventive behaviors of university students and to detect the moderating impacts of perceived risk on the structural model. Data were collected from 3693 university students at 18 universities in Beijing, China through an online survey. Structural equation modeling (SEM) and multigroup analysis were performed to examine the empirical model. The results reveal that (1) the institutional climate has a significant, direct effect on preventive behaviors for COVID-19 among university students, (2) the TPB components, namely attitudes, subjective norms and perceived behavioral control, partially mediate the relationship between the institutional climate and preventive behaviors for COVID-19, and (3) perceived risk moderates several paths in the model. Theoretical and practical implications are offered, and recommendations for future research are outlined.

Keywords: institutional climate; COVID-19 preventive behaviors; extended theory of planned behavior; university students

1. Introduction

The COVID-19 pandemic swept across the world and has been deemed the most devastating disease since the Spanish Flu in 1918–1919 [1]. By the end of January 2021, COVID-19 caused over one hundred million confirmed infections and two million deaths worldwide [2]. Although the first confirmed case was identified in Wuhan in December 2019, and the disease rapidly spread to other parts of China, through strict and effective preventive regulations and fully implemented policies, China was successful in keeping the COVID-19 pandemic under control with the efforts of the entire society.

COVID-19 prevention and control posed greater challenges and more stringent requirements for higher education institutions (HEIs) than for other social organizations. In contrast to other social systems, HEIs have a high density of people, which means that once one student gets it, large-scale pandemic transmission is likely to be triggered due to the high rate of spread of COVID-19 in crowded settlements [3]. China's health authorities responded early and quickly regarding COVID-19 prevention in HEIs. In late January 2020, soon after the outbreak of COVID-19, China's Ministry of Education (MOE) issued a series of notices requesting that all educational institutions take effective epidemic prevention and control measures and postpone the start of the 2020 spring semester. On 13 April 2020, the MOE and the National Health Commission (NHC) released the Scheme on COVID-19 Prevention and Control in HEIs and proposed that comprehensive preventive measures be implemented before, during and after students' return to campus. After campuses reopened, the Guidelines on COVID-19 Prevention and Control in HEIs for the 2020 autumn semester and for the 2021 spring semester were issued successively by the MOE and NHC. HEIs in China also actively displayed their major functions (talent training, scientific research and social services) during the COVID-19 pandemic by providing professional personnel, knowledge, skills and resources to combat COVID-19 and contribute to the research and development of definitive vaccines and forms of therapy.

Although some countries and regions, including China, have introduced a wide range of vaccinations, given the long-term complexity of the global pandemic situation, the construction and promotion of the preventive literature and behavior are critical in the "new normal" period of COVID-19 in addition to treatment and vaccine development. In fact, increasing numbers of studies added to the understanding of general public preventive behavior in many countries after the outbreak of COVID-19 [4–9]. However, few have targeted higher education systems [10,11], and most have focused on the role of knowledge and attitudes in predicting students' COVID-19 preventive behavior [12]. Thus, although HEIs are regarded as effective settings to shape specific attitudes and behaviors of students through institutional interventions [13], we still have limited knowledge about how the institutional factors of HEIs are affecting the preventive behaviors of university students and the psychological mechanism underlying this relationship during the outbreak of the COVID-19 pandemic.

To overcome the limitations of existing studies, our study explicitly identifies the impacts of the institutional climate, attitudes, subjective norms, perceived behavioral control and perceived risk of university students' COVID-19 preventive behaviors based on an extended theory of planned behavior (TPB) model. The TPB model proposed by Ajzen [14] may be one of the most influential theoretical perspectives to explain a range of health behavior intentions or actual behavior. While the TPB has been used in several recent studies of COVID-19 preventive behaviors [15], to improve the predictive capabilities of the TPB model, it is necessary to study university students' COVID-19 preventive behavior by including the institutional climate in the TPB model, because the critical role of HEIs in the prevention and control of COVID-19 has been widely reported in the literature [16]. Although the existing literature recognizes the moderating role of risk perception on a range of health behaviors [17], to the best of our knowledge, no previous study has examined the variations in the influence of institutional factors and TPB components on COVID-19 preventive behaviors in terms of different levels of risk perception.

Bearing the above considerations in mind, the key objective of the current research is to employ an extended TPB model to (1) explore the influence of the institutional climate on the COVID-19 preventive behaviors of university students, (2) test the mediating effect of three TPB elements, namely attitudes, subjective norms and perceived behavioral control toward COVID-19 prevention in the relationship between the institutional climate and university students' preventive behaviors, and (3) investigate the moderating role of perceived risk for the impacts of the institutional climate and TPB elements on university students' preventive behaviors. The results of our study will contribute to widening the reach of the application of the TPB model in COVID-19 prevention within a higher education context and improve its explanatory capacity by adding external institutional factors and internal perceived risk. Notably, with deeper knowledge of the drivers of university students' preventive behaviors, the present research can shed further light on anti-epidemic practices and measures in HEIs in China and in other areas suffering the devastating effects of COVID-19.

2. Theoretical Framework and Hypotheses

2.1. Extended TPB and Preventive Behaviors for COVID-19

Ajzen [14] introduced the TPB model as an extension and improvement of the theory of reasoned action [18]. The TPB model consists of three exogenous constructs, namely attitudes, subjective norms and perceived behavioral control. The underlying premise of the TPB model is that individuals' attitudes toward behavior, subjective norms and perceived behavioral control together can shape their behavioral intentions or actual behaviors. Since its proposal, the TPB model has been extensively used to understand behaviors in a variety of domains, including a number of health-related behaviors [19–21]. Recent studies have also provided empirical support for the utility of the TPB model in explaining COVID-19 preventive behaviors. For instance, Prasetyo et al. [22] assessed the variables that affect the perceived effectiveness of COVID-19 prevention measures in the Philippines based on TPB and protection motivation theory. Sturman et al. [23] established a modified TPB model by incorporating knowledge to better understand adherence to restrictions during the COVID-19 pandemic by respondents in metropolitan Melbourne, Australia. Furthermore, Trifiletti et al. [24] used the TPB model along with perceived risk to evaluate protective behavior against COVID-19 in adults residing in Italy. The studies mentioned above indicate that the TPB model may benefit from reasonable expansion or modification to make it suitable for preventive behaviors for COVID-19 within different contexts.

The literature in the higher education research field has explicitly elaborated the critical impact of institutional factors, such as the structures, policies and practices of HEIs, on students' experiences, beliefs, attitudes and behavioral outcomes [25,26]. After systematically comparing the TPB model and several other behavioral theories applied in the research of infection control practices, Kretzer and Larson [27] noted that real behavioral change does not happen by targeting the individual alone; the institutional context must also be taken into consideration when seeking to improve infection control practices. Based on these perspectives, our study was designed to include institutional climate in rgw TPB model as an antecedent factor of both TPB variables and preventive behaviors for COVID-19. In addition, COVID-19 has been proposed to be more dangerous and unpredictable than other infectious diseases [28], and different students may possess different levels of risk in the same environment. Therefore, we further considered perceived risk associated with COVID-19 as a moderating factor in the extended TPB model. The extended TPB model in the current study is presented in Figure 1.

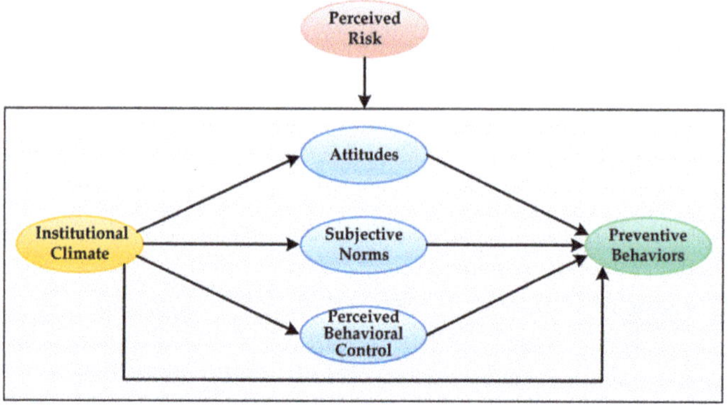

Figure 1. Research model.

2.2. Institutional Climate and Preventive Behaviors for COVID-19

Institutional climate is defined here as university students' perception of their affiliated HEI's formal policies, procedures and practices concerning the prevention and control of COVID-19 on campus [29]. According to previous research, organizational factors within the public sector play a vital role in the prevention and control of epidemics [30]. Researchers have also provided abundant empirical evidence for the relationship between institutional factors and various kinds of individuals' health-related behaviors. For example, Cheung [31] found that organizational regulation of worksite noise helped promote employees' protective behaviors for hearing loss. Ko and Kang [32] revealed that the organizational climate had a positive and significant influence on school dietitians' food safety and hygiene behaviors. Schwatka et al. [33] found that organizational safety and the health climate were positively correlated with the healthy behaviors of workers in small businesses. During the COVID-19 pandemic, although no study has directly examined the relationship between the institutional climate and preventive behaviors of COVID-19, several recent studies have provided insight into the role of institutional factors that protect against the negative effects of the COVID-19 pandemic and promote precautionary actions to minimize risk while sustaining psychological wellbeing [34,35]. In particular, Tausen et al. [36] reported that the response and support of universities combating COVID-19 increased the subjective well-being of Asian students at a predominantly white university during the COVID-19 crisis in the US. Thus, based on previous evidence, our study proposes the following hypothesis:

Hypothesis 1 (H1). *The institutional climate is positively associated with university students' preventive behaviors for COVID-19.*

2.3. Mediating Role of TPB Components

The mediation effect refers to the effect of an independent variable on a dependent variable transmitted through an intervening variable [37]. Following the definition given by Ajzen [14], attitudes refer to university students' positive or negative feelings toward and evaluations of actions against COVID-19. Subjective norms refer to university students' perceptions of social pressure to adopt or not adopt COVID-19 preventive behavior. Perceived behavioral control refers to university students' perceived ease or difficulty of adopting preventive behaviors for COVID-19. Based on the perspective of the TPB model, the more favorable students' attitudes and subjective norms are with respect to preventive behavior for COVID-19, and the greater the perceived behavioral control is, the more likely students are to perform preventive behaviors [14]. The recent literature has demonstrated the significance of the three TPB components in predicting a series of preventive behaviors for COVID-19. For example, Duong et al. [38] found that citizens' attitudes exerted a positive and significant effect on both social distancing behavior and mask wearing behavior in the U.S. Chen and Chen [39] found that attitudes and subjective norms had a significant and positive influence on individuals' preventive behaviors for COVID-19 among 1591 residents in China. Prasetyo et al. [22] revealed the positive impacts of the three TPB variables on the intention to follow preventive measures for COVID-19 in a sample in the Philippines.

Scholars have pointed out that the organizational and contextual factors connected to the formation of TPB components are not clearly represented [40]. A few studies have shed light on the understanding of the institutional factors associated with TPB components in the context of disease prevention. For example, an empirical study by Siuki et al. [41] revealed that health education interventions regarding HIV and AIDS prevention behaviors exerted a significant impact on the attitudes, subjective norms and perceived behavioral control among health volunteers in Iran. Lee and Li [42] demonstrated that organizational trust was related to individuals' perceived norms and perceived behavioral control toward social distancing behavior during the early stages of COVID-19 in the United States. Based on the extended TPB model and existing empirical evidence, we argue that the institutional climate may first influence TPB components and then enhance students' preventive behaviors for COVID-19. Thus, the following hypotheses are proposed:

Hypothesis 2a (H2a). *Attitudes mediate the relationship between the institutional climate and preventive behaviors for COVID-19.*

Hypothesis 2b (H2b). *Subjective norms mediate the relationship between the institutional climate and preventive behaviors for COVID-19.*

Hypothesis 2c (H2c). *Perceived behavioral control mediates the relationship between the institutional climate and preventive behaviors for COVID-19.*

2.4. Moderating Role of Perceived Risk

The moderating effect refers to the direction or strength of the relationship between two variables being influenced by a third variable [43]. Perceived risk is defined as one's psychological judgments and subjective feelings concerning the consequences and probability of an adverse event such as a pandemic [44]. Generally, perceived risk is a critical antecedent of individuals' health protective behaviors in empirical studies [45], whereas little is known about its possible moderating effect on specific relationships despite recent attention. For instance, Roma et al. [46] demonstrated that perceived risk can moderate the effect of the perceived efficacy of government guidelines on compliance with COVID-19 protective measures, as well as the impact of perceived efficacy on self-efficacy and the influence of self-efficacy on compliance. Consistent with these findings, we propose that the performance of preventive behaviors by university students might vary according to the level of the students' perceived risk. In other words, university students with different risk perceptions who are exposed to similar institutional climates on their campus may nonetheless engage in different preventive behaviors due to differences in how they evaluate the probability and severity of COVID-19 infection. Hence, the present study aims to test the impact of perceived risk on the link between the institutional climate and preventive behaviors with TPB components as mediating variables. Accordingly, the following hypothesis is suggested:

Hypothesis 3 (H3): *The perceived risk moderates the relationships among the institutional climate, TPB components and preventive behaviors for COVID-19.*

3. Methodology

3.1. Sample and Data Collection

Our study targeted university students in Beijing because it is the capital city and educational center of China and one of the most populous cities in the world. We used the 2021 Higher Education and Sustainability Survey (HESS) and its COVID-19-specific module. The HESS employed a random sampling design to guarantee that the resulting sample was representative of college students in Beijing. During the epidemic period, with the assistance of the student activity directors or advisors of each targeted college or department, survey questionnaires were sent to 4000 university students in 18 universities via the online survey platform Wenjuanxing (https://www.wjx.cn/ accessed date: 4 January 2021) in January and February 2021. The instruction page of the survey presented the participants with the goals of the study as well as the voluntary nature, confidentiality of participation and other matters that required attention when completing the questionnaire items. A total of 3987 questionnaires were returned. We excluded questionnaires completed in less than 3 min or with 10 consecutive identical answers to ensure that all items were clearly understood by the participants. After removing 294 invalid responses, 3693 qualified questionnaires were obtained for data analysis. Table 1 summarizes the composition of the final sample.

Table 1. Composition of the final sample.

Variable	Group	Frequency (*n*)	Percentage (%)
Gender	Female	1857	50.3
	Male	1836	49.7
Major	Science and Engineering	2782	75.3
	Humanities and Social sciences	911	24.7
Grade	Freshman	1231	33.3
	Sophomore	897	24.3
	Junior	839	22.7
	Senior	726	19.7
Ethnicity	Han	3305	89.5
	Other	388	10.5

3.2. Measures

The questionnaire included two parts: the background information of the respondents and measurement items of the constructs in the extended TPB framework. All of the scales were drawn from existing research or official documents, and a five-point Likert format was adopted for each item.

For the institutional climate toward COVID-19 prevention on campus, a six-item scale was adapted from the Guidelines on COVID-19 Prevention and Control in Higher Education Institutes recommended by the National Health Commission and Ministry of Education of China [47]. The respondents were asked about the extent to which they agreed with statements regarding the policies, procedures and practices against COVID-19 adopted by their respective universities (1 = strongly disagree, up to 5 = strongly agree).

Three items of the attitudes toward COVID-19-preventive behaviors were revised from Cheng and Ng [48] to assess the tendency of students to see the performance of COVID-19 preventive behaviors as benefits or barriers (1 = strongly disagree, up to 5 = strongly agree).

Three items derived from Sumaedi et al. [49] were utilized to evaluate respondents' subjective norms, namely the perception of social expectations from other important people to engage in COVID-19 preventive behaviors (1 = strongly disagree, up to 5 = strongly agree).

For perceived behavioral control, three items drawn from Prasetyo et al. [22] were used to measure the students' perceptions of their degree of control over the adoption of COVID-19-preventive behaviors.

COVID-19 preventive behaviors were evaluated using seven items obtained by Liu et al. [50], based on the preventive measures officially recommended by the Chinese Center for Disease Control and Prevention. We asked respondents how often they had adopted seven different COVID-19 preventive behaviors during the epidemic period (1 = never, up to 5 = always).

For the moderator, three items of the perceived risk scale were adapted from Ma [51] to measure the respondents' judgments concerning the adverse outcomes of COVID-19. Moreover, to examine the moderating role of perceived risk in the hypothesized path model, we used the median split approach to divide the sample into two subgroups of high and low risk perception students (Md = 3.33). The high risk perception group consisted of 1270 respondents, and the low risk perception group consisted of 1816 respondents. For more precise analysis, we omitted the data from respondents on the median (n = 607). We coded this as a dummy variable in the data analyses (0 = low perceived risk, 1 = high perceived risk).

As Table 2 illustrates, the Cronbach's α coefficients of the six scales ranged from 0.710 to 0.942, greater than the threshold level of 0.700 [52]. The mean score of the items ranged from 3.915 to 4.528, the standard deviation varied from 0.656 to 0.972, the absolute values of skewness ranged from 0.049 to 1.857 (less than 3), and the absolute value of kurtosis ranged from 0.224 to 7.209 (less than 10), suggesting that the distribution of all the variables and items was not significantly different from normality and that follow-up data analyses could be performed [53].

Table 2. Scale items and descriptive statistics.

Variables or Measurement Items	Mean	SD	Skewness	Kurtosis
Institutional climate (IC) (Cronbach's α = 0.942)	4.334	0.655	−1.821	7.209
IC1: Providing sufficient epidemic prevention facilities	4.242	0.814	−1.336	2.710
IC2: Strengthening education on epidemic prevention knowledge	4.361	0.725	−1.622	4.939
IC3: Expanding online and offline learning resources	4.420	0.690	−1.857	6.711
IC4: Strengthening humanistic care and psychological counseling	4.387	0.703	−1.747	5.952
IC5: Formulating effective campus epidemic prevention regulations	4.391	0.744	−1.712	4.872
IC6: Providing timely and authoritative information about COVID-19	4.206	0.783	−1.251	2.802
Attitudes (AT) (Cronbach's α = 0.781)	3.324	0.907	−0.316	−0.224
AT1: If I adopt the preventive measures, I will be less vulnerable to COVID-19 infection	3.690	1.139	−0.687	−0.403
AT2: If I adopt the preventive measures, they will cause inconvenience to me (R)	2.943	1.087	0.110	−0.922
AT3: If I adopt the preventive measures, I will become less anxious about contracting COVID-19	3.339	1.031	−0.401	−0.459
Subjective norms (SN) (Cronbach's α = 0.905)	4.313	0.637	−0.698	0.720
SN1: People who are important to me think that I should perform preventive behavior	4.323	0.720	−1.151	2.288
SN2: People who have an influence in my life think that I should perform preventive behavior	4.305	0.705	−1.042	2.052
SN3: People whose opinion matters to me think that I should perform preventive behavior	4.310	0.659	−0.795	1.383
Perceived behavior control (PBC) (Cronbach's α = 0.720)	4.010	0.625	−0.238	0.288
PBC1: I think preventive measures are easy to implement	4.085	0.741	−0.813	1.336
PBC2: I am confident that I can avoid being infected by COVID-19	3.971	0.845	−0.681	0.533
PBC3: I am confident that I have enough knowledge about COVID-19	3.974	0.754	−0.501	0.495
Preventive behaviors (BE, Cronbach's α = 0.904)	4.500	0.529	−0.935	0.761
BE1: Minimize social activities; avoid infected areas; avoid crowded public places	4.361	0.746	−1.225	1.924
BE2: Wear a single-use medical face mask when visiting public places or taking public transport	4.699	0.548	−1.927	4.487
BE3: Keep your hands clean and wash your hands frequently; minimize contact with objects in public places	4.470	0.666	−1.102	1.103
BE4: Refrain from touching your mouth, nose, and eyes with unwashed hands; cover your mouth and nose with your elbow when sneezing or coughing	4.404	0.746	−1.265	1.726
BE5: Monitor your health conditions; comply with the campus epidemic prevention regulations	4.596	0.575	−1.275	1.801
BE6: Ensure your home is adequately ventilated	4.463	0.687	−1.220	1.553
BE7: Keep distance from others in public places to reduce unnecessary infection	4.509	0.649	−1.247	1.665

Table 2. *Cont.*

Variables or Measurement Items	Mean	SD	Skewness	Kurtosis
Perceived risk (PR) (Cronbach's α = 0.710)	3.205	0.791	−0.049	0.238
PR1: Once I have cold symptoms, I will doubt whether I have been infected by COVID-19	2.920	1.065	0.186	−0.748
PR2: If there were confirmed cases in the same period of time in a place I visited, I would think I might be infected myself	3.706	0.918	−0.776	0.534
PR3: Once someone I have been in contact with has been diagnosed, I think it is only a matter of time before I get diagnosed myself	2.988	0.999	0.128	−0.344

Note: (R) = reversed item; SD = standard deviation.

3.3. Data Analysis

The hypothesized relationships in the proposed model were examined through structural equation modeling (SEM) based on the maximum likelihood estimation method. The analysis adopted the two-step approach advocated by Anderson and Gerbing [54], namely measurement model evaluation followed by structural model evaluation. The indexes that detected the goodness of fit of the model included the goodness of fit index (GFI $\geq$ 0.90), comparative fix index (CFI $\geq$ 0.90), incremental fit index (IFI $\geq$ 0.90), Tucker–Lewis index (TLI $\geq$ 0.90), standardized root mean square residual (SRMR < 0.08), root mean square error of approximation (RMSEA < 0.08) and ratio of the chi-square to the degree of freedom ($\chi^2/df \leq 5$). As χ^2/df was vulnerable to the sample size, when all 3693 responses were used, the other fit indexes mentioned above may have reflected the model fit more correctly [55]. We utilized the bootstrapping procedure with 2000 bootstrap samples to obtain bias-corrected estimates of the indirect effects of the institutional climate on preventive behavior (via attitudes, subjective norms and perceived behavioral control) and their associated 95% confidence intervals (CIs). The 95% bias-corrected bootstrap CI excluded zero, suggesting a significant mediation effect. The bootstrapping method has been found to be a more accurate test of mediation effects than other available strategies such as the Sobel test, as it enabled us to prevent type I errors that might have occurred from non-normal distributions of the mediation effects [56]. Furthermore, multigroup SEM analysis was performed to investigate the moderating effect of the perceived risk, which is regarded as a more statistically effective and powerful approach to examine structural invariance [57]. All the aforementioned analyses were conducted using the Amos 23 statistical package.

4. Results

4.1. Measurement Model

Confirmatory factor analysis (CFA) was first conducted to confirm the fitness of the measurement model to the research data before structural model testing. The measurement model included five latent constructs and 22 observed indicators. In the CFA, we allowed the latent variables to correlate with each other, and the observed indicators were restricted to load only on their associated constructs. The CFA results showed that all the fit indexes were within acceptable ranges, except the χ^2/df value (χ^2 = 2626.013; df = 199; χ^2/df = 13.196; GFI = 0.935; CFI = 0.955; IFI = 0.955; TLI = 0.947; SRMR = 0.046; and RMSEA = 0.057 (90% CI: 0.056, 0.059)). However, given the large sample size of the current study, the model fit was considered satisfactory [55]. In addition, the standardized factor loadings of all the indicators were significant and larger than the benchmark of 0.50 (from 0.609 to 0.963) [58]. Figure 2 displays the results of the measurement model.

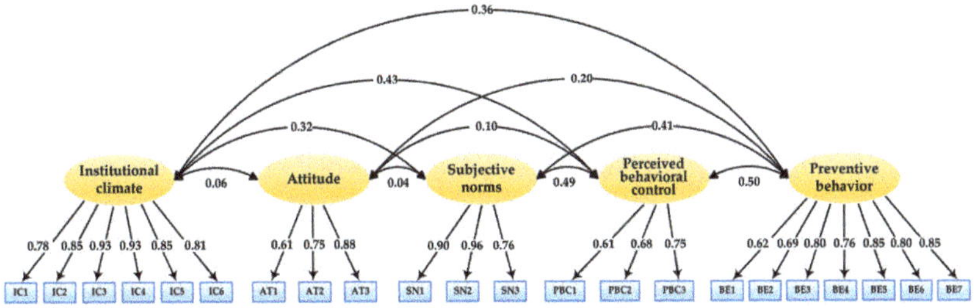

Figure 2. Results of the CFA.

Furthermore, we ran Harman's one-factor test to examine the common method variance in the data [59]. We compared the fit of a single (common method) factor model with the proposed five-factor model. The results showed that the single factor model (with all the items loaded onto one latent construct) had an unsatisfactory fit to the data (χ^2 = 28,647.504; df = 209; χ^2/df = 137.069; GFI = 0.457; CFI = 0.469; IFI = 0.469; TLI = 0.413; SRMR = 0.186; and RMSEA = 0.192 (90% CI: 0.190, 0.194)). The chi-square statistic ($\Delta\chi^2$ = 26,021.491, Δdf = 10, $p < 0.001$) also revealed that the measurement model provided a significantly better fit to the data than the single-factor model. Thus, common method variance was not significant in the present study.

Reliability and validity were assessed after the CFA analysis. As is presented in Table 3, the results for the composite reliability (CR) were between 0.724 and 0.944, which was higher than 0.7, indicating an acceptable level of internal consistency [60]. Additionally, the average variance extracted (AVE) scores ranged from 0.471 to 0.772 and were greater than the threshold value of 0.40, suggesting adequate convergent validity [61].

Table 3. Standard factor loading of items and reliability of the scales.

Variables	Items	Loadings	CR	AVE
Institutional climate (IC)	IC1	0.779	0.944	0.738
	IC2	0.853		
	IC3	0.925		
	IC4	0.925		
	IC5	0.851		
	IC6	0.812		
Attitudes (AT)	AT1	0.609	0.794	0.568
	AT2	0.751		
	AT3	0.877		
Subjective norms (SN)	SN1	0.902	0.910	0.773
	SN2	0.963		
	SN3	0.761		
Perceived behavior control (PBC)	PBC1	0.613	0.726	0.470
	PBC2	0.683		
	PBC3	0.754		
Preventive behaviors (BE)	BE1	0.617	0.910	0.593
	BE2	0.693		
	BE3	0.800		
	BE4	0.758		
	BE5	0.849		
	BE6	0.797		
	BE7	0.847		

Note: CR = composite reliability; AVE = average variance extracted.

As can be seen in Table 4, all of the correlation coefficients among the variables were significant and had the anticipated sign. Specifically, the institutional climate was positively correlated to preventive behaviors (r = 0.343, $p < 0.001$). Attitudes (r = 0.192, $p < 0.001$), subjective norms (r = 0.405, $p < 0.001$) and perceived behavior control (r = 0.407, $p < 0.001$) were each significantly associated with preventive behaviors. The institutional climate was also significantly correlated with attitudes (r = 0.055, $p < 0.01$), subjective norms (r = 0.317, $p < 0.001$) and perceived behavior control (r = 0.352, $p < 0.001$). These correlations met the conditions for mediation suggested by Baron and Kenny [62]. Moreover, as the square roots of the AVEs for all of the constructs were higher than the correlations among them, the discriminant validity of the measurement was confirmed [61].

Table 4. Discriminant validity and correlation.

Variables	1	2	3	4	5
1. Institutional climate	*0.859*				
2. Attitudes	0.055 **	*0.754*			
3. Subjective norms	0.317 ***	0.054 **	*0.879*		
4. Perceived behavior control	0.352 ***	0.088 ***	0.446 ***	*0.686*	
5. Preventive behaviors	0.343 ***	0.192 ***	0.405 ***	0.407 ***	*0.770*

Note: Diagonal elements (in italics) are the square root of the average variance extracted (AVE). ** $p < 0.01$. *** $p < 0.001$.

4.2. Structural Model

SEM analysis was employed to evaluate the hypothesized paths in the structural model. The analysis revealed an acceptable fit of the proposed structural model to the data ($\chi^2 = 3065.544$; $df = 202$; $\chi^2/df = 15.176$; GFI = 0.928; CFI = 0.946; IFI = 0.947; TLI = 0.939; SRMR = 0.069; and RMSEA = 0.062 (90% CI: 0.060, 0.064)). Then, the statistical significance of the path coefficients among the constructs was estimated. As is demonstrated in Figure 3, all the direct paths were statistically significant. First, the institutional climate had significant effects on the attitudes ($\beta = 0.057$, $t = 3.066$, $p < 0.01$), subjective norms ($\beta = 0.329$, $t = 19.026$, $p < 0.001$) and perceived behavioral control ($\beta = 0.437$, $t = 19.417$, $p < 0.001$). Second, the direct effect of the institutional climate on preventive behaviors was significant ($\beta = 0.148$, $t = 7.980$, $p < 0.01$). Third, the attitudes ($\beta = 0.163$, $t = 9.521$, $p < 0.001$), subjective norms ($\beta = 0.243$, $t = 13.351$, $p < 0.001$) and perceived behavioral control ($\beta = 0.308$, $t = 13.158$, $p < 0.001$) exerted significant impacts on preventive behaviors.

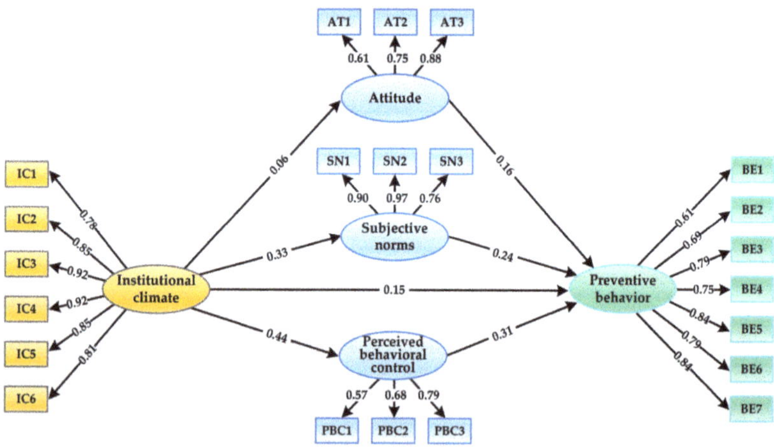

Figure 3. Results of the SEM.

We ran a bootstrapping analysis to further verify the mediation effects in the hypothesized model. As is revealed in Table 5, both the direct and indirect effects of the institutional climate on preventive behaviors were significant (all 95% bias-corrected CI did not include 0), suggesting that the link between the institutional climate and preventive behaviors was partially mediated by attitudes, subjective norms and perceived behavioral control. The results indicated that university students with high perception of the institutional climate tended to express more favorable attitudes, stronger subjective norms and greater perceived behavioral control toward COVID-19 prevention, which could promote the development and performance of preventive behavior. Thus, H1, H2a, H2b and H2c were supported.

Table 5. Results of bootstrapping.

Paths	Bootstrapping		95% Bias-Corrected CI	
	Effect	Boot S. E.	Boot LLCI	Boot ULCI
IC → AT	0.057 ***	0.019	0.021	0.094
IC → SN	0.329 ***	0.021	0.286	0.370
IC → PBC	0.437 ***	0.025	0.388	0.486
IC → BE	0.148 ***	0.022	0.104	0.193
AT → BE	0.163 ***	0.016	0.131	0.194
SN → BE	0.243 ***	0.023	0.199	0.287
PBC → BE	0.308 ***	0.024	0.262	0.355
IC → AT → BE	0.007 ***	0.002	0.002	0.011
IC → SN → BE	0.057 ***	0.007	0.044	0.072
IC → PBC → BE	0.096 ***	0.010	0.078	0.118

Note: IC = institutional climate; AT = attitudes; SN = subjective norms; PBC = perceived behavioral control; BE = preventive behaviors; LLCI = lower level confidence interval; ULCI = upper level confidence interval. *** $p < 0.001$.

4.3. Moderating Effects

Multigroup SEM analyses were employed to examine the moderating effects of perceived risk in the structural model. The sample was divided into two subgroups of high and low risk perception students using the median split approach. Next, we conducted a chi-square difference test to compare a constrained model (all the paths were restricted across the two subgroups) with an unconstrained model (all the paths were not constrained across the two subgroups). If the constrained model presented a significantly larger chi-square value than the constrained model, then this implied a potential moderating effect [60]. In each model, factor loadings between the two groups were held equivalent to ensure that the variables were measured similarly across groups; however, error variances were permitted to vary between groups [63]. The chi-square statistic demonstrated that the constrained (χ^2 = 3131.722, df = 428) and unconstrained models (χ^2 = 3037.387, df = 421) were significantly different ($\Delta\chi^2$ = 94.335, df = 7, p < 0.001), supporting the moderation effect of perceived risk on structural relationships.

To accurately detect the moderating effects of perceived risk on specific paths in the proposed model, a battery of chi-square difference tests was applied to compare the constrained models with seven diverse models separately, each retaining only one of the structural paths to be freely estimated. As is illustrated in Table 6, perceived risk significantly moderated four of the seven structural relationships. Specifically, the effect of the institutional climate on preventive behaviors was stronger for high risk perception students (β = 0.251, t = 8.594, p < 0.001) than for low risk perception students (β = 0.093, t = 3.831, p < 0.001). The effect of the institutional climate on subjective norms was stronger for high risk perception students (β = 0.379, t = 13.115, p < 0.001) than for low risk perception students (β = 0.292, t = 12.129, p < 0.001). The influence of the institutional climate on perceived behavioral control was significantly stronger among high risk perception students (β = 0.528, t = 15.177, p < 0.001) than among low risk perception students (β = 0.376, t = 13.045, p < 0.001). Moreover, high risk perception students (β = 0.281, t = 10.011, p < 0.001) exhibited a larger path effect than low risk perception students (β = 0.200, t = 8.159, p < 0.001) in the influence of subjective norms on preventive behavior. However, the results did not suggest the existence of significant differences between high and low risk perception groups regarding the effect of the institutional climate on attitudes, as well as the effect of attitudes and perceived behavioral control on preventive behaviors. Thus, H3 was partially supported.

Table 6. Results of the multigroup analysis.

	Standardized Coefficients		χ^2 (*df*)	$\Delta\chi^2$ (Δ*df*)
	Low-PR	**High-PR**		
Constrained Model	-	-	3131.722 (428)	-
IC → AT	0.082 **	0.069 *	3131.589 (427)	0.132
IC → SN	0.292 ***	0.379 ***	3116.001 (427)	15.721 ***
IC → PBC	0.376 ***	0.528 ***	3084.984 (427)	46.738 ***
IC → BE	0.093 ***	0.251 ***	3102.439 (427)	29.283 ***
AT → BE	0.175 ***	0.161 ***	3129.100 (427)	2.622
SN → BE	0.200 ***	0.281 ***	3125.790 (427)	5.932 *
PBC → BE	0.291 ***	0.350 ***	3130.303 (427)	1.419

Note: IC = institutional climate; AT = attitudes; SN = subjective norms; PBC = perceived behavioral control; BE = preventive behaviors; PR = perceived risk. * $p < 0.05$. ** $p < 0.01$. *** $p < 0.001$.

5. Discussion and Implications

The aim of the current study was to investigate the influencing factors of preventive behaviors for COVID-19 among university students in Beijing, China. With an extended TPB framework, we tested the hypothesized relationships among the institutional climate, three components of the original TPB model and preventive behaviors, as well as the moderating role of perceived risk in the structural relationships. The major research findings are summarized and discussed as follows.

Based on the extended TPB model, we found that the institutional climate was significantly associated with university students' preventive behaviors against COVID-19. Consistent with previous studies [35], the results imply that a positive institutional setting with formal policies, procedures and practices concerning COVID-19 prevention and control could enable university students to adaptively face epidemic challenges and facilitate their preventive actions against COVID-19. In addition, countries with different strengths of social norms (or cultural tightness–looseness) were varied in their effectiveness to combat COVID-19 [64]. Thus, a possible explanation for this relationship may be that an institutional climate creates social norms, duties, obligations and expectations within a specific institution that reinforce the preventive behaviors of students, especially those from tight cultures and collectivist societies such as China [48,64]. Moreover, according to the focus theory of normative conduct [65], the extent to which university students' preventive behaviors are practiced is highly dependent on the saliency and level of HEIs' COVID-19 prevention and control measures.

As expected, the results indicate that the institutional climate was significantly related to the three original TPB components, which in turn yielded a significant effect on preventive behaviors. The mediating effects of university students' attitudes, subjective norms and perceived behavioral control on the relationship between the institutional climate and preventive behaviors were supported via a bootstrapping procedure. Specifically, all three TPB components partially mediated the relationship between the institutional climate and preventive behaviors. These results indicate that attitudes, subjective norms and perceived behavioral control are critical sociopsychological factors that link institutional intervention and students' actual preventive behaviors toward COVID-19. The results suggest that with increasing emphasis on formal policies, procedures and practices concerning the prevention and control of COVID-19 on campus, university students may be expected to adopt more preventive behaviors, which requires them to possess an understanding of not only COVID-19 prevention knowledge, requirements and recommendations but also a positive emotional disposition, strong perception, substantial normative stimuli and the motivation to perform preventive behaviors; that is, the accessibility of external support, resources and information for COVID-19 prevention might lead to the enhancement of preventive behaviors by shaping the positive environment needed for university students' active precautionary beliefs to flourish.

Multigroup SEM analyses indicated that perceived risk significantly moderated several paths in the research model. We found that the impacts of the institutional climate on both subjective norms and perceived behavioral control were significantly stronger among university students with a higher level of risk perception than among those with a low level of risk perception. Our study also demonstrated that the influences of the institutional climate and subjective norms on university students' preventive behaviors were moderated by the perceived risk of COVID-19. Specifically, compared with students with a low level of perceived risk, those with a high level of perceived risk derived more benefits from the institutional climate in terms of the promotion or maintenance of preventive behaviors. These findings are highly similar to those of a recent study that found a moderating role of risk perception on the relationships among institutional factors, self-efficacy and compliance with prevention measures in Italian residents during the COVID-19 outbreak [46]. This may be explained by the fact that high risk perception students attempted to reduce their uncertainty and anxiety by resolving to accept preventive support, opinions or information from affiliated institutions and important figures and to enact preventive behaviors more strictly, while low risk perception students may have depended more on their own ability and judgment [66]. Moreover, our study revealed that the effect of the institutional climate on attitudes, as well as the influence of attitudes on preventive behaviors, remained invariant across the high and low risk perception groups. It can be concluded that, regardless of the level of university students' perception of the risk related to COVID-19, a higher level of perception of the supportive institutional climate toward COVID-19 prevention stably fostered the formation of a positive attitude toward adopting preventive behavior and, in turn, resulted in increased performance of actual behaviors.

Our study has the following theoretical implications. First, it broadens the research on individuals' preventive behaviors against COVID-19 from an institutional impact perspective with an expanded TPB model within the context of higher education. Although the institutional climate is known to be a key contextual factor for promoting individuals' disease prevention actions, empirical evidence on the association between the institutional climate and preventive behaviors for COVID-19 is limited. We examined the direct influence of the institutional climate on the preventive behaviors of university students in Beijing, China to fill this gap in the literature. Second, to the best of our knowledge, this is the first attempt to explore quantitative evidence in the potential role of TPB core constructs for bridging the relationship between institutional factors and university students' preventive behaviors toward COVID-19. Third, our study incorporates perceived risk as a moderator into the TPB model, thus providing more comprehensive insights into the influence mechanism of the institutional climate and TPB components on preventive behaviors. Moreover, our study verifies the scalability and versatility of the extended TPB model as a powerful theoretical basis for future studies of the COVID-19 preventive behaviors of other groups of people from diversified organizations around the world.

Regarding the practical implications, the findings of our study contribute to supporting HEIs' vital functions in the "new normal" period of COVID-19 in China and offer meaningful information for authorities and HEIs to encourage the adoption of preventive actions among the general public and to prevent the spread of COVID-19. First, by making COVID-19 an urgent and vital political issue, institutional actors can play a powerful and effective role in shaping the social norms of epidemic prevention [67], because political engagement and social norms represent crucial factors in facilitating prosocial behavior [68]. Accordingly, HEIs could prompt the creation of an institutional climate for COVID-19 prevention via a series of institutional interventions, including establishing effective prevention and control measures and demonstrating commitment and concrete efforts to ensure the physical and mental health and safety of students and staff on campus and to maintain the normal functions of the institutions. Second, HEIs should contribute to the management and intervention of students' positive psychological states, which will guide students in deciding which behaviors and protocols to pursue. Thus, we suggest that HEIs configure platforms to provide positive psychological interventions to students to stimulate them to enhance their knowledge, attitudes, norms and behavioral control toward COVID-19 prevention. Moreover, specific institutional interventions might be more efficient for individuals with a high level of risk perception. We propose that HEIs emphasize that more risk and crisis education is especially helpful for enhancing students' beliefs regarding the obligations of the country, institutions and themselves to make successful efforts to defeat COVID-19.

6. Conclusions

Overall, the present study demonstrated that the main variables in the research model, including the institutional climate, attitudes, subjective norms, perceived behavioral control and perceived risk, played critical roles in predicting university students' preventive behaviors against COVID-19. Thus, the TPB-based expansion model could be functionalized as an effective framework for understanding university students' preventive behaviors on campus. Although promising, there are limitations that should be noted in subsequent research. The results of our study are limited by its generalizability to HEIs and university students in other parts of China and the world because the sample data were collected from university students in Beijing. Therefore, cross-regional and cross-country studies involving university students from a broader scope of HEIs are needed in the future to enhance the generalizability and validity of research findings or revise the framework utilized to understand the influential mechanism of contextual and psychological factors on university students' preventive behaviors. Moreover, future studies should consider other potential mediation and moderation mechanisms of multiple cultural and psychological factors, through which HEIs can foster the preventive behaviors of university students due to the complexity and heterogeneity of COVID-19 spread and control around the world [69], thus producing valuable and creative theoretical and practical outcomes for combating COVID-19.

Author Contributions: Conceptualization, X.L. and J.L.; methodology, Y.Z.; software, Y.Z. and X.L.; formal analysis, X.L., J.L. and Y.Z.; investigation, J.L., M.Z., Y.D., Y.Z., M.Y., D.W., H.Z. and X.Z.; resources, D.W., H.Z. and X.Z.; data curation, J.L., M.Z. and X.L.; writing—original draft preparation, J.L. and X.L.; writing—review and editing, X.L. and Y.Z.; supervision, X.L.; project administration, X.L. and M.Y.; funding acquisition, X.L., Y.Z. and M.Y. All authors have read and agreed to the published version of the manuscript.

Funding: This research was funded by the Project of the Social Science Plan of the Beijing Municipal Education Commission (SM201910005004), Fundamental Research Funds for the Central Universities (FRF-BR-20-08A) and the Research Start-up Fund of the Capital University of Economics and Business (XRZ2021005).

Institutional Review Board Statement: The study was conducted in accordance with the Declaration of Helsinki, and the protocol was approved by the institutional review board (or ethics committee) of the Research Centre for Capital Engineering Education Development at the Beijing University of Technology (approval number: 2021001).

Informed Consent Statement: Informed consent was obtained from all subjects involved in the study.

Data Availability Statement: The data used or analyzed during the current study are available from the corresponding author on request.

Acknowledgments: We would like to thank the university students for participating in the survey and the assistance of the student activities directors or advisors of each targeted HEI in data collection.

Conflicts of Interest: The authors declare no conflict of interest.

References

1. Kunutsor, S.K.; Laukkanen, J.A. Hepatic manifestations and complications of COVID-19: A systematic review and meta-analysis. *J. Infect.* **2020**, *81*, 72–74. [CrossRef]
2. Worldometer COVID-19. Coronavirus Pandemic. Available online: https://www.worldometers.info/coronavirus/ (accessed on 17 December 2020).
3. Shaw, R.; Kim, Y.-K.; Hua, J. Governance, technology and citizen behavior in pandemic: Lessons from COVID-19 in East Asia. *Prog. Disaster Sci.* **2020**, *6*, 100090. [CrossRef] [PubMed]
4. Nguyen, N.P.T.; Hoang, T.D.; Tran, V.T.; Vu, C.T.; Fodjo, J.N.S.; Colebunders, R.; Dunne, M.P.; Van Vo, T. Preventive behavior of Vietnamese people in response to the COVID-19 pandemic. *PLoS ONE* **2020**, *15*, e0238830. [CrossRef]
5. Shinan-Altman, S.; Levkovich, I. COVID-19 precautionary behavior: The Israeli case in the initial stage of the outbreak. *BMC Public Health* **2020**, *20*, 1–7. [CrossRef] [PubMed]
6. Kim, S.; Kim, S. Analysis of the Impact of Health Beliefs and Resource Factors on Preventive Behaviors against the COVID-19 Pandemic. *Int. J. Environ. Res. Public Health* **2020**, *17*, 8666. [CrossRef] [PubMed]
7. Callaghan, T.; Lueck, J.A.; Trujillo, K.L.; Ferdinand, A.O. Rural and Urban Differences in COVID-19 Prevention Behaviors. *J. Rural Health* **2021**, *37*, 287–295. [CrossRef]
8. Kamenidou, I.E.; Stavrianea, A.; Liava, C. Achieving a Covid-19 Free Country: Citizens Preventive Measures and Communication Pathways. *Int. J. Environ. Res. Public Health* **2020**, *17*, 4633. [CrossRef]
9. Stangier, U.; Kananian, S.; Schüller, J. Perceived vulnerability to disease, knowledge about COVID-19, and changes in preventive behavior during lockdown in a German convenience sample. *Curr. Psychol.* **2021**. [CrossRef] [PubMed]
10. Alves, R.F.; Samorinha, C.; Precioso, J. Knowledge, attitudes and preventive behaviors toward COVID-19: A study among higher education students in Portugal. *J. Health Res.* **2021**, *35*, 318–328. [CrossRef]
11. Jia, Y.; Qi, Y.; Bai, L.; Han, Y.; Xie, Z.; Ge, J. Knowledge–attitude–practice and psychological status of college students during the early stage of COVID-19 outbreak in China: A cross-sectional study. *BMJ Open* **2021**, *11*, e045034. [CrossRef]
12. Roberts, J.A.; David, M.E. Improving Predictions of COVID-19 Preventive Behavior: Development of a Sequential Mediation Model. *J. Med. Internet Res.* **2021**, *23*, e23218. [CrossRef]
13. Liu, X.; Zou, Y.; Wu, J. Factors Influencing Public-Sphere Pro-Environmental Behavior among Mongolian College Students: A Test of Value–Belief–Norm Theory. *Sustainability* **2018**, *10*, 1384. [CrossRef]
14. Ajzen, I. The theory of planned behavior. *Organ. Behav. Hum. Decis. Process.* **1991**, *50*, 179–211. [CrossRef]
15. Yastica, T.V.; Salma, S.A.; Caesaron, D.; Safrudin, Y.N.; Pramadya, A.R. Application of Theory Planned Behavior (TPB) and Health Belief Model (HBM) in COVID-19 Prevention: A Literature Review. In Proceedings of the 2020 6th International Conference on Interactive Digital Media (ICIDM), Bandung, Indonesia, 14–15 December 2020; pp. 1–4.
16. Bergan, S.; Gallagher, T.; Harkavy, I.; Munck, R.; Van't Land, H. *Higher Education's Response to the Covid-19 Pandemic—Building a More Sustainable and Democratic Future*; Council of Europe Publishing: Strasbourg, France, 2021.
17. Updegraff, J.A.; Rothman, A.J. Health Message Framing: Moderators, Mediators, and Mysteries. *Soc. Pers. Psychol. Compass* **2013**, *7*, 668–679. [CrossRef]
18. Fishbein, M.; Ajzen, I. *Belief, Attitude, Intention, and Behavior: An Introduction to Theory and Research*; Addison-Wesley: Reading, MA, USA, 1975.
19. Godin, G.; Kok, G. The Theory of Planned Behavior: A Review of its Applications to Health-Related Behaviors. *Am. J. Health Promot.* **1996**, *11*, 87–98. [CrossRef] [PubMed]
20. McEachan, R.R.C.; Conner, M.; Taylor, N.J.; Lawton, R. Prospective prediction of health-related behaviours with the Theory of Planned Behaviour: A meta-analysis. *Health Psychol. Rev.* **2011**, *5*, 97–144. [CrossRef]
21. Hagger, M.S.; Chan, D.K.C.; Protogerou, C.; Chatzisarantis, N.L. Using meta-analytic path analysis to test theoretical predictions in health behavior: An illustration based on meta-analyses of the theory of planned behavior. *Prev. Med.* **2016**, *89*, 154–161. [CrossRef]
22. Prasetyo, Y.T.; Castillo, A.M.; Salonga, L.J.; Sia, J.A.; Seneta, J.A. Factors affecting perceived effectiveness of COVID-19 prevention measures among Filipinos during Enhanced Community Quarantine in Luzon, Philippines: Integrating Protection Motivation Theory and extended Theory of Planned Behavior. *Int. J. Infect. Dis.* **2020**, *99*, 312–323. [CrossRef]
23. Sturman, D.; Auton, J.C.; Thacker, J. Knowledge of social distancing measures and adherence to restrictions during the COVID-19 pandemic. *Health Promot. J. Aust.* **2021**, *32*, 344–351. [CrossRef]
24. Trifiletti, E.; Shamloo, S.E.; Faccini, M.; Zaka, A. Psychological predictors of protective behaviours during the Covid-19 pandemic: Theory of planned behaviour and risk perception. *J. Community Appl. Soc. Psychol.* **2021**. [CrossRef] [PubMed]
25. Berger, J.B.; Milem, J.F. Organizational Behavior in Higher Education and Student Outcomes. In *Higher Education: Handbook of Theory and Research*; Springer: New York, NY, USA, 2000.
26. Pascarella, E.T.; Terenzini, P.T. *How College Affects Students: A Third Decade of Research*; Jossey-Bass: San Francisco, CA, USA, 2005.
27. Kretzer, E.K.; Larson, E.L. Behavioral interventions to improve infection control practices. *Am. J. Infect. Control* **1998**, *26*, 245–253. [CrossRef]
28. Gupta, M.; Jain, R.; Taneja, S.; Chaudhary, G.; Khari, M.; Verdú, E. Real-time measurement of the uncertain epidemiological appearances of COVID-19 infections. *Appl. Soft Comput.* **2021**, *101*, 107039. [CrossRef] [PubMed]

29. Prati, G.; Albanesi, C.; Pietrantoni, L. The Reciprocal Relationship between Sense of Community and Social Well-Being: A Cross-Lagged Panel Analysis. *Soc. Indic. Res.* **2016**, *127*, 1321–1332. [CrossRef]
30. Fu, L.; Wang, X.; Wang, D.; Griffin, M.A.; Li, P. Human and organizational factors within the public sectors for the prevention and control of epidemic. *Saf. Sci.* **2020**, *131*, 104929. [CrossRef]
31. Cheung, C.-K. Organizational influence on working people's occupational noise protection in Hong Kong. *J. Saf. Res.* **2004**, *35*, 465–475. [CrossRef] [PubMed]
32. Ko, W.; Kang, H. Effect of leadership style and organizational climate on employees' food safety and hygiene behaviors in the institutional food service of schools. *Food Sci. Nutr.* **2019**, *7*, 2131–2143. [CrossRef]
33. Schwatka, N.V.; Sinclair, R.R.; Fan, W.; Dally, M.; Shore, E.; Brown, C.E.; Tenney, L.; Newman, L.S. How does Organizational Climate Motivate Employee Safe and Healthy Behavior in Small Business? *J. Occup. Environ. Med.* **2020**, *62*, 350–358. [CrossRef] [PubMed]
34. Brown, C.E.; Schwatka, N.; Dexter, L.; Dally, M.; Shore, E.; Tenney, L.; Newman, L.S. The Importance of Small Business Safety and Health Climates during COVID-19. *J. Occup. Environ. Med.* **2021**, *63*, 81–88. [CrossRef] [PubMed]
35. Corral-Verdugo, V.; Corral-Frías, N.S.; Frías-Armenta, M.; Lucas, M.Y.; Peña-Torres, E.F. Positive Environments and Precautionary Behaviors during the COVID-19 Outbreak. *Front. Psychol.* **2021**, *12*, 693. [CrossRef]
36. Tausen, B.M.; Jin, J.; Kim, P.Y.; Law, K.; Kendall, D. Academic Community Support, Campus Racial Climate, and Subjective Well-Being during the Coronavirus Outbreak among Asian American College Students. *J. Asian Am. Stud.* **2020**, *23*, 367–385. [CrossRef]
37. Aguinis, H.; Edwards, J.; Bradley, K.J. Improving Our Understanding of Moderation and Mediation in Strategic Management Research. *Organ. Res. Methods* **2016**, *20*, 665–685. [CrossRef]
38. Duong, H.T.; Nguyen, H.T.; McFarlane, S.J.; Van Nguyen, L.T. Risk perception and COVID-19 preventive behaviors: Application of the integrative model of behavioral prediction. *Soc. Sci. J.* **2021**, 1–14. [CrossRef]
39. Chen, X.; Chen, H. Differences in Preventive Behaviors of COVID-19 between Urban and Rural Residents: Lessons Learned from A Cross-Sectional Study in China. *Int. J. Environ. Res. Public Health* **2020**, *17*, 4437. [CrossRef]
40. Chan, D.K.-C.; Fung, Y.-K.; Xing, S.; Hagger, M.S. Myopia prevention, near work, and visual acuity of college students: Integrating the theory of planned behavior and self-determination theory. *J. Behav. Med.* **2013**, *37*, 369–380. [CrossRef] [PubMed]
41. Siuki, H.A.; Peyman, N.; Vahedian-Shahroodi, M.; Gholian-Aval, M.; Tehrani, H. Health Education Intervention on HIV/AIDS Prevention Behaviors among Health Volunteers in Healthcare Centers: An Applying the Theory of Planned Behavior. *J. Soc. Serv. Res.* **2019**, *45*, 582–588. [CrossRef]
42. Lee, Y.; Li, J.Q. The role of communication transparency and organizational trust in publics' perceptions, attitudes and social distancing behaviour: A case study of the COVID-19 outbreak. *J. Conting. Crisis Manag.* **2021**. [CrossRef]
43. Frazier, P.A.; Tix, A.P.; Barron, K.E. Testing Moderator and Mediator Effects in Counseling Psychology Research. *J. Couns. Psychol.* **2004**, *51*, 115–134. [CrossRef]
44. Sjoberg, L. Factors in Risk Perception. *Risk Anal.* **2000**, *20*, 1–12. [CrossRef] [PubMed]
45. Yıldırım, M.; Güler, A. Factor analysis of the COVID-19 Perceived Risk Scale: A preliminary study. *Death Stud.* **2020**, 1–8. [CrossRef] [PubMed]
46. Roma, P.; Monaro, M.; Muzi, L.; Colasanti, M.; Ricci, E.; Biondi, S.; Napoli, C.; Ferracuti, S.; Mazza, C. How to Improve Compliance with Protective Health Measures during the COVID-19 Outbreak: Testing a Moderated Mediation Model and Machine Learning Algorithms. *Int. J. Environ. Res. Public Health* **2020**, *17*, 7252. [CrossRef]
47. Chen, X.; Hu, Z. *Guidelines on COVID-19 Prevention and Control in Higher Education Institutes*; People's Medical Publishing House: Beijing, China, 2020.
48. Cheng, C.; Ng, A.-K. Psychosocial Factors Predicting SARS-Preventive Behaviors in Four Major SARS-Affected Regions. *J. Appl. Soc. Psychol.* **2006**, *36*, 222–247. [CrossRef]
49. Sumaedi, S.; Bakti, I.G.M.Y.; Rakhmawati, T.; Widianti, T.; Astrini, N.J.; Damayanti, S.; Massijaya, M.A.; Jati, R.K. Factors influencing intention to follow the "stay at home" policy during the COVID-19 pandemic. *Int. J. Health Gov.* **2020**, *26*, 13–27. [CrossRef]
50. Liu, L.; Xie, J.; Li, K.; Ji, S. Exploring How Media Influence Preventive Behavior and Excessive Preventive Intention during the COVID-19 Pandemic in China. *Int. J. Environ. Res. Public Health* **2020**, *17*, 7990. [CrossRef]
51. Ma, C. The Influence of Media Exposure on the Experiential Uncertainty of COVID-19: The Mediating Role of Risk Perception and Moderating Role of Emotional Reaction. *Shanghai J. Rev.* **2020**, *39*, 57–72. [CrossRef]
52. Nunnally, J.C. *Psychometric Theory*, 2nd ed.; McGraw-Hill: New York, NY, USA, 1978.
53. Kline, R.B. *Principles and Practice of Structural Equation Modeling*, 3rd ed.; Guilford Press: New York, NY, USA, 2011.
54. Anderson, J.C.; Gerbing, D.W. Structural equation modeling in practice: A review and recommended two-step approach. *Psychol. Bull.* **1988**, *103*, 411–423. [CrossRef]
55. Hair, J.F.; Anderson, R.E.; Tatham, R.L.; Black, W.C. *Multivariate Data Analysis*, 5th ed.; Prentice-Hall: Englewood Cliffs, NJ, USA, 1998.
56. Preacher, K.J.; Hayes, A.F. Asymptotic and resampling strategies for assessing and comparing indirect effects in multiple mediator models. *Behav. Res. Methods* **2008**, *40*, 879–891. [CrossRef] [PubMed]

57. Steenkamp, J.-B.E.M.; Baumgartner, H. Assessing Measurement Invariance in Cross-National Consumer Research. *J. Consum. Res.* **1998**, *25*, 78–90. [CrossRef]
58. Wu, M. *Structural Equation Model: Operation and Application of AMOS*; Chongqing University Press: Chongqing, China, 2009.
59. Podsakoff, P.M.; MacKenzie, S.B.; Lee, J.Y.; Podsakoff, N.P. Common method biases in behavioral research: A critical review of the literature and recommended remedies. *J. Appl. Psychol.* **2003**, *88*, 879–903. [CrossRef]
60. Wu, M. *Structural Equation Modeling: Tips for Practical Application*; Chongqing University Press: Chongqing, China, 2013.
61. Fornell, C.; Larcker, D.F. Evaluating Structural Equation Models with Unobservable Variables and Measurement Error. *J. Mark. Res.* **1981**, *18*, 39–50. [CrossRef]
62. Baron, R.M.; Kenny, D.A. The moderator–mediator variable distinction in social psychological research: Conceptual, strategic, and statistical considerations. *J. Pers. Soc. Psychol.* **1986**, *51*, 1173–1182. [CrossRef] [PubMed]
63. Augustus-Horvath, C.L.; Tylka, T.L. A test and extension of objectification theory as it predicts disordered eating: Does women's age matter? *J. Couns. Psychol.* **2009**, *56*, 253–265. [CrossRef]
64. Gelfand, M.J.; Jackson, J.C.; Pan, X.; Nau, D.; Pieper, D.; Denison, E.; Dagher, M.; Lange, P.A.M.V.; Chiu, C.-Y.; Wang, M. The relationship between cultural tightness–looseness and COVID-19 cases and deaths: A global analysis. *Lancet Planet. Health* **2021**, *5*, 135–144. [CrossRef]
65. Cialdini, R.B.; Reno, R.R.; Kallgren, C.A. A focus theory of normative conduct: Recycling the concept of norms to reduce littering in public places. *J. Pers. Soc. Psychol.* **1990**, *58*, 1015–1026. [CrossRef]
66. Rimal, R.N.; Real, K. Perceived Risk and Efficacy Beliefs as Motivators of Change. *Hum. Commun. Res.* **2003**, *29*, 370–399. [CrossRef]
67. Carvalho, A.; Burgess, J. Cultural Circuits of Climate Change in U.K. Broadsheet Newspapers, 1985–2003. *Risk Anal.* **2005**, *25*, 1457–1469. [CrossRef]
68. Ockwell, D.; Whitmarsh, L.; O'Neill, S. Reorienting Climate Change Communication for Effective Mitigation. *Sci. Commun.* **2009**, *30*, 305–327. [CrossRef]
69. Diotaiuti, P.; Valente, G.; Mancone, S. Validation study of the Italian version of Temporal Focus Scale: Psychometric properties and convergent validity. *BMC Psychol.* **2021**, *9*, 1–13. [CrossRef]

International Journal of
Environmental Research and Public Health

MDPI

Article

COVID-19 Pandemic Causing Depression in Different Sociodemographic Groups in Saudi Arabia

Hana Sonbol [1], Hadil M. Alahdal [1], Rasis A. Alanazi [2], Khawla Alsamhary [3] and Fuad Ameen [4,*]

1 Biology Department, College of Science, Princess Nourah Bint Abdulrahman University, Riyadh 11671, Saudi Arabia; HSSonbol@pnu.edu.sa (H.S.); hmalahdal@pnu.edu.sa (H.M.A.)
2 Psychology Department, College of Education, Princess Nourah Bint Abdulrahman University, Riyadh 11671, Saudi Arabia; RAAlanazi@pnu.edu.sa
3 Department of Biology, College of Science and Humanities in Al-Kharj, Prince Sattam Bin Abdulaziz University, Al-kharj 11942, Saudi Arabia; k.alsamhary@psau.edu.sa
4 Department of Botany & Microbiology, College of Science, King Saud University, Riyadh 11451, Saudi Arabia
* Correspondence: fuadameen@ksu.edu.sa

Abstract: COVID-19 disease was announced as a global pandemic in March 2020 by the World health organization (WHO). Saudi Arabia was among the first countries to enforce restriction measures such as closing schools, remote working, and a travel ban. We aim to evaluate the impact of the COVID-19 pandemic on people's depression in Saudi Arabia. A cross-sectional online survey of 1109 participants was conducted during the curfew between 18th of May and 11th of June 2020. An online questionnaire included questions about the commitment to follow the precautionary measures, knowledge on COVID-19, and depression. Depression was assessed with the Impact of Event Scale-Revised method. Females, unmarried individuals, elderly persons, parents of young children, unemployed, and small families were more likely to be depressed. Education level did not explain the differences in depression. However, the more knowledge the participants had about COVID-19 the better they followed the restrictions. A regression analysis revealed that the commitment of a person to follow the restrictions increased his/her depression symptoms. Attention should be paid to different groups of people in future psychiatric planning.

Keywords: COVID-19; depression; pandemic; precaution measures; mental health; Saudi Arabia

Citation: Sonbol, H.; Alahdal, H.M.; Alanazi, R.A.; Alsamhary, K.; Ameen, F. COVID-19 Pandemic Causing Depression in Different Sociodemographic Groups in Saudi Arabia. *Int. J. Environ. Res. Public Health* **2021**, *18*, 6955. https://doi.org/10.3390/ijerph18136955

Academic Editors: Paolo Roma, Merylin Monaro and Cristina Mazza

Received: 28 May 2021
Accepted: 23 June 2021
Published: 29 June 2021

1. Introduction

The coronavirus disease (COVID-19) first emerged in December 2019 in China and caused a global health pandemic [1,2]. The total number of COVID-19-infected people has been accelerating, and the death count is exceeding previous Middle East respiratory syndrome coronavirus (SARS-CoV) epidemics [3]. In Saudi Arabia, the first coronavirus infection was reported in March 2020 [4]. More than 470,000 people have been infected in Saudi Arabia as of June 2021.

To prevent the transmission of COVID-19 infection, significant intervention such as physical distancing and the use of face masks is widely recommended [5–7]. Saudi Arabia was one of the first countries that imposed strict measures including the limiting of outdoor activities, closing schools, minimizing social contacts, and banning mosque prayers [8]. The entire country was quarantined, and curfew was legislated in big cities.

The restrictions may have caused serious impacts on the mental health of the public. The sudden change in people's routine can predispose one to depression. COVID-19 as a new emerging virus with unique features and high infectious rates predispose people to high levels of stress. COVID-19 news in all media, the numerous hypotheses of its mode of transition and consequences, and the fear of getting the infection personally for family members can all be predisposing factors for depression. A recent study in Saudi Arabia indicated that about one-third of individuals studied had moderate to severe depression during the COVID-19 pandemic [9]. Younger people, people spending too much time thinking about the outbreak, and healthcare workers were at high risk of mental illness in China [10]. In Saudi Arabia, it is not known how and to what extent the epidemic is affecting different sociodemographic groups of people. Such studies are crucial to help determine general mental health status and anticipate possible mental disorders.

Our aim was to assess the level of depression during the COVID-19 pandemic in different sociodemographic groups and how following the precautionary measures affected depression symptoms. We measured the depression burden in adults living in Saudi Arabia during the period of curfew using a questionnaire and examined the relationship between participants' depression level and protecting factors such as commitment to follow the precautionary measures, education level, and family circumstances. Preparedness to face the virus-related mental health outcomes will help to treat the issue at an early stage.

2. Research Methodology

2.1. Study Design

A snowball sampling recruitment method was used to recruit adults living in Saudi Arabia (18–55 years old) between 18th of May and 11th of June 2020. The participants were recruited through WhatsApp chains starting from the researchers who asked their contacts first. Participants (n = 1109) completed an online survey through Google Forms in the Arabic language. It took about five minutes to complete, and communication between the researchers and the participants was possible. The participants had the freedom to stop whenever they wanted. Expedited ethics approval was obtained from the Institutional Review Board of the Princess Nourah bint Abdulrahman University (PNU) (20-0215). All respondents provided informed consent.

The public's psychological response and awareness about precautionary measures during the pandemic of COVID-19 was assessed using a cross-sectional survey design. Correct answers were given 3 points, while not knowing the answer received 2 and wrong answers received 0. The questionnaire was adopted from studies where it was pre-tested and validated [10–12]. The questionnaire about depression was from the Center for Epidemiologic Studies Depression Scale (CES-D) excluding three items [13]. The CES-D score ranged between 0–51 points, and higher scores indicated more severe depressive symptomatology [13].

All methods followed the guidelines of the National Committee of Bioethics (NCBE), Saudi Arabia. The questionnaire consisted of questions covering the following areas: (1) Sociodemographic information, (2) commitment to follow precautionary measures, and (3) feelings of depression.

The maximum score for the commitment to follow precautionary measures was 28 and for depression was 51, with higher scores indicating more severe depressive symptoms. The reliability and validity of the scale was assessed using a pilot test with 94 participants. Scale reliability was tested using a Cronbach's Alpha (α) and Spearman–Brown coefficient (0.90). The depression scale demonstrated acceptable internal consistency ($\alpha = 0.89$). The assessment was based on previous studies [14] where $\alpha > 0.70$ is acceptable in social science research.

2.2. Statistical Analysis

One-way ANOVA followed by the least significant difference test (LSD) were used to analyze the differences in the variables of precautionary measures and depression between the sociodemographic groups. The Pearson correlation was calculated, and a regression analysis was carried out between the variables of precautionary measures and depression. $p < 0.05$ was considered to be significant. SPSS Statistic 21.0 ® (IBM SPSS Statistics, Armonk, NY, USA) was used.

3. Results

3.1. Sociodemographic Characteristics

A total of 1109 participants completed the survey. The majority of respondents were female (74%, n = 824) and married (72%, n = 793). About half were under 45 years old, where 26% (n = 286) were 26–35 years old and 24% (n = 261) were 36–45 years old. Participants were mostly well educated, 65% (n = 719) had a bachelor's degree, and 21% (n = 233) had a higher degree. About half (47%, n = 516) were employed either in the private or government sectors or were entrepreneurs, while about one-third (32%, n = 351) were unemployed. Most (91%, n = 1013) belonged to families with between three and six members and about two-thirds had children (69%, n = 769). Most of the participants were from the Western Region (58%, n = 642) and the Central Region (35%, n = 391). The participants were more educated than the average population in Saudi Arabia where 23% of the population has a bachelor's degree or were at a respective level [15]. Old people were less represented than in Saudi Arabia where the demographic profile is as follows: 0–14 years: 24.8%, 15–24 years: 15.4%, 25–54 years: 50.2%, 55–64 years: 5.9% and 65 years and over: 3.6% [16].

3.2. Sociodemographic Groups and Precautionary Measures

Most of the participants always covered their mouth when coughing and sneezing (83%) and washed their hands with soap and water (77%) (Table 1). About half always avoided the sharing of utensils, washed their hands immediately after coughing or sneezing, and wore masks. About one-third (31%) of the participants felt that the COVID-19 pandemic has caused too much unnecessary panic while 77% avoided leaving their homes.

Table 1. Percentage of participants (n = 1109) following different precautionary measures. Response alternatives: 1 = never; 2 = occasionally; 3 = sometimes; 4 = most of the time; 5 = always.

Precautionary Measures	Response %				
	1	2	3	4	5
Q1: Covering mouth when coughing and sneezing	0.2	1.6	10.8	4.0	83.4
Q2: Avoiding sharing of utensils	7.6	6.1	12.0	24.0	50.3
Q3: Washing hands with soap and water	0.0	1.7	3.1	17.9	77.3
Q4: Washing hands immediately after coughing, rubbing nose, or sneezing	5.5	35.3	3.3	6.8	49.1
Q5: Wearing mask regardless of the presence or absence of symptoms	11.3	11.6	18.6	3.3	55.2
Q6: Feeling that other people are too anxious about COVID	9.0	16.4	31.0	25.2	18.4
Q7: Hours stayed at home	<9 h	10–19 h	>19 h		
	4.0	18.4	77.6		

The maximum score for precautionary measures observed was 27 and the minimum was 6. A significant difference (t-test, $p < 0.05$) in the scores of males (19.84, SD = 3.91) and females (21.17, SD = 3.82) was found (Table 2). Marital status had no effect, as no significant difference between married and unmarried participants was found. The extent of knowledge of Covid-19 presented an effect, where participants with much knowledge had a significantly higher score (21.08, SD = 3.75) than those with little knowledge (19.40, SD = 4.27). Higher education increased the commitment to precautionary measures. Undergraduate students (20.78, SD = 3.85) and post-graduates (21.36, SD = 3.42) were significantly (ANOVA, LSD, $p < 0.05$) more committed to the precautionary measures than the participants with lower education (high school participants, score 20.25, SD = 4.55). The participants who had felt concerned about the disease for three hours or more (22.18, SD = 3.60) were more likely to respond to precautionary measures than the less concerned ones (less than one hour, score 20.27, SD = 3.8) (Table 2).

Table 2. Participants (n = 1109) committed (mean, SD) to the precautionary measures in different sociodemographic groups and the p value of ANOVA indicating the significant effect of the group.

Variable	Group	*N*	Mean	SD	*p* Value
Gender	Male	285	19.84	3.91	0.010
	Female	824	21.17	3.82	
Marital Status	Married	793	20.75	3.95	0.32
	Unmarried	316	21.01	3.7	
Knowledge of COVID-19	Much	939	21.08	3.75	0.01
	Little	170	19.4	4.27	
Age	18–25	165	20.5	3.9	0.1
	26–35	261	20.93	3.57	
	36–45	286	20.9	3.82	
	46–55	220	21.27	4.01	
	>55	177	20.29	4.2	
Condition as dependent	No kids	340	20.63	3.9	0.4
	<16 years	461	21	3.84	
	>16 years	308	20.78	3.92	
Education	High school	157	20.25	4.55	0.05
	Undergraduate	719	20.78	3.85	
	Post-graduate	233	21.36	3.42	
Family Size	≤2	96	20.79	4.6	0.78
	3–5	528	20.91	3.73	
	≥6	485	20.74	3.89	
Employment Status	Student	92	20.54	4.28	0.38
	Non-employed	351	21.11	3.79	
	Retired	150	20.63	4.47	
	Employed	516	20.73	3.68	
Hours spent on COVID-19 news daily	≤1	655	20.27	3.81	0.01
	2–3	269	21.23	3.97	
	≥3	185	22.18	3.6	

3.3. Sociodemographic Groups and Depression

About half of the participants were relatively relaxed, where 52.57% had not lost their appetite, 56% felt depressed less than one day a week, 52.57% felt hopeful about the future, 68.53% did not feel that their life was a failure, 59.15% thought that people are unfriendly less than once a day, and 62.58% cried less than once a day (Table 3). About half of the participants (51.94%) felt sad, although they received support from their family and friends.

Table 3. Percentage of participants feeling different depression symptoms. Response alternatives: 1 = not at all (less than in one day a week); 2 = sometimes (in one or two days); 3 = every now and then (3–4 days), 4 = all the time (5–7 days).

Questions	Not at All (Less Than One Day)	Sometimes (a Day or Two)	Every Now and Then (3–4 Days)	All the Times (5–7) Days
	%	%	%	%
Q1. I get upset from things that normally do not upset me	37.06	7.03	44.72	11.18
Q2. I feel annoyed with things that do not annoy me usually	41.03	8.03	42.20	8.75
Q3. I lost my appetite	52.57	29.13	14.97	3.34
Q4. I feel sad despite of my family and friends support	51.94	5.14	34.45	8.48
Q5. I feel good	48.96	27.77	16.59	6.67
Q6. I feel depressed	56.00	5.41	32.46	6.13
Q7. I feel that every task I am doing is an effort	32.01	36.97	19.84	11.18
Q8. I feel hopeful about the future	44.27	31.74	17.22	6.76
Q9. I feel that my life is a failure	68.53	18.67	9.65	3.16
Q10. I feel scared	42.29	33.00	17.31	7.39
Q11. I cannot sleep at night	45.09	27.59	16.77	10.55
Q12. I feel happy	30.66	39.13	22.63	7.57
Q13. I talk less than usual	34.08	32.64	25.61	7.66
Q14. I feel lonely	48.96	24.35	17.13	9.56
Q15. People are unfriendly	59.15	23.44	12.53	4.87
Q16. I enjoy my life	39.68	29.58	22.90	7.84
Q17. I had crying spells	62.58	22.54	11.00	3.88

A significant difference was observed in the CES-D scores between married and unmarried participants, with those unmarried having higher scores (17.26, SD = 9.78) than those married (14.56, SD = 10.11) (Table 4). Females (16.25, SD = 10.23) had significantly greater scores than males (12.69, SD = 9.19). The CES-D score was not affected by the extent of knowledge of Covid-19. Participants who were concerned about the COVID-19 epidemic, spending three hours or more following the news, had higher scores than the less concerned ones. People under 55 years had higher scores (14.8–17.2) than those older than 55 years (12.21, SD = 9.97). Education had no significant effect. The number of children had a significant effect, where persons with children older than 16 years (13.45 SD = 10.06) had lower scores than people with younger children (15.84 SD = 10.23) or without children (16.34, SD = 9.72) (LSD test). Families with less than two members were significantly more depressed (17.35, SD = 10.39) than families with more than six members (14.55, SD = 9.67). Unemployed participants were significantly more depressed (16.18, SD = 10.25) than retirees (M = 12.83, SD = 9.90). The time spent engaging with COVID-19 news was reflected in the level of depression, where participants who spent more than 3 h daily had more depression (19.59, SD = 11.02) than the ones who spent one hour (13.89, SD = 9.64) or less than three hours (15.90, SD = 9.63).

Table 4. The CES-D score (mean, SD) for depression in different sociodemographic groups and the *p* value of ANOVA indicating the significant effect of the group.

Variable	Group	No. Participant	Mean	Std. Deviation	T-Value	Significant
Gender	Male	285	12.69	9.19	5.47	0.01
	Female	824	16.25	10.23		
Marital Status	Married	793	14.56	10.11	4.05	0.01
	Unmarried	316	17.26	9.78		
Knowledge of COVID-19	I know a lot	939	15.27	10.24	0.51	0.61
	I have a general knowledge	170	15.69	9.25		
Age	18–25	165	17.21	9.46	6.61	0.01
	26–35	261	16.27	9.73		
	36–45	286	15.72	10.11		
	46–55	220	14.82	10.52		
	>55	177	12.21	9.97		
Conduction as dependent	No kids	340	16.34	9.72	7.76	0.01
	16 years old child or younger	461	15.84	10.23		
	16 years child or older	308	13.45	10.06		
Education Level	High school or less	157	14.92	10.21	1.2	0.3
	Undergraduate	719	15.67	10.14		
	Graduates	233	14.57	9.85		
Family Size	≤2	96	17.35	10.39	3.7	0.05
	3–5	528	15.68	10.36		
	≥6	485	14.55	9.67		
Work Status	Student	92	15.58	9.08	3.98	0.01
	Non-employed	351	16.18	10.52		
	Retired	150	12.83	9.9		
	Employed	516	15.44	9.93		
Time spent on COVID-19 news daily	≤1	655	13.89	9.64	24.54	0.01
	2–3	269	15.9	9.63		
	≥3	185	19.59	11.02		

3.4. The Relation between the Precautionary Measures and Depression

CES-D score correlated most strongly with anxiety ($r = 0.44$) and the next strongly with wearing a mask ($r = 0.12$) (Table 5). The total scores of precautionary measures taken by the participants positively correlated with CES-D score ($r = 0.22$).

A significant regression equation was found (F (1, 1107) = 59.37, $p < 0.01$) between total precautionary score and CES-D score with anR^2 of0.051 (Table 6). CES-D score is equal to 2.61 × total precautionary score + 0.61 indicating that the participants' CES-D score increased 0.61 for each increase in precautionary measures.

Table 5. Pearson correlation coefficient (*r*) between the precautionary measures and the CES-D score describing depression ($n = 1109$, $p < 0.05$ when $r > 0.06$).

Precautionary Measures	Pearson Correlation Coefficient (*r*)
I cover the mouth when coughing and sneezing	0.003
I avoid sharing utensils	0.061
I was my hands with soap and water	0.043
I wash my hands immediately after I sneeze or after I touch my nose	0.038
I wear a mask regardless of the symptoms	0.115
I feel anxious about the spread of COVID-19	0.447
The average hours spent at home	0.015
Total scores for precautionary measures	0.226

Table 6. Regression analysis between the total scores of precautionary measures and CES-D score.

	Sum of Squares	DF	Mean Square	F	*p*	R^2
Regression Residual	6235.69 116,275.86	1 1107	6235.69 105.04	59.37	0.01	0.051
	Unstandardized Coefficients	Standardized Coefficients		T		*p*
	B	SE	Beta			
Constant	2.61	0.68		3.84		0.01
Precautionary measures	0.61	0.08	0.23	7.70		0.01

4. Discussion

The level of following good disease preventing practices was moderate to high in our study. This result was expected, as public awareness has been improved in Saudi Arabia especially with the MOH adequately updated information presented on all media channels.

Only about half of the respondents washed their hands with water and soap and covered their mouth when coughing or sneezing. About one-quarter of the participants in our study did not always, or even most of the time, avoid sharing utensils during meals. The lack of precautionary practice during meals is probably accelerating the transmission. This has been observed previously, as many disease cases originate from sharing meals [17]. Moreover, asymptomatic individuals cover their mouths when coughing and sneezing more often than symptomatic individuals [18]. The situation during the COVID-19 pandemic may worsen because of the social nature of family-oriented Saudi people with many gatherings and family activities. Thus, maintaining precautionary measures is essential. Moreover, recommendations and updates from local authorities and WHO increases people's awareness and helps people to follow precautionary measures [19–21].

In this study, married and elderly people as well as members of large families obtained lower CES-D scores measuring depression. These factors were thus protective against depression. Females appeared to be more depressed than males. This was not surprising since, according to the WHO, women are susceptible to common mental disorders such as depression and anxiety [22]. The age of children was found to be correlated with depression symptoms; the younger the children were, the more likely their parents had depression. This has been reported previously; parents of young children declare more depressive symptoms than parents of adult children [23]. In our study, unmarried individuals were more depressed than married couples. Regarding age, we found that less depression was associated with older people; participants above 55 years were less depressed. The two latter observations contradict previous studies that mostly show more depression in married and older individuals. Marriage was attributed to the great number of responsibilities [24,25]. Older people, in turn, are thought to have greater risk for depression because of their social disconnection and isolation feelings [26,27]. Our different findings might be explained by the family-oriented nature in Saudi Arabia. The conventional norms of the Saudi society also protect elderly people who mostly live with their children and not by themselves, and seldom in care houses. Additionally, bigger families protected against depression, as family members may provide support to each other.

It seems that the commitment to follow precautionary measures increased depression symptoms because a positive, although weak, correlation between the scores for CES-D and total precautionary measures was observed. The maximum score for depression in the depression scale CES-D is 51, and the cutoff score of 16 indicates a risk for clinical depression [28]. The regression analysis of our data indicated that the participants' CES-D score was increased by 0.61 units with each increase in the precautionary measures. Thus, it seems that the risk for depression is relatively high in small families, for females, unmarried, unemployed, individuals younger than 35 years old, or with no children. All these groups obtained a score higher than the cutoff of 16 in our study. This interpretation must be done with caution because the explanatory power of the regression analysis was relatively low, and the precautionary measures explained only 5% of the variation in CES-D score.

Behind the commitment to follow the precautionary measures was good knowledge about COVID-19, time spent on COVID-19 information, and high education, which were positively correlated with the commitment to follow precautionary measures. A recent study revealed that individuals with higher education had higher awareness about the precautionary measures of SARS virus [29]. Moreover, females appeared to follow precautionary practices better than males, which has been observed in some previous studies [29–31].

Lockdown and depression seem to be strongly linked. Despite that the curfew due to COVID-19 pandemic is different, it involves locking people in their houses and restricting their movements. Several studies have associated individual's lockdown with depression [32,33]. Studies have shown that limited outdoor activities can result in depression [34,35]. Outdoor activities are linked with physical exercise, which is known to improve mental health [36–38]. One important factor is light, as it provides signals to the brain to maintain circadian rhythm, which is involved in the sleep/wake cycle and is linked to the secretion of several mood and happiness hormones such as melatonin, cortisol, and serotonin [39–41]. Additionally, light exposure is linked to the maintenance of vitamin D levels, as lower levels of vitamin D are associated with depression [42,43].

The limitations of the research design have an effect on the reliability of the results. First, the survey lacks pre-COVID and post-COVID results about depression, and therefore the results must be interpreted with caution. However, several other recent articles report the increased depression symptoms and a number of psychological disorders during COVID-19 pandemic [44–47]. Moreover, the relation of the commitment of the individual to follow precautionary measures and depression symptoms can be assessed as reliable in our study. Second, the sociodemographic profile of the participants did not follow the actual profile of Saudi Arabia. Women, educated, and young people were overrepresented due to the recruiting process. However, our result that women felt more depression symptoms than men has been observed elsewhere, as reviewed [48]. One more limitation is that our cross-sectional design does not allow us to make any causal inferences. A web-based survey and snowball sampling recruitment method also create possibilities for selection bias. We were also not able to assess individuals' psychological condition before the pandemic. However, we suggest that the results show the potential of increased clinical depression cases caused by the pandemic.

5. Conclusions

We found a positive relationship between precautionary measures and depression. We also found that vulnerable individuals including elderlies and guardians with bigger families had relatively low depression levels in Saudi Arabia, which may be a benefit of a family-oriented lifestyle. It is recommended for governments and health authorities to not only provide masks, soaps, and disinfectants, but also support for mental health. Online awareness programs initiated by the government, media channels, and universities are important to increase people's knowledge about the situation and guide them through the pandemic. Free consultation services and a trauma focused-cognitive behavior therapy can be launched online for people in need. Furthermore, follow-up procedures should be taken to ensure the well-being of people. Our findings can be used to formulate psychological interventions to improve mental health and psychological resilience during the COVID-19 epidemic and to improve the precautionary measures practice.

Author Contributions: H.S.: Collection and outline the study; H.M.A.: data analysis; R.A.A.: Statistical analysis & comparing work; K.A.: Revising; F.A.: analysis, writing, revising. All authors have read and agreed to the published version of the manuscript.

Funding: This research was funded by the Deanship of Scientific Research at Princess Nourah bint Abdulrahman University through the Fast-track Research Funding Program to support publication in the top journal (Grant no. 42-FTTJ-79).

Institutional Review Board Statement: This work was approved by institutional committee of the Princess Nourah bint Abdulrahman University, Registration No. H-01-R-059.

Informed Consent Statement: Informed consent was obtained from all subjects involved in the study.

Data Availability Statement: All data related to this manuscript is incorporated in the manuscript only.

Conflicts of Interest: The authors declare no conflict of interest.

References

1. Liu, J.; Liao, X.; Qian, S.; Yuan, J.; Wang, F.; Liu, Y.; Wang, Z.; Wang, F.-S.; Liu, L.; Zhang, Z. MOH Reports First Case of Coronavirus Infection. *Emerg. Infect. Dis.* **2020**, *26*, 1320–1323. [CrossRef]
2. Nishiura, H.; Jung, S.-M.; Linton, N.M.; Kinoshita, R.; Yang, Y.; Hayashi, K.; Kobayashi, T.; Yuan, B.; Akhmetzhanov, A.R. The Extent of Transmission of Novel Coronavirus in Wuhan, China, 2020. *J. Clin. Med.* **2020**, *9*, 330. [CrossRef]
3. Petersen, E.; Koopmans, M.; Go, U.; Hamer, D.H.; Petrosillo, N.; Castelli, F.; Storgaard, M.; Al Khalili, S.; Simonsen, L. Comparing SARS-CoV-2 with SARS-CoV and influenza pandemics. *Lancet Infect. Dis.* **2020**, *20*, e238–e244. [CrossRef]
4. MOH News—MOH Reports First Case of Coronavirus Infection. (n.d.). Available online: https://www.moh.gov.sa/en/Ministry/MediaCenter/News/Pages/News-2020-03-02-002.aspx (accessed on 16 July 2020).
5. Klompas, M.; Morris, C.A.; Sinclair, J.; Pearson, M.; Shenoy, E.S. Universal Masking in Hospitals in the Covid-19 Era. *N. Engl. J. Med.* **2020**, *382*, e63. [CrossRef] [PubMed]
6. Lasry, A.; Kidder, D.; Hast, M.; Poovey, J.; Sunshine, G.; Winglee, K.; Zviedrite, N.; Ahmed, F.; Ethier, K.A.; Clodfelter, C.; et al. Timing of Community Mitigation and Changes in Reported COVID-19 and Community Mobility—Four U.S. Metropolitan Areas, 26 February–1 April 2020. *MMWR. Morb. Mortal. Wkly. Rep.* **2020**, *69*, 451–457. [CrossRef] [PubMed]
7. Mahase, E. Covid-19: What is the evidence for cloth masks? *BMJ* **2020**, *369*, m1422. [CrossRef]
8. Ebrahim, S.H.; Memish, Z.A. Saudi Arabia's drastic measures to curb the COVID-19 outbreak: Temporary suspension of the Umrah pilgrimage. *J. Travel Med.* **2020**, *27*. [CrossRef] [PubMed]
9. Alyami, H.S.; Naser, A.Y.; Dahmash, E.Z.; Alyami, M.H.; Al Meanazel, O.T.; Al-Meanazel, A.T.; Al Meanazel, O.T. Depression and anxiety during 2019 coronavirus disease pandemic in Saudi Arabia: A cross-sectional study [Preprint]. *Psychiatry Clin. Psychol.* **2020**. [CrossRef]
10. Huang, Y.; Zhao, N. Generalized anxiety disorder, depressive symptoms and sleep quality during COVID-19 outbreak in China: A web-based cross-sectional survey. *Psychiatry Res.* **2020**, *288*, 112954. [CrossRef]
11. Guan, W.J.; Ni, Z.Y.; Hu, Y.; Liang, W.H.; Ou, C.Q.; He, J.X.; Liu, L.; Shan, H.; Lei, C.L.; Hui, D.S.C.; et al. Clinical Characteristics of Coronavirus Disease 2019 in China. *N. Engl. J. Med.* **2020**, *382*, 1708–1720. [CrossRef]
12. Wang, C.; Pan, R.; Wan, X.; Tan, Y.; Xu, L.; Ho, C.S.; Ho, R.C. Immediate Psychological Responses and Associated Factors during the Initial Stage of the 2019 Coronavirus Disease (COVID-19) Epidemic among the General Population in China. *Int. J. Environ. Res. Public Health* **2020**, *17*, 1729. [CrossRef]
13. Radloff, L.S. The CES-D scale: A self-report depression scale for research in the general population. *Appl. Psychol. Meas.* **1977**, *1*, 385–401. [CrossRef]
14. Nunnally, J.C.; Nunnaly, J.C. *Psychometric Theory*; McGraw-Hill: New York, NY, USA, 1978.
15. Available online: https://gpseducation.oecd.org/CountryProfile?primaryCountry=SAU&treshold=10&topic=EO (accessed on 22 June 2021).
16. Available online: https://www.indexmundi.com/saudi_arabia/demographics_profile.html (accessed on 22 June 2021).

17. Tong, Z.-D.; Tang, A.; Li, K.-F.; Li, P.; Wang, H.-L.; Yi, J.-P.; Zhang, Y.-L.; Yan, J.-B. Potential Presymptomatic Transmission of SARS-CoV-2, Zhejiang Province, China, 2020. *Emerg. Infect. Dis.* **2020**, *26*, 1052–1054. [CrossRef] [PubMed]
18. Arons, M.M.; Hatfield, K.M.; Reddy, S.C.; Kimball, A.; James, A.; Jacobs, J.R.; Taylor, J.; Spicer, K.; Bardossy, A.C.; Oakley, L.P.; et al. Presymptomatic SARS-CoV-2 Infections and Transmission in a Skilled Nursing Facility. *N. Engl. J. Med.* **2020**, *382*, 2081–2090. [CrossRef] [PubMed]
19. Miscellaneous—Handwashing. (n.d.). Available online: https://www.moh.gov.sa/en/HealthAwareness/EducationalContent/Miscellaneous/Pages/005.aspx (accessed on 16 July 2020).
20. MOH News—MOH Advises to Avoid Gathering of More than 50 Persons. (n.d.). Available online: https://www.moh.gov.sa/en/Ministry/MediaCenter/News/Pages/News-2020-03-12-002.aspx (accessed on 16 July 2020).
21. Rothan, H.A.; Byrareddy, S.N. The epidemiology and pathogenesis of coronavirus disease (COVID-19) outbreak. *J. Autoimmun.* **2020**, *109*, 102433. [CrossRef]
22. WHO. *Gender and Women's Mental Health*; World Health Organization: Geneva, Switzerland, 2020. Available online: https://www.who.int/mental_health/prevention/genderwomen/en/ (accessed on 22 June 2021).
23. Flouri, E.; Narayanan, M.K.; Nærde, A. Stressful life events and depressive symptoms in mothers and fathers of young children. *J. Affect. Disord.* **2018**, *230*, 22–27. [CrossRef]
24. Gao, J.; Zheng, P.; Jia, Y.; Chen, H.; Mao, Y.; Chen, S.; Wang, Y.; Fu, H.; Dai, J. Mental health problems and social media exposure during COVID-19 outbreak. *PLoS ONE* **2020**, *15*, e0231924. [CrossRef]
25. Wu, X.; DeMaris, A. Gender and marital status differences in depression: The effects of chronic strains. *Sex Roles* **1996**, *34*, 299–319. [CrossRef]
26. Armitage, R.; Nellums, L.B. COVID-19 and the consequences of isolating the elderly. *Lancet Public Health* **2020**, *5*, e256. [CrossRef]
27. Yang, Y.; Li, W.; Zhang, Q.; Zhang, L.; Cheung, T.; Xiang, Y.-T. Mental health services for older adults in China during the COVID-19 outbreak. *Lancet Psychiatry* **2020**, *7*, e19. [CrossRef]
28. Lewinsohn, P.M.; Seeley, J.R.; Roberts, R.E.; Allen, N.B. Center for Epidemiologic Studies Depression Scale (CES-D) as a screening instrument for depression among community-residing older adults. *Psychol. Aging* **1997**, *12*, 277–287. [CrossRef]
29. Zhong, B.-L.; Luo, W.; Li, H.-M.; Zhang, Q.-Q.; Liu, X.-G.; Li, W.-T.; Li, Y. Knowledge, attitudes, and practices towards COVID-19 among Chinese residents during the rapid rise period of the COVID-19 outbreak: A quick online cross-sectional survey. *Int. J. Biol. Sci.* **2020**, *16*, 1745–1752. [CrossRef]
30. Alahdal, H.; Basingab, F.; Alotaibi, R. An analytical study on the awareness, attitude and practice during the COVID-19 pandemic in Riyadh, Saudi Arabia. *J. Infect. Public Health* **2020**, *13*, 1446–1452. [CrossRef]
31. Honarvar, B.; Lankarani, K.B.; Kharmandar, A.; Shaygani, F.; Zahedroozgar, M.; Haghighi, M.R.R.; Ghahramani, S.; Honarvar, H.; Daryabadi, M.M.; Salavati, Z.; et al. Knowledge, attitudes, risk perceptions, and practices of adults toward COVID-19: A population and field-based study from Iran. *Int. J. Public Health* **2020**, *65*, 731–739. [CrossRef]
32. Ozamiz-Etxebarria, N.; Dosil-Santamaria, M.; Picaza-Gorrochategui, M.; Idoiaga-Mondragon, N. Stress, anxiety, and depression levels in the initial stage of the COVID-19 outbreak in a population sample in the northern Spain. *Cad. Saúde Pública* **2020**, *36*, e00054020. [CrossRef]
33. Torales, J.; O'Higgins, M.; Castaldelli-Maia, J.M.; Ventriglio, A. The outbreak of COVID-19 coronavirus and its impact on global mental health. *Int. J. Soc. Psychiatry* **2020**, *66*, 317–320. [CrossRef] [PubMed]
34. Beyer, K.M.; Szabo, A.; Nattinger, A. Time Spent Outdoors, Depressive Symptoms, and Variation by Race and Ethnicity. *Am. J. Prev. Med.* **2016**, *51*, 281–290. [CrossRef] [PubMed]
35. Tasci, G.; Baykara, S.; Gurok, M.G.; Atmaca, M. Effect of exercise on therapeutic response in depression treatment. *Psychiatry Clin. Psychopharmacol.* **2019**, *29*, 137–143. [CrossRef]
36. Barton, J.; Pretty, J. What is the Best Dose of Nature and Green Exercise for Improving Mental Health? A Multi-Study Analysis. *Environ. Sci. Technol.* **2010**, *44*, 3947–3955. [CrossRef] [PubMed]
37. Mitchell, R. Is physical activity in natural environments better for mental health than physical activity in other environments? *Soc. Sci. Med.* **2013**, *91*, 130–134. [CrossRef]
38. Penedo, F.J.; Dahn, J.R. Exercise and well-being: A review of mental and physical health benefits associated with physical activity. *Curr. Opin. Psychiatry* **2005**, *18*, 189–193. [CrossRef]
39. Golden, R.N.; Gaynes, B.; Ekstrom, R.D.; Hamer, R.M.; Jacobsen, F.M.; Suppes, T.; Wisner, K.L.; Nemeroff, C.B. The Efficacy of Light Therapy in the Treatment of Mood Disorders: A Review and Meta-Analysis of the Evidence. *Am. J. Psychiatry* **2005**, *162*, 656–662. [CrossRef]
40. Oldham, M.A.; Ciraulo, D.A. Bright light therapy for depression: A review of its effects on chronobiology and the autonomic nervous system. *Chronobiol. Int.* **2014**, *31*, 305–319. [CrossRef]
41. Sloane, P.D.; Figueiro, M.; Cohen, L. Light as Therapy for Sleep Disorders and Depression in Older Adults. *Clin. Geriatr.* **2008**, *16*, 25–31.
42. Anglin, R.E.S.; Samaan, Z.; Walter, S.D.; McDonald, S.D. Vitamin D deficiency and depression in adults: Systematic review and meta-analysis. *Br. J. Psychiatry* **2013**, *202*, 100–107. [CrossRef] [PubMed]
43. Stewart, R.; Hirani, V. Relationship Between Vitamin D Levels and Depressive Symptoms in Older Residents From a National Survey Population. *Psychosom. Med.* **2010**, *72*, 608–612. [CrossRef] [PubMed]

44. Salari, N.; Hosseinian-Far, A.; Jalali, R.; Vaisi-Raygani, A.; Rasoulpoor, S.; Mohammadi, M.; Rasoulpoor, S.; Khaledi-Paveh, B. Prevalence of stress, anxiety, depression among the general population during the COVID-19 pandemic: A systematic review and meta-analysis. *Glob. Health* **2020**, *16*, 57. [CrossRef] [PubMed]
45. Sunjaya, D.K.; Herawati, D.M.D.; Siregar, A.Y.M. Depressive, anxiety, and burnout symptoms on health care personnel at a month after COVID-19 outbreak in Indonesia. *BMC Public Health* **2021**, *21*, 1–8. [CrossRef]
46. Pandey, U.; Corbett, G.; Mohan, S.; Reagu, S.; Kumar, S.; Farrell, T.; Lindow, S. Anxiety, Depression and Behavioural Changes in Junior Doctors and Medical Students Associated with the Coronavirus Pandemic: A Cross-Sectional Survey. *J. Obstet. Gynecol. India* **2021**, *71*, 33–37. [CrossRef]
47. Yang, X.; Zhang, Y.; Li, S.; Chen, X. Risk factors for anxiety of otolaryngology healthcare workers in Hubei province fighting coronavirus disease 2019 (COVID-19). *Soc. Psychiatry Psychiatr. Epidemiol.* **2021**, *56*, 39–45. [CrossRef] [PubMed]
48. Pappa, S.; Ntella, V.; Giannakas, T.; Giannakoulis, V.G.; Papoutsi, E.; Katsaounou, P. Prevalence of depression, anxiety, and insomnia among healthcare workers during the COVID-19 pandemic: A systematic review and meta-analysis. *Brain Behav. Immun.* **2020**, *88*, 901–907. [CrossRef] [PubMed]

International Journal of
Environmental Research and Public Health

MDPI

Article

Emotional Intelligence and Social Support: Two Key Factors in Preventing Occupational Stress during COVID-19

Giusy Danila Valenti *, Palmira Faraci and Paola Magnano

Faculty of Human and Social Sciences, University of Enna Kore, 94100 Enna, Italy; palmira.faraci@unikore.it (P.F.); paola.magnano@unikore.it (P.M.)
* Correspondence: giusy.valenti@unikore.it

Abstract: Emotional intelligence (EI) and social support are among the most investigated hypothesized variables that affect stress at work. The current study aims to evaluate the direct association between EI and occupational stress and its indirect relationship mediated by three sources of social support during the spread of the COVID-19. The total sample was composed of 367 individuals (53.7% males), aged from 20 to 68 (M = 37.84, SD = 10.39), who filled out an online questionnaire. A mediation analysis was performed to test the hypothesized relationships. Our findings showed that EI has a direct effect on psychological effects and an indirect effect on almost all the facets of occupational stress. The significant mediators were social support from both family and friends. Theoretical and practical implications are discussed and directions for future studies are suggested.

Keywords: occupational stress; emotional intelligence; social support; COVID-19

Citation: Valenti, G.D.; Faraci, P.; Magnano, P. Emotional Intelligence and Social Support: Two Key Factors in Preventing Occupational Stress during COVID-19. *Int. J. Environ. Res. Public Health* **2021**, *18*, 6918. https://doi.org/10.3390/ijerph18136918

Academic Editors: Paolo Roma, Merylin Monaro and Cristina Mazza

Received: 18 May 2021
Accepted: 22 June 2021
Published: 28 June 2021

1. Introduction

Occupational stress, also named work stress, is a psychological and physiological phenomenon, generated as a response to various external factors [1]. Resulting from insufficient coping skills with stressors at the workplace, occupational stress is a negatively perceived quality and has negative consequences on mental and physical health. This means that, prior to showing stress symptoms, at first, individuals must perceive a stressor negatively and then they must display inadequate coping abilities. That is, if a source of stress is perceived as a challenge to overcome rather than a threat to avoid, no negative outcomes will appear on mental and physical health [2].

Findings from previous studies have showed associations between high levels of stress at work and a broad range of disturbances, such as chronic fatigue, eating disorders, increased blood pressure, and the risk of cardiovascular diseases. Regarding psychological symptoms, occupational stress has been linked to depression and anxiety, mood disturbance and emotional exhaustion, and a decrease in attention and concentration [3–7].

In addition, significant positive associations were also found between occupational stress and a variety of job-related outcomes, such as intention to leave the workplace or absenteeism [6,8], whereas inverse relationships were estimated with job satisfaction, job performance, job motivation, and organizational commitment [9].

Occupational stress is considered both as a "public concern" and a "personal trouble" [10], because both job-related and individual factors influence it. Regarding job-related factors, some studies have linked occupational stress to several aspects, such as heavy workload, role ambiguity, role conflict, problematic interactions with colleagues or supervisors, inadequate training, job insecurity, low salary, and lack of career prospects [8,11,12].

With regard to individual factors, several studies have revealed significant associations with gender, age, educational level [13–15], and coping styles [16].

Owing to the complexity and heterogeneity of occupational stress, consensus about its assessment is lacking. Though some authors, such as Mensah [17], used a single item simply asking people "*Do you experience stress at work?*", occupational stress is described as a multidimensional construct, and overload, work relations, psychological symptoms and physical burdens, pay and benefits, lack of rewards, and organizational policies are among the most widely investigated indicators [8,18,19].

A relevant individual factor related to occupational stress is emotional intelligence (EI), defined as a personality predisposition associated with individuals' tendency to understand their own and others' emotions, to manage their own feelings and their relationships with others [20]. Understanding emotions helps people to be aware of their own and others' behaviors and motivations, whereas managing emotions allows the individuals to navigate their feelings constructively at work. In other words, EI is the individuals' ability to properly handle their own interpersonal and intrapersonal skills, which improves the competence in facing stressors and, consequently, enhances positive outcomes. In addition, Goleman [21] asserts that EI is twice as important as technical skills and more important than IQ in predicting positive outcomes at the workplace, suggesting that people should be judged not according to their own intelligence or professional competence, but rather by their own behaviors toward themselves and others. These premises stress the relevance of taking into account EI in working environments, both to increase productivity and efficiency and to improve workers' wellbeing, job motivation, and job satisfaction.

Indeed, recent studies [18,22–28] have reported that workers with higher EI are more productive at the workplace and can cope with stressors more efficiently. The inverse relationship between EI and occupational stress has been found in different working contexts and for different categories of workers, such as police officers [26], human service professionals [19], bank employees [18], managers [29], health care professionals [30], and college teachers [31]. These findings outline that EI negatively affects occupational stress, regardless of the specific working sector. Although there is wide agreement about the negative association between EI and stress at the workplace, some authors did not show any statistical relationships [32], suggesting that other variables, such as organizational support, are protective factors in stress management rather than EI.

Social support has long been identified as a crucial resource for mitigating threats and challenges [33,34]. It is defined as the extent to which people perceive others as attentive and responsive to their needs. Social support is considered as an important factor in maintaining wellbeing and coping with challenges [35]. It can be assessed as both a global and generalized perceived social support and by discriminating different sources, such as social support from family, friends, and significant others [36–39]. However, in the work context, work-related social support (social support from coworkers and/or supervisors) is mostly investigated because these individuals are considered as the main sources of social support for workers seeking to accomplish their goals and adjust to the workplace [40]. Actually, the results of the studies investigating the effects of work-related social support on the levels of occupational stress are incoherent and inconsistent, suggesting that the kind and the quality of interactions with coworkers and supervisors may function both as protective and risk factors [11,41]. Nevertheless, a limited number of studies examining the relationships between sources of social support and occupational stress outlined the beneficial role in mitigating the degree of stress at the workplace [42,43].

Individuals who are able to understand their own and others' feelings more likely search for support from others in challenging situations [44]. Specifically, they may need others to empathize with their situation, identify their emotional reactions, and provide social support or resources to deal with a stressful situation [45]. Social support is a key candidate to mediate EI and wellbeing. Some theorists suggested that emotional abilities contribute to acquiring social skills, thus enhancing both the quality of relationships and the availability of social support, which in turn leads to a richer sense of wellbeing [46]. Some evidence supported this hypothesis. For example, some authors showed that people with high EI reported greater social support, as well as higher levels of satisfaction and lower grades of psychological distress [36–39,47,48]. Nevertheless, the mediating role of social support in the relationship between EI and occupational stress has not yet been explored. This study aims to fill this gap.

The diffusion of the COVID-19 virus has considerably affected work conditions, leading to new job demands and pressures. Though some working sectors—such as health care professionals—are more vulnerable to occupational stress, given the higher risk of being infected and longer working hours, the current pandemic has greatly influenced each working sector without distinction. In fact, many workers have experienced—and are experiencing—different changes at work, involving an increase or a reduction of working hours, alterations in job tasks and shifts, and a transition toward smart working. In other words, many working sectors have reorganized their environments and structures to accommodate the emerging demands. All these factors may further influence how people feel in their workplaces and affect their level of occupational stress.

A large number of studies are currently examining how the pandemic is changing work conditions and affecting several job-related outcomes [17,49–51]. Among them, some authors have pointed out that both EI and social support have a strong impact in mitigating negative job-related outcomes. For example, Soto-Rubio et al. [52] have emphasized EI's key role in preventing burnout among health care professionals and in improving their levels of job satisfaction, whereas other authors [53] have stressed the influence social support has in enhancing job engagement and job retention intention.

In summary, the relationship between EI and stress has been widely studied, as well as the beneficial role of social support in maintaining health and wellbeing. Further, their protective role in decreasing the levels of stress at work is well documented. However, the joint contribution of EI and social support in reducing occupational stress has not been examined during the COVID-19 lockdown. Given the importance of EI and social support in preventing occupational stress, this study aims to analyze these relationships in the Italian context during the pandemic. Specifically, the goals of this work are (a) to examine the direct relationship between EI and occupational stress, and (b) to test the mediating role of social support (see Figure 1 for a visual representation of our hypotheses). We expect that individuals with higher levels of EI will perceive their work environment as less stressful and will experience less negative health consequences, and that social support can function as a buffer in the relationship between EI and occupational stress. Thus, we formulated the following hypotheses: (i) EI negatively affects occupational stress and (ii) social support mediates the association between EI and occupational stress. Although a similar mediation analysis has not been previously tested, the proposed model derives from the existing literature described above in which the associations between EI and social support, between social support and occupational stress, as well as between IE and occupational stress have been investigated [18,19,28–31,42–44,46].

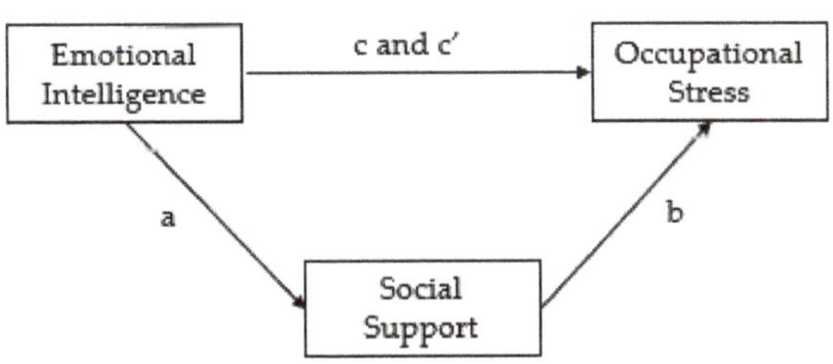

Figure 1. Conceptual model. Path a = association between EI and social support; path b = association between social support and occupational stress; path c = total effect of EI on occupational stress; c′ = direct effect of EI on occupational stress.

The current study takes into account support from family, friends, and significant others—which are little investigated in this specific field of study—to explore how not work-related sources of support affect occupational stress. This latter is defined as a broad concept in which effects on health (both psychological and physical) and work stressors (job features, career prospects, managerial role, work relationships, work–home interface, and organizational structure) are indicators. Figure 2 displays the hypothesized relationships among the investigated variables.

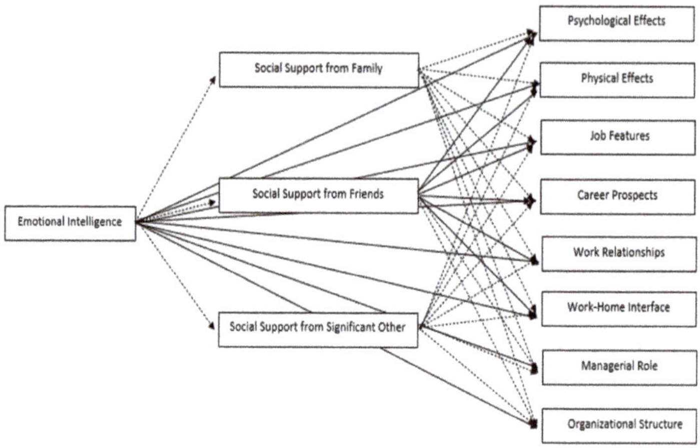

Figure 2. Hypothesized relationships among the investigated variables. Full lines indicate direct effects; dotted lines indicate indirect effects.

This research contributes to a better understanding of job-related outcomes in the current circumstances.

2. Materials and Methods

2.1. Participants

A sample of 385 individuals was recruited to fill out an online questionnaire. The inclusion criteria were age >18 and being employed. The initial screening led to eliminating 18 participants owing to their failure to complete the whole survey. We retained participants for subsequent analyses if they reported a small number of missing data, which were handled by replacing them with the mean score imputation for each considered variable. The final sample was composed of 367 individuals, aged from 20 to 68 (M = 37.84, SD = 10.39), almost equally distributed between the two genders, mostly married, and with higher education. Almost half of them (47.1%) declared not to have children, whereas the remaining (52.9%) reported having from one to five children. Participants were asked to indicate how/where they had been working during the last year (work remotely only/work remotely, but also at the workplace/work at the workplace, but also remotely/work at the workplace only), and to report the extent to which their working conditions changed after the spread of the pandemic (from "Not at all" to "Very much"). They were also asked to specify which (if any) working conditions changed, choosing the suited answers among multiple alternatives (salary increase/salary decrease, working hours increase/working hours decrease, kind of job activity, layoff, relationships with coworkers and supervisors) (see Table 1 for a more detailed description of the study sample).

Table 1. Descriptive statistics of the study sample.

Demographics	Options	N	%
Gender	Males	197	53.7%
	Females	170	46.7%
Marital status	Unmarried	127	34.6%
	Married	177	48.2%
	Divorced	20	5.4%
	Widower	1	0.3%
	Cohabitant	42	11.4%
Parental status	No children	172	47.1%
	1 child	76	20.8%
	2 children	96	26.3%
	3 children	18	4.9%
	4 children	1	0.3%
	5 children	2	0.5%
Educational	Junior high school	42	11.6%
	High school	116	32%
	Degree (Bachelor/Master)	127	35%
	Post-degree	78	21.5%
Employment status	Private sector	240	65.8%
	Public sector	100	27.4%
	Tertiary sector	25	6.8%
Way of working during COVID-19	work remotely only	80	21.8%
	work remotely, but also at the workplace	99	27%
	work at the workplace, but also remotely,	63	17.2%
	work at the workplace only	120	32.7%
Amount of changes in working conditions during COVID-19	Not at all	51	13.9%
	A little	135	13.9%
	Somewhat	101	27.5%
	Very much	64	17.4%
Working conditions changed during COVID-19	Salary increase	29	5%
	Salary decrease	78	13.4%
	Working hours increase	126	21.6%
	Working hours decrease	69	11.8%
	Kind of job activity	69	11.8%
	Layoff	26	4.5%
	Relationships with coworkers	118	20.2%
	Relationships with supervisors	49	8.4%
	Other	19	3.3%

2.2. Procedure

Data were gathered online, sharing the research link on social media, such as Facebook and LinkedIn, and through personal contacts. The introduction to the questionnaire included the researchers' institutional identity, a short explanation about the aim of the study, and an invitation to participate. Individuals were informed that their participation in the study was voluntary, and they were also assured of the confidentiality of the information obtained. Informed consent was obtained by all participants prior to answering the survey. Data were collected in February 2021. All procedures were performed in compliance with provisions from the Declaration of Helsinki regarding research on human participants, approved by the Internal Review Board of Research in Psychology of UKE (UKE-IRBPSY-03.21.02).

2.3. Measures

2.3.1. Demographics

Demographics were assessed using an ad hoc measure.

2.3.2. Emotional Intelligence

The Self-Report Emotional Intelligence Test (SREIT; [54,55]) was used to assess emotional intelligence. It is a 33-item scale (e.g., *"Emotions are one of the things that make my life worth living"*; *"I am aware of my emotions as I experience them"*) on a five-point Likert scale from 1 "strongly disagree" to 5 "strongly agree". It is a unidimensional scale, with higher scores indicating a greater level of EI. Cronbach's alpha reached 0.93.

2.3.3. Social Support

To measure perceived social support, the Italian version [56] of the Multidimensional Scale of Perceived Social Support (MSPSS; [57]) was used. The scale is composed of 12 items (e.g., *"I can tell about my problems with my family"*; *"My friends really try to help me"*) with response options on a six-point Likert-type scale, ranging from 1 "absolutely false" to 7 "absolutely true". The instrument measures support from family, friends, and significant others, which represent three distinct subscales. The reliability coefficient for each subscale was excellent, ranging from 0.89 and 0.91.

2.3.4. Occupational Stress

Occupational stress was assessed using the Occupational Stress Indicator (OSI; [58,59]). Two scales were taken into account: Sources of Stress and Effects on Health. The former is composed of 61 items distributed into six subscales: Job Factor (JF; 9 items; e.g., *"Having too much work to do"*), Managerial Factor (MF; 11 items; e.g., *"Having personal beliefs in contrast with those of the company"*), Relationships with Others Factor (RF; 10 items; e.g., *"Little encouragement from supervisors"*), Career Factor (CF; 9 items; i.e., *"Holding a position under your ability"*), Home–Work Interface Factor (IF; 11 items; e.g., *"Inability to stop working when you are at home"*), and Organizational Structure Factor (OF; 11 items; e.g., *"Luck of information and involvement in decisions"*). The latter is composed of two subscales, examining the Effects on Health from two perspectives: Psychological (PSY; 18 items; e.g., *"During a working day, do you feel irritated or agitated, though a clear reason does not always seem to be?"*) and Physical (PHY; 12 items; e.g., *"Inability to fall asleep or sleep without interruption"*) Effects. Internal reliability was excellent for each subscale, with Cronbach's alpha ranging from 0.81 to 0.92.

2.4. Statistical Analyses

Descriptive statistical analyses were used to analyze demographic data. Prior to conducting the main analyses, MANOVAs were performed to evaluate whether any significant statistical differences were estimated on the study variables according to gender differences. Mediation analyses were applied to verify whether social support functions as a buffer in the relationship between EI and occupational stress during COVID-19. The process involved examining path a, the association between EI (IV) and social support (M); path b, the impact of social support (M) on occupational stress (DV); and path c and c′, the total and direct effect of EI (IV) on occupational stress (DV). The three sources of social support (family, friends, and significant others) were considered and included in the model as three distinct mediators. Before testing the mediating model, the multivariate normality distribution of data was first examined through the Mahalanobis distance computation. Since the Mardia's coefficient (192.47) exceeded the critical value associated with twelve-degrees-of-freedom (168), the assumption of multivariate normality was not met. Therefore, we chose to apply the bootstrapping (percentiles) method, a non-parametric resampling procedure recognized as a robust and accurate method for mediation analysis [60] and the best-suited technique to perform when the multivariate normality is violated. IBM SPSS (version 20) and Jamovi (version 1.6.23) were used for the analyses.

3. Results

3.1. Preliminary Analyses

Prior to conducting the main data analyses, we carried out a correlation inspection between the study variables (see Table 2). Further, MANOVAs were performed to assess the extent to which the scores on the investigated variables differed across genders. The results of MANOVAs showed that no significant statistical differences were estimated between men and women in any of the examined variables (Wilks $\Lambda_{(12,352)} = 0.971$, $p = 0.580$, partial $\eta^2 = 0.029$), providing evidence that considering our sample as a whole for further analyses was appropriate. Table 3 depicts the scores obtained by men and women on each variable and the results of the univariate tests.

Table 2. Correlations between the study variables.

Variable	1	2	3	4	5	6	7	8	9	10	11	12
1. SREIT	-											
2. MSPSS Family	0.47 **	-										
3. MSPSS Friends	0.44 **	0.48 **	-									
4. MSPSS Significant Other	0.49 **	0.51 **	0.52 **	-								
5. OSI PSY	−0.22 **	−0.17 **	−0.12 *	0.03	-							
6. OSI PHY	−0.17 **	−0.19 **	−0.08	0.09	0.65 **	-						
7. OSI JF	−0.01	−0.04	0.07	0.01	0.55 **	0.55 **	-					
8. OSI MF	0.10	0.07	−0.08	−0.09	0.38 **	0.40 **	0.81 **	-				
9. OSI RF	0.01	0.02	−0.10 *	−0.01	0.47 **	0.50 **	0.83 **	0.84 **	-			
10. OS CF	0.03	0.01	−0.10 *	0.04	0.44 **	0.46 **	0.80 **	0.83 **	0.82 **	-		
11. OSI IF	0.09	0.10	−0.15 *	0.07	0.41 **	0.40 **	0.80 **	0.85 **	0.80 **	0.80 **	-	
12. OSI SF	0.10	0.07	0.09	0.09	0.32 **	0.37 **	0.77 **	0.89 **	0.81 **	0.81 **	0.83 **	-

Note: SREIT: Self-Report Emotional Intelligence Test; MSPSS = Multidimensional Scale of Perceived Social Support; OSI = Occupational Stress Indicator; OSI_PSY = Psychological; OSI PHY = Physical; OSI JF = Job Factor; OSI MF = Managerial Factor; OSI RF = Relational Factor; OSI CF = Career Factor; OSI IF = Work–Home Interface Factor; OSI SF = Organizational Structure Factor. * $p < 0.05$; ** $p < 0.01$.

Table 3. Scores obtained by men and women on the study variables.

	Gender	*M*	*SD*	*F*	*Sig*	*Partial* η^2
STREIT	M	116.63	16.32			
	F	116.41	15.85			
	Tot	116.53	16.08	0.018	0.895	0.000
MPSS Family	M	22.86	5.73			
	F	23.49	5.01			
	Tot	23.15	5.41	1.21	0.272	0.003
MPSS Friends	M	21.49	5.71			
	F	21.57	5.85			
	Tot	21.53	5.77	0.017	0.896	0.000
MPSS Significant Other	M	23.29	5.24			
	F	23.33	5.63			
	Tot	23.31	5.42	0.005	0.946	0.000
OSI PSY	M	55.52	15.32			
	F	56.33	12.41			
	Tot	55.89	14.04	0.301	0.584	0.001
OSY PHY	M	32.80	14.79			
	F	33.63	12.45			
	Tot	33.18	13.75	0.333	0.564	0.001
OSI JF	M	30.45	9.63			
	F	30.60	7.97			
	Tot	30.52	8.89	0.026	0.873	0.000
OSI MF	M	39.32	11.82			
	F	40.34	11.23			
	Tot	39.79	11.55	0.706	0.401	0.002
OSI CF	M	32.50	9.56			
	F	32.43	8.81			
	Tot	32.47	9.21	0.006	0.939	0.000

Table 3. *Cont.*

	Gender	*M*	*SD*	*F*	*Sig*	*Partial* η^2
OSI RF	M	34.28	10.38			
	F	33.76	9.15			
	Tot	34.04	9.82	0.251	0.617	0.001
OSI IF	M	39.86	11.03			
	F	40.30	11.02			
	Tot	40.06	11.01	0.141	0.708	0.000
OSI SF	M	40.56	11.70			
	F	40.73	11.81			
	Tot	40.64	11.74	0.020	0.888	0.000

Note: M = males; F = females; SREIT: Self-Report Emotional Intelligence Test; MSPSS = Multidimensional Scale of Perceived Social Support; OSI = Occupational Stress Indicator; OSI PSY = Psychological; OSI PHY = Physical; OSI JF = Job Factor; OSI MF = Managerial Factor; OSI RF = Relational Factor; OSI CF = Career Factor; OSI IF = Work–Home Interface Factor; OSI SF = Organizational Structure Factor.

3.2. Mediation Analyses

The significant results for mediation analyses are described in the following section. Table 4 displays all the associations among the investigated variables. Figure 3 depicts the measurement model with only significant paths.

Table 4. Relationships between emotional intelligence (EI), social support, and occupational stress.

		95% CI			
Type	**Effect**	*LL*	*UP*	β	*p*
Indirect	SREIT → MSPSS Family → OSI PSY	−0.097	−0.003	−0.06	0.036
	SREIT → MSPSS Friends → OSI PSY	0.005	0.091	−0.05	0.027
	SREIT → MSPSS Significant Other → OSI PSY	−0.055	0.042	0.00	0.800
Direct	SREIT → OSI PSY	−0.305	−0.070	−0.21	0.002
Total	SREIT → OSI PSY	−0.283	−0.108	−0.22	<0.001
Indirect	SREIT → MSPSS Family → OSI PHY	−0.094	−0.002	−0.06	0.041
	SREIT → MSPSS Friends → OSI PHY	−0.026	0.056	0.01	0.474
	SREIT → MSPSS Significant Other → OSI PHY	−0.083	0.014	−0.04	0.163
Direct	SREIT → OSI PHY	−0.195	0.036	−0.09	0.177
Total	SREIT → OSI PHY	−0.233	−0.061	−0.17	<0.001
Indirect	SREIT → MSPSS Family → OSI MF	−0.047	0.029	−0.01	0.643
	SREIT → MSPSS Friends → OSI MF	−0.011	0.059	0.03	0.175
	SREIT → MSPSS Significant Other → OSI MF	−0.014	0.068	0.04	0.192
Direct	SREIT → OSI MF	−0.072	0.123	0.04	0.609
Total	SREIT → OSI MF	−0.004	0.141	0.09	0.066
Indirect	SREIT → MSPSS Family → OSI JB	−0.052	0.007	−0.04	0.139
	SREIT → MSPSS Friends → OSI JF	0.001	0.056	−0.05	0.042
	SREIT → MSPSS Significant Other → OSI JF	−0.034	0.029	0.01	0.867
Direct	SREIT → OSI JF	−0.079	0.071	.01	0.913
Total	SREIT → OSI JF	−0.057	0.056	.01	0.980

Table 4. *Cont.*

Type	Effect	95% CI		β	*p*
		LL	*UP*		
Indirect	SREIT → MSPSS Family → OSI RF	−0.035	0.029	−0.01	0.862
	SREIT → MSPSS Friends → OSI RF	0.007	0.069	−0.06	0.015
	SREIT → MSPSS Significant Other → OSI RF	−0.055	0.015	−0.03	0.254
Direct	SREIT → OSI RF	−0.095	0.072	−0.02	0.784
Total	SREIT → OSI RF	−0.059	0.066	0.01	0.915
Indirect	SREIT → MSPSS Family → OSI CF	−0.046	0.016	−0.03	0.344
	SREIT → MSPSS Friends → OSI CF	0.001	0.059	−0.06	0.039
	SREIT → MSPSS Significant Other → OSI CF	−0.034	0.032	−0.01	0.942
Direct	SREIT → OSI CF	−0.075	0.082	0.01	0.922
Total	SREIT → OSI CF	−0.040	0.077	0.03	0.543
Indirect	SREIT → MSPSS Family → OSI IF	−0.024	0.049	0.02	0.491
	SREIT → MSPSS Friends → OSI IF	0.004	0.073	−0.05	0.026
	SREIT → MSPSS Significant Other → OSI IF	−0.049	0.029	−0.01	0.607
Direct	SREIT → OSI IF	−0.074	0.112	0.03	0.700
Total	SREIT → OSI IF	−0.009	0.129	0.09	0.092
Indirect	SREIT → MSPSS Family → OSI SF	−0.043	0.035	−0.01	0.837
	SREIT → MSPSS Friends → OSI SF	−0.062	0.056	0.02	0.278
	SREIT → MSPSS Significant Other → OSI SF	−0.034	0.049	0.01	0.738
Direct	SREIT → OSI SF	−0.029	0.170	0.09	0.167
Total	SREIT → OSI SF	−0.019	0.167	0.01	0.233

Note: SREIT: Self-Report Emotional Intelligence Test; MSPSS = Multidimensional Scale of Perceived Social Support; OSI = Occupational Stress Indicator; OSI PSY = Psychological; OSI PHY = Physical; OSI JF = Job Factor; OSI MF = Managerial Factor; OSI RF = Relational Factor; OSI CF = Career Factor; OSI IF = Work–Home Interface Factor; OSI SF = Organizational Structure Factor. CI = confidence intervals; LL = lower limit; UL = upper limit.

EI showed a significant total (β = −0.22, *p* < 0.001, 95% CI [−0.283, −0.108]) and direct (β = −0.21, *p* = 0.002, 95% CI [−0.305, −0.070]) effect on psychological effects. This relationship also indicated significant effects by adding social support as a mediator. Specifically, support from family and friends functioned as significant mediators, though the magnitude of the association between EI and psychological effects decreased (β = −0.06, *p* = 0.036, 95% CI [−0.097, −0.003], β = −0.05, *p* = 0.027, 95% CI [0.005, 0.092], respectively).

A full mediation was found in the relationship between EI and physical effects (β = −0.17, *p* < 0.001, 95% CI [−0.233, −0.061], as a direct association was not estimated. Only support from family was a significant mediator (β = −0.06, *p* = 0.041, 95% CI [−0.094, −0.002]).

Support from friends mediated the relationship between EI and job factor (β = −0.05, *p* = 0.042, 95% CI [0.001, 0.056]), as well as between EI and relational factor (β = −0.06, *p* = 0.015, 95% CI [0.007, 0.069]), between EI and career factor (β = −0.05, *p* = 0.039, 95% CI [0.001, 0.059]), and between EI and home–work interface factor (β = −0.06, *p* = 0.026, 95% CI [0.004, 0.073]).

Finally, no direct or indirect effects were estimated between EI and managerial factor and between EI and organizational structure factor.

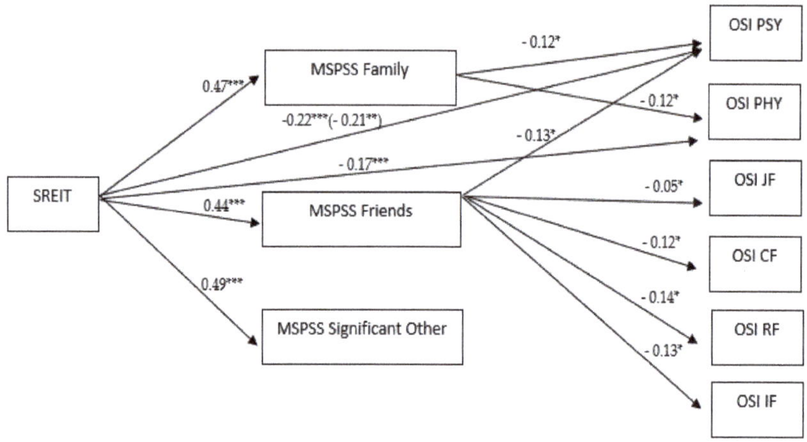

Figure 3. Measurement model testing the relationship between EI and occupational stress through social support. Only significant paths are shown. Direct effects are in parentheses. SREIT: Self-Report Emotional Intelligence Test; MSPSS = Multidimensional Scale of Perceived Social Support; OSI = Occupational Stress Indicator; OSI PSY = Psychological; OSI PHY = Physical; OSI JF = Job Factor; OSI RF = Relational Factor; OSI CF = Career Factor; OSI IF = Work–Home Interface Factor. * $p < 0.05$, ** $p < 0.01$, *** $p < 0.001$.

4. Discussion

This study's main objective was to test the direct and indirect relationship between EI and occupational stress, taking into account different sources of social support as mediators. Specifically, we hypothesized that individuals with high EI were more inclined to search for social support and, in turn, tended to experience lower levels of occupational stress. Through the mediation analyses application, all the possible paths were examined, and the associations among the aforementioned variables were verified.

To the best of our knowledge, this is the first attempt addressed to evaluate this mediation model, and the first study in which EI, social support, and occupational stress are jointly examined during the pandemic.

In line with previous research [36,47], our results supported the existence of significant associations between EI and social support, providing evidence that individuals with higher EI tend to perceive greater social support from others. In fact, EI predicted all three sources of social support. This means that individuals able to understand their own and others' emotions are more likely surrounded by positive and good relationships that strengthen their social competence, and they more easily rely on other people when facing challenging events because they think others are attentive and responsive to their own needs. These findings emphasize how the two concepts are strictly related to each other.

In the current study, three sources of social support were taken into account: social support from family members, friends, and significant others. This can be considered as an innovative aspect of the existing literature on this topic, as the majority of studies on occupational stress mainly focus on the effects of social support from coworkers and supervisors. From this point of view, our findings emphasize that, although the concept of occupational stress is associated with the inability to cope with stress at work, external variables not strictly related to work conditions can also influence the degree of occupational stress. In truth, stress is both a general and complex phenomenon in which multiple variables interact and merge into each other. This suggests that researchers should not limit the investigation of context-dependent stressors, but rather should be aware that other external variables may function both as protective and risk factors. From this perspective, our results are in line with previous research in which not work-related social support positively affected occupational [42,43].

Likewise, occupational stress was assessed considering several aspects of it, i.e., examining the effects on psychological and physical health on the one hand, and on the other, job-related stressors, such as problematic relationships with coworkers and/or supervisors, difficulties in work–home balance, incompatibilities with organizational policies, and issues linked to lacking personal and career development. Specifically, eight facets of occupational stress were identified as outcome variables. Such a distinction allowed us to examine whether the three sources of social support have a diverse impact on the different occupational stress facets and, consequently, whether or not they functioned as a mediator.

In contrast with previous studies [28,29,31] and contrary to our expectations, EI did not report direct effects on occupational stress, except for considering psychological effects as a dependent variable. From this point of view, our results supported the conclusions suggested by some authors [32], according to whom EI is not directly related to stress at the workplace, suggesting that other variables—such as organizational support—may better predict levels of occupational stress. Another plausible reason for the unexpected direct effects of EI on occupational stress dimensions may be owing to the specific critical period in which data were collected, characterized by the spread of the COVID-19 virus. Despite that EI is intended as a personality trait rather than a temporary state, participants were not adequately instructed to indicate their typical disposition toward understanding managing of their own and others' emotions. Participants' responses on some of SREIT items, such as *"I expect good things to happen"* or *"I motivate myself by imagining a good outcome to tasks I take on"*, may be biased owing to the extensive negative emotions experienced during the pandemic.

Nevertheless, significant indirect effects were estimated for almost all occupational stress facets in which social support from family and friends were found to be significant mediators. These findings provide interesting insights for interpretation that may have useful theoretical and practical implications.

From a theoretical perspective, our results indicate the relevance of considering scores on multidimensional measures' subscales separately. Previous studies on this topic have used the MSPSS for evaluating social support, combining scores obtained in each subscale into a unique total score [37–39]. This procedure represents a misuse of multidimensional measures, and we recommend applying it only if a second-order factor analysis has been performed.

In addition, using a total and global score does not allow evaluating whether the different sources of social support have a different impact on occupational stress. Indeed, our analyses' findings showed that social support from both family and friends has a beneficial effect in minimizing the effects of occupational stress, but social support from significant others did not predict any facets of the outcome variable. These results suggest adopting programs aimed at promoting and reinforcing specific sources of social support, which strengthen social competence and, in turn, have a protective function against maladaptive outcomes.

Any sources of social support had a significant impact on OSI MF and on OSI SF. A viable explanation is that both subscales are strictly related to the specific features of the workplace: the former refers to how individuals perceive others' expectancies toward themselves, and the latter is the characteristics of the structural and climate organization. Presumably, these aforementioned subscales may be better predicted by a greater sense of social support from coworkers or supervisors, rather than other sources of social support. Future studies may explore this hypothesis.

Although research on occupational stress usually takes into account work-related sources of social support as potential factors affecting or offsetting stress at work, our findings are in line with previous studies outlining how the link between social support and occupational stress is inconsistent and unclear [11]. These inconsistencies may be mainly due to the type of supporters (i.e., source), to the different functions of social support (informational, emotional, and instrumental) considered, and to the specific indicators of occupational stress investigated. From this perspective, additional research is needed that aims at evaluating whether social support (both work- and not work-related social support) differently affect the facets of occupational stress by simultaneously examining the three different functions.

In addition, further studies are also needed to have a deeper understanding of the associations between the selected variables to better justify the proposed model.

As mentioned before, the results of the present study should be considered in light of the critical period in which data were gathered and should be taken with some caution, avoiding generalizations that go beyond the pandemic period. The spread of the COVID-19 virus and the rapid and unexpected changes of habits in daily life and at workplaces may have affected the individual scores on the investigated variables.

Limitations

Some limitations should be mentioned. First, one concern addresses the missing information about the region in which the participants were living while answering the survey. Indeed, although the current pandemic extended from North to South Italy, during data collection, some regions were in a complete lockdown, whereas others had weaker restrictive measures owing to the virus's lower incidence rate. This may likely have affected the participants' response set and their scores on the investigated variables. From this point of view, we are unsure whether our participants can be considered as a representative sample of the Italian population, or whether they better reflect the situation of the country's specific regions. We suggest future studies address this issue to establish the extent to which the results obtained from the study sample can be generalized to the population to which it refers. Second, we did not explore the influence of other work-related stressors on the degree of occupational stress. For instance, we did not examine how the different changes in working conditions, such as alterations of salary, decrease in working hours, or shifts to teleworking, affected the participants' perceived level of occupational stress during the pandemic. In fact, a substantial portion of our sample declared that several working conditions changed after the outbreak of the COVID-19 pandemic, but they were taken into account purely at a descriptive level. In particular, we did not investigate the extent to which the transition toward smart working, which implies the need of new organizations and new habits into the family environment, affects occupational stress during the current circumstances. From this perspective, a broader and deeper analysis of any possible stressors generated by the new condition of working at home and by the time and spaces sharing with other family members during a working day should be conducted. Additional research should be aimed at exploring how these stressors influence occupational stress during the global emergency. A further limitation consists of the cross-sectional nature of the study, which prevents us from making inferences on the sequences of events, and there is no information on whether and how the pandemic has changed the associations among the investigated variables. Future longitudinal studies may provide a better knowledge and understanding of the relationships examined.

5. Conclusions

The present study represents the first attempt aimed at investigating the mediating role of social support in the relationship between EI and occupational stress, providing a contribution in which the three variables are jointly evaluated during the current global emergency. As the crisis that arose after the spread of the COVID-19 virus is still not under control, neither in Italy nor in other countries in the world, it is imperative to acknowledge which factors influence workers' stress in the current circumstances. Our findings offer an opportunity to better understand how these variables are related to occupational stress during the pandemic and provide useful insights to design future interventions aimed at ameliorating wellbeing in working contexts. Overall, the results of our study reported that, except for the OSI PSY, which was directly and indirectly predicted by EI, the other facets of occupational stress were negatively associated with EI only through the mediation of social support. Specifically, social support from family and friends showed a protective role in reducing occupational stress. From this perspective, our findings have practical implications, suggesting both health care services and organizations take care of employees' social relationships and promote and reinforce strong social ties. Specific interventions programs with the purpose of making workers' social relationships stronger and more solid are highly recommended, with a particular focus on the relationships with family members and friends, as both sources of social support have a relevant function in preventing negative outcomes.

Author Contributions: Conceptualization, G.D.V. and P.M.; methodology G.D.V. and P.F.; formal analysis, G.D.V.; investigation, G.D.V. and P.M.; data curation, G.D.V.; writing-original draft preparation, G.D.V.; writing-review and editing, P.F.; supervision, P.F.; project administration, G.D.V. and P.M. All authors have read and agreed to the published version of the manuscript.

Funding: This research received no external funding.

Institutional Review Board Statement: The study was conducted according to the guidelines of the Declaration of Helsinki and approved by the Institutional Review Board (or Ethics Committee) of University of Enna "Kore" (UKE-IRBPSY-03.21.02).

Informed Consent Statement: Informed consent was obtained from all participants involved in the study.

Data Availability Statement: The data presented in this study are available on request from the corresponding author.

Conflicts of Interest: The authors declare no conflict of interest.

References

1. Ganster, D.C.; Rosen, C.C. Work stress and employee health: A multidisciplinary review. *J. Manag.* **2013**, *39*, 1085–1122. [CrossRef]
2. Clarke, S.G.; Cooper, C.L. The risk management of occupational stress. *Health Risk Soc.* **2000**, *2*, 173–187. [CrossRef]
3. van der Ploeg, E.; Kleber, R.J. Acute and chronic job stressors among ambulance personnel: Predictors of health symptoms. *Occup. Environ. Med.* **2003**, *60*, 40–46. [CrossRef]
4. King, K.A.; Vidourek, R.; Schwiebert, M. Disordered eating and job stress among nurses. *J. Nurs. Manag.* **2009**, *17*, 861–869. [CrossRef]
5. Espnes, G.A.; Byrne, D.G. Occupational stress and cardiovascular disease. *Stress Health* **2008**, *24*, 231–238.
6. Bhui, K.S.; Dinos, S.; Stansfeld, S.A.; White, P.D. A Synthesis of the Evidence for Managing Stress at Work: A review of the reviews reporting on Anxiety, Depression, and Absenteeism. *J. Environ. Public Health* **2012**, 1–21. [CrossRef] [PubMed]
7. Imai, H.; Nakao, H.; Tsuchiya, M.; Kuroda, Y.; Katoh, T. Burnout and work environments of public health nurses involved in mental health care. *Occup. Environ. Med.* **2004**, *61*, 764–768. [CrossRef]
8. Mosaredaghrad, A.M. Occupational stress and its consequences: Implications for health policy and management. *Leadersh. Health Serv.* **2014**, *3*, 224–239. [CrossRef]
9. Lambert, E.; Paoline, E.A. The influence of individual, job and organizational characteristics on correctional staff job stress, job satisfaction and organizational commitment. *Crim. Justice Rev.* **2008**, *33*, 541–564. [CrossRef]
10. Kenny, D.T.; Cooper, C.L. Introduction: Occupational stress and its management. *Int. J. Stress Manag.* **2003**, *10*, 275–279. [CrossRef]
11. Beehr, T.A.; Farmer, S.; Glazer, S.; Gudanowski, D.M.; Nair, V.N. The enigma of social support and occupational stress: Source of congruence and gender tole effects. *J. Occup. Health Psych.* **2003**, *8*, 220–231. [CrossRef] [PubMed]
12. Biron, C.; Brun, J.P.; Ivers, H. Extend and sources of occupational stress in university staff. *Work* **2008**, *30*, 511–522. [PubMed]
13. Cheng, Y.; Guo, Y.L.; Yeh, W.Y. A national survey of psychosocial job stressors and their implications for health among working people in Taiwan. *Int. Arch. Occup. Environ. Health* **2001**, *74*, 495–504. [CrossRef]
14. Islam, M.I.; Alam, K.M.W.; Keramat, S.A. Working conditions and occupational stress among nurses in Bangladesh: A cross-sectional pilot study. *J. Public Health* 2021. [CrossRef]
15. Marinaccio, A.; Ferrante, P.; Corfiati, M.; Di Tecco, C.; Rondinone, B.M.; Bonafede, M.; Ronchetti, M.; Persechino, B.; Iavicoli, S. The relevance of socio-demographic and occupational variables for the assessment of work-related stress risk. *BMC Public Health* **2013**, *13*, 1157. [CrossRef]
16. Ryu, G.W.; Yang, Y.S.; Choi, M. Mediating role of coping style on the relationship between job stress and subjective well-being among Korean police officers. *BMC Public Health* **2020**, *20*, 470. [CrossRef]
17. Mensah, A. Job stress and mental well-being among working men and women in Europe: The mediating role of social support. *Int. J. Environ. Res. Public Health* **2021**, *18*, 2494. [CrossRef]
18. Leon, R.D.; Tănăsescu, R.I. Emotional intelligence and occupational stress in Romanian organizations. *Manag. Dyn. Knowl. Econ.* **2018**, *1*, 52–65. [CrossRef]
19. Ogińska-Bulik, N. Emotional intelligence in the workplace: Exploring its effects on occupational stress and health outcomes in human service workers. *Int. J. Occup. Med.* **2005**, *18*, 167–175.
20. Petrides, K.V.; Pita, R.; Kokkinaki, F. The location of trait emotional intelligence in personality factor space. *Br. J. Psychol.* **2007**, *98*, 273–289. [CrossRef]

21. Goleman, D. *Working with Emotional Intelligence*; Bantam: Bloomsbury, London, 1998.
22. Hong, E.; Lee, Y.S. The mediating effect of emotional intelligence between emotional labour, job stress, burnout and nurses' turnover intention. *Int. J. Nurs. Pract.* **2016**, *22*, 625–632. [CrossRef] [PubMed]
23. Krishnakumar, R.; Lalitha, S. A study on emotional intelligence and occupational stress. *IJMCR* **2014**, *2*, 633–636.
24. O'Connor, P.; Nguyen, J.; Anglim, J. Effectively coping with task stress: A study of the validity of the Trait Emotional Intelligence Questionnaire–Short Form (TEIQue–SF). *J. Personal. Assess.* **2017**, *99*, 304–314. [CrossRef] [PubMed]
25. Shukla, A.; Srivastava, R. Examine the relationship between emotional intelligence with Demographic profile, job stress, job satisfaction and turnover intention. *Int. J. Appl. Bus. Econ. Res.* **2016**, *14*, 4887–4900.
26. Anand, P.V. Occupational stress: Relationship with emotional intelligence and coping self-efficacy. *J. Organ. Hum. Behav.* **2019**, *8*, 33–39.
27. Lee, J.H.; Sim, I.-O. Analysis of the relationship between the psychological wellbeing, emotional intelligence, willpower, and job-efficacy of clinical nurses: A structural model application. *Int. J. Environ. Res. Public. Health* **2021**, *18*, 5582. [CrossRef]
28. Bar-On, R.; Brown, J.M.; Kirkcaldy, B.D.; Thorne, E.P. Emotional expression and implications for occupational stress: An application of the Emotional Quotient Inventory (EQ-I). *Personal. Individ. Differ.* **2000**, *28*, 1107–1118. [CrossRef]
29. King, M.; Gardner, D. Emotional intelligence and occupational stress among professional staff in New Zeland. *Int. J. Organ. Anal.* **2006**, *14*, 186–203. [CrossRef]
30. Augusto Landa, J.M.; López-Zafra, E.; Berrios Martos, M.P.; Aguilar-Luzón, M. The relationship between emotional intelligence, occupational stress and health in nurses: A questionnaire survey. *Int. J. Nurs. Stud.* **2008**, *45*, 888–901. [CrossRef]
31. Walia, P.; Tulsi, P.K. Emotional intelligence and occupational stress of college teachers. *J. Organ. Hum. Behav.* **2014**, *3*, 33–39.
32. Lartey, J.K.S.; Amponsah-Tawiah, K.; Osafo, J. Emotional intelligence and perceived organizational support as predictors of emotional exhaustion among nurses and midwives. *Int. J. Worplace Health Manag.*. ahead-of-print. [CrossRef]
33. Dinicola, G.; Julian, L.; Gregorich, S.E. The role of social support in anxiety for persons with COPD. *J. Psychosom. Res.* **2013**, *74*, 110–115. [CrossRef]
34. Ye, X.Q.; Chen, W.Q.; Lin, J.X. Effect of social support on psychological-stress-induced anxiety and depressive symptoms in patients receiving peritoneal dialysis. *J. Psychol. Res.* **2008**, *65*, 157–164. [CrossRef] [PubMed]
35. Kafetsios, K.; Sideridis, G.D. Attachment, social support and well-being in young and older adults. *J. Health Psychol.* **2006**, *11*, 863–875. [CrossRef]
36. Gallagher, E.N.; Vella-Brodrick, D.A. Social support and emotional intelligence as predictors of subjective well-being. *Personal. Individ. Differ.* **2008**, *44*, 1551–1561. [CrossRef]
37. Koydemir, S.; Simsek, Ö.F.; Schütz, A.; Tipandjan, A. Differences in how trait emotional intelligence predicts life satisfaction: The role of affect balance versus social support in India and Germany. *J. Happiness Stud.* **2013**, *14*, 51–66. [CrossRef]
38. Kong, F.; Zhao, J.; You, X. Social support mediates the impact of emotional intelligence on mental distress and life satisfaction in Chinese young adults. *Personal. Individ. Differ.* **2012**, *53*, 513–517. [CrossRef]
39. Kong, F.; Gong, X.; Sajjad, S.; Yang, K.; Zhao, J. How is emotional intelligence linked to life satisfaction? The mediating role of social support, positive affect and negative affect. *J. Happiness Stud.* **2019**, *20*, 2733–2745.
40. Yousaf, S.; Rasheed, M.I.; Hameed, Z.; Luqman, A. Occupational stress and its outcomes: The role of work-social support in the hospitality industry. *Personal. Rev.* **2019**, *49*, 755–773. [CrossRef]
41. Beehr, T.A.; Bowling, N.A.; Bennett, M.M. Occupational stress and failures of social support: When helping hurts. *J. Occup. Health Phychol.* **2010**, *15*, 45–59. [CrossRef]
42. Christo, F.; Kirti, T. Organizational role stress: Impact of manager and peer support. *J. Knowl. Glob.* **2012**, *5*, 1–28.
43. Woodhead, E.L.; Northrop, L.; Edelstein, B. Stress, social support, and burnout among long-term care nursing staff. *J. Appl. Gerontol.* **2016**, *35*, 84–105. [CrossRef] [PubMed]
44. Slaski, M.; Cartwright, S. Health, performance and emotional intelligence: An exploratory study of retail managers. *Stress Health* **2002**, *18*, 63–68. [CrossRef]
45. Jordan, D.J.; Ashkanasy, N.M.; Hartel, C.E.J. Emotional intelligence as a moderator of emotional and behavioral reactions to job insecurity. *Acad. Manag. Rev.* **2002**, *27*, 361–372. [CrossRef]
46. Salovey, P.; Rothman, A.J.; Detweiler, J.B.; Steward, W.T. Emotional states and physical health. *Am. Psychol.* **2000**, *55*, 276–285. [CrossRef]
47. Montes-Berges, B.; Augusto, J.M. Exploring the relationship between perceived emotional intelligence, coping, social support and mental health in nursing students. *J. Psychiatr. Ment. Health Nurs.* **2007**, *14*, 163–171. [CrossRef] [PubMed]
48. Ye, J.; Yeung, D.Y.; Liu, E.S.C.; Rochelle, T.L. Sequential mediating effects of provided and received social support on trait emotional intelligence and subjective happiness: A longitudinal examination in Hong Kong Chinese university students. *Int. J. Psychol.* **2019**, *54*, 478–486. [CrossRef] [PubMed]
49. Jiang, H.; Jia, H.; Zhang, J.; Li, Y.; Song, F.; Yu, X. Nurses' occupational stress and presenteeism: The mediating role of public service motivation and the moderating role of health. *Int. J. Environ. Res. Public Health* **2021**, *18*, 3523. [CrossRef]
50. Magnavita, N.; Soave, P.M.; Ricciardi, W.; Antonelli, M. Occupational stress and mental health among anestetists during the COVID-19 pandemic. *Int. J. Environ. Res. Public Health* **2020**, *17*, 8245. [CrossRef]
51. Al-Mansour, K.; Alfuzan, A.; Alsarheed, D.; Alenexi, M.; Abogazalah, F. Work-related challenges among primary health centers workers during COVID-19 in Saudi Arabia. *Int. J. Environ. Res. Public. Health* **2021**, *18*, 1898. [CrossRef]

52. Soto-Rubio, A.; Giménez-Espert, M.; Prado_Gascó, V. Effect of emotional intelligence and psychological risks of burnout, job satisfaction, and nurses' health during the COVID-19 pandemic. *Int. J. Environ. Res. Public Health* **2020**, *17*, 7998. [CrossRef]
53. Kim, Y.-J.; Lee, S.-Y.; Cho, J.-H. A study on the job retention intention of nurses based on social support in the COVID-19 Situation. *Sustainability* **2020**, *12*, 7276. [CrossRef]
54. Schutte, N.S.; Malouff, J.M.; Hall, L.E.; Haggerty, D.J.; Cooper, J.T.; Golden, C.J.; Dornheim, L. Development and validation of a measure of emotional intelligence. *Personal. Individ. Differ.* **1998**, *25*, 167–177. [CrossRef]
55. Craparo, G.; Magnano, P.; Faraci, P. Psychometric properties of the Italian version of the Self-Report Emotional Intelligence Test (SREIT). *TPM Test. Psychom.* **2014**, *21*, 121–133.
56. Di Fabio, A.; Busoni, L. Misurare il supporto sociale percepito: Proprietà psicometriche della Multidimensional Scale of Perceived Social Support (MSPSS) in un campione di studenti universitari. *Risorsa Uomo* **2008**, *14*, 339–350.
57. Zimet, G.D.; Dahlem, N.W.; Zimet, S.G.; Farley, G.K. The Multidimensional Scale of Perceived Social Support. *J. Personal. Assess.* **1988**, *52*, 30–41. [CrossRef]
58. Cooper, C.L.; Sloan, S.J.; Williams, S. *Occupational Stress Indicator*; NFERNelson: Windsor, UK, 1988.
59. Sirigatti, S.M.; Stefanile, C. *OSI: Occupational Stress Indicator*; Giunti OS-Organizzazioni Speciali: Florence, Italy, 2002.
60. Carríon, G.C.; Nitzl, C.; Roldán, J.L. *Mediation Analyses in Partial Least Squares Structural Equation Modeling: Guidelines and Empirical Examples*; Springer: New York, NY, USA, 2017.

International Journal of
Environmental Research and Public Health

MDPI

Article

Perceived Benefits Matter the Most in COVID-19 Preventive Behaviors: Empirical Evidence from Okara District, Pakistan

Gulzar H. Shah [1,*], Ansar Ali Faraz [2], Hina Khan [2] and Kristie C. Waterfield [1]

1 Department of Health Policy and Community Health, Jiann-Ping Hsu College of Public Health, Georgia Southern University, Statesboro, GA 30460, USA; kwaterfield@georgiasouthern.edu
2 Department of Statistics, Government College University, Lahore 54000, Punjab, Pakistan; ansar.ali@gcu.edu.pk (A.A.F.); hinakhan@gcu.edu.pk (H.K.)
* Correspondence: gshah@georgiasouthern.edu; Tel.: +1-912-478-2419

Abstract: The 2019 coronavirus disease (COVID-19), caused by the SARS-CoV-2 virus has affected the social determinants of health, worsening health inequities and deteriorating healthcare capacities around the globe. The objective of this study is to investigate the COVID-19 prevention behaviors within the framework of the Health Belief Model in the city of Depalpur in the Okara District of Pakistan in May 2020. Using an observational, cross-sectional, and quantitative study design, a face-to-face field survey was conducted during the epidemic of COVID-19 in district Okara, Pakistan. A sample of 500 adults was selected from the city of Depalpur the in Okara district of Pakistan, using a two-stage sampling design with cluster sampling in stage one and systematic random sampling at stage two. A COVID-19 prevention behavior scale was computed based on twelve dichotomous items. Descriptive statistics, analysis of variance (ANOVA), and negative binomial regression analyses were performed. The most common prevention behavior among study participants was avoiding going for walks in the parks (81.0%), followed by not leaving home during the lockdown (72.6%), and washing hands every day with soap and water for 20 s after going out of their home (64.0%). Fewer people exhibited prevention behaviors such as social distancing (e.g., staying at least six feet away from other people) which in the EU was recommended to be a minimum of 1.5–2 m (44.4%) and following all of the basic protective measures (e.g., hand washing, use of a face covering in public, social distancing) in order to protect against COVID-19 (33.0%). The results from the negative binomial regression analysis showed that after controlling for the other HBM constructs and sociodemographic factors, only the perceived benefits of preventative actions showed significant association with the prevention behavior scale (IRR, 1.16; CI, 1.061–1.276; $p < 0.001$). The study findings show that public health interventions attempting to control the spread of COVID-19 in Pakistan may want to affect a change in people's perceived benefits of preventative actions through mass awareness-raising campaigns.

Keywords: COVID-19 preventative behaviors; perceived susceptibility; cues to action; health belief model; health education; Okara, Pakistan

Citation: Shah, G.H.; Faraz, A.A.; Khan, H.; Waterfield, K.C. Perceived Benefits Matter the Most in COVID-19 Preventive Behaviors: Empirical Evidence from Okara District, Pakistan. *Int. J. Environ. Res. Public Health* **2021**, *18*, 6772. https://doi.org/10.3390/ijerph18136772

Academic Editors: Paolo Roma, Merylin Monaro, Cristina Mazza and Paul B. Tchounwou

Received: 22 May 2021
Accepted: 23 June 2021
Published: 24 June 2021

1. Introduction

The SARS-CoV-2 virus, which is the cause of the 2019 coronavirus disease (COVID-19) was first reported in late December 2019 in Wuhan in the Hubei province of China [1–3]. COVID-19 quickly spread globally and was declared a global pandemic by the World Health Organization (WHO) [4]. This viral disease outbreak overwhelmed global healthcare systems and adversely impacted the routine care for many chronic and ambulatory care-sensitive conditions such as cancer, diabetes, and asthma. It particularly affected resource-poor countries [2,5–9]. The intensity of the dreadful effects of coronavirus was faced by both developed and developing countries. However, in countries with weak healthcare system infrastructures, the effects appeared to be intensified [10,11]. In Pakistan, the first two positive cases of COVID-19 were reported on 26 February 2020. According to documentation, both patients had a history of recent travel to Iran [12]. As of 30 March 2021, a total number of 663,200 cases have been reported in Pakistan, a country with a population of 220.9 million people in 2020 [13], with 14,356 deaths attributable to COVID-19, which many believe is a serious under-estimation due to the severe social stigma associated with this disease [14–16].

To curb the spread of COVID-19 in Pakistan, protective measures such as social distancing, frequent hand-washing, and the use of face coverings in public were put into place and are still considered essential, given that vaccine distribution and acceptance has been challenging in subgroups with a distrust of science and western medicine [17]. To complicate the matter, global health inequities in affordability and the timing of COVID-19 vaccine sales to low-income countries (in comparison with high-income countries) still leaves preventive measures such as social distancing and face coverings as the only means to control the spread of SARS-CoV-2 [18]. A lack of trust in scientific facts, in favor of here-say and conspiracy theories, can be challenging to science-based interventions concerning COVID-19 [19]. A distrust in science may lead to an inability to learn or believe even the simplest facts about COVID-19.

In their efforts to overcome and control the spread of SARS-CoV-2, several timely measures were taken by the Pakistan government. These included the first National Coordination Committee (NCC) for COVID-19, which was established to assist with disease surveillance and data-driven decision-making. On 1 May 2020, Pakistan decided to completely close its western border with Afghanistan and Iran (reopened in August 2020). Additionally, all public gatherings and large meetings (≥250 persons or >50% of location capacity) were banned with immediate effect, and all public and private educational institutions (schools, colleges, universities), wedding halls, and cinemas were closed across the country (re-openings began in January 2021) [20,21]. A countrywide face-covering mandate took effect in Pakistan on 31 May 2020. This mandate, along with social distancing, is still in place [22]. Unfortunately, closures of businesses and a rise in unemployment has caused a negative economic impact on the Pakistani economy [23].

In Pakistan and around the globe, pandemic fatigue coupled with low health literacy has created a public health crisis that necessitates the need for broader compliance with local and global guidelines for stopping the spread of SARS-CoV-2 [19]. For public health practitioners to overcome this disease, it is necessary to understand what motivates a person's compliance with preventive measures [24,25]. To generate the practice-relevant evidence, the present study aimed to analyze the correlates of prevention behaviors concerning COVID-19 by using the Health Belief Model (HBM). HBM is one of the models widely used to convey beliefs that can be effective in shaping health protection and health promotion behaviors, including those concerning COVID-19 [26–28]. According to HBM, behavioral beliefs and modifying factors can be effective in shaping behavior, especially when someone is susceptible to the disease (perceived susceptibility), they aware of the threat of the disease to their health (perceived severity), and they also know the benefits of protective measures (perceived benefits) rather than their barriers (perceived barriers) [24]. By using this model, we aimed to determine which domains of the Health Belief Model are associated with COVID-19 prevention behaviors in Pakistan.

2. Materials and Methods

2.1. Study Design

This study used an observational, cross-sectional, and quantitative research design based on primary data collected through a face-to-face survey of the adult population in the city of Depalpur in the Okara district of Pakistan. The population of the city of Depalpur was 74,640 in 2020 [29]. The survey was based on a multi-stage sampling design, with cluster sampling in stage one, each comprising a city block. At the first stage, a total of 30 clusters were included in the sample. The systemic sampling design was used at the second stage of sample selection, with a random start, to sample 17 households per cluster from the clusters sampled at stage one, wherein at least one member of the household was above 19 years of age and was willing to participate in the survey [30].

After random selection of the first household, the subsequent 16 households in each cluster were selected using systematic sampling with equal intervals. When 17 participants (one per household) who agreed to participate in the survey were recruited in a cluster, we terminated the sample selection and moved to the next cluster, finally selecting a sample of 510 participants.

2.2. The Survey Instrument and Data Collection

A structured questionnaire (Figure S1) was constructed by the authors based on the grey literature on COVID-19 attitudes, perceptions, and preventive behaviors recommended by the WHO and other public health organizations [31–33]. For the socio-demographic and household characteristics, the authors developed questions suitable for the local context. The questionnaire was translated into Pakistan's national language, Urdu, and duly pretested and updated before using it for data collection (Figure S1). For pretesting, a convenience sample of 30 participants was recruited from the community in the actual study setting. The participants were asked to complete the questionnaire in a face-to-face setting. After each questionnaire was completed, the participants were asked about their understanding of the questions to assess their face validity. They were also asked which questions they found unclear and why. Based on information from pretesting, the questionnaire was updated. Three interviewers that were trained in face-to-face survey methodology conducted the interviews during the partial lockdown of Pakistan from 17 to 25 May 2020 using the questionnaire. Since the survey participants volunteered to participate at the sampling stage, a total of 500 adults finally participated in the survey with a response rate of 98%.

2.3. Measures

The survey items/questions were mapped to constructs of the health belief model, through research team discussion and consensus on mapping the items that could be assigned to more than one of the HBM constructs. As a result of this process, all survey questions about COVID-19-related awareness, knowledge, attitudes, motivations, and behaviors were grouped into HBM contracts (shown in Table 1).

Table 1. Descriptive Statistics for Socio-Demographic Characteristics of Study Participants, Depalpur City, Pakistan, 2020 (N = 500).

Variable Names	Variable Attributes	Frequency	Percentage
Gender			
	Male	370	74
	Female	130	26
Education			
	No Formal Education	153	30.6
	Less than High School	117	23.4
	High School Diploma	41	8.2
	Intermediate	78	15.6
	Graduation	68	13.6
	Post-Graduation	43	8.6
Age			
	Under 20	78	15.6
	20–34 years	139	27.8
	35–49 years	172	34.4
	50 years and above	111	22.2
Marital Status			
	Single or Separated/Divorced	169	33.8
	Married	331	66.2

Table 1. *Cont.*

Variable Names	Variable Attributes	Frequency	Percentage
Number of Household members			
	Less than five	139	27.8
	Five to Seven	264	52.8
	Eight to Ten	78	15.6
	More than Ten	19	3.8
Monthly Household Income (in Rupees)			
	Less than 30,000 [<$191.45] *	273	54.6
	30,000 to 60,000 [$191.45 to $382.90] *	140	28
	60,000 to 99,000 [$382.90 to $631.78] *	61	12.2
		26	5.2
Medical History			
	No	352	70.4
	Yes	148	29.6
House Ownership			
	No	175	35
	Yes	325	65
Living with Joint Family System			
	No	242	48.4
	Yes	258	51.6

* The equivalent in US Dollars. Abbreviations: N, number of study participants.

The dependent variable, COVID-19 preventive behaviors/actions, was a scale that consisted of the sum of 12 items, each coded as yes = 1 and no/don't know = 0. The other constructs of the Health Belief Model, computed the same way as the dependent variable scale, served as the independent variables which included: (a) perceived susceptibility to disease (3 items); perceived severity of disease (3 items); perceived benefits of preventative action (3 items); perceived barriers of preventative action (2 items); and cues to action (2 items). None of the survey items mapped well to the HBM construct perceived self-efficacy. The sociodemographic variable constituted the construct "modifying factors," which included gender, age, marital status, level of education, occupation, monthly income, and medical history (see supplemental digital Table S1).

2.4. Statistical Methods

Descriptive statistics were used to describe the sample characteristics. To assess the association of individual items in the independent variable scales and demographics variables with COVID-19 preventive behaviors/actions, we computed analysis of variance (ANOVA) with COVID-19 preventive behaviors/actions scale as the dependent variable (mean scale score, 95% confidence interval, and trend p values are reported in Table S1 and Table 2). To assess which constructs of HBM were associated with the COVID-19 preventive behaviors/actions score (i.e., a count variable) after controlling for other variables in the multivariable model, we performed the negative binomial regression. We ruled out the use of Poisson Regression because the dependent variable showed overdispersion (Mean = 5.83; variance = 6.49), which violated the assumption of Poisson Regression. All analyses were conducted using IBM SPSS Statistics Version 25.0 [34].

2.5. Human Subject Protection

This study protocol and materials were reviewed and approved by the Research and Ethics Committee of the Government College University [Protocol number GCU-IIB-380]. Consent was obtained from all participants with a clear declaration that the survey participation was voluntary.

Table 2. Descriptive Statistics for Items, by the Health Belief Model Constructs, Depalpur City, Pakistan, 2020 [N = 500].

Variable Names	Percent "Yes"
Perceived Susceptibility to Disease	
Are you aware of the common sign and symptoms of COVID-19?	60.2
Could people be unintentionally spreading the COVID-19 virus by touching their cell phones?	29.8
Do you think going to school, hospitals or any institution is safe for you?	32.0
Perceived Severity of Disease	
Is COVID-19 not curable in Pakistan?	79.4
Is Pakistan prepared to provide proper care to people affected by COVID-19 epidemic?	31.2
Has COVID-19 lockdown helped Pakistan prevent its spread?	53.0
Perceived Benefits of Preventative Action	
Do you think social distancing is effective in keeping you safe from COVID-19?	52.0
Do you think that the social distancing slows the rate of COVID-19?	53.2
Do you think that schools should resume quickly after the lockdown period with proper emphasis on social distancing, following the Covid-19 pandemic?	54.0
Perceived Barriers of Preventative Action	
Do you believe COVID-19 related self-isolation and social distancing affect the human body or human mind?	66.6
In your opinion, is your life/family affected negatively by social distancing?	61.6
Cues to Action	
Have you ever been tested for COVID-19?	2.6
Are most of your friends practicing the social distancing?	31.4
Individual behaviors/actions concerning COVID prevention	
Are you avoiding going for walks in the parks?	81.0
Do you not leave your home during the lockdown?	72.6
Are you washing your hands everyday with soap and water for 20 s after you go out of your home?	64.0
Are you avoiding any non-essential travel?	63.8
Are you avoiding using public transportation (except essential service workers)?	63.2
Are you avoiding all social gatherings (large and small)?	61.5
Are you avoiding going to the grocery store or pharmacy?	51.0
Are you staying/working at home rather than going to work or school?	44.6
Are you staying six feet away from the other people?	44.4
Are you self-quarantining if you have the virus or believe you have the virus?	34.8
Are you following basic protective measures (e.g., hand washing, use of mask in public, social distancing) to protect yourself against the COVID-19?	33.0
Are you wearing gloves all the time you go out of your home?	14.4

NOTE: there were no questions in the survey to reflect "Perceived Efficacy".

3. Results

3.1. Demographic Information

Table 1 shows the descriptive statistics for demographic variables. Of the 500 survey participants (one member of each household) 74.0% were male and 26.0% were female. Only 46% had at least a 10th-grade education (high school in Pakistan), whereas 30.6% had no formal education. The majority (66.2%) were married, and the remaining 33.8% were single, separated, or divorced. Houses were generally crowded as 72.2% had five or more household members. The majority had a household monthly income less than Rs 30,000 (the equivalent of United States $191). Sixty-five percent owned their homes and 51.6% were living within a joint family system.

3.2. Scale for Overall Prevention Behaviors Score

Descriptive statistics for items in the Health Belief Model, presented in Table 2, show that the most common prevention behavior shown by 81.0% of all of the survey participants was avoiding going for walks in the parks, followed by not leaving home during the lockdown (72.6%), and washing hands every day with soap and water for 20 s after going out of their home (64.0%). Avoiding any non-essential travel, and avoiding public transportation were the next most common actions, reported by 63.8%, and 63.2% of study participants, respectively. Staying six feet away from the other people (44.4%) and following all basic protective measures (e.g., hand washing, the use of a face covering in public, social distancing) to protect yourself against COVID-19 (33.0%) were other notable behaviors. Descriptive statistics for additional HBM items are also presented in Table 2.

Figure 1 shows the frequency of count variables of the overall prevention behavior scale. The distribution of COVID-19 preventive behaviors/actions score of the participants towards COVID-19 resembles the normal distribution. One in three or 32.4% of participants indicated performing eight or more preventive actions. A roughly equal proportion (31.4%) performed four or fewer prevention activities. The remaining 36.2% reported between five and seven COVID-19-related preventive actions.

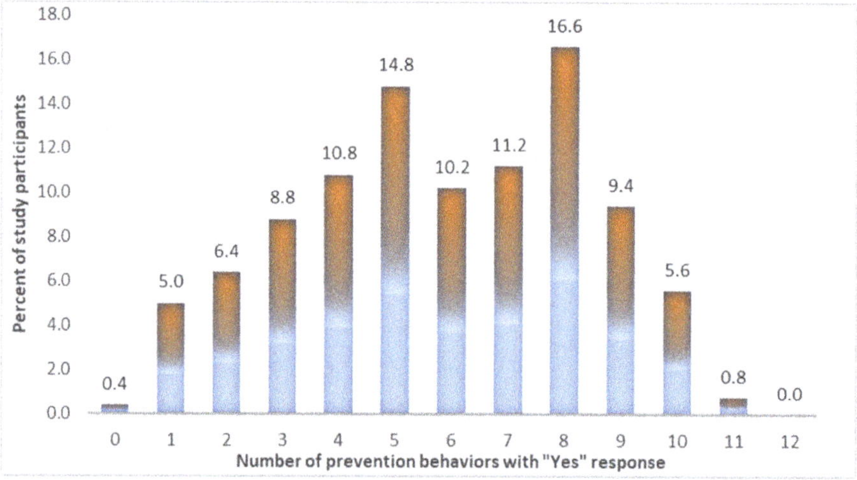

Note: Number of prevention behaviors refers to the number of "yes" responses by each study participant on prevention behaviors items listed in Table 2 under the section "Individual behaviors/actions concerning COVID prevention."

Figure 1. Percent of Study Participants by Number of Prevention Behaviors Concerning COVID-19 (with potential range from 0 to 12).

Table 3 shows the results of the ANOVA, comparing means of preventive behaviors/actions score by COVID-19-related statements representing constructs of the HBM. The mean prevention behavior scores for those answering "yes" were significantly different ($p < 0.05$) than those answering "no" for the individual items/statements representing HBM constructs. These constructs included perceived susceptibility to disease, perceived severity of the disease, perceived benefits of preventative action, perceived barriers of preventative action, and cues to action. Comparisons of means for pension behavior score by socio-demographic characteristics are available in Table S1 (supplemental digital content). The differences in prevention behavior scores were noteworthy by the number of people in the household, with smaller size households having significantly higher scores. The mean score for persons with <5 members in the household was 7.74, whereas for those with ≥10 members the mean prevention score was 3.37. Higher prevention behavior scores were observed for individuals with higher education, those younger than 34 years, single/divorced rather than married, and those who owned their homes.

Table 3. Analysis of variance for comparison of mean number of COVID-19 prevention behavior * by participants' beliefs and perceptions about COVID-19, Depalpur City, Pakistan, 2020.

COVID-19 Beliefs and Perceptions	Attribute	Mean *	95% C.I.		p
			LL	UL	
Do you believe COVID-19 related self-isolation and social distancing affect the human body or human mind?	No/unknown	5.08	4.74	5.43	**<0.001**
	Yes	6.21	6.93	6.49	
Do you think that the social distancing slows the rate of COVID-19?	No/unknown	4.59	4.32	4.85	**<0.001**
	Yes	6.93	6.64	7.22	
In your opinion, is your life/family affected negatively by social distancing?	No/unknown	6.22	5.84	6.6	**0.01**
	Yes	5.59	5.31	5.86	
Has COVID-19 lockdown helped Pakistan prevent its spread?	No/unknown	4.70	4.42	4.98	**<0.001**
	Yes	6.84	5.54	7.13	
Do you think that schools should resume quickly after the lockdown period with proper emphasis on social distancing, following the Covid-19 pandemic?	No/unknown	5.47	5.16	5.78	**0.003**
	Yes	6.14	5.83	6.45	
Do you think going to school, hospitals, or any institution is safe for you?	No/unknown	7.24	6.91	7.56	**<0.001**
	Yes	5.17	4.91	5.44	
Do you think social distancing is effective in keeping you safe from COVID-19?	No/unknown	5.01	4.72	5.3	**<0.001**
	Yes	6.59	6.28	6.9	
Are most of your friends practicing the social distancing?	No/unknown	5.45	5.19	5.71	**<0.001**
	Yes	6.67	6.26	7.08	
Could people be unintentionally spreading the COVID-19 virus by touching their cell phones?	No/unknown	5.61	5.35	5.88	**<0.001**
	Yes	6.35	5.94	6.76	
Is Pakistan prepared to provide proper care to people affected by COVID-19 epidemic?	No/unknown	6.97	6.57	7.38	**<0.001**
	Yes	5.31	5.06	5.57	
Is COVID-19 not curable in Pakistan?	No/unknown	7.29	6.8	7.78	**<0.001**
	Yes	5.45	5.21	6.69	

* Mean Score for the COVID-19 prevention behavior scale [Range 0–12]. The number of prevention behaviors refer to number of "yes" responses by each study participant on prevention behaviors items listed in Table 2 under the section "Individual behaviors/actions concerning COVID prevention". Abbreviations: CI, Confidence Interval; LL, Lower Limit; UL, Upper Limit. Note: Bolded font for p indicates the significance of differences in mean at $p < 0.05$.

3.3. Negative Binomial Regression of COVID-19 Prevention Behaviors

The results from the negative binomial regression analysis (Table 4) showed that after controlling for the other HBM constructs and sociodemographic factors (also referred to as modifying factors in the HBM), only one construct predicted the prevention behavior. The "perceived benefits of preventative actions" score was positively associated with the dependent variable, the individual behaviors/actions concerning COVID prevention (incidence rate ratio, (IRR), 1.16; confidence interval, CI, 1.061–1.276; $p < 0.001$). The IRR 1.16 indicates the estimated ratio of change in prevention behavior score, given a one unit increase in the perceived benefits of prevention score after controlling for all other variables in the model. The other constructs of the HBM, including perceived susceptibility to disease, perceived severity of the disease, perceived benefits of preventative actions, perceived barriers of preventative action, and cues to action had no significant association at $p \leq 0.05$ with the individual behaviors/actions concerning COVID-19 prevention.

Table 4. Negative binomial regression of the COVID-19 prevention behaviors (scale score) *, Depalpur City, Pakistan, 2020.

Demographic Characteristics and HBM Scales	IRR	95% CI		*p*
		LL	UL	
Gender				
Male	0.90	0.72	1.14	0.38
Female (RC)	1.00			
Education				
No Formal Education	0.96	0.59	1.56	0.87
Less than High School	0.83	0.53	1.30	0.42
High School Diploma	0.98	0.60	1.63	0.95
Intermediate	0.90	0.56	1.46	0.67
Graduation	1.04	0.64	1.67	0.89
Post-Graduation (RC)	1.00			
Age				
Under 20	1.07	0.68	1.68	0.76
20–34 years	1.03	0.72	1.48	0.87
35–49 years	0.94	0.70	1.27	0.71
50 years and above (RC)	1.00			
Marital Status				
Single or Separated/Divorced	1.07	0.80	1.44	0.63
Married (RC)	1.00			
Number of Household members				
Less than five	1.50	0.84	2.66	0.17
Five to Seven	1.33	0.77	2.32	0.31
Eight to Ten	1.35	0.74	2.47	0.33
More than Ten (RC)	1.00			
House Ownership				
No	1.15	0.91	1.45	0.24
Yes (RC)	1.00			
Perceived Susceptibility to Disease Scale (3 items)	0.90	0.78	1.05	0.18
Perceived Severity of Disease Scale (3 items)	0.96	0.82	1.12	0.62
Perceived Benefits of Preventative Actions Scale (3 items)	1.16	1.06	1.28	**<0.001**
Perceived Barriers of Preventative Action Scale (2 items)	1.03	0.87	1.22	0.71
Cues to Action Scale (2 items)	1.02	0.81	1.29	0.85

* The COVID-19 preventive behaviors/actions scale score consisted of a sum of 12 items, each coded as yes = 1 and no/don't know = 0, with potential ranges from 0 to 12. Abbreviations: IRR, Incidence Rate Ratios; CI, Confidence Interval; LL, Lower Limit; UL, Upper Limit; RC, Reference Category. Note: Bolded font for *p* indicates the significance of differences in mean at $p < 0.05$.

4. Discussion

Pakistan, like many other countries around the globe, continues to face serious life-threatening effects due to the COVID-19 pandemic, including the emergence of the 3rd wave of COVID-19 cases in late March 2021 [35]. Like many low and middle-income countries (LMICs), Pakistan faces a double jeopardy of COVID-19 vaccine resistance by masses as well as the nonavailability of vaccines. By mid-March 2021, only one million doses of vaccines had been obtained by the Government of Pakistan, with a plan to receive a donation of 10 million doses through Covax, a program co-led by the World Health Organization (WHO) for a country with a population of roughly 221 million [36,37]. With the preventive behaviors being the primary factors that assist with curbing the spread of COVID-19, this study examined the factors associated with COVID-19 prevention behavior using the Health Belief Model. The results of this study revealed that despite the survey being administered during the early months of the pandemic, the overall scores regarding COVID-19, including the perceived susceptibility and perceived severity as well as the perceived benefits and barriers of preventive measures, were high. However, despite apparently adequate levels of knowledge concerning COVID-19 and the necessary preventative measures, the cues to action and the practice of all necessary individual protective behaviors remained relatively low. For instance, social distancing was practiced by 44.4%, and basic protective measures such as handwashing, the use of a face covering in public, etc. to protect against COVID-19 were practiced by 33.0%. Only 16% showed nine or more of the twelve protective behaviors.

Perceived Benefits Matter the Most

One of our central findings is that among all constructs of the HBM, Pakistani people in Depalpur are moved by the perceived benefits of COVID-19 prevention to comply with prevention guidelines issued by the WHO and the Ministry of Health in Pakistan. When compared to recent studies, the cues to action for the study participants could have been influenced by misinformation regarding the causes and treatment of the SARS-CoV-2 virus, distrust in local government and media figures, misplaced assurance in the effectiveness of nonmedical treatments, and conspiracy narratives related to religious beliefs concerning a viral disease like COVID-19 [19,38]. A recent study in Macao, China, found that perceived susceptibility was the motivation for the participants to comply with prevention guidelines [39].

The other constructs of the HBM, such as perceived susceptibility to getting infected, perceived severity of COVID-19 disease, perceived barriers of preventative action, or cues to action did not seem to alter people's prevention behaviors. The lack of response to threats and vulnerability may be attributable to a general culture of external locus of control (i.e., that what happens is often out of people's control) since external threats are numerous and often unavoidable. The general public attitude amounts to "how worse can it get anyway", given the chronic economic and socio-cultural challenges such as high unemployment and underemployment and extreme social and health inequities.

Perceived benefits in the HBM model refer to an individual's assessment of the value or efficacy of engaging in a health-promoting behavior to decrease the risk of disease (in this case, COVID-19). The perceived barriers refer to an individual's feelings concerning the obstacles that may impede their behavior change, which means that when an individual believes a particular action will increase COVID-19 susceptibility or its seriousness, they are thus less likely to engage in preventive behavior [38,39]. Given our findings of primary drivers of behavior change, it is expected that among people of Pakistan, the perceived benefits of any COVID-19 interventions will outweigh the perceived barriers [40,41]. In this study, the perceived barriers were mainly regarding the ability to adhere to recommended social distancing and self-isolation.

In summary, while a range of health behaviors can be explained using HBM, with the exception of benefits, other constructs of HBM did not explain the study participants' health behaviors in Pakistan. In general, when considering individual behavioral change, poor knowledge and risk perceptions of the disease, illness, or situation are usually considered the main barriers to the change. While the ways in which people perceive risk does not necessarily correlate with the actual risk, their risk perception has been shown to influence their decisions to engage in individual protective behaviors [41]. According to the HBM, an increase in perceived threat (a combination of perceived severity and perceived susceptibility) to a particular health problem would increase engagement in behaviors to reduce their risk of developing the health problem [42,43]. Thus, HBM predicts that individuals who believe they are at low risk of developing an illness are more likely to engage in unhealthy, or risky, behaviors, and those that perceive a higher threat have a higher likelihood of engagement in health-promoting behaviors. In this study, the researchers found that a majority of the study participants believed that there was no cure for COVID-19 (79.4%) and doubted the Pakistani government's ability to provide proper care for those affected by the virus (68.8%). These beliefs would imply a high perceived severity of the disease and, when combined with high perceived susceptibility, would result in an overall high perceived threat of the virus among the participants.

While the cues to actions were low, the majority of the survey participants was practicing several of the protective measures such as avoiding visiting any crowded place or any social gathering, non-essential travel, and using public transportation. However, many of the participants were not following the basic protective measures (e.g., hand washing, use of face-covering in public, social distancing) when they left their homes. The lack of performing these behaviors could have been due to a number of issues such as the inability to afford soap, hand sanitizer, and/or gloves, as well as a low health literacy. The practicing of protective behaviors was the highest among those between the ages 20–34 years, females, those with at least a high school education, those in homes with less than five people, and single or separated/divorced individuals.

This study's findings should be interpreted in the context of its several limitations. First, the study is quantitative and cross-sectional. Therefore, many questions could not be answered such as why perceived benefits and not the other constructs of HBM significantly shaped our study participants' prevention behaviors. Secondly, the self-reported data may have suffered some social desirability bias, particularly because the surveys were conducted in a face-to-face setting. Third, the sample size (n = 500) and the study setting may pose limitations on the generalizability of the findings to other parts of the country. Also, we did not conduct the power test to determine the size of the sample, but instead relied on a reasonable sample size estimate. Fourth, the mapping to the HBM model was done after the data collection. It would have been better to do such mapping prior to data collection. Finally, the survey was conducted only three to four months into the COVID-19 pandemic, and some ground realities may have changed later on during the pandemic. Regardless of these limitations, this is an exploratory study that could help the Pakistan government understand the knowledge, attitudes, and practices of the general public concerning COVID-19. Also, the study findings have important implications for COVID-19 vaccine acceptance.

5. Conclusions

This study is the first to highlight the knowledge and behavior of the people of the Okara district in Pakistan towards COVID-19. The study showed that while the knowledge and the perceived threat of COVID-19 were high among the citizens of Depalpur City, Pakistan, overall the attitudes and prevention practices of the participants were lower than expected including hand washing, the use of the face-covering in public, and social distancing. While the availability of the SARS-CoV-02 vaccine is extremely limited at this time, our study findings will provide important guidelines to assist in the continued slowing of the spread of COVID-19 and in finding ways for public health professionals to overcome pandemic fatigue.

Our study implies that the government public health agencies in Pakistan should not only do more awareness-raising and health education concerning prevention practices, but that they should also continue to try to galvanize compliance to prevention guidelines by explaining the benefits of compliance with the prevention guidelines issued by the World Health Organization, Pakistan Government, and public health agencies. Although the vaccine is not broadly available currently, in anticipation of its broader availability awareness-raising is imperative about the benefits of the SARS-CoV-2 vaccine for its acceptance. To counter vaccine resistance, public health agencies may also offer benefits such as free vaccination and paid leaves for government workers on days of vaccine appointments. Educational sessions may be organized through civil society organizations in order to increase the overall health literacy of people and, more specifically, to counter the false rumors and conspiracy theories about COVID-19 prevention, management of symptoms, and benefits and side-effects of the COVID-19 vaccine.

Supplementary Materials: The following are available online at https://www.mdpi.com/article/10.3390/ijerph18136772/s1: Figure S1, Questionnaire in Urdu; Table S1, Comparison of Mean Score for the COVID-19 Prevention Behavior by Socio-Demographic Characteristics, Depalpur City, Pakistan, 2020.

Author Contributions: Conceptualization, A.A.F., H.K., and G.H.S.; methodology, G.H.S.; software, G.H.S.; validation, A.A.F., H.K., and G.H.S.; formal analysis, A.A.F., G.H.S.; investigation, A.A.F.,

H.K.; resources, A.A.F., H.K., G.H.S., and K.C.W.; data curation, A.A.F. and H.K.; writing—original draft preparation, A.A.F., H.K., G.H.S., and K.C.W.; writing—review and editing, A.A.F., H.K., G.H.S., and K.C.W.; visualization, G.H.S. and H.K.; supervision, G.H.S.; project administration, G.H.S. and H.K. All authors have read and agreed to the published version of the manuscript.

Funding: This research received no external funding.

Institutional Review Board Statement: The study was conducted according to the guidelines of the Declaration of Helsinki and approved by the Research and Ethics Committee of the Government College University [Protocol number GCU-IIB-380].

Informed Consent Statement: Informed consent was obtained from all subjects involved in the study.

Data Availability Statement: The data presented in this study are available on request from the corresponding author. The data are not publicly available due to informed consent, assuring the participants that data will not be used for any other purpose other than presenting the findings in a summary form.

Conflicts of Interest: The authors declare no conflict of interest.

References

1. Hui, D.; Azhar, E.I.; Madani, T.; Ntoumi, F.; Kock, R.; Dar, O.; Ippolito, G.; Mchugh, T.; Memish, Z.; Drosten, C.; et al. The continuing 2019-nCoV epidemic threat of novel coronaviruses to global health the latest 2019 novel coronavirus outbreak in Wuhan, China. *Int. J. Infect. Dis.* **2020**, *91*, 264–266. [CrossRef]
2. Zhou, F.; Yu, T.; Du, R.; Fan, G.; Liu, Y.; Liu, Z.; Xiang, J.; Wang, Y.; Song, B.; Gu, X.; et al. Clinical course and risk factors for mortality of adult inpatients with COVID-19 in Wuhan, China: A retrospective cohort study. *Lancet* **2020**, *395*, 1054–1062. [CrossRef]
3. Deng, C.X. The global battle against SARS-CoV-2 and COVID-19. *Int. J. Biol. Sci.* **2020**, *16*, 1676–1677. [CrossRef] [PubMed]
4. Cascella, M.; Rajnik, M.; Aleem, A.; Dulebohn, S.; Di Napoli, R. Features, Evaluation, and Treatment of Coronavirus (COVID-19). In *StatPearls*; StatPearls Publishing: Treasure Island, FL, USA, 2021.
5. Rajan, S.; Akhtar, N.; Tripathi, A.; Kumar, V.; Chaturvedi, A.; Mishra, P.; Sharma, S.; Misra, S.; Gupta, S.; Singh, M. Impact of COVID-19 pandemic on cancer surgery: Patient's perspective. *J. Surg. Oncol.* **2021**, *123*, 1188–1198. [CrossRef] [PubMed]
6. Beran, D.; Perone, S.A.; Perolini, M.C.; Chappuis, F.; Chopard, P.; Haller, D.; Jacquerioz, B.F.; Maisonneuve, H.; Perone, N.; Gastaldi, G. Beyond the virus: Ensuring continuity of care for people with diabetes during COVID-19. *Prim. Care Diabetes* **2021**, *15*, 16–17. [CrossRef] [PubMed]
7. Oreskovic, N.; Kinane, T.; Aryee, E.; Kuhlthau, K.; Perrin, J. The Unexpected Risks of COVID 19 on Asthma Control in Children. *J. Allergy Clin. Immunol. Pract.* **2020**, *8*, 2489–2491. [CrossRef]
8. Tan, E.; Song, J.; Deane, A.; Plummer, M. Global Impact of Coronavirus Disease 2019 Infection Requiring Admission to the ICU. *Chest* **2021**, *159*, 524–536. [CrossRef] [PubMed]
9. Blach, S.; Kondili, L.; Aghemo, A.; Cai, Z.; Dugan, E.; Estes, C.; Gamkrelidze, I.; Ma, S.; Pawlotsky, J.; Razavi-Shearer, D.; et al. Impact of COVID-19 on global HCV elimination efforts. *J. Hepatol.* **2021**, *74*, 31–36. [CrossRef] [PubMed]
10. Lai, C.; Wang, C.; Wang, Y.; Hsueh, S.; Ko, W.; Hsueh, P. Global epidemiology of coronavirus disease 2019 (COVID-19): Disease incidence, daily cumulative index, mortality, and their association with country healthcare resources and economic status. *Int. J. Antimicrob. Agents* **2020**, *55*, 105946. [CrossRef] [PubMed]
11. Arshad, A.S.; Baloch, M.; Ahmed, N.; Ali, A.A.; Iqbal, A. The outbreak of Coronavirus Disease 2019 (COVID-19)—An emerging global health threat. *J. Infect. Public Health* **2020**, *13*, 644–646. [CrossRef] [PubMed]
12. Ali, I. Pakistan Confirms First Two Cases of Coronavirus, Govt. Says, 'No Need to Panic'. Available online: https://www.dawn.com/news/1536792 (accessed on 6 March 2021).
13. Population Mid-2020. Available online: https://www.prb.org/international/indicator/population/table (accessed on 11 June 2021).
14. Ministry of National Health Services COVID-19 Dashboard. Available online: http://COVID.gov.pk/stats/pakistan (accessed on 6 March 2021).
15. World Health Organization. COVID-19 Transmission and Protective Measures. Available online: https://www.who.int/westernpacific/emergencies/covid-19/information/transmission-protective-measures (accessed on 11 January 2021).
16. Ransing, R.; Ramalho, R.; de Filippis, R.; Ojeahere, M.; Karaliuniene, R.; Orsolini, L.; Pinto da Costa, M.; Ullah, I.; Grandinetti, P.; Bytyçi, D.G.; et al. Infectious disease outbreak related stigma and discrimination during the COVID-19 pandemic: Drivers, facilitators, manifestations, and outcomes across the world. *Brain Behav. Immun.* **2020**, *89*, 555–558. [CrossRef] [PubMed]
17. Troiano, G.; Nardi, A. Vaccine hesitancy in the era of COVID-19. *Public Health* **2021**, *194*, 245–251. [CrossRef]
18. Wouters, O.; Shadlen, K.; Salcher-Konrad, M.; Pollard, A.; Larson, H.; Teerawattananon, Y.; Jit, M. Challenges in ensuring global access to COVID-19 vaccines: Production, affordability, allocation, and deployment. *Lancet* **2021**, *397*, 1023–1034. [CrossRef]

19. Haque, A.; Mumtaz, S.; Mumtaz, R.; Masood, F.; Buksh, H.; Ahmed, A.; Khattak, O. Assessment of Knowledge, Perceptions and Perceived Risk Concerning COVID-19 in Pakistan. *J. Epidemiol. Glob. Health* **2021**, *11*, 186–193. [CrossRef]
20. Jamal, S. 10 Steps Pakistan is Taking to Contain Coronavirus Pakistan is Taking Serious Steps to Contain Coronavirus. WORLD ASIA. Available online: https://gulfnews.com/world/asia/pakistan/10-steps-pakistan-is-taking-to-contain-coronavirus-1.70403640 (accessed on 6 March 2021).
21. CDC. *Interim Guidance: Get Your Mass Gatherings or Large Community Events Ready for Coronavirus Disease 2019 (COVID-19)*; Centers for Disease Control and Prevention: Atlanta, GA, USA, 2020.
22. OSAC. Pakistan, Countrywide Mask Mandate. Available online: https://www.osac.gov/Country/Pakistan/Content/Detail/Report/c9c53ff4-e220-4f85-8d20-1a046e0e29bf (accessed on 16 May 2021).
23. Saleem, A. How COVID-19 Crisis Is Affecting Pakistan's Economy. Available online: https://www.dw.com/en/how-the-COVID-19-crisis-is-affecting-pakistans-economy/a-54292705 (accessed on 6 March 2021).
24. Ajilore, K.; Atakiti, I.; Onyenankeya, K. College students' knowledge, attitudes, and adherence to public service announcements on Ebola in Nigeria: Suggestions for improving future Ebola prevention education programmes. *Health Educ. J.* **2017**, *76*, 648–660. [CrossRef]
25. Tachfouti, N.; Slama, K.; Berraho, M.; Nejjari, C. The impact of knowledge and attitudes on adherence to tuberculosis treatment: A case-control study in a Moroccan region. *Pan. Afr. Med. J.* **2012**, *12*, 52. [PubMed]
26. Darvishpour, A.; Vajari, S.M.; Noroozi, S. Can health belief model predict breast cancer screening behaviors? *J. Med. Sci.* **2018**, *6*, 949–953. [CrossRef] [PubMed]
27. Jose, R.; Narendran, M.; Bindu, A.; Beevi, N.; Manju, L.; Benny, P. Public perception and preparedness for the pandemic COVID 19: A Health Belief Model approach. *Clin. Epidemiol. Glob. Health* **2021**, *9*, 41–46. [CrossRef] [PubMed]
28. Wong, M.; Wong, E.; Huang, J.; Cheung, A.; Law, K.; Chong, M.; Ng, R.; Lai, C.; Boon, S.; Lau, J.; et al. Acceptance of the COVID-19 vaccine based on the health belief model: A population-based survey in Hong Kong. *Vaccine* **2021**, *39*, 1148–1156. [CrossRef] [PubMed]
29. Population of Cities in Pakistan (2021). Available online: https://worldpopulationreview.com/countries/cities/pakistan (accessed on 11 June 2021).
30. Wagner, C.; Ramsey, C. A Systematic Approach to Representative Sampling—Sampling Quality Criteria, Material Properties, Theory of Sampling. *J. AOAC Int.* **2015**, *98*, 264. [CrossRef] [PubMed]
31. WHO. *Risk Communication and Community Engagement (RCCE) Action Plan Guidance COVID-19 Preparedness and Response*; World Health Organization: Geneva, Switzerland, 2020.
32. NLM. CDC COVID-19 Community Survey Question Bank (DRAFT). Available online: https://cde.nlm.nih.gov/formView?tinyId=Kcceysolt (accessed on 30 April 2020).
33. Ministry of National Health Services Regulations and Coordination. COVID-19 Health Advisory Platform—Virus Prevention: How to Stay Safe. Available online: https://covid.gov.pk/prevention (accessed on 30 April 2020).
34. *IBM SPSS Statistics for Windows, Version 25.0*; IBM Corp: Armonk, NY, USA, 2017.
35. Gul, A. Pakistan Struggles to Contain Third COVID-19 Wave. VOA News. Available online: https://www.voanews.com/covid-19-pandemic/pakistan-struggles-contain-third-covid-19-wave (accessed on 16 May 2021).
36. Dawn News. Pakistan to Get 10 Million Doses of Vaccine under Covax. Available online: https://www.dawn.com/news/1610392/pakistan-to-get-10mdoses-of-vaccine-under-covax (accessed on 18 March 2021).
37. PRB International Data: Pakistan. Available online: https://www.prb.org/international/geography/pakistan/ (accessed on 18 March 2021).
38. Khan, Y.; Mallhi, T.; Alotaibi, N.; Alzarea, A.; Alanazi, A.; Tanveer, N.; Hashmi, F. Threat of COVID-19 Vaccine Hesitancy in Pakistan: The Need for Measures to Neutralize Misleading Narratives. *Am. J. Trop. Med. Hyg.* **2020**, *103*, 603–604. [CrossRef]
39. Tong, K.; Chen, J.; Yu, E.; Wu, A. Adherence to COVID-19 Precautionary Measures: Applying the Health Belief Model and Generalised Social Beliefs to a Probability Community Sample. *Appl. Psychol. Health Well Being* **2020**, *12*, 1205–1223. [CrossRef]
40. Janz, N.; Becker, M. The Health Belief Model: A Decade Later. *Health Educ. Q.* **1984**, *11*, 1–47. [CrossRef] [PubMed]
41. Van der Pligt, J. Risk Perception and Self-Protective Behavior. *Eur. Psychol.* **1996**, *1*, 34–43. [CrossRef]
42. Glanz, K.; Rimer, B.; Viswanath, K. *Health Behavior and Health Education: Theory, Research, and Practice*, 4th ed.; Jossey-Bass: San Francisco, CA, USA, 2008; pp. 24–40.
43. Rosenstock, I. Historical Origins of the Health Belief Model. *Health Educ. Monogr.* **1974**, *2*, 328–335. [CrossRef]

International Journal of
Environmental Research and Public Health

MDPI

Article

Get Close to the Robot: The Effect of Risk Perception of COVID-19 Pandemic on Customer–Robot Engagement

Jifei Wu [1], Xiangyun Zhang [1], Yimin Zhu [1,*] and Grace Fang Yu-Buck [2]

1 School of Business, Sun Yat-Sen University, No. 135, Xingang Xi Road, Guangzhou 510275, China; wujf8@mail2.sysu.edu.cn (J.W.); zhangxy279@mail3.sysu.edu.cn (X.Z.)
2 School of Business and Technology, University of Maryland Eastern Shore, Princess Anne, MD 21853, USA; fyu@umes.edu
* Correspondence: mnszym@mail.sysu.edu.cn

Abstract: The purpose of this study was to examine the effect of the COVID-19 pandemic on customer–robot engagement in the Chinese hospitality industry. Analysis of a sample of 589 customers using service robots demonstrated that the perceived risk of COVID-19 has a positive influence on customer–robot engagement. The positive effect is mediated by social distancing and moderated by attitudes towards risk. Specifically, the mediating effect of social distancing between the perceived risk of COVID-19 and customer–robot engagement is stronger for risk-avoiding (vs. risk-seeking) customers. Our results provide insights for hotels when they employ service robots to cope with the shock of COVID-19 pandemic.

Keywords: COVID-19 pandemic; service robot; risk perception; customer engagement; protection motivation theory; social distancing

Citation: Wu, J.; Zhang, X.; Zhu, Y.; Yu-Buck, G.F. Get Close to the Robot: The Effect of Risk Perception of COVID-19 Pandemic on Customer–Robot Engagement. *Int. J. Environ. Res. Public Health* **2021**, *18*, 6314. https://doi.org/10.3390/ijerph18126314

Academic Editors: Paolo Roma, Merylin Monaro, Cristina Mazza and Paul B. Tchounwou

Received: 13 April 2021
Accepted: 8 June 2021
Published: 10 June 2021

1. Introduction

The coronavirus disease 2019 (COVID-19) quickly became a global health emergency in 2020. Over 119 million people have contracted COVID-19, with over 2,600,000 deaths by 14 March 2021 [1]. The COVID-19 pandemic threatens not only people's physical and mental health [2,3] but also the global economy, particularly the hospitality industry [4–6]. In 2020, hotel revenue fell by nearly 50% to $84.6 billion across the United States (US) [7], the largest since the Great Depression in 1933 [8]. It is estimated that it will take five years for the US hotel industry to recover to the same level of occupancy, average daily rates, and revenue as pre-COVID-19 times [9]. Therefore, it is crucial to understand how the pandemic has and may reshape customer behavior during and after the COVID-19 pandemic [8,10,11]. During the COVID-19 pandemic, many customers changed their behavior to maintain social distancing and reduce unnecessary social contact [12]. Further, the shift in customer views regarding social contact may fundamentally change the attitudes toward and the demand for service robots without human contact in the hospitality industry [10]. According to the latest report, the sales of service robots increased 24% in 2020, which will keep increasing in the future [13]. To clarify for the rest of the paper, 'service robot(s)' is defined as systems that function as programmable tools that can sense, think, and act to enhance human productivity or engage in social interactions [14,15].

In order to meet this shift in consumer demands, some hotels began to offer contactless services, such as service robots, to replace the frontline staff or allow guests not to have to interact with frontline staff [8,14,15]. For example, Hilton and Marriott hotels across California introduced service robots to provide services, such as delivering baggage and cleaning rooms [16]. Similarly, some restaurants now employ robots to take on some traditionally human work, including ordering, cooking, and delivering dishes [17]. During the COVID-19 pandemic, employing service robots reduces the possibility of transmitting the virus, which will also help service firms improve efficiency and decrease costs [8,18].

Prior research mostly focused on the general service scenario and documented reactance against service robots and other autonomous technologies [19–23]. For instance, customers preferred human labor over robot labor in the case of services or products with higher symbolic value [19] because human (vs. robotic) labor helps consumers meet unique needs. There are some studies showing that people will express a preference in specific contexts [24,25]. For example, people tend to rely on robots in objective decision-making tasks [24,25]. In the public health emergency of COVID-19, the perceived risk of customers has attached importance to academia and industry [4,5]. Prior qualitative studies explored how perceived risk is one of the key antecedents in many customer decisions. However, there was little research focus, at least from a quantitative perspective, on perceived risk and customer decision-making during a public health emergency. Therefore, we examined the impact of the perceived risk of COVID-19 on customer–robot engagement in a quantitative way.

Protection motivation theory [26,27] posits that individuals will estimate the level of threat. They will further build coping strategies when exposed to threat information related to health with their protective motivations. Accordingly, we draw on protection motivation theory [26–28] to understand whether and how the perceived risk of the COVID-19 pandemic influences customer engagement with service robots. We specifically investigate social distancing as the mediator of the relationship between customers' perceived risk for the COVID-19 pandemic and customer–robot engagement. Finally, we explore the moderating effect of attitudes towards risk and health consciousness on the relationship between perceived risk of COVID-19 and customer engagement with service robots.

This study offers the following contributions. First, we employ protection motivation theory [26–28] to understand how the perceived risk of the COVID-19 pandemic influences consumer engagement with service robots. Previous research demonstrates that customers show negative attitudes to service robots in general service contexts [19–23]. This study finds that customers will be more engaged with service robots in public health emergencies, especially in the global pandemic of COVID-19. This study also aims to broaden the theoretical lens with regard to service robots and further expands the application scope of protection motivation theory. Second, following protection motivation theory [26,27], we explore the underlying mechanism of the relationship between the perceived risk of COVID-19 and customer engagement with service robots. The perceived risk of COVID-19 has a positive impact on social distancing and further influences customer engagement with service robots, which makes a contribution to understanding customer engagement with service robots in a public health emergency. Third, we clarify the boundary conditions of the indirect effect of COVID-19 on customer engagement with service robots. In particular, the mediating effect of social distancing between the perceived risk of COVID-19 and customer engagement with service robots is stronger for risk-avoiding customers compared to risk-seeking customers.

In the following sections, we first review the literature on service robots to develop our hypotheses. Next, we conduct a survey to test these hypotheses. Finally, we discuss theoretical contributions and managerial implications and conclude with limitations and future research directions.

2. Theoretical Framework

2.1. Perceived Risk of COVID-19 and Customer–Robot Engagement

Perceived risk is a variable connected to the probability and magnitude of the occurrence of the damage [29], which has been widely used to explain consumer behavior [8,30]. Consumer behavior researchers define perceived risk in terms of uncertainty and consequences. Perceived risk increases with higher levels of uncertainty and/or the chance of greater associated negative consequences [31,32]. For example, if a consumer is considering choosing an unfamiliar restaurant for a dinner party, the perceived risk associated with this choice could arise because he or she does not know how the dishes of the restaurant will taste (uncertainty) and is worried that guests will think poorly of him or her if it is not a good restaurant (negative consequences). In this study, we defined the perceived risk of COVID-19 as the possibility and the consequences as COVID-19 causing illness or death [32–34].

Following protection motivation theory [26,27], we propose that perceived risk triggered by COVID-19 will improve customer–robot engagement. When customers perceive the COVID-19 pandemic is riskier, they will perceive higher levels of uncertainty and infection [34,35]. Human beings are often regarded as the natural carriers of COVID-19 transmission. To reduce the risk of COVID-19, customers tend to be more avoidant of social contact with human staff than in normal times and attempt to social distance in restaurants and hotels. Indeed, choosing to engage with a service robot means a kind of avoidance to human frontline staff, which is viewed as a protection from being infected with COVID-19 [8,27,28].

Service robots can function as programmable tools which can sense, think, and act to engage in social interactions [14,15,36,37]. Prior research mostly focused on the context of general service, and this research documented reactance against service robots and autonomous technologies [19–23]. However, little focus has been on situations where customers would possibly prefer service robots and would choose to engage with a service robot [24,25]. It is necessary to explore the antecedents for consumers to engage with service robots and the underlying psychological mechanisms.

As a way to build and strengthen customer relationships, customer engagement can help companies establish a competitive advantage and achieve success [38]. In addition, it can improve customer satisfaction, customer loyalty, and company performance [38–40]. Customer engagement is a multi-dimensional concept, including cognitive, emotional, and behavioral aspects [39,41–43]. Previous research has focused on customer engagement with brand [38,40], community [41], organization [44], and other traditional objectives in marketing practice.

In the COVID-19 pandemic, there are more service robots employed in hotels and restaurants [8,15], and customers have begun to engage with these robots. Thus, we introduce the concept of customer engagement in the context of service robots. We define customer engagement with service robots (hereafter, customer–robot engagement) as the customer's personal connection to service robots that goes beyond transactions, including the reaction in cognition, emotion, and behavior [45]. Customer–robot engagement in the context of hospitality consists of attention, enthusiasm, and interaction. Attention describes the extent of customer paying attention to the service robot [46,47]; enthusiasm means how much customers are interested in and excited to be serviced by the robot [44,48]; interaction points out that customers share service robots with others or participate in online and offline activities related to a service robot [44,48,49].

In line with protection motivation theory [26,27,50], we explore the effect of the perceived risk of COVID-19 on customer–robot engagement in the hotel and restaurant industries. Protection motivation theory is a social cognitive theory that was developed to explain the influences of health threats on health attitudes and behaviors [26–28,50]. According to protection motivation theory, threat appraisal and coping appraisal are the two primary drivers of health behavior [26,27]. Threat appraisal refers to the beliefs about the severity and susceptibility of the health threat to the given person, which concerns the health threat's nature, its seriousness, and the propensity of it eventuating to affect the individual [26,34]. Coping appraisal refers to the evaluation of health-protective behavioral alternatives and responses to avoid the health threat and the negative consequences, which focuses on the effectiveness of the coping response to impede the threat [26,27,51].

When risk is salient, customers will show preference to a hotel with a service robot staff than a hotel with human staff [52]. Thus, when perceived risk is higher, the motivation is stronger to cope with uncertainty and the subsequent consequences [26,27,50]. Further, customers will be more likely to engage with the service robots. Specifically, customers will pay more attention to the service robots, will show more enthusiasm to the service robots, and will have more interactions with the service robots.

In sum, it is expected that customers who perceive a high level of risk for COVID-19 are more likely to engage with service robots in restaurant and hospitality services. Therefore, we propose the following hypotheses:

Hypothesis 1a (H1a). *Perceived risk of COVID-19 has a positive influence on customer–robot engagement, i.e., customers' attention to service robots.*

Hypothesis 1b (H1b). *Perceived risk of COVID-19 has a positive influence on customer–robot engagement, i.e., customers' enthusiasm in service robots.*

Hypothesis 1c (H1c). *Perceived risk of COVID-19 has a positive influence on customer–robot engagement, i.e., customers' interaction with service robots.*

2.2. The Mediating Role of Social Distancing

According to protection motivation theory, a higher perceived health risk will lead customers to take measures to avoid risks and protect themselves [28,51]. For example, consumers will reduce some purchase behaviors, which may bring negative consequences [53]. They will become more conservative, keeping their distance from new or risky products and services [30]. In addition, they will avoid negative consequences and take measures to protect themselves. In the COVID-19 pandemic, social distancing is a crucial measure to protect consumers when they perceive the risk of transmission of COVID-19.

Many governments promoted the prevention policies of quarantining or social distancing (i.e., maintaining a physical distance of at least 2 m (6 feet)) [54]. It is hard to keep this precise distance for most customers. A number of customers choose to reduce social contacts in order to maintain social distance and to comply with the government's prevention policy. Furthermore, many consumers have reduced their international travel and have cut down on other journeys to areas with large COVID outbreaks. In the COVID-19 pandemic, social distancing is considered an effective coping response to impede the COVID-19 threat [8,10,54]. For this reason, customers will be more willing to socially distance as a kind of protective or coping method in service places when they perceive a higher risk of COVID-19. Once they perceive higher health risks, they will be active in protective behaviors [26,51], including social distancing. Even after quarantine, many customers continued to engage in avoidance and protective behaviors in service places [55]. Therefore, we infer that the perceived risk of COVID-19 will influence customer social distancing.

If customers want to keep social distancing, they will likely embrace some options that would reduce social contact [52]. Once the intention of keeping social distancing was increased, people would decrease direct contact with humans [12], and they will be more likely to engage with services provided by robots. Even service robots can convey social meaning to customers; they are mostly functional service robots, which perform labor such as ordering or delivery in hotels and restaurants. Engagement with service robots can replace some social activities and reduce risk from social contact. Engagement with a service robot can be viewed as a protective method, which can reduce the chances of being infected with COVID-19. In addition, service robots can interact with humans, replacing some social activities [23]. Based on these functions of service robots, service robots can be an attractive consumer choice to protect themselves in the context of a public health emergency. Specifically, customers will pay more attention to service robots, show more enthusiasm to service robots, and seek out more interactions with service robots. As a result, we propose the following hypotheses:

Hypothesis 2a (H2a). *The influence of perceived risk of COVID-19 on customer–robot engagement, i.e., customers' attention to service robots.*

Hypothesis 2b (H2b). *The influence of perceived risk of COVID-19 on customer–robot engagement, i.e., customers' enthusiasm in service robots.*

Hypothesis 2c (H2c). *The influence of perceived risk of COVID-19 on customer–robot engagement, i.e., customers' interaction with service robots, is mediated by the social distancing.*

2.3. The Moderating Role of Risk Attitude

Risk attitude can reflect a decision-maker's intention to take risk or to avoid risk [56]. There are two types of attitudes towards risk: risk-seeking and risk-avoiding. Because many decisions are generally made under a certain level of risk, the optimal choice from a decision-maker's perspective will depend on their attitude towards risk [56,57]. Risk attitude has a wide-ranging influence on many types of behaviors, including trading behavior, unhealthy behavior, and work practice [58–60]. In this paper, we propose that attitude towards risk moderates the mediating effect of social distancing.

Due to the individual differences in risk attitude, some are motivated by the upside potential of risk, while others are motivated by security [61]. For risk seekers, perceived risk will not hinder their subsequent behaviors in some choices, including investment decisions and treatment choices [56,59,62]. So, risk seekers will pay less attention to service robots, show less enthusiasm to service robots, and will have fewer interactions with service robots when they perceive a high risk of COVID-19. But for the risk-averse, coping with risk is emphasized. And risk-averse individuals are less likely to engage in risky or unhealthy behavior, such as smoking and drug use [58]. If the perceived risk of COVID-19 is large, risk-averse consumers will engage in protective behavior to avoid infection, leading to social distancing and more customer–robot engagement. Thus, we propose that the positive effect of the perceived risk of COVID-19 on social distancing is stronger for risk-averse (vs. risk-seeking) customers.

Hypothesis 3a (H3a). *The mediating effect of social distancing on the relationship between the perceived risk of COVID-19 and customer–robot engagement, i.e., customers' attention to service robots.*

Hypothesis 3b (H3b). *The mediating effect of social distancing on the relationship between the perceived risk of COVID-19 and customer–robot engagement, i.e., customers' enthusiasm in service robots.*

Hypothesis 3c (H3c). *The mediating effect of social distancing on the relationship between the perceived risk of COVID-19 and customer–robot engagement, i.e., customers' interaction with service robots, is stronger for risk-averse (vs. seeking) customers.*

2.4. The Moderating Role of Health Consciousness

Health consciousness is defined as the tendency to focus on one's health [63]. Health-conscious consumers are more concerned about their health. They strive to enhance and/or sustain their healthy state by engaging in healthy behaviors [64]. Health consciousness fosters preventive health care, positive attitudes towards healthy behaviors, and purchases of health-related products [65–67]. Individuals will react to health risks differently depending on their level of health consciousness [68]. We propose that health consciousness will moderate the mediating effect of social distancing.

Health consciousness greatly impacts how people respond to health-related messages [63]. Health-conscious consumers will pay much more attention to coping with the risk related to health [64]. Researchers report a positive correlation between health consciousness and the tendency to engage in preventive health behaviors [65]. If people with high health consciousness perceive a higher level of health risk from COVID-19, they will keep social distancing and will be more likely to engage with robots. In contrast, for consumers who are not health-conscious, the effect of perceived risk on social distancing is reduced. They will also not pay more attention to service robots, they will show less enthusiasm to service robots, and they will have fewer interactions with service robots. Thus, we propose:

Hypothesis 4a (H4a). *The mediating effect of social distancing on the relationship between perceived risk of COVID-19 and customer–robot engagement, i.e., customers' attention to service robots.*

Hypothesis 4b (H4b). *The mediating effect of social distancing on the relationship between perceived risk of COVID-19 and customer–robot engagement, i.e., customers' enthusiasm in service robots.*

Hypothesis 4c (H4c). *The mediating effect of social distancing on the relationship between perceived risk of COVID-19 and customer–robot engagement, i.e., customers' interaction with service robots, is stronger for high (vs. low) health consciousness customers.*

In sum, the proposed model is summarized in Figure 1.

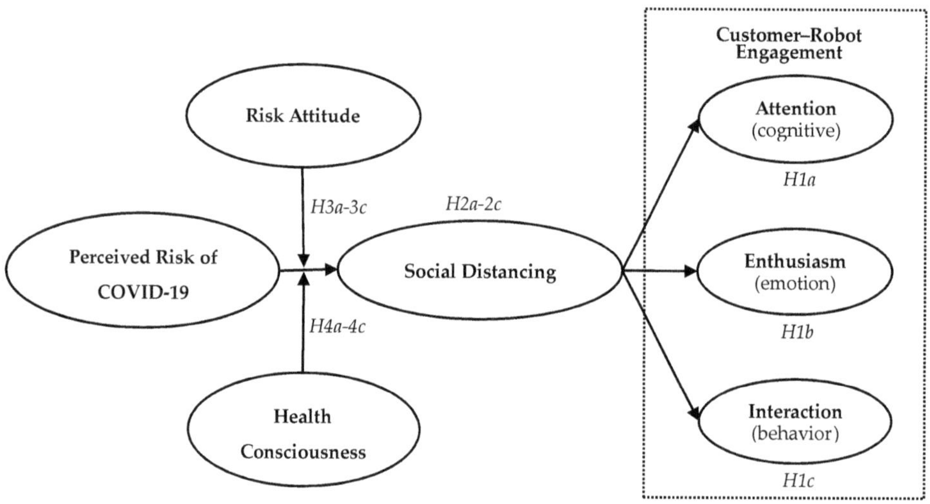

Figure 1. Conceptual model.

3. Methodology

3.1. Sample

A survey was employed to collect data to test our hypotheses. We chose the customers in Chinese hospitality with service robots as our respondents. There are two reasons. First, the early outbreak of COVID-19 caused unprecedented damage to hospitality industries in China. Second, several service robots have been introduced into hotels and restaurants in China, which provide services, such as ordering and delivering dishes, without social contact.

All multi-item constructs with existing scales were adapted from the public health, marketing, and tourism literature. Validity and reliability were ensured by back-translating the measures. Before our formal survey, we invited three professors and three Ph.D. students to examine our items. Based on their advice, we revised the items and kept the language of the items clear, specific, and simple. We also conducted a pretest and collected 53 surveys. Factor analysis was used to test the reliability and validity of the measurements to ensure the effectiveness of the follow-up survey further.

In order to guarantee the confidentiality and quality of data, we invited our respondents randomly who received service from service robots in the hospitality industry. Every responder spent about 4 min answering this survey. All respondents received RMB 4 as the payment for participating in our survey.

We invited the respondents randomly to participate in our survey through Wenjuanxing (www.wjx.cn) (accessed on 1 September 2020), the biggest survey platform in China. A total of 647 customers were invited from September to October 2020, when the outbreak of COVID-19 was largely controlled in China. In total, 36 respondents were removed because of failing to pass the attention tests or taking an unreasonably short time (i.e., less than two minutes), and 22 respondents were discarded because of incomplete data (>25% of answers omitted). In total, 589 valid respondents were used for our data analyses. The demographic profile of the sample is shown in Table 1. Approximately 51.4% of respondents were female, whereas 48.6% were male. The majority of respondents were aged 18 to 39 (97.1%) and had a bachelor's degree (68.8%). In addition, a plurality (38.5%) of respondents had yearly income between 5000 and 100,000 RMB. The second most common was an income between 10,000 and 20,000 RMB (24.7%), and third most common was less than 5000 RMB (20%).

Table 1. Demographic profile of the sample (n = 589).

Variable	Items	(%)
Gender	Male	48.6
	Female	51.4
Age	18–24	32.9
	25–29	35.5
	30–39	28.7
	40–56	2.9
Education level	High school degree	5.9
	Associate degree	11.7
	Bachelor's degree	68.8
	Graduate degree	13.6
Income level	Under RMB 5000	20.0
	RMB 5001–10,000	38.5
	RMB 10,001–20,000	24.7
	RMB 20,001–50,000	11.7
	Over RMB 50,000	5.1

3.2. Measures

We measured all multi-item constructs with existing scales drawn from the tourism, marketing, and healthcare literature (Table 2), using a seven-point Likert format (1 = strongly disagree/not at all; 7 = strongly agree/extremely) for all measures except attitude towards risk. Specifically, the perceived risk of COVID-19 was evaluated by two items adopted from Kim and Lee [69] and Gidengil et al. [68]. Customer–robot engagement was measured in terms of attention (four items), enthusiasm (four items), and interaction (four items), and this methodology was adopted from So et al. [40]. Social distancing was assessed by two items adopted from Aron [70]. Health consciousness was evaluated by four items adopted from Gineikiene et al. [71].

Table 2. Measured items and CFA results.

Variables and Items	Factor Loading	α	CR	AVE
Perceived risk	-	0.77	0.89	0.81
What are the chances of you getting infected with the COVID-19?	0.91			
What are the chances of you dying from the COVID-19 if infected?	0.89			
Social distancing	-	0.93	0.97	0.94
To what extent do you think you have an increased need to keep social distancing from others during the COVID-19?	0.97			
To what extent do you engage in social distancing during the COVID-19?	0.97			
Customer engagement				
Attention	-	0.90	0.93	0.76
I pay a lot of attention to service robots.	0.89			
I like to learn more about service robots.	0.89			
I like learning more about service robots.	0.88			
Anything related to service robots grabs my attention.	0.85			
Enthusiasm	-	0.89	0.92	0.75
I am passionate about service robots.	0.88			
I am enthusiastic about service robots.	0.90			
I feel excited about service robots.	0.87			
I love this service provided by robots.	0.83			
Interaction	-	0.87	0.91	0.72
In general, I like to get involved in service robot discussions.	0.87			
In general, I thoroughly enjoy exchanging ideas with other people about service robots.	0.86			
I often browse new topics about service robots.	0.85			
I often share my experience with service robots.	0.81			
Perceived ease of use	-	0.90	0.93	0.76
Learning to operate the robot is easy for me.	0.87			
I find it easy to get the robot to do what I want it to do.	0.85			
It is easy for me to become skillful at using the robot.	0.90			
I find the robot easy to use.	0.88			
Perceived usefulness	-	0.85	0.90	0.69
Using the robot enhances service effectiveness in the hotel.	0.80			
Using the robot enhances service productivity.	0.85			
I find the robot useful in hotel service.	0.84			
Using the robot improves service performance in hotels.	0.83			
Health consciousness	-	0.79	0.87	0.62
I reflect on my health a lot.	0.70			
I'm very self-conscious about my health.	0.80			
I am generally attentive to my inner feelings about my health.	0.84			
I am constantly examining my health.	0.80			

Notes. α, Cronbach's α; CR, composite reliability; AVE, average variance extracted.

We also measured risk attitude, which was assessed by five items adopted from Forlani and Mullins [56], i.e., please answer the following 5 items by circling the alternative ("a" or "b") you would feel most comfortable with. 1. (a) an 80% chance of winning $400, or (b) receiving $320 for sure; 2. (a) receiving $300 for sure, or (b) a 20% chance of winning $1500; 3. (a) a 90% chance of winning $200, or (b) receiving $180 for sure; 4. (a) receiving $160 for sure, or (b) a 10% chance of winning $1600; 5. (a) a 50% chance of winning $500, or (b) receiving $250 for sure.

Finally, the technology adoption model (TAM) literature deems that the customer behavior related to new technology is influenced by customer-level factors regarding the perception of the technology, such as perceived usefulness and perceived ease of use [72–74]. Therefore, we controlled for these variables to minimize omitted variable bias and account for factors that explained significant variance in customer–robot engagement. We measured perceived usefulness (four items) and perceived ease of use (four items) with scales adapted from Davis [72] and Agarwal and Karahanna [75].

3.3. Data Analysis

The marker-variable technique [76] was employed to statistically identify the threat of common method variance (CMV). Confirmatory factor analysis (CFA) was performed to evaluate the reliability and validity, and structural equation modeling (SEM) was used to examine the direct hypotheses. The bootstrapping approach based on PROCESS macro [77] was used for the mediation analysis and moderation analysis. These data analyses were conducted using SPSS 24.0 (IBM, New York, NY, USA) and Amos 24.0 (IBM, New York, NY, USA).

4. Results

4.1. Reliability and Validity

Table 2 shows the results of the CFA. The CFA resulted in good fit to the data ($\chi^2/df = 2.71$, GFI = 0.904, NFI = 0.980, CFI = 0.987, RMSEA = 0.054). The composite reliability was satisfactory as well because the scores for all constructs ranged from 0.87 to 0.97, exceeding the threshold of 0.70 [78]. Our instrument demonstrated convergent validity, as all factor loadings were between 0.70 and 0.97, greater than the recommended minimum value of 0.50; the average variance extracted (AVE) for each construct ranged from 0.62 to 0.94, greater than the threshold of 0.50 [79].

The results in Table 3 indicated strong discriminant validity, as the square roots of the AVEs were greater than the corresponding correlation coefficients between the factors [80].

Table 3. Descriptive statistics and correlation matrix of variables.

Variables	1	2	3	4	5	6	7	8	9
1. Perceived risk	**0.90**								
2. Social distancing	0.48 **	**0.97**							
3. Attention	0.52 **	0.54 **	**0.87**						
4. Enthusiasm	0.51 **	0.52 **	0.81 **	**0.87**					
5. Interaction	0.55 **	0.58 **	0.85 **	0.80 **	**0.85**				
6. Perceived ease of use	0.28 **	0.35 **	0.48 **	0.41 **	0.47 **	**0.87**			
7. Perceived usefulness	0.31 **	0.33 **	0.52 **	0.597 **	0.54 **	0.46 **	**0.83**		
8. Health consciousness	0.33 **	0.37 **	0.47 **	0.469 **	0.49 **	0.41 **	0.40 **	**0.79**	
9. Education level	−0.05	0.00	0.04	0.02	0.02	0.02	0.03	0.02	-
Mean	5.53	5.52	5.63	5.84	5.63	5.51	6.04	5.85	2.90
SD	1.07	1.27	1.08	1.01	1.04	1.11	0.81	0.86	0.69

Note. The values in the lower diagonal of the table present the correlations between the constructs, while the values in the diagonal of the table present the square roots of the AVEs of the construct. We take education level as a marker variable 3. $n = 589$; ** $p < 0.01$. Bold: the square roots of the AVE for each construct.

4.2. Common Method Biases

In addition to program control, statistical controls were employed to assess the common method biases [81]. We adopted the marker-variable technique [76] to evaluate the common method biases and took education level as a marker variable. As shown in Table 3, the correlation coefficients between education level and other variables were small and not significant ($p > 0.05$). Thus, the common method biases of the current study were not serious.

Consistent with Schwepker's study [82], we used the CFA technique to analyze potential common method biases using three steps. First, all items point to the latent variables measured by them, and carry out an eight-factor model CFA, which is called model C1. Second, all items point to the common method biases variable and carry out a one-factor model CFA, which is called model C2. Third, we compared the changes of model fit indexes of model C1 and model C2 to see if a significant difference emerged. As shown in Table 4, the model fit of model C2 was poor, and the model fix of model C1 improved fit significantly ($\Delta\chi^2 = 3735.12$, $\Delta df = 28$, $p < 0.001$), which means that the common method biases were not serious.

Table 4. The CFA model fit.

Index	χ^2	df	CFI	NFI	GFI	RMSEA
Model C1 (eight factors model)	871.85	322	0.987	0.980	0.904	0.054
Model C2 (one factor model)	4606.97	350	0.914	0.907	0.641	0.144
Δ = Model C2-Model C1	$\Delta\chi^2 = 3735.12$	$\Delta df = 28$			$p < 0.001$	

4.3. Hypotheses Test

4.3.1. Direct Effect Analysis

Figure 2 displays the results of the SEM. The fit indices ($\chi^2/df = 2.81$, GFI = 0.921, NFI = 0.945, CFI = 0.958, RMSEA = 0.073) indicated the appropriateness of the structural model [83]. The path coefficients from perceived risk of COVID-19 to customers' attention ($\beta = 0.422$, $p < 0.001$), enthusiasm ($\beta = 0.342$, $p < 0.001$), and interaction ($\beta = 0.358$, $p < 0.001$) were positively significant. Therefore, H1a, H1b and H1c, which proposed that perceived risk of COVID-19 had positive influences on customer–robot engagement (respectively, attention, enthusiasm, and interaction), were supported.

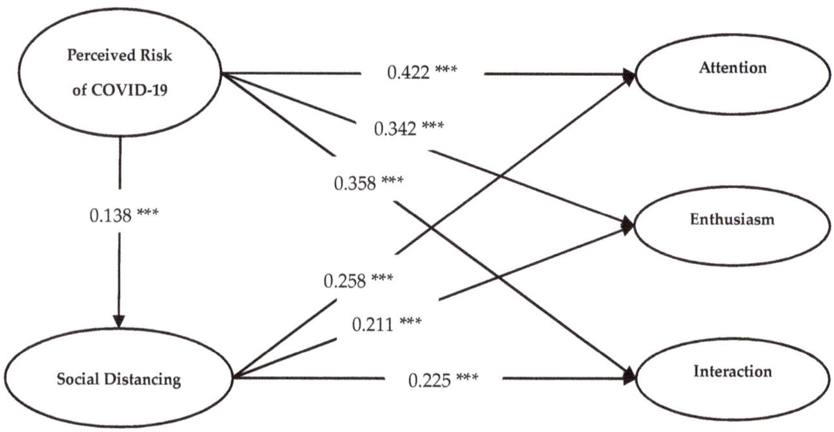

Figure 2. Results of the SEM. *** $p < 0.001$.

4.3.2. Mediation Analysis

The bootstrapping procedure suggested by Hayes [77], with a confidence level of 95% and a bootstrap sample of 5000, was conducted to examine the mediating effect of social distancing. The analysis results are shown in Table 5. All the concerned 95% confidence intervals excluded the value of 0, thereby supporting the indirect effects of perceived risk on customers' attention (effect size = 0.088, SE = 0.026, 95% CI [0.045, 0.147]), enthusiasm (effect size = 0.078, SE = 0.021, 95% CI [0.043, 0.126]) and interaction (effect size = 0.099, SE = 0.024, 95% CI [0.059, 0.151]) through social distancing. These results implied social distancing mediated the effect of perceived risk on customer–robot engagement. Therefore, H2a, H2b, and H2c were supported.

Table 5. Mediating effect analysis results ($n = 589$).

Paths	Indirect Effect	LLCI	ULCI
Perceived risk → Social distancing → Attention	0.088	0.045	0.147
Perceived risk → Social distancing → Enthusiasm	0.078	0.043	0.126
Perceived risk → Social distancing → Interaction	0.099	0.059	0.151

Note. LL = Lower limit, UL = Upper limit, CI = Confidence interval. SE, standardized error. The value of the lower limit and that of the upper limit constitutes a confidence interval.

4.3.3. Moderated Mediation Analysis

The bootstrapping procedure based on PROCESS macro suggested by Hayes [77], with a confidence level of 95% and a bootstrap sample of 5000, was conducted to examine H3a to H4c. The analysis results are shown in Table 6.

Table 6. Analysis results for the moderated mediation effect (n = 589).

DVs	Moderator	Indirect Effect of Social Distancing				Moderated Meditation Effect			
		Effect Size	SE	LLCI	ULCI	Index	SE	LLCI	ULCI
Attention	Risk attitude (seeking)	0.061	0.026	0.022	0.125	0.052	0.020	0.018	0.098
	Risk attitude (avoid)	0.113	0.032	0.060	0.182				
Enthusiasm	Risk attitude (seeking)	0.054	0.021	0.021	0.106	0.046	0.018	0.016	0.085
	Risk attitude (avoid)	0.100	0.025	0.057	0.156				
Interaction	Risk attitude (seeking)	0.069	0.025	0.029	0.128	0.059	0.022	0.019	0.104
	Risk attitude (avoid)	0.127	0.029	0.078	0.189				
Attention	Health consciousness (high)	0.088	0.026	0.050	0.149	0.006	0.010	−0.013	0.025
	Health consciousness (low)	0.077	0.027	0.035	0.139				
Enthusiasm	Health consciousness (high)	0.078	0.020	0.045	0.126	0.005	0.008	−0.012	0.021
	Health consciousness (low)	0.068	0.022	0.033	0.119				
Interaction	Health consciousness (high)	0.098	0.023	0.060	0.152	0.007	0.011	−0.015	0.027
	Health consciousness (low)	0.087	0.026	0.045	0.143				

Notes. DVs, dependent variables; SE, standardized error. Perceived risk as the independent variable, social distancing as the mediator, risk attitude, and health consciousness as moderators. Confidence interval (CI) was 95%. Bootstrap samples was 5000. Risk attitude: seeking = 0, avoiding = 1.

Using attitude towards risk as the moderator, the index of moderated mediation was significant for customers' attention (index = 0.052, SE = 0.020, 95% CI [0.018, 0.098]), enthusiasm (index = 0.046, SE = 0.016, 95% CI [0.016, 0.085]), and interaction (index = 0.059, SE = 0.022, 95% CI [0.019, 0.104]), indicating the risk attitude moderated the mediating effects of social distancing on the relationship between perceived risk and customers' attention, enthusiasm, and interaction. For risk-averse consumers, social distancing significantly mediated the effect of perceived risk on customers' attention (effect size = 0.113, SE = 0.032, 95% CI [0.060, 0.182]), enthusiasm (effect size = 0.100, SE = 0.025, 95% CI [0.057, 0.156]), and interaction (effect size = 0.127, SE = 0.029, 95% CI [0.078, 0.189]). In contrast, for risk-seeking customers, the mediating effect of social distancing on customers' attention (effect size = 0.061, SE = 0.026, 95% CI [0.022, 0.125]), enthusiasm (effect size = 0.054, SE = 0.032, 95% CI [0.060, 0.182]), and interaction (effect size = 0.069, SE = 0.025, 95% CI [0.029, 0.128]) were still significant but the effect sizes were considerably reduced (attention: from 0.113 to 0.061; enthusiasm: from 0.100 to 0.054; interaction: from 0.127 to 0.069, Figure 3A), in support of H3a, H3b, and H3c.

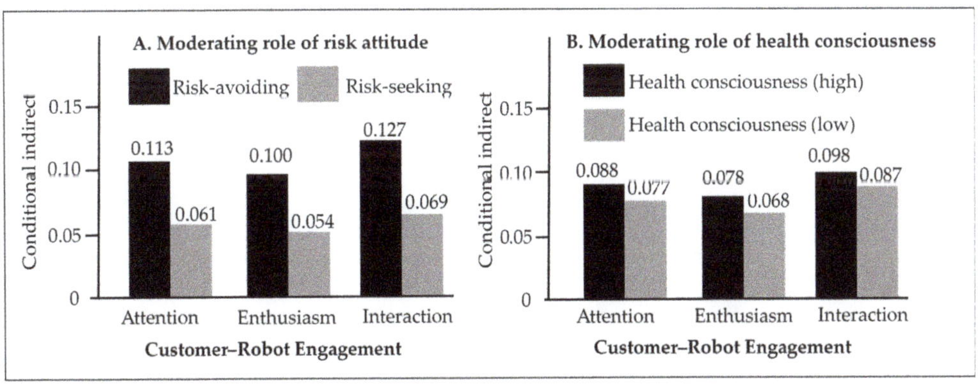

Figure 3. Conditional indirect effect. (**A**) Moderating role of risk attitude. (**B**) Moderating role of health consciousness.

Using health consciousness as the moderator, the index of moderated mediation was not significant for customers' attention (index = 0.006, SE = 0.010, 95% CI [−0.013, 0.025]), enthusiasm (index = 0.005, SE = 0.008, 95% CI [−0.012, 0.021]), and interaction (index = 0.007, SE = 0.011, 95% CI [−0.015, 0.027]), which means the mediating effect sizes were not significant difference between high and low levels of health consciousness (Figure 3B). Specifically, for high levels of health consciousness, social distancing significantly mediated the effect of perceived risk on customers' attention (effect size = 0.088, SE = 0.026, 95% CI [0.050, 0.149]), enthusiasm (effect size = 0.078, SE = 0.020, 95% CI [0.045, 0.126]), and interaction (effect size = 0.098, SE = 0.023, 95% CI [0.060, 0.152]). Similarly, for low levels of health consciousness, the mediating effect of social distancing on customers' attention (effect size = 0.077, SE = 0.027, 95% CI [0.035, 0.139]), enthusiasm (effect size = 0.068, SE = 0.022, 95% CI [0.033, 0.119]), and interaction (effect size = 0.087, SE = 0.026, 95% CI [0.045, 0.143]) were still significant. There was no significant difference between high and low levels of health consciousness (attention: from 0.088 to 0.077; enthusiasm: from 0.078 to 0.068; interaction: from 0.098 to 0.087, Figure 3B). These results showed that the health consciousness did not moderate the mediating effects of social distancing on the relationship between perceived risk and customer–robot engagement. Thus, H4a, H4b, and H4c were not supported.

5. General Discussion

5.1. Theoretical Implications

These findings of this paper have three theoretical contributions. First, most previous research suggested that people have a negative attitude toward service robots in the general service context [19–23]. In addition, prior research lacks the discussion of the role of perceived risk during the COVID-19 pandemic from a quantitative aspect [4–8]. This study focuses on the effect of the perceived risk of COVID-19 on customer–robot engagement in a public health emergency, which expands the perspective of research on service robots. Prior research on customer engagement has mostly discussed customer engagement with brand, product, and community [38,40,42,44,45]. In addition, there is some research arguing that anthropomorphism increases the intention of the customer to be close to other objects, including service robots [84,85]. The anthropomorphism of service robots provides another choice for social activities when there is a higher level of the perceived risk of COVID-19. This work discusses the impact of the perceived risk of a public health emergency on customer–robot engagement, which is rapidly developing and popular among hospitality industries. We find that the perceived risk in the COVID-19 pandemic can increase customer–robot engagement significantly, which extends the research on the antecedents of customer engagement. And the results of this study enrich the research of anthropomorphism and service robots as it replaces some human staff in hotels and restaurants.

Second, we are the first to utilize protection motivation theory [26,50] to explain how customers' perceived risk of the COVID-19 pandemic influences customer–robot engagement. Our results showed that the perceived risk of COVID-19 positively influences customer–robot engagement through the influence of social distancing, which helps deepen understanding of customer–robot engagement in a public health emergency. In line with protection motivation theory [26,50], this work demonstrated that social distancing is a critical form of coping strategy when faced with the risk of COVID-19. This research emphasized the importance of social distancing in coping with COVID-19 [12].

Third, we discussed the moderators of the indirect effect of COVID-19 on customer–robot engagement. In particular, the mediating effect of social distancing on the relationship between perceived risk of COVID-19 and customer–robot engagement is stronger for risk-averse (vs. risk-seeking) customers. This work enriches the knowledge of coping strategies for COVID-19, and it offers a new context to improve and innovate robot services.

5.2. Practical Implications

This study has important implications for how to utilize service robots to cope with a public health emergency. First, we provide some advice as to whether a company should introduce service robots into frontline service. For managers in the hospitality industry, it is one of the important decisions to employ service robots. The reason why many companies chose not to employ service robots without social contact is that previous research and reports have shown that customers have negative attitudes to service robots and other automation technologies [19–23]. The outbreak of COVID-19 had a large impact on hospitality industries whose business mainly depend on social contact. Our work found that customers tend to engage with service robots during the COVID-19 pandemic, which supports the decision for managers to introduce service robots into their hotels and restaurants. Indeed, employing service robots may help companies improve performance, reduce the risk of infection for human staff, and maintain customer relationships during the COVID-19 pandemic.

Second, this work explored the motivation of customer–robot engagement in the pandemic. When people are exposed to health threat information, their protection motivation will be enhanced [26,50], and they will increase customer–robot engagement. Thus, we suggest that hotels and restaurants should employ service robots effectively based on the protection motivation of customers. For instance, companies can emphasize the security of a service robot to cater to the customers' need for protection during and after the COVID-19 pandemic. In addition, this paper showed that social distancing is a mediator in the relationship between perceived risk and customer–robot engagement. Accordingly, hotels and restaurants may encourage, via promotional campaigns, customers to accept service from robot staff to maintain social distancing better.

Third, some references have been provided by this research for companies that aim to improve customer engagement with advanced technologies. Customer engagement can develop and strengthen customer relationships, and it can enhance customer loyalty and company performance. We demonstrated the forms of customer–robot engagement, including attention, enthusiasm, and interaction [39,41,43]. The conclusion of this paper offers guidance for designing a customer engagement approach in the hospitality industry. For example, hotels and restaurants may develop campaigns that focus on customer experience with service robots to improve attention, enthusiasm, and interaction of customers. If customers are attracted to participate in campaigns to engage with service robots, customer loyalty and company performance will be improved.

5.3. Limitations and Future Research

There are limitations and opportunities for future research. First, there are many antecedents for customers to engage with service robots. However, this study focused on one key antecedent, the perceived risk of COVID-19, and its effect on customer–robot engagement. Other antecedents for customer–robot engagement should be explored in a follow-up study.

Second, we explored the impact of the perceived risk of COVID-19 on customer–robot engagement and the underlying mechanism. However, it is worth exploring whether this effect will shift after the COVID-19 pandemic. Future research may discuss the long-term influence of the public health emergency through collecting data after the COVID-19 pandemic ends. In addition, the role of perception of social ability for service robots can be explored in the future. If customers can perceive more social closeness with service robots, they will have more intention to engage with service robots.

Finally, we deepened the understanding of the influence of the perceived risk of COVID-19 on customer–robot engagement based on protection motivation theory. And we discussed the mediation of social distancing. There are other possible theories or mechanisms to explain this influence. One future direction for research is the uncanny valley [86], which may explain the reason why customers choose to engage with a service robot or not. Moreover, the motivation of customer–robot engagement varies according to the service context. Future research may discuss customer engagement in other contexts.

6. Conclusions

Although previous research analyzed customer attitudes toward service robots in the general service context [37,87–89], little research has taken the context of public health emergencies into account. This research aimed to discuss the effect of perceived risk on customer–robot engagement in a public health emergency.

First, perceived risk has a positive impact on customer–robot engagement. Specifically, when the perceived risk of COVID-19 is at a higher level, there will be stronger protection motivation for customers. Further, customers will pay more attention to service robots, show more enthusiasm towards service robots, and have more interaction with service robots. Before the COVID-19 pandemic, most researchers found that customers preferred service to be provided by human staff rather than by service robots [37,87–89]. Some research on anthropomorphism argued that anthropomorphized robots could reduce resistance from customers [84,85]. Anthropomorphism of the robot is the attribution of human characteristics or behavior to a robot [84,85]. When customers perceived the risk of COVID-19 is at a higher level, customers have a tendency to reduce contact with human staff. Based on the anthropomorphism of service robots, people can contact service robots to replace some social activities. Service robots satisfy the social need of customers and take the place of human staff to some extent. Our findings suggest that due to the higher perceived risk of COVID-19, customers are more likely to engage with service robots in the pandemic. It demonstrates that COVID-19 may accelerate the process of acceptance of service robots without human contact, as service robots decrease the risk of COVID infection by allowing easier social distancing.

Second, our research showed that social distancing is the mediator of the effect of the perceived risk of COVID-19 on customer–robot engagement. When customers are faced with health threat information regarding COVID-19, they will appraise the health threat, including its severity and their vulnerability. When the perceived risk is high, customers will adopt a coping strategy and will strengthen social distancing, which will further enhance customer–robot engagement.

Third, risk attitude moderates the mediating effect of social distancing. The mediating effect of social distancing on the relationship between perceived risk of COVID-19 and customer–robot engagement is stronger for risk-averse (vs. risk-seeking) customers. Compared to risk-seeking customers, customers who are risk-averse attach more importance to the coping strategy of health risk. Thus, when they perceive a higher level of risk, their willingness to socially distance will be stronger, and their engagement with service robots will be enhanced.

Finally, our results showed that the moderating effect of health consciousness is not significant. The possible reason is that the direct effect of perceived risk diminishes the moderating effect of health consciousness. In the COVID-19 pandemic, customers with different levels of health consciousness perceive a high level of risk, and they would like to keep social distance and further choose to engage with service robots.

Author Contributions: Conceptualization, J.W., X.Z., G.F.Y.-B., and Y.Z.; methodology, J.W.; writing original draft preparation, J.W., G.F.Y.-B., and X.Z.; writing—review and editing, J.W. and X.Z.; visualization, J.W. and X.Z.; supervision, J.W. and Y.Z.; project administration and funding acquisition, J.W. and Y.Z. All authors have read and agreed to the published version of the manuscript.

Funding: This work was supported by the National Natural Science Foundation of China [72002225, 71672203]; the Fundamental Research Funds for the Central Universities [20wkpy12]; the China Postdoctoral Science Foundation (2020M683148), and the Natural Science Foundation of Guangdong Province (2021A1515011899, 2017A030313406).

Institutional Review Board Statement: Because of the observational nature of the study, and in the absence of any involvement of therapeutic medication, no formal approval of the Institutional Review Board of the local Ethics Committee was required. Nonetheless, all subjects were informed about the study, and participation was on a fully voluntary basis. Participants were assured of confidentiality and anonymity of the information associated with the surveys. The study was conducted according to the guidelines of the Declaration of Helsinki.

Informed Consent Statement: Informed consent has been obtained from all subjects involved in this study to publish this paper.

Data Availability Statement: The dataset used in this research are available upon request from the corresponding author. The data are not publicly available due to restrictions, i.e., privacy or ethical.

Conflicts of Interest: The authors declare no conflict of interest.

References

1. World Health Organization. WHO Coronavirus (COVID-19) Dashboard. 2021. Available online: https://covid19.who.int/ (accessed on 15 March 2021).
2. Fiorillo, A.; Gorwood, P. The consequences of the COVID-19 pandemic on mental health and implications for clinical practice. *Eur. Psychiatry* **2020**, *63*, 1–4. [CrossRef] [PubMed]
3. Warren, A.M.; Zolfaghari, K.; Fresnedo, M.; Bennett, M.; Pogue, J.; Waddimba, A.; Zvolensky, M.; Carlbring, P.; Powers, M.B. Anxiety sensitivity, COVID-19 fear, and mental health: Results from a United States population sample. *Cogn. Behav. Ther.* **2021**, *50*, 204–216. [CrossRef] [PubMed]
4. Foroudi, P.; Tabaghdehi, S.A.H.; Marvi, R. The gloom of the COVID-19 shock in the hospitality industry: A study of consumer risk perception and adaptive belief in the dark cloud of a pandemic. *Int. J. Hosp. Manag.* **2021**, *92*, 102717. [CrossRef]
5. Lazzerini, M.; Putoto, G. COVID-19 in Italy: Momentous decisions and many uncertainties. *Lancet Glob. Health* **2020**, *8*, e641–e642. [CrossRef]
6. Nicola, M.; Alsafi, Z.; Sohrabi, C.; Kerwan, A.; Al-Jabir, A.; Iosifidis, C.; Agha, M.; Agha, R. The socio-economic implications of the coronavirus pandemic (COVID-19): A review. *Int. J. Surg.* **2020**, *78*, 185–193. [CrossRef] [PubMed]
7. AHLA. AHLA's State of the Hotel Industry 2021. 2021. Available online: https://www.ahla.com/sites/default/files/2021_state_of_the_industry_0.pdf (accessed on 20 February 2021).
8. Shin, H.; Kang, J. Reducing perceived health risk to attract hotel customers in the COVID-19 pandemic era: Focused on technology innovation for social distancing and cleanliness. *Int. J. Hosp. Manag.* **2020**, *91*, 102664. [CrossRef]
9. Dobrosielski, C. HotelAVE Projects 5-Year Recovery for Hotels after COVID-19. 2020. Available online: https://www.hotelmanagement.net/asset-management/hotelave-projects-5-year-recovery-for-hotels-after-covid-19 (accessed on 20 February 2021).
10. Sheth, J. Impact of Covid-19 on consumer behavior: Will the old habits return or die? *J. Bus. Res.* **2020**, *117*, 280–283. [CrossRef]
11. Blom, V.; Lönn, A.; Ekblom, B.; Kallings, L.; Väisänen, D.; Hemmingsson, E.; Andersson, G.; Wallin, P.; Stenling, A.; Ekblom, Ö.; et al. Lifestyle Habits and Mental Health in Light of the Two COVID-19 Pandemic Waves in Sweden, 2020. *Int. J. Environ. Res. Public Health* **2021**, *18*, 3313. [CrossRef]
12. Jawaid, A. Protecting older adults during social distancing. *Science* **2020**, *368*, 145. [CrossRef]
13. Strategy Analytics. Service Robot Sales Volumes Surge as COVID-19 Pandemic Drives Demand. 2021. Available online: https://www.businesswire.com/news/home/20210223005410/en/ (accessed on 2 March 2021).
14. Jiang, Y.; Wen, J. Effects of COVID-19 on hotel marketing and management: A perspective article. *Int. J. Contemp. Hosp. Manag.* **2020**, *32*, 2563–2573. [CrossRef]
15. Jones, P.; Comfort, D. The COVID-19 crisis and sustainability in the hospitality industry. *Int. J. Contemp. Hosp. Manag.* **2020**, *32*, 3037–3050. [CrossRef]
16. Oliver, D. If You Stay at a Hotel during the Pandemic, a Robot May Deliver Wine to Your Door or Clean Your Room. 2020. Available online: https://www.usatoday.com/story/travel/hotels/2020/07/27/hotels-using-robots-delivery-cleaning-amid-covid-19-pandemic/5494472002/ (accessed on 5 March 2021).
17. Liu, Q. COVID-19 Boosting Taste for Robot Waiters, Chefs. 2020. Available online: https://www.shine.cn/news/nation/2007212570/ (accessed on 11 March 2021).
18. Rodriguez-Lizundia, E.; Marcos, S.; Zalama, E.; Gómez-García-Bermejo, J.; Gordaliza, A. A bellboy robot: Study of the effects of robot behaviour on user engagement and comfort. *Int. J. Hum. Comput. Stud.* **2015**, *82*, 83–95. [CrossRef]
19. Granulo, A.; Fuchs, C.; Puntoni, S. Preference for Human (vs. Robotic) Labor is Stronger in Symbolic Consumption Contexts. *J. Consum. Psychol.* **2021**, *31*, 72–80. [CrossRef]
20. Leung, E.; Paolacci, G.; Puntoni, S. Man Versus Machine: Resisting Automation in Identity-Based Consumer Behavior. *J. Mark. Res.* **2018**, *55*, 818–831. [CrossRef]
21. Longoni, C.; Bonezzi, A.; Morewedge, C.K. Resistance to Medical Artificial Intelligence. *J. Consum. Res.* **2019**, *46*, 629–650. [CrossRef]
22. Luo, X.; Tong, S.; Fang, Z.; Qu, Z. Frontiers: Machines vs. Humans: The Impact of Artificial Intelligence Chatbot Disclosure on Customer Purchases. *Mark. Sci.* **2019**, *38*, 937–947. [CrossRef]
23. Mende, M.; Scott, M.L.; Van Doorn, J.; Grewal, D.; Shanks, I. Service Robots Rising: How Humanoid Robots Influence Service Experiences and Elicit Compensatory Consumer Responses. *J. Mark. Res.* **2019**, *56*, 535–556. [CrossRef]
24. Castelo, N.; Bos, M.W.; Lehmann, D.R. Task-Dependent Algorithm Aversion. *J. Mark. Res.* **2019**, *56*, 809–825. [CrossRef]
25. Logg, J.M.; Minson, J.A.; Moore, D.A. Algorithm appreciation: People prefer algorithmic to human judgment. *Organ. Behav. Hum. Decis. Process.* **2019**, *151*, 90–103. [CrossRef]
26. Rogers, R.W. Cognitive and physiological processes in fear appeals and attitude change: A revised theory of protection motivation. In *Social Psychophysiology: A Sourcebook*; Cacioppo, J., Petty, R., Eds.; Guilford Press: New York, NY, USA, 1983; pp. 153–176.
27. Rogers, R.W.; Deckner, C.W. Effects of fear appeals and physiological arousal upon emotion, attitudes, and cigarette smoking. *J. Pers. Soc. Psychol.* **1975**, *32*, 222–230. [CrossRef]
28. Rippetoe, P.A.; Rogers, R.W. Effects of components of protection-motivation theory on adaptive and maladaptive coping with a health threat. *J. Pers. Soc. Psychol.* **1987**, *52*, 596–604. [CrossRef]

29. Slovic, P.; Finucane, M.L.; Peters, E.; MacGregor, D.G. Risk as Analysis and Risk as Feelings: Some Thoughts about Affect, Reason, Risk, and Rationality. *Risk Anal.* **2004**, *24*, 311–322. [CrossRef] [PubMed]
30. Hwang, J.; Choe, J.Y. Exploring perceived risk in building successful drone food delivery services. *Int. J. Contemp. Hosp. Manag.* **2019**, *31*, 3249–3269. [CrossRef]
31. Campbell, M.C.; Goodstein, R.C. The Moderating Effect of Perceived Risk on Consumers' Evaluations of Product Incongruity: Preference for the Norm: Table 1. *J. Consum. Res.* **2001**, *28*, 439–449. [CrossRef]
32. Guerhan-Canli, Z.; Batra, R. When corporate image affects product evaluations: The moderating role of perceived risk. *J. Mark. Res.* **2004**, *41*, 197–205. [CrossRef]
33. Barattucci, M.; Chirico, A.; Kuvačić, G.; de Giorgio, A. Rethinking the Role of Affect in Risk Judgment: What We Have Learned From COVID-19 During the First Week of Quarantine in Italy. *Front. Psychol.* **2020**, *11*, 554561. [CrossRef] [PubMed]
34. Carpenter, C.J. A Meta-Analysis of the Effectiveness of Health Belief Model Variables in Predicting Behavior. *Health Commun.* **2010**, *25*, 661–669. [CrossRef]
35. Itani, O.S.; Hollebeek, L.D. Light at the end of the tunnel: Visitors' virtual reality (versus in-person) attraction site tour-related behavioral intentions during and post-COVID-19. *Tour. Manag.* **2021**, *84*, 104290. [CrossRef]
36. Bartneck, C.; Forlizzi, J. A design-centred framework for social human-robot interaction. In Proceedings of the RO-MAN 2004. 13th IEEE International Workshop on Robot and Human Interactive Communication (IEEE Catalog No.04TH8759), Kurashiki, Japan, 22 September 2004; Institute of Electrical and Electronics Engineers (IEEE): Piscataway, NJ, USA, 2005; pp. 591–594.
37. Chan, A.P.H.; Tung, V.W.S. Examining the effects of robotic service on brand experience: The moderating role of hotel segment. *J. Travel Tour. Mark.* **2019**, *36*, 458–468. [CrossRef]
38. Hollebeek, L.D.; Glynn, M.S.; Brodie, R.J. Consumer Brand Engagement in Social Media: Conceptualization, Scale Development and Validation. *J. Interact. Mark.* **2014**, *28*, 149–165. [CrossRef]
39. Brodie, R.J.; Ilic, A.; Juric, B.; Hollebeek, L. Consumer engagement in a virtual brand community: An exploratory analysis. *J. Bus. Res.* **2013**, *66*, 105–114. [CrossRef]
40. So, K.K.F.; King, C.; Sparks, B. Customer engagement with tourism brands scale development and validation. *J. Hosp. Tour. Res.* **2012**, *38*, 304–329. [CrossRef]
41. Bowden, J.L. The Process of Customer Engagement: A Conceptual Framework. *J. Mark. Theory Pr.* **2009**, *17*, 63–74. [CrossRef]
42. Dessart, L.; Veloutsou, C.; Morgan-Thomas, A. Capturing consumer engagement: Duality, dimensionality and measurement. *J. Mark. Manag.* **2016**, *32*, 399–426. [CrossRef]
43. Morgan-Thomas, A.; Dessart, L.; Veloutsou, C. Digital ecosystem and consumer engagement: A socio-technical perspective. *J. Bus. Res.* **2020**, *121*, 713–723. [CrossRef]
44. Salanova, M.; Agut, S.; Peiro, J.M. Linking Organizational Resources and Work Engagement to Employee Performance and Customer Loyalty: The Mediation of Service Climate. *J. Appl. Psychol.* **2005**, *90*, 1217–1227. [CrossRef]
45. Van Doorn, J.; Lemom, K.N.; Mittal, V.; Nass, S.D.P.; Pirner, P.; Verhoef, P.C. Customer engagement behaviour: Theoretical foundations and research directions. *J. Serv. Res.* **2010**, *13*, 253–266. [CrossRef]
46. Rothbard, N.P. Enriching or Depleting? The Dynamics of Engagement in Work and Family Roles. *Adm. Sci. Q.* **2001**, *46*, 655. [CrossRef]
47. Scholer, A.A.; Higgins, E.T. Exploring the complexities of value creation: The role of engagement strength. *J. Consum. Psychol.* **2009**, *19*, 137–143. [CrossRef]
48. Schaufeli, W.; Bakker, A.B. Job demands, job resources, and their relationship with burnout and engagement: A multi-sample study. *J. Organ. Behav.* **2004**, *25*, 293–315. [CrossRef]
49. Verhoef, P.C.; Reinartz, W.J.; Krafft, M. Customer Engagement as a New Perspective in Customer Management. *J. Serv. Res.* **2010**, *13*, 247–252. [CrossRef]
50. Bui, L.; Mullan, B.; McCaffery, K. Protection motivation theory and physical activity in the general Population: A systematic literature review. *Psychol. Health Med.* **2013**, *18*, 522–542. [CrossRef] [PubMed]
51. Chen, F.; Dai, S.; Zhu, Y.; Xu, H. Will concerns for ski tourism promote pro-environmental behaviour? An implication of protection motivation theory. *Int. J. Tour. Res.* **2019**, *22*, 303–313. [CrossRef]
52. Kim, S.S.; Kim, J.; Badu-Baiden, F.; Giroux, M.; Choi, Y. Preference for robot service or human service in hotels? Impacts of the COVID-19 pandemic. *Int. J. Hosp. Manag.* **2021**, *93*, 102795. [CrossRef]
53. Lim, N. Consumers' perceived risk: Sources versus consequences. *Electron. Commer. Res. Appl.* **2003**, *2*, 216–228. [CrossRef]
54. Brindal, E.; Ryan, J.C.; Kakoschke, N.; Golley, S.; Zajac, I.T.; Wiggins, B. Individual differences and changes in lifestyle behaviours predict decreased subjective well-being during COVID-19 restrictions in an Australian sample. *J. Public Health* **2021**. [CrossRef]
55. Crandall, C.S.; Moriarty, D. Physical illness stigma and social rejection. *Br. J. Soc. Psychol.* **1995**, *34*, 67–83. [CrossRef]
56. Forlani, D.; Mullins, J.W. Perceived risks and choices in entrepreneurs' new venture decisions. *J. Bus. Ventur.* **2000**, *15*, 305–322. [CrossRef]
57. Fraenkel, L.; Bogardus, S.T.; Wittink, D.R. Risk-attitude and patient treatment preferences. *Lupus* **2003**, *12*, 370–376. [CrossRef]
58. Barsky, R.B.; Juster, F.T.; Kimball, M.S.; Shapiro, M.D. Preference Parameters and Behavioral Heterogeneity: An Experimental Approach in the Health and Retirement Study. *Q. J. Econ.* **1997**, *112*, 537–579. [CrossRef]
59. Fellner-Röhling, G.; Maciejovsky, B. Risk attitude and market behavior: Evidence from experimental asset markets. *J. Econ. Psychol.* **2007**, *28*, 338–350. [CrossRef]

60. Kulas, J.T.; Komai, M.; Grossman, P.J. Leadership, information, and risk attitude: A game theoretic approach. *Leadersh. Q.* **2013**, *24*, 349–362. [CrossRef]
61. Lopes, L.L. Between Hope and Fear: The Psychology of Risk. *Adv. Exp. Soc. Psychol.* **1987**, *20*, 255–295. [CrossRef]
62. van der Pol, M.; Ruggeri, M. Is risk attitude outcome specific within the health domain? *J. Health Econ.* **2008**, *27*, 706–717. [CrossRef] [PubMed]
63. Iversen, A.C. Does socio-economic status and health consciousness influence how women respond to health related messages in media? *Health Educ. Res.* **2006**, *21*, 601–610. [CrossRef]
64. Mai, R.; Hoffmann, S. Taste lovers versus nutrition fact seekers: How health consciousness and self-efficacy determine the way consumers choose food products. *J. Consum. Behav.* **2012**, *11*, 316–328. [CrossRef]
65. Jayanti, R.K.; Burns, A.C. The Antecedents of Preventive Health Care Behavior: An Empirical Study. *J. Acad. Mark. Sci.* **1998**, *26*, 6–15. [CrossRef]
66. Hughner, R.S.; McDonagh, P.; Prothero, A.; Shultz, C.J.; Stanton, J. Who are organic food consumers? A compilation and review of why people purchase organic food. *J. Consum. Behav.* **2007**, *6*, 94–110. [CrossRef]
67. Lockie, S.; Lyons, K.; Lawrence, G.; Mummery, K. Eating 'Green': Motivations behind organic food consumption in Australia. *Sociol. Rural.* **2002**, *42*, 23–40. [CrossRef]
68. Gidengil, C.A.; Parker, A.M.; Zikmund-Fisher, B. Trends in Risk Perceptions and Vaccination Intentions: A Longitudinal Study of the First Year of the H1N1 Pandemic. *Am. J. Public Health* **2012**, *102*, 672–679. [CrossRef] [PubMed]
69. Kim, J.; Lee, J.C. Effects of COVID-19 on preferences for private dining facilities in restaurants. *J. Hosp. Tour. Manag.* **2020**, *45*, 67–70. [CrossRef]
70. Aron, A.; Aron, E.N.; Smollan, D. Inclusion of Other in the Self Scale and the structure of interpersonal closeness. *J. Pers. Soc. Psychol.* **1992**, *63*, 596–612. [CrossRef]
71. Gineikiene, J.; Kiudyte, J.; DeGutis, M. Functional, organic or conventional? Food choices of health conscious and skeptical consumers. *Balt. J. Manag.* **2017**, *12*, 139–152. [CrossRef]
72. Davis, F.D. Perceived Usefulness, Perceived Ease of Use, and User Acceptance of Information Technology. *MIS Q.* **1989**, *13*, 319–340. [CrossRef]
73. Venkatesh, V.; Morris, M.G.; Davis, G.B.; Davis, F.D. User Acceptance of Information Technology: Toward a Unified View. *MIS Q.* **2003**, *27*, 425. [CrossRef]
74. Holzmann, P.; Schwarz, E.J.; Audretsch, D.B. Understanding the determinants of novel technology adoption among teachers: The case of 3D printing. *J. Technol. Transf.* **2018**, *45*, 259–275. [CrossRef]
75. Agarwal, R.; Karahanna, E. Time Flies When You're Having Fun: Cognitive Absorption and Beliefs about Information Technology Usage. *MIS Q.* **2000**, *24*, 665. [CrossRef]
76. Lindell, M.K.; Whitney, D.J. Accounting for common method variance in cross-sectional research designs. *J. Appl. Psychol.* **2001**, *86*, 114–121. [CrossRef]
77. Hayes, A.F. *Introduction to Mediation, Moderation, and Conditional Process Analysis: A Regression-Based Approach*; Guilford Press: New York, NY, USA, 2013.
78. Hair, J.F.; Black, W.C.; Babin, B.J.; Anderson, R.E.; Tatham, R.L. *Multivariate Data Analysis*, 6th ed.; Pearson/Prentice Hall: Upper Saddle River, NJ, USA, 2006.
79. Bagozzi, R.P. Evaluating Structural Equation Models with Unobservable Variables and Measurement Error: A Comment. *J. Mark. Res.* **1981**, *18*, 375–381. [CrossRef]
80. Bagozzi, R.P.; Yi, Y. On the evaluation of structural equation models. *J. Acad. Mark. Sci.* **1988**, *16*, 74–94. [CrossRef]
81. Podsakoff, P.M.; MacKenzie, S.B.; Lee, J.Y.; Podsakoff, N.P. Common method biases in behavioral research: A critical review of the literature and recommended remedies. *J. Appl. Psychol.* **2003**, *88*, 879–903. [CrossRef]
82. Schwepker, C.H. Strengthening Customer Value Development and Ethical Intent in the Salesforce: The Influence of Ethical Values Person–Organization Fit and Trust in Manager. *J. Bus. Ethics* **2019**, *159*, 913–925. [CrossRef]
83. Hu, L.T.; Bentler, P.M. Cutoff criteria for fit indexes in covariance structure analysis: Conventional criteria versus new alternatives. *Struct. Equ. Model. Multidiscip. J.* **1999**, *6*, 1–55. [CrossRef]
84. Epley, N.; Waytz, A.; Cacioppo, J.T. On seeing human: A three-factor theory of anthropomorphism. *Psychol. Rev.* **2007**, *114*, 864–886. [CrossRef]
85. Epley, N.; Waytz, A.; Akalis, S.; Cacioppo, J.T. When We Need a Human: Motivational Determinants of Anthropomorphism. *Soc. Cogn.* **2008**, *26*, 143–155. [CrossRef]
86. Mathur, M.B.; Reichling, D.B. Navigating a social world with robot partners: A quantitative cartography of the Uncanny Valley. *Cognition* **2016**, *146*, 22–32. [CrossRef] [PubMed]
87. Choi, Y.; Choi, M.; Oh, M.; Kim, S. Service robots in hotels: Understanding the service quality perceptions of human-robot interaction. *J. Hosp. Mark. Manag.* **2019**, *29*, 613–635. [CrossRef]
88. Kattara, H.S.; El-Said, O.A. Customers' preferences for new technology-based self-services versus human interaction services in hotels. *Tour. Hosp. Res.* **2013**, *13*, 67–82. [CrossRef]
89. Ivanov, S.; Seyitoğlu, F.; Markova, M. Hotel managers' perceptions towards the use of robots: A mixed-methods approach. *Inf. Technol. Tour.* **2020**, *22*, 505–535. [CrossRef]

International Journal of
Environmental Research and Public Health

MDPI

Article

Intention-Based Critical Factors Affecting Willingness to Adopt Novel Coronavirus Prevention in Pakistan: Implications for Future Pandemics

Munir Ahmad [1], Nadeem Akhtar [2,3,*], Gul Jabeen [4,5], Muhammad Irfan [6,7], Muhammad Khalid Anser [8], Haitao Wu [6,7] and Cem Işık [9]

1 School of Economics, Zhejiang University, Hangzhou 310058, China; munirahmad@zju.edu.cn
2 School of Urban Culture, Nanhai Campus, South China Normal University, Foshan 528225, China
3 Pakistan Center, North Minzu University, Yinchuan 750001, China
4 Research Institute of Business Analytics and Supply Chain Management, College of Management, Shenzhen University, Shenzhen 518060, China; guljabeen@ncepu.edu.cn
5 School of Economics and Management, North China Electric Power University, Beijing 102206, China
6 School of Management and Economics, Beijing Institute of Technology, Beijing 100081, China; irfansahar@bit.edu.cn (M.I.); haitao.kungfuer@gmail.com (H.W.)
7 Center for Energy and Environmental Policy Research, Beijing Institute of Technology, Beijing 100081, China
8 School of Public Administration, Xi'an University of Architecture and Technology, Xi'an 710000, China; mkhalidrao@xauat.edu.cn
9 Faculty of Tourism, Anadolu University, 26470 Tepebaşı-Eskişehir, Turkey; cemisik@anadolu.edu.tr
* Correspondence: nadeem@scnu.edu.cn; Tel.: 86-155-2102-4890

Citation: Ahmad, M.; Akhtar, N.; Jabeen, G.; Irfan, M.; Khalid Anser, M.; Wu, H.; Işık, C. Intention-Based Critical Factors Affecting Willingness to Adopt Novel Coronavirus Prevention in Pakistan: Implications for Future Pandemics. *Int. J. Environ. Res. Public Health* **2021**, *18*, 6167. https://doi.org/10.3390/ijerph18116167

Academic Editors: Paolo Roma, Merylin Monaro and Cristina Mazza

Received: 27 April 2021
Accepted: 4 June 2021
Published: 7 June 2021

Abstract: Since human beings have a long tradition of coexistence with pandemics, which may profoundly impact them, adopting preventive measures is crucial for humankind's survival. This study explores the intention-based critical factors affecting the willingness of individuals to adopt pandemic prevention. To this end, a representative sample of 931 Pakistanis filled in an online questionnaire. However, only 828 questionnaires were found to be complete and valid for path modeling analysis. The core findings are as follows: Firstly, peer groups' beliefs, self-efficacy, perceived risk, pandemic knowledge, ease of pandemic prevention adoption, and risk-averse behavior are revealed as driving forces of the individuals' willingness to adopt pandemic prevention. Contrastingly, a lack of trust in political will and mythical attitude towards pandemics are uncovered as inhibitors. Nevertheless, moral values depict a neutral role. Secondly, the peer groups' beliefs are highest ranked, followed by the lack of trust in political will and a mythical attitude towards pandemic prevention. Finally, moral values are determined as the lowest-ranked critical factor. Based on these results, the government should promote awareness campaigns on lethality and fatality of the pandemic at both centralized and decentralized levels to win people's trust at the grass-roots level and overcome the mythical attitude of individuals at all societal levels. Besides, access to personal protective gears should be made feasible since an easier pandemic prevention adoption would increase the individuals' willingness to adopt such preventative measures.

Keywords: intention-based critical factors; novel coronavirus; pandemic prevention; COVID-19; hybrid theoretical framework; path modeling; Pakistan

1. Introduction

Since human beings have a long tradition of coexistence with pandemics, which may profoundly impact them, adopting preventive measures is crucial for humankind's survival. Global pandemics are rising every day because the proper diagnosis of the right people at the right time is missing [1]. The involvement of vaccine producers, health authorities, and governments is essential for monitoring and preventing such pandemics [2].

The Coronavirus Disease 2019 (COVID-19) began in Wuhan (a Chinese city) in late December 2019. In the face of people's domestic and international mobility, the epidemic eventually turned into a worldwide pandemic. The Chinese government took strict steps to effectively curtail the epidemic outbreak [3]. As of 29 May 2021, an estimated over 169 million cases tested positive, while about 3.5 million patients lost their lives worldwide due to COVID-19 infection. The epicenter of the COVID-19 shifted from Wuhan through Iran and Italy to the United States. The U.S., with more than 33 Million confirmed cases, is the pandemic's current epicenter, followed by India with more than 27 million cases. Besides, Brazil, France, and Turkey are also among the hotspots of COVID-19 patients, with more than 16, 5.5, and 5.2 million confirmed cases, respectively [4]. Its outbreak started in Pakistan in the middle of March 2020 and reached a peak number of confirmed cases by mid-June 2020. Afterward, the number of cases reduced substantially; however, a resurgence of patients started in the last quarter of October 2020 due to the lack of prevention measures at an individual scale. As of 29 May 2021, around 913,784 cases were reported, whereas the total death toll reached 20,607. In the meantime, an estimated 835 thousand individuals have recovered, which is indeed an optimistic side of the gloomy picture.

To curtail the COVID-19 outbreak, several countries such as Italy, Spain, India, Russia, and China implemented nationwide lockdowns. However, the Pakistani government's COVID-19 containment strategy was not based on complete lockdown across the nation. Instead, smart and targeted lockdowns were imposed on locations with agglomerated patients [4]. In light of this, the individuals' willingness to adopt pandemic prevention (WAPP) becomes vital. Consequently, during a pandemic like COVID-19, the individuals' WAPP is explicitly defined by their intention-based critical factors (ICFs). The ICFs include the driving and inhibitory factors shaping the individuals' intention to accept or reject pandemic prevention. Since the individuals' intention performs a critical role in actual behavior [5], the analysis of ICFs would be imperative to understand the COVID-19 prevention measures.

The COVID-19 pandemic has become a hotly debated issue among global scholars; nevertheless, studies on ICFs affecting individuals' WAPP are scarce. In particular, no research has been identified examining the ICFs involving driving forces and inhibitors of individuals' WAPP in a hybrid theoretical framework. The previous studies were fundamentally based on the following debates: The first debate comprised the epidemiological characteristics of the epidemic, including "acquired immunodeficiency syndrome" (AIDS), dengue fever, malarial infection, and coronavirus infection [6,7]. The second debate considered the prevention and control of pandemics such as SARS-CoV 2002, MERS-CoV 2012, and COVID-19, belonging to the coronavirus family [8–10]. Simultaneously, some studies addressed epidemic prevention and control from the government's perspective [11,12]. The third debate focused on the links of COVID-19 with the sustainable supply chain [13,14] and environmental features such as humidity and temperature [15,16].

The fourth debate was based on the psychological factors interacting with COVID-19 related attributes, including the intention of being vaccinated, individuals' resilience, individual susceptibility to conspiracies, prosocial behavior, socio-political predictors, dark personality traits, and psychological entitlement, among others. In this regard, Karataş and Tagay [17] examined and revealed that no experience of trauma, satisfaction of life, and hope were positively linked with adults' resilience during the COVID-19 outbreak. Karlsson et al. [18] studied and disclosed a positive linkage between the perceived risk of COVID-19 and the intention of being vaccinated in the Finnish context. Hughes and Machan [19] assessed and concluded that Machiavellianism and psychopathy positively influenced COVID-19 related conspiracy beliefs. Jin et al. [20] empirically evaluated and found that the age factor positively impacted individuals' prosocial COVID-19 response, meaning that older individuals had a relatively higher perceived cost of being infected by the virus. In a different study, Wagerman et al. [21] investigated and revealed that anxious attachment positively determined the COVID-19 distress factor. Hardin et al. [22] analyzed and discovered that Machiavellianism and Narcissism introduced negative impacts in response to COVID-19 in the U.S. context.

Moreover, Zitek and Schlund [23] studied the psychological entitlement in the United States and revealed that the individuals were not concerned about transmitting the disease to others. Therefore, they were less likely to follow the COVID-19 prevention guidelines. Ruggieri et al. [24] investigated pre-and post-quarantine behaviors and found a rise in anxiety, stress, and loneliness, along with a decline in life satisfaction. Chan [25] studied and unveiled that fairness and caring showed compliance with all types of individual behaviors; however, sanctity merely predicted the social distancing and wearing a face mask in the United States. Next, Li et al. [26] studied the community sample in China. They discovered that high perceived risk was linked with increased donations to the COVID-19 patients and the health workers. Paredes et al. [27] examined and found that highly resilient people, who were better at overcoming stressful and traumatic situations, demonstrated relatively less impact of COVID-19 threat on prospective pandemic anxiety and stress. Malesza and Kaczmarek [28] analyzed and concluded that the factors, including a greater amount of protection recommendation, COVID-19 information from diverse sources, and a lack of belief that catching COVID-19 was determined by individuals' actions, significantly contributed to pandemic-related anxiety.

Besides, Volk et al. [29] investigated and uncovered that the demographic attributes involving income and children were directly linked to COVID-19 handling response. While age, sex, income, and children had an indirect linkage. Grossman et al. [30] studied and disclosed that COVID-19 related concerns were positively correlated with loneliness and sleeplessness. Ahmad et al. [1] studied the influencing factors of the acceptance of COVID-19 protection in China. Their findings showed that guidelines by the Chinese government boosted the epidemic protection adoption in China. However, their study included a highly educated population comprised of government employees. Therefore, the findings of their research cannot be generalized. As a further note, China's political system is different from that of other democratic nations. Hence, the findings extracted based on their sample cannot be generalized for the other democratic countries. Additionally, no research has been known to introduce the above-stated ICFs to a behavioral framework obtained by integrating the composite of planned behavior (PBST) and reasoned action schools of thought (RAST). Finally, the driving forces and inhibitors of individuals' WAPP were not previously considered. The understanding of such driving forces and inhibitors would help improve the adoption behavior substantially. Therefore, the investigation of such critical factors is timely and urgent.

To fill the aforementioned gaps, this research investigates the ICFs of individuals' WAPP in terms of driving forces and inhibitors. From the empirical side, new critical factors involving the lack of trust in political will and mythical attitude towards pandemic are included. Furthermore, a theoretical framework composite of PBST and RAST is integrated to incorporate additional ICFs that determine the WAPP. Those factors include a lack of trust in political will, mythical attitude towards pandemic, perceived risk, pandemic knowledge, the ease of pandemic prevention adoption, risk-averse behavior, and moral values. The empirical outcomes of this work are distinguished from the mainstream literature. The derived policies are equally useful for both the developing and developed nations in the world health emergency during the COVID-19 pandemic as well as potential future pandemics.

The remainder of the study is arranged as follows: Section 2 explains the extraction of a hybrid theoretical framework. Section 3 is based on data, methods, and analysis. Section 4 details the results of this work. Section 5 explains the conclusion and policy suggestions.

2. Literature Review and Hypotheses Formulation

2.1. Mythical Attitude towards Pandemic

Mythical attitude towards pandemic can be defined as the traditional way of thinking about the existence or non-existence of a pandemic and its influence on human beings. Individuals with mythical attitudes might believe that the pandemic will automatically vanish due to external factors such as high temperature. They might also believe that pandemic prevention is useless for them. In this regard, Latkin et al. [31] studied the linkages of COVID-19 skepticism with protection behavior, social distancing, conspiracy theories, and individuals' political ideas in the U.S. and revealed the highly skeptical individuals less likely to adopt COVID-19 protection. Alper [32] investigated the correlation between COVID-19 conspiracy theories and protection adoption and revealed no link between the two in the Turkish context. Research was conducted to examine the knowledge, preventive measures, and attitude of live poultry market workers regarding the avian influenza in the Chongqing district of central China by taking a sample of 216 workers of this district. The results exhibited that the workers had imperfect knowledge, took insufficient preventive measures, and had weak susceptibility perceptions [33]. In another work, Shi et al. [34] investigated the present level of evidence-based chronic disease prevention (EBCDP) by taking interviews with health practitioners and patients of different health institutes in China and found that it was at an earlier level in the implementation of prevention practices. Further, a survey was conducted in Ukraine consisting of medical, custodial, and prison administrative staff with a sample size of 243 to determine criminal justice system workers' attitudes towards drug addiction and opioid substitution therapy. The results demonstrated that the worker's attitude was negative towards drug addiction [35].

Further, Mao and Yang [36] studied the expansion of infectious diseases among human beings and prevention practices to save themselves by making two networks. This infection network deals with disease transmission and a communication network that deals with preventive measures. Moreover, Przybyla et al. [37] conducted a study to assess the attitude, knowledge, and awareness of pharmacy students regarding human immunodeficiency virus (HIV) pre-exposure prophylaxis (PrEP). It was done by using descriptive statistics and multivariate logistic regression analysis. The results explored that educational modules' progress helped increase exposure towards the attitude, information, and awareness regarding HIV and PrEP. Similarly, Ibrahim [38] investigated the expansion of HIV in Indonesia and focused on the prevention strategies to minimize it by renewing primary health care, paired with suitable economic and other risk units to health care. Given the survey of above-stated studies, the following hypothesis is formulated:

Hypothesis 1. *Mythical attitude towards pandemic is likely to have a negative association with a willingness to adopt pandemic prevention.*

2.2. Pandemic Knowledge

Pandemic knowledge refers to awareness and the collection of information gained by individuals about a pandemic's modes of transmission and prevention. It has been argued that different virus outbreaks like Ebola, Influenza, and Zika viruses could severely affect human beings, especially pregnant women. To this end, Krubiner et al. [39] explained twenty-two guidelines and recommendations that offer a road map for morally liable, socially unbiased, and deferential addition. This was done for the welfare of pregnant women and their offspring in the expansion and distribution of vaccination against pandemic outbreaks. Besides, a study was conducted in India between 2009 and 2015 to consider the impact of climate change on malarial pandemics and the influence of a specific area's population, frequency, and prevalence of malarial parasite. Further, the seasonal variations were studied by using the logistic regression model. The results showed that the climate and seasonal change influenced pandemics as summers accelerated the pandemics, while winters had a significant negative effect [40]. According to Yang et al. [41], after SARS-2003 and MERS-2012, COVID-19 appeared as a new pandemic. Its main symptoms included dry cough, flu, temperature, and body pain. The Chinese government was reportedly taking measures for prevention and control as the human-to-human transmission rate was higher than SARS and MERS. It was suggested that there was a need to develop antivirals or vaccines that would offer a big opportunity. It was further opined that the virus was affecting the nation's economy drastically. In light of these works, the following association is hypothesized:

Hypothesis 2. *Pandemic knowledge is likely to have a positive association with a willingness to adopt pandemic prevention.*

2.3. Ease of Pandemic Prevention Adoption

Ease of pandemic prevention adoption refers to the availability of protective gears to individuals and the feasibility of practicing prevention measures such as lockdown and social distancing. A study was carried out to examine the feasibility of momentary ecological assessment by taking almost 21 respondents' data. The results showed that momentary ecological assessment was easier and had no impact on behavior [42]. It has been estimated that almost 36.9 million people were affected by HIV/AIDS. Regardless of the facility of available drugs for disease treatment, lifetime therapy was required for its prevention and control and to avoid its re-emergence. Using biomedical tools, prophylaxis, and circumcision, the diffusion of HIV/AIDS could be controlled by the end of 2030 [43]. In another research, Spire et al. [44] discovered three essentials in the exertion to decrease the sexual diffusion of HIV/AIDS struggle deterrence lethargy, expand HIV checking and hostility, humiliation, and prejudice. It also contended for an indulgent damage lessening method to the deterrence of sexual diffusion of HIV that considered the clarification of danger by various persons and societies in the period of antiretroviral treatment. Lee et al. [45] analyzed the impact of information and communication technology usage on psychosocial factors by conducting a questionnaire survey from 394 U.S. residents. The feasibility of pandemic prevention was a significant contributor to future anxiety.

Moreover, Zhou et al. [46] conducted an online survey-based study in China's Wuhan city, including 728 respondents, to analyze the influence factors of wearing face masks. The availability of face masks positively affected individuals' behavior of wearing them. Intawong et al. [47] studied the role of application technology in Thailand in helping the COVID-19 patients and high-risk individuals to discover their disease symptoms through quick tracking strategies. In another work, Thomas et al. [48] assessed the role of technologies in facilitating the prevention of pandemics worldwide. To this end, social media, artificial intelligence, and other digital technologies helped to promote the ease of pandemic prevention. Clipper [49] also argued that tech solutions strengthened the healthcare systems and made prevention adoption easier through information communication. Further, Kusuma et al. [50] conducted a survey-based analysis in four South Asian countries (India, Pakistan, Bangladesh, and Sri Lanka) by recruiting 29,809 respondents to evaluate the feasibility of COVID-19 prevention adoption. The individuals were found less likely to adopt pandemic prevention due to the unavailability of protective gears. Finally, Irfan et al. [51] examined and revealed the negative impact of the unavailability of face masks on willingness to wear face masks in Pakistan. In view of the abovementioned literature, the following relationship is hypothesized:

Hypothesis 3. *Ease of pandemic prevention adoption is likely to have a positive association with a willingness to adopt pandemic prevention.*

2.4. Self-Efficacy

Self-efficacy refers to individuals' beliefs of handling or managing a certain situation. It describes individuals' ability to carry out certain actions in the needful hours. Blue [52] explored the impact of attitude, beliefs of peer groups, and self-efficacy on diabetic patients' intention to do physical activity and eat healthy food for prevention and control by taking a sample of 106 adults at risk of diabetes. The results explained that all the variables greatly influenced intentions to take a healthy diet and make oneself physically fit. Another work consisting of 147 nurses in Korea was conducted to explore the impact of attitude and self-efficacy on the nursing intention to look after patients in emerging transferrable syndromes using the theory of planned behavior. The findings indicated that the most effective variable to influence intentions was self-efficacy [53]. It has been argued that learning and forgetting behavior during pandemic disease was investigated by using the models such as the forgetting curve model (IFC), memory reception fading, and cumulating model (MRFC). It was done through sensitivity and simulation analyses. The results revealed that MRFC is more efficient and effective than IFC, which is suitable for fewer pandemics with a lower fatality rate [54]. Then, Aruta [55] analyzed and declared individuals' resilience and financial issues as the strongest determinants of psychological distress in Filipino individuals. In another work, Chen et al. [56] examined and found an adverse influence of COVID-19 on medical staff's mental health than Wuhan's general public. Given the above-discussed studies, the hypothesized association is given as follows:

Hypothesis 4. *Self-efficacy is likely to have a positive association with willingness to adopt pandemic prevention.*

2.5. Peer Groups' Beliefs

Peer groups' beliefs refer to the ways of thinking of an individual's peers, including friends, colleagues, neighbors, and other people with whom the individual is often in contact. During a pandemic, their ways of thinking might influence the behavior of an individual. It has been narrated that it would be impossible to deal with a pandemic without public cooperation, irrespective of the number of physicians, technology, health care personnel, and medical facilities available. To bring public cooperation, governments, and high authorities' participation was recommended because without considering the social dimension, it would not be possible to control the outbreak [57]. After the outbreak of SARS in 2002 to 2003, HIV/AIDS pandemics had a significant effect on the world over the subsequent decades. It exposed the substantial function of social norms, beliefs, and attitudes in determining people's lifestyles in society. It drew attention towards taking preventive measures and controlling pandemic diseases [58]. Zhang et al. [59] examined and noted the negative influence of the COVID-19 pandemic on peer groups' physical activities in the U.S. Moreover, a study consisted of Thai college undergraduate students employed via peer leaders to find how hypothetical variables function inside theory-based intermediation. It offered a concise HIV preventive measure plan to improve Thai college students' knowledge regarding HIV/AIDS prevention and improve their confidence and motivation to fight against this disease [60]. In light of these studies, the following hypothesis is formulated:

Hypothesis 5. *Peer groups' beliefs is likely to have a positive association with willingness to adopt pandemic prevention.*

2.6. Moral Values

Moral values involve an individual's sense of obligations and responsibility towards others. To illustrate, during the outbreak of a pandemic, taking care of others by helping them adopt prevention measures defines the moral values of individuals. Similarly, moral values also included an individual's cooperation with others to facilitate them get through difficult times. Concerning society's morality, a study was carried out to analyze the variations in tobacco usage and preventive measures taken by taking qualitative data from teachers of 12 schools of Maharashtra and Bihar [61]. The results discovered that tobacco usage was at a higher rate in Bihar as compared to Maharashtra as the moral norms strongly encouraged tobacco usage in Bihar. Besides, efficient functional resolutions to the difficulties between-group disagreements urged various ethical good fortune that fairly concerned Evo liberals, and not any of those social modernizations needed intervening at the stage of personal ethical capabilities. There were almost certainly believable worldwide settlements that might resolve the difficulties of anthropogenic atmospheric modification and worldwide scarcity [62]. In another research, Edmonson et al. [63] studied that eighty percent of nurses faced harassment in hospitals, and twenty-one percent of the turnover rate was also caused by bullying. There were many reasons involved, like difference in regions, gender, power, behavioral patterns, etc. The individuals experienced poor health and mental and physical stress in response to harassment. Prestia [64] examined the challenges faced by nurses during the international COVID-19 pandemic outbreak and found their pivotal role in keeping with the moral obligations to take care of patients. In the sense of contextual behaviors, Borges et al. [65] stated that the COVID-19 pandemic brought into light many moral dilemmas. Akram [66] reported that the U.S. healthcare system adopted utilitarian policies to deal with moral injuries during the COVID-19 pandemic outbreak. Liang et al. [67] studied and revealed respondents' depressive behaviors and moral collapse from China's Hubei province during the pandemic outbreak. Finally, Donnarumma and Pezzulo [68] figured out that moral collapse observed for the Italian citizens from a high outbreak region (Milan) to low outbreak regions (southern Italy) caused severe outbreak in those regions. It means moral decisions were significantly linked with the pandemic prevention measures' adoption during the outbreak. Based on the abovementioned works, the following association is hypothesized:

Hypothesis 6. *Moral values are likely to have a positive association with a willingness to adopt pandemic prevention.*

2.7. Risk-Averse Behavior

Risk-averse behavior is an individual's tendency to avoid uncertain or risky situations. To illustrate, a risk-averse individual is reluctant to indulge in events with uncertain or risky outcomes. Thus, such individuals are more inclined towards prevention adoption during a pandemic. It has been shoen that some infections stay dormant in human beings without infecting them. However, some infectious diseases not only infect the human being in which they were living but also infect other human beings who come into contact with the carrier. In order to test the persons' ability to evade the risk of the disease spreading, a pandemic spreading model was proposed by [69]. The findings showed that the cause of the expansion of disease was transforming dormant human beings into explosives. Also, self-prevention helped minimize the expansion of infectious diseases [69]. Further, Berry and Finnoff [70] investigated how individuals might react against the increasing pandemic by proposing two investment policies. Those policies included the adaptation policy (in which individuals can invest in domestic capital) and prevention policy (in which individuals can invest in foreign capital). In this way, the expansion of pandemics could be controlled. In the same vein, Lee and You [71] investigated and found a significant impact of health factors on the avoidance of healthcare use in South Korea. Hashiguchi et al. [72] analyzed the association among health risk, productivity, and work motivation among the construction workforce in Japan. The health risk was significantly associated with productivity and work motivation. Cordellieri et al. [73] studied the influence of psychological factors on COVID-19 containment and observed its negative impact. Moreover, there were three identified reasons that risk-averse behavior was considered as a distinct aim of health policy. First, public health security was a priority. Second, it was essential for societal planning. Finally, it was a suitable response towards decision-making, especially when available pieces of information were limited [74]. In light of these works, the following hypothesis is formulated:

Hypothesis 7. *Risk-averse behavior is likely to have a positive association with a willingness to adopt pandemic prevention.*

2.8. Perceived Risk

Perceived risk demonstrates an individual's subjective assessment of his/her risk of indulging in an adverse situation. In real life, perceived (subjective) risk plays a more substantial role than the actual (objective) risk in shaping the behavior of individuals [75].

Thus, the better the risk is perceived by an individual more likely he/she is to adopt pandemic prevention. It is the subjective opinion regarding the nature and magnitude of a risk encountered by the people. It is generally used for natural disasters and environmental or safety risks. Concerning this factor, Ho et al. [76] conducted a study in Taiwan in 2004 to discover the impact of perceived risk on the kind of tragedy like a flood or land sliding and characteristics of individuals (victims). The main results depicted that perceived risk has a significant influence on the type of disasters and characteristics of victims. A project named Highland Malaria Project was developed in Kenya and Uganda for early detection, control, and malaria prevention between 2001 to 2006. The main reason for this was to mitigate the risk of its expansion by detecting and curing it at an early stage [77]. From a different perspective of perceived risk, Valeeva et al. [78] studied the factors influencing the farmer's risk management strategies named biosecurity and animal health programs as well as their perception in terms of the management of disease and animal health risks by taking data from 164 participants and using a structural equation modeling approach. The results indicated that biosecurity measures are more efficient as compared to animal health programs.

Moreover, Kiviniemi et al. [79] researched the influence of the education gap in the perceived risk of HIV by taking data from 1993 to 2000 in the U.S. The findings exposed that people with a low level of education are unaware of disease and health risk compared to people with a high level of education. Hence, the perceived risk is high for highly educated people as compared to less educated people. Similarly, Raude et al. [80] unveiled the perceptions relevant to risk and behaviors in the malarial pandemic outbreak results taking the data of 434 French Guiana residents. The results showed that the perceived risk of infection considerably reduces over time. After that, Rodriguez-Besteiro et al. [81] examined and revealed a significant influence of perceived pandemic risk on nutrition, psychology, and habits of Spanish individuals. Sica et al. [82] evaluated the influence of perceived COVID-19's danger and anxiety on pandemic protection, and revealed its positive impact for 742 community members in the Italian context. In their research, Ding et al. [83] examined the COVID-risk perception in China and discovered that college students in Hubei province had a high level of risk perception. Finally, Li et al. [84] examined the impact of perceived risk on social support and the possibility of contracting COVID-19 by conducting an online questionnaire from 1970 Taiwan's residents. It was found that perceived risk mediated the impact of social support on the possibility to contract the COVID-19 disease. These studies lead to the formulation of the following hypothesis:

Hypothesis 8. *Pandemic knowledge is likely to have a positive association with willingness to adopt pandemic prevention.*

2.9. Lack of Trust in Political Will

A lack of trust in political will refers to the absence of individuals' confidence in political institutions, which damages his/her belief in the righteousness of these institutions. If such confidence is lacking, individuals would be likely to demonstrate civil disobedience and be reluctant to follow pandemic prevention guidelines by the governments. It has been suggested that the government plays a major role in reducing obesity, communicable, non-communicable diseases, and increasing the health conditions of the public. For this purpose, the monitoring and evaluation system was advised to be introduced to test the policies made by the government sector. It was done to make a healthy food environment like a government healthy food environment index developed in collaboration with international experts to maintain a hygienic food environment and reduce obesity [85]. Moreover, Yu et al. [86] analyzed the impact of government-controlled payment on the government's health services to the general public in Shanghai, China. The Shanghai government focused on developing community health services, which offered health services to the general public in 1997. Nevertheless, their main purpose was to make a profit instead of providing excellent services to the general public. In order to resolve the issue, the government introduced the government-controlled payment process that focused on providing excellent services instead of making a profit, and it positively influenced the provision of quality services to meet the health requirements of people. Moreover, health officers' hand hygiene was an important factor in preventing and controlling disease transmission from patient to patient or healthy person. Allegranzi and Pittet [87] focused on promoting hand hygiene and issues faced by health workers in adopting alcohol-based hand wash to reduce healthcare-associated infections. In light of the above reviewed literature, the following hypothesis is developed:

Hypothesis 9. *Lack of trust in political will is likely to have a negative association with willingness to adopt pandemic prevention.*

3. Materials and Methods

3.1. A Hybrid Theoretical Framework

This work extends the planned behavior (PBST) and the reasoned action school of thoughts (RAST) by incorporating new intention-based critical factors (ICFs). The new framework is called the hybrid theoretical framework. RAST was postulated by Fishbein and Ajzen [88]. They advanced the notion that the actions of individuals complied with their intentions. People anticipate the perception-based influence of their activities instead of immediately executing real actions. Hence, people tend to perform actions that they feel will contribute to positive outcomes. In this fashion, two dimensions are involved in determining the behavior based on individuals' willingness to adopt pandemic prevention: (i) mythical attitude towards pandemic and (ii) peer groups' beliefs. The attitude is defined as individuals' common sense-based confirmation or disconfirmation of behavioral intention [89]. The composition of individuals' attitudes towards pandemic prevention may stem from a set of values they have, and the appraisal of consequences associated with the behavioral intention. In addition, peer groups' beliefs can be explained as a collection of expectations of how others evaluate a person's actions and motivations [90].

Originally, RAST was thought to be entirely composed of intention-based behaviors formed by the attitude towards some action and peer groups' beliefs. Afterward, an influential opinion came forth, referring that intention was not independently developing individuals' behavior, but some control factors were also involved. In this regard, Ajzen [90] presented a modified RAST version by including a novel self-efficacy element and characterized it as PBST (Figure 1). Self-efficacy is described as the power that people feel to have for executing some action. Besides, control beliefs and feasibility are the fundamentals of self-efficacy. The control beliefs are based on individuals' intention to have or lack the ability and knowledge to do something. In parallel, feasibility involves people's judgment about the convenience of executing some action [90].

RAST and PBST are commonly used to identify multifaceted intention-based behaviors in behavioral studies [91,92]. This research advances the RAST and PBST behavioral paradigms to augment them for some novel ICFs. Among those factors, peer groups' beliefs, pandemic knowledge, self-efficacy, and attitude were used in mainstream works [91,93]. However, factors like perceived risk, risk-averse behavior, moral values, ease of pandemic prevention adoption, and lack of trust in the political will are not known to be incorporated in a behavioral framework, a combination of RAST and PBST. Thus, the present research developed this new framework incorporated those factors to demonstrate their linkages with individuals' WAPP (Figure 1). The content analysis of empirical literature was done to detail the foundation of those factors provided in the Supplementary Materials.

Using a hybrid theoretical framework, this work investigates Pakistanis' local intention-based WAPP translating it to the global context during the COVID-19 outbreak. In this regard, as per previous studies [93,94], behavioral intention has been considered instead of actually experienced behavior. Finally, the social and demographic features such as gender, age, education, and household income are taken as the controls, which partially contribute to the perceived behavioral control.

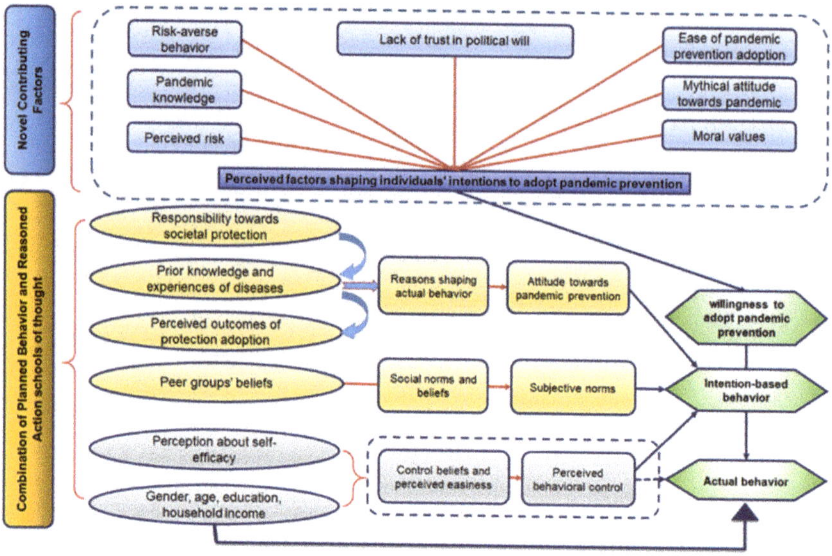

Figure 1. Modifications to the planned behavior and reasoned action schools of thought for novel contributing factors affecting individuals' willingness to adopt pandemic prevention. Source: Authors' drawing.

3.2. Survey-Based Data Compilation

A questionnaire was designed and shared with the health counselors and advisors (from the National Institute of Health), medical practitioners (from Shifa International Hospital, Pakistan Institute of Medical Sciences, and Aga Khan University Hospital), professors, and associate professors (from Quaid-i-Azam University, King Edward College, and Forman Christian College University) from the fields of Sociology, Medicine, and Psychology to obtain their expert feedback for pre-examination purposes. These expert participants played a dual role in the assessment of the questionnaire. Firstly, they commented on the contents of the questions to improve their clarity and quality. It established the content validity of the questionnaire. Secondly, they filled in the questionnaire for pilot testing to verify the functionality of the questionnaire. It established the face validity of the questionnaire [95]. The profiles of the participatory role-playing individuals are given in Appendix A (Table A1).

A questionnaire in English was combined with Urdu translation format removing any language barriers and producing informed feedback. This online survey was conducted in Pakistan during May–June 2020. In the face of the ongoing pandemic outbreak, the questionnaire was floated in numerous Facebook (Facebook Inc., Menlo Park, CA, USA) and WhatsApp (WhatsApp Inc., Menlo Park, CA, USA) groups among the social circles of friends, friends' friends, colleagues, colleagues' friends, and scholars and students from universities across universities. Ethical considerations were included by stating the research aims and scope in the questionnaire's introductory paragraph to ensure the respondents' informed consent. Furthermore, the confidentiality and anonymity of respondents were also guaranteed during the questionnaire conduction. Following Kamenidou et al. [96], the questionnaire conduction process was based on mixed non-probability sampling, which involved convenience, snowball, and criteria sampling procedures. The recruitment criterion was mainly based on the age of the respondents. Respondents below 18 years of age were advised not to fill in the questionnaire. Also, the individuals reluctant to provide their consent were excluded. (i.e., exclusion criteria). Moreover, the respondents needed to be residents of Pakistan. Further, since the questionnaire was conducted online, respondents on social media (Facebook and WhatsApp) were the only population available to generate the data sample (i.e., inclusion criteria). The respondents were from heterogeneous backgrounds in terms of occupation, qualification, and household income, among other traits. It considerably led the findings to be generalized for the population belonging to heterogeneous backgrounds. The survey was conducted from a total of 931 respondents. After initial scrutiny, 828 questionnaires were found completely and appropriately filled in by the respondents. Those questionnaires were declared valid for analysis purposes. The designed questions are presented in Appendix B (Table 2).

3.3. Data and Statistical Analysis

The partial least squares (PLS)-based path model is adopted to assess the ICFs impacting individuals' WAPP. A Likert scale consisting of five-points included 5 = "Totally agree", 4 = "Agree", 3 = "Neutral", 2 = "Disagree", and 1 = "Totally disagree." The schematic outline of the research methodology is presented in Figure 2.

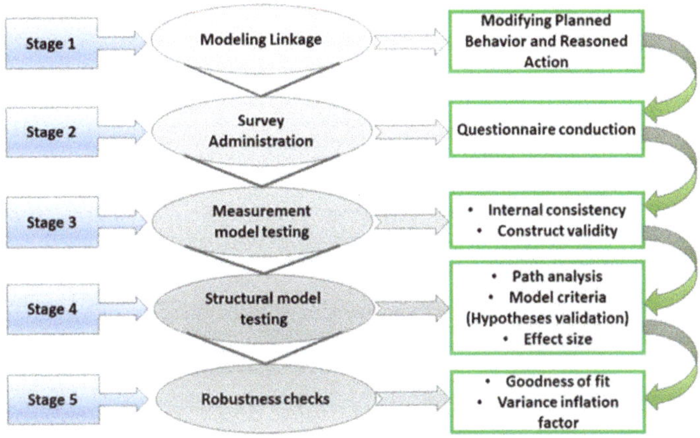

Figure 2. Schematic outline of the research methodology. Source: Authors' elaboration.

3.3.1. Demographic Data

Data on the demographic characteristics of the respondents are reported in Table 1. The participation of males (66.5%) was higher than that of females (33.4%). The proportion of urban respondents (59.3%) exceeded that of rural respondents (40.7%). The main proportion of respondents (54.7%) consisted of youth (up to 25 years old), while middle-aged individuals (26–50 years) made the second-largest age group (31.3%). The mean of respondents' age was 30.26 years, while its standard deviation was noted as 12.86. The respondents varied from illiterate (zero schooling years) to postgraduate (18 and above schooling years) in qualification. Bachelors (14 schooling years) made the largest proportion (20.9%), followed by the secondary (10 schooling years) and the higher secondary (12 schooling years) groups. The smallest proportion (4.2%) was based on illiterate respondents (zero schooling years). The largest proportion of respondents (56.6%) was unmarried, while a tiny proportion (2%) was divorced. The majority of respondents (34.2%) were employees in both public and private sectors, while students comprised the next significant share (31.3%). However, labor contributed to the smallest proportion (14.6%). The highest percentage of the respondents (43.4%) were from households with upper middle income (300,001–600,000 PRK per annum), while the lowest income households were in the smallest proportion (5.4%).

Table 1. Attributive profiles of the respondents.

Attributes	Number	Contribution (%)
Gender		
Male	551	66.5
Female	277	33.4
Resident type		
Rural (village)	337	40.7
Urban (city)	491	59.3
Age		
Youth (up to 25 years)	453	54.7
Middle aged (26–50 years)	259	31.3
Old-age (more than 50 years)	116	14.0
Qualification (schooling years)		
Illiterate (0 years)	35	4.2
Primary (5 years)	69	8.3
Middle (8 years)	112	13.5
Secondary (10 years)	151	18.2
Higher secondary (12 years)	128	15.5
Bachelor (14 years)	173	20.9
Master (16 years)	119	14.4
Postgraduate (18 years and above)	41	4.9
Marital status		
Married	342	41.3
Unmarried	469	56.6
Divorced	17	2
Profession		
Self-employed	165	19.9
Labor	121	14.6
Employees	283	34.2
Students	259	31.3
Household income (annual)		
Low (Up to 50,000 PKR)	143	17.3
Lower middle (50,001–150,000 PKR)	116	14.0
Middle (150,001–300,000 PKR)	218	26.3
Upper middle (300,001–600,000 PKR)	306	36.9
High (More than 600,000 PKR)	45	5.4

3.3.2. Statistical Measurement Model

Confirmatory factor analysis was carried out to explore whether the models were reliable and valid. The assessment of external loadings was conducted and is shown in Table 2. The external loading equivalent to or greater than 0.7 was argued to determine variations roughly surpassing 50% [97], showing that the calculated factor attained a permissible degree of reliability. As a result, external loading values above 0.7 suggest the non-exclusion of the loading factor [98].

Moreover, [99] suggested that non-external consistencies depict the reliability of a construct. In this respect, ρ-A, Cronbach-alpha (C-α), and composite reliability (CR) were employed. The range of values from 0.7 through 0.95 suggests satisfactory reliability [100]. Since C-α may understate a finite sample's efficiency, the use of an additional CR measuring tool is encouraged [101]. Furthermore, the magnitudes of ρ-A in a range between CR and Cronbach-alpha are taken to be accurate [102]. The average variance extracted (AVE) is reported in Table 2. Hair et al. [103] suggested that AVE surpassing 0.5 can be considered reliable, which is true in the present case. Thereby, the constructs in Table 2 are reliable. These findings authenticated the convergent validity and reliability of our measurement model.

Table 2. Measurement model results.

Latent Constructs	Observed Variables	External Loadings	C-α	ρ-A	CR	AVE
MAP	MAP_1	0.792	0.762	0.785	0.818	0.770
	MAP_2	0.765				
	MAP_3	0.819				
	MAP_4	0.833				
	MAP_5	0.781				
PK	PK_1	0.802	0.786	0.803	0.867	0.794
	PK_2	0.775				
	PK_3	0.793				
	PK_4	0.812				
	PK_5	0.726				
	PK_6	0.799				
	PK_7	0.845				
	PK_8	0.756				
EPPA	$EPPA_1$	0.751	0.725	0.792	0.811	0.746
	$EPPA_2$	0.773				
	$EPPA_3$	0.795				
	$EPPA_4$	0.728				
SEF	SEF_1	0.788	0.784	0.819	0.886	0.798
	SEF_2	0.823				
	SEF_3	0.795				
	SEF_4	0.776				
	SEF_5	0.861				
PGB	PGB_1	0.735	0.793	0.826	0.844	0.819
	PGB_2	0.789				
	PGB_3	0.802				
	PGB_4	0.826				
MV	MV_1	0.794	0.765	0.789	0.823	0.771
	MV_2	0.774				
	MV_3	0.832				
	MV_4	0.769				
	MV_5	0.734				
RAB	RAB_1	0.797	0.824	0.841	0.873	0.835
	RAB_2	0.824				
	RAB_3	0.800				
	RAB_4	0.775				
	RAB_5	0.730				
PR	PR_1	0.818	0.805	0.839	0.857	0.827
	PR_2	0.836				
	PR_3	0.794				
	PR_4	0.722				
	PR_5	0.765				
LTPW	$LTPW_1$	0.877	0.792	0.813	0.833	0.804
	$LTPW_2$	0.810				
	$LTPW_3$	0.848				
	$LTPW_4$	0.725				
	$LTPW_5$	0.769				
WAPP	$WAPP_1$	0.744	0.821	0.849	0.886	0.834
	$WAPP_2$	0.829				
	$WAPP_3$	0.790				
	$WAPP_4$	0.764				
	$WAPP_5$	0.893				
	$WAPP_6$	0.745				

Notes: Degree to agree with the affirmative response is classified as: 5 = "Totally agree", 4 = "Agree", 3 = "Neutral", 2 = "Disagree", 1 = "Totally disagree." C-α: Cronbach-alpha. MAP: Mythical attitude towards pandemic, PK: Pandemic knowledge, EPPA: Ease of pandemic prevention adoption, SEF: Self-efficacy, PGB: Peer groups' beliefs, MV: Moral values, RAB: Risk-averse behavior, PR: Perceived risk, LTPW: Lack of trust in political will, WAPP: Willingness to adopt pandemic prevention. AVE: average variance extracted, CR: composite reliability, ρ-A: internal consistency reliability, C-α: Cronbach-alpha.

As a step further, the confirmation of discriminant validity is crucial for assessing the scientific data's authenticity. Ketchen [104] suggested that the discriminant validity required the cross-correlations between latent constructs (LTCs) to be less than their reflective (self) correlations. In the present case, cross-correlation values of all constructs were less than their reflective correlation values (Table 3). Following Hair et al. [105], the discriminant validity is satisfied based on this criterion. Moreover, an advanced discriminant validity test by Henseler et al. [102] is used for further verification. This is known as the heterotrait-monotrait ratio (HMR) of correlations. It calculated the pairwise cross-correlations between the constructs (Table 4). At 90% confidence interval, all the cross-correlations are found within the range of confidence interval, demonstrating that the discriminant validity is established. HMR is the most recent test and it has been reported to perform better than the Fornell-Larcker [102] criterion. Since the discriminant validity is proved valid, the path analysis can be carried out.

Table 3. Discriminant validity results based on Fornell and Larcker [106] criterion.

Factors	MAP	PK	EPPA	SEF	PGB	MV	RAB	PR	LTPW	WAPP
MAP	(0.88)									
PK	0.198	(0.75)								
EPPA	0.203	0.327	(0.76)							
SEF	0.511	0.295	0.197	(0.85)						
PGB	0.136	0.189	0.205	0.329	(0.79)					
MV	0.376	0.143	0.428	0.312	0.298	(0.83)				
RA	0.281	0.451	0.365	0.408	0.156	0.396	(0.89)			
PR	0.372	0.268	0.272	0.216	0.381	0.401	0.415	(0.86)		
LTPW	0.490	0.311	0.290	0.345	0.410	0.348	0.264	0.255	(0.89)	
WAPP	0.277	0.506	0.317	0.437	0.178	0.273	0.367	0.316	0.307	(0.82)

Table 4. Discriminant validity testing based on the Heterotrait-Monotrait Ratio.

Factors	MAP	PK	EPPA	SEF	PGB	MV	RAB	PR	LTPW
MAP									
PK	0.70 $CI_{0.90}$ [0.68;0.72]								
EPPA	0.64 $CI_{0.90}$ [0.62;0.67]	0.69 $CI_{0.90}$ [0.67;0.71]							
SEF	0.65 $CI_{0.90}$ [0.63;0.68]	0.63 $CI_{0.90}$ [0.61;0.65]	0.74 $CI_{0.90}$ [0.71;0.76]						
PGB	0.76 $CI_{0.90}$ [0.73;0.78]	0.71 $CI_{0.90}$ [0.69;0.73]	0.73 $CI_{0.90}$ [0.71;0.75]	0.75 $CI_{0.90}$ [0.73;0.77]					
MV	0.68 $CI_{0.90}$ [0.66;0.70]	0.66 $CI_{0.90}$ [0.64;0.68]	0.71 $CI_{0.90}$ [0.69;0.73]	0.74 $CI_{0.90}$ [0.72;0.76]	0.69 $CI_{0.90}$ [0.67;0.71]				
RA	0.73 $CI_{0.90}$ [0.71;0.75]	0.76 $CI_{0.90}$ [0.74;0.78]	0.65 $CI_{0.90}$ [0.63;0.67]	0.62 $CI_{0.90}$ [0.60;0.64]	0.67 $CI_{0.90}$ [0.65;0.69]	0.69 $CI_{0.90}$ [0.67;0.71]			
PR	0.64 $CI_{0.90}$ [0.62;0.66]	0.67 $CI_{0.90}$ [0.65;0.69]	0.74 $CI_{0.90}$ [0.72;0.76]	0.71 $CI_{0.90}$ [0.69;0.73]	0.75 $CI_{0.90}$ [0.73;0.77]	0.69 $CI_{0.90}$ [0.67;0.71]	0.78 $CI_{0.90}$ [0.76;0.80]		
LTPW	0.81 $CI_{0.90}$ [0.79;0.83]	0.78 $CI_{0.90}$ [0.76;0.80]	0.75 $CI_{0.90}$ [0.73;0.77]	0.77 $CI_{0.90}$ [0.75;0.79]	0.73 $CI_{0.90}$ [0.71;0.75]	0.75 $CI_{0.90}$ [0.73;0.77]	0.71 $CI_{0.90}$ [0.69;0.73]	0.84 $CI_{0.90}$ [0.82;0.86]	
WAPP	0.85 $CI_{0.90}$ [0.83;0.87]	0.88 $CI_{0.90}$ [0.86;0.90]	0.84 $CI_{0.90}$ [0.82;0.86]	0.83 $CI_{0.90}$ [0.81;0.85]	0.87 $CI_{0.90}$ [0.85;0.89]	0.86 $CI_{0.90}$ [0.84;0.88]	0.79 $CI_{0.90}$ [0.77;0.81]	0.74 $CI_{0.90}$ [0.72;0.76]	0.69 $CI_{0.90}$ [0.67;0.71]

Notes: CI: confidence interval. The brackets [] contain the confidence intervals at 90%.

4. Main Results

The path modeling-based results are shown in Table 5 and Figure 3. The structural model was evaluated after the measurement model were proven to be reliable and efficient. As a primary condition, the R-square was generated for each of the constructs. R-square measures the variations captured by each of the non-exogenously discovered constructs to communicate the structural model's predictive capacity. As a rule of thumb, a magnitude no less than 0.25 has been proposed to be an average score, whereas a magnitude below 0.13 is insufficient to pass this criterion in the behavioral sciences. In contrast, the badness of outcome is exhibited by any score less than or equal to 0.03 [48]. In the present case, the R-square value is 0.807, which is well above 0.25, satisfying the path model's first criterion (Table 5).

Table 5. Path modeling analysis and post-estimation criteria results.

Hypothesis	Hypothesized Path			PC	Assessment	VIF	f-Square	R-Square	Q-Square
H1	MAP	→	WAPP	−0.581 ***	Verified	2.429	0.405	0.807	0.365
H2	PK	→	WAPP	0.509 ***	Verified	4.274	0.355		
H3	EPPA	→	WAPP	0.105 ***	Verified	1.992	0.073		
H4	SEF	→	WAPP	0.472 **	Verified	2.651	0.329		
H5	PGB	→	WAPP	0.710 ***	Verified	2.843	0.495		
H6	MV	→	WAPP	0.015	Not verified	3.701	0.010		
H7	RAB	→	WAPP	0.421 *	Verified	1.623	0.293		
H8	PR	→	WAPP	0.399 *	Verified	3.584	0.278		
H9	LTPW	→	WAPP	−0.652 ***	Verified	2.497	0.454		

Notes: PC: path coefficient. * $p < 0.05$, ** $p < 0.05$, *** $p < 0.01$, VIF: variance inflation factor.

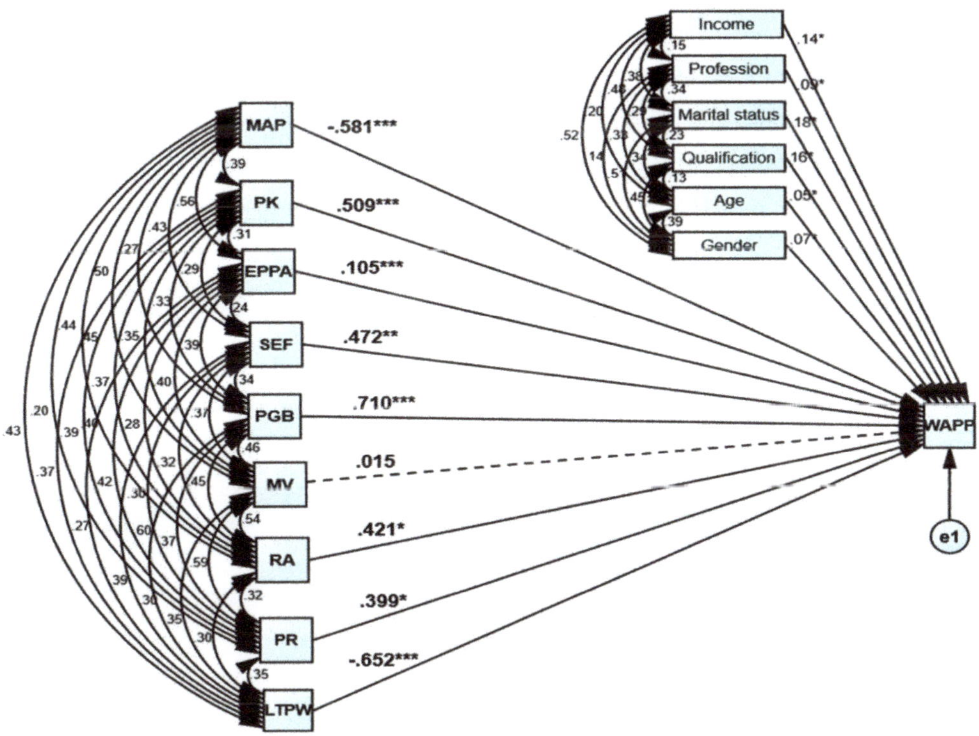

Figure 3. Path modeling-based estimation of coefficients. Notes: * $p < 0.10$, ** $p < 0.05$, *** $p < 0.01$. Solid line denotes significant path, while dashed line denotes insignificant one. Source: Authors' elaboration.

Next, Stone–Geisser's Q-square criterion was used explore the LTCs' predictive relevance [107,108]. The non-negative range score reflects the LTCs' predictive relevance [102].

Further, the predictive relevance's relative impact is given by the degree of this criterion. A Q-square > 0.35 indicates that the exogenous constructs imparted adequate prediction for their respective endogenous constructs [97]. The magnitude of the measured Q-square (0.365) proved the accuracy and precision of the structural model. The path coefficients analysis is taken as a further prerequisite. In the structural model, an approximate path coefficient score above 0.1 indicates a significant contribution of a respective variable to the dependent variable [103]. After that, f-square is obtained, determining the effect size to characterize a construct's contributing ability. Based on the f-square score, exogenous constructs define the identified differences in endogenously defined LTCs [109].

The path modeling does not require the prior existence of a normal distribution principle. Alternatively, this principle is followed by the bootstrap-based parameter estimation method to evaluate the importance of external loading and ICFs' path coefficients. The bootstrapping method scrutinizes nearly 4×10^4 samples extracted from the initial sample using the "with replacement" alternative for estimating every bootstrapped sample. This bootstrapping procedure involves generating a probability distribution for manipulating the variances and standardized residuals. To assess the validity of path coefficients, the null hypothesis of $H_1 = H_2 = H_3 = H_4 = H_5 = H_6 = H_7 = H_8 = H_9 = 0$ was assessed against the alternative of $H_1 \neq H_2 \neq H_3 \neq H_4 \neq H_5 \neq H_6 \neq H_7 \neq H_8 \neq H_9 \neq 0$. For decision-making, the probabilities equal to or less than the statistical magnitude of 0.05 are considered significant at a 5 percent level [102]. To this end, the only null hypothesis retained was $H_6 = 0$, while the remaining were successfully rejected (Table 5). In other words, all the ICFs contributed to the WAPP of individuals, except for the moral values.

The path coefficients-based relative significance of the ICFs of individuals' WAPP is depicted in Figure 4. The ICF of peer groups' beliefs is highest ranked, followed by a lack of trust in political will, mythical attitude towards pandemic, and so on. The moral values are the lowest-ranked ICF. This ranking of significance is based on the strength of the path coefficients. For illustration, the magnitudes of path coefficients are provided as peer groups' beliefs = 0.710, lack of trust in political will = 0.652, mythical attitude towards pandemic = 0.581, pandemic knowledge = 0.509, self-efficacy = 0.472, risk-averse behavior = 0.421, perceived risk = 0.399, and ease of pandemic prevention adoption = 0.105. However, the coefficient of moral values remained insignificant and lowest (0.015). And thus, moral values imparted a neutral contribution to the individuals' WAPP.

In summary, a lack of trust in the political will and a mythical attitude towards the pandemic are the dominant inhibitors of individuals' WAPP. Meanwhile, the other ICFs are revealed as the driving forces of individuals' WAPP, except moral values which highlighted a neutral role in determining the individuals' WAPP. Peer groups' beliefs and pandemic knowledge are discovered as the main driving forces of individuals' WAPP (Figure 5).

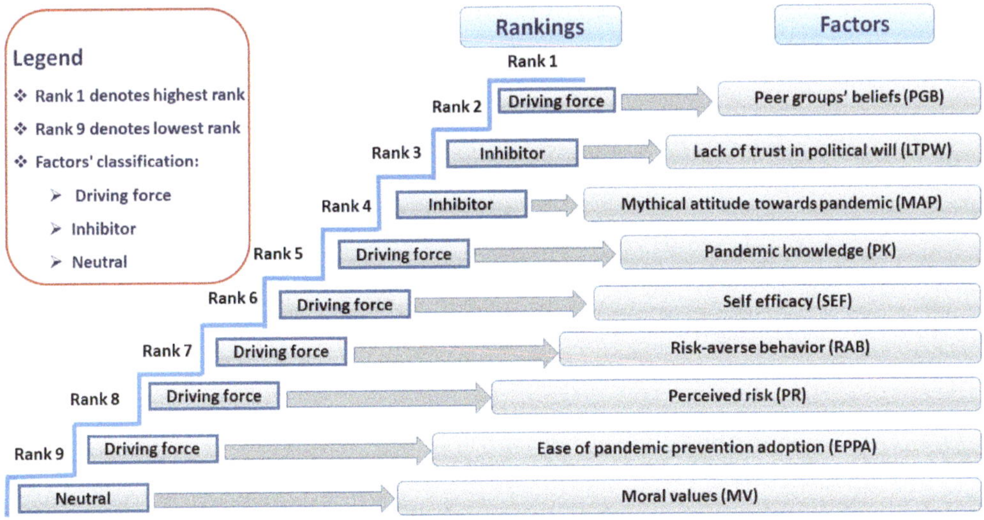

Figure 4. Ranking the significance of intention-based critical factors (ICFs) affecting individuals' willingness to adopt pandemic prevention (WAPP). Source: Authors' elaboration.

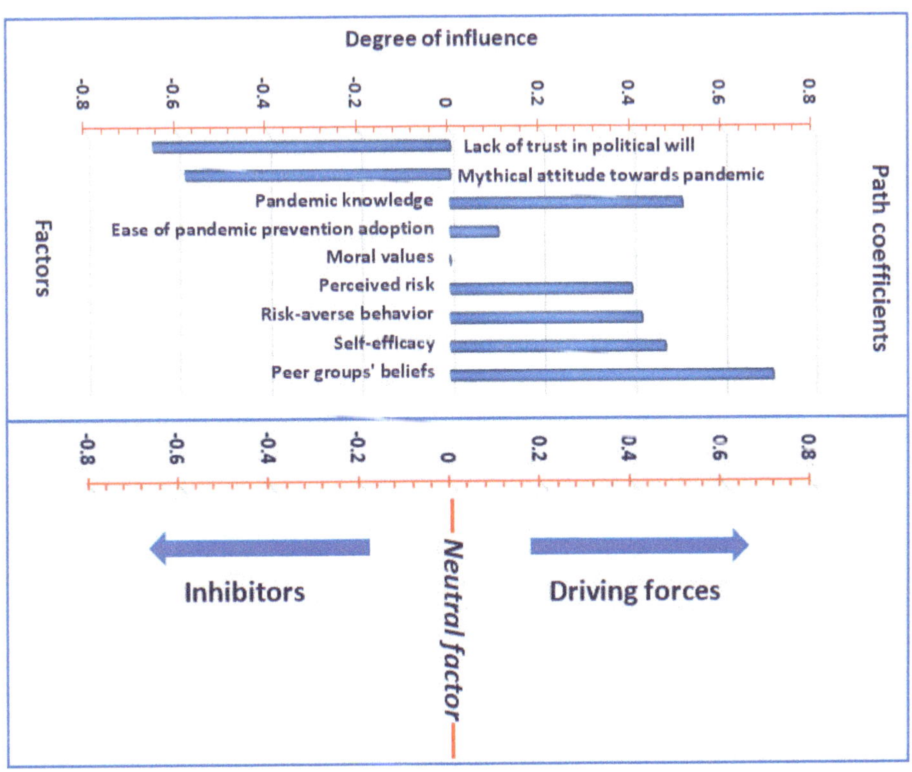

Figure 5. Path coefficients-based classification of factors into driving forces, inhibitors, and neutral factors. Source: Authors' elaboration.

5. Discussion, Limitations, and Future Research Directions

5.1. Discussion

In the present research, pandemic knowledge played a positive role in escalating the individuals' WAPP. It means that if individuals are aware of the fatal and lethal aspects of a pandemic, they are willing to protect themselves from it. In contrast, a survey-based study of 740 patients in Jordan investigated and revealed that most participants had knowledge and awareness about Chronic Kidney Disease, but half of them had the wrong information and could not detect its symptoms at the initial level. Thus, their knowledge affected the adoption of prevention practices negatively [110]. However, analogous to our results, a study on 265 Black faith leaders in the U.S. found that increased awareness regarding HIV through print and social media, church websites, and making policies of HIV prevention could help reduce the disease [111]. It was further argued that the treatment approach and treatment knowledge were essential role player in preventing the spread of HIV around the world [112]. Along these lines, the dissemination and acquisition of correct and well-informed pandemic knowledge could play an integral driving influence during pandemic outbreaks.

The Ebola virus spread through African countries in 2014, giving rise to increased fatality rates. The main reason behind the pandemic's spread was the increased population mobility worldwide (domestic and international), lack of awareness, and weak health systems. The lesson learned from the last pandemic was that a country should make its health system better. Vaccination-based treatment, safety policies, advertisement on pandemic prevention, and pandemic prevention impacts were emphasized [113]. The mythical attitude towards the pandemic proved to be a bottleneck in enhancing the individuals' WAPP. This finding was consistent with that of Khalil and Abdalrahim [110], who revealed a negative influence of attitudinal construct on disease prevention practices. Similar to the findings of the present work, Liao and Wang [114] evaluated and uncovered a supportive influence of epidemic information on China's prevention adoption. In the same vein, Ritter et al. [93] explored the ways through which farmers adopted the policies based on management practices for the prevention and control of diseases. Social relationships, social media, and farm consultants' recommendations also motivate the farmers to adopt such practices for prevention and control.

Our results revealed that peer groups' beliefs and self-efficacy positively drove the individuals' WAPP. Similarly, a different study conducted in four regions, including Toronto, Guangdong, Singapore, and Hong Kong, evaluated the beliefs of peer groups and self-efficacy on preventive behaviors to prevent and control the SARS pandemic in these regions. However, the results demonstrated that self-efficacy was not a substantial predictor for all respondents in Guangdong [115]. Additionally, successions of the cholera pandemic outbreak in Hanoi interjected a flash of financial and economic triumphalism in the past changeover. In search of the basis of a rebellious syndrome linked with scarceness and less growth and expansion, media, official groups, and residents not only found victims but also offered a way out. They also permitted specific revelations of moral conduct, the public's health, and societal order. In this regard, the beliefs of peer groups and self-efficacy strengthened the pandemic prevention adoption during the outbreaks [116].

This work has demonstrated the driving influence of perceived risk and risk-averse behavior in promoting individuals' WAPP. Along these lines, Botzen et al. [117] discovered the impact of influence factors to prevent flood damage in New York. For this purpose, the protection motivation theory was taken as a theoretical base. Their results unveiled that factors such as attitude towards risk and time preferences played a major role in individuals' decision-making regarding preventing and controlling floods in high-risk areas. It has been documented that health policy was necessary for the prevention and control of pandemics. Risk-averse behavior was considered a useful means to avoid pandemics. Further, Omodior et al. [118] investigated the impact of perceived severity and perceived susceptibility on the adoption of personnel protective behaviors (PPB) in the case of five mosquito-borne pandemics. They did it by considering a sample of 1043 respondents from the U.S. The diseases included West Nile virus, Dengue fever, Zika virus, Chikungunya, and Malaria. The outcomes disclosed that perceived severity was found among all mosquito-borne pandemics. Also, the people were more concerned about the adoption of PPB in the cases of Zika virus, Chikungunya, and Dengue fever than in the cases of West Nile virus and Malaria. Finally, Cui et al. [119] conducted a survey to bridge a gap between the linkage between risk perception about avian-influenza and adoptive biosecurity measures (ABM) by taking a sample of 426 poultry farmers in China. The results discovered that increased perceived risk induced more ABM adoption. This finding is aligned with our results since perceived risk proved to be the driving force of individuals' WAPP.

We found that ease of pandemic prevention adoption promoted the individuals' WAPP. Consistent with our results, Kusuma et al. [50] revealed that the unavailability of protective gears (mainly hand sanitizers and face masks) adversely impacted the COVID-19 prevention adoption in four South Asian countries (India, Bangladesh, Sri Lanka, and Pakistan). It means that the easier the adoption of pandemic prevention, the more that individuals will be willing to adopt it. Furthermore, Yang et al. [120] conducted an impact analysis between the feasibility of adopting good agricultural practices by the small farmers and enhancing raw milk hygiene by taking data from 34 farms. The results indicated that almost 47.73% of farmers were adopting hygienic policies for raw milk in the face of their feasible adoption.

We also revealed that a lack of trust in political inhibited the individuals' WAPP. In support of this finding, past research found that E-guidelines and price premium by the government were some factors that positively influenced the adoption of hygienic practices by building the trust of farmers in political institutions [120]. Similarly, Cui et al. [121] studied the critical factors influencing Chinese poultry farms in response to the avian influenza virus by taking semi-structured interviews from twenty-five poultry farmers between November 2016 and May 2017 using grounded theory. The results showed that the government must inform farmers regarding prevention and control at an early stage of the avian influenza virus through the proper communication networks. In contrast to our results, Paolini et al. [122] studied and discovered a positive contribution of political trust to COVID-19 distress in the Italian context. Similarly, Sarkar et al. [123] conducted a situation analysis in eight South Asian countries and confirmed that governance maximization was the optimal tool for preventing and controlling the COVID-19 epidemic.

5.2. Limitations and Future Research Directions

Since there is always room for improvement, this work has some limitations that can be overcome by future works. First, this study's sampling procedure was not purely randomized which would limit its findings' generalizability. It was not possible to make it strictly random due to the ongoing pandemic outbreak across the country. Therefore, some selected platforms were chosen to collect data through questionnaires. Future studies should overcome this limitation to make the sampling generation process purely random to gain enough generalizability of the findings. Second, this work has considered the case of intention-based factors during the ongoing pandemic outbreak; however, it cannot provide a complete picture of individuals' behavior before and after the pandemic. Therefore, future studies should conduct a pre-and post-pandemic analysis to get a clear idea of how it affects the intention-based factors influencing the individuals' adoption behavior. Third, this work analyzed the whole dataset, including rural and urban respondents. Future studies should also analyze the urban and rural samples separately to investigate the differences in individuals' intention-based factors across the two samples. This would enhance the insight of the findings, providing a deep understanding of rural-urban heterogeneity. Fourth, there might exist possible dependencies among the constructs of this study. However, we have not considered this aspect since it needs to establish a separate model to incorporate the mediation or moderation impacts. Therefore, future works should include this aspect to analyze the potential mediation or moderation among those constructs. As a final point, this work merely conducted aggregated analysis without distinguishing the demographic features of the study sample. Future studies may consider disaggregated analysis for people under different age cohorts, different income groups, and across varying levels of qualification to see the differences of response across groups of individuals with heterogeneous demographic attributes. It would provide a rich and comparative analysis for more informed and targeted public health policy outcomes.

This work's outcomes are unique in terms of reflecting the individuals' intention-based driving forces, inhibitors, and neutral factors of WAPP from the perspective of a hybrid theoretical framework based on the planned behavior and reasoned action schools of thought. The consideration of ICFs is vital in the face of the fact that these factors significantly influence the intention of individuals to adopt preventive measures during pandemic spread, such as the currently ongoing outbreak of pandemic COVID-19. During the outbreak of an infectious pandemic, everyone's participation to avoid viral transmission is critical. This work's implications are useful guidelines on ICFs to shape the WAPP of individuals in Pakistan and at the global level during the outbreak of COVID-19 and potential future pandemics.

6. Conclusions

The key conclusion points are as follows: The peer groups' beliefs, self-efficacy, risk-averse behavior, pandemic knowledge, ease of pandemic prevention adoption, and perceived risk were revealed to be the driving forces of the individuals' willingness to adopt pandemic prevention. The inhibitors included the lack of trust in political will and a mythical attitude towards pandemic. However, moral values had a neutral role. Regarding the relative significance of intention-based critical factors, peer groups' beliefs, as well as the lack of trust in the political will, were ranked the highest. Simultaneously, the moral values factor was ranked the lowest in determining individuals' willingness to adopt pandemic prevention.

Based on the empirical results, the following policies are suggested. (1) The government should play a critical role at the central level (federal/provincial level) and the decentralized levels, including divisional, district (sub-division), Tehsil (district's sub-division), and union council (Tehsil's sub-division) levels, to win the trust of people at the grass-roots level. To this end, the government needs to develop and successfully implement favorable policies to improve its image in the public's eyes. If people realize that the government is performing well, they will listen to the government's guidelines in case of potential future pandemics. (2) The mythical attitudes of individuals lead them to refuse the adoption of pandemic prevention. Therefore, awareness campaigns on lethality and fatality of the pandemic must be organized, addressing this concern at all societal levels. Testing of communicable diseases such as COVID-19 at the grass-roots level may help remove individuals' mythical attitudes regarding the disease's existence. The mythical attitude is nurtured in the roots of culture. To uproot and modify such attitudes, education is the optimal solution, reshaping the behaviors of individuals in times of pandemics like COVID-19. Pandemic knowledge is something that promotes the adoption behaviors; therefore, individuals must be educated about the existence and transmission mechanisms of this pandemic irrespective of their age groups and income classes. Moreover, the government should expand the health sector's capacity, and job creation should be enhanced. More employed individuals in this sector will help educate the people about such fatal epidemics' seriousness.

(3) Perceived risk and risk-averse behavior were found be to among the significant contributors to individuals' willingness to adopt pandemic prevention. It means that once individuals recognize the pandemic's seriousness, vulnerability, and fatality, their objective of adopting pandemic prevention is strengthened. The high level of risk perception of communicable diseases (such as COVID-19) will substantially reform the individual's willingness to adopt pandemic prevention. (4) The ease of pandemic prevention adoption was proved a significant driving force in determining the willingness of individuals to adopt the prevention. It implies that the easier the adoption of pandemic prevention, the higher

the individuals' willingness to adopt such preventative measures. Pandemic prevention gear like surgical masks, hand sanitizers, and hand wash soaps are not affordable for every individual in society. Therefore, to promote individuals' WAPP, the provision of such protective measures free of cost or at discounted rates would aid in the adoption of pandemic prevention.

Supplementary Materials: The following are available online at https://www.mdpi.com/article/10.3390/ijerph18116167/s1, S1: Informed Consent Form.

Author Contributions: Conceptualization, M.A.; Data curation, M.A., N.A., M.I. and G.J.; Formal analysis, M.A., G.J. and M.I.; Funding acquisition, N.A.; Writing—original draft, M.A.; Writing—review & editing, N.A., G.J., H.W., M.K.A. and C.I. All authors have read and agreed to the published version of the manuscript.

Funding: This work was supported by the North Minzu University Annual Research Project (Grant Number PKST2020).

Institutional Review Board Statement: This study was approved by the ethics committee of the Xi'an University of Architecture and Technology, China (No. 654-2).

Informed Consent Statement: Informed consent was obtained from all respondents during conducting the questionnaire survey.

Data Availability Statement: The data will be made available on reasonable request from the corresponding author.

Conflicts of Interest: The authors declare no potential conflicts of interest.

Appendix A

Table A1. Expert participants engaged in the assessment and testing of the questionnaire.

Sr.	Profession	Institution	Experience (Years)	Communication
1	Professors, Associate professors (Sociology, Medical, Psychology)	QAU, KEC, FCCU	10–30	Email/Telephone
2	Medical practitioners	SIH, PIMS, AKUH	10–15	Email/Telephone
3	Healthcare counselor and advisor	NIH	More than 20	Email

Notes: QAU: Quaid-i-Azam University, KEC: King Edward College, FCCU: Forman Christian College University, SIH: Shifa International Hospital, PIMS: Pakistan Institute of Medical Sciences, AKUH: Aga Khan University Hospital, NIH: National Institute of Health.

Appendix B

Table 2. List of questions included in the questionnaire survey conducted.

Constructs	Items	Degree of Agreement				
		5	4	3	2	1
Mythical attitude towards pandemic (MAP)	MAP_1: I think the adoption of preventive measures will not be helpful in pandemic containment. MAP_2: I think this pandemic (COVID-19) will vanish on its own. MAP_3: I think adopting preventive measures cannot keep me healthy. MAP_4: I think the adoption of preventive measures is useless for me because I need to go out to earn a livelihood. MAP_5: I think COVID-19 will automatically die due to high temperatures.					

Table 2. *Cont.*

Constructs	Items	Degree of Agreement				
		5	4	3	2	1
Pandemic knowledge (PK)	PK_1: The COVID-19 may transmit through human-to-human interaction. PK_2: The COVID-19 may also transmit through a common point of contact (door, table surface, etc.). PK_3: The COVID-19 may transmit through handshake and communication with the carrier of this disease. PK_4: The initial symptoms of COVID-19 include fever, dry cough, sneezing, body aches, and breathing distress, etc. PK_5: The infectious diseases may be prevented if we keep ourselves clean. PK_6: Disease (COVID-19) can be prevented through continual handwashing. PK_7: The COVID-19 enters the human body through the nasal (nose) and oral (mouth) cavity as well as the eyes. PK_8: The COVID-19 can be prevented through social distancing.					
Ease of pandemic prevention adoption (EPPA)	$EPPA_1$: I think face masks would be sufficient if there is a long-term outbreak. $EPPA_2$: I think home quarantine would be feasible if there is a long-term outbreak. $EPPA_3$: I think the food supplies would be sufficient if there is a long-term outbreak. $EPPA_4$: There is a sufficient amount of disinfectants, soaps, and hand sanitizers for the long-term outbreak.					
Self-efficacy (SEF)	SEF_1: I have the prevention instructions for the pandemic (COVID-19). SEF_2: I have the required capital (face masks, sanitizers, and disinfectants, gloves) to take preventive measures. SEF_3: I have the skills to adopt preventive measures. SEF_4: I can completely adopt the preventive measures. SEF_5: I believe I will adopt these measures until the outbreak persists.					
Peer groups' beliefs (PGB)	PGB_1: I am adopting pandemic preventive measures because my peer groups (friends, colleagues, family physicians, and health professionals) are doing so. PGB_2: I am adopting preventive measures as they are suggested by my family physician. PGB_3: I am adopting preventive measures as they are suggested by health professionals. PGB_4: I am adopting preventive measures as they are suggested by my colleagues, friends, and neighbors.					
Moral values (MV)	MV_1: I am morally responsible for preventing others from being infected because of me (if I am infected). MV_2: It is my moral obligation to provide supplies of masks and disinfectants to others if I have their excess supply. MV_3: It is my moral obligation to reduce the usage of masks and disinfectants to spare them for others. MV_4: If I have any symptoms (fever, dry cough, etc.) I am responsible for informing the relevant health authorities. MV_5: I am responsible for adopting preventive measures not only for myself but also for others.					
Risk-averse behavior (RAB)	RAB_1: I am adopting preventive measures to keep myself healthy. RAB_2: I am adopting preventive measures to keep my kids/parents/siblings/spouse healthy. RAB_3: I am advising my kids/parents/siblings/spouse to adopt preventive measures. RAB_4: I am avoiding visits to crowded places and staying at home most of the time to avoid contact with strangers. RAB_5: I am practicing social distancing to prevent COVID-19.					

Table 2. *Cont.*

Constructs	Items	Degree of Agreement				
		5	4	3	2	1
Perceived risk (PR)	PR_1: I perceive the severity of the disease (COVID-19). PR_2: I understand the susceptibility of the health risk of this disease (COVID-19). PR_3: I think this (COVID-19) is a fatal disease. PR_4: This disease (COVID-19) does not discriminate against gender, race, ethnic groups, countries, and borders. PR_5: The outbreak may persist if people are not quarantined.					
Lack of trust in political will (LTPW)	$LTPW_1$: The government does not respond timely to the economic problems. $LTPW_2$: It is not in the interest of the government to prevent people from diseases. $LTPW_3$: Government is not willing to provide better health facilities to the people. $LTPW_4$: The government is not doing enough for the people who got unemployed during the pandemic outbreak. $LTPW_5$: It is not in the interest of the government to follow transparency.					
Willingness to adopt pandemic prevention (WAPP)	$WAPP_1$: I intend to adopt preventive measures if any outbreak happens in the future. $WAPP_2$: I am ready to be quarantined to prevent the outbreak of the pandemic (COVID-19). $WAPP_3$: I intend to highly recommend the preventive measures to others. $WAPP_4$: I have the intention to adopt a healthy lifestyle even after the outbreak. $WAPP_5$: I intend to adopt preventive measures during the present outbreak of COVID-19. $WAPP_6$. If there is a long-term outbreak, I would be willing to be home quarantined for a long time.					

Notes: the degree to agree with the affirmative response is classified as: 5 = "Totally agree", 4 = "Agree", 3 = "Neutral", 2 = "Disagree", 1 = "Totally disagree."

References

1. Ahmad, M.; Iram, K.; Jabeen, G. Perception-based influence factors of intention to adopt COVID-19 epidemic prevention in China. *Environ. Res.* **2020**, *190*, 109995. [CrossRef]
2. Irfan, M.; Ahmad, M.; Fareed, Z.; Iqbal, N.; Sharif, A.; Wu, H. On the indirect environmental outcomes of COVID-19: Short-term revival with futuristic long- term implications. *Int. J. Environ. Health Res.* **2021**, 1–11. [CrossRef] [PubMed]
3. Wang, Q.; Su, M. A preliminary assessment of the impact of COVID-19 on environment—A case study of China. *Sci. Total Environ.* **2020**, *728*, 138915. [CrossRef] [PubMed]
4. World Health Organization. Available online: https://www.who.int/emergencies/diseases/novel-coronavirus-2019 (accessed on 10 February 2021).
5. Ajzen, I.; Fishbein, M. The Prediction of Behavior from Attitudinal and Normative Variables. *J. Expr. Soc. Psychol.* **1970**, *6*, 466–487. [CrossRef]
6. Zhang, D.; Li, T.; Wang, P.; Wang, W.; Feng, M.; Li, L.; Jiang, Q.; Lan, M.; Orlandini, L.C.; Li, J.; et al. Experts consensus on epidemic prevention and control in radiotherapy centers during the COVID-19 outbreak: Experiences from Sichuan Province. *Clin. Transl. Radiat. Oncol.* **2020**, *24*, 88–91. [CrossRef]
7. Ren, Y.; Liu, S.; Yang, L.; Shan, J.; Liu, Y.; Li, H.; Chen, L.H.; Chen, H. Practice and exploration of infection prevention and control measures based on risk management of surgical patients during the epidemic of corona virus disease 2019 (COVID-19). *Am. J. Infect. Control* **2020**, *49*, 151–157. [CrossRef]
8. Du, W.; Han, S.; Li, Q.; Zhang, Z. Epidemic update of COVID-19 in Hubei Province compared with other regions in China. *Int. J. Infect. Dis.* **2020**, *95*, 321–325. [CrossRef]
9. Wang, P.; Zheng, X.; Li, J.; Zhu, B. Prediction of epidemic trends in COVID-19 with logistic model and machine learning technics. *Chaos Solitons Fractals* **2020**, *139*, 110058. [CrossRef] [PubMed]
10. Yasir, A.; Hu, X.; Ahmad, M.; Rauf, A.; Shi, J.; Nasir, S.A. Modeling Impact of Word of Mouth and E-Government on Online Social Presence during COVID-19 Outbreak: A Multi-Mediation Approach. *Int. J. Environ. Res. Public Health* **2020**, *17*, 2954. [CrossRef]

11. Saez, M.; Tobias, A.; Varga, D.; Barceló, M.A. Effectiveness of the measures to flatten the epidemic curve of COVID-19. The case of Spain. *Sci. Total Environ.* **2020**, *727*, 138761. [CrossRef]
12. Zhao, Z.; Li, X.; Liu, F.; Zhu, G.; Ma, C.; Wang, L. Prediction of the COVID-19 spread in African countries and implications for prevention and control: A case study in South Africa, Egypt, Algeria, Nigeria, Senegal and Kenya. *Sci. Total Environ.* **2020**, *729*, 138959. [CrossRef] [PubMed]
13. Karmaker, C.L.; Ahmed, T.; Ahmed, S.; Ali, S.M.; Moktadir, M.A.; Kabir, G. Improving supply chain sustainability in the context of COVID-19 pandemic in an emerging economy: Exploring drivers using an integrated model. *Sustain. Prod. Consum.* **2021**, *26*, 411–427. [CrossRef]
14. Majumdar, A.; Shaw, M.; Sinha, S.K. COVID-19 debunks the myth of socially sustainable supply chain: A case of the clothing industry in South Asian countries. *Sustain. Prod. Consum.* **2020**, *24*, 150–155. [CrossRef]
15. Ali, H.; Yilmaz, G.; Fareed, Z.; Shahzad, F.; Ahmad, M. Impact of novel coronavirus (COVID-19) on daily routines and air environment: Evidence from Turkey. *Air Qual. Atmos. Health* **2021**, *26*, 411–427. [CrossRef]
16. Zhang, Z.; Xue, T.; Jin, X. Effects of meteorological conditions and air pollution on COVID-19 transmission: Evidence from 219 Chinese cities. *Sci. Total Environ.* **2020**, *741*, 140244. [CrossRef]
17. Karataş, Z.; Tagay, Ö. The relationships between resilience of the adults affected by the covid pandemic in turkey and Covid-19 fear, meaning in life, life satisfaction, intolerance of uncertainty and hope. *Personal. Individ. Differ.* **2021**, *172*, 110592. [CrossRef]
18. Karlsson, L.C.; Soveri, A.; Lewandowsky, S.; Karlsson, L.; Karlsson, H.; Nolvi, S.; Karukivi, M.; Lindfelt, M.; Antfolk, J. Fearing the Disease or the Vaccine: The Case of COVID-19. *Personal. Individ. Differ.* **2020**, *172*, 110590. [CrossRef]
19. Hughes, S.; Machan, L. It's a conspiracy: Covid-19 conspiracies link to psychopathy, Machiavellianism and collective narcissism. *Personal. Individ. Differ.* **2021**, *171*, 110559. [CrossRef] [PubMed]
20. Jin, S.; Balliet, D.; Romano, A.; Spadaro, G.; van Lissa, C.J.; Agostini, M.; Bélanger, J.J.; Gützkow, B.; Kreienkamp, J.; PsyCorona Collaboration; et al. Intergenerational conflicts of interest and prosocial behavior during the COVID-19 pandemic. *Personal. Individ. Differ.* **2021**, *171*, 1–8. [CrossRef]
21. Wagerman, S.A.; Bedikian, A.; Ross, B.S. Psychodynamic and sociopolitical predictors of COVID Distress and Gravity. *Personal. Individ. Differ.* **2020**, 110506. [CrossRef]
22. Hardin, B.S.; Smith, C.V.; Jordan, L.N. Is the COVID-19 pandemic even darker for some? Examining dark personality and affective, cognitive, and behavioral responses to the COVID-19 pandemic. *Personal. Individ. Differ.* **2021**, *171*, 110504. [CrossRef]
23. Zitek, E.M.; Schlund, R.J. Psychological entitlement predicts noncompliance with the health guidelines of the COVID-19 pandemic. *Personal. Individ. Differ.* **2021**, *171*, 110491. [CrossRef]
24. Ruggieri, S.; Ingoglia, S.; Bonfanti, R.C.; Lo Coco, G. The role of online social comparison as a protective factor for psychological wellbeing: A longitudinal study during the COVID-19 quarantine. *Personal. Individ. Differ.* **2021**, *171*, 110486. [CrossRef]
25. Chan, E.Y. Moral foundations underlying behavioral compliance during the COVID-19 pandemic. *Personal. Individ. Differ.* **2021**, *171*, 110463. [CrossRef]
26. Li, W.Q.; Li, L.M.W.; Jiang, D.; Liu, S. Fate control and ingroup bias in donation for the fight with the coronavirus pandemic: The mediating role of risk perception of COVID-19. *Personal. Individ. Differ.* **2021**, *171*, 110456. [CrossRef] [PubMed]
27. Paredes, M.R.; Apaolaza, V.; Fernandez-Robin, C.; Hartmann, P.; Yañez-Martinez, D. The impact of the COVID-19 pandemic on subjective mental well-being: The interplay of perceived threat, future anxiety and resilience. *Personal. Individ. Differ.* **2021**, *170*, 110455. [CrossRef] [PubMed]
28. Malesza, M.; Kaczmarek, M.C. Predictors of anxiety during the COVID-19 pandemic in Poland. *Personal. Individ. Differ.* **2021**, *170*, 110419. [CrossRef] [PubMed]
29. Volk, A.A.; Brazil, K.J.; Franklin-Luther, P.; Dane, A.V.; Vaillancourt, T. The influence of demographics and personality on COVID-19 coping in young adults. *Personal. Individ. Differ.* **2021**, *168*, 110398. [CrossRef]
30. Grossman, E.S.; Hoffman, Y.S.G.; Palgi, Y.; Shrira, A. COVID-19 related loneliness and sleep problems in older adults: Worries and resilience as potential moderators. *Personal. Individ. Differ.* **2021**, *168*, 110371. [CrossRef] [PubMed]
31. Latkin, C.A.; Dayton, L.; Moran, M.; Strickland, J.C.; Collins, K. Behavioral and psychosocial factors associated with COVID-19 skepticism in the United States. *Curr. Psychol.* **2021**. [CrossRef]
32. Alper, S. Psychological correlates of COVID-19 conspiracy beliefs and preventive measures: Evidence from Turkey Predictors of COVID-19 Conspiracy Beliefs. *Curr. Psychol.* **2020**, 1–10. [CrossRef]
33. Lei, X.; Jing, S.; Zeng, X.; Lin, Y.; Li, X.; Xing, Q.; Zhong, X. Knowledge, attitudes and practices towards avian in fl uenza among live poultry market workers in Chongqing, China. *Prev. Vet. Med.* **2019**, *162*, 151–159. [CrossRef] [PubMed]
34. Shi, J.; Shi, L.; Geng, J.; Liu, R.; Gong, X.; Bo, X.; Chen, N.; Liu, Q.; Yang, Y.; Wang, Z. Status of evidence-based chronic diseases prevention implementation in Shanghai, China: A qualitative study. *Int. J. Health Plan. Manag.* **2019**, *34*, 912–925. [CrossRef] [PubMed]
35. Polonsky, M.; Azbel, L.; Wickersham, J.A.; Taxman, F.S.; Grishaev, E.; Dvoryak, S.; Altice, F.L. Challenges to implementing opioid substitution therapy in Ukrainian prisons: Personnel attitudes toward addiction, treatment, and people with HIV/AIDS. *Drug Alcohol Depend.* **2015**, *148*, 47–55. [CrossRef]
36. Mao, L.; Yang, Y. Coupling infectious diseases, human preventive behavior, and networks—A conceptual framework for epidemic modeling. *Soc. Sci. Med.* **2012**, *74*, 167–175. [CrossRef]

37. Przybyla, S.M.; Parks, K.; Bleasdale, J.; Sawyer, J.; Morse, D. Awareness, knowledge, and attitudes towards human immunodeficiency virus (HIV) pre-exposure prophylaxis (PrEP) among pharmacy students. *Curr. Pharm. Teach. Learn.* **2019**, *11*, 352–360. [CrossRef]
38. Ibrahim, K. The HIV/AIDS epidemic in Indonesia: Does primary health care as a prevention. *Int. J. Nurs. Pract.* **2010**, *16*, 87–91. [CrossRef]
39. Krubiner, C.B.; Faden, R.R.; Karron, R.A.; Little, M.O.; Lyerly, A.D.; Abramson, J.S.; Beigi, R.H.; Cravioto, A.R.; Durbin, A.P.; Gellin, B.G.; et al. Pregnant women & vaccines against emerging epidemic threats: Ethics guidance for preparedness, research, and response. *Vaccine* **2019**. [CrossRef]
40. Baghbanzadeh, M.; Kumar, D.; Yavasoglu, S.I.; Manning, S.; Ali, A.; Ghasemzadeh, H.; Sikder, I.; Kumar, D.; Murmu, N.; Haque, U. Malaria epidemics in India: Role of climatic condition and control measures. *Sci. Total Environ.* **2020**, *712*. [CrossRef]
41. Yang, Y.; Peng, F.; Wang, R.; Guan, K.; Jiang, T.; Xu, G.; Sun, J.; Chang, C. The deadly coronaviruses: The 2003 SARS pandemic and the 2020 novel coronavirus epidemic in China. *J. Autoimmun.* **2020**, 102434. [CrossRef]
42. Cook, P.F.; Mcelwain, C.J.; Bradley-springer, L.A. Feasibility of a Daily Electronic Survey to Study Prevention Behavior with HIV-Infected Individuals. *Res. Nurs. Health* **2010**, 221–234. [CrossRef] [PubMed]
43. Sued, O.; Figueroa, M.I.; Cahn, P. Clinical challenges in HIV/AIDS: Hints for advancing prevention and patient management strategies. *Adv. Drug Deliv. Rev.* **2016**, *103*, 5–19. [CrossRef]
44. Spire, B.; De Zoysa, I.; Himmich, H. HIV prevention: What have we learned from community experiences in concentrated epidemics? *J. Int. AIDS Soc.* **2008**, *11*, 1–8. [CrossRef] [PubMed]
45. Lee, Y.C.; Malcein, L.A.; Kim, S.C. Information and communications technology (ICT) usage during COVID-19: Motivating factors and implications. *Int. J. Environ. Res. Public Health* **2021**, *18*, 3571. [CrossRef]
46. Zhou, M.; Long, P.; Kong, N.; Campy, K.S. Characterizing Wuhan residents' mask-wearing intention at early stages of the COVID-19 pandemic. *Patient Educ. Couns.* **2021**. [CrossRef]
47. Intawong, K.; Olson, D.; Chariyalertsak, S. Application technology to fight the COVID-19 pandemic: Lessons learned in Thailand. *Biochem. Biophys. Res. Commun.* **2021**, *538*, 231–237. [CrossRef]
48. Thomas, M.J.; Lal, V.; Baby, A.K.; Rabeeh VP, M.; James, A.; Raj, A.K. Can technological advancements help to alleviate COVID-19 pandemic? a review. *J. Biomed. Inform.* **2021**, *117*, 103787. [CrossRef]
49. Clipper, B. The Influence of the COVID-19 Pandemic on Technology: Adoption in Health Care. *Nurse Lead.* **2020**, *18*, 500–503. [CrossRef]
50. Kusuma, D.; Pradeepa, R.; Khawaja, K.I.; Hasan, M.; Siddiqui, S.; Mahmood, S.; Ali Shah, S.M.; De Silva, C.K.; de Silva, L.; Gamage, M.; et al. Low uptake of COVID-19 prevention behaviours and high socioeconomic impact of lockdown measures in South Asia: Evidence from a large-scale multi-country surveillance programme. *SSM Popul. Health* **2021**, *13*, 100751. [CrossRef]
51. Irfan, M.; Akhtar, N.; Ahmad, M.; Shahzad, F.; Elavarasan, M.; Wu, H.; Yang, C. Assessing Public Willingness to Wear Face Masks during the COVID-19 Pandemic: Fresh Insights from the Theory of Planned Behavior. *Int. J. Environ. Res. Public Health* **2021**, *18*, 4577. [CrossRef]
52. Blue, C.L. Does the Theory of Planned Behavior Identify Diabetes-Related Cognitions for Intention to Be Physically Active and Eat a Healthy Diet? *Public Health Nurs.* **2007**, *24*, 141–150. [CrossRef] [PubMed]
53. Msn, J.L.; Kang, S.J. Factors influencing nurses ' intention to care for patients with emerging infectious diseases: Application of the theory of planned behavior. *Nurs. Health Sci.* **2019**, *22*, 82–90. [CrossRef]
54. Bi, K.; Chen, Y.; Zhao, S.; Ben-arieh, D.; Wu, C.J. Computers & Industrial Engineering Modeling learning and forgetting processes with the corresponding impacts on human behaviors in infectious disease epidemics. *Comput. Ind. Eng.* **2019**, *129*, 563–577. [CrossRef]
55. Aruta, J.J.B.R. Socio-ecological determinants of distress in Filipino adults during COVID-19 crisis. *Curr. Psychol.* **2021**. [CrossRef] [PubMed]
56. Chen, B.; Li, Q.X.; Zhang, H.; Zhu, J.Y.; Yang, X.; Wu, Y.H.; Xiong, J.; Li, F.; Wang, H.; Chen, Z. tao The psychological impact of COVID-19 outbreak on medical staff and the general public. *Curr. Psychol.* **2020**. [CrossRef]
57. Quah, S.R. *Social Dimensions of Epidemics*, 2nd ed.; Elsevier: Amsterdam, The Netherlands, 2017; Volume 6, ISBN 9780128036785.
58. Quah, S.R.; Magic, T.; Hugo, V.; Mis, L.; Nickleby, D.N. Public image and governance of epidemics: Comparing HIV/AIDS and SARS. *Health Policy* **2007**, *80*, 253–272. [CrossRef]
59. Zhang, X.; Oluyomi, A.; Woodard, L.; Raza, S.A.; Fahmideh, M.A.; El-mubasher, O.; Byun, J.; Han, Y.; Amos, C.I.; Badr, H. Individual-Level Determinants of Lifestyle Behavioral Changes during COVID-19 Lockdown in the United States: Results of an Online Survey. *Int. J. Environ. Res. Public Health* **2021**, *18*, 4364. [CrossRef] [PubMed]
60. Thato, R.; Drph, J.P. Original Study A Brief, Peer-Led HIV Prevention Program for College Students in Bangkok, Thailand. *J. Pediatr. Adolesc. Gynecol.* **2013**, *26*, 58–65. [CrossRef]
61. Sorensen, G.; Gupta, P.C.; Sinha, D.N.; Shastri, S.; Kamat, M.; Pednekar, M.S.; Ramakrishnan, S. Teacher tobacco use and tobacco use prevention in two regions in India: Qualitative research findings. *Prev. Med.* **2005**, *41*, 424–432. [CrossRef]
62. Persson, I.; Savulescu, J. Moral hard-wiring and moral enhancement. *Bioethics* **2017**, *31*, 286–295. [CrossRef]
63. Edmonson, C.; Bolick, B.; Lee, J. A Moral Imperative for Nurse Leaders: Addressing Incivility and Bullying in Health Care. *Nurse Lead.* **2017**, *15*, 40–44. [CrossRef]
64. Prestia, A.S. The Moral Obligation of Nurse Leaders:: COVID-19. *Nurse Lead.* **2020**, *18*, 326–328. [CrossRef]

65. Borges, L.M.; Barnes, S.M.; Farnsworth, J.K.; Drescher, K.D.; Walser, R.D. A contextual behavioral approach for responding to moral dilemmas in the age of COVID-19. *J. Context. Behav. Sci.* **2020**, *17*, 95–101. [CrossRef]
66. Akram, F. Moral Injury and the COVID-19 Pandemic: A Philosophical Viewpoint. *Ethics Med. Public Health* **2021**, 100661. [CrossRef] [PubMed]
67. Liang, W.; Duan, Y.; Shang, B.; Hu, C.; Baker, J.S.; Lin, Z.; He, J.; Wang, Y. Precautionary behavior and depression in older adults during the covid-19 pandemic: An online cross-sectional study in Hubei, China. *Int. J. Environ. Res. Public Health* **2021**, *18*, 1853. [CrossRef]
68. Donnarumma, F.; Pezzulo, G. Moral decisions in the age of COVID-19: Your choices really matter. *Soc. Sci. Humanit. Open* **2021**, *4*, 100149. [CrossRef]
69. Han, D.; Shao, Q.; Li, D.; Sun, M. How the individuals' risk aversion affect the epidemic spreading. *Appl. Math. Comput.* **2020**, *369*, 124894. [CrossRef]
70. Berry, K.; Finnoff, D. Choosing between adaptation and prevention with an increasing probability of a pandemic. *J. Econ. Behav. Organ.* **2016**, *132*, 177–192. [CrossRef]
71. Lee, M.; You, M. Avoidance of Healthcare Utilization in South Korea during the Coronavirus Disease 2019 (COVID-19) Pandemic. *Int. J. Environ. Res. Public Health* **2021**, *18*, 4363. [CrossRef]
72. Hashiguchi, N.; Sengoku, S.; Kubota, Y.; Kitahara, S.; Lim, Y.; Kodama, K. Age-Dependent influence of intrinsic and extrinsic motivations on construction worker performance. *Int. J. Environ. Res. Public Health* **2020**, *18*, 111. [CrossRef]
73. Cordellieri, P.; Barchielli, B.; Masci, V.; Viani, F.; de Pinto, I.; Priori, A.; Torriccelli, F.D.; Cosmo, C.; Ferracuti, S.; Giannini, A.M.; et al. Psychological health status of psychiatric patients living in treatment communities before and during the covid-19 lockdown: A brief report. *Int. J. Environ. Res. Public Health* **2021**, *18*, 3567. [CrossRef]
74. Herington, J. Health Security and Risk Aversion. *Bioethics* **2016**, *30*, 479–489. [CrossRef]
75. Mitchell, V. Consumer perceived risk: Conceptualisations and models. *Eur. J. Mark.* **1999**, *33*, 163–195. [CrossRef]
76. Ho, M.C.; Shaw, D.; Lin, S.; Chiu, Y.C. How do disaster characteristics influence risk perception? *Risk Anal.* **2008**, *28*, 635–643. [CrossRef] [PubMed]
77. Jones, C.; Abeku, T.A.; Rapuoda, B.; Okia, M.; Cox, J. District-based malaria epidemic early warning systems in East Africa: Perceptions of acceptability and usefulness among key staff at health facility, district and central levels. *Soc. Sci. Med.* **2008**, *67*, 292–300. [CrossRef] [PubMed]
78. Valeeva, N.I.; van Asseldonk, M.A.P.M.; Backus, G.B.C. Perceived risk and strategy efficacy as motivators of risk management strategy adoption to prevent animal diseases in pig farming. *Prev. Vet. Med.* **2011**, *102*, 284–295. [CrossRef]
79. Kiviniemi, M.T.; Orom, H.; Waters, E.A.; McKillip, M.; Hay, J.L. Education-based disparities in knowledge of novel health risks: The case of knowledge gaps in HIV risk perceptions. *Br. J. Health Psychol.* **2018**, *23*, 420–435. [CrossRef] [PubMed]
80. Raude, J.; MCColl, K.; Flamand, C.; Apostolidis, T. Understanding health behaviour changes in response to outbreaks: Findings from a longitudinal study of a large epidemic of mosquito-borne disease. *Soc. Sci. Med.* **2019**, *230*, 184–193. [CrossRef]
81. Rodriguez-Besteiro, S.; Tornero-Aguilera, J.F.; Fernández-Lucas, J.; Clemente-Suárez, V.J. Gender differences in the covid-19 pandemic risk perception, psychology and behaviors of spanish university students. *Int. J. Environ. Res. Public Health* **2021**, *18*, 3908. [CrossRef] [PubMed]
82. Sica, C.; Caudek, C.; Cerea, S.; Colpizzi, I.; Caruso, M.; Giulini, P.; Bottesi, G. Health anxiety predicts the perceived dangerousness of covid-19 over and above intrusive illness-related thoughts, contamination symptoms, and state and trait negative affect. *Int. J. Environ. Res. Public Health* **2021**, *18*, 1933. [CrossRef]
83. Ding, Y.; Du, X.; Li, Q.; Zhang, M.; Zhang, Q.; Tan, X.; Liu, Q. Risk perception of coronavirus disease 2019 (COVID-19) and its related factors among college students in China during quarantine. *PLoS ONE* **2020**, *15*, e237626. [CrossRef] [PubMed]
84. Li, D.J.; Ko, N.Y.; Chang, Y.P.; Yen, C.F.; Chen, Y.L. Mediating effects of risk perception on association between social support and coping with covid-19: An online survey. *Int. J. Environ. Res. Public Health* **2021**, *18*, 1550. [CrossRef] [PubMed]
85. Swinburn, B.; Vandevijvere, S.; Kraak, V.; Sacks, G.; Snowdon, W.; Hawkes, C.; Barquera, S.; Friel, S.; Kelly, B.; Kumanyika, S.; et al. Monitoring and benchmarking government policies and actions to improve the healthiness of food environments: A proposed government healthy food environment policy index. *Obes. Rev.* **2013**, *14*, 24–37. [CrossRef]
86. Yu, Y.; Sun, X.; Zhuang, Y.; Dong, X.; Liu, H.; Jiang, P.; Zhang, Y.; Yu, Z. What should the government do regarding health policy-making to develop community health care in Shanghai? *Int. J. Health Plan. Manag.* **2011**, *26*, 379–435. [CrossRef]
87. Allegranzi, B.; Pittet, D. Role of hand hygiene in healthcare-associated infection prevention. *J. Hosp. Infect.* **2009**, *73*, 305–315. [CrossRef]
88. Fishbein, M.; Ajzen, I. *Belief, Attitude, Intention, and Behavior: An Introduction to Theory and Research*; Addison-Wesley: Boston, MA, USA, 1975.
89. Ajzen, I. Theory of Planned Behavior. *Organ. Behav. Hum. Decis. Process.* **1991**, *50*, 179–211. [CrossRef]
90. Ajzen, I. From Intentions to Actions: A Theory of Planned Behavior. In *Action-Control: From Cognitions to Behavior*; Springer: Berlin/Heidelberg, Germany, 1985; pp. 11–39.
91. Elyasi, M.; Lai, H.; Major, P.W.; Baker, S.R.; Amin, M. Modeling the Theory of Planned Behaviour to predict adherence to preventive dental visits in preschool children. *PLoS ONE* **2020**, *15*, e0227233. [CrossRef] [PubMed]
92. Jabeen, G.; Yan, Q.; Ahmad, M.; Fatima, N.; Qamar, S. Consumers ' intention-based in fl uence factors of renewable power generation technology utilization: A structural equation modeling approach. *J. Clean. Prod.* **2019**, *237*, 117737. [CrossRef]

93. Ritter, C.; Jansen, J.; Roche, S.; Kelton, D.F.; Adams, C.L.; Orsel, K.; Erskine, R.J.; Benedictus, G.; Lam, T.J.G.M.; Barkema, H.W. Invited review: Determinants of farmers' adoption of management-based strategies for infectious disease prevention and control. *J. Dairy Sci.* **2017**, *100*, 3329–3347. [CrossRef]
94. Fila, S.A.; Smith, C. Applying the Theory of Planned Behavior to healthy eating behaviors in urban Native American youth. *Int. J. Behav. Nutr. Phys. Act.* **2006**, *10*, 1–10. [CrossRef]
95. Hayat, K.; Rosenthal, M.; Xu, S.; Arshed, M.; Li, P.; Zhai, P.; Desalegn, G.K.; Fang, Y. View of Pakistani residents toward coronavirus disease (COVID-19) during a rapid outbreak: A rapid online survey. *Int. J. Environ. Res. Public Health* **2020**, *17*, 3347. [CrossRef]
96. Kamenidou, I.; Stavrianea, A.; Liava, C. Achieving a Covid-19 free country: Citizens preventive measures and communication pathways. *Int. J. Environ. Res. Public Health* **2020**, *17*, 4633. [CrossRef]
97. Tarka, P. An overview of structural equation modeling: Its beginnings, historical development, usefulness and controversies in the social sciences. *Qual. Quant.* **2018**, *52*, 313–354. [CrossRef] [PubMed]
98. Tan, C.S.; Ooi, H.Y.; Goh, Y.N. A moral extension of the theory of planned behavior to predict consumers' purchase intention for energy-efficient household appliances in Malaysia. *Energy Policy* **2017**, *107*, 459–471. [CrossRef]
99. Pollard, C.E. Applying the Theory of Planned Behavior to Computer Energy Saving Behavioral Intention and Use at Work. *Twenty First Am. Conf. Inf. Syst. Puerto* **2015**, 1–18. Available online: https://aisel.aisnet.org/amcis2015/GreenIS/GeneralPresentations/11/ (accessed on 30 January 2021).
100. Elmustapha, H.; Hoppe, T.; Bressers, H. Consumer renewable energy technology adoption decision-making; comparing models on perceived attributes and attitudinal constructs in the case of solar water heaters in Lebanon. *J. Clean. Prod.* **2018**, *172*, 347–357. [CrossRef]
101. Ringle, C.M.; Sarstedt, M.; Mitchell, R.; Gudergan, S.P. Partial least squares structural equation modeling in HRM research. *Int. J. Hum. Resour. Manag.* **2018**, *5192*, 1–27. [CrossRef]
102. Henseler, J.; Ringle, C.M.; Sarstedt, M. A new criterion for assessing discriminant validity in variance-based structural equation modeling. *J. Acad. Mark. Sci.* **2015**, *43*, 115–135. [CrossRef]
103. Hair, J.F.; Hult, G.T.M.; Ringle, C.M.; Sarstedt, M. *A Primer on Partial Least Squares Structural Equation Modeling (PLS-SEM)*; Sage Publications: Thousand Oaks, CA, USA, 2013; p. 165.
104. Ketchen, D.J. *A Primer on Partial Least Squares Structural Equation Modeling*; Elsevier: London, UK, 2013; Volume 46, ISBN 9781452217444.
105. Hair, J.F.; Hult, G.T.M.; Ringle, C.M. *A Primer on Partial Least Squares Structural Equation Modeling (PLS-SEM)*; Sage Publications: Thousand Oaks, CA, USA, 2016; ISBN 9781483377445.
106. Fornell, C.; Larcker, D.F. Evaluating Structural Equation Models with Unobservable Variables and Measurement Error. *J. Mark. Res.* **1981**, *18*, 39–50. [CrossRef]
107. Stone, M. Cross-Validatory Choice and Assessment of Statistical Predictions. *J. R. Stat. Soc.* **1973**, *36*, 111–147.
108. Geisser, S. Biometrika Trust A Predictive Approach to the Random Effect Model Author(s): Seymour Geisser Published by: Oxford University Press on behalf of Biometrika Trust Stable. *Biometrika Trust* **1974**, *61*, 101–107. Available online: http://www.jstor.org/stable/2334290 (accessed on 19 January 2021). [CrossRef]
109. Davison, A.; Hinkley, D. Bootstrap Methods and their Application. In *Statistical and Probabilistic Mathematics*; Cambridge University Press: Cambridge, UK, 1997; pp. 1–10.
110. Khalil, A.; Abdalrahim, M. Knowledge, attitudes, and practices towards prevention and early detection of chronic kidney disease. *Int. Nurs. Rev.* **2014**, *2010*, 237–245. [CrossRef] [PubMed]
111. Bryant-davis, T.; Ellis, M.U.; Edwards, N.; Adams, T.P.; Counts, P.; Arline-bradley, S.; Sadler, K. The Role of the Black Church in HIV Prevention: Exploring Barriers and Best Practices. *J. Community Appl. Soc. Psychol.* **2016**, *26*, 388–408. [CrossRef]
112. Parker, R.G.; Perez-brumer, A.; Garcia, J.; Gavigan, K.; Ramirez, A.; Milnor, J., Jr.; Terto, V. Review article Prevention literacy: Community-based advocacy for access and ownership of the HIV prevention toolkit. *J. Int. AIDS Soc.* **2016**, *19*, 21092. [CrossRef] [PubMed]
113. Elmahdawy, M.; Elsisi, G.H.; Carapinha, J.; Lamorde, M.; Habib, A.; Agyie-baffour, P.; Soualmi, R.; Ragab, S.; Udezi, A.W.; Usifoh, C.; et al. Ebola Virus Epidemic in West Africa: Global Health Economic Challenges, Lessons Learned, and Policy Recommendations. *Value Health Reg. Issues* **2017**, *13*, 67–70. [CrossRef]
114. Liao, H.P.; Wang, J.L. The impact of epidemic information on the public's worries and attitude toward epidemic prevention measures during the COVID-19 outbreak. *Curr. Psychol.* **2021**. [CrossRef]
115. Cheng, C.; Aik-Kwang, N. Psychosocial Factors Predicting SARS-Preventive Behaviors in Four Major SARS-Affected Regions. *J. Appl. Soc. Psychol.* **2006**, *36*, 222–247. [CrossRef]
116. Lincoln, M.L. Tainted commons, public health: The politico-moral significance of cholera in Vietnam. *Med. Anthropol. Q.* **2014**, *28*, 342–361. [CrossRef] [PubMed]
117. Botzen, W.J.W.; Kunreuther, H.; Czajkowski, J.; de Moel, H. Adoption of Individual Flood Damage Mitigation Measures in New York City: An Extension of Protection Motivation Theory. *Risk Anal.* **2019**, *39*, 2143–2159. [CrossRef]
118. Omodior, O.; Luetke, M.C.; Nelson, E.J. Mosquito-borne infectious disease, risk-perceptions, and personal protective behavior among U.S. international travelers. *Prev. Med. Rep.* **2018**, *12*, 336–342. [CrossRef]

119. Cui, B.; Liu, Z.P.; Ke, J.; Tian, Y. Determinants of highly pathogenic avian influenza outbreak information sources, risk perception and adoption of biosecurity behaviors among poultry farmers in China. *Prev. Vet. Med.* **2019**, *167*, 25–31. [CrossRef] [PubMed]
120. Yang, X.R.; Chen, K.Z.; Kong, X.Z. Factors affecting the adoption of on-farm milk safety measures in Northern China—An examination from the perspective of farm size and production type. *J. Integr. Agric.* **2019**, *18*, 471–481. [CrossRef]
121. Cui, B.; Wang, L.D.L.; Ke, J.; Tian, Y. Chinese poultry farmers' decision-making for avian influenza prevention: A qualitative analysis. *Zoonoses Public Health* **2019**, *66*, 647–654. [CrossRef] [PubMed]
122. Paolini, D.; Maricchiolo, F.; Pacilli, M.G.; Pagliaro, S. COVID-19 lockdown in Italy: The role of social identification and social and political trust on well-being and distress. *Curr. Psychol.* **2020**. [CrossRef] [PubMed]
123. Sarkar, A.; Liu, G.; Jin, Y.; Xie, Z.; Zheng, Z.-J. Public health preparedness and responses to the coronavirus disease 2019 (COVID-19) pandemic in South Asia: A situation and policy analysis. *Glob. Health J.* **2020**, *4*, 121–132. [CrossRef]

International Journal of
Environmental Research and Public Health

MDPI

Article

Precautionary Behavior Practices and Psychological Characteristics of COVID-19 Patients and Quarantined Persons

Yubin Lee [1,†], Byung-Woo Kim [2,†], Shin-Woo Kim [3], Hyunjin Son [4], Boyoung Park [5], Heeyoung Lee [6,7], Myoungsoon You [1,*] and Moran Ki [2,*]

1 Department of Public Health Sciences, Graduate School of Public Health, Seoul National University, Seoul 08826, Korea; ubeanee@snu.ac.kr
2 Department of Cancer Control and Population Health, Graduate School of Cancer Science and Policy, National Cancer Center, Goyang 10408, Korea; bero@ncc.re.kr
3 Department of Internal Medicine, School of Medicine, Kyungpook National University, Daegu 41944, Korea; ksw2kms@knu.ac.kr
4 Department of Preventive Medicine, College of Medicine, Dong-A University, Busan 49201, Korea; hjson@dau.ac.kr
5 Department of Preventive Medicine, College of Medicine, Hanyang University, Seoul 04763, Korea; hayejine@hanmail.net
6 Center for Preventive and Public Health, Seoul National University Bundang Hospital, Seongnam 13620, Korea; wanderingstone@gmail.com
7 Gyeonggi Public Health Policy Institute, Seongnam 13605, Korea
* Correspondence: msyou@snu.ac.kr (M.Y.); moranki@ncc.re.kr (M.K.)
† These authors contributed equally to this work.

Citation: Lee, Y.; Kim, B.-W.; Kim, S.-W.; Son, H.; Park, B.; Lee, H.; You, M.; Ki, M. Precautionary Behavior Practices and Psychological Characteristics of COVID-19 Patients and Quarantined Persons. *Int. J. Environ. Res. Public Health* **2021**, *18*, 6070. https://doi.org/10.3390/ijerph18116070

Academic Editors: Paolo Roma, Merylin Monaro and Cristina Mazza

Received: 10 May 2021
Accepted: 31 May 2021
Published: 4 June 2021

Abstract: Background: since the coronavirus disease (COVID-19) was first reported in 2019, South Korea has enforced isolation of patients with confirmed cases of COVID-19, as well as quarantine for close contacts of individuals diagnosed with COVID-19 and persons traveling from abroad, in order to contain its spread. Precautionary behavior practices and psychological characteristics of confirmed and quarantined persons were investigated for planning pandemic recovery and preparedness. Methods: this study was conducted with 1716 confirmed patients and quarantined persons in Daegu and Busan, regions where a high number of cases were confirmed during the early stage of the COVID-19 outbreak in South Korea. We collected online survey data from 23 April to 20 May 2020, in Daegu, and 28 April to 27 May 2020, in Busan, in cooperation with Daegu and Busan Infectious Disease Control Centers and public health centers in the regions. COVID-19 symptoms, pre-cautionary behavior practices, psychological states, and the need for improvement in isolation/quarantine environments were examined using an online survey. Results: compared to patients infected with coronavirus, quarantined persons engaged in more hygiene-related behaviors (e.g., hand washing, cough etiquette, and proper mask-wearing) and social distancing. COVID-19 patients had a strong fear of stigma, while quarantined persons had a strong fear of contracting COVID-19. Study participants responded that it was necessary to provide financial support and adequate information during isolation/quarantine. Conclusions: the study highlights the importance of precautionary behavior to prevent COVID-19 infection and the need to provide support (both psychological and financial) to patients and quarantined persons, to reinforce effective communication, social solidarity, and public health emergency preparedness (PHEP) in a pandemic situation.

Keywords: COVID-19 pandemic; quarantine; isolation; public health emergency preparedness; online survey of patients and contacts

1. Introduction

Since the first report of an emerging coronavirus in Wuhan, China, in December 2019, the virus has spread rapidly worldwide [1]. In South Korea, the first confirmed case of COVID-19 occurred on 19 January 2020 [2]. In February of the same year, beginning with a cluster infection among Shincheonji Church members, the number of COVID-19 cases rose sharply in the city of Daegu and Gyeongsangbuk Province, followed by ongoing sporadic group infections occurring nationwide [2]. To date, domestic outbreaks continue to appear, and the virus continues to spread globally.

COVID-19 symptoms include fever, cough, fatigue, body aches, headache, sore throat, diarrhea, loss of taste, and loss of smell [3]. It is reported that, in most persons infected with SARS-CoV-2, the symptoms are mild or moderate, and approximately 30% of cases are asymptomatic [4,5]. In comparison to SARS and MERS, COVID-19 has a lower mortality rate, but its basic reproduction number (R_0) is reported to be as high as 2.87 (95% CI, 2.39–3.44) [5]. As it is hard to implement pharmaceutical interventions, such as vaccines and anti-viral medications, in the pandemic, non-pharmaceutical interventions have been emphasized to prevent the spread of infection [6]. Public health authorities and experts have informed the public (and shared guidelines) on the importance of precautionary practices. A large number of countries have used interventions, such as restricting the use of public and multi-purpose facilities, prohibiting large gatherings, closing borders, and/or practicing lockdowns, although the extent of these interventions has varied across countries.

Persons confirmed with COVID-19 (or suspected of being exposed) are isolated from others and restricted in their movements in order to inhibit person-to-person transmission [7]. In South Korea, patients with moderate to critical cases are admitted to hospitals for treatment, while patients with asymptomatic or mild cases are isolated in residential treatment centers where they receive healthcare services and their symptoms are monitored. In addition, regardless of the presence or absence of symptoms, close contacts of COVID-19 patients, and anyone traveling from abroad, are required to quarantine in a residential treatment center or at home, for a period of two weeks [8].

A pandemic affects the public's physical and mental health; these health effects were also identified during the 2019 coronavirus outbreak [9–12]. In the early stage of a pandemic, people feel fear, anxiousness, and helplessness due to the lack of information and uncertainty about the new risks (as well as fear of death) [13,14]. Anxiety regarding an emerging infectious disease can lead to suspicion and distrust of others, and people often blame those who are believed to have spread the disease [13]. Therefore, isolation and quarantine are effective at reducing the number of confirmed cases and mortality, but at the same time, they have negative psychological impacts on confirmed patients and quarantined persons [15,16]. Isolated or quarantined persons may face undesirable experiences and feelings, such as guilt, embarrassment, and social stigma, during and after the isolation or quarantine period [16,17]. They may suffer from social rejection and excessive blame, as well as fear of infection [13].

As confirmed, quarantined persons are exposed to various stresses in a COVID-19 outbreak; thus, investigating their isolation/quarantine experiences and mental health statuses is important for pandemic recovery and preparedness. Previous studies on quarantine/isolation experience assessed the mental health of members of the general public who were under mass quarantine due to COVID-19, which is different from the situation of Korea [18,19]. Studies conducted in Korea assessed the mental health status of (i) caregivers at a children's hospital who were quarantined due to contact with a case of COVID-19 [20], and (ii) isolated patients in residential treatment centers [21]. To our knowledge, this paper is the first to report on the precautionary behavior practices and mental health of confirmed patients and quarantined persons, and identify the needs for improvement regarding isolation or quarantine during the early stage of the COVID-19 outbreak in Korea.

We investigated precautionary behavior practices (hygiene-related behavior and social distancing) for the two weeks before they had been confirmed or quarantined, since it is widely accepted that these practices may contribute to inhibiting the infection [22,23]. We investigated the psychological states of persons who experienced COVID-19-related isolation or quarantine, and the areas that needed improvement (in regards to isolation/quarantine); this is important to improve the care of persons in isolation or quarantine, to assist in their psychological recovery. This study was performed after the first wave of COVID-19 in South Korea, which occurred from February to March 2020, and was conducted with patients confirmed to have COVID-19 and quarantined persons in the regions where a high number of confirmed cases were initially reported (Daegu, Busan, Korea).

The study findings are expected to provide government organizations and healthcare professionals with basic data to improve policies that support persons who experience isolation or quarantine. An additional purpose of the current study is to increase public health emergency preparedness (PHEP) by promoting effective communication and emphasizing social solidarity during the persistent COVID-19 pandemic.

2. Materials and Methods

2.1. Data Collection

This study was conducted with patients confirmed to have COVID-19, and persons in Daegu and Busan who were isolated (or quarantined) and released from isolation/quarantine during the first wave of the COVID-19 outbreak in South Korea (February–March 2020). Daegu and Busan were the regions in South Korea where the virus spread accelerated during the early stages of the COVID-19 pandemic. As of 31 March 2020, 69.5% of all confirmed cases in the country had occurred in these two regions [24].

In this study, a confirmed case refers to an individual who tested positive on a re-verse transcription-polymerase chain reaction (RT-PCR) test and was treated at a hospital or residential treatment center. A quarantined person refers to an individual who quarantined for two weeks after being ordered to by health authorities, due to close contact or travel abroad, and who tested negative on the final test.

We used an online survey to investigate precautionary behavior practices, for two weeks before COVID-19 confirmation or quarantine, and to investigate COVID-19-related perceptions. The surveyed areas were Daegu and Busan, and all confirmed and quarantined persons who were released from quarantine at the time of the investigation were subject to investigation. However, since Daegu concentrated on the management of confirmed patients as the first outbreak, the management of isolated persons was difficult, so the investigation was excluded. The survey data were collected by sending text messages with a survey link to persons confirmed to have COVID-19, and quarantined persons, in cooperation with Daegu and Busan Infectious Disease Control Centers and public health centers in the regions. Of those, a total of 1716 (1130 patients and 586 quarantined persons) responded to the online survey. By region, in Daegu, the survey link was sent to 5626 patients between 23 April and 20 May 2020, and data were collected from 1100 individuals (19.6%). In Busan, the survey link was sent to 118 patients and 9500 quarantined persons between 28 April and 27 May 2020, and data were collected from 30 (25.4%) and 586 (6.2%) individuals, respectively. The study was approved by the IRB of the Korea National Cancer Center (NCC2020-0104). The data did not contain personally identifying information. All survey participants consented to participate in the study before responding to the survey.

2.2. Questionnaire

2.2.1. COVID-19 Symptoms of Confirmed Patients

COVID-19-confirmed patients were asked what COVID-19 infection-related symptoms they experienced. Specifically, they were instructed to self-report the symptoms they experienced during the period of treatment or quarantine, by selecting from the following list of symptoms: fever, chills, headache, cough, phlegm, muscle aches, sore throat, difficulty breathing, loss of smell, loss of taste, nausea, indigestion, diarrhea, and others.

2.2.2. Precautionary Behavior Practices for Two Weeks before Isolation/Quarantine

The degree to which individuals engaged in precautionary behavior practices for two weeks prior to quarantine or COVID-19 confirmation was assessed using 14 items. Of those, four items concerned handwashing (Q1. I always washed my hands after going to the bathroom; Q2. I always washed my hands (or used hand sanitizer) before eating; Q3. I washed my hands (or used hand sanitizer) if I thought that my hands might have been contaminated because I shook hands, touched the mask, or held a doorknob; Q4. I washed my hands when I returned home from outside), one concerned cough etiquette (Q1. I covered my mouth with tissue when coughing or coughed into my elbow), four concerned mask-wearing (Q1. I always wore a mask during hospital visit; Q2. I always wore a mask when talking with someone within a two-meter radius; Q3. I wore a mask by ensuring that the mouth and the nose are covered; Q4. I tried to avoid touching the surfaces of used masks), and five concerned person-to-person contact (Q1. I did not attend social gatherings; Q2. My working arrangements has changed (e.g., video or online conferences, working from home, flexible work arrangement, etc.); Q3. I tried to avoid eating out; Q4. I avoided mass gatherings that might bring me into contact with many people; Q5. I avoided contact with others when I had symptoms like fever and a cough). Survey participants self-reported in regard to their precautionary behavior practices, for two weeks before quarantine or COVID-19 confirmation, on a 5-point Likert scale (1 = "not at all" and 5 = "very often"). The item reliability analysis showed that Cronbach's α coefficients were 0.844 for hand washing, 0.866 for mask-wearing, and 0.902 for person-to-person contact (Table 1).

Table 1. Contents of the questionnaire.

Classification	Questionnaires (30)	Scale	Cronbach's α		
			Confirmed	Quarantined	Total
Symptoms *	1	Binary	n/a	–	n/a
Hand washing	4	Likert 5 points	0.831	0.823	0.844
Coughing behavior	1		n/a	n/a	n/a
Mask-wearing	4		0.888	0.856	0.886
Person-to-person contact	5		0.906	0.874	0.902
Attribution of infection	3	Likert 5 points	0.538	0.591	0.599
Fear of situation	2		0.713	0.704	0.704
Fear of stigma	2		0.759	0.711	0.759
Stress	5	Likert 4 points	0.821	0.784	0.816
Perceived daily life disruption	1	0 (completely stopped) to 10 (no change)	n/a	n/a	n/a
Needs	6	Likert 5 points	0.680	0.769	0.722

* Only confirmed patients check all symptoms at onset of infection; n/a: Questionnaires are Not Applicable.

2.2.3. Perceptions of COVID-19 Infection and Psychological States of Persons Who Experienced Isolation/Quarantine

Survey participants' perceptions of COVID-19 infection and their psychological states were assessed through seven items. Of those, three items concerned whether the respondent believed that patients were responsible for the COVID-19 infection (Q1. COVID-19 patients can prevent themselves from contracting the virus; Q2. COVID-19 patients are responsible for their own infection; Q3. It is the COVID-19 patients' own fault that they have the disease) and four concerned fears due to the COVID-19-related situation—two items regarding fear of infection (Q1. I am afraid that I will be re-infected with COVID-19 after receiving treatment; Q2. I am afraid that I will not be fully recovered) and two regarding fear of stigma (Q1. I am afraid of being blamed because I was a confirmed patient infected with COVID-19; Q2. I am afraid that if there are confirmed cases in my area, the area will be criticized or damaged for the reason). The items were all rated on a 5-point Likert scale (1 = "not at all" and 5 = "strongly agree"). The three items regarding the attribution of COVID-19 infection were developed by the researchers in reference to Mak et al. (2006) [25].

To investigate psychological states in the COVID-19 situation, we asked about physical and mental changes (Q1. I am obsessed with searching for COVID-19 news and information; Q2. I am cautious and dubious about other people because I am afraid of getting re-infected; Q3. I feel helpless and am losing interest in what I did well before; Q4. I get more easily annoyed and upset than before; Q5. I have experienced a physical response, such as headache, indigestion, and insomnia) the participants experienced after they were confirmed with COVID-19, or received an order for quarantine, as well as disruption in daily life (Q1. How much did your daily life differ because of the COVID-19 out-break?) due to COVID-19. The items were developed by the researchers with reference to a guide by the COVID-19 Integrated Mental Health Service Team (2020). Stress due to infectious disease was assessed with five items on a 4-point-Likert scale (1 = "not at all" and 4 = "strongly agree") [26]. Perceived daily life disruption due to COVID-19 was assessed by using one item on an 11-point scale (0 = "completely stopped" and 10 = "no change") [27].

The item reliability analysis revealed that Cronbach's α coefficients were 0.599 for attribution of COVID-19 infection, 0.704 for fear of infection, 0.759 for fear of stigma, and 0.816 for stress (Table 1).

2.2.4. Needs of Persons Who Experienced Isolation/Quarantine

To identify the areas in which improvements were needed in the quarantine and treatment procedures, the researchers developed the six items (Q1. Early detection of the confirmed patient; Q2. Quality of the treatment of the confirmed patient; Q3. Psychological and emotional support for the confirmed patient; Q4. Financial support for the confirmed patient; Q5. Protection of human rights and privacy for the confirmed patient; Q6. Providing adequate information for the confirmed patient) on a 5-point Likert scale (1 = "not at all" and 5 = "strongly agree"). Item reliability analysis was conducted and the Cronbach's α coefficient was 0.722 (Table 1).

2.3. Statistical Analysis

To examine the participants' characteristics, they were categorized into two groups (patients and quarantined persons) on the basis of their COVID-19 experience, and frequency analysis was performed. A chi-square test (χ^2) was performed to test for differences in the presence or absence of COVID-19-related symptoms in patients, according to sex and age group, and an independent *t*-test was performed to test for differences between the groups of patients and quarantined persons in precautionary behavior practices, psychological states, and needs. Additionally, independent t-tests and analyses of variance (ANOVA) were performed to examine differences by sex and by age group across all participants. The statistical analyses were conducted using SAS software version 9.4 (SAS Institute, Cary, NC, USA).

3. Results

3.1. Survey Participants

A total of 1716 individuals responded to the survey, of whom 1130 (65.9%) were COVID-19-confirmed patients and 586 (34.1%) were quarantined persons. Of the total participants, 600 (35%) were male and 1116 (65%) were female. The mean age was 35.8 years. By age group, 804 (46.9%) were under 29 years of age, 297 (17.3%) were 30–39, 264 (15.4%) were 40–49, 246 (14.3) were 50–59, and 105 (6.1%) were 60 years or older. A total of 471 (27.4%) participants recently entered South Korea from abroad in 2020. Of those, 33 had confirmed cases of COVID-19 and 438 were quarantined. Thus, it was found that approximately one out of every four quarantined persons was a recent traveler from abroad. A total of 417 (24.3%) participants had received a flu vaccine after October 2019. Regarding self-reported health status at the time of the study, 1045 (60.9%) participants answered "good", 529 (30.8%) responded "fair", and 142 (8.3%) answered "poor" (Table 2).

Table 2. Characteristics of survey participants *.

	COVID-19 Experience		Total (n = 1716)
	Confirmed (n = 1130)	Quarantined (n = 586)	
Sex			
Male	381 (33.7)	219 (37.4)	600 (35.0)
Female	749 (66.3)	367 (62.6)	1116 (65.0)
Age group			
≤29	519 (45.9)	285 (48.6)	804 (46.9)
30–39	170 (15.0)	127 (21.7)	297 (17.3)
40–49	177 (15.7)	87 (14.9)	264 (15.4)
50–59	202 (17.9)	44 (7.5)	246 (14.3)
≥60	62 (5.5)	43 (7.3)	105 (6.1)
Travel or visit abroad in 2020			
No	1097 (97.1)	148 (25.3)	1245 (72.6)
Yes	33 (2.9)	438 (74.7)	471 (27.4)
Flu vaccination since October 2019			
No	875 (77.4)	424 (72.4)	1299 (75.7)
Yes	255 (22.6)	162 (27.6)	417 (24.3)
Health status (Self-reported)			
Bad	129 (11.4)	13 (2.2)	142 (8.3)
Moderate	384 (34.0)	145 (24.7)	529 (30.8)
Good	617 (54.6)	428 (73.0)	1045 (60.9)

* Mean age (standard deviation) was 36.4 (13.4) for confirmed patients and 34.8 (13.0) for quarantined persons.

3.2. COVID-19 Infection Symptoms

With respect to COVID-19-related symptoms in confirmed patients, 834 (73.8%) were symptomatic and 296 (26.2%) were asymptomatic. Of the symptomatic cases, 588 (78.5%) were female and 246 (64.6%) were male, showing that the proportion of symptomatic cases was higher in women than in men ($p < 0.001$). However, the proportion did not vary according to age groups.

Of the individual COVID-19 symptoms, the most common was loss of smell (38.3%), followed by loss of taste (36.5%), cough (32.7%), muscle aches (31.3%), fever (28.4%), headache (27.6%), phlegm (26.6%), sore throat (24.4%), diarrhea (22.7%), chills (21.9%), difficulty breathing (10.0%), indigestion (9.2%), and nausea (6.8%) (Table 3).

3.3. Precautionary Behavior Practices for Two Weeks before Isolation/Quarantine

The analysis of the scores for precautionary behavior practice, for two weeks before isolation/quarantine in patients and quarantined persons, showed that the item regarding hand washing, "I always washed my hands after going to the bathroom", scored the highest in both patients and quarantined persons, with mean scores of 4.3 and 4.66, respectively. In comparison, the frequency of practice was lower for the item "I washed my hands (or used hand sanitizer) if I thought that my hands might have been contaminated because I shook hands, touched the mask, or held a doorknob", with mean scores for 3.45 in patients and 4.19 for quarantined persons. Moreover, among the items concerning correct mask-wearing, "I always wore a mask during hospital visit" showed the highest practice level with mean scores of 4.12 for confirmed persons and 4.54 for quarantined persons. Of the items concerning person-to-person contact, "I avoided contact with others when I had symptoms like fever and a cough" showed the highest practice level, with mean scores of 4.12 for confirmed persons and 4.49 for quarantined persons. Overall, the precautionary behavior practice level was higher in quarantined persons than confirmed persons for all items ($p < 0.001$) (Table 4).

Table 3. Symptoms of infection in confirmed COVID-19 patients (n = 1130).

	COVID-19 Symptoms		p-Value
	Yes	No	
Total, n (%)	834 (73.8)	296 (26.2)	
Sex			
Male	246 (64.6)	135 (35.4)	<0.001
Female	588 (78.5)	296 (21.5)	
Age Group (Mean = 35.8)			
≤29	371 (71.5)	148 (28.5)	0.131
30–39	134 (78.8)	36 (21.2)	
40–49	140 (79.1)	37 (20.9)	
50–59	146 (72.3)	56 (27.7)	
≥60	43 (69.4)	19 (30.6)	
Reported Symptoms *			
Fever	321 (28.4)	809 (71.6)	n/a
Chills	247 (21.9)	883 (78.1)	
Headache	312 (27.6)	818 (72.4)	
Cough	369 (32.7)	761 (67.3)	
Phlegm	301 (26.6)	829 (73.4)	
Muscle pain	354 (31.3)	776 (68.7)	
Sore throat	276 (24.4)	854 (75.6)	
Difficulty breathing	113 (10.0)	1017 (90.0)	
Cannot smell	433 (38.3)	697 (61.7)	
Cannot taste	413 (36.5)	717 (63.5)	
Nausea, Vomiting	77 (6.8)	1053 (93.2)	
Indigestion	104 (9.2)	1026 (90.8)	
Diarrhea	257 (22.7)	873 (77.3)	
Other symptoms	74 (6.5)	1056 (93.5)	

* Including 765 duplicate respondents; n/a: Questionnaires are Not Applicable.

Table 4. Precautionary behavioral survey response results *.

Questionnaire	Confirmed	Quarantined	p-Value
	Mean (SD)	Mean (SD)	
Hand washing (4)			
I always washed my hands after going to the bathroom.	4.30 (0.86)	4.66 (0.59)	<0.001
I always washed my hands (or used hand sanitizer) before eating.	3.75 (1.11)	4.29 (0.91)	<0.001
I washed my hands (or used hand sanitizer) if I thought that my hands might have been contaminated because I shook hands, touched the mask, or held a doorknob.	3.45 (1.22)	4.19 (0.99)	<0.001
I washed my hands when I returned home from outside.	4.15 (0.98)	4.61 (0.69)	<0.001
Coughing behavior (1)			
I covered my mouth with tissue when coughing or coughed into my elbow.	4.07 (1.02)	4.55 (0.71)	<0.001
Mask-wearing (4)			
I always wore a mask during hospital visit.	4.12 (1.15)	4.54 (0.90)	<0.001
I always wore a mask when talking with someone within a two-meter radius.	3.52 (1.30)	4.06 (1.13)	<0.001
I wore a mask by ensuring that the mouth and the nose are covered.	3.91 (1.19)	4.44 (0.91)	<0.001
I tried to avoid touching the surfaces of used masks.	3.46 (1.21)	3.94 (1.07)	<0.001
Person-to-person contact (5)			
I did not attend social gatherings.	3.74 (1.34)	4.18 (1.05)	<0.001
My working arrangements has changed (e.g., video or online conferences, working from home, flexible work arrangement, etc.).	3.14 (1.54)	3.83 (1.14)	<0.001
I tried to avoid eating out.	3.86 (1.27)	4.32 (0.97)	<0.001
I avoided mass gatherings that might bring me into contact with many people.	3.75 (1.31)	4.29 (0.96)	<0.001
I avoided contact with others when I had symptoms like fever and a cough.	4.21 (0.99)	4.49 (0.80)	<0.001

* For a period of two weeks before confirmation/being quarantined.

The analysis conducted on the difference between genders in precautionary behavior practices showed that the mean scores for hand washing and cough etiquette were higher for women than men ($p < 0.05$); in regards to mask-wearing and person-to-person contact, the results varied by item (Table 4). The age group difference was found in seven out of the total 14 items regarding precautionary behavior practices ($p < 0.05$). Of those, two items on person-to-person contact showed an opposite trend in comparison to the remaining items, which indicated higher scores as age increased (Supplementary Table S1).

3.4. Psychological States in Persons Who Experienced Isolation/Quarantine

The level of attribution, i.e., the extent to which the responsibility of infection was attributed to patients, was lower in patients than in quarantined persons ($p < 0.05$). Regarding situational fear, fear of COVID-19 reinfection in patients was higher than fear of COVID-19 confirmation in quarantined persons ($p < 0.05$). In contrast, fear of asymptomatic infection in quarantined persons was higher than patients fearing that they would not fully recover, but the difference was not significant ($p = 0.074$). In regard to fear of stigma, fears of criticism and disadvantage were higher in patients than in quarantined persons ($p < 0.05$) (Table 5).

Table 5. Psychological survey response results.

Questionnaire	Confirmed	Quarantined	p-Value
	Mean (SD)	Mean (SD)	
Attribution of infection (3)			
COVID-19 patients can prevent themselves from contracting the virus.	2.45 (1.14)	2.82 (1.19)	<0.001
COVID-19 patients are responsible for their own infection.	2.09 (0.97)	2.82 (0.97)	<0.001
It is the COVID-19 patients' own fault that they have the disease.	2.25 (1.06)	2.87 (0.9)	<0.001
Fear of situation (2)			
I am afraid that I will be re-infected with COVID-19 after receiving treatment. * I am afraid that I will be confirmed as infected with COVID-19.	3.68 (1.1)	3.46 (1.05)	<0.001
I am afraid that I will not be fully recovered. * I am afraid of being an asymptomatic infected patient.	2.9 (1.28)	3.01 (1.16)	0.074
Fear of stigma (2)			
I am afraid of being blamed because I was a confirmed patient infected with COVID-19. * I am afraid of being blamed because I was quarantined.	3.79 (1.11)	2.85 (1.32)	<0.001
I am afraid that if there are confirmed cases in my area, the area will be criticized or damaged for the reason.	3.44 (1.17)	2.91 (1.17)	<0.001
Stress (5)			
I am obsessed with searching for COVID-19 news and information.	2.56 (0.95)	2.34 (0.86)	<0.001
I am cautious and dubious about other people because I am afraid of getting re-infected. * I am cautious and dubious about other people because I am afraid of getting infected.	2.66 (0.84)	2.39 (0.82)	<0.001
I feel helpless and am losing interest in what I did well before.	2.47 (0.96)	2.1 (0.93)	<0.001
I get more easily annoyed and upset than before.	2.21 (0.93)	1.93 (0.91)	<0.001
I have experienced a physical response, such as headache, indigestion, and insomnia.	2.27 (1.01)	1.96 (0.96)	<0.001
Perceived daily life disruption due to COVID-19 out-break			
How much did your daily life differ because of the COVID-19 outbreak?	4.26 (2.83)	4.6 (2.81)	0.018

footer * For persons in quarantine due to COVID-19.

Regarding stress due to infectious disease, patients reported higher stress compared to quarantined persons for all five items ($p < 0.05$). The mean score for the item concerning perceived daily life disruption was 4.26 for confirmed persons and 4.6 for quarantined persons, showing a significant difference ($p < 0.05$). An examination of the item responses classified into three groups—high level of perceived daily life disruption (scores 0–3), medium level (4–6), and low level (7–10)—showed corresponding proportions of 49%,

25.9%, and 25.1%, respectively, for confirmed persons, and 42.3%, 29.1%, 28.6%, respectively, for quarantined persons (Table 5).

The analysis of difference between genders revealed the following. The mean score for the attribution of infection was higher in men ($p < 0.05$), whereas the mean scores for fear of the situation, fear of stigma, and stress were higher in women ($p < 0.05$). In addition, the mean score of the item concerning perceived daily life disruption was 4.94 for men and 4.07 for women, showing a significant difference ($p < 0.05$) (Supplementary Table S2).

In regards to age group differences, with the exception of the age 60 or higher group, participants were more likely to answer that patients were responsible for infection as age decreased, while fear of the situation, fear of stigma, and stress increased as age increased. Regarding perceived daily life disruption, the score was lower with a decrease in age ($p < 0.05$) (Supplementary Table S2).

3.5. Needs of Persons Who Experienced Isolation/Quarantine

The mean score for early detection of confirmed cases and persons in quarantine was high in both patients and quarantined persons, 4.51 and 4.44, respectively, and the difference was not significant ($p = 0.153$). Whereas the need for psychological/mental support, financial support, human rights protection, and adequate information was higher in patients than in quarantined persons ($p < 0.05$). However, the need for improving health management of quarantined persons (3.92) was stronger than the need for the improvement of patient treatment (3.79) ($p < 0.05$) (Table 6).

Table 6. Needs for confirmed patients and quarantined persons.

Questionnaire	Confirmed Mean (SD)	Quarantined Mean (SD)	p-Value
Needs (6)			
Early detection of the confirmed patient. * Early detection of the subject of quarantine.	4.51 (0.82)	4.44 (0.9)	0.153
Quality of the treatment of the confirmed patient. * Level of health management of the quarantined person.	3.79 (1.02)	3.92 (0.94)	0.009
Psychological and emotional support for the confirmed patient. * Psychological and emotional support for the quarantined person.	4.04 (0.94)	3.9 (0.99)	0.005
Financial support for the confirmed patient. * Financial support for the quarantined person.	4.59 (0.66)	4.06 (0.91)	<0.001
Protection of human rights and privacy for the confirmed patient.Protection of human rights and privacy for the quarantined person.	4.76 (0.58)	4.01 (1.0)	<0.001
Providing adequate information for the confirmed patient. * Providing adequate information for the quarantined person.	4.62 (0.65)	4.38 (0.84)	<0.001

footer * For persons in quarantine due to COVID-19.

The analysis was conducted to examine differences between genders but found no significant difference in either the need for financial support or appropriate COVID-19-related information. However, for the remaining items, the score was higher in women than in men ($p < 0.05$). With respect to between-age differences, the need for appropriate information was not significantly different among different age groups, but the remaining items showed significant age group differences ($p < 0.05$) (Supplementary Table S3).

4. Discussion

Participants in this study were patients with asymptomatic or mild COVID-19 cases who were treated in a hospital or residential treatment center, and persons quarantined because they had close contact with COVID-19 patients or entered the country from abroad. The participants were from Daegu and Busan, the regions in which the highest number of confirmed cases occurred during the first wave of the COVID-19 outbreak in South Korea (February–March 2020). After the new cases largely declined, we investigated COVID-19 symptoms and precautionary behavior practices (for two weeks before isolation or quarantine) and psychological states of patients and quarantined persons through a survey. Additionally, we examined the areas in which the participants felt that support would be needed during the isolation or quarantine period.

A break from daily life was the greatest change experienced by individuals due to COVID-19. This experience may have a greater significance, especially at the beginning of an infectious disease outbreak. Our study is of academic significance in that the survey investigated the isolation/quarantine experience of residents of Daegu and Busan, who experienced geographic discrimination and stigma during the first COVID-19 outbreak in South Korea, because a high number of confirmed cases occurred in these regions. Furthermore, the study has significance for the development of health policies in that lessons and implications were derived from the participants' experiences and effort was made to identify the ways to provide other forms of support in addition to treatment.

It is expected that the study findings will help understand the isolation/quarantine experience due to COVID-19 and identify factors that contribute to improving isolation and quarantine environments.

There are a few notable findings in the study. First, 26.2% of patients confirmed to have COVID-19 were asymptomatic. The proportions of asymptomatic COVID-19 patients reported varied, depending on the timing of the study and the number of study participants [28,29]. An asymptomatic case refers to a patient who tests positive on an RT-PCR test, but does not show any COVID-19-related symptoms, such as fever or a cough, either on the day of testing or for the 14 days following [30]. Because symptoms may occur a few days after a COVID-19 test (in which case, the patient is classified as pre-symptomatic), there are limitations in estimating the proportion of asymptomatic patients based on a cross-sectional study [31]. Therefore, to avoid overestimating the proportion of asymptomatic cases, a follow-up period of approximately two weeks is required. The participants in this study were those who finished the treatment and, hence, pre-symptomatic patients were not included. The proportion of asymptomatic patients in the study was similar to the findings in a previous study, in which the proportion of asymptomatic cases was estimated by following-up with patients [4].

Second, it was found that the practice of hygiene-related behaviors and social distancing were higher in participants not infected with COVID-19 (that is, quarantined persons) than those confirmed with COVID-19. Particularly, patients and quarantined persons' preventative behaviors differed among items concerning specific practices. For instance, the between-group difference was greater for the item "wearing a mask by ensuring that the mouth and the nose are covered" (3.91 for confirmed persons and 4.44 for quarantined persons) than for the item "wearing a mask during hospital visit" (4.12 for confirmed persons and 4.54 for quarantined persons). Additionally, the level of practicing precautionary behaviors was higher in women than in men, which is consistent with a previous study [32]. However, the difference between genders in practicing precautionary behaviors was not as great as the difference between infected and uninfected COVID-19 persons, and there was no significant between-gender difference in regard to practicing social distancing.

It was reported in the literature that, aside from sociodemographic factors, psychological factors also affect precautionary behavior practices during a pandemic [33]. In a study by Lee and You (2020), individuals who had a higher risk perception of COVID-19 and a higher efficacy of practicing precautionary behaviors practiced personal preventive behaviors and social distancing more rigorously [34]. Accordingly, it is highly likely that, compared to people infected with COVID-19, uninfected people more strongly perceived the severity of COVID-19 infection, and believed that infection could be prevented by practicing precautionary behaviors. Such a difference in perception may have resulted in the difference in precautionary behavior practices, and potentially the difference between infection and non-infection.

Third, the fear of COVID-19 showed different patterns in patients and quarantined persons. Patients were more afraid of social stigma, while quarantined persons feared COVID-19 infection more. In patients, the greatest fear was that they might be socially stigmatized due to the infection and the strongest need in response to COVID-19 was human rights protection. It is likely that their fear of stigma was influenced by the social awareness that individuals are responsible for having contracted the virus. In this study, the perception that patients were responsible for COVID-19 infection was higher in quarantined persons compared to the patients. Likewise, a survey conducted in Gyeonggi Province, South Korea, reported that there was a difference in perception on attribution of the disease between the general public and confirmed patients [35]. If a person believes that individuals have control over whether or not they become infected, he/she will perceive that patients are responsible for the illness [25,36]. The perception that patients are responsible for the cause of illness leads to negative emotions and behaviors toward patients confirmed to have COVID-19, even resulting in prejudice and discrimination [36]. Since stigma around COVID-19 infection affects all areas of patients' lives, the government and healthcare professionals should use public communication to reduce stigma against patients confirmed to have COVID-19, while stressing the importance of precautionary behavior practices.

Whereas, in quarantined persons, the greatest fear was COVID-19 confirmation; the strongest need in response to COVID-19 was early detection of persons who should practice quarantine. Quarantined persons' fear of a diagnosis (of infection) was also reported by Chen et al., who examined the quarantine experience of close contacts of COVID-19 patients [37]. Quarantined persons who were close contacts, not fully informed of the infectious disease, and who experienced infection-related symptoms, had a fear of infection [37,38]. The fear gradually decreased as they acquired more information on the nature of infection during quarantine and tested negative for COVID-19 [37]. However, the quarantined persons in the current study had a fear of infection, even though they did not have symptoms during quarantine and did not test positive. The finding suggests that fear of infection may be a persistent stress factor for quarantined persons regardless of the test result. Hence, central and local governments should follow-up with persons released from quarantine due to COVID-19 to understand their psychological states and support them in utilizing professional psychological intervention programs.

Finally, survey participants expressed a desire for financial support and adequate information during isolation/quarantine. Economic loss due to isolation/quarantine and insufficient information during the pandemic were identified as stress factors in another study as well [16]. If patients and quarantined persons are not guaranteed income (when they cannot work due to isolation/quarantine and afterwards), their livelihoods can be threatened. In particular, because persons with low household incomes are greatly impacted by even a temporary reduction in income, a change in income due to isolation/quarantine can significantly affect their health [39]. South Korea implemented a policy—effective as of 17 February, 2020—that workers quarantined or admitted to hospital due to COVID-19 receive paid leave from their employers, or a living allowance from the government [40]. Nevertheless, survey participants had a high level of need for financial support policy. The reason is believed to be because, in South Korea's current financial support policy, workers who cannot work due to illness are guaranteed to receive merely the minimum level of income [40]. Accordingly, the government should develop a system to help isolated or quarantined persons smoothly return to society, such as resuming work with their employer after recovery from the infection (or after release from quarantine), and not being disadvantaged by the employer's personnel decisions.

While isolated or quarantined, people want to have timely and trustworthy information regarding infection treatment and isolation/quarantine, and feel depression and fear if they do not have access to such information [41,42]. A great majority of survey participants responded that adequate information should be provided for COVID-19 patients and quarantined persons (92.1% and 85.1%, respectively). Approximately one-half of survey participants (55.3% of patients and 45.4% of quarantined persons) responded that they became overly obsessive about obtaining COVID-19 information after conformation of COVID-19 diagnosis or after receiving the quarantine order. Providing accurate information for isolated or quarantined persons to make health-related decisions, namely, empowering them, helps decrease a sense of helplessness and maintain good mental health during isolation/quarantine [42]. Thus, healthcare workers should explain the guidelines for isolation/quarantine and inform COVID-19 patients and quarantined persons of potential negative emotions that may be felt during isolation/quarantine so that they may better cope with the situation.

Our study shows the need for social solidarity and effective communication in the pandemic. COVID-19 patients and quarantined persons are often criticized, discriminated against in the community and at work, or ostracized because they are infected (or had contact) with confirmed patients [43]. An experience of physical and social isolation from society has psychological impacts, including depression, loneliness, frustration, and anxiety, which can persist even after a pandemic ends [43,44]. Not only does the stigma of infection affect personal health, but it is also unhelpful for infection management (from a social perspective). Due to the fear of social stigma, some people may hide the fact that they have COVID-19, avoid immediate use of healthcare services, or forgo adopting healthy behaviors [45]. Accordingly, it is important for public health authorities to provide accurate, persistent, and trustworthy information regarding COVID infections, while simultaneously stressing social solidarity.

From this point of view, our study highlights the importance of strengthening PHEP in a public health emergency, such as a pandemic. PHEP refers to "the capability of the public health and health care systems, communities, and individuals to prevent, protect against, quickly respond to, and recover from health emergencies" [46]. PHEP capabilities include conducting public health surveillance and epidemiological research, providing healthcare services, and performing non-pharmaceutical interventions (e.g., isolation and quarantine), as well as sharing accurate and efficient information, mental health promotion, and encouraging a return to normal daily life [47]. To develop PHEP capabilities, governments and private sectors, non-governmental organizations, and individuals should make continuous and concerted efforts [48].

The current study examined physical symptoms of COVID-19 and the psychological states and needs of patients confirmed to have COVID-19, as well as quarantined persons, and highlighted tolerance and solidarity as ways to cope with infection. The study has the following limitations. First, the study was conducted by using a self-report questionnaire after the isolation/quarantine period was over; thus, the findings may differ from those in an observational study. That is, survey participants may have not remembered the symptoms they had (recall bias) or responded that they practiced precautionary behaviors better than they actually did (social desirability bias). Second, the study findings did not reflect moderate–severe patient experiences. Considering that more than 40% of survey participants were between the ages of 20 and 29, whereas only 5.5% were 60 or older, survey participants seem biased toward younger people, the age group with a relatively higher proportion of mild patients. In addition, because the survey was conducted in the early stage of the COVID-19 outbreak, the level of precautionary behavior practices and the psychological states of the participants in a study conducted at a different time may differ, in accordance with the changes or stages of the public health emergency in South Korea.

5. Conclusions

Our findings on precautionary behavior practices emphasize the importance of hygiene-related behavior and social distancing to prevent COVID-19 infection. Compared to confirmed persons, quarantined persons showed better performance in hand washing, cough etiquette, proper mask-wearing, and social distancing. In addition, our findings suggest ways to improve the policies supporting persons isolated or quarantined due to COVID-19. In the present study, COVID-19 patients showed a strong fear of stigma, and quarantined persons had a strong fear of contracting COVID-19. Since stress can persist afterwards, the mental health of these individuals should be evaluated through a follow-up and they should be provided with opportunities to participate in counseling intervention programs. Individuals should be fully informed and financially supported during isolation or quarantine. The results of the present study emphasize the need for social and financial support for patients and quarantined persons, as well as health communication concerning precautionary behavior practices and anti-stigma and social solidity awareness during a public health emergency.

Supplementary Materials: The following are available online at https://www.mdpi.com/article/10.3390/ijerph18116070/s1, Supplementary Table S1. Precautionary behavioral survey response results, by sex and age. Supplementary Table S2. Psychological survey response results, by sex and age. Supplementary Table S3. Needs for confirmed patients and quarantined persons, by sex and age. Supplementary Table S4. Precautionary behavioral survey response results in persons quarantined, by contact or abroad *. Supplementary Table S5. Psychological survey response results in persons quarantined, by contact or abroad. Supplementary Table S6. Needs for quarantined persons, by contact or abroad.

Author Contributions: Conceptualization, M.Y. and M.K.; formal analysis, B.-W.K.; data curation, S.-W.K.; writing—original draft preparation, Y.L. and B.-W.K.; supervision, M.Y. and M.K.; project administration, H.S., H.L., and B.P. All authors have read and agreed to the published version of the manuscript.

Funding: This research was supported by the Government-wide R&D Fund Project for Infectious Disease Research (GFID), Republic of Korea (grant number: HG18C0000).

Institutional Review Board Statement: The study was conducted according to the guidelines of the Declaration of Helsinki, and approved by the National Cancer Center Institutional Review Board (IRB No. NCC2020-0104).

Informed Consent Statement: Informed consent was obtained from all subjects involved in the study.

Data Availability Statement: The data presented in this study are available on reasonable request from the corresponding author, and only after approval by the medical ethical committee. The data are not publicly available due to ethical restrictions.

Acknowledgments: The authors would like to express gratitude towards valuable cooperation from Daegu and Busan Infectious Disease Control Centers and public health centers in the regions.

Conflicts of Interest: The authors declare no conflict of interest.

References

1. Choi, M.H.; Ahn, H.; Ryu, H.S.; Kim, B.J.; Jang, J.; Jung, M.; Kim, J.; Jeong, S.H. Clinical Characteristics and Disease Progression in Early-Stage COVID-19 Patients in South Korea. *J. Clin. Med.* **2020**, *9*, 1959. [CrossRef]
2. Korean Society of Infectious Diseases; Korean Society of Pediatric Infectious Diseases; Korean Society of Epidemiology; Korean Society for Antimicrobial Therapy; Korean Society for Healthcare-associated Infection Control and Prevention; Korea Centers for Disease Control and Prevention. Report on the Epidemiological Features of Coronavirus Disease 2019 (COVID-19) Outbreak in the Republic of Korea from January 19 to March 2, 2020. *J. Korean. Med. Sci.* **2020**, *35*, e112. [CrossRef]
3. WHO. *Report of the WHO-China Joint Mission on Coronavirus Disease 2019 (COVID-19)*; 2020. Available online: https://www.who.int/publications/i/item/report-of-the-who-china-joint-mission-on-coronavirus-disease-2019-(covid-19) (accessed on 22 May 2021).
4. Kim, S.W.; Kim, S.M.; Kim, Y.K.; Kim, J.Y.; Lee, Y.M.; Kim, B.O.; Hwangbo, S.; Park, T. Clinical Characteristics and Outcomes of COVID-19 Cohort Patients in Daegu Metropolitan City Outbreak in 2020. *J. Korean Med. Sci.* **2021**, *36*, e12. [CrossRef] [PubMed]
5. Billah, M.A.; Miah, M.M.; Khan, M.N. Reproductive number of coronavirus: A systematic review and meta-analysis based on global level evidence. *PLoS ONE* **2020**, *15*, e0242128. [CrossRef] [PubMed]
6. Low, D.E. Pandemic planning: Non-pharmaceutical interventions. *Respirology* **2008**, *13* (Suppl. 1), S44–S48. [CrossRef]
7. Wilder-Smith, A.; Freedman, D.O. Isolation, quarantine, social distancing and community containment: Pivotal role for old-style public health measures in the novel coronavirus (2019-nCoV) outbreak. *J. Travel Med.* **2020**, *27*. [CrossRef] [PubMed]
8. Ministry of Health and Welfare. Patient Treatment & Management. Available online: http://ncov.mohw.go.kr/en/baroView.do?brdId=11&brdGubun=112&dataGubun=&ncvContSeq=&contSeq=&board_id= (accessed on 22 May 2021).
9. Khan, S.; Huremović, D. Psychology of the Pandemic. In *Psychiatry of Pandemics: A Mental Health Response to Infection Outbreak*; Huremović, D., Ed.; Springer International Publishing: Cham, Switzerland, 2019; pp. 37–44. [CrossRef]
10. Qiu, W.; Rutherford, S.; Mao, A.; Chu, C. The pandemic and its impacts. *Health Cult. Soc.* **2017**, *9*, 1–11. [CrossRef]
11. Robinson, E.; Boyland, E.; Chisholm, A.; Harrold, J.; Maloney, N.G.; Marty, L.; Mead, B.R.; Noonan, R.; Hardman, C.A. Obesity, eating behavior and physical activity during COVID-19 lockdown: A study of UK adults. *Appetite* **2021**, *156*, 104853. [CrossRef] [PubMed]

12. Mansfield, K.E.; Mathur, R.; Tazare, J.; Henderson, A.D.; Mulick, A.R.; Carreira, H.; Matthews, A.A.; Bidulka, P.; Gayle, A.; Forbes, H.; et al. Indirect acute effects of the COVID-19 pandemic on physical and mental health in the UK: A population-based study. *Lancet Digital Health* **2021**, *3*, e217–e230. [CrossRef]
13. KSTSS. *Guidelines on Psychosocial Care for Infectious Disease Management*; KSTSS: Gyeongsan, Korea, 2020.
14. CDC. *CERC: Psychology of a Crisis*; CDC: Atlanta, Georgia, 2019.
15. Nussbaumer-Streit, B.; Mayr, V.; Dobrescu, A.I.; Chapman, A.; Persad, E.; Klerings, I.; Wagner, G.; Siebert, U.; Christof, C.; Zachariah, C.; et al. Quarantine alone or in combination with other public health measures to control COVID-19: A rapid review. *Cochrane Database Syst. Rev.* **2020**, *4*, CD013574. [CrossRef]
16. Brooks, S.K.; Webster, R.K.; Smith, L.E.; Woodland, L.; Wessely, S.; Greenberg, N.; Rubin, G.J. The psychological impact of quarantine and how to reduce it: Rapid review of the evidence. *Lancet* **2020**, *395*, 912–920. [CrossRef]
17. Ho, C.S.; Chee, C.Y.; Ho, R.C. Mental Health Strategies to Combat the Psychological Impact of COVID-19 Beyond Paranoia and Panic. *Ann. Acad. Med. Singap.* **2020**, *49*, 155–160. [CrossRef] [PubMed]
18. Burke, T.; Berry, A.; Taylor, L.K.; Stafford, O.; Murphy, E.; Shevlin, M.; McHugh, L.; Carr, A. Increased Psychological Distress during COVID-19 and Quarantine in Ireland: A National Survey. *J. Clin. Med.* **2020**, *9*, 3481. [CrossRef] [PubMed]
19. Kaparounaki, C.K.; Patsali, M.E.; Mousa, D.-P.V.; Papadopoulou, E.V.; Papadopoulou, K.K.; Fountoulakis, K.N. University students' mental health amidst the COVID-19 quarantine in Greece. *Psychiatry Res.* **2020**, *290*, 113111. [CrossRef] [PubMed]
20. Kim, H.; Park, K.J.; Shin, Y.-W.; Lee, J.S.; Chung, S.; Lee, T.; Kim, M.-J.; Jung, J.; Lee, J.; Yum, M.-S.; et al. Psychological Impact of Quarantine on Caregivers at a Children's Hospital for Contact with Case of COVID-19. *J. Korean Med. Sci* **2020**, *35*, e255. [CrossRef]
21. Kang, E.; Lee, S.Y.; Kim, M.S.; Jung, H.; Kim, K.H.; Kim, K.-N.; Park, H.Y.; Lee, Y.J.; Cho, B.; Sohn, J.H. The Psychological Burden of COVID-19 Stigma: Evaluation of the Mental Health of Isolated Mild Condition COVID-19 Patients. *J. Korean Med. Sci.* **2021**, *36*, e33. [CrossRef]
22. Chiu, N.-C.; Chi, H.; Tai, Y.-L.; Peng, C.-C.; Tseng, C.-Y.; Chen, C.-C.; Tan, B.F.; Lin, C.-Y. Impact of Wearing Masks, Hand Hygiene, and Social Distancing on Influenza, Enterovirus, and All-Cause Pneumonia During the Coronavirus Pandemic: Retrospective National Epidemiological Surveillance Study. *J. Med. Internet Res.* **2020**, *22*, e21257. [CrossRef]
23. Jefferson, T.; Del Mar, C.; Dooley, L.; Ferroni, E.; Al-Ansary, L.A.; Bawazeer, G.A.; van Driel, M.L.; Foxlee, R.; Rivetti, A. Physical interventions to interrupt or reduce the spread of respiratory viruses: Systematic review. *BMJ* **2009**, *339*, b3675. [CrossRef]
24. KCDA. Updates on COVID-19 in Republic of Korea (as of 31 March). Available online: http://ncov.mohw.go.kr/en/tcmBoardView.do?brdId=12&brdGubun=125&dataGubun=&ncvContSeq=1662&contSeq=1662&board_id=&gubun=#. (accessed on 22 May 2021).
25. Mak, W.W.; Mo, P.K.; Cheung, R.Y.; Woo, J.; Cheung, F.M.; Lee, D. Comparative stigma of HIV/AIDS, SARS, and tuberculosis in Hong Kong. *Soc. Sci. Med.* **2006**, *63*, 1912–1922. [CrossRef]
26. COVID-19 Integrated Mental Health Service Team. *Guidance for Infectious Disease Stress Relief*; National Center for Disaster Trauma: Seoul, Korea, 2020.
27. Son, H. *The Emotional Experience of Hospital Workers and the Public in an Infectious Disease Outbreak: Implications for Disaster Management*; Seoul National University: Seoul, Korea, 2018.
28. He, J.; Guo, Y.; Mao, R.; Zhang, J. Proportion of asymptomatic coronavirus disease 2019: A systematic review and meta-analysis. *J. Med. Virol.* **2021**, *93*, 820–830. [CrossRef]
29. Oran, D.P.; Topol, E.J. Prevalence of Asymptomatic SARS-CoV-2 Infection: A Narrative Review. *Ann. Intern. Med.* **2020**, *173*, 362–367. [CrossRef] [PubMed]
30. Kimball, A.; Hatfield, K.M.; Arons, M.; James, A.; Taylor, J.; Spicer, K.; Bardossy, A.C.; Oakley, L.P.; Tanwar, S.; Chisty, Z.; et al. Asymptomatic and Presymptomatic SARS-CoV-2 Infections in Residents of a Long-Term Care Skilled Nursing Facility—King County, Washington, March 2020. *MMWR Morb Mortal Wkly. Rep.* **2020**, *69*, 377–381. [CrossRef] [PubMed]
31. Meyerowitz, E.A.; Richterman, A.; Bogoch, I.I.; Low, N.; Cevik, M. Towards an accurate and systematic characterisation of persistently asymptomatic infection with SARS-CoV-2. *Lancet Infect. Dis.* **2020**. [CrossRef]
32. Ludecke, D.; von dem Knesebeck, O. Protective Behavior in Course of the COVID-19 Outbreak-Survey Results from Germany. *Front. Public Health* **2020**, *8*, 572561. [CrossRef] [PubMed]
33. Bish, A.; Michie, S. Demographic and attitudinal determinants of protective behaviours during a pandemic: A review. *Br. J. Health Psychol.* **2010**, *15*, 797–824. [CrossRef] [PubMed]
34. Lee, M.; You, M. Psychological and Behavioral Responses in South Korea During the Early Stages of Coronavirus Disease 2019 (COVID-19). *Int. J. Environ. Res. Public Health* **2020**, *17*, 2977. [CrossRef]
35. Gyeonggi Provincial Government. Who's Responsible for the COVID-19 Infection? There is a Big Difference in Perception of Attribution of Infection between the Public and Confirmed Patients. Available online: https://gnews.gg.go.kr/briefing/brief_gongbo_view.do?BS_CODE=s017&number=44849&period_1=&period_2=&search=0&keyword=&subject_Code=BO01&page=2 (accessed on 22 May 2021).
36. Weiner, B. On sin versus sickness. A theory of perceived responsibility and social motivation. *Am. Psychol.* **1993**, *48*, 957–965. [CrossRef]
37. Chen, D.; Song, F.; Tang, L.; Zhang, H.; Shao, J.; Qiu, R.; Wang, X.; Ye, Z. Quarantine experience of close contacts of COVID-19 patients in China: A qualitative descriptive study. *Gen. Hosp. Psychiatry* **2020**, *66*, 81–88. [CrossRef]

38. Desclaux, A.; Badji, D.; Ndione, A.G.; Sow, K. Accepted monitoring or endured quarantine? Ebola contacts' perceptions in Senegal. *Soc. Sci. Med.* **2017**, *178*, 38–45. [CrossRef]
39. Mihashi, M.; Otsubo, Y.; Yinjuan, X.; Nagatomi, K.; Hoshiko, M.; Ishitake, T. Predictive factors of psychological disorder development during recovery following SARS outbreak. *Health Psychol.* **2009**, *28*, 91–100. [CrossRef]
40. OECD. *OECD Economic Surveys: Korea 2020*; OECD Publishing: Paris, France, 2020. [CrossRef]
41. Cava, M.A.; Fay, K.E.; Beanlands, H.J.; McCay, E.A.; Wignall, R. The experience of quarantine for individuals affected by SARS in Toronto. *Public Health Nurs.* **2005**, *22*, 398–406. [CrossRef] [PubMed]
42. Damir Huremović. Mental Health of Quarantine and Isolation. In *Psychiatry of Pandemics: A Mental Health Response to Infection Outbreak*; Huremović, D., Ed.; Springer: Cham, Switzerland, 2019; pp. 95–118.
43. Dubey, S.; Biswas, P.; Ghosh, R.; Chatterjee, S.; Dubey, M.J.; Chatterjee, S.; Lahiri, D.; Lavie, C.J. Psychosocial impact of COVID-19. *Diabetes Metab. Syndr.* **2020**, *14*, 779–788. [CrossRef] [PubMed]
44. Park, H.Y.; Park, W.B.; Lee, S.H.; Kim, J.L.; Lee, J.J.; Lee, H.; Shin, H.S. Posttraumatic stress disorder and depression of survivors 12 months after the outbreak of Middle East respiratory syndrome in South Korea. *BMC Public Health* **2020**, *20*, 605. [CrossRef] [PubMed]
45. WHO; IFRC; UNICEF. A Guide to Preventing and Addressing Social Stigma Associated with COVID-19. 24 February 2020. Available online: https://www.who.int/publications/m/item/a-guide-to-preventing-and-addressing-social-stigma-associated-with-covid-19 (accessed on 22 May 2021).
46. Nelson, C.; Lurie, N.; Wasserman, J.; Zakowski, S. Conceptualizing and defining public health emergency preparedness. *Am. J. Public Health* **2007**, *97* (Suppl. 1), S9–S11. [CrossRef]
47. CDC. *Public Health Emergency Preparedness and Response Capabilities: National Standards for State, Local, Tribal, and Territorial Public Health*; CDC: Atlanta, GA, USA, 2018.
48. CDC. *Public Health Preparedness: 2011 State-by-State Update on Laboratory Capabilities and Response Readiness Planning*; CDC: Atlanta, GA, USA, 2011.

International Journal of
Environmental Research and Public Health

MDPI

Article

The Impact of the COVID-19 Pandemic on Primary Emotional Systems and Emotional Regulation

Rachele Mariani [1,*], Alessia Renzi [1], Cinzia Di Monte [1], Elena Petrovska [2] and Michela Di Trani [1]

[1] Department of Dynamic and Clinical Psychology, and Health Studies Sapienza, University of Rome, 00185 Rome, Italy; alessia.renzi@uniroma1.it (A.R.); cinzia.dimonte@uniroma1.it (C.D.M.); michela.ditrani@uniroma1.it (M.D.T.)

[2] Derner School of Psychology, Adelphi University, Garden City, NY 11530-0701, USA; petre813@newschool.edu

* Correspondence: rachele.mariani@uniroma1.it

Abstract: (1) Background: The COronaVIrus Disease 2019 (COVID-19) pandemic poses a unique challenge as a severe global crisis affecting physical and psychological health. The main purpose of this work is to study the impact of a traumatic event while also observing the human ability to adapt. One of the first theories to study the adaptive importance of the evolutionary lineage of the affective systems is referred to as BrainMind (Panksepp, 2010). This study aims to explore whether primary emotional systems (PES) and emotion regulation (ER) strategies show differences between the pre- and post- lockdown period; and if positive systems and specific emotion regulation pre-pandemic act as a protective or risk factor for mental and physical wellbeing. (2) Methods: 98 participants who had participated in a previous study before the pandemic were re-contacted to refill the Affective Neuroscience Personality Scale (ANPS) and the Emotion Regulation Questionnaire (ERQ) after the outbreak of the pandemic with the addition of the Symptom Checklist-90-Revised (SCL-90R). (3) Results: The results showed that the COVID-19 lockdown rules had an impact on Emotional Regulation and on a re-balancing of PES. Moreover, pre-pandemic expressive–suppressive ERQ strategies and ANPS SADNESS scores appeared as relevant risk factors, which predicted higher Global Severity Index (GSI) scores during lockdown. (4) Conclusions: The lockdown appears to have activated PLAY and CARE as protective systems, but has detuned the ability to positively reinterpret the situation.

Keywords: coronavirus pandemic; emotion regulation; primary emotional systems; mental and physical health

Citation: Mariani, R.; Renzi, A.; Di Monte, C.; Petrovska, E.; Di Trani, M. The Impact of the COVID-19 Pandemic on Primary Emotional Systems and Emotional Regulation. *Int. J. Environ. Res. Public Health* **2021**, *18*, 5742. https://doi.org/10.3390/ijerph18115742

Academic Editors: Lorys Castelli, Paolo Roma, Merylin Monaro and Cristina Mazza

Received: 8 April 2021
Accepted: 24 May 2021
Published: 27 May 2021

1. Introduction

The Coronavirus-19 Pandemic posed a significant global challenge and particularly to Italy, as the first European country impacted by it [1]. This severe universal crisis has disrupted various crucial aspects of life and affected both the physical and psychological health of individuals facing this collective trauma [2]. COVID-19 has been defined as a cultural trauma, which in fact shared many of the characteristics that circumscribe this, including: a fundamental disruption of what is taken for granted in daily life; a potential loss of trust in leaders and social institutions; negative attribution of the media; and a contentious struggle with meaning to determine what happened and who is responsible. People have experienced the pandemic as traumatic, characterized by a loss of existential security, a biopolitical condition that can potentially create new modalities of subjection and subjectivation, shaping both collective and individual subjectivities [3]. Cultural traumas imply anxiety and suffering, but also opportunity. The latter stems from the human capacity to learn and adjust to new conditions; to reevaluate the world, as well as to live in it. COVID-19 was a real threat to human survival and the Italian government adopted isolation and social distancing as its first, and perhaps, most effective response strategy. These elements have, in turn, severely tested the stamina of individuals and contributed to a notable increase in psychopathology as a reaction to the pandemic [1,4–8].

In this context, it is of particular interest to focus on the emotional parts of personality by referring to Affective Neuroscience Theory [9,10], which is one of the most well-known theories in the emotional sciences. Panksepp was the first to coin the term, "Affective Neuroscience" [11] and posited that human personality refers to stable individual differences in emotionality, motivation, and cognition, resulting in behavioral action patterns. Furthermore, he stated that emotions are the oldest evolutionary parts of human personality which drive human personality traits and behavior. Several researchers have explained [12–14] the role of emotions in relation to personality and how they influence human relationships. Panksepp et al. looked at the brain structures that underpin human emotions using neurobiology, ethology, and evolutionary results. At the heart of human emotional processes are three positive and three negative emotional structures (capitalizations denote advanced scientific jargon) which proposed that six primary emotional systems (PES) have been equivalently conserved across the mammalian brain. These phylogenetically old systems function as tools for survival and endow mammalian species with important brain systems to successfully interact with the environment. According to Panksepp, the primary positive emotions are: SEEKING, CARE, and PLAY; whereas the primary negative ones are: FEAR, SADNESS and ANGER [15,16]. These systems reflect embedded tools for survival which are highly evolutionary; imbalances in these different systems are associated with psychopathological characteristics [17]. For example, higher FEAR/SADNESS, along with lower SEEKING levels, represent the state of depression [18].

Following this notion, emotional regulation is strictly related to the internal primary emotional system (PES) which individuals have built during their own life.

PES influences emotion regulation strategies and structures specific relationship patterns between self and others and between self and the environment. Therefore, each person, throughout the course of their lifetime, tends to establish emotional strategies that balance the basic emotional systems. A traumatic event or a completely new situation will involve a need for each person to readjust their positive and negative systems in order to ensure survival [15]. For instance, the ability to feel the support of others during social distancing is a subjective ability connected to PES [10]. Psychological health is based on the development of harmonious and balanced positive and negative emotional systems. This balance influences higher mental processes and, on the other hand, conflict or imbalance can generate psychological suffering. The pandemic is a real attack on humanity. To protect the population, the Italian government quickly instituted social distancing rules and instituted a lockdown for all the population, except for health workers involved in protecting the health of citizens.

Utilizing the framework of Affective Neuroscience, PES should contribute to the rebalancing of emotional systems in order to adapt to the imposed rules and to survive through the usage of them. Our study emphasizes how people were triggered to generate emotional and behavioral strategies in response to the fear of extinction evoked by the virus and the collective trauma surrounding it. Panksepp coined the term "BrainMind," which intentionally conflates 'brain' and 'mind' to reflect the importance of primary emotion in the influencing of attitudes, traits, and emotional strategies. We hypothesize that emotional BrainMind may detect adaptive strategies as a phylogenetically refined affective function over the course of human evolution. Furthermore, we hypothesize that diversified affective capacities can help reduce the stressful impact or, on the contrary, increase its effects. More specifically, we hypothesize that:

(1) PES and emotion regulation strategies will show differences between the pre-lockdown and lockdown period, thus highlighting possible changes in ways of coping with the critical experience of the pandemic;
(2) Both pre-pandemic PES and ER strategies will predict individuals' mental and physical wellbeing (or psychopathology symptoms) during the lockdown period, acting as protective or risk factors in dealing with this traumatic situation.

2. Materials and Methods

2.1. Participants

A total of 98 healthy participants (46 males, 52 females) took part in this study. All participants were between the ages of 18 and 70 (M = 39.3; SD = 16.6); had an adequate understanding of the Italian language and were living in Italy at the time of the lockdown; were subject to lockdown social restriction rules; and possessed the technical ability to access the online platform to complete questionnaires. Our sample was extracted from a previous database of people who had participated in a personality and PES study prior to the pandemic. We therefore excluded people who had reported psychiatric diagnoses; those who reported taking medication for psychiatric reasons; and individuals who were working as healthcare professionals during the pandemic. Healthcare professionals were in fact the only professionals excluded from the lockdown and the rule imposed by the Italian government through the use of the slogan, "stay at home".

2.2. Procedure

The participants involved in the study had taken part in a previous study about three months before the pandemic, providing the availability to be contacted for future studies. About 200 people were invited to respond to a new online questionnaire during the lockdown and 98 people answered the new questionnaire. The first administration of the test protocol took place about three months before the outbreak of the pandemic, between November and December 2019. For the first assessment the participants were enrolled using snowball sampling, and subjects were invited to participate in a study of personality and emotion regulation strategies. The surveys were made available through an online platform where participants gave their informed consent before completing the self-administered questionnaire and indicating their willingness to be contacted for a follow-up. For the second assessment during imposed lockdown in Italy (in April 2020) the participants were invited to repeat the compilation of the questionnaire. However, considering the difficult period the world was facing, in the second compilation there was an additional questionnaire which assessed mental and physical symptomatology and asked participants to share how they felt during the global health emergency lockdown. The survey protocol received ethical approval from the Department Ethics Committee.

2.3. Measures

A socio-demographic questionnaire was designed to collect information concerning age, gender, education level, relationship/social status, and current or previous clinical and mental diagnoses.

The Symptom Checklist 90-Revised (SCL-90-R) [19] is a 90-item self-report questionnaire that measures mental and physical symptoms which have occurred in the previous week. Each item is rated by respondents on a five-point Likert scale (0–4) ranging from having caused no discomfort to having caused extreme discomfort during the past week. The SCL-90-R has nine subscales, and the Global Severity Index (GSI) score reflects overall mental and physical distress. The questionnaire showed adequate test-retest reliability, internal consistency, and concurrent and discriminant validity [19]. In the present study, Cronbach's alpha of the total scale was $\alpha = 0.93$, whereas clinical subscales ranged from $\alpha = 0.72$ to $\alpha = 0.87$.

The Affective Neuroscience Personality Scale, version 2.4 (ANPS) [20] is a 112-item self-report questionnaire based on Panksepp's studies and was derived from the description of PES. The items are based on a four-point Likert scale. Six subscales, representing PES, were identified: SEEKING, CARE, PLAY, FEAR, ANGER, and SADNESS/PANIC. The questionnaire showed satisfactory internal consistency and adequate concurrent and discriminant validity [20]. In the present study, Cronbach's alpha values for the subscales were PLAY: $\alpha = 0.78$; SEEK: $\alpha = 0.72$; CARE: $\alpha = 0.71$; FEAR: $\alpha = 0.81$; ANGER: $\alpha = 0.78$; SADNESS/PANIC: $\alpha = 0.74$).

The Emotion Regulation Questionnaire (ERQ) [21] is a 10-item self-report scale designed to measure the tendency of respondents to regulate their emotions in two ways: Cognitive-Reappraisal (CR) and Expressive-Suppression (ES), which represent the subscales. Respondents answer each item on a seven-point Likert scale (1–7). The questionnaire showed good internal consistency [21]. Cronbach's alpha values for the present study were: CR: $\alpha = 0.82$ and ES: $\alpha = 0.73$.

2.4. Statistical Analysis

All statistical analyses were performed using the Statistical Package for Social Science version 25 (SPSS version 25). Data is reported as means and standard deviations for continuous variables and as percentages for discrete variables. The SCL-90 and demographic variables were analyzed using Pearson's correlation analysis. The t-test for paired samples was applied to explore differences between the pre-lockdown (Time1) and lockdown period (Time2) in the affective dimensions investigated (ERQ and ANPS). Cohen's d was computed in order to obtain standardized effect sizes. A multiple linear regression was performed in order to investigate the predictive effect of age, gender and pre-pandemic ANPS and ERQ scores on mental and physical symptomatology (GSI) evaluated during the pandemic. All the variables were entered simultaneously and were statistically significant ($p < 0.05$). Collinearity was tested (Tolerance and Variance Inflection Factor) assuming values were in the correct/accepted ranges.

3. Results

3.1. Descriptive Analysis

The participants had a mean age of 39.3 (SD = 16.6). Years of education averaged 15.5 (SD = 2.4); 45.8% had a High School Diploma, 41.7% had a Master's Degree, and 12.5% had a Bachelor's Degree. In addition, 45.8% indicated that they were married/cohabiting; 25.2% were unmarried/not cohabiting and living independently (or with roommates); 8.3% were divorced; and 20.7% were single and living with their families of origin. Age is significantly correlated to pre-pandemic and post-pandemic assessment of FEAR ($r = -0.559$, $p < 0.00$), pre-pandemic CARE ($r = -0.331$, $p < 0.01$), and not significant correlated to SCL-90R and ERQ. The same mean of SCL-90R is 0.62 (SD = 0.45) and 16% of the sample overcame the GSI clinical cut-off. More specifically, more than 30% of participants displayed elevated symptoms of depression, anxiety and obsessive compulsiveness. Primary Emotional Systems, ERQ, and SCL90 did not show any significance difference when comparing the level of education, gender assigned at birth, or relationship status.

3.2. Comparison Pre- and Post-Pandemic

In regard to changes in affective systems and emotion regulation dimensions, data analysis showed an increase in the CARE ($p = 0.001$) and PLAY ($p = 0.027$) systems of ANSP and a decrease in the cognitive-reappraisal ($p = 0.001$) dimension of the ERQ (see Table 1).

Table 1. *t* test comparison pre- and post-pandemic in ERQ and ANPS dimensions.

	Pre-Pandemic Time 1 N = 98		Lockdown Period Time 2 N = 98		T	P	Cohen's *d*
ERQ	**Mean**	**SD**	**Mean**	**SD**			
Cognitive-Reappraisal	29.52	7.89	24.46	5.68	5.284	0.001 *	0.76
Expressive-Suppression	12.35	4.65	12.06	4.85	0.567	0.574	0.09
ANPS	**Mean**	**SD**	**Mean**	**SD**			
SEEK	30.17	4.45	29.80	5.03	0.698	0.489	0.10
FEAR	24.71	6.82	24.04	7.43	1.147	0.257	0.16
CARE	29.46	5.44	32.05	4.62	−4.245	0.001 *	0.61
ANGER	17.71	7.40	17.00	6.63	1.171	0.248	0.17
PLAY	25.40	5.98	26.60	5.44	−2.290	0.027 *	0.33
SADNESS/PANIC	22.77	5.26	22.81	6.11	−0.073	0.942	0.05

t test for repeated measure, * $p < 0.05$ gf (97); ERQ = Emotion Regulation Questionnaire; ANPS = Affective Neurosciences Personality Scales; SD = Standard Deviation.

3.3. Regression Analysis

We hypothesized that PES and ERQ evaluated prior to the pandemic could predict mental and physical symptoms during the COVID-19 lockdown. To test this hypothesis, we conducted a linear regression analysis using GSI (SCL-90R) scores as dependent variables and pre-pandemic ANPS and ERQ scores, age, and gender as independent variables.

The model explains 51% of the GSI scores ($R^2 = 0.51$; adjusted $R^2 = 0.38$; $F = 3.85$; $p = 0.001$), thus indicating an adequate fit of the model tested. The independent variables that showed a significant effect were: expressive-suppression ERQ ($\beta = 0.45$; $t = 2.71$; $p < 0.001$) and SADNESS ANPS ($\beta = 0.71$; $t = 3.65$; $p < 0.001$). Age and gender did not show any statistically significant results.

4. Discussion

Consistent with previous studies regarding the impact of the COVID-19 pandemic on psychological well-being [4,5,22,23], the presence of psychopathological symptoms was found in the sample we examined. More specifically, participants displayed higher symptoms of depression, anxiety and obsessive compulsiveness. Italy was one of the first countries to be significantly affected by COVID-19 and social isolation measures were immediately enforced there. Social distancing and government-imposed lockdowns have effectively kept many people in their homes. Italy is among the countries with higher death rates from COVID-19, and with a higher average age than the rest of the world, especially during the first stage of pandemic [24]. The high number of deaths that hit the country exposed all citizens to great stress and concern for their own safety. At that time, our survey focused on detecting the psychological and physical effects of the situation, as well as understanding the modalities of emotional regulation of those who were experiencing the lockdown. The opportunity to be able to contact those who had participated in one of our research projects before the outbreak of the pandemic allowed us to verify the balance/imbalance of the PES and of the cognitive-reappraisal and expression–suppression emotional regulation strategies investigated. Elderly people were the most affected by COVID-19, and, therefore, we investigated whether age had an incidence with the variables explored and with psychopathological symptoms in the lockdown phase. The results showed that seniority is negatively related to FEAR in both pre- and post- evaluation, and also negatively related to CARE systems in pre-pandemic evaluation, which is not a significant relationship to psychological symptoms. Therefore, although the elderly is the most affected population, age does not emerge as a risk factor for psychological stress. The relationship with fear as a primary emotional system and young age is in line with the data showing that young people have suffered greatly during the pandemic, accentuated by perhaps feeling more exposed [25,26].

The results showed that COVID-19 lockdown rules had an impact on Emotional Regulation and displayed a re-balancing effect on PES. Further, during the lockdown, there was a decrease of ERQ cognitive reappraisal. Cognitive-Reappraisal (CR) generally has a buffer function which aids in the prevention of psychopathology [27]. CR is a flexible and adaptive function of emotion regulation, but the results displayed a decrease in it due to the traumatic impact of COVID-19. However, in regard to PES, we found an increase in the PLAY and CARE systems, which served as protective elements against danger. Physical PLAY is the most complex basic social emotion and persists after neo decortication [11]; CARE, or the maternal nurturance system, includes nurturance and social bonding and suggests that there is an intimate evolutionary relationship to maternal motivations. These results are consistent to studies which have shown that lower scores in the PLAY and CARE systems are linked to depression [28]. In analyzing ERQ and PES results, it could be said that the decrease in CR showed a reduction in the ability to regulate the positive reinterpretation of situations [29,30]. In other words, the results showed how people's emotions manifest during traumatic events and how this, in turn, activated a rebalancing of their positive systems in attempt to cope with the stressful situation.

The second hypothesis tested whether specific PES and ERQ factors evaluated before the pandemic predicted psychopathological symptoms. A regression model showed that pre-pandemic variables, such as SADNESS and Expressive–Suppression were a risk factor and predicted higher psychopathological symptoms of GSI during lockdown. These results are consistent with recent results obtained during the COVID-19 pandemic, which showed the protective function of the ability to cope with anxiety and stress through cognitive reappraisal. On the other hand, expressive suppression served as a risk factor for the development of psychopathological symptoms [31,32]. This result is consistent with previous studies which found that other traumatic events, such as war or abuse, suggested that PES involved SADNESS [33,34]. Several developmental studies have highlighted how the persistence of specific negative emotions in children can predict future psychopathology. It was found that higher levels of sadness in adolescents predicted internalizing symptomatology [35]. Our results confirm a significant link between the dominance of a negative primary emotional system and psychopathological manifestation.

All of these findings need to be interpreted in the light of some limitations. First, the sample size of this study is relatively small. Furthermore, the sample was composed of volunteers available to be re-selected from a previous study, which may have introduced a selection bias. A further limitation is linked to having investigated only two macro strategies for regulating emotions, instead of explaining more specific modalities that are useful in the management of psychopathology [36].

5. Conclusions

In conclusion, as proposed by Cole et al. (1994) [37], the present findings align with their assumption that psychopathology is related to an imbalance of emotional experiences (positive and negative) within an individual. The prevalence and persistence of predominantly negative feelings, without the presence of positive emotions to balance the emotional baseline, can induce a greater risk of psychopathology when facing future stressful events. The imbalanced evaluation of the environment therefore increases the perception of risk and the negative evaluations of the strength of the individual. Our results also highlight that under the stress of the pandemic, the changing emotional factors are positive, which seems to indicate that individual balancing can be achieved through positive affect, while negative emotions appear to be less flexible.

This aspect can lead to future insights confirming the incidence of the role that negative experiences during the early stages of life, as well as dysfunctional emotional regulation models learned from childhood, can impact an individual's mental health [38].

Our findings suggest that psychological interventions focused on the prevention of the imbalance of negative emotional systems can aid others in coping with negative feelings and therefore, in regulating and reinforcing resilience to stress [39].

The PES model suggests that the human adaptive capacity is able to cope with significant criticalities imposed by the environment and that flexible emotional systems are able help individuals adapt. It is recommended that all this be taken into consideration when developing the promotion of health in response to collective trauma through the reinforcement of flexible emotional regulation and the restoration of emotional balance. Our results also suggest that greater flexibility in re-establishing a good balance should be oriented towards the development of positive emotions and that the support for emotional regulation strategies should be aimed at the reappraisal of the situation.

Author Contributions: R.M. contributed to all the phases of the study from conception and design of the study, results interpretation and writing manuscript. A.R. performed the statistical analysis, contributed to results interpretation, and in writing the manuscript. C.D.M. contributed to conception, organized the database and writing manuscript. E.P. contributed to writing and editing of the manuscript. M.D.T. in results interpretation and supervision of the work. All authors have read and agreed to the published version of the manuscript.

Funding: This research received no external funding.

Institutional Review Board Statement: The study was conducted according to the guidelines of the Declaration of Helsinki, and approved by the Ethics Committee of Department of Clinical, Dynamic and Health Study Psychology, University of Rome, Sapienza (protocol code 0000323 and 16/04/2020).

Informed Consent Statement: Informed consent was obtained from all subjects involved in the study.

Data Availability Statement: Data available on request due to restrictions privacy.

Conflicts of Interest: The authors declare no conflict of interest.

References

1. Sani, G.; Janiri, D.; Di Nicola, M.; Janiri, L.; Mph, S.F.; Chieffo, D. Mental health during and after the COVID -19 emergency in Italy. *Psychiatry Clin. Neurosci.* **2020**, *74*, 372. [CrossRef] [PubMed]
2. Duan, L.; Zhu, G. Psychological interventions for people affected by the COVID-19 epidemic. *Lancet Psychiatry* **2020**, *7*, 300–302. [CrossRef]
3. Demertzis, N.; Eyerman, R. Covid-19 as cultural trauma. *Am. J. Cult. Sociol.* **2020**, *8*, 428–450. [CrossRef] [PubMed]
4. Wang, C.; Pan, R.; Wan, X.; Tan, Y.; Xu, L.; Ho, C.S.; Ho, R.C. Immediate Psychological Responses and Associated Factors during the Initial Stage of the 2019 Coronavirus Disease (COVID-19) Epidemic among the General Population in China. *Int. J. Environ. Res. Public Health* **2020**, *17*, 1729. [CrossRef] [PubMed]
5. Cao, W.; Fang, Z.; Hou, G.; Han, M.; Xu, X.; Dong, J.; Zhen, J. The psychological impact of the COVID-19 epidemic on college students in China. *Psychiatry Res.* **2020**, *287*, 112934. [CrossRef]
6. Liu, N.; Zhang, F.; Wei, C.; Jia, Y.; Shang, Z.; Sun, L.; Wu, L.; Sun, Z.; Zhou, Y.; Wang, Y.; et al. Prevalence and predictors of PTSS during COVID-19 outbreak in China hardest-hit areas: Gender differences matter. *Psychiatry Res.* **2020**, *287*, 112921. [CrossRef]
7. Mariani, R.; Renzi, A.; Di Trani, M.; Trabucchi, G.; Danskin, K.; Tambelli, R. The Impact of Coping Strategies and Perceived Family Support on Depressive and Anxious Symptomatology during the Coronavirus Pandemic (COVID-19) Lockdown. *Front. Psychiatry* **2020**, *11*, 587724. [CrossRef]
8. Mazza, M.; Marano, G.; Antonazzo, B.; Cavarretta, E.; DI Nicola, M.; Janiri, L.; Sani, G.; Frati, G.; Romagnoli, E. What about heart and mind in the COVID-19 era? *Minerva Cardiol. Angiol.* **2021**, *69*. [CrossRef] [PubMed]
9. Panksepp, J. The periconscious substrates of consciousness: Affective states and the evolutionary origins of the self. *J. Conscious. Stud.* **1998**, *5*, 566–582.
10. Davis, K.L.; Montag, C. Selected Principles of Pankseppian Affective Neuroscience. *Front. Neurosci.* **2019**, *12*, 1025. [CrossRef]
11. Panksepp, J. A critical role for "affective neuroscience" in resolving what is basic about basic emotions. *Psychol. Rev.* **1992**, *99*, 554–560. [CrossRef] [PubMed]
12. Davis, K.L.; Panksepp, J. The brain's emotional foundations of human personality and the Affective Neuro-science Personality Scales. *Neurosci. Biobehav. Rev.* **2011**, *35*, 1946–1958. [CrossRef] [PubMed]
13. Montag, C. The Brain Derived Neurotrophic Factor and Personality. *Adv. Biol.* **2014**, *2014*, 1–15. [CrossRef]
14. Montag, C.; Reuter, M. Disentangling the molecular genetic basis of personality: From monoamines to neu-ropeptides. *Neurosci. Biobehav. Rev.* **2014**, *43*, 228–239. [CrossRef]
15. Montag, C.; Panksepp, J. Primary Emotional Systems and Personality: An Evolutionary Perspective. *Front. Psychol.* **2017**, *8*, 464. [CrossRef]
16. Montag, C.; Elhai, J.D. Discussing digital technology overuse in children and adolescents during the COVID-19 pandemic and beyond: On the importance of considering Affective Neuroscience Theory. *Addict. Behav. Rep.* **2020**, *12*, 100313. [CrossRef]
17. Panksepp, J. Emotional endophenotypes in evolutionary psychiatry. *Prog. Neuro-Psychopharmacol. Biol. Psychiatry* **2006**, *30*, 774–784. [CrossRef] [PubMed]
18. Montag, C.; Hahn, E.; Reuter, M.; Spinath, F.M.; Davis, K.; Panksepp, J. The role of nature and nurture for in-dividual differences in primary emotional systems: Evidence from a twin study. *PLoS ONE* **2016**, *11*, e0151405.
19. Preti, E.; Prunas, A.; Irene, S.; Madeddu, F. *Symptom Checklist-90-R*; Giunti: Florence, Italy, 2011.
20. Giacolini, T.; Ardizzone, I.; Davis, K.L.; Ferrara, M.; Picconi, L.; Terrinoni, A.; Sabatello, U. Brain Emotional Systems: The Italian version of the ANPS-Affective Neuroscience Personality Scales 2.4 (Reliability and Validity). *Clin. Neuropsychiatry* **2017**, *14*, 263–274.
21. Balzarotti, S.; John, O.P.; Gross, J.J. An Italian Adaptation of the Emotion Regulation Questionnaire. *Eur. J. Psychol. Assess.* **2010**, *26*, 61–67. [CrossRef]
22. Sigdel, A.; Bista, A.; Bhattarai, N.; Poon, B.C.; Giri, G.; Marqusee, H. Depression, Anxiety and Depres-sion-anxiety comorbidity amid COVID-19 Pandemic: An online survey conducted during lockdown in Nepal. *MedRxiv* **2020**. [CrossRef]
23. Rodríguez-Rey, R.; Garrido-Hernansaiz, H.; Collado, S. Psychological Impact and Associated Factors During the Initial Stage of the Coronavirus (COVID-19) Pandemic Among the General Population in Spain. *Front. Psychol.* **2020**, *11*, 1540. [CrossRef]
24. Istituto nazionale di Statistica (ISTAT), Impatto Dell'epidemia COVID-19 Sulla Mortalità Totale Della Popolazione Residente Periodo Gennaio-Novembre 2020. Available online: www.iss.it/documents/20126/0/Rapp_Istat_Iss_FINALE+2020_rev.pdf (accessed on 20 February 2021).

25. Pieh, C.; Budimir, S.; Probst, T. The effect of age, gender, income, work, and physical activity on mental health during coronavirus disease (COVID-19) lockdown in Austria. *J. Psychosom. Res.* **2020**, *136*, 110186. [CrossRef] [PubMed]
26. Rossi, R.; Socci, V.; Talevi, D.; Mensi, S.; Niolu, C.; Pacitti, F.; Di Marco, A.; Rossi, A.; Siracusano, A.; Di Lorenzo, G. COVID-19 pandemic and lock-down measures impact on mental health among the general population in Italy. *Front. Psychiatry* **2020**, *11*, 790. [CrossRef]
27. Wang, X.; Zhang, R.; Chen, X.; Liu, K.; Wang, L.; Zhang, J.; Liu, X.; Feng, Z. Psychopathological Correlates and Emotion Regulation as Mediators of Approach and Avoidance Motivation in a Chinese Military Sample. *Front. Psychiatry* **2019**, *10*, 149. [CrossRef]
28. McEwen, B.S. Physiology and Neurobiology of Stress and Adaptation: Central Role of the Brain. *Physiol. Rev.* **2007**, *87*, 873–904. [CrossRef] [PubMed]
29. Hannan, S.M.; Orcutt, H.K. Emotion dysregulation as a partial mediator between reinforcement sensitivity and posttraumatic stress symptoms. *Personal. Individ. Differ.* **2013**, *55*, 574–578. [CrossRef]
30. Ochsner, K.N.; Bunge, S.A.; Gross, J.J.; Gabrieli, J.D.E. Rethinking feelings: An fMRI study of the cognitive regulation of emotion. *J. Cogn. Neurosci.* **2002**, *14*, 1215–1229. [CrossRef]
31. Lv, Z.-Y.; Yang, J.; Jiang, H.-J.; Nan, J. Psychological impacts of the COVID-19 epidemic on Chinese people: Exposure, post-traumatic stress symptom, and emotion regulation. *Asian Pac. J. Trop. Med.* **2020**, *13*, 252. [CrossRef]
32. Zhai, Y.; Xue, D. Loss and grief amidst COVID-19: A path to adaptation and resilience. *Brain Behav. Immun.* **2020**, *87*, 80–81. [CrossRef]
33. Malcolm-Smith, S.; Thomas, K.G.F.; Ipser, J.; Stein, D.; Van Honk, J.; Solms, M. Opioid Function Is Dysregulated Subsequent to Early Social Trauma: Healthy Young Adults' Response to a Buprenorphine Challenge. *Neuropsychoanalysis* **2013**, *15*, 127–143. [CrossRef]
34. Alcaro, A.; Panksepp, J. The SEEKING mind: Primal neuro-affective substrates for appetitive incentive states and their pathological dynamics in addictions and depression. *Neurosci. Biobehav. Rev.* **2011**, *35*, 1805–1820. [CrossRef] [PubMed]
35. Jenkins, J.M.; Oatley, K. Psychopathology and Short-term Emotion: The Balance of Affects. *J. Child Psychol. Psychiatry* **2000**, *41*, 463–472. [CrossRef] [PubMed]
36. Gutiérrez-Hernández, M.E.; Fanjul, L.F.; Díaz-Megolla, A.; Reyes-Hurtado, P.; Herrera-Rodríguez, J.F.; Enjuto-Castellanos, M.d.P.; Peñate, W. COVID-19 Lockdown and Mental Health in a Sample Population in Spain: The Role of Self-Compassion. *Int. J. Environ. Res. Public Health* **2021**, *18*, 2103. [CrossRef] [PubMed]
37. Cole, P.M.; Michel, M.K.; Teti, L.O.D. The development of emotion regulation and dysregulation: A clinical perspective. *Monogr. Soc. Res. Child Dev.* **1994**, *59*, 73–102. [CrossRef]
38. Vogel, A.C.; Jackson, J.J.; Barch, D.M.; Tillman, R.; Luby, J.L. Excitability and irritability in preschoolers predicts later psychopathology: The importance of positive and negative emotion dysregulation. *Dev. Psychopathol.* **2019**, *31*, 1067–1083. [CrossRef]
39. Jiménez, Ó.; Sánchez-Sánchez, L.C.; García-Montes, J.M. Psychological Impact of COVID-19 Confinement and Its Relationship with Meditation. *Int. J. Environ. Res. Public Health* **2020**, *17*, 6642. [CrossRef]

International Journal of
Environmental Research and Public Health

MDPI

Article

Older Adolescents Who Did or Did Not Experience COVID-19 Symptoms: Associations with Mental Health, Risk Perception and Social Connection

Jessica Burrai [1,2,*], Benedetta Barchielli [2], Clarissa Cricenti [1], Anna Borrelli [3], Sabina D'Amato [3], Massimo Santoro [3], Margherita Vitale [3], Stefano Ferracuti [4], Anna Maria Giannini [1] and Alessandro Quaglieri [1]

1 Department of Psychology, Sapienza University of Rome, Via dei Marsi 78, 00185 Rome, Italy; cricenticlarissa@gmail.com (C.C.); annamaria.giannini@uniroma1.it (A.M.G.); alessandro.quaglieri@uniroma1.it (A.Q.)
2 Department of Dynamic and Clinical Psychology, and Health Studies, Sapienza University of Rome, Via degli Apuli 1, 00185 Rome, Italy; benedetta.barchielli@uniroma1.it
3 Direzione Sanitaria-Servizio di Psicologia Clinica Ospedaliera A. O. U. San Giovanni e Ruggi d'Aragona, Largo Città d'ippocrate, 84131 Salerno, Italy; acquarama@libero.it (A.B.); sabinadamato@yahoo.it (S.D.); dr.massimosantoro@gmail.com (M.S.); margheritavitale79@gmail.com (M.V.)
4 Department of Human Neuroscience, Sapienza University of Rome, Viale dell'Università 30, 00185 Rome, Italy; stefano.ferracuti@uniroma1.it
* Correspondence: jessica.burrai@uniroma1.it

Citation: Burrai, J.; Barchielli, B.; Cricenti, C.; Borrelli, A.; D'Amato, S.; Santoro, M.; Vitale, M.; Ferracuti, S.; Giannini, A.M.; Quaglieri, A. Older Adolescents Who Did or Did Not Experience COVID-19 Symptoms: Associations with Mental Health, Risk Perception and Social Connection. *Int. J. Environ. Res. Public Health* **2021**, *18*, 5006. https://doi.org/10.3390/ijerph18095006

Academic Editor: Paul B. Tchounwou

Received: 14 April 2021
Accepted: 5 May 2021
Published: 9 May 2021

Publisher's Note: MDPI stays neutral with regard to jurisdictional claims in published maps and institutional affiliations.

Abstract: After a decrease in detected cases in the summer, Europe faced the emergence of a second wave of coronavirus disease 19 (COVID-19). Few studies have investigated adolescents, who may constitute a target group with possible lower compliance to public health measures, particularly the social distancing measures. A total sample of 492 participants was included in the study, and the ages of the participants ranged from 18–24 years. According to the hypothesis of our study, the sample was divided into two groups: those who experienced COVID-19 symptoms and those who did not experience COVID-19 symptoms. Demographic characteristics, knowledge, perceptions, and behaviors related to COVID-19 were investigated with ad hoc items; in addition, mood disorders, self-efficacy, and social connectedness were explored. Our results showed significant differences in the variables of risk perception, self-efficacy, and measures of belongingness among older adolescents who did or did not experience COVID-19 symptoms. In this period, adolescents experienced unprecedented disruptions in their daily lives, leading them to isolation and loneliness. Compliance with restrictive measures is considered both a proactive behavior and a social responsibility, especially if supported by prosocial reasons to prevent others from getting sick; therefore, this must be the focus of raising awareness of anti-COVID-19 compliance among adolescents.

Keywords: self-efficacy; risk-taking; social connectedness; young adult; depression; anxiety; stress

1. Introduction

At the end of February 2020, Italy faced an outbreak of coronavirus disease 19 (COVID-19), which spread quickly across most of Europe. After a decrease in detected cases in the summer, Europe faced the emergence of a second wave of COVID-19. In this context, the Italian government established a partial lockdown based on a new tiered system, classifying some areas with the highest rates of COVID-19 as high-risk red zones and maintaining preventive measures such as wearing a mask and social distancing. Previous studies on compliance with preventive measures during past epidemics and pandemics (e.g., Ebola virus disease, cholera, avian flu, severe acute respiratory syndrome, equine influenza, and Zika virus) found that factors related to compliance were knowledge of the disease [1,2], perceived effectiveness of the preventive measures [1,3,4], social influence [1], perception of risk [5], concern for self and loved ones, and perceived severity compared to other epidemics [3,6,7]. Different studies have investigated the general population, e.g., [8], psychiatric population, e.g., [9,10], and family patterns, e.g., [11]. However, few studies have investigated adolescents and young adults with ages ranging from a minimum of 15 to a maximum of 22, who may constitute a target group with possible lower compliance to public health measures, particularly with physical distancing measures [12]. However, adolescents had to face new stressors such as the fear of being infected; worrying about their parents' work (i.e., financial situation); death; restrictions on their privacy; sudden separation from schoolmates, friends, and teachers [13–16].

These factors were linked to changes in lifestyle habits, increased use of social networks, and changes in eating habits [14,17,18] and experienced emotions, such as loneliness, boredom, and sadness [19,20]; however, adolescents seem to have adapted quickly to the current situation [21].

Furthermore, studies have investigated the impact of COVID-19 on adolescents' mental health and have found an increase in both pre-existing [22] and non-pre-existing cases of major psychopathological conditions, such as depression, anxiety, and Post-Traumatic Stress Disorder [16,23–27].

On the other hand, studies have investigated the psychosocial environment of adolescents related to pandemic situations. In particular, increased time spent at home with family seems to have influenced conflict with parents, harsh discipline, and parental control [28–30]. Regarding relationships with peers and considering the decrease in face-to-face contact, adolescents appear to have increased their communication through social networking, mainly through the use of video calls [21].

During adolescence, the relationship with peers has a relevant influence on adherence to the rules, as well as negative youth-adult relationships [31,32], dysfunctional family functioning (e.g., poor family communication), poor school bonding (poor peer cohesion) [33], low levels of self-control [34], and high sensation-seeking tendencies [35,36]. In contrast, rule compliance appears to be associated with factors, such as the legitimacy of authority, justice [37], and personal factors such as self-efficacy [38].

However, adherence to protective measures during the COVID-19 pandemic was different when considering adults and younger people. Masters and colleagues [39] investigated different generations, from "Generation Z" (18–23 years) to the "Silent Generation" (≥75 years), and showed that the adoption of preventive measures, in particular distancing, increased with age: Generation Z and millennials were the least likely to comply with distancing rules.

One of the reasons that appear to support low adherence to these behaviors is the idea that "there is no alternative," while the reason that most strongly motivates young people to comply with social distancing is the desire to protect others [40,41]. In addition, young people's low adherence to COVID-19 rules seems to be associated with low-risk perception, low perception of illness severity, low acceptance of moral rules, low self-control, and peer influence, particularly the relationship with peers who do not comply with the rules [12,41–43].

In particular, with the gradual decrease in restrictive measures during the second wave, adolescents considered it no longer necessary to maintain social distancing [43].

Often, young people do not consider COVID-19 a potentially severe disease, and evidence suggests that young people are less vulnerable [44]. Indeed, the period of life between the ages of 10 and 24 years (i.e., adolescence) is often related to increased risk-taking, the need for social connection and peer acceptance, and increased sensitivity to peer influence [42]. However, it seems important to investigate the underlying characteristics of this phenomenon. The likelihood of being infected and experiencing severe COVID-19 symptoms is underestimated by young people, although the spread of COVID-19 might depend on their behaviors. To date, compliance with the rules is still essential to prevent the spread of COVID-19; therefore, the understanding of those factors could mediate the assumption of risky behaviors.

On this basis, we explored the role of social connectedness in maintaining a stable relationship with peers and the dimensions of anxiety, stress, and depression on risk perception and risk behavior in older adolescents (i.e., 18–24 years). Additionally, we explored the difference between the perceived protective behaviors and the actual behaviors to protect oneself against COVID-19 infection. Based on these considerations, the main purpose of our study was to investigate whether the experience of COVID-19 symptoms: (I) influenced risk perception, depression, anxiety and stress; (II) affected self-efficacy in terms of prevention, recognition and home management of COVID-19; and (III) whether the COVID-19 pandemic impacted the sense of belongingness and "being a part of" since the sense of connectedness emerges during adolescence and extends throughout the lifetime.

2. Materials and Methods

2.1. Participants

A total sample of 492 participants was included in the study. Of the total sample, 27.0% were male, and the ages ranged from 18 to 24 (M = 21.06, SD = 1.82). According to the hypothesis of our study, the sample was divided into two groups: those who experienced COVID-19 symptoms (CE) and those who did not experience COVID-19 symptoms (NCE). The CE sample included 211 participants (18–24 years old; M = 21.07, SD = 1.80), and 21.8% were male. The NCE sample included 281 participants (18–24 years old; M = 21.05, SD = 1.84), and 31.0% were male. With respect to the CE sample, 85.8% of the participants were university students, 3.3% were secondary school students, 7.6% were workers, and 3.3% were unemployed. With regard to the item "Who contracted COVID-19," 20.9% stated "him/herself," 14.7% stated "household members," and 64.5% stated "relatives or close friends." The full sociodemographic characteristics are described in Table 1.

Table 1. Demographic characteristics of the studied population.

Descriptive Statistics			
		CE	NCE
Sex	Male	46	87
	Female	165	194
	Total	211	281
Age	Mean	21.07	21.05
	Std. Deviation	1.80	1.84
	Range	18–24	18–24
Occupation	Unemployed	7	4
	Employed	16	8
	Second-undergraduate degree	7	16
	University degree	181	253
	Total	211	281
Who have contracted the COVID-19	Him/her-self	44	-
	Household members	31	-
	Relatives or close friends	136	-
	Total	211	-
Sport Activities	Yes	21	33
	No	190	248
	Total	211	281
Friends Meeting	Yes	80	82
	No	131	199
	Total	211	281

CE = individuals with COVID-19 symptoms experience; NCE = individuals without COVID-19 experiences.

2.2. Procedures

We collected data throughout the Qualtrics Platform online survey. This study was launched on 18 December 2020 and concluded on 5 February 2021. The survey was diffused on social networks and the university's official website. Participants agreed to participate by signing a digital informed consent form and were informed that the data collection was anonymous and data were not shared outside the current research procedures. After digitally signing the informed consent form, participants were asked to complete the different questionnaires. Demographic characteristics, knowledge, perceptions, and behaviors related to COVID-19 were investigated with ad hoc items; in addition, mood disorders, self-efficacy, and social connectedness were explored. This study was conducted according to the ethical standards of the Helsinki Declaration and was approved by the Institutional Review Board of the Department of Psychology of "Sapienza" University of Rome (protocol number 0002195/18-12-2020).

2.3. Materials

The demographic characteristics of sex, age, level of education, and COVID-19 exposure were collected. Subjects were asked to complete the following self-report measures: knowledge related to COVID-19; risk perception of COVID-19; the Depression, Anxiety, and Stress Scale–21 items (DASS-21) [45]; the COVID-19 Prevention, Recognition, and Home-Management Self-Efficacy Scale [46]; the self-reported preventive behavior and motivation to engage in preventive behavior scale [40]; and the Social Connectedness Scale (SCS) [47].

To assess the risk perception of COVID-19, ten items were designed for the purpose of this study, and participants responded to the items using a 5-point Likert scale. In this study, Cronbach's alpha was 0.66.

For this study, a specific questionnaire with six ad hoc items that evaluated the appropriate COVID-19 coping behaviors was developed. The scale showed minimally acceptable internal consistency with an alpha of 0.68.

Emotional distress was measured by the DASS-21 scale, which contains 21 items measuring three different domains: depression, anxiety, and stress. Depression (e.g., "I felt I was pretty worthless") includes dysphoria, hopelessness, devaluation of life, self-depression, lack of interest/involvement, anhedonia, and inertia; anxiety (e.g., "I felt I was close to panic") refers to autonomic nervous system arousal, skeletal musculature effects, situational anxiety, and subjective experience of anxious affects; and stress (e.g., "I felt that I was using a lot of nervous energy") relates to the presence of nonspecific arousal levels, difficulty relaxing, nervous excitement, irritability, agitation, hyperactivity, and impatience. Participants were asked to respond to questions indicating "how often the situation described has occurred in the last seven days." All subscales are rated on a 4-point Likert scale ranging from 0 (never) to 3 (almost always). The depression, anxiety, and stress subscales had Cronbach's alphas of 0.82, 0.74, and 0.85, respectively [48]. In the present study, the Cronbach's alphas were 0.88 for DASS-Depression, 0.79 for DASS-Anxiety, 0.86 for DASS-Stress, and 0.92 for the total scale.

Two instruments were used to assess self-efficacy. The first was based on previous research on SARS [49], in which a single item was used to investigate "how confident do you feel about avoiding contagion." This item is based on a 5-point Likert scale ranging from 0 (not confident) to 5 (very confident).

The second instrument was the COVID-19 Prevention, Recognition and Home-Management Self-Efficacy Scale [46]. It contains 19 items "based on the WHO's recommended behaviors to protect oneself and others from the spread of COVID-19."

The items are grouped into three categories: (i) Prevention of COVID-19 spread and contagion (e.g., "I do not touch my eyes, nose, or mouth under any circumstances"), (ii) Early recognition of COVID-19 symptoms (e.g., "I identify if I have symptoms of COVID-19 quickly after they appear"), and (iii) Home management of patients with (or suspected) COVID-19 (e.g., "Keep the door to the room of the person with symptoms closed at all times"). Scale response options ranged from 0 (completely sure that I cannot do it) to 100 (completely sure that I can do it). The COVID-19 Prevention, Recognition and Home Management Self-Efficacy Scale had a Cronbach's alpha of 0.90 and an intraclass correlation coefficient of 0.75. In the present sample, the Cronbach's alphas were 0.74 for prevention, 0.85 for recognition, 0.88 for home management, and 0.90 for the total scale.

The authors reported the internal scoring system as follows: scores below 55 indicated very low self-efficacy, scores ranging from 55 to 68 indicated low self-efficacy, scores ranging from 69 to 82 indicated moderate self-efficacy, scores ranging from 83 to 96 indicated high self-efficacy, and scores above 96 indicated very high self-efficacy.

Self-reported preventive behavior and motivation to engage in preventive behavior were investigated using a single item inspired by the study of [40]. Participants were asked, "In the past 7 days, to what extent did you engage preventive behaviors?". Six behaviors were presented: washing hands, maintaining social distancing, avoiding crowds, sneezing and coughing safely, wearing a mask, and going out only when allowed. Responses were given on a 5-point scale (1 = not at all to 5 = a great deal).

The SCS [47] measures the level of interpersonal closeness an individual feels in their social world (e.g., friends, peers, and society) and the level of difficulty in maintaining this sense of closeness. It consists of eight items using a 6-point Likert scale (1 = strongly agree to 6 = strongly disagree), and higher scores indicate a greater perceived sense of connectedness (e.g., I feel disconnected from the world around me). The SCS showed a very good internal consistency of 0.91 for social connectedness and an alpha of 0.77 for social assurance. In the present sample, Cronbach's alphas were 0.92 for social connectedness and 0.79 for social assurance. Cronbach's alpha of the total scale was 0.82.

3. Data Analysis

Statistical analyses were conducted using the Statistical Package for Social Science (SPSS; version 25.0; IBM SPSS, Armonk, NY). First, we tested the internal consistency of the instruments using Cronbach's alphas, and the results showed internal consistency with an alpha ranging from a minimum of 0.659 to a maximum of 0.924. Descriptive analyses with means and standard deviations were performed. We used independent samples *t*-tests to determine the differences between groups (conducted using SPSS). Pearson correlations were performed to explore the relationships between the main variables. Statistical significance was defined as $p < 0.05$. The distributions of all data were verified for normality. All statistical analyses were performed on de-identified data.

4. Results

The analysis of demographic characteristics showed a statistically significant results for sex ($p < 0.001$) and occupation ($p < 0.001$) and no statistically significant result for age ($p = 0.998$).

With respect to the depression t (490) = −0.271, $p = 0.787$, anxiety t (490) = −1.02, $p = 0.308$ and stress t (490) = −1.554, $p = 0.121$ dimensions of the DASS-21, there were no statistically significant differences between groups; nevertheless, CE groups reported higher overall scores in all three dimensions of the scale compared to the NCE group. With respect to the items on "COVID-19 appropriate behaviors," there were no statistically significant results between groups.

With respect to the "How confident do you feel about avoiding contagion" item, there was a statistically significant difference between groups (Table 2). The results showed a significantly higher mean in the NCE group (M = 2.95, SD = 0.805) than in the CE group (M = 2.72, SD = 0.738), t (490) = 3.25, $p < 0.01$, d = 0.296.

With regard to the items investigating "Perceived risk of COVID-19", there was a statistically significant result on "How severe would it be if you contracted COVID-19" (Table 2). The NCE had a higher mean (M = 3.70, SD = 0.762) compared to the CE group (M = 3.50, SD = 0.686), t (490) = 3.04, $p < 0.01$, d = 0.277. The item "How badly do you feel about not being able to meet the people you used to date?" had a statistically significant result (Table 2). The results showed a higher mean in the CE group (M = 4.30, SD = 0.846) than in the NCE group (M = 4.08, SD = 0.997), t (490) = −2.59, $p < 0.5$, d = 0.236. The item "How badly do you feel about having to keep a safe distance from others" yielded a statistically significant result (Table 2). Pairwise comparisons showed a higher mean in the

CE group (M = 3.94, SD = 1.08) than in the NCE group (M = 3.62, SD = 1.14), t (490) = −3.17, $p < 0.01$, d = −0.289.

Table 2. Comparison between groups (ANOVAs).

ANOVA							
Item	**t**	**df**	**Sig.**	**d**	**Multiple Comparisons**	**M**	**SE**
How confident do you feel about avoiding contagion?	3.25	490	0.01 **	0.296	NCE vs. CE	0.230	0.071
Recognition of COVID-19 symptoms.	−2.215	477	0.05 *	−0.201	CE vs. NCE	−4.28	1.93
Home management of people with COVID-19.	−3.671	490	0.001 ***	−0.334	CE vs. NCE	−6.54	1.78
Social connectedness.	−2.582	475	0.05 *	−0.235	CE vs. NCE	−2.22	0.861
How severe would it be if you contracted COVID-19?	3.041	490	0.01 **	0.277	NCE vs. CE	0.202	0.067
How badly do you feel about not being able to meet the people you used to date?	−2.586	490	0.05 *	−0.235	CE vs. NCE	−0.220	0.085
How badly do you feel about having to keep a safe distance from others?	−3.172	490	0.01 **	−0.289	CE vs. NCE	−0.324	0.102

* $p < 0.05$; ** $p < 0.01$; *** $p < 0.001$; CE = individuals with COVID-19 symptoms experience; NCE = individuals without COVID-19 experience. M = Mean; SE = Standard error.

Concerning the COVID-19 Prevention, Recognition and Home-Management Self-efficacy Scale, there was a statistically significant result for recognition of COVID-19 symptoms (Table 2), with a higher mean in the CE group (M = 77.50, SD = 19.71) than in the NCE group (M = 73.22, SD = 22.31), t (477) = −2.21, $p < 0.05$, d = −0.201. Levene's test indicated unequal variances (F = 3.88, $p = 0.049$); thus, the degrees of freedom were adjusted from 490 to 477. The home management of people with COVID-19 symptoms dimension had a statistically significant result (Table 2) in which the CE group reported a higher mean (M = 80.16, SD = 18.26) than the NCE group (M = 73.61, SD = 20.51), t (490) = −3.67, $p < 0.001$, d = −0.334. The prevention of COVID-19 contagion and spread dimension yielded no statistically significant results between groups, t (490) = −0.179, $p = 0.858$.

The social connectedness scale showed a statistically significant result concerning the "social connectedness" dimension (Table 2). The CE group reported a higher mean (M = 35.29, SD = 8.83) than the NCE group (M = 33.07, SD = 9.88), t (475) = −2.58, $p < 0.05$, d = −0.235. Levene's test indicated unequal variances (F = 5.69, $p = 0.017$); thus, the degrees of freedom were adjusted from 490 to 475. There was no statistically significant result for the "social assurance" dimension t (486) = 0.753, $p = 0.452$.

4.1. Correlations between Variables in the CE Group

Pearson correlations were calculated to explore the relationships between the main variables involved in the study. We found that "How badly do you feel about wearing a mask and not being able to see the full expression on other people's faces" was significantly and negatively correlated with prevention of COVID-19 contagion, r = −0.174, $p < 0.05$; with "Wash your hands with soap and water or alcohol-based solution," r = −0.186, $p < 0.05$; and with "Avoid gatherings of large groups of people," r = −0.166, $p < 0.05$, from the appropriate behavior scale. Additionally, "How badly do you feel about wearing a mask and not being able to see the full expression on other people's faces" was significantly and positively correlated with the DASS-Depression dimension, r = 0.185, $p < 0.01$.

We found that DASS-Depression scores were significantly and negatively correlated with the "social connectedness" dimension, r = −0.564, $p < 0.01$; and the "social assurance" dimension, r = −0.208, $p < 0.01$. DASS-Anxiety dimension scores were significantly and negatively correlated with the "social connectedness," r = −0.318, $p < 0.01$; and with the "How confident do you feel about avoiding contagion," r = −0.202, $p < 0.01$. DASS-Stress scores were significantly and negatively correlated with "How confident do you feel about avoiding contagion", r = −0.164, $p < 0.05$; "social connectedness," r = −0.325, $p < 0.01$; and "social assurance," r = −0.165, $p < 0.05$.

4.2. Correlations between Variables in the NCE Group

We found that "How badly do you feel about wearing a mask and not being able to see the full expression on other people's faces" was significantly and negatively correlated with the "social assurance" dimension, r = −0.229, $p < 0.01$; and significantly and positively correlated with the DASS-Anxiety, r = 0.171, $p < 0.01$, and DASS-Stress dimensions, r = 0.211, $p < 0.01$. We found that DASS-Depression was significantly and negatively correlated with the "social connectedness" dimension, r = −0.515, $p < 0.01$; the "social assurance" dimension, r = −0.307, $p < 0.01$; the "Recognition of COVID-19 symptoms," r = −0.205, $p < 0.01$; and with the "Home management of people with COVID-19 symptoms," r = −0.253, $p < 0.01$. The DASS-Anxiety dimension was significantly and negatively correlated with the "social connectedness" dimension, r = −0.346, $p < 0.01$; and with the "social assurance" dimension r = −0.245, $p < 0.01$. DASS-Stress dimension was significantly and negatively correlated with the "Recognition of COVID-19 symptoms," r = −0.132, $p < 0.01$; "Home management of people with COVID-19 symptoms," r = −0.184, $p < 0.01$; the "social connectedness" dimension, r = −0.387, $p < 0.01$; and the "social assurance" dimension, r = −0.216, $p < 0.01$.

5. Discussion

The main goal of this study was to better understand the condition of older adolescents during the long-term COVID-19 pandemic, considering that the extraordinary measures adopted by national governments to face the pandemic had unprecedented effects on adolescents' daily lives. In this regard, social distancing and isolation strategies have been the worldwide primary measures to prevent the risk of infection [50]. Although these measures benefit the entire community, they lead to stress, anxiety, and a sense of helplessness in everyone; for this reason, their psychological effects cannot be overlooked [51].

Our results showed significant differences in the variables of risk perception, self-efficacy, and measures of belongingness among older adolescents who experienced (CE) or did not experience (NCE) COVID-19.

With respect to the DASS-21 questionnaire, the CE and NCE groups showed no statistically significant differences. However, measures of distress along the three axes revealed "moderate" depression and "mild" anxiety for both the CE and NCE groups, "moderate" stress for the CE group and "mild" stress for the NCE group. The lack of a significant difference reported in this study could be explained by the fact that COVID-19 has long-term effects (e.g., the future perspective becomes confusing, fearful, uncertain, and distressing). In this regard, the risk and fear of contagion have changed social and interpersonal relationships, socialization opportunities, education and training systems, and physical activities, especially for younger people; furthermore, home confinement leads to uncertainty and anxiety in both children and adolescents [52]. This is true regardless of whether adolescents had direct COVID-19 experience.

Furthermore, the CE group showed a higher mean difference than the NCE group on social connectedness (one of two measures of belongingness, based on H. Kohut's [53] self-psychology theory), which focuses on the emotional distance or connection between the self and other people. Social connectedness concerns those aspects of belonging that Kohut [53] described as an "intense and pervasive sense of security" and a sense of being "human among humans." We can hypothesize that having experienced COVID-19 may increase the proximity (interest in health status) of friends and relatives; for this reason, this may have an impact on "feeling part of something."

Regarding the second measure of belongingness (i.e., social assurance), no differences between groups were found. With respect to the correlation analysis conducted, the DASS-21 depression dimension showed a negative correlation with both measures of belongingness (social connectedness and social assurance) for both the CE and NCE groups. Likewise, the anxiety and stress dimensions of the DASS-21 showed a negative correlation with social connectedness and social assurance for both the CE and NCE groups. Therefore, we can hypothesize that as anxiety, stress and depression increase, older adolescents feel more emotionally distant from friends, relatives, and society and feel less a "part of something." These data seem to be explained by prolonged isolation due to restricted home confinement, forced removal from school friends and relatives, confusing or contradictory communication on the pandemic, and the uncertainties of personal and family futures that may have led to increased anxious, stressed, and depressed responses.

Moreover, older NCE adolescents had a higher mean on the dimension of avoiding COVID-19 infection (i.e., "How confident do you feel about avoiding contagion") and scored higher than CE adolescents on the severity of being infected with COVID-19 (i.e., "How severe would it be if you contracted COVID-19"). Indeed, higher perceived self-efficacy to take preventive measures is associated with greater perceived severity of the COVID-19 disease. These data agree with the literature as risk perception is significantly related to COVID-19 severity and coronavirus self-efficacy [54]; furthermore, this result seems to agree with evidence suggesting young people are less vulnerable to the effects of COVID-19 [44]. These differences could be explained by previous knowledge of COVID-19's consequences in the CE group. The NCE group did not have direct experience with COVID-19 and therefore did not know what to expect. The NCE group perceives itself to be more effective at avoiding COVID infection as it has not yet had any experience and feels "protected" from the risk of infection. The results just discussed are also in line with further scientific literature. Indeed, people who believe that they are more vulnerable perceive a higher risk of infection and fear the virus and are also more likely to adopt preventive behaviors. This suggests that developing people's ability to cope with the impact of COVID-19 may increase the adoption of preventive behaviors. These findings suggest that risk perception, along with other factors, may influence the levels of individuals' preventive behaviors [1].

In addition, the CE group showed higher levels of bad moodiness than the NCE group and, in particular, with some measures of prevention of COVID-19 infection (e.g., "How badly do you feel about not being able to meet the people you used to date" and "How badly do you feel about having to keep a safe distance from others"). Therefore, we assumed that the CE group could consider COVID-19 infection as less serious and be more bothered by mandatory avoidance behaviors.

This is confirmed by a strong positive correlation found in the CE group between the item "How badly do you feel about wearing a mask and not being able to see the full expression on other people's faces" and the depression dimension of the DASS-21 and strong negative correlations with the COVID-19 contagion prevention item and appropriate COVID-19 coping behaviors (i.e., "Wash your hands with soap and water or alcohol-based solution" and "Avoid gatherings of large groups of people"). Thus, we can hypothesize that since CE individuals consider COVID-19 to be less severe, they may experience more discomfort in strictly adhering to protective measures and that having direct experience with the disease may have generated a false perception of invulnerability.

With respect to the COVID-19 Prevention, Recognition and Home-Management Self-efficacy Scale, the older adolescent CE group had higher means for symptom recognition and home management of COVID-19. These data are quite clear; indeed, those who experienced COVID-19 felt more capable of recognizing the symptoms of infection (e.g., fever or chills, cough, shortness of breath or difficulty breathing, fatigue, muscle or body aches, headache, loss of taste or smell, etc.) and in the home management of those infected with COVID-19 including the following: avoiding all contact with other family members, sleeping alone and staying in a dedicated room, limiting movement in house's spaces in order to avoid meeting other people, periodically measuring oxygen saturation, taking medication to control symptoms, etc. Such differences could be explained by the information that is available to an individual on COVID-19. The NCE group has less information (only the information generally acquired from media), so they may feel less effective at handling the consequences of COVID-19. Although the Protection Motivation Theory (PMT) states that self-efficacy is considered a robust predictor of various health-related behaviors [55,56], no significant differences were found between the CE and NCE groups in appropriate COVID-19 behaviors as measured by different survey items (e.g., "Always keep a distance of at least three feet between myself and others"). This can be explained by the coping-appraisal process (i.e., one of the three processes of PMT), which suggests coping as the sum of evaluations of the effectiveness and self-efficacy of responses minus any physical or psychological "costs" of adopting the recommended preventive response. Thus, our results, having been collected during the second wave, may reflect the habit of implementing certain types of protective behaviors regardless of having had experience with COVID-19.

The results showed strong correlations between "Recognition of COVID-19 symptoms" and "Home management of people with COVID-19 symptoms" and the stress and depression dimensions of the DASS in the NCE group. Self-efficacy seems to influence people's perception of themselves and may often be inconsistent with reality, resulting in a self-image that is too positive or too negative.

Stress is related to low self-efficacy, that is, beliefs about the inability to master new or challenging tasks, perform a particular behavior, or exercise control over events [57,58]. In the present study, people's self-efficacy in the prevention, detection of symptoms, and home management of COVID-19, when they had not experienced COVID-19, may have triggered a pattern in which perceived inefficacy is closely related to stress and depression. In fact, self-efficacy is an important dispositional resource that mitigates threat appraisals, state anxiety, and cortisol secretion [59].

These results offer an opportunity to reflect on the population examined here since young people tend to frequent crowded places; if they do not comply with the health measures recommended by the government, they risk spreading COVID-19. These results could highlight the importance of prosocial aspects in the management of preventive measures in adolescents for social policies. The importance of active involvement in understanding compliance with anti-COVID rules, rather than the imposition of enforcement, emerges.

However, the study has some limitations. First, it is limited by the use of online surveys and the use of self-reported questionnaires, which may have influenced the findings through well-known biases, including method biases and social desirability biases. Additionally, the study was limited by the relatively small sample size and was conducted using the online convenience sampling strategy without random sample selection. In addition, the study could not investigate comparisons between CE and NCE (i.e., regarding sex and education level) due to numerically significant differences in the sample, and using an observational design limits the generalizability of the results.

6. Conclusions

To the best of our knowledge, this study is the first to provide data on a population of older adolescents who have or have not experienced COVID-19. To prevent the spread of COVID-19, adolescents experienced unprecedented disruptions in their daily lives, leading them to isolation and loneliness. Adolescence is a stage of life in which excitement and risk-taking are experienced; thus, some adolescents may feel invulnerable and not follow guidelines regarding distancing and personal hygiene. These factors mean that adhering to social distancing rules can be especially difficult for youth and must be assertively addressed with adolescents.

Valuing adolescents' peer support system is essential. For them, it can be very important and helpful to talk to their peers about their feelings and common problems they face. It has also been found that among adolescents, compliance with restrictive measures is considered both a proactive behavior and a social responsibility, especially if supported by prosocial reasons to prevent others from getting sick; this must be the focus of raising awareness of anti-COVID-19 compliance among adolescents.

Author Contributions: Conceptualization, J.B., B.B., C.C., and A.Q.; methodology, A.Q.; formal analysis, A.Q. and J.B.; data curation, A.B., S.D., M.S., and M.V.; writing—original draft preparation, J.B., B.B., C.C., and A.Q.; writing—review and editing, S.F. and A.M.G.; supervision, S.F. and A.M.G.; All authors have read and agreed to the published version of the manuscript.

Funding: This research received no external funding.

Institutional Review Board Statement: The study was conducted according to the guidelines of the Declaration of Helsinki and approved by the Institutional Review Board of Department of Psychology, Faculty of Medicine and Psychology, "Sapienza" University of Rome (protocol number 0002195/18-12-2020).

Informed Consent Statement: Informed consent was obtained from all subjects involved in the study.

Data Availability Statement: The data presented in this study are available on request from the corresponding author. The data are not publicly available due to privacy considerations.

Conflicts of Interest: The authors declare no conflict of interest.

References

1. Gamma, A.E.; Slekiene, J.; Mosler, H.J. The Impact of Various Promotional Activities on Ebola Prevention Behaviors and Psychosocial Factors Predicting Ebola Prevention Behaviors in the Gambia Evaluation of Ebola Prevention Promotions. *Int. J. Environ. Res. Public Health* **2019**, *16*, 2020. [CrossRef] [PubMed]
2. Wong, L.P. Behavioral responses to the influenza A(H1N1) outbreak in Malaysia. *J. Behav. Med.* **2011**, *34*, 23–31. [CrossRef]
3. Lau, J.T.; Kim, J.H.; Tsui, H.Y.; Griffiths, S. Anticipated and current preventive behaviors in response to an anticipated human-to-human H5N1 epidemic in the Hong Kong Chinese general population. *BMC Infect. Dis.* **2007**, *7*. [CrossRef]
4. Contzen, N.; Mosler, H.J. Impact of different promotional channels on handwashing behaviour in an emergency context: Haiti post-earthquake public health promotions and cholera response. *J. Public Health* **2013**, *21*, 559–573. [CrossRef]
5. Lau, J.T.; Yang, X.; Tsui, H.; Kim, J.H. Monitoring community responses to the SARS epidemic in Hong Kong: From day 10 to day 62. *J. Epidemiol. Community Health* **2003**, *57*, 864–870. [CrossRef] [PubMed]
6. Lau, J.T.; Yang, X.; Tsui, H.; Pang, E.; Kim, J.H. SARS preventive and risk behaviours of Hong Kong air travellers. *Epidemiol. Infect.* **2004**, *132*, 727–736. [CrossRef]
7. Liao, Q.; Cowling, B.J.; Lam, W.W.; Ng, D.M.; Fielding, R. Anxiety, worry and cognitive risk estimate in relation to protective behaviors during the 2009 influenza A/H1N1 pandemic in Hong Kong: Ten cross-sectional surveys. *BMC Infect. Dis.* **2014**, *14*. [CrossRef] [PubMed]
8. Mazza, C.; Ricci, E.; Biondi, S.; Colasanti, M.; Ferracuti, S.; Napoli, C.; Roma, P. A nationwide survey of psychological distress among Italian people during the COVID-19 pandemic: Immediate psychological responses and associated factors. *Int. J. Environ. Res. Public Health* **2020**, *17*, 3165. [CrossRef] [PubMed]
9. Burrai, J.; Roma, P.; Barchielli, B.; Biondi, S.; Cordellieri, P.; Fraschetti, A.; Giannini, A.M. Psychological and Emotional Impact of Patients Living in Psychiatric Treatment Communities during COVID-19 Lockdown in Italy. *J. Clin. Med.* **2020**, *9*, 3787. [CrossRef]
10. Cordellieri, P.; Barchielli, B.; Masci, V.; Viani, F.; de Pinto, I.; Priori, A.; Burrai, J. Psychological Health Status of Psychiatric Patients Living in Treatment Communities before and during the COVID-19 Lockdown: A Brief Report. *Int. J. Environ. Res. Publich Health* **2021**, *18*, 3567. [CrossRef]
11. Mari, E.; Fraschetti, A.; Lausi, G.; Pizzo, A.; Baldi, M.; Paoli, E.; Avallone, F. Forced Cohabitation during Coronavirus Lockdown in Italy: A Study on Coping, Stress and Emotions among Different Family Patterns. *J. Clin. Med.* **2020**, *9*, 3906. [CrossRef] [PubMed]
12. Nivette, A.; Ribeaud, D.; Murray, A.; Steinhoff, A.; Bechtiger, L.; Hepp, U.; Shanahan, L.; Eisner, M. Non-compliance with COVID-19-related public health measures among young adults in Switzerland: Insights from a longitudinal cohort study. *Soc. Sci. Med.* **2021**, *268*, 113370. [CrossRef] [PubMed]
13. Wang, G.; Zhang, Y.; Zhao, J.; Zhang, J.; Jiang, F. Mitigate the effects of home connement on children during the COVID-19 outbreak. *Lancet* **2020**, *395*, 945–947. [CrossRef]
14. Brooks, S.K.; Webster, R.K.; Smith, L.E.; Woodland, L.; Wessely, S.; Greenberg, N.; Rubin, G.J. The psychological impact of quarantine and how to reduce it: Rapid review of the evidence. *Lancet* **2020**, *395*, 912–920. [CrossRef]
15. Jones, N.; Pincock, K.; Abu Hamad, B.; Malachowska, A.; Youssef, S.; Alheiwidi, S.; Bani Odeh, K. Ensuring No Voices Are Left Behind: The Use of Digital Storytelling and Diary-Writing in Times of Crisis. In *Researching in the Age of COVID-19*; Kara, H., Khoo, S.M., Eds.; Policy Press: Bristol, UK, 2020; Volume 2. [CrossRef]
16. Guessoum, S.B.; Lachal, J.; Radjack, R.; Carretier, E.; Minassian, S.; Benoit, L.; Moro, M.R. Adolescent psychiatric disorders during the covid19 pandemic and lockdown. *Psychiatry Res.* **2020**, *291*. [CrossRef] [PubMed]
17. Ng, K.; Cooper, J.; McHale, F.; Clifford, J.; Woods, C. Barriers and facilitators to changes in adolescent physical activity during COVID-19. *BMJ Open Sport Exerc. Med.* **2020**, *6*. [CrossRef] [PubMed]
18. Coronavirus, l'indagine di Telefono Azzurro e Doxa. Available online: https://azzurro.it/press/coronavirus-lindagine-telefono-azzurro-edoxa/ (accessed on 21 May 2020).
19. Banerjee, D.; Mayank, R. Social Isolation in COVID-19: The Impact of Loneliness. *Int. J. Soc. Psychiatry* **2020**, *66*, 525–527. [CrossRef]
20. Cohen, C.; Cadima, G.; Castellanos, D. Adolescent Well-Being and Coping during COVID-19: A US-Based Survey. *J. Pediatr. Neonatol.* **2020**, *2*, 1007.

21. Buzzi, C.; Tucci, M.; Ciprandi, R.; Brambilla, I.; Caimmi, S.; Ciprandi, G.; Marseglia, G.L. The psychosocial effects of COVID-19 on Italian adolescents' attitudes and behaviors. *Ital. J. Pediatr.* **2020**, *46*, 69. [CrossRef]
22. Chevance, A.; Gourion, D.; Hoertel, N.; Llorca, P.M.; Thomas, P.; Bocher, R.; Gaillard, R. Assurer les soins aux patients souffrant de troubles psychiques en France pendant l'épidémie à SARS-CoV-2. *Encéphale* **2020**. [CrossRef]
23. Duan, L.; Shao, X.; Wang, Y.; Huang, Y.; Miao, J.; Yang, X.; Zhu, G. An investigation of mental health status of children and adolescents in China during the outbreak of COVID-19. *J. Affect. Disord.* **2020**, *275*, 112–118. [CrossRef]
24. Zhou, S.J.; Zhang, L.G.; Wang, L.L.; Guo, Z.C.; Wang, J.Q.; Chen, J.C.; Liu, M.; Chen, X.; Chen, J.X. Prevalence and socio-demographic correlates of psychological health problems in Chinese adolescents during the outbreak of COVID-19. *Eur. Child. Adolesc. Psychiatry* **2020**, *29*, 749–758. [CrossRef] [PubMed]
25. Keles, B.; McCrae, N.; Grealish, A. A systematic review: The influence of social media on depression, anxiety and psychological distress in adolescents. *Int. J. Adolesc. Youth* **2020**, *25*, 79–93. [CrossRef]
26. Xie, X.; Xue, Q.; Zhou, Y.; Zhu, K.; Liu, Q.; Zhang, J.; Song, R. Mental health status among children in home confinement during the coronavirus disease 2019 outbreak in Hubei province, China. *JAMA Pediatr.* **2020**, *174*, 898–900. [CrossRef] [PubMed]
27. Liu, C.H.; Zhang, E.; Wong, G.T.F.; Hyun, S. Factors associated with depression, anxiety, and PTSD symptomatology during the COVID-19 pandemic: Clinical implications for US young adult mental health. *Psychiatry Res.* **2020**, *290*, 113172. [CrossRef]
28. Fegert, J.M.; Vitiello, B.; Plener, P.L.; Clemens, V. Challenges and burden of the Coronavirus 2019 (COVID-19) pandemic for child and adolescent mental health: A narrative review to highlight clinical and research needs in the acute phase and the long return to normality. *Child Adolesc. Psychiatry Ment. Health* **2020**, *14*. [CrossRef]
29. Pigaiani, Y.; Zoccante, L.; Zocca, A.; Arzenton, A.; Menegolli, M.; Fadel, S.; Ruggeri, M.; Colizzi, M. Adolescent Lifestyle Behaviors, Coping Strategies and Subjective Wellbeing during the COVID-19 Pandemic: An Online Student Survey. *Healthcare* **2020**, *8*, 472. [CrossRef] [PubMed]
30. Campbell, A.M. An increasing risk of family violence during the COVID-19 pandemic: Strengthening community collaborations to save lives. *Forensic Sci. Int. Rep.* **2020**, *2*, 100089. [CrossRef]
31. Ferguson, C.J.; San Miguel, C.; Hartley, R.D. A multivariate analysis of youth violence and aggression: The influence of family, peers, depression, and media violence. *J. Pediatr.* **2009**, *155*, 904–908. [CrossRef]
32. Cooley, J.; Fite, P.; Rubens, S.; Tunno, A. Peer Victimization, Depressive Symptoms, and Rule-Breaking Behavior in Adolescence: The Moderating Role of Peer Social Support. *J. Psychopathol. Behav. Assess.* **2015**, *37*, 512–522. [CrossRef]
33. Cordova, D.; Huang, S.; Arzon, M.; Freitas, D.; Malcolm, S.; Prado, G. The Role of Attitudes, Family, Peer and School on Alcohol Use, Rule Breaking and Aggressive Behavior in Hispanic Delinquent Adolescents. *Open Fam. Stud. J.* **2011**, *4*, 38–45. [CrossRef] [PubMed]
34. Laird, R.; Marks, L.; Marrero, M. Religiosity, self-control, and antisocial behavior: Religiosity as a promotive and protective factor. *J. Appl. Dev. Psychol.* **2011**, *32*, 78–85. [CrossRef]
35. Rolison, M.; Scherman, A. Factors influencing adolescents' decision to engage in risk-taking behavior. *Adolescence* **2002**, *37*, 585–596.
36. Sandseter, E.; Beate, H.; Breivik, G. Sensation seeking as a predictor of positive and negative risk behaviour among adolescents. *Pers. Individ. Differ.* **2001**, *30*, 627–640. [CrossRef]
37. Thomas, K.J.; Rodrigues, H.; de Oliveira, R.T.; Mangino, A.A. What Predicts Pre-adolescent Compliance with Family Rules? A Longitudinal Analysis of Parental Discipline, Procedural Justice, and Legitimacy Evaluations. *J. Youth Adolesc.* **2020**, *49*, 936–950. [CrossRef]
38. Broadhead-Fearn, D.; White, K.M. The role of self-efficacy in predicting rule-following behaviors in shelters for homeless youth: A test of the theory of planned behavior. *J. Soc. Psychol.* **2006**, *146*, 307–325. [CrossRef]
39. Masters, N.B.; Shih, S.F.; Bukoff, A.; Akel, K.B.; Kobayashi, L.C.; Miller, A.L.; Harapan, H.; Lu, Y.; Wagner, A.L. Social distancing in response to the novel coronavirus (COVID-19) in the United States. *PLoS ONE* **2020**, *15*, 0239025. [CrossRef] [PubMed]
40. Oosterhoff, B.; Palmer, C.A.; Wilson, J.; Shook, N. Adolescents' Motivations to Engage in Social Distancing During the COVID-19 Pandemic: Associations with Mental and Social Health. *J. Adolesc. Health* **2020**, *67*, 179–185. [CrossRef]
41. Yang, X.Y.; Gong, R.N.; Sassine, S.; Morsa, M.; Tchogna, A.S.; Drouin, O.; Chadi, N.; Jantchou, P. Risk Perception of COVID-19 Infection and Adherence to Preventive Measures among Adolescents and Young Adults. *Children* **2020**, *7*, 311. [CrossRef]
42. Andrews, J.L.; Foulkes, L.; Blakemore, S.J. Peer influence in adolescence: Public-health implications for COVID-19. *Trends Cogn. Sci.* **2020**, *24*, 585–587. [CrossRef] [PubMed]
43. Commodari, E.; La Rosa, V.L. Adolescents in Quarantine during COVID-19 Pandemic in Italy: Perceived Health Risk, Beliefs, Psychological Experiences and Expectations for the Future. *Front Psychol.* **2020**, *11*, 559951. [CrossRef]
44. Kolifarhood, G.; Aghaali, M.; Saadati, H.M.; Taherpour, N.; Rahimi, S.; Izadi, N.; Nazari, S.S.H. Epidemiological and clinical aspects of COVID-19; a narrative review. *Arch. Acad. Emerg. Med.* **2020**, *8*, 41. [CrossRef]
45. Lovibond, S.H.; Lovibond, P.F. *Manual for the Depression Anxiety Stress Scales*, 2nd ed.; Psychology Foundation of Australia: Sydney, Australia, 1996.
46. Hernández-Padilla, J.M.; Granero-Molina, J.; Ruiz-Fernández, M.D.; Dobarrio-Sanz, I.; López-Rodríguez, M.M.; Fernández-Medina, I.M.; Fernández-Sola, C. Design and psychometric analysis of the COVID-19 prevention, recognition and home-management self-efficacy scale. *Int. J. Environ. Res. Public Health* **2020**, *17*, 4653. [CrossRef]

47. Lee, R.M.; Robbins, S.B. Measuring belongingness: The social connectedness and the social assurance scales. *J. Couns. Psychol.* **1995**, *42*, 232. [CrossRef]
48. Bottesi, G.; Ghisi, M.; Altoè, G.; Conforti, E.; Melli, G.; Sica, C. The Italian version of the Depression Anxiety Stress Scales-21: Factor, structure and psychometric properties on community and clinical sample. *Compr. Psychiatry.* **2015**, *60*, 170–181. [CrossRef] [PubMed]
49. Zwart, O.; Veldhuijzen, I.; Elam, G.; Aro, A.; Abraham, T.; Bishop, G.; Brug, J. Perceived Threat, Risk Perception, and Efficacy Beliefs Related to SARS and Other (Emerging) Infectious Diseases: Results of an International Survey. *Int. J. Behav. Med.* **2009**, *16*, 30–40. [CrossRef] [PubMed]
50. Shen, K.; Yang, Y.; Wang, T.; Zhao, D.; Jiang, Y.; Jin, R.; Wang, Y. Global Pediatric Pulmonology Alliance. Diagnosis, Treatment, and Prevention Of 2019 Novel Coronavirus Infection. In Children: Experts' Consensus Statement. *World J. Pediatr.* **2020**, *16*, 223–231. [CrossRef]
51. Liu, J.J.; Bao, Y.; Huang, X.; Shi, J.; Lu, L. Mental health considerations for children quarantined because of COVID-19. *Lancet Child Adolesc. Health* **2020**, *4*, 347–349. [CrossRef]
52. Jiao, W.Y.; Wang, L.N.; Liu, J.; Fang, S.F.; Jiao, F.Y.; Pettoello-Mantovani, M.; Somekh, E. Behavioral and emotional disorders in children during the COVID-19 epidemic. *J. Pediatr.* **2020**, *221*, 264–266. [CrossRef] [PubMed]
53. Kohut, H. *How Does Analysis Cure?* International Universities Press: New York, NY, USA, 1984.
54. Yıldırım, M.; Geçer, E.; Akgül, Ö. The impacts of vulnerability, perceived risk, and fear on preventive behaviours against COVID-19. *Psychol. Health Med.* **2021**, *26*, 35–43. [CrossRef] [PubMed]
55. Sheeran, P.; Maki, A.; Montanaro, E.; Avishai-Yitshak, A.; Bryan, A.; Klein, W.M.; Rothman, A.J. The impact of changing attitudes, norms, and self-efficacy on health-related intentions and behavior: A meta-analysis. *Health Psychol.* **2016**, *35*, 1178. [CrossRef] [PubMed]
56. Williams, L.; Rasmussen, S.; Kleczkowski, A.; Maharaj, S.; Cairns, N. Protection motivation theory and social distancing behaviour in response to a simulated infectious disease epidemic. *Psychol. Health Med.* **2015**, *20*, 832–837. [CrossRef]
57. Bandura, A. Self-efficacy beliefs of adolescents. In *Adolescence and Education*; Pajares, F., Urdan, T., Eds.; Information Age Publishing: Greenwich, UK, 2006; pp. 307–337.
58. Pinquart, M.; Juang, L.P.; Silbereisen, R.K. Self-efficacy and successful school-to-work transition: A longitudinal study. *J. Vocat. Behav.* **2003**, *63*, 329–346. [CrossRef]
59. Minkley, N.; Westerholt, D.M.; Kirchner, W.H. Academic self-concept of ability and cortisol reactivity. *Anxiety Stress Coping* **2014**, *27*, 303–316. [CrossRef]

International Journal of
Environmental Research and Public Health

MDPI

Article

Individual-Level Determinants of Lifestyle Behavioral Changes during COVID-19 Lockdown in the United States: Results of an Online Survey

Xiaotao Zhang [1], Abiodun Oluyomi [1], LeChauncy Woodard [2,3,4], Syed Ahsan Raza [1], Maral Adel Fahmideh [1,5], Ola El-Mubasher [1], Jinyoung Byun [6], Younghun Han [6], Christopher I. Amos [1,6] and Hoda Badr [1,*]

1 Department of Medicine, Section of Epidemiology and Population Science, Baylor College of Medicine, Houston, TX 77030, USA; Xiaotao.Zhang@bcm.edu (X.Z.); Abiodun.Oluyomi@bcm.edu (A.O.); Syed.Raza@bcm.edu (S.A.R.); Maral.Adel@bcm.edu (M.A.F.); Ola.El-Mubasher@bcm.edu (O.E.-M.); chris.amos@bcm.edu (C.I.A.)
2 Department of Health Systems and Population Health Science, University of Houston College of Medicine, Houston, TX 77004, USA; lwoodard@Central.UH.EDU
3 Humana Integrated Health System Sciences Institute, University of Houston, Houston, TX 77030, USA
4 Center for Innovations in Quality, Effectiveness, and Safety (IQuESt), Houston, TX 77030, USA
5 Center for Epidemiology and Population Health, Department of Pediatrics, Baylor College of Medicine, Houston, TX 77030, USA
6 Institute for Clinical and Translational Research, Baylor College of Medicine, Houston, TX 77030, USA; Jinyoung.Byun@bcm.edu (J.B.); Younghun.Han@bcm.edu (Y.H.)
* Correspondence: hoda.badr@bcm.edu

Citation: Zhang, X.; Oluyomi, A.; Woodard, L.; Raza, S.A.; Adel Fahmideh, M.; El-Mubasher, O.; Byun, J.; Han, Y.; Amos, C.I.; Badr, H. Individual-Level Determinants of Lifestyle Behavioral Changes during COVID-19 Lockdown in the United States: Results of an Online Survey. *Int. J. Environ. Res. Public Health* **2021**, *18*, 1361. https://doi.org/10.3390/ijerph18084364

Academic Editors: Paolo Roma, Merylin Monaro and Cristina Mazza

Received: 23 March 2021
Accepted: 16 April 2021
Published: 20 April 2021

Abstract: This study examined individual-level determinants of self-reported changes in healthy (diet and physical activity) and addictive (alcohol use, smoking, and vaping) lifestyle behaviors during the initial COVID-19 lockdown period in the USA. A national online survey was administered between May and June 2020 that targeted a representative U.S. sample and yielded data from 1276 respondents, including 58% male and 50% racial/ethnic minorities. We used univariate and multivariable linear regression models to examine the associations of sociodemographic, mental health, and behavioral determinants with self-reported changes in lifestyle behaviors. Some study participants reported increases in healthy lifestyle behaviors since the pandemic (i.e., 36% increased healthy eating behaviors, and 33% increased physical activity). However, they also reported increases in addictive lifestyle behaviors including alcohol use (40%), tobacco use (41%), and vaping (46%). With regard to individual-level determinants, individuals who reported adhering to social distancing guidelines were also more likely to report increases in healthy lifestyle behaviors ($\beta = 0.12$, 95% CI 0.04 to 0.21). Conversely, women ($\beta = -0.37$, 95% CI -0.62 to -0.12), and unemployed individuals ($\beta = -0.33$, 95% CI -0.64 to -0.02) were less likely to report increases in healthy lifestyle behaviors. In addition, individuals reporting anxiety were more likely to report increases in addictive behaviors ($\beta = 0.26$, 95% CI 0.09 to 0.43). Taken together, these findings suggest that women and unemployed individuals may benefit from interventions targeting diet and physical activity, and that individuals reporting anxiety may benefit from interventions targeting smoking and alcohol cessation to address lifestyle changes during the pandemic.

Keywords: COVID-19; coronavirus; lifestyle; anxiety; behavioral determinants

1. Introduction

The coronavirus disease 2019 (COVID-19) pandemic is an unprecedented public health crisis [1]. Faced with an exponential rise in cases and deaths, and in an effort to avoid overwhelming health systems, countries around the globe have adopted protective measures to mitigate the spread of infection including social distancing and stay-at-home policies [2]. Although such interventions are necessary to mitigate transmission, they may also modify lifestyle behaviors such as diet, physical activity (PA), smoking, and alcohol use [3,4], and have significant consequences for physical health [5].

Healthy lifestyle behaviors such as observing a healthy diet and engaging in recommended amounts of PA are consistently associated with reduced all-cause mortality, and improved health and well-being [6,7]. Increased time spent at home due to adherence with mitigation policies could present an opportunity to practice healthy lifestyle behavior (e.g., by home cooking of healthy meals and engaging in regular PA). Supporting this idea, research has documented increases in population-level interest in PA during the pandemic, although actual change in PA was not ascertained [8]. Simultaneously, increased unstructured time spent at home could contribute to people feeling lonely and distressed, eating when not hungry (i.e., emotional eating), and weight gain [9]. New telework arrangements, temporary closure of fitness facilities, and the need to stay at home could also force abrupt changes in PA, increasing the likelihood of sedentary behavior and weight gain [10,11].

Addictive lifestyle behaviors such as smoking and alcohol use are major contributors to the global burden of disease [12] and are associated with poor health outcomes [13]. Emerging evidence has suggested that slight increases in these behaviors during the pandemic [14–16] could possibly be in response to the stress, boredom, and social isolation caused by COVID-19 mitigation strategies [17–19]. In fact, a market research survey conducted by Nielsen in March 2020, during the initial lockdown period in the USA, showed that alcohol sales increased by 55% in a single week [20]. This is alarming because research has shown that individuals who started abusing substances during the SARS pandemic experienced persistent substance abuse that lasted well beyond the pandemic [21]. Meanwhile, a recent cross-sectional study of 336 U.S. adults found that 28.3% reduced tobacco smoking and 24.9% reduced vaping (e-cigarettes) during the pandemic [22].

Overall, the observed changes in lifestyle behaviors during the pandemic suggest that different people have been affected in different ways. Specifically, more leisure time at home and the threat of becoming severely ill with COVID-19 may have motivated some people to engage in more healthy lifestyle behaviors, and increased distress and changes in social patterns may have driven other people to self-medicate through substance use and abuse [23,24]. Previous studies that have focused on lifestyle behaviors during the pandemic have been largely conducted in Europe and Asia [3,11,25] and with only eating and physical activity [10,26] or smoking and drinking [22,27] as the main outcomes.

In this population-based study, we examined individual-level determinants of self-reported changes in healthy (i.e., diet and physical activity) and addictive (i.e., alcohol use, smoking, and vaping) lifestyle behaviors during the initial COVID-19 lockdown period that was observed by 42 out of 50 states in the USA. Given that healthy and addictive behaviors are not mutually exclusive, we opted to take a more comprehensive approach than previous studies and assessed both healthy behavioral changes (eating and physical activity) and addictive behavioral changes (smoking, vaping, and alcohol drinking). This study also extends the existing knowledge base by evaluating individual-level determinants of lifestyle behavioral changes during the pandemic, including sociodemographic, mental health, and behavioral (e.g., adherence to mitigation strategies) factors. By elucidating individual-level determinants, at-risk groups can be identified, and targeted lifestyle interventions can be developed.

2. Materials and Methods

2.1. Sample and Setting

This study was a national, population-based survey and it was approved by the Baylor College of Medicine Institutional Review Board (H-47505) and reports on baseline data were obtained from an ongoing longitudinal cohort study of the psychosocial and health behavioral impacts of the pandemic [28]. Eligible individuals were aged ≥18 and resided in the USA. Surveys were distributed in English and Spanish via paid and unpaid social media advertisements and an online survey crowdsourcing platform, Soapbox Sample, during the initial lockdown period in the USA. The survey was initially launched on 13 April 2020 and continued through to 8 June 2020. This period of time coincided with the initial lockdown period that was observed in 42 of 50 states [29]. The U.S. states that did not institute stay-at home orders were Arkansas, Iowa, Nebraska, North Dakota, Oklahoma, South Dakota, Utah, and Wyoming. By the end of the first week in June, rates of infection in the USA had begun to slowly decline, stay-at-home orders in most states had expired, and 34 states had either reopened or were in the process of a phased, state-wide reopening [29]. In addition, governors in 8 hard-hit states had allowed counties or regions that met criteria for slowing the outbreak to open (California, Illinois, Michigan, New York, Oregon, Pennsylvania, Tennessee, and Washington) [29].

Two weeks after the initial survey launch (1 May 2020), the survey was amended to also include questions about lifestyle behaviors, as these questions were not included in the original survey. Consequently, the total survey sample size was 2222, but only 1276 individuals took the survey between 1 May 2020 and 8 June 2020, and therefore comprise the current study sample.

2.2. Procedures

Social media advertisements contained a hyperlink directing individuals to the survey website. The landing page contained a brief cover letter describing the study. If, after reading the letter, individuals were interested in participating, they were asked to check a box confirming their eligibility, understanding, and consent. The survey was administered on the Qualtrics survey platform (Provo, UT, USA) [30]. Detailed measures were shown in Appendix A-Table A1 Measures

2.2.1. Lifestyle Behavioral Change Variables

Self-reported changes in healthy (i.e., eating healthy foods and PA) and addictive (i.e., alcohol use, tobacco smoking, and vaping) lifestyle behaviors were assessed and are described as follows:

Healthy Eating. Respondents indicated a degree of agreement with the question, "Since COVID-19, I am eating more healthy foods". Response options were on a 5-point Likert-type scale from 1 = "strongly disagree" to 5 = "strongly agree".

Physical Activity. PA was assessed with the item, "Since COVID-19, I am exercising more." Response options were on a 5-point Likert-type scale from 1 = "strongly disagree" to 5 = "strongly agree".

Alcohol Use. Individuals were first asked if they drink alcohol (yes/no), and if so, whether their alcohol consumption had "increased", "decreased", or "stayed the same" since the pandemic.

Tobacco Smoking. Items were taken from the Global Adult Tobacco Survey [31]. Individuals were first asked if they currently smoke tobacco "on a daily basis", "less than daily", or "not at all". Then, they were asked if their smoking had "increased", "decreased", or "stayed the same" since the pandemic.

Vaping. Participants were first asked if they use e-cigarettes "on a daily basis", "less than daily", or "not at all". Then, they were asked if their vaping had "increased", "decreased", or "stayed the same" since the pandemic.

Lifestyle behavioral change indices.

Healthy lifestyle behavior change index. The two healthy lifestyle behavioral change variables (i.e., healthy eating and PA) were re-coded by assigning a value of +1 for affirmative responses (i.e., agree or strongly agree), −1 for negative responses (i.e., disagree or strongly disagree), and 0 for neutral responses. Then, scores for the re-coded variables were summed to yield a healthy behavioral change index with a range from −2 to +2.

Addictive lifestyle behavior index. The three addictive lifestyle behavioral change variables (i.e., alcohol use, tobacco smoking, and vaping) were re-coded as −1 = decrease in behavior, 0 = no change, or +1 = increase in behavior. Then, scores for the re-coded variables were summed to yield an addictive behavioral change index with a range from −3 to +3.

2.2.2. Individual-Level Determinants

Sociodemographic, mental health, and behavioral (i.e., degree of adherence to COVID-19 mitigation strategies) determinants were assessed.

Sociodemographics

Individuals were asked about their age, gender, race/ethnicity, education, marital status, annual household income, work status, current living arrangement (alone, or with a spouse/partner, family member, or non-family member), number of household residents, and whether they lived with someone over age 65 or younger than age 18. We also asked individuals about their postal zip codes and cross-streets. On the basis of this information, the states of residence were divided into one of 4 major U.S. census regions, i.e., Northeast, South, Midwest, and West.

Mental Health

Mental health over the past 7 days was assessed using the 4-item short-form Patient-Reported Outcome Measure Information System (PROMIS) depression [32] and anxiety measures [33]. For both measures, responses range from 1 (never) to 5 (always) and are summed to form a raw score that can then be scaled into a T-score (standardized) with a mean of 50.0 and standard deviation of 10.0. Scores >60.0 indicate the need for further psychological evaluation [34].

Behavioral Determinants

Self-reported adherence to three COVID-19 mitigation strategies (stay-at-home orders, social distancing, and hand hygiene/sanitization) were assessed. With regard to stay-at-home orders, we first asked, "Is the area where you live currently under a 'Stay-at-Home', 'Safer-at-Home', or 'Shelter-at-Home' order? (yes/no)" If participants responded, "yes", we then asked, "To what extent do you currently follow the stay-at-home order?" Response options were on an 11-point Likert-type scale from 0 = "not following the order at all" to 10 = "completely following the order". With regard to social distancing, we asked, "What amount of social distancing do you currently practice?" Response options were on an 11-point Likert-type scale from 0 = "no social distancing at all" to 10 = "complete social distancing". Finally, to assess hand hygiene/sanitization, we asked, "How often do you practice protective measures like hand washing, use of hand sanitizer, or disinfection of household surfaces to keep yourself and others you live with from contracting COVID-19?" Response options were on an 11-point Likert-type scale from 0 = "never" to 10 = "every few hours".

2.3. Statistical Analysis

Descriptive statistics for all the variables were calculated including the mean, standard deviation (SD), median, and range for continuous variables and relative frequency for categorical variables. For the main study analyses, Pearson's chi-square (χ^2) and one-way analysis of variance (ANOVA) were first used to assess univariate associations between each of the individual-level determinant variables and each of the individual lifestyle behavioral change variables (i.e., healthy eating, PA, tobacco smoking, alcohol use, and vaping). Next, univariate regression analyses were conducted to examine associations between each of the individual-level determinant variables and the two lifestyle behavioral change indices (i.e., healthy and addictive behavioral change). Then, all the variables that were associated with the behavioral change indices from the univariate regression analyses ($p < 0.10$) were entered into separate multivariable linear regression models. All statistical analyses were performed in SAS V.9.4 (SAS Institute Inc., Cary, NC, USA).

3. Results

3.1. Sample Characteristics

Data were derived from 1276 survey respondents. As shown in Table 1, the study sample was predominantly male (58%), middle aged (mean = 45.0 years, SD = 17.0 years), and college educated (79%). Half identified as racial/ethnic minorities and 51% were married. For mental health, the mean of the PROMIS depression T-score was 58.9 (SE = 10.6), which is significantly higher than the U.S. population norm (mean = 50.0, SD = 10.0, $p < 0.0001$). Thirty-nine percent of survey respondents scored above the PROMIS threshold for depression. The mean of the PROMIS anxiety T-score was 56.1 (SE = 10.1), which is also significantly higher than the U.S. population norm (mean = 50.0, SD = 10, $p < 0.0001$). About 48% of survey respondents scored above the PROMIS threshold for anxiety. Approximately 90% of survey respondents lived in an area that was under a stay-at-home order but only 34%, 32%, and 35% reported complete adherence (10 on a scale of 0 = not at all to 10 = completely) to stay-at-home, social distancing, and personal protective behavioral guidelines, respectively. With regard to healthy lifestyle behaviors, 36% of survey respondents agreed or strongly agreed that they were eating more healthy foods and 33% agreed or strongly agreed that they were exercising more since the start of the pandemic. For unhealthy lifestyle behaviors, 40% of survey respondents reported increased alcohol use, 41% reported increased tobacco smoking, and 46% reported increased vaping since the start of the pandemic.

Table 1. Descriptive analysis of participants' characteristics (n = 1276).

Sociodemographic Characteristics	n (%) [a]	Lifestyle Behaviors and Self-Reported Changes Since the Pandemic	n (%) [a]
Age, Mean (SD), years	45.0 (17.0)	Drinks alcohol	
18–30	324 (25.4)	Yes	562 (58.2)
31–50	489 (38.3)	No	404 (41.8)
51–65	264 (20.7)	Reported change in alcohol use	
>65	199 (15.6)	Increased	218 (39.5)
Gender		Decreased	87 (15.8)
Male	724 (57.5)	Stayed the same	247 (44.8)
Female	517 (41.0)	Vaping frequency	
Race/Ethnicity		Daily	108 (11.3)
White	623 (50.2)	Less than Daily	64 (6.7)
Black	238 (19.2)	Not at all	788 (82.0)
Hispanic	181 (14.6)	Reported change in vaping frequency	
Asian	35 (2.8)	Increased	78 (45.9)
Other	165 (13.3)	Decreased	31 (18.2)
Education		Stayed the same	61 (35.9)
Not college educated	263 (21.0)	Tobacco smoking frequency	
College educated	988 (79.0)	Daily	181 (19.0)
Marital status		Less than daily	61 (6.4)
Unmarried	613 (48.8)	Not at all	713 (74.7)
Married	644 (51.2)	Reported change in tobacco smoking frequency	
Annual household income		Increased	98 (41.0)
Less than $25 K	185 (19.0)	Decreased	48 (20.1)
$25 K to $74 K	382 (39.3)	Stayed the same	93 (38.9)
$75 K or more	406 (41.7)	Increase in PA frequency	

Table 1. *Cont.*

Sociodemographic Characteristics	n (%) [a]	Lifestyle Behaviors and Self-Reported Changes Since the Pandemic	n (%) [a]
Number of household residents		1 = Strongly Disagree	718 (18.6)
1	251 (20.1)	2 = Disagree	224 (23.4)
2	408 (32.6)	3 = Neutral	237 (24.8)
3–4	433 (34.6)	4 = Agree	205 (21.4)
5 or more	158 (12.6)	5 = Strongly Agree	113 (11.8)
Lives with someone > age 65		Increase in healthy eating	
Yes	281 (28.1)	1 = Strongly disagree	75 (7.8)
No	720 (71.9)	2 = Disagree	213 (22.3)
Lives with someone < age 18		3 = Neutral	324 (33.9)
Yes	452 (45.3)	4 = Agree	243 (25.4)
No	546 (54.7)	5 = Strongly agree	102 (10.7)
Work status		Mental Health	
Working full-time	460 (47.2)	Anxiety [b]	
Working part-time	128 (13.1)	T-score, mean (SE)	58.9 (10.6)
Retired	165 (16.9)	Case	423 (47.7)
Unemployed	221 (22.7)	Not a case	464 (52.3)
Living arrangement		Depression [b]	
Lives alone	229 (18.6)	T-score, mean (SE)	56.1 (10.1)
Lives with spouse/partner	679 (55.3)	Case	347 (39.1)
Lives with a family member	274 (22.3)	Not a case	541 (60.9)
Lives with a non-family member	47 (3.8)		
US region of residence		COVID-19 mitigation behaviors	
Northeast	205 (21.5)	Area of residence under stay-at-home order	
Midwest	200 (21.0)	Yes	803 (82.8)
South	365 (38.3)	No	143 (14.7)
West	184 (19.3)	Stay-at-home adherence [c]	
		Continuing life as normal	10 (1.3)
		Stay at home besides essential trips	269 (33.5)
		Social distancing adherence [d]	
		No social distancing	14 (1.5)
		Complete social distancing	299 (31.9)
		Hand hygiene/sanitization adherence [e]	
		Never	12 (1.3)
		Every few hours	327 (34.9)

[a] "Missing" was shown for reference. Missing data was not included in statistical analyses. [b] Individuals categorized as having depression or anxiety met the criteria for "caseness" (T-score > 60) on the PROMIS 4-item short-form depression and anxiety measures. [c] "Continuing life as normal" is 0 on 0 to 10 scale, "stay at home besides essential trips" is 10 on 0 to 10 scale. [d] "No social distancing" is 0 on 0 to 10 scale, "complete social distancing" is 10 on 0 to 10 scale. [e] "never" is 0 on 0 to 10 scale, "every few hours" is 10 on 0 to 10 scale.

3.2. *Changes in Healthy Lifestyle Behaviors*

3.2.1. Univariate Analyses: Healthy Lifestyle Behavioral Change

Detailed results of Pearson's chi-square (χ^2) and one-way ANOVAs to assess associations between each of the individual-level determinant variables and each of the healthy lifestyle behavioral change variables are presented in Supplemental Table S1.

3.2.2. Univariate Analyses: Healthy Behavioral Change Index

As Table 2 shows, older age, female gender, living with someone aged >65, and unemployed work status were all negatively associated with self-reported changes in healthy lifestyle behaviors. Conversely, Black and Hispanic race/ethnicity, being college educated, married, having a household income over USD 75,000, living with someone aged <18, being more adherent to stay-at-home and social distancing guidelines, and practicing more hand hygiene/sanitization were all positively associated with increases in healthy lifestyle behaviors.

Table 2. Univariate and multivariable linear regression analyses showing healthy behavioral change. Index [a] as a function of individual-level determinants [b].

Factors	Healthy Behavioral Change Index [a]					
	Crude Regression Coefficients	95% CI	*p*-Value	Adjusted Regression Coefficients [b]	95% CI	*p*-Value
Age						
One unit increase	−0.11	−0.02, −0.01	<0.001			
18–30	Ref		<0.001	Ref		0.63
31–50	0.10	−0.13, 0.33		−0.04	−0.34, 0.27	
51–65	−0.36	−0.62, −0.11		−0.23	−0.60, 0.15	
>65	−0.40	−0.68, −0.12		−0.10	−0.64, 0.44	
Gender			<0.001			
Male	Ref			Ref		
Female	−0.90	−0.57, −0.22		−0.37	−0.62, −0.12	0.003
Race			<0.001			0.35
White	Ref			Ref		
Black	0.54	0.31, 0.76		0.32	−0.02, 0.66	
Hispanic	0.33	0.06, 0.60		0.26	−0.09, 0.61	
Asian	0.45	−0.02, 0.93		0.21	−0.43, 0.85	
Other	0.27	−0.04, 0.59		0.07	−0.31, 0.45	
Education			0.02			0.12
Not college educated	Ref			Ref		
College educated	0.27	0.05, 0.49		0.24	−0.06, 0.55	
Marital status			0.006			0.34
Unmarried	Ref			Ref		
Married	0.24	0.07, 0.42		0.13	−0.13, 0.39	
Annual household income			0.002			0.24
Less than $25,000	Ref			Ref		
$25,000 to $74,000	0.14	−0.11, 0.38		−0.18	−0.53, 0.18	
$75,000 or more	0.41	0.16, 0.65		0.03	−0.34, 0.40	
Living arrangement			0.08			
Lives alone	Ref					
Lives with spouse/partner	0.27	0.03, 0.50				
Lives with family member	0.22	−0.05, 0.50				
Lives with non-family member	−0.07	−0.53, 0.38				
Number of household residents			0.22			
1	Ref					
2	0.10	−0.14, 0.35				
3–4	0.22	−0.02, 0.47				
5 or more	0.26	−0.06, 0.59				
Lives with someone > age 65			0.01			0.75
Yes	−0.29	−0.51, −0.06		0.05	−0.27, 0.37	
No	Ref			Ref		
Lives with child < age 18			<0.001			0.10
Yes	0.41	0.21, 0.60		0.22	−0.04, 0.47	
No	Ref			Ref		

Table 2. *Cont.*

Factors	Healthy Behavioral Change Index [a]					
	Crude Regression Coefficients	95% CI	*p*-Value	Adjusted Regression Coefficients [b]	95% CI	*p*-Value
Work status			<0.001			
Working full-time	Ref					0.10
Working part-time	−0.25	−0.51, −0.02		−0.18	−0.52, 0.15	
Retired	−0.71	−0.95, −0.47		−0.43	−0.88, 0.02	
Unemployed	−0.58	−0.79, −0.36		−0.33	−0.64, −0.02	
Anxiety [c]						
Case	−0.03	−0.21, 0.15				
Not a case	Ref					
Depression [c]			0.30			
Case	−0.10	−0.28, 0.09				
Not a case	Ref					
Stay-at-home adherence			0.01			0.77
One unit increase	0.06	0.01, 0.11		0.01	−0.06, 0.09	
Social distancing adherence			<0.001			0.004
One unit increase	0.09	0.04, 0.13		0.12	0.04, 0.21	
Hand hygiene/sanitization adherence						0.79
One unit increase	0.07	0.03, 0.11	0.001	0.01	−0.04, 0.06	

[a] The healthy behavioral change index includes physical activity and healthy eating, and scores range from +2 to −2. [b] Individual-level determinants include sociodemographic, mental health, and behavioral (i.e., adherence to COVID-19 mitigation strategies) factors. [c] Living arrangement was not included in the final model due to collinearity with lives with someone aged >65 and lives with child aged <18. [c] Individuals categorized as having depression or anxiety met the criteria for "caseness" (T-score > 60) on the PROMIS 4-item short-form depression and anxiety measures.

3.2.3. Multivariable Analysis: Healthy Behavioral Change Index

Multivariable regression revealed that individuals who adhered more to social distancing guidelines were more likely to engage in more healthy lifestyle behaviors (β = 0.12, 95% CI 0.04 to 0.21), relative to those who adhered less In addition, women (β = −0.37, 95% CI −0.62 to −0.12), and unemployed individuals (β = −0.33, 95% CI −0.64 to −0.02) were less likely to report engaging in more healthy lifestyle behaviors, relative to men and employed individuals (Figure 1A and Table 2).

3.3. Changes in Addictive Lifestyle Behaviors

3.3.1. Univariate Analyses: Addictive Lifestyle Behavioral Change

Detailed results of the Pearson's chi-square (χ^2) and one-way ANOVAs to assess associations between each of the individual-level determinants and each of the addictive lifestyle behavioral change variables are presented in Supplemental Table S2.

3.3.2. Univariate Analyses: Addictive Behavioral Change Index

As Table 3 shows, older aged and retired individuals were less likely to report increases in addictive behaviors, whereas individuals who lived in larger households, with someone aged <18, had anxiety or depression, were less likely to practice hand hygiene/sanitization, and were more likely to report increased addictive behaviors.

3.3.3. Multivariable Analysis: Addictive Behavioral Change Index

Multivariable liner regression analyses revealed that individuals who had anxiety were more likely to report increases in addictive behaviors since the start of the pandemic relative those who did not have anxiety (β = 0.26, 95% CI 0.09 to 0.43) (Figure 1B and Table 3).

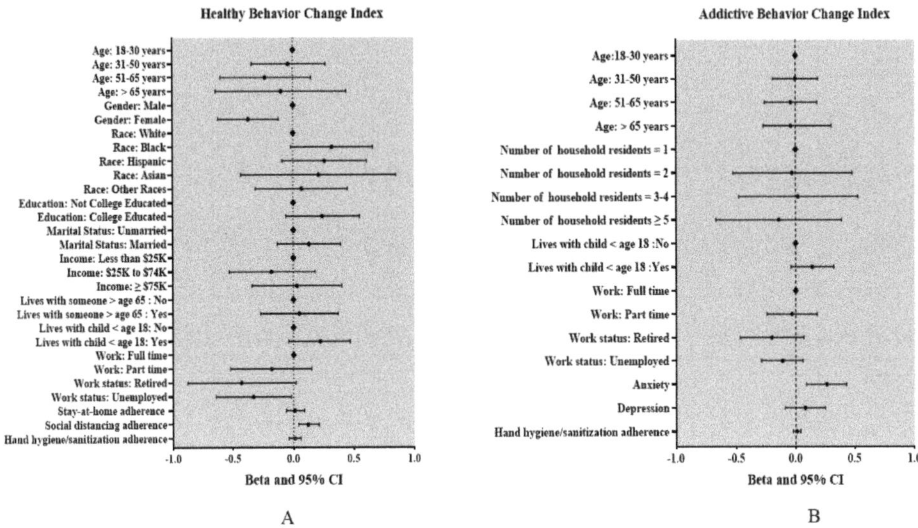

Figure 1. (**A**) Multivariable linear regression model estimating associations between explanatory variables and healthy behavioral change index. Vertical line represents null of beta. Bars denote 95% confidence interval. Healthy lifestyle behaviors include healthy eating and physical activity. Social distancing, stay-at-home adherence, and hand hygiene/sanitization adherence are in one unit increase; (**B**) multivariable linear regression model estimating associations between explanatory variables and addictive behavioral change index. Vertical line represents null of beta. Bars denote 95% confidence interval. Addictive behaviors include smoking, vaping, and drinking. Social distancing, stay-at-home adherence and hand hygiene/sanitization adherence are in one unit increase. ◆ indicate the reference groups.

Table 3. Univariate and multivariable linear regression analyses showing addictive behavior. Change index [a] as a function of individual-level determinants [b].

Factors	Addictive Behavioral Change Index [a]					
	Crude Regression Coefficients	95% CI	*p*-Value	Adjusted Regression Coefficients [c]	95% CI	*p*-Value
Age						
One unit increase	−0.005	−0.008, −0.001	0.005			
18–30	Ref		0.002			0.98
31–50	0.07	−0.08, 0.23		−0.003	−0.19, 0.19	
51–65	−0.08	−0.25, 0.09		−0.04	−0.26, 0.18	
>65	−0.19	−0.38, −0.01		0.01	−0.27, 0.30	
Gender			0.68			
Male	Ref					
Female	−0.024	−0.14, 0.09				
Race						
White	Ref					
Black	0.13	−0.03, 0.28				
Hispanic	−0.09	−0.28, 0.09				
Asian	−0.19	−0.51, 0.13				
Other	0.09	−0.12, 0.30				
Education			0.43			
Not college educated	Ref					
College Educated	0.06	−0.09, 0.21				

Table 3. *Cont.*

Factors	Addictive Behavioral Change Index [a]					
	Crude Regression Coefficients	95% CI	*p*-Value	Adjusted Regression Coefficients [c]	95% CI	*p*-Value
Marital status			0.59			
Unmarried	Ref					
Married	0.03	−0.08, 0.15				
Annual household income			0.74			
Less than $25,000	Ref					
$25,000 to $74,999	0.06	−0.10, 0.23				
$75,000 or more	0.04	−0.13, 0.20				
Living arrangement			0.04			
Lives alone	Ref					
Lives with spouse/partner	0.17	0.01, 0.32				
Lives with family member	0.11	−0.07, 0.29				
Lives with non-family member	0.40	0.10, 0.71				
Number of household residents			0.008			0.5
1	Ref			Ref		
2	0.08	−0.08, 0.24		−0.03	−0.53, 0.48	
3–4	0.26	0.10, 0.42		0.02	−0.48, 0.53	
5 or more	0.13	−0.08, 0.35		−0.14	−0.67, 0.39	
Lives with someone > age 65			0.28			
Yes	−0.08	−0.23, 0.06				
No	Ref					
Lives with child < age 18			0.004			0.12
Yes	0.19	0.06, 0.32		0.14	−0.04, 0.32	
No	Ref			Ref		
Work status						0.38
Working full-time	Ref		0.01	Ref		
Working part-time	−0.01	−0.19, 0.17		−0.03	−0.24, 0.18	
Retired	−0.27	−0.43, −0.10		−0.20	−0.47, 0.07	
Unemployed	−0.11	−0.26, 0.04		−0.11	−0.29, 0.06	
Anxiety [d]			<0.0001			0.002
Case	0.35	0.23, 0.47		0.26	0.09, 0.43	
Not a case	Ref			Ref		
Depression [d]			<0.0001			0.36
Case	0.28	0.16, 0.40		0.08	−0.09, 0.25	
Not a case	Ref			Ref		
Stay-at-home adherence						
One unit increase	−0.002	−0.037, 0.033	0.90			
Social distancing adherence						
One unit increase	0.02	−0.01, 0.05	0.19			
Hand hygiene/sanitization adherence						0.47
One unit increase	0.02	−0.16, 0.27	0.09	0.01	−0.02, 0.04	

[a] The addictive behavioral change index includes alcohol use, tobacco smoking, and vaping. Scores range from +3 to −3. [b] Individual-level determinants include sociodemographic, mental health, and behavioral (i.e., adherence to COVID-19 mitigation strategies) factors. [c] Living arrangement was not included into final model due to collinearity with number of household residents and lives with child < age 18. [d] Individuals categorized as having depression or anxiety met the criteria for "caseness" (T-score > 60) on the PROMIS 4-item short-form depression and anxiety measures.

4. Discussion

This study examined self-reported changes in healthy and addictive lifestyle behaviors during the initial COVID-19 lockdown period in the USA. Consistent with previously published pandemic-focused research [14–16], we detected a significant increase in addictive behaviors during lockdown. Nearly two in five people who smoked tobacco or drank alcohol reported increases in these behaviors and, one in two people who vaped reported increased vaping behavior. We also found a significant, albeit a smaller increase in healthy lifestyle behaviors, with about one in three people reporting more healthy eating and PA.

Overall, this study adds to the body of work on lifestyle behavioral changes during the COVID-19 pandemic. We identified sociodemographic, mental health, and behavioral determinants of behavioral changes. Specifically, we found that individuals who practiced more social distancing reported increased healthy behaviors and that women and unemployed individuals were less likely to report such increases. We also found that individuals with anxiety were more likely to report increases in addictive behaviors than individuals who did not have anxiety. Together, these findings provide important insights regarding who may be at increased risk for adopting unhealthy behaviors and could potentially benefit from lifestyle interventions.

Consistent with previous research [35,36], we found that greater adherence to social distancing guidelines was associated with self-reported improvements in healthy lifestyle behaviors. Individuals who adhered more to social distancing guidelines may have experienced an increase in leisure time and used that time to prepare healthy meals and stay physically active. Meanwhile, women were less likely to report increases in healthy lifestyle behaviors. This finding may reflect the larger societal strain and burden experienced by women during the COVID-19 pandemic [37], due in part to the closure of schools and day care centers [38]. In addition, unemployed individuals were less likely to report increases in healthy lifestyle behaviors. Being unemployed may lead to greater dependency on relatively cheaper (and unhealthy) fast foods [39], and previous research in U.S. adults has found that unemployment was associated with reductions in daily PA [40]. Overall, our findings suggest that women and unemployed individuals are at increased risk for weight gain and sedentary lifestyle during the pandemic. As such, they may benefit from interventions that emphasize healthy eating and PA and teach problem-solving and coping skills to address the additional stressors brought on by the pandemic that may be contributing to decrements in a healthy lifestyle.

Results of the multivariable analysis revealed that individuals with anxiety were more likely to report increases in addictive behaviors. Although this finding is consistent with other pandemic-focused studies [18,41], it is notable because almost half of our survey respondents scored above the PROMIS threshold and had significant anxiety symptoms. Put into context, estimates from the National Health Interview Survey from January to June 2019 showed that 8.2% of the U.S. adult population had symptoms of anxiety disorder [42], suggesting significantly elevated levels of anxiety during the COVID-19 pandemic. The substantial rise in anxiety and corresponding increase in unhealthy lifestyle behaviors may portend future behavioral and health consequences. As tobacco and alcohol are addictive substances, smoking and drinking could become the norm for substantial numbers of U.S. adults who are trying to combat pandemic-induced anxiety. Indeed, some have already called for more public health warnings about excessive substance use during this unprecedented time [43]. Although more research is needed to understand the longitudinal associations between pandemic-induced anxiety and unhealthy lifestyle behaviors, our findings suggest that individuals with high anxiety levels may be at increased risk for developing substance use problems and could potentially benefit from smoking cessation and substance use prevention interventions.

This study had some limitations. First, it was based on an online survey which excludes the possibility of verifying the data on objective grounds. However, considering the challenges of conducting such a study during pandemic lockdown, this limitation was impossible to overcome. Moreover, there is evidence that web-based surveys are equivalent to conventional face-to-face interviews in terms of data quality [44,45]. Second, given the cross-sectional nature of the data, findings represent a snapshot of lifestyle behaviors at a single moment in time. We are unable to account for how behaviors may evolve over time. Third, the descriptive and analytic inferences made are generalizable to the U.S. adult population under the assumption that non-response is unrelated to any of the sociodemographic factors examined.

This study also had some notable strengths. First, it is one of the largest studies to date to examine individual-level determinants of healthy and addictive lifestyle behavioral changes in response to the COVID-19 pandemic. Second, our study sample was racially, ethnically, socioeconomically, and geographically diverse, which increases generalizability. Third, most studies examining lifestyle changes during the COVID-19 pandemic have either focused on the magnitude of change or sought to examine the effects of a single class of determinants (e.g., mental health/well-being [4,46] or sociodemographic factors [47]) on behavioral change. This approach fails to consider the effect of other individual-level variables. Our multivariable analytic approach addresses this knowledge gap by controlling for multiple individual-level determinants of lifestyle behavioral change (i.e., sociodemographic, mental health, and behavioral).

5. Conclusions

This study provides new data on lifestyle behavioral changes during the COVID-19 pandemic lockdown in the general U.S. population. Overall, findings suggest that women, unemployed individuals, and those with high anxiety levels are at increased risk of unhealthy lifestyle behavioral changes during the COVID-19 pandemic, but that they may benefit from differently focused lifestyle interventions. Whereas women and unemployed individuals may benefit from lifestyle interventions targeting diet and physical activity, individuals with anxiety may benefit from lifestyle interventions targeting smoking and alcohol cessation. Since the COVID-19 pandemic is still ongoing, more extensive population studies of lifestyle behavioral changes are warranted to confirm our results and understand the long-term effects of the current crisis on physical health.

Supplementary Materials: The following are available online at https://www.mdpi.com/article/10.3390/ijerph18084364/s1, Table S1: Associations between individual level determinants and healthy behavioral change (physical activity and healthy eating), Table S2: Associations between individual level determinants and addictive behavioral change (tobacco smoking, alcohol use and vaping).

Author Contributions: Concept and design, H.B., C.I.A., and A.O.; Acquisition, analysis, and interpretation of data, X.Z., A.O., and H.B.; Statistical analysis, X.Z., J.B., and Y.H.; Writing—original draft preparation, X.Z., H.B., and A.O.; Supervision, H.B; Writing—review and editing, L.W., O.E.-M., M.A.F., S.A.R., J.B., Y.H., A.O., C.I.A.; All authors have read and agreed to the published version of the manuscript.

Funding: H.B. and C.I.A. were supported by NHLBI OT2HL158258 (PI, Vishwantha). X.Z., M.A.F., and S.A.R. were supported by the Research Training Award for Cancer Prevention Post-Graduate Training Program in Integrative Epidemiology from the Cancer Prevention and Research Institute of Texas (grant number RP160097, PI, M. Spitz). Finally, this work was supported by the facilities and resources of the Dan L Duncan Comprehensive Cancer Center P30 CA125123 (PI, Heslop).

Institutional Review Board Statement: This study was approved by the Baylor College of Medicine Institutional Review Board (H-47505).

Informed Consent Statement: Informed consent was obtained from all subjects involved in the study.

Data Availability Statement: The datasets generated and/or analyzed during the current study are not publicly available but are available from the corresponding author on reasonable request.

Conflicts of Interest: The authors declare no conflict of interest. The funders had no role in the design of the study; in the collection, analyses, or interpretation of data; in the writing of the manuscript, or in the decision to publish the results.

Appendix A

Table A1. Survey measures.

Construct	Measure
Sociodemographics (19 items)	Age, gender, race/ethnicity, education, marital status, annual household income, work status, current living arrangement (alone, or with a spouse/partner, family member, or non-family member), number of household residents, whether they lived with someone over age 65 or younger than age 18, zip code, and cross street.
Mental Health Impacts	
General Depression (4 items)	PROMIS Depression 4-item Short form [32]
General Anxiety (4 items)	PROMIS Anxiety 4-item Short Form [33]
Health Behavioral Impacts: COVID-19 Preventive Measures	
Adherence to Stay-at-Home Orders	"Does the area where you live have a stay-at-home Orders?" (1 = yes, 2 = no, 3 = I don't know) "To what extent do you currently follow the stay at home order?" (0 = not at all to 10 = completely)
Social Distancing	"What amount of social distancing do you currently practice?" (0 = no social distancing to 10 = complete social distancing)
Hand Hygiene	"How often do you practice protective measures like hand washing, use of hand sanitizer, or disinfection of household surfaces to keep yourself and others you live with from contracting COVID-19?" (0 = never to 10 = every few hours)
Health Behavioral Impacts: Lifestyle Behaviors	
Alcohol Use	"Has your drinking increased/decreased/stayed the same since COVID-19?"
Tobacco Use	Two items on current smoking status and type and number of tobacco products smoked per day, taken from the Global Adult Tobacco Survey [31]
Exercise	"Since COVID-19 I am exercising more." (1 = strongly disagree to 5 = strongly agree)
Diet	"Since COVID-19 I am eating more healthy foods." (1 = strongly disagree to 5 = strongly agree)

References

1. Sohrabi, C.; Alsafi, Z.; O'Neill, N.; Khan, M.; Kerwan, A.; Al-Jabir, A.; Iosifidis, C.; Agha, R. World Health Organization declares global emergency: A review of the 2019 novel coronavirus (COVID-19). *Int. J. Surg.* **2020**, *76*, 71–76. [CrossRef]
2. Balanzá–Martínez, V.; Atienza–Carbonell, B.; Kapczinski, F.; De Boni, R.B. Lifestyle behaviours during the COVID-19—Time to connect. *Acta Psychiatr. Scand.* **2020**, *141*, 399–400. [CrossRef]
3. Di Renzo, L.; Gualtieri, P.; Pivari, F.; Soldati, L.; Attinà, A.; Cinelli, G.; Leggeri, C.; Caparello, G.; Barrea, L.; Scerbo, F.; et al. Eating habits and lifestyle changes during COVID-19 lockdown: An Italian survey. *J. Transl. Med.* **2020**, *18*, 229. [CrossRef]
4. Hu, Z.; Lin, X.; Chiwanda Kaminga, A.; Xu, H. Impact of the COVID-19 Epidemic on Lifestyle Behaviors and Their Association With Subjective Well-Being Among the General Population in Mainland China: Cross-Sectional Study. *J. Med. Internet Res.* **2020**, *22*, e21176. [CrossRef]
5. Lippi, G.; Henry, B.M.; Sanchis-Gomar, F. Physical inactivity and cardiovascular disease at the time of coronavirus disease 2019 (COVID-19). *Eur. J. Prev. Cardiol.* **2020**, *27*, 906–908. [CrossRef] [PubMed]
6. Larsson, S.C.; Kaluza, J.; Wolk, A. Combined impact of healthy lifestyle factors on lifespan: Two prospective cohorts. *J. Intern. Med.* **2017**, *282*, 209–219. [CrossRef]
7. Li, Y.; Pan, A.; Wang, D.D.; Liu, X.; Dhana, K.; Franco, O.H.; Kaptoge, S.; Di Angelantonio, E.; Stampfer, M.; Willett, W.C. Impact of healthy lifestyle factors on life expectancies in the US population. *Circulation* **2018**, *138*, 345–355. [CrossRef] [PubMed]

8. Ding, D.; del Pozo Cruz, B.; Green, M.A.; Bauman, A.E. Is the COVID-19 lockdown nudging people to be more active: A big data analysis. *Br. J. Sports Med.* **2020**, *54*, 1183. [CrossRef] [PubMed]
9. Zachary, Z.; Brianna, F.; Brianna, L.; Garrett, P.; Jade, W.; Alyssa, D.; Mikayla, K. Self-quarantine and weight gain related risk factors during the COVID-19 pandemic. *Obes Res. Clin. Pr.* **2020**, *14*, 210–216. [CrossRef] [PubMed]
10. Deschasaux-Tanguy, M.; Druesne-Pecollo, N.; Esseddik, Y.; de Edelenyi, F.S.; Allès, B.; Andreeva, V.A.; Baudry, J.; Charreire, H.; Deschamps, V.; Egnell, M.; et al. Diet and physical activity during the COVID-19 lockdown period (March-May 2020): Results from the French NutriNet-Santé cohort study. *medRxiv* **2020**. [CrossRef]
11. Górnicka, M.; Drywień, M.E.; Zielinska, M.A.; Hamułka, J. Dietary and Lifestyle Changes During COVID-19 and the Subsequent Lockdowns among Polish Adults: A Cross-Sectional Online Survey PLifeCOVID-19 Study. *Nutrients* **2020**, *12*, 2324. [CrossRef]
12. Stanaway, J.D.; Afshin, A.; Gakidou, E.; Lim, S.S.; Abate, D.; Abate, K.H.; Abbafati, C.; Abbasi, N.; Abbastabar, H.; Abd-Allah, F. Global, regional, and national comparative risk assessment of 84 behavioural, environmental and occupational, and metabolic risks or clusters of risks for 195 countries and territories, 1990–2017: A systematic analysis for the Global Burden of Disease Study 2017. *Lancet* **2018**, *392*, 1923–1994.
13. Pelucchi, C.; Gallus, S.; Garavello, W.; Bosetti, C.; La Vecchia, C. Cancer risk associated with alcohol and tobacco use: Focus on upper aero-digestive tract and liver. *Alcohol Res. Health* **2006**, *29*, 193.
14. Tran, T.D.; Hammarberg, K.; Kirkman, M.; Nguyen, H.T.M.; Fisher, J. Alcohol use and mental health status during the first months of COVID-19 pandemic in Australia. *J. Affect. Disord* **2020**, *277*, 810–813. [CrossRef]
15. Yach, D. Tobacco Use Patterns in Five Countries During the COVID-19 Lockdown. *Nicotine Tob Res.* **2020**, *22*, 1671–1672. [CrossRef] [PubMed]
16. Vanderbruggen, N.; Matthys, F.; Van Laere, S.; Zeeuws, D.; Santermans, L.; Van den Ameele, S.; Crunelle, C.L. Self-reported alcohol, tobacco, and Cannabis use during COVID-19 lockdown measures: Results from a web-based survey. *Eur. Addict. Res.* **2020**, *26*, 309–315. [CrossRef] [PubMed]
17. Avery, A.R.; Tsang, S.; Seto, E.Y.W.; Duncan, G.E. Stress, Anxiety, and Change in Alcohol Use During the COVID-19 Pandemic: Findings Among Adult Twin Pairs. *Front. Psychiatry* **2020**, *11*, 571084. [CrossRef] [PubMed]
18. Stanton, R.; To, Q.G.; Khalesi, S.; Williams, S.L.; Alley, S.J.; Thwaite, T.L.; Fenning, A.S.; Vandelanotte, C. Depression, Anxiety and Stress during COVID-19: Associations with Changes in Physical Activity, Sleep, Tobacco and Alcohol Use in Australian Adults. *Int. J. Environ. Res. Public Health* **2020**, *17*, 4065. [CrossRef]
19. Ingram, J.; Maciejewski, G.; Hand, C.J. Changes in Diet, Sleep, and Physical Activity Are Associated With Differences in Negative Mood During COVID-19 Lockdown. *Front. Psychol.* **2020**, *11*, 2328. [CrossRef]
20. Bremner, J. US Alcohol Sales Increase 55 Percent in One Week Amid Coronavirus Pandemic. 2020. Available online: https://www.newsweek.com/us-alcohol-sales-increase-55-percent-one-week-amid-coronavirus-pandemic-1495510 (accessed on 13 November 2020).
21. Wu, P.; Fang, Y.; Guan, Z.; Fan, B.; Kong, J.; Yao, Z.; Liu, X.; Fuller, C.J.; Susser, E.; Lu, J. The psychological impact of the SARS epidemic on hospital employees in China: Exposure, risk perception, and altruistic acceptance of risk. *Can. J. Psychiatry* **2009**, *54*, 302–311. [CrossRef]
22. Klemperer, E.M.; West, J.C.; Peasley-Miklus, C.; Villanti, A.C. Change in Tobacco and Electronic Cigarette Use and Motivation to Quit in Response to COVID-19. *Nicotine Tob. Res.* **2020**, *22*, 1662–1663. [CrossRef] [PubMed]
23. Khantzian, E.J. The self-medication hypothesis of substance use disorders: A reconsideration and recent applications. *Harv. Rev. Psychiatry* **1997**, *4*, 231–244. [CrossRef] [PubMed]
24. Stewart, S.H.; Grant, V.V.; Mackie, C.J.; Conrod, P.J. *Comorbidity of Anxiety and Depression with Substance Use Disorders*; Oxford University Press: Oxford, UK, 2016.
25. Yang, G.Y.; Lin, X.L.; Fang, A.P.; Zhu, H.L. Eating Habits and Lifestyles during the Initial Stage of the COVID-19 Lockdown in China: A Cross-Sectional Study. *Nutrients* **2021**, *13*, 970. [CrossRef] [PubMed]
26. Tison, G.H.; Avram, R.; Kuhar, P.; Abreau, S.; Marcus, G.M.; Pletcher, M.J.; Olgin, J.E. Worldwide Effect of COVID-19 on Physical Activity: A Descriptive Study. *Ann. Intern. Med.* **2020**, *173*, 767–770. [CrossRef] [PubMed]
27. Jackson, S.E.; Garnett, C.; Shahab, L.; Oldham, M.; Brown, J. Association of the Covid-19 lockdown with smoking, drinking, and attempts to quit in England: An analysis of 2019–2020 data. *medRxiv* **2020**. [CrossRef]
28. Badr, H.; Oluyomi, A.; Adel Fahmideh, M.; Raza, S.A.; Zhang, X.; El-Mubasher, O.; Amos, C. Psychosocial and health behavioural impacts of COVID-19 pandemic on adults in the USA: Protocol for a longitudinal cohort study. *BMJ Open* **2020**, *10*, e044642. [CrossRef] [PubMed]
29. Mervosh, S.; Lee, J.; Gamio, L.; Popovich, N. See How All 50 States Are Reopening. Available online: https://www.nytimes.com/interactive/2020/us/states-reopen-map-coronavirus.html (accessed on 8 June 2020).
30. *Qualtrics [Software]*; Oxford University Press: Oxford, UK, 2020.
31. Global Adult Tobacco Survey Collaborative Group. *Tobacco Questions for Surveys: A Subset of Key Questions from the Global Adult Tobacco Survey (GATS)*; Centers for Disease Control and Prevention: Atlanta, GA, USA, 2011.
32. Cella, D.; Riley, W.; Stone, A.; Rothrock, N.; Reeve, B.; Yount, S.; Amtmann, D.; Bode, R.; Buysse, D.; Choi, S.; et al. The Patient-Reported Outcomes Measurement Information System (PROMIS) developed and tested its first wave of adult self-reported health outcome item banks: 2005–2008. *J. Clin. Epidemiol* **2010**, *63*, 1179–1194. [CrossRef] [PubMed]

33. Schalet, B.D.; Pilkonis, P.A.; Yu, L.; Dodds, N.; Johnston, K.L.; Yount, S.; Riley, W.; Cella, D. Clinical validity of PROMIS Depression, Anxiety, and Anger across diverse clinical samples. *J. Clin. Epidemiol.* **2016**, *73*, 119–127. [CrossRef]
34. Tearnan, B.H.; Lewandowski, M. The Behavioral Assessment of Pain Questionnaire: The development and validation of a comprehensive self-report instrument. *Am. J. Pain Manag.* **1992**, *2*, 181–191.
35. Bourassa, K.J.; Sbarra, D.A.; Caspi, A.; Moffitt, T.E. Social Distancing as a Health Behavior: County-Level Movement in the United States During the COVID-19 Pandemic Is Associated with Conventional Health Behaviors. *Ann. Behav. Med. A Publ. Soc. Behav. Med.* **2020**, *54*, 548–556. [CrossRef]
36. Martinez, E.Z.; Silva, F.M.; Morigi, T.Z.; Zucoloto, M.L.; Silva, T.L.; Joaquim, A.G.; Dall Agnol, G.; Galdino, G.; Martinez, M.O.Z.; Silva, W.R.d. Physical activity in periods of social distancing due to COVID-19: A cross-sectional survey. *Ciência Saúde Coletiva* **2020**, *25*, 4157–4168. [CrossRef] [PubMed]
37. Power, K. The COVID-19 pandemic has increased the care burden of women and families. *Sustain. Sci. Pract. Policy* **2020**, *16*, 67–73. [CrossRef]
38. Reichelt, M.; Makovi, K.; Sargsyan, A. The impact of COVID-19 on gender inequality in the labor market and gender-role attitudes. *Eur. Soc.* **2020**, *23*, 1–18. [CrossRef]
39. Smed, S.; Tetens, I.; Bøker Lund, T.; Holm, L.; Ljungdalh Nielsen, A. The consequences of unemployment on diet composition and purchase behaviour: A longitudinal study from Denmark. *Public Health Nutr.* **2018**, *21*, 580–592. [CrossRef] [PubMed]
40. Van Domelen, D.R.; Koster, A.; Caserotti, P.; Brychta, R.J.; Chen, K.Y.; McClain, J.J.; Troiano, R.P.; Berrigan, D.; Harris, T.B. Employment and physical activity in the U.S. *Am. J. Prev. Med.* **2011**, *41*, 136–145. [CrossRef] [PubMed]
41. Chen, D.T.-H. The psychosocial impact of the COVID-19 pandemic on changes in smoking behavior: Evidence from a nationwide survey in the UK. *Tob. Prev. Cessat.* **2020**, *6*, 1–5. [CrossRef]
42. National Center for Health Statistics. Available online: https://www.cdc.gov/nchs/covid19/pulse/mental-health.htm (accessed on 13 November 2020).
43. Clay, J.M.; Parker, M.O. Alcohol use and misuse during the COVID-19 pandemic: A potential public health crisis? *Lancet Public Health* **2020**, *5*, e259002E. [CrossRef]
44. Ekman, A.; Dickman, P.W.; Klint, A.; Weiderpass, E.; Litton, J.E. Feasibility of using web-based questionnaires in large population-based epidemiological studies. *Eur. J. Epidemiol* **2006**, *21*, 103–111. [CrossRef]
45. van Gelder, M.M.; Bretveld, R.W.; Roeleveld, N. Web-based questionnaires: The future in epidemiology? *Am. J. Epidemiol.* **2010**, *172*, 1292–1298. [CrossRef]
46. Werneck, A.O.; Silva, D.R.d.; Malta, D.C.; Souza-Júnior, P.R.B.d.; Azevedo, L.O.; Barros, M.B.d.A.; Szwarcwald, C.L. Lifestyle behaviors changes during the COVID-19 pandemic quarantine among 6,881 Brazilian adults with depression and 35,143 without depression. *Ciência Saúde Coletiva* **2020**, *25*, 4151–4156. [CrossRef]
47. Ruíz-Roso, M.B.; de Carvalho Padilha, P.; Matilla-Escalante, D.C.; Brun, P.; Ulloa, N.; Acevedo-Correa, D.; Arantes Ferreira Peres, W.; Martorell, M.; Rangel Bousquet Carrilho, T.; de Oliveira Cardoso, L. Changes of physical activity and ultra-processed food consumption in adolescents from different countries during Covid-19 pandemic: An observational study. *Nutrients* **2020**, *12*, 2289. [CrossRef] [PubMed]

International Journal of
Environmental Research and Public Health

MDPI

Article

Avoidance of Healthcare Utilization in South Korea during the Coronavirus Disease 2019 (COVID-19) Pandemic

Minjung Lee [1,2] and Myoungsoon You [1,3,*]

1 Department of Public Health Sciences, Graduate School of Public Health, Seoul National University, Seoul 08826, Korea; leciel84@snu.ac.kr
2 Office of Dental Education, School of Dentistry, Seoul National University, Seoul 08826, Korea
3 Institute of Health and Environment, Seoul National University, Seoul 08826, Korea
* Correspondence: msyou@snu.ac.kr

Abstract: Avoidance of healthcare utilization among the general population during pandemic outbreaks has been observed and it can lead to a negative impact on population health. The object of this study is to examine the influence of socio-demographic and health-related factors on the avoidance of healthcare utilization during the global outbreak of a novel coronavirus (COVID-19) in 2020. Data were collected through an online survey four weeks after the Korea Centers for Disease Control and Prevention (KCDC) confirmed the first case in South Korea; 1000 subjects were included in the analysis. The logit model for regression was used to analyze the associations between sociodemographic and health-related factors regarding the avoidance of healthcare utilization. Among the participants, 73.2% avoided healthcare utilization, and there was no significant difference in the prevalence of healthcare avoidance between groups with (72.0%) and without (74.9%) an underlying disease. Sociodemographic characteristics (e.g., gender, age, income level, and residential area) were related to healthcare avoidance. Among the investigated influencing factors, residential areas highly affected by COVID-19 (i.e., Daegu/Gyeoungbuk region) had the most significant effect on healthcare avoidance. This study found a high prevalence of healthcare avoidance among the general population who under-utilized healthcare resources during the COVID-19 outbreak. However, the results reveal that not all societal groups share the burden of healthcare avoidance equally, with it disproportionately affecting those with certain sociodemographic characteristics. This study can inform healthcare under-utilization patterns during emerging infectious disease outbreaks and provide information to public health emergency management for implementing strategies necessary to improve the preparedness of the healthcare system.

Keywords: coronavirus; COVID-19; SARS-CoV-2; healthcare utilization; healthcare avoidance; public health

Citation: Lee, M.; You, M. Avoidance of Healthcare Utilization in South Korea during the Coronavirus Disease 2019 (COVID-19) Pandemic. *Int. J. Environ. Res. Public Health* **2021**, *18*, 4363. https://doi.org/10.3390/ijerph18084363

Academic Editors: Paolo Roma, Merylin Monaro and Cristina Mazza

Received: 30 March 2021
Accepted: 14 April 2021
Published: 20 April 2021

1. Introduction

The outbreak of a novel coronavirus (COVID-19), first appeared in Wuhan [1,2] and has been a major public health threat worldwide. On 20 January, South Korea confirmed its first case [3], and an explosive increase in the number of COVID-19 patients appeared in late February in Daegu city, contributed by a religious group called Shincheonji [4]. In this time, South Korea was one of the hardest hit areas during the global outbreak of COVID-19. As the number of confirmed cases rapidly increased, the Korean government raised the alert level from orange to red on 23 February 2020, and mandated school closures [4]. As of 28 March 2020, the number of COVID-19 cases in Korea reached 9478, including 144 deaths. Among the public, the perceived risk of COVID-19 infection increased and became pervasive; widespread postponing or canceling of social events, avoiding crowded places, and reducing the use of public transportation, subsequently occurred [5].

Decrease in healthcare utilization occur frequently during pandemic outbreaks. In Korea, medical utilization (both admissions and outpatient treatments) decreased during the MERS epidemic in June and July of 2015 when compared to the numbers from 2014 and 2013 [6], along with visits to the emergency department [7]. The overall use of healthcare decreased by 18% during the peak of the Ebola Virus Disease (EVD) outbreak in West Africa [8,9]. Likewise, significant reductions in ambulatory care (23.9%), inpatient care (35.2%), and dental care (16.7%) were observed in Taiwan during the peak of the Severe Acute Respiratory Syndrome (SARS) outbreak [10]. However, a decrease in healthcare utilization patterns during outbreaks can adversely affect population health. Failure to access preventive and urgent life-saving treatments alike can lead to additional deaths [9], and the severity of illness or chronicity of disease, functional or physical disability, and even mortality, are predictable outcomes [11]. Previous studies have suggested that changes in healthcare utilization patterns due to public health emergencies have increased mortality rates from infectious disease as well as non-infectious diseases [12–14]. Moreover, increased expenditures related to healthcare as delayed diagnosis as well as more costly multimodal treatments, might be required. As a result, the burden associated with decreases in healthcare utilization may reduce the overall efficacy of a healthcare system.

Healthcare utilization may have declined for several reasons. First, the outbreak may have affected the supply of health due to closures of some health facilities during outbreaks. For example, in Korea, a 35-year-old man employed at a hospital developed symptoms of COVID-19 on February 2. He transmitted it to several patients between 2 and 17 February before he was discharged from his job. The hospital subsequently closed, and 14 additional confirmed cases from this hospital had been reported as of 2 March 2020 [4]. As another example, some hospitals were forced to close as some patients did not properly describe their symptoms of COVID-19 due to concerns of not being admitted and treated [15]. In West Africa, health workers experienced a particularly heavy death toll; many healthcare workers had died, and the supply of healthcare was affected during the EVD outbreak [9].

Second, the demand for healthcare might also have changed. Avoiding visits to healthcare facilities even when sick, or healthcare avoidance behavior, can negatively affect the population's well-being [11]. It might impede positive health-seeking behaviors and delay care, lead to non-adherence with treatment regimens, or result in a total lack of access to the healthcare system. According to a study in Korea, 34.5% of respondents reported that they avoided hospital visits even when they were ill during the MERS outbreak [16]. Potential patients may have avoided seeking care at health facilities because they feared contracting an infectious disease if they visited during outbreaks. Several studies have reported that concerns about the potential for nosocomial transmission of the disease led to beliefs that health facilities should be avoided. For instance, a Taiwanese study showed that the public's fears of SARS strongly influenced access to care [10] and a study of Hong Kong residents in the initial stage of the H1N1 outbreak reported that 63.4% of respondents avoided visiting hospitals due to perceived high risk [17].

The potentially severe impact of COVID-19 outbreak on people's access to healthcare is an important area of study. A critical challenge is to determine how healthcare agencies should respond to changes in healthcare utilization and possible barriers to access healthcare facilities for the public created by the COVID-19 outbreak. Moreover, the lessons learned from the MERS experience in Korea [6] and other countries demonstrate the importance of understanding the community response [17–23]. To our knowledge, no other study has evaluated the impact of COVID-19 on the demand of healthcare utilization among the general population. In this study, we focus on the avoidance of healthcare utilization or changes in healthcare-seeking behaviors of the public during the COVID-19 outbreak. The aims of the study are two-fold. First, we examine the prevalence of healthcare avoidance among the general population during the COVID-19 outbreak. Second, we investigate the factors associated with healthcare avoidance and identify the vulnerable populations. The results of this study can inform healthcare utilization patterns during infectious disease outbreaks and understanding the factors which affect the access of timely care will inform public health emergency management for implementing strategies necessary to improve the preparedness of the healthcare system.

2. Materials and Methods

2.1. Study Design

We adopted a cross-sectional survey design to evaluate the public's avoidance of healthcare utilization during the COVID-19 epidemic using an anonymous online questionnaire. The survey was conducted via an online platform from a research company called Korea Research. The company recruited respondents by sending survey invitations containing general information about the survey, such as its aim and consent statement via e-mail or text message, to registered survey panel members who met the inclusion criteria. The inclusion criteria were as follows: (1) aged 18 years or older, (2) a resident in South Korea, and (3) a Korean speaker. The company sampled respondents using age, sex, and a geographic region-based proportional and quota sampling process. The respondents provided electronic informed consent which appeared on the first page of the survey, and the company protects the confidentiality of anonymous respondents. The target sample size was 999, determined by identifying the smallest acceptable size of a demographic subgroup with a ±3.1% margin of error and a confidence level of 95% [24,25].

Over 1000 subjects completed the surveys, and 1000 were included in the analysis after excluding incomplete responses. The data collection took place over three days (25–27 March), two months after the Korea Centers for Disease Control and Prevention (KCDC) confirmed the first case at the early stage of the epidemic and just before 10,000 cases had been reported (3 April).

2.2. Measurements

The outcome variable was the avoidance of healthcare utilization, which respondents self-reported. Respondents self-reported the frequency of the action—"I avoided visiting hospitals even when I was sick"—they have taken during the previous week using a 4-point Likert-type scale (never, sometimes, often, and always). To conduct a logistic regression analysis, we converted the responses into binary answers (never = 0 and otherwise = 1).

Independent variables were categorized into two groups: sociodemographic and health-related factors. Sociodemographic factors included gender (1 = male, 2 = female), age, family size (i.e., living alone, more than 2 persons), marital status (i.e., married, single, divorced, bereaved), and the presence of children younger than elementary school at home (yes = 1, none = 0). We also assessed the education level (1 = middle school or below to 3 = college and above) and the monthly household income in Korean won (KRW) (1 = 200 million KRW or below to 4 = 600 million KRW or above). We collected information about the respondents' residences (urban = 1, rural = 2) and residential areas, including Seoul, Incheon/Gyeonggi, Daejeon/Sejong/Chungcheong, Gwangju/Jeolla, Daegu/Gyeongbuk, Busan/Ulsan/Gyeongnam, and Gangwon/Jeju regions. The occupation status included whether the respondent was a salary earner, self-employed, or if the respondent was unemployed.

Subjective health status (very poor = 1, poor = 2, moderate = 3, good = 4, Excellent = 5) was investigated to assess health-related factors. To conduct a logistic regression analysis, we converted the responses into ternary answers (poor = 1, moderate = 2, good = 3). We also investigated the presence of underlying disease (e.g., hypertension, dyslipidemia, diabetes, chronic cardiac disease, asthma, and cancer, and others) (Table 1).

Table 1. General characteristics of the study participants.

Characteristics	Total (n = 1000)	
Socio-Demographics	n	%
Gender		
Male	478	47.8
Female	522	52.2

Table 1. *Cont.*

Characteristics	**Total (*n* = 1000)**	
Socio-Demographics	*n*	%
Age (year)	M = 47.04	SD = 15.04
18–29	165	16.5
30–39	157	15.7
40–49	197	19.7
50–59	205	20.5
≥60	276	27.6
Family size, No.		
1(living alone)	99	9.9
more than 2	901	90.1
Education level		
Middle school or below	29	2.9
High school graduate	481	48.1
College and above	490	49.0
Marital status		
Married	649	64.9
Single/divorced/bereaved	351	35.1
Presence of children		
None	903	90.3
More than 1	97	9.7
Monthly household income		
Under 200	129	12.9
200–400	315	31.5
400–600	262	26.2
≥600	294	29.4
Residence		
Urban	880	88.0
Rural	120	12.0
Residential areas		
Seoul	193	19.3
Incheon/Gyeonggi	308	30.8
Daejeon/Sejong/Chungcheong	105	10.5
Gwangju/Jeolla	95	9.5
Daegu/Gyeongbuk	99	9.9
Busan/Ulsan/Gyeongnam	159	15.9
Gangwon/Jeju	41	4.1
Occupation status		
Salary earner	473	47.3
Self-employed	131	13.1
Out of labor	396	39.6
Health-related factors	*n*	%
Subjective health		
Bad	116	11.6
Moderate	442	44.2
Good	442	44.2
Underlying disease		
None	589	58.9
More than 1	411	41.1
Avoidance of healthcare utilization	*n*	%
Never	268	26.8%
Sometimes	266	26.6%
Often	223	22.3%
Always	243	24.3%

2.3. Statistical Analysis

We conducted statistical analyses using R version 3.5.1 (R Foundation for Statistical Computing, Vienna, Austria). All the results of quantitative variables were reported by mean (M), standard deviation (SD), or frequency (%) (Table 1). To determine the role of sociodemographic and health-related factors on healthcare utilization avoidance, differences in socio-demographics and health-related factors were compared with the healthcare utilization avoidance using the chi-square statistics (Table 2). The logit model for regression analyzed the associations between sociodemographic factors (e.g., gender, age, family size, education, marital status, income, and employment) and health-related factors (i.e., subjective health and presence of underlying disease) toward one's avoidance of healthcare utilization. Confounding factors were explored by comparing the differences between the adjusted odds ratio (aOR) in multivariate analysis and the crude odds ratio (OR) in a bivariate analysis of each independent variable on healthcare utilization avoidance (Table 3). Additionally, to examine the moderating effect of gender and the presence of an underlying disease, the same logit model for regression was performed among subgroup participants along with gender (Table 4) and the presence of underlying disease (Table 5).

Table 2. Chi-square statistics for variables related to healthcare utilization avoidance.

Variables	Sample Size (*n*)	Avoid Healthcare Utilization		
		"Never"	"Otherwise"	*p*-Value
Socio-demographics				
Gender				<0.001
Male	478	156 (32.6%)	322 (67.4%)	
Female	522	112 (21.5%)	410 (78.5%)	
Age				<0.001
18–29	165	63 (38.2%)	102 (61.8%)	
30–39	157	34 (21.7%)	123 (78.3%)	
40–49	197	56 (28.4%)	141 (71.6%)	
50–59	205	46 (22.4%)	159 (77.6%)	
≥60	276	69 (25.0%)	207 (75.0%)	
Family size, No.				0.29
1(living alone)	99	31 (31.3%)	68 (68.7%)	
more than 2	901	237 (26.3%)	664 (73.7%)	
Education level				0.38
Middle school or below	29	7 (24.1%)	22 (75.9%)	
High school graduate	481	120 (24.9%)	361 (75.1%)	
College and above	490	141 (28.8%)	349 (71.2%)	
Marital status				0.02
Married	649	158 (24.3%)	491 (75.7%)	
Single/divorced/bereaved	351	110 (31.3%)	241 (68.7%)	
Presence of children				0.15
None	903	248 (27.5%)	655 (72.5%)	
More than 1	97	20 (20.6%)	77 (79.4%)	
Monthly household income				0.12
Under 200	129	32 (24.8%)	97 (75.2%)	
200–400	315	71 (22.5%)	244 (77.5%)	
400–600	262	75 (28.6%)	187 (71.4%)	
≥600	294	90 (30.6%)	204 (69.4%)	
Residence				0.53
Urban	880	233 (26.5%)	647 (73.5%)	
Rural	120	35 (29.2%)	85 (70.8%)	
Residential area				0.01
Seoul	193	66 (34.2%)	127 (65.8%)	
Incheon/Gyeonggi	308	86 (27.9%)	222 (72.1%)	
Daejeon/Sejong/Chungcheong	105	23 (21.9%)	82 (78.1%)	
Gwangju/Jeolla	95	25 (26.3%)	70 (73.7%)	

Table 2. *Cont.*

Variables	Sample Size (*n*)	Avoid Healthcare Utilization		
		"Never"	"Otherwise"	*p*-Value
Socio-demographics				
Daegu/Gyeongbuk	99	15 (15.2%)	84 (84.8%)	
Busan/Ulsan/Gyeongnam	159	46 (28.9%)	113 (71.1%)	
Gangwon/Jeju	41	7 (17.1%)	34 (82.9%)	
Occupation status				0.56
Salary earner	473	122 (25.8%)	351 (74.2%)	
Self-employed or other job	131	40 (30.5%)	91 (69.5%)	
Out of labor	396	106 (26.8%)	290 (73.2%)	
Health-related factors				
Subjective health				0.08
Bad	116	27 (23.3%)	89 (76.7%)	
Moderate	442	107 (24.2%)	335 (75.8%)	
Good	442	134 (30.3%)	308 (69.7%)	
Underlying disease				0.30
None	589	165 (28.0%)	424 (72.0%)	
More than 1	411	103 (25.1%)	308 (74.9%)	

Table 3. Influencing factors associated with healthcare utilization avoidance ($n = 1000$).

Variables	Unadjusted		Adjusted	
	OR (95%CI)	*p*-Value	Adjusted OR (95%CI)	*p*-Value
Socio-demographics				
Gender				
Male	Ref.		Ref.	
Female	1.79 (1.34–2.38)	<0.001	1.91 (1.40–2.62)	<0.001
Age (year)				
18–29	Ref.		Ref.	
30–39	2.19 (1.33–3.60)	<0.001	1.85 (1.05–3.27)	0.03
40–49	1.53 (0.98–2.38)	0.06	1.26 (0.72–2.21)	0.42
50–59	2.09 (1.32–3.31)	<0.001	1.93 (1.06–3.50)	0.03
≥60	1.85 (1.21–2.83)	<0.001	1.46 (0.82–2.60)	0.2
Family size, No.				
1(living alone)	Ref.		Ref.	
more than 2	1.25 (0.79–1.97)	0.34	1.46 (0.83–2.56)	0.19
Education level				
Under middle school	Ref.		Ref.	
High school graduate	1.04 (0.43–2.51)	0.93	1.06 (0.42–2.69)	0.9
College and above	0.82 (0.34–1.97)	0.66	1.06 (0.41–2.74)	0.9
Marital status				
Married	Ref.		Ref.	
Single/divorced/bereaved	0.71 (0.53–0.95)	0.02	0.91 (0.58–1.42)	0.66
Presence of children				
None	Ref.		Ref.	
More than 1	1.42 (0.85–2.37)	0.18	1.19 (0.66–2.15)	0.57
Household monthly income				
Under 200	Ref.		Ref.	
200–400	1.07 (0.66–1.74)	0.79	0.98 (0.58–1.68)	0.95
400–600	0.79 (0.49–1.29)	0.35	0.65 (0.37–1.15)	0.14
≥600	0.69 (0.43–1.12)	0.13	0.61 (0.35–1.08)	0.09

Table 3. *Cont.*

Variables	Unadjusted		Adjusted	
	OR (95%CI)	*p*-Value	Adjusted OR (95%CI)	*p*-Value
Residential area				
Urban	Ref.		Ref.	
Town	0.86 (0.57–1.31)	0.49	0.65 (0.41–0.99)	0.05
Residential area2				
Seoul	Ref.		Ref.	
Incheon/Gyeonggi-do	1.30 (0.88–1.91)	0.19	1.37 (0.92–2.06)	0.12
Daejeon/Sejong/Chungcheong-do	1.80 (1.04–3.12)	0.04	2.04 (1.14–3.65)	0.02
Gwangju/Jeolla-do	1.45 (0.83–2.52)	0.19	1.49 (0.84–2.63)	0.17
Daegu/Gyeongbuk region	2.75 (1.47–5.16)	<0.001	3.10 (1.62–5.94)	<0.001
Busan/Ulsan/Gyeongnam region	1.29 (0.82–2.05)	0.27	1.30 (0.81–2.09)	0.28
Gangwon/Jeju	2.38 (1.00–5.67)	0.05	2.78 (1.12–6.88)	0.03
Occupation status				
Salary earner	Ref.		Ref.	
Self-employed or other job	0.78 (0.51–1.20)	0.26	0.77 (0.50–1.21)	0.26
Out of labor	0.96 (0.71–1.31)	0.81	0.75 (0.52–1.08)	0.13
Health-related factors				
Subjective health				
Bad	Ref.		Ref.	
Moderate	0.98 (0.60–1.59)	0.93	1.01 (0.61–1.69)	0.96
Good	0.71 (0.44–1.15)	0.17	0.79 (0.47–1.34)	0.39
Underlying disease				
None	Ref.		Ref.	
More than 1	1.17 (0.87–1.56)	0.3	0.97 (0.69–1.38)	0.88

Table 4. Influencing factors associated with healthcare utilization avoidance among subgroup participants along with gender.

Variables	Adjusted OR (95%CI)	*p*-Value	Adjusted OR (95%CI)	*p*-Value
	Male Subgroup (*n* = 478)		Female Subgroup (*n* = 522)	
Socio-demographics				
Age (year)				
18–29	Ref.		Ref.	
30–39	1.71 (0.76 3.84)	0.19	2.01 (0.85–4.74)	0.11
40–49	0.83 (0.36–1.92)	0.67	1.73 (0.77–3.88)	0.18
50–59	1.08 (0.44–2.62)	0.87	3.05 (1.27–7.30)	0.01
≥60	0.66 (0.28–1.57)	0.34	2.90 (1.23–6.82)	0.01
Family size, No.				
1(living alone)	Ref.		Ref.	
2 or more	1.63 (0.74–3.58)	0.22	1.70 (0.71–4.11)	0.24
Education level				
Middle school or below	Ref.		Ref.	
High school graduate	3.15 (0.88–11.26)	0.08	0.30 (0.04–2.44)	0.26
College and above	2.89 (0.79–10.60)	0.11	0.34 (0.04–2.81)	0.32
Marital status				
Married	Ref.		Ref.	
Single/divorced/bereaved	0.58 (0.30–1.14)	0.12	1.25 (0.64–2.46)	0.51
Presence of children				
None	Ref.		Ref.	
More than 1	1.25 (0.49–3.19)	0.64	1.23 (0.55–2.74)	0.62

Table 4. *Cont.*

Variables	Adjusted OR (95%CI)	p-Value	Adjusted OR (95%CI)	p-Value
	Male Subgroup (n = 478)		Female Subgroup (n = 522)	
Household income/mo.				
Under 200	Ref.		Ref.	
200–400	0.91 (0.41–2.02)	0.81	0.85 (0.39–1.84)	0.68
400–600	0.43 (0.18–0.98)	0.05	0.74 (0.32–1.71)	0.48
≥600	0.45 (0.19–0.99)	0.05	0.62 (0.27–1.40)	0.25
Residence				
Urban	Ref.		Ref.	
Rural	0.53 (0.28–1.01)	0.05	0.87 (0.44–1.74)	0.70
Residential area				
Seoul	Ref.		Ref.	
Incheon/Gyeonggi	2.02 (1.14–3.58)	0.02	0.86 (0.47–1.58)	0.63
Daejeon/Sejong/Chungcheong	2.93 (1.30–6.57)	0.01	1.37 (0.57–3.28)	0.48
Gwangju/Jeolla	2.80 (1.23–6.36)	0.01	0.82 (0.35–1.89)	0.64
Daegu/Gyeongbuk	4.87 (1.93–12.28)	0.00	1.88 (0.73–4.87)	0.19
Busan/Ulsan/Gyeongnam	1.50 (0.77–2.91)	0.24	1.11 (0.54–2.31)	0.77
Gangwon/Jeju	4.97 (1.36–18.07)	0.02	1.69 (0.44–6.54)	0.45
Occupation status				
Salary earner	Ref.		Ref.	
Self-employed or other job	0.68 (0.37–1.24)	0.21	1.00 (0.48–2.10)	1.00
Out of labor	0.71 (0.40–1.27)	0.25	0.87 (0.52–1.44)	0.58
Health-related factors				
Subjective health				
Bad	Ref.		Ref.	
Moderate	1.44 (0.65–3.19)	0.36	0.76 (0.37–1.56)	0.46
Good	0.85 (0.38–1.88)	0.68	0.81 (0.39–1.68)	0.57
Underlying disease				
None	Ref.			
More than 1	0.90 (0.67–1.23)	0.88	0.78(0.54–1.05)	0.27

Table 5. Influencing factors associated with the avoidance of healthcare utilization among subgroup participants according to the presence of an underlying disease.

Variables	Adjusted OR (95%CI)	p-Value	Adjusted OR (95%CI) (95%CI)	p-Value
	With Underlying Disease (n = 411)		Without Underlying Disease (n = 589)	
Socio-demographics				
Gender				
Male	Ref.		Ref.	
Female	1.58 (0.94–2.65)	0.09	2.02 (1.34–3.04)	<0.001
Age (year)				
18–29	Ref.		Ref.	
30–39	0.69 (0.20–2.41)	0.56	2.52 (1.29–4.93)	0.01
40–49	1.12 (0.32–4.02)	0.86	1.22 (0.63–2.34)	0.56
50–59	1.63 (0.49–5.43)	0.43	1.87 (0.89–3.92)	0.10
≥60	1.11 (0.35–3.55)	0.86	1.54 (0.73–3.26)	0.26
Family size, No.				
1(living alone)	Ref.		Ref.	
more than 2	0.80 (0.25–2.54)	0.71	1.92 (1.00–3.77)	0.05

Table 5. *Cont.*

Variables	Adjusted OR (95%CI)	*p*-Value	Adjusted OR (95%CI) (95%CI)	*p*-Value
	With Underlying Disease (n = 411)		Without Underlying Disease (n = 589)	
Education level				
Middle school or below	Ref.		Ref.	
High school graduate	1.33 (0.43–4.12)	0.62	1.18 (0.20–7.03)	0.86
College and above	0.85 (0.27–2.70)	0.78	1.49 (0.25–8.98)	0.66
Marital status				
Married	Ref.		Ref.	
Single/divorced/bereaved	0.94 (0.43–2.04)	0.87	0.92 (0.52–1.63)	0.77
Presence of children				
None	Ref.		Ref.	
More than 1	1.31 (0.42–4.14)	0.64	2.00 (1.07–3.73)	0.03
Monthly household income				
Under 200	Ref.		Ref.	
200–400	1.04 (0.47–2.34)	0.92	1.01 (0.49–2.09)	0.97
400–600	0.90 (0.37–2.22)	0.82	0.61 (0.29–1.29)	0.20
≥600	0.61 (0.26–1.48)	0.28	0.68 (0.32–1.44)	0.31
Residence				
Urban	Ref.		Ref.	
Rural	0.76 (0.37–1.59)	0.47	0.52 (0.28–0.96)	0.04
Residential area				
Seoul	Ref.		Ref.	
Incheon/Gyeonggi	1.41 (0.75–2.68)	0.29	1.27 (0.74–2.18)	0.38
Daejeon/Sejong/Chungcheong	2.01 (0.80–5.05)	0.14	2.14 (1.00–4.62)	0.05
Gwangju/Jeolla	1.94 (0.74–5.10)	0.18	1.37 (0.66–2.85)	0.40
Daegu/Gyeongbuk	4.26 (1.45–12.51)	0.01	2.51 (1.10–5.76)	0.03
Busan/Ulsan/Gyeongnam	1.56 (0.74–3.27)	0.24	1.11 (0.59–2.09)	0.76
Gangwon/Jeju	3.67 (0.75–18.01)	0.11	2.30 (0.72–7.36)	0.16
Occupation status				
Salary earner	Ref.		Ref.	
Self-employed or other job	0.83 (0.41–1.68)	0.61	0.69 (0.38–1.27)	0.24
Out of labor	0.96 (0.53–1.73)	0.88	0.67 (0.42–1.08)	0.10
Health-related factors				
Subjective health				
Bad	Ref.		Ref.	
Moderate	1.44 (0.77–2.67)	0.25	0.50 (0.16–1.58)	0.24
Good	1.00 (0.51–1.96)	0.99	0.42 (0.13–1.33)	0.14

3. Results

3.1. Sociodemographic and Health-Related Characteristics

Among the 1000 respondents, there were 478 men (47.8%) and 522 women (52.2%), with a mean age of 47.04 years (M = 47.04, SD = 15.04) (Table 1). The majority of respondents had a family size of more than two persons (90.1%), and 64.9% were married. Half of the respondents had at least some college education (49.0%), followed by those with only a high school education (48.1%). The most common monthly household income was approximately 2.00–3.99 million KRW ($1688–$3369; 31.5%), followed by over 6.00 million KRW ($5065; 29.4%) and 4.00–5.99 million KRW ($3377–$5057; 26.2%) (Table 1). Among the respondents, 88.0% lived in urban areas, and about 9.7% had young children in the home. Regarding occupation status, 47.3% were salary earners, 39.6% were unemployed, and 13.1% were self-employed or held other jobs.

3.2. Avoidance of Healthcare Utilization

Among the respondents, 26.8% reported that they never avoided visiting hospitals when they were sick (Figure 1). However, 26.6% reported that they did sometimes, 22.3%

often, and 24.3% reported that they "always" avoided healthcare utilization when they were unwell. Table 2 reports the Chi-square statistics for variables related to the avoidance of healthcare utilization and describes the group differences in avoidance behavior. Women ($p < 0.001$) and married respondents ($p = 0.02$) were more likely to avoid healthcare. Group differences among age ($p < 0.001$) and residential area ($p = 0.01$) were statistically significant. Among the residential areas, respondents in the Daegu/Gyeongbuk region reported the highest rate of healthcare avoidance (84.8%). However, group differences between respondents with more than one or no underlying disease were not statistically significant (Figure 1).

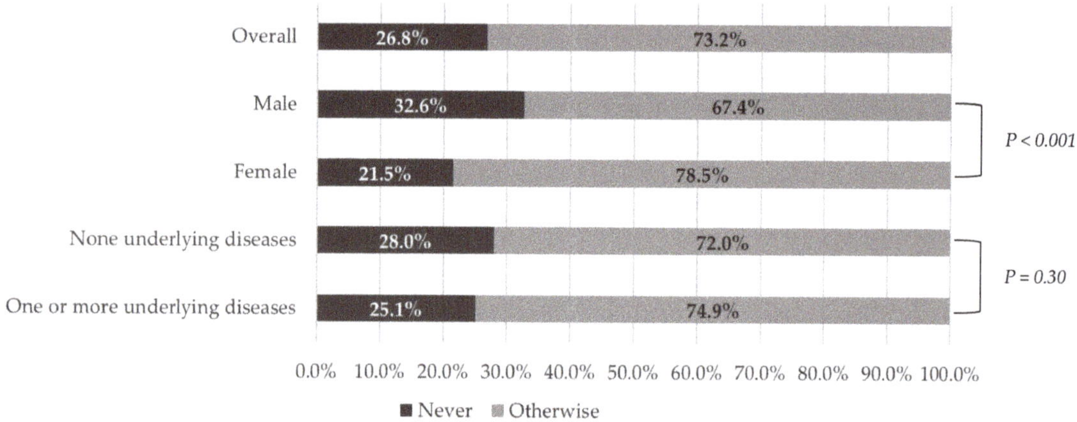

Figure 1. Healthcare utilization avoidance among subgroup participants based on gender and the presence of an underlying disease.

3.3. Factors Influencing the Avoidance of Healthcare Utilization

We used logit regression models to test the association between the avoidance of healthcare utilization and respondents' sociodemographic factors and health-related factors (Table 3). Out of the sociodemographic factors, female sex (odds ratio (OR), 1.91; 95% confidence interval (CI), 1.40–2.62; $p < 0.001$), age in 50 s (OR, 1.93; 95% CI, 1.06–3.50; $p = 0.03$) and living in rural area (OR, 0.65; 95% CI, 0.41–0.99; $p = 0.05$) were significant individual predictors of healthcare avoidance. Among residential areas, respondents who live in the Daegu/Gyeongbuk region (OR, 3.10; 95% CI, 1.62–5.94; $p < 0.001$), Gangwon/Jeju (OR, 2.78; 95% CI, 1.12–6.88; $p = 0.03$) and Daejeon/Sejong/Chungcheong-do (OR, 2.04; 95% CI, 1.14–3.65; $p = 0.02$) were more likely to practice avoidance than those living in Seoul, the capital city of South Korea. Interestingly, none of the health-related factors were associated significantly with the dependent variable. Respondents who are women in their 50s living in urban and residential areas (especially the Daegu/Gyeongbuk region) are vulnerable in healthcare utilization.

Tables 4 and 5 provide the results of the subgroup analysis, which show a moderate effect of gender and presence of underlying disease. Among men ($n = 478$), sociodemographic factors such as monthly household income level 4.00–5.99 million KRW (OR = 0.43; 95% CI, 0.18–0.98; $p = 0.05$), and over 6.00 million KRW (OR = 0.45; 95% CI, 0.19–0.99; $p = 0.05$) and residential area were associated significantly with healthcare avoidance. However, among women ($n = 522$), in their 50 s (OR = 3.05; 95% CI, 1.27–7.30; $p = 0.01$) or older than 60 (OR = 2.90; 95% CI, 1.23–6.82; $p = 0.01$) significantly influenced their healthcare avoidance. Factors that made people vulnerable differed among gender groups. When we restricted the respondents to those with an underlying disease ($n = 411$), only the respondents' residential area, Daegu/Gyeongbuk-region (OR = 4.26; 95% CI, 1.45–12.51; $p = 0.01$), was significantly related to their healthcare utilization. Among the respondents with no underlying disease, the following groups were more likely to avoid healthcare: females (OR = 2.02; 95% CI, 1.34–3.04; $p < 0.001$), those in their 30s (OR = 2.52; 95% CI, 1.29–4.93; $p = 0.01$), families of two or more (OR = 1.92; 95% CI, 1.00–3.77; $p = 0.05$), those with young children in the home (OR = 2.00; 95% CI, 1.07–3.73; $p = 0.03$), and those living in Daejeon/Sejong/Chungcheong-do (OR = 2.14; 95% CI, 1.00–4.62; $p = 0.05$) and Daegu/Gyeongbuk (OR = 2.51; 95% CI, 1.10–5.76; $p = 0.03$).

4. Discussion

Our findings provide useful insights for understanding the under-utilization of healthcare services in terms of demand by investigating the avoidance of healthcare associated with the COVID-19 pandemic, an emerging infectious disease. Among respondents, 73.2% avoided healthcare utilization, while only 26.8% did not. There was no statistically significant difference in the prevalence of healthcare avoidance between those with (72.0%) and without (74.9%) an underlying disease. The results indicate that the general population avoided visiting health facilities as a response to the COVID-19 outbreak, regardless of whether public health authorities recommended that they do so. We also identified sociodemographic factors (i.e., gender, age, income level, residential area) influencing the avoidance of healthcare utilization. The present study shows that not all societal groups share the burden of healthcare avoidance equally, as it disproportionately affects those with certain sociodemographic characteristics.

A few interesting findings should be highlighted. First, avoiding hospitals was prominent during the peak of the COVID-19 outbreak, which can potentially damage the overall health of the population and disrupt daily life. During the outbreak, the Korean government and public health authorities had not given any public health advice about postponing or avoiding visits to hospitals. Instead, officials made efforts to ensure access to safe and reliable care by encouraging the public to utilize healthcare when needed. The Korean government has designated a "National Relief Hospital," that operates a screening clinic to separate potential COVID-19 infected patients and treats patients with respiratory infections in a separate place. Moreover, the transmission of the COVID-19 virus mostly occurred by community-acquired infection, not in hospitals.

Widespread healthcare avoidance might relate to the South Koreans' experience with the Middle East Respiratory Syndrome (MERS) in 2015, as the COVID-19 outbreak brings back memories of MERS. Between the first documented occurrence of MERS infection (20 May 2015) and diagnosis of the last case (4 July 2015), there were 186 confirmed cases, with 38 deaths and 16,752 people quarantined [26]. All confirmed cases of MERS were suspected to be hospital-acquired infections except for one case of household transmission, and hospital-to-hospital transmission occurred in 17 hospitals, all of which originated in one hospital [26]. Avoiding hospitals even when sick during the 2015 South Korean MERS outbreak may have been a strategy for reducing the perceived risk of infection, as most MERS infections occurred at hospitals; the uncertainty about viral spread was very high. However, unlike the MERS virus, the spread of the COVID-19 virus has occurred primarily in communities. Although there is a distinct difference between the two viruses, the public might fear a nosocomial infection, and hold other misconceptions about the virus. This should be investigated further.

Second, socio-demographic characteristics (i.e., gender, age, income level) and especially residential area, were highly related to healthcare avoidance. Women, older people, those with a lower income level, and those living in highly affected residential areas were more likely to avoid healthcare utilization than other groups were. These results are similar to prior research investigating the association between social determinants and healthcare avoidance during public health emergencies such as epidemic outbreaks [18,23,27]. Therefore, the avoidance of behaviors of subpopulation members during a pandemic warrant the attention of health policy officers and public health authorities. Especially, elderly people in need of care need the support of family and friends or caregivers [27].

Among the investigated influencing factors, residential area had the most significant effect on healthcare avoidance. In particular, living in Daegu or Gyeongbuk (North Gyeongsang Province) regions, where COVID-19-confirmed patients exploded at the time of this study, have been found to be the strongest influencing factor in avoiding hospital visits. For example, among men, respondents living in the Daegu and Gyeoungbuk region were 4.87 times more likely to avoid healthcare than those living in Seoul. In the peak of the outbreak, the daily new patient count in Daegu had reached 741 by February 29, and thousands waited for hospital beds as cases surged [28]. At the time of this study, cumulative cases in Daegu had reached 6456 (25 March). One can reasonably expect that citizens of Daegu/Gyeongbuk were at increased risk due to healthcare under-utilization during the COVID-19 outbreak. Fortunately, many medical staff and volunteers both local and from all over the country have come and participated voluntarily to help overcome the crisis in Daegu [15].

There are a number of implications that have emerged from this study. First, health authorities must make efforts to sustain the efficacy of the healthcare systems by providing sufficient support for the public to utilize proper healthcare services on both the demand-side and the supply-side. For the demand-side, instructions on how and when to visit the hospital should be provided to patients with non-infectious diseases in order to prevent inappropriate healthcare avoidance. While controlling the spread of infectious disease quickly is the urgent primary goal of the public health authorities, guidelines for people in terms of maintaining their health is also very important [29]. At the same time, standards and procedures should be prepared to treat non-infected patients in all possible clinical situations. On the supply-side, human resources of medical experts, experts in public health and epidemics, along with new policies are needed to improve the resilience of highly affected communities. Second, it is expected that the number of patients visiting hospitals has drastically decreased, causing financial losses in the healthcare facilities. Negative financial impacts of outbreaks have been reported in previous studies [30,31]. Various support plans should be prepared, including financial arrangements to compensate for the loss of medical institutions.

Our study has several limitations. First, the analyses did not extensively explore psychological factors such as the perceived risk or fear of visiting hospitals and trust in public health authorities. Therefore, we did not investigate the psychological factors influencing healthcare avoidance, so further research is needed. Second, we could not identify whether healthcare avoidance resulted from misconceptions about the spread of COVID-19, which some might perceive as a nosocomial infection. Future studies should measure and analyze knowledge of the virus as an independent variable. Third, this study is based on questionnaires which investigated the self-reported healthcare service avoidance. Moreover, this study design is cross-sectional and is not available to examine the trend of healthcare avoidance during the pandemic. Further research using national data, such as Korea National Health Insurance (KNHI) Claims Database, would be able to investigate actual numbers of healthcare utilization and change over time during the pandemic. Finally, this study did not investigate the avoidance of healthcare service for reasons other than COVID-19, which can confound the findings of this study.

5. Conclusions

In conclusion, the results of this study documented that a noticeable proportion of the public avoided healthcare visits who under-utilized healthcare resources that had not been advised by the government during the COVID-19 outbreak. Subgroups who were more likely to avoid visiting hospitals were identified, with residential areas playing a significant role in respondents' behaviors. This study offers guidance for developing public health policy making to establish customized healthcare utilization policies and health promotion for specific groups of individuals. Prioritizing policies and efforts will be necessary for these vulnerable populations to reduce unmet healthcare needs. Understanding the patterns of healthcare utilization during infectious disease outbreaks would be valuable for facilitating appropriate responses and reducing the negative impact on population health.

Author Contributions: M.L. and M.Y. conceptualized the study. M.L. was responsible for the methodology and conducted a formal analysis. M.Y. was responsible for data acquisition. M.L. wrote the initial draft of the manuscript, and M.Y. assisted with the writing, review, and editing of the manuscript. Both authors have read and agreed to the published version of the manuscript.

Funding: This work was supported by the National Research Foundation of Korea (BK21 Center for Integrative Response to Health Disasters, Graduate School of Public Health, Seoul National University); National Research Foundation of Korea Grant funded by the Korean Government (No. 21B20151213037); and Rainbow Communication and Consulting.

Institutional Review Board Statement: The present study protocol was reviewed and approved by the Institutional Review Board (IRB) at Seoul National University (IRB No. 2003/002-005). Informed consent was submitted by all subjects when they were enrolled.

Informed Consent Statement: Informed consent was obtained from all subjects involved in the study.

Data Availability Statement: The datasets used and analyzed in the current study are available from the corresponding author on reasonable request.

Acknowledgments: We would like to thank Hyemin Yeo, Junghoon Shin, and Yeunhoon Jang for assistance with survey development and data collection.

Conflicts of Interest: The authors declare no conflict of interest.

References

1. Li, Q.; Guan, X.; Wu, P.; Wang, X.; Zhou, L.; Tong, Y.; Ren, R.; Leung, K.S.; Lau, E.H.; Wong, J.Y.; et al. Early transmission dynamics in Wuhan, China, of Novel Coronavirus—Infected pneumonia. *N. Engl. J. Med.* **2020**, *382*, 1199–1207. [CrossRef] [PubMed]
2. Zhu, N.; Zhang, D.; Wang, W.; Li, X.; Yang, B.; Song, J.; Zhao, X.; Huang, B.; Shi, W.; Lu, R.; et al. A Novel Coronavirus from Patients with Pneumonia in China, 2019. *N. Engl. J. Med.* **2020**, *382*, 727–733. [CrossRef]
3. Kim, J.Y.; Choe, P.G.; Oh, Y.; Oh, K.J.; Kim, J.; Park, S.J.; Park, J.H.; Na, H.K.; Oh, M.-D. The First Case of 2019 Novel Coronavirus Pneumonia Imported into Korea from Wuhan, China: Implication for Infection Prevention and Control Measures. *J. Korean Med. Sci.* **2020**, *35*, e61. [CrossRef] [PubMed]
4. Yoo, J.; Chung, M.; Kim, J.; Ko, J.; Kim, Y.; Kim, Y.; Kim, J.; Chung, Y.; Kim, H.; Han, M. Report on the Epidemiological Features of Coronavirus Disease 2019 (COVID-19) Outbreak in the Republic of Korea from January 19 to March 2, 2020. *J. Korean Med. Sci.* **2020**, *35*, e112.
5. Lee, M.; You, M. Psychological and Behavioral Responses in South Korea During the Early Stages of Coronavirus Disease 2019 (COVID-19). *Int. J. Environ. Res. Public Health* **2020**, *17*, 2977. [CrossRef] [PubMed]
6. Lee, H.; Park, J. Changes in health care utilization during the MERS epidemic. *Int. J. Infect. Dis.* **2018**, *73*, 187. [CrossRef]
7. Paek, S.H.; Kim, D.K.; Lee, J.H.; Kwak, Y.H. The Impact of Middle East Respiratory Syndrome Outbreak on Trends in Emergency Department Utilization Patterns. *J. Korean Med. Sci.* **2017**, *32*, 1576–1580. [CrossRef]
8. Wagenaar, B.H.; Augusto, O.; Beste, J.; Toomay, S.J.; Wickett, E.; Dunbar, N.; Bawo, L.; Wesseh, C.S. The 2014–2015 Ebola virus disease outbreak and primary healthcare delivery in Liberia: Time-series analyses for 2010–2016. *PLoS Med.* **2018**, *15*, e1002508. [CrossRef]
9. Wilhelm, J.A.; Helleringer, S. Utilization of non-Ebola health care services during Ebola outbreaks: A systematic review and meta-analysis. *J. Glob. Health* **2019**, *9*, 010406.
10. Chang, H.-J.; Huang, N.; Lee, C.-H.; Hsu, Y.-J.; Hsieh, C.-J.; Chou, Y.-J. The Impact of the SARS Epidemic on the Utilization of Medical Services: SARS and the Fear of SARS. *Am. J. Public Health* **2004**, *94*, 562–564. [CrossRef]
11. Byrne, S.K. Healthcare avoidance: A critical review. *Holist. Nurs. Pract.* **2008**, *22*, 280–292. [CrossRef]
12. Janz, N.K.; Becker, M.H. The Health Belief Model: A Decade Later. *Health Educ. Q.* **1984**, *11*, 1–47. [CrossRef]
13. Takahashi, S.; Metcalf, C.J.E.; Ferrari, M.J.; Moss, W.J.; Truelove, S.A.; Tatem, A.J.; Grenfell, B.T.; Lessler, J. Reduced vaccination and the risk of measles and other childhood infections post-Ebola. *Science* **2015**, *347*, 1240–1242. [CrossRef] [PubMed]
14. Walker, P.G.T.; White, M.T.; Griffin, J.T.; Reynolds, A.; Ferguson, N.M.; Ghani, A.C. Malaria morbidity and mortality in Ebola-affected countries caused by decreased health-care capacity, and the potential effect of mitigation strategies: A modelling analysis. *Lancet Infect. Dis.* **2015**, *15*, 825–832. [CrossRef]
15. Yum, H.-K. Suggestions to Prepare for the Second Epidemic of COVID-19 in Korea. *J. Korean Med. Sci.* **2020**, *35*, e191. [CrossRef] [PubMed]
16. Lee, M.; Ju, Y.; You, M. The Effects of Social Determinants on Public Health Emergency Preparedness Mediated by Health Communication: The 2015 MERS Outbreak in South Korea. *Health Commun.* **2020**, *35*, 1396–1406. [CrossRef]
17. Lau, J.T.F.; Griffiths, S.; Choi, K.C.; Tsui, H.Y. Avoidance behaviors and negative psychological responses in the general population in the initial stage of the H1N1 pandemic in Hong Kong. *BMC Infect. Dis.* **2010**, *10*, 139. [CrossRef]
18. Lau, J.T.F.; Yang, X.; Tsui, H.; Kim, J.H. Monitoring community responses to the SARS epidemic in Hong Kong: From day 10 to day 62. *J. Epidemiol. Commun. Health* **2003**, *57*, 864–870. [CrossRef]

19. Lau, J.T.; Tsui, H.; Kim, J.H.; Griffiths, S. Perceptions about status and modes of H5N1 transmission and associations with immediate behavioral responses in the Hong Kong general population. *Prev. Med.* **2006**, *43*, 406–410. [CrossRef]
20. Sadique, M.Z.; Edmunds, W.J.; Smith, R.D.; Meerding, W.J.; De Zwart, O.; Brug, J.; Beutels, P. Precautionary Behavior in Response to Perceived Threat of Pandemic Influenza. *Emerg. Infect. Dis.* **2007**, *13*, 1307–1313. [CrossRef] [PubMed]
21. Tang, C.S.-K.; Wong, C.-Y. Factors influencing the wearing of facemasks to prevent the severe acute respiratory syndrome among adult Chinese in Hong Kong. *Prev. Med.* **2004**, *39*, 1187–1193. [CrossRef] [PubMed]
22. Ozdemir, S.; Ng, S.; Chaudhry, I.; Finkelstein, E.A. Adoption of Preventive Behaviour Strategies and Public Perceptions About COVID-19 in Singapore. *Int. J. Health Policy Manag.* **2020**. [CrossRef]
23. Hung, K.K.; Walline, J.H.; Chan, E.Y.Y.; Huang, Z.; Lo, E.S.K.; Yeoh, E.K.; Graham, C.A. Health Service Utilization in Hong Kong During the COVID-19 Pandemic—A Cross-sectional Public Survey. *Int. J. Health. Policy Manag.* **2020**. [CrossRef]
24. Conroy, R. Sample Size. A Rough Guide. 2015. Available online: http://www.beaumontethics.ie/docs/application/samplesizecalculation.pdf (accessed on 10 January 2021).
25. Israel, G.D. *Determining Sample Size*; Institute of Food and Agriculture Sciences: Dade City, FL, USA, 1992.
26. Ki, M. 2015 MERS outbreak in Korea: Hospital-to-hospital transmission. *Epidemiol. Health* **2015**, *37*, e2015033. [CrossRef] [PubMed]
27. Fischer, F.; Raiber, L.; Boscher, C.; Winter, M.H.-J. COVID-19 and the Elderly: Who Cares? *Front. Public Health* **2020**, *8*, e151. [CrossRef]
28. Ricci, F.; Izzicupo, P.; Moscucci, F.; Sciomer, S.; Maffei, S.; Di Baldassarre, A.; Mattioli, A.V.; Gallina, S. Recommendations for Physical Inactivity and Sedentary Behavior During the Coronavirus Disease (COVID-19) Pandemic. *Front. Public Health* **2020**, *8*, 199. [CrossRef]
29. Kim, S.-W.; Lee, K.S.; Kim, K.; Lee, J.J.; Kim, J.-Y.; Daegu Medical Association. A Brief Telephone Severity Scoring System and Therapeutic Living Centers Solved Acute Hospital-Bed Shortage during the COVID-19 Outbreak in Daegu, Korea. *J. Korean Med. Sci.* **2020**, *35*, e152. [CrossRef]
30. Braithwaite, S.; Friedman, B.; Mutter, R.; Handrigan, M. Microsimulation of Financial Impact of Demand Surge on Hospitals: The H1N1 Influenza Pandemic of Fall 2009. *Health Serv. Res.* **2013**, *48*, 735–752. [CrossRef]
31. Matheny, J.; Toner, E.; Waldhorn, R. Financial effects of an influenza pandemic on US hospitals. *J. Health Care Financ.* **2007**, *34*, 58.

International Journal of
Environmental Research and Public Health

MDPI

Article

Gender Differences in the COVID-19 Pandemic Risk Perception, Psychology, and Behaviors of Spanish University Students

Stephanie Rodriguez-Besteiro [1], José Francisco Tornero-Aguilera [1,2], Jesús Fernández-Lucas [3,4] and Vicente Javier Clemente-Suárez [1,2,5,*]

1 Faculty of Sports Sciences, Universidad Europea de Madrid, Tajo Street, s/n, 28670 Madrid, Spain; stephanie.rodriguez@universidadeuropea.es (S.R.-B.); josefrancisco.tornero@universidadeuropea.es (J.F.T.-A.)
2 Studies Centre in Applied Combat (CESCA), 45007 Toledo, Spain
3 Applied Biotechnology Group, European University of Madrid, c/ Tajo s/n, Villaviciosa de Odón, 28670 Madrid, Spain; jesus.fernandez2@universidadeuropea.es
4 Grupo de Investigación en Ciencias Naturales y Exactas, GICNEX, Universidad de la Costa, CUC, 080002 Barranquilla, Colombia
5 Grupo de Investigación en Cultura, Educación y Sociedad, Universidad de la Costa, 080002 Barranquilla, Colombia
* Correspondence: vctxente@yahoo.es

Citation: Rodriguez-Besteiro, S.; Tornero-Aguilera, J.F.; Fernández-Lucas, J.; Clemente-Suárez, V.J. Gender Differences in the COVID-19 Pandemic Risk Perception, Psychology, and Behaviors of Spanish University Students. *Int. J. Environ. Res. Public Health* **2021**, *18*, 3908. https://doi.org/10.3390/ijerph18083908

Academic Editors: Paolo Roma, Merylin Monaro, Cristina Mazza and Paul B. Tchounwou

Received: 2 March 2021
Accepted: 2 April 2021
Published: 8 April 2021

Abstract: The actual COVID-19 pandemic scenario has generated a context of uncertainty, helplessness, and inequality. Yet, the perception of COVID-19 risk has influenced nutritional, psychological, and physical activity patterns depending on gender. We conducted the present research with the aim of studying gender differences of university students in the perceived risk of the COVID-19 pandemic, and in psychological, nutritional, oral health, and physical activity habits. To reach the study's aim, 300 volunteer university students completed an online questionnaire which analyzed variables of perceived risk of the COVID-19 pandemic, psychological profiles, and nutritional, oral health, and physical activity habits. Results showed that females presented a higher perception of danger to the COVID-19 virus than males but showed no differences in how the pandemic has affected personal lives. Females showed higher values of anxiety, conscientiousness, neuroticism, and openness to experience, while males presented higher values of extraversion. Nutritionally, males presented greater consumption of soft drinks, meat, and pasta or rice, and lower buccal hygiene. Yet, no differences were found regarding physical activity patterns. Results from the present study could be used by various educational institutions to implement multidisciplinary interventions to reduce the stress and risk perception.

Keywords: gender differences; COVID-19; students; risk perception; anxiety; personality

1. Introduction

Originating in Wuhan (Hubei, China) in December 2019 as a cluster of unexplained cases of pneumonia, the World Health Organization classified the SARS-Cov-2 outbreak as a pandemic in March 2020, affecting multiple countries, with more than 110 million confirmed cases and more than 2.5 million deaths [1]. On 26 February 2020, the first case of COVID-19 was detected in Spain. Due to the large increase in the number of cases, on 14 March, the Spanish government declared a state of alarm throughout the country. Beyond impacting millions of lives around the world, the pandemic has dealt a blow to the economy on a global level. The COVID-19 health crisis has posed a complex scenario for economy not only because of the shock it has produced, but also because its repercussions will be significant [2]. The world economy is facing its greatest challenge since the Great Recession. The state of alarm in Spain has resulted in the confinement of millions of people and, for this reason, the Spanish economy was forced to establish urgent measures to avoid the paralysis of both public and private administrative activity. In this way, many companies were forced to implement teleworking quickly so that their employees could continue to carry out their duties from home. Similarly, universities also moved 75% of their students [3] to online learning so that they could continue their studies [4]. However, not all companies have been able to adapt to this new modality, so they have been forced to permanently or temporarily suspend all or part of their activity, exercising Temporary Employment Regulation Files or on many occasions to dismiss their employees.

Because of the interactions between biological factors and social determinants, including gender stereotypes, differences and roles, social stigma, and social autonomy [5], inequities are expected to appear in the context of COVID-19. Indeed, COVID-19 has affected males and females differently, presenting higher fatality rates, a worse prognosis, and a higher risk of death in males [6]. Yet, despite fatality rates, females have a higher prevalence and severity of anxiety, depression, and acute stress symptoms [7]. However, females have experienced a greater number of psychological alterations that can be associated with isolated symptoms and complex disorders, which are related to a deterioration in functionality and the development of anxiety, insomnia, depression, or post-traumatic stress disorder (PTSD). In addition, gender moderates the relationship between emotional disturbances (e.g., psychological distress) and personal strengths such as resilience and social support in students. Thus, differences in psychometric and emotional profiles are key elements to understand the striking differences between males and females regarding COVID-19 beliefs and behaviors.

In this line, the authors hypothesize that females are more likely to take the pandemic seriously. In March, 59% of female respondents considered COVID-19 to be a very serious health problem compared to 49% of males. In mid-April, both numbers decreased, but the gender difference remained: 40% of females still saw the virus as a very serious risk compared to 33% of males. This difference is present among studied countries [8]. Indeed, the authors postulate that gender differences regarding perception risk are echoed in behavioral differences between male and female leaders. Countries which are led by females have responded with greater effectiveness to the pandemic than countries led by males [9]. For example, Germany, Iceland, New Zealand, and Denmark, which have female leaders, have used a more democratic and inclusive style of leadership, with decisive and clear communication strategies. Meanwhile, countries with male leaders such as the US, Brazil, and the UK have experienced the worst COVID-19 outcomes [9].

Yet, one of the most affected by the COVID-19 pandemic groups are students, since their welfare and mental health is threatened. Previous research on COVID-19's psychological effect on university students indicates that the economic situation, as well as delays in academic activities, are risk factors for developing anxiety, with depressive symptoms, stress, and anxiety being the most commonly identified psychological effects [10]. When compared to other collectives, such as professors, students seem to present higher scores of stress and anxiety [11], with females presenting higher ratios and a growing and greater prevalence of depression among male students [12]. However, the psychological and emotional profiles and the behavioral responses depend greatly on both contextual and multifactorial factors such as nutritional status, oral health, and the amount of physical exercise [13]. All of these factors are influenced by gender [14], and previous authors have remarked that these factors may be influenced by the pandemic situation (-) and lockdown (-).

In this line, researchers have established an association between the way people eat and their mood. Thus, eating patterns can affect the way people feel [15]. During the period of confinement, nutritional habits changed dramatically in parallel with the increase in anxiety and stress values among the population [16]. Previous authors have found that the most frequent changes related to an increased consumption of fruit (27%), eggs (25.4%), legumes (22.5%), vegetables (21%), and fish (20%), and a reduced consumption of processed meats (35.5%) and sugary drinks (32.8%), with clear differences according to age and gender. Physical activity can be a contextual factor for the psychological profile. Students who are physically active tend to have a healthier and more balanced diet than those who are not physically active. University students practice an average 40 min of physical activity per day, being significantly higher in males than in females [17]. Along these lines, male university students tend to opt for sporting activities in their leisure time, while females give greater importance to other social activities and personal hobbies in detriment of physical activity [18]. Few studies have focused on gender differences regarding the impact of the COVID-19 outbreak countries like Spain, where mortality remains one of the highest worldwide, especially when considering a wide range of multifactorial variables. Thus, we conducted the present research with the aim of studying gender differences in university student regarding the perceived risk of the COVID-19 pandemic and in psychological, nutritional, oral health, and physical activity habits. The initial hypotheses were: (i) There are gender differences in the perceived risk of the COVID-19 pandemic, and (ii) there are gender differences in the psychological, nutritional, oral health, and physical activity habits of students.

2. Materials and Methods

In the current study, 300 university students residing in Spain, aged between 17 and 51 years (according to the sample obtained), were interviewed via online questionnaire in a period of 3 months, from October 2020 to December 2020. Our inclusion criteria were: Enrollment in the current academic year, currently living in Spain, and either graduate or undergraduate students from any field/area of expertise. In order to prevent double responses from the same person, students had to include their Student ID, which was required to match with the university database. Furthermore, data were considered strictly confidential. This research complied with the Helsinki declarations (revised in Brazil, 2013), on human research and was approved by the University Ethics Committee (CIPI/18/074).

All of the participants digitally signed a consented participation where the aims and procedure of the study was explained. To reach the aim of the present research, a cross-sectional study was developed. The following parameters were analyzed.

2.1. Sociodemographic Factors

Age (years), height (cm), weight (kg), and Body Mass Index (BMI, Kg/m^2) were analyzed, along with the degree of compliance with the confinement due to the COVID-19 crisis using a Likert scale, where 0 means the least and 10 the most. The question, "How many people you have lived with during the confinement?" was measured on a self-perception scale, indicating the number of people with which the student lived.

2.2. Economic Variables

We analyzed whether the university students performed any type of paid work. If so, we then asked whether this had been affected by the COVID-19 crisis. The options were: Not affected, reduced working hours and income reduced, and job loss.

2.3. Psychological Profile

We analyzed the students' perceived danger of the COVID-19 virus using a Likert scale from 0 to 10, where 0 means the least and 10 is the most. A Likert scale was also used to measure how the COVID-19 crisis has affected the participant personally, where 0 means the least and 10 the most. A reduced version of the Spanish version of the Big Five Inventory [19] was used to measure personality traits, including openness to experience, conscientiousness, extraversion, agreeableness, and neuroticism. The reduced version is composed of 10 items that are answered on a 5-point Likert scale, where 1 means completely disagree and 5 means completely agree. A reduced version of the Spanish version of Spielberger State-Trait Anxiety Inventory [20], composed of 6 items assessing anxiety that are answered on a 4-point Likert scale where 1 means not at all and 4 means very much, was used to measure anxiety. The Spanish version of the Acceptance and Action Questionnaire II [21] was used to analyze the experiential avoidance or psychological inflexibility through 7 items answered by a 7-point Likert scale, where 0 means never true and 7 means always true. The Spanish version of the UCLA Loneliness Scale [22] was used to scale measures loneliness. In the present study, we used a condensed version which consists of 3 items answered by a 3-point Likert scale, where 1 means never and 3 means frequently. The Spanish version of Zung Depression Scale [23] was used to measure depression in relation to the COVID-19 crisis. The Zung Depression Scale uses a self-applied scale for depression, which has a sensitivity and specificity greater than 80% and consists of 20 items formulated in positive and negative terms. Somatic and cognitive symptoms are highly relevant, with 8 items for each group. The scale also includes 2 items referring to mood and 2 to psychomotor symptoms.

2.4. Health-Related Factors

Hours of sleep per day were measured on a self-perception scale, indicating the number of hours the student sleep per day. The quality of the parcipants' last sleep was measured using a Likert scale, where 1 means very poor sleep quality and 10 means very good sleep quality. Average number of steps per day in the last week was measured on a self-perception scale, indicating the number of steps the student had taken in the last week. Nutritional habits were analyzed using an adapted previously used questionnaire. The first 2 questions were related to eating habits. The rest of questions to the consumption frequency of different food groups, including fish, vegetables, legumes, meat, fast food, soft drinks, in which answers ranged from "less than two per week" to "seven or more per week." For oral health, a previously used questionnaire consisting of 4 items related to oral health was used. For the first question ("How many times a day do you brush your teeth?"), the answers ranged from "none" to "more than four per day." For the question "Do you smoke?", answers ranged from "no" to "more than five cigarettes per day." The rest of questions were answered by "yes," "sometimes," or "no." Physical activity habits were measured with a questionnaire used in line with previous research. We evaluated the psychophysiological stress response in high psychologically demanding contexts using a questionnaire which included the items: "Did you do any physical activity in the last 7 days?", "If so, time in minutes of cyclic and/or aerobic activity (cycling, treadmill, Zumba) adding up all the sessions of the 7 days", "If so, time in minutes of activity with self-loads (sit-ups, push-ups, squats...) or weights (gym machines, weights...) adding up all the sessions of the 7 days."

2.5. Statistical Analysis

Statistical analyses were analyzed using the Statistical Package for the Social Sciences (SPSS) version 24.0 (SPSS Inc., Chicago, IL, USA). Descriptive statistics (mean and standard deviation) were calculated for each variable. Kolmogorov–Smirnov tests were performed to analyze normality and homogeneity of each variable. To analyze gender differences in sociodemographic, academic, and psychological variables, an independent T test was conducted. To analyze gender differences in economic, health-related, and oral health variables, the Chi-square test was used. The level of significance was set at $p \leq 0.05$.

3. Results

Data are presented as mean ± standard deviation. Anthropometrical differences were found regarding height, weight, and BMI (Table 1).

Table 1. Gender differences in sociodemographic factors.

Variable	Male	Female	*t*	*p*
Age (yrs)	23.86 ± 5.45	24.40 ± 6.95	0.711	0.477
Height (cm)	178.17 ± 6.46	162.45 ± 17.10	−10.158	0.000
Weight (Kg)	79.98 ± 55.29	59.33 ± 8.44	−4.082	0.000
Body Mass Index (BMI)	23.65 ± 2.93	21.92 ± 2.87	−4.787	0.000
Degree of confinement compliance due to the COVID-19 crisis	8.65 ± 1.69	8.91 ± 1.68	1.218	0.224
How many people have you lived with in confinement?	2.74 ± 1.24	2.57 ± 1.19	−1.141	0.255

Regarding economic variables, no gender differences were found in how the COVID-19 pandemic has affected employment (Table 2).

Table 2. Gender differences in economic variables.

Variable	Male	Female	Chi-Squared	*p*
Do you perform any paid work?	1.46 ± 0.65	1.54 ± 0.71	0.469	0.333
Regarding your work. have you been affected by the COVID-19 crisis?	1.46 ± 0.65	1.59 ± 0.67	0.272	0.177

According to the academic variables, no gender differences were found in how the COVID-19 pandemic has affected studies.

According to the psychological profile, females showed a higher perception of danger to the COVID-19 virus than males. Females presented higher values in conscientiousness, neuroticism, openness to experience, and stress than males. However, males presented higher values of extraversion than females. Yet, no gender differences were seen for psychological traits such as depression, loneliness, and experiential avoidance (Table 3). Reliability was estimated through Cronbach's alpha, obtaining 0.729 for Big Five factors, 0.810 for the Acceptance and Action Questionnaire II (AAQII), 0.870 for the UCLA Loneliness Scale (UCLA), 0.854 for the Spielberger State-Trait Anxiety Inventory (STAI), and 0.793 for the Zung Depression Scale (ZUNG).

Table 3. Gender differences in psychological profiles.

Variable	Male	Female	*t*	*p*
Level of perceived danger in the COVID-19 Pandemic	6.49 ± 2.03	7.20 ± 1.65	3.089	0.002
Extraversion	5.88 ± 1.71	5.27 ± 1.69	−2.906	0.004
Agreeableness	6.24 ± 1.55	6.56 ± 1.577	1.673	0.096
Conscientiousness	6.39 ± 1.89	7.08 ± 1.69	3.132	0.002
Neuroticism	5.74 ± 2.12	6.72 ± 2.27	3.609	0.000
Openness to experience	6.96 ± 1.69	7.48 ± 1.76	2.471	0.014
AAQII	23.36 ± 8.90	24.22 ± 11.04	0.702	0.483
UCLA	4.47 ± 1.76	4.47 ± 1.61	−0.033	0.974
ZUNG	41.73 ± 4.47	42.70 ± 5.23	31.945	0.234

AAQII (Acceptance and Action Questionnaire II); UCLA (UCLA Loneliness Scale); STAI (Spielberger State-Trait Anxiety Inventory); ZUNG (Zung Depression Scale).

Regarding the health-related factors, males presented a higher weekly consumption of soft drinks, meat, and pasta or rice than females. Females showed higher values in daily tooth brushing and dry mouth than males. No gender differences were found in the physical activity habits analyzed (Table 4).

Table 4. Gender differences in the health-related factors.

Variable	Male	Female	Chi-Squared	*p*
How many meals did you take on average during your confinement?	4.28 ± 1.25	4.50 ± 1.39	13.168	0.155
How many glasses of water do you drink per day?	4.89 ± 1.34	4.80 ± 1.43	5.262	0.385
Juices	1.63 ± 0.97	1.52 ± 0.90	2.458	0.483
Alcoholic Beverage	1.06 ± 0.27	1.04 ± 0.23	1.153	0.562
Fermented beverage	1.37 ± 0.70	1.30 ± 0.60	1.707	0.635
Soft drinks	1.58 ± 0.87	1.38 ± 0.69	4.118	0.042
Energy Drink	1.16 ± 0.44	1.12 ± 0.43	3.730	0.155
Fruit	2.68 ± 1.06	2.83 ± 1.01	3.230	0.357
Bakery/Sweets	1.72 ± 0.83	1.76 ± 0.89	2.931	0.402
Meat	2.87 ± 0.75	2.28 ± 0.95	34.075	0.000
Fish	2.00 ± 0.79	1.87 ± 0.81	6.846	0.077
Legume	2.21 ± 0.82	2.00 ± 0.84	11.721	0.008
Pasta or rice	2.69 ± 0.80	2.16 ± 0.89	26.040	0.000
Vegetables	2.55 ± 0.95	2.75 ± 0.98	3.826	0.281
Bread	2.70 ± 1.14	2.61 ± 1.18	1.669	0.644
Fast food	1.37 ± 0.63	1.28 ± 0.53	2.596	0.458
Do you smoke?	1.18 ± 0.60	1.29 ± 0.79	6.369	0.095
Do you suffer from gastritis or heartburn?	2.17 ± 0.49	2.20 ± 0.48	0.617	0.735
How many times do you brush your teeth per day?	2.39 ± 0.87	2.71 ± 0.80	3.078	0.002
Does your mouth often feel dry as if it lacks saliva?	2.11 ± 0.53	2.25 ± 0.59	2.057	0.041
Minutes of cyclic and/or aerobic activity	276.97 ± 243.24	227.77 ± 239.74	45.267	0.227
Minutes of activity with self-loading or weights	217.68 ± 209.87	236.36 ± 254.01	35.254	0.760

4. Discussion

The aim of the present research was to study gender differences among university students regarding the perceived risk of the COVID-19 pandemic and in psychological, nutritional, oral health, and physical activity habits. The initial hypothesis was partially confirmed, since female students showed higher scores on the level of perceived risk of the COVID-19 pandemic than male students. However, significant differences between genders were found in some psychological and nutritional variables but not in oral health and physical activity variables.

In the present study, females presented higher perceived risks level of the COVID-19 pandemic than males. Authors have suggested that there a is a gender difference in the psychological experience, somatization, and impact of the COVID-19 pandemic and the emotions it provokes, suggesting that women are more emotionally vulnerable to the effects of COVID-19 context than men [24]. This may be related to the greater levels of state-trait anxiety reached in this study, where females presented higher levels than males in lin with previous literature [25]. This may also explain the greater emotional vulnerability of females [26]. Indeed, there are also gender differences in stress coping among university students [27], where females have shown greater stress and lower stress coping abilities than male [28], thus supporting our results.

The psychometric profile and personality trait differences between genders may explain the stronger influence of perceived risk and anxiety in females. Within these personality traits, our data suggest that male students have higher levels of extraversion than females, while females present higher values in conscientiousness and neuroticism, which is in lineprevious research conducted in female professors [29]. The present data suggest that females have greater openness to experience, contrary to the results of Castañeiras et al. (2006), where males showed higher levels of openness to experience than females [30]. However, these differences could be attributed to the difference in the socio-cultural context (Latin America-Europe), as well as the context of the sample, since our sample was students.

Regarding the nutritional profile, no gender differences were found among the consumption of fruit, legume, or vegetables, which is contrary to previous studies. Authors have suggested that male's poorer nutrition knowledge explains a significant part of their lower intake of fruit and vegetables [31], with a tendency for fat and protein rich foods breweries as beer, spirits, and sweet carbonated drinks [32], in line with our data. Yet, it has been reported that students have poor nutrition habits [33], reflecting a significant gender difference in weight status with the percentage of overweight/obese males being more than double that of females [34]. However, no gender differences were seen in the present study as in previous research in the COVID-19 pandemic [35].

According to oral health profile, females showed significantly higher values for daily tooth brushing, dry mouth, and gastritis than males. This high frequency in daily tooth brushing is consequent with previous research and may be related to the higher values of neuroticism and conscientiousness shown by females [36]. However, no significant relationships have been found between toothbrushing and psychological factors [37]. In the same way, dry mouth or lack of saliva has also been related to increased stress perception and the somatization of anxiety and depression, conforming to a psych emotional profile and stress perception of the analyzed female sample. Thus, a relationship was found between stress and oral health, where females tended to suffer more than males despite the high frequency of brushing, which coincides with the literature found in other groups such as teachers [38].

Regarding the physical activity profile, no gender differences were found, which is in line with previous literature among university students [39]. Yet, values or physical exercise were still down considering the minimum requirements of daily/weekly physical exercise, which is in line with data found in gender and university students in previous research [40,41]. Indeed, authors have suggested that students who do not engage in physical exercise or sport present greater stress reactions [42]. Yet, authors have suggested that younger students present better performance in physical exercise, academics, and work, demonstrating a good lifestyle compared to older students [43].

The multifactorial analysis of factors related to the perception of risk level of COVID-19 may be a useful tool to measure the associated stress in university students to explain and prevent the psychological consequences of the COVID-19 pandemic. In addition, the use of questionnaires allows significant information to be collected in a short period of time. Knowledge of these related factors could be used by various educational institutions to implement multidisciplinary interventions to reduce this perception and, thus, students' stress in the face of the virus. The present research also presents some limitations, with the main limitation being the lack of biological measurement due to COVID-19 and the impossibility of measuring stress hormones (cortisol, adrenaline, alpha amylase …). Other limitations were that anthropometrical data were self-declared, which may lead to a serious risk of bias. However, since this was an online questionnaire, no other further methods of evaluations were possible. Future studies may address this issue. As a future research line, we propose analyzing the influence of cultural differences in the levels of perceived danger from the COVID-19 virus. In addition, this study could be extended to other degrees, as well as to other educational levels such as primary and secondary school.

5. Conclusions

We can conclude that female university students presented higher levels of perceived danger from the COVID-19 virus than male university students. Males showed higher levels of extraversion than females, but females showed higher levels of conscientiousness, neuroticism, and openness to experience. Females showed higher levels of perceived anxiety than males. Regarding the nutritional profile, males showed a higher frequency of consumption of soft drinks, meat, pasta, or rice. Regarding oral health, females showed a higher number of times they brushed their teeth, as well as a higher frequency of dry mouth or lack of saliva. In the physical activity profile, no significant results were found in either gender.

The multifactorial analysis of factors related to the perception of the level of danger to COVID-19 may be a useful tool to measure the associated stress in university students to explain and prevent the psychological consequences of the COVID-19 pandemic. In addition, the use of questionnaires allows significant information to be collected in a short period of time. Awareness of these related factors could be used by various educational institutions to implement multidisciplinary interventions to reduce this perception and, thus, students' stress in response to the virus.

Author Contributions: Conceptualization, V.J.C.-S. and J.F.T.-A.; methodology, J.F.-L.; software, J.F.-L. and S.R.-B.; validation, S.R.-B., J.F.T.-A., J.F.-L., V.J.C.-S.; formal analysis, V.J.C.-S. and S.R.-B.; investigation, V.J.C.-S., J.F.-L. and S.R.-B.; writing—S.R.-B., J.F.T.-A., J.F.-L., V.J.C.-S. All authors have read and agreed to the published version of the manuscript.

Funding: This research received no external funding.

Institutional Review Board Statement: The study was conducted according to the guidelines of the Declaration of Helsinki, and approved by the European University Ethics Committee (CIPI/18/074).

Informed Consent Statement: Informed consent was obtained from all subjects involved in the study.

Data Availability Statement: All data are presented in the manuscript.

Conflicts of Interest: The authors declare no conflict of interest.

References

1. WHO—World Health Organization. *Coronavirus Disease (COVID-19) Dashboard*; WHO: Cham, Switzerland, 2020.
2. Torres, R.; Fernández, M.J. La política económica española y el COVID-19. *Funcas Cuad. Inf. Económica* **2020**, *275*, 1–7.
3. Secretaría General de Universidades. *Datos y Cifras del Sistema Universitario Español*; Publicación 2018–2019; Secretaría General Técnica del Ministerio de Ciencia, Innovación y Universidad: Madrid, Spain, 2019; pp. 10–13.
4. Díaz, A.L.; Prados, J.S.F.; Canos, V.F.; Martínez, A.M.M. Impactos del confinamiento por el COVID-19 entre universitarios: Satisfacción Vital, Resiliencia y Capital Social Online. *RISE* **2020**, *9*, 79–104. [CrossRef]
5. Hou, F.; Bi, F.; Jiao, R.; Luo, D.; Song, K. Gender differences of depression and anxiety among social media users during the COVID-19 outbreak in China: A cross-sectional study. *BMC Public Health* **2020**. [CrossRef] [PubMed]
6. Spagnolo, P.A.; Manson, J.E.; Joffe, H. Sex and Gender Differences in Health: What the COVID-19 Pandemic Can Teach Us. *Ann. Intern. Med.* **2020**, *173*, 385–386. [CrossRef] [PubMed]
7. Liu, N.; Zhang, F.; Wei, C.; Jia, Y.; Shang, Z.; Sun, L.; Liu, W.; Wu, L.; Sun, Z.; Zhou, Y.; et al. Prevalence and predictors of PTSS during COVID-19 outbreak in China hardest-hit areas: Gender differences matter. *Psychiatry Res.* **2020**, *287*, 112921. [CrossRef] [PubMed]
8. Galasso, V.; Pons, V.; Profeta, P.; Becher, M.; Brouard, S.; Foucault, M. Gender differences in COVID-19 related attitudes and behavior: Evidence from a panel survey in eight OECD countries. *Proc. Natl. Acad. Sci. USA* **2020**, *117*, 27285–27291. [CrossRef] [PubMed]
9. Garikipati, S.; Kambhampati, U. *Women Leaders are Better Fighting at the Pandemic*; Vox Eu: London, UK, 2020.
10. Cobo-Rendón, R.; Vega-Valenzuela, A.; García-Álvarez, D. Consideraciones institucionales sobre la Salud Mental en estudiantes universitarios durante la pandemia de COVID-19. *CienciAmérica* **2020**, *9*, 277–284. [CrossRef]
11. Odriozola-González, P.; Planchuelo-Gómez, Á.; Irurtia, M.J.; de Luis-García, R. Psychological effects of the COVID-19 outbreak and lockdown among students and workers of a Spanish university. *Psychiatry Res.* **2020**, *290*, 113108. [CrossRef]
12. Gao, W.; Ping, S.; Liu, X. Gender differences in depression, anxiety, and stress among college students: A longitudinal study from China. *J. Affect. Disord.* **2020**, *263*, 292–300. [CrossRef]
13. Belinchón-deMiguel, P.; Tornero-Aguilera, J.F.; Dalamitros, A.A.; Nikolaidis, P.T.; Rosemann, T.; Knechtle, B.; Clemaleste-Suárez, V.J. Multidisciplinary analysis of differences between finisher and non-finisher ultra-endurance mountain athletes. *Front. Physiol.* **2020**, *10*, 1507. [CrossRef]
14. Sharkey, T.; Whatnall, M.C.; Hutchesson, M.J.; Haslam, R.L.; Bezzina, A.; Collins, C.E.; Ashton, L.M. Effectiveness of gender-targeted versus gender-neutral interventions aimed at improving dietary intake, physical activity and/or overweight/obesity in young adults (aged 17–35 years): A systematic review and meta-analysis. *Nutr. J.* **2020**, *19*, 1–20. [CrossRef]
15. Soh, N.L.; Walter, G.; Baur, L.; Collins, C. Nutrition, mood and behaviour: A review. *Acta Neuropsychiatr.* **2009**, *21*, 214–227. [CrossRef] [PubMed]
16. Clemente-Suárez, V.J.; Dalamitros, A.A.; Beltran-Velasco, A.I.; Mielgo-Ayuso, J.; Tornero-Aguilera, J.F. Social and psychophysiological consequences of the COVID-19 pandemic: An extensive literature review. *Front. Psychol.* **2020**, *11*, 3077. [CrossRef] [PubMed]

17. Práxedes, A.; Moreno, A.; Sevil, J.; Del Villar, F.; García-González, L. Niveles de Actividad Física en Estudiantes Universitarios: Diferencias en Función del Género, la Edad y los Estados de Cambio. In *Revista Iberoamericana De Psicología Del Ejercicio Y Ei Deporte*; 2016; Volume 11, pp. 123–132. Available online: https://www.redalyc.org/pdf/3111/311143051014.pdf (accessed on 7 April 2021).
18. Lores, A.P.; Murcia, J.A.M. Actitud de los universitarios ante la práctica físico-deportiva: Diferencias por géneros. *Rev. Psicol. Deporte* **2008**, *17*, 7–23.
19. Rammstedt, B.; John, O.P. Measuring personality in one minute or less: A 10-item short version of the Big Five Inventory in English and German. *J. Res. Personal.* **2007**, *41*, 203–212. [CrossRef]
20. Van Knippenberg, F.C.E.; Duivenvoorden, H.J.; Bonke, B.; Passchier, J. Shortening the state-trait anxiety inventory. *J. Clin. Epidemiol.* **1990**, *43*, 995–1000. [CrossRef]
21. Bond, F.W.; Hayes, S.C.; Baer, R.A.; Carpenter, K.M.; Guenole, N.; Orcutt, H.K.; Waltz, T.; Zettle, R.D. Preliminary psychometric properties of the Acceptance and Action Questionnaire–II: A revised measure of psychological inflexibility and experiential avoidance. *Behav. Ther.* **2011**, *42*, 676–688. [CrossRef]
22. Russell, D.W. UCLA Loneliness Scale (Version 3): Reliability, validity, and factor structure. *J. Personal. Assess.* **1996**, *66*, 20–40. [CrossRef]
23. Zung, W.W. A self-rating depression scale. *Arch. Gen. Psychiatry* **1965**, *12*, 63–70. [CrossRef] [PubMed]
24. Sandín, B.; Valiente, R.M.; García-Escalera, J.; Chorot, P. Impacto psicológico de la pandemia de COVID-19: Efectos negativos y positivos en población española asociados al periodo de confinamiento nacional. *Rev. Psicopatología Psicol. Clínica* **2020**, *25*. [CrossRef]
25. Matud, M.P. Gender differences in stress and coping styles. *Personal. Individ. Differ.* **2004**, *37*, 1401–1415. [CrossRef]
26. Pine, D.S.; Mogg, K.; Bradley, B.P.; Montgomery, L.; Monk, C.S.; McClure, E.; Guyer, A.; Ernst, M.; Charney, D.; Kaufman, J. Attention bias to threat in maltreated children: Implications for vulnerability to stress-related psychopathology. *Am. J. Psychiatry* **2005**, *162*, 291–296. [CrossRef] [PubMed]
27. Cabanach, R.G.; Fariña, F.; Freire, C.; González, P.; del Mar Ferradás, M. Diferencias en el afrontamiento del estrés en estudiantes universitarios hombres y mujeres. *Eur. J. Educ. Psychol.* **2015**, *6*. [CrossRef]
28. Pacheco, N.; Durán, A.; Rey, L. Inteligencia emocional y su relación con los niveles de burnout, engagement y estrés en estudiantes universitarios. *Rev. Educ.* **2007**, *342*, 239–256.
29. Redondo-Flórez, L.; Tornero-Aguilera, J.F.; Ramos-Campo, D.J.; Clemente-Suárez, V.J. Gender Differences in Stress-and Burnout-Related Factors of University Professors. *Biomed. Res. Int.* **2020**, *2020*. [CrossRef]
30. Castañeiras, C.; Posada, M.C. Estilos de personalidad y su relación con medidas de ansiedad y depresión: Datos normativos para el Inventario MIPS en adultos marplatenses. *Rev. Iberoam. Diagnóstico Evaluación-Avaliação Psicológica* **2006**, *1*, 127–147.
31. Baker, A.H.; Wardle, J. Sex differences in fruit and vegetable intake in older adults. *Appetite* **2003**, *40*, 269–275. [CrossRef]
32. Varì, R.; Scazzocchio, B.; Del Papa, S. Dietary habits and gender differences. *Ital. J. Gend. Specif. Med.* **2017**, *3*, 55–58.
33. Barzegari, A.; Ebrahimi, M.; Azizi, M.; Ranjbar, K. A study of nutrition knowledge, attitudes and food habits of college students. *World Appl. Sci. J.* **2011**, *15*, 1012–1017.
34. Yahia, N.; Wang, D.; Rapley, M.; Dey, R. Assessment of weight status, dietary habits and beliefs, physical activity, and nutritional knowledge among university students. *Perspect. Public Health* **2016**, *136*, 231–244. [CrossRef]
35. Moreno, C.O.S.; Lomelí, D.G.; Valencia, D.G.G. Actividad física y hábitos alimenticios en universitarios durante la pandemia por COVID-19. In *Memorias de Extenso*; Modalidad Virtual; University of Sonora: Sonora, Mexico, 2020.
36. Tachalov, V.V.; Orekhova, L.Y.; Kudryavtseva, T.V.; Isaeva, E.R.; Loboda, E.S. Manifestations of personal characteristics in individual oral care. *EPMA J.* **2016**, *7*, 1–5. [CrossRef] [PubMed]
37. Alkan, A.; Cakmak, O.; Yilmaz, S.; Cebi, T.; Gurgan, C. Relationship between psychological factors and oral health status and behaviours. *Oral Health Prev. Dent.* **2015**, *13*, 331–339. [CrossRef] [PubMed]
38. Redondo-Flórez, L.; Fernández-Lucas, J.; Clemente-Suárez, V.J. Cultural differences in stress-related psychological, nutrition, physical activity and oral health factors of professors. *Nutrients* **2020**, *12*, 3644. [CrossRef] [PubMed]
39. Von Bothmer, M.I.; Fridlund, B. Gender differences in health habits and in motivation for a healthy lifestyle among Swedish university students. *Nurs. Health Sci.* **2005**, *7*, 107–118. [CrossRef] [PubMed]
40. Clemente, F.M.; Nikolaidis, P.T.; Martins, F.M.L.; Mendes, R.S. Physical activity patterns in university students: Do they follow the public health guidelines? *PLoS ONE* **2016**, *11*, e0152516. [CrossRef] [PubMed]
41. Bebetsos, E.; Antoniou, P. University students' differences on attitudes towards computer use. Comparison with students' attitudes towards physical activity. *Interact. Educ. Multimed.* **2008**, *17*, 20–28.
42. Valenzuela, M.C.S.; Gallegos, L.I.F.; Baca, L.R.L.; López, H.L.M.; Rico, F.J.F. Estrés académico en universitarios y la práctica de ejercicio físico-deportivo. *Rev. Publicando* **2021**, *8*, 1–8. [CrossRef]
43. Goenaga, A.N.M.; Marín, A.R. Factores asociados a los estilos de vida en los estudiantes universitarios. Una aplicación del instrumento fantástico. *Rev. Digit. Act. Física Deporte* **2020**, *6*, 87–108.

International Journal of
Environmental Research and Public Health

MDPI

Article

Information and Communications Technology (ICT) Usage during COVID-19: Motivating Factors and Implications

Yi-Ching Lee [1,*], Lindsey A. Malcein [1] and Sojung Claire Kim [2]

1 Department of Psychology, George Mason University, 4400 University Drive, Fairfax, VA 22030, USA; lmalcein@masonlive.gmu.edu
2 Department of Communication, George Mason University, 4400 University Drive, Fairfax, VA 22030, USA; skim205@gmu.edu
* Correspondence: YLEE65@gmu.edu; Tel.: +1-703-993-6216

Abstract: This study was designed to investigate the roles information and communications technology (ICT) played during the current COVID-19 pandemic. Specifically, we focused on the relationships between ICT use and perceived importance of social connectedness and future anxiety, while considering relevant personality and psychosocial factors. A U.S. sample of 394 adults answered questions about ICT use, pandemic-related reactions and actions, demographics, and psychosocial factors via an online survey. Using logistic regression, findings indicated that personality (extraversion and conscientiousness) and psychosocial (need to belong and perceived attachment to phone) factors, types of ICT as news source, and gender were associated with perceived importance of social connectedness. Neuroticism, time spent on ICT for social purposes, and perceived threat of COVID-19 were associated with future anxiety. In addition, using Mann–Whitney U test, people who rated higher on importance of social connectedness had higher ICT use, both in terms of types and time spent on ICT. Overall, results are consistent with the idea that technology is a coping tool during the pandemic and balanced use can lead to feelings of social connectedness and less future anxiety. Therefore, it is important for authorities to align their messaging and outreach with people's psychosocial, personality, and health considerations through ICT channels while empowering ICT users to be responsible for their interactions with the technology.

Keywords: Information and Communications Technology (ICT); COVID-19; social connectedness; future anxiety; social media; technology and society

Citation: Lee, Y.-C.; Malcein, L.A.; Kim, S.C. Information and Communications Technology (ICT) Usage during COVID-19: Motivating Factors and Implications. *Int. J. Environ. Res. Public Health* **2021**, *18*, 3571. https://doi.org/10.3390/ijerph18073571

Academic Editors: Paolo Roma, Merylin Monaro and Cristina Mazza

Received: 1 February 2021
Accepted: 25 March 2021
Published: 30 March 2021

1. Introduction

In early January of 2020 the World Health Organization (WHO) reported that an outbreak of pneumonia-like cases in Wuhan, China, had been determined to be caused by a novel coronavirus. With evidence of human-to-human transmission, the virus started to spread and many nations across the globe started to report their own cases. On January 30th the WHO declared the coronavirus outbreak a Public Health Emergency of International Concern, and on February 3rd, the United States (U.S.) declared a Public Health Emergency due to the outbreak. The disease caused by the novel coronavirus was officially named COVID-19 on February 11th. On March 11th WHO declared COVID-19 a Pandemic [1], and two days later the U.S. declared COVID-19 a National Emergency. As a way to slow the spread of transmission, most countries around the world implemented social distancing, quarantine, and lockdown guidelines. Due to these health and safety measures, global citizens faced unprecedented changes to their daily routines, including stay-at-home orders, travel bans, and closures of educational institutions and entertainment-related locales.

One change affecting many people was in their use of Information and Communications Technology (ICT). ICTs are broadly defined as products that can digitally store, retrieve, manipulate, transmit, or receive information, such as personal computers, televisions, telephones, email systems, robotic and smart devices, and other internet-enabled systems, including traditional media and social media [2–4]. For example, with regard to television use, during the week of March 16th of 2020, viewership of the four largest broadcasts networks in the U.S. increased nearly 19% compared to the same week during 2019. In terms of news consumption during the week of March 16th, viewership of cable news networks increased 73% from 2019 to 2020 and increased 40% compared to the week of February 17th of 2020. During the week of March 16th, number of digital visits to news websites in the U.S. increased by 68% and the number of digital visits to government sources (e.g., WHO) increased by 299% compared to the week of February 17th [5]. In regard to cell phone usage, data collected in May 2020 from the U.S. suggested that people have become more dependent on their phone service: 37% increase in texting, 36% increase in social media, 23% increase in the use of shopping apps, and 32% increase in video calling [6]. Similarly, Zoom, Google Classroom, and Microsoft Teams have documented increased use of video calling during the first half of March [7]. Mobile, contactless payments and online food ordering have also seen increased use in tandem with social distancing measures [8,9].

Empirical studies have also reported an increasing trend of ICT use and higher risk of excessive internet use during COVID-19 quarantine or lockdown [10]. The increased use of ICT can ultimately be associated with various physical, psychosocial, and mental health outcomes [11,12]. This increased use may be driven by disrupted daily routine, need for telework and online schooling, anxiety due to uncertainty about the future, and need for entertainment, news, and social connectedness. Individual differences such as personality traits may also affect feelings about and responses to COVID-19 safety measures and social connectedness. This paper aimed to investigate the relationships among ICT use, social connectedness, and feelings about the pandemic. Relevant literature related to the connection between ICT use and COVID-19 as well as the associated feelings about social connectedness and the future will be reviewed in the next section.

2. Literature Review

2.1. ICT Use during the Pandemic

Engagement with ICT during the COVID-19 pandemic has received mixed reporting. On the one hand, ICT facilitates the dissemination of information and facts about the disease while allowing people to access and search for related updates [13]. Given the evolving nature of the pandemic, the practical challenge is how to best transfer and deliver the latest information efficiently. Traditional methods of dissemination and communication, such as static websites and even email are considered slower than the use of news media and social media [14]. For example, the use of educational materials and infographics via social media has been viewed as a speedier way of information dissemination compared to traditional methods [13,15]. Additionally, large scale working from home and online schooling has become possible due to the use of ICT and other internet-enabled technologies [16–18]. Similarly, telehealth services can provide feasible on-going or new treatment options via online means during the pandemic [19,20]. Staying socially connected with families and friends and having access to virtual physical exercise materials and entertainment during stay-at-home orders are realized through ICT [20,21], as these strategies are recommended for mental health by the WHO [22].

However, the use of ICT can also be problematic. Among children and university students, excessive screen time and limited outdoor activities during the pandemic have potential worrisome outcomes in relation to myopia [23], sedentary behaviors [24], disrupted sleep routines [25], and reduced physical activity [26], just to name a few. Adults also report worse depression, loneliness, and stress being associated with increased screen time and reduced physical activity [27]. These lifestyle changes during the pandemic have been linked to poor mental health [27], thus confirming the established association between excessive screen time and negative mental health outcomes from pre-pandemic times [28,29]. Another downside of ICT use is related to the lack of in-person social interactions. Even for people who do not live alone, they may still feel lonely if their contact with others, such as through the means of ICT during quarantines, does not provide a sufficient sense of social connectedness [30]. In addition, with the amount of information about COVID-19 that is available through various ICT channels, some people have expressed feelings of information overload and fatigue [31,32], while, at the same time, having feelings of anxiety and uncertainty about the future and especially about how the pandemic will end [33].

2.2. Social Connectedness during the Pandemic

One consequence of COVID-19 and the associated social-distancing measures has been accompanied by psychosocial implications, including increased risk of social isolation and loneliness [30]. Social isolation—the objective lack of interactions with others or the wider community [34]—even as short as 10 days, can have negative long-term effects three years later [35]. Loneliness—the subjective feeling of the lack of social networks or companions [34]—can be triggered by social isolation, or vice versa [36]. Prolonged social isolation and feelings of loneliness, characterized by reduced social connections and contact, have been linked to reduced psychological and physiological functioning and increased morbidity and mortality [37,38]. Therefore, public health agencies and clinicians emphasize the importance of maintaining social contact during this pandemic for the purpose of improving feelings of social connectedness and decreasing loneliness [30].

Psychoactive substance use and other reinforcing behaviors such as video gaming, TV watching, using social media, gambling, and surfing the internet are often used to reduce anxiety and depression [10], but increased ICT consumption can also lead to negative health outcomes, as have been observed during COVID-19 [27,39]. For example, one study investigated the impact of COVID-19 on online gambling during the week of April 21st, 2020 and found that individuals with higher levels of anxiety and depression were more likely to have gambled than individuals with no symptoms [40]. Among a sample of adolescents and young adults across several countries, COVID-related worries, compulsive internet use, social media use, and gaming addiction predicted scores of escapism, depression, and loneliness [41]. A study conducted during June 2020 found that college students had excessive use of social networking sites and lack of personal control to disengage themselves from those sites [42]; this tendency was also associated with the use of alcohol, tobacco, cannabis, and sedative without a doctor's prescription. Another study conducted in March and April 2020 in the U.S. suggested that exposure to COVID-19 information, via Twitter, Instagram, and Facebook, and increased alcohol use in March contributed to more frequent alcohol consumption in April, especially those working or studying from home [43]. These empirical studies suggest that even though ICT provides a means of social connection with one's social networks and the wider community, moderate and responsible use is important in maintaining a healthy approach to it.

Personality traits have also been linked to COVID-19 stress, coping, and concerns. Extraverts—compared to introverts—tend to have larger social network sizes [44] and these network connections can serve as a buffer during the pandemic [45]. Arguably, extraverts may suffer more due to COVID-19 travel bans and restrictions on social gatherings. An online study conducted in late March and early April 2020 across 47 countries investigated the associations among the level of stringency of safety measures, extraversion, and depression [46]: Results showed that, after controlling for country-level factors, introverts were doing better in terms of depressive symptoms when facing stringent social-distancing measures, but the stringent measures only had limited, non-significant effects on extraverts' depressive symptoms. Other aspects of personality traits were also examined: using an adult sample collected in late March 2020 from the U.S., individuals higher on neuroticism and lower on conscientiousness had more pandemic-related concerns, especially health-related concerns; however, individuals higher on neuroticism and extraversion had more relationship-related concerns [47]. Higher conscientiousness was associated with more precautious behaviors (such as hand washing) to avoid contracting COVID-19 but fewer preparatory behaviors (such as buying face masks). However, older individuals who were higher on conscientiousness had more preparatory behaviors. In terms of estimates of the pandemic duration, individuals higher on neuroticism had a more negative feeling about the pandemic (i.e., longer duration), but individuals higher on extraversion and conscientiousness had more optimistic estimates [47]. These findings shed some light on the associations between personality traits and behaviors related to COVID-19; however, other aspects of behavioral and psychosocial responses, such as social connectedness in the context of ICT use and its relation to personality, have not been widely explored.

ICT plays an important role in helping people adapt to restrictions on in-person gatherings. Many organizations in the public, private, and philanthropic sectors have developed messaging and outreach programs to specifically promote social connections and reduce loneliness via emails, websites, or smart phone applications. ICT serves as communication channels and social interaction media between sources of information and receivers. Although online interactions—both on the giving and the receiving ends—can foster a sense of connection, there is conflicting evidence about the role ICT plays in enhancing the feeling of social connectedness during the COVID-19 pandemic. This paper was designed to further investigate this open question.

2.3. Feelings About the Future during the Pandemic

At the time of writing, the pandemic is still ongoing and affecting people's lives holistically. While the prospect of a vaccine provides a sense of relief for some, there is still a lot of anxiety and uncertainty about when and how the pandemic is going to end and whether lives will return to the pre-pandemic normal. These feelings are not easy to tease apart, as they are deeply intertwined with the economic, societal, and psychological consequences of the pandemic [48].

These feelings are also related to the perceived threat of the pandemic. An online study conducted in June 2020 during a lockdown measure investigated the relationships among perceived threat of COVID-19, future anxiety, and subjective well-being [49]. Results indicated that perceived threat negatively predicted subjective well-being, and this relationship was mediated by anxious feelings about the future. Another online study conducted in early May 2020 investigated the relationships among personality traits, perceived stress during the pandemic, perceived threat of contracting COVID-19, and perceived efficacy to prevent COVID-19 [50]. Results showed that higher neuroticism was associated with higher levels of pandemic-related stress, and this relationship was mediated by perceived threat and efficacy. Similarly, higher extraversion was associated with higher pandemic-related stress.

There have also been studies that examined the effect of media exposure on COVID-related fear and worries. An online study conducted in mid-March 2020 investigated the relationships among fear of COVID-19, intolerance of uncertainty, worry, anxiety, personal relevance of the threat, and media exposure (sources of COVID-19 information); results indicated that media exposure through regular and social media, tendency to worry about health, and risk for loved ones predicted increased fear of COVID-19 [51]. Another study conducted in early April 2020 had participants recall their media sources (i.e., government, commercial, foreign, and social media) from late January to February during the pandemic in China while responding to questions about media traumatization and anxiety due to the pandemic. Most of the survey respondents spent 1-3 h per day watching or hearing COVID-19 information and repeated media exposure led to higher levels of anxiety as well as media traumatization [52]. These findings suggest that the subjective feelings about the pandemic, such as anxiety, may be influenced by a number of psychosocial factors, personality traits, and media exposure. This paper was designed to further investigate the influence of media types for news information or social purposes on subjective feelings about the pandemic.

2.4. Study Objectives

Based on the past literature, this paper focused on two consequences of ICT use during the pandemic: social connectedness and feelings about the future. Specifically, we explored how ICT use, behavioral and psychosocial responses during the pandemic, personality traits, and demographic factors influenced perceived importance of social connectedness and perceived future anxiety.

3. Materials and Methods

An online, anonymous survey was used for this work. This study received the Institution Review Board approval from the authors' university. This survey was posted on Mechanical Turk during the afternoon of April 21st and the morning of April 22nd, 2020; during this time, 42 states and territories in the U.S. had issued mandatory stay-at-home orders [53].

3.1. Participants

Individuals who were Amazon Mechanical Turk workers and held the status of a Master [54] (workers who have demonstrated high performance over time and meet the performance requirements put forth by Mechanical Turk) were invited to participate. Other inclusion criteria included being an adult (18 years of age or older) and residing in the U.S. A total of 402 participants completed the survey and received the compensation of USD 7. Eight of them provided at least one invalid answer to the three attention check questions (e.g., answering 1978 when the survey asked for the current year, answering February when the survey asked for the current month) and were removed from the dataset; therefore, the final sample size was 394.

3.2. Procedure

Individuals who chose to take part would first read the consent page and must agree to the requirement of completing the entire survey. Once they indicated consent, they read the instructions as well as the definitions of the terminology (e.g., ICT) used in the survey. The instructions also emphasized that there were no right or wrong answers and that participants were asked to answer the survey questions honestly. Participants saw one question at a time and were encouraged to answer all the questions, although they could skip questions if they chose to. At the end of the survey, participants were encouraged to leave comments and feedback about the survey and report any technical issues during the study. On average, participants took 16 min to complete the survey.

3.3. Key Measures

The survey was programed in Qualtrics software (see Supplementary Materials for the survey items). About half of the items were previously validated psychosocial scales: The Need to Belong Scale [55], the Fear of Missing Out Scale [56], Perceived Attachment to Phone Scale [57], Habitual Smartphone/Internet Behavior Scale [58,59], the Self Regulation Scale [60], the Boredom Proneness Scale [61,62], and the Abbreviated version of the Big Five Inventory [63]. The rest of the survey items were developed by the authors and are detailed below.

3.3.1. Information and Communications Technology (ICT)

There were 6 questions about the ICT. ICT was defined as "the integration of telecommunications and computers as well as necessary software, hardware, and audiovisual systems that enable users to access, store, transmit, and manipulate information and to communicate in a digital form." These questions were about (1) overall ICT devices used on a daily basis, (2) time spent using ICTs for obtaining news on a daily basis, and (3) the sources for obtaining news on a daily basis (e.g., news channels, radio, etc.). These questions were presented twice—for participants to indicate their answers from two time periods: before the pandemic and during the pandemic.

3.3.2. Reactions Related to the Pandemic

There were 3 questions about the reactions related to the pandemic. One question asked participants to rate their feeling after reading or hearing the news about the pandemic. A second question asked whether the participants considered the current pandemic situation a threat to their health and safety. Another question asked whether they think the news conveyed the current pandemic situation correctly.

3.3.3. Actions Related to the Pandemic

There were 4 questions about the actions that have been taken as the result of the pandemic. Two questions asked whether participants took actions about the pandemic and what the actions were (e.g., social distancing). Another set of questions asked for the time spent on applications (e.g., social media, email, etc.) for the purpose of staying connected with their social network as well as the importance of staying connected with friends, family, and social networks.

3.3.4. Demographic Questionnaire

There were 8 questions. These items asked for participants' age, gender, residence, state of residence, race and ethnicity, education, income, and employment status.

3.3.5. Attention Check Questions

Three attention check questions were included in the survey. They were added to help identify inattentive participants and to provide progress status, as they appeared after each quarter (1/4, 1/2, and 3/4) in the survey.

3.4. Analytic Strategy

A few additional variables were calculated to answer the proposed research questions: (1) Types of ICT devices used on a daily basis: participants could check all that apply from 11 options (e.g., Computer for non-internet use, Computer for internet use, Cable TV, etc.) and write in additional items. These types were then added to reflect the overall total types of devices used. These steps were used for the before and during pandemic periods. (2) Types of ICT as news sources about what is happening on a daily basis: participants could check all that apply from 8 options (e.g., Social media, TV news channels, Radio, etc.) and write in additional items. These types were then added to reflect the overall total types of sources. These steps were used for the before and during pandemic periods. (3) Average hours spent on using applications and systems for the purpose of staying connected with social networks on a daily basis: participants used a sliding bar to indicate the hours for social media, telecommunication, and email and had the options to write in two additional items and then indicate the hours. These hours were then averaged across the items to reflect the average hours spent daily for virtually staying connected with social networks.

To answer our first research question, a logistic regression was used to model the relationship between the perceived importance of social connectedness (low vs. high) and the psychosocial, ICT use, and demographic variables. To answer our second research question, a logistic regression was used to model the relationship between participants' feeling about the future (positive vs. negative) and the psychosocial, ICT use, and demographic variables.

A non-parametric Mann–Whitney U test was used to compare the distributions of responses due to the non-normality of our data distribution. Correlations of the variables were checked and there was no evidence of multicollinearity (all the Spearman correlation coefficients were smaller than 0.6). SPSS version 26 was used for the analyses.

4. Results

4.1. Sample Characteristics

The sample consisted of 219 men and 175 women in the U.S., with ages ranging from 20 to 76 and the average being 40.89 (SD = 11.21) years. The participants came from all of the states, except Alaska, Arkansas, North Dakota, South Dakota, and Vermont. In terms of primary residence, 190 indicated suburban areas, 125 indicated urban areas, 77 indicated rural areas, and 2 chose other. The majority of the participants identified their race and ethnicity as White (n = 307) (61 as Asian, 20 as Black, 12 as Hispanic/Latino/Spanish origin, 11 as American Indian/Alaska Native, 1 as Native Hawaiian/Other Pacific Islander, and 2 as Other). As for education level, most of participants reported having a college degree (n = 219), followed by having some college (n = 70), having a graduate degree (n = 56), having a high school diploma (n = 47), and having some high school education (n = 2). The annual household income item included five options: most of participants selected the 45 K–70 K (n = 115) and 25 K–45 K (n = 105) options, followed by the 70 K–110 K option (n = 69), <25 K option (n = 62), and >110K option (n = 43). Most of them currently had a full-time job (n = 258) (22 worked part-time, 82 were self-employed, 3 were a student, 27 were unemployed). The statistics of the psychosocial scales are listed in Table 1.

Table 1. Statistics of the psychosocial scales.

Scales	Mean	SD	Cronbach's Alpha
Need to belong	26.77	7.93	0.88
Fear of missing out	20.28	8.18	0.91
Perceived attachment to phones	15.80	5.51	0.87
Habitual smartphone/internet behavior—Smartphone	27.45	7.39	0.95
Habitual smartphone/internet behavior—Internet	31.96	3.52	0.80
Self regulation	31.06	6.03	0.90
Boredom proneness—Lack of internal stimulation	30.95	6.01	0.81
Boredom proneness—Lack of external stimulation	20.12	7.20	0.81
Abbreviated version of the big five—Extraversion	5.49	2.49	0.76
Abbreviated version of the big five—Agreeableness	11.23	2.73	0.67
Abbreviated version of the big five—Conscientiousness	8.17	1.83	0.63
Abbreviated version of the big five—Neuroticism	4.86	2.36	0.79
Abbreviated version of the big five—Openness	7.47	2.06	0.60

Almost all of the participants (n = 391) indicated that they actively took actions about the current pandemic situation (e.g., social distancing, working from home, etc.). The majority of them thought that the news correctly conveyed the current pandemic situation (n = 308) and that the current pandemic situation was a threat to their health and safety (n = 315). Slightly less than half of the participants rated their feeling about the pandemic upon reading the news as "Positive—it's going to be ok" (n = 181), while the rest felt "Negative—it's not going to be ok."

4.2. *Importance of Social Connectedness*

In answering our first research question, one survey item asked about the importance of staying connected with friends, family members, and social networks. Participants rated from not at all important to extremely important. Given the uneven distribution of the rated responses (see Figure 1), this variable was dichotomized to reflect two levels of importance: low (combined from "not at all important," "slightly important," and "moderately important") and high (combined from "very important" and "extremely important") importance, having n = 192 and 202, respectively, in each level. Using this dichotomized importance as the grouping variable, Mann–Whitney U test suggested that types of ICT devices used and types of ICT as news source were higher in the high-importance group for both before and during pandemic periods. Hours spent on ICTs for obtaining news before the pandemic were not different between the low-and high-importance groups; however, hours were higher in the high-importance group during the pandemic (see Table 2).

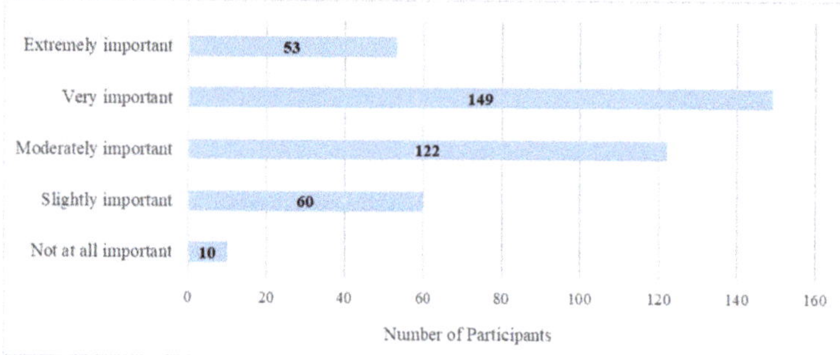

Figure 1. Response distributions for the importance of the social connectedness variable.

Table 2. Comparison of information and communications technology (ICT) use variables between low- and high-importance groups.

	Low-Importance: Mean (SD)	High-Importance: Mean (SD)	U Test	Sig.
Type of ICT use—before pandemic	4.51 (1.67)	4.96 (1.56)	16507	<0.01
Type of ICT use—during pandemic	4.59 (1.68)	5.09 (1.52)	16207	<0.01
Type of ICT as news source—before pandemic	2.43 (1.24)	3.14 (1.53)	14334	<0.001
Type of ICT as news source—during pandemic	3.04 (1.49)	3.99 (1.73)	13352	<0.001
Hours of ICT—before pandemic	2.81 (3.45)	3.12 (3.70)	18414	0.37
Hours of ICT—during pandemic	4.52 (4.10)	5.40 (4.31)	16285	<0.01

Subsequently, a logistic regression was used to model the relationship between the perceived importance of social connectedness (low vs. high) and the psychosocial, ICT use, and demographic variables. These variables were entered in three blocks, with block 1 consisting of psychosocial variables, block 2 consisting of ICT use variables, and block 3 consisting of demographic variables. Insignificant variables were removed with each iteration. The final model had a Nagelkerke R of 0.36 and a Hosmer and Lemeshow Test of χ^2 (8, N = 394) = 11.55, p = 0.17, indicating a good fit to the data. The classification accuracy was 68.80% for predicting low-importance and 76.70% for predicting high-importance, with the overall accuracy being 72.80%. Table 3 shows the logistic regression coefficient, Wald test, and odds ratio for each of the predictors for the importance of the social connectedness variable. Employing a 0.05 criterion of statistical significance, ratings of extraversion, conscientiousness, need to belong, and perceived attachment to phone, types of ICT as news source, and gender had significant partial effects. For each one-point increase on the five-point extraversion and conscientiousness scales there were odds of higher rating of importance of social connectedness by a multiplicative factor of 1.34, and 1.47, respectively. Similarly, for each one-point increase on the five-point need to belong and perceived attachment to phones scales there were odds of higher rating by a multiplicative factor of 1.11 and 1.33, respectively. For each one additional type of ICT that was used for obtaining news there were odds of higher rating by a factor of 1.31. As for the gender variable (women coded as one), women were 2.17 times more likely than men to report higher rating on importance of social connectedness.

Table 3. Significant predictors for the perceived importance of social connectedness variable (n = 394).

Variables	B	Wald	Sig.	Odds Ratio
Extraversion	0.31	9.24	<0.01	1.36
Conscientiousness	0.38	7.24	<0.01	1.47
Need to belong scale	0.11	33.33	<0.001	1.11
Perceived attachment to phones scale	0.29	5.98	0.02	1.33
Type of ICT as news source	0.27	12.75	<0.001	1.31
Gender	0.78	10.40	<0.001	2.17

4.3. Feelings about the Future

In answering our second research question, one survey item asked participants to rate their feelings (positive vs. negative) upon reading about the current pandemic situation. Using this as the grouping variable, the Mann–Whitney U test suggested that types of ICT devices used, types of ICT as news source, and hours spent on ICTs for obtaining news were about the same in both feeling groups before and during the pandemic periods.

The same modeling approach was used to develop a logistic regression model to predict the feelings (negative feeling coded as one) about the pandemic. The final model had a Nagelkerke R of 0.21 and a Hosmer and Lemeshow Test of χ^2 (8, N = 392) = 3.21, p = 0.92, indicating good fit to the data. The classification accuracy was 82.10% for predicting the negative feeling and 50.60% for predicting the positive feeling, with the overall accuracy being 67.60%. Table 4 shows the logistic regression coefficient, Wald test, and odds ratio for each of the predictors for the feeling variable. Employing a 0.05 criterion of statistical significance, rating of neuroticism, hours spent on using virtual means for the purpose of staying socially connected with people, and viewing the pandemic situation as a threat had significant partial effects. For each one-point increase on the five-point neuroticism scale there were odds of feeling negatively by a multiplicative factor of 1.41. With one hour increase in using social media, emails, etc. to stay socially connected, participants were 1.10 times less likely to rate the feeling as negative. Participants who thought the current pandemic situation was a threat to their health and safety (yes coded as one) were 6.51 times more likely to rate their feeling about the pandemic negatively.

Table 4. Significant predictors for the feeling about the future variable (n = 392).

Variables	B	Wald	Sig.	Odds Ratio
Neuroticism	0.35	12.34	<0.001	1.41
Openness	−0.20	3.37	0.07	0.82
Hours spent on virtually staying connected	−0.09	5.32	0.02	0.91
Threat	1.87	35.65	<0.001	6.51

5. Discussion

This study was conducted in the early phase of the pandemic in the U.S. and was designed to examine the role ICT played—in terms of daily use for receiving news and staying in contact with social networks—in people's feelings about social connectedness and future anxiety while taking into account relevant personality and psychosocial factors. The results showed that the use of ICT was associated with a number of personality, health, and social factors.

Participants who rated higher on importance of social connectedness had higher ICT use, both in terms of types of ICT and time spent on ICT. This is consistent with the concept of using technology as a coping tool [30]. Social-distancing measures and stay-at-home orders took away many forms of communications and social interactions, but thanks to technology, some of them can be supplemented by ICT. Our findings also suggest that we need to have a balanced perspective on monitoring ICT use while allowing users to take advantage of the technology [10,20]. Using social media has been regarded as a negative practice as there is evidence of addiction and excessive usage [41,42]. However, when it is used for staying socially engaged and connected during COVID-19, our finding showed that people had less negative feelings about the future. Therefore, meaningful and responsible use of ICT during this pandemic, in particular social media and email, is likely to help people handle the anxiety and stress in the long run.

Prior empirical work suggests that feelings of social connectedness during COVID-19 stay-at-home orders is associated with reduced stress [30,64], and the WHO and other authorities have issued recommendations for enhancing positive feelings about being socially distanced from others [32]. Consistent with results from prior work, our findings showed that individuals higher on extraversion, belongingness, and attachment to one's phone rated staying socially connected to be more important [45,57,65]. Even though prior work did not study the relationship between conscientiousness and social connection in the context of ICT, individuals higher on conscientiousness tend to be more cautious about health-related behaviors (e.g., exercise more) [66] and take more precautions to avoid contracting COVID-19 [47]. We argue that this approach to health and safety translates to feelings about social networks that individuals higher on conscientiousness may value the importance of and take more active actions about staying connected with others compared to those lower on conscientiousness. In addition, individuals higher on neuroticism had more future anxiety, and this finding is consistent with prior research that neuroticism was associated with more concerns and longer duration estimates of the pandemic [47]. Similarly, individuals who thought the pandemic was a threat to their safety had more future anxiety, and this finding parallels prior work that perceived threat undermines mental well-being [49].

There have been mixed results about the association between gender and COVID-19-related feelings, stress, and actions. For example, women had more COVID-related worries than men but had about the same level of perceived stress and perceived chance of contracting COVID-19 with men [64]. When it comes to using social media to share information about COVID-19, women were 1.58 times more likely to do so than men [67]. Our finding suggests that women were 2.17 times more likely than men to report higher rating on the perceived importance of social connectedness, potentially explaining the reason for women's higher rate of sharing information on social media.

This study has a few limitations. Arguably, the level and form of human–ICT interaction may be different for each type of ICT [3]. For example, traditional media, such as television channels, may be used for information seeking purposes, whereas social media, such as Facebook, may be used for information seeking purposes as well as maintaining social connectedness. This variability may also differ from one user to another. The current paper broadly defined ICT as digital communication technology that allows users to interact and receive information and did not specify the application environment or users' prior experience with each ICT. We also did not consider multi-user interactions or devices, such as the case of video gaming applications. In the context of pandemic response, prior research has highlighted the benefits of using digital communication technologies for diagnostic efforts, risk communication practices, and coordination processes [4], and future research should examine the level and form of human–ICT interaction in each of the use categories.

Second, given the nature of data collection, some potential threats to external validity of the study are discussed. First of all, the sample might not be representative of the general U.S. public. The sample size was small and participants were recruited through Mechanical Turk, a crowdsourcing platform developed by Amazon. Walters and colleagues [68] have found that although MTurk workers were similar to the representative national sample, MTurk users tended to be younger, more likely to have a college degree, and less likely to report excellent health status. Additionally, the data were collected around the early phase of the COVID-19 pandemic. With new COVID-19 vaccines and related media, political and economic adjustments, the degree to which the study results will stay the same as the pandemic enters a more advanced stage remains an open question. In addition, only self-reported survey instruments were used; there might have been overreporting, underreporting, or social desirability bias, especially for socially sensitive questions [69]. Although indirect questioning was used to the extent possible (such as the phrasing of third-person wording, as opposed to first-person wording), some direct questioning was unavoidable. Future research should compare these wording differences in the context of a global pandemic and pandemic response in survey-based study design.

Despite the limitations of having a small sample size and the use of self-reported instruments, our findings contribute to the literature by highlighting the role ICTs play during the early phase of the pandemic: they are used for information seeking and social contact. These usage patterns are associated with various feelings about the pandemic. Therefore, it is important for authorities, clinicians, researchers, policy makers, and employers to align their messaging and outreach activities with people's psychosocial, personality, and health considerations through ICT channels while empowering ICT users to be responsible for their interactions with the technology [70].

6. Conclusions

This study was designed to examine the roles ICTs played during the early phase of the COVID-19 pandemic. Adults from a U.S. sample completed questions about their reactions, actions, feelings about the pandemic as well as their personality and psychosocial characteristics via an online survey. We argue that ICTs played multiple roles during the pandemic. Notably, ICTs are broadly defined in this study as the focus is on digital communication technology. Our results suggest that users interact with ICTs for the purposes of information seeking and staying socially connected with their families, friends, and social networks. These findings are in line with the idea that technology is used as a coping tool; however, as the society's reliance on technology increases during the pandemic and potentially post-pandemic, we need to constructively and mindfully leverage technology to improve our health and safety and reduce anxiety and stress. Users are to pay attention to their usage habits, and responsible interactions with ICT are critical in improving feelings of social connectedness while minimizing feelings of future anxiety.

Supplementary Materials: The following are available online at https://www.mdpi.com/article/10.3390/ijerph18073571/s1, File S1: A copy of the survey items.

Author Contributions: Conceptualization, Y.-C.L.; methodology, Y.-C.L.; formal analysis, Y.-C.L.; data curation, Y.-C.L. and L.A.M.; writing—original draft preparation, L.A.M., Y.-C.L. and S.C.K.; writing—review and editing, Y.-C.L. and S.C.K.; visualization, Y.-C.L. and L.A.M.; supervision, Y.-C.L. All authors have read and agreed to the published version of the manuscript.

Funding: This research received no external funding. Publication of this article was funded by the George Mason University Libraries Open Access Publishing Fund.

Institutional Review Board Statement: The study was conducted according to the guidelines of the Declaration of Helsinki, and approved by the Institutional Review Board of George Mason University (protocol # 1589810 on 14 April 2020).

Informed Consent Statement: Informed consent was obtained from all subjects involved in the study.

Data Availability Statement: The data presented in this study are available on request from the corresponding author. The data are not publicly available due to privacy considerations.

Conflicts of Interest: The authors declare no conflict of interest.

References

1. World Health Organization. Timeline: WHO's COVID-19 Response 2020. Available online: https://www.who.int/emergencies/diseases/novel-coronavirus-2019/interactive-timeline (accessed on 8 December 2020).
2. Ziemba, E. The contribution of ICT adoption to the sustainable information society. *J. Comput. Inf. Syst.* **2019**, *59*, 116–126. [CrossRef]
3. Baranyi, P.; Csapo, A.; Sallai, G. Definitions, concepts and assumptions. In *Cognitive Infocommunications (CogInfoCom)*; Baranyi, P., Csapo, A., Sallai, G., Eds.; Springer International Publishing: Cham, Switzerland, 2015; pp. 13–22. Available online: https://doi.org/10.1007/978-3-319-19608-4_2 (accessed on 23 March 2021).
4. Wilson, C.; Jumbert, M.G. The new informatics of pandemic response: Humanitarian technology, efficiency, and the subtle retreat of national agency. *J. Int. Humanit Action* **2018**, *3*, 8. [CrossRef]
5. Sarault, J. Understanding media consumption during the Coronavirus Pandemic. Comscore, Inc. 2020. Available online: https://www.comscore.com/Insights/Presentations-and-Whitepapers/2020/Understanding-Media-Consumption-During-the-Coronavirus-Pandemic (accessed on 8 December 2020).
6. Twigby.com. U.S. Study Finds COVID-19 Pandemic Transforms Cell Phone Usage. 2020. Available online: https://www.prnewswire.com/news-releases/us-study-finds-covid-19-pandemic-transforms-cell-phone-usage-301066502.html (accessed on 7 December 2020).

7. National Initiative for Cybersecurity Careers and Studies. The Evolution of Smartphones during a Global Pandemic. 2020. Available online: https://niccs.cisa.gov/about-niccs/featured-stories/evolution-smartphones-during-global-pandemic (accessed on 7 December 2020).
8. Walden, S. Banking after COVID-19: The Rise of Contactless Payments in the U.S. Forbes Advisor. 2020. Available online: https://www.forbes.com/advisor/banking/banking-after-covid-19-the-rise-of-contactless-payments-in-the-u-s/ (accessed on 7 December 2020).
9. DeGrasse, M. 4 Ways COVID-19 Is Changing Mobile Phone Usage. FierceWireless. 2020. Available online: https://www.fiercewireless.com/wireless/three-ways-covid-19-changing-mobile-phone-usage (accessed on 7 December 2020).
10. Király, O.; Potenza, M.N.; Stein, D.J.; King, D.L.; Hodgins, D.C.; Saunders, J.B.; Griffiths, M.D.; Gjoneska, B.; Billieux, J.; Brand, M.; et al. Preventing problematic internet use during the COVID-19 pandemic: Consensus guidance. *Compr. Psychiatry* **2020**, *100*, 152180. [CrossRef]
11. Forsman, A.K.; Nordmyr, J. Psychosocial links between Internet use and mental health in later life: A systematic review of quantitative and qualitative evidence. *J. Appl. Gerontol.* **2017**, *36*, 1471–1518. [CrossRef] [PubMed]
12. Thomée, S.; Lissner, L.; Hagberg, M.; Grimby-Ekman, A. Leisure time computer use and overweight development in young adults—A prospective study. *BMC Public Health* **2015**, *15*, 1–14. [CrossRef]
13. Chan, A.K.M.; Nickson, C.P.; Rudolph, J.W.; Lee, A.; Joynt, G.M. Social media for rapid knowledge dissemination: Early experience from the COVID-19 pandemic. *Anaesthesia* **2020**, *75*, 1579–1582. [CrossRef] [PubMed]
14. Brownson, R.C.; Eyler, A.A.; Harris, J.K.; Moore, J.B.; Tabak, R.G. Getting the word out: New approaches for disseminating public health science. *J. Public Health Manag. Pr.* **2018**, *24*, 102–111. [CrossRef]
15. Bhatt, N.R.; Czarniecki, S.W.; Borgmann, H.; Van Oort, I.M.; Esperto, F.; Pradere, B.; Van Gurp, M.; Bloemberg, J.; Darraugh, J.; Rouprêt, M.; et al. A systematic review of the use of social media for dissemination of clinical practice guidelines. *Eur. Urol. Focus.* 7 November 2020. Available online: http://www.sciencedirect.com/science/article/pii/S2405456920302923 (accessed on 8 December 2020).
16. Bick, A.; Blandin, A.; Mertens, K. *Work from Home after the Covid-19 Outbreak [Internet]*; Report No.: ID 3650114; Social Science Research Network: Rochester, NY, USA, July 2020. Available online: https://papers.ssrn.com/abstract=3650114 (accessed on 8 December 2020).
17. Johnson, N.; Veletsianos, G.; Seaman, J. U.S. faculty and administrators' experiences and approaches in the early weeks of the COVID-19 Pandemic. *Online Learn.* **2020**, *24*, 6–21. [CrossRef]
18. De Mendonça, W.L.; Costa, P.H.; Cançado, E.C.; Lima, F.; Canedo, E.D.; Bonifácio, R.; Amaral, L.H. From dusk till dawn: Reflections on the impact of COVID-19 on the development practices of a R&D project. In Proceedings of the 34th Brazilian Symposium on Software Engineering, New York, NY, USA, 19–23 October 2020; pp. 596–605. Available online: https://doi.org/10.1145/3422392.3422446 (accessed on 18 March 2021).
19. Zhou, X.; Snoswell, C.L.; Harding, L.E.; Bambling, M.; Edirippulige, S.; Bai, X.; Smith, A.C. The role of telehealth in reducing the mental health burden from COVID-19. *Telemed. e-Health* **2020**, *26*, 377–379. [CrossRef]
20. Garfin, D.R. Technology as a coping tool during the coronavirus disease 2019 (COVID-19) pandemic: Implications and recommendations. *Stress Health* **2020**, *36*, 555–559. [CrossRef]
21. Bentlage, E.; Ammar, A.; How, D.; Ahmed, M.; Trabelsi, K.; Chtourou, H.; Brach, M. Practical recommendations for maintaining active lifestyle during the COVID-19 Pandemic: A systematic literature review. *Int. J. Environ. Res. Public Health* **2020**, *17*, 6265. [CrossRef]
22. World Health Organization. Mental Health and Psychosocial Considerations during the COVID-19 Outbreak. 2020. Available online: https://www.who.int/publications-detail-redirect/WHO-2019-nCoV-MentalHealth-2020.1 (accessed on 8 December 2020).
23. Wong, C.W.; Tsai, A.; Jonas, J.B.; Ohno-Matsui, K.; Chen, J.; Ang, M.; Ting, D.S. Digital screen time during COVID-19 pandemic: Risk for a further myopia boom? *Am. J. Ophthalmol.* 30 July 2020. Available online: http://www.sciencedirect.com/science/article/pii/S0002939420303925 (accessed on 7 December 2020).
24. Romero-Blanco, C.; Rodríguez-Almagro, J.; Onieva-Zafra, M.D.; Parra-Fernández, M.L.; Prado-Laguna, M.D.C.; Hernández-Martínez, A. Physical activity and sedentary lifestyle in university students: Changes during confinement due to the COVID-19 Pandemic. *Int. J. Environ. Res. Public Health* **2020**, *17*, 6567. [CrossRef] [PubMed]
25. Majumdar, P.; Biswas, A.; Sahu, S. COVID-19 pandemic and lockdown: Cause of sleep disruption, depression, somatic pain, and increased screen exposure of office workers and students of India. *Chronobiol. Int.* **2020**, *37*, 1191–1200. [CrossRef] [PubMed]
26. Bates, L.; Zieff, G.; Stanford, K.; Moore, J.; Kerr, Z.; Hanson, E.; Gibbs, B.B.; Kline, C.; Stoner, L. COVID-19 impact on behaviors across the 24-hour day in children and adolescents: Physical activity, sedentary behavior, and sleep. *Children* **2020**, *7*, 138. [CrossRef]
27. Meyer, J.; McDowell, C.; Lansing, J.; Brower, C.; Smith, L.; Tully, M.; Herring, M. Changes in physical activity and sedentary behavior in response to COVID-19 and their associations with mental health in 3052 US adults. *Int. J. Environ. Res. Public Health* **2020**, *17*, 6469. [CrossRef] [PubMed]
28. Teychenne, M.; A Costigan, S.; Parker, K. The association between sedentary behaviour and risk of anxiety: A systematic review. *BMC Public Health* **2015**, *15*, 1–8. [CrossRef]
29. Hoare, E.; Milton, K.; Foster, C.; Allender, S. The associations between sedentary behaviour and mental health among adolescents: A systematic review. *Int. J. Behav. Nutr. Phys. Act.* **2016**, *13*, 1–22. [CrossRef] [PubMed]

30. Pantell, M.S.; Shields-Zeeman, L. Maintaining social connections in the setting of COVID-19 social distancing: A call to action. *Am. J. Public Health* **2020**, *110*, 1367–1368. [CrossRef]
31. Farooq, A.; Laato, S.; Islam, A.K.M.N. Impact of online information on self-isolation intention during the COVID-19 Pandemic: Cross-Sectional Study. *J. Med. Internet Res.* **2020**, *22*, e19128. [CrossRef]
32. Laato, S.; Islam, A.K.M.N.; Islam, M.N.; Whelan, E. What drives unverified information sharing and cyberchondria during the COVID-19 pandemic? *Eur. J. Inf. Syst.* **2020**, *29*, 288–305. [CrossRef]
33. Sauer, K.S.; Jungmann, S.M.; Witthöft, M. Emotional and behavioral consequences of the COVID-19 Pandemic: The role of health anxiety, intolerance of uncertainty, and distress (in)tolerance. *Int. J. Environ. Res. Public Health* **2020**, *17*, 7241. [CrossRef]
34. Leigh-Hunt, N.; Bagguley, D.; Bash, K.; Turner, V.; Turnbull, S.; Valtorta, N.; Caan, W. An overview of systematic reviews on the public health consequences of social isolation and loneliness. *Public Health* **2017**, *152*, 157–171. [CrossRef]
35. Brooks, S.K.; Webster, R.K.; Smith, L.E.; Woodland, L.; Wessely, S.; Greenberg, N.; Rubin, G.J. The psychological impact of quarantine and how to reduce it: Rapid review of the evidence. *Lancet* **2020**, *395*, 912–920. [CrossRef]
36. Shankar, A.; McMUNN, A.; Banks, J.; Steptoe, A. Loneliness, social isolation, and behavioral and biological health indicators in older adults. *Health Psychol.* **2011**, *30*, 377–385. [CrossRef] [PubMed]
37. Hawkley, L.C.; Cacioppo, J.T. Loneliness matters: A theoretical and empirical review of consequences and mechanisms. *Ann. Behav. Med.* **2010**, *40*, 218–227. [CrossRef] [PubMed]
38. Bhatti, A.B.; ul Haq, A. The pathophysiology of perceived social isolation: Effects on health and mortality. *Cureus* **2017**, *9*. Available online: https://www.ncbi.nlm.nih.gov/pmc/articles/PMC5367921/ (accessed on 9 December 2020). [CrossRef]
39. Figueroa, C.A.; Aguilera, A. The need for a mental health technology revolution in the COVID-19 pandemic. *Front. Psychiatry* **2020**, *11*. Available online: https://www.ncbi.nlm.nih.gov/pmc/articles/PMC7283500/ (accessed on 24 November 2020). [CrossRef]
40. Price, A. Online gambling in the midst of COVID-19: A nexus of mental health concerns, substance use and financial stress. *Int. J. Ment. Health Addict.* **2020**. Available online: https://doi.org/10.1007/s11469-020-00366-1 (accessed on 24 November 2020). [CrossRef] [PubMed]
41. Fernandes, B.; Biswas, U.N.; Mansukhani, R.T.; Casarín, A.V.; Essau, C.A. The impact of COVID-19 lockdown on internet use and escapism in adolescents. *Rev. Psicol. Clín. Con. Niños Adolesc.* **2020**, *7*, 59–65.
42. Gómez-Galán, J.; Martínez-López, J.Á.; Lázaro-Pérez, C.; Sarasola Sánchez-Serrano, J.L. Social networks consumption and addiction in college students during the COVID-19 pandemic: Educational approach to responsible use. *Sustainability* **2020**, *12*, 7737. [CrossRef]
43. Chartier, K.G.; Guidry, J.P.D.; Lee, C.A. At home and online during the early months of the COVID-19 pandemic and the relationship to alcohol consumption in a national sample of U.S. adults. *medRxiv* **2020**. [CrossRef]
44. Pollet, T.V.; Roberts, S.G.B.; Dunbar, R.I.M. Extraverts have larger social network layers: But do not feel emotionally closer to individuals at any layer. *J. Individ. Differ.* **2011**, *32*, 161–169. [CrossRef]
45. Folk, D.; Okabe-Miyamoto, K.; Dunn, E.; Lyubomirsky, S. Did social connection decline during the first wave of COVID-19?: The role of extraversion. *Collabra Psychol.* **2020**, *6*. Available online: https://go.gale.com/ps/i.do?p=HRCA&sw=w&issn=24747394&v=2.1&it=r&id=GALE%7CA631235444&sid=googleScholar&linkaccess=abs (accessed on 9 December 2020). [CrossRef]
46. Wijngaards, I.; De Zilwa, S.C.M.S.; Burger, M.J. Extraversion moderates the relationship between the stringency of COVID-19 protective measures and depressive symptoms. *Front. Psychol.* **2020**, *11*, 568907. [CrossRef]
47. Aschwanden, D.; Strickhouser, J.E.; Sesker, A.A.; Lee, J.H.; Luchetti, M.; Stephan, Y.; Sutin, A.R.; Terracciano, A. Psychological and behavioural responses to Coronavirus disease 2019: The role of personality. *Eur. J. Pers.* **2021**, *35*, 51–66. [CrossRef] [PubMed]
48. Van Bavel, J.J.; Baicker, K.; Boggio, P.S.; Capraro, V.; Cichocka, A.; Cikara, M.; Crockett, M.J.; Crum, A.J.; Douglas, K.M.; Druckman, J.N.; et al. Using social and behavioural science to support COVID-19 pandemic response. *Nat. Hum. Behav.* **2020**, *4*, 460–471. [CrossRef]
49. Paredes, M.R.; Apaolaza, V.; Fernandez-Robin, C.; Hartmann, P.; Yañez-Martinez, D. The impact of the COVID-19 pandemic on subjective mental well-being: The interplay of perceived threat, future anxiety and resilience. *Pers. Individ. Differ.* **2021**, *170*, 110455. [CrossRef]
50. Liu, S.; Lithopoulos, A.; Zhang, C.-Q.; Garcia-Barrera, M.A.; Rhodes, R.E. Personality and perceived stress during COVID-19 pandemic: Testing the mediating role of perceived threat and efficacy. *Pers. Individ. Differ.* **2021**, *168*, 110351. [CrossRef] [PubMed]
51. Mertens, G.; Gerritsen, L.; Duijndam, S.; Salemink, E.; Engelhard, I.M. Fear of the coronavirus (COVID-19): Predictors in an online study conducted in March 2020. *J. Anxiety Disord.* **2020**, *74*, 102258. [CrossRef]
52. Liu, C.; Liu, Y. Media exposure and anxiety during COVID-19: The ediation effect of media vicarious traumatization. *Int. J. Environ. Res. Public Health* **2020**, *17*. Available online: https://www.ncbi.nlm.nih.gov/pmc/articles/PMC7370076/ (accessed on 7 November 2020).
53. Moreland, A. Timing of state and territorial COVID-19 stay-at-home orders and changes in population movement—United States, March 1–May 31, 2020. *MMWR Morb. Mortal Wkly. Rep.* **2020**, *69*. Available online: https://www.cdc.gov/mmwr/volumes/69/wr/mm6935a2.htm (accessed on 12 January 2021). [CrossRef]
54. Lovett, M.; Bajaba, S.; Simmering, M.J. Data quality from crowdsourced surveys: A mixed method inquiry into perceptions of Amazon's Mechanical Turk masters. *Appl. Psychol.* **2017**, *67*, 339–366. [CrossRef]
55. Baumeister, R.F.; Leary, M.R. The need to belong: Desire for interpersonal attachments as a fundamental human motivation. *Psychol. Bull.* **1995**, *117*, 497–529. [CrossRef]

56. Przybylski, A.K.; Murayama, K.; DeHaan, C.R.; Gladwell, V. Motivational, emotional, and behavioral correlates of fear of missing out. *Comput. Hum. Behav.* **2013**, *29*, 1841–1848. [CrossRef]
57. Weller, J.A.; Shackleford, C.; Dieckmann, N.; Slovic, P. Possession attachment predicts cell phone use while driving. *Health Psychol.* **2013**, *32*, 379–387. [CrossRef]
58. Van Deursen, A.J.A.M.; Bolle, C.L.; Hegner, S.M.; Kommers, P.A.M. Modeling habitual and addictive smartphone behavior: The role of smartphone usage types, emotional intelligence, social stress, self-regulation, age, and gender. *Comput. Hum. Behav.* **2015**, *45*, 411–420. [CrossRef]
59. Limayenm, M.; Hirt, S.; Cheung, C. Habit in the context of IS continuance: Theory extension and scale development. ECIS 2003 Proc. 1 January 2003. Available online: https://aisel.aisnet.org/ecis2003/90 (accessed on 7 December 2020).
60. Diehl, M.; Semegon, A.B.; Schwarzer, R. Assessing attention control in goal pursuit: A component of dispositional self-regulation. *J. Pers. Assess.* **2006**, *86*, 306–317. [CrossRef] [PubMed]
61. Farmer, R.; Sundberg, N.D. Boredom Proneness—The development and correlates of a new scale. *J. Pers. Assess.* **1986**, *50*, 4–17. [CrossRef] [PubMed]
62. Vodanovich, S.J.; Wallace, J.C.; Kass, S.J. A confirmatory approach to the factor structure of the Boredom Proneness Scale: Evidence for a two-factor short form. *J. Pers. Assess.* **2005**, *85*, 295–303. [CrossRef] [PubMed]
63. Rammstedt, B.; John, O.P. Measuring personality in one minute or less: A 10-item short version of the Big Five Inventory in English and German. *J. Res. Pers.* **2007**, *41*, 203–212. [CrossRef]
64. Nitschke, J.P.; Forbes, P.A.G.; Ali, N.; Cutler, J.; Apps, M.A.J.; Lockwood, P.L.; Lamm, C. Resilience during uncertainty? Greater social connectedness during COVID-19 lockdown is associated with reduced distress and fatigue. *Br. J. Health Psychol.* **2020**. Available online: https://bpspsychub.onlinelibrary.wiley.com/doi/abs/10.1111/bjhp.12485 (accessed on 10 December 2020). [CrossRef]
65. Leary, M.R.; Kelly, K.M.; Cottrell, C.A.; Schreindorfer, L.S. Construct validity of the Need to Belong Scale: Mapping the nomological network. *J. Pers. Assess.* **2013**, *95*, 610–624. [CrossRef] [PubMed]
66. Wilson, K.E.; Dishman, R.K. Personality and physical activity: A systematic review and meta-analysis. *Pers. Individ. Differ.* **2015**, *72*, 230–242. [CrossRef]
67. Campos-Castillo, C.; I Laestadius, L. Racial and ethnic digital divides in posting COVID-19 content on social media among US adults: Secondary survey analysis. *J. Med. Internet Res.* **2020**, *22*, e20472. [CrossRef]
68. Walters, K.; Christakis, D.A.; Wright, D.R. Are Mechanical Turk worker samples representative of health status and health behaviors in the U.S.? *PLoS ONE* **2018**, *13*, e0198835. [CrossRef] [PubMed]
69. Fisher, R.J. Social desirability bias and the validity of indirect questioning. *J. Consum. Res.* **1993**, *20*, 303–315. [CrossRef]
70. Hawkins, R.P.; Kreuter, M.; Resnicow, K.; Fishbein, M.; Dijkstra, A. Understanding tailoring in communicating about health. *Health Educ. Res.* **2008**, *23*, 454–466. [CrossRef] [PubMed]

International Journal of
Environmental Research and Public Health

MDPI

Article

Psychological Health Status of Psychiatric Patients Living in Treatment Communities before and during the COVID-19 Lockdown: A Brief Report

Pierluigi Cordellieri [1], Benedetta Barchielli [2], Valeria Masci [3], Francesca Viani [3], Ivan de Pinto [3], Andrea Priori [3], Felice Damiano Torriccelli [3], Chiara Cosmo [4], Stefano Ferracuti [4], Anna Maria Giannini [1] and Jessica Burrai [1,2,*]

1 Department of Psychology, Sapienza University of Rome, Via dei Marsi 78, 00185 Rome, Italy; pierluigi.cordellieri@uniroma1.it (P.C.); annamaria.giannini@uniroma1.it (A.M.G.)
2 Department of Dynamic and Clinical Psychology, and Health Studies, Sapienza University of Rome, Via degli Apuli 1, 00185 Rome, Italy; benedetta.barchielli@gmail.com
3 Association of Therapeutic Communities "Reverie", Via Località Passo Cavallone 4, 00060 Capena, Italy; masci.valeria@gmail.com (V.M.); francescaviani93@gmail.com (F.V.); ivandp94@libero.it (I.d.P.); andreapriori7@gmail.com (A.P.); feldatorr@gmail.com (F.D.T.)
4 Department of Human Neuroscience, Sapienza University of Rome, Viale dell'Università 30, 00185 Rome, Italy; chiaracosmo@hotmail.it (C.C.); Stefano.ferracuti@uniroma1.it (S.F.)
* Correspondence: jessica.burrai@uniroma1.it

Citation: Cordellieri, P.; Barchielli, B.; Masci, V.; Viani, F.; de Pinto, I.; Priori, A.; Torriccelli, F.D.; Cosmo, C.; Ferracuti, S.; Giannini, A.M.; et al. Psychological Health Status of Psychiatric Patients Living in Treatment Communities before and during the COVID-19 Lockdown: A Brief Report. *Int. J. Environ. Res. Public Health* **2021**, *18*, 3567. https://doi.org/10.3390/ijerph18073567

Academic Editor: Paul B. Tchounwou

Received: 25 February 2021
Accepted: 28 March 2021
Published: 30 March 2021

Publisher's Note: MDPI stays neutral with regard to jurisdictional claims in published maps and institutional affiliations.

Abstract: Many studies investigated the psychological impact of lockdown measures on the general population, while few studies focused on the psychiatric population. This study aimed to investigate the role of therapeutic communities in the management and containment of symptoms of patients with psychosis living in psychiatric residential facilities. Data were collected at two different points: November 2019 (Coronavirus disease 19 had not yet spread) and April 2020 (during the lockdown in Italy). Twenty-two study participants were recruited from three residential accredited psychiatric facilities. During lockdown, the patients showed a small increase in symptomatology in terms of emotional isolation. In addition, it was been observed significant differences in certain functional areas of the behavior, measured as lower inclination towards violent behaviors during lockdown, and higher scores in substance abuse and medical impairment. The lockdown condition could represent a form of containment; daily routines, along with adequate social support, are important aspects of the stability and the level of behavioral functioning of psychiatric patients. Social support and continuity of care offered by psychiatric communities can be an effective safeguard against the psychological impact of the COVID-19 epidemic.

Keywords: COVID-19; psychiatric patients; mental illness; cognitive function; psychiatric symptoms; risk perception; social support; lockdown

1. Introduction

Residential facilities are a key resource for the Italian Mental Health Department; the facilities are dedicated to the treatment of patients suffering from mental illness who require therapeutic rehabilitation or social and health support interventions in residential settings. Nonmedical residential care facilities (RCFs) are a common residential setting for many people with mental illness, especially those with limited social support and greater supervision and care needs. Residential service models emerged as alternatives to deinstitutionalization, and RCFs base their work on the continuity of care; patients who moved back and forth between different care settings were most likely to change residence and to have the highest number of short admissions [1], while the continuity of the care setting could play a role in containment and help in the management of symptomatology [2].

Therapeutic psychiatric communities are complex organisms with a complex care path defined spatially and temporally. The path begins at the initial moment of reception in individual interventions, group interventions, or interventions with family members, and it is a path of inclusion, attachment, and detachment with involvement in the social network; great importance is given to the daily life and climate of the patient [3].

Indeed, residential programs in therapeutic psychiatric communities are often based on the integration of educational, psychiatric, and psychotherapeutic treatments within a therapeutic setting [4]. The assumptions of therapeutic psychiatric communities are represented by the shared construction of a therapeutic project between the patient, family, sending service, and community staff, and, moreover, by the therapeutic alliance that is built after a preliminary phase and that each community must try to guarantee [5,6].

Community-based residential mental health services are judged to be less restrictive and regimented models of care; for these reasons, they are considered less isolating and stigmatizing than other models of care [7]. Clinical intervention in the healthcare organization involves overcoming an individualistic conception [8] derived from the medical model, according to which the only patient is the individual. In addition, over time, increasing importance has been given to relational and intersubjective conceptions, highlighting the importance of social ties for the mental health of individuals and groups.

The group constitutes the modality through which the community of care can operate to achieve its aims [9]; that is, it is a space for the sharing and symbolic re-elaboration of experiences of suffering and the sharing of experiences, which are nourished by the transformative and "generative" capacity characteristic of "group thought" [10]. Despite growing evidence for their effectiveness, little research has been conducted to establish how therapeutic communities (TCs) work to produce positive outcomes. Pearce and Pickad [11] argued that there are two specific factors that, in combination, contribute to TC effectiveness: the promotion of a sense of belongingness and the capacity for responsible agency. Although both factors are found in other therapeutic approaches and are important to the psychosocial aspects of psychiatric care, the authors argued that their combination, extent, and emphasis are unique to TCs [11]. These characteristics could be considered crucial during the lockdown implemented to avoid the spread of coronavirus disease 19 (COVID-19). Patients living in psychiatric treatment communities during the COVID-19 lockdown showed unchanged depressive, anxious, and stressful symptoms; in particular, residential patients had lower perceived stress scores due to the COVID-19 situation compared to those of the general population, and the uninterrupted care provided by the residential community was considered to be an important protective factor [12]. In contrast, psychiatric patients, a population that could be considered at greater risk of distress and psychosocial pathological responses to exposure to a stressful situation such as a COVID-19 lockdown, were underinvestigated [13]. In people with preexisting mental illness, the impact of COVID-19 may be different than that for the general population. A rapid review of the literature on the potential impact of COVID-19 on psychotic patients during past epidemics and pandemics (e.g., Severe acute respiratory syndrome, SARS; Swine influenza, H1N1; Ebolavirus disease, EVD; Middle east respiratory syndrome coronavirus infection, MERS-CoV, and Equine influenza) highlighted that individuals with preexisting psychosis appeared to be less compliant with measures to prevent the spread of the virus (e.g., physical distancing and personal hygiene) [14]. Even in the healthy population, compliance factors are important in preventing the spread of the virus, although they are not often applied [15].

To the best of our knowledge, a comparison between symptomatology before and during the pandemic situation in the psychiatric population has not yet been performed. Aiming to address this gap, we compared clinical conditions of the psychiatric population living in health facilities before and during the COVID-19 pandemic in several domains, such as psychological impairment, social skills, and psychiatric symptoms. The study aimed to investigate the role of therapeutic communities in the management and containment of symptoms of patients with psychosis living in psychiatric residential facilities. The first data collection was conducted in November 2019 (COVID-19 had not yet spread), and the second was conducted in April 2020 (during the lockdown in Italy).

2. Materials and Methods

2.1. Participants

Twenty-two study participants were recruited from three residential accredited psychiatric facilities in Rome and Capena (Italy). These facilities are psychiatric communities that provide healthcare assistance through qualified personnel 24 h per day. Various professional figures work closely with psychiatric patients within the communities: psychologists, psychiatrists, educators, nurses, and social assistants. The therapeutic model of these communities evolved from the work of Wilfred Bion and John Rickman [16], and more generally from the first British therapeutic communities [17,18]. All patients carry out individual and group activities involving pharmacological, psychotherapeutic, rehabilitation, and socialization interventions. During the lockdown, all the professionals continued to work in the communities, guaranteeing the psychiatric patients' continuity of care and treatment. Positive reinforcement techniques were used to encourage participation in therapy groups to prepare the patients to face social isolation and emotional flattening.

All participants voluntarily responded to the anonymous survey and provided their informed consent. The sample included 12 males (54.5%) and 10 females aged between 19 and 45 years, with a mean age of 31.82 (SD = 6.69). The descriptive statistics and participant diagnoses are reported in Table 1. The exclusion criteria were (a) an inability to provide informed consent (i.e., Mini Mental State Examination < 8) and (b) a disease affecting the central nervous system (CNS). The study was approved by the Institutional Board of the Department of Human Neuroscience, Faculty of Medicine and Dentistry, "Sapienza" University of Rome (IRB-2020-6), in conformity with the principles of the Declaration of Helsinki. The descriptive statistics of the sample (Table 1) are reported.

Table 1. Descriptive statistics of the study sample.

Characteristic	Group	Psychiatric Patients *N* (%) = 22
Age	*M* (*SD*)	31.82 (6.96)
	Min–Max	19–45
Gender	Female	10 (45.5%)
	Male	12 (54.5%)
Education	Middle school diploma	8 (36.4%)
	High school diploma	12 (54.5%)
	Graduate	2 (9.1%)
Diagnostic Criteria	Schizophrenia	6
	Delusional Disorder	5
	Schizoaffective Disorder	5
	Depressive Disorders	1
	Bipolar and Related Disorders	1
	Personality Disorders	4

2.2. Procedures

The first data collection (T1) was conducted in November 2019 (non-COVID time, hereinafter NoCoT). The patients were evaluated using the following clinical scales: the Mini Mental State Examination (MMSE), Brief Psychiatric Rating Scale (BPRS), and Kennedy Axis V (K Axis). The second data collection (T2) was conducted in April 2020 (COVID time, CoT). The patients were evaluated with the same scales as those at T1, but specific items were added on COVID-19 to investigate the psychiatric patients' knowledge and risk perception about the COVID-19 pandemic. Information on COVID-19 was collected through self-report items (i.e., "How did you become aware of the spread of COVID-19?"; "What is COVID-19?"; "Did you participate in community training sessions on this health emergency?").

2.3. Materials

Sociodemographic information was collected with a questionnaire developed ad hoc that included items on gender, age, marital status, education level, substance use, socioeconomic status, psychiatric diagnosis, presence of any other pathology, time spent in the community, and relationships with family.

Validated and reliable measures were used to assess the patients' cognitive functions, psychiatric symptoms, and several specific areas of functioning. Cognitive domains (orientation to time and space, registration of three words, attention, and calculation, recall of three words, language, and visual construction) were measured with the MMSE [19]. Psychiatric symptoms were measured with the 24-item Brief Psychiatric Rating Scale [20]. The K Axis [21] was used to measure the patients' overall functioning and functioning in several specific areas, with each area of functioning scored on a continuum of 100 points according to a decreasing order of severity (0 = very severe compression; 100 = high function). The investigated areas were as follows: (1) Psychological impairment; (2) Social skills; (3) Violence; (4) ADL-Occupational skills (5) Substance abuse; (6) Compromising of physical conditions: Medical impairment; (7) Ancillary impairment (legal, financial, milieu).

COVID-19 risk perception was measured with three items adapted from Cho and Lee [22]. Five items evaluated negative mood due to restrictive measures carried out in the community.

For social support, the shorter version of the Multidimensional Scale of Perceived Social Support (MSPSS) [23] was used. The short version used in the present research contains three items ranked from 1 (not agree at all) to 7 (agree at all).

2.4. Statistical Analyses

ANOVA with repeated measures was used to compare the scores of the clinical scales in two different periods (NoCot vs. Cot). Statistical analyses were performed using Statistical Package for Social Science (SPSS; version 25.0; IBM SPSS, Armonk, NY, USA). In the pairwise comparisons, the Bonferroni correction for alpha inflation was performed.

3. Results

The descriptive statistics of the sample (Table 1), risk perception, negative mood, and social support (Table 2) are reported.

Table 2. Descriptive statistic of COVID information and risk perception, bad mood, and social support during the quarantine.

Dimension	M (*SD*) Min-Max	Cronbach's Alpha (*a*)	*N* (%)
Participation informative meetings about COVID-19	Yes		22 (100%)
Risk perception	11.87 (2.27) 3–15	0.725	22 (100%)
Bad mood due to restrictive measures	16.06 (3.68) 5–25	0.72	22 (100%)
Social support	14.56 (4.95) 3–21	0.818	22 (100%)

As shown in Table 3, we did not find statistically significant differences between the BPRS scores measured in November (T1; NoCoT) and April (T2; CoT). During lockdown, the patients showed a small increase in symptomatology ($T1_{NoCoT}$ M = 2.50, T2CoT M = 2.79) in terms of emotional isolation, but differences in other symptoms were not found. The MMSE also did not show a significant difference (Table 3).

Table 3. Between administration-time differences (ANOVA).

Clinical Scale							
Dimension	**F**	***p***	**η_p^2**	**Multiple Comparisons**	**Mean Difference**	**Std. Error**	**Sig.**
MMSE	1.56	0.234	0.107	T1 vs. T2			
BPRS	0.296	0.596	0.022	T1 vs. T2			
K_Axis	3.157	0.008	0.195	T1 vs. T2			
PI				T1 vs. T2	1.25	1.821	-
SS				T1 vs. T2	3.194	3.051	-
Vi				T1 vs. T2	−13.333	5.090	0.05 *
OI				T1 vs. T2	−5.556	0.021	-
SA				T1 vs. T2	−4.861	0.265	0.05 *
CPC				T1 vs. T2	−7.917	0.004	0.01 **
AI				T1 vs. T2	0.000	1.00	-
GAF Eq.	4.316	0.058	0.249	T1 vs. T2			
GAF K	0.671	0.428	0.049	T1 vs. T2			
DL	0.985	0.339	0.070	T1 vs. T2			

* $p < 0.05$. ** $p < 0.01$; K_Axis = Kennedy Axis V; PI = Psychological impairment; SS = Social skills; Vi = Violence; OI = ADL-Occupational Skills; SA = Substance abuse; CPC = Compromising of physical conditions: Medical impairment; AI = Ancillary impairment; GAF Eq = Global Evaluation Functioning Equivalent, a score that provides an average and global representation of the patient's functioning. It is obtained from the average of the first four Kennedy Axis V scales; GAF K = Global assessment of functioning. Global functioning obtained by selecting the lowest of the scores from the first four areas; DL = Danger level, this index identifies the highest risk score among those obtained in the seven areas.

Otherwise, the K Axis scores showed a significant main effect ($F_{(1,6)} = 9.996$, $p < 0.001$; $\eta_p^2 = 0.0435$) and significant interaction effect of K Axis*Session ($F_{(1,12)} = 3.157$, $p < 0.01$; $\eta_p^2 = 0.195$). We observed significant differences in certain functional areas of the behavior measured by the K Axis between the two time points (Table 3). The comparisons revealed significant differences for violence (Area 3). Pairwise comparisons showed that the mean of T1 was lower (M = −13.333, SE = 0.09, $p < 0.05$) compared to the T2. Specifically, the patients showed a lower inclination towards violent behaviors during lockdown (higher scores indicate a lower level of criticality in this area).

A significant difference was also observed for area 5, substance abuse. Pairwise comparisons showed higher mean difference in the T2 compared to the T1 (M = −4.861, SE = 0.265, $p < 0.05$). This functional area seemed to improve during the lockdown (higher scores indicate a lower level of criticality in this area).

Finally, there were significant differences for medical impairment (Area 6). Pairwise comparisons showed a significant higher mean difference in the T2 compared with T1 (M = −7.917, SE = 0.004, $p < 0.05$). The physical condition of the patients improved during the lockdown (higher scores indicate a lower level of criticality in this area). No gender differences were found for any dimensions assessed.

4. Discussion

Several recent studies have demonstrated a significant impact of the COVID-19 pandemic on psychological health, particularly as a result of the lockdown [24–26], but few studies have investigated this impact on specific populations, such as psychiatric patients.

The present study compared the psychiatric symptoms and functioning in several specific areas of patients living in residential communities before and during the lockdown in Italy. An important result emerged from the comparison between the clinical evaluations from November 2019 (before the lockdown in Italy) and April 2020 (during the lockdown in Italy). According to our data, the patients did not show an increase in psychiatric symptoms; the only exception was a small increase in emotional isolation. The increased feeling of emotional isolation may have been linked to the isolation imposed by the necessary containment of COVID-19. Although social isolation is part of the symptomatology of many psychiatric disorders [27], the limitations imposed during the lockdown may have exacerbated the sense of loneliness and despair due to the imposed distance from loved ones but also staff and other psychiatric patients in the community. In contrast, different functional areas of behavior showed improvements: there was a lower propensity for violent behaviors, lower rates of substance abuse, and better physical conditions.

These findings may seem to contrast with those of numerous studies that have indicated concerns about the pandemic or reported that a period of isolation can lead to an increase in psychopathologies, including psychotic psychopathologies [28]. Systematic reviews and specific studies have shown significant effects of the COVID-19 pandemic on the psychiatric population [29–31]. Forced quarantine to combat the spread of COVID-19 has produced forms of acute panic, anxiety, obsessive behavior, paranoia, and depression in psychiatric patients.

In the same studies, however, it was recognized that acute pathological conditions increase with concomitant causes of stressors, such as psychological vulnerability, social isolation, unemployment, relational rupture, etc. In particular, social isolation seems to be the variable that "carries the most weight" for the psychiatric population. For example, Giallonardo and colleagues [32] showed that if protracted, social isolation may increase the risk of recurrences of episodes of mental disorders beyond triggering the onset of new mental disorders in the most vulnerable people. Moreover, objective social isolation and subjective feelings of loneliness are associated with a higher risk of suicidal ideation and suicide attempts. For many persons with mental disorders, being alone is a heavy burden, far greater than that experienced by many other persons. Moesmann and colleagues [27] reported that in their nonresidential clinics, some patients went from a high level of functioning to a need for hospitalization due to the rupture of their weekly routines. In some cases, telepsychiatry and other cutting-edge technologies have been effective tools in bridging social distance and ensuring continuity in mental health assistance [33].

Research has shown the importance of ensuring social support and mental health care for patients with mental disorders [34]. In the literature, differences between psychiatric outpatients and inpatients have been reported. Outpatients have been shown to experience greater psychological impact on their mental health, with higher depression, anxiety, and stress scores than healthy controls [29,35] due to the interruption of some psychiatric services and the difficulties accessing these services due to the lockdown. Therefore, continuous monitoring of the medical and psychological health of patients receiving mental health services is essential to design and respond to problems arising from the lockdown and the spread of the virus [36]. On the other hand, inpatients have been found to experience greater confidence in being protected from virus than control groups, as they feel protected by hospital staff [37]. However, inpatient psychiatric settings have faced new challenges: close contact between staff and patients, the restriction of visitors, and the recommendation of improved hygiene [38].

In our study, the subjects were residential patients in therapeutic communities and were therefore protected from different social stressors, such as relational continuity and low exposure to mass and/or social media. During quarantine, the patients' days were spent engaging in routine activities. Twice a week, the patients could call their families to ensure their health. The peer group or community psychologists provided ongoing social support. Therefore, we believe that the patients in our study did not have worsening symptoms due to the continuity of social support and medical care.

We observed that some functional areas of behavior improved. These behavioral areas were mainly linked with containment aspects [39]. "Containment" is a broader term that includes a wide variety of strategies, including pharmacological treatment and nonpharmacological interventions or techniques, such as increased observation levels, locked wards, de-escalation techniques, the use of behavioral agreements and increased staffing levels. In this study, we refer to the conditions imposed due to COVID-19 outbreak: an inability for patients to leave the community, the use of only telephone meetings with family and friends, etc. Paradoxically, for the patients in our study, these measures likely resulted in less exposure to social stressors. Indeed, the family environment can either play a protective and detrimental role [40] and for psychiatric patients, not being embedded in dysfunctional family dynamics (e.g., low family cohesion and low caregiver warmth) may have contributed to a stability in symptom severity.

Our hypothesis is that the lockdown condition represented a further form of containment. Daily routines, along with adequate social support, are important aspects of the stability and the level of behavioral functioning of psychiatric patients, in particular for those with anxiety, violent acts, and substance abuse. In summary, we believe that social support and continuity of care offered by psychiatric communities can be an effective safeguard against the psychological impact of the COVID-19 epidemic.

We are aware of the limitations of our research. The limited number of subjects could not ensure the external validity of our research. In addition, our investigation involved patients from a single community association. It could also be very interesting to extend our results to other residential contexts. We believe, however, that our results provide interesting insight and may be a stimulus for further research on the severe psychiatric patient population during COVID-19 and in directing further research on patients living in treatment communities.

5. Conclusions

Lockdown measures are still the best available containment strategy in limiting the spread of viruses despite their negative long-lasting psychological impact related to isolation and loneliness.

The impact of COVID-19 may differ from the general population in psychiatry patients; however, the responses to exposure to a stressful situation, such as a COVID-19 lockdown, in psychiatric patients have been underinvestigated.

The present study compared the psychiatric symptoms and functioning in several specific areas of patients living in residential communities before and during the lockdown in Italy. Lockdown measure may be an additional form of containment along with daily routines and adequate social support that can be an effective safeguard against the psychological impact of the COVID-19 outbreak.

Author Contributions: Conceptualization, P.C., J.B., B.B., and A.M.G.; methodology, P.C.; formal analysis, P.C.; data curation, I.d.P., V.M., A.P., F.V., and F.D.T.; writing—original draft preparation, P.C., J.B., and B.B.; writing—review and editing, S.F., A.M.G., and C.C.; supervision, A.M.G. and S.F. All authors have read and agreed to the published version of the manuscript.

Funding: This research received no external funding.

Institutional Review Board Statement: The study was conducted according to the guidelines of the Declaration of Helsinki and approved by the Institutional Review Board of Department of Human Neuroscience, Faculty of Medicine and Dentistry, "Sapienza" University of Rome (IRB-2020-6 approved on 23/03/2020).

Informed Consent Statement: Informed consent was obtained from all subjects involved in the study. Written informed consent has been obtained from the patient(s) to publish this paper.

Data Availability Statement: The data presented in this study are available on request from the corresponding author. The data are not publicly available due to request from Mental Community where data have been collected.

Acknowledgments: The data of this study were collected thanks to participation of the Manager and Staff of Community Mental Health Service "Reverie".

Conflicts of Interest: The authors declare no conflict of interest.

References

1. De Mooij, L.D.; Kikkert, M.; Lommerse, N.M.; Theunissen, J.; de Koning, M.B.; de Haan, L.; Beekman, A.T.F.; Duurkoop, W.R.A.; Dekker, J.J.M. Homesick: Residential and care patterns in patients with severe mental illness. *BMC Psychiatry* **2016**, *16*, 1–10. [CrossRef]
2. Freeman, G.; Hughes, J. *Continuity of Care and the Patient Experience*; King's Fund: London, UK, 2010.
3. Moos, R.H.; Houts, P.S. Differential effects of the social atmosphere of psychiatric wards. *Hum. Relat.* **1970**, *23*, 47–60. [CrossRef]

4. Salvi, V.; Boccardo, F.; Giannini, P.; Corulli, M. Gli esiti del trattamento riabilitativo in comunità terapeutica: Uno studio di follow-up. *Riv. Psichiatr.* **2016**, *51*, 66–71. [CrossRef] [PubMed]
5. Priebe, S.; Gruyters, T. The role of the helping alliance in psychiatric community care: A prospective study. *J. Nerv. Ment. Dis.* **1993**. [CrossRef] [PubMed]
6. McCabe, R.; Priebe, S. The therapeutic relationship in the treatment of severe mental illness: A review of methods and findings. *Int. J. Soc. Psychiatry* **2006**, *50*, 115–128. [CrossRef] [PubMed]
7. Parker, S.; Siskind, D.; Harris, M. Community based residential mental health services: What do we need to know? *Aust. N. Z. J. Psychiatry* **2015**, *49*, 86–87. [CrossRef] [PubMed]
8. Montesarchio, G.; Venuleo, C. L'attraversamento è un Costrutto Postmoderno. Attraversando il Maestro. In *Falgares (a cura di). Psicologia Psicologica. Scritti in Onore di Franco Di Maria*; Di Nuovo, G.S., Ed.; Franco Angeli: Milano, Italy, 2008; pp. 299–319.
9. Neri, C. *Gruppo*; Borla: Roma, Italy, 1996.
10. Laurora, E. Gruppalità e Istituzione curante. In *Il Lavoro Della Cura Nelle Istituzioni*; Vigorelli, M., Ed.; Franco Angeli: Milano, Italy, 2005.
11. Pearce, S.; Pickard, H. How therapeutic communities work: Specific factors related to positive outcome. *Int. J. Soc. Psychiatry* **2013**, *59*, 636–645. [CrossRef]
12. Burrai, J.; Roma, P.; Barchielli, B.; Biondi, S.; Cordellieri, P.; Fraschetti, A.; Pizzimenti, A.; Mazza, C.; Ferracuti, S.; Giannini, A.M. Psychological and Emotional Impact of Patients Living in Psychiatric Treatment Communities during Covid-19 Lockdown in Italy. *J. Clin. Med.* **2020**, *9*, 3787. [CrossRef]
13. Yao, H.; Chen, J.H.; Xu, Y.F. Patients with mental health disorders in the COVID-19 epidemic. *Lancet Psychiatry* **2020**, *7*, e21. [CrossRef]
14. Brown, E.; Gray, R.; Lo Monaco, S.; O'Donoghue, B.; Nelson, B.; Thompson, A.; Francey, S.; McGorry, P. The potential impact of COVID-19 on psychosis: A rapid review of contemporary epidemic and pandemic research. *Schizophr. Res.* **2020**. [CrossRef]
15. Roma, P.; Monaro, M.; Muzi, L.; Colasanti, M.; Ricci, E.; Biondi, S.; Napoli, C.; Ferracuti, S.; Mazza, C. How to improve compliance with protective health measures during the covid-19 outbreak: Testing a moderated mediation model and machine learning algorithms. *Int. J. Environ. Res. Public Health* **2020**, *17*, 7252. [CrossRef]
16. Bion, W.R.; Rickman, J. Intra-group tensions in therapy; their study as the task of the group. *Lancet* **1943**. [CrossRef]
17. Foulkes, S.H. *Therapeutic Group Analysis*; Routledge: Oxon, UK, 2018.
18. Harrison, T. *Bion, Rickman, Foulkes, and the Northfield Experiments: Advancing on a Different Front*; Jessica Kingsley Publishers: London, UK, 2000; Volume 5.
19. Folstein, M.F.; Folstein, S.E.; McHugh, P.R. "Mini-mental state". A practical method for grading the cognitive state of patients for the clinician. *J. Psychiatr. Res.* **1971**, *12*, 189–198. [CrossRef]
20. Overall, J.E.; Gorham, D.R. The Brief Psychiatric Rating Scale. *Psychol. Rep.* **1962**, *10*, 799–812. [CrossRef]
21. Kennedy, J.A. *Il Funzionamento del Paziente Psichiatrico: Manuale di Valutazione. Verso un Nuovo Asse V del DSM.*; Trad. it. Raffaello Cortina Editore: Milano, Italy, 2007.
22. Cho, H.; Lee, J.S. The influence of self-efficacy, subjective norms, and risk perception on behavioral intentions related to the H1N1 flu pandemic: A comparison between Korea and the US. *Asian J. Soc. Psychol.* **2015**, *18*, 311–324. [CrossRef]
23. Zimet, G.D.; Dahlem, N.W.; Zimet, S.G.; Farley, G.K. The multidimensional scale of perceived social support. *J. Pers. Assess.* **1988**, *52*, 30–41. [CrossRef]
24. Roma, P.; Monaro, M.; Colasanti, M.; Ricci, E.; Biondi, S.; Di Domenico, A.; Verrocchio, M.C.; Napoli, C.; Ferracuti, S.; Mazza, C. A 2-Month Follow-Up Study of Psychological Distress among Italian People during the COVID-19 Lockdown. *Int. J. Environ. Res. Public Health* **2020**, *17*, 8180. [CrossRef]
25. Mazza, C.; Ricci, E.; Biondi, S.; Colasanti, M.; Ferracuti, S.; Napoli, C.; Roma, P.A. Nationwide Survey of Psychological Distress among Italian People during the COVID-19 Pandemic: Immediate Psychological Responses and Associated Factors. *Int. J. Environ. Res. Public Health* **2020**, *17*, 3165. [CrossRef]
26. Wang, C.; Pan, R.; Wan, X.; Tan, Y.; Xu, L.; Ho, C.S.; Ho, R.C. Immediate psychological responses and associated factors during the initial stage of the 2019 coronavirus disease (COVID-19) epidemic among the general population in China. *Int. J. Environ. Res. Public Health* **2020**, *17*, 1729. [CrossRef]
27. Moesmann, M.M.; Dines, D.; Hieronymus, F. Optimizing psychiatric care during the COVID-19 pandemic. *Acta Psychiatr. Scand.* **2020**, *142*, 70–71. [CrossRef]
28. Anglin, D.M.; Galea, S.; Bachman, P. Going upstream to advance psychosis prevention and improve public health. *JAMA Psychiatry* **2020**, *77*, 665–666. [CrossRef]
29. Hao, F.; Tan, W.; Jiang, L.; Zhang, L.; Zhao, X.; Zou, Y.; Hu, Y.; Luo, X.; Jiang, X.; McIntyre, R.S.; et al. Do psychiatric patients experience more psychiatric symptoms during COVID-19 pandemic and lockdown? A case-control study with service and research implications for immunopsychiatry. *Brain Behav. Immun.* **2020**, *87*, 100–106. [CrossRef] [PubMed]
30. Anjum, S.; Ullah, R.; Rana, M.S.; Ali Khan, H.; Memon, F.S.; Ahmed, Y.; Jabeen, S.; Faryal, R. COVID-19 Pandemic: A Serious Threat for Public Mental Health Globally. *Psychiatr. Danub.* **2020**, *32*, 245–250. [CrossRef] [PubMed]
31. Capuzzi, E.; Di Brita, C.; Caldiroli, A.; Colmegna, F.; Nava, R.; Buoli, M.; Clerici, M. Psychiatric emergency care during Coronavirus 2019 (COVID 19) pandemic lockdown: Results from a Department of Mental Health and Addiction of northern Italy. *Psychiatr. Res.* **2020**, *293*, 113463. [CrossRef] [PubMed]

32. Giallonardo, V.; Sampogna, G.; Del Vecchio, V.; Luciano, M.; Albert, U.; Carmassi, C.; Carrà, G.; Cirulli, F.; Dell'Osso, B.; Nanni, M.G.; et al. The impact of quarantine and physical distancing following COVID-19 on mental health: Study protocol of a multicentric Italian population trial. *Front Psychiatry* **2020**, *11*, 533. [CrossRef] [PubMed]
33. Di Carlo, F.; Sociali, A.; Picutti, E.; Pettorruso, M.; Vellante, F.; Verrastro, V.; Martinotti, G.; di Giannantonio, M. Telepsychiatry and other cutting-edge technologies in COVID-19 pandemic: Bridging the distance in mental health assistance. *Int. J. Clin. Prat.* **2020**, *75*. [CrossRef]
34. Chevance, A.; Gourion, D.; Hoertel, N.; Llorca, P.M.; Thomas, P.; Bocher, R.; Moro, M.-R.; Laprévote, V.; Benyamina, A.; Fossati, P.; et al. Ensuring mental health care during the SARS-CoV-2 epidemic in France: A narrative review. *L'encephale* **2020**, *46*, 193–201. [CrossRef]
35. Iasevoli, F.; Fornaro, M.; D'Urso, G.; Galletta, D.; Casella, C.; Paternoster, M.; Buccelli, C.; De Bartolomeis, A. Psychological distress in patients with serious mental illness during the COVID-19 outbreak and one-month mass quarantine in Italy. *Psychol. Med.* **2020**, 1–3. [CrossRef]
36. Anmella, G.; Arbelo, N.; Fico, G.; Murru, A.; Llach, C.D.; Madero, S.; Gomes-da-Costa, S.; Imaz, M.L.; López-Pelayo, H.; Vieta, E.; et al. COVID-19 inpatients with psychiatric disorders: Real-world clinical recommendations from an expert team in consultation-liaison psychiatry. *J. Affect. Disord.* **2020**, *274*, 1062–1067. [CrossRef]
37. Iancu, I.; Strous, R.; Poreh, A.; Kotler, M.; Chelben, Y. Psychiatric Inpatients' Reactions to the SARS Epidemic: An Israeli Survey. *ISR J. Psychiatry Relat. Sci.* **2005**, *42*, 258–262.
38. Li, L.; Li, F.; Fortunati, F.; Krystal, J.H. Association of a prior psychiatric diagnosis with mortality among hospitalized patients with Coronavirus disease 2019 (COVID-19) Infection. *JAMA Netw. Open* **2020**, *3*, e2023282. [CrossRef] [PubMed]
39. Rubio-Valera, M.; Luciano, J.V.; Ortiz, J.M.; Salvador-Carulla, L.; Gracia, A.; Serrano-Blanco, A. Health service use and costs associated with aggressiveness or agitation and containment in adult psychiatric care: A systematic review of the evidence. *BMC Psychiatry* **2015**, *15*, 1–13. [CrossRef] [PubMed]
40. Gurak, K.; de Mamani, A.W. Risk and Protective Factors, Perceptions of Family Environment, Ethnicity, and Schizophrenia Symptoms. *J. Nerv. Ment. Dis.* **2016**, *204*, 570–577. [CrossRef] [PubMed]

International Journal of
Environmental Research and Public Health

MDPI

Article

Health Anxiety Predicts the Perceived Dangerousness of COVID-19 over and above Intrusive Illness-Related Thoughts, Contamination Symptoms, and State and Trait Negative Affect

Claudio Sica [1], Corrado Caudek [2], Silvia Cerea [3], Ilaria Colpizzi [1], Maria Caruso [1], Paolo Giulini [1] and Gioia Bottesi [3,*]

[1] Department of Health Sciences, Psychology Section, University of Firenze, Via San Salvi, 12, 50135 Firenze, Italy; claudio.sica@unifi.it (C.S.); ilaria.colpizzi@unifi.it (I.C.); mcaruso260@gmail.com (M.C.); paolo.guglielmo.giulini@gmail.com (P.G.)
[2] Department of Neurosciences, Psychology, Drug Research, and Child Health, University of Firenze, Via San Salvi, 12, 50135 Firenze, Italy; corrado.caudek@unifi.it
[3] Department of General Psychology, University of Padova, Via Venezia, 8, 35131 Padova, Italy; silvia.cerea@unipd.it
* Correspondence: gioia.bottesi@unipd.it; Tel.: +39-049-827-6631

Abstract: This study sought to evaluate the specificity of health anxiety, relative to other forms of psychopathology, in perceptions of COVID-19 as dangerous. Measures of health anxiety, COVID-19 perceived dangerousness, negative affect, anxiety, depression, stress, contamination-related obsessions and compulsions, and intrusive illness-related thoughts were administered online to 742 community individuals during the Italian national lockdown. Results showed that, after controlling for demographic variables and other internalizing problems, health anxiety was the single most important factor associated with the perceived dangerousness of COVID-19. Moreover, a comparison between the current sample's scores on various symptom measures and scores from prepandemic Italian samples revealed that, whereas other internalizing symptoms increased by a large or very large magnitude during the pandemic, levels of health anxiety and negative affect increased by a medium amount. This result may indicate that health anxiety is relatively trait-like, increasing the likelihood that our correlational data support the model of health anxiety as a vulnerability rather than an outcome. Together, these results indicate that health anxiety may be a specific risk factor for COVID-related maladjustment and support the distinction of health anxiety from other psychological problems.

Keywords: health anxiety; intrusive thoughts; contamination; negative affect; pandemic; psychopathology

Citation: Sica, C.; Caudek, C.; Cerea, S.; Colpizzi, I.; Caruso, M.; Giulini, P.; Bottesi, G. Health Anxiety Predicts the Perceived Dangerousness of COVID-19 over and above Intrusive Illness-Related Thoughts, Contamination Symptoms, and State and Trait Negative Affect. *Int. J. Environ. Res. Public Health* **2021**, *18*, 1933. https://doi.org/10.3390/ijerph18041933

Academic Editor: Paolo Roma
Received: 10 January 2021
Accepted: 12 February 2021
Published: 17 February 2021

1. Introduction

In late 2019, a respiratory syndrome called coronavirus disease (COVID-19) began to spread, posing a mortal threat to the health of people around the globe [1,2]. Generally, COVID-19 has an incubation period of 1–14 days, and its symptoms include mild to severe fever, cough, dyspnea, and pneumonia [3,4]. The fatality rate is between 1% and 2%. The World Health Organization classified COVID-19 as a pandemic in March 2020. Due to a sharp increase in the number of confirmed cases and deaths, many governments around the world declared a state of emergency and advised people to practice social distancing to minimize contact with others, including self-isolating at home [1,2,5].

Beyond the impact on physical health, ongoing uncertainty related to the pandemic and the dramatic changes in behavior required by social distancing efforts may uniquely and profoundly impact mental health, and these problems may be more likely among individuals with certain psychological conditions [6–8]. Specifically, pre-existing health anxiety (although recently changed to "illness anxiety" in the fifth edition of the Diagnostic and

Statistical Manual of Mental Disorders [9], "health anxiety" is still in common use by mental health researchers and clinicians and is the term used in the ubiquitous cognitive behavioral model of health anxiety (for a discussion, see Bailer et al. [10])) may represent an important vulnerability factor contributing to heightened concerns about the COVID-19 pandemic. The essential feature of health anxiety, according to the Diagnostic and Statistical Manual of Mental Disorders, fifth edition (DSM-5) [9], is the presence of worries, concerns, or fears of having or acquiring a serious physical disease or other health-related issues [11,12]. Individuals with health anxiety are extremely preoccupied with bodily sensations and functions and with anything that may appear to be a sign of a pathological condition. They may excessively scrutinize medical and health information and frequently look up symptoms and diseases on the Internet (known as cyberchondria) [13,14]. This behavior may lead them to misinterpret trivial symptoms as reflecting serious ailments [15,16].

The aims of the current study were (1) to investigate how health anxiety, relative to other clinical problems, is associated with perceptions of COVID-19 dangerousness and (2) to determine whether the onset of COVID-19 has influenced the prevalence of health anxiety.

1.1. Health Anxiety and Epidemics

Few studies have been carried out to evaluate the associations between health anxiety and the fear of infection during an epidemic. This is a surprising limitation, given that one might expect the general tendency toward health-related worries to be associated with heightened concern in the context of disease outbreaks [15]. Blakey and Abramowitz [17] investigated psychological predictors (including health anxiety) of virus-related anxiety in 216 adults during the 2015–2016 Zika outbreak. Overestimations of the likelihood of contamination and greater factual knowledge about Zika emerged as the only variables predicting Zika-related anxiety. Wheaton and colleagues [18] examined the psychological processes associated with swine-flu-related anxiety in 315 college students during the H1N1 influenza pandemic of 2009–2010. Regression analysis indicated that health anxiety symptoms were the third significant predictor ($\beta = 0.21$) of swine-flu-related anxiety, after contamination fears and disgust sensitivity (both $\beta s = 0.28$).

More recently, Jungmann and Witthöft [19] conducted an online survey with 1615 individuals to investigate the roles of health anxiety, cyberchondria, and coping in COVID-19-related anxiety. Health anxiety showed positive relationships with virus anxiety ($r = 0.34$), distress caused by Internet research ($r = 0.48$), and maladaptive emotion regulation ($r = 0.17$). In addition, individuals with heightened health anxiety reported an increase in virus-related anxiety in recent months, according to a retrospective report. Importantly, however, findings from this last study do not allow for firm conclusions to be drawn about the specificity of the relationship between health anxiety and COVID-19-related anxiety, since other potentially relevant psychological variables—such as depression, contamination compulsions, and general anxiety—were not taken into account.

Similarly, Cannito and colleagues [20] found that during the national lockdown in Italy, health anxiety predicted attentional bias toward virus-related objects [21]. However, as in the study above, it was not possible to rule out the influence of general psychological distress or other clinical variables. Indeed, attentional bias toward threats is a common phenomenon among anxious populations [22], so it is unclear if health anxiety plays a specific role in disease-related cognitive processing.

1.2. The Current Study

The current study sought to extend prior research on health anxiety during disease outbreaks through the following main aims:

(1) To clarify the specific role of health anxiety in disease-related cognition, over and above other forms of psychopathology. Because health-related worries occur in other psychological disorders beyond health anxiety [23–28], it is not clear to what extent health anxiety symptoms contribute to perceptions of COVID-19 as dangerous, over and above

general distress and symptoms of generalized anxiety disorder, obsessive-compulsive disorder, and depressive disorders. In addition, during a disease outbreak, transient illness-related intrusive thoughts are fairly common [29,30] and do not necessarily indicate the presence of clinical health anxiety. Therefore, we also wanted to rule out the possibility that the purported link between health anxiety and perceptions of COVID-19 dangerousness were driven by these transient thoughts.

(2) To compare levels of health anxiety during the COVID-19 pandemic to prepandemic statistics. The literature suggests that health anxiety is relatively chronic, but it may also fluctuate in relation to life events [31]. Therefore, we also hoped to ascertain whether, on average, people reported more health anxiety symptoms during the pandemic than in pandemic-free periods, suggesting a prominent effect of stressful life events, or if reported health anxiety symptoms remained consistent, suggesting a more stable course.

Drawing on the scarce extant literature, the following hypotheses were tested: (1) health anxiety, negative affect, contamination compulsions, generalized anxiety, depression symptoms, and intrusive illness-related thoughts should be all related to the perceived dangerousness of COVID-19, and (2) health anxiety should be uniquely associated with perceived dangerousness of COVID-19, over and above the other psychological variables. Because of the variability of the prior literature, we had no a priori hypotheses about how the level of health anxiety reported by our participants would compare to prepandemic levels in similar samples.

2. Materials and Methods

2.1. Participants and Procedures

Data for the current study were collected in Italy during the period of maximal national restrictions in response to COVID-19 (i.e., from 10 March 2020 to 2 June 2020). An online battery of questionnaires was advertised through social media platforms (Facebook, Twitter, and Instagram). There were no exclusionary criteria, and the online battery took about one hour to complete. Of note, the sample consisted of community members and was not selected for elevated health anxiety. We believe this to be a strength, as health anxiety represents a continuum ranging from the absence of health concerns to pathological health anxiety [32,33]. When examining the psychological processes surrounding health anxiety, it is beneficial to use large, unselected samples that include a full range of symptoms, rather than focusing exclusively on samples of individuals with severe levels of health anxiety [10,33].

Ethical approval was obtained from the Institutional Board of the University of Firenze, in accordance with the principles of the Declaration of Helsinki. All participants were informed about the study's aims and provided informed consent before completing the survey.

2.2. Measures

A sociodemographic questionnaire was administered to collect background information such as sex, age, level of education, marital status, and place of residence. Participants were also asked if they, a close family member, or a significant other had contracted COVID-19.

The Perceived Dangerousness of Infection Questionnaire (PDIQ) was developed for the purposes of the current study to assess participants' perceptions of the dangerousness of COVID-19. Items were designed to assess participants' perceptions of the extent of the threat posed by COVID-19, including both the likelihood they would contract COVID-19 and the anticipated degree of personal harm an infection would cause [34]. As a first step, a pool of 10 items was collaboratively developed by a group of clinicians and researchers with experience in evaluating and treating individuals with anxiety disorders and somatization. Next, 30 individuals from the community rated the degree of intelligibility and clarity of the provisional items, using two separate five-point Likert scales ranging from 0 ("poor") to 4 ("excellent"). Comments by each participant about the items were also recorded. Only the items that received a mean rating of 3 or higher for both intelligibility and clarity were included in the final questionnaire. The final version of the PDIQ comprised nine items, which participants rated on a Likert scale ranging from 1 ("I do not agree at all") to 4 ("I fully agree"). Sample items included, "When I think of Coronavirus, I feel much more nervous than usual" and "I don't understand why people care so much about Coronavirus". A total score was created by reversing items keyed in the direction of low dangerousness, such that a higher total score indicated elevated perception of the dangerousness of COVID-19. In the current sample, internal consistency reliability for the PDIQ total score was acceptable (Cronbach's $\alpha = 0.71$).

The Health Anxiety Questionnaire (HAQ) [35] is a 21-item questionnaire measuring the main manifestations of health anxiety. Cluster and factor analyses have revealed four factors: worry and health preoccupation, fear of illness and death, reassurance-seeking behavior, and the extent to which symptoms interfere with a person's life. Prior studies indicate that the HAQ has appropriate reliability and discriminant validity in both the original and the Italian [36] versions. In the current sample, internal consistency for the HAQ total score was excellent (Cronbach's $\alpha = 0.93$).

To compare health anxiety to other forms of psychopathology in predicting COVID-19 perceptions, we also administered the following self-report instruments:

The Questionnaire of Unpleasant Intrusive Thoughts (QUIT) [37] is a measure assessing cognitive intrusions of various types. The QUIT begins with a detailed definition of unwanted mental intrusions and the different ways they can be experienced (i.e., as images, thoughts/doubts, impulses, or physical sensations). After the initial description, four separate sets of intrusions are presented: obsessional (i.e., related to obsessive-compulsive disorder; 12 items), appearance-related (i.e., related to body dysmorphic disorder; 9 items), illness and death-related (i.e., related to health anxiety; 10 items) and eating-related (i.e., related to eating disorders; 8 items). Respondents are then requested to evaluate each intrusion for frequency from 0 ("never") to 6 ("always, frequently throughout the day") and the discomfort it produces when it occurs from 0 ("not at all") to 4 ("extremely disturbing"). The QUIT was validated in a cross-cultural study [32] carried out in Europe (including Italy), the Middle East, and South America. In the current study, only the discomfort score associated with health anxiety-related intrusions (e.g., "For no particular reason, I have intrusive thoughts such as 'I could die of a serious illness,' for example, cancer, AIDS, etc.") was used, given the high correlation between discomfort and frequency (r=0.90). In the current sample, internal consistency for this scale was very good (Cronbach's $\alpha = 0.90$).

The Obsessive-Compulsive Inventory-Revised (OCI-R) [38] is a widely used 18-item self-report questionnaire measuring the severity of obsessive-compulsive symptoms on a five-point Likert scale. Items are grouped into six subscales (washing/contamination, checking, ordering, obsessing, hoarding, and mental neutralizing). Reliability and validity of this instrument are supported both in the original and in the Italian [39] versions. In the current study, we used the washing/contamination scale only (which was consistently related to pandemic-related problems [17,18]) and the Cronbach's α was 0.70.

The Depression Anxiety Stress Scale-21 (DASS-21) [40] is a 21-item measure assessing depression (lack of incentive, low self-esteem, and dysphoria), anxiety (somatic and subjective symptoms of anxiety as well as acute responses of fear), and stress (irritability, impatience, tension, and persistent arousal) over the previous week on a four-point Likert scale. Good psychometric properties have been reported for both the original and the Italian [41] versions. In the current study, Cronbach's αs for depression, anxiety, and stress were all above 0.90.

The personality inventory for DSM-5 personality disorders (PID-5) [42] consists of 220 items rated on a four-point Likert scale assessing 25 facet traits that that load onto five higher-order dimensions: antagonism, detachment, disinhibition, negative affect, and psychoticism. The PID-5 has adequate psychometric properties in its original version [43,44] as well as in the Italian translation [45,46]. In the current study, we used the negative affect scale only, and its internal consistency was excellent (Cronbach's $\alpha = 0.91$). We chose a measure of negative affect as an index of general internalizing psychopathology, since it is thought to subsume most internalizing symptoms, and it is strictly related to neuroticism [47].

2.3. Statistical Analyses

Zero-order correlations (Pearson's *rs*) were computed to evaluate the associations among all study variables. Following Cohen's classification [48], large correlations were defined as 0.50 and above, medium correlations between 0.30 and 0.49, and small correlations between 0.10 and 0.29. In addition, Steiger's *z* test was used to evaluate magnitude differences between correlations.

To evaluate the unique association between the HAQ score and the PDIQ (Aim 1), we used a multiple regression analysis. In the first block, age, education, and gender (dummy coded: 1 = males, 2 = females) were entered to control for any effect of demographic variables. In the second block, all the symptom variables that were found to correlate with the PDIQ were entered, apart from the HAQ. In the third and final block, the HAQ score was included. In this way, we were able to evaluate the association between health anxiety and perceived COVID-19 dangerousness, over and above the other psychopathology variables.

To address Aim 2, independent-samples *t*-tests were run to compare the average scores on each symptom measure in our sample, collected during the COVID-19 lockdown, versus the previously published Italian validation samples (i.e., pre- versus peri-COVID-19 scores). Hedges' *g* coefficients were computed to evaluate the effect size of the differences. These effects are considered small at or below 0.2, medium around 0.5, and large above 0.8 [48]. All the statistical analyses were conducted using IBM SPSS, version 26.

3. Results

Of the 743 adults who enrolled in the study, 742 (99.8%) completed all questionnaires. The mean age of this final sample was 30.7 years (SD = 14.0), and 73% was female. Their mean education was 14.4 years (SD = 3.5); 69% of the sample was single, 26% was married or cohabitating, and 4% was separated or divorced. Geographically, 23% lived in Northern Italy, 65% in Central Italy, and 12% in Southern Italy. None of the participants reported being ill or infected by COVID-19 themselves, but 65 (8.7%) reported that a close family member or significant other had contracted the virus.

Bivariate correlations among all study variables are presented in Table 1.

Table 1. Bivariate correlations (Pearson's *rs*) among psychopathological variables (*N* = 742).

Measure	1	2	3	4	5	6	7	8
1. PDIQ		**0.26** **	0.21 **	0.04	0.13 **	0.13 **	0.18 **	0.14 **
2. HAQ			**0.40** **	**0.21** **	**0.26** **	**0.26** **	**0.16** **	**0.41** **
3. PID 5 Negative Affect				0.46 **	0.38 **	0.51 **	0.26 **	0.42 **
4. DASS-21 Depression					0.58 **	0.70 **	0.12 **	0.20 **
5. DASS-21 Anxiety						0.67 **	0.21 **	0.27 **
6. DASS-21 Stress							0.15 **	0.30 **
7. OCI-R Washing/Contamination								0.28 **
8. QUIT Health Discomfort								

PDIQ = Perceived Dangerousness of Infection Questionnaire, HAQ = Health Anxiety Questionnaire, PID-5 = Personality Inventory for DSM-5 Personality Disorders, DASS-21 = Depression Anxiety Stress Scale-21, OCI-R = Obsessive-Compulsive Inventory-Revised, and QUIT = Questionnaire of Unpleasant Intrusive Thoughts. ** $p < 0.001$; figures for the HAQ are bolded.

All the variables were significantly related to the PDIQ at a small magnitude, except for the DASS-21 Depression scale, which showed a negligible correlation coefficient. In turn, the HAQ was significantly associated with all the other variables at a small size, except for the QUIT Health Discomfort score ($r = 0.41$, $p < 0.001$) and PID-5 Negative Affect scale ($r = 0.40$, $p < 0.001$). According to the Steiger's *z* test, the latter two correlation coefficients were significantly larger than the correlations between the HAQ and all the other variables ($p < 0.001$). Unsurprisingly, the PID-5 Negative Affect score appeared, on average, as the largest association with all the other variables (mean $r = 0.36$).

Findings from the multiple regression analysis are shown in Table 2. Because DASS-21 Depression was not correlated with PDIQ scores, it was not included in the model. Inspection of the final model indicated that multicollinearity was not a problem [49].

Table 2. Results of linear regression analysis predicting Perceived Dangerousness of Infection Questionnaire score.

Predictors	*B*	*SE B*	*β*	*t*	*ΔR2*	*F*	*df1*	*df2*
Step 1					0.03 **	8.05	3	738
(Constant)	27.01	0.99		27.16 **				
Age	−0.02	0.01	−0.08	−2.17 *				
Gender	1.34	0.34	0.15	4.00 **				
Education	−0.03	0.05	−0.02	−0.58				
Step 2					0.07 **	8.38	8	733
(Constant)	24.59	1.06		23.25 **				
Age	−0.02	0.01	−0.08	−2.07 *				
Gender	1.05	0.33	0.11	3.17 *				
Education	0.03	0.05	0.02	0.60				
PID-5 Negative Affect	0.04	0.01	0.13	2.80 *				
DASS-21 Anxiety	0.02	0.02	0.04	0.91				
DASS-21 Stress	−0.01	0.02	−0.02	−0.33				
OCI-R Washing/Contamination	0.20	0.06	0.14	3.60 **				
QUIT Health Discomfort	0.01	0.02	0.03	0.66				
Step 3					0.11 **	10.83	9	732
(Constant)	22.43	1.12		20.09 **				
Age	−0.02	0.01	−0.08	−2.16 *				
Gender	1.11	0.33	0.12	3.42 *				
Education	0.03	0.05	0.02	0.52				
PID-5 Negative Affect	0.02	0.02	0.07	1.54				
DASS-21 Anxiety	0.01	0.02	0.02	0.41				
DASS-21 Stress	−0.00	0.02	−0.01	−0.21				
OCI-R Washing/Contamination	0.20	0.06	0.14	3.67 **				
QUIT Health Discomfort	−0.02	0.02	−0.03	−0.79				
HAQ	0.08	0.02	0.21	5.29 **				

PID-5 = Personality Inventory for DSM-5 Personality Disorders, DASS-21 = Depression Anxiety Stress Scale-21, OCI-R = Obsessive-Compulsive Inventory-Revised, QUIT = Questionnaire of Unpleasant Intrusive Thoughts, and HAQ = Health Anxiety Questionnaire.
* $p < 0.05$, ** $p < 0.001$.

Results showed that each successive step of the regression added significantly to the overall prediction of PDIQ scores (ΔR^2). In the final model, female gender, younger age, the OCI-R Washing/Contamination scale, and the HAQ score were the only significant predictors of the PDIQ. Overall, the final model explained 12% of the variance in PDIQ scores; the HAQ explained 4% of the variance in PDIQ score beyond that explained by the other variables.

Lastly, we compared the average scores on all questionnaires completed by the current sample with the normative values reported in the Italian standardization studies (Table 3).

Results showed that all symptom scores were significantly higher in the current COVID-19 sample than in the pre-COVID-19 Italian validation samples, except for QUIT Health Discomfort scores, which were surprisingly significantly lower than in the pre-COVID-19 sample. Hedges' *g* was medium-sized for HAQ, QUIT, and PID-5 Negative Affect scores and large for OCI-R Washing/Contamination and each of the DASS-21 scale scores.

Table 3. Comparison between the current sample and the original Italian standardization sample on various measures of psychopathology.

	HAQ	QUIT Health Discomfort	OCI-R Washing/Contamination	DASS-21 Depression	DASS-21 Anxiety	DASS-21 Stress	PID-5 Negative Affect
Current sample	39.9 (11.1)	12.6 (9.0)	12 (2.8)	12.9 (10.3)	11.1 (9.3)	18.6 (10.2)	29.9 (12.5)
Pre-COVID sample	33.8 (9.2)	19.5 (9.9)	0.9 (1.5)	3.5 (3.2)	2.4 (2.6)	6.4 (3.8)	23.2 (9.9)
t-test outcome	7.8 *	−7.5 *	68.7 *	18.4 *	18.7 *	23.5 *	9.2 *
Hedges' *g*	0.57	0.75	4.5	1.11	1.14	1.58	0.57

Standard deviation in parentheses. HAQ = Health Anxiety Questionnaire (pre-COVID-19 sample N = 252 community individuals [36]), QUIT = Questionnaire of Unpleasant Intrusive Thoughts (pre-COVID-19 sample N = 114 undergraduates [37]), OCI-R = Obsessive-Compulsive Inventory-Revised (pre-COVID-19 sample N = 340 community individuals [39]), DASS-21 = Depression Anxiety Stress Scale-21 (pre-COVID-19 sample N = 417 community individuals [41]), and PID-5 = Personality Inventory for DSM-5 Personality Disorders (pre-COVID-19 sample N = 389 community individuals [45]). * $p < 0.01$.

4. Discussion

Correlational findings showed that all the variables examined in this study were relevant to the perceived dangerousness of COVID-19, except for depression. Depression may be more closely related to the consequences of the pandemic (e.g., living in quarantine) than concerns about its dangerousness [50,51]. Consistent with the high comorbidity of health anxiety [10], different psychopathological symptoms were significantly linked to HAQ scores. For example, illness-related intrusions were moderately associated with health anxiety, demonstrating that these two phenomena are related but not overlapping. While transient intrusive thoughts about illness and its consequences may occur in any individual during a pandemic, excessive preoccupation and concern about one's health—which are characteristic of health anxiety and reflected in HAQ scores—appear more relevant to perceptions of COVID-19 dangerousness.

Regression results indicated that health anxiety, as measured by the HAQ, was the single most important factor associated to the perceived dangerousness of COVID-19. This result is an important step beyond the existing literature given that, in this study, other relevant psychopathological variables were taken in account. Even though recent studies have stressed the role of general tendencies toward health anxiety in COVID-19-related concerns [19], this is one of the first studies demonstrating a specific association between health anxiety and the perceived dangerousness of COVID-19, over and above other forms of internalizing.

In addition to health anxiety, the present study suggests that individuals with obsessive-compulsive symptoms related to washing and contamination may also be sensitive and vulnerable to COVID-19 fears. This finding is consistent with the literature and suggests that these individuals may be at risk of exacerbation of obsessive-compulsive symptoms during COVID-19 [52,53]. Importantly, this vulnerability appears independent from health anxiety, given that our regression analyses elucidated the *unique* contributions of each variable of interest to perceptions of COVID-19 dangerousness.

Regarding demographic variables, younger individuals and females appeared to be more concerned about the dangerousness of COVID-19, indicating that these individuals may be more prone to developing distressing symptoms during a pandemic [51].

The results summarized above suggest that in disease-threat situations, individuals with high levels of health anxiety may react differently than people with low levels of health anxiety. For instance, Höfling and Weck [54] reported that processes such as worries about one's health, perception of others as unsupportive of the respondent's illness concerns, tendency toward reassurance-seeking behavior with regard to illness concerns, and preoccupation with bodily sensations were more intense for patients with hypochondriasis in contrast to those with panic disorder or social phobia [55,56]. Consistent with this finding, current theoretical conceptualizations emphasize the importance of cognitive processes in the maintenance of severe health anxiety [14,21,57]. The link between health anxiety and perceptions of COVID-19 as dangerous, as found in the current study, should not be overlooked. For instance, anxiety about becoming ill with COVID-19 could lead people to visit health care facilities excessively and often, thereby increasing the risk of transmission and hindering the provision of necessary medical care to patients in real need. Moreover, individuals who are highly concerned about being infected may undertake excessive or iatrogenic protective measures. In addition, excessive control and reassurance-seeking among people who are overly concerned about their health may place a significant burden on the health care system and trigger socially disruptive behaviors [58].

The unique nature of health anxiety is also demonstrated by the comparison between the scores of our community sample during COVID-19 lockdown with those obtained in similar samples before the pandemic. Whereas symptom scores such as generalized anxiety, stress, depression, and contamination-related intrusive thoughts increased by a large or very large magnitude, HAQ and PID-5 Negative Affect scores increased by a medium amount only. This result may indicate that health anxiety symptoms are approximately as stable as a personality trait like negative affect, even in a crisis context when other clinical symptoms are increasing drastically. In contrast, the distress linked to intrusive thoughts about illness was lower during the pandemic than in the pre-COVID-19 period. This result may be due to the difference between samples, as the QUIT validation sample [37] tested in the prepandemic period included only college students, whereas our community sample had a higher mean age and lower mean educational attainment. Another possible explanation regards habituation mechanisms. Indeed, frequent and inescapable news and government warnings about the infection might have acted as a form of exposure to intrusive thoughts, resulting in less distress. In any case, the contrasting patterns of pre- to peri-COVID scores seem to further demonstrate that intrusive thoughts about illness and health anxiety are qualitatively different phenomena.

The specific role of health anxiety demonstrated in this study adds robustness to the distinction of health anxiety from other psychopathological conditions, as illustrated by the placement of illness anxiety disorder in a separate section named "Somatic Symptom and Related Disorders" in both DSM-5 [9] and in the Psychodynamic Diagnostic Manual [54,59]. Health anxiety has long held an uncertain place in prominent taxonomies of mental illness. This fact is illustrated in recent changes to the Hierarchical Taxonomy of Psychopathology (HiTOP), a quantitative-empirical nosology initiative. Initially, health anxiety was provisionally considered to fall under the Somatoform Spectrum in HiTOP, separate from the other major spectra (i.e., Internalizing, Thought Disorder, Disinhibited Externalizing, Antagonistic Externalizing, and Detachment) [60]. However, in more recent HiTOP studies based on updated structural models, health anxiety is considered a "syndrome" falling under the Somatic Anxiety Sub-Subfactor of the Fear Subfactor, which is contained within Internalizing Spectrum [61]. Given these recent changes, the placement of health anxiety in taxonomies of psychopathology remains to be clarified. Further research on the specific cognitive processes that produce health anxiety and differentiate it from other forms of internalizing could contribute to these efforts [62].

Some study limitations warrant mention. The cross-sectional nature of this investigation precludes us from drawing causal inferences regarding the relationships between the symptom variables and concerns about the COVID-19 pandemic. Nonetheless, the finding of relative stability of health anxiety between pre- and peri-COVID samples, compared with other forms of psychopathology, lends initial support to the theoretical model described here, wherein pre-existing health anxiety makes an individual more likely to perceive COVID-19 as dangerous. Another limitation is that, in the current study, a large portion of variance in the perceived dangerousness of COVID-19 remains unexplained, thereby requiring more research about the factors associated with COVID-19-related perceptions. Future studies using a longitudinal design could consider the System Dynamics approach as a means to model the various influences on perceptions of COVID-19 as dangerous [63,64]. In addition, the use of an Italian sample may limit generalizability to other countries, as results may not be identical for individuals with different backgrounds and pandemic-related stressors or in countries with different government responses. Lastly, given that frequency and/or duration of online health research correlates consistently with health anxiety and often provokes anxiety [19,65], it will be important for future research to investigate the role of the Internet in the association between health anxiety and perceived dangerousness of COVID-19.

5. Conclusions

Notwithstanding the above-mentioned limitations, the present study contributes to the existing literature by demonstrating the specific influence of health anxiety on perceptions of COVID-19 as dangerous. Our results have potential clinical implications. Although our data are correlational, they are consistent with the idea that individuals with health anxiety symptoms could be especially vulnerable to anxiety about ongoing disease threats, especially in the context of ongoing media and governmental advisories to employ stringent precautionary measures. Clinicians can help these individuals to respond to this information in a more adaptive way by challenging their perceptions of the likelihood and severity of infection, thus reducing excessive and pathological fear and avoidance behaviors. In general, cognitive-behavioral therapy components such as psychoeducation, cognitive restructuring, and exposure therapy have shown utility in health anxiety management [31]. Additionally, given the inability to fully avoid aversive and anxiety-provoking information during a global pandemic, acceptance-based approaches such as Acceptance and Commitment Therapy [66] could be employed to increase one's willingness to experience uncomfortable thoughts and feelings about COVID-19 dangerousness without trying to avoid or struggle with them [67].

Author Contributions: Conceptualization, C.S., C.C., I.C., and G.B.; Formal analysis, C.S., C.C., and I.C.; Investigation, C.C., S.C., I.C., M.C., and P.G.; Methodology, C.C. and I.C.; Project administration, C.S., C.C., and I.C.; Supervision, C.S. and G.B.; Writing—original draft, C.S. and G.B.; Writing—review & editing, C.S. and G.B. All authors have read and agreed to the published version of the manuscript.

Funding: This research received no external funding.

Institutional Review Board Statement: The study was conducted according to the guidelines of the Declaration of Helsinki and was approved by the Institutional Review Board of the University of Firenze (protocol code: 97, date of approval: 29 May 2020)

Informed Consent Statement: Informed consent was obtained from all subjects involved in the study.

Data Availability Statement: The data presented in this study are available on request from the corresponding author. The data are not publicly available due to their use in other ongoing works.

Acknowledgments: The Authors wish to thank Emily R. Perkins for her precious theoretical suggestions and for the revision of the manuscript. This work was carried out within the scope of the project "Use-Inspired Basic Research," for which the Department of General Psychology of the University of Padova has been recognized as "Dipartimento di eccellenza" by the Ministry of University and Research.

Conflicts of Interest: The authors declare no conflict of interest.

References

1. World Health Organization. Coronavirus Disease (COVID-19) Pandemic. 2020. Available online: https://www.who.int/emergencies/diseases/novel-coronavirus-2019 (accessed on 16 November 2020).
2. The Novel Coronavirus Pneumonia Emergency Response Epidemiology Team. The epidemiological characteristics of an outbreak of 2019 novel coronavirus diseases (COVID-19) in China. *China CDC Wkly* **2020**, *2*, 113–122. [CrossRef]
3. Centers for Disease Control and Prevention. About COVID-19. 2020. Available online: https://www.cdc.gov/coronavirus/2019-ncov/cdcresponse/about-COVID-19.html (accessed on 16 November 2020).
4. Huang, C.; Wang, Y.; Li, X.; Ren, L.; Zhao, J.; Hu, Y.; Zhang, L.; Fan, G.; Xu, J.; Gu, X.; et al. Clinical features of patients infected with 2019 novel coronavirus in Wuhan, China. *Lancet* **2020**, *395*, 497–506. [CrossRef]

5. Kucharski, A.J.; Russell, T.W.; Diamond, C.; Liu, Y.; Edmunds, J.; Funk, S.; Eggo, R.M. Early dynamics of transmission and control of COVID-19: ADS mathematical modelling study. *Lancet Infect. Dis.* **2020**, *20*, 553–558. [CrossRef]
6. Cao, W.; Fang, Z.; Hou, G.; Han, M.; Xu, X.; Dong, J.; Zheng, J. The psychological impact of the COVID-19 epidemic on college students in China. *Psychiatry Res.* **2020**, *287*, 112934. [CrossRef] [PubMed]
7. Cénat, J.M.; Blais-Rochette, C.; Kokou-Kpolou, C.K.; Noorishad, P.G.; Mukunzi, J.N.; McIntee, S.E.; Dalexis, R.D.; Goulet, M.A.; Labelle, P.R. Prevalence of symptoms of depression, anxiety, insomnia, posttraumatic stress disorder, and psychological distress among populations affected by the COVID-19 pandemic: A systematic review and meta-analysis. *Psychiatry Res.* **2020**, *295*, 113599. [CrossRef]
8. Pfefferbaum, B.; North, C.S. Mental Health and the Covid-19 Pandemic. *N. Engl. J. Med.* **2020**, *383*, 510–512. [CrossRef]
9. American Psychiatric Association. *Diagnostic and Statistical Manual of Mental Disorders (DSM-5)*; American Psychiatric Association Publishing: Washington, DC, USA, 2013.
10. Bailer, J.; Kerstner, T.; Witthöft, M.; Diener, C.; Mier, D.; Rist, F. Health anxiety and hypochondriasis in the light of DSM-5. *Anxiety Stress Coping* **2016**, *29*, 219–239. [CrossRef]
11. Tyrer, P. Recent advances in the understanding and treatment of health anxiety. *Curr. Psychiatry Rep.* **2018**, *20*, 49. [CrossRef]
12. Bobevski, I.; Clarke, D.M.; Meadows, G. Health anxiety and its relationship to disability and service use: Findings from a large epidemiological survey. *Psychosom. Med.* **2016**, *78*, 13–25. [CrossRef] [PubMed]
13. McMullan, R.D.; Berle, D.; Arnáez, S.; Starcevic, V. The relationships between health anxiety, online health information seeking, and cyberchondria: Systematic review and meta-analysis. *J. Affect. Disord.* **2019**, *245*, 270–278. [CrossRef] [PubMed]
14. Witthoft, M.; Hiller, W. Psychological approaches to origins and treatments of somatoform disorders. *Annu. Rev. Clin. Psychol.* **2010**, *6*, 257–283. [CrossRef] [PubMed]
15. Tyrer, P. Why health anxiety needs to be recognised in hospital practice. *Clin. Med.* **2020**, *20*, 339–342. [CrossRef]
16. Salkovskis, P.M.; Warwick, H.C. Making sense of hypochondriasis: A cognitive model of health anxiety. In *Health Anxiety: Clinical and Research Perspectives on Hypochondriasis and Related Conditions*; Asmundson, G.J.G., Taylor, S., Cox, B.J., Eds.; John Wiley & Sons: Hoboken, NJ, USA, 2001.
17. Blakey, S.M.; Abramowitz, J.S. Psychological predictors of health anxiety in response to the Zika virus. *J. Clin. Psychol. Med. Settings* **2017**, *24*, 270–278. [CrossRef]
18. Wheaton, M.G.; Abramowitz, J.S.; Berman, N.C.; Fabricant, L.E.; Olatunji, B.O. Psychological predictors of anxiety in response to the H1N1 (swine flu) pandemic. *Cogn. Ther. Res.* **2011**, *36*, 210–218. [CrossRef]
19. Jungmann, S.M.; Witthöft, M. Health anxiety, cyberchondria, and coping in the current COVID-19 pandemic: Which factors are related to coronavirus anxiety? *J. Anxiety Disord.* **2020**, *73*, 102239. [CrossRef]
20. Cannito, L.; Di Crosta, A.; Palumbo, R.; Ceccato, I.; Anzani, S.; La Malva, P.; Di Domenico, A. Health anxiety and attentional bias toward virus-related stimuli during the COVID-19 pandemic. *Sci. Rep.* **2020**, *10*, 1–8. [CrossRef]
21. Marcus, D.K.; Gurley, J.R.; Marchi, M.M.; Bauer, C. Cognitive and perceptual variables in hypochondriasis and health anxiety: A systematic review. *Clin. Psychol. Rev.* **2007**, *27*, 127–139. [CrossRef] [PubMed]
22. Bar-Haim, Y.; Lamy, D.; Pergamin, L.; Bakermans-Kranenburg, M.J.; Van Ijzendoorn, M.H. Threat-related attentional bias in anxious and nonanxious individuals: A meta-analytic study. *Psychol. Bull.* **2007**, *133*, 1–24. [CrossRef] [PubMed]
23. Asmundson, G.J.; Abramowitz, J.S.; Richter, A.A.; Whedon, M. Health anxiety: Current perspectives and future directions. *Curr. Psychiatry Rep.* **2010**, *12*, 306–312. Available online: https://pubmed.ncbi.nlm.nih.gov/20549396/ (accessed on 17 November 2020). [CrossRef] [PubMed]
24. Olatunji, B.O.; Deacon, B.J.; Abramowitz, J.S. Is hypochondriasis an anxiety disorder? *Br. J. Psychiatry* **2009**, *194*, 481–482. [CrossRef]
25. Sakai, R.; Nestoriuc, Y.; Nolido, N.V.; Barsky, A.J. The prevalence of personality disorders in hypochondriasis. *J. Clin. Psychiatry* **2010**, *71*, 41–47. [CrossRef] [PubMed]
26. Sunderland, M.; Newby, J.M.; Andrews, G. Health anxiety in Australia: Prevalence, comorbidity, disability and service use. *Br. J. Psychiatry* **2013**, *202*, 56–61. [CrossRef]
27. Taylor, S.; McKay, D.; Abramowitz, J.S. Hypochondriasis and Health-Related Anxiety. In *Handbook of Evidence-Based Practice in Clinical Psychology*; Sturmey, P., Hersen, M., Eds.; John Wiley & Sons: Hoboken, NJ, USA, 2012; Volume 2.
28. McClure, E.B.; Lilienfeld, S.O. Personality traits and health anxiety. In *Health Anxiety: Clinical and Research Perspectives on Hypochondriasis and Related Conditions*; Asmundson, G.J.G., Taylor, S., Cox, B.J., Eds.; John Wiley & Sons: Hoboken, NJ, USA, 2001.
29. Barsky, A.J.; Fama, J.M.; Bailey, E.D.; Ahern, D.K. A Prospective 4- to 5-Year Study of DSM-III-R Hypochondriasis. *Arch. Gen. Psychiatry* **1998**, *55*, 737–744. [CrossRef] [PubMed]
30. Simon, G.E.; Gureje, O.; Fullerton, C. Course of hypochondriasis in an international primary care study. *Gen. Hosp. Psychiatry* **2001**, *23*, 51–55. [CrossRef]
31. Taylor, S.; Asmundson, G.J. *Treating Health Anxiety: A Cognitive-Behavioral Approach*; Guilford Press: New York, NY, USA, 2004.
32. Ferguson, E. A taxometric analysis of health anxiety. *Psychol. Med.* **2009**, *39*, 277–285. [CrossRef]
33. Norbye, A.D.; Abelsen, B.; Førde, O.H.; Ringberg, U. Distribution of health anxiety in a general adult population and associations with demographic and social network characteristics. *Psychol. Med.* **2020**, 1–8. [CrossRef]
34. Freeston, M.H.; Tiplady, A.; Mawn, L.; Bottesi, G.; Thwaites, S. Towards a model of uncertainty distress in the context of Coronavirus (Covid-19). *Cogn. Behav. Ther.* **2020**, *13*, E31. [CrossRef]

35. Lucock, M.P.; Morley, S. The health anxiety questionnaire. *Br. J. Health Psychol.* **1996**, *1*, 137–150. [CrossRef]
36. Melli, G.; Coradeschi, D.; Smurra, R. The Italian version of Health Anxiety Questionnaire: Reliability and factorial analysis. *Psicoter. Cogn. Comport.* **2007**, *13*, 37–48.
37. Pascual-Vera, B.; Akin, B.; Belloch, A.; Bottesi, G.; Clark, D.A.; Doron, G.; Fernández-Alvarez, H.; Ghisi, M.; Gómez, B.; Inozu, M.; et al. The cross-cultural and transdiagnostic nature of unwanted mental intrusions. *Int. J. Clin. Health Psychol.* **2019**, *19*, 85–96. [CrossRef]
38. Foa, E.B.; Huppert, J.D.; Leiberg, S.; Langner, R.; Kichic, R.; Hajcak, G.; Salkovskis, P.M. The Obsessive-Compulsive Inventory: Development and validation of a short version. *Psychol. Assess.* **2002**, *14*, 485–496. [CrossRef]
39. Sica, C.; Ghisi, M.; Altoè, G.; Chiri, L.R.; Franceschini, S.; Coradeschi, D.; Melli, G. The Italian version of the Obsessive Compulsive Inventory: Its psychometric properties on community and clinical samples. *J. Anxiety Disord.* **2009**, *23*, 204–211. [CrossRef] [PubMed]
40. Lovibond, P.F.; Lovibond, S.H. The structure of negative emotional states: Comparison of the Depression Anxiety Stress Scales (DASS) with the Beck Depression and Anxiety Inventories. *Behav. Res. Ther.* **1995**, *33*, 335–343. [CrossRef]
41. Bottesi, G.; Ghisi, M.; Altoè, G.; Conforti, E.; Melli, G.; Sica, C. The Italian version of the Depression Anxiety Stress Scales-21: Factor structure and psychometric properties on community and clinical samples. *Compr. Psychiatry* **2015**, *60*, 170–181. [CrossRef]
42. Krueger, R.F.; Derringer, J.; Markon, K.E.; Watson, D.; Skodol, A.E. Initial construction of a maladaptive personality trait model and inventory for DSM-5. *Psychol. Med.* **2012**, *42*, 1879–1890. [CrossRef] [PubMed]
43. Al-Dajani, N.; Gralnick, T.M.; Bagby, R.M. A psychometric review of the Personality Inventory for DSM–5 (PID–5): Current status and future directions. *J. Personal. Assess.* **2016**, *98*, 62–81. [CrossRef]
44. Krueger, R.F.; Markon, K.E. The Role of the DSM-5 Personality Trait Model in Moving Toward a Quantitative and Empirically Based Approach to Classifying Personality and Psychopathology. *Annu. Rev. Clin. Psychol.* **2014**, *10*, 477–501. [CrossRef]
45. Fossati, A.; Krueger, R.F.; Markon, K.E.; Borroni, S.; Maffei, C. Reliability and validity of the Personality Inventory for DSM-5 (PID-5) predicting DSM-IV personality disorders and psychopathy in community-dwelling Italian adults. *Assessment* **2013**, *20*, 689–708. [CrossRef] [PubMed]
46. Bottesi, G.; Ghisi, M.; Martignon, A.; Sica, C. Self-other agreement in DSM-5 Section III Dimensional Personality Traits: A study on Italian community individuals. *Personal. Individ. Differ.* **2018**, *130*, 135–140. [CrossRef]
47. Kotov, R.; Krueger, R.F.; Watson, D.; Achenbach, T.M.; Althoff, R.R.; Bagby, R.M.; Brown, T.A.; Carpenter, W.T.; Caspi, A.; Clark, L.A.; et al. The Hierarchical Taxonomy of Psychopathology (HiTOP): A dimensional alternative to traditional nosologies. *J. Abnorm. Psychol.* **2017**, *126*, 454–477. [CrossRef]
48. Cohen, J. *Statistical Power Analysis for the Behavioral Sciences*, 2nd ed.; Lawrence Erlbaum Associates: Mahwah, NJ, USA, 1988.
49. Hair, J.F.; Black, W.C.; Babin, B.J.; Anderson, R.E.; Tatham, R.L. *Multivariate Data Analysis*, 6th ed.; Pearson Prentice Hall: Upper Saddle River, NJ, USA, 2006.
50. Brooks, S.K.; Webster, R.K.; Smith, L.E.; Woodland, L.; Wessely, S.; Greenberg, N.; Rubin, G.J. The psychological impact of quarantine and how to reduce it: Rapid review of the evidence. *Lancet* **2020**, *395*, 912–920. [CrossRef]
51. Luo, M.; Guo, L.; Yu, M.; Jiang, W.; Wang, H. The Psychological and Mental Impact of Coronavirus Disease 2019 (COVID-19) on Medical Staff and General Public—A systematic Review and Meta-analysis. *Psychiatry Res.* **2020**, *291*, 113190. [CrossRef] [PubMed]
52. Matsunaga, H.; Mukai, K.; Yamanishi, K. Acute impact of COVID-19 pandemic on phenomenological features in fully or partially remitted patients with obsessive–compulsive disorder. *Psychiatry Clin. Neurosci.* **2020**, *74*, 565–566. [CrossRef]
53. Khosravani, V.; Asmundson, G.J.G.; Taylor, S.; Bastan, F.S.; Ardestani, S.M.S. The Persian COVID stress scales (Persian-CSS) and COVID-19-related stress reactions in patients with obsessive-compulsive and anxiety disorders. *J. Obsessive Compuls. Relat. Disord.* **2021**, *28*, 100615. [CrossRef] [PubMed]
54. Höfling, V.; Weck, F. Hypochondriasis Differs from Panic Disorder and Social Phobia: Specific Processes Identified Within Patient Groups. *J. Nerv. Ment. Dis.* **2017**, *205*, 227–233. [CrossRef] [PubMed]
55. Noyes, R.; Stuart, S.; Watson, D.B.; Langbehn, D.R. Distinguishing between hypochondriasis and somatization disorder: A review of the existing literature. *Psychother. Psychosom.* **2006**, *75*, 270–281. [CrossRef]
56. Rief, W.; Hessel, A.; Braehler, E. Somatization symptoms and hypochondriacal features in the general population. *Psychosom. Med.* **2001**, *63*, 595–602. [CrossRef] [PubMed]
57. Norris, L.A.; Marcus, D.K. Cognition in health anxiety and hypochondriasis: Recent advances. *Curr. Psychiatry Rev.* **2014**, *10*, 44–49. [CrossRef]
58. Tyrer, P.; Tyrer, H. Health anxiety: Detection and treatment. *BJPsych Adv.* **2018**, *24*, 66–72. [CrossRef]
59. Lingiardi, V.; McWilliams, N. *Psychodynamic Diagnostic Manual: PDM-2*, 2nd ed.; Guilford Press: New York, NY, USA, 2017.
60. Kotov, R.; Ruggero, C.J.; Krueger, R.F.; Watson, D.; Yuan, Q.; Zimmerman, M. New dimensions in the quantitative classification of mental illness. *Arch. Gen. Psychiatry* **2011**, *68*, 1003–1011. [CrossRef] [PubMed]
61. Forbes, M.K.; Sunderland, M.; Rapee, R.M.; Batterham, P.J.; Calear, A.L.; Carragher, N.; Ruggero, C.; Zimmerman, M.; Baillie, A.J.; Lynch, S.J.; et al. A Detailed Hierarchical Model of Psychopathology: From Individual Symptoms Up to the General Factor of Psychopathology. Available online: https://osf.io/3dp6f/ (accessed on 25 November 2020).
62. Hedman-Lagerlöf, E. *The Clinician's Guide to Treating Health Anxiety: Diagnosis, Mechanisms, and Effective Treatment*; Academic Press: Cambridge, MA, USA, 2019.

63. Di Nardo, M.; Madonna, M.; Murino, T.; Castagna, F. Modelling a Safety Management System Using System Dynamics at the Bhopal Incident. *Appl. Sci.* **2020**, *10*, 903. [CrossRef]
64. Golenia, L.; Schoemaker, M.M.; Otten, E.; Mouton, L.J.; Bongers, R.M. What the Dynamic Systems Approach Can Offer for Understanding Development: An Example of Mid-childhood Reaching. *Front. Psychol.* **2017**, *8*, 1774. [CrossRef]
65. Brown, R.J.; Skelly, N.; Chew-Graham, C.A. Online health research and health anxiety: A systematic review and conceptual integration. *Clin. Psychol.* **2020**, *27*, e12299. [CrossRef]
66. Hayes, S.C.; Strosahl, K.D.; Wilson, K.G. *Acceptance and Commitment Therapy: The Process and Practice of Mindful Change*; Guilford Press: New York, NY, USA, 2011.
67. Eilenberg, T.; Fink, P.; Jensen, J.S.; Rief, W.; Frostholm, L. Acceptance and Commitment Group Therapy (ACT-G) for health anxiety: A randomized controlled trial. *Psychol. Med.* **2016**, *46*, 103–115. [CrossRef]

International Journal of
Environmental Research and Public Health

MDPI

Article

Precautionary Behavior and Depression in Older Adults during the COVID-19 Pandemic: An Online Cross-Sectional Study in Hubei, China

Wei Liang [1,2], Yanping Duan [1,2,3,*], Borui Shang [4], Chun Hu [5], Julien Steven Baker [1,2], Zhihua Lin [6], Jiali He [3] and Yanping Wang [7]

1 Center for Health and Exercise Science Research, Hong Kong Baptist University, Hong Kong, China; wliang1020@hkbu.edu.hk (W.L.); jsbaker@hkbu.edu.hk (J.S.B.)
2 Department of Sport, Physical Education and Health, Hong Kong Baptist University, Hong Kong, China
3 Wuhan Institute of Physical Education, College of Health Sciences, Wuhan 430000, China; h13163386915@163.com
4 Department of Kinesiology, Hebei Institute of Physical Education, Shijiazhuang 050000, China; boruishang@hepec.edu.cn
5 Student Mental Health Education Center, Northwestern Polytechnical University, Xi'an 710000, China; huchun52@163.com
6 Sport Section, Wuhan University, Wuhan 430000, China; zhihualin_wu@163.com
7 The National Physical Fitness Lab, Hubei Institute of Sport Sciences, Wuhan 430000, China; yanniswyp@163.com
* Correspondence: duanyp@hkbu.edu.hk

Citation: Liang, W.; Duan, Y.; Shang, B.; Hu, C.; Baker, J.S.; Lin, Z.; He, J.; Wang, Y. Precautionary Behavior and Depression in Older Adults during the COVID-19 Pandemic: An Online Cross-Sectional Study in Hubei, China. *Int. J. Environ. Res. Public Health* **2021**, *18*, 1853. https://doi.org/10.3390/ijerph18041853

Academic Editors: Paolo Roma, Merylin Monaro and Cristina Mazza

Received: 6 January 2021
Accepted: 10 February 2021
Published: 14 February 2021

Abstract: The large-scale COVID-19 pandemic has not only resulted in the risk of death but also augmented the levels of depression in community-dwelling older adults. The present study aimed to investigate the characteristics of depression in Chinese older adults during the COVID-19 pandemic, to examine the association of individual precautionary behavior with older adults' depression levels, and to identify the moderating role of socioeconomic indicators in the aforementioned association. Five hundred and sixteen older adults were recruited from five cities of Hubei province in China. They were asked to complete an online questionnaire survey. Results showed that 30.8% of participants indicated a significant depressive symptom during the pandemic. Older adults' depression levels differed significantly in marital status, living situation, education level, household income, subjective health status, and infected cases of acquaintances. Precautionary behavior change showed significant inverse associations with older adults' depression levels, where household income moderated this relationship. This is the first study to investigate the characteristics, behavioral correlates, and moderators of depression among Chinese older adults during the COVID-19 pandemic. Research findings may provide new insights into interventions and policy-making on individual precautionary behavior and mental health among older adults for future pandemics.

Keywords: COVID-19; older adults; depression; precautionary behavior; socioeconomic status; online survey; mental health

1. Introduction

Since the beginning of December 2019, a novel coronavirus disease (COVID-19), which was first recognized in Wuhan, Hubei province of China, quickly spread globally, infecting millions of people [1]. In China, there were 91,388 confirmed cases and 4746 fatality cases recorded by 13 October 2020 [2,3]. As a serious pandemic, the COVID-19 imposed enormous burdens on the medical system and exerted catastrophic impacts on social economics [4]. For individuals, the epidemic not only led to the risk of death from the viral infection but also augmented the comorbidity of mental illnesses (e.g., depressive symptoms) [5,6]. As a vulnerable group that accounted for the highest percentage of deaths from COVID-19 (approximately 75%), older adults have indicated a high risk of mental problems during the pandemic [7,8]. With the ongoing COVID-19 pandemic, older adults were more likely to experience fear of becoming ill or dying. This was accompanied by feelings of helplessness and stigma [8,9]. These feelings might result in an increased risk of depressive symptoms imposing profound negative influences on the health and well-being of older adults [8,9]. Previous studies have indicated a high prevalence of depressive symptoms from 22.3% to 39.1% among older adults during the COVID-19 outbreak [10–13]. Given the lack of relevant research, this emphasizes an urgent need for addressing the characteristics, correlates, and moderators of depression among older adults during the COVID-19 [13].

Since there has been very limited success in vaccination prevention for COVID-19, individual precautionary actions, such as hand washing, facemask wearing, and social distancing play a crucial role in inhibiting the human-to-human transmission of COVID-19 [14–16]. In addition, recent studies have indicated a significantly positive impact of precautionary behaviors on lessening the depressive symptoms among non-infected adolescents, adult populations, and adults with mental illnesses during the outbreak of COVID-19 [5,17]. The findings may generate urgently needed insights into the association of precautionary behaviors with mental health in the general population. However, to the best of our knowledge, there are limited studies examining the impact of COVID-19 precautionary behaviors on depression in older adults.

Socioeconomic status (SES) indicators, including education level, employment status, and household income, have been shown to be important predictors for precautionary behaviors and depression levels in the general population, respectively [17–22]. For instance, evidence has indicated a significantly positive association of education level and household income with the engagement of COVID-19 precautionary behaviors [15,19]. In addition, low education levels, unemployment status, and low household income have been demonstrated to be significantly correlated with a higher level or an increased risk of depression in previous studies [18,20,23]. The SES indicators have been considered to moderate the impact of certain health behaviors (e.g., physical activity, smoking, and social activities) on depression levels [24–27], whereas the moderating effects of SES in the relationship between COVID-19 precautionary behaviors and depression among older adults is still unknown. This deserves further examination, as identifying the socioeconomic characteristics associated with older adults' depression levels is important. The effects of SES indicators on the relationships between precautionary behaviors and depression will help to develop tailored approaches to tackle the depression problems of the elderly population during the COVID-19 outbreak and future pandemics. In addition, the effects of specific SES indicators may also provide practical policy implications and enable the efficiency and feasibility of potential policy interventions to help combat COVID-19 and future pandemics [28].

The current study aimed to (1) investigate the characteristics of depression among Chinese older adults during the COVID-19 pandemic; (2) examine the association between individual precautionary behavior and older adults' depression levels; and (3) identify the role of SES indicators (education level, occupational status, and household income) in moderating the association between individual precautionary behavior and depression levels in Chinese older adults. We hypothesized that (1) older adult's depression levels would differ significantly for demographic characteristics, such as age, gender, marital status, and socioeconomic indicators; (2) taking up more COVID-19 precautionary behavior would be significantly associated with lower depression levels in older adults; (3) certain SES indicators would significantly moderate the association between individual precautionary behavior and depression levels in Chinese older adults.

2. Materials and Methods

2.1. Study Design and Participants

This study used a cross-sectional design using a snowball sampling approach. The online survey was conducted from 15 June to 10 July 2020 (the lockdown had been withdrawn for around two months). We contacted 727 Chinese older adults from five cities (e.g., Wuhan, Xiaogan, Jingzhou, Shiyan, and Xiangyang) in the Hubei province of China. A total of 609 participants (609/727, 83.8% response rate) agreed to participate in the survey. All of the participants who were community-dwelling older adults ($\geq$60 years) met the eligibility criteria, which included: (1) not having been infected with COVID-19; (2) not having any cognitive disorders or impairments; (3) having access to a mobile phone or laptop; and (4) having sufficient reading and listening skills in Chinese. For those older adults who had difficulties in mobile phone or laptop operation, their family members and friends were invited to assist them in completing the online survey. Finally, there were 516 eligible participants (516/727, 71.0%), including 299 females (57.9%) and 217 males (42.1%), aged from 60 to 89 years (mean = 67.55 years, SD = 6.60).

2.2. Procedure

To minimize face-to-face interaction as recommended by the Chinese government, the questionnaire survey was constructed and administered using an online survey platform in China, namely, SOJUMP (Changsha Ranxing Information Technology Co., Ltd., Changsha, China). Four older adults (two males and two females) were invited to complete a pilot test with the purpose of (1) improving the layout of the electronic questionnaires (e.g., using the large font and highlighting the key information), and (2) modifying the grammar and any typographical errors while ensuring the scale items were more understandable [29]. All recruitment posters and the hyperlink for the survey were disseminated via mobile short message service (SMS) and popular social media platforms in China (e.g., WeChat, Weibo, and QQ). There were three approaches used for recruiting participants. (1) Relying on the researchers' social networks in five cities of Hubei province, the eligible family members, friends, and relatives of researchers were invited. The participants then encouraged their friends to join the survey. (2) Researchers contacted the directors of community neighborhood committees in Wuhan and Xiaogan, respectively, and sought their collaboration and support. Upon receiving the agreement of directors, researchers were permitted to enter into their community neighborhood WeChat groups to recruit eligible participants. (3) Researchers contacted officials who were in charge of the retirement in two universities in Wuhan. With the support of officials, a recruitment poster and survey hyperlink were delivered to their internal WeChat group, especially for retirement colleagues.

To increase the engagement of participation, each participant who completed the online survey was eligible for 30 RMB by electronic transfer as an incentive. Participants were asked to sign an informed consent form on the first page of the survey platform prior to completing the questionnaires. Ethical approval for conducting the study was obtained from the Research Ethics Committee of Hong Kong Baptist University (REC/19-20/0490).

2.3. Measurement

2.3.1. Demographic Information

Demographic characteristics included age, gender (male/female), marital status (single/married/divorced or widowed), living situation (alone/with spouse, partners or children), medical history of chronic diseases (e.g., heart diseases, diabetes, cancer, respiratory illnesses, liver or kidney diseases), and three key indicators of socioeconomic status (SES) [18,20,23,28]. These included education level (primary school or below/middle or high school/college or above), occupational status (unemployed/pensioner or retired/part-time or full-time employment), and household income (below average/average/above average). Participants were also asked to report their body weight and height for the calculation of body mass index (BMI), using the formula "BMI = body weight (kg)/body height squared (m^2)". Based on previous literature, the BMI was categorized by four levels for Chinese people (underweight: BMI < 18.5; healthy weight: 18.5 ≤ BMI < 23; overweight: 23 ≤ BMI < 26; and obesity: BMI ≥ 26) [30].

2.3.2. Covariates

The acquaintances' disease status and subjective health status served as important covariates for older adult's depression [31,32]. Participants were asked to report the infection situation of COVID-19 of their acquaintances (e.g., friends, family members, and neighbors), as well as their subjective health status (bad/satisfactory/excellent).

2.3.3. Precautionary Behaviors

As recommended by the WHO, the precautionary behaviors for COVID-19 include hand washing, facemask wearing, and social distancing [14]. A six-item structured scale was used to measure the COVID-19 precautionary behaviors, with two items for each of the three behaviors. For example, the items for hand washing were "during the previous week, I adhered to washing my hands with soap and water or alcohol-based hand rub (for at least 20 s, on all surfaces of the hands)" followed by two situations including "(a) in a daily life situation, e.g., before eating, and (b) in a disease-related situation, e.g., after caring for the sick." The items for facemask wearing were "during the previous week, I adhered to wearing a face mask properly" followed by two different situations including "(a) when visiting public places, and (b) when caring for the sick". The items for the social distancing were "during the previous week, I adhered to social distancing" followed by two items including "(a) staying out of crowded places and avoiding mass gatherings when going outside of my home, and (b) keeping space (at least 1.5 m) between myself and other people who are coughing or sneezing." All responses were indicated on a four-point Likert scale ranging from "1 = strongly disagree" to "4 = strongly agree". A mean score of the total six items was calculated.

Participants were also invited to recall their precautionary behaviors before the outbreak of COVID-19 during seasonal influenza (i.e., past precautionary behaviors) using the same scale.

2.3.4. Depression

Depression levels were measured using the Chinese version of the Epidemiologic Studies Short Depression Scale (CESD-10) [33,34]. The questions were asked: "In the past week, how often I feel", followed by 10 items such as "I had trouble keeping my mind on what I was doing". The responses were given on a four-point Likert scale, ranging from "0 = rarely (less than 1 day)" to "3 = for most of the time (5–7 days)". The total score of the 10 items was calculated (≥10 indicating significant depressive symptoms) [35]. The CESD-10 has demonstrated satisfactory validity and internal consistency reliability among Chinese older adults (Cronbach's alpha = 0.78–0.82) [33,34].

The package of questionnaires was delivered on the online survey platform, and all participants were asked to complete the survey using their mobile phones or laptops. The duration to complete the online survey was around 20 min.

2.4. Statistical Analysis

IBM SPSS 26.0 (Armonk, NY, USA) was used for data analyses. The diagnostic testing (e.g., outlier screening and distribution checking) was first conducted, and all data adhered to the normal distribution that the absolute values of skewness and kurtosis were <2. Descriptive statistics (e.g., mean, standard deviation, percentage) were used to describe baseline characteristics. The characteristics of depression were examined by independent T-test and one-way analysis of variance (ANOVA). Hierarchical linear regression models were used to explore the association of precautionary behaviors with depression. To control the influence of past precautionary behaviors, residualized change scores (RCS; calculated by conducting linear regression between past behaviors and current behaviors) were used [36]. In Model 1, the demographic variables were set as predictors for the depression level.

Subsequently, two covariates were added to the regression analysis in Model 2. Finally, the RCS of COVID-19 precautionary behaviors was included as a predictor in Model 3, controlled for the significant demographics and covariates. The role of the SES indicators in moderating the behavior–depression association was examined using IBM SPSS Process (Model 1), and the 95% confidence intervals (CIs) of the standardized effects were estimated using the bias-corrected bootstrap approach (5000 resample). The 5% level (two-tailed) was taken as the statistical significance cutoff point.

3. Results

3.1. Sample Characteristics

The descriptive characteristics of the sample are presented in Table 1. The data of 516 eligible older adults were included in the analysis. Most participants were females (57.9%) and were aged between 60 and 69 years (68.6%). The majority of the older adults were married (83.7%) and lived with their spouse, partners, or children (90.7%). In terms of the medical histories, about half of the participants have suffered from chronic diseases (e.g., heart diseases, diabetes, or cancer). For SES indicators, only a small percentage of participants were illiterate or semi-illiterate (8.7%), the majority of participants were pensioners/retired (92.6%), and more than half of the sample indicated an average level of household income (57.9%). In terms of BMI, a considerable proportion of elderly participants were overweight or obese (52.1%). In addition, most participants perceived their health status as good or excellent (52.7%), and only 9.7% of participants reported that their family members, friends, or neighbors had been infected with the COVID-19. According to the cutoff point for depression (CESD-10 $\geq$ 10) [35], 30.8% of the participants indicated significant depressive symptoms during the outbreak of COVID-19.

Table 1. Descriptive characteristics of the study sample (n = 516).

	n (%)
Age (years), mean (SD): 67.55 (6.60)	
60–69	354 (68.6)
70–79	128 (24.8)
80 and above	34 (6.6)
Gender	
Male	217 (42.1)
Female	299 (57.9)
Marital status	
Single	14 (2.7)
Married	432 (83.7)
Divorced or widowed	70 (13.6)
Living situation	
Alone	48 (9.3)
With spouse/partners/Children	468 (90.7)
Medical history of chronic diseases	
Yes	262 (50.8)
No	254 (49.2)
Education level	
Primary school or below	45 (8.7)
Middle or high school	231 (44.8)
College or above	240 (46.5)
Occupational status	
Unemployed	22 (4.3)
Pensioner or retired	478 (92.6)
Part-time or full-time employment	16 (3.1)

Table 1. *Cont.*

	n (%)
Household income	
Below average	113 (21.9)
Average	299 (57.9)
Above average	104 (20.2)
BMI (kg/m^2), mean (SD): 23.06 (2.67)	
<18.5	19 (3.7)
18.5 ≤ BMI < 23	228 (44.2)
23 ≤ BMI < 26	206 (39.9)
≥26	63 (12.2)
Subjective health status	
Bad	48 (9.3)
Satisfactory	196 (38.0)
Excellent	272 (52.7)
Infected cases of acquaintances	
Yes	50 (9.7)
No	466 (90.3)
Depression, mean (SD): 7.34 (5.23)	
No depressive symptom	357 (69.2)
Have depressive symptoms	159 (30.8)
Precautionary behaviors	
Before the outbreak of COVID-19, mean (SD): 3.12 (0.67)	
During the outbreak of COVID-19, mean (SD): 3.61 (0.40)	

Note. SD = standard deviation.

3.2. Characteristics of Depression

As shown in Table 2, older adult's depression differed significantly for different characteristics. There were no significant differences in depression levels for gender, medical history of chronic diseases, occupational status, and BMI intervals (p = 0.10–0.95). The results indicated that older adults who were divorced/widowed and lived alone showed significantly higher depression levels than those who were married ($p < 0.001$) and lived with their spouse, partners, and children ($p = 0.035$). The depression level was significantly lower for participants who had higher educational levels ($p = 0.001$) and higher household income ($p < 0.001$) relative to those with poorer socioeconomic status. In addition, older adults who perceived their health status as bad and poor ($p < 0.001$) and who had acquaintances infected with COVID-19 ($p = 0.003$) indicated significantly higher depression levels than those in the other categories.

Table 2. Characteristics of depression (n = 516).

Factors	Depression Mean (SD)	Significance
Age span		
60–69	7.06 (5.04)	$F_{2, 513} = 1.78$, $p = 0.17$
70–79	7.88 (5.45)	
80 and above	8.29 (6.08)	
Gender		
Male	7.33 (5.43)	$t_{514} = -0.06$, $p = 0.95$
Female	7.35 (5.09)	
Marital status		
Single	9.07 (5.80)	$F_{2, 513} = 7.87$, $p < 0.001$
Married	6.96 (5.07)	
Divorced or widowed	9.57 (5.56)	

Table 2. *Cont.*

Factors	Depression Mean (SD)	Significance
Living situation		
Alone	8.85 (5.34)	$t_{514} = 2.11$, $p = 0.035$
With spouse/partners/Children	7.19 (5.20)	
Medical history of chronic diseases		
Yes	7.72 (5.26)	$t_{514} = 1.66$, $p = 0.10$
No	6.96 (5.17)	
Education level		
Primary school or below	10.07 (5.94)	$F_{2, 513} = 7.32$, $p = 0.001$
Middle or high school	7.12 (5.02)	
College or above	6.86 (5.13)	
Occupational status		
Unemployed	9.01 (6.18)	$F_{2, 513} = 1.24$, $p = 0.29$
Pensioner or retired	7.29 (5.22)	
Part-time or full-time employment	6.75 (3.73)	
Household income		
Below average	9.06 (5.72)	$F_{2, 513} = 9.09$, $p < 0.001$
Average	7.08 (5.07)	
Above average	6.24 (4.70)	
Body mass index (BMI) intervals	23.06 (2.67)	
BMI < 18.5 kg/m^2	6.37 (4.70)	$F_{3, 512} = 0.62$, $p = 0.60$
18.5 kg/m^2 ≤ BMI < 23 kg/m^2	7.62 (5.60)	
23 kg/m^2 ≤ BMI < 26 kg/m^2	7.08 (4.88)	
BMI ≥ 26 kg/m^2	7.48 (5.10)	
Subjective health status		
Bad	10.44 (6.01)	$F_{2, 513} = 17.25$, $p < 0.001$
Satisfactory	8.09 (5.32)	
Excellent	6.26 (4.69)	
Infected cases of acquaintances		
Yes	9.40 (6.18)	$t_{514} = 2.95$, $p = 0.003$
No	7.12 (5.07)	

Note. SD = standard deviation.

3.3. *Association of Individual Precautionary Behaviors with Depression*

Based on the characteristics of depression, all demographic variables that have shown significant differences in the depression levels were included as predictors in the hierarchical linear regression models [31]. Dummy variables were generated for all polynomial predictors. Results revealed that two demographic variables were significant predictors for older adult's depression levels, including education level and household income, which aggregately accounted for 7% of the variance in the depression level ($p < 0.001$). In terms of the covariates, both subjective health status and infected cases of participants' acquaintances significantly predicted the depression level among participants, coupled with the demographics contributing to the explanation for 12 % of the variance in the depression levels ($p < 0.001$). After controlling for the demographic factors and covariates, changes in COVID-19 precautionary behaviors significantly predicted the depression of older adults ($\beta = -0.18$, 95%CI = −1.24 to −0.62, $p < 0.001$), contributing to a significant improvement in the variance explanation ($\Delta R^2 = 0.03$, $p < 0.001$). The total model accounted for 15% of the variance in depression level ($p < 0.001$). Details of multiple linear regression analyses are shown in Table 3.

Table 3. Results of hierarchical linear regression models ($n = 516$).

Predictors of Depression	Model 1			Model 2			Model 3		
	β	95% CI	*p*	β	95% CI	*p*	β	95% CI	*p*
Marital status									
Single (reference group)	N/A	N/A	N/A	N/A	N/A	N/A	N/A	N/A	N/A
Married	−0.08	−3.08, 0.80	0.25	−0.05	−2.60, 1.18	0.46	−0.03	−2.28, 1.45	0.66
Divorces or widowed	0.04	−1.41, 2.77	0.53	0.05	−1.24, 2.84	0.44	0.07	−1.01, 3.00	0.33
Living situation									
Alone (reference group)	N/A	N/A	N/A	N/A	N/A	N/A	N/A	N/A	N/A
With spouse/partners/children	<0.01	−0.58, 0.65	0.91	−0.01	−0.66, 0.53	0.83	0.01	−0.50, 0.68	0.76
Education level									
Primary school or below (reference group)	N/A	N/A	N/A	N/A	N/A	N/A	N/A	N/A	N/A
Middle or high school	−0.18	−3.06, −0.65	0.003	−0.17	−2.95, −0.60	0.003	−00.16	−2.81, −0.49	0.005
College or above	−0.19	−3.18, −0.75	0.002	−0.19	−3.17, −0.79	0.001	−0.16	−2.80, −0.45	0.007
Household income									
Below average (reference group)	N/A	N/A	N/A	N/A	N/A	N/A	N/A	N/A	N/A
Average	−0.15	−3.28, −1.27	<0.001	−0.11	−1.98, −0.40	0.003	−0.08	−1.66, −0.10	0.027
Above average	−0.18	−3.28, −1.27	<0.001	−0.13	−2.65, −0.66	0.001	−0.10	−2.33, −0.36	0.008
Subjective health status									
Bad (reference group)	N/A	N/A	N/A	N/A	N/A	N/A	N/A	N/A	N/A
Satisfactory	N/A	N/A	N/A	−0.16	−2.87, −0.63	0.002	−0.16	−2.85, −0.64	0.002
Excellent	N/A	N/A	N/A	−0.33	−4.53, −2.33	<0.001	−0.33	−4.55, −2.39	<0.001
Infected cases of acquaintances									
Yes (reference group)	N/A	N/A	N/A	N/A	N/A	N/A	N/A	N/A	N/A
No	N/A	N/A	N/A	−0.10	−1.44, −0.40	0.001	−0.11	−1.47, −0.45	<0.001
Precautionary behaviors [a]	N/A	N/A	N/A	N/A	N/A	N/A	−0.18	−1.24, −0.62	<0.001
R^2		$0.07, p < 0.001$			$0.12, p < 0.001$			$0.15, p < 0.001$	
ΔR^2		N/A			$0.05, p < 0.001$			$0.03, p < 0.001$	

Note. [a] Residualized change scores were used for the calculation.

3.4. Moderating Effect of Socioeconomic Status

As the occupational status was not significantly associated with depression in our previous examination ($r = -0.04$, $p = 0.32$), only education level and household income were included in the moderation analysis. The interaction of socioeconomic variables with precautionary behaviors was first examined and the results showed that education level was not significantly related with precautionary behaviors for predicting older adult's depression ($\beta_1 = 0.12$, $t_{510} = 0.78$, $p = 0.44$, 95%CI = −0.93 to 2.14; $\beta_2 = 0.04$, $t_{510} = 0.23$, $p = 0.82$, 95%CI = −1.42 to 1.79). For the household income, a significant moderation effect was identified in the analysis (See Figure 1). Results indicated a significant interaction between household income (average vs. below average) and precautionary behaviors ($\beta_1 = 0.26$, $t_{510} = 2.53$, $p = 0.012$, 95%CI = 0.31 to 2.44), as well as between household income (above average vs. below average) and precautionary behaviors ($\beta_2 = 0.39$, $t_{510} = 3.01$, $p = 0.003$, 95%CI = 0.70 to 3.34). The interaction contributed to a significant change in the variance explanation ($\Delta R^2 = 0.02$, $p = 0.007$). The total moderation model accounted for 9% of the variance in depression ($p < 0.001$). The descriptive plot of the moderating effects of household income on the relationship between COVID-19 precautionary behavior change and depression level among older adults is presented in Figure 2. For older adults with higher levels of household income, there was only a slight negative association between precautionary behavior change and depression level, whereas for those with average and lower levels of household income, prominent associations between behavior change and depression levels occurred.

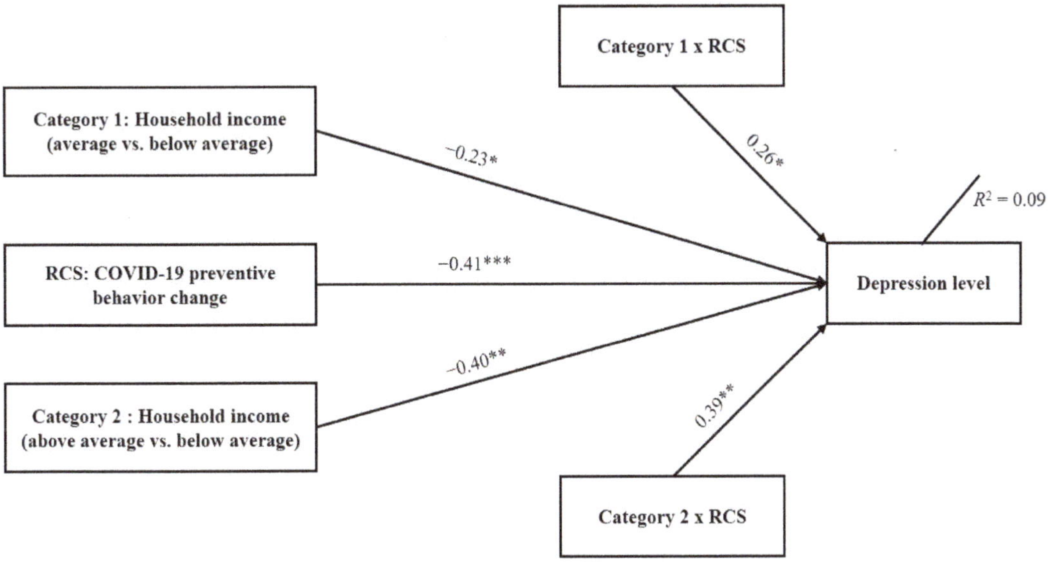

Figure 1. Moderation effect of household income on behavior-depression association ($n = 516$). RCS = Residualized change score; * $p < 0.05$; ** $p < 0.01$; *** $p < 0.001$.

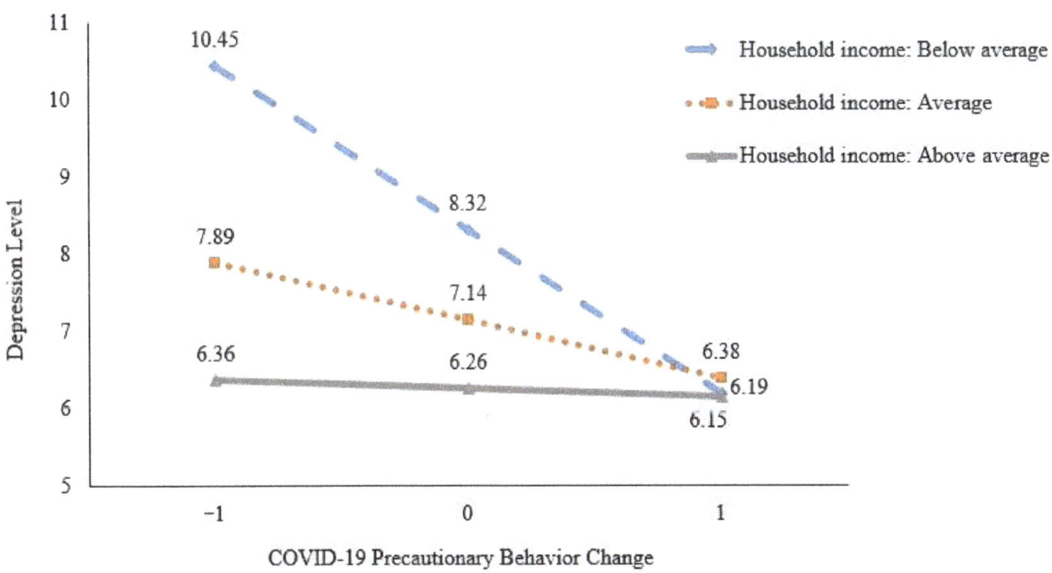

Figure 2. Plot of simple slopes showing the association between COVID-19 precautionary behavior change and depression level at different categories of household income.

4. Discussion

To the best of our knowledge, this is the first online cross-sectional study to explore the characteristics of depression, to examine the association between COVID-19 precautionary behaviors and depression levels, and to identify the role of SES in moderating the behavior–depression association among Chinese older adults during the COVID-19 pandemic. The findings from the study have fully supported the hypotheses. In particular, during the outbreak of COVID-19, older adults' depression levels differed significantly in a series of characteristics, including marital status, living situation, SES indicators (education level and household income), as well as subjective health status and infected cases of acquaintances. After controlling for the demographic covariates, COVID-19 precautionary behaviors showed a significant inverse association with older adults' depression levels. Of the three SES indicators, only household income significantly moderated the association between COVID-19 precautionary behaviors and depression levels among Chinese older adults.

In terms of the characteristics of depression, as suggested in previous studies, individuals who lack social support from families and friends showed significantly higher levels of depression than those with sufficient social support from families and friends [37–39]. Therefore, it is not surprising that in this study, older adults who have married and lived with their spouse, partners, or children indicated a prominent lower depression level. The findings also revealed that older adults who perceived their health status as poor and had acquaintances being infected showed a significantly higher level of depression. These findings are consistent with previous studies, where older adults with these characteristics may experience greater fear of being infected or dying themselves, leading to higher depression levels [32,37,38]. In line with previous evidence in Chinese adolescents and adults, the findings showed that older adults who had higher education levels and higher household income might be less influenced by the COVID-19 pandemic, indicating a comparative lower depression level [5,22]. The discrepancy with previous evidence occurred in the indicator of occupational status [23,24], where no significant difference was found in the current study. This may be attributed to the reason that the majority of our participants were retired older adults (92.6%).

In terms of the association of individual precautionary behavior towards COVID-19 with depression levels, our findings were consistent with previous studies among Chinese non-infected adolescent and adult populations [5], and with a recent study among Japanese adults with depressive symptoms [17]. Older adults who adopted more precautionary behaviors (e.g., hand washing, facemask wearing, and social distancing) were more likely to have lower depression levels during the COVID-19 epidemic. It is worth noting that the change in COVID-19 precautionary behaviors accounted for 3% of the variance in depression levels, while the SES indicators (education levels and household income) and covariates (infected cases of acquaintances, subjective health status), also played a critical role in predicting older adults' depressive states. These findings emphasize the significance of promoting precautionary behaviors during the COVID-19 pandemic among older adults, as well as the importance of considering the socio-demographic characteristics when designing psychological interventions and making relevant policies to improve mental health outcomes among older adults.

In terms of the moderating effect of SES indicators on the behavior–depression association, household income was found to be a significant moderator. This result agrees with previous studies [25], which indicate that the economic dependency significantly interacted with social activity and depression among older adults ($\beta = -0.16$, SE = 0.01, $p < 0.001$) [25]. The findings of the current study support the moderating role of household income in the behavior depression association, revealing that when we motivate older adults to take COVID-19 precautionary behaviors to reduce their depression levels, we need to especially focus on older adults who are at an economically disadvantaged level. From the government's perspective, the findings indicate the importance and necessity of providing relief funding for low-income households to ease the stress of the pandemic. These findings also bear considerable implications for future preventive measures of epidemics among older adults.

This study has several limitations. First, given the urgency of the research needed on the COVID-19 pandemic and the limited resources available, we have to apply an online cross-sectional approach using snowball sampling, so the participants may vary in relation to the actual patterns of the general elderly population (e.g., in the illiterate or semi-illiterate samples). Moreover, all the variables were measured by self-reported scales, which might lead to recall bias, self-perception bias, and social desirability effects [22,40]. However, the bias has been found to be lower in anonymous online surveys than in telephone or face-to-face paper surveys [15,41]. In spite of online methodologies being an efficient means and cost-effective method to conduct surveys, we adopted several strategies to ensure that the online survey was easy-to-operate. However, many elderly participants were confronted with difficulties in the process of the survey (e.g., operational functionality, submission setting). Further actions are needed to make online surveys more user-friendly for elderly populations. Additionally, the demographic and behavioral factors identified in the present study only explained 15% of the variance of depression levels, so other factors need to be investigated in future studies. In addition, the depression levels did not significantly differ in gender, whereas other studies have found a prominent role for the gender variable in the psychological responses towards the pandemic [21,22]. This point deserves further investigation. Finally, the findings of the present study were obtained from a specific age group within a Chinese context; therefore, it is unclear whether these findings would be generalizable to other age groups and different cultural contexts. Notwithstanding the aforementioned limitations, this study provides invaluable information on the characteristics of depression, and the impact of COVID-19 precautionary behaviors when considering depression levels. The study also provides detail relating to the role of SES indicators in moderating the behavior–depression association among Chinese older adults during the COVID-19 pandemic. The research findings presented here could be used as a meaningful reference, adding knowledge and giving new insights into future research promoting precautionary behaviors and relationships between mental health and older adults during the COVID-19 outbreak and potential future pandemics.

5. Conclusions

The current study investigated the characteristics of depression between Chinese older adults during the COVID-19 pandemic. The study also examined the association between older adult's individual precautionary behaviors and their depression levels, and identified the role of SES indicators in moderating the behavior–depression relationship. All of the study hypotheses were supported. The depression levels of older adults differed significantly for marital status, living situations, education levels, household income, subjective health status, and infected cases of acquaintances. The inverse association between precautionary behavior change and depression levels was also identified in the current study. Of the three SES indicators, only household income significantly moderated the impacts of COVID-19 precautionary behaviors on older adults' depression levels. The research findings highlight the potential for embracing COVID-19 precautionary behaviors on mitigating depression levels among older adults. The findings also revealed the importance of considering socioeconomic disparities when promoting precautionary behaviors for mental health. These findings could be important in influencing relevant social policy decisions that target older adults.

Author Contributions: Y.D. and W.L. conceived and designed the study. Y.D., W.L., C.H., and J.H. contributed to the preparation of study materials. Y.D., W.L., Z.L., J.H., Y.W., and C.H. collected the data. W.L., B.S., and J.H. screened and analyzed the data. W.L. drafted the manuscript. Y.D., J.S.B., and B.S. revised and polished the manuscript. Y.D. and W.L. had full access to all study data and take responsibility for the integrity of the data and the accuracy of the data analysis. All authors have read and agreed to the published version of the manuscript.

Funding: This research was supported by the Start-Up Grant and Strategic Development Fund (SDF) of Hong Kong Baptist University. The funding organization had no role in the study design, study implementation, data collection, data analysis, manuscript preparation, or publication decision. The work is the responsibility of the authors.

Institutional Review Board Statement: Ethical approval for conducting the study was obtained from the Research Ethics Committee of Hong Kong Baptist University (REC/19-20/0490).

Informed Consent Statement: Informed consent was obtained from all subjects involved in the study.

Conflicts of Interest: The authors declare no conflict of interest.

References

1. WHO Coronavirus Disease (COVID-19) Dashboard. Available online: https://covid19.who.int/ (accessed on 20 August 2020).
2. Center for Systems Science and Engineering (CSSE) at Johns Hopkins University, USA. Available online: https://gisanddata.maps.arcgis.com/apps/opsdashboard/index.html#/bda7594740fd40299423467b48e9ecf6 (accessed on 15 October 2020).
3. National Health Commission of China. Update on the New Coronavirus Cases. Available online: http://health.people.com.cn/GB/26466/431463/431576/index.html (accessed on 15 October 2020).
4. Sachs, J.D.; Horton, R.; Bagenal, J.; Amor, Y.B.; Caman, O.K.; Lafortune, G. The Lancet COVID-19 Commission. *Lancet* **2020**, *396*, 454–455. [CrossRef]
5. Wang, C.; Pan, R.; Wan, X.; Tan, Y.; Xu, L.; Ho, C.S.; Ho, R.C. Immediate psychological responses and associated factors during the initial stage of the 2019 coronavirus disease (COVID-19) epidemic among the general population in China. *Int. J. Environ. Res. Public Health* **2020**, *17*, 1729. [CrossRef] [PubMed]
6. Ahmed, M.Z.; Ahmed, O.; Aibao, Z.; Hanbin, S.; Siyu, L.; Ahmad, A. Epidemic of COVID-19 in China and associated Psychological Problems. *Asian J. Psychiatry* **2020**, *14*, 102092. [CrossRef] [PubMed]
7. World Health Organization. Coronavirus Disease (COVID-19) Pandemic. Available online: https://www.who.int/emergencies/diseases/novel-coronavirus-2019 (accessed on 15 October 2020).
8. Shahid, Z.; Kalayanamitra, R.; McClafferty, B.; Kepko, D.; Ramgobin, D.; Patel, R.; Aggarwal, C.S.; Vunnam, R.; Sahu, N.; Bhatt, D.; et al. COVID-19 and older adults: What we know. *J. Am. Geriatr. Soc.* **2020**, *68*, 926–929. [CrossRef]
9. Khan, K.S.; Mamun, M.A.; Griffiths, M.D.; Ullah, I. The mental health impact of the COVID-19 pandemic across different cohorts. *Int. J. Ment. Health Addict.* **2020**, *9*, 1–7. [CrossRef] [PubMed]
10. Othman, N. Depression, Anxiety, and Stress in the Time of COVID-19 Pandemic in Kurdistan Region, Iraq. *Kurd. J. Appl. Res.* **2020**, *5*, 37–44. [CrossRef]
11. Salari, N.; Hosseinian-Far, A.; Jalali, R.; Vaisi-Raygani, A.; Rasoulpoor, S.; Mohammadi, M.; Rasoulpoor, S.; Khaledi-Paveh, B. Prevalence of stress, anxiety, depression among the general population during the COVID-19 pandemic: A systematic review and meta-analysis. *Glob. Health* **2020**, *16*, 1. [CrossRef]
12. Guo, Y.; Cheng, C.; Zeng, Y.; Li, Y.; Zhu, M.; Yang, W.; Xu, H.; Li, X.; Leng, J.; Monroe-Wise, A.; et al. Mental health disorders and associated risk factors in quarantined adults during the COVID-19 outbreak in China: Cross-sectional study. *J. Med. Internet Res.* **2020**, *22*, e20328. [CrossRef]
13. Yang, Y.; Li, W.; Zhang, Q.; Zhang, L.; Cheung, T.; Xiang, Y.T. Mental health services for older adults in China during the COVID-19 outbreak. *Lancet Psychiatry* **2020**, *7*, e19. [CrossRef]
14. World Health Organization. Coronavirus Disease (COVID-19) Advice for the Public. Available online: https://www.who.int/emergencies/diseases/novel-coronavirus-2019/advice-for-public (accessed on 30 May 2020).
15. Li, S.; Feng, B.; Liao, W.; Pan, W. Internet use, risk awareness, and demographic characteristics associated with engagement in preventive behaviors and testing: Cross-sectional survey on COVID-19 in the United States. *J. Med. Internet Res.* **2020**, *22*, e19782. [CrossRef]
16. Chiu, N.C.; Chi, H.; Tai, Y.L.; Peng, C.C.; Tseng, C.Y.; Chen, C.C.; Tan, B.F.; Lin, C.Y. Impact of wearing masks, hand hygiene, and social distancing on influenza, enterovirus, and all-cause pneumonia during the coronavirus pandemic: Retrospective national epidemiological surveillance study. *J. Med. Internet Res.* **2020**, *22*, e21257. [CrossRef] [PubMed]
17. Stickley, A.; Matsubayashi, T.; Sueki, H.; Ueda, M. COVID-19 preventive behaviours among people with anxiety and depressive symptoms: Findings from Japan. *Public Health* **2020**. [CrossRef] [PubMed]
18. Jin, Y.; Luo, Y.; He, P. Hypertension, socioeconomic status and depressive symptoms in Chinese middle-aged and older adults: Findings from the China health and retirement longitudinal study. *J. Affect. Disord.* **2019**, *252*, 237–244. [CrossRef]
19. Niu, Z.; Wang, T.; Hu, P.; Mei, J.; Tang, Z. Chinese Public's Engagement in Preventive and Intervening Health Behaviors During the Early Breakout of COVID-19: Cross-Sectional Study. *J. Med. Internet Res.* **2020**, *22*, e19995. [CrossRef]
20. Domènech-Abella, J.; Mundó, J.; Leonardi, M.; Chatterji, S.; Tobiasz-Adamczyk, B.; Koskinen, S.; Haro, J.M. The association between socioeconomic status and depression among older adults in Finland, Poland and Spain: A comparative cross-sectional study of distinct measures and pathways. *J. Affect. Disord.* **2018**, *241*, 311–318. [CrossRef]
21. Flesia, L.; Monaro, M.; Mazza, C.; Fietta, V.; Colicino, E.; Segatto, B.; Roma, P. Predicting perceived stress related to the Covid-19 outbreak through stable psychological traits and machine learning models. *J. Clin. Med.* **2020**, *9*, 3350. [CrossRef]
22. Adamson, M.M.; Phillips, A.; Seenivasan, S.; Martinez, J.; Grewal, H.; Kang, X.; Coetzee, J.; Luttenbacher, I.; Jester, A.; Harris, O.A.; et al. International prevalence and correlates of psychological stress during the global CoViD-19 pandemic. *Int. J. Environ. Res. Public Health* **2020**, *17*, 9248. [CrossRef]
23. Yoo, K.B.; Park, E.C.; Jang, S.Y.; Kwon, J.A.; Kim, S.J.; Cho, K.H.; Park, S. Association between employment status change and depression in Korean adults. *BMJ Open* **2016**, *6*. [CrossRef] [PubMed]
24. Segel-Karpas, D.; Ayalon, L.; Lachman, M.E. Loneliness and depressive symptoms: The moderating role of the transition into retirement. *Aging Ment. Health* **2018**, *22*, 135–140. [CrossRef] [PubMed]

25. Bhandari, P.; Paswan, B. Lifestyle Behaviours and Mental Health Outcomes of Elderly: Modification of Socio-Economic and Physical Health Effects. *Ageing Int.* **2020**, 1–35. [CrossRef]
26. Mezuk, B.; Rafferty, J.A.; Kershaw, K.N.; Hudson, D.; Abdou, C.M.; Lee, H.; Jackson, J.S. Reconsidering the role of social disadvantage in physical and mental health: Stressful life events, health behaviors, race, and depression. *Am. J. Epidemiol.* **2010**, *172*, 1238–1249. [CrossRef] [PubMed]
27. Jacka, F.N.; Cherbuin, N.; Anstey, K.J.; Butterworth, P. Dietary patterns and depressive symptoms over time: Examining the relationships with socioeconomic position, health behaviours and cardiovascular risk. *PLoS ONE.* **2014**, *9*, e87657. [CrossRef] [PubMed]
28. Fiske, A.; Wetherell, J.L.; Gatz, M. Depression in older adults. *Ann. Rev. Clinical. Psychol.* **2009**, *5*, 363–389. [CrossRef] [PubMed]
29. Rasche, P.; Wille, M.; Bröhl, C.; Theis, S.; Schäfer, K.; Knobe, M.; Mertens, A. Prevalence of health app use among older adults in Germany: National survey. *JMIR mHealth uHealth* **2018**, *6*, e26. [CrossRef]
30. Ko, G.T.; Tang, J.; Chan, J.C.; Sung, R.; Wu, M.M.; Wai, H.P.; Chen, R. Lower BMI cut-off value to define obesity in Hong Kong Chinese: An analysis based on body fat assessment by bioelectrical impedance. *Br. J. Nutr.* **2001**, *85*, 239–242. [CrossRef] [PubMed]
31. Steiner, P.M.; Cook, T.D.; Shadish, W.R.; Clark, M.H. The importance of covariate selection in controlling for selection bias in observational studies. *Psychol. Methods* **2010**, *15*, 250. [CrossRef]
32. Park, J.I.; Park, T.W.; Yang, J.C.; Chung, S.K. Factors associated with depression among elderly Koreans: The role of chronic illness, subjective health status, and cognitive impairment. *Psychogeriatrics* **2016**, *16*, 62–69. [CrossRef]
33. Rankin, S.H.; Galbraith, M.E.; Johnson, S. Reliability and validity data for a Chinese translation of the Center for Epidemiological Studies-Depression. *Psychol. Rep.* **1993**, *73* (Suppl. 3), 1291–1298. [CrossRef]
34. Duan, Y.P.; Liang, W.; Guo, L.; Wienert, J.; Si, G.Y.; Lippke, S. Evaluation of a web-based intervention for multiple health behavior changes in patients with coronary heart disease in home-based rehabilitation: Pilot randomized controlled trial. *J. Med. Internet Res.* **2018**, *20*, e12052. [CrossRef]
35. Andresen, E.M.; Malmgren, J.A.; Carter, W.B.; Patrick, D.L. Screening for depression in well older adults: Evaluation of a short form of the CES-D. *Am. J. Prev. Med.* **1994**, *10*, 77–84. [CrossRef]
36. Castro-Schilo, L.; Grimm, K.J. Using residualized change versus difference scores for longitudinal research. *J. Soc. Pers. Relatsh.* **2018**, *35*, 32–58. [CrossRef]
37. Miller, K.J.; Mesagno, C.; McLaren, S.; Grace, F.; Yates, M.; Gomez, R. Exercise, mood, self-efficacy, and social support as predictors of depressive symptoms in older adults: Direct and interaction effects. *Front. Psychol.* **2019**, *10*, 2145. [CrossRef] [PubMed]
38. Ahn, S.; Kim, S.; Zhang, H. Changes in depressive symptoms among older adults with multiple chronic conditions: Role of positive and negative social support. *Int. J. Environ. Res. Public Health* **2017**, *14*, 16. [CrossRef]
39. Barnett, A.; Zhang, C.J.; Johnston, J.M.; Cerin, E. Relationships between the neighborhood environment and depression in older adults: A systematic review and meta-analysis. *Int. Psychogeriatr.* **2018**, *30*, 1153–1176. [CrossRef]
40. Liang, W.; Duan, Y.P.; Shang, B.R.; Wang, Y.P.; Hu, C.; Lippke, S. A web-based lifestyle intervention program for Chinese college students: Study protocol and baseline characteristics of a randomized placebo-controlled trial. *BMC Public Health* **2019**, *19*, 1–11. [CrossRef] [PubMed]
41. Keeter, S.; McGeeney, K.; Igielnik, R.; Mercer, A.; Mathiowetz, N. From telephone to the web: The challenge of mode of interview effects in public opinion polls. Pew Research Center. Available online: http://www.aapor.org/AAPOR_Main/media/AnnualMeetingProceedings/2015/I2-1-Keeter.pdf (accessed on 13 May 2015).

International Journal of
Environmental Research and Public Health

MDPI

Article

Mediating Effects of Risk Perception on Association between Social Support and Coping with COVID-19: An Online Survey

Dian-Jeng Li [1,2,3], Nai-Ying Ko [4], Yu-Ping Chang [5], Cheng-Fang Yen [1,6,*] and Yi-Lung Chen [7,8,*]

1 Graduate Institute of Medicine, College of Medicine, Kaohsiung Medical University, Kaohsiung City 80708, Taiwan; u108800004@kmu.edu.tw
2 Department of Nursing, Meiho University, Pingtung 91202, Taiwan
3 Department of Addiction Science, Kaohsiung Municipal Kai-Syuan Psychiatric Hospital, Kaohsiung City 802211, Taiwan
4 Department of Nursing, College of Medicine, National Cheng Kung University, Tainan City 70140, Taiwan; nyko@mail.ncku.edu.tw
5 School of Nursing, The State University of New York, University at Buffalo, Buffalo, NY 14260, USA; yc73@buffalo.edu
6 Department of Psychiatry, Kaohsiung Medical University Hospital, Kaohsiung City 80708, Taiwan
7 Department of Healthcare Administration, Asia University, Taichung City 41354, Taiwan
8 Department of Psychology, Asia University, Taichung City 41354, Taiwan
* Correspondence: chfaye@cc.kmu.edu.tw (C.-F.Y.); elong@asia.edu.tw (Y.-L.C.); Tel.: +886-7-312-1101 (ext. 6822) (C.-F.Y.); +886-4-2332-3456 (ext. 20106) (Y.-L.C.); Fax: +886-7-313-4761 (C.-F.Y.); +886-4-2332-1206 (Y.-L.C.)

Abstract: Coronavirus disease 2019 (COVID-19) is a novel infectious disease which has had a great impact on the public. Further investigations are, therefore, needed to investigate how the public copes with COVID-19. This study aimed to develop a model to estimate the mediating effects of risk perception and confidence on the association between perceived social support and active coping with the COVID-19 pandemic among people in Taiwan. The data of 1970 participants recruited from a Facebook advertisement were analyzed. Perceived social support, active coping with COVID-19, risk perception and confidence were evaluated using self-administered questionnaires. Structural equation modeling was used to verify the direct and indirect effects between variables. The mediation model demonstrated that lower perceived social support was significantly associated with a higher level of active coping with COVID-19, and this was mediated by a higher level of risk perception. The present study identified the importance of risk perception on the public's coping strategies during the COVID-19 pandemic.

Keywords: risk perception; confidence; social support; coping strategy; COVID-19; SARS-CoV-2

Citation: Li, D.-J.; Ko, N.-Y.; Chang, Y.-P.; Yen, C.-F.; Chen, Y.-L. Mediating Effects of Risk Perception on Association between Social Support and Coping with COVID-19: An Online Survey. *Int. J. Environ. Res. Public Health* **2021**, *18*, 1550. https://doi.org/10.3390/ijerph18041550

Academic Editors: Paolo Roma, Merylin Monaro and Cristina Mazza

Received: 18 January 2021
Accepted: 2 February 2021
Published: 6 February 2021

1. Introduction

1.1. Golobal Scenario of COVID-19 and Coping Strategies for Infective Respiratory Disease Pandemics

Coronavirus disease 2019 (COVID-19) is a novel infectious respiratory disease caused by a novel coronavirus (SARS-CoV-2). It causes physical symptoms including severe pneumonia, pulmonary edema and multiple organ failure [1]. It emerged at the end of 2019 and soon became a major public health burden worldwide [2]. On 11 March 2020, the WHO declared the COVID-19 outbreak a pandemic due to the rapid virus spread and high death toll over the world [3]. As of 29 January 2021, there were up to one hundred million confirmed cases and over two million deaths in over 200 countries [4].

People may change their daily routines due to the adoption of protective behaviors against COVID-19 and search for additional information on the disease. Understanding how the public cope with a pandemic can help health professionals better understand the impact it has on their daily lives, the adequacy of policy for infection control, and the future outcomes of the pandemic. For instance, handwashing is the behavior most recommended by the World Health Organization to protect individuals from contracting COVID-19 [5]. Several coping strategies during infectious disease pandemic were frequently used, such as active coping (seeking social support), problem-focused coping (seeking alternatives, problem-solving), and emotion-focused coping (avoidance) [6]. A longitudinal study recruiting publics during COVID-19 also indicated that several coping strategies, specifically seeking social support, engaging in distractions, and seeking professional help, were used more frequently by those with more pandemic/lockdown distress [7].

In contrast with negative/passive coping, active coping is a stress-management strategy in which a person directly works to control a stressor through targeted behavior [8]. It is generally considered adaptive, having been associated with fewer mood disturbances, and enhanced self-efficacy [8]. Different types of coping strategies are associated with diversities of psychological impacts. During the severe acute respiratory syndrome (SARS) pandemic, active coping was positively related to perceived general health and life satisfaction [9]. It was also reported to be associated with positively subjective wellbeing in COVID-19 pandemic [10]. On the other hand, a web-based survey of people in China reported that those with negative/passive coping strategies, such as do nothing or substance abuse, had a higher level of psychological distress during the COVID-19 epidemic [11]. Moreover, individuals who have negative coping strategies for the COVID-19 pandemic have a higher risk of being infected. For example, people with cognitive impairment and mental illness are more vulnerable to COVID-19 infection as they have little awareness of the risk and maladaptive coping strategies regarding personal protection [12]. Therefore, investigations into factors that predict how the public actively cope with the COVID-19 pandemic are crucial to estimate the multi-dimensional impacts of COVID-19.

1.2. *Influence of Perceived Social Support, Risk Perception, and Confidence with Active Coping*

Whether perceived social support affects individuals' coping strategies against the threat of COVID-19 remains unclear. Chao reported that higher social support was positively associated with problem-focused coping among the elderly who experienced Typhoon Morakot in Taiwan [13]. In addition, a study in the US revealed that support via financial security was a predictor of adherence to the Centers for Disease Control and Prevention (CDC) guidelines for infection control of COVID-19 [14]. However, how perceived social support influences coping strategies against COVID-19 is not clear. Therefore, further studies are needed to investigate whether there are factors that mediate the association between perceived social support and active coping with the COVID-19 pandemic.

A meta-analysis of experimental studies demonstrated that people's intentions and behavior change following heightened risk appraisal, including risk perception [15]. Several psychological or social factors are reported to be associated with risk perceptions of COVID-19. Improving perceptions about infectious diseases in society could lead to a significant improvement in a patient's well-being and decrease in discrimination [16]. In addition, prosocial values, trust in government, science, and medical professionals, and personal knowledge of COVID-19 were all significant predictors of risk perception [17]. Estimating the level of risk perception may be important for the public because that it will affect the public's behaviors or coping with COVID-19. It was reported that social distancing and hand washing were strongly predicted by the perceived probability of personally being infected, which is a kind of risk perception [18]. Another cross-sectional study in Mexico demonstrated that both higher level of perceived susceptibility and perceived severity of COVID-19 were associated with protective behaviors of staying home [19]. On the other hand, confidence in coping with the COVID-19 pandemic may be associated with active coping with COVID-19. Confidence in coping is similar to self-efficacy, representing the individuals' beliefs that they have the ability to do specific tasks in the future [20]. Previous studies have reported significant associations between having more knowledge about disease and self-efficacy in coping with SARS [21] along with COVID-19 [22]. Therefore, further studies are warranted to investigate whether risk perception and confidence mediate the association between social support and active coping with COVID-19.

1.3. Aims of the Current Study

Adopting adequate coping strategies for infective respiratory disease pandemics affects both personal health and also the efficacy of infection control for society as a whole. The aims of the present study were to identify any associations between perceived social support and active coping with the COVID-19 pandemic, and the potentially mediating effects of risk perception and confidence. According to above reviews of literatures, it is hypothesized that perceived social support may be associated with active coping with the COVID-19 pandemic. Moreover, either confidence or risk perception may be partial or full mediated the association between perceived social support and active coping with COVID-19.

2. Methods

2.1. Participants and Procedures

The current study was based on dataset of the Survey of Health Behaviors During the COVID-19 Pandemic in Taiwan, which was initially reported elsewhere [22]. The expert meeting was held to develop questionnaires, which were used in this study. In brief, Facebook users aged ≥20 years and living in Taiwan were recruited into this study between 10 April and 23 April 2020. A Facebook advertisement was posted, which included a headline, main text, pop-up banner and weblink to the research questionnaire website. The recruiting advertisement was designed to appear in the "News Feed" of Facebook, which is a streaming list of updates from the user's connections (e.g., friends) and advertisers. A previous study indicated that News Feed advertisements are more effective in terms of recruitment metrics for research studies [23]. In order to increase its visibility, we also posted the online advertisement to Line and Facebook groups.

This study was approved by the Institutional Review Board of Kaohsiung Medical University Hospital (approval no. KMUHIRB-EXEMPT(I)20200011). Although the participants were not given any incentive for their participation, at the end of the questionnaire we provided them with weblinks to the online COVID-19 Information Centers of the Taiwanese CDC, Kaohsiung Medical University Hospital, and the Medical College of National Cheng Kung University so they could search for useful information.

2.2. Questionnaires

2.2.1. Perceived Social Support

We estimated the levels of satisfaction with perceived social support using three questions: "In the past week, did you receive satisfactory support from your (1) family, (2) friends, and (3) colleagues or classmates?" The responses were graded on a five-point Likert scale, with scores ranging from 0 (entirely disappointed) to 4 (extremely satisfied). Higher total scores indicated more satisfaction with their level of perceived social support during the COVID-19 pandemic. This instrument is reliable and well-validated according to the supplementary material of previous publication [24].

2.2.2. Active Coping with COVID-19

Liao et al. [25] developed several questionnaires to estimate the protective behavior in the 2009 influenza A/H1N1 pandemic in Hong Kong. In reference to the above study, we developed 7 questions to assess the respondents' level of active coping with the threat of COVID-19 during their daily lives [26]. The active coping with COVID-19 represented the coping strategies of problem solving (protective behaviors) against the threat of COVID-19. These questions asked participants if they: (1) avoided going to crowded places, (2) maintained good indoor ventilation, (3) cleaned or disinfected their house more often, (4) washed their hands more often, (5) wore a mask, (6) searched for information on COVID-19, and (7) avoided clinic visits or had missed appointments at clinics in the past week. The responses were scored as 0 ("no" or "yes, but not due to COVID-19") and 1 ("yes, due to COVID-19").

2.2.3. Risk Perception toward COVID-19

According to Liao et al. [25], we developed the following question to assess the severity of current worry towards COVID-19: "Please rate your level of current worry towards COVID-19." The severity of current worry towards COVID-19 was rated from 1 (minimal) to 10 (extremely severe). We also developed four additional questions to evaluate different categories of risk perception: (1) "If you developed flu-like symptoms tomorrow, would you be worried? Reply: 1 (not at all) to 5 (extremely)", (2) "In the past week, have you worried about catching COVID-19? Reply: 1 (not at all) to 5 (extremely)", (3) "How likely do you think it is that you will contract COVID-19 over the next month? Reply: 1 (impossible) to 7 (guaranteed)", and (4) "What do you think your chances are of getting COVID-19 over the next month compared with others outside your family? Reply: 1 (impossible) to 7 (guaranteed)". The current measurement is reported to be reliable and well-validated according to the supplementary material of previous publication [24].

2.2.4. Confidence against COVID-19

Self-confidence about COVID-19 and perceived confidence in the local government's ability to control the COVID-19 pandemic were assessed using the following 2 questions: (1) "How confident are you that you will overcome the threats of the COVID-19 pandemic?" and (2) "How confident are you that your city is controlling the COVID-19 pandemic?" The responses were scored on a five-point Likert scale as follows: 0 (not at all confident), 1 (not very confident), 2 (neutral), 3 (confident), and 4 (very confident). Higher scores indicated that the individual was more confident about overcoming the COVID-19 pandemic.

2.2.5. Statistical Analysis

To examine the hypothesized multiple mediation model for the association between perceived social support and active coping with COVID-19, which was mediated by risk perception or confidence (Figure 1), the following analyses were conducted using SPSS and AMOS version 23.0 for Windows (SPSS Inc., Chicago, IL, USA). We examined bivariate associations among the variables using Pearson's correlation coefficient (r), followed by two steps of structural equation modeling (SEM). First, confirmatory factor analysis (CFA) was used to verify the association between latent variables and their indicators in the measurement model. Each question was composed of observed variables (indicators) and latent variables, which indicated perceived social support, active coping with COVID-19, risk perception, and confidence. Factor loading was used as an index to assess the scale reliability between indicators and the corresponding latent variables in the CFA. In addition, Cronbach's α was calculated to examine the internal consistency reliability. The range was considered acceptable if Cronbach's α was >0.5 [27]. To estimate the sample adequacy of "active coping with COVID-19" in factor analysis, the Kaiser–Mayer–Olkin (KMO) measure of sampling adequacy and Bartlett testing were applied. A KMO value of >0.60 and statistically significant value of $p < 0.05$ from Bartlett testing indicated the data was adequate for factor analysis [28]. Then, the total variance explained (%) was also estimated through EFA to estimate the validity of "active coping with COVID-19".

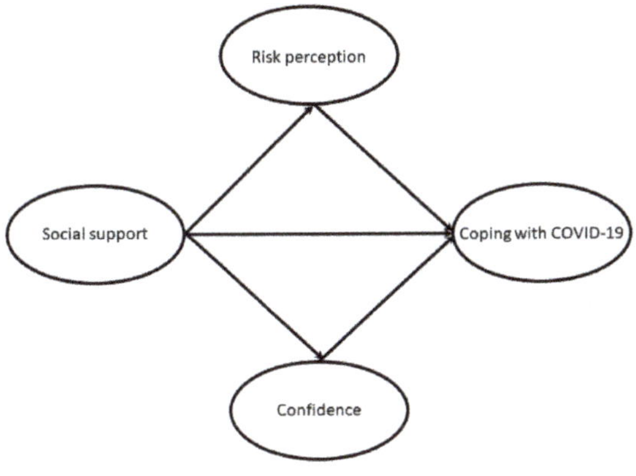

Figure 1. The conceptual model of mediating effect.

Latent variable path analysis with maximum likelihood parameter estimations was used to estimate the model adequacy and the direct/indirect effects of perceived social support on active coping with COVID-19 through risk perception or confidence [29]. Bootstrapping method with 5000 samples was applied in the path analysis due to the non-normality of the data (Kolmogorov-Smirnov test; $p < 0.001$). As a multiple mediator model, both mediators were applied into the model to assess and compare the mediating effects. As there was a relatively high proportion of females in the study cohort and as the Kolmogorov-Smirnov test ($p < 0.001$) for age was significant, indicating non-normal distribution, age and gender were also included in the multiple mediators' model as covariates to adjust for their effects on the latent variables. Gender (female, male and transgender) was transformed into two dichotomous dummy variables (male vs. female; and transgender vs. female) for the analysis. The standardized estimates (beta coefficient; β) were reported for the predictive strength explained in the model.

We used the Sobel test to verify the mediating effect [30]. Furthermore, to test the adequacy of the model, multiple indices were applied to verify the goodness of fit. For each of these fit indices, the values indicating an acceptable model fit were as follows: Goodness of Fit Index (GFI ≥ 0.9); Adjusted Goodness of Fit Index (AGFI ≥ 0.9); root mean square error of approximation (RMSEA < 0.08); and standardized root mean square residual (SRMR ≤ 0.08) [31,32].

3. Results

3.1. Descriptive Statistics, Factor Analysis, and the Correlation Matrix

Initially, 2031 respondents filled in the online questionnaire. After excluding those with missing values ($n = 31$) and those aged below 20 years ($n = 30$), a total of 1970 participants (1305 females, 650 males, and 15 transgender) were included in the analysis. The mean age of the participants was 37.81 $\pm$ 11.00 years. The correlation matrix with significance, mean and standard deviation for each indicator is shown in Table 1. In general, active coping with COVIDD-19 is postively correlated with risk perception, but negatively correlated with perceived social support. The values of Cronbach's α of all questionnares were above 0.5, indicating acceptable range [27]. Regarding the EFA of "active coping with COVID-19", the value of the KMO coefficient was 0.70, and the Bartletts' test of sphericity reached statistical significance ($p < 0.01$). It supported the adequeacy of the sample. The total variance explained (%) of "active coping with COVID-19" was at 43.29%, which was close to the acceptable range of 50% [33].

Table 1. The correlation matrix of observed variables.

Varaible	Mean	SD	2	3	4	5	6	7	8	9	10	11	12	13	14	15	16	17
1	0.94	0.23	0.13 *	0.14 *	0.16 *	0.18 *	0.09 *	0.06 *	0.18 *	0.1 *	0.18 *	0.11 *	0.04	−0.1 *	−0.05 *	0.01	<0.01	−0.01
2	0.88	0.32	-	0.24 *	0.15 *	0.12 *	0.14 *	0.09 *	0.05 *	0.05 *	0.12 *	0.04	<0.01	−0.02	0.01	−0.01	−0.02	−0.001
3	0.67	0.47		-	0.27 *	0.19 *	0.22 *	0.15 *	0.16 *	0.21 *	0.23 *	0.09 *	0.04	−0.09 *	−0.07 *	−0.02	−0.04	−0.06 *
4	0.92	0.28			-	0.39 *	0.18 *	0.07 *	0.16 *	0.15 *	0.16 *	0.08 *	0.07 *	−0.05 *	−0.04	0.03	−0.01	−0.02
5	0.89	0.31				-	0.21 *	0.1 *	0.18 *	0.18 *	0.22 *	0.13 *	0.12 *	−0.07 *	−0.04	0.02	−0.004	−0.02
6	0.76	0.43					-	0.12 *	0.18 *	0.17 *	0.21 *	0.11 *	0.05 *	−0.9 *	−0.05 *	−0.04	−0.05 *	−0.004
7	0.17	0.37						-	0.07 *	0.13 *	0.09 *	0.08 *	0.03	−0.1 *	−0.04	−0.05 *	−0.07 *	−0.06 *
8	3.93	0.92							-	0.45 *	0.48 *	0.27 *	0.18 *	−0.22 *	−0.13 *	0.01	−0.02	<0.01
9	2.59	0.99								-	0.55 *	0.46 *	0.33 *	−0.31 *	−0.23 *	−0.06 *	−0.1 *	−0.1 *
10	6.14	2.25									-	0.37 *	0.23 *	−0.32 *	−0.24 *	−0.02	−0.05 *	−0.06 *
11	3.47	1.14										-	0.57 *	−0.39 *	−0.27 *	−0.09 *	−0.09 *	−0.09 *
12	3.53	1.28											-	−0.23 *	−0.17 *	−0.04	−0.02	−0.05 *
13	2.41	0.84												-	−0.54 *	0.16 *	0.18 *	0.18 *
14	2.32	0.95													-	0.12 *	0.13 *	0.17 *
15	2.98	0.80														-	0.62 *	0.51 *
16	2.90	0.72															-	0.67 *
17	2.71	0.83																-

*: $p < 0.05$; 1 = Coping-1; 2 = Coping-2; 3 = Coping-3; 4 = Coping-4; 5 = Coping-5; 6 = Coping-6; 7 = Coping-7; 8 = Risk-1; 9 = Risk-2; 10 = Risk-3; 11 = Risk-4; 12 = Risk-5; 13 = Con-1; 14 = Con-2; 15 = Support-1; 16 = Support-2; 17 = Support-3; details of abbreviations are listed in Table 2.

Table 2. Principle component analysis for factors in the conceptual model.

Latent Variables/Observed Variables	Factor Loading	Cronbach's Alpha
Active coping with COIVD-19		0.56
Avoid going to crowded places (Coping-1)	0.32	
Keep good indoor ventilation (Coping-2)	0.33	
Disinfect house more often (Coping-3)	0.50	
Wash hands more often (Coping-4)	0.55	
Wear a mask (Coping-5)	0.53	
Search information of COVID-19 (Coping-6)	0.40	
Prevent clinic visits or lost follow up (Coping-7)	0.23	
Risk perception		0.71
Develop flu-like symptoms tomorrow (Risk-1)	0.57	
Worried about catching COVID-19 last week (Risk-2)	0.76	
Rate current level of your worry to COVID-19 (Risk-3)	0.71	
How likely you will contract COVID-19 (Risk-4)	0.61	
Chances of getting COVID-19 next 1 month (Risk-5)	0.46	
Confidence against COVID-19		0.70
Self-confidence overcoming threats of COVID-19 (Con-1)	0.89	
Perceived confidence of regional government (Con-2)	0.61	
Perceived social support		0.81
Family members (Support-1)	0.69	
Friends (Support-2)	0.89	
Colleagues or classmates (Support-3)	0.75	

3.2. Tests for the Mediation Model and Estimated Coefficient Paths

The first step of the SEM estimated the factor loadings through CFA (Table 2). The results of the reliability test are also presented, which indicated an acceptable range of reliability. After adjusting for age and gender, the multiple mediator model was used to estimate the indirect and direct effects, and the estimated path coefficients are illustrated in Figure 2. We found that an indirect effect at a value of −0.06 reached statistical significance (Sobel test: $Z = -4.05$; $p < 0.05$), and this was based on the product terms of the path from perceived social support to risk perception ($\beta = -0.13$, $p < 0.001$) and the path from risk perception to active coping with COVID-19 ($\beta = 0.49$, $p < 0.001$). On the other hand, the mediating effect of confidence on the path between perceived social support and active coping with COVID-19 was not significant (Sobel test: $Z = 0.99$; $p = 0.32$). Moreover, the direct effect from perceived social support to active coping with COVID-19 was not statistically significant. The significance of the path analysis did not change after adjusting for age and gender.

These results confirmed the mediating effect of risk perception on the association between perceived social support and active coping with COVID-19. Based on the model fit index, the hypothesized model had an adequate model fit index for RMESA (0.068), GFI (0.927), AGFI (0.902), and SRMR (0.069), indicating the good fit of our hypothesized mediation model.

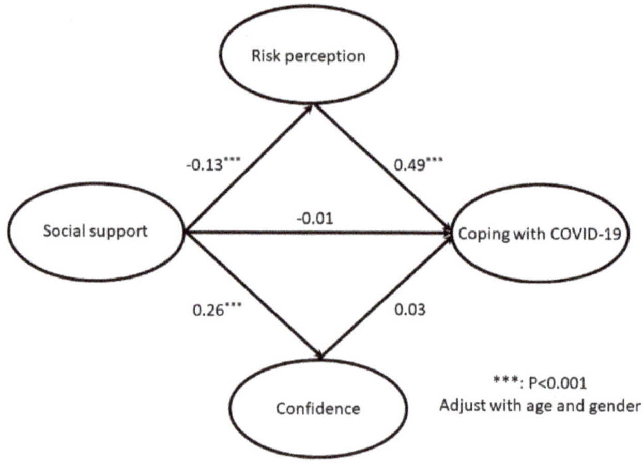

Figure 2. Final model of mediating effect indicating the estimated coefficients of the paths.

4. Discussion

4.1. Main Findings of the Current Study

In the current study, an indirect effect was found in that lower perceived support was significantly associated with a higher level of coping with COVID-19, which was mediated by a higher level of risk perception. In addition, a direct effect of perceived social support on coping with COVID-19 and another indirect effect mediated by confidence against COVID-19 did not reach statistical significance.

4.2. Mediating Effect of Risk Perception on the Association between Perceived Social Support and Active Coping with COVID-19

A higher level of risk perception fully mediated the association between lower perceived support and a higher level of active coping with COVID-19. Although a previous study indicated that financial security predicted better coping strategies against COVID-19 [14], the association between perceived social support and active coping with COVID-19 may be different. Perceived social support represents satisfaction with the general support provided by family, friends, and colleagues/classmates, and this represents broader domains than financial support. In addition, although it did not investigate infective respiratory diseases, a previous study demonstrated that a higher level of social support was associated with a lower perceived risk of breast cancer [34]. O'Sullivan reported that individuals with a higher level of perceived social support may feel that they are relatively safe, leading to optimism bias, which causes them to believe that they are less likely to experience negative events [35]. Individuals with such bias may underestimate their risk of COVID-19; however, further studies are needed to test the effects of optimism bias on risk perception.

In the current study, we found that a higher level of risk perception was associated with a higher level of active coping with COVID-19. A previous study investigated the association between risk perception and coping strategies in patients with diabetes, and found that those who had a low premorbid perception of risks often engaged in diabetes-related risky behaviors [36]. In addition, a systematic review demonstrated that healthcare workers' risk perception influenced their behavior towards patients and facilitated risk-mitigating strategies for emerging acute respiratory infection diseases [37]. Further prospective studies may provide a better understanding of the temporal relationship between risk perception and active coping in relation to infective respiratory diseases.

The above findings revealed the importance of risk perception on active coping with COVID-19; however, perceived social support can compromise the level of risk perception, leading the interference in active coping with COVID-19. It manifested the controversial role of perceived social support. Previous study reported that higher level of perceived social support was associated with less sleep disturbance and suicidal thought, indicating the protective effect of perceived social support from mental burden [26]. It implicated that interventions in risk perception and perceived social support are both important for publics during the COVID-19 pandemic. Specific support to facilitate social interaction is crucial for those who are socially isolated or quarantined due to infection. Telecommunication or online gathering should also be promoted for the time in need of social distancing. Whereas, intervention to enhance publics' risk perception should not be neglected. Medical information, news, and governmental policies regarding COVID-19 pandemic should also be announced widely to enhance the risk perception of publics [17].

4.3. The Non-Significant Mediating Effect of Confidence on the Association between Perceived Social Support and Active Coping with COVID-19

We found that perceived social support was positively associated with confidence, whereas the association between confidence and coping with COVID-19 was not significant. A cross-sectional observational study on medical staff treating patients with COVID-19 in China demonstrated that levels of social support were significantly associated with self-efficacy [38]. Self-efficacy represents how well one can execute courses of action required to deal with prospective situations, and indicates an individual's belief that they can overcome obstacles [39]. Although confidence against COVID-19 cannot be entirely compared with self-efficacy, the association between perceived social support and confidence observed in the current study deserves further investigation to explore the potential effect of social support on self-efficacy.

On the other hand, the insignificant association between confidence and active coping with COVID-19 means that confidence failed to significantly mediate the association between perceived social support and active coping with COVID-19. Since previous studies have emphasized the significant association between gathering information and confidence [22,40], gathering information was only considered as part of active coping with COVID-19 in the current study. This unexpected finding violated the hypothesis of the current study. Several factors may implicate this insignificant association. First, it is possible that other factors involved in active coping with COVID-19 interfered with the association. On the other hand, the questionnaires of confidence in the current study may be insufficient to entirely measure the self-efficacy of participants. Therefore, further development of conceptual model with comprehensively psychological factors and detailed questionnaires measuring self-efficacy may be helpful to determine the detailed interactions between confidence and coping strategies against COVID-19.

4.4. Limitations

There are several limitations to the present study. First, possible selection bias may have confounded the results, as the participants were only recruited through a Facebook advertisement. Second, causality could only be inferred among the variables due to the cross-sectional design of this study. Third, several measurements which were crucial in this scenario were not estimated in the questionnaires, such as level of stigma [16], psychological distress, and symptoms of post-traumatic stress disorder (PTSD). Finally, COVID-19 had a limited impact in Taiwan in comparison with other countries, so whether our results can be generalized to other countries is unclear and warrants further investigation.

5. Conclusions

In the present study, we found that lower perceived social support was indirectly associated with increased active coping against COVID-19, and that this association was mediated by higher risk perception. However, we did not identify a mediating effect of confidence or a direct effect between perceived social support and active coping with COVID-19. The implication of the current study is that intervention to enhance both perceived social support and risk perception are necessary for public during COVID-19 pandemic. Moreover, risk perception could be more effective to enhance active coping with

COVID-19 than the confidence against COVID-19. The subjects who were satisfied with their social support might have had optimism bias that weakened their risk perception and had a compromising effect on their motivation to cope with COVID-19. Since the inversed association between perceived social support and risk perception, it is critical to reduce the effect of optimism bias resulting from perceived social support but not reduce the social support. To enhance perceived social support, specific resources to facilitate social interaction are warranted under adequate infection control. Regarding the impact of the problematic internet use, it is still necessary to promote the telecommunication, online gathering, or programs of social interaction at the difficult time of social distancing. In order to strengthen the risk perception and weaken the effect of optimism bias, facilitation of individuals' recognition to this pandemic may be beneficial. Timely and correct information about current threats, policies, and strategies against COVID-19 are necessary and should be announced by the authorities through traditional (newspapers or television news) and digital media, such as news feed or livestream thought social software. Public education on infection control is also necessary both during infectious disease outbreaks and at other times.

We have several suggestions for further research, which could help extend the findings of the present study. A paper-and-pencil questionnaire as opposed to a digital questionnaire, along with printed advertisements posted in public areas would be beneficial to also include non-netizens in the study population. Additional psycho-social factors should also be considered, such as stigma, discrimination, psychological distress, and symptoms of post-traumatic stress disorder. Moreover, further studies investigating optimism bias and self-efficacy using the General Self-Efficacy Scale [41] may be helpful to explore how people cope with the threats of COVID-19. Finally, the prospective cohort study estimating the self-efficacy, risk perception, coping with COVID-19, perceived support and related psycho-social factors (stigma, discrimination, symptoms of PTSD, psychological distress, vaccine hesitancy, etc.) at different stages of this pandemic are warranted. Importantly, attitude or hesitancy of vaccine may be associated with risk perception or coping with COVID-19. Measurements at different stages will be helpful to verify the conceptual model.

Author Contributions: D.-J.L.: Conceptualization, methodology, formal analysis, investigation, writing—original draft. N.-Y.K.: Formal analysis, data curation, conceptualization. Y.-P.C.: Methodology, data curation. C.-F.Y.: Conceptualization, methodology, formal analysis, project administration, writing—review and editing. Y.-L.C.: Formal analysis, writing—review and editing. All authors have read and agreed to the published version of the manuscript.

Funding: This research received no external funding.

Institutional Review Board Statement: This study was approved by the Institutional Review Board of Kaohsiung Medical University Hospital (approval no. KMUHIRB-EXEMPT(I)20200011).

Informed Consent Statement: Patient consent was waived due to the design of on-line survey. Participation in the online survey was voluntary and survey responses were anonymous.

Data Availability Statement: The data presented in this study are available on request from the corresponding author.

Conflicts of Interest: The authors declare no conflict of interest.

References

1. Huang, C.; Wang, Y.; Li, X.; Ren, L.; Zhao, J.; Hu, Y.; Zhang, L.; Fan, G.; Xu, J.; Gu, X.; et al. Clinical features of patients infected with 2019 novel coronavirus in Wuhan, China. *Lancet* **2020**, *395*, 497–506. [CrossRef]
2. Wang, C.; Horby, P.W.; Hayden, F.G.; Gao, G.F. A novel coronavirus outbreak of global health concern. *Lancet* **2020**, *395*, 470–473. [CrossRef]
3. World Health Organization. Coronavirus Disease 2019 (COVID-19) Situation Report-51. Available online: https://www.who.int/docs/default-source/coronaviruse/situation-reports/20200311-sitrep-51-covid-19.pdf?sfvrsn=1ba62e57_10 (accessed on 12 January 2021).

4. World Health Organization. Coronavirus Disease (COVID-19) Weekly Epidemiological Update and Weekly Operational Update. Available online: https://www.who.int/docs/default-source/coronaviruse/situation-reports/20210127_weekly_epi_update_24.pdf?sfvrsn=a8d660fc_9&download=true (accessed on 29 January 2021).
5. World Health Organization. Coronavirus Disease (COVID-19) Advice for Public. Available online: https://www.who.int/emergencies/diseases/novel-coronavirus-2019/advice-for-public (accessed on 11 January 2021).
6. Chew, Q.H.; Wei, K.C.; Vasoo, S.; Chua, H.C.; Sim, K. Narrative synthesis of psychological and coping responses towards emerging infectious disease outbreaks in the general population: Practical considerations for the COVID-19 pandemic. *Singap. Med. J.* **2020**, *61*, 350–356. [CrossRef] [PubMed]
7. Shanahan, L.; Steinhoff, A.; Bechtiger, L.; Murray, A.L.; Nivette, A.; Hepp, U.; Ribeaud, D.; Eisner, M. Emotional distress in young adults during the COVID-19 pandemic: Evidence of risk and resilience from a longitudinal cohort study. *Psychol. Med.* **2020**, 1–10. [CrossRef]
8. Brown, G.K.; Nicassio, P.M. Development of a questionnaire for the assessment of active and passive coping strategies in chronic pain patients. *Pain®* **1987**, *31*, 53–64. [CrossRef]
9. Main, A.; Zhou, Q.; Ma, Y.; Luecken, L.J.; Liu, X. Relations of SARS-related stressors and coping to Chinese college students' psychological adjustment during the 2003 Beijing SARS epidemic. *J. Couns. Psychol.* **2011**, *58*, 410–423. [CrossRef] [PubMed]
10. Zacher, H.; Rudolph, C.W. Individual differences and changes in subjective wellbeing during the early stages of the COVID-19 pandemic. *Am. Psychol.* **2021**, *76*, 50–62. [CrossRef] [PubMed]
11. Wang, H.; Xia, Q.; Xiong, Z.; Li, Z.; Xiang, W.; Yuan, Y.; Liu, Y.; Li, Z. The psychological distress and coping styles in the early stages of the 2019 coronavirus disease (COVID-19) epidemic in the general mainland Chinese population: A web-based survey. *PLoS ONE* **2020**, *15*, e0233410. [CrossRef]
12. Yao, H.; Chen, J.H.; Xu, Y.F. Patients with mental health disorders in the COVID-19 epidemic. *Lancet Psychiatry* **2020**, *7*, e21. [CrossRef]
13. Chao, S.F. Social support, coping strategies and their correlations with older adults' relocation adjustments after natural disaster. *Geriatr. Gerontol. Int.* **2017**, *17*, 1006–1014. [CrossRef]
14. Park, C.L.; Russell, B.S.; Fendrich, M.; Finkelstein-Fox, L.; Hutchison, M.; Becker, J. Americans' COVID-19 Stress, Coping, and Adherence to CDC Guidelines. *J. Gen. Intern. Med.* **2020**, *35*, 2296–2303. [CrossRef]
15. Sheeran, P.; Harris, P.R.; Epton, T. Does heightening risk appraisals change people's intentions and behavior? A meta-analysis of experimental studies. *Psychol. Bull.* **2014**, *140*, 511–543. [CrossRef]
16. Baldassarre, A.; Giorgi, G.; Alessio, F.; Lulli, L.G.; Arcangeli, G.; Mucci, N. Stigma and Discrimination (SAD) at the Time of the SARS-CoV-2 Pandemic. *Int. J. Environ. Res. Public Health* **2020**, *17*, 6341. [CrossRef]
17. Dryhurst, S.; Schneider, C.R.; Kerr, J.; Freeman, A.L.J.; Recchia, G.; van der Bles, A.M.; Spiegelhalter, D.; van der Linden, S. Risk perceptions of COVID-19 around the world. *J. Risk Res.* **2020**, *23*, 994–1006. [CrossRef]
18. Wise, T.; Zbozinek, T.D.; Michelini, G.; Hagan, C.C.; Mobbs, D. Changes in risk perception and self-reported protective behaviour during the first week of the COVID-19 pandemic in the United States. *R. Soc. Open Sci.* **2020**, *7*, 200742. [CrossRef]
19. Irigoyen-Camacho, M.E.; Velazquez-Alva, M.C.; Zepeda-Zepeda, M.A.; Cabrer-Rosales, M.F.; Lazarevich, I.; Castano-Seiquer, A. Effect of Income Level and Perception of Susceptibility and Severity of COVID-19 on Stay-at-Home Preventive Behavior in a Group of Older Adults in Mexico City. *Int. J. Environ. Res. Public Health* **2020**, *17*, 7418. [CrossRef]
20. Bandura, A. Self-efficacy: Toward a unifying theory of behavioral change. *Psychol. Rev.* **1977**, *84*, 191–215. [CrossRef]
21. Voeten, H.A.; de Zwart, O.; Veldhuijzen, I.K.; Yuen, C.; Jiang, X.; Elam, G.; Abraham, T.; Brug, J. Sources of information and health beliefs related to SARS and avian influenza among Chinese communities in the United Kingdom and The Netherlands, compared to the general population in these countries. *Int. J. Behav. Med.* **2009**, *16*, 49–57. [CrossRef]
22. Wang, P.W.; Lu, W.H.; Ko, N.Y.; Chen, Y.L.; Li, D.J.; Chang, Y.P.; Yen, C.F. COVID-19-Related Information Sources and the Relationship With Confidence in People Coping with COVID-19: Facebook Survey Study in Taiwan. *J. Med. Internet Res.* **2020**, *22*, e20021. [CrossRef] [PubMed]
23. Ramo, D.E.; Rodriguez, T.M.; Chavez, K.; Sommer, M.J.; Prochaska, J.J. Facebook Recruitment of Young Adult Smokers for a Cessation Trial: Methods, Metrics, and Lessons Learned. *Internet Interv.* **2014**, *1*, 58–64. [CrossRef] [PubMed]
24. Li, D.J.; Ko, N.Y.; Chen, Y.L.; Wang, P.W.; Chang, Y.P.; Yen, C.F. Confidence in coping with COVID-19 and its related factors among the public in Taiwan. *Psychiatry Clin. Neurosci.* **2020**, *74*, 608–610. [CrossRef]
25. Liao, Q.; Cowling, B.J.; Lam, W.W.; Ng, D.M.; Fielding, R. Anxiety, worry and cognitive risk estimate in relation to protective behaviors during the 2009 influenza A/H1N1 pandemic in Hong Kong: Ten cross-sectional surveys. *BMC Infect. Dis.* **2014**, *14*, 169. [CrossRef] [PubMed]
26. Li, D.-J.; Ko, N.-Y.; Chen, Y.-L.; Wang, P.-W.; Chang, Y.-P.; Yen, C.-F.; Lu, W.-H. COVID-19-Related Factors Associated with Sleep Disturbance and Suicidal Thoughts among the Taiwanese Public: A Facebook Survey. *Int. J. Environ. Res. Public Health* **2020**, *17*, 4479. [CrossRef]
27. Hinton, P.R. *SPSS Explained*; Routledge: London, UK; New York, NY, USA, 2004; pp. 363–364.
28. Tabachnick, B.G.; Fidell, L.S. *Using Multivariate Statistics*, 5th ed.; Allyn and Bacon: New York, NY, USA, 2007.
29. Kline, T. *Psychological Testing: A Practical Approach to Design and Evaluation*; Sage Publications: Thousand Oaks, CA, USA, 2005; pp. 356–357.
30. Sobel, M.E. Asymptotic Confidence Intervals for Indirect Effects in Structural Equation Models. *Sociol. Methodol.* **1982**, *13*, 290. [CrossRef]
31. Hu, L.T.; Bentler, P.M. Cutoff criteria for fit indexes in covariance structure analysis: Conventional criteria versus new alternatives. *Struct. Equ. Model. A Multidiscip. J.* **1999**, *6*, 1–55. [CrossRef]

32. McDonald, R.P.; Ho, M.H. Principles and practice in reporting structural equation analyses. *Psychol. Methods* **2002**, *7*, 64–82. [CrossRef]
33. Beavers, A.S.; Lounsbury, J.W.; Richards, J.K.; Huck, S.W.; Skolits, G.; Esquivel, S.L. Practical considerations for using exploratory factor analysis in educational research. *Pract. Assess. Res. Eval.* **2013**, *18*, 6.
34. Kinsinger, S.W.; McGregor, B.A.; Bowen, D.J. Perceived breast cancer risk, social support, and distress among a community-based sample of women. *J. Psychosoc. Oncol.* **2009**, *27*, 230–247. [CrossRef]
35. O'Sullivan, O.P. The Neural Basis of Always Looking on the Bright Side. *Dialogues Philos. Ment. Neuro Sci.* **2015**, *8*, 11–15.
36. Tabong, P.T.; Bawontuo, V.; Dumah, D.N.; Kyilleh, J.M.; Yempabe, T. Premorbid risk perception, lifestyle, adherence and coping strategies of people with diabetes mellitus: A phenomenological study in the Brong Ahafo Region of Ghana. *PLoS ONE* **2018**, *13*, e0198915. [CrossRef]
37. Koh, Y.; Hegney, D.G.; Drury, V. Comprehensive systematic review of healthcare workers' perceptions of risk and use of coping strategies towards emerging respiratory infectious diseases. *Int. J. Evid. Based Healthc.* **2011**, *9*, 403–419. [CrossRef] [PubMed]
38. Xiao, H.; Zhang, Y.; Kong, D.; Li, S.; Yang, N. The Effects of Social Support on Sleep Quality of Medical Staff Treating Patients with Coronavirus Disease 2019 (COVID-19) in January and February 2020 in China. *Med. Sci. Monit.* **2020**, *26*, e923549. [CrossRef] [PubMed]
39. Bandura, A. Self-efficacy mechanism in human agency. *Am. Psychol.* **1982**, *37*, 122–147. [CrossRef]
40. Zhong, B.L.; Luo, W.; Li, H.M.; Zhang, Q.Q.; Liu, X.G.; Li, W.T.; Li, Y. Knowledge, attitudes, and practices towards COVID-19 among Chinese residents during the rapid rise period of the COVID-19 outbreak: A quick online cross-sectional survey. *Int. J. Biol. Sci.* **2020**, *16*, 1745–1752. [CrossRef]
41. Zhang, X.; Zhan, Y.; Liu, J.; Chai, S.; Xu, L.; Lei, M.; Koh, K.W.L.; Jiang, Y.; Wang, W. Chinese translation and psychometric testing of the cardiac self-efficacy scale in patients with coronary heart disease in mainland China. *Health Qual. Life Outcomes* **2018**, *16*, 43. [CrossRef]

MDPI
St. Alban-Anlage 66
4052 Basel
Switzerland
Tel. +41 61 683 77 34
Fax +41 61 302 89 18
www.mdpi.com

International Journal of Environmental Research and Public Health Editorial Office
E-mail: ijerph@mdpi.com
www.mdpi.com/journal/ijerph

www.ingramcontent.com/pod-product-compliance
Lightning Source LLC
Chambersburg PA
CBHW061504220926
51850CB00004B/166
9783036530154